W9-DFU-966

EIGHTH EDITION

International Financial Management

Jeff Madura
Florida Atlantic University

Australia · Canada · Mexico · Singapore · Spain · United Kingdom · United States

International Financial Management, 8e
Jeff Madura

VP/Editorial Director:
Jack W. Calhoun

VP/Editor-in-Chief:
Dave Shaut

Executive Editor:
Michael R. Reynolds

Senior Developmental Editor:
Trish Taylor

Marketing Manager:
Heather MacMaster

Production Editor:
Amy McGuire

Technology Project Editor:
John Barans

Web Coordinator:
Karen Schaffer

Manufacturing Coordinator:
Sandee Milewski

Production House:
G&S Typesetters, Inc.

Printer:
RR Donnelley
Willard Manufacturing Division

Art Director:
Chris Miller

Internal Designer:
Craig Ramsdell, Ramsdell Design

Cover Designer:
Chris Miller

Cover Images:
Corbis

Printed in the United States of America
4 5 08 07
SE PKG ISBN-13: 978-0-324-28841-4
ISBN-10: 0-324-28841-7
SE TEXT ISBN-13: 978-0-324-31948-4
ISBN-10: 0-324-31948-7
IE PKG ISBN-13: 978-0-324-39543-3
ISBN-10: 0-324-39543-4
IE TEXT ISBN-13: 978-0-324-39542-6
ISBN-10: 0-324-39542-6
Library of Congress Control Number: 2004 111825

For more information contact Thomson Higher Education, 5191 Natorp Boulevard, Mason, Ohio 45040 USA
Or you can visit our Internet site at: http://www.swlearning.com

Asia (including India)
Thomson Learning
5 Shenton Way
#01-01 UIC Building
Singapore 068808

Canada
Thomson Nelson
1120 Birchmount Road
Toronto, Ontario
Canada M1K 5G4

Australia/New Zealand
Thomson Learning Australia
102 Dodds Street
Southbank, Victoria 3006
Australia

UK/Europe/Middle East/Africa
Thomson Learning
High Holborn House
50–51 Bedford Road
London WC1R 4LR
United Kingdom

Latin America
Thomson Learning
Seneca, 53
Colonia Polanco
11560 Mexico
D.F. Mexico

Spain (including Portugal)
Thomson Paraninfo
Calle Magallanes, 25
28015 Madrid, Spain

Dedication

To My Parents

About the Author

Jeff Madura is presently the SunTrust Bank Professor of Finance at Florida Atlantic University. He has written several textbooks, including *Financial Markets and Institutions.* His research on international finance has been published in numerous journals, including *Journal of Financial and Quantitative Analysis, Journal of Money, Credit and Banking, Journal of Banking and Finance, Journal of International Money and Finance, Journal of Financial Research, Financial Review, Journal of Multinational Financial Management,* and *Global Finance Journal.* He has received awards for excellence in teaching and research, and has served as a consultant for international banks, securities firms, and other multinational corporations. He has served as a director for the Southern Finance Association and Eastern Finance Association, and also served as president of the Southern Finance Association.

Brief Contents

Contents

PART 4

Long-Term Asset and Liability Management

CHAPTER 13

Direct Foreign Investment 392

CHAPTER 14

Multinational Capital Budgeting 411

PART 5
Short-Term Asset and Liability Management

CHAPTER 20

Short-Term Financing 582

CHAPTER 21

International Cash Management 605

APPENDIX 21

Investing in a Portfolio of Currencies 629

Preface

Multinational corporations (MNCs) continue to expand their operations globally. They must not only be properly managed to apply their comparative advantages in foreign countries, but must also manage their exposure to many forms and sources of risk. These firms' exposure is especially pronounced in developing countries, where currency values and economies are volatile. As international conditions change, so do opportunities and risk. Those MNCs that are most capable of responding to changes in the international financial environment will be rewarded. The same can be said for today's students who may become the MNC managers of the future.

Intended Market

This text presumes an understanding of basic corporate finance. It is suitable for both undergraduate and master's level courses in international financial management. For master's courses, the more challenging questions, problems, and cases in each chapter are recommended, along with special projects.

Organization of the Text

This text is organized first to provide a background on the international environment and then to focus on the managerial aspects from a corporate perspective. MNC managers need to understand the international financial environment before they can manage within it.

The first two parts of the text provide the macroeconomic framework for the text. Part 1 (Chapters 1 to 5) introduces the major markets that facilitate international business. Part 2 (Chapters 6 to 8) describes relationships among exchange rates and economic variables and explains the forces that influence these relationships.

The remainder of the text provides a microeconomic framework, with a focus on the managerial aspects of international financial management. Part 3 (Chapters 9 to 12) explains the measurement and management of exchange rate risk. Part 4 (Chapters 13 to 18) describes the management of long-term assets and liabilities, including motives for direct foreign investment, multinational capital budgeting, country risk analysis, and capital structure decisions. Part 5 (Chapters 19 to 21) concentrates on MNCs' management of short-term assets and liabilities, including trade financing, other short-term financing, and international cash management.

Each chapter is self-contained so that professors can use classroom time to focus on the more comprehensive topics and rely on the text to cover any other concepts. Long-term asset management (chapters on direct foreign investment, multinational capital budgeting, multinational restructuring, and country risk analysis) is covered before long-term liability management (chapters on capital structure and long-term financing), because financing decisions depend on the investments that they support. Nevertheless, concepts are explained with an emphasis on how to integrate long-term assets with long-term liabilities. For example, multinational capital budgeting analysis demonstrates how the feasibility of a foreign project may depend on the financing mix available.

The strategic aspects, such as motives for direct foreign investment, are covered before the operational aspects such as short-term financing or investment. For professors who prefer to cover MNCs' management of short-term assets and liabilities before MNCs' management of long-term assets and liabilities, the parts can be rearranged because they are self-contained.

Approach of the Text

International Financial Management focuses upon management decisions that maximize the firm's value. The book recognizes that professors have unique styles for reinforcing key concepts within a course. Numerous methods of reinforcing these concepts are provided in the text so that professors can select the methods and features that fit their teaching styles. Key concepts are reinforced in the following ways:

1. PART-OPENING DIAGRAM: A diagram at the beginning of each part illustrates in general terms how the key concepts covered in that part relate to one another. This offers some intuition about the organization of chapters in that part.
2. OBJECTIVES: Key concepts are identified within a bulleted list of objectives at the beginning of each chapter.
3. EMPHASIS: Key concepts are thoroughly described in the chapter and supported by examples and illustrations.
4. MANAGING FOR VALUE: This feature illustrates how one or more key concepts relate to MNC valuation.
5. EXAMPLES: Numerous examples illustrate key concepts in each chapter.
6. USING THE WEB: Websites that provide useful information related to key concepts are identified.
7. SUMMARY: The key concepts are summarized at the end of the chapter in a bulleted list that corresponds to the list of objectives at the beginning of the chapter.
8. POINT COUNTER-POINT: A controversial topic is introduced, two opposing views are provided, and students must decide which view they support and explain why.
9. SELF TESTS: A "Self Test" at the end of each chapter challenges students on the key concepts. The answers to these questions are provided in Appendix A.
10. QUESTIONS AND APPLICATIONS: Many of the questions and other applications at the end of the chapter test students' knowledge of the key concepts in the chapter. Near the end of this section is the "Internet Application," which identifies a specific website related to key concepts and requires students to access the website to answer questions about the concepts.
11. CONTINUING CASE: At the end of each chapter, the continuing case allows students to use the key concepts to solve problems experienced by a firm called Blades, Inc. (a producer of roller blades). By working on cases related to the same MNC over a school term, students recognize how an MNC's decisions are integrated.
12. SMALL BUSINESS DILEMMA: The Small Business Dilemma at the end of each chapter places students in a position where they must use concepts introduced in the chapter to make decisions about a small MNC called Sports Exports Company.

13. INTEGRATIVE PROBLEM: The Integrative Problem at the end of each part integrates the key concepts across chapters within that part.
14. SUPPLEMENTAL CASES: Supplemental cases allow students to apply chapter concepts to a specific situation of an MNC. All supplemental cases are located in Appendix B at the end of the text.
15. RUNNING YOUR OWN MNC: This project (provided at **http://maduraxtra.swlearning.com**) allows each student to create a small international business and apply key concepts from each chapter to run the business throughout the school term.
16. ONLINE ANALYSIS OF AN MNC: This project (provided at **http://maduraxtra.swlearning.com**) allows each student to select an MNC and determine how the key concepts from each chapter apply to that MNC throughout the school term.
17. INTERNATIONAL INVESTING PROJECT: This project (provided at **http://maduraxtra.learning.com** and in Appendix D) allows students to simulate investing in stocks of MNCs and foreign companies and requires them to assess how the values of these stocks change during the school term in response to international economic conditions.
18. DISCUSSION IN THE BOARDROOM: This project (in Appendix E) allows students to play the role of managers or board members of a small MNC that that they created and make decisions about that firm.

Online Resources

Numerous online resources are available for both students and instructors:

- **Madura Xtra!** The Madura Xtra! website, available at **http://maduraxtra.swlearning.com,** provides numerous resources for students:
  - **Online Quizzes.** Online Quizzes reinforce student comprehension of chapter concepts. They provide answers with immediate feedback so that students know why the correct answer is correct. The quizzes may be sent to the student's instructor for grading or credit.
  - **PowerPoint Lecture Slides.** PowerPoint slides, created by Yee-Tien Fu of National Cheng-Chi University, are available.
  - **Plus** Running your Own MNC, Online Analysis of an MNC, and the International Investing Project!
- **Product support website.** The free product support website, available at **http://madura.swlearning.com,** contains supplements restricted to qualified instructors as well as updated links to websites listed in each chapter.

Other Supplements

The following supplements are available to students and instructors:
For the Student

- **South-Western Finance Resource Center (http://finance.swlearning.com)**. The South-Western Finance Resource Center provides unique features, customer service information, and links to book-related websites. Learn about valuable products and services to help with your finance studies, contact the finance editors, and more.

For the Instructor

- **Instructor's Manual/Test Bank.** The Instructor's Manual contains the chapter theme, topics to stimulate class discussion, and answers to end-of-chapter Questions, Case Problems, Continuing Cases (Blades, Inc.), Small Business Dilemmas, Integrative Problems, and Supplemental Cases. An expanded Test Bank contains a large set of questions in multiple choice or true/false format, including content questions as well as problems.

- **ExamView™ Computerized Testing.** The ExamView™ computerized testing program contains all of the questions in the printed Test Bank. ExamView™ is an easy-to-use test creation software compatible with Microsoft Windows. Instructors can add or edit questions, instructions, and answers and select questions by previewing them on the screen—selecting them randomly or by number. Instructors can also create and administer quizzes online, whether over the Internet, a local area network (LAN), or a wide area network (WAN).
- **PowerPoint Presentation Slides.** Revised for this edition by Yee-Tien Fu of National Cheng-Chi University, these PowerPoint slides are intended to enhance lectures and provide a guide for student note taking.
- **South-Western Finance Resource Center (http://finance.swlearning.com).** The South-Western Finance Resource Center provides unique features, including NewsWire: Finance in the News, FinanceLinks Online, and more, as well as customer service information and relevant product information and links. You may learn how to become an author with South-Western, request review copies, contact the finance editors, and more.

Acknowledgments

Several people have contributed to this textbook. First, the motivation to write the textbook was primarily due to encouragement from Professors Robert L. Conn (Miami University of Ohio), E. Joe Nosari and William Schrode (Florida State University), Anthony E. Scaperlanda (Northern Illinois University), and Richard A. Zuber (University of North Carolina at Charlotte).

Many of the revisions and expanded sections contained in this edition are due to comments and suggestions from students who used previous editions. In addition, many professors reviewed various editions of the text and had a major influence on its content and organization. All are acknowledged in alphabetical order:

Raj Aggarwal, *Kent State University*
Alan Alford, *Northeastern University*
H. David Arnold, *Auburn University*
Robert Aubey, *University of Wisconsin*
Bruce D. Bagamery, *Central Washington University*
James C. Baker, *Kent State University*
Gurudutt Baliga, *University of Delaware*
Laurence J. Belcher, *Stetson University*
Bharat B. Bhalla, *Fairfield University*
Rita Biswas, *State University of New York at Albany*
Steve Borde *(University of Central Florida)*
Sarah Bryant, *George Washington University*
Francisco Carrada-Bravo, *American Graduate School of International Management*
Andreas C. Christofi, *Azusa Pacific University*
Alan Cook, *Baylor University*
W. P. Culbertson, *Louisiana State University*
Maria E. DeBoyrie, *New Mexico State University*
Andrea L. DeMaskey, *Villanova University*
Mike Dosal, *SunTrust Bank (Orlando)*
Robert Driscill, *Ohio State University*
Larry Fauver, *University of Miami*
Paul Fenton, *Bishop's University*
Robert G. Fletcher, *California State University–Bakersfield*

Stuart Fletcher, *Appalachian State University*
Jennifer Foo, *Stetson University*
Robert D. Foster, *American Graduate School of International Management*
Hung-Gay Fung, *University of Baltimore*
Juli-Ann E. Gasper, *Texas A&M University*
Farhad F. Ghannadian, *Mercer University*
Kimberly Gleason, *Florida Atlantic University*
Deborah W. Gregory, *Bentley College*
Nicholas Gressis, *Wright State University*
Indra Guertler, *Babson College*
Ann M. Hackert, *Idaho State University*
Joel Harper, *Oklahoma State University*
John M. Harris, Jr., *Clemson University*
Andrea J. Heuson, *University of Miami*
Ghassem Homaifar, *Middle Tennessee State University*
Nathaniel Jackendoff, *Temple University*
Kurt R. Jesswein, *Texas A&M International*
Steve A. Johnson, *University of Texas at El Paso*
Manuel L. Jose, *University of Akron*
Rauv Kalra, *Morehead State University*
Ho-Sang Kang, *University of Texas at Dallas*
Frederick J. Kelly, *Seton Hall University*
Robert Kemp, *University of Virginia*
Coleman S. Kendall, *University of Illinois–Chicago*
Dara Khambata, *American University*
Suresh Krishman, *Pennsylvania State University*
Boyden E. Lee, *New Mexico State University*
Jeong W. Lee, *University of North Dakota*
Charmen Loh, *Rider University*
Carl Luft, *DePaul University*
K. Christopher Ma, *KCM Investment Co.*
Richard D. Marcus, *University of Wisconsin–Milwaukee*
Anna D. Martin, *Fairfield University*
Ike Mathur, *Washington University*
Wendell McCulloch, Jr., *California State University–Long Beach*
Carl McGowan, *University of Michigan at Flint*
Fraser McHaffie *(Marietta College)*
Stuart Michelson, *Stetson University*
Edward Omberg, *San Diego State University*
Prasad Padmanabhan, *San Diego State University*
Ali M. Parhizgari, *Florida International University*
Anne Perry, *American University*
Larry Prather, *East Tennessee State University*
Frances A. Quinn, *Merrimack College*
S. Ghon Rhee, *University of Rhode Island*
William J. Rieber, *Butler University*
Ashok Robin, *Rochester Institute of Technology*
Tom Rosengarth, *Westminster College*
Kevin Scanlon, *Indiana University at South Bend*
Oliver Schnusenberg, *University of North Florida*
Jacobus T. Severiens, *Kent State University*
Peter Sharp, *California State University–Sacramento*
Dilip K. Shome, *Virginia Tech University*
Joseph Singer, *University of Missouri–Kansas City*
Naim Sipra, *University of Colorado at Denver*
Jacky So, *Southern Illinois University at Edwardsville*
Luc Soenen, *California Polytechnic State University–San Luis Obisbo*
Ahmad Sohrabian, *California State Polytechnic University–Pomona*
Caroline Spencer, *Dowling College*
Angelo Tarallo, *Ramapo College*
Amir Tavakkol, *Kansas State University*
Stephen G. Timme, *Georgia State University*
Mahmoud S. Wahab, *University of Hartford*
Ralph C. Walter III, *Northeastern Illinois University*
Elizabeth Webbink, *Rutgers University*
Ann Marie Whyte, *University of Central Florida*
Marilyn Wiley, *Florida Atlantic University*
Rohan Williamson, *Georgetown University*
Larry Wolken, *Texas A&M University*
Glenda Wong, *DePaul University*
Mike Yarmuth, *Sullivan University*
Yeomin Yoon, *Seton Hall University*
David Zalewski, *Providence College*
Emilio Zarruk, *Florida Atlantic University*
Stephen Zera, *California State University–San Marcos*

Beyond the suggestions provided by reviewers, this edition also benefited from the input of many people from outside the United States who were willing to share their views about international financial management. In addition, I thank my colleagues at Florida Atlantic University, including John Bernardin, Juan Dempere, Antoine Giannetti, Kim Gleason, and Emilio Zarruk. I also thank Joel Harper (Oklahoma State University), Victor Kalafa (Cross Country, Inc.), Oliver Schnusenberg (University of North Florida), and Alan Tucker (Pace University) for their suggestions.

I acknowledge the help and support from the people at South-Western, including Mike Reynolds (Executive Editor) and Trish Taylor (Senior Developmental Editor). I wish to thank Kaila Wyllys at G&S Typesetters for her production services. Special thanks are due to Amy McGuire (Production Editor) and Pat Lewis (Copy Editor) for their efforts to ensure a quality final product.

Finally, I wish to thank my wife, Mary, and my parents, Arthur and Irene Madura, for their moral support.

Jeff Madura
Florida Atlantic University

PART 1

The International Financial Environment

Part 1 (Chapters 1 through 5) provides an overview of the multinational corporation (MNC) and the environment in which it operates. Chapter 1 explains the goals of the MNC, along with the motives and risks of international business. Chapter 2 describes the international flow of funds between countries. Chapter 3 describes the international financial markets and how these markets facilitate ongoing operations. Chapter 4 explains how exchange rates are determined, while Chapter 5 provides a background on the currency futures and options markets. Managers of MNCs must understand the international environment described in these chapters in order to make proper decisions.

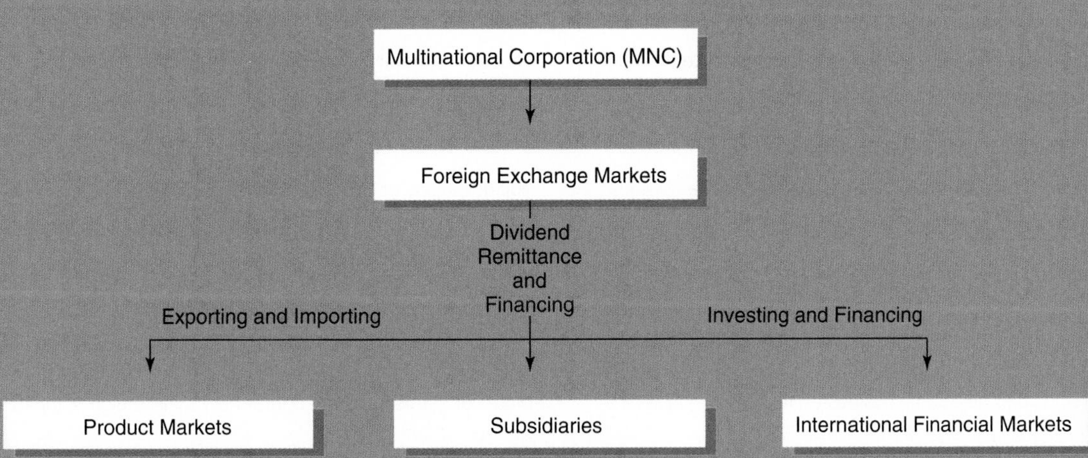

CHAPTER 1

Multinational Financial Management: An Overview

The commonly stated goal of a firm is to maximize its value and thereby maximize shareholder wealth. This goal is applicable not only to firms that focus on domestic business, but also to firms that focus on international business. In fact, many firms have expanded their international business as a means of enhancing their value. Since foreign markets can be distinctly different from local markets, they create opportunities for improving the firm's cash flows. Many barriers to entry into foreign markets have been reduced or removed recently, thereby encouraging firms to pursue international business (producing and/or selling goods in foreign countries). Consequently, many firms have evolved into multinational corporations (MNCs), which are defined as firms that engage in some form of international business. Their managers conduct international financial management, which involves international investing and financing decisions that are intended to enhance the value of the MNC.

Initially, firms may merely attempt to export products to a particular country or import supplies from a foreign manufacturer. Over time, however, many of them recognize additional foreign opportunities and eventually establish subsidiaries in foreign countries. Dow Chemical, IBM, Nike, and many other firms have more than half of their assets in foreign countries. Some businesses, such as ExxonMobil, American Brands, and Colgate-Palmolive, commonly generate more than half of their sales in foreign countries. A prime example is the Coca-Cola Co., which distributes its products in more than 160 countries and uses 40 different currencies. Over 60 percent of its total annual operating income is typically generated outside the United States.

An understanding of international financial management is crucial not only for the largest MNCs with numerous foreign subsidiaries but also for other firms that conduct international business. Even smaller U.S. firms commonly generate more than 20 percent of their sales in foreign markets, including AMSCO International (Pennsylvania), Ferro (Ohio), Interlake (Illinois), Medtronic (Minnesota), Sybron (Wisconsin), and Synoptics (California). These U.S. firms that conduct international business tend to focus on the niches that have made them successful in the United States. They tend to penetrate specialty markets where they will not have to compete with large firms that could capitalize on economies of scale. While some small firms have established subsidiaries, many of them penetrate foreign markets through exports. Seventy-five percent of U.S. firms that export have fewer than 100 employees.

International financial management is important even to companies that have no international business because these companies must recognize how their foreign competitors will be affected by movements in exchange rates, foreign interest rates, labor costs, and inflation. Such economic characteristics can affect the foreign competitors' costs of production and pricing policies.

Companies must also recognize how domestic competitors that obtain foreign supplies or foreign financing will be affected by economic conditions in foreign countries. If these domestic competitors are able to reduce their costs by capitalizing on opportunities in international markets, they may be able to reduce their prices without reducing their profit margins. This could allow them to increase market share at the expense of the purely domestic companies.

This chapter provides a background on the goals of an MNC and the potential risk and returns from engaging in international business.

The specific objectives of this chapter are to:

- identify the main goal of the MNC and potential conflicts with that goal,
- describe the key theories that justify international business, and
- explain the common methods used to conduct international business.

Goal of the MNC

The commonly accepted goal of an MNC is to maximize shareholder wealth. Developing a goal is necessary because all decisions should contribute to its accomplishment. Some MNCs based outside the United States, however, tend to focus more on satisfying the respective goals of their governments, banks, or employees than on maximizing shareholder wealth.

The focus of this text is on MNCs whose parents wholly own any foreign subsidiaries, which means that the U.S. parent is the sole owner of the subsidiaries. This is the most common form of ownership of U.S.-based MNCs, and it enables financial managers throughout the MNC to have a single goal of maximizing the value of the entire MNC instead of maximizing the value of any particular foreign subsidiary.

Conflicts with the MNC Goal

It has often been argued that managers of a firm may make decisions that conflict with the firm's goal to maximize shareholder wealth. For example, a decision to establish a subsidiary in one location versus another may be based on the location's appeal to a particular manager rather than on its potential benefits to shareholders. A decision to expand may be determined by a manager's desire to make the division grow in order to receive more responsibility and compensation. When a firm has only one owner who is also the sole manager, such a conflict of goals does not occur. However, when a corporation's shareholders differ from its managers, a conflict of goals can exist. This conflict is often referred to as the **agency problem**.

The costs of ensuring that managers maximize shareholder wealth (referred to as *agency costs*) are normally larger for MNCs than for purely domestic firms for several reasons. First, MNCs with subsidiaries scattered around the world may experience larger agency problems because monitoring managers of distant subsidiaries in foreign countries is more difficult. Second, foreign subsidiary managers raised in different cultures may not follow uniform goals. Third, the sheer size of the larger MNCs can also create large agency problems. Fourth, some non-U.S. managers tend to downplay the short-term effects of decisions, which may result in decisions for foreign subsidiaries of the U.S.-based MNCs that are inconsistent with maximizing shareholder wealth.

Financial managers of an MNC with several subsidiaries may be tempted to make decisions that maximize the values of their respective subsidiaries. This objective will not necessarily coincide with maximizing the value of the overall MNC.

EXAMPLE

A subsidiary manager obtained financing from the parent firm (headquarters) to develop and sell a new product. The manager estimated the costs and benefits of the project from the subsidiary's perspective and determined that the project was feasible. However, the manager neglected to realize that any earnings from this project remitted to the parent would be heavily taxed by the host government. The estimated after-tax benefits received by the parent were more than offset by the cost of financing the project. While the subsidiary's individual value was enhanced, the MNC's overall value was reduced.

If financial managers are to maximize the wealth of their MNC's shareholders, they must implement policies that maximize the value of the overall MNC rather than the value of their respective subsidiaries. Many MNCs require major decisions by subsidiary managers to be approved by the parent. However, it is difficult for the parent to monitor all decisions made by subsidiary managers.

Impact of Management Control

The magnitude of agency costs can vary with the management style of the MNC. A centralized management style, as illustrated in the top section of Exhibit 1.1, can reduce agency costs because it allows managers of the parent to control foreign subsidiaries and therefore reduces the power of subsidiary managers. However, the parent's managers may make poor decisions for the subsidiary if they are not as informed as subsidiary managers about financial characteristics of the subsidiary.

Alternatively, an MNC can use a decentralized management style, as illustrated in the bottom section of Exhibit 1.1. This style is more likely to result in higher agency costs because subsidiary managers may make decisions that do not focus on maximizing the value of the entire MNC. Yet, this style gives more control to those managers who are closer to the subsidiary's operations and environment. To the extent that subsidiary managers recognize the goal of maximizing the value of the overall MNC and are compensated in accordance with that goal, the decentralized management style may be more effective.

Given the obvious tradeoff between centralized and decentralized management styles, some MNCs attempt to achieve the advantages of both styles. That is, they allow subsidiary managers to make the key decisions about their respective operations, but the parent's management monitors the decisions to ensure that they are in the best interests of the entire MNC.

How the Internet Facilitates Management Control. The Internet is making it easier for the parent to monitor the actions and performance of its foreign subsidiaries.

Exhibit 1.1 Management Styles of MNCs

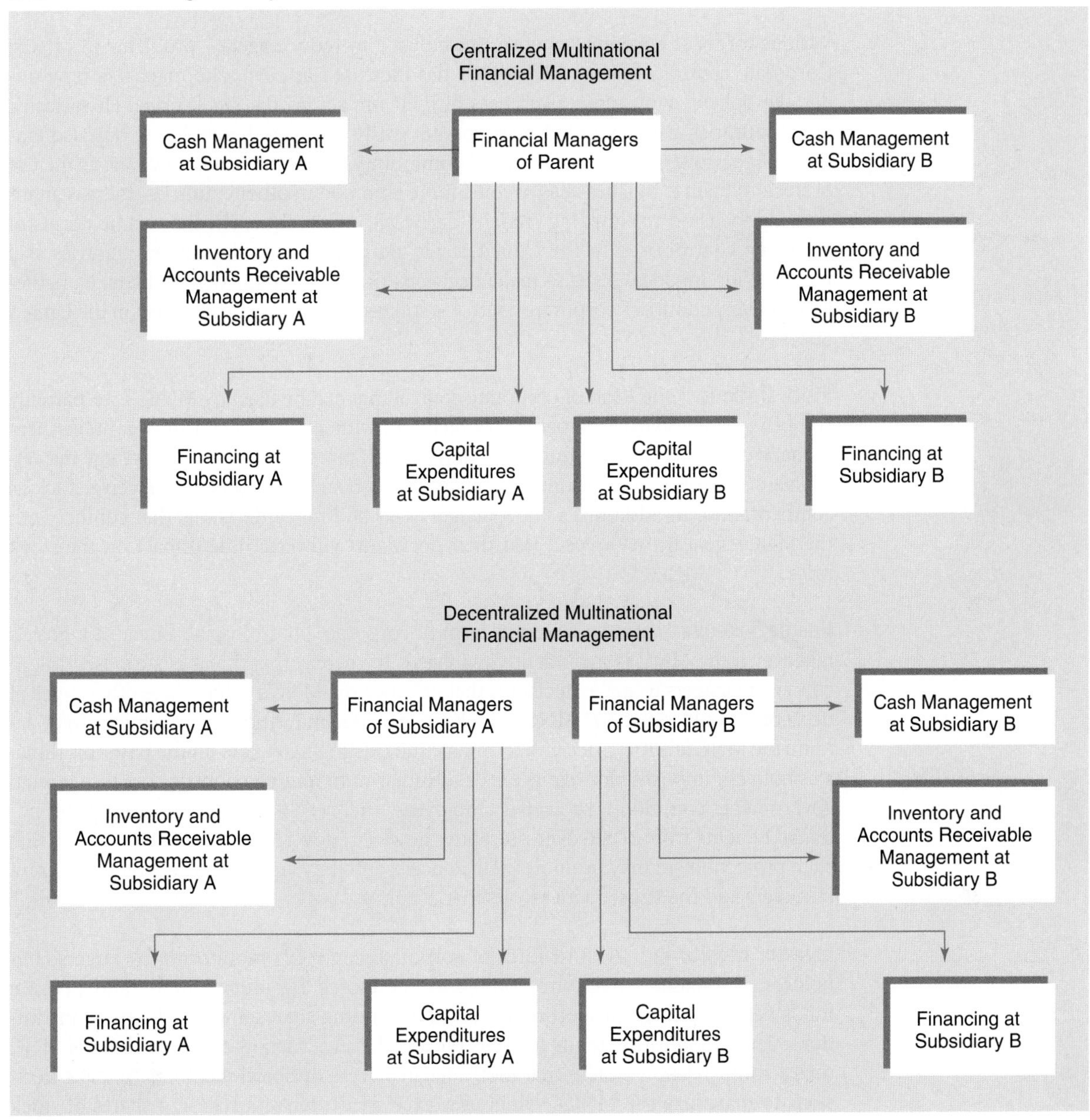

EXAMPLE

The parent of Jersey, Inc., has subsidiaries in Australia and Italy. The subsidiaries are in different time zones, so communicating frequently by phone is inconvenient and expensive. In addition, financial reports and designs of new products or plant sites cannot be easily communicated over the phone. The Internet allows the foreign subsidiaries to e-mail updated information in a standardized format to avoid language problems and to send images of financial reports and product designs. The parent can easily track inventory, sales, expenses, and earnings of each subsidiary on a weekly or monthly basis. Thus, the use of the Internet can reduce agency costs due to international business.

Impact of Corporate Control

Various forms of corporate control can be used to reduce agency problems in MNCs. Corporate control of U.S.-based MNCs has increased as corporate managers now undertake policies with more awareness of their impact on the stock price. Historically, other countries have expected managers to satisfy not just shareholders, but also employees, the government, and the local community. In recent years, however, as the use of stock to finance business has become more common in other countries, there is an increasing focus on maximizing shareholder wealth. Consequently, the various forms of corporate control used in the United States are being adopted in other countries as a means of forcing local firms to make decisions that satisfy their shareholders. Nonetheless, in many countries corporate control is still used to a lesser degree than in the United States.

Stock Options. One form of corporate control that can be used by MNCs is to partially compensate the board members and executives with stock, which can encourage them to make decisions that maximize the MNC's stock price. However, this strategy may effectively control only decisions by managers and board members who receive stock as compensation. In addition, some managers may still make decisions that conflict with the MNC's goal if they expect that their decisions will have little impact on the stock price.

Hostile Takeover Threat. A second form of corporate control is the threat of a hostile takeover if the MNC is inefficiently managed. In theory, this threat is supposed to encourage managers to make decisions that enhance the MNC's value, since other types of decisions would cause the MNC's stock price to decline. Another firm might then acquire the MNC at a low price and terminate the existing managers. In the past, this threat was not very imposing for managers of subsidiaries in foreign countries because foreign governments commonly protected employees, thereby effectively eliminating the potential benefits from a takeover. Recently, however, governments have recognized that such protectionism may promote inefficiencies, and they are now more willing to accept takeovers and the subsequent layoffs that occur.

Investor Monitoring. A third form of corporate control is monitoring by large shareholders. U.S.-based MNCs are commonly monitored by mutual funds and pension funds because a large proportion of their outstanding shares are held by these institutions. Their monitoring tends to focus on broad issues such as ensuring that the MNC uses a compensation system that motivates managers or board members to make decisions to maximize the MNC's value; uses excess cash for repurchasing shares of stock rather than investing in questionable projects; and does not insulate itself from the threat of a takeover (by implementing anti-takeover amendments, for example). An MNC whose decisions appear inconsistent with maximizing shareholder wealth will be subjected to shareholder activism as pension funds and other large institutional shareholders lobby for management changes or other changes. MNCs that have been subjected to various forms of shareholder activism include Eastman Kodak, IBM, and Sears Roebuck.

Like U.S. mutual funds and pension funds, foreign-owned banks also maintain large stock portfolios (unlike U.S. commercial banks, which do not use deposited funds to purchase stocks). The foreign banks are large and hold a sufficient proportion of shares of numerous firms (including some U.S.-based MNCs) to have some influence on key corporate policies. Their additional role as a lender to many of these firms enhances their ability to monitor corporate policies. To date, however, these banks have not played a major role in corporate control. In general, they do not attempt to intervene unless a particular firm is experiencing major financial problems.

Constraints Interfering with the MNC's Goal

When financial managers of MNCs attempt to maximize their firm's value, they are confronted with various constraints that can be classified as environmental, regulatory, or ethical in nature.

Environmental Constraints. Each country enforces its own environmental constraints. Some countries may enforce more of these restrictions on a subsidiary whose parent is based in a different country. Building codes, disposal of production waste materials, and pollution controls are examples of restrictions that force subsidiaries to incur additional costs. Many European countries have recently imposed tougher antipollution laws as a result of severe pollution problems.

Regulatory Constraints. Each country also enforces its own regulatory constraints pertaining to taxes, currency convertibility, earnings remittance, employee rights, and other policies that can affect cash flows of a subsidiary established there. Because these regulations can influence cash flows, financial managers must consider them when assessing policies. Also, any change in these regulations may require revision of existing financial policies, so financial managers should monitor the regulations for any potential changes over time.

To recognize the potential impact of regulations, consider the regulation of employee rights. Although it is understandable that every country attempts to ensure employee rights, some countries may prevent maximization of firm value if the protection of employees is excessive.

EXAMPLE

Eurenza, a manufacturing firm in Eastern Europe, is struggling financially. The firm's stock price has declined in the last two years, as its sales have declined while its expenses remain very high. One problem is that many of its employees are unproductive. Eurenza would like to lay off some of these employees, a move that would reduce its expenses and increase earnings. Its existing shareholders would be better off if the employees were laid off. Yet, the government will not allow Eurenza to lay off employees, even if they are not productive. The government is concerned that such a complete focus on shareholder wealth will be detrimental to the labor force.

Ideally, managers attempt to reward employees for efficient production so that the goals of labor and shareholders will be closely aligned.

Ethical Constraints. There is no consensus standard of business conduct that applies to all countries. A business practice that is perceived to be unethical in one country may be totally ethical in another. For example, U.S.-based MNCs are well aware that certain business practices that are accepted in some less developed countries would be illegal in the United States. Bribes to governments in order to receive special tax breaks or other favors are common in some countries. A recent report presented to Congress estimated that U.S. firms lost out on at least $36 billion of international business transactions because of bribes paid by foreign competitors. The MNCs face a dilemma. If they do not participate in such practices, they may be at a competitive disadvantage. Yet, if they do participate, their reputations will suffer in countries that do not approve of such practices.

Managing within the Constraints. Some U.S.-based MNCs have made the costly choice to refrain from business practices that are legal in certain foreign countries but not legal in the United States. Thus, they follow a worldwide code of ethics. This may enhance their worldwide credibility, which can increase global demand for their products. Recently, McKinsey & Co. found that investors assigned a higher value to firms that exhibit high corporate governance standards and are likely to obey ethical constraints. The premiums that investors would pay for these firms averaged 12 percent in North America, 20 to 25 percent in Asia and Latin America, and more than 30 percent in Europe.

Theories of International Business

The commonly held theories as to why firms become motivated to expand their business internationally are (1) the theory of comparative advantage, (2) the imperfect markets theory, and (3) the product cycle theory. The three theories overlap to a degree and can complement each other in developing a rationale for the evolution of international business.

Theory of Comparative Advantage

Multinational business has generally increased over time. Part of this growth is due to the heightened realization that specialization by countries can increase production efficiency. Some countries, such as Japan and the United States, have a technology advantage, while other countries, such as Jamaica, Mexico, and South Korea, have an advantage in the cost of basic labor. Since these advantages cannot be easily transported, countries tend to use their advantages to specialize in the production of goods that can be produced with relative efficiency. This explains why countries such as Japan and the United States are large producers of computer components, while countries such as Jamaica and Mexico are large producers of agricultural and handmade goods.

When a country specializes in some products, it may not produce other products, so trade between countries is essential. This is the argument made by the classical theory of **comparative advantage**. Comparative advantages allow firms to penetrate foreign markets. Many of the Virgin Islands, for example, specialize in tourism and rely completely on international trade for most products. Although these islands could produce some goods, it is more efficient for them to specialize in tourism. That is, the islands are better off using some revenues earned from tourism to import products rather than attempting to produce all the products that they need.

Imperfect Markets Theory

Countries differ with respect to resources available for the production of goods. Yet, even with such comparative advantages, the volume of international business would be limited if all resources could be easily transferred among countries. If markets were perfect, factors of production (except land) would be mobile and freely transferable. The unrestricted mobility of factors would create equality in costs and returns and remove the comparative cost advantage, the rationale for international trade and investment. However, the real world suffers from **imperfect market** conditions where factors of production are somewhat immobile. There are costs and often restrictions related to the transfer of labor and other resources used for production. There may also be restrictions on transferring funds and other resources among countries. Because markets for the various resources used in production are "imperfect," firms often capitalize on a foreign country's resources. Imperfect markets provide an incentive for firms to seek out foreign opportunities.

Product Cycle Theory

One of the more popular explanations as to why firms evolve into MNCs is the **product cycle theory**. According to this theory, firms become established in the home market as a result of some perceived advantage over existing competitors, such as a need by the market for at least one more supplier of the product. Because information about markets and competition is more readily available at home, a firm is likely to establish itself first in its home country. Foreign demand for the firm's product will initially be accommodated by exporting. As time passes, the firm may feel the only way to retain its advantage over competition in foreign countries is to produce the product in foreign markets, thereby reducing its transportation costs. The competition in the foreign markets may increase as other producers become more familiar with the firm's product. The firm may develop strategies to prolong the foreign demand for its product. A common approach is to attempt to differentiate the product so that other competitors cannot offer exactly the same product. These phases of the cycle are illustrated in Exhibit 1.2. As an example, 3M Co. uses one new product to penetrate foreign markets. After entering the market, it expands its product line.

Exhibit 1.2
International Product Life Cycle

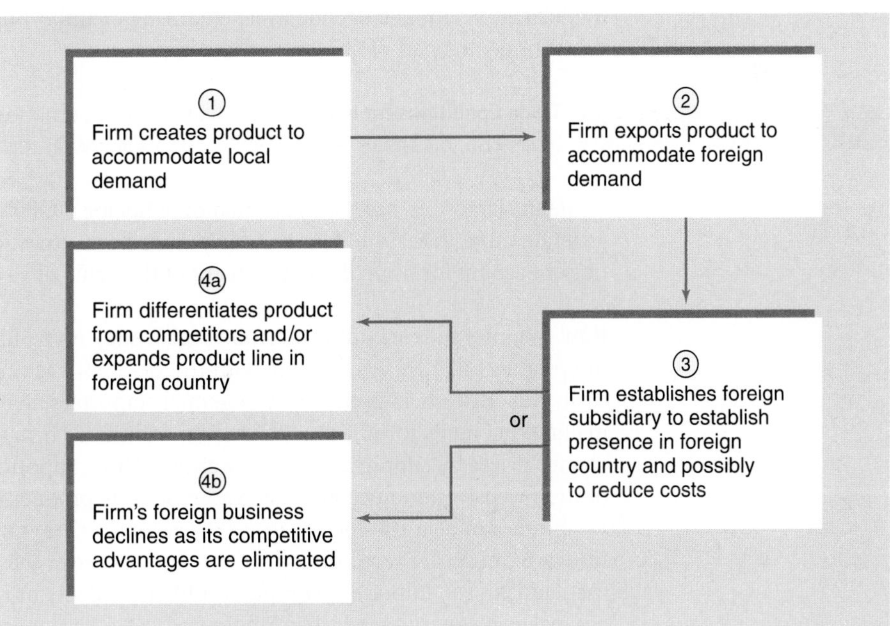

There is more to the product cycle theory than is summarized here. This discussion merely suggests that, as a firm matures, it may recognize additional opportunities outside its home country. Whether the firm's foreign business diminishes or expands over time will depend on how successful it is at maintaining some advantage over its competition. The advantage could represent an edge in its production or financing approach that reduces costs or an edge in its marketing approach that generates and maintains a strong demand for its product.

International Business Methods

Firms use several methods to conduct international business. The most common methods are these:

- International trade
- Licensing
- Franchising
- Joint ventures
- Acquisitions of existing operations
- Establishing new foreign subsidiaries

Each method is discussed in turn, with some emphasis on its risk and return characteristics.

International Trade

International trade is a relatively conservative approach that can be used by firms to penetrate markets (by exporting) or to obtain supplies at a low cost (by importing). This approach entails minimal risk because the firm does not place any of its capital at risk. If the firm experiences a decline in its exporting or importing, it can normally reduce or discontinue this part of its business at a low cost.

USING THE WEB

Trade Conditions for Industries An outlook of international trade conditions for each of several industries is provided at http://www.ita.doc.gov/td/industry/otea.

Many large U.S.-based MNCs, including Boeing, DuPont, General Electric, and IBM, generate more than $4 billion in annual sales from exporting. Nonetheless, small businesses account for more than 20 percent of the value of all U.S. exports.

How the Internet Facilitates International Trade. Many firms use their websites to list the products that they sell, along with the price for each product. This allows them to easily advertise their products to potential importers anywhere in the world without mailing brochures to various countries. In addition, a firm can add to its product line or change prices by simply revising its website. Thus, importers need only monitor an exporter's website periodically to keep abreast of its product information.

Firms can also use their websites to accept orders online. Some products such as software can be delivered directly to the importer over the Internet in the form of a file that lands in the importer's computer. Other products must be shipped, but the Internet makes it easier to track the shipping process. An importer can transmit its order for products via e-mail to the exporter. The exporter's warehouse fills orders. When the warehouse ships the products, it can send an e-mail message to the importer and to the exporter's headquarters. The warehouse may even use technology to monitor its inventory of products so that suppliers are automatically notified to send more supplies once the inventory is reduced to a specific level. If the exporter uses multiple warehouses, the Internet allows them to work as a network so that if one warehouse cannot fill an order, another warehouse will.

Licensing

Licensing obligates a firm to provide its technology (copyrights, patents, trademarks, or trade names) in exchange for fees or some other specified benefits. For example, AT&T and Verizon Communications have licensing agreements to build and operate parts of India's telephone system. Sprint Corp. has a licensing agreement to develop telecommunications services in the United Kingdom. Eli Lilly & Co. has a licensing agreement to produce drugs for Hungary and other countries. IGA, Inc., which operates more than 3,000 supermarkets in the United States, has a licensing agreement to operate supermarkets in China and Singapore. Licensing allows firms to use their technology in foreign markets without a major investment in foreign countries and without the transportation costs that result from exporting. A major disadvantage of licensing is that it is difficult for the firm providing the technology to ensure quality control in the foreign production process.

How the Internet Facilitates Licensing. Some firms with an international reputation use their brand name to advertise products over the Internet. They may use manufacturers in foreign countries to produce some of their products subject to their specifications.

EXAMPLE

Springs, Inc., has set up a licensing agreement with a manufacturer in the Czech Republic. When Springs receives orders for its products from customers in Eastern Europe, it relies on this manufacturer to produce and deliver the products ordered. This expedites the delivery process and may even allow Springs to have the products manufactured at a lower cost than if it produced them itself.

Franchising

Franchising obligates a firm to provide a specialized sales or service strategy, support assistance, and possibly an initial investment in the franchise in exchange for periodic fees. For example, McDonald's, Pizza Hut, Subway Sandwiches, Blockbuster Video, and Dairy Queen have franchises that are owned and managed by local residents in many foreign countries. Like licensing, franchising allows firms to penetrate foreign markets without a major investment in foreign countries. The recent relaxation of barriers in foreign countries throughout Eastern Europe and South America has resulted in numerous franchising arrangements.

Joint Ventures

A **joint venture** is a venture that is jointly owned and operated by two or more firms. Many firms penetrate foreign markets by engaging in a joint venture with firms that reside in those markets. Most joint ventures allow two firms to apply their respective comparative advantages in a given project. For example, General Mills, Inc., joined in a venture with Nestlé SA, so that the cereals produced by General Mills could be sold through the overseas sales distribution network established by Nestlé.

Xerox Corp. and Fuji Co. (of Japan) engaged in a joint venture that allowed Xerox Corp. to penetrate the Japanese market and allowed Fuji to enter the photocopying business. Sara Lee Corp. and SBC Communications have engaged in joint ventures with Mexican firms to gain entry to Mexico's markets. Joint ventures between automobile manufacturers are numerous, as each manufacturer can offer its technological advantages. General Motors has ongoing joint ventures with automobile manufacturers in several different countries, including Hungary and the former Soviet states.

Acquisitions of Existing Operations

Firms frequently acquire other firms in foreign countries as a means of penetrating foreign markets. For example, American Express recently acquired offices in London, while Procter & Gamble purchased a bleach company in Panama. Acquisitions allow firms to have full control over their foreign businesses and to quickly obtain a large portion of foreign market share.

EXAMPLE

In 2001, Home Depot acquired the second largest home improvement business in Mexico. This acquisition was Home Depot's first in Mexico, but allowed it to expand its business after establishing name recognition there. Home Depot is expanding in Mexico just as it did in Canada throughout the 1990s.

An acquisition of an existing corporation is subject to the risk of large losses, however, because of the large investment required. In addition, if the foreign operations perform poorly, it may be difficult to sell the operations at a reasonable price.

Some firms engage in partial international acquisitions in order to obtain a stake in foreign operations. This requires a smaller investment than full international acquisitions and therefore exposes the firm to less risk. On the other hand, the firm will not have complete control over foreign operations that are only partially acquired.

Establishing New Foreign Subsidiaries

Firms can also penetrate foreign markets by establishing new operations in foreign countries to produce and sell their products. Like a foreign acquisition, this method requires a large investment. Establishing new subsidiaries may be preferred to foreign acquisitions because the operations can be tailored exactly to the firm's needs. In addition, a smaller investment may be required than would be needed to purchase existing operations. However, the firm will not reap any rewards from the investment until the subsidiary is built and a customer base established.

Summary of Methods

The methods of increasing international business extend from the relatively simple approach of international trade to the more complex approach of acquiring foreign firms or establishing new subsidiaries. Any method of increasing international business that requires a direct investment in foreign operations normally is referred to as a **direct foreign investment (DFI)**. International trade and licensing usually are not considered to be DFI because they do not involve direct investment in foreign operations. Franchising and joint ventures tend to require some investment in foreign operations, but to a limited degree. Foreign acquisitions and the establishment of new foreign subsidiaries require substantial investment in foreign operations and represent the largest portion of DFI.

Many MNCs use a combination of methods to increase international business. Motorola and IBM, for example, have substantial direct foreign investment, but also derive some of their foreign revenue from various licensing agreements, which require less DFI to generate revenue.

EXAMPLE

The evolution of Nike began in 1962, when Phil Knight, a business student at Stanford's business school, wrote a paper on how a U.S. firm could use Japanese technology to break the German dominance of the athletic shoe industry in the United States. After graduation, Knight visited the Unitsuka Tiger shoe company in Japan. He made a licensing agreement with that company to produce a shoe that he sold in the United States under the name Blue Ribbon Sports (BRS). In 1972, Knight exported his shoes to Canada. In 1974, he expanded his operations into Australia. In 1977, the firm licensed factories in Taiwan and Korea to produce athletic shoes and then sold the shoes in Asian countries. In 1978, BRS became Nike, Inc., and began to export shoes to Europe and South America. As a result of its exporting and its direct foreign investment, Nike's international sales reached $1 billion by 1992 and were about $5 billion by 2004.

International Opportunities

http://

Visit http://lcweb2.loc.gov/frd/cs/cshome.html, a page of the Library of Congress's website, for detailed studies of 85 countries.

Because of possible cost advantages from producing in foreign countries or possible revenue opportunities from demand by foreign markets, the growth potential becomes much greater for firms that consider international business. Exhibit 1.3 illustrates how a firm's growth can be affected by foreign investment and financing opportunities.

Investment Opportunities

Exhibit 1.3 shows hypothetical investment opportunities for both a purely domestic firm and an MNC with similar operating characteristics. Each horizontal step represents a specific project. Each project is expected to generate a marginal return to the firm.

Moving from left to right in Exhibit 1.3, the projects are prioritized according to marginal return. Assume that these projects are independent of each other and that their expected returns as shown have been adjusted to account for risk. With these assumptions, a firm would select the project with the highest marginal return as the most feasible and would undertake this project. Then, it would undertake the proposed project with the next highest marginal return, and so on. The marginal returns on projects for the MNC are above those of the purely domestic firm because the MNC has an expanded opportunity set of possible projects from which to select.

Exhibit 1.3
Cost-Benefit Evaluation for Purely Domestic Firms versus MNCs

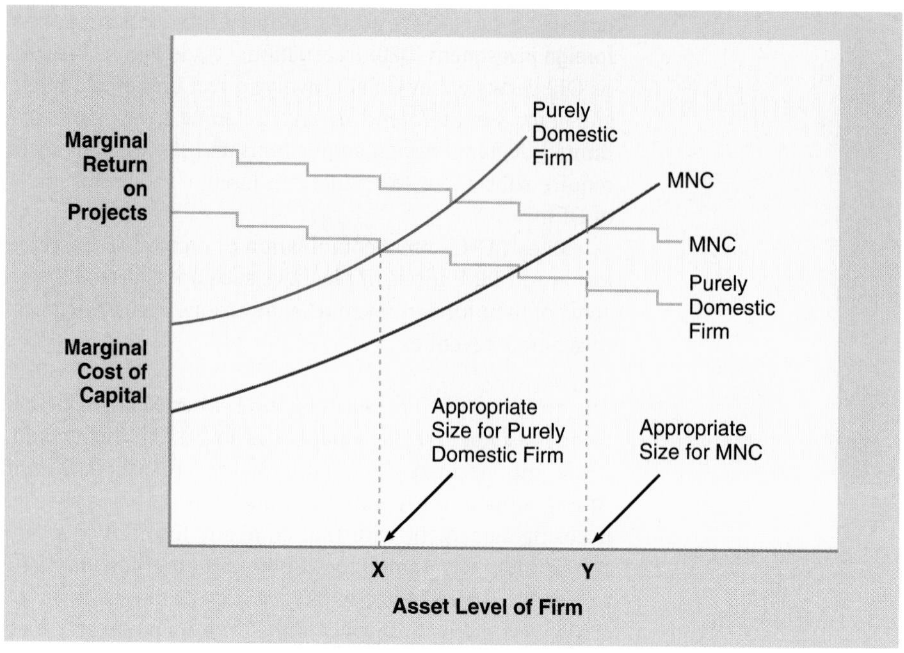

Financing Opportunities

Exhibit 1.3 also displays cost-of-capital curves for the MNC and the purely domestic firm. The exhibit shows the cost of capital increasing with asset size for either type of firm. This is based on the premise that creditors or shareholders require a higher rate of return as the firm grows. Growth in asset size requires increased debt, which forces the firm to increase its periodic interest payments to creditors. Consequently, the firm has a greater probability of being unable to meet its debt obligations. To the extent that creditors and shareholders require a higher return for a more highly indebted firm, the cost of capital to the firm rises with its volume of assets. The exhibit shows that the MNC can obtain capital funding at a lower cost than the purely domestic firm can. This advantage is due to the MNC's larger opportunity set of funding sources around the world.

Once the marginal cost of financing projects exceeds the marginal return on projects, the firm should not pursue such projects. As shown in Exhibit 1.3, a purely domestic firm will continue to accept projects up to point X. After that point, the marginal cost of additional projects exceeds the expected benefits.

When foreign resources, funds, and potential projects are considered, the firm's volume of feasible projects is greater. The MNC's projects become unacceptable after point Y. This optimal level of assets exceeds that of the purely domestic firm due to cost advantages and opportunities in foreign countries. This comparison illustrates why firms may desire to become internationalized.

The concept illustrated in Exhibit 1.3 has several limitations. In some cases, a firm may not have any feasible foreign opportunities. In addition, an argument could be made that foreign projects are riskier than domestic projects and therefore result in a higher cost of capital. Firms that diversify their business internationally, however, reduce the sensitivity of their performance to the home country conditions. For example, while a U.S. recession may lower the U.S. demand for a firm's product, the non-U.S. demand may be unaffected. The optimal size of a given firm will typically be greater if that firm considers foreign opportunities.

Opportunities in Europe

Over time, economic and political conditions can change, creating new opportunities in international business. Four events have had a major impact on opportunities in Europe: (1) the Single European Act, (2) the removal of the Berlin Wall, (3) the inception of the euro, and (4) the expansion of the European Union.

Single European Act. In the late 1980s, industrialized countries in Europe agreed to make regulations more uniform and to remove many taxes on goods traded between these countries. This agreement, supported by the Single European Act of 1987, was followed by a series of negotiations among the countries to achieve uniform policies by 1992. The act allows firms in a given European country greater access to supplies from firms in other European countries.

Many firms, including European subsidiaries of U.S.-based MNCs, have capitalized on the agreement by attempting to penetrate markets in border countries. By producing more of the same product and distributing it across European countries, firms are now better able to achieve economies of scale. Best Foods (now part of Unilever) was one of many MNCs that increased efficiency by streamlining manufacturing operations as a result of the reduction in barriers.

Removal of the Berlin Wall. In 1989, another historic event occurred in Europe when the Berlin Wall separating East Germany from West Germany was torn down. This was symbolic of new relations between East Germany and West Germany and was followed by the reunification of the two countries. In addition, it encouraged free enterprise in all Eastern European countries and the privatization of businesses that were owned by the government. A key motive for pursuing opportunities in Eastern Europe was the lack of products available there. Coca-Cola Co., Reynolds Metals Co., General Motors, and numerous other MNCs aggressively pursued expansion in Eastern Europe as a result of the momentum toward free enterprise.

While the Single European Act of 1987 and the move toward free enterprise in Eastern Europe offered new opportunities to MNCs, they also posed new risks. Firms doing business in Europe were subjected to more competition. As in other historical examples of deregulation, the more efficient firms have benefited at the expense of less efficient firms.

Inception of the Euro. In 1999, several European countries adopted the euro as their currency for business transactions between these countries. The euro was phased in as a currency for other transactions during 2001 and completely replaced the currencies of the participating countries on January 1, 2002. Consequently, only the euro is used for transactions in these countries, so firms (including European subsidiaries of U.S.-based MNCs) no longer face the costs and risks associated with converting one currency to another. The single currency system in most of Europe should definitely encourage more trade among European countries. In addition, the use of a single currency allows for a single monetary policy in those countries. Therefore, in assessing the economic growth in Europe, MNCs can focus on only one monetary policy rather than the country-specific monetary policies that were prevalent before 1999.

USING THE WEB

Updated Euro Information An update of information on the euro is provided at http://www.ecb.int.

Expansion of the European Union. In the late 1990s, the European Union (EU) made plans to allow more countries to become members. In 2004, the plans became a reality, as Cyprus, the Czech Republic, Estonia, Hungary, Latvia, Lithuania, Malta, Poland, Slovakia, and Slovenia were admitted to the EU. These countries continued to use their own currencies, but may be able to adopt the euro as their currency in the future if they meet specified guidelines regarding budget deficits and other financial conditions. Nevertheless, their admission into the EU is relevant because restrictions on their trade with Western Europe will be reduced. Since wages in these countries are substantially lower than in Western European countries, many MNCs have established manufacturing plants there to produce products and export them to Western Europe. The governments in some of the new EU countries have reduced corporate tax rates and offered other incentives to encourage MNCs to establish facilities there.

Opportunities in Latin America

Like Europe, Latin America offers more business opportunities now because of a reduction in restrictions.

NAFTA. As a result of the North American Free Trade Agreement (NAFTA) of 1993, trade barriers between the United States and Mexico were eliminated. Some U.S. firms attempted to capitalize on this by exporting goods that had previously been restricted by barriers to Mexico. Other firms established subsidiaries in Mexico to produce their goods at a lower cost than was possible in the United States and then sell the goods in the United States. The removal of trade barriers essentially allowed U.S. firms to penetrate product and labor markets that previously had not been accessible.

The removal of trade barriers between the United States and Mexico allows Mexican firms to export some products to the United States that were previously restricted. Thus, U.S. firms that produce these goods are now subject to competition from Mexican exporters. Given the low cost of labor in Mexico, some U.S. firms have lost some of their market share. The effects are most pronounced in the labor-intensive industries.

Within a month after the NAFTA accord, the momentum for free trade continued with a GATT (General Agreement on Tariffs and Trade) accord. This accord was the conclusion of trade negotiations from the so-called Uruguay Round that had begun seven years earlier. It called for the reduction or elimination of trade restrictions on specified imported goods over a ten-year period across 117 countries. The accord has generated more international business for firms that had previously been unable to penetrate foreign markets because of trade restrictions.

Removal of Investment Restrictions. Many Latin American countries have made it easier for MNCs to engage in direct foreign investment there by allowing MNCs more ownership rights if they acquire a local company. MNCs with technological advantages are now able to capitalize on their comparative advantages in Latin America. The flow of direct foreign investment into Latin America has not only been beneficial to MNCs, but has also improved the level of technology there.

Opportunities in Asia

MNCs have commonly identified Asia as having tremendous business potential because of its large population base. Yet, MNCs had difficulty pursuing growth opportunities in Asia because of excessive restrictions on investment there. Some of the restrictions were explicit, while others were implicit (major bureaucratic delays).

Removal of Investment Restrictions. During the 1990s, many Asian countries reduced the restrictions imposed on investment by MNCs based in other countries. Consequently, MNCs can now acquire companies in Asia more easily or create licensing agreements with Asian companies without government interference.

Since the reduction in restrictions, U.S. firms such as PepsiCo, Coca-Cola Co., Apple Computer, and International Paper have increased their international business in Asia. Many U.S. firms view China as the country with the most potential for growth. General Motors, Ford Motor Co., Procter & Gamble, and AT&T have invested billions of dollars in China to capitalize on the expected growth.

Many U.S. breweries have expanded into China to capitalize on the large increase in the demand for beer in that market. Pabst Blue Ribbon, which has lost much of its market share in the United States, has been very successful in China. Heilman Brewing has also had success with its Lone Star Beer, as the American cowboy image has been a useful marketing tool in China. Miller High Life has expanded into China through a licensing agreement, while Anheuser-Busch (producer of Budweiser) has partially acquired a Chinese beer company.

http://

This website provides a background on the Asian crisis: http://www.asienhaus.org/links/crisis.htm

Impact of the Asian Crisis. In 1997, several Asian countries including Indonesia, Malaysia, and Thailand experienced severe economic problems. Many local companies went bankrupt, and concerns about the countries caused financial outflows of funds. These outflows left limited funds to support the economy. Interest rates increased because of the outflow of funds; this placed even more strain on firms that needed to borrow money. This so-called Asian crisis lingered into 1998 and adversely affected numerous U.S.-based MNCs that conducted business in these countries.

Yet, the crisis also created international business opportunities. The values of local firms were depressed, and Asian governments reduced restrictions on acquisitions, which allowed MNCs from the United States and other countries to pursue acquisitions in the Asian countries. Some U.S.-based MNCs were able to purchase local companies at a relatively low cost, improve the efficiency of the firms, and benefit from future economic growth. For example, during the Asian crisis in 1997–1998, South Korea's large conglomerate firms (called *chaebols*) experienced financial problems and began to sell many of their business units to obtain cash. General Electric, Procter & Gamble, and Coca-Cola Co. were among the U.S.-based MNCs that acquired business units in Asia during this period.

Exposure to International Risk

Although international business can reduce an MNC's exposure to its home country's economic conditions, it usually increases an MNC's exposure to (1) exchange rate movements, (2) foreign economic conditions, and (3) political risk. Each of these forms of exposure is briefly described here and is discussed in more detail in later sections of the text. MNCs that plan to pursue international business should consider these potential risks.

Exposure to Exchange Rate Movements

Most international business results in the exchange of one currency for another to make payment. Since exchange rates fluctuate over time, the cash outflows required to make payments change accordingly. Consequently, the number of units of a firm's home currency needed to purchase foreign supplies can change even if the suppliers have not adjusted their prices.

Similarly, even if an exporter denominates its exports in its own currency, exchange rate fluctuations may affect the foreign demand for the firm's product. When the home currency strengthens, products denominated in that currency become more expensive to foreign customers, which may cause a decline in demand and, therefore, a decline in cash inflows.

For MNCs with subsidiaries in foreign countries, exchange rate fluctuations affect the value of cash flows remitted by subsidiaries to the parent. When the parent's home currency is strong, the remitted funds will convert to a smaller amount of the home currency.

http://

Visit the Fed's data bank at http://research.stlouisfed.org/fred2 for numerous economic and financial time series, e.g., on balance of payment statistics, interest rates, and foreign exchange rates.

Exposure to Foreign Economies

When MNCs enter foreign markets to sell products, the demand for these products is dependent on the economic conditions in those markets. Thus, the cash flows of the MNC are subject to foreign economic conditions. For example, U.S.-based MNCs such as Nike and 3M Co. that conducted business in Asia were adversely affected by the Asian crisis in 1998, as the weak Asian economies reduced the Asian demand for products. In the 2000–2002 period, U.S. firms such as DuPont and IBM experienced lower-than-expected cash flows because of weak European economies.

Exposure to Political Risk

When MNCs establish subsidiaries in foreign countries, they become exposed to **political risk**, which arises because the host government or the public may take actions that affect the MNC's cash flows (political risk is often viewed as a subset of **country risk**, which is discussed in detail in a later chapter). For example, the host government may impose higher taxes on U.S.-based subsidiaries in retaliation for actions by the U.S. government. Alternatively, the host government may decide to buy out a subsidiary at whatever price it decides is fair. Milder forms of risk include actions by the host government that place foreign firms at a disadvantage. For example, the Mexican government was slow to respond to the request of United Parcel Service (UPS) to use its large vehicles for providing delivery services.

Terrorism and War. One form of an exposure to political risk is terrorism. A terrorist attack can affect a firm's operations or its employees. The September 11, 2001 terrorist attack on the World Trade Center reminded MNCs around the world of the exposure to terrorism. MNCs from more than 50 countries were directly affected because they occupied space in the World Trade Center. In addition, other MNCs were also affected because they engage in trade or have direct foreign investment in foreign countries that may also experience an increase in terrorism.

Wars can also adversely affect an MNC's cash flows. During the war in Iraq in 2003, anti-American protests against the war in countries in the Middle East and elsewhere forced some U.S.-based MNCs to temporarily shut down their operations in some countries. In addition, the protests led to a decline in the demand for products produced by some U.S.-based MNCs.

Overview of an MNC's Cash Flows

Most U.S.-based MNCs have some local business within the United States, similar to other purely domestic firms. Because of the MNCs' international operations, however, their cash flow streams differ from those of purely domestic firms. Exhibit 1.4 shows cash flow diagrams for three common profiles of MNCs. Profile A in this exhibit reflects an MNC whose only international business is international trade. Thus, its international cash flows result from either paying for imported supplies or receiving payment in exchange for products that it exports.

Profile B reflects an MNC that engages in both international trade and some international arrangements (which can include international licensing, franchising, or joint ventures). Any of these international arrangements can require cash outflows by the MNC in foreign countries to comply with the arrangement, such as the expenses incurred from transferring technology or funding partial investment in a franchise or joint venture. These arrangements generate cash flows to the MNC in the form of fees for services (such as technology or support assistance) it provides.

Profile C reflects an MNC that engages in international trade, international arrangements, and direct foreign investment. This type of MNC has one or more foreign subsidiaries. There can be cash outflows from the U.S. parent to its foreign subsidiaries in the form of invested funds to help finance the operations of the foreign subsidiaries. There are also cash flows from the foreign subsidiaries to the U.S. parent in the form of remitted earnings and fees for services provided by the parent, which can all be classified as remitted funds from the foreign subsidiaries. In general, the cash outflows associated with international business by the U.S. parent are to pay for imports, to comply with its international arrangements, or to support the creation or expansion of foreign subsidiaries. Conversely, it will receive cash flows in the form of payment for its exports, fees for the services it provides within its international arrangements, and remitted funds from the foreign subsidiaries.

Many MNCs initially conduct international business in the manner illustrated by Profile A. Some of these MNCs develop international arrangements and foreign subsidiaries over time; others are content to focus on exporting or importing as their only method of international business. Although the three profiles vary, they all show how international business generates cash flows. These cash flows represent the cash inflows received by the MNC minus the cash outflows.

Exhibit 1.4
Cash Flow Diagrams for MNCs

Valuation Model for an MNC

The value of an MNC is relevant to its shareholders and its debtholders. When managers make decisions that maximize the value of the firm, they maximize shareholder wealth (assuming that the decisions are not intended to maximize the wealth of debtholders at the expense of shareholders). Since international financial management should be conducted with the goal of increasing the value of the MNC, it is useful to review some basics of valuation. There are numerous methods of valuing an MNC, and some methods will lead to the same valuation. The one valuation method described here can be used to understand the key factors that affect an MNC's value in a general sense.

MANAGING FOR VALUE

Yahoo!'s Decision to Expand Internationally

Many U.S.-based MNCs have penetrated foreign markets in recent years. Like domestic projects, foreign projects involve an investment decision and a financing decision. The investment decision to engage in a foreign project results in revenue and expenses that are denominated in a foreign currency. The decision of how to finance a foreign project affects the MNC's cost of capital. Most foreign projects are assessed on the basis of their potential to attract new demand and therefore generate additional cash flows. Consider Yahoo!, which has expanded its portal services in numerous foreign countries. For example, it has established main pages in Canada, Latin America, Europe, and Asia. It generates cash inflows from these foreign projects in the form of advertising fees paid by local merchants who purchase space on Yahoo!'s website. It incurs cash outflows from these foreign projects in the form of expenses incurred from providing information. It needs funding to finance these foreign projects and hopes that its cash flows will generate a return that exceeds the cost of financing.

Every foreign project considered by Yahoo! is subject to conditions specific to that country, resulting in a unique estimate of net cash flows. Every foreign project is also subject to a cost of financing that is specific to the country. Thus, Yahoo!'s decision regarding a possible project in Argentina may not necessarily be the same as its decision regarding a similar project in Australia.

Once an MNC such as Yahoo! has decided to pursue a foreign project, it must continually consider a set of multinational finance decisions, such as these:

- How to forecast exchange rates of the currencies it uses.
- How to assess its exposure to exchange rate movements.
- Whether and how to hedge its exposure to exchange rate movements.
- How to pursue additional foreign expansion.
- How to finance its foreign expansion.
- How to manage its international cash and liquidity.

These are the key multinational finance decisions that are made by Yahoo! and other MNCs, and they are therefore given much attention in this text. To the extent that Yahoo!'s managers can make multinational finance decisions that increase the overall present value of its future cash flows, they can maximize the firm's value.

Before financial managers of Yahoo! and other MNCs make these multinational finance decisions, they need to understand how international financial markets can facilitate their business and must recognize the forces that affect exchange rates. These macroeconomic concepts, which are discussed in the first two parts of the text, set the stage for understanding how the performance of any business is influenced by local country conditions. Then, in the last three parts of the text, multinational finance decisions are examined.

Domestic Model

Before modeling an MNC's value, consider the valuation of a purely domestic firm that does not engage in any foreign transactions. The value (V) of a purely domestic firm in the United States is commonly specified as the present value of its expected cash flows, where the discount rate used reflects the weighted average cost of capital and represents the required rate of return by investors:

$$V = \sum_{t=1}^{n} \left\{ \frac{[E(CF_{\$,t})]}{(1+k)^t} \right\}$$

where $E(CF_{\$,t})$ represents expected cash flows to be received at the end of period t, n represents the number of periods into the future in which cash flows are received, and k represents the required rate of return by investors. The dollar cash flows in period t represent funds received by the firm minus funds needed to pay expenses or taxes, or to reinvest in the firm (such as an investment to replace old computers or machinery). The expected cash flows are estimated from knowledge about various existing projects as well as other projects that will be implemented in the future. A firm's decisions about how it should invest funds to expand its business can affect its expected future cash flows and therefore can affect the firm's value. Holding other factors constant, an increase in expected cash flows over time should increase the value of the firm.

The required rate of return (k) in the denominator of the valuation equation represents the cost of capital (including both the cost of debt and the cost of equity) to the firm and is essentially a weighted average of the cost of capital based on all of the firm's projects. As the firm makes decisions that affect its cost of debt or its cost of equity for one or more projects, it affects the weighted average of its cost of capital and therefore affects the required rate of return. For example, if the firm's credit rating is suddenly lowered, its cost of capital will probably increase and so will its required rate of return. Holding other factors constant, an increase in the firm's required rate of return will reduce the value of the firm, because expected cash flows must be discounted at a higher interest rate. Conversely, a decrease in the firm's required rate of return will increase the value of the firm because expected cash flows are discounted at a lower required rate of return.

Valuing International Cash Flows

An MNC's value can be specified in the same manner as a purely domestic firm's. However, consider that the expected cash flows generated by a U.S.-based MNC's parent in the period t may be coming from various countries and may therefore be denominated in different foreign currencies. The foreign currency cash flows will be converted into dollars. Thus, the expected dollar cash flows to be received at the end of period t are equal to the sum of the products of cash flows denominated in each currency j times the expected exchange rate at which currency j could be converted into dollars by the MNC at the end of period t.

$$E(CF_{\$,t}) = \sum_{j=1}^{m} [E(CF_{j,t}) \times E(ER_{j,t})]$$

where $CF_{j,t}$ represents the amount of cash flow denominated in a particular foreign currency j at the end of period t, and $ER_{j,t}$ represents the exchange rate at which the foreign currency (measured in dollars per unit of the foreign currency) can be converted to dollars at the end of period t.

For example, an MNC that does business in two currencies could measure its expected dollar cash flows in any period by multiplying the expected cash flow in each currency times the expected exchange rate at which that currency could be converted to dollars and then summing those two products. If the firm does not use various techniques (discussed later in the text) to hedge its transactions in foreign currencies, the expected exchange rate in a given period would be used in the valuation equation to estimate the corresponding expected exchange rate at which the foreign currency can be converted into dollars in that period. Conversely, if the MNC hedges these transactions, the exchange rate at which it can hedge would be used in the valuation equation.

It may help to think of an MNC as a portfolio of currency cash flows, one for each currency in which it conducts business. The expected dollar cash flows derived from each of those currencies can be combined to determine the total expected dollar cash flows in each future period. The present value of those cash flows serves as the estimate of the MNC's value. It is easier to derive an expected dollar cash flow value for each currency before combining the cash flows among currencies within a given period, because each currency's cash flow amount must be converted to a common unit (the dollar) before combining the amounts.

EXAMPLE

To illustrate how the dollar cash flows of an MNC can be measured, consider a U.S. firm that had expected cash flows of \$100,000 from local business and 1,000,000 Mexican pesos from business in Mexico at the end of period t. Assuming that the peso's value is expected to be \$.09, the expected dollar cash flows are:

$$\begin{aligned} E(CF_{\$,t}) &= [E(CF_{j,t}) \times E(ER_{j,t})] \\ &= [\$100{,}000] + [1{,}000{,}000 \text{ pesos } \times (\$.09)] \\ &= [\$100{,}000] + \$[90{,}000] \\ &= \$190{,}000. \end{aligned}$$

The cash flows of \$100,000 from U.S. business were already denominated in U.S. dollars and therefore did not have to be converted.

The MNC's dollar cash flows at the end of every period in the future can be estimated in the same manner. Then, the MNC's value can be measured by determining the present value of the expected dollar cash flows, which is the sum of the discounted dollar cash flows that are expected in all future periods. This example uses only two currencies, but if the MNC had transactions involving 40 currencies, the same process could be used. The expected dollar cash flows for each of the 40 currencies would be estimated separately for each future period. The expected dollar cash flows for each of the 40 currencies within each period could then be combined to derive the total dollar cash flows per period. Finally, the cash flows in each period would be discounted to derive the value of the MNC.

The general formula for the dollar cash flows received by an MNC in any particular period can be written as:

$$E(CF_{\$,t}) = \sum_{j=1}^{m} [E(CF_{j,t}) \times E(ER_{j,t})]$$

The value of an MNC can be more clearly differentiated from the value of a purely domestic firm by substituting the expression $[E(CF_{j,t}) \times E(ER_{j,t})]$ for $E(CF_{\$,t})$ in the valuation model, as shown here:

$$V = \sum_{t=1}^{n} \left\{ \frac{\sum_{j=1}^{m} [E(CF_{j,t}) \times E(ER_{j,t})]}{(1 + k)^t} \right\}$$

where $CF_{j,t}$ represents the cash flow denominated in a particular currency (including dollars), and $ER_{j,t}$ represents the exchange rate at which the MNC can convert the foreign currency at the end of period t. Thus, the value of an MNC can be affected by a change in expectations about $CF_{j,t}$ or $ER_{j,t}$. Only those cash flows that are to be received by the MNC's parent in the period of concern should be counted. To avoid double-counting, cash flows of the MNC's subsidiaries are considered in the valuation model only when they reflect transactions with the U.S. parent. Thus, any expected cash flows received by foreign subsidiaries should not be counted in the valuation equation until they are expected to be remitted to the parent.

The denominator of the valuation model for the MNC remains unchanged from the original valuation model for the purely domestic firm. However, recognize that the weighted average cost of capital for the MNC is based on funding some projects that reflect business in different countries. Thus, any decision by the MNC's parent that affects the cost of its capital supporting projects in a specific country can affect its weighted average cost of capital (and its required rate of return) and therefore can affect its value.

In general, the valuation model shows that an MNC's value can be affected by forces that influence the amount of its cash flows in a particular currency (CF_j), the exchange rate at which that currency is converted into dollars (ER_j), or the MNC's weighted average cost of capital (k).

Impact of Financial Management and International Conditions on Value

U.S.-based MNCs recognize that they may increase their value by increasing their dollar cash flows or by reducing their cost of capital. Hence, their challenge is to make decisions that will accomplish one or both of these objectives. An MNC's financial decisions include how much business to conduct in each country and how much financing to obtain in each currency. Its financial decisions determine its exposure to the international environment. If it conducts very little international business, its potential for enhancing its value is limited, but so is its vulnerability to changes in exchange rate movements or other international conditions. Conversely, if an MNC pursues substantial international business in markets where there are opportunities, it may be able to substantially increase its dollar cash flows and therefore increase its value, but it will be highly exposed to exchange rate effects, economic conditions, and political conditions in these markets.

The uncertainty surrounding a U.S.-based MNC's dollar cash flows is influenced by the composition of its international business, as well as by the amount of that business. Exchange rates, economic conditions, and political conditions are much more volatile in some countries than in others. Therefore, two MNCs of the same size and in the same industry may have the same volume of foreign business, but one of them might be less risky because it conducts business in more stable countries.

Though an MNC does not have control over a country's exchange rate, economic conditions, or political conditions, it can control its degree of exposure to those conditions with its financial management. Two MNCs of the same size and in the same industry could have the exact same composition of international business, but one of them might be less risky because it makes financial decisions that reduce its exposure to exchange rates, economic conditions, or political conditions.

Organization of the Text

The organization of the chapters in this text is shown in Exhibit 1.5. Chapters 2 through 8 discuss international markets and conditions from a macroeconomic perspective, focusing on external forces that can affect the value of an MNC. Though financial managers may not have control over these forces, they do have some control over their degree of exposure to these forces. These macroeconomic chapters provide the background necessary to make financial decisions.

Chapters 9 through 21 take a microeconomic perspective and focus on how the financial management of an MNC can affect its value. Financial decisions by MNCs are commonly classified as either investing decisions or financing decisions. In general, investing decisions by an MNC tend to affect the numerator of the valuation model because such decisions affect expected cash flows. In addition, if investing decisions by the MNC's parent alter the firm's weighted average cost of capital, they may also affect the

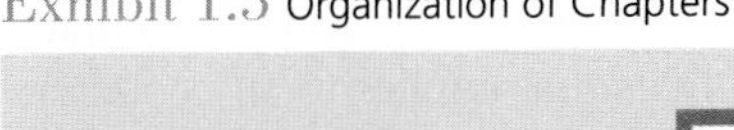
Exhibit 1.5 Organization of Chapters

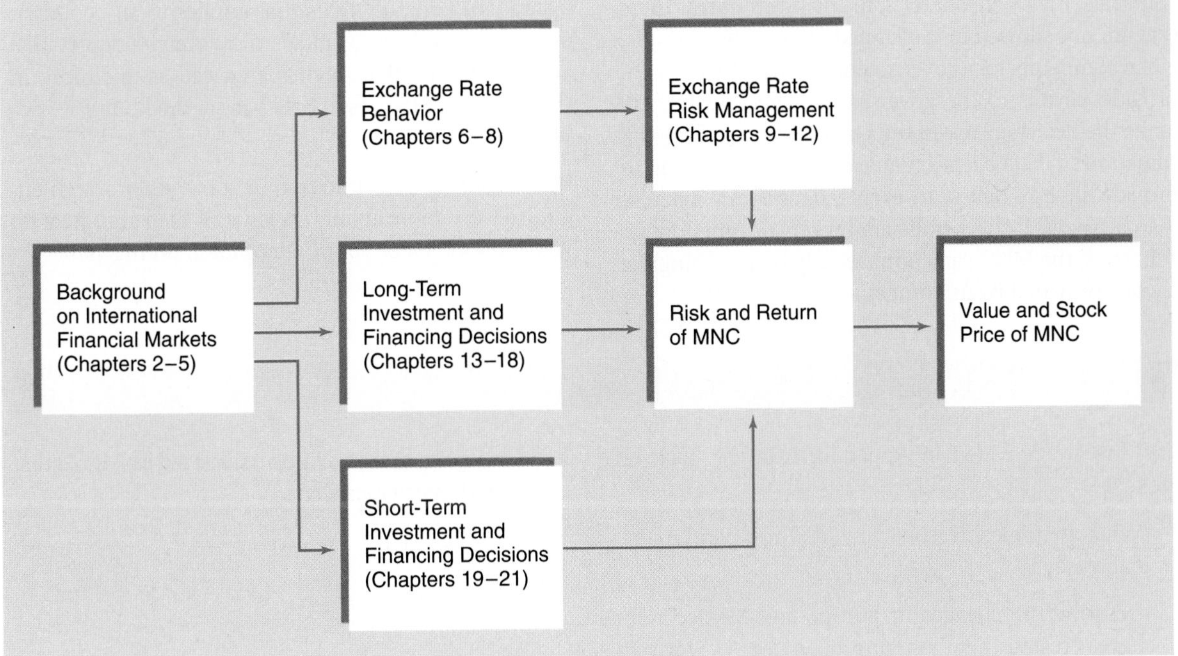

denominator of the valuation model. Long-term financing decisions by an MNC's parent tend to affect the denominator of the valuation model because they affect the MNC's cost of capital.

SUMMARY

- The main goal of an MNC is to maximize shareholder wealth. When managers are tempted to serve their own interests instead of those of shareholders, an agency problem exists. Managers also face environmental, regulatory, and ethical constraints that can conflict with the goal of maximizing shareholder wealth.
- International business is justified by three key theories. The theory of comparative advantage suggests that each country should use its comparative advantage to specialize in its production and rely on other countries to meet other needs. The imperfect markets theory suggests that because of imperfect markets, factors of production are immobile, which encourages countries to specialize based on the resources they have. The product cycle theory suggests that after firms are established in their home countries, they commonly expand their product specialization in foreign countries.
- The most common methods by which firms conduct international business are international trade, licensing, franchising, joint ventures, acquisitions of foreign firms, and formation of foreign subsidiaries. Methods such as licensing and franchising involve little capital investment but distribute some of the profits to other parties. The acquisition of foreign firms and formation of foreign subsidiaries require substantial capital investments but offer the potential for large returns.

POINT COUNTER-POINT

Should an MNC Reduce Its Ethical Standards to Compete Internationally?

Point Yes. When a U.S.-based MNC competes in some countries, it may encounter some business norms there that are not allowed in the United States. For example, when competing for a government contract, firms might provide payoffs to the government officials who will make the decision. Yet, in the United States, a firm will sometimes take a client on an expensive golf outing or provide skybox tickets to events. This is no different than a payoff. If the payoffs are bigger in some foreign countries, the MNC can compete only by matching the payoffs provided by its competitors.

Counter-Point No. A U.S.-based MNC should maintain a standard code of ethics that applies to any country, even if it is at a disadvantage in a foreign country that allows activities that might be viewed as unethical. In this way, the MNC establishes more credibility worldwide.

Who Is Correct? Use InfoTrac or some other search engine to learn more about this issue. Which argument do you support? Offer your own opinion on this issue.

SELF TEST

Answers are provided in Appendix A at the back of the text.

1. What are typical reasons why MNCs expand internationally?
2. Describe the changes in Europe and Mexico that have created new opportunities for U.S.-based MNCs.
3. Identify the more obvious risks faced by MNCs that expand internationally.

QUESTIONS AND APPLICATIONS

1. **Agency Problems of MNCs.**

   a. Explain the agency problem of MNCs.

   b. Why might agency costs be larger for an MNC than for a purely domestic firm?

2. **Comparative Advantage.**

   a. Explain how the theory of comparative advantage relates to the need for international business.

   b. Explain how the product cycle theory relates to the growth of an MNC.

3. **Imperfect Markets.**

   a. Explain how the existence of imperfect markets has led to the establishment of subsidiaries in foreign markets.

   b. If perfect markets existed, would wages, prices, and interest rates among countries be more similar or less similar than under conditions of imperfect markets? Why?

4. **International Opportunities.**

   a. How does access to international opportunities affect the size of corporations?

   b. Describe a scenario in which the size of a corporation is not affected by access to international opportunities.

   c. Explain why MNCs such as Coca-Cola and PepsiCo, Inc., still have numerous opportunities for international expansion.

5. **International Opportunities Due to the Internet.**

   a. What factors cause some firms to become more internationalized than others?

   b. Offer your opinion on why the Internet may result in more international business.

6. **Impact of the Euro.** Explain how the adoption of the euro as the single currency by European countries could be beneficial to MNCs based in Europe and to MNCs based in the United States.

7. **Benefits and Risks of International Business.** As an overall review of this chapter, identify possible reasons for growth in international business. Then, list the various disadvantages that may discourage international business.

8. **Motives of an MNC.** Describe constraints that interfere with an MNC's objective.

9. **Centralization and Agency Costs.** Would the agency problem be more pronounced for Berkely Corp., which has its parent company make most major decisions for its foreign subsidiaries, or Oakland Corp., which uses a decentralized approach?

10. **Global Competition.** Explain why more standardized product specifications across countries can increase global competition.

11. **Impact of the Euro on U.S. Subsidiaries.** McCanna Corp. has a French subsidiary that produces wine and exports to various European countries. Explain how the subsidiary's business may have been affected since the conversion of many European currencies into a single European currency (the euro) in 1999.

12. **Macro versus Micro Topics.** Review the table of contents and indicate whether each of the chapters from Chapter 2 through Chapter 21 has a macro or micro perspective.

13. **Methods Used to Conduct International Business.** Duve, Inc., desires to penetrate a foreign market with either a licensing agreement with a foreign firm or by acquiring a foreign firm. Explain the differences in potential risk and return between a licensing agreement with a foreign firm and the acquisition of a foreign firm.

14. **International Business Methods.** Snyder Golf Co., a U.S. firm that sells high-quality golf clubs in the United States, wants to expand internationally by selling the same golf clubs in Brazil.

    a. Describe the tradeoffs that are involved for each method (such as exporting, direct foreign investment, etc.) that Snyder could use to achieve its goal.

    b. Which method would you recommend for this firm? Justify your recommendation.

15. **Impact of Political Risk.** Explain why political risk may discourage international business.

16. **Impact of September 11.** Following the terrorist attack on the United States, the valuations of many MNCs declined by more than 10 percent. Explain

why the expected cash flows of MNCs were reduced, even if they were not directly hit by the terrorist attacks.

ADVANCED QUESTIONS

17. **International Joint Venture.** Anheuser-Busch, the producer of Budweiser and other beers, has recently expanded into Japan by engaging in a joint venture with Kirin Brewery, the largest brewery in Japan. The joint venture enables Anheuser-Busch to have its beer distributed through Kirin's distribution channels in Japan. In addition, it can utilize Kirin's facilities to produce beer that will be sold locally. In return, Anheuser-Busch provides information about the American beer market to Kirin.

    a. Explain how the joint venture can enable Anheuser-Busch to achieve its objective of maximizing shareholder wealth.

    b. Explain how the joint venture can limit the risk of the international business.

    c. Many international joint ventures are intended to circumvent barriers that normally prevent foreign competition. What barrier in Japan is Anheuser-Busch circumventing as a result of the joint venture? What barrier in the United States is Kirin circumventing as a result of the joint venture?

    d. Explain how Anheuser-Busch could lose some of its market share in countries outside Japan as a result of this particular joint venture.

18. **Impact of Eastern European Growth.** The managers of Loyola Corp. recently had a meeting to discuss new opportunities in Europe as a result of the recent integration among Eastern European countries. They decided not to penetrate new markets because of their present focus on expanding market share in the United States. Loyola's financial managers have developed forecasts for earnings based on the 12 percent market share (defined here as its percentage of total European sales) that Loyola currently has in Eastern Europe. Is 12 percent an appropriate estimate for next year's Eastern European market share? If not, does it likely overestimate or underestimate the actual Eastern European market share next year?

19. **Valuation of an MNC.** Birm Co., based in Alabama, considers several international opportunities in Europe that could affect the value of its firm. The valuation of its firm is dependent on four factors: (1) expected cash flows in dollars, (2) expected cash flows in euros that are ultimately converted into dollars, (3) the rate at which it can convert euros to dollars, and (4) Birm's weighted average cost of capital. For each opportunity, identify the factors that would be affected.

    a. Birm plans a licensing deal in which it will sell technology to a firm in Germany for $3,000,000; the payment is invoiced in dollars, and this project has the same risk level as its existing businesses.

    b. Birm plans to acquire a large firm in Portugal that is riskier than its existing businesses.

    c. Birm plans to discontinue its relationship with a U.S. supplier so that it can import a small amount of supplies (denominated in euros) at a lower cost from a Belgian supplier.

    d. Birm plans to export a small amount of materials to Ireland that are denominated in euros.

20. **Assessing Motives for International Business.** Fort Worth, Inc., specializes in manufacturing some basic parts for sports utility vehicles that are produced and sold in the United States. Its main advantage in the United States is that its production is efficient and less costly than that of some other unionized manufacturers. It has a substantial market share in the United States. Its manufacturing process is labor-intensive. It pays relatively low wages compared to U.S. competitors, but has guaranteed the local workers that their job positions will not be eliminated for the next 30 years. It hired a consultant to determine whether it should set up a subsidiary in Mexico, where the parts would be produced. The consultant suggested that Fort Worth should expand for the following reasons. Offer your opinion on whether the consultant's reasons are logical.

    a. Theory of Competitive Advantage: There are not many SUVs sold in Mexico, so Fort Worth, Inc., would not have to face much competition there.

    b. Imperfect Markets Theory: Fort Worth cannot easily transfer workers to Mexico, but it can establish a subsidiary there in order to penetrate a new market.

    c. Product Cycle Theory: Fort Worth has been successful in the United States. It has limited growth opportunities because it already controls much of the U.S. market for the parts it produces. Thus, the natural next step is to conduct the same business in a foreign country.

d. Exchange Rate Risk: The exchange rate of the peso has weakened recently, so this would allow Fort Worth to build a plant at a very low cost (by exchanging dollars for the cheap pesos to build the plant).

e. Political Risk: The political conditions in Mexico have stabilized in the last few months, so Fort Worth should attempt to penetrate the Mexican market now.

21. **Valuation of Wal-Mart's International Business.** In addition to all of its stores in the United States, Wal-Mart has 11 stores in Argentina, 24 stores in Brazil, 214 stores in Canada, 29 stores in China, 92 stores in Germany, 15 stores in South Korea, 611 stores in Mexico, and 261 stores in the United Kingdom. Consider the value of Wal-Mart as being composed of two parts, a U.S. part (due to business in the United States) and a non-U.S. part (due to business in other countries). Explain how to determine the present value (in dollars) of the non-U.S. part assuming that you had access to all the details of Wal-Mart businesses outside the United States.

22. **Impact of International Business on Cash Flows and Risk.** Nantucket Travel Agency specializes in tours for American tourists. Until recently, all of its business was in the United States. It just established a subsidiary in Athens, Greece, which provides tour services in the Greek islands for American tourists. It rented a shop near the port of Athens. It also hired residents of Athens, who could speak English and provide tours of the Greek islands. The subsidiary's main costs are rent and salaries for its employees and the lease of a few large boats in Athens that it uses for tours. American tourists pay for the entire tour in dollars at Nantucket's main U.S. office before they depart for Greece.

    a. Explain why Nantucket may be able to effectively capitalize on international opportunities such as the Greek island tours.

    b. Nantucket is privately owned by owners who reside in the United States and work in the main office. Explain possible agency problems associated with the creation of a subsidiary in Athens, Greece. How can Nantucket attempt to reduce these agency costs?

    c. Greece's cost of labor and rent are relatively low. Explain why this information is relevant to Nantucket's decision to establish a tour business in Greece.

    d. Explain how the cash flow situation of the Greek tour business exposes Nantucket to exchange rate risk. Is Nantucket favorably or unfavorably affected when the euro (Greece's currency) appreciates against the dollar? Explain.

    e. Nantucket plans to finance its Greek tour business. Its subsidiary could obtain loans in euros from a bank in Greece to cover its rent, and its main office could pay off the loans over time. Alternatively, its main office could borrow dollars and would periodically convert dollars to euros to pay the expenses in Greece. Does either type of loan reduce the exposure of Nantucket to exchange rate risk? Explain.

    f. Explain how the Greek island tour business could expose Nantucket to country risk.

INTERNET APPLICATION

23. **Assessing Direct Foreign Investment Trends.** The website address of the Bureau of Economic Analysis is **http://www.bea.doc.gov**.

    a. Use this website to assess recent trends in direct foreign investment (DFI) abroad by U.S. firms. Compare the DFI in the United Kingdom with the DFI in France. Offer a possible reason for the large difference.

    b. Based on the recent trends in DFI, are U.S.-based MNCs pursuing opportunities in Asia? In Eastern Europe? In Latin America?

DISCUSSION IN THE BOARDROOM

This exercise can be found in Appendix E at the back of this textbook.

RUNNING YOUR OWN MNC

This exercise can be found on the Xtra! website at **http://maduraxtra.swlearning.com**.

BLADES, INC. CASE

Decision to Expand Internationally

Blades, Inc., is a U.S.-based company that has been incorporated in the United States for three years. Blades is a relatively small company, with total assets of only $200 million. The company produces a single type of product, roller blades. Due to the booming roller blade market in the United States at the time of the company's establishment, Blades has been quite successful. For example, in its first year of operation, it reported a net income of $3.5 million. Recently, however, the demand for Blades' "Speedos," the company's primary product in the United States, has been slowly tapering off, and Blades has not been performing well. Last year, it reported a return on assets of only 7 percent. In response to the company's annual report for its most recent year of operations, Blades' shareholders have been pressuring the company to improve its performance; its stock price has fallen from a high of $20 per share three years ago to $12 last year. Blades produces high-quality roller blades and employs a unique production process, but the prices it charges are among the top 5 percent in the industry.

In light of these circumstances, Ben Holt, the company's chief financial officer (CFO), is contemplating his alternatives for Blades' future. There are no other cost-cutting measures that Blades can implement in the United States without affecting the quality of its product. Also, production of alternative products would require major modifications to the existing plant setup. Furthermore, and because of these limitations, expansion within the United States at this time seems pointless.

Ben Holt is considering the following: If Blades cannot penetrate the U.S. market further or reduce costs here, why not import some parts from overseas and/or expand the company's sales to foreign countries? Similar strategies have proved successful for numerous companies that expanded into Asia in recent years to increase their profit margins. The CFO's initial focus is on Thailand. Thailand has recently experienced weak economic conditions, and Blades could purchase components there at a low cost. Ben Holt is aware that many of Blades' competitors have begun importing production components from Thailand.

Not only would Blades be able to reduce costs by importing rubber and/or plastic from Thailand due to the low costs of these inputs, but it might also be able to augment weak U.S. sales by exporting to Thailand, an economy still in its infancy and just beginning to appreciate leisure products such as roller blades. While several of Blades' competitors import components from Thailand, few are exporting to the country. Long-term decisions would also eventually have to be made; maybe Blades, Inc., could establish a subsidiary in Thailand and gradually shift its focus away from the United States if its U.S. sales do not rebound. Establishing a subsidiary in Thailand would also make sense for Blades due to its superior production process. Ben Holt is reasonably sure that Thai firms could not duplicate the high-quality production process employed by Blades. Furthermore, if the company's initial approach of exporting works well, establishing a subsidiary in Thailand would preserve Blades' sales before Thai competitors are able to penetrate the Thai market.

As a financial analyst for Blades, Inc., you are assigned to analyze international opportunities and risk resulting from international business. Your initial assessment should focus on the barriers and opportunities that international trade may offer. Ben Holt has never been involved in international business in any form and is unfamiliar with any constraints that may inhibit his plan to export to and import from a foreign country. Mr. Holt has presented you with a list of initial questions you should answer.

1. What are the advantages Blades could gain from importing from and/or exporting to a foreign country such as Thailand?
2. What are some of the disadvantages Blades could face as a result of foreign trade in the short run? In the long run?
3. Which theories of international business described in this chapter apply to Blades, Inc., in the short run? In the long run?
4. What long-range plans other than establishment of a subsidiary in Thailand are an option for Blades and may be more suitable for the company?

SMALL BUSINESS DILEMMA

Developing a Multinational Sporting Goods Corporation

In every chapter of this text, some of the key concepts are illustrated with an application to a small sporting goods firm that conducts international business. These "Small Business Dilemma" features allow students to recognize the dilemmas and possible decisions that firms (such as this sporting goods firm) may face in a global environment. For this chapter, the application is on the development of the sporting goods firm that would conduct international business.

Last month, Jim Logan completed his undergraduate degree in finance and decided to pursue his dream of managing his own sporting goods business. Jim had worked in a sporting goods shop while going to college, and he had noticed that many customers wanted to purchase a low-priced football. However, the sporting goods store where he worked, like many others, sold only top-of-the-line footballs. From his experience, Jim was aware that top-of-the-line footballs had a high markup and that a low-cost football could possibly penetrate the U.S. market. He also knew how to produce footballs. His goal was to create a firm that would produce low-priced footballs and sell them on a wholesale basis to various sporting goods stores in the United States. Unfortunately, many sporting goods stores began to sell low-priced footballs just before Jim was about to start his business. The firm that began to produce the low-cost footballs already provided many other products to sporting goods stores in the United States and therefore had already established a business relationship with these stores. Jim did not believe that he could compete with this firm in the U.S. market.

Rather than pursue a different business, Jim decided to implement his idea on a global basis. While football (as it is played in the United States) has not been a traditional sport in foreign countries, it has become more popular in some foreign countries in recent years. Furthermore, the expansion of cable networks in foreign countries would allow for much more exposure to U.S. football games in those countries in the future. To the extent that this would increase the popularity of football (U.S. style) as a hobby in the foreign countries, it would result in a demand for footballs in foreign countries. Jim asked many of his foreign friends from college days if they recalled seeing footballs sold in their home countries. Most of them said they rarely noticed footballs being sold in sporting goods stores but that they expected the demand for footballs to increase in their home countries. Consequently, Jim decided to start a business of producing low-priced footballs and exporting them to sporting goods distributors in foreign countries. Those distributors would then sell the footballs at the retail level. Jim planned to expand his product line over time once he identified other sports products that he might sell to foreign sporting goods stores. He decided to call his business "Sports Exports Company." To avoid any rent and labor expenses, Jim planned to produce the footballs in his garage and to perform the work himself. Thus, his main business expenses were the cost of the material used to produce footballs and expenses associated with finding distributors in foreign countries who would attempt to sell the footballs to sporting goods stores.

1. Is Sports Exports Company a multinational corporation?
2. Why are the agency costs lower for Sports Exports Company than for most MNCs?
3. Does Sports Exports Company have any comparative advantage over potential competitors in foreign countries that could produce and sell footballs there?
4. How would Jim Logan decide which foreign markets he would attempt to enter? Should he initially focus on one or many foreign markets?
5. The Sports Exports Company has no immediate plans to conduct direct foreign investment. However, it might consider other less costly methods of establishing its business in foreign markets. What methods might the Sports Exports Company use to increase its presence in foreign markets by working with one or more foreign companies?

CHAPTER 2

International Flow of Funds

International business is facilitated by markets that allow for the flow of funds between countries. The transactions arising from international business cause money flows from one country to another. The balance of payments is a measure of international money flows and is discussed in this chapter.

Financial managers of MNCs monitor the balance of payments so that they can determine how the flow of international transactions is changing over time. The balance of payments can indicate the volume of transactions between specific countries and may even signal potential shifts in specific exchange rates.

The specific objectives of this chapter are to:

- explain the key components of the balance of payments,
- explain how the international trade flows are influenced by economic factors and other factors, and
- explain how the international capital flows are influenced by country characteristics.

Balance of Payments

The **balance of payments** is a summary of transactions between domestic and foreign residents for a specific country over a specified period of time. It represents an accounting of a country's international transactions for a period, usually a quarter or a year. It accounts for transactions by businesses, individuals, and the government.

A balance-of-payments statement can be broken down into various components. Those that receive the most attention are the current account and the capital account. The **current account** represents a summary of the flow of funds between one specified country and all other countries due to purchases of goods or services, or the provision of income on financial assets. The **capital account** represents a summary of the flow of funds resulting from the sale of assets between one specified country and all other countries over a specified period of time. Thus, it compares the new foreign investments made by a country with the foreign investments within a country over a particular time period. Transactions that reflect inflows of funds generate positive numbers (credits) for the country's balance, while transactions that reflect outflows of funds generate negative numbers (debits) for the country's balance.

Current Account

A key component of the current account is the **balance of trade**, which is simply the difference between exports and imports. Merchandise exports and imports represent tangible products, such as computers and clothing, that are transported between countries. Service exports and imports represent tourism and other services, such as legal, insurance, and consulting services, provided for customers based in other countries. Service exports by the United States result in an inflow of funds to the United States, while service imports by the United States result in an outflow of funds.

A deficit in the balance of trade means that the value of goods and services exported by the United States is less than the value of goods and services imported by the United States. Before 1993, the balance of trade focused on only merchandise exports and imports. In 1993, it was redefined to include service exports and imports as well. The value of U.S. service exports usually exceeds the value of U.S. service imports. However, the value of U.S. merchandise exports is typically much smaller than the value of U.S. merchandise imports. Overall, the United States normally has a negative balance of trade.

A second component of the current account is **factor income**, which represents income (interest and dividend payments) received by investors on foreign investments in financial assets (securities). Thus, factor income received by U.S. investors reflects an inflow of funds into the United States. Factor income paid by the United States reflects an outflow of funds from the United States.

A third component of the current account is transfer payments, which represent aid, grants, and gifts from one country to another. Exhibit 2.1 shows several examples of transactions that would be reflected in the current account.

Notice in the exhibit that every transaction that generates a U.S. cash inflow (exports and income receipts by the United States) represents a credit to the current account, while every transaction that generates a U.S. cash outflow (imports and income payments by the United States) represents a debit to the current account. Therefore, a large current account deficit indicates that the United States is sending more cash abroad to buy goods and services or to pay income than it is receiving for those same reasons.

The U.S. current account balance in the year 2003 is summarized in Exhibit 2.2. Notice that the exports of goods were valued at $712 billion, while imports of goods by the United States were valued at $1,263 billion. Total U.S. exports of goods and services and income receipts amounted to $1,279 billion, while total U.S. imports of goods and services and income payments amounted to $1,768 billion. The bottom of the exhibit shows that net transfers (which include grants and gifts provided to other countries) were −$68 billion. The negative number for net transfers represents a cash outflow from the United States.

Exhibit 2.2 shows that the current account balance can be derived as the difference between total U.S. exports and income receipts (line 4) and the total U.S. imports and income payments (line 8), with an adjustment for net transfer payments (line 9). This is logical, since the total U.S. exports and income receipts represent U.S. cash inflows while the total U.S. imports and income payments and the net transfers represent U.S. cash outflows. The negative current account balance means that the United States spent more on trade, income, and transfer payments than it received in the year 2003.

Exhibit 2.1
Examples of Current Account Transactions

International Trade Transaction	U.S. Cash Flow Position	Entry on U.S. Balance-of-Payments Account
J.C. Penney purchases stereos produced in Indonesia that it will sell in its U.S. retail stores.	U.S. cash outflow	Debit
Individuals in the U.S. purchase CDs over the Internet from a firm based in China.	U.S. cash outflow	Debit
The Mexican government pays a U.S. consulting firm for consulting services provided by the firm.	U.S. cash inflow	Credit
IBM headquarters in the U.S. purchases computer chips from Singapore that it uses in assembling computers.	U.S. cash outflow	Debit
A university book store in Ireland purchases textbooks produced by a U.S. publishing company.	U.S. cash inflow	Credit
U.S. tourists purchase jewelry in Budapest, Hungary.	U.S. cash outflow	Debit
International Income Transaction	**U.S. Cash Flow Position**	**Entry on U.S. Balance-of-Payments Account**
A U.S. investor receives a dividend payment from a French firm in which she purchased stock.	U.S. cash inflow	Credit
The U.S. Treasury sends an interest payment to a German insurance company that purchased U.S. Treasury bonds one year ago.	U.S. cash outflow	Debit
A Mexican company that borrowed dollars from a bank based in the U.S. sends an interest payment to that bank.	U.S. cash inflow	Credit

Capital Account

The key components of the capital account are direct foreign investment, portfolio investment, and other capital investment. Direct foreign investment represents the investment in fixed assets in foreign countries that can be used to conduct business operations. Examples of direct foreign investment include a firm's acquisition of a foreign company, its construction of a new manufacturing plant, or its expansion of an existing plant in a foreign country.

Portfolio investment represents transactions involving long-term financial assets (such as stocks and bonds) between countries that do not affect the transfer of control. Thus, a purchase of Heineken (Netherlands) stock by a U.S. investor is classified as portfolio investment because it represents a purchase of foreign financial assets without changing control of the company. If a U.S. firm purchased all of Heineken's stock in an acquisition, this transaction would result in a transfer of control and therefore would be classified as direct foreign investment instead of portfolio investment.

A third component of the capital account consists of other capital investment, which represents transactions involving short-term financial assets (such as money market se-

Exhibit 2.2
Summary of U.S. Current Account in the Year 2003 (in billions of $)

(1)	U.S. exports of goods	+ $712
+ (2)	U.S. exports of services	+ 292
+ (3)	U.S. income receipts	+ 275
= (4)	Total U.S. exports and income receipts	= $1,279
(5)	U.S. imports of goods	− $1,263
+ (6)	U.S. imports of services	− 246
+ (7)	U.S. income payments	− 259
= (8)	Total U.S. imports and income payments	= $1,768
(9)	Net transfers by the U.S.	− $68
(10)	Current account balance = (4) − (8) − (9)	− $557

curities) between countries. In general, direct foreign investment measures the expansion of firms' foreign operations, whereas portfolio investment and other capital investment measure the net flow of funds due to financial asset transactions between individual or institutional investors.

International Trade Flows

Canada, France, Germany, and other European countries rely more heavily on trade than the United States does. Canada's trade volume of exports and imports per year is valued at more than 50 percent of its annual gross domestic product (GDP). The trade volume of European countries is typically between 30 and 40 percent of their respective GDPs. The trade volume of the United States and Japan is typically between 10 and 20 percent of their respective GDPs. Nevertheless, for all countries, the volume of trade has grown over time.

Distribution of U.S. Exports and Imports

The dollar value of U.S. exports to various countries during 2003 is shown in Exhibit 2.3. The amounts of U.S. exports are rounded to the nearest billion. For example, exports to Canada were valued at $170 billion.

The proportion of total U.S. exports to various countries is shown at the top of Exhibit 2.4. About 24 percent of all U.S. exports are to Canada, while 14 percent of U.S. exports are to Mexico.

The proportion of total U.S. imports from various countries is shown at the bottom of Exhibit 2.4. Canada, China, Mexico, and Japan are the key exporters to the United States: together, they are responsible for more than half of the value of all U.S. imports.

USING THE WEB

Updated Trade Conditions An update of the current account balance and international trade balance is provided at http://www.whitehouse.gov/fsbr/international.html.

Exhibit 2.3

Distribution of U.S. Exports across Countries (in billions of $)

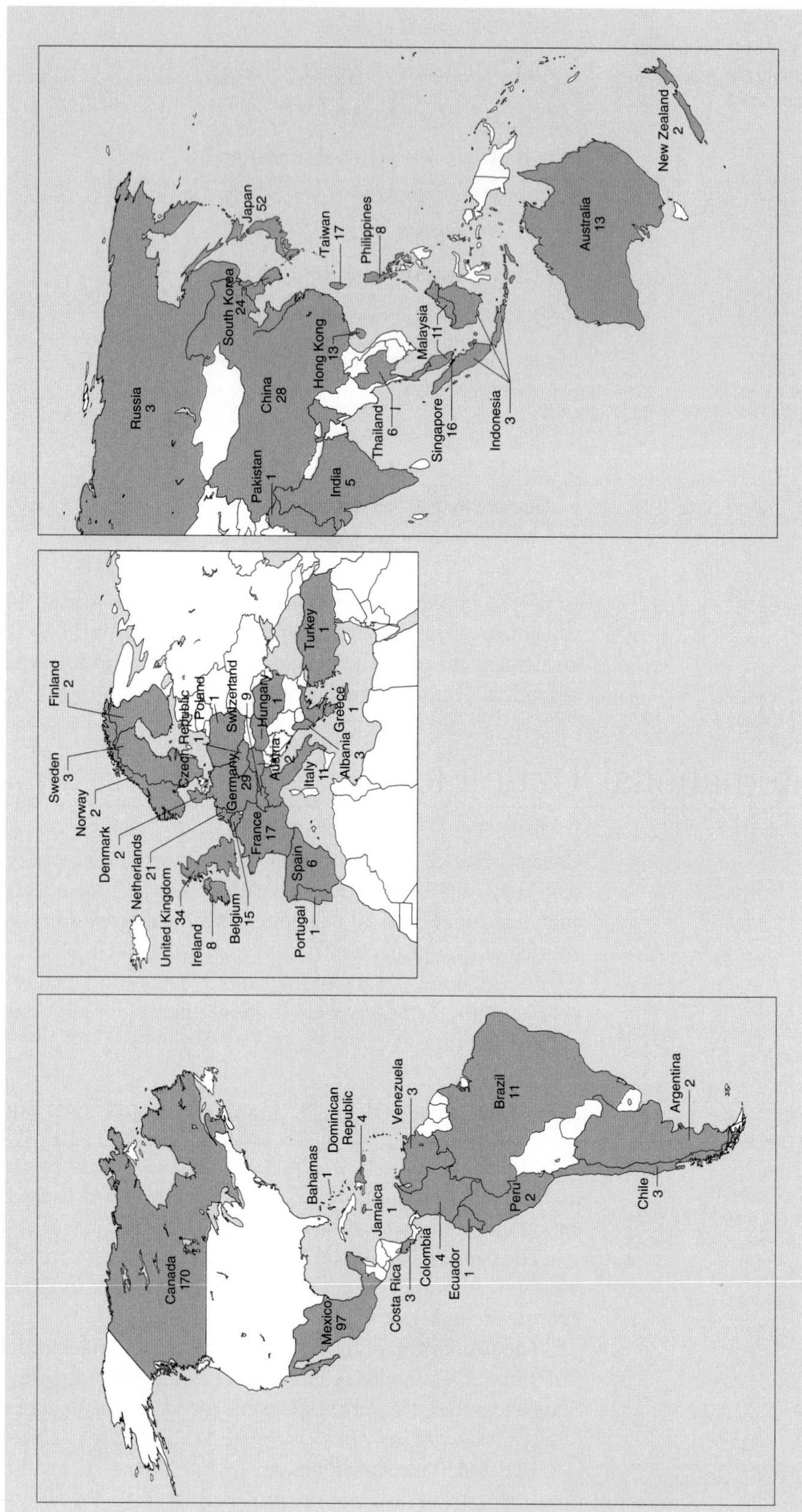

Source: U.S. Census Bureau, 2003.

Exhibit 2.4
2003 Distribution of U.S. Exports and Imports

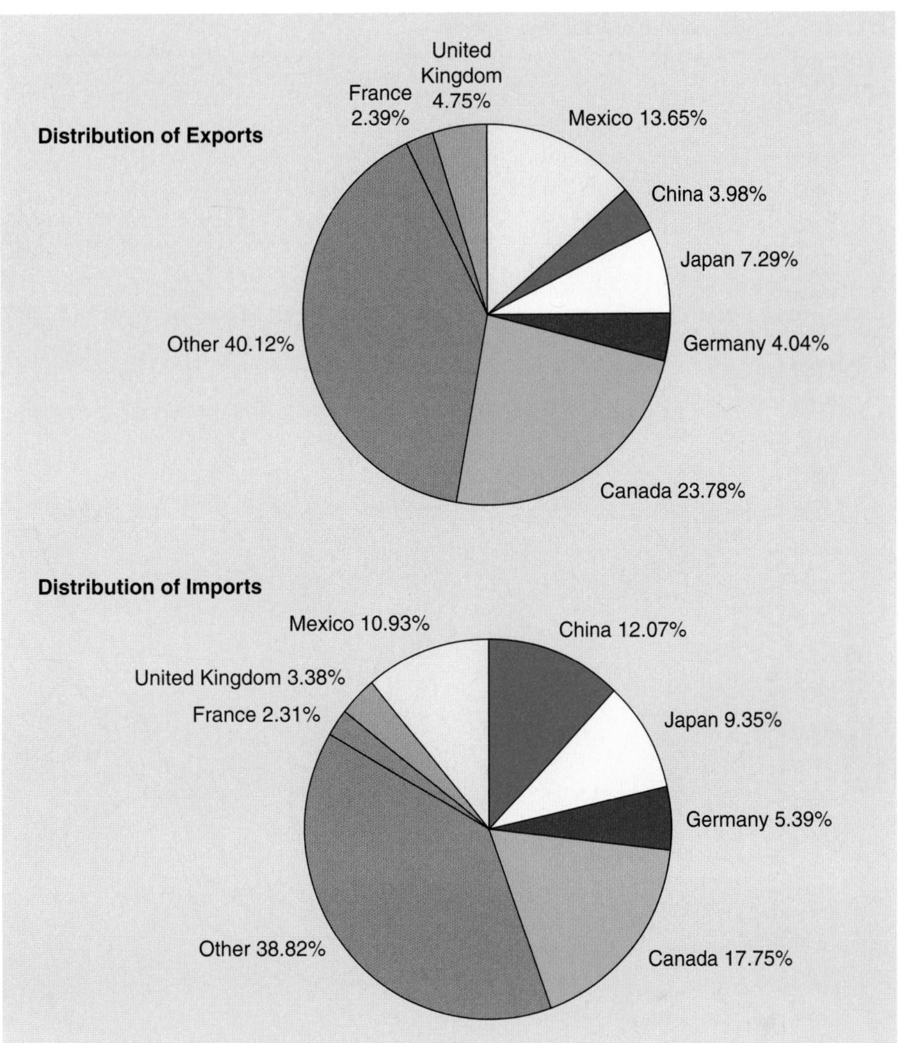

Source: Federal Reserve Bank of St. Louis, 2004.

U.S. Balance of Trade Trend

http://

The International Trade Administration's site at http://www.ita.doc.gov provides access to a variety of trade-related country and sector statistics.

Recent trends for U.S. exports, U.S. imports, and the U.S. balance of trade are shown in Exhibit 2.5. Notice that the value of U.S. exports and U.S. imports has grown substantially over time. Since 1976, the value of U.S. imports has exceeded the value of U.S. exports, causing a balance of trade deficit. Much of the trade deficit is due to a trade imbalance with just two countries, China and Japan. The United States has had an annual trade deficit of about $60 billion with Japan and an annual trade deficit of more than $40 billion with China. Thus, U.S. trade with these two countries results in an annual balance of trade deficit of more than $100 billion.

Any country's balance of trade can change substantially over time. Shortly after World War II, the United States experienced a large balance of trade surplus because Europe relied on U.S. exports as it was rebuilt. During the last decade, the United States has experienced balance of trade deficits because of strong U.S. demand for imported products that are produced at a lower cost than similar products can be produced in the United States.

Exhibit 2.5 U.S. Balance of Trade over Time

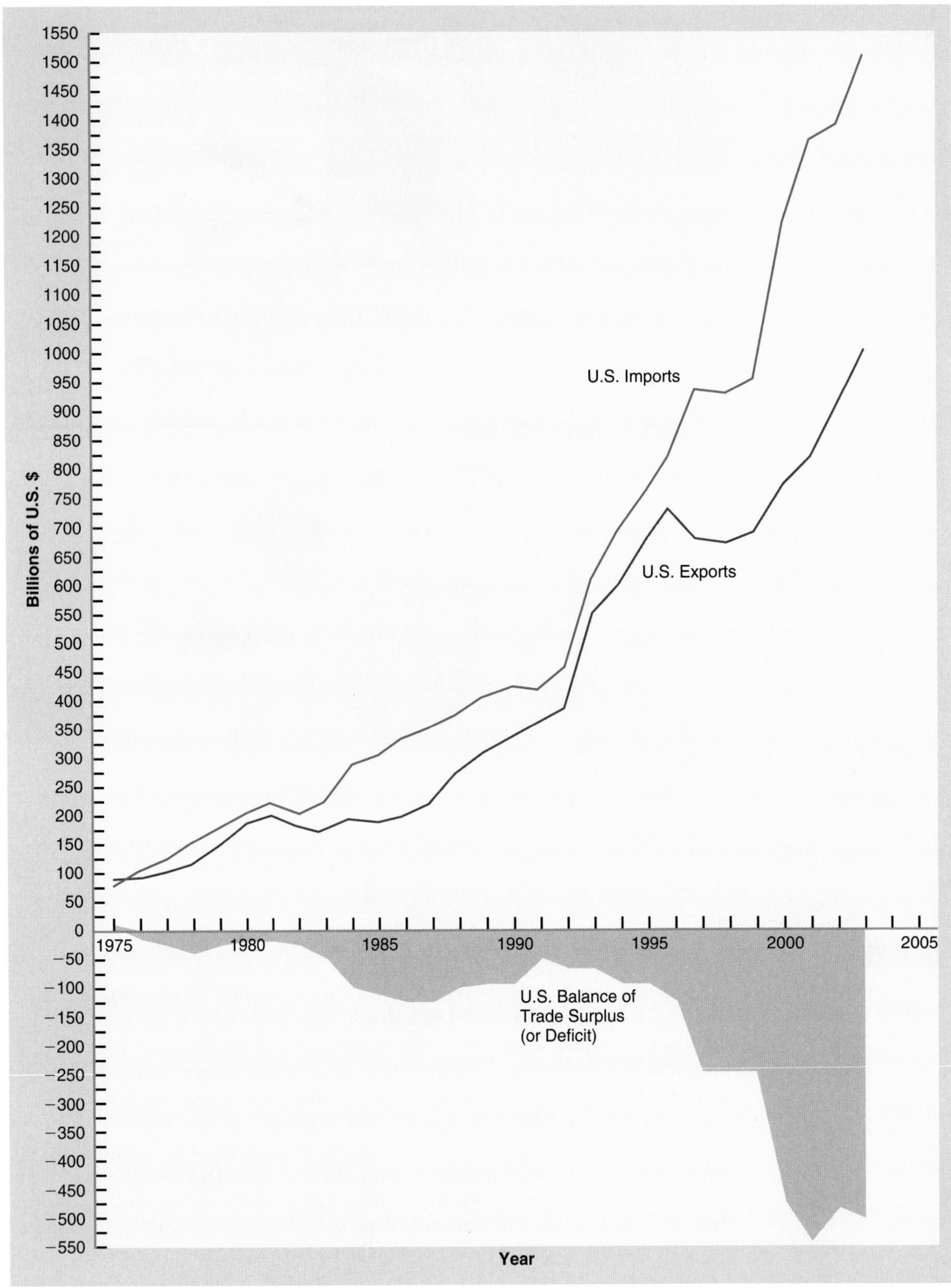

USING THE WEB

U.S. Balance of Trade with Each Country The U.S. balance of trade with each individual country is updated monthly and provided at http://www.census.gov/foreign-trade/www/index.html. Click on Balance with U.S., and then click on a specific country. The balance of trade with the country you specify is shown for several recent months.

USING THE WEB

U.S. Balance of Trade in Aggregate The trend of the U.S. balance of trade in aggregate is provided at http://www.census.gov/foreign-trade/www/index.html. Click on U.S. International Trade in Goods and Services. There are several links here to additional details about the U.S. balance of trade.

Trade Agreements

Many trade agreements have occurred over the years in an effort to reduce trade restrictions. In January 1988, the United States and Canada agreed to a free trade pact, which was completely phased in by 1998. This agreement reduced trade barriers on many products and increased global competition within some industries. In December 1993, a General Agreement on Tariffs and Trade (GATT) accord among 117 nations called for lower tariffs around the world. In addition, the North American Free Trade Agreement (NAFTA) was enacted, removing numerous restrictions on trade between Canada, Mexico, and the United States. The agreement was an extension of a 1989 treaty that reduced trade barriers. NAFTA also reduced some restrictions on direct foreign investment in Mexico.

Throughout the 1990s, trade restrictions between European countries were removed. One implicit trade barrier was the different regulations among countries. MNCs were unable to sell products across all European countries because each country required different specifications (related to the size or composition of the products). The standardization of product specifications throughout Europe during the 1990s removed a very large trade barrier. The adoption of the euro as a single currency in much of Europe also encouraged trade between European countries. It removed the transaction costs associated with the conversion of one currency to another. It also removed concerns about exchange rate risk for producers or customers based in Europe that were selling to other countries in Europe.

In June 2003, the United States and Chile signed a free trade agreement to remove tariffs on more than 90 percent of the products traded between the two countries. The United States has also established trade agreements with many other countries.

Trade Disagreements

International trade policies partially determine which firms get most of the market share within an industry. These policies affect each country's unemployment level, income level, and economic growth. Even though trade treaties have reduced tariffs and quotas over time, most countries still impose some type of trade restrictions on particular products in order to protect their local firms.

An easy way to start an argument among students (or professors) is to ask what they think the policy on international trade should be. People whose job prospects are highly influenced by international trade tend to have very strong opinions about international trade policy. On the surface, most people agree that free trade can be beneficial because it encourages more intense competition among firms, which enables consumers to obtain products where the quality is highest and the prices are low. Free trade should cause a shift in production to those countries where it can be done most efficiently. Each country's government wants to increase its exports because more exports result in a higher level of production and income and may create jobs. However, a job created in one country may be lost in another, which causes countries to battle for a greater share of the world's exports.

People disagree on the type of strategies a government should be allowed to use to increase its respective country's share of the global market. They may agree that a tariff or quota on imported goods prevents free trade and gives local firms an unfair advantage in their own market. Yet, they disagree on whether governments should be allowed to use other more subtle trade restrictions against foreign firms or provide incentives that give local firms an unfair advantage in the battle for global market share. Consider the following situations that commonly occur:

1. The firms based in one country are not subject to environmental restrictions and, therefore, can produce at a lower cost than firms in other countries.
2. The firms based in one country are not subject to child labor laws and are able to produce products at a lower cost than firms in other countries by relying mostly on children to produce the products.
3. The firms based in one country are allowed by their government to offer bribes to large customers when pursuing business deals in a particular industry. They have a competitive advantage over firms in other countries that are not allowed to offer bribes.
4. The firms in one country receive subsidies from the government, as long as they export the products. The exporting of products that were produced with the help of government subsidies is commonly referred to as **dumping**. These firms may be able to sell their products at a lower price than any of their competitors in other countries.
5. The firms in one country receive tax breaks if they are in specific industries. This practice is not necessarily a subsidy, but it still is a form of government financial support.

http://

Trade statistics within a specific trading block are provided at http://www.worldbank.org/data/wdi2000/pdfs/tab6_5.pdf.

In all of these situations, firms in one country may have an advantage over firms in other countries. Every government uses some strategies that may give its local firms an advantage in the fight for global market share. Thus, the playing field in the battle for global market share is probably not even across all countries. Yet, there is no formula that will ensure a fair battle for market share. Regardless of the progression of international trade treaties, governments will always be able to find strategies that can give their local firms an edge in exporting. Suppose, as an extreme example, that a new international treaty outlawed all of the strategies described above. One country's government could still try to give its local firms a trade advantage by attempting to maintain a relatively weak currency. This strategy can increase foreign demand for products produced locally because products denominated in a weak currency can be purchased at a low price.

Using the Exchange Rate as a Policy. At any given point in time, a group of exporters may claim that they are being mistreated and lobby their government to adjust the currency so that their exports will not be so expensive for foreign purchasers. In 1999, U.S. exporters claimed that they were at a disadvantage because the dollar was too strong (expensive for importers). In 2004, European exporters claimed that they were at a disadvantage because the euro was too strong. Meanwhile, U.S. exporters still claimed that they could not compete with China because the Chinese currency (yuan) was maintained at an artificially weak level.

Outsourcing. One of the most recent issues related to trade is the outsourcing of services. For example, technology support of computer systems used in the United States may be outsourced to India, Bulgaria, China, or other countries where labor costs are low. Outsourcing affects the balance of trade because it means that a service is purchased in another country. This form of international trade allows MNCs to conduct operations at a lower cost. However, it shifts jobs to other countries and is criticized by the people who lose their jobs due to the outsourcing. Many people have opinions about outsourcing, which are often inconsistent with their own behavior.

EXAMPLE

As a U.S. citizen, Rick says he is embarrassed by U.S. firms that outsource their labor services to other countries as a means of increasing their value, because this practice eliminates jobs in the United States. Rick is president of Atlantic Company and says the company will never outsource its services. Atlantic Company imports most of its materials from a foreign company. It also owns a factory in Mexico, and the clothing produced in Mexico is exported to the United States.

Rick recognizes that outsourcing may replace jobs in the United States. Yet, he does not realize that importing materials or operating a factory in Mexico may also have replaced jobs in the United States. If questioned about his use of foreign labor markets for materials or production, he would likely explain that the high manufacturing wages in the United States force him to rely on lower cost labor in foreign countries. Yet, the same argument could be used by other U.S. firms that outsource services.

Rick owns a Toyota, a Nokia cell phone, a Toshiba computer, and Adidas clothing. He argues that these non-U.S. products are a better value for the money than U.S. products. Nicole, a friend of Rick, suggests that his consumption choices are inconsistent with his "create U.S. jobs" philosophy. She explains that she only purchases U.S. products. She owns a Ford (produced in Mexico), a Motorola telephone (components produced in Asia), a Compaq computer (produced in China), and Nike clothing (produced in Indonesia).

Using Trade Policies for Political Reasons. International trade policy issues have become even more contentious over time as people have come to expect that trade policies will be used to punish countries for various actions. People expect countries to restrict imports from countries that fail to enforce environmental laws or child labor laws, initiate war against another country, or are unwilling to participate in a war against an unlawful dictator of another country. Every international trade convention now attracts a large number of protesters, all of whom have their own agendas. International trade may not even be the focus of each protest, but it is often thought to be the potential solution to the problem (at least in the mind of that protester). Although all of the protesters are clearly dissatisfied with existing trade policies, there is no consensus as to what trade policies should be. These different views are similar to the disagreements that occur between government representatives when they try to negotiate international trade policy.

The managers of each MNC cannot be responsible for resolving these international trade policy conflicts. However, they should at least recognize how international trade policy affects their competitive position in the industry and how changes in policy could affect their position in the future.

Disagreements within the European Union. In 2004, ten countries from eastern Europe joined the European Union (EU). Firms based in these newer participating countries in the EU are now subject to reduced trade barriers on EU-related trade. However, these countries are now also subject to the EU tariffs on products that enter the EU. For example, the EU places a 75 percent tax (tariff) on bananas that are imported by all EU countries. Consequently, the retail price of bananas will likely increase, as the tax is passed on to the consumers. This type of tariff has caused some friction between EU countries that commonly import products and other EU countries.

The philosophy behind the EU trade agreements is that firms within the EU can compete on a level playing field with zero or standardized restrictions across countries. However, governments still claim that some countries have advantages over others. For example, the German government suggested that firms in Poland have an unfair advantage because the Polish government imposes a relatively lower corporate tax rate on its corporations than other EU countries impose on their corporations.

Factors Affecting International Trade Flows

Because international trade can significantly affect a country's economy, it is important to identify and monitor the factors that influence it. The most influential factors are:

- Inflation
- National income
- Government restrictions
- Exchange rates

Impact of Inflation

http://

Visit http://www.census.gov for access to the latest economic, financial, socioeconomic, and political surveys and statistics.

If a country's inflation rate increases relative to the countries with which it trades, its current account will be expected to decrease, other things being equal. Consumers and corporations in that country will most likely purchase more goods overseas (due to high local inflation), while the country's exports to other countries will decline.

Impact of National Income

If a country's income level (national income) increases by a higher percentage than those of other countries, its current account is expected to decrease, other things being equal. As the real income level (adjusted for inflation) rises, so does consumption of goods. A percentage of that increase in consumption will most likely reflect an increased demand for foreign goods.

USING THE WEB

International Trade Information about international trade, international transactions, and the balance of trade is provided at http://research.stlouisfed.org/fred2.

Impact of Government Restrictions

A country's government can prevent or discourage imports from other countries. By imposing such restrictions, the government disrupts trade flows. Among the most commonly used trade restrictions are tariffs and quotas.

USING THE WEB

Import Controls Information about tariffs on imported products is provided at http://www.dataweb.usitc.gov. Click on any country listed, and then click on Trade Regulations. Review the import controls set by that country's government.

MANAGING FOR VALUE

Impact of Trade Policies on Firm Value

The values of steel companies and chemical exporting companies in the United States are affected by U.S. trade policies, but in different ways. U.S. steel companies rely on U.S. demand for their products. They tend to lobby the U.S. government to impose trade barriers to protect jobs in the steel industry. Chemical exporting companies rely on European demand for their products. They must always be concerned with potential European retaliation in response to U.S. government–imposed tariffs on U.S. imports. Periodically, the U.S. government imposes tariffs on steel imports in an effort to protect U.S. jobs in the steel industry. Such tariffs are often imposed shortly before or within an election year as a means of appealing to the voting power of the steel industry. If European governments retaliate against the steel tariff by imposing a tariff on chemical products, the U.S. chemical companies experience a loss in sales and value. Meanwhile, any jobs saved in the U.S. steel industry may be lost in the U.S. chemical industry.

Tariffs and Quotas. If a country's government imposes a tax on imported goods (often referred to as a **tariff**), the prices of foreign goods to consumers are effectively increased. Tariffs imposed by the U.S. government are on average lower than those imposed by other governments. Some industries, however, are more highly protected by tariffs than others. American apparel products and farm products have historically received more protection against foreign competition through high tariffs on related imports.

USING THE WEB

Tariff Rates Detailed information about tariffs imposed by each country is provided at http://www.worldbank.org/data/wdi2000/pdfs/tab6_6.pdf.

In addition to tariffs, a government can reduce its country's imports by enforcing a **quota**, or a maximum limit that can be imported. Quotas have been commonly applied to a variety of goods imported by the United States and other countries.

USING THE WEB

Import Restrictions General information about import restrictions and other trade-related information is provided at http://www.commerce.gov.

Other Types of Restrictions. Some trade restrictions may be imposed on products for health and safety reasons.

EXAMPLE

In 2001, an outbreak of foot-and-mouth disease occurred in the United Kingdom and eventually spread to several other European countries. This disease can spread by direct or indirect contact with infected animals. The U.S. government imposed trade restrictions on some products produced in the United Kingdom for health reasons. Consequently, U.K. exports to the United States declined abruptly.

This example illustrates how uncontrollable factors besides inflation, national income, tariffs and quotas, and exchange rates can affect the balance of trade between two countries.

USING THE WEB

Trade Sanctions An update of sanctions imposed by the U.S. government on specific countries is provided at http://www.treas.gov/ofac.

Impact of Exchange Rates

Each country's currency is valued in terms of other currencies through the use of exchange rates, so that currencies can be exchanged to facilitate international transactions. The values of most currencies can fluctuate over time because of market and government forces (as discussed in detail in Chapter 4). If a country's currency begins to rise in value against other currencies, its current account balance should decrease, other things being equal. As the currency strengthens, goods exported by that country will become more expensive to the importing countries. As a consequence, the demand for such goods will decrease.

A tennis racket that sells in the United States for $100 will require a payment of C$125 by the Canadian importer if the Canadian dollar is valued at C$1 = $.80. If C$1 = $.70, it would require a payment of C$143, which might discourage the Canadian demand for U.S. tennis rackets. A strong local currency is expected to reduce the current account balance if the traded goods are **price-elastic** (sensitive to price changes).

Using the tennis racket example above, consider the possible effects if currencies of several countries depreciate simultaneously against the dollar (the dollar strengthens). The U.S. balance of trade can decline substantially.

During the 1997–1998 Asian crisis, the exchange rates of Asian currencies declined substantially against the dollar, which caused the prices of Asian products to decline from the perspective of the United States and many other countries. Consequently, the demand for Asian products increased and sometimes replaced the demand for products of other countries. For example, the weakness of the Thai baht during this period caused an increase in the global demand for fish from Thailand and a decline in the demand for similar products from the United States (Seattle).

Just as a strong dollar is expected to cause a lower (or more negative) U.S. balance of trade as explained above, a weak dollar is expected to cause a higher balance of trade. The dollar's weakness lowers the price paid for U.S. goods by foreign customers and can lead to an increase in the demand for U.S. products. A weak dollar also tends to increase the dollar price paid for foreign goods and thus reduces the U.S. demand for foreign goods.

Interaction of Factors

Because the factors that affect the balance of trade interact, their simultaneous influence on the balance of trade is complex. For example, as a high U.S. inflation rate reduces the current account, it places downward pressure on the value of the dollar (as discussed in detail in Chapter 4). Since a weaker dollar can improve the current account, it may partially offset the impact of inflation on the current account.

Correcting a Balance of Trade Deficit

A balance of trade deficit is not necessarily a problem, as it may enable a country's consumers to benefit from imported products that are less expensive than locally produced products. However, the purchase of imported products implies less reliance on domestic production in favor of foreign production. Thus, it may be argued that a large balance of trade deficit causes a transfer of jobs to some foreign countries. Consequently, a country's government may attempt to correct a balance of trade deficit.

By reconsidering some of the factors that affect the balance of trade, it is possible to develop some common methods for correcting a deficit. Any policy that will increase foreign demand for the country's goods and services will improve its balance of trade position. Foreign demand may increase if export prices become more attractive. This can occur when the country's inflation is low or when its currency's value is reduced, thereby making the prices cheaper from a foreign perspective.

A floating exchange rate could possibly correct any international trade imbalances in the following way. A deficit in a country's balance of trade suggests that the country is spending more funds on foreign products than it is receiving from exports to foreign countries. Because it is selling its currency (to buy foreign goods) in greater volume than the foreign demand for its currency, the value of its currency should decrease. This decrease in value should encourage more foreign demand for its goods in the future.

While this theory seems rational, it does not always work as just described. It is possible that, instead, a country's currency will remain stable or appreciate even when the country has a balance of trade deficit.

EXAMPLE

The United States normally experiences a large balance of trade deficit, which should place downward pressure on the value of the dollar. Yet, in some years, there is substantial investment in dollar-denominated securities by foreign investors. This foreign demand for the dollar places upward pressure on its value, thereby offsetting the downward pressure caused by the trade imbalance. Thus, a balance of trade deficit will not always be corrected by a currency adjustment.

Why a Weak Home Currency Is Not a Perfect Solution

Even if a country's home currency weakens, its balance of trade deficit will not necessarily be corrected for the following reasons.

Counterpricing by Competitors. When a country's currency weakens, its prices become more attractive to foreign customers, and many foreign companies lower their prices to remain competitive with the country's firms.

Impact of Other Weak Currencies. The currency does not necessarily weaken against all currencies at the same time.

EXAMPLE

When the dollar weakens in Europe, the dollar's exchange rates with the currencies of Hong Kong, Singapore, South Korea, and Taiwan may remain more stable. As some U.S. firms reduce their demand for supplies produced in European countries, they tend to increase their demand for goods produced in Asian countries. Consequently, the dollar's weakness in European countries causes a change in international trade behavior but does not eliminate the U.S. trade deficit.

Prearranged International Transactions. Many international trade transactions are prearranged and cannot be immediately adjusted. Thus, non-U.S. importing companies may be attracted to U.S. firms as a result of a weaker dollar but cannot immediately sever their relationships with suppliers from other countries. Over time, they may begin to take advantage of the weaker dollar by purchasing U.S. imports, if they believe that the

Exhibit 2.6
J-Curve Effect

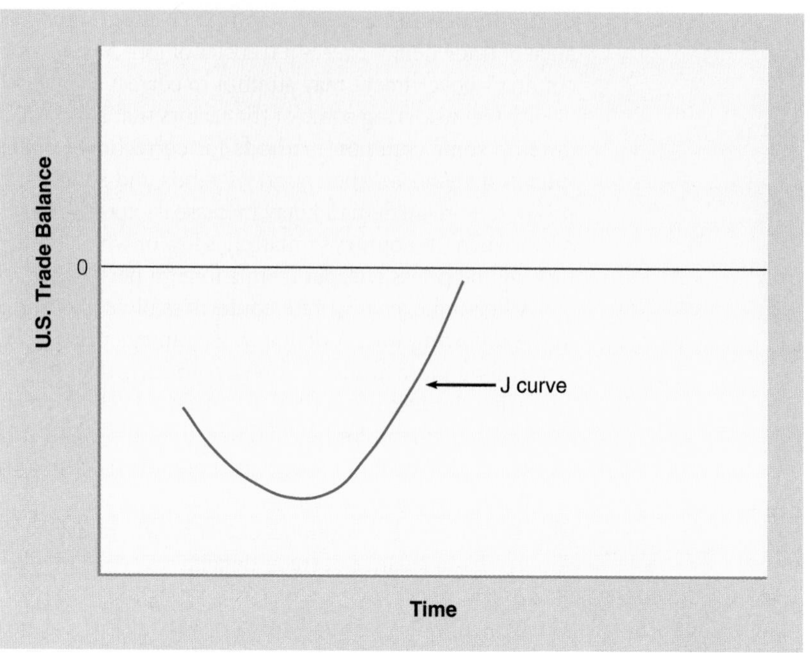

weakness will continue. The lag time between the dollar's weakness and the non-U.S. firms' increased demand for U.S. products has sometimes been estimated to be 18 months or even longer.

The U.S. balance of trade may actually deteriorate in the short run as a result of dollar depreciation. It only improves when U.S. and non-U.S. importers respond to the change in purchasing power that is caused by the weaker dollar. This pattern is called the **J-curve effect**, and it is illustrated in Exhibit 2.6. The further decline in the trade balance before a reversal creates a trend that can look like the letter J.

Intercompany Trade. A fourth reason why a weak currency will not always improve a country's balance of trade is that importers and exporters that are under the same ownership have unique relationships. Many firms purchase products that are produced by their subsidiaries in what is referred to as **intracompany trade**. This type of trade makes up more than 50 percent of all international trade. The trade between the two parties will normally continue regardless of exchange rate movements. Thus, the impact of exchange rate movements on intracompany trade patterns is limited.

International Capital Flows

Capital flows between the United States and other countries are illustrated in Exhibit 2.7. The total capital flows are shown in the upper left graph. Notice that U.S. capital inflows exceed capital outflows. The difference has increased over time. The components that make up the total flows are shown in the other three graphs in Exhibit 2.7. The inflows from portfolio investment (lower left graph) in the United States are much larger than the outflows. At one point in 2002, the graph shows negative portfolio investment outflows from the United States, which implies that the value of foreign securities sold exceeded the value of new investment in foreign securities. U.S. direct

Exhibit 2.7 International Capital Flows (quarterly numbers, annualized; in billions of $)

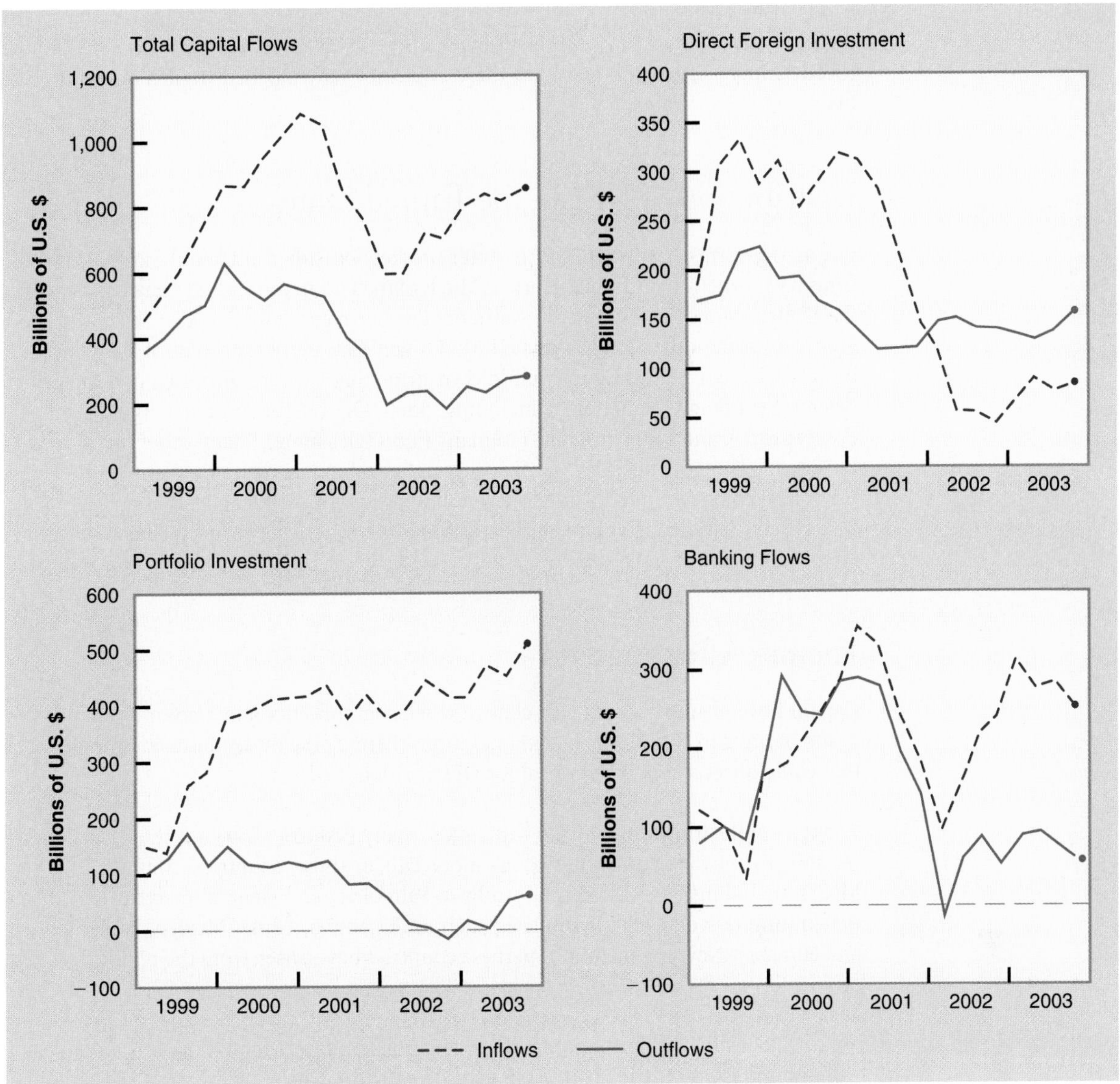

Source: Federal Reserve.

foreign investment (upper right graph) in other countries has been somewhat stable, but direct foreign investment in the United States declined substantially when the U.S. economy weakened in recent years. The capital flows of funds into U.S. banks (lower right graph) have been much larger than U.S. capital flows of funds into foreign banks.

Distribution of DFI by U.S. Firms

Many U.S.-based MNCs have recently increased their DFI in foreign countries. For example, ExxonMobil, IBM, and Hewlett-Packard have at least 50 percent of their assets in foreign countries. The United Kingdom and Canada are the biggest targets. Europe as a whole receives more than 50 percent of all DFI by U.S. firms. Another 30 percent of DFI is focused on Latin America and Canada, while about 16 percent is concentrated in the Asia and Pacific region. The DFI by U.S. firms in Latin American and Asian countries has increased substantially as these countries have opened their markets to U.S. firms.

Distribution of DFI in the United States

Just as U.S. firms have used DFI to enter markets outside the United States, non-U.S. firms have penetrated the U.S. market. Much of the DFI in the United States comes from the United Kingdom, Japan, the Netherlands, Germany, and Canada. Seagram, Food Lion, and some other foreign-owned MNCs generate more than half of their revenue from the United States. Many well-known firms that operate in the United States are owned by foreign companies, including Shell Oil (Netherlands), Citgo Petroleum (Venezuela), Canon (Japan), and Fireman's Fund (Germany). Many other firms operating in the United States are partially owned by foreign companies, including MCI Communications (United Kingdom), and Northwest Airlines (Netherlands). While U.S.-based MNCs consider expanding in other countries, they must also compete with foreign firms in the United States.

Factors Affecting DFI

Capital flows resulting from DFI change whenever conditions in a country change the desire of firms to conduct business operations there. Some of the more common factors that could affect a country's appeal for DFI are identified here.

Changes in Restrictions. During the 1990s, many countries lowered their restrictions on DFI, thereby opening the way to more DFI in those countries. Many U.S.-based MNCs, including Bausch & Lomb, Colgate-Palmolive, and General Electric, have been penetrating less developed countries such as Argentina, Chile, Mexico, India, China, and Hungary. New opportunities in these countries have arisen from the removal of government barriers.

USING THE WEB

DFI Regulations Information about regulations on direct foreign investment in each country is provided at http://biz.yahoo.com/ifc/. Click on any country listed, then click on Foreign Regulations, and then click on Incoming Direct Investment. Review the restrictions set by that country's government.

Privatization. Several national governments have recently engaged in **privatization**, or the selling of some of their operations to corporations and other investors. Privatization is popular in Brazil and Mexico, in Eastern European countries such as Poland and Hungary, and in such Caribbean territories as the Virgin Islands. It allows for greater international business as foreign firms can acquire operations sold by national governments.

Privatization was used in Chile to prevent a few investors from controlling all the shares and in France to prevent a possible reversion to a more nationalized economy. In the United Kingdom, privatization was promoted to spread stock ownership across investors, which allowed more people to have a direct stake in the success of British industry.

http://

Visit http://www.privatization.org for information about privatizations around the world, commentaries, and related publications.

The primary reason that the market value of a firm may increase in response to privatization is the anticipated improvement in managerial efficiency. Managers in a privately owned firm can focus on the goal of maximizing shareholder wealth, whereas in a state-owned business, the state must consider the economic and social ramifications of any business decision. Also, managers of a privately owned enterprise are more motivated to ensure profitability because their careers may depend on it. For these reasons, privatized firms will search for local and global opportunities that could enhance their value. The trend toward privatization will undoubtedly create a more competitive global marketplace.

Potential Economic Growth. Countries that have greater potential for economic growth are more likely to attract DFI because firms recognize that they may be able to capitalize on that growth by establishing more business there.

Tax Rates. Countries that impose relatively low tax rates on corporate earnings are more likely to attract DFI. When assessing the feasibility of DFI, firms estimate the after-tax cash flows that they expect to earn.

Exchange Rates. Firms typically prefer to direct DFI to countries where the local currency is expected to strengthen against their own. Under these conditions, they can invest funds to establish their operations in a country while that country's currency is relatively cheap (weak). Then, earnings from the new operations can periodically be converted back to the firm's currency at a more favorable exchange rate.

Factors Affecting International Portfolio Investment

The desire by individual or institutional investors to direct international portfolio investment to a specific country is influenced by the following factors.

Tax Rates on Interest or Dividends. Investors normally prefer to invest in a country where the taxes on interest or dividend income from investments are relatively low. Investors assess their potential after-tax earnings from investments in foreign securities.

Interest Rates. Portfolio investment can also be affected by interest rates. Money tends to flow to countries with high interest rates, as long as the local currencies are not expected to weaken.

Exchange Rates. When investors invest in a security in a foreign country, their return is affected by (1) the change in the value of the security and (2) the change in the value of the currency in which the security is denominated. If a country's home currency is expected to strengthen, foreign investors may be willing to invest in the country's securities to benefit from the currency movement. Conversely, if a country's home currency is expected to weaken, foreign investors may decide to purchase securities in other countries. In a period such as 2003, U.S. investors that invested in foreign securities benefited from the change in exchange rates. Since the foreign currencies strengthened against the dollar over time, the foreign securities were ultimately converted to more dollars when they were sold at the end of the year.

USING THE WEB

Capital Flows Information on capital flows and international transactions is provided at http://www.worldbank.org.

Agencies That Facilitate International Flows

A variety of agencies have been established to facilitate international trade and financial transactions. These agencies often represent a group of nations. A description of some of the more important agencies follows.

International Monetary Fund

http://

The home page of the IMF at http://www.imf.org makes the latest international economic news, data, and surveys available.

The United Nations Monetary and Financial Conference held in Bretton Woods, New Hampshire, in July 1944, was called to develop a structured international monetary system. As a result of this conference, the **International Monetary Fund (IMF)** was formed. The major objectives of the IMF, as set by its charter, are to (1) promote cooperation among countries on international monetary issues, (2) promote stability in exchange rates, (3) provide temporary funds to member countries attempting to correct imbalances of international payments, (4) promote free mobility of capital funds across countries, and (5) promote free trade. It is clear from these objectives that the IMF's goals encourage increased internationalization of business.

The IMF is overseen by a Board of Governors, composed of finance officers (such as the head of the central bank) from each of the 184 member countries. It also has an executive board composed of 24 executive directors representing the member countries. This board is based in Washington, D.C., and meets at least three times a week to discuss ongoing issues.

One of the key duties of the IMF is its **compensatory financing facility (CFF)**, which attempts to reduce the impact of export instability on country economies. Although it is available to all IMF members, this facility is used mainly by developing countries. A country experiencing financial problems due to reduced export earnings must demonstrate that the reduction is temporary and beyond its control. In addition, it must be willing to work with the IMF in resolving the problem.

Each member country of the IMF is assigned a quota based on a variety of factors reflecting that country's economic status. Members are required to pay this assigned quota. The amount of funds that each member can borrow from the IMF depends on its particular quota.

The financing by the IMF is measured in **special drawing rights (SDRs)**. The SDR is not a currency but simply a unit of account. It is an international reserve asset created by the IMF and allocated to member countries to supplement currency reserves. The SDR's value fluctuates in accordance with the value of major currencies.

The IMF played an active role in attempting to reduce the adverse effects of the Asian crisis. In 1997 and 1998, it provided funding to various Asian countries in exchange for promises from the respective governments to take specific actions intended to improve economic conditions.

Funding Dilemma of the IMF. The IMF typically specifies economic reforms that a country must satisfy to receive IMF funding. In this way, the IMF attempts to ensure that the country uses the funds properly. However, some countries want funding without adhering to the economic reforms required by the IMF.

During the Asian crisis, the IMF agreed to provide $43 billion to Indonesia. The negotiations were tense, as the IMF demanded that President Suharto break up some of the monopolies run by his friends and family members and close some weak banks. Citizens of Indonesia interpreted the bank closures as a banking crisis and began to withdraw their deposits from all banks. In January 1998, the IMF demanded many types of economic reform, and Suharto agreed to them. The reforms may have been overly ambitious, however, and Suharto failed to institute them. The IMF agreed to renegotiate the terms in March 1998 in a continuing effort to rescue Indonesia, but this effort signaled that a country did not have to meet the terms of its agreement to obtain funding. A new agreement was completed in April, and the IMF resumed its payments to support a bailout of Indonesia. In May 1998, Suharto abruptly discontinued subsidies for gasoline and food, which led to riots. Suharto blamed the riots on the IMF and on foreign investors who wanted to acquire assets in Indonesia at depressed prices.

World Bank

http://

See http://www.worldbank.org, the website of The World Bank Group.

The **International Bank for Reconstruction and Development (IBRD)**, also referred to as the **World Bank**, was established in 1944. Its primary objective is to make loans to countries to enhance economic development. For example, the World Bank recently extended a loan to Mexico for about $4 billion over a ten-year period for environmental projects to facilitate industrial development near the U.S. border. Its main source of funds is the sale of bonds and other debt instruments to private investors and governments. The World Bank has a profit-oriented philosophy. Therefore, its loans are not subsidized but are extended at market rates to governments (and their agencies) that are likely to repay them.

A key aspect of the World Bank's mission is the **Structural Adjustment Loan (SAL)**, established in 1980. The SALs are intended to enhance a country's long-term economic growth. For example, SALs have been provided to Turkey and to some less developed countries that are attempting to improve their balance of trade.

Because the World Bank provides only a small portion of the financing needed by developing countries, it attempts to spread its funds by entering into **cofinancing agreements**. Cofinancing is performed in the following ways:

- *Official aid agencies.* Development agencies may join the World Bank in financing development projects in low-income countries.
- *Export credit agencies.* The World Bank cofinances some capital-intensive projects that are also financed through export credit agencies.
- *Commercial banks.* The World Bank has joined with commercial banks to provide financing for private-sector development. In recent years, more than 350 banks from all over the world have participated in cofinancing, including Bank of America, J.P. Morgan Chase, and Citigroup.

The World Bank recently established the **Multilateral Investment Guarantee Agency (MIGA)**, which offers various forms of political risk insurance. This is an additional means (along with its SALs) by which the World Bank can encourage the development of international trade and investment.

The World Bank is one of the largest borrowers in the world; its borrowings have amounted to the equivalent of $70 billion. Its loans are well diversified among numerous currencies and countries. It has received the highest credit rating (AAA) possible.

World Trade Organization

The **World Trade Organization (WTO)** was created as a result of the Uruguay Round of trade negotiations that led to the GATT accord in 1993. This organization was established to provide a forum for multilateral trade negotiations and to settle trade disputes related to the GATT accord. It began its operations in 1995 with 81 member countries, and more countries have joined since then. Member countries are given voting rights that are used to make judgments about trade disputes and other issues.

International Financial Corporation

In 1956 the **International Financial Corporation (IFC)** was established to promote private enterprise within countries. Composed of a number of member nations, the IFC works to promote economic development through the private rather than the government sector. It not only provides loans to corporations but also purchases stock, thereby becoming part owner in some cases rather than just a creditor. The IFC typically provides 10 to 15 percent of the necessary funds in the private enterprise projects in which it invests, and the remainder of the project must be financed through other sources. Thus, the IFC acts as a catalyst, as opposed to a sole supporter, for private enterprise development projects. It traditionally has obtained financing from the World Bank but can borrow in the international financial markets.

International Development Association

The **International Development Association (IDA)** was created in 1960 with country development objectives somewhat similar to those of the World Bank. Its loan policy is more appropriate for less prosperous nations, however. The IDA extends loans at low interest rates to poor nations that cannot qualify for loans from the World Bank.

Bank for International Settlements

The **Bank for International Settlements (BIS)** attempts to facilitate cooperation among countries with regard to international transactions. It also provides assistance to countries experiencing a financial crisis. The BIS is sometimes referred to as the "central banks' central bank" or the "lender of last resort." It played an important role in supporting some of the less developed countries during the international debt crisis in the early and mid-1980s. It commonly provides financing for central banks in Latin American and Eastern European countries.

Regional Development Agencies

Several other agencies have more regional (as opposed to global) objectives relating to economic development. These include, for example, the Inter-American Development Bank (focusing on the needs of Latin America), the Asian Development Bank (established to enhance social and economic development in Asia), and the African Development Bank (focusing on development in African countries).

In 1990, the European Bank for Reconstruction and Development was created to help the Eastern European countries adjust from communism to capitalism. Twelve Western European countries hold a 51 percent interest, while Eastern European countries hold a 13.5 percent interest. The United States is the biggest shareholder, with a 10 percent interest. There are 40 member countries in aggregate.

How International Trade Affects an MNC's Value

An MNC's value can be affected by international trade in several ways. The cash flows (and therefore the value) of an MNC's subsidiaries that export to a specific country are typically expected to increase in response to a higher inflation rate (causing local substitutes to be more expensive) or a higher national income (which increases the level of spending) in that country. The expected cash flows of the MNC's subsidiaries that export or import may increase as a result of country trade agreements that reduce tariffs or other trade barriers.

Cash flows to a U.S.-based MNC that occur in the form of payments for exports manufactured in the United States are expected to increase as a result of a weaker dollar because the demand for its dollar-denominated exports should increase. However, cash flows of U.S.-based importers may be reduced by a weaker dollar because it will take more dollars (increased cash outflows) to purchase the imports. A stronger dollar will have the opposite effects on cash flows of U.S.-based MNCs involved in international trade.

SUMMARY

- The key components of the balance of payments are the current account and the capital account. The current account is a broad measure of the country's international trade balance. The capital account is a measure of the country's long-term and short-term capital investments, including direct foreign investment and investment in securities (portfolio investment).
- A country's international trade flows are affected by inflation, national income, government restrictions, and exchange rates. High inflation, a high national income, low or no restrictions on imports, and a strong local currency tend to result in a strong demand for imports and a current account deficit. Although some countries attempt to correct current account deficits by reducing the value of their currencies, this strategy is not always successful.
- A country's international capital flows are affected by any factors that influence direct foreign investment or portfolio investment. Direct foreign investment tends to occur in those countries that have no restrictions and much potential for economic growth. Portfolio investment tends to occur in those countries where taxes are not excessive, where interest rates are high, and where the local currencies are not expected to weaken.

POINT COUNTER-POINT

Should Trade Restrictions Be Used to Influence Human Rights Issues?

Point Yes. Some countries do not protect human rights in the same manner as the United States. At times, the United States should threaten to restrict U.S. imports from or investment in a particular country if it does not correct human rights violations. The United States should use its large international trade and investment as leverage to ensure that human rights violations do not occur. Other countries with a history of human rights violations are more likely to honor human rights if their economic conditions are threatened.

Counter-Point No. International trade and human rights are two separate issues. International trade should not be used as the weapon to enforce human rights. Firms engaged in international trade should not be penalized by the human rights violations of a government. If the United States imposes trade restrictions to enforce human rights, the country will retaliate. Thus, the U.S. firms that export to that foreign country will be adversely affected. By imposing trade sanctions, the U.S. government is indirectly penalizing the MNCs that are attempting to conduct business in specific foreign countries. Trade sanctions cannot solve every difference in beliefs or morals between the more developed countries and the developing countries. By restricting trade, the United States will slow down the economic progress of developing countries.

Who Is Correct? Use InfoTrac or some other search engine to learn more about this issue. Which argument do you support? Offer your own opinion on this issue.

SELF TEST

Answers are provided in Appendix A at the back of the text.

1. Briefly explain how changes in various economic factors affect the U.S. current account balance.
2. Explain why U.S. tariffs may change the composition of U.S. exports but will not necessarily reduce a U.S. balance of trade deficit.
3. Explain how the Asian crisis affected trade between the United States and Asia.

QUESTIONS AND APPLICATIONS

1. **Balance of Payments.**

   a. What is the current account generally composed of?

   b. What is the capital account generally composed of?

2. **Inflation Effect on Trade.**

   a. How would a relatively high home inflation rate affect the home country's current account, other things being equal?

   b. Is a negative current account harmful to a country? Discuss.

3. **Government Restrictions.** How can government restrictions affect international payments among countries?

4. **IMF.**

   a. What are some of the major objectives of the IMF?

   b. How is the IMF involved in international trade?

5. **Exchange Rate Effect on Trade Balance.** Would the U.S. balance of trade deficit be larger or smaller if the dollar depreciates against all currencies, versus depreciating against some currencies but appreciating against others? Explain.

6. **Demand for Exports.** A relatively small U.S. balance of trade deficit is commonly attributed to a strong demand for U.S. exports. What do you think is the underlying reason for the strong demand for U.S. exports?

7. **September 11 Effects on Trade.** Why do you think international trade volume could be reduced as a result of the terrorist attacks on the United States on September 11, 2001? Are there any products for which international trade may increase?

8. **Effects of the Euro.** Explain how the existence of the euro may affect U.S. international trade.

9. **Currency Effects.** When South Korea's export growth stalled, some South Korean firms suggested that South Korea's primary export problem was the weakness in the Japanese yen. How would you interpret this statement?

10. **Effects of Tariffs.** Assume a simple world in which the United States exports soft drinks and beer to France and imports wine from France. If the United States imposes large tariffs on the French wine, explain the likely impact on the values of the U.S. beverage firms, U.S. wine producers, the French beverage firms, and the French wine producers.

ADVANCED QUESTIONS

11. **Free Trade.** There has been considerable momentum to reduce or remove trade barriers in an effort to achieve "free trade." Yet, one disgruntled executive of an exporting firm stated, "Free trade is not conceivable; we are always at the mercy of the exchange rate. Any country can use this mechanism to impose trade barriers." What does this statement mean?

12. **International Investments.** In recent years many U.S.-based MNCs have increased their investments in foreign securities, which are not as susceptible to negative shocks in the U.S. market. Also, when MNCs believe that U.S. securities are overvalued, they can pursue non-U.S. securities that are driven by a different market. Moreover, in periods of low U.S. interest rates, U.S. corporations tend to seek investments in foreign securities. In general, the flow of funds into foreign countries tends to decline when U.S. investors anticipate a strong dollar.

    a. Explain how expectations of a strong dollar can affect the tendency of U.S. investors to invest abroad.

    b. Explain how low U.S. interest rates can affect the tendency of U.S.-based MNCs to invest abroad.

    c. In general terms, what is the attraction of foreign investments to U.S. investors?

13. **Exchange Rate Effects on Trade.**

    a. Explain why a stronger dollar could enlarge the U.S. balance of trade deficit. Explain why a weaker dollar could affect the U.S. balance of trade deficit.

    b. It is sometimes suggested that a floating exchange rate will adjust to reduce or eliminate any current account deficit. Explain why this adjustment would occur.

    c. Why does the exchange rate not always adjust to a current account deficit?

INTERNET APPLICATION

14. **U.S. Balance of Trade** The website address of the Bureau of Economic Analysis is **http://www.bea.doc.gov**.

    a. Use this website to assess recent trends in exporting and importing by U.S. firms. How has the balance of trade changed over the last 12 months?

    b. Offer possible reasons for this change in the balance of trade.

DISCUSSION IN THE BOARDROOM

This exercise can be found in Appendix E at the back of this textbook.

RUNNING YOUR OWN MNC

This exercise can be found on the Xtra! website at **http://maduraxtra.swlearning.com**.

BLADES, INC. CASE

Exposure to International Flow of Funds

Ben Holt, chief financial officer (CFO) of Blades, Inc., has decided to counteract the decreasing demand for "Speedos" roller blades by exporting this product to Thailand. Furthermore, due to the low cost of rubber and plastic in Southeast Asia, Holt has decided to import some of the components needed to manufacture "Speedos" from Thailand. Holt feels that importing rubber and plastic components from Thailand will provide Blades with a cost advantage (the components imported from Thailand are about 20 percent cheaper than similar components in the United States). Currently, approximately $20 million, or 10 percent, of Blades' sales are contributed by its sales in Thailand. Only about 4 percent of Blades' cost of goods sold is attributable to rubber and plastic imported from Thailand.

Blades faces little competition in Thailand from other U.S. roller blades manufacturers. Those competitors that export roller blades to Thailand invoice their exports in U.S. dollars. Currently, Blades follows a policy of invoicing in Thai baht (Thailand's currency). Ben

Holt felt that this strategy would give Blades a competitive advantage, since Thai importers can plan more easily when they do not have to worry about paying differing amounts due to currency fluctuations. Furthermore, Blades' primary customer in Thailand (a retail store) has committed itself to purchasing a certain amount of "Speedos" annually if Blades will invoice in baht for a period of three years. Blades' purchases of components from Thai exporters are currently invoiced in Thai baht.

Ben Holt is rather content with current arrangements and believes the lack of competitors in Thailand, the quality of Blades' products, and its approach to pricing will ensure Blades' position in the Thai roller blade market in the future. Holt also feels that Thai importers will prefer Blades over its competitors because Blades invoices in Thai baht.

You, Blades' financial analyst, have doubts as to Blades' "guaranteed" future success. Although you believe Blades' strategy for its Thai sales and imports is sound, you are concerned about current expectations for the Thai economy. Current forecasts indicate a high level of anticipated inflation, a decreasing level of national income, and a continued depreciation of the Thai baht. In your opinion, all of these future developments could affect Blades financially given the company's current arrangements with its suppliers and with the Thai importers. Both Thai consumers and firms might adjust their spending habits should certain developments occur.

In the past, you have had difficulty convincing Ben Holt that problems could arise in Thailand. Consequently, you have developed a list of questions for yourself, which you plan to present to the company's CFO after you have answered them. Your questions are listed here:

1. How could a higher level of inflation in Thailand affect Blades (assume U.S. inflation remains constant)?
2. How could competition from firms in Thailand and from U.S. firms conducting business in Thailand affect Blades?
3. How could a decreasing level of national income in Thailand affect Blades?
4. How could a continued depreciation of the Thai baht affect Blades? How would it affect Blades relative to U.S. exporters invoicing their roller blades in U.S. dollars?
5. If Blades increases its business in Thailand and experiences serious financial problems, are there any international agencies that the company could approach for loans or other financial assistance?

SMALL BUSINESS DILEMMA

Identifying Factors That Will Affect the Foreign Demand at the Sports Exports Company

Recall from Chapter 1 that Jim Logan planned to pursue his dream of establishing his own business (called the Sports Exports Company) of exporting footballs to one or more foreign markets. Jim has decided to initially pursue the market in the United Kingdom because British citizens appear to have some interest in football as a possible hobby, and no other firm has capitalized on this idea in the United Kingdom. (The sporting goods shops in the United Kingdom do not sell footballs but might be willing to sell them.) Jim has contacted one sporting goods distributor that has agreed to purchase footballs on a monthly basis and distribute (sell) them to sporting goods stores throughout the United Kingdom. The distributor's demand for footballs is ultimately influenced by the demand for footballs by British citizens who shop in British sporting goods stores. The Sports Exports Company will receive British pounds when it sells the footballs to the distributor and will then convert the pounds into dollars. Jim recognizes that products (such as the footballs his firm will produce) exported from U.S. firms to foreign countries can be affected by various factors.

Identify the factors that affect the current account balance between the United States and the United Kingdom. Explain how each factor may possibly affect the British demand for the footballs that are produced by the Sports Exports Company.

CHAPTER 3

International Financial Markets

Due to growth in international business over the last 30 years, various international financial markets have been developed. Financial managers of MNCs must understand the various international financial markets that are available so that they can use those markets to facilitate their international business transactions.

The specific objectives of this chapter are to describe the background and corporate use of the following international financial markets:

- foreign exchange market,
- international money market,
- international credit market,
- international bond market, and
- international stock markets.

Motives for Using International Financial Markets

Several barriers prevent the markets for real or financial assets from becoming completely integrated; these barriers include tax differentials, tariffs, quotas, labor immobility, cultural differences, financial reporting differences, and significant costs of communicating information across countries. Nevertheless, the barriers can also create unique opportunities for specific geographic markets that will attract foreign creditors and investors. For example, barriers such as tariffs, quotas, and labor immobility can cause a given country's economic conditions to be distinctly different from others. Investors and creditors may want to do business in that country to capitalize on favorable conditions unique to that country. The existence of imperfect markets has precipitated the internationalization of financial markets.

Motives for Investing in Foreign Markets

Investors invest in foreign markets for one or more of the following motives:

- *Economic conditions.* Investors may expect firms in a particular foreign country to achieve more favorable performance than those in the investor's home country. For example, the loosening of restrictions in Eastern European countries created favorable economic conditions there. Such conditions attracted foreign investors and creditors.
- *Exchange rate expectations.* Some investors purchase financial securities denominated in a currency that is expected to appreciate against their own. The performance of such an investment is highly dependent on the currency movement over the investment horizon.
- *International diversification.* Investors may achieve benefits from internationally diversifying their asset portfolio. When an investor's entire portfolio does not depend solely on a single country's economy, cross-border differences in economic conditions can allow for risk-reduction benefits. A stock portfolio representing firms across European countries is less risky than a stock portfolio representing firms in any single European country. Furthermore, access to foreign markets allows investors to spread their funds across a more diverse group of industries than may be available domestically. This is especially true for investors residing in countries where firms are concentrated in a relatively small number of industries.

Motives for Providing Credit in Foreign Markets

Creditors (including individual investors who purchase debt securities) have one or more of the following motives for providing credit in foreign markets:

http://

Visit http://www.bloomberg.com for the latest information from financial markets around the world.

- *High foreign interest rates.* Some countries experience a shortage of loanable funds, which can cause market interest rates to be relatively high, even after considering default risk. Foreign creditors may attempt to capitalize on the higher rates, thereby providing capital to overseas markets. Often, however, relatively high interest rates are perceived to reflect relatively high inflationary expectations in that country. To the extent that inflation can cause depreciation of the local currency against others, high interest rates in the country may be somewhat offset by a weakening of the local currency over the time period of concern. The relation between a country's expected inflation and its local currency movements is not precise, however, because several other factors can influence currency movements as well. Thus, some creditors may believe that the interest rate advantage in a particular country will not be offset by a local currency depreciation over the period of concern.
- *Exchange rate expectations.* Creditors may consider supplying capital to countries whose currencies are expected to appreciate against their own. Whether the form of the transaction is a bond or a loan, the creditor benefits when the currency of denomination appreciates against the creditor's home currency.
- *International diversification.* Creditors can benefit from international diversification, which may reduce the probability of simultaneous bankruptcy across borrowers. The effectiveness of such a strategy depends on the correlation between the economic conditions of countries. If the countries of concern tend to experience somewhat similar business cycles, diversification across countries will be less effective.

Motives for Borrowing in Foreign Markets

Borrowers may have one or more of the following motives for borrowing in foreign markets:

- *Low interest rates.* Some countries have a large supply of funds available compared to the demand for funds, which can cause relatively low interest rates. Borrowers may attempt to borrow funds from creditors in these countries because the interest rate charged is lower. A country with relatively low interest rates is often expected to have a relatively low rate of inflation, which can place upward pressure on the foreign currency's value and offset any advantage of lower interest rates. The relation between expected inflation differentials and currency movements is not precise, however, so some borrowers will choose to borrow from a market where nominal interest rates are low, since they do not expect an adverse currency movement to fully offset this advantage.
- *Exchange rate expectations.* When a foreign subsidiary of a U.S.-based MNC remits funds to its U.S. parent, the funds must be converted to dollars and are subject to exchange rate risk. The MNC will be adversely affected if the foreign currency depreciates at that time. If the MNC expects that the foreign currency may depreciate against the dollar, it can reduce the exchange rate risk by having the subsidiary borrow funds locally to support its business. The subsidiary will remit less funds to the parent if it must pay interest on local debt before remitting the funds. Thus, the amount of funds converted to dollars will be smaller, resulting in less exposure to exchange rate risk.

If the U.S. parent needs to borrow funds for its own purposes, it may pursue a more aggressive strategy and borrow a foreign currency that is expected to depreciate. In this case, the parent would borrow that currency and convert it to dollars for use. The value of the foreign currency when converted to dollars would exceed the value when the MNC repurchases the currency to repay the loan. The favorable currency effect can offset part or all of the interest owed on the funds borrowed. Such a strategy may be especially desirable if the foreign currency has a low interest rate compared to the U.S. interest rate.

Foreign Exchange Market

When MNCs or other participants invest or borrow in foreign markets, they commonly rely on the foreign exchange market to obtain the currencies that they need. Thus, the act of borrowing or investing internationally typically requires the use of the foreign exchange market. By allowing currencies to be exchanged, the **foreign exchange market** facilitates international trade and financial transactions. MNCs rely on the foreign exchange market to exchange their home currency for a foreign currency that they need to purchase imports or to use for direct foreign investment. Alternatively, they may need the foreign exchange market to exchange a foreign currency that they receive into their home currency. The system for establishing exchange rates has changed over time.

History of Foreign Exchange

The system used for exchanging foreign currencies has evolved from the gold standard, to an agreement on fixed exchange rates, to a floating rate system.

Gold Standard. From 1876 to 1913, exchange rates were dictated by the **gold standard**. Each currency was convertible into gold at a specified rate. Thus, the exchange rate between two currencies was determined by their relative convertibility rates per ounce of gold. Each country used gold to back its currency.

When World War I began in 1914, the gold standard was suspended. Some countries reverted to the gold standard in the 1920s but abandoned it as a result of a banking panic in the United States and Europe during the Great Depression. In the 1930s, some countries attempted to peg their currency to the dollar or the British pound, but there were frequent revisions. As a result of the instability in the foreign exchange market and the severe restrictions on international transactions during this period, the volume of international trade declined.

Agreements on Fixed Exchange Rates. In 1944, an international agreement (known as the **Bretton Woods Agreement**) called for fixed exchange rates between currencies. This agreement lasted until 1971. During this period, governments would intervene to prevent exchange rates from moving more than 1 percent above or below their initially established levels.

By 1971, the U.S. dollar appeared to be overvalued; the foreign demand for U.S. dollars was substantially less than the supply of dollars for sale (to be exchanged for other currencies). Representatives from the major nations met to discuss this dilemma. As a result of this conference, which led to the **Smithsonian Agreement**, the U.S. dollar was devalued relative to the other major currencies. The degree to which the dollar was devalued varied with each foreign currency. Not only was the dollar's value reset, but exchange rates were also allowed to fluctuate by 2.25 percent in either direction from the newly set rates. This was the first step in letting market forces (supply and demand) determine the appropriate price of a currency. Although boundaries still existed for exchange rates, they were widened, allowing the currency values to move more freely toward their appropriate levels.

Floating Exchange Rate System. Even after the Smithsonian Agreement, governments still had difficulty maintaining exchange rates within the stated boundaries. By March 1973, the more widely traded currencies were allowed to fluctuate in accordance with market forces, and the official boundaries were eliminated.

Foreign Exchange Transactions

The "foreign exchange market" should not be thought of as a specific building or location where traders exchange currencies. Companies normally exchange one currency for another through a commercial bank over a telecommunications network.

Spot Market. The most common type of foreign exchange transaction is for immediate exchange at the so-called **spot rate**. The market where these transactions occur is known as the **spot market**. The average daily foreign exchange trading by banks around the world now exceeds $1.5 trillion. The average daily foreign exchange trading in the United States alone exceeds $200 billion.

USING THE WEB

Historical Exchange Rates Historical exchange rate movements are provided at http://www.oanda.com. Data are available on a daily basis for most currencies.

The U.S. dollar is not part of every transaction. Foreign currencies can be traded for each other. For example, a Japanese firm may need British pounds to pay for imports from the United Kingdom. Although banks in London, New York, and Tokyo, the three largest foreign exchange trading centers, conduct much of the foreign exchange trading, many foreign exchange transactions occur outside these trading centers. Banks in virtually every major city facilitate foreign exchange transactions between MNCs. Commercial transactions between countries are often done electronically, but the exchange rate at the time affects the amount of funds involved in the transaction.

EXAMPLE

Indiana Co. purchases supplies priced at 100,000 euros (€) from Belgo, a Belgian supplier, on the first day of every month. Indiana instructs its bank to transfer funds from its account to the supplier's account on the first day of each month. It only has dollars in its account, whereas Belgo's account is in euros. When payment was made one month ago, the euro was worth $1.08, so Indiana Co. needed $108,000 to pay for the supplies (€100,000 × $1.08 = $108,000). The bank reduced Indiana's account balance by $108,000, which was exchanged at the bank for €100,000. The bank then sent the €100,000 electronically to Belgo by increasing Belgo's account balance by €100,000. Today, a new payment needs to be made. The euro is currently valued at $1.12, so the bank will reduce Indiana's account balance by $112,000 (€100,000 × $1.12 = $112,000) and exchange it for €100,000, which will be sent electronically to Belgo.

The bank not only executes the transactions but also serves as the foreign exchange dealer. Each month the bank receives dollars from Indiana Co. in exchange for the euros it provides. In addition, the bank facilitates other transactions for MNCs in which it receives euros in exchange for dollars. The bank maintains an inventory of euros, dollars, and other currencies to facilitate these foreign exchange transactions. If the transactions cause it to buy as many euros as it sells to MNCs, its inventory of euros will not change. If the bank sells more euros than it buys, however, its inventory of euros will be reduced.

Other intermediaries also serve the foreign exchange market. Some other financial institutions such as securities firms can provide the same services described in the previous example. In addition, most major airports around the world have foreign exchange centers, where individuals can exchange currencies. In many cities, there are retail foreign exchange offices where tourists and other individuals can exchange currencies.

Use of the Dollar in the Spot Market. Many foreign transactions do not require an exchange of currencies but allow a given currency to cross country borders. For example, the U.S. dollar is commonly accepted as a medium of exchange by merchants in many countries, especially in countries such as Bolivia, Brazil, China, Cuba, Indonesia, Russia, and Vietnam where the home currency is either weak or subject to foreign exchange restrictions. Many merchants accept U.S. dollars because they can use them to purchase goods from other countries. The U.S. dollar is the official currency of Ecuador, Liberia, and Panama.

Spot Market Structure. Hundreds of banks facilitate foreign exchange transactions, but the top 20 handle about 50 percent of the transactions. Deutsche Bank (Germany), Citibank (a subsidiary of Citigroup, U.S.), and J.P. Morgan Chase are the largest traders of foreign exchange. Some banks and other financial institutions have formed alliances (one example is FX Alliance LLC) to offer currency transactions over the Internet.

At any given point in time, the exchange rate between two currencies should be similar across the various banks that provide foreign exchange services. If there is a large discrepancy, customers or other banks will purchase large amounts of a currency from whatever bank quotes a relatively low price and immediately sell it to whatever bank quotes a relatively high price. Such actions cause adjustments in the exchange rate quotations that eliminate any discrepancy.

If a bank begins to experience a shortage in a particular foreign currency, it can purchase that currency from other banks. This trading between banks occurs in what is often referred to as the **interbank market**. Within this market, banks can obtain quotes, or they can contact brokers who sometimes act as intermediaries, matching one bank desiring to sell a given currency with another bank desiring to buy that currency. About 10 foreign exchange brokerage firms handle much of the interbank transaction volume.

Although foreign exchange trading is conducted only during normal business hours in a given location, these hours vary among locations due to different time zones. Thus, at any given time on a weekday, somewhere around the world a bank is open and ready to accommodate foreign exchange requests.

When the foreign exchange market opens in the United States each morning, the opening exchange rate quotations are based on the prevailing rates quoted by banks in London and other locations where the foreign exchange markets have opened earlier. Suppose the quoted spot rate of the British pound was $1.80 at the previous close of the U.S. foreign exchange market, but by the time the market opens the following day, the opening spot rate is $1.76. News occurring in the morning before the U.S. market opened could have changed the supply and demand conditions for British pounds in the London foreign exchange market, reducing the quoted price for the pound.

With the newest electronic devices, foreign currency trades are negotiated on computer terminals, and a push of a button confirms the trade. Traders now use electronic trading boards that allow them to instantly register transactions and check their bank's positions in various currencies. Also, several U.S. banks have established night trading desks. The largest banks initiated night trading to capitalize on foreign exchange movements at night and to accommodate corporate requests for currency trades. Even some medium-sized banks now offer night trading to accommodate corporate clients.

Spot Market Liquidity. The spot market for each currency can be described by its liquidity, which reflects the level of trading activity. The more willing buyers and sellers there are, the more liquid a market is. The spot markets for heavily traded currencies such as the euro, the British pound, and the Japanese yen are very liquid. Conversely, the spot markets for currencies of less developed countries are less liquid. A currency's liquidity affects the ease with which an MNC can obtain or sell that currency. If a currency is illiquid, the number of willing buyers and sellers is limited, and an MNC may be unable to quickly purchase or sell that currency at a reasonable exchange rate.

Forward Transactions. In addition to the spot market, a forward market for currencies enables an MNC to lock in the exchange rate (called a **forward rate**) at which it will buy or sell a currency. A **forward contract** specifies the amount of a particular currency that will be purchased or sold by the MNC at a specified future point in time and at a specified exchange rate. Commercial banks accommodate the MNCs that desire forward contracts. MNCs commonly use the forward market to hedge future payments that they expect to make or receive in a foreign currency. In this way, they do not have to worry about fluctuations in the spot rate until the time of their future payments. The liquidity of the forward market varies among currencies. The forward market for euros is very liquid because many MNCs take forward positions to hedge their future payments in euros. In contrast, the forward markets for Latin American and Eastern European currencies are less liquid because there is less international trade with those countries and therefore MNCs take fewer forward positions. For some currencies, there is no forward market.

Attributes of Banks That Provide Foreign Exchange. The following characteristics of banks are important to customers in need of foreign exchange:

1. *Competitiveness of quote.* A savings of 1¢ per unit on an order of one million units of currency is worth $10,000.
2. *Special relationship with the bank.* The bank may offer cash management services or be willing to make a special effort to obtain even hard-to-find foreign currencies for the corporation.
3. *Speed of execution.* Banks may vary in the efficiency with which they handle an order. A corporation needing the currency will prefer a bank that conducts the transaction promptly and handles any paperwork properly.
4. *Advice about current market conditions.* Some banks may provide assessments of foreign economies and relevant activities in the international financial environment that relate to corporate customers.
5. *Forecasting advice.* Some banks may provide forecasts of the future state of foreign economies, the future value of exchange rates, and the like.

This list suggests that a corporation needing a foreign currency should not automatically choose a bank that will sell that currency at the lowest price. Most corporations that often need foreign currencies develop a close relationship with at least one major bank in case they ever need favors from a bank.

USING THE WEB

Currency Accounts for Individuals Individuals can open an FDIC-insured money market account or a CD account in a foreign currency. The details are provided at http://www.everbank.com. Look for the link to FDIC-Insured Deposits in Foreign Currencies.

MANAGING FOR VALUE

Intel's Currency Trading

When Intel needs to exchange foreign currency, it no longer calls a bank to request an exchange of currencies. Instead, it logs on to an online currency trader that serves as an intermediary between Intel and member banks. One popular online currency trader is Currenex, which conducts more than $300 million in foreign exchange transactions per day. If Intel needs to purchase a foreign currency, it logs on and specifies its order. Currenex relays the order to various banks that are members of its system and are allowed to bid for the orders. When Currenex relays the order, member banks have 25 seconds to specify a quote online for the currency that the customer (Intel) desires. Then, Currenex displays the quotes on a screen, ranked from highest to lowest. Intel has 5 seconds to select one of the quotes provided, and the deal is completed. This process is much more transparent than traditional foreign exchange market transactions because Intel can review quotes of many competitors at one time. By enabling Intel to make sure that it does not overpay for a currency, this system enhances the company's value.

Bid/Ask Spread of Banks. Commercial banks charge fees for conducting foreign exchange transactions. At any given point in time, a bank's **bid** (buy) quote for a foreign currency will be less than its ask (**sell**) quote. The **bid/ask spread** represents the differential between the bid and ask quotes, and is intended to cover the costs involved in accommodating requests to exchange currencies. The bid/ask spread is normally expressed as a percentage of the ask quote.

EXAMPLE

To understand how a bid/ask spread could affect you, assume you have $1,000 and plan to travel from the United States to the United Kingdom. Assume further that the bank's bid rate for the British pound is $1.52 and its ask rate is $1.60. Before leaving on your trip, you go to this bank to exchange dollars for pounds. Your $1,000 will be converted to 625 pounds (£), as follows:

$$\frac{\text{Amount of U.S. dollars to be converted}}{\text{Price charged by bank per pound}} = \frac{\$1{,}000}{\$1.60} = £625$$

Now suppose that because of an emergency you cannot take the trip, and you reconvert the £625 back to U.S. dollars, just after purchasing the pounds. If the exchange rate has not changed, you will receive

$$£625 \times (\text{Bank's bid rate of } \$1.52 \text{ per pound}) = \$950.$$

Due to the bid/ask spread, you have $50 (5 percent) less than what you started with. Obviously, the dollar amount of the loss would be larger if you originally converted more than $1,000 into pounds.

USING THE WEB

Bid and Ask Quotations Bid and ask quotations are provided for all major currencies at http://www.sonnet-financial.com/rates/full.asp. This website provides exchange rates for many currencies. The table can be customized to focus on the currencies of interest to you.

Comparison of Bid/Ask Spread among Currencies. The differential between a bid quote and an ask quote will look much smaller for currencies that have a smaller value. This differential can be standardized by measuring it as a percentage of the currency's spot rate.

EXAMPLE

Charlotte Bank quotes a bid price for yen of $.007 and an ask price of $.0074. In this case, the nominal bid/ask spread is $.0074 − $.007, or just four-hundredths of a penny. Yet, the bid/ask spread in percentage terms is actually slightly higher for the yen in this example than for the pound in the previous example. To prove this, consider a traveler who sells $1,000 for yen at the bank's ask price of $.0074. The traveler receives about ¥135,135 (computed as $1,000/$.0074). If the traveler cancels the trip and converts the yen back to dollars, then, assuming no changes in the bid/ask quotations, the bank will buy these yen back at the bank's bid price of $.007 for a total of about $946 (computed by ¥135,135 × $.007), $54 (or 5.4 percent) less than what the traveler started with. This spread exceeds that of the British pound (5 percent in the previous example).

A common way to compute the bid/ask spread in percentage terms follows:

$$\text{Bid/ask spread} = \frac{\text{Ask rate} - \text{Bid rate}}{\text{Ask rate}}$$

Exhibit 3.1
Computation of the Bid/Ask Spread

Currency	Bid Rate	Ask Rate	$\frac{\text{Ask Rate} - \text{Bid Rate}}{\text{Ask Rate}}$	=	Bid/Ask Percentage Spread
British pound	$1.52	$1.60	$\frac{\$1.60 - \$1.52}{\$1.60}$	=	.05 *or* 5%
Japanese yen	$ .0070	$ .0074	$\frac{\$.0074 - \$.007}{\$.0074}$	=	.054 *or* 5.4%

Using this formula, the bid/ask spreads are computed in Exhibit 3.1 for both the British pound and the Japanese yen.

Notice that these numbers coincide with those derived earlier. Such spreads are common for so-called retail transactions serving consumers. For larger so-called wholesale transactions between banks or for large corporations, the spread will be much smaller. The bid/ask spread for small retail transactions is commonly in the range of 3 to 7 percent; for wholesale transactions requested by MNCs, the spread is between .01 and .03 percent. The spread is normally larger for illiquid currencies that are less frequently traded. Commercial banks are normally exposed to more exchange rate risk when maintaining these currencies.

The bid/ask spread as defined here represents the discount in the bid rate as a percentage of the ask rate. An alternative bid/ask spread uses the bid rate as the denominator instead of the ask rate and measures the percentage markup of the ask rate above the bid rate. The spread is slightly higher when using this formula because the bid rate used in the denominator is always less than the ask rate.

In the following discussion and in examples throughout much of the text, the bid/ask spread will be ignored. That is, only one price will be shown for a given currency to allow you to concentrate on understanding other relevant concepts. These examples depart slightly from reality because the bid and ask prices are, in a sense, assumed to be equal. Although the ask price will always exceed the bid price by a small amount in reality, the implications from examples should nevertheless hold, even though the bid/ask spreads are not accounted for. In particular examples where the bid/ask spread can contribute significantly to the concept, it will be accounted for.

Various websites, including bloomberg.com, provide bid/ask quotations. To conserve space, some quotations show the entire bid price followed by a slash and then only the last two or three digits of the ask price.

EXAMPLE

Assume that the prevailing quote for wholesale transactions by a commercial bank for the euro is $1.0876/78. This means that the commercial bank is willing to pay $1.0876 per euro. Alternatively, it is willing to sell euros for $1.0878. The bid/ask spread in this example is:

$$\text{Bid/ask spread} = \frac{\$1.0878 - \$1.0876}{\$1.0878}$$

$$= \text{about } .000184 \text{ or } .0184\%.$$

Factors That Affect the Spread. The spread on currency quotations is influenced by the following factors:

$$\text{Spread} = f(\underset{+}{\text{Order costs}}, \underset{+}{\text{Inventory costs}}, \underset{-}{\text{Competition}}, \underset{-}{\text{Volume}}, \underset{+}{\text{Currency risk}})$$

- *Order costs.* Order costs are the costs of processing orders, including clearing costs and the costs of recording transactions.
- *Inventory costs.* Inventory costs are the costs of maintaining an inventory of a particular currency. Holding an inventory involves an opportunity cost because the funds could have been used for some other purpose. If interest rates are relatively high, the opportunity cost of holding an inventory should be relatively high. The higher the inventory costs, the larger the spread that will be established to cover these costs.
- *Competition.* The more intense the competition, the smaller the spread quoted by intermediaries. Competition is more intense for the more widely traded currencies because there is more business in those currencies.
- *Volume.* More liquid currencies are less likely to experience a sudden change in price. Currencies that have a large trading volume are more liquid because there are numerous buyers and sellers at any given time. This means that the market has sufficient depth that a few large transactions are unlikely to cause the currency's price to change abruptly.
- *Currency risk.* Some currencies exhibit more volatility than others because of economic or political conditions that cause the demand for and supply of the currency to change abruptly. For example, currencies in countries that have frequent political crises are subject to abrupt price movements. Intermediaries that are willing to buy or sell these currencies could incur large losses due to an abrupt change in the values of these currencies.

Interpreting Foreign Exchange Quotations

Exchange rate quotations for widely traded currencies are published in *The Wall Street Journal* and in business sections of many newspapers on a daily basis. With some exceptions, each country has its own currency. In 1999, several European countries (including Germany, France, and Italy) adopted the euro as their new currency for commercial transactions, replacing their own currencies. Their own currencies were phased out by the year 2002.

Quotations of Forward Rates. Some quotations of exchange rates include forward rates for the most widely traded currencies. Other forward rates are not quoted in business newspapers but are quoted by the banks that offer forward contracts in various currencies.

Direct versus Indirect Quotations. The quotations of exchange rates for currencies normally reflect the ask prices for large transactions. Since exchange rates change throughout the day, the exchange rates quoted in a newspaper reflect only one specific point in time during the day. Quotations that represent the value of a foreign currency in dollars (number of dollars per currency) are referred to as **direct quotations**. Conversely, quotations that represent the number of units of a foreign currency per dollar are referred to as **indirect quotations**. The indirect quotation is the reciprocal of the corresponding direct quotation.

EXAMPLE

The spot rate of the euro is quoted this morning at $1.031. This is a direct quotation, as it represents the value of the foreign currency in dollars. The indirect quotation of the euro is the reciprocal of the direct quotation:

$$\begin{aligned}\text{Indirect quotation} &= 1/\text{Direct quotation}\\ &= 1/\$1.031\\ &= .97, \text{ which means } .97 \text{ euros} = \$1.\end{aligned}$$

If you initially received the indirect quotation, you can take the reciprocal of it to obtain the direct quote. Since the indirect quotation for the euro is $.97, the direct quotation is:

$$\text{Direct quotation} = 1/\text{Indirect quotation}$$
$$= 1/.97$$
$$= \$1.031.$$

A comparison of direct and indirect exchange rates for two points in time appears in Exhibit 3.2. Columns 2 and 3 provide quotes at the beginning of the semester, while columns 4 and 5 provide quotes at the end of the semester. For each currency, the indirect quotes at the beginning and end of the semester (columns 3 and 5) are the reciprocals of the direct quotes at the beginning and end of the semester (columns 2 and 4).

The exhibit illustrates how the indirect quotation adjusts in response to changes in the direct quotation.

Based on Exhibit 3.2, the Canadian dollar's direct quotation changed from $.66 to $.70 over the semester. This change reflects an appreciation of the Canadian dollar, as the currency's value increased over the semester. Notice that the Canadian dollar's indirect quotation decreased from 1.51 to 1.43 over the semester. This means that it takes fewer Canadian dollars to obtain a U.S. dollar at the end of the semester than it took at the beginning. This change also confirms that the Canadian dollar's value has strengthened, but it can be confusing because the decline in the indirect quote over time reflects an appreciation of the currency.

Notice that the Mexican peso's direct quotation changed from $.12 to $.11 over the semester. This reflects a depreciation of the peso. The indirect quotation increased over the semester, which means that it takes more pesos at the end of the semester to obtain a U.S. dollar than it took at the beginning. This change also confirms that the peso has depreciated over the semester.

The examples illustrate that the direct and indirect quotations for a given currency move in opposite directions over a particular period. This relationship should be obvious by now: as one quotation moves in one direction, the reciprocal of that quotation must

Exhibit 3.2 Direct and Indirect Exchange Rate Quotations

(1) Currency	(2) Direct Quotation as of Beginning of Semester	(3) Indirect Quotation (number of units per dollar) as of Beginning of Semester	(4) Direct Quotation as of End of Semester	(5) Indirect Quotation (number of units per dollar) as of End of Semester
Canadian dollar	$.66	1.51	$.70	1.43
Euro	$1.031	.97	$1.064	.94
Japanese yen	$.009	111.11	$.0097	103.09
Mexican peso	$.12	8.33	$.11	9.09
Swiss franc	$.62	1.61	$.67	1.49
U.K. pound	$1.50	.67	$1.60	.62

move in the opposite direction. If you are doing any extensive analysis of exchange rates, you should first convert all exchange rates into direct quotations. In this way, you can more easily compare currencies and are less likely to make a mistake in determining whether a currency is appreciating or depreciating over a particular period.

Discussions of exchange rate movements can be confusing if some comments refer to direct quotations while others refer to indirect quotations. For consistency, this text uses direct quotations unless an example can be clarified by the use of indirect quotations. Direct quotations are easier to link with comments about any foreign currency.

Cross Exchange Rates. Most tables of exchange rate quotations express currencies relative to the dollar, but in some instances, a firm will be concerned about the exchange rate between two nondollar currencies. For example, if a Canadian firm needs Mexican pesos to buy Mexican goods, it wants to know the Mexican peso value relative to the Canadian dollar. The type of rate desired here is known as a **cross exchange rate**, because it reflects the amount of one foreign currency per unit of another foreign currency. Cross exchange rates can be easily determined with the use of foreign exchange quotations. The value of any nondollar currency in terms of another is its value in dollars divided by the other currency's value in dollars.

EXAMPLE

If the peso is worth \$.07, and the Canadian dollar is worth \$.70, the value of the peso in Canadian dollars (C\$) is calculated as follows:

$$\text{Value of peso in C\$} = \frac{\text{Value of peso in \$}}{\text{Value of C\$ in \$}} = \$.07 \,/\, \$.70 = \text{C\$}.10$$

Thus, a Mexican peso is worth C\$.10. The exchange rate can also be expressed as the number of pesos equal to one Canadian dollar. This figure can be computed by taking the reciprocal: .70/.07 = 10.0, which indicates that a Canadian dollar is worth 10.0 pesos according to the information provided.

USING THE WEB

Cross Exchange Rates Cross exchange rates for several currencies are provided at http://www.bloomberg.com.

Currency Futures and Options Markets

A **currency futures contract** specifies a standard volume of a particular currency to be exchanged on a specific settlement date. Some MNCs involved in international trade use the currency futures markets to hedge their positions.

EXAMPLE

Memphis Co. has ordered supplies from European countries that are denominated in euros. It expects the euro to increase in value over time and therefore desires to hedge its payables in euros. Memphis buys futures contracts on euros to lock in the price that it will pay for euros at a future point in time. Meanwhile, it will receive Mexican pesos in the future and wants to hedge these receivables. Memphis sells futures contracts on pesos to lock in the dollars that it will receive when it sells the pesos at a specified point in the future.

Futures contracts are somewhat similar to forward contracts except that they are sold on an exchange whereas forward contracts are offered by commercial banks. Additional details on futures contracts, including other differences from forward contracts, are provided in Chapter 5.

Currency options contracts can be classified as calls or puts. A **currency call option** provides the right to buy a specific currency at a specific price (called the **strike price** or **exercise price**) within a specific period of time. It is used to hedge future payables. A **currency put option** provides the right to sell a specific currency at a specific price within a specific period of time. It is used to hedge future receivables.

Currency call and put options can be purchased on an exchange. They offer more flexibility than forward or futures contracts because they do not require any obligation. That is, the firm can elect not to exercise the option.

Currency options have become a popular means of hedging. The Coca-Cola Co. has replaced about 30 to 40 percent of its forward contracting with currency options. FMC, a U.S. manufacturer of chemicals and machinery, now hedges its foreign sales with currency options instead of forward contracts. A recent study by the Whitney Group found that 85 percent of U.S.-based MNCs use currency options. Additional details about currency options, including other differences from futures and forward contracts, are provided in Chapter 5.

International Money Market

Financial markets exist in every country to ensure that funds are transferred efficiently from surplus units (savers) to deficit units (borrowers). These markets are overseen by various regulators that attempt to enhance the markets' safety and efficiency. The financial institutions that serve these financial markets exist primarily to provide information and expertise. The increase in international business has resulted in the development of an international money market. Financial institutions in this market serve MNCs by accepting deposits and offering loans in a variety of currencies. In general, the international money market is distinguished from domestic money markets by the types of transactions between the participating financial institutions and the MNCs. The financial transactions are in a wide variety of currencies, and large, often the equivalent of $1 million or more.

Origins and Development

The international money market includes large banks in countries around the world. Large U.S. financial institutions such as Citigroup and J.P. Morgan Chase are major participants. Two other important elements of the international money market are the European money market and the Asian money market.

European Money Market. The origins of the European money market can be traced to the Eurocurrency market that developed during the 1960s and 1970s. As MNCs expanded their operations during that period, international financial intermediation emerged to accommodate their needs. Because the U.S. dollar was widely used even by foreign countries as a medium for international trade, there was a consistent need for dollars in Europe and elsewhere. To conduct international trade with European countries, corporations in the United States deposited U.S. dollars in European banks. The banks were willing to accept the deposits because they could lend the dollars to corporate customers based in Europe. These dollar deposits in banks in Europe (and on other continents as well) came to be known as **Eurodollars**, and the market for Eurodollars came to be known as the **Eurocurrency market**. ("Eurodollars" and "Eurocurrency" should not be confused with the "euro," which is the currency of many European countries today.)

The growth of the Eurocurrency market was stimulated by regulatory changes in the United States. For example, when the United States limited foreign lending by U.S. banks in 1968, foreign subsidiaries of U.S.-based MNCs could obtain U.S. dollars from banks in Europe via the Eurocurrency market. Similarly, when ceilings were placed on the interest rates paid on dollar deposits in the United States, MNCs transferred their funds to European banks, which were not subject to the ceilings.

The growing importance of the Organization of Petroleum Exporting Countries (OPEC) also contributed to the growth of the Eurocurrency market. Because OPEC generally requires payment for oil in dollars, the OPEC countries began to use the Eurocurrency market to deposit a portion of their oil reserves. These dollar-denominated deposits are sometimes known as **petrodollars**. Oil revenues deposited in banks have sometimes been lent to oil-importing countries that are short of cash. As these countries purchase more oil, funds are again transferred to the oil-exporting countries, which in turn create new deposits. This recycling process has been an important source of funds for some countries.

Today, the term *Eurocurrency market* is not used as often as in the past because several other international financial markets have been developed. The European money market is still an important part of the network of international money markets, however.

Asian Money Market. Like the European money market, the Asian money market originated as a market involving mostly dollar-denominated deposits. Hence, it was originally known as the **Asian dollar market**. The market emerged to accommodate the needs of businesses that were using the U.S. dollar (and some other foreign currencies) as a medium of exchange for international trade. These businesses could not rely on banks in Europe because of the distance and different time zones. Today, the Asian money market, as it is now called, is centered in Hong Kong and Singapore, where large banks accept deposits and make loans in various foreign currencies.

Functions of the International Money Market. Today, both the Asian money market and the European money market are key components of the international money market. The primary function of banks in this market is to channel funds from depositors to borrowers. For example, the major sources of deposits in the Asian money market are MNCs with excess cash and government agencies. Manufacturers are major borrowers in this market. Another function is interbank lending and borrowing. Banks that have more qualified loan applicants than they can accommodate use the interbank market to obtain additional funds. Banks in the Asian money market commonly borrow from or lend to banks in the European market.

Standardizing Global Bank Regulations

The growing standardization of regulations around the world has contributed to the trend toward globalization in the banking industry. Three of the more significant regulatory events allowing for a more competitive global playing field are (1) the Single European Act, (2) the Basel Accord, and (3) the Basel II Accord.

Single European Act. One of the most significant events affecting international banking was the **Single European Act**, which was phased in by 1992 throughout the European Union (EU) countries. The following are some of the more relevant provisions of the Single European Act for the banking industry:

- Capital can flow freely throughout Europe.
- Banks can offer a wide variety of lending, leasing, and securities activities in the EU.
- Regulations regarding competition, mergers, and taxes are similar throughout the EU.
- A bank established in any one of the EU countries has the right to expand into any or all of the other EU countries.

As a result of this act, banks have expanded across European countries. Efficiency in the European banking markets has increased because banks can more easily cross countries without concern for country-specific regulations that prevailed in the past.

Another key provision of the act is that banks entering Europe receive the same banking powers as other banks there. Similar provisions apply to non-U.S. banks that enter the United States.

Basel Accord. Before 1987, capital standards imposed on banks varied across countries, which allowed some banks to have a comparative global advantage over others. As an example, suppose that banks in the United States were required to maintain more capital than foreign banks. Foreign banks would grow more easily, as they would need a relatively small amount of capital to support an increase in assets. Despite their low capital, such banks were not necessarily perceived as too risky because the governments in those countries were likely to back banks that experienced financial problems. Therefore, some non-U.S. banks had globally competitive advantages over U.S. banks, without being subject to excessive risk. In December 1987, 12 major industrialized countries attempted to resolve the disparity by proposing uniform bank standards. In July 1988, in the **Basel Accord**, central bank governors of the 12 countries agreed on standardized guidelines. Under these guidelines, banks must maintain capital equal to at least 4 percent of their assets. For this purpose, banks' assets are weighted by risk. This essentially results in a higher required capital ratio for riskier assets. Off-balance sheet items are also accounted for so that banks cannot circumvent capital requirements by focusing on services that are not explicitly shown as assets on a balance sheet.

Basel II Accord. Banking regulators that form the so-called Basel Committee are working on a new accord (called Basel II) to correct some inconsistencies that still exist. For example, banks in some countries have required better collateral to back their loans. The Basel II accord is attempting to account for such differences among banks. In addition, this accord will account for operational risk, which is defined by the Basel Committee as the risk of losses resulting from inadequate or failed internal processes or systems. The Basel Committee wants to encourage banks to improve their techniques for controlling operational risk, which could reduce failures in the banking system. The Basel Committee also plans to require banks to provide more information to existing and prospective shareholders about their exposure to different types of risk.

International Credit Market

Multinational corporations and domestic firms sometimes obtain medium-term funds through term loans from local financial institutions or through the issuance of notes (medium-term debt obligations) in their local markets. However, MNCs also have access to medium-term funds through banks located in foreign markets. Loans of one year or longer extended by banks to MNCs or government agencies in Europe are commonly called Eurocredits or **Eurocredit loans**. These loans are provided in the so-called **Eurocredit market**. The loans can be denominated in dollars or many other currencies and commonly have a maturity of five years.

Because banks accept short-term deposits and sometimes provide longer-term loans, their asset and liability maturities do not match. This can adversely affect a bank's performance during periods of rising interest rates, since the bank may have locked in a rate on its longer-term loans while the rate it pays on short-term deposits is rising over time. To avoid this risk, banks commonly use floating rate loans. The loan rate floats in accordance with the movement of some market interest rate, such as the **London Interbank Offer Rate (LIBOR)**, which is the rate commonly charged for loans between banks. For example, a Eurocredit loan may have a loan rate that adjusts every six months and is set at "LIBOR plus 3 percent." The premium paid above LIBOR will depend on the credit risk of the borrower. The LIBOR varies among currencies because the market supply of and demand for funds vary among currencies.

The international credit market is well developed in Asia and is developing in South America. Periodically, some regions are affected by an economic crisis, which increases the credit risk. Financial institutions tend to reduce their participation in those markets when credit risk increases. Thus, even though funding is widely available in many markets, the funds tend to move toward the markets where economic conditions are strong and credit risk is tolerable.

Syndicated Loans

Sometimes a single bank is unwilling or unable to lend the amount needed by a particular corporation or government agency. In this case, a **syndicate** of banks may be organized. Each bank within the syndicate participates in the lending. A lead bank is responsible for negotiating terms with the borrower. Then the lead bank organizes a group of banks to underwrite the loans. The syndicate of banks is usually formed in about six weeks, or less if the borrower is well known because the credit evaluation can then be conducted more quickly.

Borrowers that receive a syndicated loan incur various fees besides the interest on the loan. Front-end management fees are paid to cover the costs of organizing the syndicate and underwriting the loan. In addition, a commitment fee of about .25 percent or .50 percent is charged annually on the unused portion of the available credit extended by the syndicate.

Syndicated loans can be denominated in a variety of currencies. The interest rate depends on the currency denominating the loan, the maturity of the loan, and the creditworthiness of the borrower. Interest rates on syndicated loans are commonly adjustable according to movements in an interbank lending rate, and the adjustment may occur every six months or every year.

Syndicated loans not only reduce the default risk of a large loan to the degree of participation for each individual bank, but they can also add an extra incentive for the borrower to repay the loan. If a government defaults on a loan to a syndicate, word will quickly spread among banks, and the government will likely have difficulty obtaining future loans. Borrowers are therefore strongly encouraged to repay syndicated loans promptly. From the perspective of the banks, syndicated loans increase the probability of prompt repayment.

International Bond Market

Although MNCs, like domestic firms, can obtain long-term debt by issuing bonds in their local markets, MNCs can also access long-term funds in foreign markets. MNCs may choose to issue bonds in the international bond markets for three reasons. First, issuers recognize that they may be able to attract a stronger demand by issuing their bonds in a particular foreign country rather than in their home country. Some countries have a limited investor base, so MNCs in those countries seek financing elsewhere. Second, MNCs may prefer to finance a specific foreign project in a particular currency and therefore may attempt to obtain funds where that currency is widely used. Third, financing in a foreign currency with a lower interest rate may enable an MNC to reduce its cost of financing, although it may be exposed to exchange rate risk (as explained in later chapters). Some institutional investors prefer to invest in international bond markets rather than their respective local markets when they can earn a higher return on bonds denominated in foreign currencies.

International bonds are typically classified as either foreign bonds or Eurobonds. A **foreign bond** is issued by a borrower foreign to the country where the bond is placed. For example, a U.S. corporation may issue a bond denominated in Japanese yen, which is sold to investors in Japan. In some cases, a firm may issue a variety of bonds in various countries. The currency denominating each type of bond is determined by the country where it is sold. These foreign bonds are sometimes specifically referred to as **parallel bonds**.

Eurobond Market

Eurobonds are bonds that are sold in countries other than the country of the currency denominating the bonds. The emergence of the Eurobond market was partially the result of the **Interest Equalization Tax (IET)** imposed by the U.S. government in 1963 to discourage U.S. investors from investing in foreign securities. Thus, non-U.S. borrowers that historically had sold foreign securities to U.S. investors began to look elsewhere for funds. Further impetus to the market's growth came in 1984 when the U.S. government abolished a withholding tax that it had formerly imposed on some non-U.S. investors and allowed U.S. corporations to issue bearer bonds directly to non-U.S. investors.

Eurobonds have become very popular as a means of attracting funds, perhaps in part because they circumvent registration requirements. U.S.-based MNCs such as McDonald's and Walt Disney commonly issue Eurobonds. Non-U.S. firms such as Guinness, Nestlé, and Volkswagen also use the Eurobond market as a source of funds.

In recent years, governments and corporations from emerging markets such as Croatia, Ukraine, Romania, and Hungary have frequently utilized the Eurobond market.

New corporations that have been established in emerging markets rely on the Eurobond market to finance their growth. They have to pay a risk premium of at least three percentage points annually above the U.S. Treasury bond rate on dollar-denominated Eurobonds.

Features of Eurobonds. Eurobonds have several distinctive features. They are usually issued in bearer form, and coupon payments are made yearly. Some Eurobonds carry a convertibility clause allowing them to be converted into a specified number of shares of common stock. An advantage to the issuer is that Eurobonds typically have few, if any, protective covenants. Furthermore, even short-maturity Eurobonds include call provisions. Some Eurobonds, called **floating rate notes (FRNs)**, have a variable rate provision that adjusts the coupon rate over time according to prevailing market rates.

Denominations. Eurobonds are commonly denominated in a number of currencies. Although the U.S. dollar is used most often, denominating 70 to 75 percent of Eurobonds, the euro will likely also be used to a significant extent in the future. Recently, some firms have issued debt denominated in Japanese yen to take advantage of Japan's extremely low interest rates. Because interest rates for each currency and credit conditions change constantly, the popularity of particular currencies in the Eurobond market changes over time.

Underwriting Process. Eurobonds are underwritten by a multinational syndicate of investment banks and simultaneously placed in many countries, providing a wide spectrum of fund sources to tap. The underwriting process takes place in a sequence of steps. The multinational managing syndicate sells the bonds to a large underwriting crew. In many cases, a special distribution to regional underwriters is allocated before the bonds finally reach the bond purchasers. One problem with the distribution method is that the second- and third-stage underwriters do not always follow up on their promise to sell the bonds. The managing syndicate is therefore forced to redistribute the unsold bonds or to sell them directly, which creates "digestion" problems in the market and adds to the distribution cost. To avoid such problems, bonds are often distributed in higher volume to underwriters that have fulfilled their commitments in the past at the expense of those that have not. This has helped the Eurobond market maintain its desirability as a bond placement center.

Secondary Market. Eurobonds also have a secondary market. The market makers are in many cases the same underwriters who sell the primary issues. A technological advance called **Euro-clear** helps to inform all traders about outstanding issues for sale, thus allowing a more active secondary market. The intermediaries in the secondary market are based in 10 different countries, with those in the United Kingdom dominating the action. They can act not only as brokers but also as dealers that hold inventories of Eurobonds. Many of these intermediaries, such as Bank of America International, Salomon Smith Barney, and Citicorp International, are subsidiaries of U.S. corporations.

Before the adoption of the euro in much of Europe, MNCs in European countries commonly preferred to issue bonds in their own local currency. The market for bonds in each currency was limited. Now, with the adoption of the euro, MNCs from many different countries can issue bonds denominated in euros, which allows for a much larger and more liquid market. MNCs have benefited because they can more easily obtain debt by issuing bonds, as investors know that there will be adequate liquidity in the secondary market.

Development of Other Bond Markets

Bond markets have developed in Asia and South America. Government agencies and MNCs in these regions use international bond markets to issue bonds when they believe they can reduce their financing costs. Investors in some countries use international bond markets because they expect their local currency to weaken in the future and prefer to invest in bonds denominated in a strong foreign currency. The South American bond market has experienced limited growth because the interest rates in some countries there are usually high. MNCs and government agencies in those countries are unwilling to issue bonds when interest rates are so high, so they rely heavily on short-term financing.

Comparing Interest Rates among Currencies

Recently quoted annualized interest rates are shown in Exhibit 3.3. Notice the wide disparity among interest rates of different countries. At one extreme, Japan's annualized interest rate was about 1 percent, whereas Brazil's annualized interest rate was 19 percent.

The interest rates in debt markets are crucial because they affect the MNC's cost of financing. Since interest rates can vary substantially among currencies, the cost of local financing for foreign projects varies among countries. The interest rate on a debt instrument denominated in a specific currency is determined by the demand for funds denominated in that currency and the supply of funds available in that currency.

EXAMPLE

The supply and demand schedules for the U.S. dollar and for Mexico's currency (the peso) are compared for a given point in time in Exhibit 3.4. The demand schedule for loanable funds is downward sloping for any currency, which simply means that the quantity of funds demanded at any point in time is inversely related to the interest rate level. That is, the total amount of loanable funds demanded (borrowed) at a given point in time is higher if the cost of borrowing is lower.

The supply schedule for loanable funds denominated in a given currency is upward sloping, which means that the total amount of loanable funds supplied (such as savings by individuals) at a given point in time is positively related to the interest rate level. That is, the total amount of loanable funds supplied to the market is higher if the interest rate offered on savings accounts is higher.

Though the demand schedule for loanable funds should be downward sloping for every currency and the supply schedule of loanable funds should be upward sloping for every currency, the actual positions of these schedules vary among currencies. First, notice that the demand and supply curves are further to the right for the dollar than for the Mexican peso. The amount of dollar-denominated loanable funds supplied and demanded is much greater than the amount of peso-denominated loanable funds because the U.S. economy is much larger than Mexico's economy.

Also notice that the positions of the demand and supply schedules for loanable funds are much higher for the Mexican peso than for the dollar. The supply schedule for loanable funds denominated in Mexican peso shows that hardly any amount of savings would be supplied at low interest rate levels because the high inflation in Mexico encourages households to spend all of their disposable income before prices increase more. It discourages households from saving unless the interest rate is sufficiently high. In addition, the demand for loanable funds in pesos shows that borrowers are willing to

Exhibit 3.3

Comparison of Annualized Short-Term Interest Rates among Countries in 2004 (Rates are rounded to the nearest percent.)

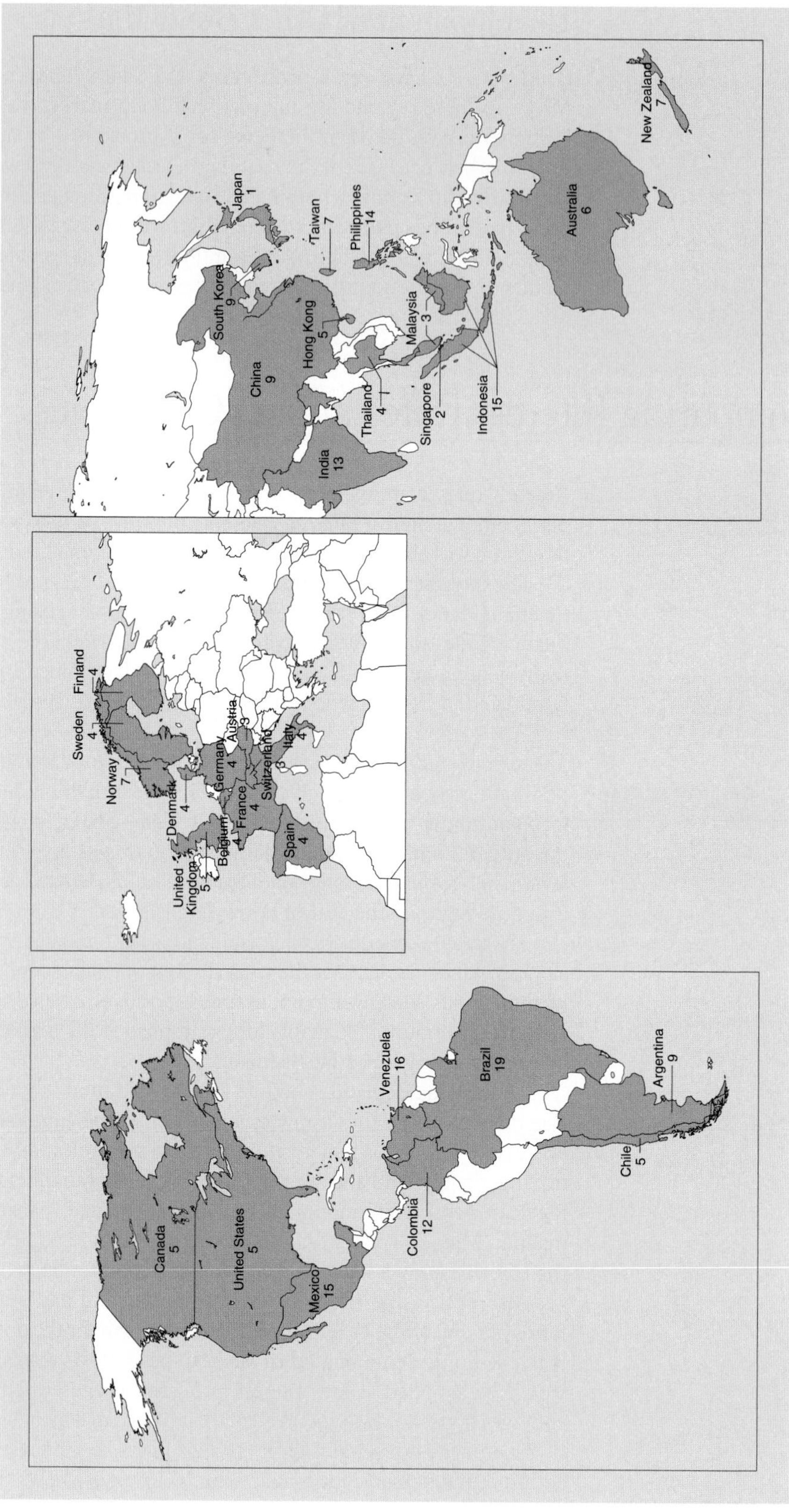

borrow even at very high rates of interest because they would rather borrow funds to make purchases now before prices increase.

Because of the differences in the positions of the demand and supply schedules for the two currencies shown in Exhibit 3.4, the equilibrium interest rate for the Mexican peso is much higher than for the dollar.

As the demand and supply schedules change over time for a specific currency, so will the equilibrium interest rate.

EXAMPLE

Suppose that Mexico's government is able to substantially reduce the local inflation. In that case, the supply schedule of loanable funds denominated in pesos would shift out (to the right). Conversely, the demand schedule of loanable funds denominated in pesos would shift in (to the left). The two shifts would result in a lower equilibrium interest rate.

One might think that investors from other countries should invest in savings accounts in high-inflation countries. However, the currencies of these high-inflation countries usually weaken over time, which may more than offset the interest rate advantage as explained later in the text. Second, savings deposits in some of these countries are not insured, which presents another risk to foreign investors. Third, some emerging countries impose restrictions that discourage investors from investing funds there.

Supply and demand conditions can explain the relative interest rate for any currency. Japan's very low interest rate is attributed to a large supply of savings by Japanese households relative to a weak demand for funds because of a weak economy (limited borrowing). The relatively high interest rate in Brazil is attributed to both high inflation, which encourages firms and consumers to borrow and make purchases before prices increase further, and to excessive borrowing by the government.

A change in one currency's interest rate can have an impact on another within the same day, week, or month. The point is that the freedom to transfer funds across countries causes the demand and supply conditions for funds to be somewhat integrated, which can cause interest rate movements to be integrated. Interest rates in the European countries participating in the euro are similar because they are subject to the same money supply and demand conditions.

Exhibit 3.4

Why U.S. Dollar Interest Rates Differ from Mexican Peso Interest Rates

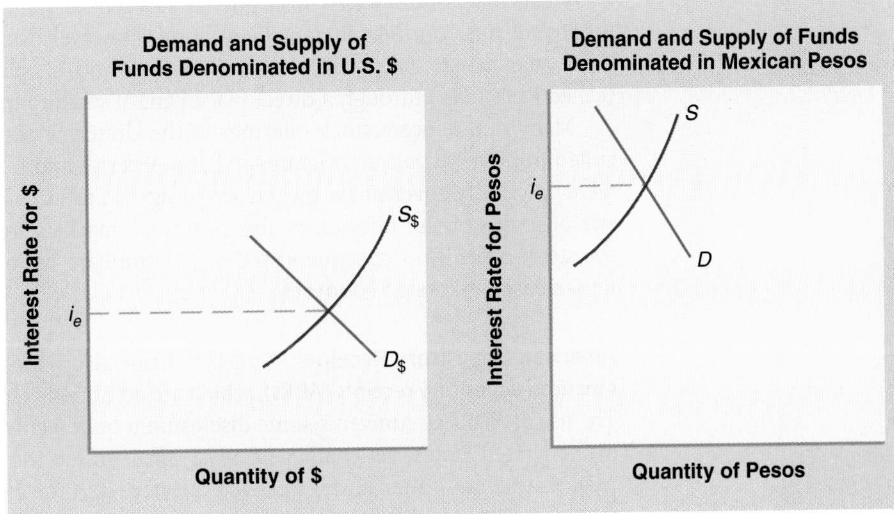

International Stock Markets

http://

Visit http://www.stockmarkets.com for information about stock markets around the world.

MNCs and domestic firms commonly obtain long-term funding by issuing stock locally. Yet, MNCs can also attract funds from foreign investors by issuing stock in international markets. The stock offering may be more easily digested when it is issued in several markets. In addition, the issuance of stock in a foreign country can enhance the firm's image and name recognition there.

The recent conversion of many European countries to a single currency (the euro) has resulted in more stock offerings in Europe by U.S.- and European-based MNCs. In the past, an MNC needed a different currency in every country where it conducted business and therefore borrowed currencies from local banks in those countries. Now, it can use the euro to finance its operations across several European countries and may be able to obtain all the financing it needs with one stock offering in which the stock is denominated in euros. The MNCs can then use a portion of the revenue (in euros) to pay dividends to shareholders who have purchased the stock.

Issuance of Foreign Stock in the United States

Non-U.S. corporations or governments that need large amounts of funds sometimes issue stock in the United States (these are called **Yankee stock offerings**) due to the liquidity of the new-issues market there. In other words, a foreign corporation or government may be more likely to sell an entire issue of stock in the U.S. market, whereas in other, smaller markets, the entire issue may not necessarily sell.

When a non-U.S. firm issues stock in its own country, its shareholder base is quite limited, as a few large institutional investors may own most of the shares. By issuing stock in the United States, such a firm diversifies its shareholder base, which can reduce share price volatility caused when large investors sell shares.

The U.S. investment banks commonly serve as underwriters of the stock targeted for the U.S. market and receive underwriting fees representing about 7 percent of the value of stock issued. Since many financial institutions in the United States purchase non-U.S. stocks as investments, non-U.S. firms may be able to place an entire stock offering within the United States.

Firms that issue stock in the United States typically are required to satisfy stringent disclosure rules on their financial condition. However, they are exempt from some of these rules when they qualify for a Securities and Exchange Commission guideline (called Rule 144a) through a direct placement of stock to institutional investors.

Many of the recent stock offerings in the United States by non-U.S. firms have resulted from privatization programs in Latin America and Europe. Thus, businesses that were previously government owned are being sold to U.S. shareholders. Given the large size of some of these businesses, the local stock markets are not large enough to digest the stock offerings. Consequently, U.S. investors are financing many privatized businesses based in foreign countries.

American Depository Receipts. Non-U.S. firms also obtain equity financing by using **American depository receipts (ADRs)**, which are certificates representing bundles of stock. The use of ADRs circumvents some disclosure requirements imposed on stock offerings in the United States, yet enables non-U.S. firms to tap the U.S. market for funds. The ADR market grew after businesses were privatized in the early 1990s, as some of these businesses issued ADRs to obtain financing.

Since ADR shares can be traded just like shares of a stock, the price of an ADR changes each day in response to demand and supply conditions. Over time, however, the value of an ADR should move in tandem with the value of the corresponding stock that is listed on the foreign stock exchange, after adjusting for exchange rate effects. The formula for calculating the price of an ADR is:

$$P_{ADR} = P_{fs} \times S$$

where P_{ADR} represents the price of the ADR, P_{fs} represents the price of the foreign stock measured in foreign currency, and S is the spot rate of the foreign currency.

EXAMPLE

A share of the ADR of the French firm Pari represents one share of this firm's stock that is traded on a French stock exchange. The share price of Pari was 20 euros when the French market closed. As the U.S. stock market opens, the euro is worth \$1.05, so the ADR price should be:

$$\begin{aligned} P_{ADR} &= P_{fs} \times S \\ &= 20 \times \$1.05 \\ &= \$21. \end{aligned}$$

If there is a discrepancy between the ADR price and the price of the foreign stock (after adjusting for the exchange rate), investors can use arbitrage to capitalize on the discrepancy between the prices of the two assets. The act of arbitrage should realign the prices.

EXAMPLE

Assume no transaction costs. If $P_{ADR} < (P_{fs} \times S)$, then ADR shares will flow back to France. They will be converted to shares of the French stock and will be traded in the French market. Investors can engage in arbitrage by buying the ADR shares in the United States, converting them to shares of the French stock, and then selling those shares on the French stock exchange where the stock is listed.

The arbitrage will (1) reduce the supply of ADRs traded in the U.S. market, thereby putting upward pressure on the ADR price, and (2) increase the supply of the French shares traded in the French market, thereby putting downward pressure on the stock price in France. The arbitrage will continue until the discrepancy in prices disappears.

The preceding example assumed a conversion rate of one ADR share per share of stock. Some ADRs are convertible into more than one share of the corresponding stock. Under these conditions, arbitrage will occur only if:

$$P_{ADR} = Conv \times P_{fs} \times S$$

where *Conv* represents the number of shares of foreign stock that can be obtained for the ADR.

EXAMPLE

If the Pari ADR from the previous example is convertible into two shares of stock, the ADR price should be:

$$\begin{aligned} P_{ADR} &= 2 \times 20 \times \$1.05 \\ &= \$42. \end{aligned}$$

In this case, the ADR shares will be converted into shares of stock only if the ADR price is less than \$42.

In reality, some transaction costs are associated with converting ADRs to foreign shares. Thus, arbitrage will occur only if the potential arbitrage profit exceeds the transaction costs.

Issuance of Stock in Foreign Markets

Although the U.S. market can be advantageous for new stock issues due to its size, the registration requirements can sometimes cause delays in selling the new issues. For this reason, some U.S. firms have issued new stock in foreign markets in recent years. Other U.S. firms issue stock in foreign markets simply to enhance their global image. The existence of various markets for new issues provides corporations in need of equity with a choice. This competition among various new-issues markets should increase the efficiency of new issues.

The locations of an MNC's operations can influence the decision about where to place its stock, as the MNC may desire a country where it is likely to generate enough future cash flows to cover dividend payments. The stocks of some U.S.-based MNCs are widely traded on numerous stock exchanges around the world. For example, the Coca-Cola Co., IBM, and many other U.S.-based MNCs have their stock listed on several different stock exchanges overseas. When an MNC's stock is listed on foreign stock exchanges, it can easily be traded by foreign investors who have access to those exchanges.

Impact of the Euro. The adoption of the euro by many European countries has encouraged MNCs based in Europe to issue stock. Investors throughout Europe are more willing to invest in stocks when they do not have to worry about exchange rate effects. For example, a German insurance company may be more willing to buy a stock issued by a firm in Portugal now that the same currency is used in both countries. The secondary market for stocks denominated in euros is more liquid as a result of the participation by investors from several different countries that have adopted the euro.

http://

The site at http://finance.yahoo.com/? provides access to various domestic and international financial markets and financial market news, as well as links to national financial news servers.

Comparison of Stock Markets. Exhibit 3.5 provides a summary of the major stock markets, but there are numerous other exchanges. Some foreign stock markets are much smaller than the U.S. markets because their firms have relied more on debt financing than equity financing in the past. Recently, however, firms outside the United States have been issuing stock more frequently, which has resulted in the growth of non-U.S. stock markets. The percentage of individual versus institutional ownership of shares varies across stock markets. Financial institutions and other firms own a large proportion of the shares outside the United States, while individual investors own a relatively small proportion of shares.

Large MNCs have begun to float new stock issues simultaneously in various countries. Investment banks underwrite stocks through one or more syndicates across countries. The global distribution of stock can reach a much larger market, so greater quantities of stock can be issued at a given price.

USING THE WEB **Stock Market Trading Information** Information about the market capitalization, stock trading volume, and turnover for each stock market is provided at http://www.worldbank.org/data.

In 2000, the Amsterdam, Brussels, and Paris stock exchanges merged to create the Euronext market. Since then, the Lisbon stock exchange has joined as well. As of 2004, the Euronext market had about 1,500 firms listed, about 300 of them from other countries. Most of the largest firms based in Europe have listed their stock on the Euronext market. This market is likely to grow over time as other stock exchanges may join it. A

Exhibit 3.5
Stock Exchanges around the World

Country	Stock Market Capitalization (in millions of $)	Country	Stock Market Capitalization (in millions of $)
Argentina	$ 192,499	Netherlands	640,456
Australia	372,974	New Zealand	18,613
Austria	29,935	Nigeria	5,404
Belgium	182,481	Norway	65,034
Brazil	186,238	Pakistan	4,944
Chile	56,310	Peru	11,134
Finland	293,635	Philippines	41,523
France	1,146,634	Poland	26,017
Germany	1,270,243	Portugal	60,681
Greece	86,538	South Africa	139,750
Hungary	10,637	Spain	504,219
India	110,396	Sweden	328,339
Indonesia	23,006	Switzerland	792,316
Ireland	81,882	Thailand	36,340
Israel	55,964	Turkey	47,150
Italy	768,364	United Kingdom	2,576,992
Japan	3,157,222	United States	15,104,037
Luxembourg	34,016	Yugoslavia	10,817
Malaysia	120,007	Zimbabwe	7,972
Mexico	121,403		

Source: International Bank for Reconstruction and Development, 2002.

single European stock market with similar guidelines for all stocks regardless of their home country would make it easier for those investors who prefer to do all of their trading in one market.

In recent years, many new stock markets have been developed. These so-called emerging markets enable foreign firms to raise large amounts of capital by issuing stock. These markets may enable U.S. firms doing business in emerging markets to raise funds by issuing stock there and listing their stock on the local stock exchanges. Market characteristics such as the amount of trading relative to market capitalization and the applicable tax rates can vary substantially among emerging markets.

Comparison of International Financial Markets

Exhibit 3.6 illustrates the foreign cash flow movements of a typical MNC. These cash flows can be classified into four corporate functions, all of which generally require use of the foreign exchange markets. The spot market, forward market, currency futures market, and currency options market are all classified as foreign exchange markets.

Exhibit 3.6 Foreign Cash Flow Chart of an MNC

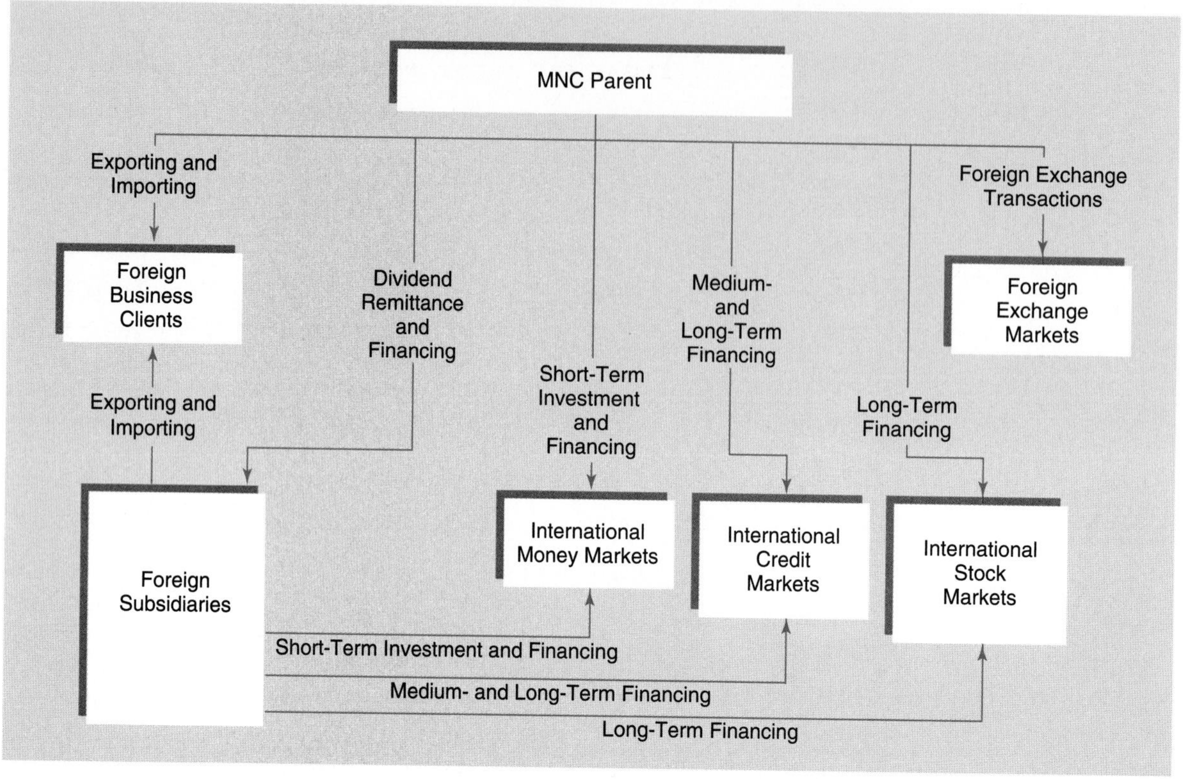

The first function is foreign trade with business clients. Exports generate foreign cash inflows, while imports require cash outflows. A second function is direct foreign investment, or the acquisition of foreign real assets. This function requires cash outflows but generates future inflows through remitted dividends back to the MNC parent or the sale of these foreign assets. A third function is short-term investment or financing in foreign securities. A fourth function is longer-term financing in the international bond or stock markets.

How Financial Markets Affect an MNC's Value

Since interest rates commonly vary among countries, an MNC's parent may use international money or bond markets to obtain funds at a lower cost than they can be obtained locally. By doing so, it reduces its cost of debt and therefore reduces its weighted average cost of capital, which results in a higher valuation.

An MNC's parent may be able to achieve a lower weighted average cost of capital by issuing equity in some foreign markets rather than issuing equity in its local market. If the MNC achieves a lower cost of capital, it can achieve a higher valuation.

SUMMARY

- The existence of market imperfections prevents markets from being completely integrated. Consequently, investors and creditors can attempt to capitalize on unique characteristics that make foreign markets more attractive than domestic markets. This motivates the international flow of funds and results in the development of international financial markets.
- The foreign exchange market allows currencies to be exchanged in order to facilitate international trade or financial transactions. Commercial banks serve as financial intermediaries in this market. They stand ready to exchange currencies on the spot or at a future point in time with the use of forward contracts.
- The international money markets are composed of several large banks that accept deposits and provide short-term loans in various currencies. This market is used primarily by governments and large corporations. The European market is a part of the international money market.
- The international credit markets are composed of the same commercial banks that serve the international money market. These banks convert some of the deposits received into loans (for medium-term periods) to governments and large corporations.
- The international bond markets facilitate international transfers of long-term credit, thereby enabling governments and large corporations to borrow funds from various countries. Theinternational bond market is facilitated by multinational syndicates of investment banks that help to place the bonds.
- International stock markets enable firms to obtain equity financing in foreign countries. Thus, these markets have helped MNCs finance their international expansion.

POINT COUNTER-POINT

Should Firms That Go Public Engage in International Offerings?

Point Yes. When a U.S. firm issues stock to the public for the first time in an initial public offering (IPO), it is naturally concerned about whether it can place all of its shares at a reasonable price. It will be able to issue its stock at a higher price by attracting more investors. It will increase its demand by spreading the stock across countries. The higher the price at which it can issue stock, the lower is its cost of using equity capital. It can also establish a global name by spreading stock across countries.

Counter-Point No. If a U.S. firm spreads its stock across different countries at the time of the IPO, there will be less publicly traded stock in the United States. Thus, it will not have as much liquidity in the secondary market. Investors desire stocks that they can easily sell in the secondary market, which means that they require that the stocks have liquidity. To the extent that a firm reduces its liquidity in the United States by spreading its stock across countries, it may not attract sufficient U.S. demand for the stock. Thus, its efforts to create global name recognition may reduce its name recognition in the United States.

Who Is Correct? Use InfoTrac or some other search engine to learn more about this issue. Which argument do you support? Offer your own opinion on this issue.

SELF TEST

Answers are provided in Appendix A at the back of the text.

1. Stetson Bank quotes a bid rate of $.784 for the Australian dollar and an ask rate of $.80. What is the bid/ask percentage spread?
2. Fullerton Bank quotes an ask rate of $.190 for the Peruvian currency (new sol) and a bid rate of $.188. Determine the bid/ask percentage spread.
3. Briefly explain how MNCs can make use of each international financial market described in this chapter.

QUESTIONS AND APPLICATIONS

1. **Motives for Investing in Foreign Money Markets.** Explain why an MNC may invest funds in a financial market outside its own country.

2. **Motives for Providing Credit in Foreign Markets.** Explain why some financial institutions prefer to provide credit in financial markets outside their own country.

3. **Exchange Rate Effects on Investing.** Explain how the appreciation of the Australian dollar against the U.S. dollar would affect the return to a U.S. firm that invested in an Australian money market security.

4. **Exchange Rate Effects on Borrowing.** Explain how the appreciation of the Japanese yen against the U.S. dollar would affect the return to a U.S. firm that borrowed Japanese yen and used the proceeds for a U.S. project.

5. **Bank Services.** List some of the important characteristics of bank foreign exchange services that MNCs should consider.

6. **Bid/Ask Spread.** Utah Bank's bid price for Canadian dollars is $.7938 and its ask price is $.81. What is the bid/ask percentage spread?

7. **Bid/Ask Spread.** Compute the bid/ask percentage spread for Mexican peso retail transactions in which the ask rate is $.11 and the bid rate is $.10.

8. **Forward Contract.** The Wolfpack Corporation is a U.S. exporter that invoices its exports to the United Kingdom in British pounds. If it expects that the pound will appreciate against the dollar in the future, should it hedge its exports with a forward contract? Explain.

9. **Euro.** Explain the foreign exchange situation for countries that use the euro when they engage in international trade among themselves.

10. **Indirect Exchange Rate.** If the direct exchange rate of the euro is worth $1.25, what is the indirect rate of the euro? That is, what is the value of a dollar in euros?

11. **Cross Exchange Rate.** Assume Poland's currency (the zloty) is worth $.17 and the Japanese yen is worth $.008. What is the cross rate of the zloty with respect to yen? That is, how many yen equal a zloty?

12. **Syndicated Loans.** Explain how syndicated loans are used in international markets.

13. **Loan Rates.** Explain the process used by banks in the Eurocredit market to determine the rate to charge on loans.

14. **International Markets.** What is the function of the international money markets? Briefly describe the reasons for the development and growth of the European money market. Explain how the international money, credit, and bond markets differ from one another.

15. **Evolution of Floating Rates.** Briefly describe the historical developments that led to floating exchange rates as of 1973.

16. **International Diversification.** Explain how the Asian crisis would have affected the returns to a U.S. firm investing in the Asian stock markets as a means of international diversification. [See the chapter appendix.]

17. **Eurocredit Loans.**

    a. With regard to Eurocredit loans, who are the borrowers?

    b. Why would a bank desire to participate in syndicated Eurocredit loans?

    c. What is LIBOR, and how is it used in the Eurocredit market?

18. **Foreign Exchange.** You just came back from Canada, where the Canadian dollar was worth $.70. You still have C$200 from your trip and could exchange them for dollars at the airport, but the airport foreign exchange desk will only buy them for $.60. Next week, you will be going to Mexico and will need pesos. The airport foreign exchange desk will sell you pesos for $.10 per peso. You met a tourist at the airport who is from Mexico and is on his way to Canada. He is willing to buy your C$200 for 130 pesos. Should you accept the offer or cash the Canadian dollars in at the airport? Explain.

19. **Foreign Stock Markets.** Explain why firms may issue stock in foreign markets. Why might U.S. firms issue more stock in Europe since the conversion to a single currency in 1999?

20. **Stock Market Integration.** Bullet, Inc., a U.S. firm, is planning to issue new stock in the United States during this month. The only decision still to be made is the specific day on which the stock will be issued. Why do you think Bullet monitors results of the Tokyo stock market every morning?

ADVANCED QUESTIONS

21. **Effects of September 11.** Why do you think the terrorist attack on the United States was expected to cause a decline in U.S. interest rates? Given the expectations for a decline in U.S. interest rates and stock prices, how were capital flows between the United States and other countries likely affected?

22. **International Financial Markets.** Recently, Wal-Mart established two retail outlets in the city of Shanzen, China, which has a population of 3.7 million. These outlets are massive and contain products purchased locally as well as imports. As Wal-Mart generates earnings beyond what it needs in Shanzen, it may remit those earnings back to the United States. Wal-Mart is likely to build additional outlets in Shanzen or in other Chinese cities in the future.

    a. Explain how the Wal-Mart outlets in China would use the spot market in foreign exchange.

    b. Explain how Wal-Mart might utilize the international money markets when it is establishing other Wal-Mart stores in Asia.

    c. Explain how Wal-Mart could use the international bond market to finance the establishment of new outlets in foreign markets.

23. **Interest Rates.** Why do interest rates vary among countries? Why are interest rates normally similar for those European countries that use the euro as their currency? Offer a reason why the government interest rate of one country could be slightly higher than that of the government interest rate of another country, even though the euro is the currency used in both countries.

INTERNET APPLICATION

24. **Market Information on the Internet** The Bloomberg website provides quotations of various exchange rates and stock market indexes. Its website address is **http://www.bloomberg.com**.

    a. Use this website to determine the cross exchange rate between the Japanese yen and the Australian dollar. That is, determine how many yen must be converted to an Australian dollar for Japanese importers that purchase Australian products today.

    b. Use this website to review how stock markets performed today. (This relates to the appendix of this chapter.) Does it appear that returns on Asian stock markets today are related? Does it appear that the returns on European stock markets today are related?

DISCUSSION IN THE BOARDROOM

This exercise can be found in Appendix E at the back of this textbook.

RUNNING YOUR OWN MNC

This exercise can be found on the Xtra! website at **http://maduraxtra.swlearning.com**.

BLADES, INC. CASE

Decisions to Use International Financial Markets

As a financial analyst for Blades, Inc., you are reasonably satisfied with Blades' current setup of exporting "Speedos" (roller blades) to Thailand. Due to the unique arrangement with Blades' primary customer in Thailand, forecasting the revenue to be generated there is a relatively easy task. Specifically, your customer has agreed to purchase 180,000 pairs of Speedos annually, for a period of three years, at a price of THB4,594 (THB = Thai baht) per pair. The current direct quotation of the dollar-baht exchange rate is $0.024.

The cost of goods sold incurred in Thailand (due to imports of the rubber and plastic components from Thailand) runs at approximately THB2,871 per pair of Speedos, but Blades currently only imports materials sufficient to manufacture about 72,000 pairs of Speedos. Blades' primary reasons for using a Thai supplier are the high quality of the components and the low cost, which has been facilitated by a continuing depreciation of the Thai baht against the U.S. dollar. If the dollar cost of buying components becomes more expensive in Thailand than in the United States, Blades is contemplating providing its U.S. supplier with the additional business.

Your plan is quite simple; Blades is currently using its Thai-denominated revenues to cover the cost of goods sold incurred there. During the last year, excess revenue was converted to U.S. dollars at the prevailing exchange rate. Although your cost of goods sold is not fixed contractually as the Thai revenues are, you expect them to remain relatively constant in the near future. Consequently, the baht-denominated cash inflows are fairly predictable each year because the Thai customer has committed to the purchase of 180,000 pairs of Speedos at a fixed price. The excess dollar revenue resulting from the conversion of baht is used either to support the U.S. production of Speedos if needed or to invest in the United States. Specifically, the revenues are used to cover cost of goods sold in the U.S. manufacturing plant, located in Omaha, Nebraska.

Ben Holt, Blades' CFO, notices that Thailand's interest rates are approximately 15 percent (versus 8 percent in the United States). You interpret the high interest rates in Thailand as an indication of the uncertainty resulting from Thailand's unstable economy. Holt asks you to assess the feasibility of investing Blades' excess funds from Thailand operations in Thailand at an interest rate of 15 percent. After you express your opposition to his plan, Holt asks you to detail the reasons in a detailed report.

1. One point of concern for you is that there is a trade-off between the higher interest rates in Thailand and the delayed conversion of baht into dollars. Explain what this means.
2. If the net baht received from the Thailand operation are invested in Thailand, how will U.S. operations be affected? (Assume that Blades is currently paying 10 percent on dollars borrowed and needs more financing for its firm.)
3. Construct a spreadsheet to compare the cash flows resulting from two plans. Under the first plan, net baht-denominated cash flows (received today) will be invested in Thailand at 15 percent for a one-year period, after which the baht will be converted to dollars. The expected spot rate for the baht in one year is about $0.022 (Ben Holt's plan). Under the second plan, net baht-denominated cash flows are converted to dollars immediately and invested in the United States for one year at 8 percent. For this question, assume that all baht-denominated cash flows are due today. Does Holt's plan seem superior in terms of dollar cash flows available after one year? Compare the choice of investing the funds versus using the funds to provide needed financing to the firm.

SMALL BUSINESS DILEMMA

Use of the Foreign Exchange Markets by the Sports Exports Company

Each month, the Sports Exports Company (a U.S. firm) receives an order for footballs from a British sporting goods distributor. The monthly payment for the footballs is denominated in British pounds, as requested by the British distributor. Jim Logan, owner of the Sports Exports Company, must convert the pounds received into dollars.

1. Explain how the Sports Exports Company could utilize the spot market to facilitate the exchange of currencies. Be specific.
2. Explain how the Sports Exports Company is exposed to exchange rate risk and how it could use the forward market to hedge this risk.

APPENDIX 3

Investing in International Financial Markets

http://

Visit http://money.cnn.com for current national and international market data and analyses.

The trading of financial assets (such as stocks or bonds) by investors in international financial markets has a major impact on MNCs. First, this type of trading can influence the level of interest rates in a specific country (and therefore the cost of debt to an MNC) because it affects the amount of funds available there. Second, it can affect the price of an MNC's stock (and therefore the cost of equity to an MNC) because it influences the demand for the MNC's stock. Third, it enables MNCs to sell securities in foreign markets. So, even though international investing in financial assets is not the most crucial activity of MNCs, international investing by individual and institutional investors can indirectly affect the actions and performance of an MNC. Consequently, an understanding of the motives and methods of international investing is necessary to anticipate how the international flow of funds may change in the future and how that change may affect MNCs.

Background on International Stock Exchanges

The international trading of stocks has grown over time but has been limited by three barriers: transaction costs, information costs, and exchange rate risk. In recent years, however, these barriers have been reduced as explained here.

USING THE WEB

Stock Exchange Information A summary of links to stock exchanges around the world is provided at http://123world.com/stockexchanges.

Reduction in Transaction Costs

Most countries tend to have their own stock exchanges, where the stocks of local publicly held companies are traded. In recent years, exchanges have been consolidated within a country, which has increased efficiency and reduced transaction costs. Some European stock exchanges now have extensive cross-listings so that investors in a given European country can easily purchase stocks of companies based in other European countries.

In particular, because of its efficiency, the stock exchange of Switzerland may serve as a model that will be applied to many other stock exchanges around the world. The Swiss stock exchange is now fully computerized, so a trading floor is not needed. Orders by investors to buy or sell flow to financial institutions that are certified members of the Swiss stock exchange. These institutions are not necessarily based in Switzerland. The details of the orders, such as the name of the stock, the number of shares to be bought or sold, and the price at which the investor is willing to buy or sell, are fed into a computer system. The system matches buyers and sellers and then sends information confirming the transaction to the financial institution, which informs the investor that the transaction is completed.

When there are many more buy orders than sell orders for a given stock, the computer is unable to accommodate all orders. Some buyers will then increase the price they are willing to pay for the stock. Thus, the price adjusts in response to the demand (buy orders) for the stock and the supply (sell orders) of the stock for sale recorded by the computer system. Similar dynamics occur when a trading floor is used, but the computerized system has documented criteria by which it prioritizes the execution of orders; traders on a trading floor may execute some trades in ways that favor themselves at the expense of investors.

In recent years, electronic communications networks (ECNs) have been created in many countries to match orders between buyers and sellers. Like the Swiss stock exchange, ECNs do not have a visible trading floor: the trades are executed by a computer network. Examples of popular ECNs include Archipelago, Instinet, and Tradebook. With an ECN, investors can place orders on their computers that are then executed by the computer system and confirmed through the Internet to the investor. Thus, all parts of the trading process from the placement of the order to the confirmation that the transaction has been executed are conducted by computer. The ease with which such orders can occur, regardless of the locations of the investor and the stock exchange, is sure to increase the volume of international stock transactions in the future.

Impact of Alliances. Several stock exchanges have created international alliances with the stock exchanges of other countries, thereby enabling firms to more easily cross-list their shares among various stock markets. This gives investors easier and cheaper access to foreign stocks. The alliances also allow greater integration between markets. At some point in the future, there may be one global stock market in which any stock of any country can be easily purchased or sold by investors around the world. A single global stock market would allow U.S. investors to easily purchase any stock, regardless of where the corporation is based or the currency in which the stock is denominated. The international alliances are a first step toward a single global stock market. The costs of international stock transactions have already been substantially reduced as a result of some of the alliances.

Reduction in Information Costs

The Internet provides investors with access to much information about foreign stocks, enabling them to make more informed decisions without having to purchase information about these stocks. Consequently, investors should be more comfortable assessing foreign stocks. Although differences in accounting rules still limit the degree to which financial data about foreign companies can be interpreted or compared to data about firms in other countries, there is some momentum toward making accounting standards uniform across some countries.

Exchange Rate Risk

When investing in a foreign stock that is denominated in a foreign currency, investors are subject to the possibility that the currency denominating the stock may depreciate against the investor's currency over time.

The potential for a major decline in the stock's value simply because of a large degree of depreciation is more likely for emerging markets, such as Indonesia or Russia, where the local currency can change by 10 percent or more on a single day.

Measuring the Impact of Exchange Rates. The return to a U.S. investor from investing in a foreign stock is influenced by the return on the stock itself (R), which includes the dividend, and the percentage change in the exchange rate (e), as shown here:

$$R_{\$} = (1 + R)(1 + e) - 1$$

EXAMPLE

A year ago, Rob Grady invested in the stock of Vopka, a Russian company. Over the last year, the stock increased in value by 35 percent. Over this same period, however, the Russian ruble's value declined by 30 percent. Rob sold the Vopka stock today. His return is:

$$\begin{aligned} R_{\$} &= (1 + R)(1 + e) - 1 \\ &= (1 + .35)[1 + (-.30)] - 1 \\ &= -.055 \text{ or } -5.5\%. \end{aligned}$$

Even though the return on the stock was more pronounced than the exchange rate movement, Rob lost money on his investment. The reason is that the exchange rate movement of −30 percent wiped out not only 30 percent of his initial investment but also 30 percent of the stock's return.

As the preceding example illustrates, investors should consider the potential influence of exchange rate movements on foreign stocks before investing in those stocks. Foreign investments are especially risky in developing countries, where exchange rates tend to be very volatile.

Reducing Exchange Rate Risk of Foreign Stocks. One method of reducing exchange rate risk is to take short positions in the foreign currencies denominating the foreign stocks. For example, a U.S. investor holding Mexican stocks who expects the stocks to be worth 10 million Mexican pesos one year from now could sell forward contracts (or futures contracts) representing 10 million pesos. The stocks could be liquidated at that time, and the pesos could be exchanged for dollars at a locked-in price.

Although hedging the exchange rate risk of an international stock portfolio can be effective, it has three limitations. First, the number of foreign currency units to be converted to dollars at the end of the investment horizon is unknown. If the units received from liquidating the foreign stocks are more (less) than the amount hedged, the investor has a net long (short) position in that foreign currency, and the return will be unfavorably affected by its depreciation (appreciation). Nevertheless, though the hedge may not be perfect for this reason, investors normally should be able to hedge most of their exchange rate risk.

A second limitation of hedging exchange rate risk is that the investors may decide to retain the foreign stocks beyond the initially planned investment horizon. Of course, they can create another short position after the initial short position is terminated. If they ever decide to liquidate the foreign stocks prior to the forward delivery date, the hedge will be less effective. They could use the proceeds to invest in foreign money market securities denominated in that foreign currency in order to postpone conversion to dollars until the forward delivery date. But this prevents them from using the funds for other opportunities until that delivery date.

A third limitation of hedging is that forward rates for currencies that are less widely traded may not exist or may exhibit a large discount.

International Stock Diversification

A substantial amount of research has demonstrated that investors in stocks can benefit by diversifying internationally. The stocks of most firms are highly influenced by the countries where those firms reside (although some firms are more vulnerable to economic conditions than others).

Since stock markets partially reflect the current and/or forecasted state of their countries' economies, they do not move in tandem. Thus, particular stocks of the various markets are not expected to be highly correlated. This contrasts with a purely domestic portfolio, in which most stocks often move in the same direction and by a somewhat similar magnitude.

The risk of a stock portfolio can be measured by its volatility. Investors prefer a stock portfolio that has a lower degree of volatility because the future returns of a less volatile portfolio are subject to less uncertainty. The volatility of a single stock is commonly measured by its standard deviation of returns over a recent period. The volatility of a stock portfolio can also be measured by its standard deviation of returns over a recent period. The standard deviation of a stock portfolio is determined by the standard deviation of returns for each individual stock along with the correlations of returns between each pair of stocks in the portfolio, as shown below for a two-stock portfolio:

$$\sigma_p = \sqrt{w_X^2\sigma_X^2 + w_Y^2\sigma_Y^2 + 2w_Xw_Y\sigma_X\sigma_Y(CORR_{XY})}$$

where w_X is the proportion of funds invested in stock X, w_Y is the proportion of funds invested in stock Y, σ_X is the standard deviation of returns for stock X, σ_Y is the standard deviation of returns for stock Y, and $CORR_{XY}$ is the correlation coefficient of returns between stock X and stock Y. From this equation, it should be clear that the standard deviation of returns (and therefore the risk) of a stock portfolio is positively related to the standard deviation of the individual stocks included within the portfolio and is also positively related to the correlations between individual stock returns.

Much research has documented that stock returns are driven by their country market conditions. Therefore, individual stocks within a given country tend to be highly correlated. If country economies are segmented, their stock market returns should not be highly correlated, and therefore, the individual stocks of one country should not be highly correlated with individual stocks of other countries. Thus, investors should be able to reduce the risk of their stock portfolio by investing in stocks among different countries.

Limitations of International Diversification

In general, correlations between stock indexes have been higher in recent years than they were several years ago. The general increase in correlations among stock market returns may have implications for MNCs that attempt to diversify internationally. To the extent that stock prices in each market reflect anticipated earnings, the increased correlations may suggest that more highly correlated anticipated earnings are expected among countries. Thus, the potential risk-reduction benefits to an MNC that diversifies its business may be limited.

USING THE WEB

Stock Market Performance Charts showing recent stock market performance for each market can be found at http://finance.yahoo.com/intlindices?u. The prevailing stock index level is shown for each country, as well as the performance of each market during the previous day. For some markets, you can assess the performance over the last year by clicking on Chart next to the country's name.

One reason for the increased correlations among stock market returns is increased integration of business between countries. Increased integration results in more intercountry trade flows and capital flows, which causes each country to have more influence on other countries. In particular, many European countries have become more integrated as regulations have been standardized throughout Europe to facilitate trade between countries. In addition, the adoption of the euro has removed exchange rate risk due to trade between participating countries.

The conversion to the euro also allows portfolio managers in European countries to invest in stocks of other participating European countries without concern for exchange rate risk, because these stocks are also denominated in euros. This facilitates a more regional approach for European investors, who are not restricted to stocks within their respective countries.

Since some stock market correlations may become more pronounced during a crisis, international diversification will not necessarily be as effective during a downturn as it is during more favorable conditions. Two events that had an adverse effect on many markets are the 1987 crash and the Asian crisis, which are discussed next.

Market Movements during the 1987 Crash. Further evidence on the relationships between stock markets is obtained by assessing market movements during the stock market crash in October 1987. Exhibit 3A.1 shows the stock market movements for four major countries during the crash. While the magnitude of the decline was not exactly the same, all four markets were adversely affected. When institutional investors anticipated a general decline in stocks, they sold some stocks from all markets, instead of just the U.S. market.

Many stock markets experienced larger declines in prices than U.S. stock markets did. For example, during the month of October 1987, the U.S. market index declined by about 21 percent, while the German market index declined by about 23 percent and the United Kingdom index by 26 percent. The stock market indexes of Australia and Hong Kong decreased by more than 50 percent over this same month.

Market Movements during the Asian Crisis. In the summer of 1997, Thailand experienced severe economic problems, which were followed by economic downturns in several other Asian countries. Investors revalued stocks downward because of weakened

Exhibit 3A.1 Integration among Foreign Stock Markets during the 1987 Crash

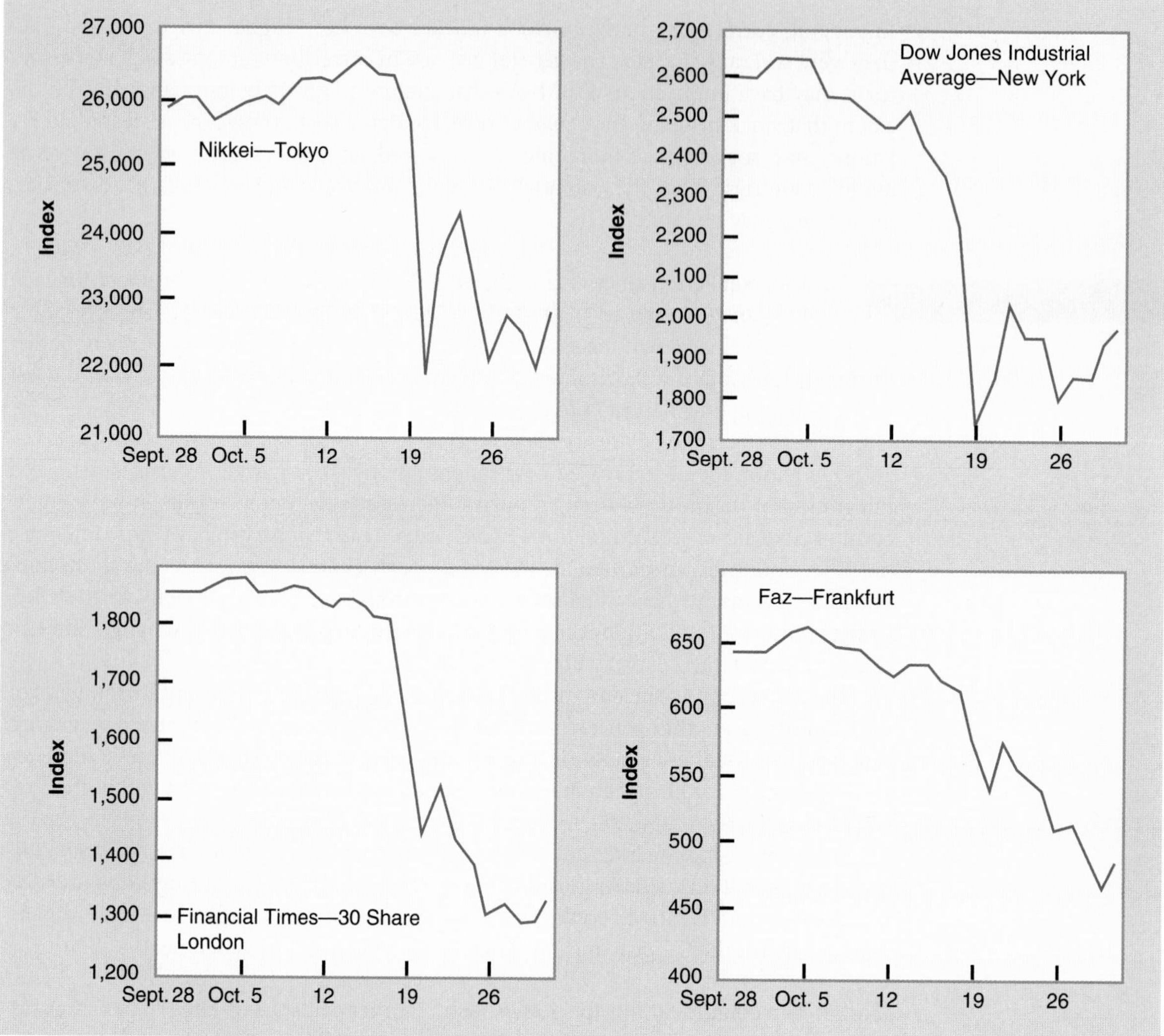

Source: *Economic Trends,* Federal Reserve Bank of Cleveland (November 1987), p. 17.

economic conditions, more political uncertainty, and a lack of confidence that the problems would be resolved. The effects during the first year of the Asian crisis are summarized in Exhibit 3A.2. This crisis demonstrated how quickly stock prices could adjust to changing conditions and how adverse market conditions could spread across countries. Thus, diversification across Asia did not effectively insulate investors during the Asian crisis. Diversification across all continents would have been a more effective method of diversification during the crisis.

Although there has not been another world stock market crash since 1987, there have been several mini-crashes. For example, on August 27, 1998 (referred to as "Bloody Thursday"), Russian stock and currency values declined abruptly in response to severe financial problems in Russia, and most stock markets around the world experienced losses on that day. U.S. stocks declined by more than 4 percent on this day. The adverse

Exhibit 3A.2
How Stock Market Levels Changed during the Asian Crisis from a U.S. Perspective

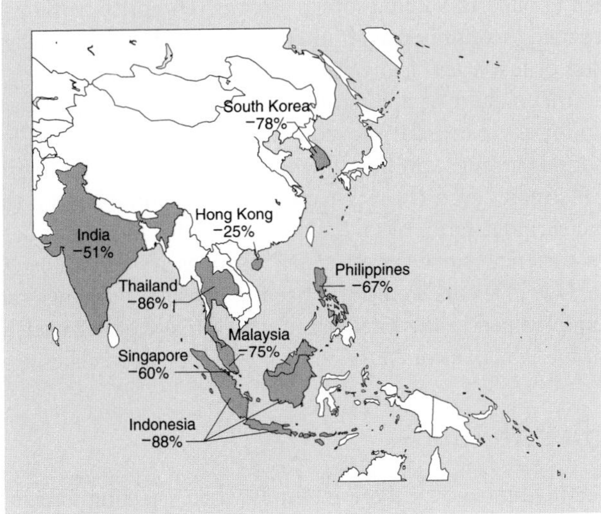

effects extended beyond stocks that would be directly affected by financial problems in Russia as paranoia caused investors to sell stocks across all markets due to fears that all stocks might be overvalued.

In response to the September 11, 2001, terrorist attacks on the United States, many stock markets experienced declines of more than 10 percent over the following week. Diversification among markets was not very effective in reducing risk in this case.

Valuation of Foreign Stocks

When investors consider investing in foreign stocks, they need methods for valuing those stocks.

Dividend Discount Model

One possibility is to use the dividend discount model with an adjustment to account for expected exchange rate movements. Foreign stocks pay dividends in the currency in which they are denominated. Thus, the cash flow per period to U.S. investors is the dividend (denominated in the foreign currency) multiplied by the value of that foreign currency in dollars. The dividend can normally be forecasted with more accuracy than the value of the foreign currency. Because of exchange rate uncertainty, the value of the foreign stock from a U.S. investor's perspective is subject to much uncertainty.

Price-Earnings Method

An alternative method of valuing foreign stocks is to apply price-earnings ratios. The expected earnings per share of the foreign firm are multiplied by the appropriate price-earnings ratio (based on the firm's risk and industry) to determine the appropriate price of the firm's stock. Although this method is easy to use, it is subject to some limitations when applied to valuing foreign stocks. The price-earnings ratio for a given industry may change continuously in some foreign markets, especially when the industry is composed of just a few firms. Thus, it is difficult to determine the proper price-earnings ratio that should be applied to a specific foreign firm. In addition, the price-earnings ratio for any particular industry may need to be adjusted for the firm's country, since reported earnings can be influenced by the firm's accounting guidelines and tax laws. Furthermore, even if U.S. investors are comfortable with their estimate of the proper price-earnings ratio, the value derived by this method is denominated in the local foreign currency (since the estimated earnings are denominated in that currency). Therefore, U.S. investors would still need to consider exchange rate effects. Even if the stock is undervalued in the foreign country, it may not necessarily generate a reasonable return for U.S. investors if the foreign currency depreciates against the dollar.

Other Methods

Some investors adapt these methods when selecting foreign stocks. For example, they may first assess the macroeconomic conditions of all countries to screen out those countries that are expected to experience poor conditions in the future. Then, they use other methods such as the dividend discount model or the price-earnings method to value specific firms within the countries that are appealing.

Why Perceptions of Stock Valuation Differ among Countries

A stock that appears undervalued to investors in one country may seem overvalued to investors in another country. Some of the more common reasons why perceptions of a stock's valuation may vary among investors in different countries are identified here.

Required Rate of Return. Some investors attempt to value a stock according to the present value of the future cash flows that it will generate. The dividend discount model is one of many models that use this approach. The required rate of return that is used to discount the cash flows can vary substantially among countries. It is based on the prevailing risk-free interest rate available to investors, plus a risk premium. For investors in the United States, the risk-free rate is typically below 10 percent. Thus, U.S. investors would apply a required rate of return of 12 to 15 percent in some cases. In contrast, investors in a country such as Brazil would not be willing to accept such a low rate because their risk-free interest rate is commonly above 25 percent. If they can earn an annual return of 25 percent by investing in a risk-free asset, they would require a higher return than that before they would invest in risky assets such as stocks.

Exchange Rate Risk. The exposure of investors to exchange rate risk from investing in foreign stocks is dependent on their home country. Investors in the United States who invest in a Brazilian stock are highly exposed to exchange rate risk, as the Brazilian currency (the real) has depreciated substantially against the dollar over time. Brazilian investors are not as exposed to exchange rate risk when investing in U.S. stocks, however, because there is less chance of a major depreciation in the dollar against the Brazilian real. In fact, Brazilian investors normally benefit from investing in U.S. stocks because of the dollar's appreciation against the Brazilian real. Indeed, the appreciation of the dollar is often necessary to generate an adequate return for Brazilian investors, given their high required return when investing in foreign stocks.

Taxes. The tax effects of dividends and capital gains also vary among countries. The lower a country's tax rates, the greater the proportion of the pre-tax cash flows received that the investor can retain. Other things being equal, investors based in low-tax countries should value stocks higher.

The valuation of stocks by investors within a given country changes in response to changes in tax laws. Before 2003, dividend income received by U.S. investors was taxed at ordinary income tax rates, which could be nearly 40 percent for some taxpayers. Consequently, many U.S. investors may have placed higher valuations on foreign stocks that paid low or no dividends (especially if the investors did not rely on the stocks to provide periodic income). Before 2003, the maximum tax on long-term capital gains was 20 percent, a rate that made foreign stocks that paid no dividends but had high potential for large capital gains very attractive. In 2003, however, the maximum tax rate on both dividends and long-term capital gains was set at 15 percent. Consequently, U.S. investors became more willing to consider foreign stocks that paid high dividends.

Methods Used to Invest Internationally

For investors attempting international stock diversification, five common approaches are available:

- Direct purchases of foreign stocks
- Investment in MNC stocks
- American depository receipts (ADRs)
- Exchange-traded funds (ETFs)
- International mutual funds (IMFs)

Each approach is discussed in turn.

Direct Purchases of Foreign Stocks

Foreign stocks can be purchased on foreign stock exchanges. This requires the services of brokerage firms that can contact floor brokers who work on the foreign stock exchange of concern. However, this approach is inefficient because of market imperfections such as insufficient information, transaction costs, and tax differentials among countries.

An alternative method of investing directly in foreign stocks is to purchase stocks of foreign companies that are sold on the local stock exchange. In the United States, for example, Royal Dutch Shell (of the Netherlands), Sony (of Japan), and many other foreign stocks are sold on U.S. stock exchanges. Because the number of foreign stocks listed on any local stock exchange is typically quite limited, this method by itself may not be adequate to achieve the full benefits of international diversification.

Investment in MNC Stocks

The operations of an MNC represent international diversification. Like an investor with a well-managed stock portfolio, an MNC can reduce risk (variability in net cash flows) by diversifying sales not only among industries but also among countries. In this sense, the MNC as a single firm can achieve stability similar to that of an internationally diversified stock portfolio.

the MNC as a single firm can achieve stability similar to that of an internationally diversified stock portfolio.

If MNC stocks behave like an international stock portfolio, then they should be sensitive to the stock markets of the various countries in which they operate. The sensitivity of returns of MNCs based in a particular country to specific international stock markets can be measured as:

$$R_{MNC} = a_o + a_1 R_L + b_1 R_{I,1} + b_2 R_{I,2} + \cdots + b_n R_{I,n} + u,$$

where R_{MNC} is the average return on a portfolio of MNCs from the same country, a_o is the intercept, R_L is the return on the local stock market, $R_{I,1}$ through $R_{I,n}$ are returns on foreign stock indices I_1 through I_n, and u is an error term. The regression coefficient a_1 measures the sensitivity of MNC returns to their local stock market, while coefficients b_1 through b_n measure the sensitivity of MNC returns to the various foreign stock markets. Studies have applied the time series regression model specified here and found that MNCs based in a particular country were typically affected only by their respective local stock markets and were not affected by other stock market movements. This suggests that the diversification benefits from investing in an MNC are limited.

American Depository Receipts

Another approach is to purchase American depository receipts (ADRs), which are certificates representing ownership of foreign stocks. More than 1,000 ADRs are available in the United States, primarily traded on the over-the-counter (OTC) stock market. An investment in ADRs may be an adequate substitute for direct investment in foreign stocks. Only a limited number of ADRs are available, however.

USING THE WEB

ADR Performance The performance of ADRs is provided at http://www.adr.com. Click on Industry to review the stock performance of ADRs within each industry. The website provides a table that shows information about the industry, including the number of ADRs in that industry, and the 6-month and 12-month returns. Click on any particular industry of interest to review the performance of individual ADRs in that industry.

Exchange-Traded Funds (ETFs)

Although investors have closely monitored international stock indexes for years, they were typically unable to invest directly in these indexes. The index was simply a measure of performance for a set of stocks but was not traded. Exchange-traded funds (ETFs) represent indexes that reflect composites of stocks for particular countries; they were created to allow investors to invest directly in a stock index representing any one of several countries. ETFs are sometimes referred to as world equity benchmark shares (WEBS) or as iShares.

International Mutual Funds

A final approach to consider is purchasing shares of **international mutual funds (IMFs)**, which are portfolios of stocks from various countries. Several investment firms, such as Fidelity, Vanguard, and Merrill Lynch, have constructed IMFs for their customers. Like domestic mutual funds, IMFs are popular due to (1) the low minimum investment necessary to participate in the funds, (2) the presumed expertise of the portfolio managers, and (3) the high degree of diversification achieved by the portfolios' inclusion of several stocks. Many investors believe an IMF can better reduce risk than a purely domestic mutual fund because the IMF includes foreign securities. An IMF represents a prepackaged portfolio, so investors who use it do not need to construct their own portfolios. Although some investors prefer to construct their own portfolios, the existence of numerous IMFs on the market today allows investors to select the one that most closely resembles the type of portfolio they would have constructed on their own. Moreover, some investors feel more comfortable with a professional manager managing the international portfolio.

CHAPTER 4

Exchange Rate Determination

Financial managers of MNCs that conduct international business must continuously monitor exchange rates because their cash flows are highly dependent on them. They need to understand what factors influence exchange rates so that they can anticipate how exchange rates may change in response to specific conditions. This chapter provides a foundation for understanding how exchange rates are determined.

The specific objectives of this chapter are to:

- explain how exchange rate movements are measured,
- explain how the equilibrium exchange rate is determined, and
- examine factors that affect the equilibrium exchange rate.

Measuring Exchange Rate Movements

Exchange rate movements affect an MNC's value because they can affect the amount of cash inflows received from exporting or from a subsidiary, and the amount of cash outflows needed to pay for imports. An exchange rate measures the value of one currency in units of another currency. As economic conditions change, exchange rates can change substantially. A decline in a currency's value is often referred to as **depreciation**. When the British pound depreciates against the U.S. dollar, this means that the U.S. dollar is strengthening relative to the pound. The increase in a currency value is often referred to as **appreciation**.

When a foreign currency's spot rates at two specific points in time are compared, the spot rate at the more recent date is denoted as S and the spot rate at the earlier date is denoted as S_{t-1}. The percentage change in the value of the foreign currency is computed as follows:

$$\text{Percent } \Delta \text{ in foreign currency value} = \frac{S - S_{t-1}}{S_{t-1}}$$

http://

Visit http://www.federalreserve.gov/releases/ for current and historic exchange rates.

A positive percentage change indicates that the foreign currency has appreciated, while a negative percentage change indicates that it has depreciated. The values of some currencies have changed as much as 5 percent over a 24-hour period.

On some days, most foreign currencies appreciate against the dollar, although by different degrees. On other days, most currencies depreciate against the dollar, but by different degrees. There are also days when some currencies appreciate while others depreciate against the dollar; the media describe this scenario by stating that "the dollar was *mixed* in trading."

Exhibit 4.1 illustrates how the euro changed on an annual basis from 2000 to 2004. Some currencies that are less frequently traded are even more volatile. The changes in a currency's value can have a major impact on costs and revenue.

EXAMPLE

Consider the impact of the euro's change in value from the beginning of 2003 to the beginning of 2004. Assume that a hotel in Europe charged 100 euros for a room on these two dates. If you had visited Europe and stayed in that hotel, your cost would have been $105 at the beginning of 2003 and $126 in 2004. The hotel receives the same amount of euros on both dates, but your cost in dollars was 20 percent more in 2004 because the euro appreciated by 20 percent. Meanwhile, Europeans who visited the United States would have paid less for a hotel in 2004 than in 2003 because it took fewer euros to obtain a given number of dollars in 2004. In 2004, the euro was referred to as "strong" because of its high value.

Now consider the effect of the euro's fluctuation on an MNC. If a U.S.-based MNC purchased products priced at 1 million euros at the beginning of 2003, the dollar cost was $1.05 million. If it purchased the same products at the beginning of 2004 (assuming no change in the euro price), the dollar cost was $1.26 million. The cost in 2004 was 20 percent higher because the euro's value was 20 percent higher. Meanwhile an MNC based in Europe would have been able to buy dollar-denominated products with fewer euros in 2004 than 2003 because of the euro's strength.

The potential impact of exchange rate movements on an MNC's costs and revenue is obvious and is reinforced throughout the text. Consequently, it is important to understand the forces that can cause an exchange rate to change over time. MNCs that

Exhibit 4.1
Annual Changes in the Value of the Euro

Date	Exchange Rate	Annual Percentage Change
01/01/2000	$1.001	—
01/01/2001	$.94	−6.1%
01/01/2002	$.89	−5.3%
01/01/2003	$1.05	+18.0%
01/01/2004	$1.26	+20.0%

understand how currencies might be affected by existing forces can prepare for possible adverse effects on their expenses or revenue and may be able to reduce their exposure.

Exchange Rate Equilibrium

Although it is easy to measure the percentage change in the value of a currency, it is more difficult to explain why the value changed or to forecast how it may change in the future. To achieve either of these objectives, the concept of an **equilibrium exchange rate** must be understood, as well as the factors that affect the equilibrium rate.

Before considering why an exchange rate changes, realize that an exchange rate at a given point in time represents the *price* of a currency. Like any other products sold in markets, the price of a currency is determined by the demand for that currency relative to supply. Thus, for each possible price of a British pound, there is a corresponding demand for pounds and a corresponding supply of pounds for sale. At any point in time, a currency should exhibit the price at which the demand for that currency is equal to supply, and this represents the equilibrium exchange rate. Of course, conditions can change over time, causing the supply or demand for a given currency to adjust, and thereby causing movement in the currency's price. This topic is more thoroughly discussed in this section.

Demand for a Currency

The British pound is used here to explain exchange rate equilibrium. The United Kingdom has not adopted the euro as its currency and continues to use the pound. Exhibit 4.2 shows a hypothetical number of pounds that would be demanded under various possibilities for the exchange rate. At any one point in time, there is only one exchange rate. The exhibit shows the quantity of pounds that would be demanded at

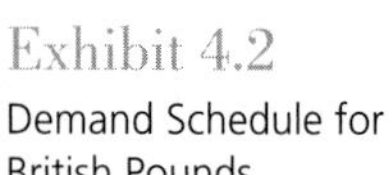

Exhibit 4.2
Demand Schedule for British Pounds

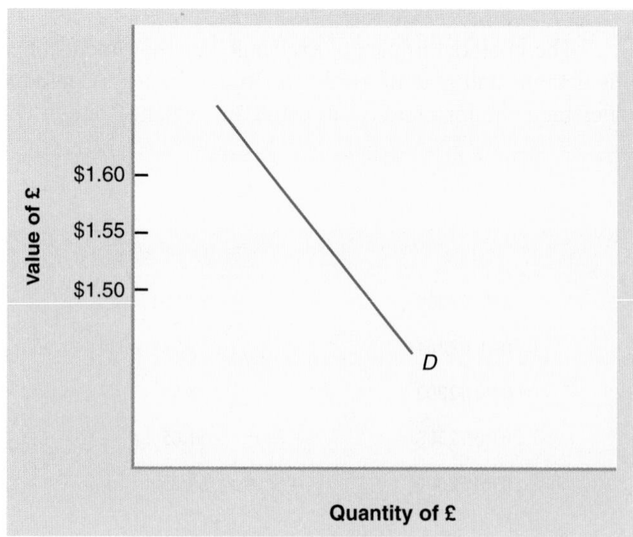

various exchange rates. The demand schedule is downward sloping because U.S. corporations will be encouraged to purchase more British goods when the pound is worth less, as it will take fewer dollars to obtain the desired amount of pounds.

Supply of a Currency for Sale

Up to this point, only the U.S. demand for pounds has been considered, but the British demand for U.S. dollars must also be considered. This can be referred to as a British *supply of pounds for sale*, since pounds are supplied in the foreign exchange market in exchange for U.S. dollars.

A supply schedule of pounds for sale in the foreign exchange market can be developed in a manner similar to the demand schedule for pounds. Exhibit 4.3 shows the quantity of pounds for sale (supplied to the foreign exchange market in exchange for dollars) corresponding to each possible exchange rate. Notice from the supply schedule in Exhibit 4.3 that there is a positive relationship between the value of the British pound and the quantity of British pounds for sale (supplied), which can be explained as follows. When the pound is valued high, British consumers and firms are more likely to purchase U.S. goods. Thus, they supply a greater number of pounds to the market, to be exchanged for dollars. Conversely, when the pound is valued low, the supply of pounds for sale is smaller, reflecting less British desire to obtain U.S. goods.

Equilibrium

The demand and supply schedules for British pounds are combined in Exhibit 4.4. At an exchange rate of $1.50, the quantity of pounds demanded would exceed the supply of pounds for sale. Consequently, the banks that provide foreign exchange services would experience a shortage of pounds at that exchange rate. At an exchange rate of $1.60, the quantity of pounds demanded would be less than the supply of pounds for sale. Therefore, banks providing foreign exchange services would experience a surplus

Exhibit 4.3
Supply Schedule of British Pounds for Sale

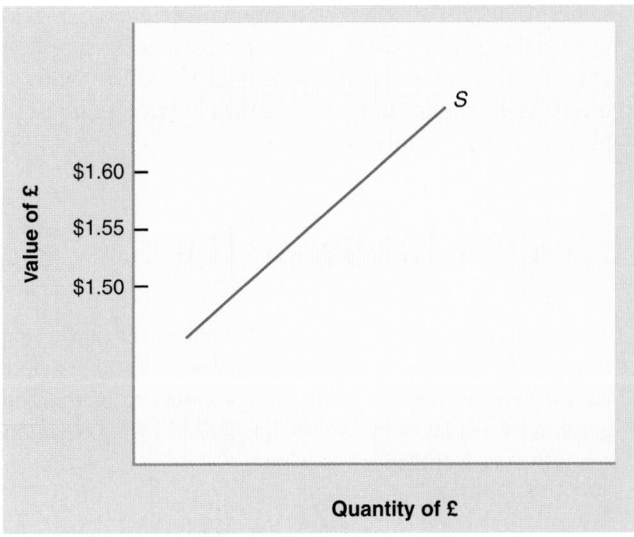

Exhibit 4.4
Equilibrium Exchange Rate Determination

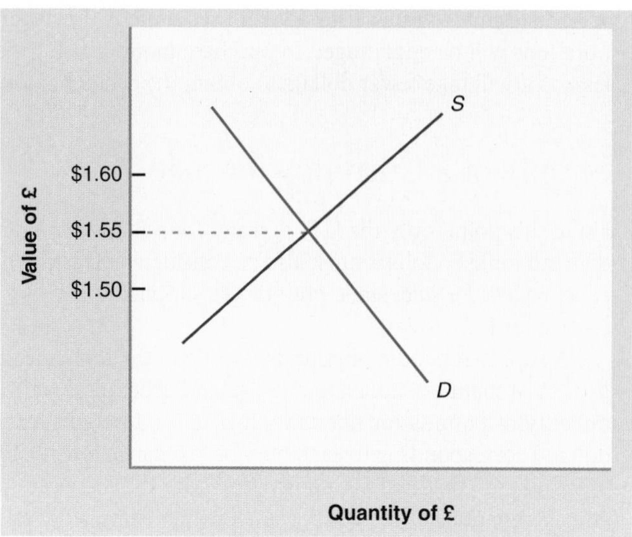

of pounds at that exchange rate. According to Exhibit 4.4, the equilibrium exchange rate is $1.55 because this rate equates the quantity of pounds demanded with the supply of pounds for sale.

Impact of Liquidity. For all currencies, the equilibrium exchange rate is reached through transactions in the foreign exchange market, but for some currencies, the adjustment process is more volatile than for others. The liquidity of a currency affects the sensitivity of the exchange rate to specific transactions. If the currency's spot market is liquid, its exchange rate will not be highly sensitive to a single large purchase or sale of the currency. Therefore, the change in the equilibrium exchange rate will be relatively small. With many willing buyers and sellers of the currency, transactions can be easily accommodated. Conversely, if the currency's spot market is illiquid, its exchange rate may be highly sensitive to a single large purchase or sale transaction. There are not sufficient buyers or sellers to accommodate a large transaction, which means that the price of the currency must change to rebalance the supply and demand for the currency. Consequently, illiquid currencies tend to exhibit more volatile exchange rate movements, as the equilibrium prices of their currencies adjust to even minor changes in supply and demand conditions.

Factors That Influence Exchange Rates

The equilibrium exchange rate will change over time as supply and demand schedules change. The factors that cause currency supply and demand schedules to change are discussed here by relating each factor's influence to the demand and supply schedules graphically displayed in Exhibit 4.4. The following equation summarizes the factors that can influence a currency's spot rate:

$$e = f(\Delta INF, \Delta INT, \Delta INC, \Delta GC, \Delta EXP)$$

where

e = percentage change in the spot rate

ΔINF = change in the differential between U.S. inflation and the foreign country's inflation

ΔINT = change in the differential between the U.S. interest rate and the foreign country's interest rate

ΔINC = change in the differential between the U.S. income level and the foreign country's income level

ΔGC = change in government controls

ΔEXP = change in expectations of future exchange rates

Relative Inflation Rates

Changes in relative inflation rates can affect international trade activity, which influences the demand for and supply of currencies and therefore influences exchange rates.

EXAMPLE

Consider how the demand and supply schedules displayed in Exhibit 4.4 would be affected if U.S. inflation suddenly increased substantially while British inflation remained the same. (Assume that both British and U.S. firms sell goods that can serve as substitutes for each other.) The sudden jump in U.S. inflation should cause an increase in the U.S. demand for British goods and therefore also cause an increase in the U.S. demand for British pounds.

In addition, the jump in U.S. inflation should reduce the British desire for U.S. goods and therefore reduce the supply of pounds for sale. These market reactions are illustrated in Exhibit 4.5. At the previous equilibrium exchange rate of $1.55, there will be a shortage of pounds in the foreign exchange market. The increased U.S. demand for pounds and the reduced supply of pounds for sale place upward pressure on the value of the pound. According to Exhibit 4.5, the new equilibrium value is $1.57.

Exhibit 4.5

Impact of Rising U.S. Inflation on the Equilibrium Value of the British Pound

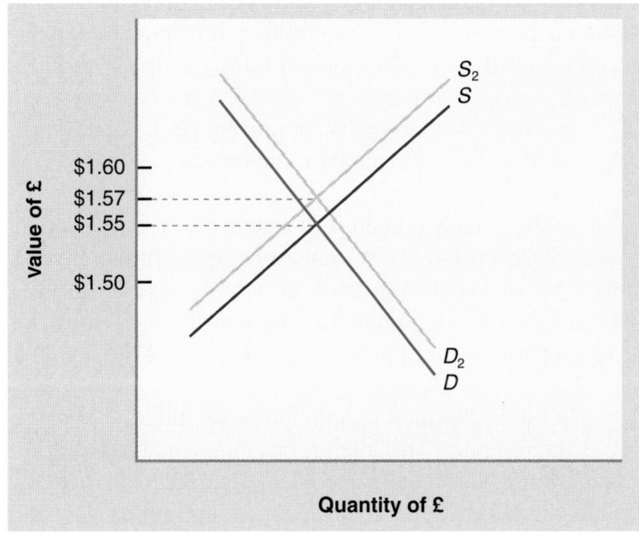

If British inflation increased (rather than U.S. inflation), the opposite forces would occur.

EXAMPLE

Assume there is a sudden and substantial increase in British inflation while U.S. inflation is low. Based on this information, answer the following questions: (1) How is the demand schedule for pounds affected? (2) How is the supply schedule of pounds for sale affected? (3) Will the new equilibrium value of the pound increase, decrease, or remain unchanged? Based on the information given, the answers are (1) the demand schedule for pounds should shift inward, (2) the supply schedule of pounds for sale should shift outward, and (3) the new equilibrium value of the pound will decrease. Of course, the actual amount by which the pound's value will decrease depends on the magnitude of the shifts. There is not enough information to determine their exact magnitude.

In reality, the actual demand and supply schedules, and therefore the true equilibrium exchange rate, will reflect several factors simultaneously. The point of the preceding example is to demonstrate how to logically work through the mechanics of the effect that higher inflation in a country can have on an exchange rate. Each factor is assessed one at a time to determine its separate influence on exchange rates, holding all other factors constant. Then, all factors can be tied together to fully explain why an exchange rate moves the way it does.

Relative Interest Rates

Changes in relative interest rates affect investment in foreign securities, which influences the demand for and supply of currencies and therefore influences exchange rates.

Assume that U.S. interest rates rise while British interest rates remain constant. In this case, U.S. investors will likely reduce their demand for pounds, since U.S. rates are now more attractive relative to British rates, and there is less desire for British bank deposits. Because U.S. rates will now look more attractive to British investors with excess cash, the supply of pounds for sale by British investors should increase as they establish more bank deposits in the United States. Due to an inward shift in the demand for pounds and an outward shift in the supply of pounds for sale, the equilibrium exchange rate should decrease. This is graphically represented in Exhibit 4.6. If U.S. interest rates decreased relative to British interest rates, the opposite shifts would be expected.

http://

Visit http://www.bloomberg.com for the latest information from financial markets around the world.

In some cases, an exchange rate between two countries' currencies can be affected by changes in a third country's interest rate.

When the Canadian interest rate increases, it can become more attractive to British investors than the U.S. rate. This encourages British investors to purchase fewer dollar-denominated securities. Thus, the supply of pounds to be exchanged for dollars would be smaller than it would have been without the increase in Canadian interest rates, which places upward pressure on the value of the pound against the U.S. dollar.

In the 1999–2000 period, European interest rates were relatively low compared to U.S. interest rates. This interest rate differential encouraged European investors to invest money in dollar-denominated debt securities. This activity resulted in a large supply of euros in the foreign exchange market and put downward pressure on the euro. In the 2002–2003 period, U.S. interest rates were lower than European interest rates. Conse-

Exhibit 4.6
Impact of Rising U.S. Interest Rates on the Equilibrium Value of the British Pound

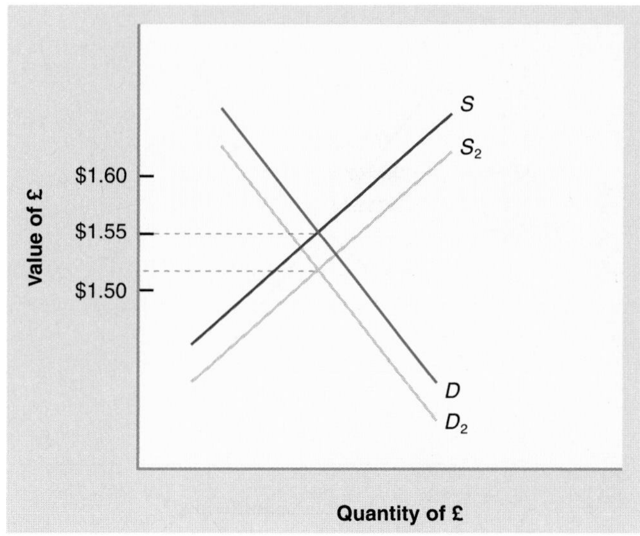

quently, there was a large U.S. demand for euros to capitalize on the higher interest rates, which placed upward pressure on the euro.

http://

Visit the Fed's data bank at http://research.stlouisfed.org/fred2 for numerous economic and financial time series, e.g., on balance-of-payment statistics and interest rates.

Real Interest Rates. Although a relatively high interest rate may attract foreign inflows (to invest in securities offering high yields), the relatively high interest rate may reflect expectations of relatively high inflation. Because high inflation can place downward pressure on the local currency, some foreign investors may be discouraged from investing in securities denominated in that currency. For this reason, it is helpful to consider the **real interest rate**, which adjusts the nominal interest rate for inflation:

$$\text{Real interest rate} \cong \text{Nominal interest rate} - \text{Inflation rate}$$

This relationship is sometimes called the Fisher effect.

The real interest rate is commonly compared among countries to assess exchange rate movements because it combines nominal interest rates and inflation, both of which influence exchange rates. Other things held constant, there should be a high correlation between the real interest rate differential and the dollar's value.

Relative Income Levels

A third factor affecting exchange rates is relative income levels. Because income can affect the amount of imports demanded, it can affect exchange rates.

EXAMPLE

Assume that the U.S. income level rises substantially while the British income level remains unchanged. Consider the impact of this scenario on (1) the demand schedule for pounds, (2) the supply schedule of pounds for sale, and (3) the equilibrium exchange rate. First, the demand schedule for pounds will shift outward, reflecting the increase in U.S. income and therefore increased demand for British goods. Second, the supply schedule of pounds for sale is not expected to change. Therefore, the equilibrium exchange rate of the pound is expected to rise, as shown in Exhibit 4.7.

Exhibit 4.7

Impact of Rising U.S. Income Levels on the Equilibrium Value of the British Pound

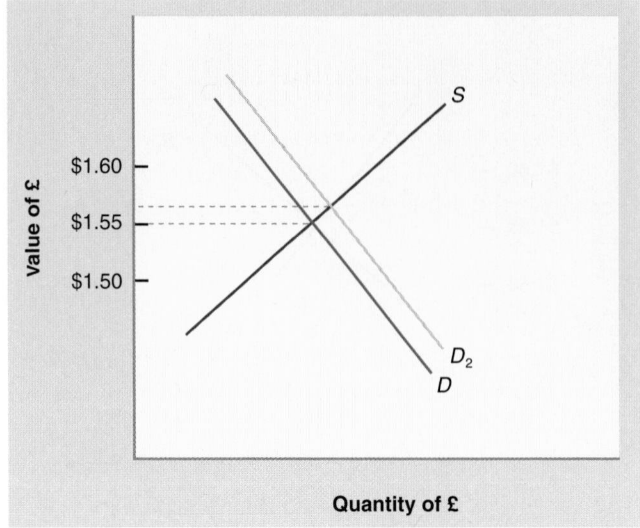

Changing income levels can also affect exchange rates indirectly through effects on interest rates. When this effect is considered, the impact may differ from the theory presented here, as will be explained shortly.

Government Controls

A fourth factor affecting exchange rates is government controls. The governments of foreign countries can influence the equilibrium exchange rate in many ways, including (1) imposing foreign exchange barriers, (2) imposing foreign trade barriers, (3) intervening (buying and selling currencies) in the foreign exchange markets, and (4) affecting macro variables such as inflation, interest rates, and income levels. Chapter 6 covers these activities in detail.

Recall the example in which U.S. interest rates rose relative to British interest rates. The expected reaction was an increase in the British supply of pounds for sale to obtain more U.S. dollars (in order to capitalize on high U.S. money market yields). Yet, if the British government placed a heavy tax on interest income earned from foreign investments, this could discourage the exchange of pounds for dollars.

Expectations

A fifth factor affecting exchange rates is market expectations of future exchange rates. Like other financial markets, foreign exchange markets react to any news that may have a future effect. News of a potential surge in U.S. inflation may cause currency traders to sell dollars, anticipating a future decline in the dollar's value. This response places immediate downward pressure on the dollar.

Many institutional investors (such as commercial banks and insurance companies) take currency positions based on anticipated interest rate movements in various countries.

Investors may temporarily invest funds in Canada if they expect Canadian interest rates to increase. Such a rise may cause further capital flows into Canada, which could place upward pressure on the Canadian dollar's value. By taking a position based on expectations, investors can fully benefit from the rise in the Canadian dollar's value because they will have purchased Canadian dollars before the change occurred. Although the investors face an obvious risk here that their expectations may be wrong, the point is that expectations can influence exchange rates because they commonly motivate institutional investors to take foreign currency positions.

http://

http://www.ny.frb.org contains links to information on economic conditions that affect foreign exchange rates and potential speculation in the foreign exchange market.

Impact of Signals on Currency Speculation. Day-to-day speculation on future exchange rate movements is commonly driven by signals of future interest rate movements, but it can also be driven by other factors. Signals of the future economic conditions that affect exchange rates can change quickly, so the speculative positions in currencies may adjust quickly, causing unclear patterns in exchange rates. It is not unusual for the dollar to strengthen substantially on a given day, only to weaken substantially on the next day. This can occur when speculators overreact to news on one day (causing the dollar to be overvalued), which results in a correction on the next day. Overreactions occur because speculators are commonly taking positions based on signals of future actions (rather than the confirmation of actions), and these signals may be misleading.

When speculators speculate on currencies in emerging markets, they can have a substantial impact on exchange rates. Those markets have a smaller amount of foreign exchange trading for other purposes (such as international trade) and therefore are less liquid than the larger markets.

EXAMPLE

The abrupt decline in the Russian ruble on some days during 1998 was partially attributed to speculative trading (although the decline might have occurred anyway over time). The decline in the ruble created a lack of confidence in other emerging markets as well and caused speculators to sell off other emerging market currencies, such as those of Poland and Venezuela. The market for the ruble is not very active, so a sudden shift in positions by speculators can have a substantial impact.

Interaction of Factors

Transactions within the foreign exchange markets facilitate either trade or financial flows. Trade-related foreign exchange transactions are generally less responsive to news. Financial flow transactions are very responsive to news, however, because decisions to hold securities denominated in a particular currency are often dependent on anticipated changes in currency values. Sometimes trade-related factors and financial factors interact and simultaneously affect exchange rate movements.

EXAMPLE

An increase in income levels sometimes causes expectations of higher interest rates. So, even though a higher income level can result in more imports, it may also indirectly attract more financial inflows (assuming interest rates increase). Because the favorable financial flows may overwhelm the unfavorable trade flows, an increase in income levels is frequently expected to strengthen the local currency.

Exhibit 4.8 separates payment flows between countries into trade-related and finance-related flows and summarizes the factors that affect these flows. Over a particular period, some factors may place upward pressure on the value of a foreign currency while other factors place downward pressure on the currency's value.

Exhibit 4.8 Summary of How Factors Can Affect Exchange Rates

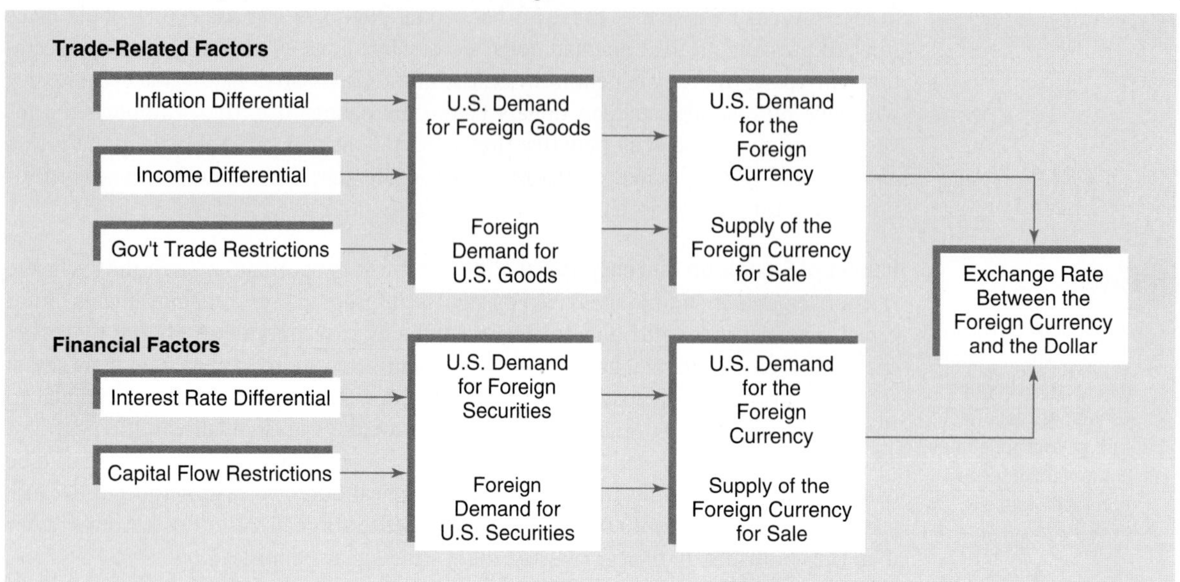

EXAMPLE

Assume the simultaneous existence of (1) a sudden increase in U.S. inflation and (2) a sudden increase in U.S. interest rates. If the British economy is relatively unchanged, the increase in U.S. inflation will place upward pressure on the pound's value while the increase in U.S. interest rates places downward pressure on the pound's value.

The sensitivity of an exchange rate to these factors is dependent on the volume of international transactions between the two countries. If the two countries engage in a large volume of international trade but a very small volume of international capital flows, the relative inflation rates will likely be more influential. If the two countries engage in a large volume of capital flows, however, interest rate fluctuations may be more influential.

EXAMPLE

Assume that Morgan Co., a U.S.-based MNC, commonly purchases supplies from Venezuela and Japan and therefore desires to forecast the direction of the Venezuelan bolivar and the Japanese yen. Morgan's financial analysts have developed the following one-year projections for economic conditions:

Factor	United States	Venezuela	Japan
Change in interest rates	−1%	−2%	−4%
Change in inflation	+2%	−3%	−6%

Assume that the United States and Venezuela conduct a large volume of international trade but engage in minimal capital flow transactions. Also assume that the United States and Japan conduct very little international trade but frequently engage in capital flow transactions. What should Morgan expect regarding the future value of the Venezuelan bolivar and the Japanese yen?

MANAGING FOR VALUE

Impact of Exchange Rate Determinants on Coca-Cola's Cash Flows

When financial managers develop cash flow forecasts for their firms, they should recognize the potential impact of exchange rate determinants on cash flows. As these determinants affect exchange rates, the exchange rate movements affect the present value of future cash flows to be received by the MNC. For example, consider the Coca-Cola Co., which derives a large proportion of its earnings from foreign countries. As earnings are remitted from foreign subsidiaries to the parent, the foreign currencies are converted into dollars. The dollar value of the remitted earnings is dependent on the exchange rate at the time the earnings are remitted, which is influenced by the inflation rate, interest rates, trade restrictions, and government intervention in that foreign country. Coca-Cola's financial managers can anticipate changes in the exchange rate by monitoring these factors for each country from which funds will be remitted.

Although it is impossible to predict exchange rate movements with perfect accuracy, financial managers may be able to at least anticipate the general movement of a particular currency against the dollar. For example, when Latin American countries experience a very high rate of inflation, there is a high probability that their currencies will depreciate against the dollar over time. Therefore, the earnings remitted to Coca-Cola will be converted at a less favorable exchange rate, which will result in a lower amount of cash flow. By anticipating general movements in exchange rates, financial managers may adjust the timing of their exchange of currencies, which may enable them to increase the values of their MNCs.

The bolivar should be influenced most by trade-related factors because of Venezuela's assumed heavy trade with the United States. The expected inflationary changes should place upward pressure on the value of the bolivar. Interest rates are expected to have little direct impact on the bolivar because of the assumed infrequent capital flow transactions between the United States and Venezuela.

The Japanese yen should be most influenced by interest rates because of Japan's assumed heavy capital flow transactions with the United States. The expected interest rate changes should place downward pressure on the yen. The inflationary changes are expected to have little direct impact on the yen because of the assumed infrequent trade between the two countries.

Capital flows have become larger over time and can easily overwhelm trade flows. For this reason, the relationship between the factors (such as inflation and income) that affect trade and exchange rates is not always as strong as one might expect.

An understanding of exchange rate equilibrium does not guarantee accurate forecasts of future exchange rates because that will depend in part on how the factors that affect exchange rates will change in the future. Even if analysts fully realize how factors influence exchange rates, they may not be able to predict how those factors will change.

Speculating on Anticipated Exchange Rates

Many commercial banks attempt to capitalize on their forecasts of anticipated exchange rate movements in the foreign exchange market, as illustrated in this example.

- Chicago Bank expects the exchange rate of the New Zealand dollar (NZ$) to appreciate from its present level of $.50 to $.52 in 30 days.

- Chicago Bank is able to borrow $20 million on a short-term basis from other banks.
- Present short-term interest rates (annualized) in the interbank market are as follows:

Currency	Lending Rate	Borrowing Rate
U.S. dollars	6.72%	7.20%
New Zealand dollars (NZ$)	6.48%	6.96%

Because brokers sometimes serve as intermediaries between banks, the lending rate differs from the borrowing rate. Given this information, Chicago Bank could

1. Borrow $20 million.
2. Convert the $20 million to NZ$40 million (computed as $20,000,000/$.50).
3. Lend the New Zealand dollars at 6.48 percent annualized, which represents a .54 percent return over the 30-day period [computed as 6.48% × (30/360)]. After 30 days, the bank will receive NZ$40,216,000 [computed as NZ$40,000,000 × (1 + .0054)].
4. Use the proceeds from the New Zealand dollar loan repayment (on Day 30) to repay the dollars borrowed. The annual interest on the U.S. dollars borrowed is 7.2 percent, or .6 percent over the 30-day period [computed as 7.2% × (30/360)]. The total U.S. dollar amount necessary to repay the loan is therefore $20,120,000 [computed as $20,000,000 × (1 + .006)].

Assuming that the exchange rate on Day 30 is $.52 per New Zealand dollar as anticipated, the number of New Zealand dollars necessary to repay the dollar loan is NZ$38,692,308 (computed as $20,120,000/$.52 per New Zealand dollar). Given that the bank accumulated NZ$40,216,000 from its New Zealand dollar loan, it would earn a speculative profit of NZ$1,523,692, which is the equivalent of $792,320 (given a spot rate of $.52 per New Zealand dollar on Day 30). The bank would earn this speculative profit without using any funds from deposit accounts because the funds would have been borrowed through the interbank market.

If, instead, Chicago Bank expects that the New Zealand dollar will depreciate, it can attempt to make a speculative profit by taking positions opposite to those just described. To illustrate, assume that the bank expects an exchange rate of $.48 for the New Zealand dollar on Day 30. It can borrow New Zealand dollars, convert them to U.S. dollars, and lend the U.S. dollars out. On Day 30, it will close out these positions. Using the rates quoted in the previous example, and assuming the bank can borrow NZ$40 million, the bank takes the following steps:

1. Borrow NZ$40 million.
2. Convert the NZ$40 million to $20 million (computed as NZ$40,000,000 × $.50).
3. Lend the U.S. dollars at 6.72 percent, which represents a .56 percent return over the 30-day period. After 30 days, the bank will receive $20,112,000 [computed as $20,000,000 × (1 + .0056)].
4. Use the proceeds of the U.S. dollar loan repayment (on Day 30) to repay the New Zealand dollars borrowed. The annual interest on the New Zealand dollars borrowed is 6.96 percent, or .58 percent over the 30-day period [computed as 6.96 × (30/360)]. The total New Zealand dollar amount necessary to repay the loan is therefore NZ$40,232,000 [computed as NZ$40,000,000 × (1 + .0058)].

Assuming that the exchange rate on Day 30 is \$.48 per New Zealand dollar as anticipated, the number of U.S. dollars necessary to repay the NZ\$ loan is \$19,311,360 (computed as NZ\$40,232,000 × \$.48 per New Zealand dollar). Given that the bank accumulated \$20,112,000 from its U.S. dollar loan, it would earn a speculative profit of \$800,640 without using any of its own money (computed as \$20,112,000 − \$19,311,360).

Most money center banks continue to take some speculative positions in foreign currencies. In fact, some banks' currency trading profits have exceeded \$100 million per quarter lately.

The potential returns from foreign currency speculation are high for banks that have large borrowing capacity. Nevertheless, foreign exchange rates are very volatile, and a poor forecast could result in a large loss. One of the best-known bank failures, Franklin National Bank in 1974, was primarily attributed to massive speculative losses from foreign currency positions.

SUMMARY

- Exchange rate movements are commonly measured by the percentage change in their values over a specified period, such as a month or a year. MNCs closely monitor exchange rate movements over the period in which they have cash flows denominated in the foreign currencies of concern.
- The equilibrium exchange rate between two currencies at any point in time is based on the demand and supply conditions. Changes in the demand for a currency or the supply of a currency for sale will affect the equilibrium exchange rate.
- The key economic factors that can influence exchange rate movements through their effects on demand and supply conditions are relative inflation rates, interest rates, and income levels, as well as government controls. As these factors cause a change in international trade or financial flows, they affect the demand for a currency or the supply of currency for sale and therefore affect the equilibrium exchange rate.
- The two factors that are most closely monitored by foreign exchange market participants are relative inflation and interest rates:

  If a foreign country experiences high inflation (relative to the United States), its exports to the United States should decrease (U.S. demand for its currency decreases), its imports should increase (supply of its currency to be exchanged for dollars increases), and there is downward pressure on its currency's equilibrium value.

  If a foreign country experiences an increase in interest rates (relative to U.S. interest rates), the inflow of U.S. funds to purchase its securities should increase (U.S. demand for its currency increases), the outflow of its funds to purchase U.S. securities should decrease (supply of its currency to be exchanged for U.S. dollars decreases), and there is upward pressure on its currency's equilibrium value.
- All relevant factors must be considered simultaneously to assess the likely movement in a currency's value.

POINT COUNTER-POINT

How Can Persistently Weak Currencies Be Stabilized?

Point The currencies of some Latin American countries depreciate against the U.S. dollar on a consistent basis. The governments of these countries need to attract more capital flows by raising interest rates and making their currencies more attractive. They also need to insure bank deposits so that foreign investors who invest in large bank deposits do not need to worry about default risk. In addition, they could impose capital restrictions on local investors to prevent capital outflows.

Counter-Point Some Latin American countries have had high inflation, which encourages local firms and consumers to purchase products from the United States instead. Thus, these countries could relieve the downward pressure on their local currencies by reducing inflation. To reduce inflation, a country may have to reduce economic growth temporarily. These countries should not raise their interest rates in order to attract foreign investment, because they will still not attract funds if investors fear that there will be large capital outflows upon the first threat of continued depreciation.

Who Is Correct? Use InfoTrac or some other search engine to learn more about this issue. Which argument do you support? Offer your own opinion on this issue.

SELF TEST

Answers are provided in Appendix A at the back of the text.

1. Briefly describe how various economic factors can affect the equilibrium exchange rate of the Japanese yen's value with respect to that of the dollar.
2. A recent shift in the interest rate differential between the United States and Country A had a large effect on the value of Currency A. However, the same shift in the interest rate differential between the United States and Country B had no effect on the value of Currency B. Explain why the effects may vary.
3. Smart Banking Corp. can borrow $5 million at 6 percent annualized. It can use the proceeds to invest in Canadian dollars at 9 percent annualized over a six-day period. The Canadian dollar is worth $.95 and is expected to be worth $.94 in six days. Based on this information, should Smart Banking Corp. borrow U.S. dollars and invest in Canadian dollars? What would be the gain or loss in U.S. dollars?

QUESTIONS AND APPLICATIONS

1. **Percentage Depreciation.** Assume the spot rate of the British pound is $1.73. The expected spot rate one year from now is assumed to be $1.66. What percentage depreciation does this reflect?
2. **Inflation Effects on Exchange Rates.** Assume that the U.S. inflation rate becomes high relative to Canadian inflation. Other things being equal, how should this affect the (a) U.S. demand for Canadian dollars, (b) supply of Canadian dollars for sale, and (c) equilibrium value of the Canadian dollar?
3. **Interest Rate Effects on Exchange Rates.** Assume U.S. interest rates fall relative to British interest rates. Other things being equal, how should this affect the (a) U.S. demand for British pounds, (b) supply of pounds for sale, and (c) equilibrium value of the pound?
4. **Income Effects on Exchange Rates.** Assume that the U.S. income level rises at a much higher rate than does the Canadian income level. Other things being equal, how should this affect the (a) U.S. demand for Canadian dollars, (b) supply of Canadian dollars for sale, and (c) equilibrium value of the Canadian dollar?
5. **Trade Restriction Effects on Exchange Rates.** Assume that the Japanese government relaxes its controls on imports by Japanese companies. Other things being equal, how should this affect the (a) U.S. demand for Japanese yen, (b) supply of yen for sale, and (c) equilibrium value of the yen?
6. **Effects of Real Interest Rates.** What is the expected relationship between the relative real interest rates of two countries and the exchange rate of their currencies?
7. **Speculative Effects on Exchange Rates.** Explain why a public forecast by a respected economist about future interest rates could affect the value of the dollar today. Why do some forecasts by well-respected economists have no impact on today's value of the dollar?

8. **Factors Affecting Exchange Rates.** What factors affect the future movements in the value of the euro against the dollar?

9. **Interaction of Exchange Rates.** Assume that there are substantial capital flows among Canada, the United States, and Japan. If interest rates in Canada decline to a level below the U.S. interest rate, and inflationary expectations remain unchanged, how could this affect the value of the Canadian dollar against the U.S. dollar? How might this decline in Canada's interest rates possibly affect the value of the Canadian dollar against the Japanese yen?

10. **Trade Deficit Effects on Exchange Rates.** Every month, the U.S. trade deficit figures are announced. Foreign exchange traders often react to this announcement and even attempt to forecast the figures before they are announced.

    a. Why do you think the trade deficit announcement sometimes has such an impact on foreign exchange trading?

    b. In some periods, foreign exchange traders do not respond to a trade deficit announcement, even when the announced deficit is very large. Offer an explanation for such a lack of response.

11. **Comovements of Exchange Rates.** Explain why the value of the British pound against the dollar will not always move in tandem with the value of the euro against the dollar.

12. **Factors Affecting Exchange Rates.** In the 1990s, Russia was attempting to import more goods but had little to offer other countries in terms of potential exports. In addition, Russia's inflation rate was high. Explain the type of pressure that these factors placed on the Russian currency.

13. **National Income Effects.** Analysts commonly attribute the appreciation of a currency to expectations that economic conditions will strengthen. Yet, this chapter suggests that when other factors are held constant, increased national income could increase imports and cause the local currency to weaken. In reality, other factors are not constant. What other factor is likely to be affected by increased economic growth and could place upward pressure on the value of the local currency?

14. **Factors Affecting Exchange Rates.** If the Asian countries experience a decline in economic growth (and experience a decline in inflation and interest rates as a result), how will their currency values (relative to the U.S. dollar) be affected?

15. **Impact of Crises.** Why do you think most crises in countries (such as the Asian crisis) cause the local currency to weaken abruptly? Is it because of trade or capital flows?

16. **Impact of September 11.** The terrorist attacks on the United States on September 11, 2001, were expected to weaken U.S. economic conditions and reduce U.S. interest rates. How do you think the weaker U.S. economic conditions would have affected trade flows? How would this have affected the value of the dollar (holding other factors constant)? How do you think the lower U.S. interest rates would have affected the value of the U.S. dollar (holding other factors constant)?

ADVANCED QUESTIONS

17. **Measuring Effects on Exchange Rates.** Tarheel Co. plans to determine how changes in U.S. and Mexican real interest rates will affect the value of the U.S. dollar. (See Appendix C.)

    a. Describe a regression model that could be used to achieve this purpose. Also explain the expected sign of the regression coefficient.

    b. If Tarheel Co. thinks that the existence of a quota in particular historical periods may have affected exchange rates, how might this be accounted for in the regression model?

18. **Factors Affecting Exchange Rates.** Mexico tends to have much higher inflation than the United States and also much higher interest rates than the United States. Inflation and interest rates are much more volatile in Mexico than in industrialized countries. The value of the Mexican peso is typically more volatile than the currencies of industrialized countries from a U.S. perspective; it has typically depreciated from one year to the next, but the degree of depreciation has varied substantially. The bid/ask spread tends to be wider for the peso than for currencies of industrialized countries.

    a. Identify the most obvious economic reason for the persistent depreciation of the peso.

    b. High interest rates are commonly expected to strengthen a country's currency because they can encourage foreign investment in securities in that country, which results in the exchange of other currencies for that currency. Yet, the peso's value has declined against the dollar over most years even though Mexican interest rates are typically much higher than U.S. interest rates. Thus, it appears that the high Mexican interest rates do not attract substantial U.S. investment in Mexico's securities. Why do you think U.S. investors do not try to capitalize on the high interest rates in Mexico?

c. Why do you think the bid/ask spread is higher for pesos than for currencies of industrialized countries? How does this affect a U.S. firm that does substantial business in Mexico?

19. **Aggregate Effects on Exchange Rates.** Assume that the United States invests heavily in government and corporate securities of Country K. In addition, residents of Country K invest heavily in the United States. Approximately $10 billion worth of investment transactions occur between these two countries each year. The total dollar value of trade transactions per year is about $8 million. This information is expected to also hold in the future.

Because your firm exports goods to Country K, your job as international cash manager requires you to forecast the value of Country K's currency (the "krank") with respect to the dollar. Explain how each of the following conditions will affect the value of the krank, holding other things equal. Then, aggregate all of these impacts to develop an overall forecast of the krank's movement against the dollar.

a. U.S. inflation has suddenly increased substantially, while Country K's inflation remains low.

b. U.S. interest rates have increased substantially, while Country K's interest rates remain low. Investors of both countries are attracted to high interest rates.

c. The U.S. income level increased substantially, while Country K's income level has remained unchanged.

d. The United States is expected to impose a small tariff on goods imported from Country K.

e. Combine all expected impacts to develop an overall forecast.

20. **Speculation.** Blue Demon Bank expects that the Mexican peso will depreciate against the dollar from its spot rate of $.15 to $.14 in 10 days. The following interbank lending and borrowing rates exist:

Currency	Lending Rate	Borrowing Rate
U.S. dollar	8.0%	8.3%
Mexican peso	8.5%	8.7%

Assume that Blue Demon Bank has a borrowing capacity of either $10 million or 70 million pesos in the interbank market, depending on which currency it wants to borrow.

a. How could Blue Demon Bank attempt to capitalize on its expectations without using deposited funds? Estimate the profits that could be generated from this strategy.

b. Assume all the preceding information with this exception: Blue Demon Bank expects the peso to appreciate from its present spot rate of $.15 to $.17 in 30 days. How could it attempt to capitalize on its expectations without using deposited funds? Estimate the profits that could be generated from this strategy.

21. **Speculation.** Diamond Bank expects that the Singapore dollar will depreciate against the dollar from its spot rate of $.43 to $.42 in 60 days. The following interbank lending and borrowing rates exist:

Currency	Lending Rate	Borrowing Rate
U.S. dollar	7.0%	7.2%
Singapore dollar	22.0%	24.0%

Diamond Bank considers borrowing 10 million Singapore dollars in the interbank market and investing the funds in dollars for 60 days. Estimate the profits (or losses) that could be earned from this strategy. Should Diamond Bank pursue this strategy?

INTERNET APPLICATION

22. **Exchange Rates Online** The website of the Federal Reserve Bank of St. Louis provides exchange rate trends of various currencies. Its address is **http://www.federalreserve.gov/releases/**.

a. Use this Web page to determine how exchange rates of various currencies have changed in recent months. Note that most of these currencies (except the British pound) are quoted in units per dollar.

In general, have most currencies strengthened or weakened against the dollar over the last three months? Offer one or more reasons to explain the recent general movements in currency values against the dollar.

b. Does it appear that the Asian currencies move in the same direction relative to the dollar? Does it appear that the Latin American currencies move in the same direction against the dollar? Explain.

DISCUSSION IN THE BOARDROOM

This exercise can be found in Appendix E at the back of this textbook.

RUNNING YOUR OWN MNC

This exercise can be found on the Xtra! website at **http://maduraxtra.swlearning.com**.

BLADES, INC. CASE

Assessment of Future Exchange Rate Movements

As the chief financial officer of Blades, Inc., Ben Holt is pleased that his current system of exporting "Speedos" to Thailand seems to be working well. Blades' primary customer in Thailand, a retailer called Entertainment Products, has committed itself to purchasing a fixed number of Speedos annually for the next three years at a fixed price denominated in baht, Thailand's currency. Furthermore, Blades is using a Thai supplier for some of the components needed to manufacture Speedos. Nevertheless, Holt is concerned about recent developments in Asia. Foreign investors from various countries had invested heavily in Thailand to take advantage of the high interest rates there. As a result of the weak economy in Thailand, however, many foreign investors have lost confidence in Thailand and have withdrawn their funds.

Ben Holt has two major concerns regarding these developments. First, he is wondering how these changes in Thailand's economy could affect the value of the Thai baht and, consequently, Blades. More specifically, he is wondering whether the effects on the Thai baht may affect Blades even though its primary Thai customer is committed to Blades over the next three years.

Second, Holt believes that Blades may be able to speculate on the anticipated movement of the baht, but he is uncertain about the procedure needed to accomplish this. To facilitate Holt's understanding of exchange rate speculation, he has asked you, Blades' financial analyst, to provide him with detailed illustrations of two scenarios. In the first, the baht would move from a current level of $0.022 to $0.020 within the next 30 days. Under the second scenario, the baht would move from its current level to $0.025 within the next 30 days.

Based on Holt's needs, he has provided you with the following list of questions to be answered:

1. How are percentage changes in a currency's value measured? Illustrate your answer numerically by assuming a change in the Thai baht's value from a value of $0.022 to $0.026.
2. What are the basic factors that determine the value of a currency? In equilibrium, what is the relationship between these factors?
3. How might the relatively high levels of inflation and interest rates in Thailand have affected the baht's value? (Assume a constant level of U.S. inflation and interest rates.)
4. How do you think the loss of confidence in the Thai baht, evidenced by the withdrawal of funds from Thailand, affected the baht's value? Would Blades be affected by the change in value, given the primary Thai customer's commitment?
5. Assume that Thailand's central bank wishes to prevent a withdrawal of funds from its country in order to prevent further changes in the currency's value. How could it accomplish this objective using interest rates?
6. Construct a spreadsheet illustrating the steps Blades' treasurer would need to follow in order to speculate on expected movements in the baht's value over the next 30 days. Also show the speculative profit (in dollars) resulting from each scenario. Use both of Ben Holt's examples to illustrate possible speculation. Assume that Blades can borrow either $10 million or the baht equivalent of this amount. Furthermore, assume that the following short-term interest rates (annualized) are available to Blades:

Currency	Lending Rate	Borrowing Rate
Dollars	8.10%	8.20%
Thai baht	14.80%	15.40%

SMALL BUSINESS DILEMMA

Assessment by the Sports Exports Company of Factors That Affect the British Pound's Value

Because the Sports Exports Company (a U.S. firm) receives payments in British pounds every month and converts those pounds into dollars, it needs to closely monitor the value of the British pound in the future. Jim Logan, owner of the Sports Exports Company, expects that inflation will rise substantially in the United Kingdom, while inflation in the United States will remain low. He also expects that the interest rates in both countries will rise by about the same amount.

1. Given Jim's expectations, forecast whether the pound will appreciate or depreciate against the dollar over time.
2. Given Jim's expectations, will the Sports Exports Company be favorably or unfavorably affected by the future changes in the value of the pound?

CHAPTER 5

Currency Derivatives

This chapter is devoted entirely to currency derivatives, often used by speculators interested in trading currencies simply to achieve profits but also used by firms to cover their foreign currency positions. A currency derivative is a contract whose price is partially derived from the value of the underlying currency that it represents. Some individuals and financial firms take positions in currency derivatives to speculate on future exchange rate movements. MNCs commonly take positions in currency derivatives to hedge their exposure to exchange rate risk. Their managers must understand how these derivatives can be used to achieve corporate goals.

The specific objectives of this chapter are to:

- explain how forward contracts are used to hedge based on anticipated exchange rate movements,
- describe how currency futures contracts are used to speculate or hedge based on anticipated exchange rate movements, and
- explain how currency options contracts are used to speculate or hedge based on anticipated exchange rate movements.

Forward Market

The forward market facilitates the trading of forward contracts on currencies. A **forward contract** is an agreement between a corporation and a commercial bank to exchange a specified amount of a currency at a specified exchange rate (called the **forward rate**) on a specified date in the future. When multinational corporations (MNCs) anticipate a future need for or future receipt of a foreign currency, they can set up forward contracts to lock in the rate at which they can purchase or sell a particular foreign currency. Virtually all large MNCs use forward contracts. Some MNCs have forward contracts outstanding worth more than $100 million to hedge various positions.

Because forward contracts accommodate large corporations, the forward transaction will often be valued at $1 million or more. Forward contracts normally are not used by consumers or small firms. In cases when a bank does not know a corporation well or fully trust it, the bank may request that the corporation make an initial deposit to assure that it will fulfill its obligation. Such a deposit is called a compensating balance and typically does not pay interest.

The most common forward contracts are for 30, 60, 90, 180, and 360 days, although other periods (including longer periods) are available. The forward rate of a given currency will typically vary with the length (number of days) of the forward period.

How MNCs Use Forward Contracts

MNCs use forward contracts to hedge their imports. They can lock in the rate at which they obtain a currency needed to purchase imports.

EXAMPLE

Turz, Inc., is an MNC based in Chicago that will need 1,000,000 Singapore dollars in 90 days to purchase Singapore imports. It can buy Singapore dollars for immediate delivery at the spot rate of $.50 per Singapore dollar (S$). At this spot rate, the firm would need $500,000 (computed as S$1,000,000 × $.50 per Singapore dollar). However, it does not have the funds right now to exchange for Singapore dollars. It could wait 90 days and then exchange dollars for Singapore dollars at the spot rate existing at that time. But Turz does not know what the spot rate will be at that time. If the rate rises to $.60 by then, Turz will need $600,000 (computed as S$1,000,000 × $.60 per Singapore dollar), an additional outlay of $100,000 due to the appreciation of the Singapore dollar.

To avoid exposure to exchange rate risk, Turz can lock in the rate it will pay for Singapore dollars 90 days from now without having to exchange dollars for Singapore dollars immediately. Specifically, Turz can negotiate a forward contract with a bank to purchase S$1,000,000 90 days forward.

The ability of a forward contract to lock in an exchange rate can create an opportunity cost in some cases.

EXAMPLE

Assume that in the previous example, Turz negotiated a 90-day forward rate of $.50 to purchase S$1,000,000. If the spot rate in 90 days is $.47, Turz will have paid $.03 per unit or $30,000 (1,000,000 units × $.03) more for the Singapore dollars than if it did not have a forward contract.

Corporations also use the forward market to lock in the rate at which they can sell foreign currencies. This strategy is used to hedge against the possibility of those currencies depreciating over time.

EXAMPLE

Scanlon, Inc., based in Virginia, exports products to a French firm and will receive payment of €400,000 in four months. It can lock in the amount of dollars to be received from this transaction by selling euros forward. That is, Scanlon can negotiate a forward contract with a bank to sell the €400,000 for dollars at a specified forward rate today. Assume the prevailing four-month forward rate on euros is $1.10. In four months, Scanlon will exchange its €400,000 for $440,000 (computed as €400,000 × $1.10 = $440,000).

Bid/Ask Spread. Like spot rates, forward rates have a bid/ask spread. For example, a bank may set up a contract with one firm agreeing to sell the firm Singapore dollars 90 days from now at $.510 per Singapore dollar. This represents the ask rate. At the same time, the firm may agree to purchase (bid) Singapore dollars 90 days from now from some other firm at $.505 per Singapore dollar.

The spread between the bid and ask prices is wider for forward rates of currencies of developing countries, such as Chile, Mexico, South Korea, Taiwan, and Thailand. Because these markets have relatively few orders for forward contracts, banks are less able to match up willing buyers and sellers. This lack of liquidity causes banks to widen the bid/ask spread when quoting forward contracts. The contracts in these countries are generally available only for short-term horizons.

Premium or Discount on the Forward Rate. The difference between the forward rate (F) and the spot rate (S) at a given point in time is measured by the premium:

$$F = S(1 + p)$$

where p represents the forward premium, or the percentage by which the forward rate exceeds the spot rate.

EXAMPLE

If the euro's spot rate is $1.03, and its one-year forward rate has a forward premium of 2 percent, the one-year forward rate is:

$$\begin{aligned} F &= S(1 + p) \\ &= \$1.03(1 + .02) \\ &= \$1.0506. \end{aligned}$$

Given quotations for the spot rate and the forward rate at a given point in time, the premium can be determined by rearranging the above equation:

$$\begin{aligned} F &= S(1 + p) \\ F/S &= 1 + p \\ (F/S) - 1 &= p \end{aligned}$$

EXAMPLE

If the euro's one-year forward rate is quoted at $1.0506 and the euro's spot rate is quoted at $1.03, the euro's forward premium is:

$$\begin{aligned} (F/S) - 1 &= p \\ (\$1.0506/\$1.03) - 1 &= p \\ 1.02 - 1 &= .02 \text{ or 2 percent.} \end{aligned}$$

When the forward rate is less than the prevailing spot rate, the forward premium is negative, and the forward rate exhibits a discount.

EXAMPLE

If the euro's one-year forward rate is quoted at $1.00 and the euro's spot rate is quoted at $1.03, the euro's forward premium is:

$$\begin{aligned} (F/S) - 1 &= p \\ (\$1.00/\$1.03) - 1 &= p \\ .9709 - 1 &= -.0291 \text{ or } -2.91 \text{ percent.} \end{aligned}$$

Since p is negative, the forward rate contains a discount.

EXAMPLE

Assume the forward exchange rates of the British pound for various maturities as shown in the second column of Exhibit 5.1. Based on each forward exchange rate, the forward discount can be computed on an annualized basis, as shown in Exhibit 5.1.

In some situations, a firm may prefer to assess the premium or discount on an unannualized basis. In this case, it would not include the fraction that represents the number of periods per year in the formula.

Arbitrage. Forward rates typically differ from the spot rate for any given currency. If the forward rate were the same as the spot rate, and interest rates of the two countries differed, it would be possible for some investors (under certain assumptions) to use **arbitrage** to earn higher returns than would be possible domestically without incurring additional risk (as explained in Chapter 7). Consequently, the forward rate usually contains a premium (or discount) that reflects the difference between the home interest rate and the foreign interest rate.

Movements in the Forward Rate over Time. If the forward rate's premium remained constant, the forward rate would move in perfect tandem with the movements in the corresponding spot rate over time. For example, if the spot rate of the euro increased by 4 percent from a month ago until today, the forward rate would have to increase by 4 percent as well over the same period in order to maintain the same premium. In reality, the forward premium is influenced by the interest rate differential between the two countries (as explained in Chapter 7) and can change over time. Most of the movement in a currency's forward rate over time is due to movements in that currency's spot rate.

USING THE WEB

Forward Rates Forward rates of the Canadian dollar, British pound, euro, and Japanese yen are provided for various periods at http://www.bmo.com/economic/regular/fxrates.html. The website shows the forward rate of the Canadian dollar for many time horizons. It also shows the forward rate of the British pound, the euro, and the Japanese yen against the Canadian dollar and against the U.S. dollar.

Offsetting a Forward Contract. In some cases, an MNC may desire to offset a forward contract that it previously created.

EXAMPLE

On March 10, Green Bay, Inc., hired a Canadian construction company to expand its office and agreed to pay C$200,000 for the work on September 10. It negotiated a six-month forward contract to obtain C$200,000 at $.70 per unit, which would be used to pay the Canadian firm in six months. On April 10, the construction company informed Green Bay that it would not be able to perform the work as promised. Therefore, Green Bay offset its existing contract by negotiating a forward contract to sell C$200,000 for the date of September 10. However, the spot rate of the Canadian dollar had decreased over the last month, and the prevailing forward contract price for September 10 is $.66. Green Bay now has a forward contract to sell C$200,000 on September 10, which offsets the other contract it has to buy C$200,000 on September 10. The forward rate was $.04 per unit less on its forward sale than on its forward purchase, resulting in a cost of $8,000 (C$200,000 × $.04).

If Green Bay in the preceding example negotiates the forward sale with the same bank where it negotiated the forward purchase, it may simply be able to request that its

Exhibit 5.1
Computation of Forward Rate Premiums or Discounts

Type of Exchange Rate for £	Value	Maturity	Forward Rate Premium or Discount for £
Spot rate	$1.681		
30-day forward rate	$1.680	30 days	$\frac{\$1.680 - \$1.681}{\$1.681} \times \frac{360}{30} = -.71\%$
90-day forward rate	$1.677	90 days	$\frac{\$1.677 - \$1.681}{\$1.681} \times \frac{360}{90} = -.95\%$
180-day forward rate	$1.672	180 days	$\frac{\$1.672 - \$1.681}{\$1.681} \times \frac{360}{180} = -1.07\%$

initial forward contract be offset. The bank will charge a fee for this service, which will reflect the difference between the forward rate at the time of the forward purchase and the forward rate at the time of the offset. Thus, the MNC cannot just ignore its obligation, but must pay a fee to offset its original obligation.

Using Forward Contracts for Swap Transactions. A swap transaction involves a spot transaction along with a corresponding forward contract that will ultimately reverse the spot transaction. Many forward contracts are negotiated for this purpose.

Soho, Inc., needs to invest 1 million Chilean pesos in its Chilean subsidiary for the production of additional products. It wants the subsidiary to repay the pesos in one year. Soho wants to lock in the rate at which the pesos can be converted back into dollars in one year, and it uses a one-year forward contract for this purpose. Soho contacts its bank and requests the following swap transaction:

1. *Today:* The bank should withdraw dollars from Soho's U.S. account, convert the dollars to pesos in the spot market, and transmit the pesos to the subsidiary's account.
2. *In one year:* The bank should withdraw 1 million pesos from the subsidiary's account, convert them to dollars at today's forward rate, and transmit them to Soho's U.S. account.

Soho, Inc., is not exposed to exchange rate movements due to the transaction because it has locked in the rate at which the pesos will be converted back to dollars. If the one-year forward rate exhibits a discount, however, Soho will receive fewer dollars in one year than it invested in the subsidiary today. It may still be willing to engage in the swap transaction under these circumstances in order to remove uncertainty about the dollars it will receive in one year.

Non-Deliverable Forward Contracts

A new type of forward contract called a **non-deliverable forward contract (NDF)** is frequently used for currencies in emerging markets. Like a regular forward contract, an NDF represents an agreement regarding a position in a specified amount of a specified currency, a specified exchange rate, and a specified future settlement date. However, an NDF does not result in an actual exchange of the currencies at the future date. That is, there is no delivery. Instead, one party to the agreement makes a payment to the other party based on the exchange rate at the future date.

EXAMPLE

Jackson, Inc., an MNC based in Wyoming, determines as of April 1 that it will need 100 million Chilean pesos to purchase supplies on July 1. It can negotiate an NDF with a local bank as follows. The NDF will specify the currency (Chilean peso), the settlement date (90 days from now), and a so-called reference rate, which identifies the type of exchange rate that will be marked to market at the settlement. Specifically, the NDF will contain the following information:

- Buy 100 million Chilean pesos.
- Settlement date: July 1.
- Reference index: Chilean peso's closing exchange rate (in dollars) quoted by Chile's central bank in 90 days.

Assume that the Chilean peso (which is the reference index) is currently valued at $.0020, so the dollar amount of the position is $200,000 at the time of the agreement. At the time of the settlement date (July 1), the value of the reference index is determined, and a payment is made between the two parties to settle the NDF. For example, if the peso value increases to $.0023 by July 1, the value of the position specified in the NDF will be $230,000 ($.0023 × 100 million pesos). Since the value of Jackson's NDF position is $30,000 higher than when the agreement was created, Jackson will receive a payment of $30,000 from the bank.

Recall that Jackson needs 100 million pesos to buy imports. Since the peso's spot rate rose from April 1 to July 1, Jackson will need to pay $30,000 more for the imports than if it had paid for them on April 1. At the same time, however, Jackson will have received a payment of $30,000 due to its NDF. Thus, the NDF hedged the exchange rate risk.

If the Chilean peso had depreciated to $.0018 instead of rising, Jackson's position in its NDF would have been valued at $180,000 (100 million pesos × $.0018) at the settlement date, which is $20,000 less than the value when the agreement was created. Therefore, Jackson would have owed the bank $20,000 at that time. However, the decline in the spot rate of the peso means that Jackson would pay $20,000 less for the imports than if it had paid for them on April 1. Thus, an offsetting effect would also occur in this example.

As these examples show, although an NDF does not involve delivery, it can effectively hedge future foreign currency payments that are anticipated by an MNC.

Since an NDF can specify that any payments between the two parties be in dollars or some other available currency, firms can even use NDFs to hedge existing positions of foreign currencies that are not convertible. Consider an MNC that expects to receive payment in a foreign currency that cannot be converted into dollars. Though the MNC may use the currency to make purchases in the local country of concern, it still may desire to hedge against a decline in the value of the currency over the period before it receives payment. It takes a sell position in an NDF and uses the closing exchange rate of that currency as of the settlement date as the reference index. If the currency depreciates against the dollar over time, the firm will receive the difference between the dollar value of the position when the NDF contract was created and the dollar value of the position as of the settlement date. Thus, it will receive a payment in dollars from the NDF to offset any depreciation in the currency over the period of concern.

Currency Futures Market

http://

The *Futures* magazine website at http://www.futuresmag.com/library/contents.html covers various aspects of derivatives trading such as new products, strategies, and market analyses.

http://

Visit the Chicago Mercantile Exchange site at http://www.cme.com for a time series on financial futures and option prices. The site also allows for the generation of historic price charts.

Currency futures contracts are contracts specifying a standard volume of a particular currency to be exchanged on a specific settlement date. Thus, currency futures contracts are similar to forward contracts in terms of their obligation, but differ from forward contracts in the way they are traded. They are commonly used by MNCs to hedge their foreign currency positions. In addition, they are traded by speculators who hope to capitalize on their expectations of exchange rate movements. A buyer of a currency futures contract locks in the exchange rate to be paid for a foreign currency at a future point in time. Alternatively, a seller of a currency futures contract locks in the exchange rate at which a foreign currency can be exchanged for the home currency. In the United States, currency futures contracts are purchased to lock in the amount of dollars needed to obtain a specified amount of a particular foreign currency; they are sold to lock in the amount of dollars to be received from selling a specified amount of a particular foreign currency.

Contract Specifications

Currency futures contracts are available for several widely traded currencies at the Chicago Mercantile Exchange (CME); the contract for each currency specifies a standardized number of units (see Exhibit 5.2).

Exhibit 5.2

Currency Futures Contracts Traded on the Chicago Mercantile Exchange

Currency	Units per Contract
Australian dollar	100,000
Brazilian real	100,000
British pound	62,500
Canadian dollar	100,000
Euro	125,000
Japanese yen	12,500,000
Mexican peso	500,000
New Zealand dollar	100,000
Norwegian krone	2,000,000
Russian ruble	2,500,000
South African rand	500,000
Swedish krona	2,000,000
Swiss franc	125,000
Czech koruna*	4,000,000
Polish zloty*	500,000
Hungarian forint*	30,000,000

* These countries joined the European Union in 2004 but will still use their currencies until at least 2006.

The typical currency futures contract is based on a currency value in terms of U.S. dollars. However, futures contracts are also available on some cross-rates, such as the exchange rate between the Australian dollar and the Canadian dollar. Thus, speculators who expect that the Australian dollar will move substantially against the Canadian dollar can take a futures position to capitalize on their expectations. In addition, Australian firms that have exposure in Canadian dollars or Canadian firms that have exposure in Australian dollars may use this type of futures contract to hedge their exposure. See http://www.cme.com/prd/fx/crossrate2625.html for more information about futures on cross exchange rates.

Currency futures contracts typically specify the third Wednesday in March, June, September, or December as the settlement date. There is also an over-the-counter currency futures market, where various financial intermediaries facilitate trading of currency futures contracts with specific settlement dates. Contracts have to be standardized, or floor trading would slow down considerably while brokers assessed contract specifications.

Trading Futures

Firms or individuals can execute orders for currency futures contracts by calling brokerage firms that serve as intermediaries. The order to buy or sell a currency futures contract for a specific currency and a specific settlement date is communicated to the brokerage firm, which in turn communicates the order to the CME. A floor broker at the CME who specializes in that type of currency futures contract stands at a specific spot at the trading pit where that type of contract is traded and attempts to find a counterparty to fulfill the order. For example, if an MNC wants to purchase a Mexican peso futures contract with a December settlement date, the floor broker assigned to execute this order will look for another floor broker who has an order to sell a Mexican peso futures contract with a December settlement date.

Trading on the floor (in the trading pits) of the CME takes place from 7:20 A.M. to 2:00 P.M. (Chicago time) Monday through Friday. Currency futures contracts can also be traded on the CME's automated order-entry and matching system called GLOBEX, which typically is open 23 hours per day (closed from 4 P.M. to 5 P.M.). The GLOBEX system matches buy and sell orders for each type of currency futures contract. E-mini futures for some currencies are also traded on the GLOBEX system; they specify half the number of units of the standard futures contract.

When participants in the currency futures market take a position, they need to establish an initial margin, which may represent as little as 10 percent of the contract value. The margin required is in the form of cash for small investors or Treasury securities for institutional investors. In addition to the initial margin, participants are subject to a variation margin, which is intended to accumulate a sufficient amount of funds to back the futures position. Full-service brokers typically charge a commission of about \$50 for a round-trip trade in currency futures, while discount brokers charge a commission of about \$20. Some Internet brokers also trade currency futures.

EXAMPLE

Assume that as of February 10, a futures contract on 62,500 British pounds with a March settlement date is priced at \$1.50 per pound. Consider the positions of two different firms on the opposite sides of this contract. The buyer of this currency futures contract will receive £62,500 on the March settlement date and will pay $93,750 for the pounds (computed as £62,500 × $1.50 per pound). The seller of this contract is obligated to sell £62,500 at a price of $1.50 per pound and therefore will receive $93,750 on the settlement date.

Comparison of Currency Futures and Forward Contracts

Currency futures contracts are similar to forward contracts in that they allow a customer to lock in the exchange rate at which a specific currency is purchased or sold for a specific date in the future. Nevertheless, there are some differences between currency futures contracts and forward contracts, which are summarized in Exhibit 5.3. Currency futures contracts are sold on an exchange, while each forward contract is negotiated between a firm and a commercial bank over a telecommunications network. Thus, forward contracts can be tailored to the needs of the firm, while currency futures contracts are standardized.

Corporations that have established relationships with large banks tend to use forward contracts rather than futures contracts because forward contracts are tailored to the precise amount of currency to be purchased or sold in the future and the precise forward date that they prefer. Conversely, small firms and individuals who do not have established relationships with large banks or prefer to trade in smaller amounts tend to use currency futures contracts.

Exhibit 5.3 Comparison of the Forward and Futures Markets

	Forward	Futures
Size of contract	**Tailored to individual needs.**	**Standardized.**
Delivery date	**Tailored to individual needs.**	**Standardized.**
Participants	**Banks, brokers, and multinational companies. Public speculation not encouraged.**	**Banks, brokers, and multinational companies. Qualified public speculation encouraged.**
Security deposit	**None as such, but compensating bank balances or lines of credit required.**	**Small security deposit required.**
Clearing operation	**Handling contingent on individual banks and brokers. No separate clearinghouse function.**	**Handled by exchange clearinghouse. Daily settlements to the market price.**
Marketplace	**Over the telephone worldwide.**	**Central exchange floor with worldwide communications.**
Regulation	**Self-regulating.**	**Commodity Futures Trading Commission; National Futures Association.**
Liquidation	**Most settled by actual delivery. Some by offset, at a cost.**	**Most by offset, very few by delivery.**
Transaction costs	**Set by "spread" between bank's buy and sell prices.**	**Negotiated brokerage fees.**

Source: Chicago Mercantile Exchange.

Pricing Currency Futures

The price of currency futures normally will be similar to the forward rate for a given currency and settlement date. This relationship is enforced by the potential arbitrage activity that would occur if there were significant discrepancies.

EXAMPLE

Assume that the currency futures price on the pound is $1.50 and that forward contracts for a similar period are available for $1.48. Firms may attempt to purchase forward contracts and simultaneously sell currency futures contracts. If they can exactly match the settlement dates of the two contracts, they can generate guaranteed profits of $.02 per unit. These actions will place downward pressure on the currency futures price. The futures contract and forward contracts of a given currency and settlement date should have the same price, or else guaranteed profits are possible (assuming no transaction costs).

The currency futures price differs from the spot rate for the same reasons that a forward rate differs from the spot rate. If a currency's spot and futures prices were the same and the currency's interest rate were higher than the U.S. rate, U.S. speculators could lock in a higher return than they would receive on U.S. investments. They could purchase the foreign currency at the spot rate, invest the funds at the attractive interest rate, and simultaneously sell currency futures to lock in the exchange rate at which they could reconvert the currency back to dollars. If the spot and futures rates were the same, there would be neither a gain nor a loss on the currency conversion. Thus, the higher foreign interest rate would provide a higher yield on this type of investment. The actions of investors to capitalize on this opportunity would place upward pressure on the spot rate and downward pressure on the currency futures price, causing the futures price to fall below the spot rate.

USING THE WEB

Futures Prices Currency futures prices can be obtained on the website of the Chicago Mercantile Exchange, http://www.cme.com. Information is provided on each of the currencies for which futures contracts are traded on that exchange. The information includes the open price, high and low prices for the day, closing (last) price, and trading volume.

Credit Risk of Currency Futures Contracts

Each currency futures contract represents an agreement between a client and the exchange clearinghouse, even though the exchange has not taken a position. To illustrate, assume you call a broker to request the purchase of a British pound futures contract with a March settlement date. Meanwhile, another person unrelated to you calls a broker to request the sale of a similar futures contract. Neither party needs to worry about the credit risk of the counterparty. The exchange clearinghouse assures that you will receive whatever is owed to you as a result of your currency futures position.

To minimize its risk in such a guarantee, the CME imposes **margin requirements** to cover fluctuations in the value of a contract, meaning that the participants must make a deposit with their respective brokerage firms when they take a position. The initial margin requirement is typically between $1,000 and $2,000 per currency futures contract. However, if the value of the futures contract declines over time, the buyer may be asked to add to the initial margin. Margin requirements are not always required for forward contracts due to the more personal nature of the agreement; the bank knows the firm it is dealing with and may trust it to fulfill its obligation.

Speculation with Currency Futures

Currency futures contracts are sometimes purchased by speculators who are simply attempting to capitalize on their expectation of a currency's future movement.

EXAMPLE

Assume that speculators expect the British pound to appreciate in the future. They can purchase a futures contract that will lock in the price at which they buy pounds at a specified settlement date. On the settlement date, they can purchase their pounds at the rate specified by the futures contract and then sell these pounds at the spot rate. If the spot rate has appreciated by this time in accordance with their expectations, they will profit from this strategy.

Currency futures are often sold by speculators who expect that the spot rate of a currency will be less than the rate at which they would be obligated to sell it.

EXAMPLE

Assume that as of April 4, a futures contract specifying 500,000 Mexican pesos and a June settlement date is priced at \$.09. On April 4, speculators who expect the peso will decline sell futures contracts on pesos. Assume that on June 17 (the settlement date), the spot rate of the peso is \$.08. The transactions are shown in Exhibit 5.4 (the margin deposited by the speculators is not considered). The gain on the futures position is \$5,000, which represents the difference between the amount received (\$45,000) when selling the pesos in accordance with the futures contract versus the amount paid (\$40,000) for those pesos in the spot market.

Of course, expectations are often incorrect. It is because of different expectations that some speculators decide to purchase futures contracts while other speculators decide to sell the same contracts at a given point in time.

Currency Futures Market Efficiency. If the currency futures market is efficient, the futures price for a currency at any given point in time should reflect all available

Exhibit 5.4
Source of Gains from Buying Currency Futures

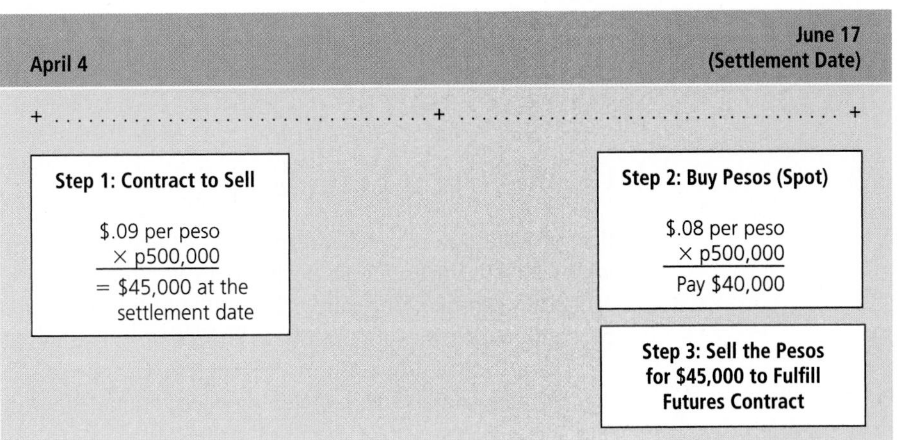

information. That is, it should represent an unbiased estimate of the respective currency's spot rate on the settlement date. Thus, the continual use of a particular strategy to take positions in currency futures contracts should not lead to abnormal profits. Some positions will likely result in gains while others will result in losses, but over time, the gains and losses should offset. Research has found that in some years, the futures price has consistently exceeded the corresponding price as of the settlement date, while in other years, the futures price has consistently been below the corresponding price as of the settlement date. This suggests that the currency futures market may be inefficient. However, the patterns are not necessarily observable until after they occur, which means that it may be difficult to consistently generate abnormal profits from speculating in currency futures.

How Firms Use Currency Futures

Corporations that have open positions in foreign currencies can consider purchasing or selling futures contracts to offset their positions.

Purchasing Futures to Hedge Payables. The purchase of futures contracts locks in the price at which a firm can purchase a currency.

EXAMPLE

Teton Co. orders Canadian goods and upon delivery will need to send C$500,000 to the Canadian exporter. Thus, Teton purchases Canadian dollar futures contracts today, thereby locking in the price to be paid for Canadian dollars at a future settlement date. By holding futures contracts, Teton does not have to worry about changes in the spot rate of the Canadian dollar over time.

Selling Futures to Hedge Receivables. The sale of futures contracts locks in the price at which a firm can sell a currency.

EXAMPLE

Karla Co. sells futures contracts when it plans to receive a currency from exporting that it will not need (it accepts a foreign currency when the importer prefers that type of payment). By selling a futures contract, Karla Co. locks in the price at which it will be able to sell this currency as of the settlement date. Such an action can be appropriate if Karla expects the foreign currency to depreciate against Karla's home currency.

The use of futures contracts to cover, or **hedge**, a firm's currency positions is described more thoroughly in Chapter 11.

Closing Out a Futures Position

If a firm holding a currency futures contract decides before the settlement date that it no longer wants to maintain its position, it can close out the position by selling an identical futures contract. The gain or loss to the firm from its previous futures position is dependent on the price of purchasing futures versus selling futures.

The price of a futures contract changes over time in accordance with movements in the spot rate and also with changing expectations about the spot rate's value as of the settlement date.

If the spot rate of a currency increases substantially over a one-month period, the futures price will likely increase by about the same amount. In this case, the purchase and subsequent sale of a futures contract would be profitable. Conversely, a decline in the spot rate over time will correspond with a decline in the currency futures price, meaning that the purchase and subsequent sale of a futures contract would result in a loss. While the purchasers of the futures contract could decide not to close out their position under such conditions, the losses from that position could increase over time.

EXAMPLE

On January 10, Tacoma Co. anticipates that it will need Australian dollars (A$) in March when it orders supplies from an Australian supplier. Consequently, Tacoma purchases a futures contract specifying A$100,000 and a March settlement date (which is March 19 for this contract). On January 10, the futures contract is priced at $.53 per A$. On February 15, Tacoma realizes that it will not need to order supplies because it has reduced its production levels. Therefore, it has no need for A$ in March. It sells a futures contract on A$ with the March settlement date to offset the contract it purchased in January. At this time, the futures contract is priced at $.50 per A$. On March 19 (the settlement date), Tacoma has offsetting positions in futures contracts. However, the price when the futures contract was purchased was higher than the price when an identical contract was sold, so Tacoma incurs a loss from its futures positions. Tacoma's transactions are summarized in Exhibit 5.5. Move from left to right along the time line to review the transactions. The example does not include margin requirements.

Sellers of futures contracts can close out their positions by purchasing currency futures contracts with similar settlement dates. Most currency futures contracts are closed out before the settlement date.

Transaction Costs of Currency Futures

Brokers that fulfill orders to buy or sell futures contracts charge a transaction or brokerage fee in the form of a bid/ask spread. That is, they buy a futures contract for one price (their "bid" price) and simultaneously sell the contract to someone else for a slightly higher price (their "ask" price). The difference between a bid and an ask price on a futures contract may be as little as $7.50. Yet, even this amount is larger in percentage terms than the transaction fees for forward contracts.

Exhibit 5.5 Closing Out a Futures Contract

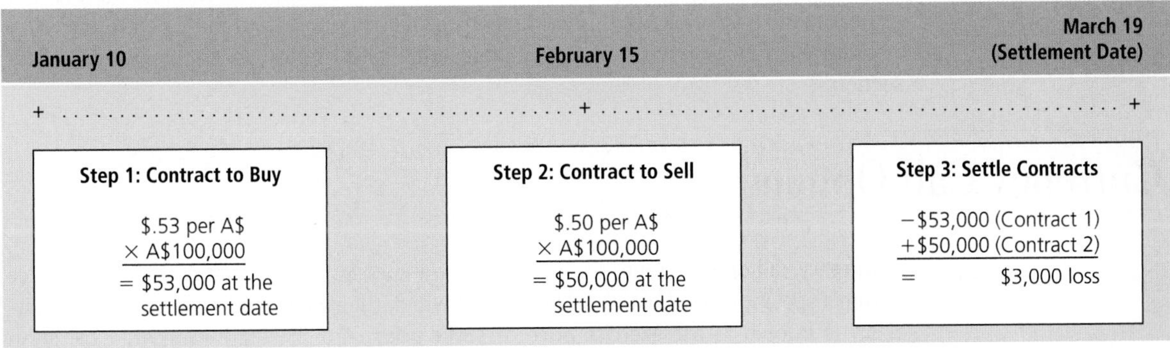

Currency Options Market

Currency options provide the right to purchase or sell currencies at specified prices. They are available for many currencies, including the Australian dollar, British pound, Brazilian real, Canadian dollar, euro, Japanese yen, Mexican peso, New Zealand dollar, Russian ruble, South African rand, and Swiss franc.

Option Exchanges

In late 1982, exchanges in Amsterdam, Montreal, and Philadelphia first allowed trading in standardized foreign currency options. Since that time, options have been offered on the Chicago Mercantile Exchange and the Chicago Board Options Exchange. Currency options are traded through the GLOBEX system at the Chicago Mercantile Exchange, even after the trading floor is closed. Thus, currency options are traded virtually around the clock.

The options exchanges in the United States are regulated by the Securities and Exchange Commission. Options can be purchased or sold through brokers for a commission. The commission per transaction is commonly \$30 to \$60 for a single currency option, but it can be much lower per contract when the transaction involves multiple contracts. Brokers require that a margin be maintained during the life of the contract. The margin is increased for clients whose option positions have deteriorated. This protects against possible losses if the clients do not fulfill their obligations.

Over-the-Counter Market

In addition to the exchanges where currency options are available, there is an over-the-counter market where currency options are offered by commercial banks and brokerage firms. Unlike the currency options traded on an exchange, currency options are tailored to the specific needs of the firm. Since these options are not standardized, all the terms must be specified in the contracts. The number of units, desired strike price, and expiration date can be tailored to the specific needs of the client. When currency options are not standardized, there is less liquidity and a wider bid/ask spread.

The minimum size of currency options offered by financial institutions is normally about \$5 million. Since these transactions are conducted with a specific financial institution rather than an exchange, there are no credit guarantees. Thus, the agreement made is only as safe as the parties involved. For this reason, financial institutions may require some collateral from individuals or firms desiring to purchase or sell currency options. Currency options are classified as either **calls** or **puts**, as discussed in the next section.

Currency Call Options

A **currency call option** grants the right to buy a specific currency at a designated price within a specific period of time. The price at which the owner is allowed to buy that currency is known as the **exercise price** or **strike price**, and there are monthly expiration dates for each option.

Call options are desirable when one wishes to lock in a maximum price to be paid for a currency in the future. If the spot rate of the currency rises above the strike price, owners of call options can "exercise" their options by purchasing the currency at the strike price, which will be cheaper than the prevailing spot rate. This strategy is somewhat similar to that used by purchasers of futures contracts, but the futures contracts require an obligation, while the currency option does not. The owner can choose to let the option expire on the expiration date without ever exercising it. Owners of expired call options will have lost the premium they initially paid, but that is the most they can lose.

Currency options quotations are summarized each day in *The Wall Street Journal* and other business newspapers. Although currency options typically expire near the middle of the specified month, some of them expire at the end of the specific month and are designated as EOM. Some options are listed as "European Style," which means that they can be exercised only upon expiration.

A currency call option is said to be *in the money* when the present exchange rate exceeds the strike price, *at the money* when the present exchange rate equals the strike price, and *out of the money* when the present exchange rate is less than the strike price. For a given currency and expiration date, an in-the-money call option will require a higher premium than options that are at the money or out of the money.

Factors Affecting Currency Call Option Premiums

http://

Visit http://www.ino.com for the latest information and prices of options and financial futures as well as the corresponding historic price charts.

The premium on a call option represents the cost of having the right to buy the underlying currency at a specified price. For MNCs that use currency call options to hedge, the premium reflects a cost of insurance or protection to the MNCs.

The call option premium (referred to as C) is primarily influenced by three factors:

$$C = f(\underset{+}{S - X}, \underset{+}{T}, \underset{+}{\sigma})$$

where $S - X$ represents the difference between the spot exchange rate (S) and the strike or exercise price (X), T represents the time to maturity, and σ represents the volatility of the currency, as measured by the standard deviation of the movements in the currency. The relationships between the call option premium and these factors are summarized next.

- *Level of existing spot price relative to strike price.* The higher the spot rate relative to the strike price, the higher the option price will be. This is due to the higher probability of buying the currency at a substantially lower rate than what you could sell it for. This relationship can be verified by comparing premiums of options for a specified currency and expiration date that have different strike prices.
- *Length of time before the expiration date.* It is generally expected that the spot rate has a greater chance of rising high above the strike price if it has a longer period of time to do so. A settlement date in June allows two additional months beyond April for the spot rate to move above the strike price. This explains why June option prices exceed April option prices given a specific strike price. This relationship can be verified by comparing premiums of options for a specified currency and strike price that have different expiration dates.
- *Potential variability of currency.* The greater the variability of the currency, the higher the probability that the spot rate will be above the strike price. Thus, more volatile

currencies have higher call option prices. For example, the Canadian dollar is more stable than most other currencies. If all other factors are similar, Canadian call options should be less expensive than call options on other foreign currencies.

The potential currency variability can also vary over time for a particular currency. For example, at the beginning of the Asian crisis in 1997, the Asian countries experienced financial problems, and their currency values were subject to much more uncertainty. Consequently, the premium on over-the-counter options of Asian currencies such as the Thai baht, Indonesian rupiah, and Korean won increased. The higher premium was necessary to compensate those who were willing to sell options in these currencies, as the risk to sellers had increased because the currencies had become more volatile.

How Firms Use Currency Call Options

Corporations with open positions in foreign currencies can sometimes use currency call options to cover these positions.

Using Call Options to Hedge Payables. MNCs can purchase call options on a currency to hedge future payables.

EXAMPLE

When Pike Co. of Seattle orders Australian goods, it makes a payment in Australian dollars to the Australian exporter upon delivery. An Australian dollar call option locks in a maximum rate at which Pike can exchange dollars for Australian dollars. This exchange of currencies at the specified strike price on the call option contract can be executed at any time before the expiration date. In essence, the call option contract specifies the maximum price that Pike must pay to obtain these Australian dollars. If the Australian dollar's value remains below the strike price, Pike can purchase Australian dollars at the prevailing spot rate when it needs to pay for its imports and simply let its call option expire.

Options may be more appropriate than futures or forward contracts for some situations. Intel Corp. uses options to hedge its order backlog in semiconductors. If an order is canceled, it has the flexibility to let the option contract expire. With a forward contract, it would be obligated to fulfill its obligation even though the order was canceled.

Using Call Options to Hedge Project Bidding. U.S.-based MNCs that bid for foreign projects may purchase call options to lock in the dollar cost of the potential expenses.

EXAMPLE

Kelly Co. is an MNC based in Fort Lauderdale that has bid on a project sponsored by the Canadian government. If the bid is accepted, Kelly will need approximately C$500,000 to purchase Canadian materials and services. However, Kelly will not know whether the bid is accepted until three months from now. In this case, it can purchase call options with a three-month expiration date. Ten call option contracts will cover the entire amount of potential exposure. If the bid is accepted, Kelly can use the options to purchase the Canadian dollars needed. If the Canadian dollar has depreciated over time, Kelly will likely let the options expire.

Assume that the exercise price on Canadian dollars is $.70 and the call option premium is $.02 per unit. Kelly will pay $1,000 per option (since there are 50,000 units per Canadian dollar option), or $10,000 for the 10 option contracts. With the options, the maximum amount necessary to purchase the C$500,000 is $350,000 (computed as $.70 per Canadian dollar × C$500,000). The amount of U.S. dollars needed would be less if the Canadian dollar's spot rate were below the exercise price at the time the Canadian dollars were purchased.

Even if Kelly's bid is rejected, it will exercise the currency call option if the Canadian dollar's spot rate exceeds the exercise price before the option expires and sell the Canadian dollars in the spot market. Any gain from exercising may partially or even fully offset the premium paid for the options.

This type of example is quite common. When Air Products and Chemicals was hired to perform some projects, it needed capital equipment from Germany. The purchase of equipment was contingent on whether the firm was hired for the projects. The company used options to hedge this possible future purchase.

Using Call Options to Hedge Target Bidding. Firms can also use call options to hedge a possible acquisition.

EXAMPLE

Morrison Co. is attempting to acquire a French firm and has submitted its bid in euros. Morrison has purchased call options on the euro because it will need euros to purchase the French company's stock. The call options hedge the U.S. firm against the potential appreciation of the euro by the time the acquisition occurs. If the acquisition does not occur and the spot rate of the euro remains below the strike price, Morrison Co. can let the call options expire. If the acquisition does not occur and the spot rate of the euro exceeds the strike price, Morrison Co. can exercise the options and sell the euros in the spot market. Alternatively, Morrison Co. can sell the call options it is holding. Either of these actions may offset part or all of the premium paid for the options.

Speculating with Currency Call Options

Because this text focuses on multinational financial management, the corporate use of currency options is more important than the speculative use. The use of options for hedging is discussed in detail in Chapter 11. Speculative trading is discussed here in order to provide more of a background on the currency options market.

Individuals may speculate in the currency options market based on their expectation of the future movements in a particular currency. Speculators who expect that a foreign currency will appreciate can purchase call options on that currency. Once the spot rate of that currency appreciates, the speculators can exercise their options by purchasing that currency at the strike price and then sell the currency at the prevailing spot rate.

Just as with currency futures, for every buyer of a currency call option there must be a seller. A seller (sometimes called a **writer**) of a call option is obligated to sell a specified currency at a specified price (the strike price) up to a specified expiration date. Speculators may sometimes want to sell a currency call option on a currency that they expect will depreciate in the future. The only way a currency call option will be exercised is if the spot rate is higher than the strike price. Thus, a seller of a currency call option will receive the premium when the option is purchased and can keep the entire amount if the option is not exercised. When it appears that an option will be exercised, there will still be sellers of options. However, such options will sell for high premiums due to the high risk that the option will be exercised at some point.

The net profit to a speculator who purchases call options on a currency is based on a comparison of the selling price of the currency versus the exercise price paid for the currency and the premium paid for the call option.

EXAMPLE

Jim is a speculator who buys a British pound call option with a strike price of $1.40 and a December settlement date. The current spot price as of that date is about $1.39. Jim pays a premium of $.012 per unit for the call option. Assume there are no brokerage fees. Just before the expiration date, the spot rate of the British pound reaches $1.41. At this time, Jim exercises the call option and then immediately sells the pounds at the spot rate to a bank. To determine Jim's profit or loss, first compute his revenues from selling the currency. Then, subtract from this amount the purchase price of pounds when exercising the option, and also subtract the purchase price of the option. The computations follow. Assume one option contract specifies 31,250 units.

	Per Unit	Per Contract
Selling price of £	$1.41	$44,063 ($1.41 × 31,250 units)
− Purchase price of £	−1.40	−43,750 ($1.40 × 31,250 units)
− Premium paid for option	−.012	−375 ($.012 × 31,250 units)
= Net profit	−$.002	−$62 (−$.002 × 31,250 units)

Assume that Linda was the seller of the call option purchased by Jim. Also assume that Linda would purchase British pounds only if and when the option was exercised, at which time she must provide the pounds at the exercise price of $1.40. Using the information in this example, Linda's net profit from selling the call option is derived here:

	Per Unit	Per Contract
Selling price of £	$1.40	$43,750 ($1.40 × 31,250 units)
− Purchase price of £	−1.41	−44,063 ($1.41 × 31,250 units)
+ Premium received	+.012	+375 ($.012 × 31,250 units)
= Net profit	$.002	$62 ($.002 × 31,250 units)

As a second example, assume the following information:

- Call option premium on Canadian dollars (C$) = $.01 per unit.
- Strike price = $.70.
- One option contract represents C$50,000.

A speculator who had purchased this call option decided to exercise the option shortly before the expiration date, when the spot rate reached $.74. The speculator immediately sold the Canadian dollars in the spot market. Given this information, the net profit to the speculator is computed as follows:

	Per Unit	Per Contract
Selling price of C$	$.74	$37,000 ($.74 × 50,000 units)
− Purchase price of C$	−.70	−35,000 ($.70 × 50,000 units)
− Premium paid for option	−.01	−500 ($.01 × 50,000 units)
= Net profit	$.03	$1,500 ($.03 × 50,000 units)

If the seller of the call option did not obtain Canadian dollars until the option was about to be exercised, the net profit to the seller of the call option was

	Per Unit	Per Contract
Selling price of C$	$.70	$35,000 ($.70 × 50,000 units)
− Purchase price of C$	−.74	−37,000 ($.74 × 50,000 units)
+ Premium received	+.01	+500 ($.01 × 50,000 units)
= Net profit	−$.03	−$1,500 (−$.03 × 50,000 units)

When brokerage fees are ignored, the currency call purchaser's gain will be the seller's loss. The currency call purchaser's expenses represent the seller's revenues, and the purchaser's revenues represent the seller's expenses. Yet, because it is possible for purchasers and sellers of options to close out their positions, the relationship described here will not hold unless both parties begin and close out their positions at the same time.

An owner of a currency option may simply sell the option to someone else before the expiration date rather than exercising it. The owner can still earn profits, since the option premium changes over time, reflecting the probability that the option can be exercised and the potential profit from exercising it.

Break-Even Point from Speculation. The purchaser of a call option will break even if the revenue from selling the currency equals the payments for (1) the currency (at the strike price) and (2) the option premium. In other words, regardless of the number of units in a contract, a purchaser will break even if the spot rate at which the currency is sold is equal to the strike price plus the option premium.

EXAMPLE

Based on the information in the previous example, the strike price is $.70 and the option premium is $.01. Thus, for the purchaser to break even, the spot rate existing at the time the call is exercised must be $.71 ($.70 + $.01). Of course, speculators will not purchase a call option if they think the spot rate will only reach the break-even point and not go higher before the expiration date. Nevertheless, the computation of the break-even point is useful for a speculator deciding whether to purchase a currency call option.

Currency Put Options

The owner of a **currency put option** receives the right to sell a currency at a specified price (the strike price) within a specified period of time. As with currency call options, the owner of a put option is not obligated to exercise the option. Therefore, the maximum potential loss to the owner of the put option is the price (or premium) paid for the option contract.

A currency put option is said to be *in the money* when the present exchange rate is less than the strike price, *at the money* when the present exchange rate equals the strike price, and *out of the money* when the present exchange rate exceeds the strike price. For a given currency and expiration date, an in-the-money put option will require a higher premium than options that are at the money or out of the money.

Factors Affecting Currency Put Option Premiums

The put option premium (referred to as P) is primarily influenced by three factors:

$$P = f(\underset{-}{S - X}, \underset{+}{T}, \underset{+}{\sigma})$$

where $S - X$ represents the difference between the spot exchange rate (S) and the strike or exercise price (X), T represents the time to maturity, and σ represents the volatility of the currency, as measured by the standard deviation of the movements in the currency. The relationships between the put option premium and these factors, which also influence call option premiums as described earlier, are summarized next.

First, the spot rate of a currency relative to the strike price is important. The lower the spot rate relative to the strike price, the more valuable the put option will be, because there is a higher probability that the option will be exercised. Recall that just the opposite relationship held for call options. A second factor influencing put option premium is the length of time until the expiration date. As with currency call options, the longer the time to expiration, the greater the put option premium will be. A longer period creates a higher probability that the currency will move into a range where it will be feasible to exercise the option (whether it is a put or a call). These relationships can be verified by assessing quotations of put option premiums for a specified currency. A third factor that influences the put option premium is the variability of a currency. As with currency call options, the greater the variability, the greater the put option premium will be, again reflecting a higher probability that the option may be exercised.

Hedging with Currency Put Options

Corporations with open positions in foreign currencies can use currency put options in some cases to cover these positions.

EXAMPLE

Assume Duluth Co. has exported products to Canada and invoiced the products in Canadian dollars (at the request of the Canadian importers). Duluth is concerned that the Canadian dollars it is receiving will depreciate over time. To insulate itself against possible depreciation, Duluth purchases Canadian dollar put options, which entitle it to sell Canadian dollars at the specified strike price. In essence, Duluth locks in the minimum rate at which it can exchange Canadian dollars for U.S. dollars over a specified period of time. If the Canadian dollar appreciates over this time period, Duluth can let the put options expire and sell the Canadian dollars it receives at the prevailing spot rate.

Speculating with Currency Put Options

Individuals may speculate with currency put options based on their expectations of the future movements in a particular currency. For example, speculators who expect that the British pound will depreciate can purchase British pound put options, which will entitle them to sell British pounds at a specified strike price. If the pound's spot rate depreciates as expected, the speculators can then purchase pounds at the spot rate and exercise their put options by selling these pounds at the strike price.

Speculators can also attempt to profit from selling currency put options. The seller of such options is obligated to purchase the specified currency at the strike price from the owner who exercises the put option. Speculators who believe the currency will appreciate (or at least will not depreciate) may sell a currency put option. If the currency appreciates over the entire period, the option will not be exercised. This is an ideal situation for put option sellers, since they keep the premiums received when selling the options and bear no cost.

The net profit to a speculator from purchasing put options on a currency is based on a comparison of the exercise price at which the currency can be sold versus the purchase price of the currency and the premium paid for the put option.

MANAGING FOR VALUE

Cisco's Dilemma When Hedging with Put Options

When Cisco Systems' European subsidiaries remit funds to their U.S. parent, Cisco may consider purchasing put options to lock in the rate at which the euros will convert to dollars. The put options also offer the flexibility of letting the options expire if the prevailing exchange rate of the euro is higher than the options' exercise price. Several put options are available to Cisco and other MNCs that wish to hedge their currency positions. At a given point in time, some put options are deep out of the money, meaning that the prevailing exchange rate is high above the exercise price. These options are cheaper (have a lower premium), as they are unlikely to be exercised because their exercise price is too low. At the same time, other put options have an exercise price that is currently above the prevailing exchange rate and are therefore more likely to be exercised. Consequently, these options are more expensive.

Cisco must weigh the tradeoff when using put options to hedge. It can create a hedge that is cheap, but the options can be exercised only if the currency's spot rate declines substantially. Alternatively, Cisco can create a hedge that can be exercised at a more favorable exchange rate, but it must pay a higher premium for the options. If Cisco's goal in using put options is simply to prevent a major loss if the currency weakens substantially, it may be willing to use an inexpensive put option (low exercise price, low premium). However, if its goal is to ensure that the currency can be exchanged at a more favorable exchange rate, Cisco will use a more expensive put option (high exercise price, high premium). By selecting currency options with an exercise price and premium that fits their objectives, Cisco and other MNCs can increase their value.

EXAMPLE

A put option contract on British pounds specifies the following information:

- Put option premium on British pound (£) = $.04 per unit.
- Strike price = $1.40.
- One option contract represents £31,250.

A speculator who had purchased this put option decided to exercise the option shortly before the expiration date, when the spot rate of the pound was $1.30. The speculator purchased the pounds in the spot market at that time. Given this information, the net profit to the purchaser of the put option is calculated as follows:

	Per Unit	Per Contract
Selling price of £	$1.40	$43,750 ($1.40 × 31,250 units)
− Purchase price of £	−1.30	−40,625 ($1.30 × 31,250 units)
− Premium paid for option	−.04	−1,250 ($.04 × 31,250 units)
= Net profit	$.06	$ 1,875 ($.06 × 31,250 units)

Assuming that the seller of the put option sold the pounds received immediately after the option was exercised, the net profit to the seller of the put option is calculated as follows:

	Per Unit	Per Contract
Selling price of £	$1.30	$40,625 ($1.30 × 31,250 units)
− Purchase price of £	−1.40	−43,750 ($1.40 × 31,250 units)
+ Premium received	+.04	+1,250 ($.04 × 31,250 units)
= Net profit	−$.06	−$1,875 (−$.06 × 31,250 units)

The seller of the put options could simply refrain from selling the pounds (after being forced to buy them at $1.40 per pound) until the spot rate of the pound rises. However, there is no guarantee that the pound will reverse its direction and begin to appreciate. The seller's net loss could potentially be greater if the pound's spot rate continued to fall, unless the pounds were sold immediately.

Whatever an owner of a put option gains, the seller loses, and vice versa. This relationship would hold if brokerage costs did not exist and if the buyer and seller of options entered and closed their positions at the same time. Brokerage fees for currency options exist, however, and are very similar in magnitude to those of currency futures contracts.

Speculating with Combined Put and Call Options. For volatile currencies, one possible speculative strategy is to create a **straddle**, which uses both a put option and a call option at the same exercise price. This may seem unusual because owning a put option is appropriate for expectations that the currency will depreciate while owning a call option is appropriate for expectations that the currency will appreciate. However, it is possible that the currency will depreciate (at which time the put is exercised) and then reverse direction and appreciate (allowing for profits when exercising the call).

USING THE WEB

Options Prices Information on currency options can be obtained on the website of the Philadelphia Stock Exchange. In particular, the link http://www.phlx.com/products/currency/currency.html provides contract specifications and volume information for the currency options contracts that are traded on that exchange.

Also, a speculator might anticipate that a currency will be substantially affected by current economic events yet be uncertain of the exact way it will be affected. By purchasing a put option and a call option, the speculator will gain if the currency moves substantially in either direction. Although two options are purchased and only one is exercised, the gains could more than offset the costs.

Currency Options Market Efficiency. If the currency options market is efficient, the premiums on currency options properly reflect all available information. Under these conditions, it may be difficult for speculators to consistently generate abnormal profits when speculating in this market. Research has found that the currency options market is efficient after controlling for transaction costs. Although some trading strategies could have generated abnormal gains in specific periods, they would have generated large losses if implemented in other periods. It is difficult to know which strategy would generate abnormal profits in future periods.

Contingency Graphs for Currency Options

A contingency graph for currency options illustrates the potential gain or loss for various exchange rate scenarios.

Contingency Graph for a Purchaser of a Call Option

A contingency graph for a purchaser of a call option compares the price paid for the call option to potential payoffs to be received with various exchange rate scenarios.

EXAMPLE

A British pound call option is available, with a strike price of $1.50 and a call premium of $.02. The speculator plans to exercise the option on the expiration date (if appropriate at that time) and then immediately sell the pounds received in the spot market. Under these conditions, a **contingency graph** can be created to measure the profit or loss per unit (see the upper-left graph in Exhibit 5.6). Notice that if the future spot rate is $1.50 or less, the net gain per unit is −$.02 (ignoring transaction costs). This represents the loss of the premium per unit paid for the option, as the option would not be exercised. At $1.51, $.01 per unit would be earned by exercising the option, but considering the $.02 premium paid, the net gain would be −$.01.

At $1.52, $.02 per unit would be earned by exercising the option, which would offset the $.02 premium per unit. This is the break-even point. At any rate above this point, the gain from exercising the option would more than offset the premium, resulting in a positive net gain. The maximum loss to the speculator in this example is the premium paid for the option.

Exhibit 5.6 Contingency Graphs for Currency Options

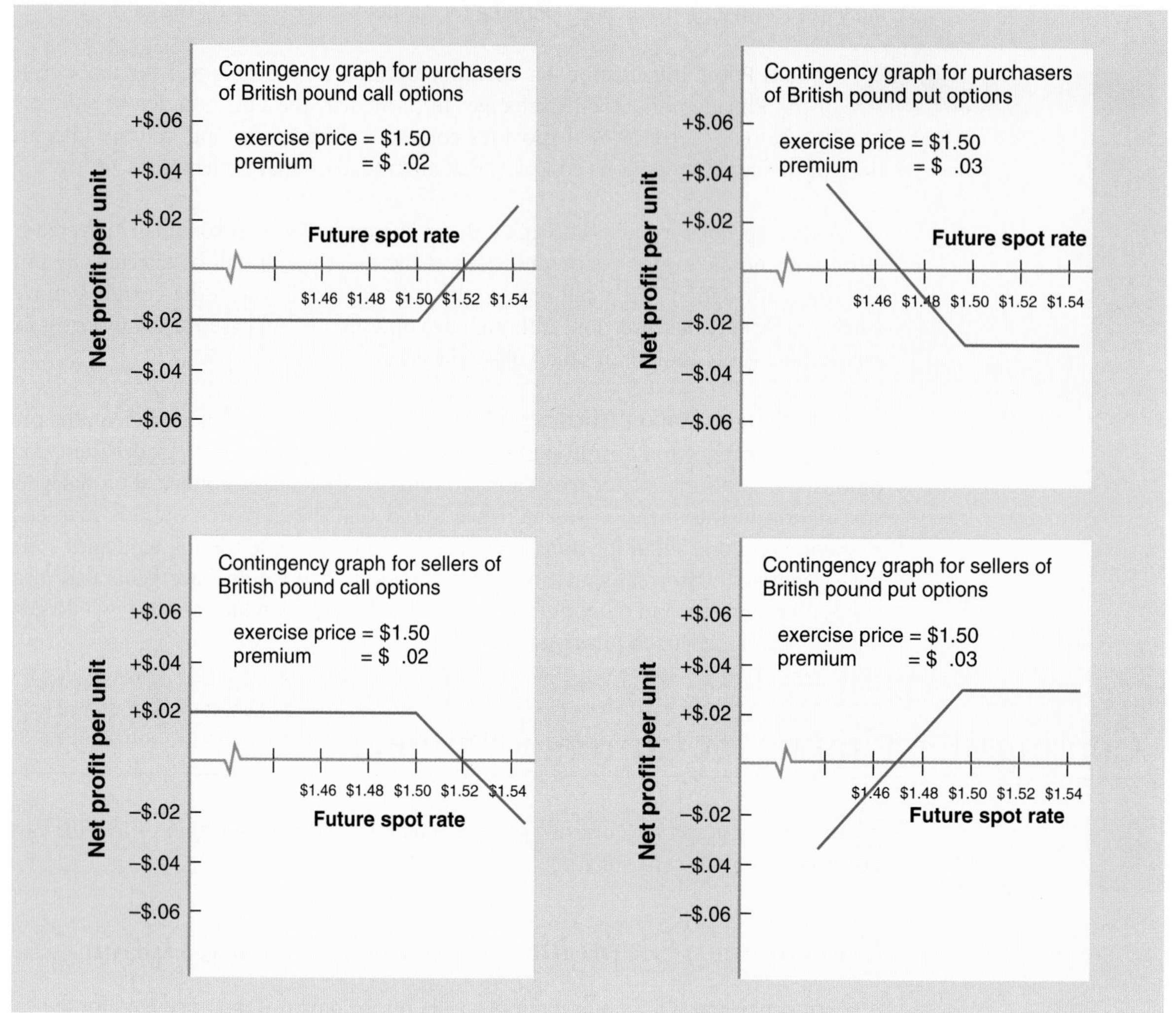

Contingency Graph for a Seller of a Call Option

A contingency graph for the seller of a call option compares the premium received from selling a call option to the potential payoffs made to the buyer of the call option for various exchange rate scenarios.

EXAMPLE

The lower-left graph shown in Exhibit 5.6 provides a contingency graph for a speculator who sold the call option described in the previous example. It assumes that this seller would purchase the pounds in the spot market just as the option was exercised (ignoring transaction costs). At future spot rates of less than $1.50, the net gain to the seller would be the premium of $.02 per unit, as the option would not have been exercised. If the future spot rate is $1.51, the seller would lose $.01 per unit on the option transaction (paying $1.51 for pounds in the spot market and selling pounds for $1.50 to fulfill the exercise request). Yet, this loss would be more than offset by the premium of $.02 per unit received, resulting in a net gain of $.01 per unit.

The break-even point is at $1.52, and the net gain to the seller of a call option becomes negative at all future spot rates higher than that point. Notice that the contingency graphs for the buyer and seller of this call option are mirror images of one another.

Contingency Graph for a Buyer of a Put Option

A contingency graph for a buyer of a put option compares the premium paid for the put option to potential payoffs received for various exchange rate scenarios.

EXAMPLE

The upper-right graph in Exhibit 5.6 shows the net gains to a buyer of a British pound put option with an exercise price of $1.50 and a premium of $.03 per unit. If the future spot rate is above $1.50, the option will not be exercised. At a future spot rate of $1.48, the put option will be exercised. However, considering the premium of $.03 per unit, there will be a net loss of $.01 per unit. The break-even point in this example is $1.47, since this is the future spot rate that will generate $.03 per unit from exercising the option to offset the $.03 premium. At any future spot rates of less than $1.47, the buyer of the put option will earn a positive net gain.

Contingency Graph for a Seller of a Put Option

A contingency graph for the seller of this put option compares the premium received from selling the option to the possible payoffs made to the buyer of the put option for various exchange rate scenarios. The graph is shown in the lower-right graph in Exhibit 5.6. It is the mirror image of the contingency graph for the buyer of a put option.

For various reasons, an option buyer's net gain will not always represent an option seller's net loss. The buyer may be using call options to hedge a foreign currency, rather than to speculate. In this case, the buyer does not evaluate the options position taken by measuring a net gain or loss; the option is used simply for protection. In addition, sellers of call options on a currency in which they currently maintain a position will not need to purchase the currency at the time an option is exercised. They can simply liquidate their position in order to provide the currency to the person exercising the option.

Conditional Currency Options

A currency option can be structured with a conditional premium, meaning that the premium paid for the option is conditioned on the actual movement in the currency's value over the period of concern.

EXAMPLE

Jensen Co., a U.S.-based MNC, needs to sell British pounds that it will receive in 60 days. It can negotiate a traditional currency put option on pounds in which the exercise price is $1.70 and the premium is $.02 per unit.

Alternatively, it can negotiate a conditional currency option with a commercial bank, which has an exercise price of $1.70 and a so-called trigger of $1.74. If the pound's value falls below the exercise price by the expiration date, Jensen will exercise the option, thereby receiving $1.70 per pound, and it will not have to pay a premium for the option.

If the pound's value is between the exercise price ($1.70) and the trigger ($1.74), the option will not be exercised, and Jensen will not need to pay a premium. If the pound's value exceeds the trigger of $1.74, Jensen will pay a premium of $.04 per unit. Notice that this premium may be higher than the premium that would be paid for a basic put option. Jensen may not mind this outcome, however, because it will be receiving a high dollar amount from converting its pound receivables in the spot market.

Jensen must determine whether the potential advantage of the conditional option (avoiding the payment of a premium under some conditions) outweighs the potential disadvantage (paying a higher premium than the premium for a traditional put option on British pounds).

The potential advantage and disadvantage are illustrated in Exhibit 5.7. At exchange rates less than or equal to the trigger level ($1.74), the conditional option results in a larger payment to Jensen by the amount of the premium that would have been paid for the basic option. Conversely, at exchange rates above the trigger level, the conditional option results in a lower payment to Jensen, as its premium of $.04 exceeds the premium of $.02 per unit paid on a basic option.

The choice of a basic option versus a conditional option is dependent on expectations of the currency's exchange rate over the period of concern. A firm that was very confident that the pound's value would not exceed $1.74 in the previous example would prefer the conditional currency option.

Conditional currency options are also available for U.S. firms that need to purchase a foreign currency in the near future.

Exhibit 5.7
Comparison of Conditional and Basic Currency Options

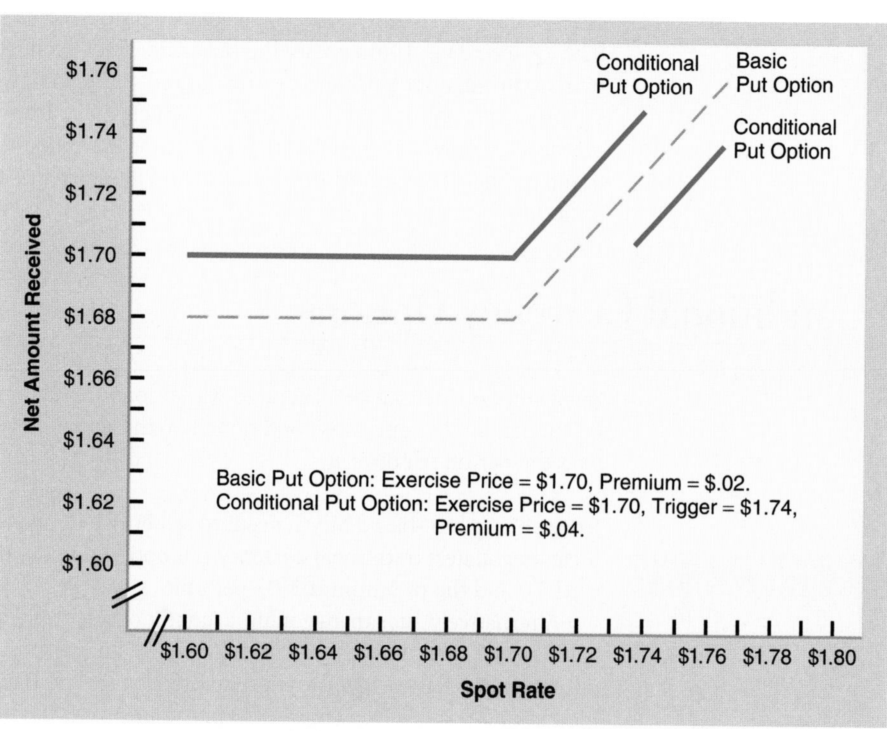

EXAMPLE

A conditional call option on pounds may specify an exercise price of $1.70 and a trigger of $1.67. If the pound's value remains above the trigger of the call option, a premium will not have to be paid for the call option. However, if the pound's value falls below the trigger, a large premium (such as $.04 per unit) will be required. Some conditional options require a premium if the trigger is reached anytime up until the expiration date; others require a premium only if the exchange rate is beyond the trigger as of the expiration date.

Firms also use various combinations of currency options. For example, a firm may purchase a currency call option to hedge payables and finance the purchase of the call option by selling a put option on the same currency.

European Currency Options

The discussion of currency options up to this point has dealt solely with American-style options. European-style currency options are also available for speculating and hedging in the foreign exchange market. They are similar to American-style options except that they must be exercised on the expiration date if they are to be exercised at all. Consequently, they do not offer as much flexibility; however, this is not relevant to some situations. For example, firms that purchase options to hedge future foreign currency cash flows will probably not desire to exercise their options before the expiration date anyway. If European-style options are available for the same expiration date as American-style options and can be purchased for a slightly lower premium, some corporations may prefer them for hedging.

SUMMARY

- A forward contract specifies a standard volume of a particular currency to be exchanged on a particular date. Such a contract can be purchased by a firm to hedge payables or sold by a firm to hedge receivables.
- A currency futures contract can be purchased by speculators who expect the currency to appreciate. Conversely, it can be sold by speculators who expect that currency to depreciate. If the currency depreciates, the value of the futures contract declines, allowing those speculators to benefit when they close out their positions.
- Futures contracts on a particular currency can be purchased by corporations that have payables in that currency and wish to hedge against the possible appreciation of that currency. Conversely, these contracts can be sold by corporations that have receivables in that currency and wish to hedge against the possible depreciation of that currency.
- Currency options are classified as call options or put options. Call options allow the right to purchase a specified currency at a specified exchange rate by a specified expiration date. Put options allow the right to sell a specified currency at a specified exchange rate by a specified expiration date.
- Call options on a specific currency can be purchased by speculators who expect that currency to appreciate. Put options on a specific currency can be purchased by speculators who expect that currency to depreciate.
- Currency call options are commonly purchased by corporations that have payables in a currency that is expected to appreciate. Currency put options are commonly purchased by corporations that have receivables in a currency that is expected to depreciate.

POINT COUNTER-POINT

Should Speculators Use Currency Futures or Options?

Point Speculators should use currency futures because they can avoid a substantial premium. To the extent that they are willing to speculate, they must have confidence in their expectations. If they have sufficient confidence in their expectations, they should bet on their expectations without having to pay a large premium to cover themselves if they are wrong. If they do not have confidence in their expectations, they should not speculate at all.

Counter-Point Speculators should use currency options to fit the degree of their confidence. For example, if they are very confident that a currency will appreciate substantially, but want to limit their investment, they can buy deep out-of-the-money options. These options have a high exercise price but a low premium, and therefore require a small investment. Alternatively, they can buy options that have a lower exercise price (higher premium), which will likely generate a greater return if the currency appreciates. Speculation involves risk. Speculators must recognize that their expectations may be wrong. While options require a premium, the premium is worthwhile to limit the potential downside risk. Options enable speculators to select the degree of downside risk that they are willing to tolerate.

Who Is Correct? Use InfoTrac or some other search engine to learn more about this issue. Which argument do you support? Offer your own opinion on this issue.

SELF TEST

Answers are provided in Appendix A at the back of the text.

1. A call option on Canadian dollars with a strike price of $.60 is purchased by a speculator for a premium of $.06 per unit. Assume there are 50,000 units in this option contract. If the Canadian dollar's spot rate is $.65 at the time the option is exercised, what is the net profit per unit to the speculator? What is the net profit for one contract? What would the spot rate need to be at the time the option is exercised for the speculator to break even? What is the net profit per unit to the seller of this option?
2. A put option on Australian dollars with a strike price of $.80 is purchased by a speculator for a premium of $.02. If the Australian dollar's spot rate is $.74 on the expiration date, should the speculator exercise the option on this date or let the option expire? What is the net profit per unit to the speculator? What is the net profit per unit to the seller of this put option?
3. Longer-term currency options are becoming more popular for hedging exchange rate risk. Why do you think some firms decide to hedge by using other techniques instead of purchasing long-term currency options?

QUESTIONS AND APPLICATIONS

1. **Forward versus Futures Contracts.** Compare and contrast forward and futures contracts.
2. **Using Currency Futures.**

   a. How can currency futures be used by corporations?

   b. How can currency futures be used by speculators?
3. **Currency Options.** Differentiate between a currency call option and a currency put option.
4. **Forward Premium.** Compute the forward discount or premium for the Mexican peso whose 90-day forward rate is $.102 and spot rate is $.10. State whether your answer is a discount or premium.

5. **Effects of a Forward Contract.** How can a forward contract backfire?

6. **Hedging with Currency Options.** When would a U.S. firm consider purchasing a call option on euros for hedging? When would a U.S. firm consider purchasing a put option on euros for hedging?

7. **Speculating with Currency Options.** When should a speculator purchase a call option on Australian dollars? When should a speculator purchase a put option on Australian dollars?

8. **Currency Call Option Premiums.** List the factors that affect currency call option premiums and briefly explain the relationship that exists for each. Do you think an at-the-money call option in euros has a higher or lower premium than an at-the-money call option in British pounds (assuming the expiration date and the total dollar value represented by each option are the same for both options)?

9. **Currency Put Option Premiums.** List the factors that affect currency put options and briefly explain the relationship that exists for each.

10. **Speculating with Currency Call Options.** Randy Rudecki purchased a call option on British pounds for $.02 per unit. The strike price was $1.45, and the spot rate at the time the option was exercised was $1.46. Assume there are 31,250 units in a British pound option. What was Randy's net profit on this option?

11. **Speculating with Currency Put Options.** Alice Duever purchased a put option on British pounds for $.04 per unit. The strike price was $1.80, and the spot rate at the time the pound option was exercised was $1.59. Assume there are 31,250 units in a British pound option. What was Alice's net profit on the option?

12. **Selling Currency Call Options.** Mike Suerth sold a call option on Canadian dollars for $.01 per unit. The strike price was $.76, and the spot rate at the time the option was exercised was $.82. Assume Mike did not obtain Canadian dollars until the option was exercised. Also assume that there are 50,000 units in a Canadian dollar option. What was Mike's net profit on the call option?

13. **Selling Currency Put Options.** Brian Tull sold a put option on Canadian dollars for $.03 per unit. The strike price was $.75, and the spot rate at the time the option was exercised was $.72. Assume Brian immediately sold off the Canadian dollars received when the option was exercised. Also assume that there are 50,000 units in a Canadian dollar option. What was Brian's net profit on the put option?

14. **Forward versus Currency Option Contracts.** What are the advantages and disadvantages to a U.S. corporation that uses currency options on euros rather than a forward contract on euros to hedge its exposure in euros? Explain why an MNC may use forward contracts to hedge committed transactions and use currency options to hedge contracts that are anticipated but not committed. Why might forward contracts be advantageous for committed transactions, and currency options be advantageous for anticipated transactions?

15. **Speculating with Currency Futures.** Assume that the euro's spot rate has moved in cycles over time. How might you try to use futures contracts on euros to capitalize on this tendency? How could you determine whether such a strategy would have been profitable in previous periods?

16. **Hedging with Currency Derivatives.** Assume that the transactions listed in the first column of the following table are anticipated by U.S. firms that have no other foreign transactions. Place an "X" in the table wherever you see possible ways to hedge each of the transactions.

17. **Price Movements of Currency Futures.** Assume that on November 1, the spot rate of the British pound was $1.58 and the price on a December futures contract was $1.59. Assume that the pound depreciated during November so that by November 30 it was worth $1.51.

    a. What do you think happened to the futures price over the month of November? Why?

    b. If you had known that this would occur, would you have purchased or sold a December futures contract in pounds on November 1? Explain.

18. **Speculating with Currency Futures.** Assume that a March futures contract on Mexican pesos was available in January for $.09 per unit. Also assume that forward contracts were available for the same settlement date at a price of $.092 per peso. How could speculators capitalize on this situation, as-

	Forward Contract		Futures Contract		Options Contract	
	Forward Purchase	Forward Sale	Buy Futures	Sell Futures	Purchase a Call	Purchase a Put
a. Georgetown Co. plans to purchase Japanese goods denominated in yen.						
b. Harvard, Inc., will sell goods to Japan, denominated in yen.						
c. Yale Corp. has a subsidiary in Australia that will be remitting funds to the U.S. parent.						
d. Brown, Inc., needs to pay off existing loans that are denominated in Canadian dollars.						
e. Princeton Co. may purchase a company in Japan in the near future (but the deal may not go through).						

suming zero transaction costs? How would such speculative activity affect the difference between the forward contract price and the futures price?

19. **Speculating with Currency Call Options.** LSU Corp. purchased Canadian dollar call options for speculative purposes. If these options are exercised, LSU will immediately sell the Canadian dollars in the spot market. Each option was purchased for a premium of $.03 per unit, with an exercise price of $.75. LSU plans to wait until the expiration date before deciding whether to exercise the options. Of course, LSU will exercise the options at that time only if it is feasible to do so. In the following table, fill in the net profit (or loss) per unit to LSU Corp. based on the listed possible spot rates of the Canadian dollar on the expiration date.

Possible Spot Rate of Canadian Dollar on Expiration Date	Net Profit (Loss) per Unit to LSU Corp.
$.76	
.78	
.80	
.82	
.85	
.87	

20. **Speculating with Currency Put Options.** Auburn Co. has purchased Canadian dollar put options for speculative purposes. Each option was purchased for a premium of $.02 per unit, with an exercise price of $.86 per unit. Auburn Co. will purchase the Canadian dollars just before it exercises the options (if it is feasible to exercise the options). It plans to wait until the expiration date before deciding whether to exercise the options. In the following table, fill in the net profit (or loss) per unit to Auburn Co. based on the listed possible spot rates of the Canadian dollar on the expiration date.

Possible Spot Rate of Canadian Dollar on Expiration Date	Net Profit (Loss) per Unit to Auburn Co.
$.76	
.79	
.84	
.87	
.89	
.91	

21. **Speculating with Currency Call Options.** Bama Corp. has sold British pound call options for speculative purposes. The option premium was $.06 per unit,

and the exercise price was $1.58. Bama will purchase the pounds on the day the options are exercised (if the options are exercised) in order to fulfill its obligation. In the following table, fill in the net profit (or loss) to Bama Corp. if the listed spot rate exists at the time the purchaser of the call options considers exercising them.

Possible Spot Rate at the Time Purchaser of Call Options Considers Exercising Them	Net Profit (Loss) per Unit to Bama Corp.
$1.53	
1.55	
1.57	
1.60	
1.62	
1.64	
1.68	

22. **Speculating with Currency Put Options.** Bulldog, Inc., has sold Australian dollar put options at a premium of $.01 per unit, and an exercise price of $.76 per unit. It has forecasted the Australian dollar's lowest level over the period of concern as shown in the following table. Determine the net profit (or loss) per unit to Bulldog, Inc., if each level occurs and the put options are exercised at that time.

Possible Value of Australian Dollar	Net Profit (Loss) to Bulldog, Inc. If Value Occurs
$.72	
.73	
.74	
.75	
.76	

23. **Hedging with Currency Derivatives.** A U.S. professional football team plans to play an exhibition game in the United Kingdom next year. Assume that all expenses will be paid by the British government, and that the team will receive a check for 1 million pounds. The team anticipates that the pound will depreciate substantially by the scheduled date of the game. In addition, the National Football League must approve the deal, and approval (or disapproval) will not occur for three months. How can the team hedge its position? What is there to lose by waiting three months to see if the exhibition game is approved before hedging?

ADVANCED QUESTIONS

24. **Risk of Currency Futures.** Currency futures markets are commonly used as a means of capitalizing on shifts in currency values, because the value of a futures contract tends to move in line with the change in the corresponding currency value. Recently, many currencies appreciated against the dollar. Most speculators anticipated that these currencies would continue to strengthen and took large buy positions in currency futures. However, the Fed intervened in the foreign exchange market by immediately selling foreign currencies in exchange for dollars, causing an abrupt decline in the values of foreign currencies (as the dollar strengthened). Participants that had purchased currency futures contracts incurred large losses. One floor broker responded to the effects of the Fed's intervention by immediately selling 300 futures contracts on British pounds (with a value of about $30 million). Such actions caused even more panic in the futures market.

    a. Explain why the central bank's intervention caused such panic among currency futures traders with buy positions.

    b. Explain why the floor broker's willingness to sell 300 pound futures contracts at the going market rate aroused such concern. What might this action signal to other brokers?

    c. Explain why speculators with short (sell) positions could benefit as a result of the central bank's intervention.

    d. Some traders with buy positions may have responded immediately to the central bank's intervention by selling futures contracts. Why would some speculators with buy positions leave their positions unchanged or even increase their positions by purchasing more futures contracts in response to the central bank's intervention?

25. **Currency Straddles.** Reska, Inc., has constructed a long euro straddle. A call option on euros with an exercise price of $1.10 has a premium of $.025 per unit. A euro put option has a premium of $.017 per unit. Some possible euro values at option expiration are shown in the following table. (See Appendix B in this chapter.)

	Value of Euro at Option Expiration			
	$.90	$1.05	$1.50	$2.00
Call				
Put				
Net				

a. Complete the worksheet and determine the net profit per unit to Reska, Inc., for each possible future spot rate.

b. Determine the break-even point(s) of the long straddle. What are the break-even points of a short straddle using these options?

26. **Currency Straddles.** Refer to the previous question, but assume that the call and put option premiums are $.02 per unit and $.015 per unit, respectively. (See Appendix B in this chapter.)

a. Construct a contingency graph for a long euro straddle.

b. Construct a contingency graph for a short euro straddle.

27. **Currency Option Contingency Graphs.** (See Appendix B in this chapter.) The current spot rate of the Singapore dollar (S$) is $.50. The following option information is available:

- Call option premium on Singapore dollar (S$) = $.015
- Put option premium on Singapore dollar (S$) = $.009
- Call and put option strike price = $.55
- One option contract represents S$70,000.

Construct a contingency graph for a short straddle using these options.

28. **Speculating with Currency Straddles.** Maggie Hawthorne is a currency speculator. She has noticed that recently the euro has appreciated substantially against the U.S. dollar. The current exchange rate of the euro is $1.15. After reading a variety of articles on the subject, she believes that the euro will continue to fluctuate substantially in the months to come. Although most forecasters believe that the euro will depreciate against the dollar in the near future, Maggie thinks that there is also a good possibility of further appreciation. Currently, a call option on euros is available with an exercise price of $1.17 and a premium of $.04. A euro put option with an exercise price of $1.17 and a premium of $.03 is also available. (See Appendix B in this chapter.)

a. Describe how Maggie could use straddles to speculate on the euro's value.

b. At option expiration, the value of the euro is $1.30. What is Maggie's total profit or loss from a long straddle position?

c. What is Maggie's total profit or loss from a long straddle position if the value of the euro is $1.05 at option expiration?

d. What is Maggie's total profit or loss from a long straddle position if the value of the euro at option expiration is still $1.15?

e. Given your answers to the questions above, when is it advantageous for a speculator to engage in a long straddle? When is it advantageous to engage in a short straddle?

29. **Currency Strangles.** (See Appendix B in this chapter.) Assume the following options are currently available for British pounds (£):

- Call option premium on British pounds = $.04 per unit
- Put option premium on British pounds = $.03 per unit
- Call option strike price = $1.56
- Put option strike price = $1.53
- One option contract represents £31,250.

a. Construct a worksheet for a long strangle using these options.

b. Determine the break-even point(s) for a strangle.

c. If the spot price of the pound at option expiration is $1.55, what is the total profit or loss to the strangle buyer?

d. If the spot price of the pound at option expiration is $1.50, what is the total profit or loss to the strangle writer?

30. **Currency Straddles.** Refer to the previous question, but assume that the call and put option premiums are $.035 per unit and $.025 per unit, respectively. (See Appendix B in this chapter.)

    a. Construct a contingency graph for a long pound straddle.

    b. Construct a contingency graph for a short pound straddle.

31. **Currency Strangles.** The following information is currently available for Canadian dollar (C$) options (see Appendix B in this chapter):

    - Put option exercise price = $.75
    - Put option premium = $.014 per unit
    - Call option exercise price = $.76
    - Call option premium = $.01 per unit
    - One option contract represents C$50,000.

    a. What is the maximum possible gain the purchaser of a strangle can achieve using these options?

    b. What is the maximum possible loss the writer of a strangle can incur?

    c. Locate the break-even point(s) of the strangle.

32. **Currency Strangles.** For the following options available on Australian dollars (A$), construct a worksheet and contingency graph for a long strangle. Locate the break-even points for this strangle. (See Appendix B in this chapter.)

    - Put option strike price = $.67
    - Call option strike price = $.65
    - Put option premium = $.01 per unit
    - Call option premium = $.02 per unit.

33. **Speculating with Currency Options.** Barry Egan is a currency speculator. Barry believes that the Japanese yen will fluctuate widely against the U.S. dollar in the coming month. Currently, one-month call options on Japanese yen (¥) are available with a strike price of $.0085 and a premium of $.0007 per unit. One-month put options on Japanese yen are available with a strike price of $.0084 and a premium of $.0005 per unit. One option contract on Japanese yen contains ¥6.25 million. (See Appendix B in this chapter.)

    a. Describe how Barry Egan could utilize these options to speculate on the movement of the Japanese yen.

    b. Assume Barry decides to construct a long strangle in yen. What are the break-even points of this strangle?

    c. What is Barry's total profit or loss if the value of the yen in one month is $.0070?

    d. What is Barry's total profit or loss if the value of the yen in one month is $.0090?

34. **Currency Bull spreads and Bear spreads.** A call option on British pounds (£) exists with a strike price of $1.56 and a premium of $.08 per unit. Another call option on British pounds has a strike price of $1.59 and a premium of $.06 per unit. (See Appendix B in this chapter.)

    a. Complete the worksheet for a bull spread below.

	Value of British Pound at Option Expiration			
	$1.50	**$1.56**	**$1.59**	**$1.65**
Call @ $1.56				
Call @ $1.59				
Net				

    b. What is the break-even point for this bull spread?

    c. What is the maximum profit of this bull spread? What is the maximum loss?

    d. If the British pound spot rate is $1.58 at option expiration, what is the total profit or loss for the bull spread?

    e. If the British pound spot rate is $1.55 at option expiration, what is the total profit or loss for a bear spread?

35. **Bull spreads and Bear spreads.** Two British pound (£) put options are available with exercise prices of $1.60 and $1.62. The premiums associated with these options are $.03 and $.04 per unit, respectively. (See Appendix B in this chapter.)

    a. Describe how a bull spread can be constructed using these put options. What is the difference between using put options versus call options to construct a bull spread?

    b. Complete the following worksheet.

Value of British Pound at Option Expiration				
	$1.55	$1.60	$1.62	$1.67
Put @ $1.60				
Put @ $1.62				
Net				

c. At option expiration, the spot rate of the pound is $1.60. What is the bull spreader's total gain or loss?

d. At option expiration, the spot rate of the pound is $1.58. What is the bear spreader's total gain or loss?

36. **Profits from Using Currency Options and Futures.** On July 2, the two-month futures rate of the Mexican peso contained a 2 percent discount (unannualized). There was a call option on pesos with an exercise price that was equal to the spot rate. There was also a put option on pesos with an exercise price equal to the spot rate. The premium on each of these options was 3 percent of the spot rate at that time. On September 2, the option expired. Go to **http://www.oanda.com** (or any website that has foreign exchange rate quotations) and determine the direct quote of the Mexican peso. You exercised the option on this date if it was feasible to do so.

a. What was your net profit per unit if you had purchased the call option?

b. What was your net profit per unit if you had purchased the put option?

c. What was your net profit per unit if you had purchased a futures contract on July 2 that had a settlement date of September 2?

d. What was your net profit per unit if you sold a futures contract on July 2 that had a settlement date of September 2?

INTERNET APPLICATION

37. **Currency Futures Online.** The website of the Chicago Mercantile Exchange provides information about currency futures and options. Its address is **http://www.cme.com**.

a. Use this website to review the prevailing prices of currency futures contracts. Do today's futures prices (for contracts with the closest settlement date) generally reflect an increase or decrease from the day before? Is there any news today that might explain the change in the futures prices?

b. Does it appear that futures prices among currencies (for the closest settlement date) are changing in the same direction? Explain.

c. If you purchase a British pound futures contract with the closest settlement date, what is the futures price? Given that a contract is based on 62,500 pounds, what is the dollar amount you will need at the settlement date to fulfill the contract?

DISCUSSION IN THE BOARDROOM

This exercise can be found in Appendix E at the back of this textbook.

RUNNING YOUR OWN MNC

This exercise can be found on the Xtra! website at **http://maduraxtra.swlearning.com**.

BLADES, INC. CASE

Use of Currency Derivative Instruments

Blades, Inc., needs to order supplies two months ahead of the delivery date. It is considering an order from a Japanese supplier that requires a payment of 12.5 million yen payable as of the delivery date. Blades has two choices:

- Purchase two call options contracts (since each option contract represents 6,250,000 yen).
- Purchase one futures contract (which represents 12.5 million yen).

The futures price on yen has historically exhibited a slight discount from the existing spot rate. However, the firm would like to use currency options to hedge payables in Japanese yen for transactions two months in advance. Blades would prefer hedging its yen payable position because it is uncomfortable leaving the position open given the historical volatility of the yen. Nevertheless, the firm would be willing to remain unhedged if the yen becomes more stable someday.

Ben Holt, Blades' chief financial officer (CFO), prefers the flexibility that options offer over forward contracts or futures contracts because he can let the options expire if the yen depreciates. He would like to use an exercise price that is about 5 percent above the existing spot rate to ensure that Blades will have to pay no more than 5 percent above the existing spot rate for a transaction two months beyond its order date, as long as the option premium is no more than 1.6 percent of the price it would have to pay per unit when exercising the option.

In general, options on the yen have required a premium of about 1.5 percent of the total transaction amount that would be paid if the option is exercised. For example, recently the yen spot rate was $0.0072, and the firm purchased a call option with an exercise price of $0.00756, which is 5 percent above the existing spot rate. The premium for this option was $0.0001134, which is 1.5 percent of the price to be paid per yen if the option is exercised.

A recent event caused more uncertainty about the yen's future value, although it did not affect the spot rate or the forward or futures rate of the yen. Specifically, the yen's spot rate was still $0.0072, but the option premium for a call option with an exercise price of $0.00756 was now $0.0001512. An alternative call option is available with an expiration date of two months from now; it has a premium of $0.0001134 (which is the size of the premium that would have existed for the option desired before the event), but it is for a call option with an exercise price of $.00792.

The table below summarizes the option and futures information available to Blades:

	Before Event	After Event	
Spot rate	**$.0072**	**$.0072**	**$.0072**
Option Information:			
Exercise price ($)	**$.00756**	**$.00756**	**$.00792**
Exercise price (% above spot)	**5%**	**5%**	**10%**
Option premium per yen ($)	**$.0001134**	**$.0001512**	**$.0001134**
Option premium (% of exercise price)	**1.5%**	**2.0%**	**1.5%**
Total premium ($)	**$1,417.50**	**$1,890.00**	**$1,417.50**
Amount paid for yen if option is exercised (not including premium)	**$94,500**	**$94,500**	**$99,000**
Futures Contract Information:			
Futures price	**$.006912**	**$.006912**	

As an analyst for Blades, you have been asked to offer insight on how to hedge. Use a spreadsheet to support your analysis of questions 4 and 6.

1. If Blades uses call options to hedge its yen payables, should it use the call option with the exercise price of $0.00756 or the call option with the exercise price of $0.00792? Describe the tradeoff.

2. Should Blades allow its yen position to be unhedged? Describe the tradeoff.

3. Assume there are speculators who attempt to capitalize on their expectation of the yen's movement over the two months between the order and delivery dates by either buying or selling yen futures now and buying or selling yen at the future spot rate. Given this information, what is the *expectation* on the order date of the yen spot rate by the delivery date? (Your answer should consist of one number.)

4. Assume that the firm shares the market consensus of the future yen spot rate. Given this expectation and given that the firm makes a decision (i.e., option, futures contract, remain unhedged) purely on a cost basis, what would be its optimal choice?

5. Will the choice you made as to the optimal hedging strategy in question 4 definitely turn out to be the lowest-cost alternative in terms of actual costs incurred? Why or why not?

6. Now assume that you have determined that the historical standard deviation of the yen is about $0.0005. Based on your assessment, you believe it is highly unlikely that the future spot rate will be more than two standard deviations above the expected spot rate by the delivery date. Also assume that the futures price remains at its current level of $0.006912. Based on this expectation of the future spot rate, what is the optimal hedge for the firm?

SMALL BUSINESS DILEMMA

Use of Currency Futures and Options by the Sports Exports Company

The Sports Exports Company receives pounds each month as payment for the footballs that it exports. It anticipates that the pound will depreciate over time against the dollar.

1. How can the Sports Exports Company use currency futures contracts to hedge against exchange rate risk? Are there any limitations of using currency futures contracts that would prevent the Sports Exports Company from locking in a specific exchange rate at which it can sell all the pounds it expects to receive in each of the upcoming months?
2. How can the Sports Exports Company use currency options to hedge against exchange rate risk? Are there any limitations of using currency options contracts that would prevent the Sports Exports Company from locking in a specific exchange rate at which it can sell all the pounds it expects to receive in each of the upcoming months?
3. Jim Logan, owner of the Sports Exports Company, is concerned that the pound may depreciate substantially over the next month, but he also believes that the pound could appreciate substantially if specific situations occur. Should Jim use currency futures or currency options to hedge the exchange rate risk? Is there any disadvantage of selecting this method for hedging?

APPENDIX 5A

Currency Option Pricing

The premiums paid for currency options depend on various factors that must be monitored when anticipating future movements in currency option premiums. Since participants in the currency options market typically take positions based on their expectations of how the premiums will change over time, they can benefit from understanding how options are priced.

Boundary Conditions

The first step in pricing currency options is to recognize boundary conditions that force the option premium to be within lower and upper bounds.

Lower Bounds

The call option premium (C) has a lower bound of at least zero or the spread between the underlying spot exchange rate (S) and the exercise price (X), whichever is greater, as shown below:

$$C = \text{MAX}(0, S - X)$$

This floor is enforced by arbitrage restrictions. For example, assume that the premium on a British pound call option is \$.01, while the spot rate of the pound is \$1.62 and the exercise price is \$1.60. In this example, the spread ($S - X$) exceeds the call premium, which would allow for arbitrage. One could purchase the call option for \$.01 per unit, immediately exercise the option at \$1.60 per pound, and then sell the pounds in the spot market for \$1.62 per unit. This would generate an immediate profit of \$.01 per unit. Arbitrage would continue until the market forces realigned the spread ($S - X$) to be less than or equal to the call premium.

The put option premium (P) has a lower bound of zero or the spread between the exercise price (X) and the underlying spot exchange rate (S), whichever is greater, as shown below:

$$P = \text{MAX}(0, X - S)$$

This floor is also enforced by arbitrage restrictions. For example, assume that the premium on a British pound put option is \$.02, while the spot rate of the pound is \$1.60 and the exercise price is \$1.63. One could purchase the pound put option for \$.02 per unit, purchase pounds in the spot market at \$1.60, and immediately exercise the option by selling the pounds at \$1.63 per unit. This would generate an immediate profit of \$.01 per unit. Arbitrage would continue until the market forces realigned the spread $(X - S)$ to be less than or equal to the put premium.

Upper Bounds

The upper bound for a call option premium is equal to the spot exchange rate (S):

$$C = S$$

If the call option premium ever exceeds the spot exchange rate, one could engage in arbitrage by selling call options for a higher price per unit than the cost of purchasing the underlying currency. Even if those call options are exercised, one could provide the currency that was purchased earlier (the call option was covered). The arbitrage profit in this example is the difference between the amount received when selling the premium and the cost of purchasing the currency in the spot market. Arbitrage would occur until the call option's premium was less than or equal to the spot rate.

The upper bound for a put option is equal to the option's exercise price (X):

$$P = X$$

If the put option premium ever exceeds the exercise price, one could engage in arbitrage by selling put options. Even if the put options are exercised, the proceeds received from selling the put options exceed the price paid (which is the exercise price) at the time of exercise.

Given these boundaries that are enforced by arbitrage, option premiums lie within these boundaries.

Application of Pricing Models

Although boundary conditions can be used to determine the possible range for a currency option's premium, they do not precisely indicate the appropriate premium for the option. However, pricing models have been developed to price currency options. Based on information about an option (such as the exercise price and time to maturity) and about the currency (such as its spot rate, standard deviation, and interest rate), pricing models can derive the premium on a currency option. The currency option pricing model of Biger and Hull[1] is shown below:

$$C = e^{-r^*T}S \cdot N(d_1) - e^{-rT}X \cdot N(d_1 - \sigma\sqrt{T})$$

[1]Nahum Biger and John Hull, "The Valuation of Currency Options," *Financial Management* (Spring 1983), 24–28.

where

$d_1 = \{[\ln(S/X) + (r - r^* + (\sigma^2/2))T]/\sigma\sqrt{T}\}$
C = price of the currency call option
S = underlying spot exchange rate
X = exercise price
r = U.S. riskless rate of interest
r^* = foreign riskless rate of interest
σ = instantaneous standard deviation of the return on a holding of foreign currency
T = option's time maturity expressed as a fraction of a year
$N(\cdot)$ = standard normal cumulative distribution function

This equation is based on the stock option pricing model (OPM) when allowing for continuous dividends. Since the interest gained on holding a foreign security (r^*) is equivalent to a continuously paid dividend on a stock share, this version of the OPM holds completely. The key transformation in adapting the stock OPM to value currency options is the substitution of exchange rates for stock prices. Thus, the percentage change of exchange rates is assumed to follow a diffusion process with constant mean and variance.

Bodurtha and Courtadon[2] have tested the predictive ability of the currency option of the pricing model. They computed pricing errors from the model using 3,326 call options. The model's average percentage pricing error for call options was −6.90 percent, which is smaller than the corresponding error reported for the dividend-adjusted Black-Scholes stock OPM. Hence, the currency option pricing model has been more accurate than the counterpart stock OPM.

The model developed by Biger and Hull is sometimes referred to as the European model because it does not account for early exercise. European currency options do not allow for early exercise (before the expiration date), while American currency options do allow for early exercise. The extra flexibility of American currency options may justify a higher premium on American currency options than on European currency options with similar characteristics. However, there is not a closed-form model for pricing American currency options. Although various techniques are used to price American currency options, the European model is commonly applied to price American currency options because the European model can be just as accurate.

Bodurtha and Courtadon found that the application of an American currency options pricing model does not improve predictive accuracy. Their average percentage pricing error was −7.07 percent for all sample call options when using the American model.

Given all other parameters, the currency option pricing model can be used to impute the standard deviation σ. This implied parameter represents the option's market assessment of currency volatility over the life of the option.

[2] James Bodurtha and Georges Courtadon, "Tests of an American Option Pricing Model on the Foreign Currency Options Market," *Journal of Financial Quantitative Analysis* (June 1987): 153–168.

Pricing Currency Put Options According to Put-Call Parity

Given the premium of a European call option (called *C*), the premium for a European put option (called *P*) on the same currency and same exercise price (*X*) can be derived from put-call parity, as shown below:

$$P = C + Xe^{-rT} - Se^{-r^{*}T}$$

where

r = U.S. riskless rate of interest

r^{*} = foreign riskless rate of interest

T = option's time to maturity expressed as a fraction of the year

If the actual put option premium is less than what is suggested by the put-call parity equation above, arbitrage can be conducted. Specifically, one could (1) buy the put option, (2) sell the call option, and (3) buy the underlying currency. The purchases are financed with the proceeds from selling the call option and from borrowing at the rate r. Meanwhile, the foreign currency that was purchased can be deposited to earn the foreign rate r^{*}. Regardless of the scenario for the path of the currency's exchange rate movement over the life of the option, the arbitrage will result in a profit. First, if the exchange rate is equal to the exercise price such that each option expires worthless, the foreign currency can be converted in the spot market to dollars, and this amount will exceed the amount required to repay the loan. Second, if the foreign currency appreciates and therefore exceeds the exercise price, there will be a loss from the call option being exercised. Although the put option will expire, the foreign currency will be converted in the spot market to dollars, and this amount will exceed the amount required to repay the loan and the amount of the loss on the call option. Third, if the foreign currency depreciates and therefore is below the exercise price, the amount received from exercising the put option plus the amount received from converting the foreign currency to dollars will exceed the amount required to repay the loan. Since the arbitrage generates a profit under any exchange rate scenario, it will force an adjustment in the option premiums so that put-call parity is no longer violated.

If the actual put option premium is more than what is suggested by put-call parity, arbitrage would again be possible. The arbitrage strategy would be the reverse of that used when the actual put option premium was less than what is suggested by put-call parity (as just described). The arbitrage would force an adjustment in option premiums so that put-call parity is no longer violated. The arbitrage that can be applied when there is a violation of put-call parity on American currency options differs slightly from the arbitrage applicable to European currency options. Nevertheless, the concept still holds that the premium of a currency put option can be determined according to the premium of a call option on the same currency and the same exercise price.

APPENDIX 5B

Currency Option Combinations

In addition to the basic call and put options just discussed, a variety of currency option combinations are available to the currency speculator and hedger. A **currency option combination** uses simultaneous call and put option positions to construct a unique position to suit the hedger's or speculator's needs. A currency option combination may include both long and short positions and will itself be either long or short. Typically, a currency option combination will result in a unique contingency graph.

Currency option combinations can be used both to hedge cash inflows and outflows denominated in a foreign currency and to speculate on the future movement of a foreign currency. More specifically, both MNCs and individual speculators can construct a currency option combination to accommodate expectations of either appreciating or depreciating foreign currencies.

In this appendix, two of the most popular currency option combinations are discussed. These are **straddles** and **strangles**. For each of these combinations, the following topics will be discussed:

- The composition of the combination
- The worksheet and contingency graph for the long combination
- The worksheet and contingency graph for the short combination
- Uses of the combination to speculate on the movement of a foreign currency

The two main types of currency option combinations are discussed next.

Currency Straddles

Long Currency Straddle

To construct a long straddle in a foreign currency, an MNC or individual would buy (take a long position in) both a call option and a put option for that currency; the call and the put option have the same expiration date and striking price.

When constructing a long straddle, the buyer purchases both the right to buy the foreign currency and the right to sell the foreign currency. Since the call option will become profitable if the foreign currency appreciates, and the put option will become profitable if the foreign currency depreciates, a long straddle becomes profitable when the foreign currency *either* appreciates or depreciates. Obviously, this is a huge advantage for the individual or entity that constructs a long straddle, since it appears that it would benefit from the position as long as the foreign currency exchange rate does not remain constant. The disadvantage of a long straddle position is that it is expensive to construct, because it involves the purchase of two separate options, each of which requires payment of the option premium. Therefore, a long straddle becomes profitable only if the foreign currency appreciates or depreciates substantially.

Long Currency Straddle Worksheet. To determine the profit or loss associated with a long straddle (or any combination), it is easiest to first construct a profit or loss worksheet for several possible currency values at option expiration. The worksheet can be set up to show each individual option position and the net position. The worksheet will also help in constructing a contingency graph for the combination.

EXAMPLE

Put and call options are available for euros (€) with the following information:

- Call option premium on euro = $.03 per unit
- Put option premium on euro = $.02 per unit
- Strike price = $1.05
- One option contract represents €62,500.

To construct a long straddle, the buyer would purchase both a euro call and a euro put option, paying $.03 + $.02 = $.05 per unit. If the value of the euro at option expiration is above the strike price of $1.05, the call option is in the money, but the put option is out of the money. Conversely, if the value of the euro at option expiration is below $1.05, the put option is in the money, but the call option is out of the money.

A possible worksheet for the long straddle that illustrates the profitability of the individual components is shown below:

	Value of Euro at Option Expiration					
	$.95	$1.00	$1.05	$1.10	$1.15	$1.20
Own a call	−$.03	−$.03	−$.03	+$.02	+$.07	+$.12
Own a put	+$.08	+$.03	−$.02	−$.02	−$.02	−$.02
Net	+$.05	$.00	−$.05	$.00	+$.05	+$.10

Long Currency Straddle Contingency Graph. A contingency graph for the long currency straddle is shown in Exhibit 5B.1. This graph includes more extreme possible outcomes than are shown in the table. Either the call or put option on the foreign currency will be in the money at option expiration as long as the foreign currency value at option expiration differs from the strike price.

There are two break-even points for a long straddle position—one below the strike price and one above the strike price. The lower break-even point is equal to the strike price less both premiums; the higher break-even point is equal to the strike price plus both premiums. Thus, for the above example, the two break-even points are located at $1.00 = $1.05 − $.05 and at $1.10 = $1.05 + $.05.

The maximum loss for the long straddle in the example occurs at a euro value at option expiration equal to the strike price, when both options are at the money. At that point, the straddle buyer would lose both option premiums. The maximum loss for the straddle buyer is thus equal to $.05 = $.03 + $.02.

Exhibit 5B.1
Contingency Graph for a Long Currency Straddle

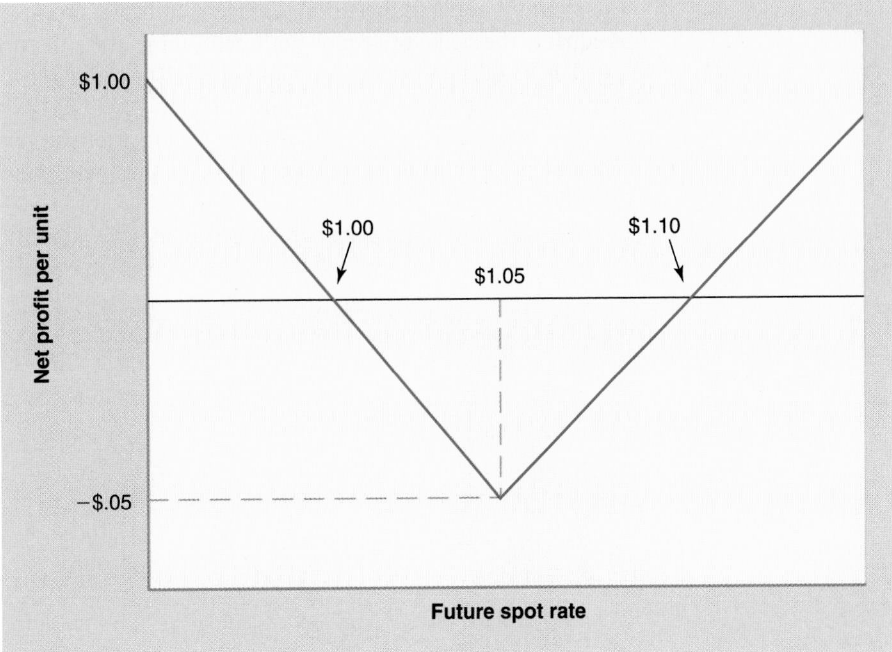

Short Currency Straddle

Constructing a short straddle in a foreign currency involves selling (taking a short position in) both a call option and a put option for that currency. As in a long straddle, the call and put option have the same expiration date and strike price.

The advantage of a short straddle is that it provides the option writer with income from two separate options. The disadvantage is the possibility of substantial losses if the underlying currency moves substantially away from the strike price.

Short Currency Straddle Worksheet and Contingency Graph. A short straddle results in a worksheet and contingency graph that are exactly opposite to those of a long straddle.

EXAMPLE

Assuming the same information as in the previous example, a short straddle would involve writing both a call option on euros and a put option on euros. A possible worksheet for the resulting short straddle is shown below:

	Value of Euro at Option Expiration					
	$.95	$1.00	$1.05	$1.10	$1.15	$1.20
Sell a call	+$.03	+$.03	+$.03	−$.02	−$.07	−$.12
Sell a put	−$.08	−$.03	+$.02	+$.02	+$.02	+$.02
Net	−$.05	$.00	+$.05	$.00	−$.05	−$.10

The worksheet also illustrates that there are two break-even points for a short straddle position—one below the strike price and one above the strike price. The lower break-even point is equal to the strike price less both premiums; the higher break-even point is equal to the strike price plus both premiums. Thus, the two break-even points are located at $1.00 = $1.05 − $.05 and at $1.10 = $1.05 + $.05. This is the same relationship as for the long straddle position.

The maximum gain occurs at a euro value at option expiration equal to the strike price of $1.05 and is equal to the sum of the two option premiums ($.03 + $.02 = $.05).

The resulting contingency graph is shown in Exhibit 5B.2.

Exhibit 5B.2

Contingency Graph for a Short Currency Straddle

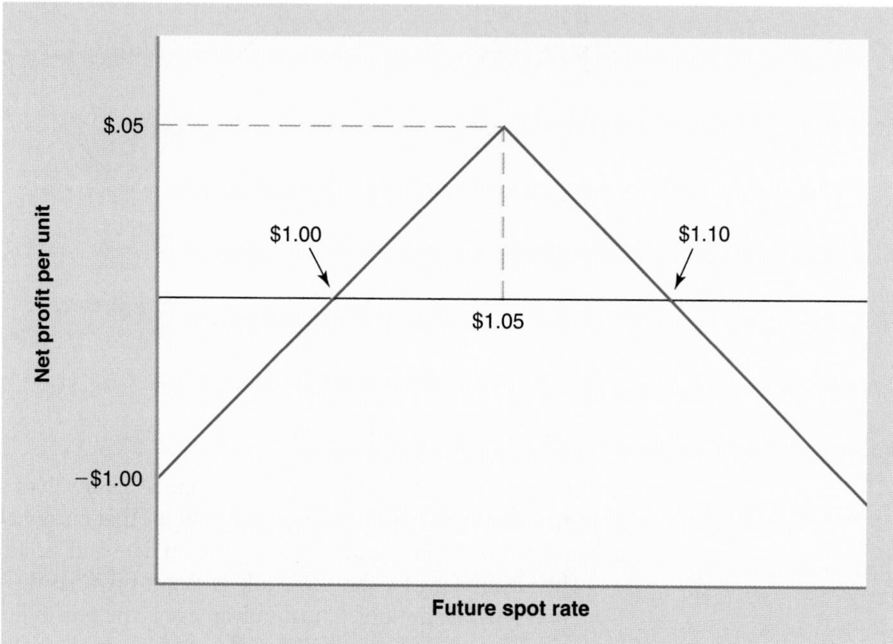

Speculating with Currency Straddles

Individuals can speculate using currency straddles based on their expectations of the future movement in a particular foreign currency. For example, speculators who expect that the British pound will appreciate or depreciate substantially can buy a straddle. If the pound appreciates substantially, the speculator will let the put option expire and exercise the call option. If the pound depreciates substantially, the speculator will let the call option expire and exercise the put option.

Speculators may also profit from short straddles. The writer of a short straddle believes that the value of the underlying currency will remain close to the exercise price until option expiration. If the value of the underlying currency is equal to the strike price at option expiration, the straddle writer would collect premiums from both options. However, this is a rather risky position; if the currency appreciates or depreciates substantially, the straddle writer will lose money. If the currency appreciates substantially, the straddle writer will have to sell the currency for the strike price, since the call option will be exercised. If the currency depreciates substantially, the straddle writer has to buy the currency for the strike price, since the put option will be exercised.

EXAMPLE

Call and put option contracts on British pounds (£) are available with the following information:

- Call option premium on British pounds = $.035
- Put option premium on British pounds = $.025
- Strike price = $1.50
- One option contract represents £31,250.

At expiration, the spot rate of the pound is $1.40. A speculator who had bought a straddle will therefore exercise the put option but let the call option expire. Therefore, the speculator will buy pounds at the prevailing spot rate and sell them for the exercise price. Given this information, the net profit to the straddle buyer is calculated as follows:

	Per Unit	Per Contract
Selling price of £	+$1.50	$46,875 ($1.50 × 31,250 units)
− Purchase price of £	−1.40	−43,750 ($1.40 × 31,250 units)
− Premium paid for call option	−.035	−1,093.75 ($.035 × 31,250 units)
− Premium paid for put option	−.025	−781.25 ($.025 × 31,250 units)
= Net profit	$.04	$1,250 ($.04 × 31,250 units)

The straddle writer will have to purchase pounds for the exercise price. Assuming the speculator immediately sells the acquired pounds at the prevailing spot rate, the net profit to the straddle writer will be:

	Per Unit	Per Contract
Selling price of £	+$1.40	$43,750 ($1.40 × 31,250 units)
− Purchase price of £	−1.50	−46,875 ($1.50 × 31,250 units)
+ Premium received for call option	+.035	1,093.75 ($.035 × 31,250 units)
+ Premium received for put option	+.025	781.25 ($.025 × 31,250 units)
= Net profit	−$.04	−$1,250 ($.04 × 31,250 units)

As with an individual short put position, the seller of the straddle could simply refrain from selling the pounds (after being forced to buy them at the exercise price of $1.50) until the spot rate of the pound rises. However, there is no guarantee that the pound will appreciate in the near future.

Note from the above example and discussion that the straddle writer gains what the straddle buyer loses, and vice versa. Consequently, the straddle writer's gain or loss is the straddle buyer's loss or gain. Thus, the same relationship that applies to individual call and put options also applies to option combinations.

Currency Strangles

Currency strangles are very similar to currency straddles, with one important difference: the call and put options of the underlying foreign currency have different exercise prices. Nevertheless, the underlying security and the expiration date for the call and put options are identical.

Long Currency Strangle

Since the call and put options used in a strangle can have different exercise prices, a long strangle can be constructed in a variety of ways. For example, a strangle could be constructed in which the call option has a higher exercise price than the put option and vice versa. The most common type of strangle, and the focus of this section, is a strangle that involves buying a put option with a lower strike price than the call option that is purchased. To construct a long strangle in a foreign currency, an MNC or individual would thus take a long position in a call option and a long position in a put option for that currency. The call option has the higher exercise price.

An advantage of a long strangle relative to a comparable long straddle is that it is cheaper to construct. From previous sections, recall that there is an inverse relationship between the spot price of the currency relative to the strike price and the call option premium: the lower the spot price relative to the strike price, the lower the option premium will be. Therefore, if a long strangle involves purchasing a call option with a relatively high exercise price, it should be cheaper to construct than a comparable straddle, everything else being equal.

The disadvantage of a strangle relative to a straddle is that the underlying currency has to fluctuate more prior to expiration. As with a long straddle, the reason for constructing a long strangle is the expectation of a substantial currency fluctuation in either direction prior to the expiration date. However, since the two options involved in a strangle have different exercise prices, the underlying currency has to fluctuate to a larger extent before the strangle is in the money at future spot prices.

Long Currency Strangle Worksheet. The worksheet for a long currency strangle is similar to the worksheet for a long currency straddle, as the following example shows.

EXAMPLE

Put and call options are available for euros (€) with the following information:

- Call option premium on euro = \$.025 per unit
- Put option premium on euro = \$.02 per unit
- Call option strike price = \$1.15
- Put option strike price = \$1.05
- One option contract represents €62,500.

Note that this example is almost identical to the earlier straddle example, except that the call option has a higher exercise price than the put option and the call option premium is slightly lower.

A possible worksheet for the long strangle is shown here:

	Value of Euro at Option Expiration					
	$.95	$1.00	$1.05	$1.10	$1.15	$1.20
Own a call	−$.025	−$.025	−$.025	−$.025	−$.025	+$.025
Own a put	+$.08	+$.03	−$.02	−$.02	−$.02	−$.02
Net	+$.055	+$.005	−$.045	−$.045	−$.045	+$.005

Long Currency Strangle Contingency Graph. Exhibit 5B.3 shows a contingency graph for the long currency strangle. Again, the graph includes more extreme values than are shown in the worksheet. The call option will be in the money when the foreign currency value is higher than its strike price at option expiration, and the put option will be in the money when the foreign currency value is below the put option strike price at option expiration. Thus, the long call position is in the money at euro values above the $1.15 call option exercise price at option expiration. Conversely, the put option is in the money at euro values below the put option exercise price of $1.05.

The two break-even points for a long strangle position are located below the put option premium and above the call option premium. The lower break-even point is equal to the put option strike price less both premiums ($1.005 = $1.05 − $.045); the higher break-even point is equal to the call option strike price plus both premiums ($1.195 = $1.15 + $.045).

The maximum loss for a long strangle occurs at euro values at option expiration between the two strike prices. At any future spot price between the two exercise prices, the straddle buyer would lose both option premiums (−$.045 = −$0.25 − $.02).

The contingency graph for the long strangle illustrates that the euro must fluctuate more widely than with a straddle before the position becomes profitable. However, the maximum loss is only $.045 per unit, whereas it was $.05 per unit for the long straddle.

Exhibit 5B.3

Contingency Graph for a Long Currency Strangle

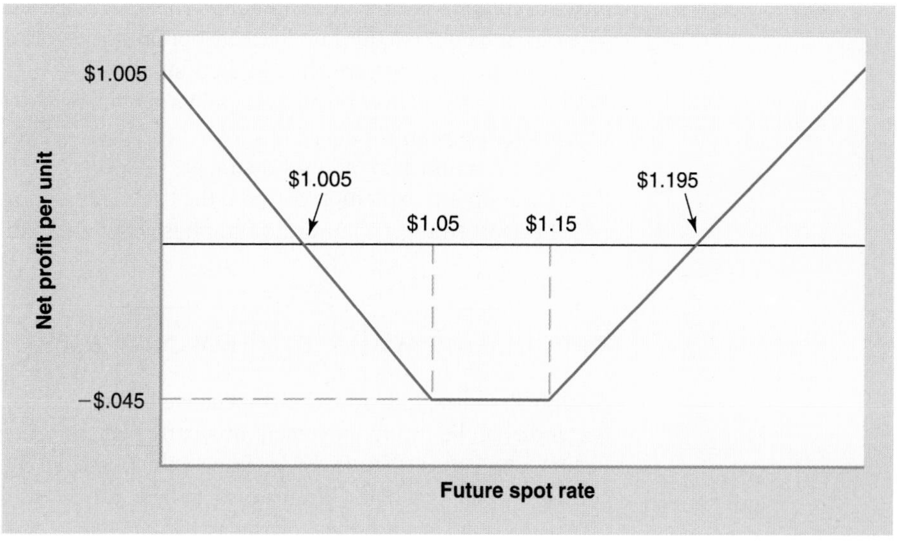

Short Currency Strangle

Analogous to a short currency straddle, a short strangle involves taking a short position in both a call option and a put option for that currency. As with a short straddle, the call and put options have the same expiration date. However, the call option has the higher exercise price in a short strangle.

Relative to a short straddle, the disadvantage of a short strangle is that it provides less income, since the call option premium will be lower, everything else being equal. However, the advantage of a short strangle relative to a short straddle is that the underlying currency has to fluctuate more before the strangle writer is in danger of losing money.

Short Currency Strangle Worksheet and Contingency Graph. The euro example is next used to show that the worksheet and contingency graph for the short strangle are exactly opposite to those of a long strangle.

EXAMPLE

Continuing with the information in the preceding example, a short strangle can be constructed by writing a call option on euros and a put option on euros. The resulting worksheet is shown below:

	Value of Euro at Option Expiration					
	$.95	$1.00	$1.05	$1.10	$1.15	$1.20
Sell a call	+$.025	+$.025	+$.025	+$.025	+$.025	−$.025
Sell a put	−$.08	−$.03	+$.02	+$.02	+$.02	+$.02
Net	−$.055	−$.005	+$.045	+$.045	+$.045	−$.005

The table shows that there are two break-even points for the short strangle. The lower break-even point is equal to the put option strike price less both premiums; the higher break-even point is equal to the call option strike price plus both premiums. The two break-even points are thus located at $1.005 = $1.05 − $.045 and at $1.195 = $1.15 + $.045. These break-even points are identical to the break-even points for the long strangle position.

The maximum gain for a short strangle ($.045 = $.025 + $.02) occurs at a value of the euro at option expiration between the two exercise prices.

The short strangle contingency graph is shown in Exhibit 5B.4.

Speculating with Currency Strangles

As with straddles, individuals can speculate using currency strangles based on their expectations of the future movement in a particular foreign currency. For instance, speculators who expect that the Swiss franc will appreciate or depreciate substantially can construct a long strangle. Speculators can benefit from short strangles if the future spot price of the underlying currency is between the two exercise prices.

Exhibit 5B.4

Contingency Graph for a Short Currency Strangle

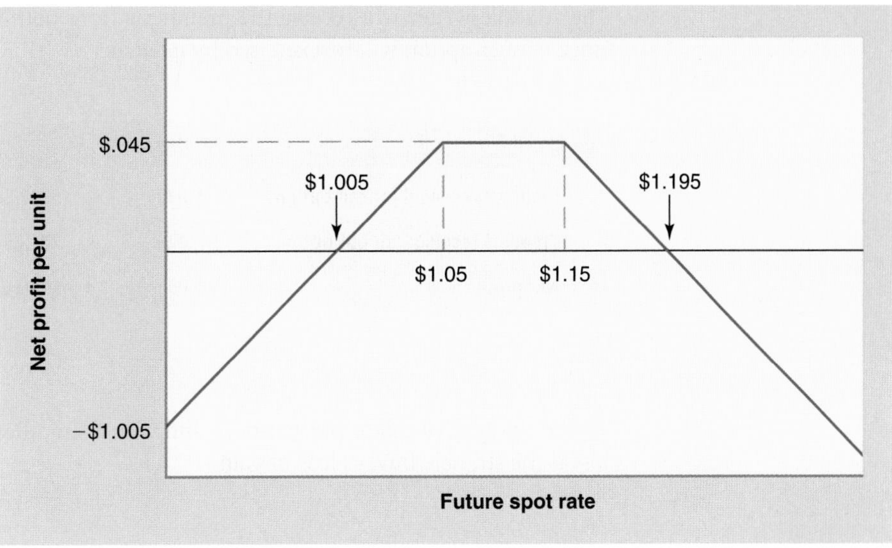

Compared to a straddle, the speculator who buys a strangle believes that the underlying currency will fluctuate even more widely prior to expiration. In return, the speculator pays less to construct the long strangle. A speculator who writes a strangle will receive both option premiums as long as the future spot price is between the two exercise prices. Compared to a straddle, the total amount received from writing the two options is less. However, the range of future spot prices between which no option is exercised is much wider for a short strangle.

EXAMPLE

Call and put option contracts on British pounds (£) are available with the following information:

- Call option premium on British pounds = $.030
- Put option premium on British pounds = $.025
- Call option strike price = $1.60
- Put option strike price = $1.50
- One option contract represents £31,250.

The spot rate of the pound on the expiration date is $1.52. With a long strangle, the speculator will let both options expire, since both the call and the put option are out of the money. Consequently, the strangle buyer will lose both option premiums:

	Per Unit	Per Contract
− Premium paid for call option	−$.030	−$937.50 ($.030 × 31,250 units)
− Premium paid for put option	−.025	−781.25 ($.025 × 31,250 units)
= Net profit	−$.055	−$1,718.75 (−$.055 × 31,250 units)

The straddle writer will receive the premiums from both the call and the put option, since neither option will be exercised by its owner:

	Per Unit	Per Contract
+ Premium received for call option	+\$.030	\$937.50 (\$.030 × 31,250 units)
+ Premium received for put option	+.025	781.25 (\$.025 × 31,250 units)
= Net profit	+\$.055	\$1,718.75 (\$.055 × 31,250 units)

As with individual call or put positions and with a straddle, the strangle writer's gain or loss is the strangle buyer's loss or gain.

Currency Spreads

A variety of currency spreads exist that can be used by both MNCs and individuals to hedge cash inflows or outflows or to profit from an anticipated movement in a foreign currency. This section covers two of the most popular types of spreads: bull spreads and bear spreads. Bull spreads are profitable when a foreign currency appreciates, whereas bear spreads are profitable when a foreign currency depreciates.

Currency Bull Spreads with Call Options

A currency bull spread is constructed by buying a call option for a particular underlying currency and simultaneously writing a call option for the same currency with a higher exercise price. A bull spread can also be constructed using currency put options, as will be discussed shortly.

With a bull spread, the spreader believes that the underlying currency will appreciate modestly, but not substantially.

EXAMPLE

Assume two call options on Australian dollars (A\$) are currently available. The first option has a strike price of \$.64 and a premium of \$.019. The second option has a strike price of \$.65 and a premium of \$.015. The bull spreader buys the \$.64 option and sells the \$.65 option. An option contract on Australian dollars consists of 50,000 units.

Consider the following scenarios:

1. The Australian dollar appreciates to \$.645, a spot price between the two exercise prices. The bull spreader will exercise the option he bought. Assuming the bull spreader immediately sells the Australian dollars for the \$.645 spot rate after purchasing them for the \$.64 exercise price, he will gain the difference. The bull spreader will also collect the premium on the second option he wrote, but that option will not be exercised by the (unknown) buyer:

	Per Unit	Per Contract
Selling price of A$	+$.645	$32,250 ($.645 × 50,000 units)
− Purchase price of A$	−.64	−32,000 ($.64 × 50,000 units)
− Premium paid for call option	−.019	−950 ($.019 × 50,000 units)
+ Premium received for call option	+.015	+750 ($.015 × 50,000 units)
= Net profit	$.001	$50 ($.001 × 50,000 units)

Under this scenario, note that the bull spreader would have incurred a net loss of $.645 − $.64 − $.019 = −$.014/A$ if he had purchased only the first option. By writing the second call option, the spreader increased his net profit by $.015/A$.

2. The Australian dollar appreciates to $.70, a value above the higher exercise price. Under this scenario, the bull spreader will exercise the option he purchased, but the option he wrote will also be exercised by the (unknown) buyer. Assuming the bull spreader immediately sells the Australian dollars purchased with the first option and buys the Australian dollars he has to sell to the second option buyer for the spot rate, he will incur the following cash flows:

	Per Unit	Per Contract
Selling price of A$	+$.70	$35,000 ($.70 × 50,000 units)
− Purchase price of A$	−.64	−32,000 ($.64 × 50,000 units)
− Premium paid for call option	−.019	−950 ($.019 × 50,000 units)
+ Selling price of A$	+$.65	+32,500 ($.65 × 50,000 units)
− Purchase price of A$	−.70	−35,000 ($.70 × 50,000 units)
+ Premium received for call option	+.015	+750 ($.015 × 50,000 units)
= Net profit	$.006	$300 ($.006 × 50,000 units)

The important point to understand here is that the net profit to the bull spreader will remain $.006/A$ no matter how much more the Australian dollar appreciates. This is because the bull spreader will always sell the Australian dollars he purchased with the first option for the spot price and purchase the Australian dollars needed to meet his obligation for the second option. The two effects always cancel out, so the bull spreader will net the difference in the two strike prices less the difference in the two premiums ($.65 − $.64 − $.019 + $.015 = $.006). Therefore, the net profit to the bull spreader will be $.006 per unit at any future spot price above $.65.

Equally important to understand is the tradeoff involved in constructing a bull spread. The bull spreader in effect forgoes the benefit from a large currency appreciation by collecting the premium from writing a currency option with a higher exercise price and ensuring a constant profit at future spot prices above the higher exercise price; if he had not written the second option with the higher exercise price, he would have benefited substantially under this scenario, netting $.70 − $.64 − $.019 = $.041/A$ as a result of exercising the call option with the $.64 strike price. This is the reason the bull spreader expects that the underlying currency will appreciate modestly so that he gains from the option he buys and collects the premium from the option he sells without incurring any opportunity costs.

3. The Australian dollar depreciates to $.62, a value below the lower exercise price. If the future spot price is below the lower exercise price, neither call option will be exercised, as they are both out of the money. Consequently, the net profit to the bull spreader is the difference between the two option premiums:

	Per Unit	Per Contract
− Premium paid for call option	−$.019	−$950 ($.019 × 50,000 units)
+ Premium received for call option	+.015	+750 ($.015 × 50,000 units)
= Net profit	−$.004	−$200 ($.004 × 50,000 units)

Similar to the scenario where the Australian dollar appreciates modestly between the two exercise prices, the bull spreader's loss in this case is reduced by the premium received from writing the call option with the higher exercise price.

Currency Bull Spread Worksheet and Contingency Graph. For the Australian dollar example above, a worksheet and contingency graph can be constructed. One possible worksheet is shown below:

	Value of Australian Dollar at Option Expiration				
	$.60	$.64	$.645	$.65	$.70
Buy a call	−$.019	−$.019	−$.014	−$.009	+$.041
Sell a call	+$.015	+$.015	+$.015	+$.015	−$.035
Net	−$.004	−$.004	+$.001	+$.006	+$.006

Exhibit 5B.5 shows the corresponding contingency graph.

Exhibit 5B.5

Contingency Graph for a Currency Bull Spread

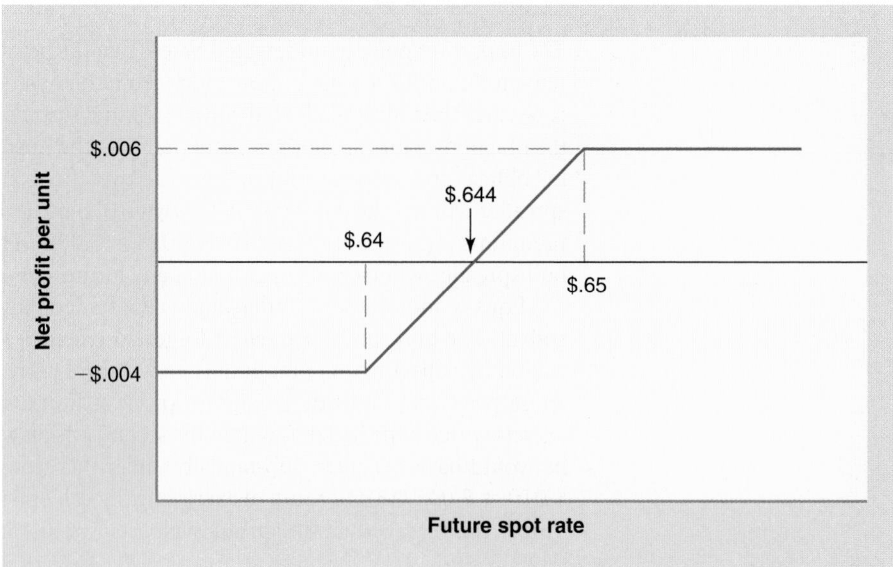

The worksheet and contingency graph show that the maximum loss for the bull spreader is limited to the difference between the two option premiums of −$.004 = −$.019 + $.015. This maximum loss occurs at future spot prices equal to the lower strike price or below.

Also note that for a bull spread the gain is limited to the difference between the strike prices less the difference in the option premiums and is equal to $.006 = $.65 − $.64 − $.004. This maximum gain occurs at future spot prices equal to the higher exercise price or above.

The break-even point for the bull spread is located at the lower exercise price plus the difference in the two option premiums and is equal to $.644 = $.64 + $.004.

Currency Bull Spreads with Put Options

As mentioned previously, currency bull spreads can be constructed just as easily with put options as with call options. To construct a put bull spread, the spreader would again buy a put option with a lower exercise price and write a put option with a higher exercise price. The basic arithmetic involved in constructing a put bull spread is thus essentially the same as for a call bull spread, with one important difference, as discussed next.

Recall that there is a positive relationship between the level of the existing spot price relative to the strike price and the call option premium. Consequently, the option with the higher exercise price that is written in a call bull spread will have the lower option premium, everything else being equal. Thus, buying the call option with the lower exercise price and writing the call option with the higher exercise price involves a cash outflow for the bull spreader. For this reason, call bull spreads fall into a broader category of spreads called debit spreads. Also recall that the lower the spot rate relative to the strike price, the higher the put option premium will be. Consequently, the option with the higher strike price that is written in a put bull spread will have the higher option premium, everything else being equal. Thus, buying the put option with the lower exercise price and writing the put option with the higher exercise price in a put bull spread results in a cash inflow for the bull spreader. For this reason, put bull spreads fall into a broader category of spreads called credit spreads.

Speculating with Currency Bull Spreads

The speculator who constructs a currency bull spread trades profit potential for a reduced cost of establishing the position. Ideally, the underlying currency will appreciate to the higher exercise price but not far above it. Although the speculator would still realize the maximum gain of the bull spread in this case, he or she would incur significant opportunity costs if the underlying currency appreciates much above the higher exercise price. Speculating with currency bull spreads is appropriate for currencies that are expected to appreciate slightly until the expiration date. Since the bull spread involves both buying and writing options for the underlying currency, bull spreads can be relatively cheap to construct and will not result in large losses if the currency depreciates. Conversely, bull spreads are useful tools to generate additional income for speculators.

Currency Bear Spreads

The easiest way to think about a currency bear spread is as a short bull spread. That is, a currency bear spread involves taking exactly the opposite positions involved in a bull spread. The bear spreader writes a call option for a particular underlying currency and simultaneously buys a call option for the same currency with a higher exercise price. Consequently, the bear spreader anticipates a modest depreciation in the foreign currency.

Currency Bear Spread Worksheet and Contingency Graph. For the Australian dollar example above, the bear spreader writes the \$.64 option and buys the \$.65 option. A worksheet and contingency graph can be constructed. One possible worksheet is shown below:

	Value of Australian Dollar at Option Expiration				
	\$.60	\$.64	\$.645	\$.65	\$.70
Sell a call	+\$.019	+\$.019	+\$.014	+\$.009	−\$.041
Buy a call	−\$.015	−\$.015	−\$.015	−\$.015	+\$.035
Net	+\$.004	+\$.004	−\$.001	−\$.006	−\$.006

The corresponding contingency graph is shown in Exhibit 5B.6.

Exhibit 5B.6

Contingency Graph for a Currency Bear Spread

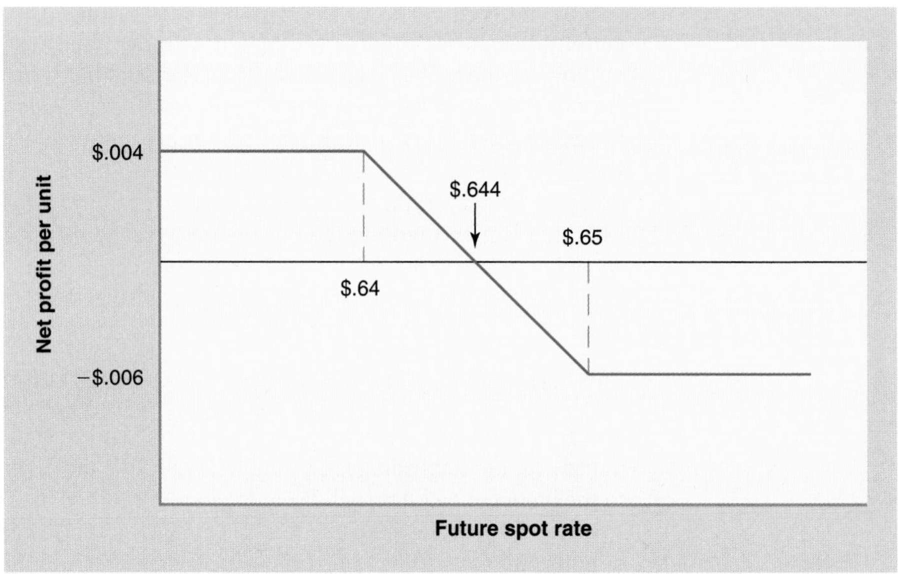

Notice that the worksheet and contingency graph for the bear spread are the mirror image of the worksheet and contingency graph for the bull spread. Consequently, the maximum gain for the bear spreader is limited to the difference between the two exercise prices of $\$.004 = \$.019 - \$.015$, and the maximum loss for a bear spread ($-\$.006 = -\$.65 + \$.64 + \$.004$) occurs when the Australian dollar's value is equal to or above the exercise price at option expiration.

Also, the break-even point is located at the lower exercise price plus the difference in the two option premiums and is equal to \$.644 = \$.64 + \$.004, which is the same break-even point as for the bull spread.

It is evident from the above illustration that the bear spreader hopes for a currency depreciation. An alternative way to profit from a depreciation would be to buy a put option for the currency. A bear spread, however, is typically cheaper to construct, since it involves buying one call option and writing another call option. The disadvantage of the bear spread compared to a long put position is that opportunity costs can be significant if the currency depreciates dramatically. Consequently, the bear spreader hopes for a modest currency depreciation.

PART 1

Integrative Problem

The International Financial Environment

Mesa Co. specializes in the production of small fancy picture frames, which are exported from the United States to the United Kingdom. Mesa invoices the exports in pounds and converts the pounds to dollars when they are received. The British demand for these frames is positively related to economic conditions in the United Kingdom. Assume that British inflation and interest rates are similar to the rates in the United States. Mesa believes that the U.S. balance of trade deficit from trade between the United States and the United Kingdom will adjust to changing prices between the two countries, while capital flows will adjust to interest rate differentials. Mesa believes that the value of the pound is very sensitive to changing international capital flows and is moderately sensitive to changing international trade flows. Mesa is considering the following information:

- The U.K. inflation rate is expected to decline, while the U.S. inflation rate is expected to rise.
- British interest rates are expected to decline, while U.S. interest rates are expected to increase.

Questions

1. Explain how the international trade flows should initially adjust in response to the changes in inflation (holding exchange rates constant). Explain how the international capital flows should adjust in response to the changes in interest rates (holding exchange rates constant).
2. Using the information provided, will Mesa expect the pound to appreciate or depreciate in the future? Explain.
3. Mesa believes international capital flows shift in response to changing interest rate differentials. Is there any reason why the changing interest rate differentials in this example will not necessarily cause international capital flows to change significantly? Explain.
4. Based on your answer to question 2, how would Mesa's cash flows be affected by the expected exchange rate movements? Explain.
5. Based on your answer to question 4, should Mesa consider hedging its exchange rate risk? If so, explain how it could hedge using forward contracts, futures contracts, and currency options.

PART 2

Exchange Rate Behavior

Part 2 (Chapters 6 through 8) focuses on critical relationships pertaining to exchange rates. Chapter 6 explains how governments can influence exchange rate movements and how such movements can affect economic conditions. Chapter 7 explores the relationships among foreign currencies. It also explains how the forward exchange rate is influenced by the differential between interest rates of any two countries. Chapter 8 discusses prominent theories regarding the impact of inflation on exchange rates and the impact of interest rate movements on exchange rates.

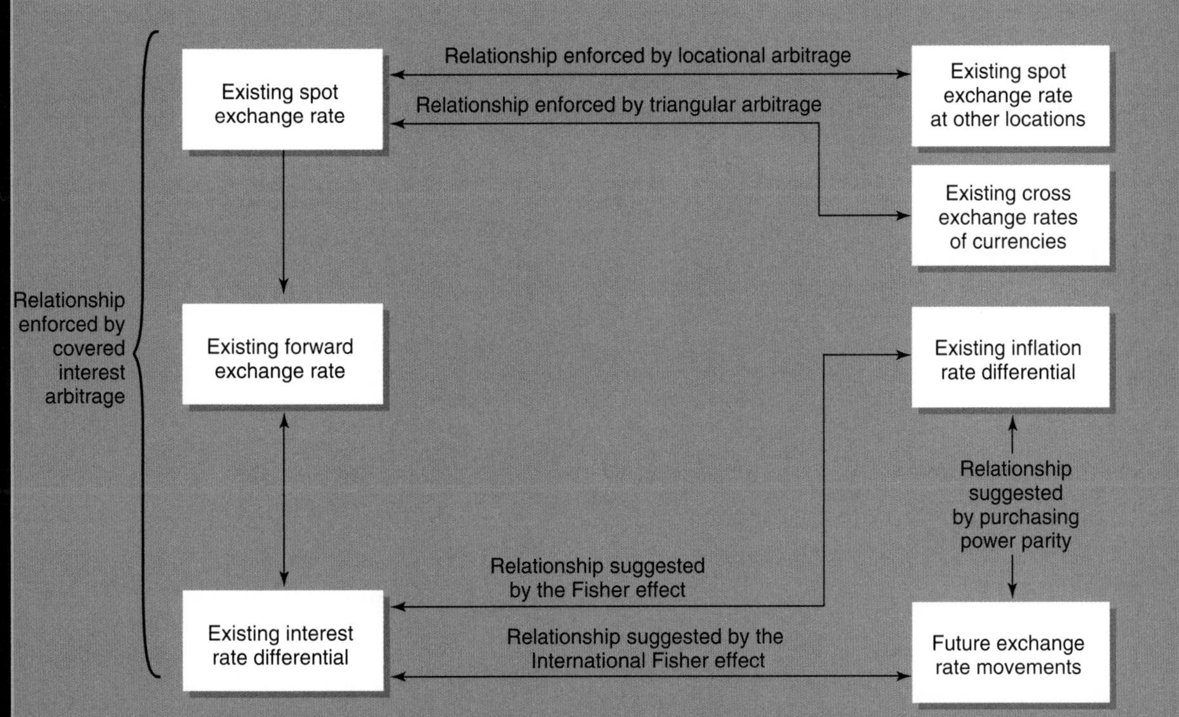

CHAPTER 6

Government Influence on Exchange Rates

Government policies affect exchange rates, which can influence a country's economy and financial markets. Because the performance of an MNC is affected by both the economy and exchange rates, financial managers need to understand how the government affects exchange rates.

The specific objectives of this chapter are to:

- describe the exchange rate systems used by various governments,
- explain how governments can use direct intervention to influence exchange rates,
- explain how governments can use indirect intervention to influence exchange rates, and
- explain how government intervention in the foreign exchange market can affect economic conditions.

Exchange Rate Systems

Exchange rate systems can be classified according to the degree by which exchange rates are controlled by the government. Exchange rate systems normally fall into one of the following categories:

- Fixed
- Freely floating
- Managed float
- Pegged

Each of these exchange rate systems is discussed in turn.

Fixed Exchange Rate System

In a **fixed exchange rate system**, exchange rates are either held constant or allowed to fluctuate only within very narrow boundaries. If an exchange rate begins to move too much, governments intervene to maintain it within the boundaries. In some situations, a government will **devalue** or reduce the value of its currency against other currencies. In other situations, it will **revalue** or increase the value of its currency against other currencies. A central bank's actions to devalue a currency in a fixed exchange rate system is referred to as **devaluation**. The term *devaluation* is normally used in a different context than depreciation. Devaluation refers to a downward adjustment of the exchange rate by the central bank. **Revaluation** refers to an upward adjustment of the exchange rate by the central bank. The methods used by governments to alter the value of a currency are discussed later in this chapter.

Bretton Woods Agreement. From 1944 to 1971, exchange rates were typically fixed according to a system planned at the Bretton Woods conference (held in Bretton Woods, New Hampshire, in 1944) by representatives from various countries. Because this arrangement, known as the **Bretton Woods Agreement**, lasted from 1944 to 1971, that period is sometimes referred to as the Bretton Woods era. Each currency was valued in terms of gold; for example, the U.S. dollar was valued as 1/35 ounce of gold. Since all currencies were valued in terms of gold, their values with respect to each other were fixed. Governments intervened in the foreign exchange markets to ensure that exchange rates drifted no more than 1 percent above or below the initially set rates.

Smithsonian Agreement. During the Bretton Woods era, the United States often experienced balance of trade deficits, an indication that the dollar's value may have been too strong, since the use of dollars for foreign purchases exceeded the demand by foreign countries for dollar-denominated goods. By 1971, it appeared that some currency values would need to be adjusted to restore a more balanced flow of payments between countries. In December 1971, a conference of representatives from various countries concluded with the **Smithsonian Agreement**, which called for a devaluation of the U.S. dollar by about 8 percent against other currencies. In addition, boundaries for the currency values were expanded to within 2.25 percent above or below the rates initially set by the agreement. Nevertheless, international payments imbalances continued, and as of February 1973, the dollar was again devalued. By March 1973, most governments of the major countries were no longer attempting to maintain their home currency values within the boundaries established by the Smithsonian Agreement.

Advantages of a Fixed Exchange Rate System. In a fixed exchange rate environment, MNCs may be able to engage in international trade without worrying about the future exchange rate. Consequently, the managerial duties of an MNC are less difficult.

When General Motors (GM) imported materials from foreign countries during the Bretton Woods era, it could anticipate the amount of dollars it would need to pay for the imports. When the dollar was devalued in the 1970s, however, GM needed more dollars to purchase the imports.

Disadvantages of a Fixed Exchange Rate System. One disadvantage of a fixed exchange rate system is that there is still risk that the government will alter the value of a specific currency. Although an MNC is not exposed to continual movements in an exchange rate, it does face the possibility that its government will devalue or revalue its currency.

A second disadvantage is that from a macro viewpoint, a fixed exchange rate system may make each country more vulnerable to economic conditions in other countries.

EXAMPLE

Assume that there are only two countries in the world: the United States and the United Kingdom. Also assume a fixed exchange rate system, and that these two countries trade frequently with each other. If the United States experiences a much higher inflation rate than the United Kingdom, U.S. consumers should buy more goods from the United Kingdom and British consumers should reduce their imports of U.S. goods (due to the high U.S. prices). This reaction would force U.S. production down and unemployment up. It could also cause higher inflation in the United Kingdom due to the excessive demand for British goods relative to the supply of British goods produced. Thus, the high inflation in the United States could cause high inflation in the United Kingdom. In the mid- and late 1960s, the United States experienced relatively high inflation and was accused of "exporting" that inflation to some European countries.

Alternatively, a high unemployment rate in the United States will cause a reduction in U.S. income and a decline in U.S. purchases of British goods. Consequently, productivity in the United Kingdom may decrease and unemployment may rise. In this case, the United States may "export" unemployment to the United Kingdom.

Freely Floating Exchange Rate System

In a **freely floating exchange rate system**, exchange rate values are determined by market forces without intervention by governments. Whereas a fixed exchange rate system allows no flexibility for exchange rate movements, a freely floating exchange rate system allows complete flexibility. A freely floating exchange rate adjusts on a continual basis in response to demand and supply conditions for that currency.

Advantages of a Freely Floating Exchange Rate System. One advantage of a freely floating exchange rate system is that a country is more insulated from the inflation of other countries.

EXAMPLE

Continue with the previous example in which there are only two countries, but now assume a freely floating exchange rate system. If the United States experiences a high rate of inflation, the increased U.S. demand for British goods will place upward pressure on the value of the British pound. As a second consequence of the high U.S. inflation, the reduced British demand for U.S. goods will result in a reduced supply of pounds for sale (exchanged for dollars), which will also place upward pressure on the British pound's value. The pound will appreciate due to these market forces (it was not allowed to appreciate under the fixed rate system). This appreciation will make British goods more expensive for U.S. consumers, even though British producers did not raise their prices. The higher prices will simply be due to the pound's appreciation; that is, a greater number of U.S. dollars are required to buy the same number of pounds as before.

In the United Kingdom, the actual price of the goods as measured in British pounds may be unchanged. Even though U.S. prices have increased, British consumers will continue to purchase U.S. goods because they can exchange their pounds for more U.S. dollars (due to the British pound's appreciation against the U.S. dollar).

Another advantage of freely floating exchange rates is that a country is more insulated from unemployment problems in other countries.

EXAMPLE

Under a floating rate system, the decline in U.S. purchases of British goods will reflect a reduced U.S. demand for British pounds. Such a shift in demand can cause the pound to depreciate against the dollar (under the fixed rate system, the pound would not be allowed to depreciate). The depreciation of the pound will make British goods look cheap to U.S. consumers, offsetting the possible reduction in demand for these goods resulting from a lower level of U.S. income. As was true with inflation, a sudden change in unemployment will have less influence on a foreign country under a floating rate system than under a fixed rate system.

As these examples illustrate, in a freely floating exchange rate system, problems experienced in one country will not necessarily be contagious. The exchange rate adjustments serve as a form of protection against "exporting" economic problems to other countries.

An additional advantage of a freely floating exchange rate system is that a central bank is not required to constantly maintain exchange rates within specified boundaries. Therefore, it is not forced to implement an intervention policy that may have an unfavorable effect on the economy just to control exchange rates. Furthermore, governments can implement policies without concern as to whether the policies will maintain the exchange rates within specified boundaries. Finally, if exchange rates were not allowed to float, investors would invest funds in whatever country had the highest interest rate. This would likely cause governments in countries with low interest rates to restrict investors' funds from leaving the country. Thus, there would be more restrictions on capital flows, and financial market efficiency would be reduced.

Disadvantages of a Freely Floating Exchange Rate System. In the previous example, the United Kingdom is somewhat insulated from the problems experienced in the United States due to the freely floating exchange rate system. Although this is an advantage for the country that is protected (the United Kingdom), it can be a disadvantage for the country that initially experienced the economic problems.

EXAMPLE

If the United States experiences high inflation, the dollar may weaken, thereby insulating the United Kingdom from the inflation, as discussed earlier. From the U.S. perspective, however, a weaker U.S. dollar causes import prices to be higher. This can increase the price of U.S. materials and supplies, which will in turn increase U.S. prices of finished goods. In addition, higher foreign prices (from the U.S. perspective) can force U.S. consumers to purchase domestic products. As U.S. producers recognize that their foreign competition has been reduced due to the weak dollar, they can more easily raise their prices without losing their customers to foreign competition.

In a similar manner, a freely floating exchange rate system can adversely affect a country that has high unemployment.

EXAMPLE

If the U.S. unemployment rate is rising, U.S. demand for imports will decrease, putting upward pressure on the value of the dollar. A stronger dollar will then cause U.S. consumers to purchase foreign products rather than U.S. products because the foreign products can be purchased cheaply. Yet, such a reaction can actually be detrimental to the United States during periods of high unemployment.

As these examples illustrate, a country's economic problems can sometimes be compounded by freely floating exchange rates. Under such a system, MNCs will need to devote substantial resources to measuring and managing exposure to exchange rate fluctuations. Nonetheless, since exchange rate movements can affect economic conditions within a country, most governments want the flexibility to directly or indirectly control their exchange rates when necessary.

Managed Float Exchange Rate System

The exchange rate system that exists today for some currencies lies somewhere between fixed and freely floating. It resembles the freely floating system in that exchange rates are allowed to fluctuate on a daily basis and there are no official boundaries. It is similar to the fixed rate system in that governments can and sometimes do intervene to prevent their currencies from moving too far in a certain direction. This type of system is known as a **managed float** or "dirty" float (as opposed to a "clean" float where rates float freely without government intervention). The various forms of intervention used by governments to manage exchange rate movements are discussed later in this chapter.

At times, the governments of various countries including Brazil, Russia, South Korea, and Venezuela have imposed bands around their currency to limit its degree of movement. Later, however, they removed the bands when they found that they could not maintain the currency's value within the bands.

Criticism of a Managed Float System. Critics suggest that a managed float system allows a government to manipulate exchange rates in a manner that can benefit its own country at the expense of others. For example, a government may attempt to weaken its currency to stimulate a stagnant economy. The increased aggregate demand for products that results from such a policy may reflect a decreased aggregate demand for products in other countries, as the weakened currency attracts foreign demand. Although this criticism is valid, it could apply as well to the fixed exchange rate system, where governments have the power to devalue their currencies.

Pegged Exchange Rate System

Some countries use a **pegged exchange rate** arrangement, in which their home currency's value is pegged to a foreign currency or to some unit of account. While the home currency's value is fixed in terms of the foreign currency (or unit of account) to which it is pegged, it moves in line with that currency against other currencies.

Some Asian countries such as Malaysia and Thailand had pegged their currency's value to the dollar. During the Asian crisis, though, they were unable to maintain the peg and allowed their currencies to float against the dollar.

Creation of Europe's Snake Arrangement. One of the best-known pegged exchange rate arrangements was established by several European countries in April 1972. Their goal was to maintain their currencies within established limits of each other. This arrangement became known as the **snake**. The snake was difficult to maintain, however, and market pressure caused some currencies to move outside their established limits. Consequently, some members withdrew from the snake arrangement, and some currencies were realigned.

Creation of the European Monetary System (EMS). Due to continued problems with the snake arrangement, the European Monetary System (EMS) was pushed into operation in March 1979. The EMS concept was similar to the snake, but the specific characteristics differed. Under the EMS, exchange rates of member countries were held together within specified limits and were also tied to the European Currency Unit (ECU), which was a unit of account. Its value was a weighted average of exchange rates of the member countries; each weight was determined by a member's relative gross national product and activity in intra-European trade. The currencies of these member countries were allowed to fluctuate by no more than 2.25 percent (6 percent for some currencies) from the initially established par values.

The method of linking European currency values with the ECU was known as the **exchange rate mechanism (ERM)**. The participating governments intervened in the foreign exchange markets to maintain the exchange rates within boundaries established by the ERM.

Demise of the European Monetary System. In the fall of 1992, however, the exchange rate mechanism experienced severe problems, as economic conditions and goals began to vary among European countries. The German government was mostly concerned about inflation because its economy was relatively strong. It increased local interest rates to prevent excessive spending and inflation. Other European governments, however, were more concerned about stimulating their economies to lower their high unemployment levels, so they wanted to reduce interest rates. In October 1992, the British and Italian governments suspended their participation in the ERM because they could not achieve their own goals for a stronger economy while their interest rates were so highly influenced by German interest rates.

In 1993, the ERM boundaries were widened substantially, allowing more fluctuation in exchange rates between European currencies. The demise of the exchange rate mechanism caused European countries to realize that a pegged system would work in Europe only if it was set permanently. This provided momentum for the single European currency (the euro), which began in 1999 and is discussed later in this chapter.

http://

Visit the European Union site at http://europa.eu.int/index_en.htm for access to the server of the European Union's Parliament, Council, Commission, Court of Justice, and other bodies. It includes basic information on all related political and economic issues.

How Mexico's Pegged System Led to the Mexican Peso Crisis. In 1994, Mexico's central bank used a special pegged exchange rate system that linked the peso to the U.S. dollar but allowed the peso's value to fluctuate against the dollar within a band. The Mexican central bank enforced the link through frequent intervention. In fact, it partially supported its intervention by issuing short-term debt securities denominated in dollars and using the dollars to purchase pesos in the foreign exchange market. Limiting the depreciation of the peso was intended to reduce inflationary pressure that can be caused by a very weak home currency. Mexico experienced a large balance of trade deficit in 1994, however, perhaps because the peso was stronger than it should have been and encouraged Mexican firms and consumers to buy an excessive amount of imports.

Many speculators based in Mexico recognized that the peso was being maintained at an artificially high level, and they speculated on its potential decline by investing their funds in the United States. They planned to liquidate their U.S. investments if and when the peso's value weakened so that they could convert the dollars from their U.S. investments into pesos at a favorable exchange rate. Ironically, the flow of funds from Mexico to the United States that was motivated by the potential devaluation in the peso put even more downward pressure on the peso, because the speculators were converting pesos into dollars to invest in the United States.

By December 1994, there was substantial downward pressure on the peso. On December 20, 1994, Mexico's central bank devalued the peso by about 13 percent. Mexico's stock prices plummeted, as many foreign investors sold their shares and withdrew their funds from Mexico in anticipation of further devaluation of the peso. On December 22, the central bank allowed the peso to float freely, and it declined by 15 percent. This was the beginning of the so-called Mexican peso crisis. In an attempt to discourage foreign investors from withdrawing their investments in Mexico's debt securities, the central bank increased interest rates, but the higher rates increased the cost of borrowing for Mexican firms and consumers, thereby slowing economic growth.

As Mexico's short-term debt obligations denominated in dollars matured, the Mexican central bank used its weak pesos to obtain dollars and repay the debt. Since the peso had weakened, the effective cost of financing with dollars was very expensive for the central bank. Mexico's financial problems caused investors to lose confidence in peso-denominated securities, so they liquidated their peso-denominated securities and transferred their funds to other countries. These actions put additional downward pressure on the peso. In the four months after December 20, 1994, the value of the peso declined by more than 50 percent. Over time, Mexico's economy improved, and the paranoia that had led to the withdrawal of funds by foreign investors subsided. The Mexican crisis might not have occurred if the peso had been allowed to float throughout 1994, because the peso would have gravitated toward its natural level. The crisis illustrates that central bank intervention will not necessarily be able to overwhelm market forces; thus, the crisis may serve as an argument for letting a currency float freely.

Currency Boards

A currency board is a system for pegging the value of the local currency to some other specified currency. The board must maintain currency reserves for all the currency that it has printed.

EXAMPLE

Hong Kong has tied the value of its currency (the Hong Kong dollar) to the U.S. dollar (HK$7.80 = $1.00) since 1983. Every Hong Kong dollar in circulation is backed by a U.S. dollar in reserve. In 2000, El Salvador set its currency (the colon) to be valued at 8.75 per dollar.

A currency board can stabilize a currency's value. This is important because investors generally avoid investing in a country if they expect the local currency will weaken substantially. If a currency board is expected to remain in place for a long period, it may reduce fears that the local currency will weaken and thus may encourage investors to maintain their investments within the country. However, a currency board is worth considering only if the government can convince investors that the exchange rate will be maintained.

EXAMPLE

When Indonesia was experiencing financial problems during the 1997–1998 Asian crisis, businesses and investors sold the local currency (rupiah) because of expectations that it would weaken further. Such actions perpetuated the weakness, as the exchange of rupiah for other currencies placed more downward pressure on the value of the rupiah. Indonesia considered implementing a currency board to stabilize its currency and discourage the flow of funds out of the country. Businesses and investors had no confidence in the Indonesian government's ability to maintain a fixed exchange rate, however, and feared that economic pressures would ultimately lead to a decline in the rupiah's value. Thus, Indonesia's government did not implement a currency board.

A currency board is effective only if investors believe that it will last. If investors expect that market forces will prevent a government from maintaining the local currency's exchange rate, they will attempt to move their funds to other countries where they expect the local currency to be stronger. When foreign investors withdraw their funds from a country and convert the funds into a different currency, they place downward pressure on the local currency's exchange rate. If the supply of the currency for sale continues to exceed the demand, the government will be forced to devalue its currency.

EXAMPLE

In 1991, Argentina established a currency board that pegged the Argentine peso to the dollar. In 2002, Argentina was suffering from major economic problems, and its government was unable to repay its debt. Foreign investors and local investors began to transfer their funds to other countries because they feared that their investments would earn poor returns. These actions required the exchange of pesos into other currencies such as the dollar and caused an excessive supply of pesos for sale in the foreign exchange market. The government could not maintain the exchange rate of 1 peso = 1 dollar, because the supply of pesos for sale exceeded the demand at that exchange rate. In March 2002, the government devalued the peso to 1 peso = \$.71 (1.4 pesos per dollar). Even at this new exchange rate, the supply of pesos for sale exceeded the demand, so the Argentine government decided to let the peso's value float in response to market conditions rather than set the peso's value.

Exposure of a Pegged Currency to Interest Rate Movements. A country that uses a currency board does not have complete control over its local interest rates, because its rates must be aligned with the interest rates of the currency to which it is tied.

EXAMPLE

Recall that the Hong Kong dollar is pegged to the U.S. dollar. If Hong Kong lowers its interest rates to stimulate its economy, its interest rate would then be lower than U.S. interest rates. Investors based in Hong Kong would be enticed to exchange Hong Kong dollars for U.S. dollars and invest in the United States where interest rates are higher. Since the Hong Kong dollar is tied to the U.S. dollar, the investors could exchange the proceeds of their investment back to Hong Kong dollars at the end of the investment period without concern about exchange rate risk because the exchange rate is fixed.

If the United States raises its interest rates, Hong Kong would be forced to raise its interest rates (on securities with similar risk as those in the United States). Otherwise, investors in Hong Kong could invest their money in the United States and earn a higher rate.

Even though a country may not have control over its interest rate when it establishes a currency board, its interest rate may be more stable than if it did not have a currency board. Its interest rate will move in tandem with the interest rate of the currency to which it is tied. The interest rate may include a risk premium that could reflect either default risk or the risk that the currency board will be discontinued.

EXAMPLE

While the Hong Kong interest rate moves in tandem with the U.S. interest rate, specific investment instruments may have a slightly higher interest rate in Hong Kong than in the United States. For example, a Treasury bill may offer a slightly higher rate in Hong Kong than in the United States. While this allows for possible arbitrage by U.S. investors who wish to invest in Hong Kong, they will face two forms of risk. First, some investors may believe that there is a slight risk that the Hong Kong government could default on its debt. Second, if there is sudden downward pressure on the Hong Kong dollar, the currency board could be discontinued. In this case, the Hong Kong dollar's value would be reduced, and U.S. investors would earn a lower return than they could have earned in the United States.

Exposure of a Pegged Currency to Exchange Rate Movements. A currency that is pegged to another currency cannot be pegged against all other currencies. If it is pegged to the U.S. dollar, it is forced to move in tandem with the dollar against other currencies. Since a country cannot peg its currency to all currencies, it is exposed to movements of currencies against the currency to which it is pegged.

EXAMPLE

As mentioned earlier, from 1991 to 2002, the Argentine peso's value was set to equal one U.S. dollar. Thus, if the dollar strengthened against the Brazilian real by 10 percent in a particular month, the Argentine peso strengthened against the Brazilian real by the exact same amount. During the 1991–2002 period, the dollar commonly strengthened against the Brazilian real and some other currencies in South America; therefore, the Argentine peso also strengthened against those currencies. Many exporting firms in Argentina were adversely affected by the strong Argentine peso, however, because it made their products too expensive for importers. Now that Argentina's currency board has been eliminated, the Argentine peso is no longer forced to move in tandem with the dollar against other currencies.

Meanwhile, the Chinese yuan continues to be pegged to the dollar. During 2003, the U.S. dollar weakened against the euro and some other currencies. By remaining pegged to the dollar during this period, the Chinese yuan weakened against those currencies as well. China benefited from this effect because the demand for its exports increased. Some of its trading partners were adversely affected, however, because their export prices increased, and China's demand for their products declined.

Dollarization

Dollarization is the replacement of a foreign currency with U.S. dollars. This process is a step beyond a currency board, because it forces the local currency to be replaced by the U.S. dollar. Although dollarization and a currency board both attempt to peg the local currency's value, the currency board does not replace the local currency with dollars. The decision to use U.S. dollars as the local currency cannot be easily reversed because the country no longer has a local currency.

EXAMPLE

From 1990 to 2000, Ecuador's currency (the sucre) depreciated by about 97 percent against the dollar. The weakness of the currency caused unstable trade conditions, high inflation, and volatile interest rates. In 2000, in an effort to stabilize trade and economic conditions, Ecuador replaced the sucre with the U.S. dollar as its currency. By November 2000, inflation had declined and economic growth had increased. Thus, it appeared that dollarization had favorable effects.

Classification of Exchange Rate Arrangements

Exhibit 6.1 identifies the currencies and exchange rate arrangements used by various countries. Many countries allow the value of their currency to float against others but intervene periodically to influence its value. Several small countries peg their currencies to the U.S. dollar.

The Mexican peso has a controlled exchange rate that applies to international trade and a floating market rate that applies to tourism. The floating market rate is influenced by central bank intervention. Chile intervenes to maintain its currency within 10 per-

Exhibit 6.1
Exchange Rate Arrangements

Floating Rate System			
Country	**Currency**	**Country**	**Currency**
Afghanistan	new afghani	Norway	krone
Argentina	peso	Paraguay	guarani
Australia	dollar	Peru	new sol
Bolivia	boliviano	Poland	zloty
Brazil	real	Romania	leu
Canada	dollar	Russia	ruble
Chile	peso	Singapore	dollar
Euro participants (12 European countries)	euro	South Africa	rand
Hungary	forint	South Korea	won
India	rupee	Sweden	krona
Indonesia	rupiah	Switzerland	franc
Israel	new shekel	Taiwan	new dollar
Jamaica	dollar	Thailand	baht
Japan	yen	United Kingdom	pound
Mexico	peso	Venezuela	bolivar

Pegged Rate System		
The following currencies are pegged to a currency or a composite of currencies.		
Country	**Currency**	**Currency Is Pegged to**
Bahamas	dollar	U.S. dollar
Barbados	dollar	U.S. dollar
Bermuda	dollar	U.S. dollar
China	yuan	U.S. dollar
Hong Kong	dollar	U.S. dollar
Saudi Arabia	riyal	U.S. dollar

cent of a specified exchange rate with respect to major currencies. Venezuela intervenes to limit exchange rate fluctuations within wide bands.

Some Eastern European countries that recently opened their markets have tied their currencies to a single widely traded currency. The arrangement was sometimes temporary, as these countries were searching for the proper exchange rate that would stabilize or enhance their economic conditions. For example, the government of Slovakia devalued its currency (the koruna) in an attempt to increase foreign demand for its goods and reduce unemployment.

Many governments attempt to impose exchange controls to prevent their exchange rates from fluctuating. When these governments remove the controls, however, the exchange rates abruptly adjust to a new market-determined level. For example, in October 1994, the Russian authorities allowed the Russian ruble to fluctuate, and the ruble depreciated by 27 percent against the dollar on that day. In April 1996, Venezuela's government removed controls on the bolivar (its currency), and the bolivar depreciated by 42 percent on that day.

After the 2001 war in Afghanistan, an exchange rate system was needed there. In October 2002, a new currency, called the new afghani, was created to replace the old afghani. The old currency was exchanged for the new money at a ratio of 1,000 to 1. Thus, 30,000 old afghanis were exchanged for 30 new afghanis. The new money was printed with watermarks to deter counterfeits.

At the end of the 2003 war in Iraq, an exchange rate system was also needed there. At that time, three different currencies were being used in Iraq. The Swiss dinar (so called because it was designed in Switzerland) was created before the Gulf War, but had not been printed since then. It traded at about 8 dinars per dollar and was used by the Kurds in northern Iraq. The Saddam dinar, which was used extensively before 2003, was printed in excess to finance Iraq's military budget and was easy to counterfeit. Its value relative to the dollar was very volatile over time. The U.S. dollar was frequently used in the black market in Iraq even before the 2003 war. Just after the war, the dollar was used more frequently, as merchants were unwilling to accept Saddam dinars out of fear that their value was declining.

A Single European Currency

In 1991, the Maastricht Treaty called for the establishment of a single European currency. As of January 1, 1999, the euro replaced the national currencies of 11 European countries for the purpose of commercial transactions executed through electronic transfers and other forms of payment. By June 1, 2002, when the national currencies were to be withdrawn from the financial system and replaced with the euro, a twelfth country had qualified for the euro.

Membership

The agreement to adopt the euro was a major historical event. Countries that had previously been at war with each other at various times in the past were now willing to work together toward a common cause. Of the 25 countries that are members of the European Union (EU), 12 countries participate in the euro: Austria, Belgium, Finland, France, Germany, Greece, Ireland, Italy, Luxembourg, the Netherlands, Portugal, and Spain. Together, the participating countries comprise almost 20 percent of the world's gross domestic product—a proportion similar to that of the United States. Three countries that were members of the EU in 1999 (the United Kingdom, Denmark, and Sweden) decided not to adopt the euro at that time. The 10 countries in Eastern Europe (including the Czech Republic and Hungary) that joined the EU in 2004 will be eligible to participate in the euro in the future if they meet specific economic goals. Countries that participate in the EU are supposed to abide by the Stability and Growth pact before they adopt the euro. This pact requires that the country's budget deficit be less than 3 percent of its gross domestic product. However, there is already some question about the budget deficit exceeding the limit of the EU countries that presently participate in the euro.

Four of the 10 countries that became part of the EU in May 2004 (Cyprus, Estonia, Lithuania, and Slovenia) are planning to take the first step in adopting the euro. To do so, they must restrict the movements of the euro relative to their home currency within a range of plus or minus 15 percent from an initially set exchange rate. This will allow them to monitor the exchange movements within this range before they permanently convert their currency into euros at a particular exchange rate. Assuming that they also comply with other specified macroeconomic conditions, such as limiting inflation and their budget deficit, these countries could adopt the euro in 2007.

Impact on European Monetary Policy

The euro allows for a single money supply throughout much of Europe, rather than a separate money supply for each participating currency. Thus, European monetary policy is consolidated, because any effects on the money supply will have an impact on all European countries using the euro as their form of money. The implementation of a common monetary policy may promote more political unity among European countries with similar national defense and foreign policies.

European Central Bank. The European Central Bank (ECB) is based in Frankfurt and is responsible for setting monetary policy for all participating European countries. Its objective is to control inflation in the participating countries and to stabilize (within reasonable boundaries) the value of the euro with respect to other major currencies. Thus, the ECB's monetary goals of price stability and currency stability are similar to those of individual countries around the world, but differ in that they are focused on a group of countries instead of a single country.

Implications of a European Monetary Policy. Although a single European monetary policy may allow for more consistent economic conditions across countries, it prevents any individual European country from solving local economic problems with its own unique monetary policy. European governments may disagree on the ideal monetary policy to enhance their local economies, but they must agree on a single European monetary policy. Any given policy used in a particular period may enhance conditions in some countries and adversely affect others. Each participating country is still able to apply its own fiscal policy (tax and government expenditure decisions), however. The use of a common currency may someday create more political harmony among European countries.

Impact on Business within Europe

The euro enables residents of participating countries to engage in cross-border trade flows and capital flows throughout the so-called euro zone (of participating countries) without converting to a different currency. The elimination of currency movements among European countries also encourages more long-term business arrangements between firms of different countries, as they no longer have to worry about adverse effects due to currency movements. Thus, firms in different European countries are increasingly engaging in all types of business arrangements including licensing, joint ventures, and acquisitions.

Prices of products are now more comparable among European countries, as the exchange rate between the countries is fixed. Thus, buyers can more easily determine where they can obtain products at the lowest cost.

Trade flows between the participating European countries have increased because exporters and importers can conduct trade without concern about exchange rate movements. To the extent that there are more trade flows between these countries, economic conditions in each of these countries should have a larger impact on the other European countries, and economies of these countries may become more integrated.

Impact on the Valuation of Businesses in Europe

When firms consider acquiring targets in Europe, they can more easily compare the prices (market values) of targets among countries because their values are denominated in the same currency (the euro). In addition, the future currency movements of the target's currency against any non-European currency will be the same. Therefore, U.S. firms can more easily conduct valuations of firms across the participating European countries because when funds are remitted to the U.S. parent from any of the participating countries, the level of appreciation or depreciation will be the same for a particular period and there will be no differences in exchange rate effects.

European firms face more pressure to perform well because they can be measured against all other firms in the same industry throughout the participating countries, not just within its own country. Therefore, these firms are more focused on meeting various performance goals.

Impact on Financial Flows

A single European currency forces the interest rate offered on government securities to be similar across the participating European countries. Any discrepancy in rates would encourage investors within these European countries to invest in the currency with the highest rate, which would realign the interest rates among these countries. However, the rate may still vary between two government securities with the same maturity if they exhibit different levels of credit risk.

Stock prices are now more comparable among the European countries because they are denominated in the same currency. Investors in the participating European countries are now able to invest in stocks throughout these countries without concern about exchange rate risk. Thus, there is more cross-border investing than there was in the past.

http://

The website http://www.ecb.int/home/html/index.en.html provides information on the euro and monetary policy conducted by the European Central Bank.

Since stock market prices are influenced by expectations of economic conditions, the stock prices among the European countries may become more highly correlated if economies among these countries become more highly correlated. Investors from other countries who invest in European countries may not achieve as much diversification as in the past because of the integration and because the exchange rate effects will be the same for all markets whose stocks are denominated in euros. Stock markets in these European countries are also likely to consolidate over time now that they use the same currency.

Bond investors based in these European countries can now invest in bonds issued by governments and corporations in these countries without concern about exchange rate risk, as long as the bonds are denominated in euros. Some European governments have already issued bonds that are redenominated in euros, because the secondary market for some bonds issued in Europe with other currency denominations is now less active. The bond yields in participating European countries are not necessarily similar even though they are now denominated in the same currency; the credit risk may still be higher for issuers in a particular country.

Impact on Exchange Rate Risk

One major advantage of a single European currency is the complete elimination of exchange rate risk between the participating European countries, which could encourage more trade and capital flows across European borders. In addition, foreign exchange transaction costs associated with transactions between European countries have been eliminated. The single European currency is consistent with the goal of the Single European Act to remove trade barriers between European borders, since exchange rate risk is an implicit trade barrier.

The euro's value with respect to the dollar changes continuously. The euro's value is influenced by the trade flows and capital flows between the set of participating European countries and the United States, since these flows affect supply and demand conditions. Its value with respect to the Japanese yen is influenced by the trade flows and capital flows between the set of participating European countries and Japan.

European countries that participate in the euro are still affected by movements in its value with respect to other currencies such as the dollar. Furthermore, many U.S. firms are still affected by movements in the euro's value with respect to the dollar.

Status Report on the Euro

The euro has experienced a volatile ride since it was introduced in 1999. Its value initially declined substantially against the British pound, the dollar, and many other currencies. In October 2001, for example, 33 months after it was introduced, its value was $.88, or about 27 percent less than its initial value. The weakness was partially attributed to capital outflows from Europe. By June 2004, however, the euro was valued at $1.22, or 42 percent above its value in October 2001. The strength in the euro was partially due to the relatively high European interest rates compared to U.S. interest rates in this period, which attracted capital inflows into Europe.

Government Intervention

Each country has a central bank that may intervene in the foreign exchange markets to control its currency's value. In the United States, for example, the central bank is the Federal Reserve System (the Fed). Central banks have other duties besides intervening in the foreign exchange market. In particular, they attempt to control the growth of the money supply in their respective countries in a way that will favorably affect economic conditions.

USING THE WEB

Central Bank Website Links The Bank for International Settlements website http://www.bis.org/cbanks.htm provides links to websites of central banks around the world. Some of the websites are in English.

Reasons for Government Intervention

The degree to which the home currency is controlled, or "managed," varies among central banks. Central banks commonly manage exchange rates for three reasons:

- To smooth exchange rate movements.
- To establish implicit exchange rate boundaries.
- To respond to temporary disturbances.

Smooth Exchange Rate Movements. If a central bank is concerned that its economy will be affected by abrupt movements in its home currency's value, it may attempt to smooth the currency movements over time. Its actions may keep business cycles less volatile. The central bank may also encourage international trade by reducing exchange rate uncertainty. Furthermore, smoothing currency movements may reduce fears in the financial markets and speculative activity that could cause a major decline in a currency's value.

Establish Implicit Exchange Rate Boundaries. Some central banks attempt to maintain their home currency rates within some unofficial, or implicit, boundaries. Analysts are commonly quoted as forecasting that a currency will not fall below or rise above a particular benchmark value because the central bank would intervene to prevent that. The Federal Reserve periodically intervenes to reverse the U.S. dollar's upward or downward momentum.

Respond to Temporary Disturbances. In some cases, a central bank may intervene to insulate a currency's value from a temporary disturbance. In fact, the stated objective of the Fed's intervention policy is to counter disorderly market conditions.

EXAMPLE

News that oil prices might rise could cause expectations of a future decline in the value of the Japanese yen because Japan exchanges yen for dollars to purchase oil from oil-exporting countries. Foreign exchange market speculators may exchange yen for dollars in anticipation of this decline. Central banks may therefore intervene to offset the immediate downward pressure on the yen caused by such market transactions.

Several studies have found that government intervention does not have a permanent impact on exchange rate movements. In many cases, intervention is overwhelmed by market forces. In the absence of intervention, however, currency movements would be even more volatile.

Direct Intervention

http://

The Federal Reserve Bank of New York website http://www.ny.frb.org/markets/foreignex.html provides information on its recent direct intervention in the foreign exchange market.

To force the dollar to depreciate, the Fed can intervene directly by exchanging dollars that it holds as reserves for other foreign currencies in the foreign exchange market. By "flooding the market with dollars" in this manner, the Fed puts downward pressure on the dollar. If the Fed desires to strengthen the dollar, it can exchange foreign currencies for dollars in the foreign exchange market, thereby putting upward pressure on the dollar.

The effects of direct intervention on the value of the British pound are illustrated in Exhibit 6.2. To strengthen the pound's value (or to weaken the dollar), the Fed exchanges dollars for pounds, which causes an outward shift in the demand for pounds in

Exhibit 6.2 Effects of Direct Central Bank Intervention in the Foreign Exchange Market

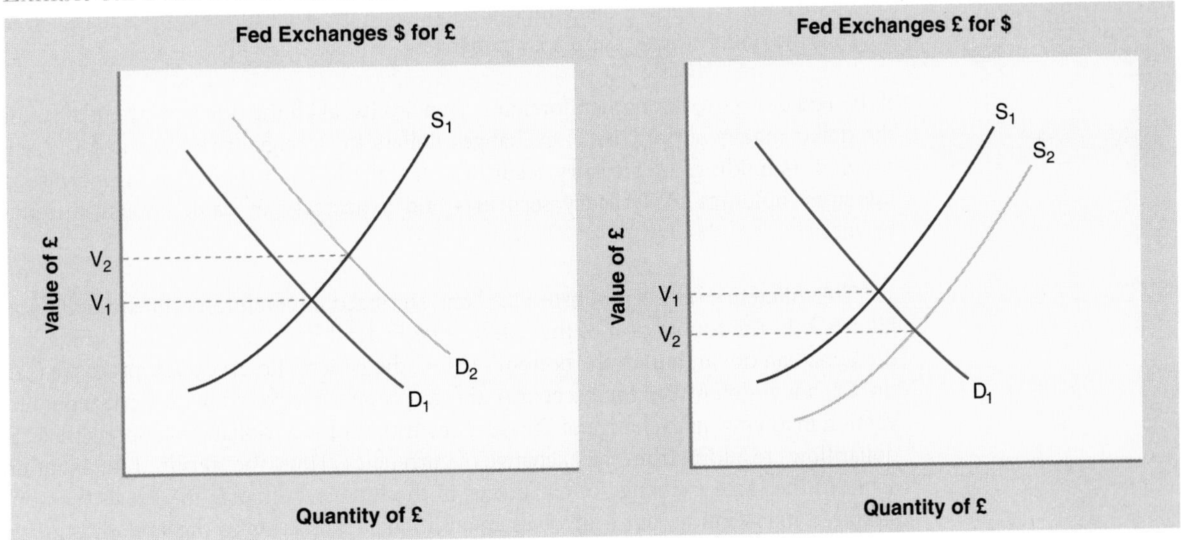

the foreign exchange market (as shown in the graph on the left). Conversely, to weaken the pound's value (or to strengthen the dollar), the Fed exchanges pounds for dollars, which causes an outward shift in the supply of pounds for sale in the foreign exchange market (as shown in the graph on the right).

During early 2004, Japan's central bank, the Bank of Japan, intervened on several occasions to lower the value of the yen. In the first two months of 2004, the Bank of Japan sold yen in the foreign exchange market in exchange for $100 billion. Then, on March 5, 2004, the Bank of Japan sold yen in the foreign exchange market in exchange for $20 billion, which put immediate downward pressure on the value of the yen.

Direct intervention is usually most effective when there is a coordinated effort among central banks. If all central banks simultaneously attempt to strengthen or weaken the currency in the manner just described, they can exert greater pressure on the currency's value.

Reliance on Reserves. The potential effectiveness of a central bank's direct intervention is the amount of reserves it can use. If the central bank has a low level of reserves, it may not be able to exert much pressure on the currency's value. Market forces would likely overwhelm its actions.

As foreign exchange activity has grown, central bank intervention has become less effective. The volume of foreign exchange transactions on a single day now exceeds the combined values of reserves at all central banks. Consequently, the number of direct interventions has declined. In 1989, for example, the Fed intervened on 97 different days. Since then, the Fed has not intervened on more than 20 days in any year.

Nonsterilized versus Sterilized Intervention. When the Fed intervenes in the foreign exchange market without adjusting for the change in the money supply, it is engaging in a **nonsterilized intervention**. For example, if the Fed exchanges dollars for foreign currencies in the foreign exchange markets in an attempt to strengthen foreign currencies (weaken the dollar), the dollar money supply increases.

In a **sterilized intervention**, the Fed intervenes in the foreign exchange market and simultaneously engages in offsetting transactions in the Treasury securities markets. As a result, the dollar money supply is unchanged.

EXAMPLE

If the Fed desires to strengthen foreign currencies (weaken the dollar) without affecting the dollar money supply, it (1) exchanges dollars for foreign currencies and (2) sells some of its holdings of Treasury securities for dollars. The net effect is an increase in investors' holdings of Treasury securities and a decrease in bank foreign currency balances.

The difference between nonsterilized and sterilized intervention is illustrated in Exhibit 6.3. In the top section of the exhibit, the Federal Reserve attempts to strengthen the Canadian dollar, and in the bottom section, the Federal Reserve attempts to weaken the Canadian dollar. For each scenario, the graph on the right shows a sterilized intervention involving an exchange of Treasury securities for U.S. dollars that offsets the U.S. dollar flows resulting from the exchange of currencies. Thus, the sterilized intervention achieves the same exchange of currencies in the foreign exchange market as the nonsterilized intervention, but it involves an additional transaction to prevent adjustments in the U.S. dollar money supply.

Speculating on Direct Intervention. Some traders in the foreign exchange market attempt to determine when Federal Reserve intervention is occurring, and the extent of the intervention, in order to capitalize on the anticipated results of the intervention effort. Normally, the Federal Reserve attempts to intervene without being noticed. However, dealers at the major banks that trade with the Fed often pass the information to other market participants. Also, when the Fed deals directly with numerous commercial banks, markets are well aware that the Fed is intervening. To hide its strategy,

Exhibit 6.3

Forms of Central Bank Intervention in the Foreign Exchange Market

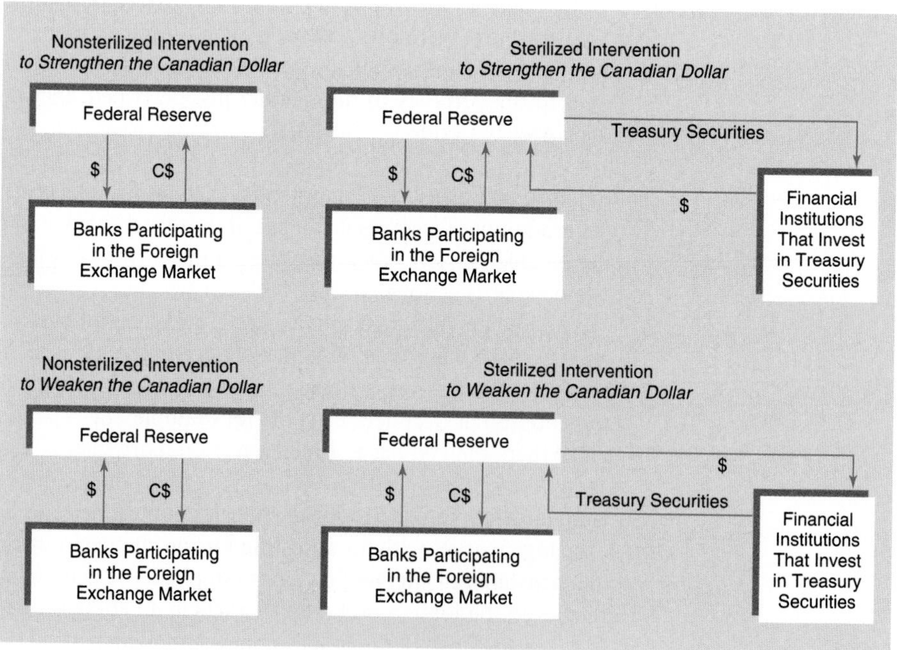

the Fed may pretend to be interested in selling dollars when it is actually buying dollars, or vice versa. It calls commercial banks and obtains both bid and ask quotes on currencies, so the banks will not know whether the Fed is considering purchases or sales of these currencies.

Intervention strategies vary among central banks. Some arrange for one large order when they intervene; others use several smaller orders equivalent to $5 million to $10 million. Even if traders determine the extent of central bank intervention, they still cannot know with certainty what impact it will have on exchange rates.

Indirect Intervention

The Fed can also affect the dollar's value indirectly by influencing the factors that determine it. Recall that the change in a currency's spot rate is influenced by the following factors:

$$e = f(\Delta INF, \Delta INT, \Delta INC, \Delta GC, \Delta EXP)$$

where:

e = percentage change in the spot rate

ΔINF = change in the differential between U.S. inflation and the foreign country's inflation

ΔINT = change in the differential between the U.S. interest rate and the foreign country's interest rate

ΔINC = change in the differential between the U.S. income level and the foreign country's income level

ΔGC = change in government controls

ΔEXP = change in expectations of future exchange rates

The central bank can influence all of these variables, which in turn can affect the exchange rate. Since these variables will likely have a more lasting impact on a spot rate than direct intervention, a central bank may use indirect intervention by influencing these variables. Although the central bank can influence all of these variables, it is likely to focus on interest rates or government controls when using indirect intervention.

Government Adjustment of Interest Rates. When countries experience substantial net outflows of funds (which places severe downward pressure on their currency), they commonly intervene indirectly by raising interest rates to discourage excessive outflows of funds and therefore limit any downward pressure on the value of their currency. However, this strategy adversely affects local borrowers (government agencies, corporations, and consumers) and may weaken the economy.

EXAMPLE

The Fed can attempt to lower interest rates by increasing the U.S. money supply (assuming that inflationary expectations are not affected). Lower U.S. interest rates tend to discourage foreign investors from investing in U.S. securities, thereby placing downward pressure on the value of the dollar. Or, to boost the dollar's value, the Fed can attempt to increase interest rates by reducing the U.S. money supply. It has commonly used this strategy along with direct intervention in the foreign exchange market.

EXAMPLE

In October 1997, there was concern that the Asian crisis might adversely affect Brazil and other Latin American countries. Speculators pulled funds out of Brazil and reinvested them in other countries, causing major capital outflows and therefore placing extreme downward pressure on the Brazilian currency (the real). The central bank of Brazil responded at the end of October by doubling its interest rates from about 20 percent to about 40 percent. This action discouraged investors from pulling funds out of Brazil because they could now earn twice the interest from investing in some securities there. Although the bank's action was successful in defending the real, it reduced economic growth because the cost of borrowing funds was too high for many firms.

In another example, during the Asian crisis in 1997 and 1998, central banks of some Asian countries increased their interest rates to prevent their currencies from weakening. The higher interest rates were expected to make the local securities more attractive and therefore encourage investors to maintain their holdings of securities, which would reduce the exchange of the local currency for other currencies. This effort was not successful for most Asian countries, although it worked for China and Hong Kong.

As a third example, in May 1998, the Russian currency (the ruble) had consistently declined, and Russian stock prices had fallen by more than 50 percent from their level four months earlier. Fearing that the lack of confidence in Russia's currency and stocks would cause massive outflows of funds, the Russian central bank attempted to prevent further outflows by tripling interest rates (from about 50 percent to 150 percent). The ruble was temporarily stabilized, but stock prices continued to decline because investors were concerned that the high interest rates would reduce economic growth.

Government Use of Foreign Exchange Controls. Some governments attempt to use foreign exchange controls (such as restrictions on the exchange of the currency) as a form of indirect intervention to maintain the exchange rate of their currency. Under severe pressure, however, they tend to let the currency float temporarily toward its market-determined level and set new bands around that level.

EXAMPLE

During the mid-1990s, Venezuela imposed foreign exchange controls on its currency (the bolivar). In April 1996, Venezuela removed its controls on foreign exchange, and the bolivar declined by 42 percent the next day. This result suggests that the market-determined exchange rate of the bolivar was substantially lower than the exchange rate at which the government artificially set the bolivar.

Exchange Rate Target Zones

In recent years, many economists have criticized the present exchange rate system because of the wide swings in exchange rates of major currencies. Some have suggested that **target zones** be used for these currencies. An initial exchange rate would be established, with specific boundaries surrounding that rate. Such a target zone is similar to the bands used in a fixed exchange rate system, but would likely be wider. Proponents of the target zone system suggest that it would stabilize international trade patterns by reducing exchange rate volatility.

Implementing a target zone system could be complicated, however. First, what initial exchange rate should be established for each country? Second, how wide should the

MANAGING FOR VALUE

How Yahoo! Is Exposed to Exchange Rate Systems and Intervention

When Yahoo! conducts business in foreign countries, it recognizes that its future dollar cash flows are dependent on the exchange rate movements in those countries. Its concerns about exchange rate movements vary with the exchange rate system enforced by the local government. When doing business in Europe, Yahoo! focuses on the day-to-day fluctuations in the value of the euro against the dollar. It is concerned that the exchange rate could wander from its prevailing level in a manner that would adversely affect the company's cash flows in the near future. When doing business in countries such as Hong Kong, Yahoo! is concerned that the fixed exchange rate between the local currency and the U.S. dollar could be revised. Even though the exchange rate is fixed, Yahoo! recognizes that the government could abruptly adjust the exchange rate in response to currency flow imbalances.

Like other MNCs, Yahoo! must also closely monitor central bank interventions aimed at correcting local economic conditions. In particular, emerging countries are susceptible to capital outflows of funds when they experience severe economic conditions, as investors move their money out of the country. These actions place downward pressure on the local currency, and central banks commonly attempt to discourage the outflows by raising interest rates to offer a higher return on investments. MNCs like Yahoo! that finance a portion of their foreign operations with local borrowed funds are adversely affected by this type of government intervention. By anticipating such actions, Yahoo! and other MNCs may reduce their exposure before the intervention occurs.

target zone be? The ideal target zone would allow exchange rates to adjust to economic factors without causing wide swings in international trade and arousing fear in financial markets.

If target zones were implemented, governments would be responsible for intervening to maintain their currencies within the zones. If the zones were sufficiently wide, government intervention would rarely be necessary; however, such wide zones would basically resemble the exchange rate system as it exists today. Governments tend to intervene when a currency's value moves outside some implicitly acceptable zone.

Unless governments could maintain their currency's value within the target zone, this system could not ensure stability in international markets. A country experiencing a large balance of trade deficit might intentionally allow its currency to float below the lower boundary in order to stimulate foreign demand for its exports. Wide swings in international trade patterns could result. Furthermore, financial market prices would be more volatile because financial market participants would expect some currencies to move outside their zones. The result would be a system no different from what exists today.

In February 1987, representatives of the United States, Japan, West Germany, France, Canada, Italy, and the United Kingdom (also known as the Group of Seven or G-7 countries) signed the **Louvre Accord** to establish acceptable ranges (not disclosed to the public) for the dollar's value relative to other currencies. The Federal Reserve intervened heavily in the foreign exchange market for two years after the Louvre Accord, but it has generally intervened only in small doses in recent years. Thus, recent central bank intervention policy has been similar to the policy that existed before the Louvre Accord.

Intervention as a Policy Tool

The government of any country can implement its own fiscal and monetary policies to control its economy. In addition, it may attempt to influence the value of its home currency in order to improve its economy, weakening its currency under some conditions and strengthening it under others. In essence, the exchange rate becomes a tool, like tax laws and the money supply, that the government can use to achieve its desired economic objectives.

Influence of a Weak Home Currency on the Economy

A weak home currency can stimulate foreign demand for products. A weak dollar, for example, can substantially boost U.S. exports and U.S. jobs. In addition, it may also reduce U.S. imports.

Though a weak currency can reduce unemployment at home, it can lead to higher inflation. In the early 1990s, the U.S. dollar was weak, causing U.S. imports from foreign countries to be highly priced. This situation priced firms such as Bayer, Volkswagen, and Volvo out of the U.S. market. Under these conditions, U.S. companies were able to raise their domestic prices because it was difficult for foreign producers to compete. In addition, U.S. firms that are heavy exporters, such as Goodyear Tire & Rubber Co., Litton Industries, Merck, and Maytag Corp., also benefit from a weaker dollar.

Influence of a Strong Home Currency on the Economy

A strong home currency can encourage consumers and corporations of that country to buy goods from other countries. This situation intensifies foreign competition and forces domestic producers to refrain from increasing prices. Therefore, the country's overall inflation rate should be lower if its currency is stronger, other things being equal.

Though a strong currency is a possible cure for high inflation, it may cause higher unemployment due to the attractive foreign prices that result from a strong home currency. The ideal value of the currency depends on the perspective of the country and the officials who must make these decisions. The strength or weakness of a currency is just one of many factors that influence a country's economic conditions.

By combining this discussion of how exchange rates affect inflation with the discussion in Chapter 4 of how inflation can affect exchange rates, a more complete picture of the dynamics of the exchange rate–inflation relationship can be achieved. A weak dollar places upward pressure on U.S. inflation, which in turn places further downward pressure on the value of the dollar. A strong dollar places downward pressure on inflation and on U.S. economic growth, which in turn places further upward pressure on the dollar's value.

The interaction among exchange rates, government policies, and economic factors is illustrated in Exhibit 6.4. As already mentioned, factors other than the home currency's strength affect unemployment and/or inflation. Likewise, factors other than unemployment and the inflation level influence a currency's strength. The cycles that have been described here will often be interrupted by these other factors and therefore will not continue indefinitely.

Exhibit 6.4
Impact of Government Actions on Exchange Rates

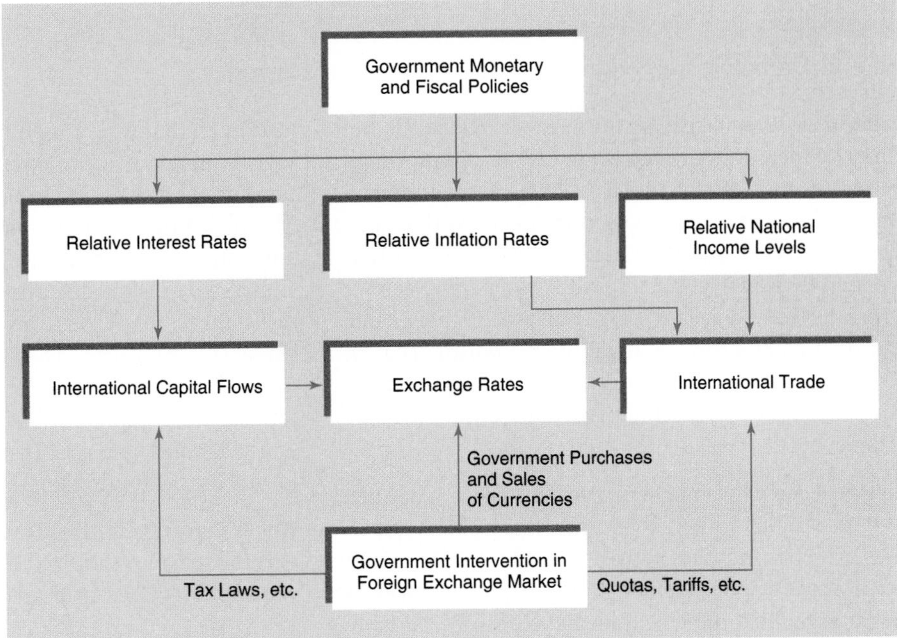

SUMMARY

- Exchange rate systems can be classified as fixed rate, freely floating, managed float, and pegged. In a fixed exchange rate system, exchange rates are either held constant or allowed to fluctuate only within very narrow boundaries. In a freely floating exchange rate system, exchange rate values are determined by market forces without intervention. In a managed float system, exchange rates are not restricted by boundaries but are subject to government intervention. In a pegged exchange rate system, a currency's value is pegged to a foreign currency or a unit of account and moves in line with that currency (or unit of account) against other currencies.

- Governments can use direct intervention by purchasing or selling currencies in the foreign exchange market, thereby affecting demand and supply conditions and, in turn, affecting the equilibrium values of the currencies. When a government purchases a currency in the foreign exchange market, it puts upward pressure on the currency's equilibrium value. When a government sells a currency in the foreign exchange market, it puts downward pressure on the currency's equilibrium value.

- Governments can use indirect intervention by influencing the economic factors that affect equilibrium exchange rates.

- When government intervention is used to weaken the U.S. dollar, the weak dollar can stimulate the U.S. economy by reducing the U.S. demand for imports and increasing the foreign demand for U.S. exports. Thus, the weak dollar tends to reduce U.S. unemployment, but it can increase U.S. inflation.

  When government intervention is used to strengthen the U.S. dollar, the strong dollar can increase the U.S. demand for imports, thereby intensifying foreign competition. The strong dollar can reduce U.S. inflation but may cause a higher level of U.S. unemployment.

POINT COUNTER-POINT

Should China Be Forced to Alter the Value of Its Currency?

Point In 2004, some U.S. politicians wanted to pressure China to increase the value of the Chinese yuan, which is tied to the U.S. dollar. They claimed that the yuan was the cause of the large U.S. trade deficit with China. This issue is periodically raised not only with currencies tied to the dollar, but also with currencies that have a floating rate. Some critics argue that the exchange rate can be used as a form of trade protectionism. That is, a country can discourage or prevent imports and encourage exports by keeping the value of its currency artificially low.

Counter-Point China might counter that its large balance of trade surplus with the United States has been due to the difference in prices between the two countries and that it should not be blamed for the high U.S. prices. It might argue that the U.S. trade deficit can be partially attributed to the very high prices in the United States, which are necessary to cover the excessive compensation for executives and other employees at U.S. firms. The high prices in the United States encourage firms and consumers to purchase goods from China. Even if China's yuan is revalued upward, this does not necessarily mean that U.S. firms and consumers will purchase U.S. products. They may shift their purchases from China to Indonesia or other low-wage countries rather than buy more U.S. products. Thus, the underlying dilemma is not China, but any country that has lower costs of production than the United States.

Who Is Correct? Use InfoTrac or some other search engine to learn more about this issue. Which argument do you support? Offer your own opinion on this issue.

SELF TEST

Answers are provided in Appendix A at the back of the text.

1. Explain why it would be virtually impossible to set an exchange rate between the Japanese yen and the dollar and to maintain a fixed exchange rate.
2. Assume the Federal Reserve believes that the dollar should be weakened against the Mexican peso. Explain how the Fed could use direct and indirect intervention to weaken the dollar's value with respect to the peso. Assume that future inflation in the United States is expected to be low, regardless of the Fed's actions.
3. Briefly explain why the Federal Reserve may attempt to weaken the dollar.

QUESTIONS AND APPLICATIONS

1. **Exchange Rate Systems.** Compare and contrast the fixed, freely floating, and managed float exchange rate systems. What are some advantages and disadvantages of a freely floating exchange rate system versus a fixed exchange rate system?
2. **Intervention with Euros.** Assume that Belgium, one of the European countries that uses the euro as its currency, would prefer that its currency depreciate against the dollar. Can it apply central bank intervention to achieve this objective? Explain.
3. **Direct Intervention.** How can a central bank use direct intervention to change the value of a currency? Explain why a central bank may desire to smooth exchange rate movements of its currency.
4. **Indirect Intervention.** How can a central bank use indirect intervention to change the value of a currency?
5. **Intervention Effects.** Assume there is concern that the United States may experience a recession. How

should the Federal Reserve influence the dollar to prevent a recession? How might U.S. exporters react to this policy (favorably or unfavorably)? What about U.S. importing firms?

6. **Currency Effects on Economy.** What is the impact of a weak home currency on the home economy, other things being equal? What is the impact of a strong home currency on the home economy, other things being equal?

7. **Feedback Effects.** Explain the potential feedback effects of a currency's changing value on inflation.

8. **Indirect Intervention.** Why would the Fed's indirect intervention have a stronger impact on some currencies than others? Why would a central bank's indirect intervention have a stronger impact than its direct intervention?

9. **Effects on Currencies Tied to the Dollar.** The Hong Kong dollar's value is tied to the U.S. dollar. Explain how the following trade patterns would be affected by the appreciation of the Japanese yen against the dollar: (a) Hong Kong exports to Japan and (b) Hong Kong exports to the United States.

10. **Intervention Effects on Bond Prices.** U.S. bond prices are normally inversely related to U.S. inflation. If the Fed planned to use intervention to weaken the dollar, how might bond prices be affected?

11. **Direct Intervention in Europe.** If most countries in Europe experience a recession, how might the European Central Bank use direct intervention to stimulate economic growth?

12. **Sterilized Intervention.** Explain the difference between sterilized and nonsterilized intervention.

13. **Effects of Indirect Intervention.** Suppose that the government of Chile reduces one of its key interest rates. The values of several other Latin American currencies are expected to change substantially against the Chilean peso in response to the news.

    a. Explain why other Latin American currencies could be affected by a cut in Chile's interest rates.

    b. How would the central banks of other Latin American countries likely adjust their interest rates? How would the currencies of these countries respond to the central bank interventions?

    c. How would a U.S. firm that exports products to Latin American countries be affected by the central bank interventions? (Assume the exports are denominated in the corresponding Latin American currency for each country.)

14. **Freely Floating Exchange Rates.** Should the governments of Asian countries allow their currencies to float freely? What would be the advantages of letting their currencies float freely? What would be the disadvantages?

15. **Indirect Intervention.** During the Asian crisis, some Asian central banks raised their interest rates to prevent their currencies from weakening. Yet, the currencies weakened anyway. Offer your opinion as to why the central banks' efforts at indirect intervention did not work.

ADVANCED QUESTIONS

16. **Monitoring of the Fed's Intervention.** Why do foreign market participants attempt to monitor the Fed's direct intervention efforts? How does the Fed attempt to hide its intervention actions? The media frequently report that "the dollar's value strengthened against many currencies in response to the Federal Reserve's plan to increase interest rates." Explain why the dollar's value may change even before the Federal Reserve affects interest rates.

17. **Effects of September 11.** Within a few days after the September 11, 2001 terrorist attack on the United States, the Federal Reserve reduced short-term interest rates to stimulate the U.S. economy. How might this action have affected the foreign flow of funds into the United States and affected the value of the dollar? How could such an effect on the dollar have increased the probability that the U.S. economy would strengthen?

18. **Intervention Effects on Corporate Performance.** Assume you have a subsidiary in Australia. The subsidiary sells mobile homes to local consumers in Australia, who buy the homes using mostly borrowed funds from local banks. Your subsidiary purchases all of its materials from Hong Kong. The Hong Kong dollar is tied to the U.S. dollar. Your subsidiary borrowed funds from the U.S. parent, and must pay the parent $100,000 in interest each month. Australia has just raised its interest rate in order to boost the value of its currency (Australian dollar, A$). The Australian dollar appreciates against the dollar as a result. Explain whether

these actions would increase, reduce, or have no effect on:

a. The volume of your subsidiary's sales in Australia (measured in A$).

b. The cost to your subsidiary of purchasing materials (measured in A$).

c. The cost to your subsidiary of making the interest payments to the U.S. parent (measured in A$).

Briefly explain each answer.

19. **Pegged Currencies.** Why do you think a country suddenly decides to peg its currency to the dollar or some other currency? When a currency is unable to maintain the peg, what do you think are the typical forces that break the peg?

20. **Impact of Intervention on Currency Option Premiums.** Assume that the central bank of the country Zakow periodically intervenes in the foreign exchange market to prevent large upward or downward fluctuations in its currency (called the zak) against the U.S. dollar. Today, the central bank announced that it will no longer intervene in the foreign exchange market. The spot rate of the zak against the dollar was not affected by this news. Will the news affect the premium on currency call options that are traded on the zak? Will the news affect the premium on currency put options that are traded on the zak? Explain.

INTERNET APPLICATION

21. **Bank of Japan.** The website for Japan's central bank, the Bank of Japan, provides information about its mission and its policy actions. Its address is **http://www.boj.or.jp/en/index.htm**.

a. Use this website to summarize the mission of the Bank of Japan. How does this mission relate to intervening in the foreign exchange market?

b. Review the minutes of recent meetings by Bank of Japan officials. Summarize at least one recent meeting that was associated with possible or actual intervention to affect the yen's value.

c. Why might the foreign exchange intervention strategies of the Bank of Japan be relevant to the U.S. government and to U.S.-based MNCs?

DISCUSSION IN THE BOARDROOM

This exercise can be found in Appendix E at the back of this textbook.

RUNNING YOUR OWN MNC

This exercise can be found on the Xtra! website at **http://maduraxtra.swlearning.com**.

BLADES, INC. CASE

Assessment of Government Influence on Exchange Rates

Recall that Blades, the U.S. manufacturer of roller blades, generates most of its revenue and incurs most of its expenses in the United States. However, the company has recently begun exporting roller blades to Thailand. The company has an agreement with Entertainment Products, Inc., a Thai importer, for a three-year period. According to the terms of the agreement, Entertainment Products will purchase 180,000 pairs of "Speedos," Blades' primary product, annually at a fixed price of 4,594 Thai baht per pair. Due to quality and cost considerations, Blades is also importing certain rubber and plastic components from a Thai exporter. The cost of these components is approximately 2,871 Thai baht per pair of Speedos. No contractual agreement exists between Blades, Inc., and the Thai exporter. Consequently, the cost of the rubber and plastic components imported from Thailand is subject not only to exchange rate considerations but to economic conditions (such as inflation) in Thailand as well.

Shortly after Blades began exporting to and importing from Thailand, Asia experienced weak economic conditions. Consequently, foreign investors in Thailand feared the baht's potential weakness and withdrew their investments, resulting in an excess supply of Thai baht for sale. Because of the resulting downward pressure on the baht's value, the Thai government attempted to stabilize the baht's exchange rate. To maintain the baht's value, the Thai government intervened in the foreign exchange market. Specifically, it swapped its baht reserves for dollar reserves at other central banks and then used its dollar reserves to purchase the baht in the foreign exchange market. However, this agreement required Thailand to reverse this transaction by exchanging dollars for baht at a future date. Unfortunately, the Thai government's intervention was unsuccessful, as it was overwhelmed by market forces. Consequently, the Thai government ceased its intervention efforts, and the value of the Thai baht declined substantially against the dollar over a three-month period.

When the Thai government stopped intervening in the foreign exchange market, Ben Holt, Blades' CFO, was concerned that the value of the Thai baht would continue to decline indefinitely. Since Blades generates net inflow in Thai baht, this would seriously affect the company's profit margin. Furthermore, one of the reasons Blades had expanded into Thailand was to appease the company's shareholders. At last year's annual shareholder meeting, they had demanded that senior management take action to improve the firm's low profit margins. Expanding into Thailand had been Holt's suggestion, and he is now afraid that his career might be at stake. For these reasons, Holt feels that the Asian crisis and its impact on Blades demand his serious attention. One of the factors Holt thinks he should consider is the issue of government intervention and how it could affect Blades in particular. Specifically, he wonders whether the decision to enter into a fixed agreement with Entertainment Products was a good idea under the circumstances. Another issue is how the future completion of the swap agreement initiated by the Thai government will affect Blades. To address these issues and to gain a little more understanding of the process of government intervention, Holt has prepared the following list of questions for you, Blades' financial analyst, since he knows that you understand international financial management.

1. Did the intervention effort by the Thai government constitute direct or indirect intervention? Explain.
2. Did the intervention by the Thai government constitute sterilized or nonsterilized intervention? What is the difference between the two types of intervention? Which type do you think would be more effective in increasing the value of the baht? Why? (Hint: Think about the effect of nonsterilized intervention on U.S. interest rates.)
3. If the Thai baht is virtually fixed with respect to the dollar, how could this affect U.S. levels of inflation? Do you think these effects on the U.S. economy will be more pronounced for companies such as Blades that operate under trade arrangements involving commitments or for firms that do not? How are companies such as Blades affected by a fixed exchange rate?
4. What are some of the potential disadvantages for Thai levels of inflation associated with the floating exchange rate system that is now used in Thailand? Do you think Blades contributes to these disadvantages to a great extent? How are companies such as Blades affected by a freely floating exchange rate?
5. What do you think will happen to the Thai baht's value when the swap arrangement is completed? How will this affect Blades?

SMALL BUSINESS DILEMMA

Assessment of Central Bank Intervention by the Sports Exports Company

Jim Logan, owner of the Sports Exports Company, is concerned about the value of the British pound over time because his firm receives pounds as payment for footballs exported to the United Kingdom. He recently read that the Bank of England (the central bank of the United Kingdom) is likely to intervene directly in the foreign exchange market by flooding the market with British pounds.

1. Forecast whether the British pound will weaken or strengthen based on the information provided.
2. How would the performance of the Sports Exports Company be affected by the Bank of England's policy of flooding the foreign exchange market with British pounds (assuming that it does not hedge its exchange rate risk)?

APPENDIX 6

Government Intervention during the Asian Crisis

From 1990 to 1997, Asian countries achieved higher economic growth than any other countries. They were viewed as models for advances in technology and economic improvement. In the summer and fall of 1997, however, they experienced financial problems, leading to what is commonly referred to as the "Asian crisis," and resulting in bailouts of several countries by the International Monetary Fund (IMF).

Much of the crisis is attributed to the substantial depreciation of Asian currencies, which caused severe financial problems for firms and governments throughout Asia, as well as some other regions. This crisis demonstrated how exchange rate movements can affect country conditions and therefore affect the firms that operate in those countries.

The specific objectives of this appendix are to describe the conditions in the foreign exchange market that contributed to the Asian crisis, explain how governments intervened in an attempt to control their exchange rates, and describe the consequences of their intervention efforts.

Crisis in Thailand

Until July 1997, Thailand was one of the world's fastest growing economies. In fact, Thailand grew faster than any other country over the 1985-1994 period. Thai consumers spent freely, which resulted in lower savings compared to other Southeast Asian countries. The high level of spending and low level of saving put upward pressure on prices of real estate and products and on the local interest rate. Normally, countries with high inflation tend to have weak currencies because of forces from purchasing power parity. Prior to July 1997, however, Thailand's currency was linked to the dollar, which made Thailand an attractive site for foreign investors; they could earn a high interest rate on invested funds while being protected (until the crisis) from a large depreciation in the baht.

Bank Lending Situation

Normally, countries desire a large inflow of funds because it can help support the country's growth. In Thailand's case, however, the inflow of funds provided Thai banks with more funds than the banks could use for making loans. Consequently, in an attempt to use all the funds, the banks made many very risky loans. Commercial developers borrowed heavily without having to prove that the expansion was feasible. Lenders were willing to lend large sums of money based on the previous success of the developers. The loans may have seemed feasible based on the assumption that the economy would continue its high growth, but such high growth could not last forever. The corporate structure of Thailand also led to excessive lending. Many corporations are tied in with banks, such that some bank lending is not an "arms-length" business transaction, but a loan to a friend that needs funds.

Flow of Funds Situation

In addition to the lending situation, the large inflow of funds made Thailand more susceptible to a massive outflow of funds if foreign investors ever lost confidence in the Thai economy. Given the large amount of risky loans and the potential for a massive outflow of funds, Thailand was sometimes described as a "house of cards," waiting to collapse.

While the large inflow of funds put downward pressure on interest rates, the supply was offset by a strong demand for funds as developers and corporations sought to capitalize on the growth economy by expanding. Thailand's government was also borrowing heavily to improve the country's infrastructure. Thus, the massive borrowing was occurring at relatively high interest rates, making the debt expensive to the borrowers.

Export Competition

During the first half of 1997, the dollar strengthened against the Japanese yen and European currencies, which reduced the prices of Japanese and European imports. Although the dollar was linked to the baht over this period, Thailand's products were not priced as competitively to U.S. importers.

Pressure on the Thai Baht

The baht experienced downward pressure in July 1997 as some foreign investors recognized its potential weakness. The outflow of funds expedited the weakening of the baht, as foreign investors exchanged their baht for their home currencies. The baht's value relative to the dollar was pressured by the large sale of baht in exchange for dollars. On July 2, 1997, the baht was detached from the dollar. Thailand's central bank then attempted to maintain the baht's value by intervention. Specifically, it swapped its baht reserves for dollar reserves at other central banks and then used its dollar reserves to purchase the baht in the foreign exchange market (this swap agreement required Thailand to reverse this exchange by exchanging dollars for baht at a future date). The intervention was intended to offset the sales of baht by foreign investors in the foreign exchange market, but market forces overwhelmed the intervention efforts. As the supply of baht for sale exceeded the demand for baht in the foreign exchange market, the government eventually had to surrender in its effort to defend the baht's value. In July 1997, the value of the baht plummeted. Over a five-week period, it declined by more than 20 percent against the dollar.

Damage to Thailand

Thailand's central bank used more than $20 billion to purchase baht in the foreign exchange market as part of its direct intervention efforts. Due to the decline in the value of the baht, Thailand needed more baht to be exchanged for the dollars to repay the other central banks.

Thailand's banks estimated the amount of their defaulted loans at over $30 billion. Meanwhile, some corporations in Thailand had borrowed funds in other currencies (including the dollar) because the interest rates in Thailand were relatively high. This strategy backfired because the weakening of the baht forced these corporations to exchange larger amounts of baht for the currencies needed to pay off the loans. Consequently, the corporations incurred a much higher effective financing rate (which accounts for the exchange rate effect to determine the true cost of borrowing) than they would have paid if they had borrowed funds locally in Thailand. The higher borrowing cost was an additional strain on the corporations.

Rescue Package for Thailand

On August 5, 1997, the IMF and several countries agreed to provide Thailand with a $16 billion rescue package. Japan provided $4 billion, while the IMF provided $4 billion. At the time, this was the second largest bailout plan ever put together for a single country (Mexico had received a $50 billion bailout in 1994). In return for this monetary support, Thailand agreed to reduce its budget deficit, prevent inflation from rising above 9 percent, raise its value-added tax from 7 percent to 10 percent, and clean up the financial statements of the local banks, which had many undisclosed bad loans.

The rescue package took time to finalize because Thailand's government was unwilling to shut down all the banks that were experiencing financial problems as a result of their overly generous lending policies. Many critics have questioned the efficacy of the rescue package because some of the funding was misallocated due to corruption in Thailand.

Spread of the Crisis throughout Southeast Asia

The crisis in Thailand was contagious to other countries in Southeast Asia. The Southeast Asian economies are somewhat integrated because of the trade between countries. The crisis was expected to weaken Thailand's economy, which would result in a reduction in the demand for products produced in the other countries of Southeast Asia. As the demand for those countries' products declined, so would their national income and their demand for products from other Southeast Asian countries. Thus, the effects could perpetuate. Like Thailand, the other Southeast Asian countries had very high growth in recent years, which had led to overly optimistic assessments of future economic conditions and thus to excessive loans being extended for projects that had a high risk of default.

These countries were also similar to Thailand in that they had relatively high interest rates, and their governments tended to stabilize their currencies. Consequently, these countries had attracted a large amount of foreign investment as well. Thailand's crisis made foreign investors realize that such a crisis could also hit the other countries in Southeast Asia. Consequently, they began to withdraw funds from these countries.

Effects on Other Asian Currencies

In July and August of 1997, the values of the Malaysian ringgit, Singapore dollar, Philippine peso, Taiwan dollar, and Indonesian rupiah also declined. The Philippine peso was devalued in July. Malaysia initially attempted to maintain the ringgit's value within a narrow band but then surrendered and let the ringgit float to its market-determined level.

In August 1997, Bank Indonesia (the central bank) used more than $500 million in direct intervention to purchase rupiah in the foreign exchange market in an attempt to boost the value of the rupiah. By mid-August, however, it gave up its effort to maintain the rupiah's value within a band and let the rupiah float to its natural level. This decision by Bank Indonesia to let the rupiah float may have been influenced by the failure of Thailand's costly efforts to maintain the baht. The market forces were too strong and could not be offset by direct intervention. On October 30, 1997, a rescue package for Indonesia was announced, but the IMF and Indonesia's government did not agree on the terms of the $43 billion package until the spring of 1998. One of the main points of contention was that President Suharto wanted to peg the rupiah's exchange rate, but the IMF believed that Bank Indonesia would not be able to maintain the rupiah's exchange rate at a fixed level and that it would come under renewed speculative attack.

As the Southeast Asian countries gave up their fight to maintain their currencies within bands, they imposed restrictions on their forward and futures markets to prevent excessive speculation. For example, Indonesia and Malaysia imposed a limit on the size of forward contracts created by banks for foreign residents. These actions limited the degree to which speculators could sell these currencies forward based on expectations that the currencies would weaken over time. In general, efforts to protect the currencies failed because investors and firms had no confidence that the fundamental factors causing weakness in the currencies were being corrected. Therefore, the flow of funds out of the Asian countries continued; this outflow led to even more sales of Asian currencies in exchange for other currencies, which put additional downward pressure on the values of the currencies.

Effects on Financing Expenses

As the values of the Southeast Asian currencies declined, speculators responded by withdrawing more of their funds from these countries, which led to further weakness in the currencies. As in Thailand, many corporations had borrowed in other countries (such as the United States) where interest rates were relatively low. The decline in the values of their local currencies caused the corporations' effective rate of financing to be excessive, which strained their cash flow situation.

Due to the integration of Southeast Asian economies, the excessive lending by the local banks across the countries, and the susceptibility of all these countries to massive fund outflows, the crisis was not really focused on one country. What was initially referred to as the Thailand crisis became the Asian crisis.

Impact of the Asian Crisis on Hong Kong

On October 23, 1997, prices in the Hong Kong stock market declined by 10.2 percent on average; considering the three trading days before that, the cumulative four-day effect was a decline of 23.3 percent. The decline was primarily attributed to speculation that Hong Kong's currency might be devalued and that Hong Kong could experience financial problems similar to the Southeast Asian countries. The fact that the market value of Hong Kong companies could decline by almost one-fourth over a four-day period demonstrated the perceived exposure of Hong Kong to the crisis.

During this period, Hong Kong maintained its pegged exchange rate system with the Hong Kong dollar tied to the U.S. dollar. However, it had to increase interest rates to discourage investors from transferring their funds out of the country.

Impact of the Asian Crisis on Russia

The Asian crisis caused investors to reconsider other countries where similar effects might occur. In particular, they focused on Russia. As investors lost confidence in the Russian currency (the ruble), they began to transfer funds out of Russia. In response to the downward pressure this outflow of funds placed on the ruble, the central bank of Russia engaged in direct intervention by using dollars to purchase rubles in the foreign exchange market. It also used indirect intervention by raising interest rates to make Russia more attractive to investors, thereby discouraging additional outflows.

In July 1998, the IMF (with some help from Japan and the World Bank) organized a loan package worth $22.6 billion for Russia. The package required that Russia boost its tax revenue, reduce its budget deficit, and create a more capitalist environment for its businesses.

During August 1998, Russia's central bank commonly intervened to prevent the ruble from declining substantially. On August 26, however, it gave up its fight to defend the ruble's value, and market forces caused the ruble to decline by more than 50 percent against most currencies on that day. This led to fears of a new crisis, and the next day (called "Bloody Thursday"), paranoia swept stock markets around the world. Some stock markets (including the U.S. stock market) experienced declines of more than 4 percent.

Impact of the Asian Crisis on South Korea

By November 1997, seven of South Korea's conglomerates (called *chaebols*) had collapsed. The banks that financed the operations of the chaebols were stuck with the equivalent of $52 billion in bad debt as a result. Like banks in the Southeast Asian countries, South Korea's banks had been too willing to provide loans to corporations (especially the chaebols) without conducting a thorough credit analysis. The banks had apparently engaged in such risky lending because they assumed that economic growth would continue at a rapid pace and therefore exaggerated the future cash flows that borrowers would have available to pay off their loans. In addition, South Korean banks had traditionally extended loans to the conglomerates without assessing whether the loans could be repaid. In November, South Korea's currency (the won) declined substantially, and the central bank attempted to use its reserves to prevent a free fall in the won but with little success. Meanwhile, the credit ratings of several banks were downgraded because of their bad loans.

On December 3, 1997, the IMF agreed to enact a $55 billion dollar rescue package for South Korea. The World Bank and the Asian Development Bank joined with the IMF to provide a standby credit line of $35 billion. If that amount was not sufficient, other countries (including Japan and the United States) had agreed to provide a credit line of $20 billion. The total available credit (assuming it was all used) exceeded the credit provided in the Mexican bailout of 1994 and made this the largest bailout ever. In exchange for the funding, South Korea agreed to reduce its economic growth and to restrict the conglomerates from excessive borrowing. This restriction resulted in some bankruptcies and unemployment, as the banks could not automatically provide loans to all conglomerates needing funds unless the funding was economically justified.

Impact of the Asian Crisis on Japan

Japan was also affected by the Asian crisis because it exports products to these countries, and many of its corporations have subsidiaries in these countries so their business performance is affected by the local economic conditions. Japan had also been experiencing its own problems. Its financial industry had been struggling, primarily because of defaulted loans. In November 1997, one of Japan's 20 largest banks failed. A week later, Yamaichi Securities Co. (a brokerage firm) announced that it would shut down. Yamaichi was the largest firm to fail in Japan since World War II. The news was shocking because the Japanese government had historically bailed out large firms such as Yamaichi because of the possible adverse effects on other firms. Yamaichi's collapse made market participants question the potential failure of other large financial institutions that were previously perceived to be protected ("too big to fail"). The continued weakening of the Japanese yen against the dollar during the spring of 1998 put more pressure on other Asian currencies; Asian countries wanted to gain a competitive advantage in exporting to the United States as a result of their weak currencies. In April 1998, the Bank of Japan used more than $20 billion to purchase yen in the foreign exchange market. This effort to boost the yen's value was unsuccessful. In July 1998, Prime Minister Hashimoto resigned, causing more uncertainty about the outlook for Japan.

Impact of the Asian Crisis on China

Ironically, China did not experience the adverse economic effects of the Asian crisis because it had grown less rapidly than the Southeast Asian countries in the years prior to the crisis. The Chinese government had more control over economic conditions because it still owned most real estate and still controlled most of the banks that provided credit to support growth. Thus, there were fewer bankruptcies resulting from the crisis in China. In addition, China's government was able to maintain the value of the yuan against the dollar, which limited speculative flows of funds out of China. Though interest rates increased during the crisis, they remained relatively low. Consequently Chinese firms could obtain funding at a reasonable cost and could continue to meet their interest payments.

Nevertheless, concerns about China mounted because it relies heavily on exports to stimulate its economy; China was now at a competitive disadvantage relative to the Southeast Asian countries whose currencies had depreciated. Thus, importers from the United States and Europe shifted some of their purchases to those countries. In addition, the decline in the other Asian currencies against the Chinese yuan encouraged Chinese consumers to purchase imports instead of locally manufactured products.

Impact of the Asian Crisis on Latin American Countries

The Asian crisis also affected Latin American countries. Countries such as Chile, Mexico, and Venezuela were adversely affected because they export products to Asia, and the weak Asian economies resulted in a lower demand for the Latin American exports. In addition, the Latin American countries lost some business to other countries that switched to Asian products because of the substantial depreciation of the Asian currencies, which made their products cheaper than those of Latin America.

The adverse effects on Latin American countries put pressure on Latin American currency values, as there was concern that speculative outflows of funds would weaken these currencies in the same way that Asian currencies had weakened. In particular, there was pressure on Brazil's currency (the real) in late October 1997. Some speculators believed that since most Asian countries could not maintain their currencies within bands under the existing conditions, Brazil would be unable to stabilize the value of its currency.

The central bank of Brazil used about $7 billion of reserves in a direct intervention to buy the real in the foreign exchange market and protect the real from depreciation. It also used indirect intervention by raising short-term interest rates in Brazil. This encouraged foreign investment in Brazil's short-term securities to capitalize on the high interest rates and also encouraged local investors to invest locally rather than in foreign markets. The adjustment of interest rates to maintain the value of the real signaled that the central bank of Brazil was serious about maintaining the currency's stability. The intervention was costly, however, because it increased the cost of borrowing for households, corporations, and government agencies in Brazil and thus could reduce economic growth. If Brazil's currency had weakened, the speculative forces might have spread to the other Latin American currencies as well.

The Asian crisis also caused bond ratings of many large corporations and government agencies in Latin America to be downgraded. Rumors that banks were dumping Asian bonds caused fears that all emerging market debt would be dumped in the bond markets. Furthermore, there was concern that many banks experiencing financial problems (because their loans were not being paid back) would sell bond holdings in the secondary market in order to raise funds. Consequently, prices of bonds issued in emerging markets declined, including those of Latin American countries.

Impact of the Asian Crisis on Europe

During the Asian crisis, European countries were experiencing strong economic growth. Many European firms, however, were adversely affected by the crisis. Like firms in Latin America, some firms in Europe experienced a reduced demand for their exports to Asia during the crisis. In addition, they lost some exporting business to Asian exporters as a result of the weakened Asian currencies that reduced Asian prices from an importer's perspective. European banks were especially affected by the Asian crisis because they had provided large loans to numerous Asian firms that defaulted.

Impact of the Asian Crisis on the United States

The effects of the Asian crisis were even felt in the United States. Stock values of U.S. firms, such as 3M Co., Motorola, Hewlett-Packard, and Nike, that conducted much business in Asia declined. Many U.S. engineering and construction firms were adversely affected as Asian countries reduced their plans to improve infrastructure. Stock values of U.S. exporters to those countries fell because of the decline in spending by consumers and corporations in Asian countries and because of the weakening of the Asian currencies, which made U.S. products more expensive. Some large U.S. commercial banks experienced significant stock price declines because of their exposure (primarily loans and bond holdings) to Asian countries.

Lessons about Exchange Rates and Intervention

The Asian crisis demonstrated the degree to which currencies could depreciate in response to a lack of confidence by investors and firms in a central bank's ability to stabilize its local currency. If investors and firms had believed the central banks could prevent the free fall in currency values, they would not have transferred their funds to other countries, and Southeast Asian currency values would not have experienced such downward pressure.

Exhibit 6A.1 shows how exchange rates of some Asian currencies changed against the U.S. dollar during one year of the crisis (from June 1997 to June 1998). In particular, the currencies of Indonesia, Malaysia, South Korea, and Thailand declined substantially.

The Asian crisis also demonstrated how interest rates could be affected by flows of funds out of countries. Exhibit 6A.2 illustrates how interest rates changed from June 1997 (just before the crisis) to June 1998 for various Asian countries. The increase in interest rates can be attributed to the indirect interventions intended to prevent the local currencies from depreciating further, or to the massive outflows of funds, or to both of these conditions. In particular, interest rates of Indonesia, Malaysia, and Thailand increased substantially from their pre-crisis levels. Those countries whose local currencies experienced more depreciation had higher upward adjustments. Since the substantial increase in interest rates (which tends to reduce economic growth) may have been caused by the outflow of funds, it may have been indirectly due to the lack of confidence by investors and firms in the ability of the Asian central banks to stabilize the local currencies.

Exhibit 6A.1

How Exchange Rates Changed during the Asian Crisis (June 1997–June 1998)

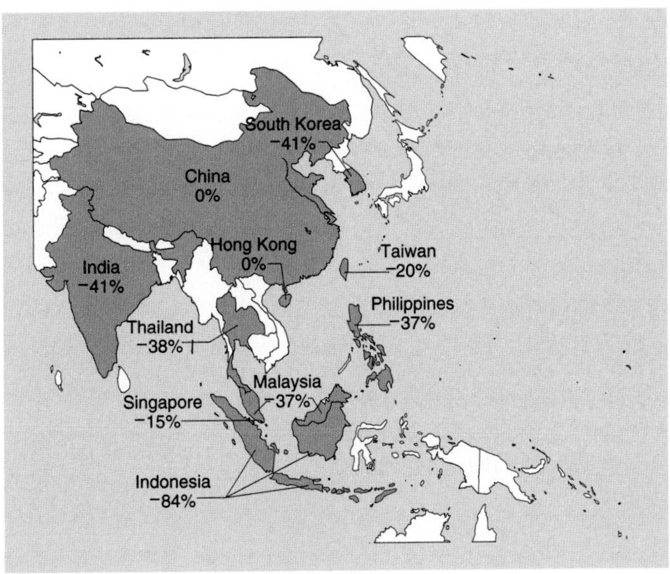

Exhibit 6A.2

How Interest Rates Changed during the Asian Crisis (Number before slash represents annualized interest rate as of June 1997; number after slash represents annualized interest rate as of June 1998)

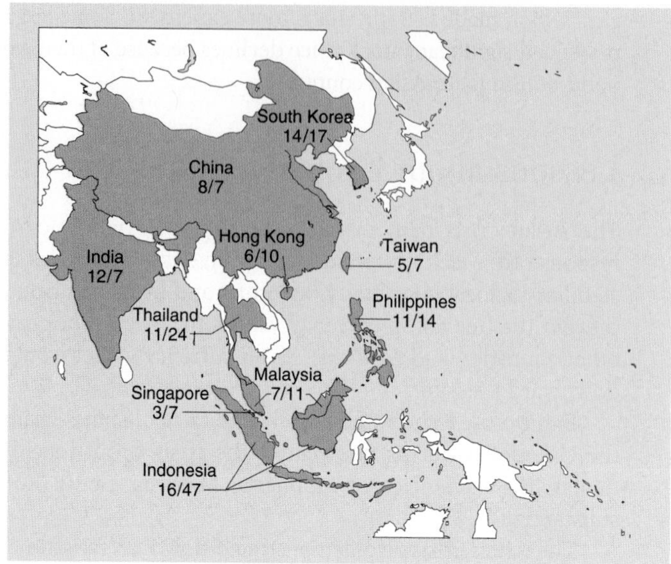

Finally, the Asian crisis demonstrated how integrated country economies are, especially during a crisis. Just as the U.S. and European economies can affect emerging markets, they are susceptible to conditions in emerging markets. Even if a central bank can withstand the pressure on its currency caused by conditions in other countries, it cannot necessarily insulate its economy from other countries that are experiencing financial problems.

DISCUSSION QUESTIONS

The following discussion questions related to the Asian crisis illustrate how the foreign exchange market conditions are integrated with the other financial markets around the world. Thus, participants in any of these markets must understand the dynamics of the foreign exchange market. These discussion questions can be used in several ways. They may serve as an assignment on a day that the professor is unable to attend class. They are especially useful for group exercises. The class could be segmented into small groups; each group is asked to assess all of the issues and determine a solution. Each group should have a spokesperson. For each issue, one of the groups will be randomly selected and asked to present their solution, and then other students not in that group may suggest alternative answers if they feel that the answer can be improved. Some of the issues have no perfect solution, which allows for different points of view to be presented by students.

1. Was the depreciation of the Asian currencies during the Asian crisis due to trade flows or capital flows? Why do you think the degree of movement over a short period may depend on whether the reason is trade flows or capital flows?
2. Why do you think the Indonesian rupiah was more exposed to an abrupt decline in value than the Japanese yen during the Asian crisis (even if their economies experienced the same degree of weakness)?
3. During the Asian crisis, direct intervention did not prevent depreciation of currencies. Offer your explanation for why the interventions did not work.
4. During the Asian crisis, some local firms in Asia borrowed dollars rather than local currency to support local operations. Why would they borrow dol-

lars when they really needed their local currency to support operations? Why did this strategy backfire?

5. The Asian crisis showed that a currency crisis could affect interest rates. Why did the crisis put upward pressure on interest rates in Asian countries? Why did it put downward pressure on U.S. interest rates?

6. According to the international Fisher effect, high interest rates reflect high expected inflation, and can signal future weakness in a currency. Based on this theory, how would expectations of Asian exchange rates change after interest rates in Asia increased? Why? Is the underlying reason logical?

7. During the Asian crisis, why did the discount of the forward rate of Asian currencies change? Do you think it increased or decreased? Why?

8. During the Hong Kong crisis, the Hong Kong stock market declined substantially over a four-day period due to concerns in the foreign exchange market. Why would stock prices decline due to concerns in the foreign exchange market? Why would some countries be more susceptible to this type of situation than others?

9. On August 26, 1998, the day that Russia decided to let the ruble float freely, the ruble declined by about 50 percent. On the following day, called "Bloody Thursday," stock markets around the world (including the United States) declined by more than 4 percent. Why do you think the decline in the ruble had such a global impact on stock prices? Was the markets' reaction rational? Would the effect have been different if the ruble's plunge had occurred in an earlier time period, such as four years earlier? Why?

10. Normally, a weak local currency is expected to stimulate the local economy. Yet, it appeared that the weak currencies of Asia adversely affected their economies. Why do you think the weakening of the currencies did not initially improve their economies during the Asian crisis?

11. During the Asian crisis, Hong Kong and China successfully intervened (by raising their interest rates) to protect their local currencies from depreciating. Nevertheless, these countries were also adversely affected by the Asian crisis. Why do you think the actions to protect the values of their currencies affected these countries' economies? Why do you think the weakness of other Asian currencies against the dollar and the stability of the Chinese and Hong Kong currencies against the dollar adversely affected their economies?

12. Why do you think the values of bonds issued by Asian governments declined during the Asian crisis? Why do you think the values of Latin American bonds declined in response to the Asian crisis?

13. Why do you think the depreciation of the Asian currencies adversely affected U.S. firms? (There are at least three reasons, each related to a different type of exposure of some U.S. firms to exchange rate risk.)

14. During the Asian crisis, the currencies of many Asian countries declined even though their governments attempted to intervene with direct intervention or by raising interest rates. Given that the abrupt depreciation of the currencies was attributed to an abrupt outflow of funds in the financial markets, what alternative Asian government action might have been more successful in preventing a substantial decline in the currencies' values? Are there any possible adverse effects of your proposed solution?

CHAPTER 7

International Arbitrage and Interest Rate Parity

If discrepancies occur within the foreign exchange market, with quoted prices of currencies varying from what the market prices should be, certain market forces will realign the rates. The realignment occurs as a result of international arbitrage. Financial managers of MNCs must understand how international arbitrage realigns exchange rates because it has implications for how they should use the foreign exchange market to facilitate their international business.

The specific objectives of this chapter are to:

- explain the conditions that will result in various forms of international arbitrage, along with the realignments that will occur in response to various forms of international arbitrage, and
- explain the concept of interest rate parity and how it prevents arbitrage opportunities.

International Arbitrage

Arbitrage can be loosely defined as capitalizing on a discrepancy in quoted prices by making a riskless profit. In many cases, the strategy does not require an investment of funds to be tied up for a length of time and does not involve any risk.

EXAMPLE

Two coin shops buy and sell coins. If Shop A is willing to sell a particular coin for $120, while Shop B is willing to buy that same coin for $130, a person can execute arbitrage by purchasing the coin at Shop A for $120 and selling it to Shop B for $130. The prices at coin shops can vary because demand conditions may vary among shop locations. If two coin shops are not aware of each other's prices, the opportunity for arbitrage may occur.

The act of arbitrage will cause prices to realign. In our example, arbitrage would cause Shop A to raise its price (due to high demand for the coin). At the same time, Shop B would reduce its bid price after receiving a surplus of coins as arbitrage occurs. The type of arbitrage discussed in this chapter is primarily international in scope; it is applied to foreign exchange and international money markets and takes three common forms:

- Locational arbitrage
- Triangular arbitrage
- Covered interest arbitrage

Each form will be discussed in turn.

Locational Arbitrage

Commercial banks providing foreign exchange services normally quote about the same rates on currencies, so shopping around may not necessarily lead to a more favorable rate. If the demand and supply conditions for a particular currency vary among banks, the banks may price that currency at different rates, and market forces will force realignment.

When quoted exchange rates vary among locations, participants in the foreign exchange market can capitalize on the discrepancy. Specifically, they can use **locational arbitrage**, which is the process of buying a currency at the location where it is priced cheap and immediately selling it at another location where it is priced higher.

EXAMPLE

Akron Bank and Zyn Bank serve the foreign exchange market by buying and selling currencies. Assume that there is no bid/ask spread. The exchange rate quoted at Akron Bank for a British pound is $1.60, while the exchange rate quoted at Zyn Bank is $1.61. You could conduct locational arbitrage by purchasing pounds at Akron Bank for $1.60 per pound and then selling them at Zyn Bank for $1.61 per pound. Under the condition that there is no bid/ask spread and there are no other costs to conducting this arbitrage strategy, your gain would be $.01 per pound. The gain is risk-free in that you knew when you purchased the pounds how much you could sell them for. Also, you did not have to tie your funds up for any length of time.

Locational arbitrage is normally conducted by banks or other foreign exchange dealers whose computers can continuously monitor the quotes provided by other banks. If other banks noticed a discrepancy between Akron Bank and Zyn Bank, they would quickly engage in locational arbitrage to earn an immediate risk-free profit. Since banks have a bid/ask spread on currencies, this next example accounts for the spread.

EXAMPLE

The information on British pounds at both banks is revised to include the bid/ask spread in Exhibit 7.1. Based on these quotes, you can no longer profit from locational arbitrage. If you buy pounds from Akron Bank at $1.61 (the bank's ask price) and then sell the pounds at Zyn Bank at its bid price of $1.61, you just break even. As this example demonstrates, even when the bid or ask prices of two banks are different, locational arbitrage will not always be possible. To achieve profits from locational arbitrage, the bid price of one bank must be higher than the ask price of another bank.

Exhibit 7.1
Currency Quotes for Locational Arbitrage Example

	Akron Bank			Zyn Bank	
	Bid	Ask		Bid	Ask
British pound quote	$1.60	$1.61	British pound quote	$1.61	$1.62

Gains from Locational Arbitrage. Your gain from locational arbitrage is based on the amount of money that you use to capitalize on the exchange rate discrepancy, along with the size of the discrepancy.

The quotations for the New Zealand dollar (NZ$) at two banks are shown in Exhibit 7.2. You can obtain New Zealand dollars from North Bank at the ask price of $.640 and then sell New Zealand dollars to South Bank at the bid price of $.645. This represents one "round-trip" transaction in locational arbitrage. If you start with $10,000 and conduct one round-trip transaction, how many U.S. dollars will you end up with? The $10,000 is initially exchanged for NZ$15,625 ($10,000/$.640 per New Zealand dollar) at North Bank. Then the NZ$15,625 are sold for $.645 each, for a total of $10,078. Thus, your gain from locational arbitrage is $78.

Your gain may appear to be small relative to your investment of $10,000. However, consider that you did not have to tie up your funds. Your round-trip transaction could take place over a telecommunications network within a matter of seconds. Also, if you could use a larger sum of money for the transaction, your gains would be larger. Finally, you could continue to repeat your round-trip transactions until North Bank's ask price is no longer less than South Bank's bid price.

This example is not intended to suggest that you can pay for your education through part-time locational arbitrage. As mentioned earlier, foreign exchange dealers compare quotes from banks on computer terminals, which immediately signal any opportunity to employ locational arbitrage.

Exhibit 7.2
Locational Arbitrage

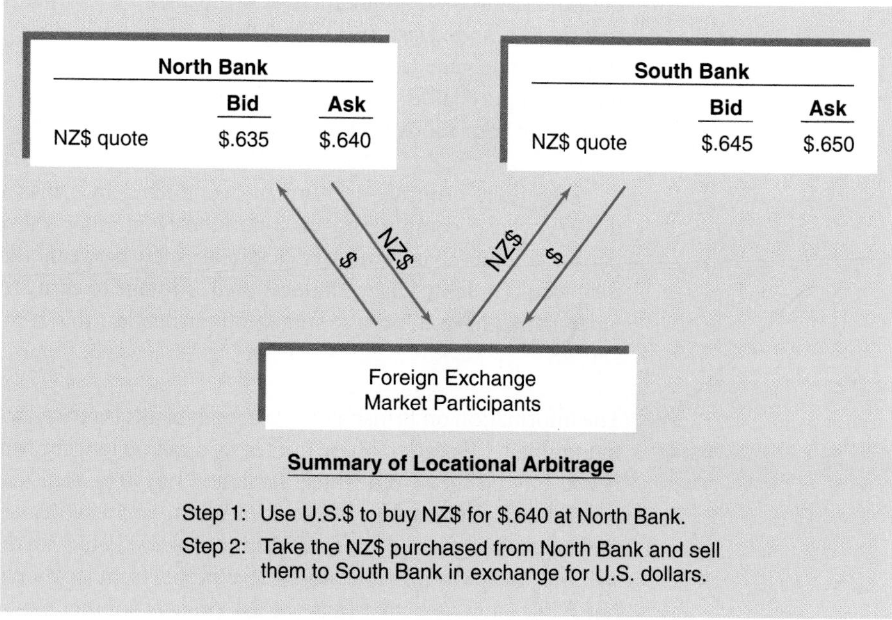

Realignment due to Locational Arbitrage. Quoted prices will react to the locational arbitrage strategy used by you and other foreign exchange market participants.

EXAMPLE

In the previous example, the high demand for New Zealand dollars at North Bank (resulting from arbitrage activity) will cause a shortage of New Zealand dollars there. As a result of this shortage, North Bank will raise its ask price for New Zealand dollars. The excess supply of New Zealand dollars at South Bank (resulting from sales of New Zealand dollars to South Bank in exchange for U.S. dollars) will force South Bank to lower its bid price. As the currency prices are adjusted, gains from locational arbitrage will be reduced. Once the ask price of North Bank is not any lower than the bid price of South Bank, locational arbitrage will no longer occur. Prices may adjust in a matter of seconds or minutes from the time when locational arbitrage occurs.

The concept of locational arbitrage is relevant in that it explains why exchange rate quotations among banks at different locations normally will not differ by a significant amount. This applies not only to banks on the same street or within the same city but to all banks across the world. Technology allows banks to be electronically connected to foreign exchange quotations at any time. Thus, banks can ensure that their quotes are in line with those of other banks. They can also immediately detect any discrepancies among quotations as soon as they occur, and capitalize on those discrepancies. Thus, technology enables more consistent prices among banks and reduces the likelihood of significant discrepancies in foreign exchange quotations among locations.

The site at http://finance.yahoo.com/currency?u provides a currency converter for over 100 currencies with frequent daily foreign exchange rate updates.

Triangular Arbitrage

Cross exchange rates represent the relationship between two currencies that are different from one's base currency. In the United States, the term *cross exchange rate* refers to the relationship between two nondollar currencies.

EXAMPLE

If the British pound (£) is worth \$1.60, while the Canadian dollar (C\$) is worth \$.80, the value of the British pound with respect to the Canadian dollar is calculated as follows:

$$\text{Value of £ in units of C\$} = \$1.60/\$.80 = 2.0$$

The value of the Canadian dollar in units of pounds can also be determined from the cross exchange rate formula:

$$\text{Value of C\$ in units of £} = \$.80/\$1.60 = .50$$

Notice that the value of a Canadian dollar in units of pounds is simply the reciprocal of the value of a pound in units of Canadian dollars.

If a quoted cross exchange rate differs from the appropriate cross exchange rate (as determined by the preceding formula), you can attempt to capitalize on the discrepancy. Specifically, you can use **triangular arbitrage**, in which currency transactions are conducted in the spot market to capitalize on a discrepancy in the cross exchange rate between two currencies.

EXAMPLE

Assume that a bank has quoted the British pound (£) at $1.60, the Malaysian ringgit (MYR) at $.20, and the cross exchange rate at £1 = MYR8.1. Your first task is to use the pound value in U.S. dollars and Malaysian ringgit value in U.S. dollars to develop the cross exchange rate that should exist between the pound and the Malaysian ringgit. The cross rate formula in the previous example reveals that the pound should be worth MYR8.0.

When quoting a cross exchange rate of £1 = MYR8.1, the bank is exchanging too many ringgit for a pound and is asking for too many ringgit in exchange for a pound. Based on this information, you can engage in triangular arbitrage by purchasing pounds with dollars, converting the pounds to ringgit, and then exchanging the ringgit for dollars. If you have $10,000, how many dollars will you end up with if you implement this triangular arbitrage strategy? To answer the question, consider the following steps:

1. Determine the number of pounds received for your dollars: $10,000 = £6,250, based on the bank's quote of $1.60 per pound.
2. Determine how many ringgit you will receive in exchange for pounds: £6,250 = MYR50,625, based on the bank's quote of 8.1 ringgit per pound.
3. Determine how many U.S. dollars you will receive in exchange for the ringgit: MYR50,625 = $10,125 based on the bank's quote of $.20 per ringgit (5 ringgit to the dollar). The triangular arbitrage strategy generates $10,125, which is $125 more than you started with.

Like locational arbitrage, triangular arbitrage does not tie up funds. Also, the strategy is risk-free, since there is no uncertainty about the prices at which you will buy and sell the currencies.

Accounting for the Bid/Ask Spread. The previous example is simplified in that it does not account for transaction costs. In reality, there is a bid and ask quote for each currency, which means that the arbitrageur incurs transaction costs that can reduce or even eliminate the gains from triangular arbitrage. The following example illustrates how bid and ask prices can affect arbitrage profits.

EXAMPLE

Using Exhibit 7.3, you can determine whether triangular arbitrage is possible by starting with some fictitious amount (say, $10,000) of U.S. dollars and estimating the number of dollars you would generate by implementing the strategy. Exhibit 7.3 differs from the previous example only in that bid/ask spreads are now considered.

Recall that the previous triangular arbitrage strategy involved exchanging dollars for pounds, pounds for ringgit, and then ringgit for dollars. Apply this strategy to the bid and ask quotations in Exhibit 7.3. Your initial $10,000 will be converted into £6,211 (based on the bank's ask price of $1.61 per pound). Then the £6,211 are converted into MYR50,310 (based on the bank's bid price for pounds of MYR8.1 per pound, £6,211 × 8.1 = MYR50,309). Next, the MYR50,310 are converted to $10,062 (based on the bank's bid price of $.200). The profit is $10,062 − $10,000 = $62. The profit is lower here than in the previous example because bid and ask quotations are used.

Exhibit 7.3

Currency Quotes for a Triangular Arbitrage Example

	Quoted Bid Price	Quoted Ask Price
Value of a British pound in U.S. dollars	$1.60	$1.61
Value of a Malaysian ringgit (MYR) in U.S. dollars	$.200	$.201
Value of a British pound in Malaysian ringgit (MYR)	MYR8.10	MYR8.20

Exhibit 7.4
Impact of Triangular Arbitrage

Activity	Impact
1. Participants use dollars to purchase pounds.	Bank increases its ask price of pounds with respect to the dollar.
2. Participants use pounds to purchase Malaysian ringgit.	Bank reduces its bid price of the British pound with respect to the ringgit; that is, it reduces the number of ringgit to be exchanged per pound received.
3. Participants use Malaysian ringgit to purchase U.S. dollars.	Bank reduces its bid price of ringgit with respect to the dollar.

Realignment due to Triangular Arbitrage. The realignment that results from the triangular arbitrage activity is summarized in the second column of Exhibit 7.4. The realignment will likely occur quickly to prevent continued benefits from triangular arbitrage. The discrepancies assumed here are unlikely to occur within a single bank. More likely, triangular arbitrage would require three transactions at three separate banks.

Given three currencies, the exchange rate between each pair is displayed in Exhibit 7.5. If any two of these three exchange rates are known, the exchange rate of the third pair can be determined. When the actual cross exchange rate differs from the appropriate cross exchange rate, the exchange rates of the currencies are not in equilibrium. Triangular arbitrage would force the exchange rates back into equilibrium.

Like locational arbitrage, triangular arbitrage is a strategy that few of us can ever take advantage of because the computer technology available to foreign exchange dealers can easily detect misalignments in cross exchange rates. The point of this discussion is that because of triangular arbitrage, cross exchange rates are usually aligned correctly. If they are not, triangular arbitrage will take place until the rates are aligned correctly.

Covered Interest Arbitrage

Covered interest arbitrage is the process of capitalizing on the interest rate differential between two countries while covering your exchange rate risk. The logic of the term *covered interest arbitrage* becomes clear when it is broken into two parts: "interest arbitrage" refers to the process of capitalizing on the difference between interest rates between two countries; "covered" refers to hedging your position against exchange rate risk.

Exhibit 7.5
Relationship among Three Currencies

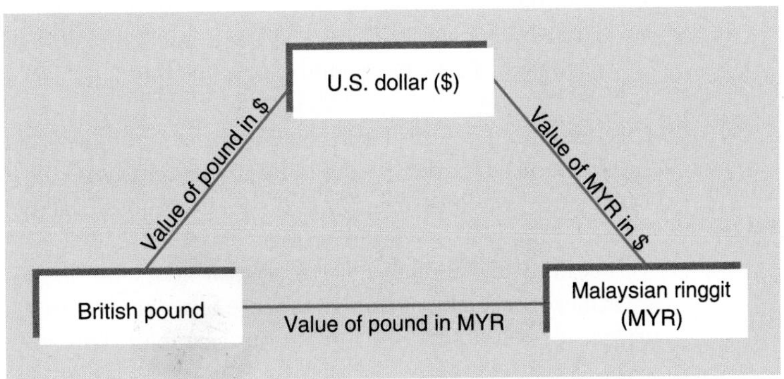

Covered interest arbitrage is sometimes interpreted to mean that the funds to be invested are borrowed locally. In this case, the investors are not tying up any of their own funds. In another interpretation, however, the investors use their own funds. In this case, the term *arbitrage* is loosely defined since there is a positive dollar amount invested over a period of time. The following discussion is based on this latter meaning of covered interest arbitrage; under either interpretation, however, arbitrage should have a similar impact on currency values and interest rates.

EXAMPLE

You desire to capitalize on relatively high rates of interest in the United Kingdom and have funds available for 90 days. The interest rate is certain; only the future exchange rate at which you will exchange pounds back to U.S. dollars is uncertain. You can use a forward sale of pounds to guarantee the rate at which you can exchange pounds for dollars at a future point in time. This actual strategy is as follows:

1. On day 1, convert your U.S. dollars to pounds and set up a 90-day deposit account in a British bank.
2. On day 1, engage in a forward contract to sell pounds 90 days forward.
3. In 90 days when the deposit matures, convert the pounds to U.S. dollars at the rate that was agreed upon in the forward contract.

If the proceeds from engaging in covered interest arbitrage exceed the proceeds from investing in a domestic bank deposit, and assuming neither deposit is subject to default risk, covered interest arbitrage is feasible. The feasibility of covered interest arbitrage is based on the interest rate differential and the forward rate premium. To illustrate, consider the following numerical example.

EXAMPLE

Assume the following information:

- You have $800,000 to invest.
- The current spot rate of the pound is $1.60.
- The 90-day forward rate of the pound is $1.60.
- The 90-day interest rate in the United States is 2 percent.
- The 90-day interest rate in the United Kingdom is 4 percent.

Based on this information, you should proceed as follows:

1. On day 1, convert the $800,000 to £500,000 and deposit the £500,000 in a British bank.
2. On day 1, sell £520,000 90 days forward. By the time the deposit matures, you will have £520,000 (including interest).
3. In 90 days when the deposit matures, you can fulfill your forward contract obligation by converting your £520,000 into $832,000 (based on the forward contract rate of $1.60 per pound).

This reflects a 4 percent return over the three-month period, which is 2 percent above the return on a U.S. deposit. In addition, the return on this foreign deposit is known on day 1, since you know when you make the deposit exactly how many dollars you will get back from your 90-day investment.

Recall that locational and triangular arbitrage do not tie up funds; thus, any profits are achieved instantaneously. In the case of covered interest arbitrage, the funds are tied up for a period of time (90 days in our example). This strategy would not be advantageous if it earned 2 percent or less, since you could earn 2 percent on a domestic deposit. The term *arbitrage* here suggests that you can guarantee a return on your funds that exceeds the returns you could achieve domestically.

Realignment due to Covered Interest Arbitrage. As with the other forms of arbitrage, market forces resulting from covered interest arbitrage will cause a market realignment. Once the realignment takes place, excess profits from arbitrage are no longer possible.

In the previous examples, four variables (pound spot rate, British interest rate, U.S. interest rate, and pound forward rate) could be affected by covered interest arbitrage. It is difficult to forecast the exact magnitude of each change. Nevertheless, as should be clear, each change reduces the excess return initially achieved from covered interest arbitrage.

EXAMPLE

Using the information from the previous example, Exhibit 7.6 summarizes the impact of covered interest arbitrage on exchange rates and interest rates. If we assume no adjustment in interest rates, covered interest arbitrage will be feasible until the forward rate of the pound is sufficiently below the spot rate to offset the interest rate advantage. Given that the British interest rate is 2 percent above the U.S. interest rate, U.S. investors can benefit from covered interest arbitrage until the forward rate is about 2 percent less than the spot rate.

Now assume that the exchange rates change in response to covered interest arbitrage as shown in Exhibit 7.7. With these new rates, further efforts to conduct covered interest arbitrage no longer provide a return to U.S. investors that is higher than the prevailing U.S. interest rate. This can be shown by computing the return earned from covered interest arbitrage, as follows (assume an initial investment of $800,000):

1. Convert $800,000 to pounds:

$$\$800{,}000/\$1.62 = £493{,}827$$

2. Calculate accumulated pounds over 90 days at 4 percent:

$$£493{,}827 \times 1.04 = £513{,}580$$

3. Reconvert pounds to dollars (at the forward rate of $1.5888) after 90 days:

$$£513{,}580 \times \$1.5888 = \$815{,}976$$

4. Determine the yield earned from covered interest arbitrage:

$$(\$815{,}976 - \$800{,}000)/\$800{,}000 = .02, \text{ or } 2\%$$

As this example shows, those individuals who initially conduct covered interest arbitrage cause exchange rates and possibly interest rates to move in such a way that future attempts at covered interest arbitrage provide a return that is no better than what is possible domestically. Due to the market forces from covered interest arbitrage, a relationship between the forward rate premium and interest rate differentials should exist. This relationship is discussed shortly.

Exhibit 7.6
Impact of Covered Interest Arbitrage

Activity	Impact
1. Use dollars to purchase pounds in the spot market.	Upward pressure on the spot rate of the pound.
2. Engage in a forward contract to sell pounds forward.	Downward pressure on the forward rate of the pound.
3. Invest funds from the United States in the United Kingdom.	Possible upward pressure on U.S. interest rates and downward pressure on British interest rates.

Exhibit 7.7
Adjustments in Exchange Rates due to Covered Interest Arbitrage

	Original Value	Value after Being Affected by Covered Interest Arbitrage
British pound spot rate in U.S. dollars	$1.60	$1.6200
British pound 90-day forward rate in U.S. dollars	1.60	1.5888

Consideration of Spreads. One more example is provided to illustrate the effects of the spread between the bid and ask quotes and the spread between deposit and loan rates.

EXAMPLE

The following exchange rates and one-year interest rates exist.

	Bid Quote	Ask Quote
Euro spot	$1.12	$1.13
Euro one-year forward	1.12	1.13
	Deposit Rate	**Loan Rate**
Interest rate on dollars	6.0%	9.0%
Interest rate on euros	6.5%	9.5%

You have $100,000 to invest for one year. Would you benefit from engaging in covered interest arbitrage?

Notice that the quotes of the euro spot and forward rates are exactly the same, while the deposit rate on euros is .5 percent higher than the deposit rate on dollars. So it may seem that covered interest arbitrage is feasible. However, U.S. investors would be subjected to the ask quote when buying euros (€) in the spot market, versus the bid quote when selling the euros through a one-year forward contract.

1. Convert $100,000 to euros (ask quote):

$$\$100{,}000/\$1.13 = €88{,}496$$

2. Calculate accumulated euros over one year at 6.5 percent:

$$€88{,}496 \times 1.065 = €94{,}248$$

3. Sell euros for dollars at the forward rate (bid quote):

$$€94{,}248 \times \$1.12 = \$105{,}558$$

4. Determine the yield earned from covered interest arbitrage:

$$(\$105{,}557 - \$100{,}000)/\ \$100{,}000 = .05557,\ \text{or}\ 5.557\%$$

The yield is less than you would have earned if you had invested the funds in the United States. Thus, covered interest arbitrage is not feasible.

Comparison of Arbitrage Effects

Exhibit 7.8 provides a comparison of the three types of arbitrage. The threat of locational arbitrage ensures that quoted exchange rates are similar across banks in different locations. The threat of triangular arbitrage ensures that cross exchange rates are properly set. The threat of covered interest arbitrage ensures that forward exchange rates are properly set. Any discrepancy will trigger arbitrage, which should eliminate the discrepancy. Thus, arbitrage tends to allow for a more orderly foreign exchange market.

Exhibit 7.8
Comparing Arbitrage Strategies

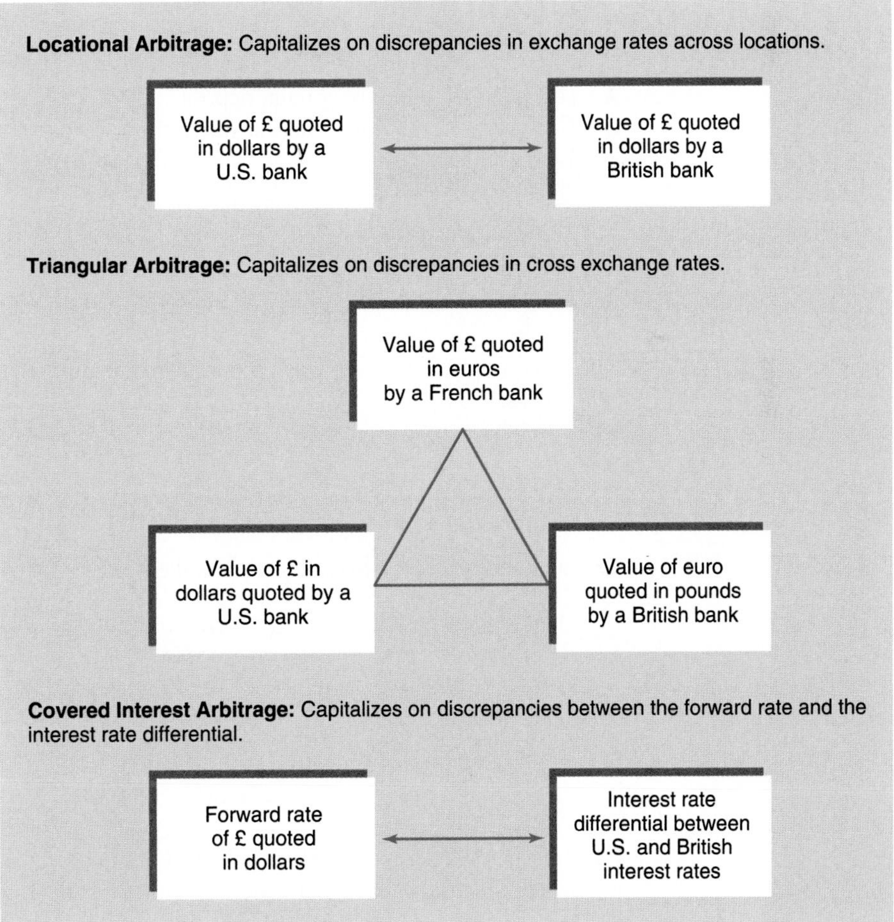

Interest Rate Parity (IRP)

Once market forces cause interest rates and exchange rates to adjust such that covered interest arbitrage is no longer feasible, there is an equilibrium state referred to as **interest rate parity (IRP)**. In equilibrium, the forward rate differs from the spot rate by a sufficient amount to offset the interest rate differential between two currencies. In the previous example, the U.S. investor receives a higher interest rate from the foreign investment, but there is an offsetting effect because the investor must pay more per unit of foreign currency (at the spot rate) than is received per unit when the currency is sold forward (at the forward rate). Recall that when the forward rate is less than the spot rate, this implies that the forward rate exhibits a discount.

Derivation of Interest Rate Parity

The relationship between a forward premium (or discount) of a foreign currency and the interest rates representing these currencies according to IRP can be determined as follows. Consider a U.S. investor who attempts covered interest arbitrage. The investor's return from using covered interest arbitrage can be determined given the following:

- The amount of the home currency (U.S. dollars in our example) that is initially invested (A_h).
- The spot rate (S) in dollars when the foreign currency is purchased.
- The interest rate on the foreign deposit (i_f).
- The forward rate (F) in dollars at which the foreign currency will be converted back to U.S. dollars.

The amount of the home currency received at the end of the deposit period due to such a strategy (called A_n) is:

$$A_n = (A_h/S)(1 + i_f)F$$

Since F is simply S times one plus the forward premium (called p), we can rewrite this equation as:

$$\begin{aligned} A_n &= (A_h/S)(1 + i_f)[S(1 + p)] \\ &= A_h(1 + i_f)(1 + p) \end{aligned}$$

The rate of return from this investment (called R) is as follows:

$$\begin{aligned} R &= \frac{A_n - A_h}{A_h} \\ &= \frac{[A_h(1 + i_f)(1 + p)] - A_h}{A_h} \\ &= (1 + i_f)(1 + p) - 1 \end{aligned}$$

If IRP exists, then the rate of return achieved from covered interest arbitrage (R) should be equal to the rate available in the home country. Set the rate that can be achieved from using covered interest arbitrage equal to the rate that can be achieved from an investment in the home country (the return on a home investment is simply the home interest rate called i_h):

$$R = i_h$$

By substituting into the formula the way in which R is determined, we obtain:

$$(1 + i_f)(1 + p) - 1 = i_h$$

By rearranging terms, we can determine what the forward premium of the foreign currency should be under conditions of IRP:

$$(1 + i_f)(1 + p) - 1 = i_h$$

$$(1 + i_f)(1 + p) = 1 + i_h$$

$$1 + p = \frac{1 + i_h}{1 + i_f}$$

$$p = \frac{1 + i_h}{1 + i_f} - 1$$

Determining the Forward Premium

Using the information just presented, the forward premium can be measured based on the interest rate differential under conditions of IRP.

EXAMPLE

Assume that the Mexican peso exhibits a six-month interest rate of 6 percent, while the U.S. dollar exhibits a six-month interest rate of 5 percent. From a U.S. investor's perspective, the U.S. dollar is the home currency. According to IRP, the forward rate premium of the peso with respect to the U.S. dollar should be:

$$p = \frac{1 + .05}{1 + .06} - 1$$

$$= -.0094, \text{ or } -.94\% \text{ (not annualized)}$$

Thus, the peso should exhibit a forward discount of about .94 percent. This implies that U.S. investors would receive .94 percent less when selling pesos six months from now (based on a forward sale) than the price they pay for pesos today at the spot rate. Such a discount would offset the interest rate advantage of the peso. If the peso's spot rate is \$.10, a forward discount of .94 percent means that the six-month forward rate is as follows:

$$F = S(1 + p)$$

$$= \$.10(1 - .0094)$$

$$= \$.09906$$

Relationship between Forward Premium and Interest Rate Differential. The relationship between the forward premium (or discount) and the interest rate differential according to IRP is simplified in an approximated form as follows:

$$p = \frac{F - S}{S} \cong i_h - i_f$$

where

p = forward premium (or discount)
F = forward rate in dollars
S = spot rate in dollars
i_h = home interest rate
i_f = foreign interest rate

This approximated form provides a reasonable estimate when the interest rate differential is small. The variables in this equation are not annualized. In our previous example, the U.S. (home) interest rate is less than the foreign interest rate, so the forward rate contains a discount (the forward rate is less than the spot rate). The larger the degree by which the foreign interest rate exceeds the home interest rate, the larger will be the forward discount of the foreign currency specified by the IRP formula.

If the foreign interest rate is less than the home interest rate, the IRP relationship suggests that the forward rate should exhibit a premium.

Implications. If the forward premium is equal to the interest rate differential as explained above, covered interest arbitrage will not be feasible.

EXAMPLE

Use the information on the spot rate, the six-month forward rate of the peso, and Mexico's interest rate from the preceding example to determine a U.S. investor's return from using covered interest arbitrage. Assume the investor begins with $1,000,000 to invest.

Step 1. On the first day, the U.S. investor converts $1,000,000 into pesos (MXP) at $.10 per peso:

$1,000,000/$.10 per peso = MXP10,000,000

Step 2. On the first day, the U.S. investor also sells pesos six months forward. The number of pesos to be sold forward is the anticipated accumulation of pesos over the six-month period, which is estimated as:

MXP10,000,000 × (1 + .06) = MXP10,600,000

Step 3. After six months, the U.S. investor withdraws the initial deposit of pesos along with the accumulated interest, amounting to a total of 10,600,000 pesos. The investor converts the pesos into dollars in accordance with the forward contract agreed upon six months earlier. The forward rate was $.09906, so the number of U.S. dollars received from the conversion is:

MXP10,600,000 × ($.09906 per peso) = $1,050,036

In this case, the investor's covered interest arbitrage achieves a return of about 5 percent. Rounding the forward discount to .94 percent causes the slight deviation from the 5 percent return. The results suggest that, in this instance, using covered interest arbitrage generates a return that is about what the investor would have received anyway by simply investing the funds domestically. This confirms that covered interest arbitrage is not worthwhile if IRP exists.

Graphic Analysis of Interest Rate Parity

http://

Visit http://www.bloomberg.com for the latest information from financial markets around the world.

The interest rate differential can be compared to the forward premium (or discount) with the use of a graph. All the possible points that represent interest rate parity are plotted on Exhibit 7.9 by using the approximation expressed earlier and plugging in numbers.

Points Representing a Discount. For all situations in which the foreign interest rate exceeds the home interest rate, the forward rate should exhibit a discount approximately equal to that differential. When the foreign interest rate (i_f) exceeds the home interest rate (i_h) by 1 percent ($i_h - i_f = -1\%$), then the forward rate should exhibit a discount of 1 percent. This is represented by point A on the graph. If the foreign interest rate exceeds the home rate by 2 percent, then the forward rate should exhibit a discount of 2 percent, as represented by point B on the graph, and so on.

Points Representing a Premium. For all situations in which the foreign interest rate is less than the home interest rate, the forward rate should exhibit a premium approximately equal to that differential. For example, if the home interest rate exceeds the foreign rate by 1 percent ($i_h - i_f = 1\%$), then the forward premium should be 1 percent, as represented by point C. If the home interest rate exceeds the foreign rate by 2 percent ($i_h - i_f = 2\%$), then the forward premium should be 2 percent, as represented by point D, and so on.

Exhibit 7.9

Illustration of Interest Rate Parity

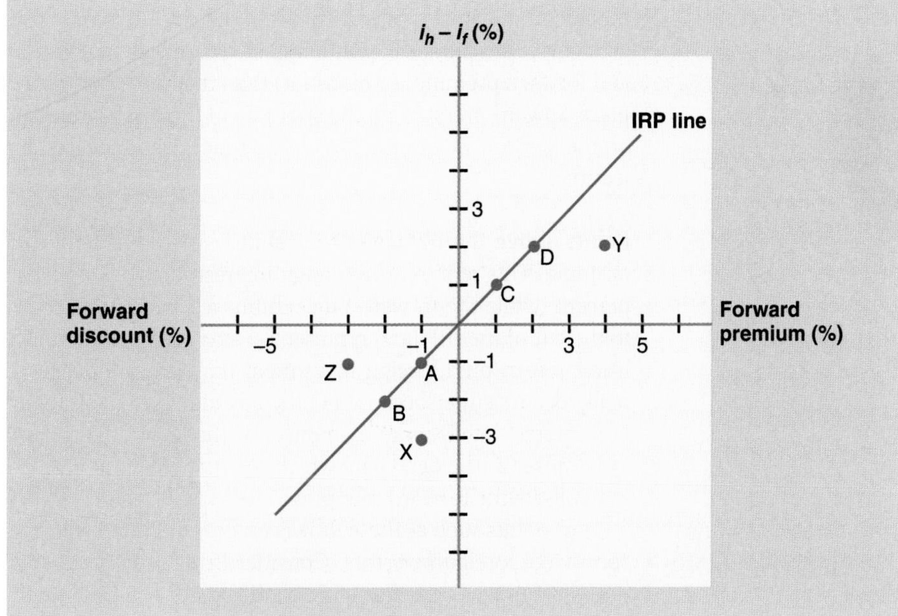

Points Representing IRP. Any points lying on the diagonal line cutting the intersection of the axes represent IRP. For this reason, that diagonal line is referred to as the **interest rate parity (IRP) line**. Covered interest arbitrage is not possible for points along the IRP line.

An individual or corporation can at any time examine all currencies to compare forward rate premiums (or discounts) to interest rate differentials. From a U.S. perspective, interest rates in Japan are usually lower than the home interest rates. Consequently, the forward rate of the Japanese yen usually exhibits a premium and may be represented by points such as C or D or even points above D along the diagonal line in Exhibit 7.9. Conversely, the United Kingdom often has higher interest rates than the United States, so the pound's forward rate often exhibits a discount, represented by point A or B.

Exhibit 7.9 can be used whether or not you annualize the rates, as long as you are consistent. That is, if you annualize the interest rates to determine the interest rate differential, you should also annualize the forward premium or discount.

Points below the IRP Line. What if a three-month deposit represented by a foreign currency offers an annualized interest rate of 10 percent versus an annualized interest rate of 7 percent in the home country? Such a scenario is represented on the graph by $i_h - i_f = -3\%$. Also assume that the foreign currency exhibits an annualized forward discount of 1 percent. The combined interest rate differential and forward discount information can be represented by point X on the graph. Since point X is not on the IRP line, we should expect that covered interest arbitrage will be beneficial for some investors. The investor attains an additional 3 percentage points for the foreign deposit, and this advantage is only partially offset by the 1 percent forward discount.

Assume that the annualized interest rate for the foreign currency is 5 percent, as compared to 7 percent for the home country. The interest rate differential expressed on the graph is $i_h - i_f = 2\%$. However, assume that the forward premium of the foreign currency is 4 percent (point Y in Exhibit 7.9). Thus, the high forward premium more than makes up what the investor loses on the lower interest rate from the foreign investment.

If the current interest rate and forward rate situation is represented by point X or Y, home country investors can engage in covered interest arbitrage. By investing in a foreign currency, they will earn a higher return (after considering the foreign interest rate and forward premium or discount) than the home interest rate. This type of activity will place upward pressure on the spot rate of the foreign currency, and downward pressure on the forward rate of the foreign currency, until covered interest arbitrage is no longer feasible.

Points above the IRP Line. Now shift to the left side of the IRP line. Take point Z, for example. This represents a foreign interest rate that exceeds the home interest rate by 1 percent, while the forward rate exhibits a 3 percent discount. This point, like all points to the left of the IRP line, represents a situation in which U.S. investors would achieve a lower return on a foreign investment than on a domestic one. This lower return normally occurs either because (1) the advantage of the foreign interest rate relative to the U.S. interest rate is more than offset by the forward rate discount (reflected by point Z), or because (2) the degree by which the home interest rate exceeds the foreign rate more than offsets the forward rate premium.

For points such as these, however, covered interest arbitrage is feasible from the perspective of foreign investors. Consider British investors in the United Kingdom, whose interest rate is 1 percent higher than the U.S. interest rate, and the forward rate (with respect to the dollar) contains a 3 percent discount (as represented by point Z). British investors will sell their foreign currency in exchange for dollars, invest in dollar-denominated securities, and engage in a forward contract to purchase pounds forward. Though they earn 1 percent less on the U.S. investment, they are able to purchase their home currency for 3 percent less than what they initially sold it for. This type of activity will place downward pressure on the spot rate of the pound and upward pressure on the pound's forward rate, until covered interest arbitrage is no longer feasible.

How to Test Whether Interest Rate Parity Exists

An investor or firm can plot all realistic points for various currencies on a graph such as that in Exhibit 7.9 to determine whether gains from covered interest arbitrage can be achieved. The location of the points provides an indication of whether covered interest arbitrage is worthwhile. For points to the right of the IRP line, investors in the home country should consider using covered interest arbitrage, since a return higher than the home interest rate (i_h) is achievable. Of course, as investors and firms take advantage of such opportunities, the point will tend to move toward the IRP line. Covered interest arbitrage should continue until the interest rate parity relationship holds.

Interpretation of Interest Rate Parity

Interest rate parity should be interpreted with caution. It does not imply that investors from different countries will earn the same returns. It is focused on the comparison of a foreign investment and a domestic investment in interest-bearing securities by a particular investor.

Assume that the United States has a 10 percent interest rate, while the United Kingdom has a 14 percent interest rate. U.S. investors can achieve 10 percent domestically or attempt to use covered interest arbitrage. If they attempt covered interest arbitrage while IRP exists, then the result will be a 10 percent return, the same as they could achieve in the United States. If British investors attempt covered interest arbitrage while IRP exists, then the result will be a 14 percent return, the same as they could achieve in the United Kingdom. Thus, U.S. investors and British investors do *not* achieve the same nominal return here, even though IRP exists. An appropriate summary explanation of IRP is that if IRP exists, investors cannot use covered interest arbitrage to achieve higher returns than those achievable in their respective home countries.

Does Interest Rate Parity Hold?

To determine conclusively whether interest rate parity holds, it is necessary to compare the forward rate (or discount) with interest rate quotations occurring at the same time. If the forward rate and interest rate quotations do not reflect the same time of day, then results could be somewhat distorted. Due to limitations in access to data, it is difficult to obtain quotations that reflect the same point in time.

A comparison of annualized forward rate premiums and annualized interest rate differentials for seven widely traded currencies as of February 10, 2004, is provided in Exhibit 7.10 from a U.S. perspective. At this time, the U.S. interest rate was higher than the Japanese interest rate and lower than the interest rates in other countries. The exhibit shows that the yen exhibited a forward premium, while all other currencies exhibited a

Exhibit 7.10

Forward Rate Premiums and Interest Rate Differentials for Seven Currencies

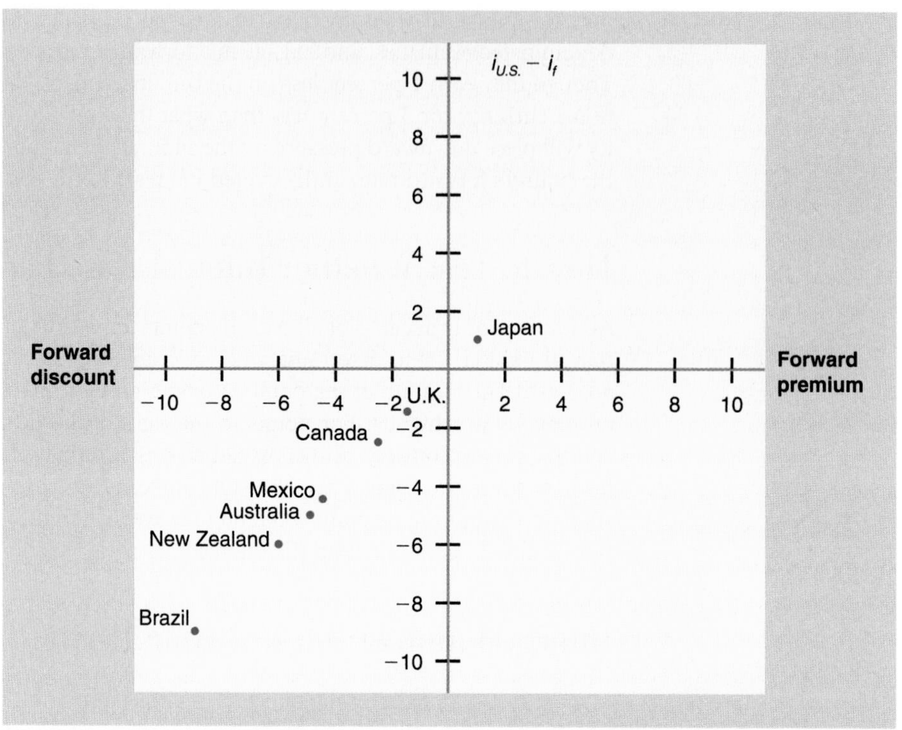

Note: The data are as of February 10, 2004. The forward rate premium is based on the six-month forward rate and is annualized. The interest rate differential represents the difference between the six-month annualized U.S. interest rate and the six-month foreign interest rate.

discount. The Brazilian real exhibited the most pronounced forward discount, which is attributed to its relatively high interest rate. The forward premium or discount of each currency is in line with the interest rate differential and therefore reflects IRP.

At different points in time, the position of a country may change. For example, if Mexico's interest rate increased while other countries' interest rates stayed the same, Mexico's position would move down along the *y*-axis. Yet, its forward discount would likely be more pronounced (farther to the left along the *x*-axis) as well, since covered interest arbitrage would occur otherwise. Therefore, its new point would be farther to the left but would still be along the 45-degree line.

Numerous academic studies have conducted empirical examination of IRP in several periods. The actual relationship between the forward rate premium and interest rate differentials generally supports IRP. Although there are deviations from IRP, they are often not large enough to make covered interest arbitrage worthwhile, as we will now discuss in more detail.

Considerations When Assessing Interest Rate Parity

If interest rate parity does not hold, covered interest arbitrage deserves consideration. Nevertheless, covered interest arbitrage still may not be worthwhile due to various characteristics of foreign investments, including transaction costs, political risk, and differential tax laws.

Exhibit 7.11
Potential for Covered Interest Arbitrage When Considering Transaction Costs

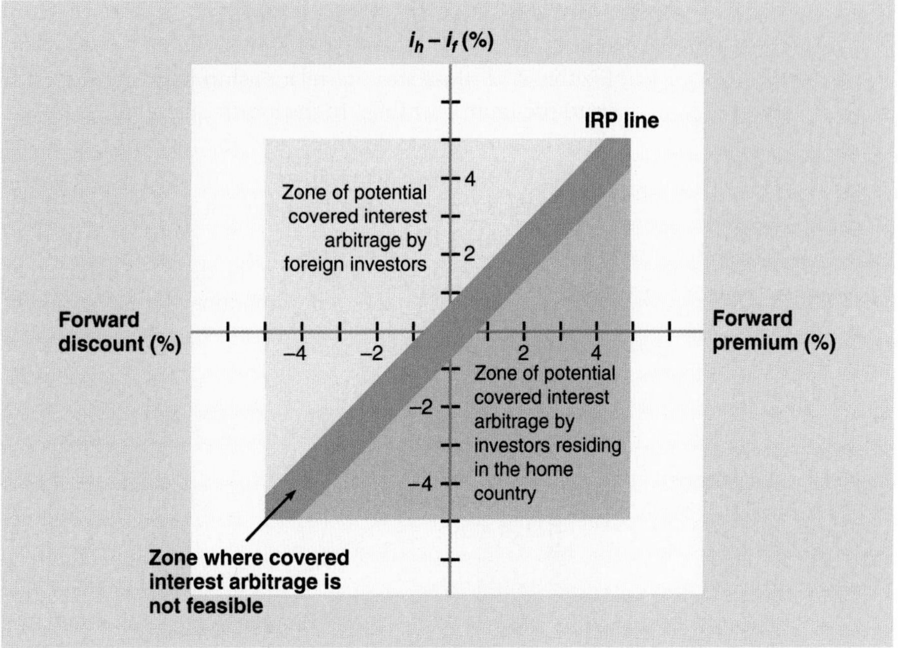

Transaction Costs. If an investor wishes to account for transaction costs, the actual point reflecting the interest rate differential and forward rate premium must be farther from the IRP line to make covered interest arbitrage worthwhile. Exhibit 7.11 identifies the areas that reflect potential for covered interest arbitrage *after* accounting for transaction costs. Notice the band surrounding the IRP line. For points not on the IRP line but within this band, covered interest arbitrage is not worthwhile (because the excess return is offset by costs). For points to the right of (or below) the band, investors residing in the home country could gain through covered interest arbitrage. For points to the left of (or above) the band, foreign investors could gain through covered interest arbitrage.

Political Risk. Even if covered interest arbitrage appears feasible after accounting for transaction costs, investing funds overseas is subject to political risk. Though the forward contract locks in the rate at which the foreign funds should be reconverted, there is no guarantee that the foreign government will allow the funds to be reconverted. A crisis in the foreign country could cause its government to restrict any exchange of the local currency for other currencies. In this case, the investor would be unable to use these funds until the foreign government eliminated the restriction.

Investors may also perceive a slight default risk on foreign investments such as foreign Treasury bills, since they may not be assured that the foreign government will guarantee full repayment of interest and principal upon default. Therefore, because of concern that the foreign Treasury bills may default, they may accept a lower interest rate on their domestic Treasury bills rather than engage in covered interest arbitrage in an effort to obtain a slightly higher expected return.

Differential Tax Laws. Because tax laws vary among countries, investors and firms that set up deposits in other countries must be aware of the existing tax laws. Covered interest arbitrage might be feasible when considering before-tax returns but not necessarily when considering after-tax returns. Such a scenario would be due to differential tax rates.

Changes in Forward Premiums

Exhibit 7.12 illustrates the relationship between interest rate differentials and the forward premium over time. In the fourth quarter of 2000, the U.S. interest rate was higher than the interest rate on euros, and the forward rate of the euro exhibited a premium. During the next two years, the U.S. interest rate declined to a greater degree than the euro's interest rate. As the U.S. interest rate declined below the euro's interest rate in 2001, the euro's forward rate exhibited a discount, as the forward rate was lower than the prevailing spot rate. The larger the degree to which the euro's interest rate exceeded the U.S. interest rate, the more pronounced was the euro's forward discount.

Exhibit 7.12

Relationship between Interest Rate Differentials and Forward Rate Premiums over Time

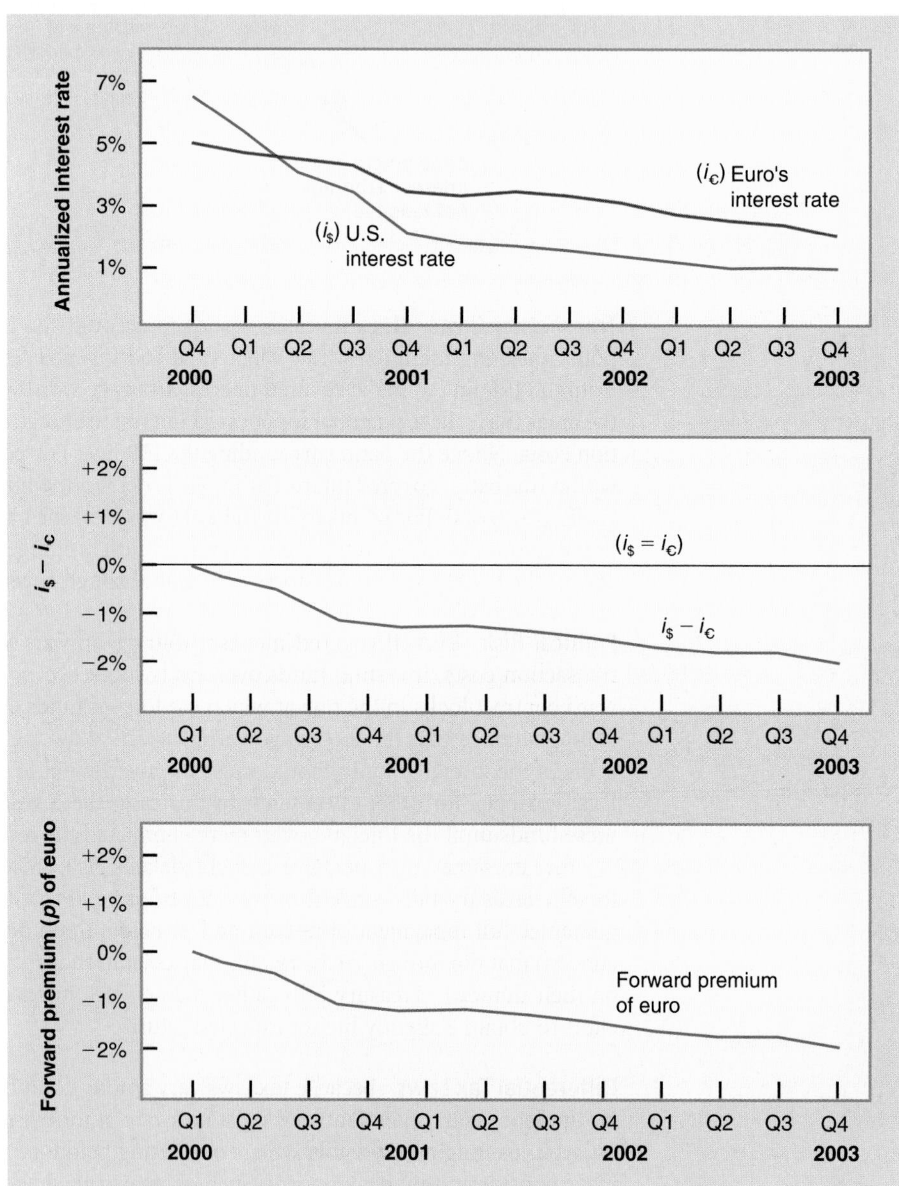

MANAGING FOR VALUE

How Interest Rate Parity Affects IBM's Hedge

Like many U.S.-based MNCs, IBM has some foreign subsidiaries based in Brazil. Since the Brazilian real has historically depreciated against the dollar, IBM naturally considers hedging any funds that its Brazilian subsidiaries plan to remit to the parent. Forward and futures contracts can be used to hedge the future transactions in which the Brazilian real will be converted into dollars. Due to interest rate parity, however, the forward or futures rate of the Brazilian real is unfavorable relative to its spot rate. Since the Brazilian interest rate is higher than the U.S. interest rate, IRP forces the forward rate of the Brazilian real to exhibit a discount. The discount is especially pronounced when the Brazilian interest rate is very high. Thus, if IBM hedges its future conversions of Brazilian real to dollars, it must accept a heavily discounted exchange rate for conversion in the future. This exchange rate may not be as favorable as the prevailing spot rate at that future time, even if today's spot rate declines over time. This is an important cost of doing business in countries with high interest rates. Since high interest rates are usually caused by a high level of expected inflation, this example illustrates the indirect effect that a foreign country's expected inflation can have on an MNC. IBM and other MNCs can increase their value by identifying countries that will have a high degree of expected inflation and limiting their exchange rate exposure in those countries.

During the 2000–2003 period, the interest rate on the Japanese yen was near .5 percent. The U.S. interest rate exceeded the Japanese interest rate throughout this entire period, which caused the Japanese yen's forward rate to exhibit a premium throughout the period. Yet, as the U.S. interest rate declined during the period, the differential between the Japanese and U.S. interest rates narrowed, and the yen's forward rate premium declined as a result.

USING THE WEB

Forward Rates Forward rates of the Canadian dollar, British pound, euro, and Japanese yen are provided for various periods at http://www.bmo.com/economic/regular/fxrates.html.

SUMMARY

- Locational arbitrage may occur if foreign exchange quotations differ among banks. The act of locational arbitrage should force the foreign exchange quotations of banks to become realigned, and locational arbitrage will no longer be possible.
- Triangular arbitrage is related to cross exchange rates. A cross exchange rate between two currencies is determined by the values of these two currencies with respect to a third currency. If the actual cross exchange rate of these two currencies differs from the rate that should exist, triangular arbitrage is possible. The act of triangular arbitrage should force cross exchange rates to become realigned, at which time triangular arbitrage will no longer be possible.
- Covered interest arbitrage is based on the relationship between the forward rate premium and the interest rate differential. The size of the premium or discount exhibited by the forward rate of a currency should be about the same as the differential between the interest rates of the two countries of concern. In general terms, the forward rate of the foreign currency will contain a discount (premium) if its interest rate is higher (lower) than the U.S. interest rate. If the forward premium deviates substantially from the interest rate differential, covered interest arbitrage is possible. In this type of arbitrage, a foreign short-term investment in a foreign currency is covered by a forward sale of that foreign currency in the future. In this manner, the investor

is not exposed to fluctuation in the foreign currency's value.

- Interest rate parity (IRP) is a theory that states that the size of the forward premium (or discount) should be equal to the interest rate differential between the two countries of concern. When IRP exists, covered interest arbitrage is not feasible because any interest rate advantage in the foreign country will be offset by the discount on the forward rate. Thus, the act of covered interest arbitrage would generate a return that is no higher than what would be generated by a domestic investment.

POINT COUNTER-POINT

Does Arbitrage Destabilize Foreign Exchange Markets?

Point Yes. Large financial institutions have the technology to recognize when one participant in the foreign exchange market is trying to sell a currency for a higher price than another participant. They also recognize when the forward rate does not properly reflect the interest rate differential. They use arbitrage to capitalize on these situations, which results in large foreign exchange transactions. In some cases, their arbitrage involves taking large positions in a currency and then reversing their positions a few minutes later. This jumping in and out of currencies can cause abrupt price adjustments of currencies and may create more volatility in the foreign exchange market. Regulations should be created that would force financial institutions to maintain their currency positions for at least one month. This would result in a more stable foreign exchange market.

Counter-Point No. When financial institutions engage in arbitrage, they create pressure on the price of a currency that will remove any pricing discrepancy. If arbitrage did not occur, pricing discrepancies would become more pronounced. Consequently, firms and individuals who use the foreign exchange market would have to spend more time searching for the best exchange rate when trading a currency. The market would become fragmented, and prices could differ substantially among banks in a region, or among regions. If the discrepancies became large enough, firms and individuals might even attempt to conduct arbitrage themselves. The arbitrage conducted by banks allows for a more integrated foreign exchange market, which ensures that foreign exchange prices quoted by any institution are in line with the market.

Who Is Correct? Use InfoTrac or some other search engine to learn more about this issue. Which argument do you support? Offer your own opinion on this issue.

SELF TEST

Answers are provided in Appendix A at the back of the text.

1. Assume that the following spot exchange rates exist today:

   £1 = \$1.50
   C\$ = \$.75
   £1 = C\$2

   Assume no transaction costs. Based on these exchange rates, can triangular arbitrage be used to earn a profit? Explain.

2. Assume the following information:

   Spot rate of £ = \$1.60
   180-day forward rate of £ = \$1.56
   180-day British interest rate = 4%
   180-day U.S. interest rate = 3%

   Based on this information, is covered interest arbitrage by U.S. investors feasible? Explain.

3. Using the information in the previous question, does interest rate parity exist? Explain.

4. Explain in general terms how various forms of arbitrage can remove any discrepancies in the pricing of currencies.

5. Assume that the British pound's one-year forward rate exhibits a discount. Assume that interest rate parity continually exists. Explain how the discount on the British pound's one-year forward discount would change if British one-year interest rates rose by 3 percentage points while U.S. one-year interest rates rose by 2 percentage points.

QUESTIONS AND APPLICATIONS

1. **Locational Arbitrage.** Explain the concept of locational arbitrage and the scenario necessary for it to be plausible.

2. **Locational Arbitrage.** Assume the following information:

	Beal Bank	Yardley Bank
Bid price of New Zealand dollar	$.401	$.398
Ask price of New Zealand dollar	$.404	$.400

   Given this information, is locational arbitrage possible? If so, explain the steps involved in locational arbitrage, and compute the profit from this arbitrage if you had $1,000,000 to use. What market forces would occur to eliminate any further possibilities of locational arbitrage?

3. **Triangular Arbitrage.** Explain the concept of triangular arbitrage and the scenario necessary for it to be plausible.

4. **Triangular Arbitrage.** Assume the following information:

	Quoted Price
Value of Canadian dollar in U.S. dollars	$.90
Value of New Zealand dollar in U.S. dollars	$.30
Value of Canadian dollar in New Zealand dollars	NZ$3.02

   Given this information, is triangular arbitrage possible? If so, explain the steps that would reflect triangular arbitrage, and compute the profit from this strategy if you had $1,000,000 to use. What market forces would occur to eliminate any further possibilities of triangular arbitrage?

5. **Covered Interest Arbitrage.** Explain the concept of covered interest arbitrage and the scenario necessary for it to be plausible.

6. **Covered Interest Arbitrage.** Assume the following information:

Spot rate of Canadian dollar	= $.80
90-day forward rate of Canadian dollar	= $.79
90-day Canadian interest rate	= 4%
90-day U.S. interest rate	= 2.5%

   Given this information, what would be the yield (percentage return) to a U.S. investor who used covered interest arbitrage? (Assume the investor invests $1,000,000.) What market forces would occur to eliminate any further possibilities of covered interest arbitrage?

7. **Covered Interest Arbitrage.** Assume the following information:

Spot rate of Mexican peso	= $.100
180-day forward rate of Mexican peso	= $.098
180-day Mexican interest rate	= 6%
180-day U.S. interest rate	= 5%

   Given this information, is covered interest arbitrage worthwhile for Mexican investors who have pesos to invest? Explain your answer.

8. **Effects of September 11.** The terrorist attack on the United States on September 11, 2001, caused expectations of a weaker U.S. economy. Explain how such expectations could have affected U.S. interest rates and therefore have affected the forward rate premium (or discount) on various foreign currencies.

9. **Interest Rate Parity.** Explain the concept of interest rate parity. Provide the rationale for its possible existence.

10. **Inflation Effects on the Forward Rate.** Why do you think currencies of countries with high inflation rates tend to have forward discounts?

11. **Covered Interest Arbitrage in Both Directions.** Assume that the existing U.S. one-year interest rate is 10 percent and the Canadian one-year interest rate is 11 percent. Also assume that interest rate parity exists. Should the forward rate of the Canadian dollar exhibit a discount or a premium? If U.S. investors attempt covered interest arbitrage, what will be their return? If Canadian investors attempt covered interest arbitrage, what will be their return?

12. **Interest Rate Parity.** Why would U.S. investors consider covered interest arbitrage in France when the interest rate on euros in France is lower than the U.S. interest rate?

13. **Interest Rate Parity.** Consider investors who invest in either U.S. or British one-year Treasury bills. Assume zero transaction costs and no taxes.

    a. If interest rate parity exists, then the return for U.S. investors who use covered interest arbitrage will be the same as the return for U.S. investors who invest in U.S. Treasury bills. Is this statement true or false? If false, correct the statement.

    b. If interest rate parity exists, then the return for British investors who use covered interest arbitrage will be the same as the return for British investors who invest in British Treasury bills. Is this statement true or false? If false, correct the statement.

14. **Changes in Forward Premiums.** Assume that the Japanese yen's forward rate currently exhibits a premium of 6 percent and that interest rate parity exists. If U.S. interest rates decrease, how must this premium change to maintain interest rate parity? Why might we expect the premium to change?

15. **Changes in Forward Premiums.** Assume that the forward rate premium of the euro was higher last month than it is today. What does this imply about interest rate differentials between the United States and Europe today compared to those last month?

16. **Interest Rate Parity.** If the relationship that is specified by interest rate parity does not exist at any period but does exist on average, then covered interest arbitrage should not be considered by U.S. firms. Do you agree or disagree with this statement? Explain.

17. **Covered Interest Arbitrage in Both Directions.** The one-year interest rate in New Zealand is 6 percent. The one-year U.S. interest rate is 10 percent. The spot rate of the New Zealand dollar (NZ$) is $.50. The forward rate of the New Zealand dollar is $.54. Is covered interest arbitrage feasible for U.S. investors? Is it feasible for New Zealand investors? In each case, explain why covered interest arbitrage is or is not feasible.

18. **Limitations of Covered Interest Arbitrage.** Assume that the one-year U.S. interest rate is 11 percent, while the one-year interest rate in Malaysia is 40 percent. Assume that a U.S. bank is willing to purchase the currency of that country from you one year from now at a discount of 13 percent. Would covered interest arbitrage be worth considering? Is there any reason why you should not attempt covered interest arbitrage in this situation? (Ignore tax effects.)

19. **Covered Interest Arbitrage in Both Directions.** Assume that the annual U.S. interest rate is currently 8 percent and Germany's annual interest rate is currently 9 percent. The euro's one-year forward rate currently exhibits a discount of 2 percent.

    a. Does interest rate parity exist?

    b. Can a U.S. firm benefit from investing funds in Germany using covered interest arbitrage?

    c. Can a German subsidiary of a U.S. firm benefit by investing funds in the United States through covered interest arbitrage?

20. **Covered Interest Arbitrage.** The South African rand has a one-year forward premium of 2 percent. One-year interest rates in the United States are 3 percentage points higher than in South Africa. Based on this information, is covered interest arbitrage possible for a U.S. investor if interest rate parity holds?

21. **Deriving the Forward Rate.** Assume that annual interest rates in the United States are 4 percent, while interest rates in France are 6 percent.

    a. According to IRP, what should the forward rate premium or discount of the euro be?

b. If the euro's spot rate is $1.10, what should the one-year forward rate of the euro be?

22. **Covered Interest Arbitrage in Both Directions.** The following information is available:
    - You have $500,000 to invest.
    - The current spot rate of the Moroccan dirham is $.110.
    - The 60-day forward rate of the Moroccan dirham is $.108.
    - The 60-day interest rate in the United States is 1 percent.
    - The 60-day interest rate in Morocco is 2 percent.

    a. What is the yield to a U.S. investor who conducts covered interest arbitrage? Did covered interest arbitrage work for the investor in this case?

    b. Would covered interest arbitrage be possible for a Moroccan investor in this case?

ADVANCED QUESTIONS

23. **Economic Effects on the Forward Rate.** Assume that Mexico's economy has expanded significantly, causing a high demand for loanable funds there by local firms. How might these conditions affect the forward discount of the Mexican peso?

24 **Differences among Forward Rates.** Assume that the 30-day forward premium of the euro is −1 percent, while the 90-day forward premium of the euro is 2 percent. Explain the likely interest rate conditions that would cause these premiums. Does this ensure that covered interest arbitrage is worthwhile?

25. **Testing Interest Rate Parity.** Describe a method for testing whether interest rate parity exists. Why are transaction costs, currency restrictions, and differential tax laws important when evaluating whether covered interest arbitrage can be beneficial?

26. **Deriving the Forward Rate.** Before the Asian crisis began, Asian central banks were maintaining a somewhat stable value for their respective currencies. Nevertheless, the forward rate of Southeast Asian currencies exhibited a discount. Explain.

27. **Interpreting Changes in the Forward Premium.** Assume that interest rate parity holds. At the beginning of the month, the spot rate of the Canadian dollar is $.70, while the one-year forward rate is $.68. Assume that U.S. interest rates increase steadily over the month. At the end of the month, the one-year forward rate is higher than it was at the beginning of the month. Yet, the one-year forward discount is larger (the one-year premium is more negative) at the end of the month than it was at the beginning of the month. Explain how the relationship between the U.S. interest rate and the Canadian interest rate changed from the beginning of the month until the end of the month.

28. **Interpreting a Large Forward Discount.** The interest rate in Indonesia is commonly higher than the interest rate in the United States, which reflects a high expected rate of inflation there. Why should Nike consider hedging its future remittances from Indonesia to the U.S. parent even when the forward discount on the currency (rupiah) is so large?

29. **Change in the Forward Premium.** At the end of this month, you (owner of a U.S. firm) are meeting with a Japanese firm to which you will try to sell supplies. If you receive an order from that firm, you will obtain a forward contract to hedge the future receivables in yen. As of this morning, the forward rate of the yen and spot rate are the same. You believe that interest rate parity holds.

    This afternoon, news occurs that makes you believe that the U.S. interest rates will increase substantially by the end of this month, and that the Japanese interest rate will not change. However, your expectations of the spot rate of the Japanese yen are not affected at all in the future. How will your expected dollar amount of receivables from the Japanese transaction be affected (if at all) by the news that occurred this afternoon? Explain.

30. **Testing IRP.** The one-year interest rate in Singapore is 11 percent. The one-year interest rate in the United States is 6 percent. The spot rate of the Singapore dollar (S$) is $0.50 and the forward rate of the S$ is $0.46. Assume zero transactions costs.

    a. Does interest rate parity exist?

    b. Can a U.S. firm benefit from investing funds in Singapore using covered interest arbitrage?

INTERNET APPLICATION

31. **Cross Rates Online.** The Bloomberg website provides quotations in foreign exchange markets. Its address is **http://www.bloomberg.com**.

    Use this web page to determine the cross exchange rate between the Canadian dollar and the

Japanese yen. Notice that the value of the pound (in dollars) and the value of the yen (in dollars) are also disclosed. Based on these values, is the cross rate between the Canadian dollar and the yen what you expected it to be? Explain.

DISCUSSION IN THE BOARDROOM

This exercise can be found in Appendix E at the back of this textbook.

RUNNING YOUR OWN MNC

This exercise can be found on the Xtra! website at **http://maduraxtra.swlearning.com**.

BLADES, INC. CASE

Assessment of Potential Arbitrage Opportunities

Recall that Blades, a U.S. manufacturer of roller blades, has chosen Thailand as its primary export target for "Speedos," Blades' primary product. Moreover, Blades' primary customer in Thailand, Entertainment Products, has committed itself to purchase 180,000 Speedos annually for the next three years at a fixed price denominated in baht, Thailand's currency. Because of quality and cost considerations, Blades also imports some of the rubber and plastic components needed to manufacture Speedos.

Lately, Thailand has experienced weak economic growth and political uncertainty. As investors lost confidence in the Thai baht as a result of the political uncertainty, they withdrew their funds from the country. This resulted in an excess supply of baht for sale over the demand for baht in the foreign exchange market, which put downward pressure on the baht's value. As foreign investors continued to withdraw their funds from Thailand, the baht's value continued to deteriorate. Since Blades has net cash flows in baht resulting from its exports to Thailand, a deterioration in the baht's value will affect the company negatively.

Ben Holt, Blades' CFO, would like to ensure that the spot and forward rates Blades' bank has quoted are reasonable. If the exchange rate quotes are reasonable, then arbitrage will not be possible. If the quotations are not appropriate, however, arbitrage may be possible. Under these conditions, Holt would like Blades to use some form of arbitrage to take advantage of possible mispricing in the foreign exchange market. Although Blades is not an arbitrageur, Holt believes that arbitrage opportunities could offset the negative impact resulting from the baht's depreciation, which would otherwise seriously affect Blades' profit margins.

Ben Holt has identified three arbitrage opportunities as profitable and would like to know which one of them is the most profitable. Thus, he has asked you, Blades' financial analyst, to prepare an analysis of the arbitrage opportunities he has identified. This would allow Holt to assess the profitability of arbitrage opportunities very quickly.

1. The first arbitrage opportunity relates to locational arbitrage. Holt has obtained spot rate quotations from two banks in Thailand: Minzu Bank and Sobat Bank, both located in Bangkok. The bid and ask prices of Thai baht for each bank are displayed in the table below:

	Minzu Bank	Sobat Bank
Bid	$0.0224	$0.0228
Ask	$0.0227	$0.0229

   Determine whether the foreign exchange quotations are appropriate. If they are not appropriate, determine the profit you could generate by withdrawing $100,000 from Blades' checking account and engaging in arbitrage before the rates are adjusted.

2. Besides the bid and ask quotes for the Thai baht provided in the previous question, Minzu Bank has provided the following quotations for the U.S. dollar and the Japanese yen:

	Quoted Bid Price	Quoted Ask Price
Value of a Japanese yen in U.S. dollars	$0.0085	$0.0086
Value of a Thai baht in Japanese yen	¥2.69	¥2.70

Determine whether the cross exchange rate between the Thai baht and Japanese yen is appropriate. If it is not appropriate, determine the profit you could generate for Blades by withdrawing $100,000 from Blades' checking account and engaging in triangular arbitrage before the rates are adjusted.

3. Ben Holt has obtained several forward contract quotations for the Thai baht to determine whether covered interest arbitrage may be possible. He was quoted a forward rate of $0.0225 per Thai baht for a 90-day forward contract. The current spot rate is $0.0227. Ninety-day interest rates available to Blades in the United States are 2 percent, while 90-day interest rates in Thailand are 3.75 percent (these rates are not annualized). Holt is aware that covered interest arbitrage, unlike locational and triangular arbitrage, requires an investment of funds. Thus, he would like to be able to estimate the dollar profit resulting from arbitrage over and above the dollar amount available on a 90-day U.S. deposit.

   Determine whether the forward rate is priced appropriately. If it is not priced appropriately, determine the profit you could generate for Blades by withdrawing $100,000 from Blades' checking account and engaging in covered interest arbitrage. Measure the profit as the excess amount above what you could generate by investing in the U.S. money market.

4. Why are arbitrage opportunities likely to disappear soon after they have been discovered? To illustrate your answer, assume that covered interest arbitrage involving the immediate purchase and forward sale of baht is possible. Discuss how the baht's spot and forward rates would adjust until covered interest arbitrage is no longer possible. What is the resulting equilibrium state called?

SMALL BUSINESS DILEMMA

Assessment of Prevailing Spot and Forward Rates by the Sports Exports Company

As the Sports Exports Company exports footballs to the United Kingdom, it receives British pounds. The check (denominated in pounds) for last month's exports just arrived. Jim Logan (owner of the Sports Exports Company) normally deposits the check with his local bank and requests that the bank convert the check to dollars at the prevailing spot rate (assuming that he did not use a forward contract to hedge this payment). Jim's local bank provides foreign exchange services for many of its business customers who need to buy or sell widely traded currencies. Today, however, Jim decided to check the quotations of the spot rate at other banks before converting the payment into dollars.

1. Do you think Jim will be able to find a bank that provides him with a more favorable spot rate than his local bank? Explain.

2. Do you think that Jim's bank is likely to provide more reasonable quotations for the spot rate of the British pound if it is the only bank in town that provides foreign exchange services? Explain.

3. Jim is considering using a forward contract to hedge the anticipated receivables in pounds next month. His local bank quoted him a spot rate of $1.65 and a one-month forward rate of $1.6435. Before Jim decides to sell pounds one month forward, he wants to be sure that the forward rate is reasonable, given the prevailing spot rate. A one-month Treasury security in the United States currently offers a yield (not annualized) of 1 percent, while a one-month Treasury security in the United Kingdom offers a yield of 1.4 percent. Do you believe that the one-month forward rate is reasonable given the spot rate of $1.65?

CHAPTER 8

Relationships among Inflation, Interest Rates, and Exchange Rates

Inflation rates and interest rates can have a significant impact on exchange rates (as explained in Chapter 4) and therefore can influence the value of MNCs. Financial managers of MNCs must understand how inflation and interest rates can affect exchange rates so that they can anticipate how their MNCs may be affected. Given their potential influence on MNC values, inflation and interest rates deserve to be studied more closely.

The specific objectives of this chapter are to:

- explain the purchasing power parity (PPP) theory and its implications for exchange rate changes,
- explain the international Fisher effect (IFE) theory and its implications for exchange rate changes, and
- compare the PPP theory, the IFE theory, and the theory of interest rate parity (IRP), which was introduced in the previous chapter.

Purchasing Power Parity (PPP)

In Chapter 4, the expected impact of relative inflation rates on exchange rates was discussed. Recall from this discussion that when a country's inflation rate rises, the demand for its currency declines as its exports decline (due to its higher prices). In addition, consumers and firms in that country tend to increase their importing. Both of these forces place downward pressure on the high-inflation country's currency. Inflation rates often vary among countries, causing international trade patterns and exchange rates to adjust accordingly. One of the most popular and controversial theories in international finance is the **purchasing power parity (PPP) theory**, which attempts to quantify the inflation–exchange rate relationship.

Interpretations of Purchasing Power Parity

There are two popular forms of PPP theory, each of which has its own implications.

Absolute Form of PPP. The **absolute form of PPP** is based on the notion that without international barriers, consumers shift their demand to wherever prices are lower. It suggests that prices of the same basket of products in two different countries should be equal when measured in a common currency. If a discrepancy in prices as measured by a common currency exists, the demand should shift so that these prices converge.

EXAMPLE

If the same basket of products is produced by the United States and the United Kingdom, and the price in the United Kingdom is lower when measured in a common currency, the demand for that basket should increase in the United Kingdom and decline in the United States. Consequently, the actual price charged in each country may be affected, and/or the exchange rate may adjust. Both forces would cause the prices of the baskets to be similar when measured in a common currency.

Realistically, the existence of transportation costs, tariffs, and quotas may prevent the absolute form of PPP. If transportation costs were high in the preceding example, the demand for the baskets of products might not shift as suggested. Thus, the discrepancy in prices would continue.

Relative Form of PPP. The **relative form of PPP** accounts for the possibility of market imperfections such as transportation costs, tariffs, and quotas. This version acknowledges that because of these market imperfections, prices of the same basket of products in different countries will not necessarily be the same when measured in a common currency. It does state, however, that the rate of change in the prices of the baskets should be somewhat similar when measured in a common currency, as long as the transportation costs and trade barriers are unchanged.

EXAMPLE

Assume that the United States and the United Kingdom trade extensively with each other and initially have zero inflation. Now assume that the United States experiences a 9 percent inflation rate, while the United Kingdom experiences a 5 percent inflation rate. Under these conditions, PPP theory suggests that the British pound should appreciate by approximately 4 percent, the differential in inflation rates. Thus, the exchange rate should adjust to offset the differential in the inflation rates of the two countries. If this occurs, the prices of goods in the two countries should appear similar to consumers. That is, the relative purchasing power when buying products in one country is similar to when buying products in the other country.

Rationale behind Purchasing Power Parity Theory

If two countries produce products that are substitutes for each other, the demand for the products should adjust as inflation rates differ. In our previous example, the relatively high U.S. inflation should cause U.S. consumers to increase imports from the United Kingdom and British consumers to lower their demand for U.S. goods (since prices of British goods have increased by a lower rate). Such forces place upward pressure on the British pound's value.

The shifting in consumption from the United States to the United Kingdom will continue until the British pound's value has appreciated to the extent that (1) the prices paid for British goods by U.S. consumers are no lower than the prices for comparable products made in the United States and (2) the prices paid for U.S. goods by British consumers are no higher than the prices for comparable products made in the United Kingdom. To achieve this new equilibrium situation, the pound will need to appreciate by approximately 4 percent, as will be verified here.

Given British inflation of 5 percent and the pound's appreciation of 4 percent, U.S. consumers will be paying about 9 percent more for the British goods than they paid in the initial equilibrium state. This is equal to the 9 percent increase in prices of U.S. goods from the U.S. inflation.

Consider a situation in which the pound appreciated by only 1 percent in response to the inflation differential. In this case, the increased price of British goods to U.S. consumers will be approximately 6 percent (5 percent inflation and 1 percent appreciation in the British pound), which is less than the 9 percent increase in the price of U.S. goods to U.S. consumers. Thus, we would expect U.S. consumers to continue to shift their consumption to British goods. Purchasing power parity suggests that the increasing U.S. consumption of British goods by U.S. consumers would persist until the pound appreciated by about 4 percent. Any level of appreciation lower than this would represent more attractive British prices relative to U.S. prices from the U.S. consumer's viewpoint.

From the British consumer's point of view, the price of U.S. goods would have initially increased by 4 percent more than British goods. Thus, British consumers would continue to reduce imports from the United States until the pound appreciated enough to make U.S. goods no more expensive than British goods. Once the pound appreciated by 4 percent, this would partially offset the increase in U.S. prices of 9 percent from the British consumer's perspective. To be more precise, the net effect is that the prices of U.S. goods would increase by approximately 5 percent to British consumers (9 percent inflation minus the 4 percent savings to British consumers due to the pound's 4 percent appreciation).

Derivation of Purchasing Power Parity

Assume that the price indexes of the home country (h) and a foreign country (f) are equal. Now assume that over time, the home country experiences an inflation rate of I_h, while the foreign country experiences an inflation rate of I_f. Due to inflation, the price index of goods in the consumer's home country (P_h) becomes

$$P_h(1 + I_h)$$

The price index of the foreign country (P_f) will also change due to inflation in that country:

$$P_f(1 + I_f)$$

If $I_h > I_f$, and the exchange rate between the currencies of the two countries does not change, then the consumer's purchasing power is greater on foreign goods than on home goods. In this case, PPP does not exist. If $I_h < I_f$, and the exchange rate between the currencies of the two countries does not change, then the consumer's purchasing power is greater on home goods than on foreign goods. In this case also, PPP does not exist.

The PPP theory suggests that the exchange rate will not remain constant but will adjust to maintain the parity in purchasing power. If inflation occurs and the exchange rate of the foreign currency changes, the foreign price index from the home consumer's perspective becomes

$$P_f(1 + I_f)(1 + e_f)$$

where e_f represents the percentage change in the value of the foreign currency. According to PPP theory, the percentage change in the foreign currency (e_f) should change to maintain parity in the new price indexes of the two countries. We can solve for e_f under conditions of PPP by setting the formula for the new price index of the foreign country equal to the formula for the new price index of the home country, as follows:

$$P_f(1 + I_f)(1 + e_f) = P_h(1 + I_h)$$

Solving for e_f, we obtain

$$(1 + e_f) = \frac{P_h(1 + I_h)}{P_f(1 + I_f)}$$

$$e_f = \frac{P_h(1 + I_h)}{P_f(1 + I_f)} - 1$$

Since P_h equals P_f (because price indexes were initially assumed equal in both countries), they cancel, leaving

$$e_f = \frac{(1 + I_h)}{(1 + I_f)} - 1$$

This formula reflects the relationship between relative inflation rates and the exchange rate according to PPP. Notice that if $I_h > I_f$, e_f should be positive. This implies that the foreign currency will appreciate when the home country's inflation exceeds the foreign country's inflation. Conversely, if $I_h < I_f$, then e_f should be negative. This implies that the foreign currency will depreciate when the foreign country's inflation exceeds the home country's inflation.

Using PPP to Estimate Exchange Rate Effects

The relative form of PPP can be used to estimate how an exchange rate will change in response to differential inflation rates between countries.

EXAMPLE

Assume that the exchange rate is in equilibrium initially. Then the home currency experiences a 5 percent inflation rate, while the foreign country experiences a 3 percent inflation rate. According to PPP, the foreign currency will adjust as follows:

$$\begin{aligned} e_f &= \frac{1 + I_h}{1 + I_f} - 1 \\ &= \frac{1 + .05}{1 + .03} - 1 \\ &= .0194, \text{ or } 1.94\% \end{aligned}$$

Thus, according to this example, the foreign currency should appreciate by 1.94 percent in response to the higher inflation of the home country relative to the foreign country. If this exchange rate change does occur, the price index of the foreign country will be as high as the index in the home country from the perspective of home country consumers. Even though inflation is lower in the foreign country, appreciation of the foreign currency pushes the foreign country's price index up from the perspective of consumers in the home country. When considering the exchange rate effect, price indexes of both countries rise by 5 percent from the home country perspective. Thus, consumers' purchasing power is the same for foreign goods and home goods.

EXAMPLE

This example examines the situation when foreign inflation exceeds home inflation. Assume that the exchange rate is in equilibrium initially. Then the home country experiences a 4 percent inflation rate, while the foreign country experiences a 7 percent inflation rate. According to PPP, the foreign currency will adjust as follows:

$$\begin{aligned} e_f &= \frac{(1 + I_h)}{(1 + I_f)} - 1 \\ &= \frac{1 + .04}{1 + .07} - 1 \\ &= -.028, \text{ or } -2.8\% \end{aligned}$$

Thus, according to this example, the foreign currency should depreciate by 2.8 percent in response to the higher inflation of the foreign country relative to the home country. Even though the inflation is lower in the home country, the depreciation of the foreign currency places downward pressure on the foreign country's prices from the perspective of consumers in the home country. When considering the exchange rate impact, prices of both countries rise by 4 percent. Thus, PPP still exists due to the adjustment in the exchange rate.

Using a Simplified PPP Relationship. A simplified but less precise relationship based on PPP is

$$e_f \cong I_h - I_f$$

That is, the percentage change in the exchange rate should be approximately equal to the differential in inflation rates between the two countries. This simplified formula is appropriate only when the inflation differential is small.

Graphic Analysis of Purchasing Power Parity

Using PPP theory, we should be able to assess the potential impact of inflation on exchange rates. Exhibit 8.1 is a graphic representation of PPP theory. The points on the exhibit suggest that given an inflation differential between the home and the foreign country of X percent, the foreign currency should adjust by X percent due to that inflation differential.

PPP Line. The diagonal line connecting all these points together is known as the **PPP line**. Point A represents our earlier example in which the U.S. (considered the home country) and British inflation rates were assumed to be 9 percent and 5 percent, respectively, so

Exhibit 8.1
Illustration of Purchasing Power Parity

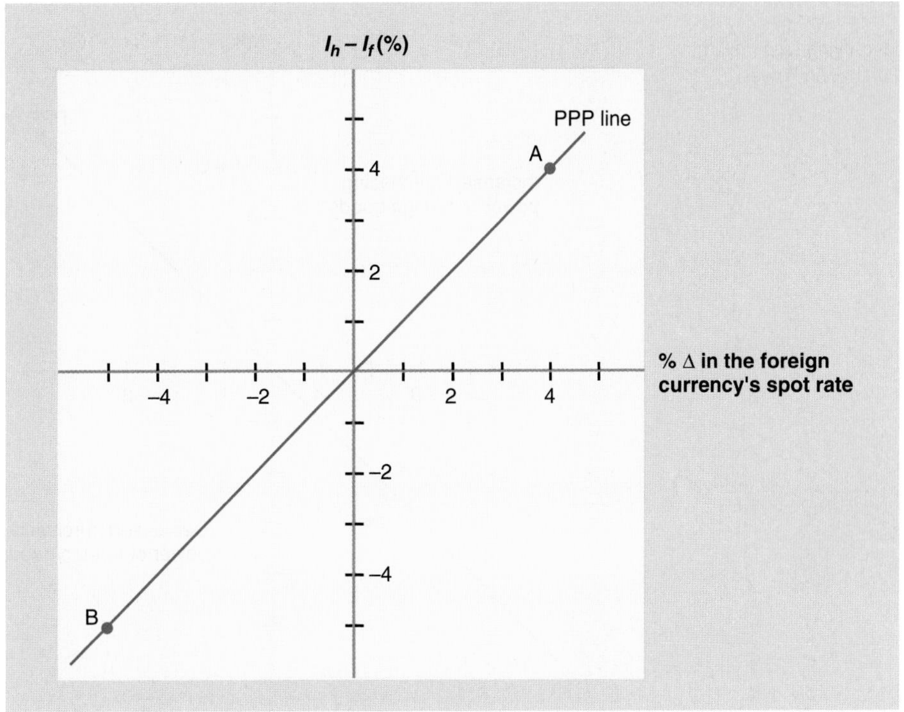

that $I_h - I_f = 4\%$. Recall that this led to the anticipated appreciation in the British pound of 4 percent, as illustrated by point A. Point B reflects a situation in which the U.S. and foreign inflation rates are 1 percent and 6 percent, respectively, so that $I_h - I_f = -5\%$. This leads to anticipated depreciation of the foreign currency by 5 percent, as illustrated by point B. If the exchange rate does respond to inflation differentials as PPP theory suggests, the actual points should lie on or close to the PPP line.

Purchasing Power Disparity. Exhibit 8.2 identifies areas of purchasing power disparity. Assume an initial equilibrium situation, then a change in the inflation rates of the two countries. If the exchange rate does not move as PPP theory suggests, there is a disparity in the purchasing power of the two countries.

Point C in Exhibit 8.2 represents a situation where home inflation (I_h) exceeds foreign inflation (I_f) by 4 percent. Yet, the foreign currency appreciated by only 1 percent in response to this inflation differential. Consequently, purchasing power disparity exists. Home country consumers' purchasing power for foreign goods has become more favorable relative to their purchasing power for the home country's goods. The PPP theory suggests that such a disparity in purchasing power should exist only in the short run. Over time, as the home country consumers take advantage of the disparity by purchasing more foreign goods, upward pressure on the foreign currency's value will cause point C to move toward the PPP line. All points to the left of (or above) the PPP line represent more favorable purchasing power for foreign goods than for home goods.

Point D in Exhibit 8.2 represents a situation where home inflation is 3 percent below foreign inflation. Yet, the foreign currency has depreciated by only 2 percent. Again, purchasing power disparity exists. The purchasing power for foreign goods has become less favorable relative to the purchasing power for the home country's goods. The PPP

Exhibit 8.2
Identifying Disparity in Purchasing Power

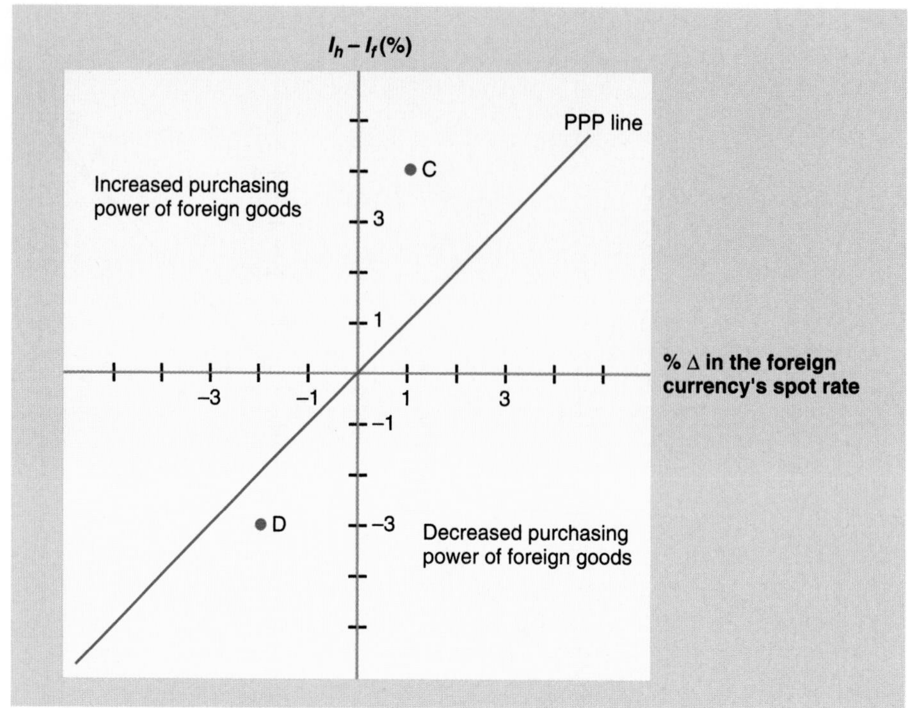

theory suggests that the foreign currency in this example should have depreciated by 3 percent to fully offset the 3 percent inflation differential. Since the foreign currency did not weaken to this extent, the home country consumers may cease purchasing foreign goods, causing the foreign currency to weaken to the extent anticipated by PPP theory. If so, point D would move toward the PPP line. All points to the right of (or below) the PPP line represent more favorable purchasing power for home country goods than for foreign goods.

Testing the Purchasing Power Parity Theory

The PPP theory not only provides an explanation of how relative inflation rates between two countries can influence an exchange rate, but it also provides information that can be used to forecast exchange rates.

Conceptual Tests of PPP. One way to test the PPP theory is to choose two countries (say, the United States and a foreign country) and compare the differential in their inflation rates to the percentage change in the foreign currency's value during several time periods. Using a graph similar to Exhibit 8.2, we could plot each point representing the inflation differential and exchange rate percentage change for each specific time period and then determine whether these points closely resemble the PPP line as drawn in Exhibit 8.2. If the points deviate significantly from the PPP line, then the percentage change in the foreign currency is not being influenced by the inflation differential in the manner PPP theory suggests.

As an alternative test, several foreign countries could be compared with the home country over a given time period. Each foreign country will exhibit an inflation differential relative to the home country, which can be compared to the exchange rate change during the period of concern. Thus, a point can be plotted on a graph such as Exhibit 8.2 for each foreign country analyzed. If the points deviate significantly from the PPP line, then the exchange rates are not responding to the inflation differentials in accordance with PPP theory. The PPP theory can be tested for any countries on which inflation information is available.

Statistical Test of PPP. A somewhat simplified statistical test of PPP can be developed by applying regression analysis to historical exchange rates and inflation differentials (see Appendix C for more information on regression analysis). To illustrate, let's focus on one particular exchange rate. The quarterly percentage changes in the foreign currency value (e_f) can be regressed against the inflation differential that existed at the beginning of each quarter, as shown here:

$$e_f = a_0 + a_1\left[\frac{(1 + I_{U.S.})}{(1 + I_f)} - 1\right] + \mu$$

where a_0 is a constant, a_1 is the slope coefficient, and μ is an error term. Regression analysis would be applied to quarterly data to determine the regression coefficients. The hypothesized values of a_0 and a_1 are 0 and 1.0, respectively. These coefficients imply that for a given inflation differential, there is an equal offsetting percentage change in the exchange rate, on average. The appropriate *t*-test for each regression coefficient requires a comparison to the hypothesized value and division by the standard error (s.e.) of the coefficient as follows:

$$\text{Test for } a_0 = 0: \qquad \text{Test for } a_1 = 1$$

$$t = \frac{a_0 - 0}{\text{s.e. of } a_0} \qquad t = \frac{a_1 - 1}{\text{s.e. of } a_1}$$

Then the *t*-table is used to find the critical *t*-value. If either *t*-test finds that the coefficients differ significantly from what is expected, the relationship between the inflation differential and the exchange rate differs from that stated by PPP theory. It should be mentioned that the appropriate lag time between the inflation differential and the exchange rate is subject to controversy.

Results of Tests of PPP. Much research has been conducted to test whether PPP exists. Studies by Mishkin, Adler and Dumas, and Abuaf and Jorion[1] found evidence of significant deviations from PPP that persisted for lengthy periods. A related study by Adler and Lehman[2] provided evidence against PPP even over the long term.

Hakkio,[3] however, found that when an exchange rate deviated far from the value that would be expected according to PPP, it moved toward that value. Although the

[1] Frederic S. Mishkin, "Are Real Interest Rates Equal Across Countries? An Empirical Investigation of International Parity Conditions," *Journal of Finance* (December 1984): 1345–1357; Michael Adler and Bernard Dumas, "International Portfolio Choice and Corporate Finance: A Synthesis," *Journal of Finance* (June 1983): 925–984; Niso Abuaf and Philippe Jorion, "Purchasing Power in the Long Run," *Journal of Finance* (March 1990): 157–174.

[2] Michael Adler and Bruce Lehman, "Deviations from Purchasing Power Parity in the Long Run," *Journal of Finance* (December 1983): 1471–1487.

[3] Craig S. Hakkio, "Interest Rates and Exchange Rates—What Is the Relationship?" *Economic Review*, Federal Reserve Bank of Kansas City (November 1986): 33–43.

relationship between inflation differentials and exchange rates is not perfect even in the long run, it supports the use of inflation differentials to forecast long-run movements in exchange rates.

http://

The site at http://www.singstat.gov.sg compares the actual values of foreign currencies with the value that should exist under conditions of purchasing power parity.

Tests of PPP for Each Currency. To further examine whether PPP is valid, Exhibit 8.3 illustrates the relationship between relative inflation rates and exchange rate movements over time. The inflation differential shown in each of the four graphs (each graph represents one foreign currency) is measured as the U.S. inflation rate minus the foreign inflation rate. The annual differential in inflation between the United States and each foreign country is represented on the vertical axis. The annual percentage change in the exchange rate of each foreign currency (relative to the U.S. dollar) is represented on the horizontal axis. The annual inflation differentials and percentage changes in exchange rates from 1982 to 2004 are plotted. If PPP existed during the period examined, the points plotted on the graph should be near an imaginary 45-degree line, which would split the axes (like the PPP line shown in Exhibit 8.2).

Exhibit 8.3 Comparison of Annual Inflation Differentials and Exchange Rate Movements for Four Major Countries

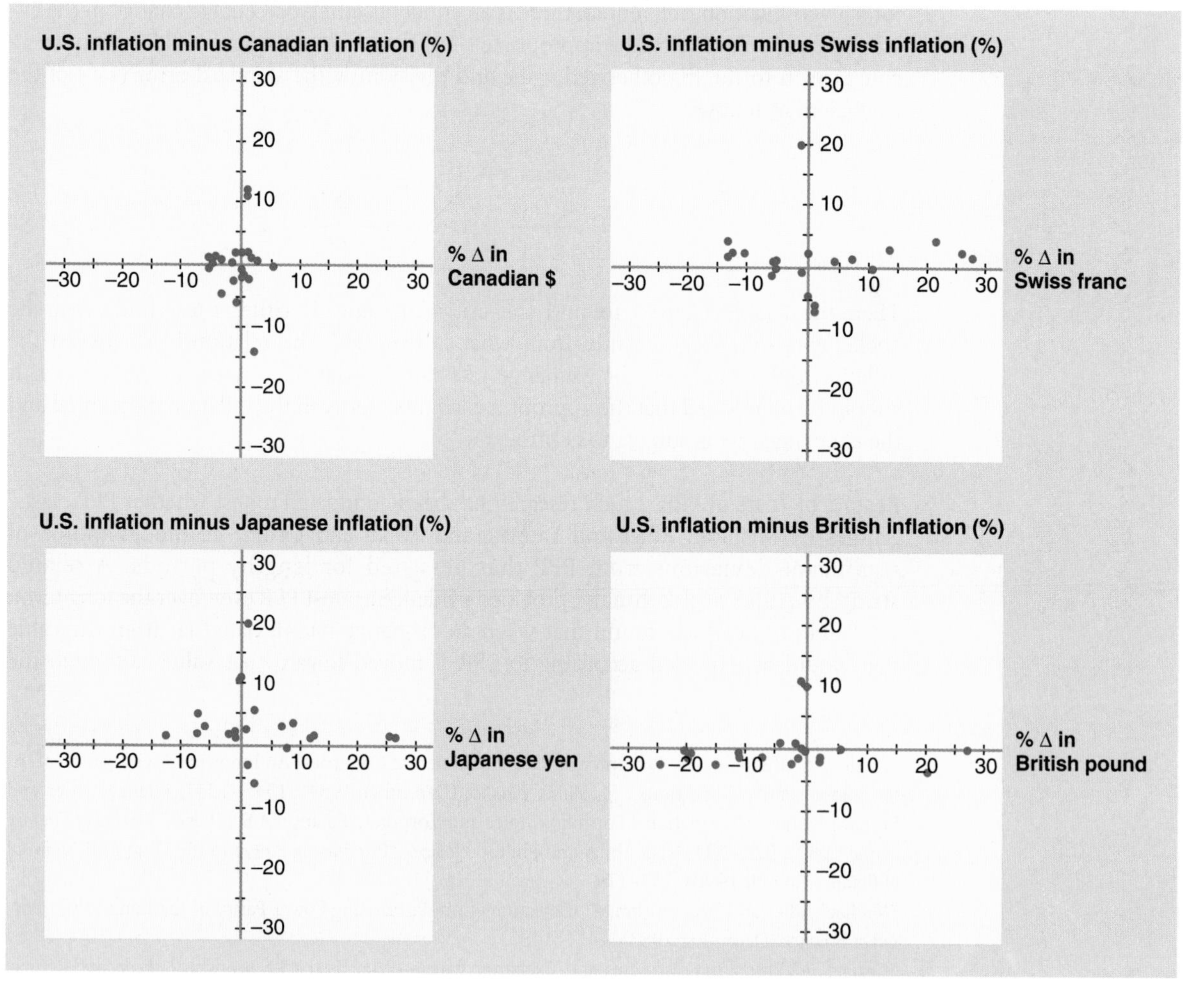

Although each graph shows different results, some general comments apply to all four graphs. The percentage changes in exchange rates are typically much more volatile than the inflation differentials. Thus, the exchange rates are changing to a greater degree than PPP theory would predict. In some years, even the direction of a currency could not have been anticipated by PPP theory. The results in Exhibit 8.3 suggest that the relationship between inflation differentials and exchange rate movements often becomes distorted.

Limitation of PPP Tests. A limitation in testing PPP theory is that the results will vary with the base period used. For example, if 1978 is used as a base period, most subsequent periods will show a relatively overvalued dollar; by contrast, if 1984 is used, the dollar may appear undervalued in subsequent periods.

The base period chosen should reflect an equilibrium position, since subsequent periods are evaluated in comparison to it. Unfortunately, it is difficult to choose such a base period. In fact, one of the main reasons for abolishing fixed exchange rates was the difficulty in identifying an appropriate equilibrium exchange rate.

USING THE WEB

Country Inflation Rates Information about inflation for each country is provided at http://biz.yahoo.com/ifc/. Click on any country listed, then click on Country Fact Sheet. The inflation rate in the recent year is reported, along with the average annual inflation rate over the last five years.

Why Purchasing Power Parity Does Not Occur

Purchasing power parity does not consistently occur because of confounding effects and because of a lack of substitutes for some traded goods. These reasons are explained next.

Confounding Effects. The PPP theory presumes that exchange rate movements are driven completely by the inflation differential between two countries. Yet, recall from Chapter 4 that a change in a currency's spot rate is influenced by the following factors:

$$e = f(\Delta INF, \Delta INT, \Delta INC, \Delta GC, \Delta EXP)$$

where

e = percentage change in the spot rate
ΔINF = change in the differential between U.S. inflation and the foreign country's inflation
ΔINT = change in the differential between the U.S. interest rate and the foreign country's interest rate
ΔINC = change in the differential between the U.S. income level and the foreign country's income level
ΔGC = change in government controls
ΔEXP = change in expectations of future exchange rates

Since the exchange rate movement is not driven solely by ΔINF, the relationship between the inflation differential and the exchange rate movement is not as simple as suggested by PPP.

EXAMPLE

Assume that Venezuela's inflation rate is 5 percent above the U.S. inflation rate. From this information, PPP theory would suggest that the Venezuelan bolivar should depreciate by about 5 percent against the U.S. dollar. Yet, if the government of Venezuela imposes trade barriers against U.S. exports, Venezuela's consumers and firms will not be able to adjust their spending in reaction to the inflation differential. Therefore, the exchange rate will not adjust as suggested by PPP.

No Substitutes for Traded Goods. The idea behind PPP theory is that as soon as the prices become relatively higher in one country, consumers in the other country will stop buying imported goods and shift to purchasing domestic goods instead. This shift influences the exchange rate. But, if substitute goods are not available domestically, consumers may not stop buying imported goods.

EXAMPLE

Reconsider the previous example in which Venezuela's inflation is 5 percent higher than the U.S. inflation rate. If U.S. consumers do not find suitable substitute goods at home, they may continue to buy the highly priced goods from Venezuela, and the bolivar may not depreciate as expected according to PPP theory.

Purchasing Power Parity in the Long Run

Purchasing power parity can be tested over the long run by assessing a "real" exchange rate between two currencies over time. The real exchange rate is the actual exchange rate adjusted for inflationary effects in the two countries of concern. In this way, the exchange rate serves as a measure of purchasing power. If a currency weakens by 10 percent but its home inflation is 10 percent more than inflation in the foreign country, the real exchange rate has not changed. The degree of weakness in the currency is offset by the lower inflationary effects on foreign goods.

If the real exchange rate reverts to some mean level over time, this suggests that it is constant in the long run, and any deviations from the mean are temporary. Conversely, if the real exchange rate follows a random walk, this implies that it moves randomly without any predictable pattern. That is, it does not tend to revert to some mean level and therefore cannot be viewed as constant in the long run. Under these conditions, the notion of PPP is rejected because the movements in the real exchange rate appear to be more than temporary deviations from some equilibrium value.

The study by Abuaf and Jorion,[4] mentioned earlier, tested PPP by assessing the long-run pattern of the real exchange rate. Abuaf and Jorion state that the typical findings rejecting PPP in previous studies are questionable because of limitations in the methods used to test PPP. They suggest that deviations from PPP are substantial in the short run but are reduced by about half in three years. Thus, even though exchange rates deviate from the levels predicted by PPP in the short run, their deviations are reduced over the long run.

USING THE WEB

Inflation and Exchange Rate Forecasts Information about anticipated inflation and exchange rates for each country is available at http://biz.yahoo.com/ifc/. Information is provided about various economic indicators, including inflation. A general inflation forecast is normally provided.

[4] Abuaf and Jorion, "Purchasing Power in the Long Run."

MANAGING FOR VALUE

Indirect Impact of Purchasing Power Parity on MNCs

The purchasing power parity relationship, though not exact, can explain how some events can have major effects on MNCs through their impact on exchange rates. One common example is the impact of oil prices on inflation and therefore on exchange rates. During the year 2000, the market price of oil increased substantially, placing upward pressure on inflation rates in countries that import oil. The European countries that participate in the euro import oil and were subjected to the higher prices of oil. Since the United Kingdom produces its own oil, it was not directly affected by the higher market price of oil. Its MNCs, however, were adversely affected as a result of their business with the other European countries. Inflation increased in Europe during 2000, which placed downward pressure on the euro relative to the British pound. MNCs in the United Kingdom that export to these euro-zone countries were adversely affected because the pound became more expensive relative to the euro, reducing the demand for British products.

MNCs based in euro-zone countries were also affected. Those that export to the United Kingdom benefited because their products became cheaper to British consumers. However, the inflation in the euro-zone countries caused the European Central Bank to raise interest rates in an attempt to reduce the inflationary pressure. Consequently, the economies of these countries weakened, and the local demand for the products produced by the MNCs was reduced.

MNCs that recognize their susceptibility to foreign inflation rates are motivated to monitor foreign inflation and limit their exposure to countries that may experience an abrupt increase in inflation.

International Fisher Effect (IFE)

Along with PPP theory, another major theory in international finance is the **international Fisher effect (IFE)** theory. It uses interest rate rather than inflation rate differentials to explain why exchange rates change over time, but it is closely related to the PPP theory because interest rates are often highly correlated with inflation rates. According to the so-called **Fisher effect**, nominal risk-free interest rates contain a real rate of return and anticipated inflation. If investors of all countries require the same real return, interest rate differentials between countries may be the result of differentials in expected inflation.

Relationship with Purchasing Power Parity

Recall that PPP theory suggests that exchange rate movements are caused by inflation rate differentials. If real rates of interest are the same across countries, any difference in nominal interest rates could be attributed to the difference in expected inflation. The IFE theory suggests that foreign currencies with relatively high interest rates will depreciate because the high nominal interest rates reflect expected inflation. The nominal interest rate would also incorporate the *default risk* of an investment. The following examples focus on investments that are risk-free so that default risk will not have to be accounted for.

EXAMPLE

The nominal interest rate is 8 percent in the United States. Investors in the United States expect a 6 percent rate of inflation, which means that they expect to earn a real return of 2 percent over one year. The nominal interest rate in Canada is 13 percent. Given that investors in Canada also require a real return of 2 percent, the expected inflation rate in

Canada must be 11 percent. According to PPP theory, the Canadian dollar is expected to depreciate by approximately 5 percent against the U.S. dollar (since the Canadian inflation rate is 5 percent higher). Therefore, U.S. investors would not benefit from investing in Canada because the 5 percent interest rate differential would be offset by investing in a currency that is expected to be worth 5 percent less by the end of the investment period. U.S. investors would earn 8 percent on the Canadian investment, which is the same as they could earn in the United States.

The IFE theory disagrees with the notion introduced in Chapter 4 that a high interest rate may entice investors from various countries to invest there and could place upward pressure on the currency. One way to reconcile the difference is to consider the possible effects on two currencies, one of which is subject to extreme interest rate and inflation conditions.

EXAMPLE

Brazil's prevailing nominal interest rate is frequently very high because of the high inflation there. With inflation levels sometimes exceeding 100 percent annually, people tend to spend now before prices rise. Rather than saving, they are very willing to borrow even at high interest rates to buy products now because the alternative is to defer the purchase and have to pay a much higher price later. Thus, the high nominal interest rate is attributed to the high expected inflation. Given these expectations of high inflation, even interest rates exceeding 50 percent will not entice U.S. investors because they recognize that high inflation could cause Brazil's currency (the Brazilian real) to decline by more than 50 percent in a year, fully offsetting the high interest rate. Thus, the high interest rate in Brazil does not attract investment from U.S. investors and therefore will not cause the Brazilian real to strengthen. Instead, the high interest rate in Brazil may indicate potential depreciation of the Brazilian real, which places downward pressure on the currency's value. This example of Brazil supports the IFE theory.

Now consider a second currency, the Chilean peso. The nominal interest rate in Chile is usually only a few percentage points higher than the nominal interest rate in the United States. Chile normally has relatively low inflation, so U.S. investors are not as concerned that the Chilean peso's value will decline due to inflationary pressure. Therefore, they may attempt to capitalize on the higher interest rate in Chile. In this case, the U.S. investment in Chile may even cause the Chilean peso's value to increase, at least temporarily. This example of Chile does not support the IFE theory.

To reinforce the IFE concept, consider the outcome that would occur if the U.S. investors believed the IFE applied to Chile. The U.S. investors would assume that the slight interest advantage in Chile versus the United States reflected a slightly higher degree of expected inflation in Chile. The slightly higher inflation in Chile would be expected to cause a slight depreciation in the Chilean peso, which would offset the interest rate advantage. Thus, the return to U.S. investors from investing in Chile would be no higher than what they could earn from investing in the United States.

Implications of the IFE for Foreign Investors

The implications are similar for foreign investors who attempt to capitalize on relatively high U.S. interest rates. The foreign investors will be adversely affected by the effects of a relatively high U.S. inflation rate if they try to capitalize on the high U.S. interest rates.

EXAMPLE

The nominal interest rate is 8 percent in the United States and 5 percent in Japan. The expected real rate of return is 2 percent in each country. The U.S. inflation rate is expected to be 6 percent, while the inflation rate in Japan is expected to be 3 percent.

According to PPP theory, the Japanese yen is expected to appreciate by the expected inflation differential of 3 percent. If the exchange rate changes as expected, Japanese investors who attempt to capitalize on the higher U.S. interest rate will earn a return similar to what they could have earned in their own country. Though the U.S. interest rate is 3 percent higher, the Japanese investors will repurchase their yen at the end of the investment period for 3 percent more than the price at which they sold yen. Therefore, their return from investing in the United States is no better than what they would have earned domestically.

The IFE theory can be applied to any exchange rate, even exchange rates that involve two non-U.S. currencies.

EXAMPLE

Given the information in two previous examples, the expected inflation differential between Canada and Japan is 8 percent. According to PPP theory, this inflation differential suggests that the Canadian dollar should depreciate by 8 percent against the yen. Therefore, even though Japanese investors would earn an additional 8 percent interest on a Canadian investment, the Canadian dollar would be valued at 8 percent less by the end of the period. Under these conditions, the Japanese investors would earn a return of 5 percent, which is the same as what they would earn on an investment in Japan.

These possible investment opportunities, along with some others, are summarized in Exhibit 8.4. Note that wherever investors of a given country invest their funds, the expected nominal return is the same.

Derivation of the International Fisher Effect

http://

http://www.ny.frb.org/research/global_economy/index.html provides exchange rate and interest rate data for various countries.

The precise relationship between the interest rate differential of two countries and the expected exchange rate change according to the IFE can be derived as follows. First, the actual return to investors who invest in money market securities (such as short-term bank deposits) in their home country is simply the interest rate offered on those securities. The actual return to investors who invest in a foreign money market security, however, depends on not only the foreign interest rate (i_f) but also the percentage change in the value of the foreign currency (e_f) denominating the security. The formula for the actual or "effective" (exchange-rate-adjusted) return on a foreign bank deposit (or any money market security) is

$$r = (1 + i_f)(1 + e_f) - 1$$

According to the IFE, the effective return on a foreign investment should, on average, be equal to the effective return on a domestic investment. Therefore, the IFE suggests that the expected return on a foreign money market investment is equal to the interest rate on a local money market investment:

$$E(r) = i_h$$

where r is the effective return on the foreign deposit and i_h is the interest rate on the home deposit. We can determine the degree by which the foreign currency must change

Exhibit 8.4 Illustration of the International Fisher Effect (IFE) from Various Investor Perspectives

Investors Residing in	Attempt to Invest in	Expected Inflation Differential (Home Inflation Minus Foreign Inflation)	Expected Percentage Change in Currency Needed by Investors	Nominal Interest Rate to Be Earned	Return to Investors after Considering Exchange Rate Adjustment	Inflation Anticipated in Home Country	Real Return Earned by Investors
Japan	Japan		—	5%	5%	3%	2%
	U.S.	3% − 6% = −3%	−3%	8	5	3	2
	Canada	3% − 11% = −8%	−8	13	5	3	2
U.S.	Japan	6% − 3% = 3%	3	5	8	6	2
	U.S.		—	8	8	6	2
	Canada	6% − 11% = −5%	−5	13	8	6	2
Canada	Japan	11% − 3% = 8%	8	5	13	11	2
	U.S.	11% − 6% = 5%	5	8	13	11	2
	Canada		—	13	13	11	2

in order to make investments in both countries generate similar returns. Take the previous formula for what determines r, and set it equal to i_h as follows:

$$r = i_h$$
$$(1 + i_f)(1 + e_f) - 1 = i_h$$

Now solve for e_f:

$$(1 + i_f)(1 + e_f) = (1 + i_h)$$
$$(1 + e_f) = \frac{(1 + i_h)}{(1 + i_f)}$$
$$e_f = \frac{(1 + i_h)}{(1 + i_f)} - 1$$

As verified here, the IFE theory contends that when $i_h > i_f$, e_f will be positive because the relatively low foreign interest rate reflects relatively low inflationary expectations in the foreign country. That is, the foreign currency will appreciate when the foreign interest rate is lower than the home interest rate. This appreciation will improve the foreign return to investors from the home country, making returns on foreign securities similar to returns on home securities. Conversely, when $i_f > i_h$, e_f will be negative. That is, the foreign currency will depreciate when the foreign interest rate exceeds the home interest rate. This depreciation will reduce the return on foreign securities from the perspective of investors in the home country, making returns on foreign securities no higher than returns on home securities.

Numerical Example Based on the Derivation of IFE. Given two interest rates, the value of e_f can be determined from the formula that was just derived, and used to forecast the exchange rate.

EXAMPLE

Assume that the interest rate on a one-year insured home country bank deposit is 11 percent, and the interest rate on a one-year insured foreign bank deposit is 12 percent. For the actual returns of these two investments to be similar from the perspective of investors in the home country, the foreign currency would have to change over the investment horizon by the following percentage:

$$e_f = \frac{(1 + i_h)}{(1 + i_f)} - 1$$
$$= \frac{1 + .11}{1 + .12} - 1$$
$$= -.0089, \text{ or } -.89\%$$

The implications are that the foreign currency denominating the foreign deposit would need to depreciate by .89 percent to make the actual return on the foreign deposit equal to 11 percent from the perspective of investors in the home country. This would make the return on the foreign investment equal to the return on a domestic investment.

Simplified Relationship. A more simplified but less precise relationship specified by the IFE is

$$e_f \cong i_h - i_f$$

That is, the percentage change in the exchange rate over the investment horizon will equal the interest rate differential between two countries. This approximation provides reasonable estimates only when the interest rate differential is small.

Graphic Analysis of the International Fisher Effect

Exhibit 8.5 displays the set of points that conform to the argument behind IFE theory. For example, point E reflects a situation where the foreign interest rate exceeds the home interest rate by three percentage points. Yet, the foreign currency has depreciated by 3 percent to offset its interest rate advantage. Thus, an investor setting up a deposit in the foreign country achieves a return similar to what is possible domestically. Point F represents a home interest rate 2 percent above the foreign interest rate. If investors from the home country establish a foreign deposit, they are at a disadvantage regarding the foreign interest rate. However, IFE theory suggests that the currency should appreciate by 2 percent to offset the interest rate disadvantage.

Point F in Exhibit 8.5 also illustrates the IFE from a foreign investor's perspective. The home interest rate will appear attractive to the foreign investor. However, IFE theory suggests that the foreign currency will appreciate by 2 percent, which, from the foreign investor's perspective, implies that the home country's currency denominating the investment instruments will depreciate to offset the interest rate advantage.

Exhibit 8.5
Illustration of IFE Line (When Exchange Rate Changes Perfectly Offset Interest Rate Differentials)

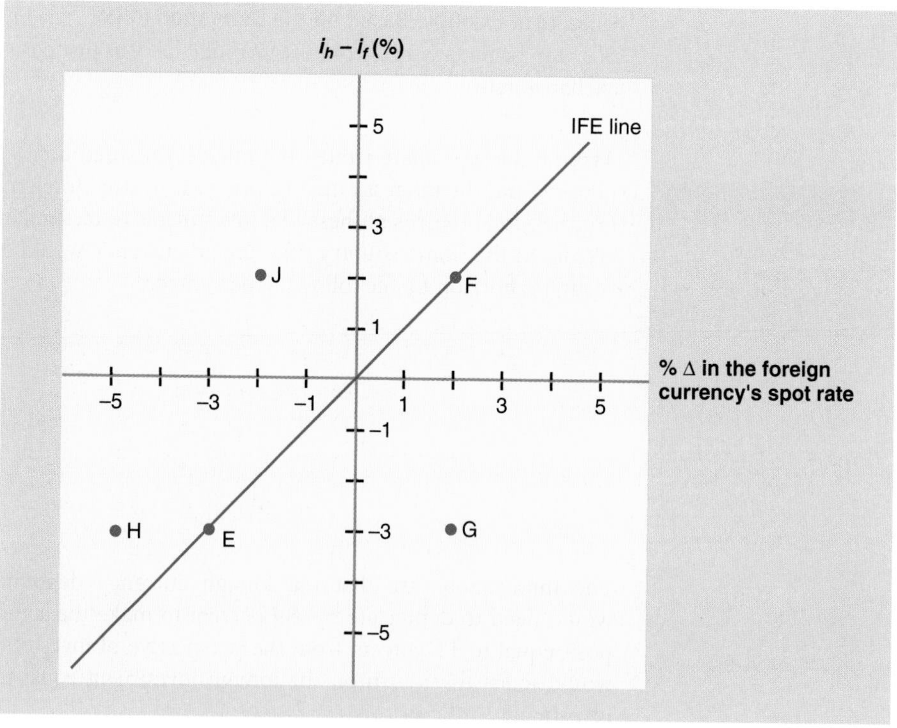

Points on the IFE Line. All the points along the so-called **IFE line** in Exhibit 8.5 reflect exchange rate adjustments to offset the differential in interest rates. This means investors will end up achieving the same yield (adjusted for exchange rate fluctuations) whether they invest at home or in a foreign country.

To be precise, IFE theory does not suggest that this relationship will exist continuously over each time period. The point of IFE theory is that if a corporation periodically makes foreign investments to take advantage of higher foreign interest rates, it will achieve a yield that is sometimes above and sometimes below the domestic yield. Periodic investments by a U.S. corporation in an attempt to capitalize on the higher interest rates will, on average, achieve a yield similar to that by a corporation simply making domestic deposits periodically.

Points below the IFE Line. Points below the IFE line generally reflect the higher returns from investing in foreign deposits. For example, point G in Exhibit 8.5 indicates that the foreign interest rate exceeds the home interest rate by 3 percent. In addition, the foreign currency has appreciated by 2 percent. The combination of the higher foreign interest rate plus the appreciation of the foreign currency will cause the foreign yield to be higher than what is possible domestically. If actual data were compiled and plotted, and the vast majority of points were below the IFE line, this would suggest that investors of the home country could consistently increase their investment returns by establishing foreign bank deposits. Such results would refute the IFE theory.

Points above the IFE Line. Points above the IFE line generally reflect returns from foreign deposits that are lower than the returns possible domestically. For example, point H reflects a foreign interest rate that is 3 percent above the home interest rate. Yet, point H also indicates that the exchange rate of the foreign currency has depreciated by 5 percent, more than offsetting its interest rate advantage.

As another example, point J represents a situation in which an investor of the home country is hampered in two ways by investing in a foreign deposit. First, the foreign interest rate is lower than the home interest rate. Second, the foreign currency depreciates during the time the foreign deposit is held. If actual data were compiled and plotted, and the vast majority of points were above the IFE line, this would suggest that investors of the home country would receive consistently lower returns from foreign investments as opposed to investments in the home country. Such results would refute the IFE theory.

Tests of the International Fisher Effect

http://

http://www.economagic.com/fedstl.htm provides U.S. inflation and exchange rate data.

If the actual points (one for each period) of interest rates and exchange rate changes were plotted over time on a graph such as Exhibit 8.5, we could determine whether the points are systematically below the IFE line (suggesting higher returns from foreign investing), above the line (suggesting lower returns from foreign investing), or evenly scattered on both sides (suggesting a balance of higher returns from foreign investing in some periods and lower foreign returns in other periods).

Exhibit 8.6 is an example of a set of points that tend to support the IFE theory. It implies that returns from short-term foreign investments are, on average, about equal to the returns that are possible domestically. Notice that each individual point reflects a change in the exchange rate that does not exactly offset the interest rate differential. In some cases, the exchange rate change does not fully offset the interest rate differential. In other cases, the exchange rate change more than offsets the interest rate

Exhibit 8.6

Illustration of IFE Concept (When Exchange Rate Changes Offset Interest Rate Differentials on Average)

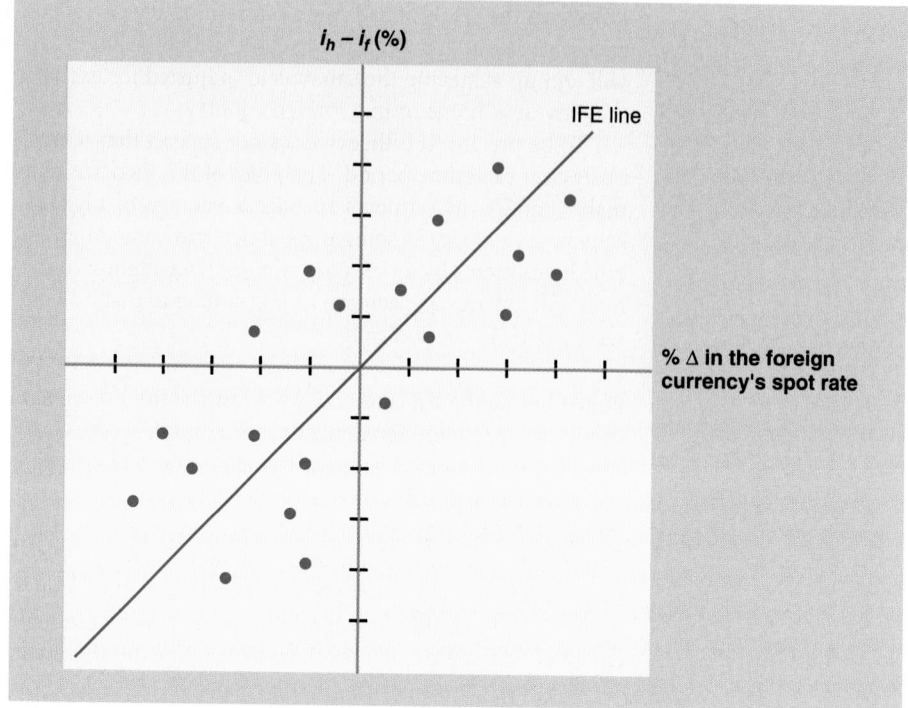

differential. Overall, the results balance out such that the interest rate differentials are, *on average*, offset by changes in the exchange rates. Thus, foreign investments have generated yields that are, on average, equal to those of domestic investments.

If foreign yields are expected to be about equal to domestic yields, a U.S. firm would probably prefer the domestic investments. The firm would know the yield on domestic short-term securities (such as bank deposits) in advance, whereas the yield to be attained from foreign short-term securities would be uncertain because the firm would not know what spot exchange rate would exist at the securities' maturity. Investors generally prefer an investment whose return is known over an investment whose return is uncertain, assuming that all other features of the investments are similar.

Results from Testing the IFE. Whether the IFE holds in reality depends on the particular time period examined. Although the IFE theory may hold during some time frames, there is evidence that it does not consistently hold. A study by Thomas[5] tested the IFE theory by examining the results of (1) purchasing currency futures contracts of currencies with high interest rates that contained discounts (relative to the spot rates) and (2) selling futures on currencies with low interest rates that contained premiums. If the high-interest-rate currencies depreciated and the low-interest-rate currencies appreciated to the extent suggested by the IFE theory, this strategy would not generate significant profits. However, 123 (57 percent) of the 216 transactions created by this strategy were profitable. In addition, the average gain was much higher than the average loss. This study indicates that the IFE does not hold.

[5]Lee R. Thomas, "A Winning Strategy for Currency-Futures Speculation," *Journal of Portfolio Management* (Fall 1985): 65–69.

Statistical Test of the IFE. A somewhat simplified statistical test of the IFE can be developed by applying regression analysis to historical exchange rates and the nominal interest rate differential:

$$e_f = a_0 + a_1\left[\frac{(1 + i_{U.S.})}{(1 + i_f)} - 1\right] + \mu$$

where a_0 is a constant, a_1 is the slope coefficient, and μ is an error term. Regression analysis would determine the regression coefficients. The hypothesized values of a_0 and a_1 are 0 and 1.0, respectively.

The appropriate t-test for each regression coefficient requires a comparison to the hypothesized value and then division by the standard error (s.e.) of the coefficients, as follows:

Test for $a_0 = 0$	Test for $a_1 = 1$
$t = \frac{a_0 - 0}{\text{s.e. of } a_0}$	$t = \frac{a_1 - 1}{\text{s.e. of } a_1}$

The t-table is then used to find the critical t-value. If either t-test finds that the coefficients differ significantly from what was hypothesized, the IFE is refuted.

Why the International Fisher Effect Does Not Occur

As mentioned earlier in this chapter, purchasing power parity (PPP) has not held over certain periods. Since the IFE is based on purchasing power parity, it does not consistently hold either. Because exchange rates can be affected by factors other than inflation, exchange rates do not always adjust in accordance with the inflation differential. Assume a nominal interest rate in a foreign country that is 3 percent above the U.S. rate because expected inflation in that country is 3 percent above expected U.S. inflation. Even if these nominal rates properly reflect inflationary expectations, the exchange rate of the foreign currency will react to other factors in addition to the inflation differential. If these other factors put upward pressure on the foreign currency's value, they will offset the downward pressure from the inflation differential. Consequently, foreign investments will achieve higher returns for the U.S. investors than domestic investments will.

Comparison of the IRP, PPP, and IFE Theories

At this point, it may be helpful to compare three related theories of international finance: (1) interest rate parity (IRP), discussed in Chapter 7, (2) purchasing power parity (PPP), and (3) the international Fisher effect (IFE). Exhibit 8.7 summarizes the main themes of each theory. Note that although all three theories relate to the determination of exchange rates, they have different implications. The IRP theory focuses on why the forward rate differs from the spot rate and on the degree of difference that should exist. It relates to a specific point in time. In contrast, the PPP theory and IFE theory focus on how a currency's spot rate will change over time. Whereas PPP theory suggests that the spot rate will change in accordance with inflation differentials, IFE theory suggests that it will change in accordance with interest rate differentials. Nevertheless, PPP is related to IFE

Exhibit 8.7
Comparison of the IRP, PPP, and IFE Theories

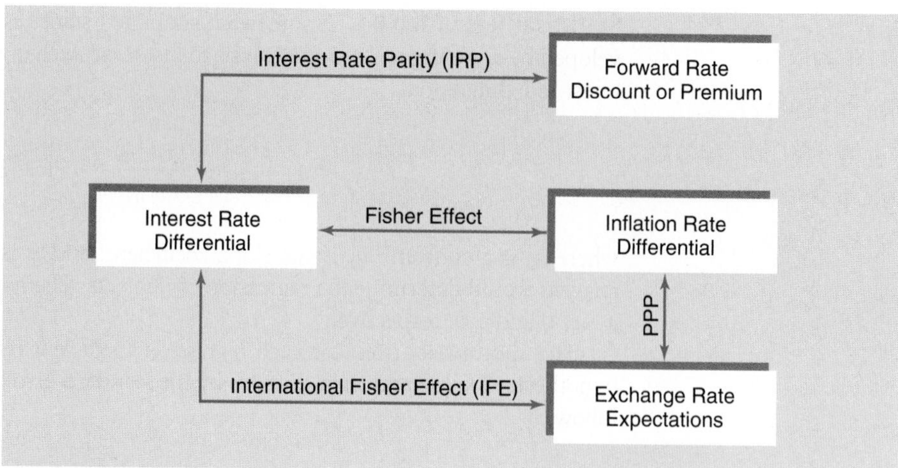

Theory	Key Variables of Theory		Summary of Theory
Interest rate parity (IRP)	Forward rate premium (or discount)	Interest rate differential	The forward rate of one currency with respect to another will contain a premium (or discount) that is determined by the differential in interest rates between the two countries. As a result, covered interest arbitrage will provide a return that is no higher than a domestic return.
Purchasing power parity (PPP)	Percentage change in spot exchange rate	Inflation rate differential	The spot rate of one currency with respect to another will change in reaction to the differential in inflation rates between the two countries. Consequently, the purchasing power for consumers when purchasing goods in their own country will be similar to their purchasing power when importing goods from the foreign country.
International Fisher effect (IFE)	Percentage change in spot exchange rate	Interest rate differential	The spot rate of one currency with respect to another will change in accordance with the differential in interest rates between the two countries. Consequently, the return on uncovered foreign money market securities will, on average, be no higher than the return on domestic money market securities from the perspective of investors in the home country.

because expected inflation differentials influence the nominal interest rate differentials between two countries.

Some generalizations about countries can be made by applying these theories. High-inflation countries tend to have high nominal interest rates (due to the Fisher effect). Their currencies tend to weaken over time (because of the PPP and IFE), and the forward rates of their currencies normally exhibit large discounts (due to IRP).

SUMMARY

- Purchasing power parity (PPP) theory specifies a precise relationship between relative inflation rates of two countries and their exchange rate. In inexact terms, PPP theory suggests that the equilibrium exchange rate will adjust by the same magnitude as the differential in inflation rates between two countries. Though PPP continues to be a valuable concept, there is evidence of sizable deviations from the theory in the real world.
- The international Fisher effect (IFE) specifies a precise relationship between relative interest rates of two countries and their exchange rates. It suggests that an investor who periodically invests in foreign interest-bearing securities will, on average, achieve a return similar to what is possible domestically. This implies that the exchange rate of the country with high interest rates will depreciate to offset the interest rate advantage achieved by foreign investments. However, there is evidence that during some periods the IFE does not hold. Thus, investment in foreign short-term securities may achieve a higher return than what is possible domestically. If a firm attempts to achieve this higher return, however, it does incur the risk that the currency denominating the foreign security might depreciate against the investor's home currency during the investment period. In this case, the foreign security could generate a lower return than a domestic security, even though it exhibits a higher interest rate.
- The PPP theory focuses on the relationship between the inflation rate differential and future exchange rate movements. The IFE focuses on the interest rate differential and future exchange rate movements. The theory of interest rate parity (IRP) focuses on the relationship between the interest rate differential and the forward rate premium (or discount) at a given point in time.
- If IRP exists, it is not possible to benefit from covered interest arbitrage. Investors can still attempt to benefit from high foreign interest rates if they remain uncovered (do not sell the currency forward). But IFE suggests that this strategy will not generate higher returns than what are possible domestically because the exchange rate is expected to decline, on average, by the amount of the interest rate differential.

POINT COUNTER-POINT

Does PPP Eliminate Concerns about Long-Term Exchange Rate Risk?

Point Yes. Studies have shown that exchange rate movements are related to inflation differentials in the long run. Based on PPP, the currency of a high-inflation country will depreciate against the dollar. A subsidiary in that country should generate inflated revenue from the inflation, which will help offset the adverse exchange effects when its earnings are remitted to the parent. If a firm is focused on long-term performance, the deviations from PPP will offset over time. In some years, the exchange rate effects may exceed the inflation effects, and in other years the inflation effects will exceed the exchange rate effects.

Counter-Point No. Even if the relationship between inflation and exchange rate effects is consistent, this does not guarantee that the effects on the firm will be offsetting. A subsidiary in a high-inflation country will not necessarily be able to adjust its price level to keep up with the increased costs of doing business there. The effects vary with each MNC's situation. Even if the subsidiary can raise its prices to match the rising costs, there are short-term deviations from PPP. The investors who invest in an MNC's stock may be concerned about short-term deviations from PPP, because they will not necessarily hold the stock for the long term. Thus, investors may prefer that firms manage in a manner that reduces the volatility in their performance in short-run and long-run periods.

Who Is Correct? Use InfoTrac or some other search engine to learn more about this issue. Which argument do you support? Offer your own opinion on this issue.

SELF TEST

Answers are provided in Appendix A at the back of the text.

1. A U.S. importer of Japanese computer components pays for the components in yen. The importer is not concerned about a possible increase in Japanese prices (charged in yen) because of the likely offsetting effect caused by purchasing power parity (PPP). Explain what this means.

2. Use what you know about tests of PPP to answer this question. Using the information in the first question, explain why the U.S. importer of Japanese computer components should be concerned about its future payments.

3. Use PPP to explain how the values of the currencies of Eastern European countries might change if those countries experience high inflation, while the United States experiences low inflation.

4. Assume that the Canadian dollar's spot rate is \$.85 and that the Canadian and U.S. inflation rates are similar. Then assume that Canada experiences 4 percent inflation, while the United States experiences 3 percent inflation. According to PPP, what will be the new value of the Canadian dollar after it adjusts to the inflationary changes? (You may use the approximate formula to answer this question.)

5. Assume that the Australian dollar's spot rate is \$.90 and that the Australian and U.S. one-year interest rates are initially 6 percent. Then assume that the Australian one-year interest rate increases by 5 percentage points, while the U.S. one-year interest rate remains unchanged. Using this information and the international Fisher effect (IFE) theory, forecast the spot rate for one year ahead.

6. In the previous question, the Australian interest rates increased from 6 percent to 11 percent. According to the IFE, what is the underlying factor that would cause such a change? Give an explanation based on the IFE of the forces that would cause a change in the Australian dollar. If U.S. investors believe in the IFE, will they attempt to capitalize on the higher Australian interest rates? Explain.

QUESTIONS AND APPLICATIONS

1. **PPP.** Explain the theory of purchasing power parity (PPP). Based on this theory, what is a general forecast of the values of currencies in countries with high inflation?

2. **Rationale of PPP.** Explain the rationale of the PPP theory.

3. **Testing PPP.** Explain how you could determine whether PPP exists. Describe a limitation in testing whether PPP holds.

4. **Testing PPP.** Inflation differentials between the United States and other industrialized countries have typically been a few percentage points in any given year. Yet, in many years annual exchange rates between the corresponding currencies have changed by 10 percent or more. What does this information suggest about PPP?

5. **Limitations of PPP.** Explain why PPP does not hold.

6. **Implications of IFE.** Explain the international Fisher effect (IFE). What is the rationale for the existence of the IFE? What are the implications of the IFE for firms with excess cash that consistently invest in foreign Treasury bills? Explain why the IFE may not hold.

7. **Implications of IFE.** Assume U.S. interest rates are generally above foreign interest rates. What does this suggest about the future strength or weakness of the dollar based on the IFE? Should U.S. investors invest in foreign securities if they believe in the IFE? Should foreign investors invest in U.S. securities if they believe in the IFE?

8. **Comparing Parity Theories.** Compare and contrast interest rate parity (discussed in the previous chapter), purchasing power parity (PPP), and the international Fisher effect (IFE).

9. **Real Interest Rate.** One assumption made in developing the IFE is that all investors in all countries have the same real interest rate. What does this mean?

10. **Interpreting Inflationary Expectations.** If investors in the United States and Canada require the same real interest rate, and the nominal rate of interest is 2 percent higher in Canada, what does this imply about expectations of U.S. inflation and Canadian inflation? What do these inflationary expectations suggest about future exchange rates?

11. **PPP Applied to the Euro.** Assume that several European countries that use the euro as their currency experience higher inflation than the United States, while two other European countries that use the euro as their currency experience lower inflation than the United States. According to PPP, how will the euro's value against the dollar be affected?

12. **Source of Weak Currencies.** Currencies of some Latin American countries, such as Brazil and Venezuela, frequently weaken against most other currencies. What concept in this chapter explains this occurrence? Why don't all U.S.-based MNCs use forward contracts to hedge their future remittances of funds from Latin American countries to the United States if they expect depreciation of the currencies against the dollar?

13. **PPP.** Japan has typically had lower inflation than the United States. How would one expect this to affect the Japanese yen's value? Why does this expected relationship not always occur?

14. **IFE.** Assume that the nominal interest rate in Mexico is 48 percent and the interest rate in the United States is 8 percent for one-year securities that are free from default risk. What does the IFE suggest about the differential in expected inflation in these two countries? Using this information and the PPP theory, describe the expected nominal return to U.S. investors who invest in Mexico.

15. **IFE.** Shouldn't the IFE discourage investors from attempting to capitalize on higher foreign interest rates? Why do some investors continue to invest overseas, even when they have no other transactions overseas?

16. **Changes in Inflation.** Assume that the inflation rate in Brazil is expected to increase substantially. How will this affect Brazil's nominal interest rates and the value of its currency (called the real)? If the IFE holds, how will the nominal return to U.S. investors who invest in Brazil be affected by the higher inflation in Brazil? Explain.

17. **Comparing PPP and IFE.** How is it possible for PPP to hold if the IFE does not?

18. **Estimating Depreciation Due to PPP.** Assume that the spot exchange rate of the British pound is $1.73. How will this spot rate adjust according to PPP if the United Kingdom experiences an inflation rate of 7 percent while the United States experiences an inflation rate of 2 percent?

19. **Forecasting the Future Spot Rate Based on IFE.** Assume that the spot exchange rate of the Singapore dollar is $.70. The one-year interest rate is 11 percent in the United States and 7 percent in Singapore. What will the spot rate be in one year according to the IFE? (You may use the approximate formula to answer this question.)

20. **Deriving Forecasts of the Future Spot Rate.** As of today, assume the following information is available:

	U.S.	Mexico
Real rate of interest required by investors	2%	2%
Nominal interest rate	11%	15%
Spot rate	—	$.20
One-year forward rate	—	$.19

a. Use the forward rate to forecast the percentage change in the Mexican peso over the next year.

b. Use the differential in expected inflation to forecast the percentage change in the Mexican peso over the next year.

c. Use the spot rate to forecast the percentage change in the Mexican peso over the next year.

21. **Inflation and Interest Rate Effects.** The opening of Russia's market has resulted in a highly volatile Russian currency (the ruble). Russia's inflation has commonly exceeded 20 percent per month. Russian interest rates commonly exceed 150 percent, but this is sometimes less than the annual inflation rate in Russia.

a. Explain why the high Russian inflation has put severe pressure on the value of the Russian ruble.

b. Does the effect of Russian inflation on the decline in the ruble's value support the PPP theory? How might the relationship be distorted by political conditions in Russia?

c. Does it appear that the prices of Russian goods will be equal to the prices of U.S. goods from the perspective of Russian consumers (after considering exchange rates)? Explain.

d. Will the effects of the high Russian inflation and the decline in the ruble offset each other for U.S. importers? That is, how will U.S. importers of Russian goods be affected by the conditions?

22. **IFE Application to Asian Crisis.** Before the Asian crisis, many investors attempted to capitalize on the high interest rates prevailing in the Southeast Asian countries although the level of interest rates primarily reflected expectations of inflation. Explain why investors behaved in this manner. Why does the IFE suggest that the Southeast Asian countries would not have attracted foreign investment before the Asian crisis despite the high interest rates prevailing in those countries?

23. **IFE Applied to the Euro.** Given the recent conversion of several European currencies to the euro, explain what would cause the euro's value to change against the dollar according to the IFE.

ADVANCED QUESTIONS

24. **IFE.** Beth Miller does not believe that the international Fisher effect (IFE) holds. Current one-year interest rates in Europe are 5 percent, while one-year interest rates in the United States are 3 percent. Beth converts $100,000 to euros and invests them in Germany. One year later, she converts the euros back to dollars. The current spot rate of the euro is $1.10.

    a. According to the IFE, what should the spot rate of the euro in one year be?

    b. If the spot rate of the euro in one year is $1.00, what is Beth's percentage return from her strategy?

    c. If the spot rate of the euro in one year is $1.08, what is Beth's percentage return from her strategy?

    d. What must the spot rate of the euro be in one year for Beth's strategy to be successful?

25. **Integrating IRP and IFE.** Assume the following information is available for the United States and Europe:

	U.S.	Europe
Nominal interest rate	4%	6%
Expected inflation	2%	5%
Spot rate	—	$1.13
One-year forward rate	—	$1.10

    a. Does IRP hold?

    b. According to PPP, what is the expected spot rate of the euro in one year?

    c. According to the IFE, what is the expected spot rate of the euro in one year?

    d. Reconcile your answers to parts (a) and (c).

26. **IRP.** The one-year risk-free interest rate in Mexico is 10 percent. The one-year risk-free rate in the United States is 2 percent. Assume that interest rate parity exists. The spot rate of the Mexican peso is $.14.

    a. What is the forward rate premium?

    b. What is the one-year forward rate of the peso?

    c. Based on the international Fisher effect, what is the expected change in the spot rate over the next year?

    d. If the spot rate changes as expected according to the IFE, what will be the spot rate in one year?

    e. Compare your answers to (b) and (d) and explain the relationship.

27. **Testing the PPP.** How could you use regression analysis to determine whether the relationship specified by PPP exists on average? Specify the model, and describe how you would assess the regression results to determine if there is a *significant* difference from the relationship suggested by PPP.

28. **Testing the IFE.** Describe a statistical test for the IFE.

29. **Impact of Barriers on PPP and IFE.** Would PPP be more likely to hold between the United States and Hungary if trade barriers were completely removed and if Hungary's currency were allowed to float without any government intervention? Would the IFE be more likely to hold between the United

States and Hungary if trade barriers were completely removed and if Hungary's currency were allowed to float without any government intervention? Explain.

30. **Interactive Effects of PPP.** Assume that the inflation rates of the countries that use the euro are very low, while other European countries that have their own currencies experience high inflation. Explain how and why the euro's value could be expected to change against these currencies according to the PPP theory.

31. **Applying IRP and IFE.** Assume that Mexico has a one-year interest rate that is higher than the U.S. one-year interest rate. Assume that you believe in the international Fisher effect (IFE) and interest rate parity. Assume zero transactions costs.

    Ed is based in the United States and attempts to speculate by purchasing Mexican pesos today, investing the pesos in a risk-free asset for a year, and then converting the pesos to dollars at the end of one year. Ed did not cover his position in the forward market.

    Maria is based in Mexico and attempts covered interest arbitrage by purchasing dollars today and simultaneously selling dollars one year forward, investing the dollars in a risk-free asset for a year, and then converting the dollars back to pesos at the end of one year.

    Do you think the rate of return on Ed's investment will be higher than, lower than, or the same as the rate of return on Maria's investment? Explain.

32. **Arbitrage and PPP.** Assume that locational arbitrage ensures that spot exchange rates are properly aligned. Also assume that you believe in purchasing power parity. The spot rate of the British pound is $1.80. The spot rate of the Swiss franc is 0.3 pounds. You expect that the one-year inflation rate is 7 percent in the United Kingdom, 5 percent in Switzerland, and 1 percent in the United States. The one-year interest rate is 6 percent in the United Kingdom, 2 percent in Switzerland, and 4 percent in the United States. What is your expected spot rate of the Swiss franc in one year with respect to the U.S. dollar? Show your work.

33. **IRP Versus IFE.** You believe that interest rate parity and the international Fisher effect hold. Assume that the U.S. interest rate is presently much higher than the New Zealand interest rate. You have receivables of 1 million New Zealand dollars that you will receive in one year. You could hedge the receivables with the one-year forward contract. Or, you could decide to not hedge. Is your expected U.S. dollar amount of the receivables in one year from hedging higher, lower, or the same as your expected U.S. dollar amount of the receivables without hedging? Explain.

34. **IRP, PPP, and Speculating in Currency Derivatives.** The U.S. three-month interest rate (unannualized) is 1 percent. The Canadian three-month interest rate (unannualized) is 4 percent. Interest rate parity exists. The expected inflation over this period is 5 percent in the United States and 2 percent in Canada. A call option with a three-month expiration date on Canadian dollars is available for a premium of $.02 and a strike price of $.64. The spot rate of the Canadian dollar is $.65. Assume that you believe in purchasing power parity.

    a. Determine the dollar amount of your profit or loss from buying a call option contract specifying C$100,000.

    b. Determine the dollar amount of your profit or loss from buying a futures contract specifying C$100,000.

INTERNET APPLICATION

35. **Currency Interest Rates** The "Market" section of the Bloomberg website provides interest rate quotations for numerous currencies. Its address is **http://www.bloomberg.com**.

    a. Go to the "Markets" section and then to "International Yield Curves." Determine the prevailing one-year interest rate of the Australian dollar, the Japanese yen, and the British pound. Assuming a 2 percent real rate of interest for savers in any country, determine the expected rate of inflation over the next year in each of these countries that is implied by the nominal interest rate (according to the Fisher effect).

    b. What is the approximate expected percentage change in the value of each of these currencies against the dollar over the next year, when applying PPP to the inflation level of each of these currencies versus the dollar?

DISCUSSION IN THE BOARDROOM

This exercise can be found in Appendix E at the back of this textbook.

RUNNING YOUR OWN MNC

This exercise can be found on the Xtra! website at **http://maduraxtra.swlearning.com**.

BLADES, INC. CASE

Assessment of Purchasing Power Parity

Blades, the U.S.-based roller blades manufacturer, is currently both exporting to and importing from Thailand. The company has chosen Thailand as an export target for its primary product, "Speedos," because of Thailand's growth prospects and the lack of competition from both Thai and U.S. roller blade manufacturers in Thailand. Under an existing arrangement, Blades sells 180,000 pairs of Speedos annually to Entertainment Products, Inc., a Thai retailer. The arrangement involves a fixed, baht-denominated price and will last for three years. Blades generates approximately 10 percent of its revenue in Thailand.

Blades has also decided to import certain rubber and plastic components needed to manufacture Speedos because of cost and quality considerations. Specifically, the weak economic conditions in Thailand resulting from recent events have allowed Blades to import components from the country at a relatively low cost. However, Blades did not enter into a long-term arrangement to import these components and pays market prices (in baht) prevailing in Thailand at the time of purchase. Currently, Blades incurs about 4 percent of its cost of goods sold in Thailand.

Although Blades has no immediate plans for expansion in Thailand, it may establish a subsidiary there in the future. Moreover, even if Blades does not establish a subsidiary in Thailand, it will continue exporting to and importing from the country for several years. Due to these considerations, Blades' management is very concerned about recent events in Thailand and neighboring countries, as they may affect both Blades' current performance and its future plans.

Ben Holt, Blades' CFO, is particularly concerned about the level of inflation in Thailand. Blades' export arrangement with Entertainment Products, while allowing for a minimum level of revenue to be generated in Thailand in a given year, prevents Blades from adjusting prices according to the level of inflation in Thailand. In retrospect, Holt is wondering whether Blades should have entered into the export arrangement at all. Because Thailand's economy was growing very fast when Blades agreed to the arrangement, strong consumer spending there resulted in a high level of inflation and high interest rates. Naturally, Blades would have preferred an agreement whereby the price per pair of Speedos would be adjusted for the Thai level of inflation. However, to take advantage of the growth opportunities in Thailand, Blades accepted the arrangement when Entertainment Products insisted on a fixed price level. Currently, however, the baht is freely floating, and Holt is wondering how a relatively high level of Thai inflation may affect the baht-dollar exchange rate and, consequently, Blades' revenue generated in Thailand.

Ben Holt is also concerned about Blades' cost of goods sold incurred in Thailand. Since no fixed-price arrangement exists and the components are invoiced in Thai baht, Blades has been subject to increases in the prices of rubber and plastic. Holt is wondering how a potentially high level of inflation will impact the baht-dollar exchange rate and the cost of goods sold incurred in Thailand now that the baht is freely floating.

When Holt started thinking about future economic conditions in Thailand and the resulting impact on Blades, he found that he needed your help. In particular, Holt is vaguely familiar with the concept of purchasing power parity (PPP) and is wondering about this theory's implications, if any, for Blades. Furthermore, Holt also remembers that relatively high interest rates in Thailand will attract capital flows and put upward pressure on the baht.

Because of these concerns, and to gain some insight into the impact of inflation on Blades, Ben Holt has asked you to provide him with answers to the following questions:

1. What is the relationship between the exchange rates and relative inflation levels of the two countries? How will this relationship affect Blades' Thai revenue and costs given that the baht is freely floating? What is the net effect of this relationship on Blades?

2. What are some of the factors that prevent PPP from occurring in the short run? Would you expect PPP to hold better if countries negotiate trade arrangements under which they commit themselves to the purchase or sale of a fixed number of goods over a specified time period? Why or why not?

3. How do you reconcile the high level of interest rates in Thailand with the expected change of the baht-dollar exchange rate according to PPP?

4. Given Blades' future plans in Thailand, should the company be concerned with PPP? Why or why not?

5. PPP may hold better for some countries than for others. Given that the Thai baht has been freely floating for only a short period of time, how do you think Blades can gain insight into whether PPP will hold for Thailand?

SMALL BUSINESS DILEMMA

Assessment of the IFE by the Sports Exports Company

Every month, the Sports Exports Company receives a payment denominated in British pounds for the footballs it exports to the United Kingdom. Jim Logan, owner of the Sports Exports Company, decides each month whether to hedge the payment with a forward contract for the following month. Now, however, he is questioning whether this process is worth the trouble. He suggests that if the international Fisher effect (IFE) holds, the pound's value should change (on average) by an amount that reflects the differential between the interest rates of the two countries of concern. Since the forward premium reflects that same interest rate differential, the results from hedging should equal the results from not hedging on average.

1. Is Jim's interpretation of the IFE theory correct?

2. If you were in Jim's position, would you spend time trying to decide whether to hedge the receivables each month, or do you believe that the results would be the same (on average) whether you hedged or not?

PART 2

Integrative Problem

Exchange Rate Behavior

Questions

1. As an employee of the foreign exchange department for a large company, you have been given the following information:

   Beginning of Year

   Spot rate of £ = $1.596

   Spot rate of Australian dollar (A$) = $.70

   Cross exchange rate: £1 = A$2.28

   One-year forward rate of A$ = $.71

   One-year forward rate of £ = $1.58004

   One-year U.S. interest rate = 8.00%

   One-year British interest rate = 9.09%

   One-year Australian interest rate = 7.00%

   Determine whether triangular arbitrage is feasible and, if so, how it should be conducted to make a profit.

2. Using the information in question 1, determine whether covered interest arbitrage is feasible and, if so, how it should be conducted to make a profit.

3. Based on the information in question 1 for the beginning of the year, use the international Fisher effect (IFE) theory to forecast the annual percentage change in the British pound's value over the year.

4. Assume that at the beginning of the year, the pound's value is in equilibrium. Assume that over the year the British inflation rate is 6 percent, while the U.S. inflation rate is 4 percent. Assume that any change in the pound's value due to the inflation differential has occurred by the end of the year. Using this information and the information provided in question 1, determine how the pound's value changed over the year.

5. Assume that the pound's depreciation over the year was attributed directly to central bank intervention. Explain the type of direct intervention that would place downward pressure on the value of the pound.

PART 3

Exchange Rate Risk Management

Part 3 (Chapters 9 through 12) explains the various functions involved in managing exposure to exchange rate risk. Chapter 9 describes various methods used to forecast exchange rates and explains how to assess forecasting performance. Chapter 10 demonstrates how to measure exposure to exchange rate movements. Given a firm's exposure and forecasts of future exchange rates, Chapters 11 and 12 explain how to hedge that exposure.

Information on existing and anticipated economic conditions of various countries and on historical exchange rate movements

Forecasting exchange rates

Information on existing and anticipated cash flows in each currency at each subsidiary

Measuring exposure to exchange rate fluctuations

Managing exposure to exchange rate fluctuations

- How exposure will affect cash flows based on forecasted exchange rates.
- Whether to hedge any of the exposure and which hedging technique to use.

CHAPTER 9

Forecasting Exchange Rates

Many decisions of MNCs are influenced by exchange rate projections. Financial managers must understand how to forecast exchange rates so that they can make decisions that maximize the value of their MNCs.

The specific objectives of this chapter are to:

- explain how firms can benefit from forecasting exchange rates,
- describe the common techniques used for forecasting, and
- explain how forecasting performance can be evaluated.

Why Firms Forecast Exchange Rates

Virtually every operation of an MNC can be influenced by changes in exchange rates. The following are some of the corporate functions for which exchange rate forecasts are necessary:

- *Hedging decision.* MNCs constantly face the decision of whether to hedge future payables and receivables in foreign currencies. Whether a firm hedges may be determined by its forecasts of foreign currency values.

EXAMPLE

Laredo Co., based in the United States, plans to pay for clothing imported from Mexico in 90 days. If the forecasted value of the peso in 90 days is sufficiently below the 90-day forward rate, the MNC may decide not to hedge. Forecasting may enable the firm to make a decision that will increase its cash flows.

- *Short-term financing decision.* When large corporations borrow, they have access to several different currencies. The currency they borrow will ideally (1) exhibit a low interest rate and (2) weaken in value over the financing period.

EXAMPLE

Westbury Co. considers borrowing Japanese yen to finance its U.S. operations because the yen has a low interest rate. If the yen depreciates against the U.S. dollar over the financing period, the firm can pay back the loan with fewer dollars (when converting those dollars in exchange for the amount owed in yen). The decision of whether to finance with yen or dollars is dependent on a forecast of the future value of the yen.

- *Short-term investment decision.* Corporations sometimes have a substantial amount of excess cash available for a short time period. Large deposits can be established in several currencies. The ideal currency for deposits will (1) exhibit a high interest rate and (2) strengthen in value over the investment period.

EXAMPLE

Lafayette Co. has excess cash and considers depositing the cash into a British bank account. If the British pound appreciates against the dollar by the end of the deposit period when pounds will be withdrawn and exchanged for U.S. dollars, more dollars will be received. Thus, the firm can use forecasts of the pound's exchange rate when determining whether to invest the short-term cash in a British account or a U.S. account.

- *Capital budgeting decision.* When an MNC's parent assesses whether to invest funds in a foreign project, the firm takes into account that the project may periodically require the exchange of currencies. The capital budgeting analysis can be completed only when all estimated cash flows are measured in the parent's local currency.

EXAMPLE

Evansville Co. wants to determine whether to establish a subsidiary in Thailand. Forecasts of the future cash flows used in the capital budgeting process will be dependent on the future exchange rate of Thailand's currency (the baht) against the dollar. This dependency can be due to (1) future inflows denominated in baht that will require conversion to dollars and/or (2) the influence of future exchange rates on demand for the subsidiary's products. Accurate forecasts of currency values will improve the estimates of the cash flows and therefore enhance the MNC's decision making.

- *Earnings assessment.* The parent's decision about whether a foreign subsidiary should reinvest earnings in a foreign country or remit earnings back to the parent may be influenced by exchange rate forecasts. If a strong foreign currency is expected to weaken substantially against the parent's currency, the parent may prefer to expedite the remittance of subsidiary earnings before the foreign currency weakens.

  Exchange rate forecasts are also useful for forecasting an MNC's earnings. When earnings of an MNC are reported, subsidiary earnings are consolidated and translated into the currency representing the parent firm's home country.

EXAMPLE

Monroe Co. has its home office in the United States and subsidiaries in Canada and the United Kingdom. It must decide whether its Canadian and U.K. subsidiaries should remit their earnings. This involves comparing the amount of dollar cash flows that would be received today (if the subsidiaries remit the earnings) to the potential dollar cash flows that would be received in the future (if the subsidiaries reinvest the earnings). The decision is influenced by Monroe's forecast of the value of the Canadian dollar and the British pound at the time when the future earnings of the subsidiaries would be remitted.

For accounting purposes, the Canadian subsidiary's earnings in Canadian dollars must be measured by translating them to U.S. dollars. The British subsidiary's earnings in pounds must also be measured by translation to U.S. dollars. "Translation" does not mean that the earnings are physically converted to U.S. dollars. It is simply a periodic recording process so that consolidated earnings can be reported in a single currency. In this case, appreciation of the Canadian dollar will boost the Canadian subsidiary's earnings when they are reported in (translated to) U.S. dollars. Forecasts of exchange rates thus play an important role in the overall forecast of an MNC's consolidated earnings.

- *Long-term financing decision*. Corporations that issue bonds to secure long-term funds may consider denominating the bonds in foreign currencies. They prefer that the currency borrowed depreciate over time against the currency they are receiving from sales. To estimate the cost of issuing bonds denominated in a foreign currency, forecasts of exchange rates are required.

EXAMPLE

Bryce Co. needs long-term funds to support its U.S. business. It can issue 10-year bonds denominated in Japanese yen at a 1 percent coupon rate, which is 5 percentage points less than the prevailing coupon rate on dollar-denominated bonds. However, Bryce will need to convert dollars to make the coupon or principal payments on the yen-denominated bond, so if the yen's value rises, the yen-denominated bond could be more costly to Bryce than the U.S. bond. Bryce's decision to issue yen-denominated bonds versus dollar-denominated bonds will be dependent on its forecast of the yen's exchange rate over the 10-year period.

Although most forecasting is applied to currencies whose exchange rates fluctuate continuously, forecasts are also derived for currencies whose exchange rates are fixed.

EXAMPLE

Even though the Argentine peso's value was still tied to the U.S. dollar in 2001, some U.S.-based MNCs created forecasts for the peso at that time because they anticipated that it would be devalued. The peso was devalued in 2002, and its exchange rate is no longer tied to the U.S. dollar. The Hong Kong dollar has been tied to the U.S. dollar since 1983, but some MNCs still prepare long-term forecasts of the Hong Kong dollar in anticipation that it may be revalued.

An MNC's motives for forecasting exchange rates are summarized in Exhibit 9.1. The motives are distinguished according to whether they can enhance the MNC's value by influencing its cash flows or its cost of capital. The need for accurate exchange rate projections should now be clear. The following section describes the forecasting methods available.

Exhibit 9.1
Corporate Motives for Forecasting Exchange Rates

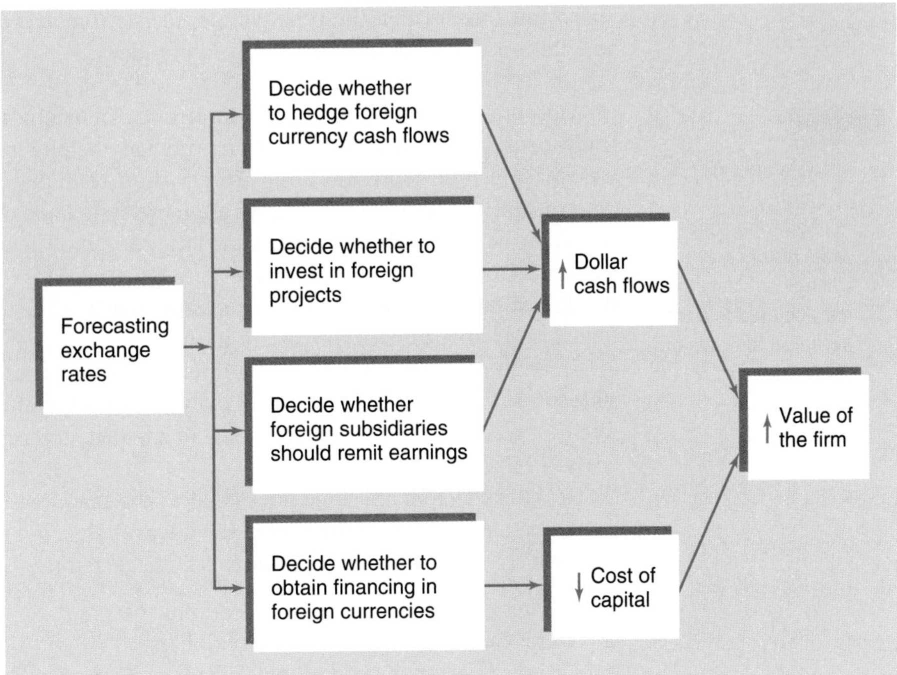

Forecasting Techniques

The numerous methods available for forecasting exchange rates can be categorized into four general groups: (1) technical, (2) fundamental, (3) market-based, and (4) mixed.

Technical Forecasting

Technical forecasting involves the use of historical exchange rate data to predict future values.

EXAMPLE

Tomorrow Kansas Co. has to pay 10 million Mexican pesos for supplies that it recently received from Mexico. Today, the peso has appreciated by 3 percent against the dollar. Kansas Co. could send the payment today so that it would avoid the effects of any additional appreciation tomorrow. Based on an analysis of historical time series, Kansas has determined that whenever the peso appreciates against the dollar by more than 1 percent, it experiences a reversal of about 60 percent on the following day. That is,

$$e_{t+1} = e_t \times (-60\%) \text{ when } e_t > 1\%$$

Applying this tendency to the current situation in which the peso appreciated by 3 percent today, Kansas Co. forecasts that tomorrow's exchange rate will change by

$$\begin{aligned} e_{t+1} &= e_t \times (-60\%) \\ &= (3\%) \times (-60\%) \\ &= -1.8\% \end{aligned}$$

Given this forecast that the peso will depreciate tomorrow, Kansas Co. decides that it will make its payment tomorrow instead of today.

http://

http://www.ny.frb.org/markets/foreignex.html provides historical exchange rate data that may be used to create technical forecasts of exchange rates.

Corporations tend to make only limited use of technical forecasting because it typically focuses on the near future, which is not very helpful for developing corporate policies. Most technical forecasts apply to very short-term periods such as one day because patterns in exchange rate movements are more systematic over such periods. Since patterns may be less reliable for forecasting long-term movements over a quarter, a year, or five years from now, technical forecasts are less useful for forecasting exchange rates in the distant future. Thus, technical forecasting may not be suitable for firms that need to forecast exchange rates in the distant future.

In addition, technical forecasting rarely provides point estimates or a range of possible future values. Because technical analysis typically cannot estimate future exchange rates in precise terms, it is not, by itself, an adequate forecasting tool for financial managers of MNCs.

Technical factors are sometimes cited as the main reason for changing speculative positions that cause an adjustment in the dollar's value. For example, headlines often attribute a change in the dollar's value to technical factors:

- Technical factors overwhelmed economic news.
- Technical factors triggered sales of dollars.
- Technical factors indicated that dollars had been recently oversold, triggering purchases of dollars.

As these examples suggest, technical forecasting appears to be widely used by speculators who attempt to capitalize on day-to-day exchange rate movements.

Technical forecasting models have helped some speculators in the foreign exchange market at various times. However, a model that has worked well in one particular period will not necessarily work well in another. With the abundance of technical models existing today, some are bound to generate speculative profits in any given period. If the pattern of currency values over time appears to be random, then technical forecasting is

MANAGING FOR VALUE

How DuPont's Earnings Forecasts Are Based on Currency Forecasts

Like many publicly traded companies, DuPont periodically announces its expectations of future earnings. Because much of its business is international, the company considers movements in exchange rates when deriving expectations of its earnings. In particular, the euro's value is closely monitored because of DuPont's major presence in Europe. When the euro's value changes over a quarter, the translated earnings generated by DuPont's European subsidiaries are affected. Thus, DuPont's forecast of its consolidated earnings requires a forecast of earnings generated by subsidiaries in each country along with a forecast of the exchange rate at which those earnings will be translated into dollars. Given the uncertainty of exchange rates and other factors that affect earnings, DuPont uses a range when forecasting its earnings. The low end allows for the possibility of a weak euro (European earnings translated at low exchange rates), while the high end allows for the possibility of a strong euro (European earnings translated at high exchange rates).

Investors attempting to value DuPont's stock use the company's earnings forecasts to derive its expected future cash flows. Because DuPont's forecast of its consolidated earnings captures possible exchange rate movements, investors should not be surprised if a weakened euro adversely affects DuPont's earnings.

not appropriate. Unless historical trends in exchange rate movements can be identified, examination of past movements will not be useful for indicating future movements.

Many foreign exchange participants argue that even if a particular technical forecasting model is shown to lead consistently to speculative profits, it will no longer be useful once other participants begin to use it. Trading based on the model's recommendation will push the currency value to a new position immediately. Speculators using technical exchange rate forecasting often incur large transaction costs due to their frequent trading. In addition, monitoring currency movements in search of a systematic pattern can be time-consuming. Furthermore, speculators need sufficient capital to absorb losses that may occur.

Fundamental Forecasting

Fundamental forecasting is based on fundamental relationships between economic variables and exchange rates. Recall from Chapter 4 that a change in a currency's spot rate is influenced by the following factors:

$$e = f(\Delta INF, \Delta INT, \Delta INC, \Delta GC, \Delta EXT)$$

where

e = percentage change in the spot rate

ΔINF = change in the differential between U.S. inflation and the foreign country's inflation

ΔINT = change in the differential between the U.S. interest rate and the foreign country's interest rate

ΔINC = change in the differential between the U.S. income level and the foreign country's income level

ΔGC = change in government controls

ΔEXT = change in expectations of future exchange rates

Given current values of these variables along with their historical impact on a currency's value, corporations can develop exchange rate projections.

A forecast may arise simply from a subjective assessment of the degree to which general movements in economic variables in one country are expected to affect exchange rates. From a statistical perspective, a forecast would be based on quantitatively measured impacts of factors on exchange rates. Although some of the full-blown fundamental models are beyond the scope of this text, a simplified discussion follows.

EXAMPLE

The focus here is on only two of the many factors that affect currency values. Before identifying them, consider that the corporate objective is to forecast the percentage change (rate of appreciation or depreciation) in the British pound with respect to the U.S. dollar during the next quarter. For simplicity, assume the firm's forecast for the British pound is dependent on only two factors that affect the pound's value:

1. Inflation in the United States relative to inflation in the United Kingdom.
2. Income growth in the United States relative to income growth in the United Kingdom (measured as a percentage change).

The first step is to determine how these variables have affected the percentage change in the pound's value based on historical data. This is commonly achieved with regression analysis. First, quarterly data are compiled for the inflation and income growth levels of both the United Kingdom and the United States. The dependent variable is the quarterly percentage change in the British pound value (called *BP*). The independent (influential) variables may be set up as follows:

1. Previous quarterly percentage change in the inflation differential (U.S. inflation rate minus British inflation rate), referred to as INF_{t-1}.
2. Previous quarterly percentage change in the income growth differential (U.S. income growth minus British income growth), referred to as INC_{t-1}.

The regression equation can be defined as

$$BP_t = b_0 + b_1 INF_{t-1} + b_2 INC_{t-1} + \mu_t$$

where b_0 is a constant, b_1 measures the sensitivity of BP_t to changes in INF_{t-1}, b_2 measures the sensitivity of BP_t to changes in INC_{t-1}, and μ_t represents an error term. A set of historical data is used to obtain previous values of *BP*, *INF*, and *INC*. Using this data set, regression analysis will generate the values of the regression coefficients (b_0, b_1, and b_2). That is, regression analysis determines the direction and degree to which *BP* is affected by each independent variable. The coefficient b_1 will exhibit a positive sign if, when INF_{t-1} changes, BP_t changes in the same direction (other things held constant). A negative sign indicates that BP_t and INF_{t-1} move in opposite directions. In the equation given, b_1 is expected to exhibit a positive sign because when U.S. inflation increases relative to inflation in the United Kingdom, upward pressure is exerted on the pound's value.

The regression coefficient b_2 (which measures the impact of INC_{t-1} on BP_t) is expected to be positive because when U.S. income growth exceeds British income growth, there is upward pressure on the pound's value. These relationships have already been thoroughly discussed in Chapter 4.

Once regression analysis is employed to generate values of the coefficients, these coefficients can be used to forecast. To illustrate, assume the following values: $b_0 = .002$, $b_1 = .8$, and $b_2 = 1.0$. The coefficients can be interpreted as follows. For a one-unit percentage change in the inflation differential, the pound is expected to change by .8 percent in the same direction, other things held constant. For a one-unit percentage change in the income differential, the British pound is expected to change by 1.0 percent in the same direction, other things held constant. To develop forecasts, assume that the most recent quarterly percentage change in INF_{t-1} (the inflation differential) is 4 percent, and that INC_{t-1} (the income growth differential) is 2 percent. Using this information along with our estimated regression coefficients, the forecast for BP_t is

$$\begin{aligned} BP_t &= b_0 + b_1 INF_{t-1} + b_2 INC_{t-1} \\ &= .002 + .8(4\%) + 1(2\%) \\ &= .2\% + 3.2\% + 2\% \\ &= 5.4\% \end{aligned}$$

Thus, given the current figures for inflation rates and income growth, the pound should appreciate by 5.4 percent during the next quarter.

This example is simplified to illustrate how fundamental analysis can be implemented for forecasting. A full-blown model might include many more than two factors, but the application would still be similar. A large time series database would be necessary to warrant any confidence in the relationships detected by such a model.

Use of Sensitivity Analysis for Fundamental Forecasting. When a regression model is used for forecasting, and the values of the influential factors have a lagged impact on exchange rates, the actual value of those factors can be used as input for the forecast. For example, if the inflation differential has a lagged impact on exchange rates, the inflation differential in the previous period may be used to forecast the percentage change in the exchange rate over the future period. Some factors, however, have an instantaneous influence on exchange rates. Since these factors obviously cannot be known, forecasts must be used. Firms recognize that poor forecasts of these factors can cause poor forecasts of the exchange rate movements, so they may attempt to account for the uncertainty by using **sensitivity analysis**, which considers more than one possible outcome for the factors exhibiting uncertainty.

EXAMPLE

Phoenix Corp. develops a regression model to forecast the percentage change in the Mexican peso's value. It believes that the real interest rate differential and the inflation differential are the only factors that affect exchange rate movements, as shown in this regression model:

$$e_t = a_0 + a_1 INT_t + a_2 INF_{t-1} + \mu_t$$

where

e_t = percentage change in the peso's exchange rate over period t

INT_t = real interest rate differential over period t

INF_{t-1} = inflation differential in the previous period t

a_0, a_1, a_2 = regression coefficients

μ_t = error term

Historical data are used to determine values for e_t along with values for INT_t and INF_{t-1} for several periods (preferably, 30 or more periods are used to build the database). The length of each historical period (quarter, month, etc.) should match the length of the period for which the forecast is needed. The historical data needed per period for the Mexican peso model are (1) the percentage change in the peso's value, (2) the U.S. real interest rate minus the Mexican real interest rate, and (3) the U.S. inflation rate in the previous period minus the Mexican inflation rate in the previous period. Assume that regression analysis has provided the following estimates for the regression coefficients:

Regression Coefficient	Estimate
a_0	.001
a_1	−.7
a_2	.6

The negative sign of a_1 indicates a negative relationship between INT_t and the peso's movements, while the positive sign of a_2 indicates a positive relationship between INF_{t-1} and the peso's movements.

To forecast the peso's percentage change over the upcoming period, INT_t and INF_{t-1} must be estimated. Assume that INF_{t-1} was 1 percent. However, INT_t is not known at the beginning of the period and must therefore be forecasted. Assume that Phoenix Corp. has developed the following probability distribution for INT_t:

Probability	Possible Outcome
20%	−3%
50%	−4%
30%	−5%
100%	

A separate forecast of e_t can be developed from each possible outcome of INT_t as follows:

Forecast of *INT*	Forecast of e_t	Probability
−3%	.1% + (−.7)(−3%) + .6(1%) = 2.8%	20%
−4%	.1% + (−.7)(−4%) + .6(1%) = 3.5%	50%
−5%	.1% + (−.7)(−5%) + .6(1%) = 4.2%	30%

If the firm needs forecasts for other currencies, it can develop the probability distributions of their movements over the upcoming period in a similar manner.

EXAMPLE

Phoenix Corp. can forecast the percentage change in the Japanese yen by regressing historical percentage changes in the yen's value against (1) the differential between U.S. real interest rates and Japanese real interest rates and (2) the differential between U.S. inflation in the previous period and Japanese inflation in the previous period. The regression coefficients estimated by regression analysis for the yen model will differ from those for the peso model. The firm can then use the estimated coefficients along with estimates for the interest rate differential and inflation rate differential to develop a forecast of the percentage change in the yen. Sensitivity analysis can be used to reforecast the yen's percentage change based on alternative estimates of the interest rate differential.

Use of PPP for Fundamental Forecasting. Recall that the theory of purchasing power parity (PPP) specifies the fundamental relationship between the inflation differential and the exchange rate. In simple terms, PPP states that the currency of the relatively inflated country will depreciate by an amount that reflects that country's inflation differential. Recall that according to PPP, the percentage change in the foreign currency's value (e) over a period should reflect the differential between the home inflation rate (I_h) and the foreign inflation rate (I_f) over that period.

EXAMPLE

The U.S. inflation rate is expected to be 1 percent over the next year, while the Australian inflation rate is expected to be 6 percent. According to PPP, the Australian dollar's exchange rate should change as follows:

$$\begin{aligned} e_f &= \frac{(1 + I_{U.S.})}{(1 + I_f)} - 1 \\ &= \frac{1.01}{1.06} - 1 \\ &\cong -4.7\% \end{aligned}$$

This forecast of the percentage change in the Australian dollar can be applied to its existing spot rate to forecast the future spot rate at the end of one year. If the existing spot rate (S_t) of the Australian dollar is $.50, the expected spot rate at the end of one year, $E(S_{t+1})$, will be about $.4765:

$$\begin{aligned} E(S_{t+1}) &= S_t(1 + e_f) \\ &= \$.50[1 + (-.047)] \\ &= \$.4765 \end{aligned}$$

In reality, the inflation rates of two countries over an upcoming period are uncertain and therefore would have to be forecasted when using PPP to forecast the future exchange rate at the end of the period. This complicates the use of PPP to forecast future exchange rates. Even if the inflation rates in the upcoming period were known with certainty, PPP might not be able to forecast exchange rates accurately.

If the PPP theory were accurate in reality, there would be no need to even consider alternative forecasting techniques. However, using the inflation differential of two countries to forecast their exchange rate is not always accurate. Problems arise for several reasons: (1) the timing of the impact of inflation fluctuations on changing trade patterns, and therefore on exchange rates, is not known with certainty; (2) data used to measure relative prices of two countries may be somewhat inaccurate; (3) barriers to trade can disrupt the trade patterns that should emerge in accordance with PPP theory; and (4) other factors, such as the interest rate differential between countries, can also affect exchange rates. For these reasons, the inflation differential by itself is not sufficient to accurately forecast exchange rate movements. Nevertheless, it should be included in any fundamental forecasting model.

Limitations of Fundamental Forecasting. Although fundamental forecasting accounts for the expected fundamental relationships between factors and currency values, the following limitations exist:

1. The precise timing of the impact of some factors on a currency's value is not known. It is possible that the full impact of inflation on exchange rates will not occur until two, three, or four quarters later. The regression model would need to be adjusted accordingly.
2. As mentioned earlier, some factors exhibit an immediate impact on exchange rates. They can be usefully included in a fundamental forecasting model only if forecasts can be obtained for them. Forecasts of these factors should be developed for a period that corresponds to the period for which a forecast of exchange rates is

necessary. In this case, the accuracy of the exchange rate forecasts will be somewhat dependent on the accuracy of these factors. Even if a firm knows exactly how movements in these factors affect exchange rates, its exchange rate projections may be inaccurate if it cannot predict the values of the factors.

3. Some factors that deserve consideration in the fundamental forecasting process cannot be easily quantified. For example, what if large Australian exporting firms experience an unanticipated labor strike, causing shortages? This will reduce the availability of Australian goods for U.S. consumers and therefore reduce U.S. demand for Australian dollars. Such an event, which would put downward pressure on the Australian dollar value, normally is not incorporated into the forecasting model.
4. Coefficients derived from the regression analysis will not necessarily remain constant over time. In the previous example, the coefficient for INF_{t-1} was .6, suggesting that for a one-unit change in INF_{t-1}, the Mexican peso would appreciate by .6 percent. Yet, if the Mexican or U.S. governments imposed new trade barriers, or eliminated existing barriers, the impact of the inflation differential on trade (and therefore on the Mexican peso's exchange rate) could be affected.

These limitations of fundamental forecasting have been discussed to emphasize that even the most sophisticated forecasting techniques (fundamental or otherwise) cannot provide consistently accurate forecasts. MNCs that develop forecasts must allow for some margin of error and recognize the possibility of error when implementing corporate policies.

Market-Based Forecasting

The process of developing forecasts from market indicators, known as **market-based forecasting**, is usually based on either (1) the spot rate or (2) the forward rate.

Use of the Spot Rate. Today's spot rate may be used as a forecast of the spot rate that will exist on a future date. To see why the spot rate can serve as a market-based forecast, assume the British pound is expected to appreciate against the dollar in the very near future. This expectation will encourage speculators to buy the pound with U.S. dollars today in anticipation of its appreciation, and these purchases can force the pound's value up immediately. Conversely, if the pound is expected to depreciate against the dollar, speculators will sell off pounds now, hoping to purchase them back at a lower price after they decline in value. Such actions can force the pound to depreciate immediately. Thus, the current value of the pound should reflect the expectation of the pound's value in the very near future. Corporations can use the spot rate to forecast, since it represents the market's expectation of the spot rate in the near future.

http://

See http://www.cme.com for quotes on currency futures that can be used to create market-based forecasts.

Use of the Forward Rate. A forward rate quoted for a specific date in the future is commonly used as the forecasted spot rate on that future date. That is, a 30-day forward rate provides a forecast for the spot rate in 30 days, a 90-day forward rate provides a forecast of the spot rate in 90 days, and so on. Recall that the forward rate is measured as

$$F = S(1 + p)$$

where p represents the forward premium. Since p represents the percentage by which the forward rate exceeds the spot rate, it serves as the expected percentage change in the exchange rate:

$$\begin{aligned} E(e) &= p \\ &= (F/S) - 1 \text{ [by rearranging terms]} \end{aligned}$$

EXAMPLE

If the one-year forward rate of the Australian dollar is \$.63, while the spot rate is \$.60, the expected percentage change in the Australian dollar is

$$\begin{aligned} E(e) &= p \\ &= (F/S) - 1 \\ &= (.63/.60) - 1 \\ &= .05 \text{ or } 5\% \end{aligned}$$

Rationale for Using the Forward Rate. To understand why the forward rate can serve as a forecast of the future spot rate, consider the following example.

EXAMPLE

If speculators expect the spot rate of the British pound in 30 days to be \$1.45, and the prevailing forward rate is \$1.40, they might buy pounds 30 days forward at \$1.40 and then sell them when received (in 30 days) at the spot rate existing then. If a large number of speculators implement this strategy, the substantial forward purchases of pounds will cause the forward rate to increase until this speculative demand stops.

Perhaps this speculative demand will terminate when the forward rate reaches \$1.45, since at this rate, no profits will be expected by implementing the strategy. Thus, the forward rate should move toward the market's general expectation of the future spot rate. In this sense, the forward rate serves as a market-based forecast, since it reflects the market's expectation of the spot rate at the end of the forward horizon (30 days from now in this example).

Although the focus of this chapter is on corporate forecasting rather than speculation, it is speculation that helps to push the forward rate to the level that reflects the general expectation of the future spot rate. If corporations are convinced that the forward rate is a reliable indicator of the future spot rate, they can simply monitor this publicly quoted rate to develop exchange rate projections.

Long-Term Forecasting with Forward Rates. Long-term exchange rate forecasts can be derived from long-term forward rates.

EXAMPLE

Assume that the spot rate of the euro is currently \$1.00, while the five-year forward rate of the euro is \$1.06. This forward rate can serve as a forecast of \$1.06 for the euro in five years, which reflects a 6 percent appreciation in the euro over the next five years.

Forward rates are normally available for periods of two to five years or even longer, but the bid/ask spread is wide because of the limited trading volume. Although such rates are rarely quoted in financial newspapers, the quoted interest rates on risk-free instruments of various countries can be used to determine what the forward rates would be under conditions of interest rate parity.

EXAMPLE

The U.S. five-year interest rate is currently 10 percent, annualized, while the British five-year interest rate is 13 percent. The five-year compounded return on investments in each of these countries is computed as follows:

Country	Five-Year Compounded Return
United States	$(1.10)^5 - 1 = 61\%$
United Kingdom	$(1.13)^5 - 1 = 84\%$

Thus, the appropriate five-year forward rate premium (or discount) of the British pound would be

$$
\begin{aligned}
p &= \frac{(1 + i_{U.S.})}{(1 + i_{U.K.})} - 1 \\
&= \frac{1.61}{1.84} - 1 \\
&= -.125, \text{ or } -12.5\%
\end{aligned}
$$

The results of this comparison suggest that the five-year forward rate of the pound should contain a 12.5 percent discount. That is, the spot rate of the pound is expected to depreciate by 12.5 percent over the five-year period for which the forward rate is used to forecast.

The governments of some emerging markets (such as those in Latin America) do not issue long-term fixed-rate bonds very often. Consequently, long-term interest rates are not available, and long-term forward rates cannot be derived in the manner shown here.

USING THE WEB

Forward Rates as Forecasts Forward rates are available for the euro, British pound, Canadian dollar, and Japanese yen for 1-month, 3-month, 6-month, and 12-month maturities at http://www.bmo.com/economic/regular/fxrates.html. These forward rates may serve as forecasts of future spot rates.

The forward rate is easily accessible and therefore serves as a convenient and free forecast. Like any method of forecasting exchange rates, the forward rate is typically more accurate when forecasting exchange rates for short-term horizons than for long-term horizons. Exchange rates tend to wander farther from expectations over longer periods of time.

Implications of the IFE and IRP for Forecasts Using the Forward Rate. Recall that if interest rate parity (IRP) holds, the forward rate premium reflects the interest rate differential between two countries. Also recall that if the international Fisher effect (IFE) holds, a currency that has a higher interest rate than the U.S. interest rate should depreciate against the dollar because the higher interest rate implies a higher level of expected inflation in that country than in the United States. Since the forward rate captures the nominal interest rate (and therefore the expected inflation rate) between two countries, it should provide more accurate forecasts for currencies in high-inflation countries than the spot rate.

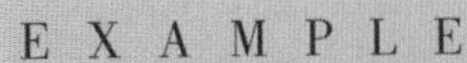

Alves, Inc., is a U.S. firm that does business in Brazil, and it needs to forecast the exchange rate of the Brazilian real for one year ahead. It considers using either the spot rate or the forward rate to forecast the real. The spot rate of the Brazilian real is $.40. The one-year interest rate in Brazil is 20 percent, versus 5 percent in the United States. The one-year forward rate is $.35, which reflects a discount to offset the interest rate differential according to IRP (check this yourself). Alves believes that the future exchange rate of the real will be driven by the inflation differential between Brazil and the United States. It also believes that the real rate of interest in both Brazil and the United States is 3 percent. This implies that the expected inflation rate for next year is 17 percent in Brazil and 2 percent in the United States. The forward rate discount is based on the interest rate differential, which in turn is related to the inflation differential. In this example, the forward rate of the Brazilian real reflects a large discount, which means that it implies a forecast of substantial depreciation of the real. Conversely, using the spot rate of the real as a forecast would imply that the exchange rate at the end of the year will be what it is today. Since the forward rate forecast indirectly captures the differential in expected inflation rates, it is a more appropriate forecast method than the spot rate.

Firms may not always believe that the forward rate provides more accurate forecasts than the spot rate. If a firm is forecasting over a very short-term horizon such as a day or a week, the interest rate (and therefore expected inflation) differential may not be as influential. Second, some firms may believe that the interest rate differential may not even be influential in the long run. Third, if the foreign country's interest rate is usually similar to the U.S. rate, the forward rate premium or discount will be close to zero, meaning that the forward rate and spot rate will provide similar forecasts.

Mixed Forecasting

Because no single forecasting technique has been found to be consistently superior to the others, some MNCs prefer to use a combination of forecasting techniques. This method is referred to as **mixed forecasting**. Various forecasts for a particular currency value are developed using several forecasting techniques. The techniques used are assigned weights in such a way that the weights total 100 percent, with the techniques considered more reliable being assigned higher weights. The actual forecast of the currency is a weighted average of the various forecasts developed.

EXAMPLE

College Station, Inc., needs to assess the value of the Mexican peso because it is considering expanding its business in Mexico. The conclusions drawn from each forecasting technique are shown in Exhibit 9.2. Notice that, in this example, the forecasted direction of the peso's value is dependent on the technique used. The fundamental forecast predicts the peso will appreciate, but the technical forecast and the market-based forecast predict it will depreciate. Also, notice that even though the fundamental and market-based forecasts are both driven by the same factor (interest rates), the results are distinctly different.

Sometimes MNCs assign one technique a lower weight when forecasting in one period, but a higher weight when forecasting in a later period. Some firms even weight a given technique more for some currencies than for others at a given point in time. For example, a firm may decide that a market-based forecast provides the best prediction for

Exhibit 9.2 Forecasts of the Mexican Peso Drawn from Each Forecasting Technique

	Factors Considered	Situation	Forecast
Technical Forecast	Recent movement in peso	The peso's value declined below a specific threshold level in the last few weeks.	The peso's value will continue to fall now that it is beyond the threshold level.
Fundamental Forecast	Economic growth, inflation, interest rates	Mexico's interest rates are high, and inflation should remain low.	The peso's value will rise as U.S. investors capitalize on the high interest rates by investing in Mexican securities.
Market-Based Forecast	Spot rate, forward rate	The peso's forward rate exhibits a significant discount, which is attributed to Mexico's relatively high interest rates.	Based on the forward rate, which provides a forecast of the future spot rate, the peso's value will decline.

the pound, but that fundamental forecasting works best for the New Zealand dollar, and technical forecasting for the Mexican peso.

While each forecasting method has its merits, some changes in exchange rates are not anticipated by any method.

EXAMPLE

During the Asian crisis, the Indonesian rupiah depreciated by more than 80 percent against the dollar within a nine-month period. Before the rupiah's decline, neither technical factors, nor fundamental factors, nor the forward rate indicated any potential weakness. The depreciation of the rupiah was primarily attributed to concerns by institutional investors about the safety of their investments in Indonesia, which encouraged them to liquidate the investments and convert the rupiah into other currencies, putting downward pressure on the rupiah.

USING THE WEB

Exchange Rate Forecasts Exchange rate forecasts for the currency of each country are provided at http://biz.yahoo.com/ifc/. Click on Country Outlook; then click on Exchange Rates to review exchange rate forecasts. The forecast is based on a consensus of experts. The website summarizes the forecasts for various time horizons and reports a mean, high, and low forecast for those horizons.

Weakness in some currencies may best be anticipated by a subjective assessment of conditions in a particular country and not by the quantitative methods described here. Thus, MNCs may benefit from using the methods described in this chapter along with their own sense of the conditions in a particular country. Nevertheless, it is still difficult to anticipate that a currency will weaken before a speculative outflow occurs. By that time, the currency will have weakened as a result of the outflow.

Forecasting Services

The corporate need to forecast currency values has prompted the emergence of several forecasting service firms, including Business International, Conti Currency, Predex, and Wharton Econometric Forecasting Associates. In addition, some large investment banks such as Goldman Sachs and commercial banks such as Citigroup offer forecasting services. Many consulting services use at least two different types of analysis to generate separate forecasts and then determine the weighted average of the forecasts. Some forecasting services focus on technical forecasting, while others focus on fundamental forecasting.

Forecasts are even provided for currencies that are not widely traded. Forecasting service firms provide forecasts on any currency for time horizons of interest to their clients, ranging from one day to 10 years from now. In addition, some firms offer advice on international cash management, assessment of exposure to exchange rate risk, and hedging. Many of the firms provide their clients with forecasts and recommendations monthly, or even weekly, for an annual fee.

Performance of Forecasting Services

Given the recent volatility in foreign exchange markets, it is quite difficult to forecast currency values. One way for a corporation to determine whether a forecasting service is valuable is to compare the accuracy of its forecasts to that of publicly available and free forecasts. The forward rate serves as a benchmark for comparison here, since it is quoted in many newspapers and magazines.

Some studies have compared several forecasting services' forecasts for different currencies to the forward rate, and found that the forecasts provided by services are no better than using the forward rate. Such results are frustrating for the corporations that have paid substantial amounts for expert opinions.

Perhaps some corporate clients of these forecasting services believe the fee is justified even when the forecasting performance is poor, if other services (such as cash management) are included in the package. It is also possible that a corporate treasurer, in recognition of the potential for error in forecasting exchange rates, may prefer to pay a forecasting service firm for its forecasts. Then the treasurer is not directly responsible for corporate problems that result from inaccurate currency forecasts. Not all MNCs hire forecasting service firms to do their forecasting. For example, Kodak, Inc., once used a service but became dissatisfied with it and has now developed its own forecasting system.

Evaluation of Forecast Performance

An MNC that forecasts exchange rates must monitor its performance over time to determine whether the forecasting procedure is satisfactory. For this purpose, a measurement of the forecast error is required. There are various ways to compute forecast errors. One popular measurement will be discussed here and is defined as follows:

$$\text{Absolute forecast error as a percentage of the realized value} = \frac{\left| \begin{array}{c}\text{Forecasted} \\ \text{value}\end{array} - \begin{array}{c}\text{Realized} \\ \text{value}\end{array} \right|}{\begin{array}{c}\text{Realized} \\ \text{value}\end{array}}$$

The error is computed using an absolute value because this avoids a possible offsetting effect when determining the mean forecast error. If the forecast error is .05 in the first period and −.05 in the second period (if the absolute value is not taken), the mean error is zero. Yet, that is misleading because the forecast was not perfectly accurate in either period. The absolute value avoids such a distortion.

When comparing a forecasting technique's performance among different currencies, it is often useful to adjust for their relative sizes.

EXAMPLE

Consider the following forecasted and realized values by New Hampshire Co. during one period:

	Forecasted Value	Realized Value
British pound	$1.35	$1.50
Mexican peso	$ .12	$ .10

In this case, the difference between the forecasted value and the realized value is \$.15 for the pound versus \$.02 for the peso. This does not necessarily mean that the forecast for the peso is more accurate. When the size of what is forecasted is considered (by dividing the difference by the realized value), one can see that the British pound has been predicted with more accuracy on a percentage basis. With the data given, the forecasting error (as defined earlier) of the British pound is

$$\frac{|\$1.35 - \$1.50|}{\$1.50} = \frac{\$.15}{\$1.50} = .10, \text{ or } 10\%$$

In contrast, the forecast error of the Mexican peso is

$$\frac{|.12 - .10|}{.10} = \frac{.02}{.10} = .20, \text{ or } 20\%$$

Thus, the peso has been predicted with less accuracy.

Forecast Accuracy over Time

MNCs are likely to have more confidence in their measurement of the forecast error when they measure it over each of several periods. The absolute forecast error as a percentage of the realized value can be estimated for each period to derive the mean error over all of these periods. If an MNC is most interested in forecasting the value of a currency 90 days (one quarter) from now, it will assess errors from the application of various forecast procedures over the last several quarters.

Have forecasts improved in recent years? The answer depends on the method used to develop forecasts. Exhibit 9.3 shows the magnitude of the absolute errors when the forward rate is used as a predictor for the British pound over time. The size of the errors changes over time. The errors are larger in periods when the pound's value was more volatile.

Forecast Accuracy among Currencies

The ability to forecast currency values may vary with the currency of concern. The Canadian dollar stands out as the currency most accurately predicted. Its mean error is typically less than the mean absolute forecast errors for other major currencies because its

Exhibit 9.3 Absolute Forecast Errors over Time for the British Pound (Using the Forward Rate to Forecast)

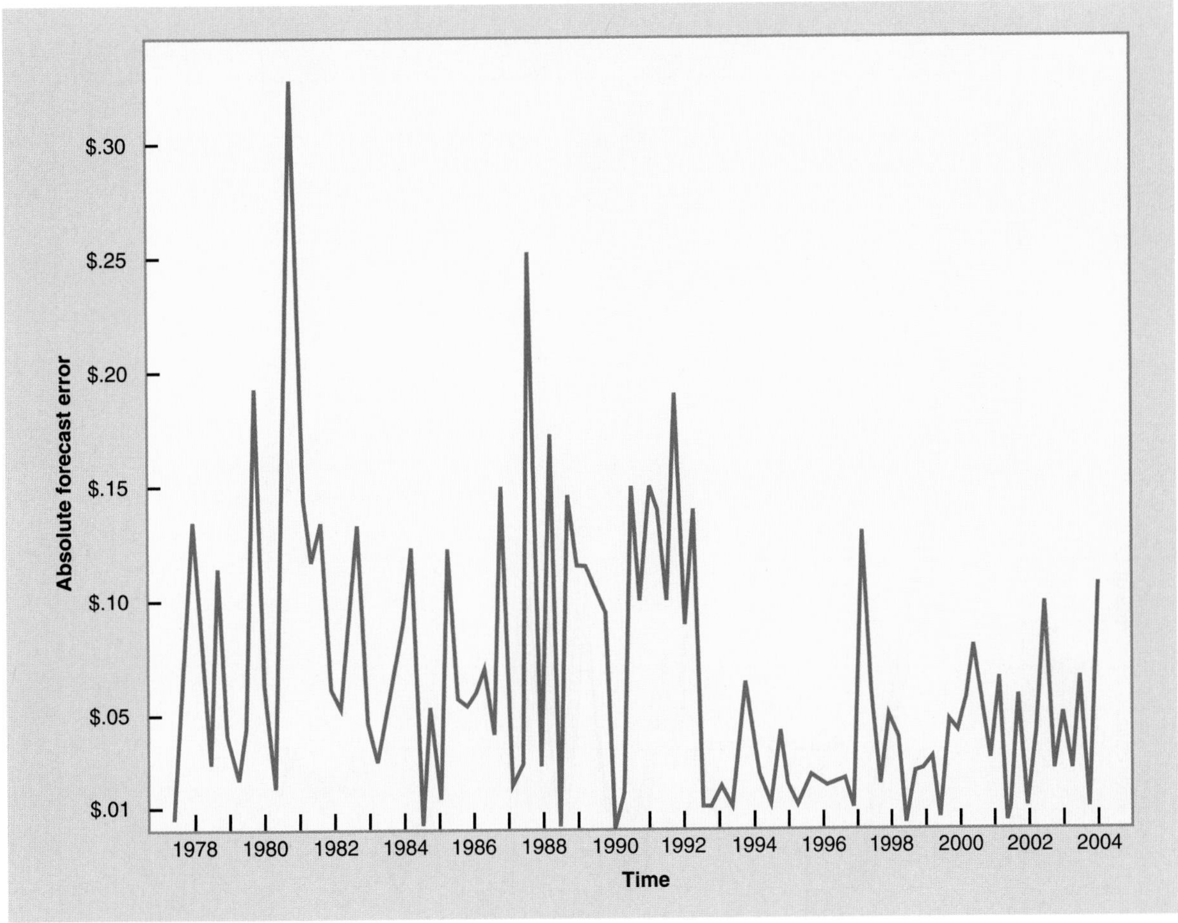

value is more stable over time. This information is important because it means that a financial manager of a U.S. firm can feel more confident about the number of dollars to be received (or needed) on Canadian transactions.

The absolute forecast errors of currencies can change over time. The absolute forecast error of each currency is lower, on average, in periods when the currency is more stable.

Search for Forecast Bias

The difference between the forecasted and realized exchange rates for a given point in time is a nominal forecast error. A time series of nominal forecast errors for the British pound is illustrated in Exhibit 9.4. Negative errors over time indicate underestimating, while positive errors indicate overestimating. If the errors are consistently positive or negative over time, then a bias in the forecasting procedure does exist. It appears that a bias did exist in distinct periods. During the strong-pound periods, the forecasts underestimated, while in weak-pound periods, the forecasts overestimated.

Exhibit 9.4 Comparison of Forecasted and Realized Spot Rates over Time for the British Pound (Using the Forward Rate to Forecast)

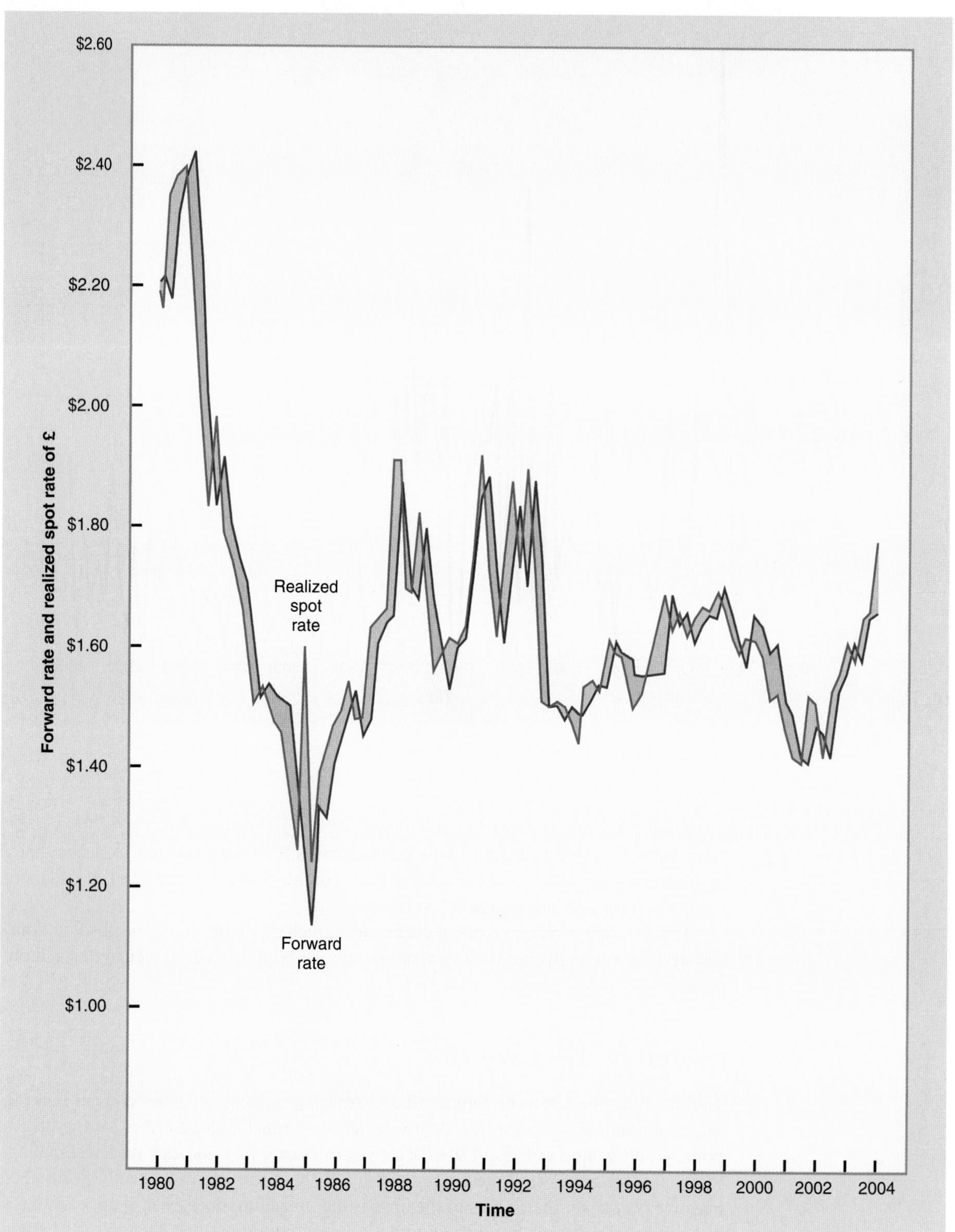

Statistical Test of Forecast Bias

If the forward rate is a biased predictor of the future spot rate, this implies that there is a systematic forecast error, which could be corrected to improve forecast accuracy. If the forward rate is unbiased, it fully reflects all available information about the future spot rate. In any case, any forecast errors would be the result of events that could not have been anticipated from existing information at the time of the forecast. A conventional method of testing for a forecast bias is to apply the following regression model to historical data:

$$S_t = a_0 + a_1 F_{t-1} + \mu_t$$

where

$$\begin{aligned} S_t &= \text{spot rate at time } t \\ F_{t-1} &= \text{forward rate at time } t-1 \\ \mu_t &= \text{error term} \\ a_0 &= \text{intercept} \\ a_1 &= \text{regression coefficient} \end{aligned}$$

If the forward rate is unbiased, the intercept should equal zero, and the regression coefficient a_1 should equal 1.0. The t-test for a_1 is

$$t = \frac{a_1 - 1}{\text{Standard error of } a_1}$$

If $a_0 = 0$ and a_1 is significantly less than 1.0, this implies that the forward rate is systematically overestimating the spot rate. For example, if $a_0 = 0$ and $a_1 = .90$, the future spot rate is estimated to be 90 percent of the forecast generated by the forward rate.

Conversely, if $a_0 = 0$ and a_1 is significantly greater than 1.0, this implies that the forward rate is systematically underestimating the spot rate. For example, if $a = 0$ and $a_1 = 1.1$, the future spot rate is estimated to be 1.1 times the forecast generated by the forward rate.

When a bias is detected and anticipated to persist in the future, future forecasts may incorporate that bias. For example, if $a_1 = 1.1$, future forecasts of the spot rate may incorporate this information by multiplying the forward rate by 1.1 to create a forecast of the future spot rate.

By detecting a bias, an MNC may be able to adjust for the bias so that it can improve its forecasting accuracy. For example, if the errors are consistently positive, an MNC could adjust today's forward rate downward to reflect the bias. Over time, a forecasting bias can change (from underestimating to overestimating, or vice versa). Any adjustment to the forward rate used as a forecast would need to reflect the anticipated bias for the period of concern.

Graphic Evaluation of Forecast Performance

Forecast performance can be examined with the use of a graph that compares forecasted values with the realized values for various time periods.

EXAMPLE

For eight quarters, Tunek Co. used the three-month forward rate of Currency Q to forecast Q's value three months ahead. The results from this strategy are shown in Exhibit 9.5, and the predicted and realized exchange rate values in Exhibit 9.5 are compared graphically in Exhibit 9.6.

The 45-degree line in Exhibit 9.6 represents perfect forecasts. If the realized value turned out to be exactly what was predicted over several periods, all points would be located on that 45-degree line in Exhibit 9.6. For this reason, the 45-degree line is referred to as the **perfect forecast line.** The closer the points reflecting the eight periods are vertically to the 45-degree line, the better the forecast. The vertical distance between

Exhibit 9.5
Evaluation of Forecast Performance

Period	Predicted Value of Currency Q for End of Period	Realized Value of Currency Q as of End of Period
1	$.20	$.16
2	.18	.14
3	.24	.16
4	.26	.22
5	.30	.28
6	.22	.26
7	.16	.14
8	.14	.10

Exhibit 9.6
Graphic Evaluation of Forecast Performance

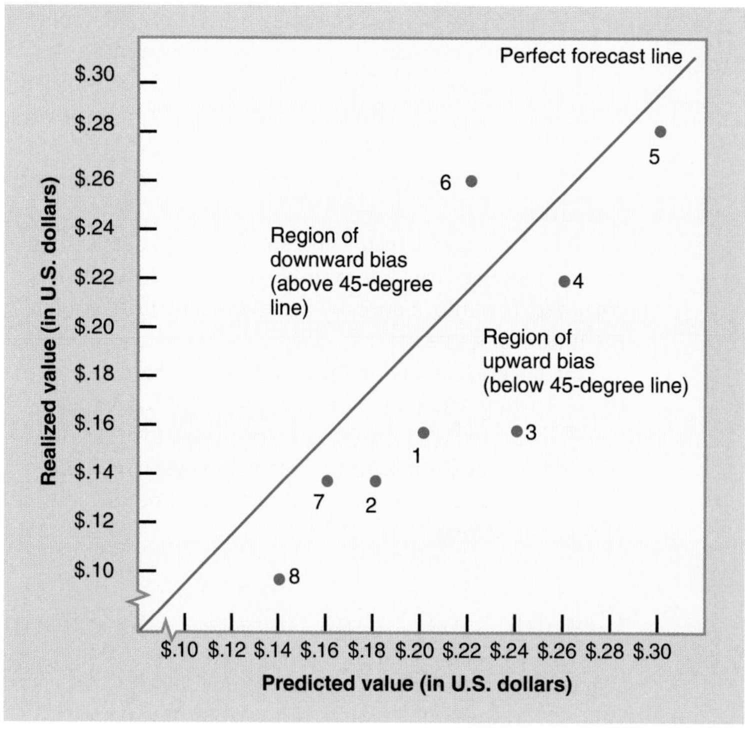

each point and the 45-degree line is the forecast error. If the point is \$.04 above the 45-degree line, this means that the realized spot rate was \$.04 higher than the exchange rate forecasted. All points above the 45-degree line reflect underestimation, while all points below the 45-degree line reflect overestimation.

If points appear to be scattered evenly on both sides of the 45-degree line, then the forecasts are said to be *unbiased*, since they are not consistently above or below the realized values. Whether evaluating the size of forecast errors or attempting to search for a bias, more reliable results are obtained when examining a large number of forecasts.

A more thorough assessment of a forecast bias can be conducted by separating the entire period into subperiods as shown in Exhibit 9.7 for the British pound. Each graph reflects a particular subperiod. Some graphs show a general underestimation while others show overestimation, which means that the forecast bias changed from one subperiod to another.

Comparison of Forecasting Methods

An MNC can compare forecasting methods by plotting the points relating to two methods on a graph similar to Exhibit 9.6. The points pertaining to each method can be distinguished by a particular mark or color. The performance of the two methods can be evaluated by comparing distances of points from the 45-degree line. In some cases, neither forecasting method may stand out as superior when compared graphically. If so, a more precise comparison can be conducted by computing the forecast errors for all periods for each method and then comparing these errors.

Xavier Co. uses a fundamental forecasting method to forecast the Polish currency (zloty), which it will need to purchase to buy imports from Poland. Xavier also derives a second forecast for each period based on an alternative forecasting model. Its previous forecasts of the zloty, using Model 1 (the fundamental method) and Model 2 (the alternative method), are shown in Columns 2 and 3, respectively, of Exhibit 9.8, along with the realized value of the zloty in Column 4.

The absolute forecast errors of forecasting with Model 1 and Model 2 are shown in Columns 5 and 6, respectively. Notice that Model 1 outperformed Model 2 in six of the eight periods. The mean absolute forecast error when using Model 1 is \$.04, meaning that forecasts with Model 1 are off by \$.04 on the average. Although Model 1 is not perfectly accurate, it does a better job than Model 2, whose mean absolute forecast error is \$.07. Overall, predictions with Model 1 are on the average \$.03 closer to the realized value.

For a complete comparison of performance among forecasting methods, an MNC should evaluate as many periods as possible. Only eight periods are used in our example because that is enough to illustrate how to compare forecasting performance. If the MNC has a large number of periods to evaluate, it could statistically test for significant differences in forecasting errors.

Forecasting under Market Efficiency

The efficiency of the foreign exchange market also has implications for forecasting. If the foreign exchange market is **weak-form efficient**, then historical and current exchange rate information is not useful for forecasting exchange rate movements because today's

Exhibit 9.7 Graphic Comparison of Forecasted and Realized Spot Rates in Different Subperiods for the British Pound (Using the Forward Rate as the Forecast)

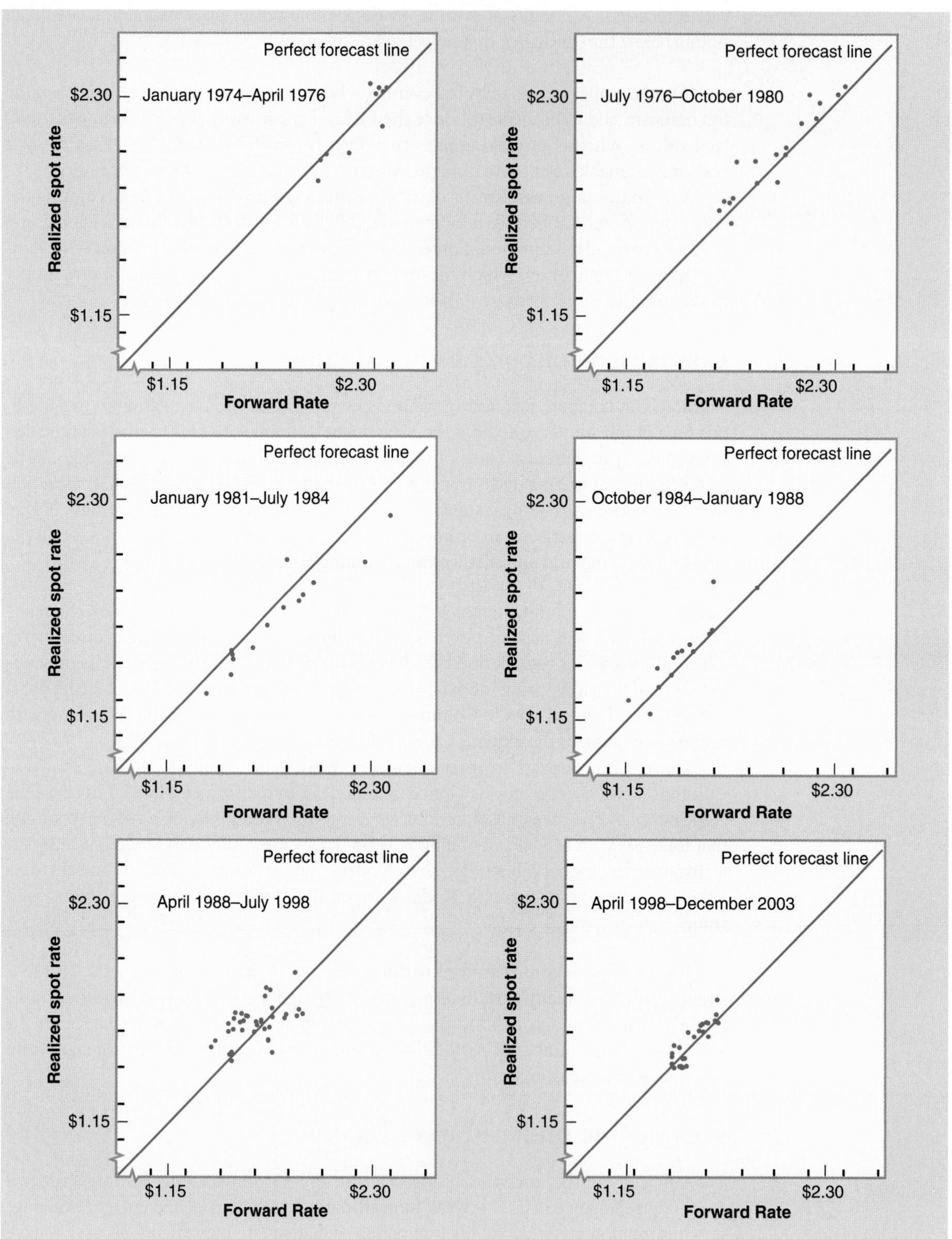

Exhibit 9.8 Comparison of Forecast Techniques

(1)	(2)	(3)	(4)	(5)	(6)	(7) = (5) − (6)
Period	Predicted Value of Zloty by Model 1	Predicted Value of Zloty by Model 2	Realized Value of Zloty	Absolute Forecast Error Using Model 1	Absolute Forecast Error Using Model 2	Difference in Absolute Forecast Errors (Model 1 − Model 2)
1	$.20	$.24	$.16	$.04	$.08	$−.04
2	.18	.20	.14	.04	.06	−.02
3	.24	.20	.16	.08	.04	.04
4	.26	.20	.22	.04	.02	.02
5	.30	.18	.28	.02	.10	−.08
6	.22	.32	.26	.04	.06	−.02
7	.16	.20	.14	.02	.06	−.04
8	.14	.24	.10	.04	.14	−.10
				Sum = .32 Mean = .04	Sum = .56 Mean = .07	Sum = −.24 Mean = −.03

exchange rates reflect all of this information. That is, technical analysis would not be capable of improving forecasts. If the foreign exchange market is **semistrong-form efficient**, then all relevant public information is already reflected in today's exchange rates. If today's exchange rates fully reflect any historical trends in exchange rate movements, but not other public information on expected interest rate movements, the foreign exchange market is weak-form efficient, but not semistrong-form efficient. Much research has tested the efficient market hypothesis for foreign exchange markets. Research suggests that foreign exchange markets appear to be weak-form efficient and semistrong-form efficient. However, there is some evidence of inefficiencies for some currencies in specific periods.

If foreign exchange markets are **strong-form efficient**, then all relevant public and private information is already reflected in today's exchange rates. This form of efficiency cannot be tested because private information is not available.

Even though foreign exchange markets are generally found to be at least semistrong-form efficient, forecasts of exchange rates by MNCs may still be worthwhile. Their goal is not necessarily to earn speculative profits but to use reasonable exchange rate forecasts to implement policies. When MNCs assess proposed policies, they usually prefer to develop their own forecasts of exchange rates over time rather than simply use market-based rates as a forecast of future rates. MNCs are often interested in more than a point estimate of an exchange rate one year, three years, or five years from now. They prefer to develop a variety of scenarios and assess how exchange rates may change for each scenario. Even if today's forward exchange rate properly reflects all available information, it does not indicate to the MNC the possible deviation of the realized future exchange rate from what is expected. MNCs need to determine the range of various possible exchange rate movements in order to assess the degree to which their operating performance could be affected.

Exchange Rate Volatility

MNCs recognize that it is nearly impossible to predict future exchange rates with perfect accuracy. For this reason, they may specify a range around their forecast.

EXAMPLE

Harp, Inc., based in Oklahoma, imports products from Canada. It uses the spot rate of the Canadian dollar (currently $.70) to forecast the value of the Canadian dollar one month from now. It also specifies a range around its forecasts, based on the historical volatility of the Canadian dollar. The more volatile the currency, the more likely it is to wander far from the forecasted value in the future (the larger is the expected forecast error). Harp determines that the standard deviation of the Canadian dollar's movements over the last 12 months is 2 percent. Thus, assuming the movements are normally distributed, it expects that there is a 68 percent chance that the actual value will be within 1 standard deviation (2 percent) of its forecast, which results in a range from $.686 to $.714. In addition, it expects that there is a 95 percent chance that the Canadian dollar will be within 2 standard deviations (4 percent) of the predicted value, which results in a range from $.672 to $.728. By specifying a range, Harp can more properly anticipate how far the actual value of the currency might deviate from its predicted value. If the currency was more volatile, its standard deviation would be larger, and the range surrounding the forecast would also be larger.

As this example shows, the measurement of a currency's volatility is useful for specifying a range around a forecast. However, a currency's volatility can change over time, which means that past volatility levels will not necessarily be the optimal method of establishing a range around a forecast. Therefore, MNCs may prefer to forecast exchange rate volatility to determine the potential range surrounding their forecast.

The first step in forecasting exchange rate volatility is to determine the relevant period of concern. If an MNC is forecasting the value of the Canadian dollar each day over the next quarter, it may also attempt to forecast the standard deviation of daily exchange rate movements over this quarter. This information could be used along with the point estimate forecast of the Canadian dollar for each day to derive confidence intervals around each forecast.

Methods of Forecasting Exchange Rate Volatility

The volatility of exchange rate movements for a future period can be forecast using (1) recent exchange rate volatility, (2) historical time series of volatilities, and (3) the implied standard deviation derived from currency option prices.

Use of the Recent Volatility Level. The volatility of historical exchange rate movements over a recent period can be used to forecast the future. In our example, the standard deviation of monthly exchange rate movements in the Canadian dollar during the previous 12 months could be used to estimate the future volatility of the Canadian dollar over the next month.

Use of a Historical Pattern of Volatilities. Since historical volatility can change over time, the standard deviation of monthly exchange rate movements in the last 12 months is not necessarily an accurate predictor of the volatility of exchange rate movements in the next month. To the extent that there is a pattern to the changes in exchange rate volatility over time, a series of time periods may be used to forecast volatility in the next period.

EXAMPLE

The standard deviation of monthly exchange rate movements in the Canadian dollar can be determined for each of the last several years. Then, a time series trend of these standard deviation levels can be used to form an estimate for the volatility of the Canadian dollar over the next month. The forecast may be based on a weighting scheme such as 60 percent times the standard deviation in the last year, plus 30 percent times the standard deviation in the year before that, plus 10 percent times the standard deviation in the year before that. This scheme places more weight on the most recent data to derive the forecast but allows data from the last three years to influence the forecast. Normally, the weights that achieved the most accuracy (lowest forecast error) over previous periods and the number of previous periods (lags) would be used when applying this method.

Various economic and political factors can cause exchange rate volatility to change abruptly, however, so even sophisticated time series models do not necessarily generate accurate forecasts of exchange rate volatility. This method differs from the first method in that it uses information from periods beyond the previous 12 months.

Implied Standard Deviation. A third method for forecasting exchange rate volatility is to derive the exchange rate's implied standard deviation (ISD) from the currency option pricing model. Recall that the premium on a call option for a currency is dependent on factors such as the relationship between the spot exchange rate and the exercise (strike) price of the option, the number of days until the expiration date of the option, and the anticipated volatility of the currency's exchange rate movements.

There is a currency option pricing model for estimating the call option premium based on various factors. The actual values of each of these factors are known, except for the anticipated volatility. By plugging in the prevailing option premium paid by investors for that specific currency option, however, it is possible to derive the market's anticipated volatility for that currency. The volatility is measured by the standard deviation, which can be used to develop a probability distribution surrounding the forecast of the currency's exchange rate.

USING THE WEB

Implied Volatilities Implied volatilities of major currencies are provided at http://www.fednewyork.org/markets/impliedvolatility.html. The implied volatility can be used to measure the market's expectations of a specific currency's volatility in the future. Implied volatilities are shown for different expiration dates, which allows for forecasts of volatility over periods up to those expiration dates.

SUMMARY

- Multinational corporations need exchange rate forecasts to make decisions on hedging payables and receivables, short-term financing and investment, capital budgeting, and long-term financing.
- The most common forecasting techniques can be classified as (1) technical, (2) fundamental, (3) market-based, and (4) mixed. Each technique has limitations, and the quality of the forecasts produced varies. Yet, due to the high variability in exchange rates, it should not be surprising that forecasts are not always accurate.
- Forecasting methods can be evaluated by comparing the actual values of currencies to the values predicted by the forecasting method. To be mean-

ingful, this comparison should be conducted over several periods. Two criteria used to evaluate performance of a forecast method are bias and accuracy. When comparing the accuracy of forecasts for two currencies, the absolute forecast error should be divided by the realized value of the currency to control for differences in the relative values of currencies.

POINT COUNTER-POINT

What Should an MNC Use to Forecast When Budgeting?

Point Use the spot rate to forecast. When a U.S.-based MNC firm conducts financial budgeting, it must estimate the values of its foreign currency cash flows that will be received by the parent. Since it is well documented that firms cannot accurately forecast future values, MNCs should use the spot rate for budgeting. Changes in economic conditions are difficult to predict, and the spot rate reflects the best guess of the future spot rate if there are no changes in economic conditions.

Counter-Point Use the forward rate to forecast. The spot rates of some currencies do not represent accurate or even unbiased estimates of the future spot rates. Many currencies of developing countries have generally declined over time. These currencies tend to be in countries that have high inflation rates. If the spot rate had been used for budgeting, the dollar cash flows resulting from cash inflows in these currencies would have been highly overestimated. The expected inflation in a country can be accounted for by using the nominal interest rate. A high nominal interest rate implies a high level of expected inflation. Based on interest rate parity, these currencies will have pronounced discounts. Thus, the forward rate captures the expected inflation differential between countries because it is influenced by the nominal interest rate differential. Since it captures the inflation differential, it should provide a more accurate forecast of currencies, especially those currencies in high-inflation countries.

Who Is Correct? Use InfoTrac or some other search engine to learn more about this issue. Which argument do you support? Offer your own opinion on this issue.

SELF TEST

Answers are provided in Appendix A at the back of the text.

1. Assume that the annual U.S. return is expected to be 7 percent for each of the next four years, while the annual interest rate in Mexico is expected to be 20 percent. Determine the appropriate four-year forward rate premium or discount on the Mexican peso, which could be used to forecast the percentage change in the peso over the next four years.

2. Consider the following information:

Currency	90-Day Forward Rate	Spot Rate That Occurred 90 Days Later
Canadian dollar	$.80	$.82
Japanese yen	$.012	$.011

   Assuming the forward rate was used to forecast the future spot rate, determine whether the Canadian dollar or the Japanese yen was forecasted with more accuracy, based on the absolute forecast error as a percentage of the realized value.

3. Assume that the forward rate and spot rate of the Mexican peso are normally similar at a given point in time. Assume that the peso has depreciated consistently and substantially over the last three years. Would the forward rate have been biased over this period? If so, would it typically have overestimated or underestimated the future spot rate of the peso (in dollars)? Explain.

4. An analyst has stated that the British pound seems to increase in value over the two weeks following announcements by the Bank of England (the British central bank) that it will raise interest rates. If this

statement is true, what are the inferences regarding weak-form or semistrong-form efficiency?

5. Assume that Mexican interest rates are much higher than U.S. interest rates. Also assume that interest rate parity (discussed in Chapter 7) exists. If you use the forward rate of the Mexican peso to forecast the Mexican peso's future spot rate, would you expect the peso to appreciate or depreciate? Explain.

6. Warden Co. is considering a project in Venezuela, which will be very profitable if the local currency (bolivar) appreciates against the dollar. If the bolivar depreciates, the project will result in losses. Warden Co. forecasts that the bolivar will appreciate. The bolivar's value historically has been very volatile. As a manager of Warden Co., would you be comfortable with this project? Explain.

QUESTIONS AND APPLICATIONS

1. **Motives for Forecasting.** Explain corporate motives for forecasting exchange rates.

2. **Technical Forecasting.** Explain the technical technique for forecasting exchange rates. What are some limitations of using technical forecasting to predict exchange rates?

3. **Fundamental Forecasting.** Explain the fundamental technique for forecasting exchange rates. What are some limitations of using a fundamental technique to forecast exchange rates?

4. **Market-Based Forecasting.** Explain the market-based technique for forecasting exchange rates. What is the rationale for using market-based forecasts? If the euro appreciates substantially against the dollar during a specific period, would market-based forecasts have overestimated or underestimated the realized values over this period? Explain.

5. **Mixed Forecasting.** Explain the mixed technique for forecasting exchange rates.

6. **Detecting a Forecast Bias.** Explain how to assess performance in forecasting exchange rates. Explain how to detect a bias in forecasting exchange rates.

7. **Measuring Forecast Accuracy.** You are hired as a consultant to assess a firm's ability to forecast. The firm has developed a point forecast for two different currencies presented in the following table. The firm asks you to determine which currency was forecasted with greater accuracy.

Period	Yen Forecast	Actual Yen Value	Pound Forecast	Actual Pound Value
1	$.0050	$.0051	$1.50	$1.51
2	.0048	.0052	1.53	1.50
3	.0053	.0052	1.55	1.58
4	.0055	.0056	1.49	1.52

8. **Limitations of a Fundamental Forecast.** Syracuse Corp. believes that future real interest rate movements will affect exchange rates, and it has applied regression analysis to historical data to assess the relationship. It will use regression coefficients derived from this analysis, along with forecasted real interest rate movements, to predict exchange rates in the future. Explain at least three limitations of this method.

9. **Consistent Forecasts.** Lexington Co. is a U.S.-based MNC with subsidiaries in most major countries. Each subsidiary is responsible for forecasting the future exchange rate of its local currency relative to the U.S. dollar. Comment on this policy. How might Lexington Co. ensure consistent forecasts among the different subsidiaries?

10. **Forecasting with a Forward Rate.** Assume that the four-year annualized interest rate in the United States is 9 percent and the four-year annualized interest rate in Singapore is 6 percent. Assume interest rate parity holds for a four-year horizon. Assume that the spot rate of the Singapore dollar is $.60. If the forward rate is used to forecast exchange rates, what will be the forecast for the Singapore dollar's spot rate in four years? What percentage appreciation or depreciation does this forecast imply over the four-year period?

11. **Foreign Exchange Market Efficiency.** Assume that foreign exchange markets were found to be weak-form efficient. What does this suggest about utilizing

technical analysis to speculate in euros? If MNCs believe that foreign exchange markets are strong-form efficient, why would they develop their own forecasts of future exchange rates? That is, why wouldn't they simply use today's quoted rates as indicators about future rates? After all, today's quoted rates should reflect all relevant information.

12. **Forecast Error.** The director of currency forecasting at Champaign-Urbana Corp. says, "The most critical task of forecasting exchange rates is not to derive a point estimate of a future exchange rate but to assess how wrong our estimate might be." What does this statement mean?

13. **Forecasting Exchange Rates of Currencies That Previously Were Fixed.** When some countries in Eastern Europe initially allowed their currencies to fluctuate against the dollar, would the fundamental technique based on historical relationships have been useful for forecasting future exchange rates of these currencies? Explain.

14. **Forecast Error.** Royce Co. is a U.S. firm with future receivables one year from now in Canadian dollars and British pounds. Its pound receivables are known with certainty, and its estimated Canadian dollar receivables are subject to a 2 percent error in either direction. The dollar values of both types of receivables are similar. There is no chance of default by the customers involved. Royce's treasurer says that the estimate of dollar cash flows to be generated from the British pound receivables is subject to greater uncertainty than that of the Canadian dollar receivables. Explain the rationale for the treasurer's statement.

15. **Forecasting the Euro.** Cooper, Inc., a U.S.-based MNC, periodically obtains euros to purchase German products. It assesses U.S. and German trade patterns and inflation rates to develop a fundamental forecast for the euro. How could Cooper possibly improve its method of fundamental forecasting as applied to the euro?

16. **Forward Rate Forecast.** Assume that you obtain a quote for a one-year forward rate on the Mexican peso. Assume that Mexico's one-year interest rate is 40 percent, while the U.S. one-year interest rate is 7 percent. Over the next year, the peso depreciates by 12 percent. Do you think the forward rate overestimated the spot rate one year ahead in this case? Explain.

17. **Forecasting Based on PPP versus the Forward Rate.** You believe that the Singapore dollar's exchange rate movements are mostly attributed to purchasing power parity. Today, the nominal annual interest rate in Singapore is 18 percent. The nominal annual interest rate in the United States is 3 percent. You expect that annual inflation will be about 4 percent in Singapore and 1 percent in the United States. Assume that interest rate parity holds. Today the spot rate of the Singapore dollar is $.63. Do you think the one-year forward rate would underestimate, overestimate, or be an unbiased estimate of the future spot rate in one year? Explain.

18. **Interpreting an Unbiased Forward Rate.** Assume that the forward rate is an unbiased but not necessarily accurate forecast of the future exchange rate of the yen over the next several years. Based on this information, do you think Raven Co. should hedge its remittance of expected Japanese yen profits to the U.S. parent by selling yen forward contracts? Why would this strategy be advantageous? Under what conditions would this strategy backfire?

ADVANCED QUESTIONS

19. **Probability Distribution of Forecasts.** Assume that the following regression model was applied to historical quarterly data:

$$e_t = a_0 + a_1 INT_t + a_2 INF_{t-1} + \mu_t$$

where e_t = percentage change in the exchange rate of the Japanese yen in period t

INT_t = average real interest rate differential (U.S. interest rate minus Japanese interest rate) over period t

INF_{t-1} = inflation differential (U.S. inflation rate minus Japanese inflation rate) in the previous period

a_0, a_1, a_2 = regression coefficients

μ_t = error term

Assume that the regression coefficients were estimated as follows:

$$a_0 = 0.0$$
$$a_1 = 0.9$$
$$a_2 = 0.8$$

Also assume that the inflation differential in the most recent period was 3 percent. The real interest rate differential in the upcoming period is forecasted as follows:

Interest Rate Differential	Probability
0%	30%
1	60
2	10

If Stillwater, Inc., uses this information to forecast the Japanese yen's exchange rate, what will be the probability distribution of the yen's percentage change over the upcoming period?

20. **Testing for a Forecast Bias.** You must determine whether there is a forecast bias in the forward rate. You apply regression analysis to test the relationship between the actual spot rate and the forward rate forecast (F):

$$S = a_0 + a_1(F)$$

The regression results are as follows:

Coefficient	Standard Error
$a_0 = .006$	.011
$a_1 = .800$	.05

Based on these results, is there a bias in the forecast? Verify your conclusion. If there is a bias, explain whether it is an overestimate or an underestimate.

21. **Effect of September 11 on Forward Rate Forecasts.** The September 11, 2001 terrorist attack on the United States was quickly followed by lower interest rates in the United States. How would this affect a fundamental forecast of foreign currencies? How would this affect the forward rate forecast of foreign currencies?

22. **Interpreting Forecast Bias Information**. The treasurer of Glencoe, Inc., detected a forecast bias when using the 30-day forward rate of the euro to forecast future spot rates of the euro over various periods. He believes he can use this information to determine whether imports ordered every week should be hedged (payment is made 30 days after each order). Glencoe's president says that in the long run the forward rate is unbiased and that the treasurer should not waste time trying to "beat the forward rate" but should just hedge all orders. Who is correct?

23. **Forecasting Latin American Currencies.** The value of each Latin American currency relative to the dollar is dictated by supply and demand conditions between that currency and the dollar. The values of Latin American currencies have generally declined substantially against the dollar over time. Most of these countries have high inflation rates and high interest rates. The data on inflation rates, economic growth, and other economic indicators are subject to error, as limited resources are used to compile the data.

a. If the forward rate is used as a market-based forecast, will this rate result in a forecast of appreciation, depreciation, or no change in any particular Latin American currency? Explain.

b. If technical forecasting is used, will this result in a forecast of appreciation, depreciation, or no change in the value of a specific Latin American currency? Explain.

c. Do you think that U.S. firms can accurately forecast the future values of Latin American currencies? Explain.

24. **Selecting between Forecast Methods.** Bolivia currently has a nominal one-year risk-free interest rate of 40 percent, which is primarily due to the high level of expected inflation. The U.S. nominal one-year risk-free interest rate is 8 percent. The spot rate of Bolivia's currency (called the boliviana) is $.14. The one-year forward rate of the boliviana is $.108. What is the forecasted percentage change in the boliviana if the spot rate is used as a one-year forecast? What is the forecasted percentage change in the boliviana if the one-year forward rate is used as a one-year forecast? Which forecast do you think will be more accurate? Why?

25. **Comparing Market-based Forecasts.** For all parts of this question, assume that interest rate parity exists, the prevailing one-year U.S. nominal interest rate is low, and that you expect U.S. inflation to be low this year.

a. Assume that the country Dinland engages in much trade with the United States and the trade involves many different products. Dinland has had a zero trade balance with the United States (the value of exports and imports is about the same) in the past. Assume that you expect a high level of inflation (about 40 percent) in Dinland over the next year because of a large increase in the prices of many products that Dinland produces. Dinland presently has a one-year risk-free interest rate of more than 40 percent. Do you think that the prevailing spot rate or the one-year forward rate would result in a more accurate forecast of Dinland's currency (the din) one year from now? Explain.

b. Assume that the country Freeland engages in much trade with the United States and the trade involves many different products. Freeland has had a zero trade balance with the United States (the value of exports and imports is about the same) in the past. You expect high inflation (about 40 percent) in Freeland over the next year because of a large increase in the cost of land (and therefore housing) in Freeland. You believe that the prices of products that Freeland produces will not be affected. Freeland presently has a one-year risk-free interest rate of more than 40 percent. Do you think that the prevailing one-year forward rate of Freeland's currency (the fre) would overestimate, underestimate, or be a reasonably accurate forecast of the spot rate one year from now? [Presume a direct quotation of the exchange rate, so that if the forward rate underestimates, it means that its value is less than the realized spot rate in one year. If the forward rate overestimates, it means that its value is more than the realized spot rate in one year.]

INTERNET APPLICATION

26. **CME Exchange Rates** The website of the Chicago Mercantile Exchange (CME) provides information about the exchange and the futures contracts offered on the exchange. Its address is **http://www.cme.com**.

a. Go to the section on "Prices" and then to the "Daily and Weekly Charts." Describe the trend of a peso futures contract over the last few months. What does this trend suggest about changes in forecasts of the peso over the period assessed (assuming that the futures rate was used as a forecasting method)? What do you think caused the futures prices to change over the last few months?

b. Select a peso futures contract that has at least one month until its settlement date. Determine whether that futures contract would have underestimated or overestimated the spot rate as of the settlement date if it had been used to forecast the future spot rate. Was the forecast accurate?

DISCUSSION IN THE BOARDROOM

This exercise can be found in Appendix E at the back of this textbook.

RUNNING YOUR OWN MNC

This exercise can be found on the Xtra! website at **http://maduraxtra.swlearning.com**.

BLADES, INC. CASE

Forecasting Exchange Rates

Recall that Blades, Inc., the U.S.-based manufacturer of roller blades, is currently both exporting to and importing from Thailand. Ben Holt, Blades' chief financial officer (CFO), and you, a financial analyst at Blades, Inc., are reasonably happy with Blades' current performance in Thailand. Entertainment Products, Inc., a Thai retailer for sporting goods, has committed itself to purchase a minimum number of Blades' "Speedos" annually. The agreement will terminate after three years. Blades also imports certain components needed to manufacture its products from Thailand. Both Blades' imports and exports are denominated in Thai baht. Because of these arrangements, Blades generates approximately 10 percent of its revenue and 4 percent of its cost of goods sold in Thailand.

Currently, Blades' only business in Thailand consists of this export and import trade. Ben Holt, however, is thinking about using Thailand to augment

Blades' U.S. business in other ways as well in the future. For example, Holt is contemplating establishing a subsidiary in Thailand to increase the percentage of Blades' sales to that country. Furthermore, by establishing a subsidiary in Thailand, Blades will have access to Thailand's money and capital markets. For instance, Blades could instruct its Thai subsidiary to invest excess funds or to satisfy its short-term needs for funds in the Thai money market. Furthermore, part of the subsidiary's financing could be obtained by utilizing investment banks in Thailand.

Due to Blades' current arrangements and future plans, Ben Holt is concerned about recent developments in Thailand and their potential impact on the company's future in that country. Economic conditions in Thailand have been unfavorable recently. Movements in the value of the baht have been highly volatile, and foreign investors in Thailand have lost confidence in the baht, causing massive capital outflows from Thailand. Consequently, the baht has been depreciating.

When Thailand was experiencing a high economic growth rate, few analysts anticipated an economic downturn. Consequently, Holt never found it necessary to forecast economic conditions in Thailand even though Blades was doing business there. Now, however, his attitude has changed. A continuation of the unfavorable economic conditions prevailing in Thailand could affect the demand for Blades' products in that country. Consequently, Entertainment Products may not renew its commitment for another three years.

Since Blades generates net cash inflows denominated in baht, a continued depreciation of the baht could adversely affect Blades, as these net inflows would be converted into fewer dollars. Thus, Blades is also considering hedging its baht-denominated inflows.

Because of these concerns, Holt has decided to reassess the importance of forecasting the baht-dollar exchange rate. His primary objective is to forecast the baht-dollar exchange rate for the next quarter. A secondary objective is to determine which forecasting technique is the most accurate and should be used in future periods. To accomplish this, he has asked you, a financial analyst at Blades, for help in forecasting the baht-dollar exchange rate for the next quarter.

Holt is aware of the forecasting techniques available. He has collected some economic data and conducted a preliminary analysis for you to use in your analysis. For example, he has conducted a time series analysis for the exchange rates over numerous quarters. He then used this analysis to forecast the baht's value next quarter. The technical forecast indicates a depreciation of the baht by 6 percent over the next quarter from the baht's current level of \$.023 to \$.02162. He has also conducted a fundamental forecast of the baht-dollar exchange rate using historical inflation and interest rate data. The fundamental forecast, however, depends on what happens to Thai interest rates during the next quarter and therefore reflects a probability distribution. There is a 30 percent chance that Thai interest rates will be such that the baht will depreciate by 2 percent, a 15 percent chance that the baht will depreciate by 5 percent, and a 55 percent chance that the baht will depreciate by 10 percent.

Ben Holt has asked you to answer the following questions:

1. Considering both Blades' current practices and future plans, how can it benefit from forecasting the baht-dollar exchange rate?
2. Which forecasting technique (i.e., technical, fundamental, or market-based) would be easiest to use in forecasting the future value of the baht? Why?
3. Blades is considering using either current spot rates or available forward rates to forecast the future value of the baht. Available forward rates currently exhibit a large discount. Do you think the spot or the forward rate will yield a better market-based forecast? Why?
4. The current 90-day forward rate for the baht is \$.021. By what percentage is the baht expected to change over the next quarter according to a market-based forecast using the forward rate? What will be the value of the baht in 90 days according to this forecast?
5. Assume that the technical forecast has been more accurate than the market-based forecast in recent weeks. What does this indicate about market efficiency for the baht-dollar exchange rate? Do you think this means that technical analysis will always be superior to other forecasting techniques in the future? Why or why not?
6. What is the expected percentage change in the value of the baht during the next quarter based on the fundamental forecast? What is the forecasted value of the baht using this forecast? If the value of the baht 90 days from now turns out to be \$.022,

which forecasting technique is the most accurate? (Use the absolute forecast error as a percentage of the realized value to answer the last part of this question.)

7. Do you think the technique you have identified in question 6 will always be the most accurate? Why or why not?

SMALL BUSINESS DILEMMA

Exchange Rate Forecasting by the Sports Exports Company

The Sports Exports Company converts British pounds into dollars every month. The prevailing spot rate is about $1.65, but there is much uncertainty about the future value of the pound. Jim Logan, owner of the Sports Exports Company, expects that British inflation will rise substantially in the future. In previous years when British inflation was high, the pound depreciated. The prevailing British interest rate is slightly higher than the prevailing U.S. interest rate. The pound has risen slightly over each of the last several months. Jim wants to forecast the value of the pound for each of the next 20 months.

1. Explain how Jim can use technical forecasting to forecast the future value of the pound. Based on the information provided, do you think that a technical forecast will predict future appreciation or depreciation in the pound?
2. Explain how Jim can use fundamental forecasting to forecast the future value of the pound. Based on the information provided, do you think that a fundamental forecast will predict appreciation or depreciation in the pound?
3. Explain how Jim can use a market-based forecast to forecast the future value of the pound. Do you think the market-based forecast will predict appreciation, depreciation, or no change in the value of the pound?
4. Does it appear that all of the forecasting techniques will lead to the same forecast of the pound's future value? Which technique would you prefer to use in this situation?

CHAPTER 10

Measuring Exposure to Exchange Rate Fluctuations

Exchange rate risk can be broadly defined as the risk that a company's performance will be affected by exchange rate movements. Multinational corporations (MNCs) closely monitor their operations to determine how they are exposed to various forms of exchange rate risk. Financial managers must understand how to measure the exposure of their MNCs to exchange rate fluctuations so that they can determine whether and how to protect their companies from that exposure.

The specific objectives of this chapter are to:

- discuss the relevance of an MNC's exposure to exchange rate risk,
- explain how transaction exposure can be measured,
- explain how economic exposure can be measured, and
- explain how translation exposure can be measured.

Is Exchange Rate Risk Relevant?

Some have argued that exchange rate risk is irrelevant. These contentions, in turn, have resulted in counterarguments, as summarized here.

Purchasing Power Parity Argument

One argument for exchange rate irrelevance is that, according to purchasing power parity (PPP) theory, exchange rate movements are just a response to differentials in price changes between countries. Therefore, the exchange rate effect is offset by the change in prices.

Franklin Co. is a U.S. exporter that denominates its exports in euros. If the euro weakens by 3 percent due to purchasing power parity, that implies that European inflation is about 3 percent higher than U.S. inflation. If European competitors raise their prices in line with European inflation, Franklin can increase its prices without losing any customers. Thus, the increase in its price offsets the reduction in the value of the euro.

PPP does not necessarily hold, however, so the exchange rate will not necessarily change in accordance with the inflation differential between the two countries. Since a perfect offsetting effect is unlikely, the firm's competitive capabilities may indeed be influenced by exchange rate movements. Even if PPP did hold over a very long period of time, this would not comfort managers of MNCs that are focusing on the next quarter or year.

The Investor Hedge Argument

A second argument for exchange rate irrelevance is that investors in MNCs can hedge exchange rate risk on their own. The investor hedge argument assumes that investors have complete information on corporate exposure to exchange rate fluctuations as well as the capabilities to correctly insulate their individual exposure. To the extent that investors prefer that corporations perform the hedging for them, exchange rate exposure is relevant to corporations. An MNC may be able to hedge at a lower cost than individual investors. In addition, it has more information about its exposure and can more effectively hedge its exposure.

Currency Diversification Argument

Another argument is that if a U.S.-based MNC is well diversified across numerous countries, its value will not be affected by exchange rate movements because of offsetting effects. It is naive, however, to presume that exchange rate effects will offset each other just because an MNC has transactions in many different currencies.

Stakeholder Diversification Argument

Some critics also argue that if stakeholders (such as creditors or stockholders) are well diversified, they will be somewhat insulated against losses experienced by an MNC due to exchange rate risk. Many MNCs are similarly affected by exchange rate movements, however, so it is difficult to compose a diversified portfolio of stocks that will be insulated from exchange rate movements.

Response from MNCs

Creditors that provide loans to MNCs can experience large losses if the MNCs experience financial problems. Thus, creditors may prefer that the MNCs maintain low exposure to exchange rate risk. Consequently, MNCs that hedge their exposure to risk may be able to borrow funds at a lower cost.

To the extent that MNCs can stabilize their earnings over time by hedging their exchange rate risk, they may also reduce their general operating expenses over time (by avoiding costs of downsizing and restructuring). Many MNCs, including Colgate-

Palmolive, Eastman Kodak, and Merck, have attempted to stabilize their earnings with hedging strategies because they believe exchange rate risk is relevant. Further evidence that MNCs consider exchange rate risk to be relevant can be found in annual reports. The following comments from annual reports of MNCs are typical:

The primary purpose of the Company's foreign currency hedging program is to manage the volatility associated with foreign currency purchases of materials and other assets and liabilities created in the normal course of business. Corporate policy prescribes a range of allowable hedging activity.

Procter & Gamble Co.

The Company enters into foreign exchange contracts and options to hedge various currency exposures. . . . the primary business objective of the activity is to optimize the U.S. dollar value of the Company's assets, liabilities, and future cash flows with respect to exchange rate fluctuations.

Dow Chemical Co.

Types of Exposure

As mentioned in the previous chapter, exchange rates cannot be forecasted with perfect accuracy, but the firm can at least measure its exposure to exchange rate fluctuations. If the firm is highly exposed to exchange rate fluctuations, it can consider techniques to reduce its exposure. Such techniques are identified in the following chapter. Before choosing among them, the firm should first measure its degree of exposure.

Exposure to exchange rate fluctuations comes in three forms:

- Transaction exposure
- Economic exposure
- Translation exposure

Each type of exposure will be discussed in turn.

Transaction Exposure

The value of a firm's cash inflows received in various currencies will be affected by the respective exchange rates of these currencies when they are converted into the currency desired. Similarly, the value of a firm's cash outflows in various currencies will be dependent on the respective exchange rates of these currencies. The degree to which the value of future cash transactions can be affected by exchange rate fluctuations is referred to as **transaction exposure**.

Transaction exposure can have a substantial impact on a firm's earnings. It is not unusual for a currency to change by as much as 10 percent in a given year. If an exporter denominates its exports in a foreign currency, a 10 percent decline in that currency will reduce the dollar value of its receivables by 10 percent. This effect could possibly eliminate any profits from exporting.

To assess transaction exposure, an MNC needs to (1) estimate its net cash flows in each currency and (2) measure the potential impact of the currency exposure.

Estimating "Net" Cash Flows in Each Currency

MNCs tend to focus on transaction exposure over an upcoming short-term period (such as the next month or the next quarter) for which they can anticipate foreign currency cash flows with reasonable accuracy. Since MNCs commonly have foreign subsidiaries spread around the world, they need an information system that can track their currency positions. The Internet enables all subsidiaries to tap into the same network and provide information on their existing and expected future currency positions.

To measure its transaction exposure, an MNC needs to project the consolidated net amount in currency inflows or outflows for all its subsidiaries, categorized by currency. One foreign subsidiary may have inflows of a foreign currency while another has outflows of that same currency. In that case, the MNC's net cash flows of that currency overall may be negligible. If most of the MNC's subsidiaries have future inflows in another currency, however, the net cash flows in that currency could be substantial. Estimating the consolidated net cash flows per currency is a useful first step when assessing an MNC's exposure because it helps to determine the MNC's overall position in each currency.

EXAMPLE

Miami Co. conducts its international business in four currencies. Its objective is to first measure its exposure in each currency in the next quarter and then estimate its consolidated cash flows for one quarter ahead, as shown in Exhibit 10.1. For example, Miami expects Canadian dollar inflows of C$12,000,000 and outflows of C$2,000,000 over the next quarter. Thus, Miami expects net inflows of C$10,000,000. Given an expected exchange rate of $.80 at the end of the quarter, it can convert the expected net inflow of Canadian dollars into an expected net inflow of $8,000,000 (estimated as C$10,000,000 × $.80).

The same process is used to determine the net cash flows of each of the other three currencies. Notice from the last column of Exhibit 10.1 that the expected net cash flows in three of the currencies are positive, while the net cash flows in Swedish kronar are negative (reflecting cash outflows). Thus, Miami will be favorably affected by appreciation of the pound, Canadian dollar, and Mexican peso. Conversely, it will be adversely affected by appreciation of the krona.

The information in Exhibit 10.1 needs to be converted into dollars so that Miami Co. can assess the exposure of each currency by using a standardized measure. For each currency, the net cash flows are converted into dollars to determine the dollar amount of exposure. Notice that Miami has a smaller dollar amount of exposure in Mexican pe-

Exhibit 10.1 Consolidated Net Cash Flow Assessment of Miami Co.

Currency	Total Inflow	Total Outflow	Net Inflow or Outflow	Expected Exchange Rate at End of Quarter	Net Inflow or Outflow as Measured in U.S. Dollars
British pound	£17,000,000	£7,000,000	+£10,000,000	$1.50	+$15,000,000
Canadian dollar	C$12,000,000	C$2,000,000	+C$10,000,000	$ .80	+$ 8,000,000
Swedish krona	SK20,000,000	SK120,000,000	−SK100,000,000	$ .15	−$15,000,000
Mexican peso	MXP90,000,000	MXP10,000,000	+MXP80,000,000	$ .10	+$ 8,000,000

Exhibit 10.2 Estimating the Range of Net Inflows or Outflows for Miami Co.

Currency	Net Inflow or Outflow	Range of Possible Exchange Rates at End of Quarter	Range of Possible Net Inflows or Outflows in U.S. Dollars (Based on Range of Possible Exchange Rates)
British pound	+£10,000,000	$1.40 to $1.60	+$14,000,000 to +$16,000,000
Canadian dollar	+C$10,000,000	$.79 to $.81	+$ 7,900,000 to +$ 8,100,000
Swedish krona	−SK100,000,000	$.14 to $.16	−$14,000,000 to −$16,000,000
Mexican peso	+MXP80,000,000	$.06 to $.11	+$ 4,800,000 to +$ 8,800,000

sos and Canadian dollars than in the other currencies. However, this does not necessarily mean that Miami will be less affected by these exposures, as will be explained shortly.

Recognize that the net inflows or outflows in each foreign currency and the exchange rates at the end of the period are uncertain. Thus, Miami might develop a range of possible exchange rates for each currency, as shown in Exhibit 10.2, instead of a point estimate. In this case, there is a range of net cash flows in dollars rather than a point estimate. Notice that the range of dollar cash flows resulting from Miami's peso transactions is wide, reflecting the high degree of uncertainty surrounding the peso's value over the next quarter. In contrast, the range of dollar cash flows resulting from the Canadian dollar transactions is narrow because the Canadian dollar is expected to be relatively stable over the next quarter.

Miami Co. assessed its net cash flow situation for only one quarter. It could also derive its expected net cash flows for other periods, such as a week or a month. Some MNCs assess their transaction exposure during several periods by applying the methods just described to each period. The further into the future an MNC attempts to measure its transaction exposure, the less accurate will be the measurement due to the greater uncertainty about inflows or outflows in each foreign currency, as well as future exchange rates, over periods further into the future. An MNC's overall exposure can be assessed only after considering each currency's variability and the correlations among currencies. The overall exposure of Miami Co. will be assessed after the following discussion of currency variability and correlations.

Measuring the Potential Impact of the Currency Exposure

The net cash flows of an MNC can be viewed as a portfolio of currencies. The exposure of the portfolio of currencies can be measured by the standard deviation of the portfolio, which indicates how the portfolio's value may deviate from what is expected. Consider an MNC that will receive payments in two foreign currencies. The risk (as measured by the standard deviation of monthly percentage changes) of a two-currency portfolio (σ_p) can be estimated as follows:

$$\sigma_p = \sqrt{W_X^2\sigma_X^2 + W_Y^2\sigma_Y^2 + 2W_XW_Y\sigma_X\sigma_Y CORR_{XY}}$$

where

W_X = proportion of total portfolio value that is in currency X
W_Y = proportion of total portfolio value that is in currency Y
σ_X = standard deviation of monthly percentage changes in currency X
σ_Y = standard deviation of monthly percentage changes in currency Y
$CORR_{XY}$ = correlation coefficient of monthly percentage changes between currencies X and Y

The equation shows that an MNC's exposure to multiple currencies is influenced by the variability of each currency and the correlation of movements between the currencies. The volatility of a currency portfolio is positively related to a currency's volatility and positively related to the correlation between currencies. Each component in the equation that affects a currency portfolio's risk can be measured using a series of monthly percentage changes in each currency. These components are described in more detail next.

http://

http://www.fednewyork.org/markets/impliedvolatility.html provides a measure of exchange rate volatility.

Measurement of Currency Variability. The standard deviation statistic measures the degree of movement for each currency. In any given period, some currencies clearly fluctuate much more than others. For example, the standard deviations of the monthly movements in the Japanese yen and the Swiss franc are typically more than twice that of the Canadian dollar. Based on this information, the potential for substantial deviations from the projected future values is greater for the yen and the Swiss franc than for the Canadian dollar (from a U.S. firm's perspective). Some currencies in emerging markets are very volatile.

Currency Variability over Time. The variability of a currency will not necessarily remain consistent from one time period to another. Nevertheless, an MNC can at least identify currencies whose values are *most likely* to be stable or highly variable in the future. For example, the Canadian dollar consistently exhibits lower variability than other currencies, regardless of the period that is assessed.

Measurement of Currency Correlations. The correlations among currency movements can be measured by their *correlation coefficients*, which indicate the degree to which two currencies move in relation to each other. The extreme case is perfect positive correlation, which is represented by a correlation coefficient equal to 1.00. Correlations can also be negative, reflecting an inverse relationship between individual movements, the extreme case being −1.00.

Exhibit 10.3 shows the correlation coefficients (based on quarterly data) for several currency pairs. It is clear that some currency pairs exhibit a much higher correlation than others. The European currencies are highly correlated, whereas the Canadian dollar has a relatively low correlation with other currencies. Currency correlations are generally positive; this implies that currencies tend to move in the same direction against the U.S. dollar (though by different degrees). The positive correlation may not always occur on a day-to-day basis, but it appears to hold over longer periods of time for most currencies.

Applying Currency Correlations to Net Cash Flows. The implications of currency correlations for a particular MNC depend on the cash flow characteristics of that MNC.

The equation for a portfolio's standard deviation suggests that positive cash flows in highly correlated currencies result in higher exchange rate risk for the MNC. However, many MNCs have negative net cash flow positions in some currencies; in these

Exhibit 10.3 Correlations among Exchange Rate Movements

	British Pound	Canadian Dollar	Euro	Japanese Yen	Swedish Krona
British pound	1.00				
Canadian dollar	.35	1.00			
Euro	.91	.48	1.00		
Japanese yen	.71	.12	.67	1.00	
Swedish krona	.83	.57	.92	.64	1.00

Exhibit 10.4 Impact of Cash Flow and Correlation Conditions on an MNC's Exposure

If the MNC's Expected Cash Flow Situation Is:	And the Currencies Are:	The MNC's Exposure Is Relatively:
Equal amounts of net inflows in two currencies	Highly correlated	High
Equal amounts of net inflows in two currencies	Slightly positively correlated	Moderate
Equal amounts of net inflows in two currencies	Negatively correlated	Low
A net inflow in one currency and a net outflow of about the same amount in another currency	Highly correlated	Low
A net inflow in one currency and a net outflow of about the same amount in another currency	Slightly positively correlated	Moderate
A net inflow in one currency and a net outflow of about the same amount in another currency	Negatively correlated	High

situations, the correlations can have different effects on the MNC's exchange rate risk. Exhibit 10.4 illustrates some common situations for an MNC that has exposure to only two currencies.

The concept of currency correlations can be applied to the earlier example of Miami Co.'s net cash flows, as displayed in Exhibit 10.2. Recall that Miami Co. anticipates cash inflows in British pounds equivalent to $15 million and cash outflows in Swedish kronar equivalent to $15 million. Thus, if a weak-dollar cycle occurs, Miami will be adversely affected by its exposure to the krona, but favorably affected by its pound exposure. During a strong-dollar cycle, it will be adversely affected by the pound exposure but favorably affected by its krona exposure. If Miami expects that these two currencies will move in the same direction and by about the same degree over the next period, its exposures to these two currencies are partially offset.

Miami may not be too concerned about its exposure to the Canadian dollar's movements because the Canadian dollar is somewhat stable with respect to the U.S. dollar over time; risk of substantial depreciation of the Canadian dollar is low. However, the company should be concerned about its exposure to the Mexican peso's movements because the peso is quite volatile and could depreciate substantially within a short period of time. Miami has no exposure to another currency that will offset the exposure to the peso. Therefore, Miami should seriously consider whether to hedge its expected net cash flow position in pesos.

Currency Correlations over Time. Exhibit 10.5 shows the trends of exchange rate movements of various currencies against the dollar. Notice how correlations and volatility levels of currencies vary among currencies and over time. The Chinese yuan's value has been stable because it has been pegged to the dollar since 1994. After declining consistently for a number of years, the value of the Indian rupee has been fairly stable recently, while the value of other currencies has increased in some periods and declined in others.

An MNC cannot use previous correlations to predict future correlations with perfect accuracy. Nevertheless, some general relationships tend to hold over time. For example, movements in the values of the pound, the euro, and other European currencies against the dollar tend to be highly correlated in most periods. In addition, the Canadian dollar tends to move independently of other currency movements.

Assessing Transaction Exposure Based on Value-at-Risk

A related method for assessing exposure is the value-at-risk (VAR) method, which incorporates volatility and currency correlations to determine the potential maximum one-day loss on the value of positions of an MNC that is exposed to exchange rate movements.

EXAMPLE

Celia Co. will receive 10 million Mexican pesos (MXP) tomorrow as a result of providing consulting services to a Mexican firm. It wants to determine the maximum one-day loss due to a potential decline in the value of the peso, based on a 95 percent confidence level. It estimates the standard deviation of daily percentage changes of the Mexican peso to be 1.2 percent over the last 100 days. If these daily percentage changes are normally distributed, the maximum one-day loss is determined by the lower boundary (the left tail) of the probability distribution, which is about 1.65 standard deviations away from the expected percentage change in the peso. Assuming an expected percentage change of 0 percent (implying no expected change in the peso) during the next day, the maximum one-day loss is

$$\begin{aligned}\text{Maximum one-day loss} &= E(e_t) - (1.65 \times \sigma_{MXP}) \\ &= 0\% - (1.65 \times 1.2\%) \\ &= -.0198, \text{ or } -1.98\%.\end{aligned}$$

Assume the spot rate of the peso is \$.09. The maximum one-day loss of −1.98 percent implies a peso value of

$$\begin{aligned}\text{Peso value based on maximum one-day loss} &= S \times [1 + E(e_t)] \\ &= \$.09 \times [1 + (-.0198)] \\ &= \$.088218.\end{aligned}$$

Thus, if the maximum one-day loss occurs, the peso's value will have declined to \$.088218. The dollar value of this maximum one-day loss is dependent on Celia's position in Mexican pesos. For example, if Celia has MXP10 million, this represents a value of \$900,000 (at \$.09 per peso), so a decline in the peso's value of −.198 percent would result in a loss of \$900,000 × −1.98% = −\$17,820.

Factors That Affect the Maximum One-day Loss. The maximum one-day loss of a currency is dependent on three factors. First, it is dependent on the expected percentage

Exhibit 10.5 Movements of Major Currencies against the Dollar

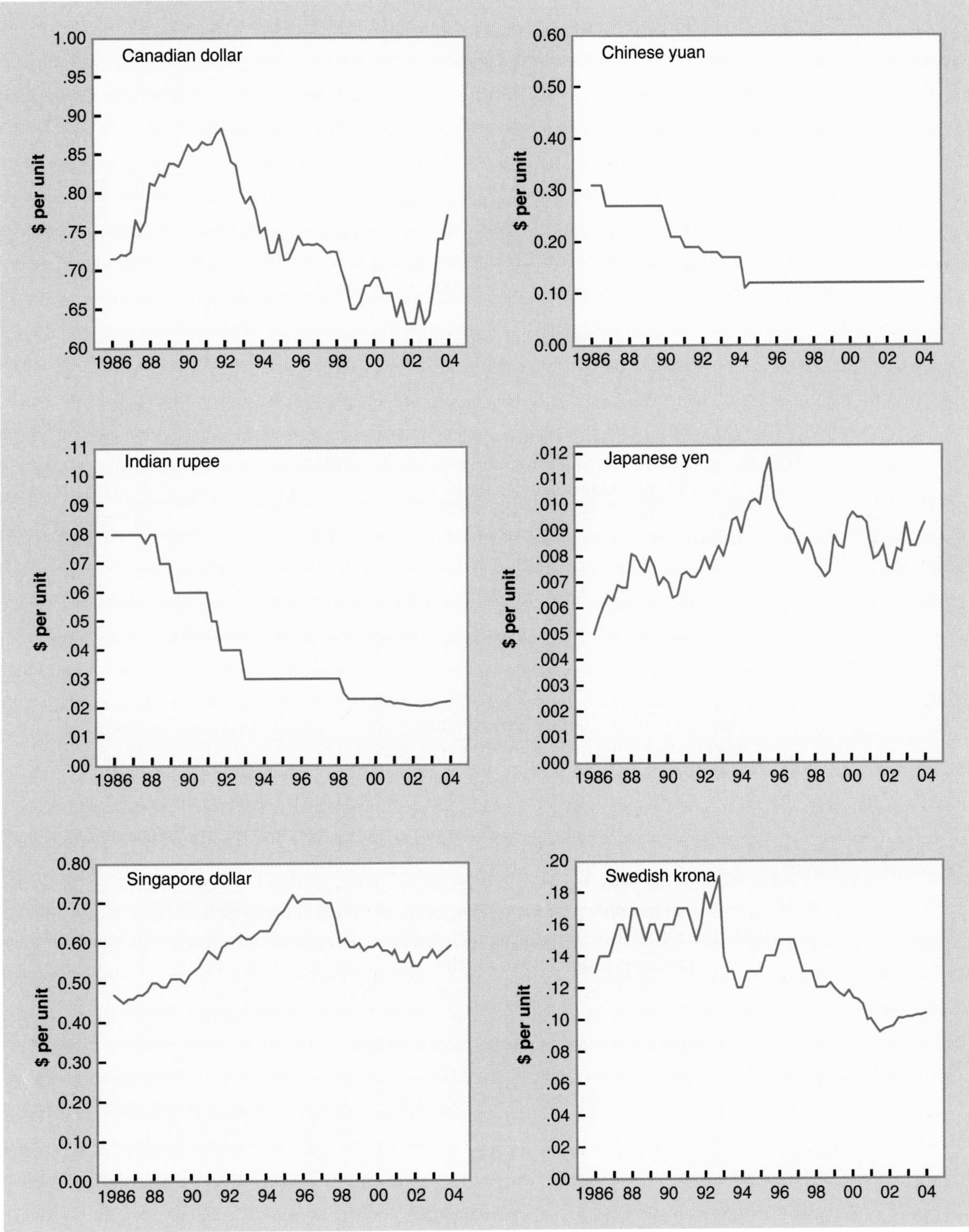

change in the currency for the next day. If the expected outcome in the previous example is −.2 percent instead of 0 percent, the maximum loss over the one-day period is

$$\begin{aligned}\text{Maximum one-day loss} &= E(e_t) - (1.65 \times \sigma_{MXP}) \\ &= -.2\% - (1.65 \times 1.2\%) \\ &= -.0218, \text{ or } -2.18\%.\end{aligned}$$

Second, the maximum one-day loss is dependent on the confidence level used. A higher confidence level will cause a more pronounced maximum one-day loss, holding other factors constant. If the confidence level in the example is 97.5 percent instead of 95 percent, the lower boundary is 1.96 standard deviations from the expected percentage change in the peso. Thus, the maximum one-day loss is

$$\begin{aligned}\text{Maximum one-day loss} &= E(e_t) - (1.96 \times \sigma_{MXP}) \\ &= 0\% - (1.96 \times 1.2\%) \\ &= -.02352, \text{ or } -2.352\%.\end{aligned}$$

Third, the maximum one-day loss is dependent on the standard deviation of the daily percentage changes in the currency over a previous period. If the peso's standard deviation in the example is 1 percent instead of 1.2 percent, the maximum one-day loss is

$$\begin{aligned}\text{Maximum one-day loss} &= E(e_t) - (1.65 \times \sigma_{MXP}) \\ &= 0\% - (1.65 \times 1\%) \\ &= -.0165, \text{ or } -1.65\%.\end{aligned}$$

Applying VAR to Longer Time Horizons. The VAR method can also be used to assess exposure over longer time horizons. The standard deviation should be estimated over the time horizon in which the maximum loss is to be measured.

Lada, Inc., expects to receive Mexican pesos in one month for products that it exported. It wants to determine the maximum one-month loss due to a potential decline in the value of the peso, based on a 95 percent confidence level. It estimates the standard deviation of monthly percentage changes of the Mexican peso to be 6 percent over the last 40 months. If these monthly percentage changes are normally distributed, the maximum one-month loss is determined by the lower boundary (the left tail) of the probability distribution, which is about 1.65 standard deviations away from the expected percentage change in the peso. Assuming an expected percentage change of −1 percent during the next month, the maximum one-month loss is

$$\begin{aligned}\text{Maximum one-month loss} &= E(e_t) - (1.65 \times \sigma_{MXP}) \\ &= -1\% - (1.65 \times 6\%) \\ &= -.109, \text{ or } -10.9\%.\end{aligned}$$

If Lada, Inc., is uncomfortable with the magnitude of the potential loss, it can hedge its position as explained in the next chapter.

Applying VAR to Transaction Exposure of a Portfolio. Since MNCs are commonly exposed to more than one currency, they may apply the VAR method to a currency portfolio. When considering multiple currencies, software packages can be used to perform the computations. An example of applying VAR to a two-currency portfolio is provided here.

EXAMPLE

Benou, Inc., a U.S. exporting firm, expects to receive substantial payments denominated in Indonesian rupiah and Thai baht in one month. Based on today's spot rates, the dollar value of the funds to be received is estimated at $600,000 for the rupiah and $400,000 for the baht. Thus, Benou is exposed to a currency portfolio weighted 60 percent in rupiah and 40 percent in baht. Benou wants to determine the maximum one-month loss due to a potential decline in the value of these currencies, based on a 95 percent confidence level. Based on data for the last 20 months, it estimates the standard deviation of monthly percentage changes to be 7 percent for the rupiah and 8 percent for the baht, and a correlation coefficient of .50 between the rupiah and baht. The portfolio's standard deviation is

$$\begin{aligned}\sigma_p &= \sqrt{(.36)(.0049) + (.16)(.0064) + 2(.60)(.40)(.07)(.08)(.50)}\\ &= \text{about } .0643, \text{ or about } 6.43\%.\end{aligned}$$

If the monthly percentage changes of each currency are normally distributed, the monthly percentage changes of the portfolio should be normally distributed. The maximum one-month loss of the currency portfolio is determined by the lower boundary (the left tail) of the probability distribution, which is about 1.65 standard deviations away from the expected percentage change in the currency portfolio. Assuming an expected percentage change of 0 percent for each currency during the next month (and therefore an expected change of zero for the portfolio), the maximum one-month loss is

$$\begin{aligned}\text{Maximum one-month loss of currency portfolio} &= E(e_t) - (1.65 \times \sigma_p)\\ &= 0\% - (1.65 \times 6.43\%)\\ &= \text{about } -.1061, \text{ or about } -10.61\%.\end{aligned}$$

Compare this maximum one-month loss to that of the rupiah or the baht:

$$\begin{aligned}\text{Maximum one-month loss of rupiah} &= 0\% - (1.65 \times 7\%)\\ &= -.1155, \text{ or } -11.55\%.\\ \text{Maximum one-month loss of baht} &= 0\% - (1.65 \times 8\%)\\ &= -.132, \text{ or } -13.2\%.\end{aligned}$$

Notice that the maximum one-month loss for the portfolio is lower than the maximum loss for either individual currency, which is attributed to the diversification effects. Even if one currency experiences its maximum loss in a given month, the other currency is not likely to experience its maximum loss in that same month. The lower the correlation between the movements in the two currencies, the greater are the diversification benefits.

Given the maximum losses calculated here, Benou, Inc., may decide to hedge its rupiah position, its baht position, neither position, or both positions. The decision of whether to hedge is discussed in the next chapter.

Economic Exposure

The degree to which a firm's present value of future cash flows can be influenced by exchange rate fluctuations is referred to as **economic exposure** to exchange rates. All types of anticipated future transactions that cause transaction exposure also cause economic exposure because these transactions represent cash flows that can be influenced by exchange rate fluctuations. In addition, other types of business that do not cause transaction exposure can cause economic exposure.

Intel invoices about 65 percent of its chip exports in U.S. dollars. Although Intel is not subject to transaction exposure for its dollar-denominated exports, it is subject to economic exposure. If the euro weakens against the dollar, the European importers of those chips from Intel will need more euros to pay for them. These importers are subject to transaction exposure and economic exposure. As their costs of importing the chips increase in response to the weak euro, they may decide to purchase chips from European manufacturers instead. Consequently, Intel's cash flows from its exports will be reduced, even though these exports are invoiced in dollars.

Some of the more common international business transactions that typically subject an MNC's cash flows to economic exposure are listed in the first column of Exhibit 10.6. Transactions listed in the exhibit that require conversion of currencies, and thus reflect transaction exposure, include exports denominated in foreign currency, interest received from foreign investments, imports denominated in foreign currency, and interest owed on foreign loans. The other transactions, which do not require conversion of currencies and therefore do not reflect transaction exposure, are also a form of economic exposure because the cash flows resulting from these transactions can be influenced by exchange rate movements. Exchange rate movements can have as large an effect on cash flows from these transactions as on cash flows from transactions that require currency conversion.

Exhibit 10.6 Economic Exposure to Exchange Rate Fluctuations

Transactions That Influence the Firm's Local Currency Inflows	Impact of Local Currency Appreciation on Transactions	Impact of Local Currency Depreciation on Transactions
Local sales (relative to foreign competition in local markets)	Decrease	Increase
Firm's exports denominated in local currency	Decrease	Increase
Firm's exports denominated in foreign currency	Decrease	Increase
Interest received from foreign investments	Decrease	Increase
Transactions That Influence the Firm's Local Currency Outflows		
Firm's imported supplies denominated in local currency	No change	No change
Firm's imported supplies denominated in foreign currency	Decrease	Increase
Interest owed on foreign funds borrowed	Decrease	Increase

The second and third columns of Exhibit 10.6 indicate how each transaction can be affected by the appreciation and depreciation, respectively, of the firm's home (local) currency. The next sections discuss these effects in turn.

Economic Exposure to Local Currency Appreciation

The following discussion is related to the second column of Exhibit 10.6. With regard to the firm's cash inflows, its local sales (in the firm's home country) are expected to decrease if the local (home) currency appreciates because the firm will face increased foreign competition. Local customers will be able to obtain foreign substitute products cheaply with their strengthened currency. The extent of the decline in local sales will depend on the degree of foreign competition in the domestic market.

Cash inflows from exports denominated in the local currency will also likely be reduced as a result of appreciation in that currency. The reason is that foreign importers will need more of their own currency to pay for these products.

EXAMPLE

Mariah Corp, a U.S. firm, arranged to sell software to Mexican customers. Recently, the Mexican peso depreciated against the dollar, substantially increasing the price of the software to Mexican customers. Consequently, some Mexican customers shifted their purchases to Mexican software producers, and Mariah Corp.'s sales to Mexico declined.

Exports and investment income denominated in the foreign currency also will likely result in reduced cash inflows, but for a different reason. Inflows received in a currency that has depreciated will convert to a reduced amount of dollars. Similarly, any interest or dividends received from foreign investments will also convert to a reduced amount if the local currency has strengthened.

With regard to the firm's cash outflows, the cost of imported supplies denominated in the local currency will not be directly affected by changes in exchange rates. If the local currency appreciates, however, the cost of imported supplies denominated in the foreign currency will be reduced. In addition, any interest to be paid on financing in foreign currencies will be reduced (in terms of the local currency) if the local currency appreciates because the strengthened local currency will be exchanged for the foreign currency to make the interest payments.

Thus, appreciation in the firm's local currency causes a reduction in both cash inflows and outflows. The impact on a firm's net cash flows will depend on whether the inflow transactions are affected more or less than the outflow transactions. If, for example, the firm is in the exporting business but obtains its supplies and borrows funds locally, its inflow transactions will be reduced by a greater degree than its outflow transactions. In this case, net cash flows will be reduced. Conversely, cash inflows of a firm concentrating its sales locally with little foreign competition will not be severely reduced by appreciation of the local currency. If such a firm obtains supplies and borrows funds overseas, its outflows will be reduced. Overall, this firm's net cash flows will be enhanced by the appreciation of its local currency.

Economic Exposure to Local Currency Depreciation

If the firm's local currency depreciates (see the third column of Exhibit 10.6), its transactions will be affected in a manner opposite to the way they are influenced by appreciation. Local sales should increase due to reduced foreign competition, because prices

MANAGING FOR VALUE

Caterpillar's Exposure to Exchange Rate Risk

Caterpillar, Inc., relies heavily on exports for a large portion of its sales. The weakening of the dollar reduces the price importers must pay for Caterpillar's products. When the dollar is relatively weak, the demand for Caterpillar's exports increases, and so does Caterpillar's performance. Caterpillar's exposure to exchange rates works in both directions, however. When the dollar is strong, importers incur a higher cost of importing from Caterpillar because it takes more of their currency to obtain the dollars to purchase Caterpillar's products. Caterpillar is especially vulnerable to the value of the dollar because its key competitor is Komatsu of Japan, whose exports are denominated in Japanese yen. Thus, when the dollar is expensive, Caterpillar's customers can switch to a competitor whose prices are not denominated in dollars.

During the 1999–2000 period, many currencies weakened against the dollar but strengthened against the yen. Consequently, Caterpillar's performance declined in response to the decline in the foreign demand for its product, and its stock price fell.

Just as Caterpillar's value is adversely affected by a strong dollar, it may be enhanced by a weak dollar. In 2003, the dollar declined substantially against many currencies, and Caterpillar performed very well. Other U.S. firms that rely heavily on exports typically have the same type of exposure, especially when their competitors are based outside the United States.

denominated in strong foreign currencies will seem high to the local customers. The firm's exports denominated in the local currency will appear cheap to importers, thereby increasing foreign demand for those products. Even exports denominated in the foreign currency can increase cash flows because a given amount in foreign currency inflows to the firm will convert to a larger amount of the local currency. In addition, interest or dividends from foreign investments will now convert to more of the local currency.

With regard to cash outflows, imported supplies denominated in the local currency will not be directly affected by any change in exchange rates. The cost of imported supplies denominated in the foreign currency will rise, however, because more of the weakened local currency will be required to obtain the foreign currency needed. Any interest payments paid on financing in foreign currencies will increase.

In general, depreciation of the firm's local currency causes an increase in both cash inflows and outflows. A firm that concentrates on exporting and obtains supplies and borrows funds locally will likely benefit from a depreciated local currency. This is the case for Caterpillar, Ford, and General Motors in periods when the dollar weakens substantially against most major currencies. Conversely, a firm that concentrates on local sales, has very little foreign competition, and obtains foreign supplies (denominated in foreign currencies) will likely be hurt by a depreciated local currency.

Economic Exposure of Domestic Firms

Although our focus is on the financial management of MNCs, even purely domestic firms are affected by economic exposure.

EXAMPLE

Burlington, Inc., is a U.S. manufacturer of steel that purchases all of its supplies locally and sells all of its steel locally. Because its transactions are solely in the local currency, Burlington is not subject to transaction exposure. It is subject to economic exposure, however, because it faces foreign competition in its local markets. If the exchange rate of the foreign competitor's invoice currency depreciates against the dollar, customers interested in steel products will shift their purchases toward the foreign steel producer. Consequently, demand for Burlington's steel will likely decrease, and so will its net cash inflows. Thus, Burlington is subject to economic exposure even though it is not subject to transaction exposure.

Measuring Economic Exposure

Since MNCs are affected by economic exposure, they should assess the potential degree of exposure that exists and then determine whether to insulate themselves against it.

Sensitivity of Earnings to Exchange Rates. One method of measuring an MNC's economic exposure is to classify the cash flows into different income statement items and subjectively predict each income statement item based on a forecast of exchange rates. Then an alternative exchange rate scenario can be considered and the forecasts for the income statement items revised. By reviewing how the earnings forecast in the income statement changes in response to alternative exchange rate scenarios, the firm can assess the influence of currency movements on its earnings and cash flows. This procedure is especially useful for firms that have more expenses than revenue in a particular foreign currency as illustrated next.

EXAMPLE

Madison, Inc., is a U.S.-based MNC that conducts a portion of its business in Canada. Its U.S. sales are denominated in U.S. dollars, while its Canadian sales are denominated in Canadian dollars. Its pro forma income statement for next year is shown in Exhibit 10.7. The income statement items are segmented into those for the United States and for Canada. Assume that Madison, Inc., desires to assess how its income statement items would be affected by three possible exchange rate scenarios for the Canadian dollar over the period of concern: (1) \$.75, (2) \$.80, and (3) \$.85. These scenarios are separately analyzed in the second, third, and fourth columns of Exhibit 10.8.

If the U.S. sales are unaffected by the possible exchange rates, the impact of exchange rates on all income statement items can be assessed from the information

Exhibit 10.7

Revenue and Cost Estimates: Madison, Inc. (in Millions of U.S. Dollars and Canadian Dollars)

	U.S. Business	Canadian Business
Sales	\$304.00	C\$ 4
Cost of goods sold	50.00	200
Gross profit	\$254.00	C\$−196
Operating expenses:		
Fixed	\$ 30.00	—
Variable	30.72	—
Total	\$ 60.72	—
Earnings before interest and taxes (EBIT)	\$193.28	C\$−196
Interest expense	3.00	10
Earnings before taxes (EBT)	\$190.28	C\$−206

Exhibit 10.8 Impact of Possible Exchange Rate Movements on Earnings of Madison, Inc. (in Millions)

	Exchange Rate Scenario					
	C$ = $.75		C$ = $.80		C$ = $.85	
Sales:						
(1) U.S.		$300.0		$304.00		$307.00
(2) Canadian	C$4 =	3.0	C$4 =	3.20	C$4 =	3.40
(3) Total		$303.0		$307.20		$310.40
Cost of goods sold:						
(4) U.S.		$ 50.0		$ 50.00		$ 50.00
(5) Canadian	C$200 =	150.0	C$200 =	160.00	C$200 =	170.00
(6) Total		$200.0		$210.00		$220.00
(7) Gross profit		$103.0		$ 97.20		$ 90.40
Operating expenses:						
(8) U.S.: Fixed		$ 30.0		$ 30.00		$ 30.00
(9) U.S.: Variable (10% of total sales)		30.3		30.72		31.04
(10) Total		$ 60.3		$ 60.72		$ 61.04
(11) EBIT		$ 42.7		$ 36.48		$ 29.36
Interest expense:						
(12) U.S.		$ 3.0		$ 3.00		$ 3.00
(13) Canadian	C$10 =	7.5	C$10 =	8.00	C$10 =	8.50
(14) Total		$ 10.5		$ 11.00		$ 11.50
(15) EBT		$ 32.2		$ 25.48		$ 17.86

contained in Exhibit 10.7. However, Madison's sales in the United States are higher when the Canadian dollar (C$) is stronger because Canadian competitors are priced out of the U.S. market. To be specific, assume the following forecasts for U.S. sales corresponding to each possible exchange rate scenario:

Possible Exchange Rate of C$	Forecasted U.S. Sales (in Millions)
$.75	$300
.80	304
.85	307

The impact of an exchange rate on local sales for any firm will depend on the foreign competition of concern. Historical data can be used to assess how local sales were affected by exchange rates in the past. For our example, the impact of the exchange rate on local sales is given, so there is no need to assess historical data.

Given this information, Madison, Inc., can determine how its pro forma statement would be affected by each exchange rate scenario, as shown in Exhibit 10.8. The assumed impact of exchange rates on U.S. sales is shown in row 1. Row 2 shows the amount in U.S. dollars to be received as a result of Canadian sales (after converting the forecasted C$4 million of Canadian sales into U.S. dollars). Row 3 shows the estimated U.S. dollars to be received from total sales, which is determined by combining rows 1 and 2. Row 4 shows the cost of goods sold in the United States. Row 5 converts the estimated C$200 million cost of goods sold into U.S. dollars for each exchange rate scenario. Row 6 measures the estimated U.S. dollars needed to cover the total cost of goods sold, which is determined by combining rows 4 and 5. Row 7 estimates the gross profit in U.S. dollars, determined by subtracting row 6 from row 3. Rows 8 through 10 show estimated operating expenses, and row 11 subtracts total operating expenses from gross profit to determine earnings before interest and taxes (EBIT). Row 12 estimates the interest expenses paid in the United States, while row 13 estimates the U.S. dollars needed to make interest payments in Canada. Row 14 combines rows 12 and 13 to estimate total U.S. dollars needed to make all interest payments. Row 15 shows earnings before taxes (EBT), estimated by subtracting row 14 from row 11.

The effect of exchange rates on Madison's revenues and costs can now be reviewed. Exhibit 10.8 illustrates how both U.S. sales and the dollar value of Canadian sales would increase as a result of a stronger Canadian dollar. Because Madison's Canadian cost of goods sold exposure (C$200 million) is much greater than its Canadian sales exposure (C$4 million), a strong Canadian dollar has a negative overall impact on gross profit. The total amount in U.S. dollars needed to make interest payments is also higher when the Canadian dollar is stronger. In general, Madison, Inc., would be adversely affected by a stronger Canadian dollar. It would be favorably affected by a weaker Canadian dollar because the reduced value of total revenue would be more than offset by the reduced cost of goods sold and interest expenses.

A general conclusion from this example is that firms with more (less) in foreign costs than in foreign revenue will be unfavorably (favorably) affected by a stronger foreign currency. The precise anticipated impact, however, can be determined only by utilizing the procedure described here or some alternative procedure. The example is based on a one-period time horizon. If firms have developed forecasts of sales, expenses, and exchange rates for several periods ahead, they can assess their economic exposure over time. Their economic exposure will be affected by any change in operating characteristics over time.

Sensitivity of Cash Flows to Exchange Rates. A firm's economic exposure to currency movements can also be assessed by applying regression analysis to historical cash flow and exchange rate data as follows:

$$PCF_t = a_0 + a_1 e_t + \mu_t$$

where

PCF_t = percentage change in inflation-adjusted cash flows measured in the firm's home currency over period t

e_t = percentage change in the exchange rate of the currency over period t

μ_t = random error term

a_0 = intercept

a_1 = slope coefficient

The regression coefficient a_1, estimated by regression analysis, indicates the sensitivity of PCF_t to e_t. If the firm anticipates no major adjustments in its operating structure, it will expect the sensitivity detected from regression analysis to be somewhat similar in the future.

This regression model can be revised to handle more complex situations. For example, if additional currencies are to be assessed, they can be included in the model as additional independent variables. Each currency's impact is measured by estimating its respective regression coefficient. If an MNC is influenced by numerous currencies, it can measure the sensitivity of PCF_t to an index (or composite) of currencies.

The analysis just described for a single currency can also be extended over separate subperiods, as the sensitivity of a firm's cash flows to a currency's movements may change over time. This would be indicated by a shift in the regression coefficient, which may occur if the firm's exposure to exchange rate movements changes.

Some MNCs may prefer to use their stock price as a proxy for the firm's value and then assess how their stock price changes in response to currency movements. Regression analysis could also be applied to this situation by replacing PCF_t with the percentage change in stock price in the model specified here.

Some researchers, including Adler and Dumas,[1] suggest the use of regression analysis for this purpose. By assigning stock returns as the dependent variable, regression analysis can indicate how the firm's value is sensitive to exchange rate fluctuations.

Some companies may assess the impact of exchange rates on particular corporate characteristics, such as earnings, exports, or sales.

Toyota Motor Corp. measures the sensitivity of its exports to the yen exchange rate (relative to the U.S. dollar). Consequently, it can determine how the level of exports may change in response to potential changes in the value of the yen. This information is useful when Toyota determines its production level and manages its inventory.

Translation Exposure

An MNC creates its financial statements by consolidating all of its individual subsidiaries' financial statements. A subsidiary's financial statement is normally measured in its local currency. To be consolidated, each subsidiary's financial statement must be translated into the currency of the MNC's parent. Since exchange rates change over time, the translation of the subsidiary's financial statement into a different currency is affected by exchange rate movements. The exposure of the MNC's consolidated financial statements to exchange rate fluctuations is known as **translation exposure**. In particular, subsidiary earnings translated into the reporting currency on the consolidated income statement are subject to changing exchange rates.

To translate earnings, MNCs use a process established by the Financial Accounting Standards Board (FASB). The prevailing guidelines are set by FASB 52 for translation and by FASB 133 for valuing existing currency derivative contracts.

[1]Michael Adler and Bernard Dumas, "Exposure to Currency Risk: Definition and Measurement," *Financial Management*, 13, no. 2 (Summer 1984): 41–50.

Does Translation Exposure Matter?

The relevance of translation exposure can be argued based on a cash flow perspective or a stock price perspective.

Cash Flow Perspective. Translation of financial statements for consolidated reporting purposes does not by itself affect an MNC's cash flows. The subsidiary earnings do not actually have to be converted into the parent's currency. If a subsidiary's local currency is currently weak, the earnings could be retained rather than converted and sent to the parent. The earnings could be reinvested in the subsidiary's country if feasible opportunities exist.

An MNC's parent, however, may rely on funding from periodic remittances of earnings by the subsidiary. Even if the subsidiary does not need to remit any earnings today, it will remit earnings at some point in the future. To the extent that today's spot rate serves as a forecast of the spot rate that will exist when earnings are remitted, a weak foreign currency today results in a forecast of a weak exchange rate at the time that the earnings are remitted. In this case, the expected future cash flows are affected by the prevailing weakness of the foreign currency.

Stock Price Perspective. Many investors tend to use earnings when valuing firms, either by deriving estimates of expected cash flows from previous earnings or by applying a price-earnings (P/E) ratio to expected annual earnings to derive a value per share of stock. Since an MNC's translation exposure affects its consolidated earnings, it can affect the MNC's valuation.

Determinants of Translation Exposure

Some MNCs are subject to a greater degree of translation exposure than others. An MNC's degree of translation exposure is dependent on the following:

- The proportion of its business conducted by foreign subsidiaries
- The locations of its foreign subsidiaries
- The accounting methods that it uses

Proportion of Its Business Conducted by Foreign Subsidiaries. The greater the percentage of an MNC's business conducted by its foreign subsidiaries, the larger the percentage of a given financial statement item that is susceptible to translation exposure.

EXAMPLE

Locus Co. and Zeuss Co. each generate about 30 percent of their sales from foreign countries. However, Locus Co. generates all of its international business by exporting, whereas Zeuss Co. has a large Mexican subsidiary that generates all of its international business. Locus Co. is not subject to translation exposure (although it is subject to economic exposure), while Zeuss has substantial translation exposure.

Locations of Foreign Subsidiaries. The locations of the subsidiaries can also influence the degree of translation exposure because the financial statement items of each subsidiary are typically measured by the home currency of the subsidiary's country.

EXAMPLE

Zeuss Co. and Canton Co. each have one large foreign subsidiary that generates about 30 percent of their respective sales. However, Zeuss Co. is subject to a much higher degree of translation exposure because its subsidiary is based in Mexico, and the peso's value is subject to a large decline. In contrast, Canton's subsidiary is based in Canada, and the Canadian dollar is very stable against the U.S. dollar.

Accounting Methods. An MNC's degree of translation exposure can be greatly affected by the accounting procedures it uses to translate when consolidating financial statement data. Many of the important consolidated accounting rules for U.S.-based MNCs are based on FASB 52:

1. The functional currency of an entity is the currency of the economic environment in which the entity operates.
2. The current exchange rate as of the reporting date is used to translate the assets and liabilities of a foreign entity from its functional currency into the reporting currency.
3. The weighted average exchange rate over the relevant period is used to translate revenue, expenses, and gains and losses of a foreign entity from its functional currency into the reporting currency.
4. Translated income gains or losses due to changes in foreign currency values are not recognized in current net income but are reported as a second component of stockholder's equity; an exception to this rule is a foreign entity located in a country with high inflation.
5. Realized income gains or losses due to foreign currency transactions are recorded in current net income, although there are some exceptions.

Under FASB 52, consolidated earnings are sensitive to the functional currency's weighted average exchange rate.

EXAMPLE

A British subsidiary of Providence, Inc., earned £10,000,000 in Year 1 and £10,000,000 in Year 2. When these earnings are consolidated along with other subsidiary earnings, they are translated into dollars at the weighted average exchange rate in that year. Assume the weighted average exchange rate is $1.70 in Year 1 and $1.50 in Year 2. The translated earnings for each reporting period in U.S. dollars are determined as follows:

Reporting Period	Local Earnings of British Subsidiary	Weighted Average Exchange Rate of Pound over the Reporting Period	Translated U.S. Dollar Earnings of British Subsidiary
Year 1	£10,000,000	$1.70	$17,000,000
Year 2	£10,000,000	$1.50	$15,000,000

Notice that even though the subsidiary's earnings in pounds were the same each year, the translated consolidated dollar earnings were reduced by $2 million in Year 2. The discrepancy here is due to the change in the weighted average of the British pound exchange rate. The drop in earnings is not the fault of the subsidiary, but rather of the weakened British pound that makes its Year 2 earnings look small (when measured in U.S. dollars).

Examples of Translation Exposure

Consolidated earnings of Black & Decker, The Coca-Cola Company, and other MNCs are very sensitive to exchange rates because more than a third of their assets and sales are overseas. Their earnings in foreign countries are reduced when foreign currencies depreciate against the dollar.

In the 2000–2001 period, the weakness of the euro caused several U.S.-based MNCs to report lower earnings than they had expected. In September 2000, when DuPont announced that its consolidated earnings would be affected by its translation exposure to the euro, investors responded quickly by dumping DuPont's shares. The stock price of DuPont declined 10 percent on that day. Other MNCs including Colgate-Palmolive, Gillette, Goodyear, and McDonald's followed with similar announcements.

In 2002 and 2003, however, the euro strengthened, and the consolidated income statements of U.S.-based MNCs improved as a result. IBM stated that in the first quarter of 2003, more than half of its 11 percent increase in revenue was attributed to favorable translation effects. In that same quarter, translation effects accounted for more than two-thirds of Colgate-Palmolive's 20 percent increase in revenue.

SUMMARY

- MNCs with less risk can obtain funds at lower financing costs. Since they may experience more volatile cash flows because of exchange rate movements, exchange rate risk can affect their financing costs. Thus, MNCs may benefit from hedging exchange rate risk.
- Transaction exposure is the exposure of an MNC's future cash transactions to exchange rate movements. MNCs can measure their transaction exposure by determining their future payables and receivables positions in various currencies, along with the variability levels and correlations of these currencies. From this information, they can assess how their revenue and costs may change in response to various exchange rate scenarios.
- Economic exposure is any exposure of an MNC's cash flows (direct or indirect) to exchange rate movements. MNCs can attempt to measure their economic exposure by determining the extent to which their cash flows will be affected by their exposure to each foreign currency.
- Translation exposure is the exposure of an MNC's consolidated financial statements to exchange rate movements. To measure translation exposure, MNCs can forecast their earnings in each foreign currency and then determine the potential exchange rate movements of each currency relative to their home currency.

POINT COUNTER-POINT

Should Investors Care about an MNC's Translation Exposure?

Point No. The present value of an MNC's cash flows is based on the cash flows that the parent receives. Any impact of the exchange rates on the financial statements is not important unless cash flows are affected. MNCs should focus their energy on assessing the exposure of their cash flows to exchange rate movements and should not be concerned with the exposure of their financial statements to exchange rate movements. Value is about cash flows, and investors focus on value.

Counter-Point Investors do not have sufficient financial data to derive cash flows. They commonly use earnings as a base, and if earnings are distorted, so will be their estimates of cash flows. If they underestimate cash flows because of how exchange rates affected the reported earnings, they may underestimate the value of the MNC. Even if the value is corrected in the future once the market realizes how the earnings were distorted, some investors may have sold their stock by the time the correction occurs. Investors should be concerned about an MNC's translation exposure. They should recognize that the earnings of MNCs with large translation exposure may be more distorted than the earnings of MNCs with low translation exposure.

Who Is Correct? Use InfoTrac or some other search engine to learn more about this issue. Which argument do you support?

SELF TEST

Answers are provided in Appendix A at the back of the text.

1. Given that shareholders can diversify away an individual firm's exchange rate risk by investing in a variety of firms, why are firms concerned about exchange rate risk?
2. Bradley, Inc., considers importing its supplies from either Canada (denominated in C$) or Mexico (denominated in pesos) on a monthly basis. The quality is the same for both sources. Once the firm completes the agreement with a supplier, it will be obligated to continue using that supplier for at least three years. Based on existing exchange rates, the dollar amount to be paid (including transportation costs) will be the same. The firm has no other exposure to exchange rate movements. Given that the firm prefers to have less exchange rate risk, which alternative is preferable? Explain.
3. Assume your U.S. firm currently exports to Mexico on a monthly basis. The goods are priced in pesos. Once material is received from a source, it is quickly used to produce the product in the United States, and then the product is exported. Currently, you have no other exposure to exchange rate risk. You have a choice of purchasing the material from Canada (denominated in C$), from Mexico (denominated in pesos), or from within the United States (denominated in U.S. dollars). The quality and your expected cost are similar across the three sources. Which source is preferable, given that you prefer minimal exchange rate risk?
4. Using the information in the previous question, consider a proposal to price the exports to Mexico in dollars and to use the U.S. source for material. Would this proposal eliminate the exchange rate risk?
5. Assume that the dollar is expected to strengthen against the euro over the next several years. Explain how this will affect the consolidated earnings of U.S.-based MNCs with subsidiaries in Europe.

QUESTIONS AND APPLICATIONS

1. **Transaction versus Economic Exposure.** Compare and contrast transaction exposure and economic exposure. Why would an MNC consider examining only its "net" cash flows in each currency when assessing its transaction exposure?
2. **Assessing Transaction Exposure.** Your employer, a large MNC, has asked you to assess its transaction exposure. Its projected cash flows are as follows for the next year:

Currency	Total Inflow	Total Outflow	Current Exchange Rate in U.S. Dollars
Danish krone (DK)	DK50,000,000	DK40,000,000	$.15
British pound (£)	£2,000,000	£1,000,000	$1.50

Assume that the movements in the Danish krone and the pound are highly correlated. Provide your assessment as to your firm's degree of transaction exposure (as to whether the exposure is high or low). Substantiate your answer.

3. **Factors That Affect a Firm's Transaction Exposure.** What factors affect a firm's degree of transaction exposure in a particular currency? For each factor, explain the desirable characteristics that would reduce transaction exposure.

4. **Currency Correlations.** Kopetsky Co. has net receivables in several currencies that are highly correlated with each other. What does this imply about the firm's overall degree of transaction exposure? Are currency correlations perfectly stable over time? What does your answer imply about Kopetsky Co. or any other firm using past data on correlations as an indicator for the future?

5. **Currency Effects on Cash Flows.** How should appreciation of a firm's home currency generally affect its cash inflows? How should depreciation of a firm's home currency generally affect its cash outflows?

6. **Transaction Exposure.** Fischer, Inc., exports products from Florida to Europe. It obtains supplies and borrows funds locally. How would appreciation of the euro likely affect its net cash flows? Why?

7. **Exposure of Domestic Firms.** Why are the cash flows of a purely domestic firm exposed to exchange rate fluctuations?

8. **Measuring Economic Exposure.** Memphis Co. hires you as a consultant to assess its degree of economic exposure to exchange rate fluctuations. How would you handle this task? Be specific.

9. **Factors That Affect a Firm's Translation Exposure.** What factors affect a firm's degree of translation exposure? Explain how each factor influences translation exposure.

10. **Translation Exposure.** Consider a period in which the U.S. dollar weakens against the euro. How will this affect the reported earnings of a U.S.-based MNC with European subsidiaries? Consider a period in which the U.S. dollar strengthens against most foreign currencies. How will this affect the reported earnings of a U.S.-based MNC with subsidiaries all over the world?

11. **Transaction Exposure.** Aggie Co. produces chemicals. It is a major exporter to Europe, where its main competition is from other U.S. exporters. All of these companies invoice the products in U.S. dollars. Is Aggie's transaction exposure likely to be significantly affected if the euro strengthens or weakens? Explain. If the euro weakens for several years, can you think of any change that might occur in the global chemicals market?

12. **Economic Exposure.** Longhorn Co. produces hospital equipment. Most of its revenues are in the United States. About half of its expenses require outflows in Philippine pesos (to pay for Philippine materials). Most of Longhorn's competition is from U.S. firms that have no international business at all. How will Longhorn Co. be affected if the peso strengthens?

13. **Economic Exposure.** Lubbock, Inc., produces furniture and has no international business. Its major competitors import most of their furniture from Brazil and then sell it out of retail stores in the United States. How will Lubbock, Inc., be affected if Brazil's currency (the real) strengthens over time?

14. **Economic Exposure.** Sooner Co. is a U.S. wholesale company that imports expensive high-quality luggage and sells it to retail stores around the United States. Its main competitors also import high-quality luggage and sell it to retail stores. None of these competitors hedge their exposure to exchange rate movements. The treasurer of Sooner Co. told the board of directors that the firm's performance would be more volatile over time if it hedged its exchange rate exposure. How could a firm's cash flows be more stable as a result of such high exposure to exchange rate fluctuations?

15. **PPP and Economic Exposure.** Boulder, Inc., exports chairs to Europe (invoiced in U.S. dollars) and competes against local European companies. If purchasing power parity exists, why would Boulder not benefit from a stronger euro?

16. **Measuring Changes in Economic Exposure.** Toyota Motor Corp. measures the sensitivity of its exports to the yen exchange rate (relative to the U.S. dollar). Explain how regression analysis could be used for such a task. Identify the expected sign of the regression coefficient if Toyota primarily exports to

the United States. If Toyota established plants in the United States, how might the regression coefficient on the exchange rate variable change?

17. **Impact of Exchange Rates on Earnings.** Cieplak, Inc., is a U.S.-based MNC that has expanded into Asia. Its U.S. parent exports to some Asian countries, with its exports denominated in the Asian currencies. It also has a large subsidiary in Malaysia that serves that market. Offer at least two reasons related to exposure to exchange rates why Cieplak's earnings were reduced during the Asian crisis.

ADVANCED QUESTIONS

18. **Speculating Based on Exposure.** During the Asian crisis in 1998, there were rumors that China would weaken its currency (the yuan) against the U.S. dollar and many European currencies. This caused investors to sell stocks in Asian countries such as Japan, Taiwan, and Singapore. Offer an intuitive explanation for such an effect. What types of Asian firms would have been affected the most?

19. **Effect of September 11.** Explain how the September 11, 2001 terrorist attack caused lower U.S. interest rates. Explain how this effect on the value of the dollar could have adversely affected some MNCs that were subject to transaction exposure. Based on your expectations, would U.S. exporters or importers have been more adversely affected?

20. **Using Regression Analysis to Measure Exposure.**

    a. How can a U.S. company use regression analysis to assess its economic exposure to fluctuations in the British pound?

    b. In using regression analysis to assess the sensitivity of cash flows to exchange rate movements, what is the purpose of breaking the database into subperiods?

    c. Assume the regression coefficient based on assessing economic exposure was much higher in the second subperiod than in the first subperiod. What does this tell you about the firm's degree of economic exposure over time? Why might such results occur?

21. **Transaction Exposure.** Vegas Corp. is a U.S. firm that exports most of its products to Canada. It historically invoiced its products in Canadian dollars to accommodate the importers. However, it was adversely affected when the Canadian dollar weakened against the U.S. dollar. Since Vegas did not hedge, its Canadian dollar receivables were converted into a relatively small amount of U.S. dollars. After a few more years of continual concern about possible exchange rate movements, Vegas called its customers and requested that they pay for future orders with U.S. dollars instead of Canadian dollars. At this time, the Canadian dollar was valued at $.81. The customers decided to oblige, since the number of Canadian dollars to be converted into U.S. dollars when importing the goods from Vegas was still slightly smaller than the number of Canadian dollars that would be needed to buy the product from a Canadian manufacturer. Based on this situation, has transaction exposure changed for Vegas Corp.? Has economic exposure changed? Explain.

22. **Measuring Economic Exposure.** Using the following cost and revenue information shown for DeKalb, Inc., determine how the costs, revenue, and earnings items would be affected by three possible exchange rate scenarios for the New Zealand dollar (NZ$): (1) NZ$ = $.50, (2) NZ$ = $.55, and (3) NZ$ = $.60. (Assume U.S. sales will be unaffected by the exchange rate.) Assume that NZ$ earnings will be remitted to the U.S. parent at the end of the period.

Revenue and Cost Estimates: DeKalb, Inc.
(in millions of U.S. dollars and New Zealand dollars)

	U.S. Business	New Zealand Business
Sales	$800	NZ$800
Cost of goods sold	500	100
Gross profit	$300	NZ$700
Operating expenses	300	0
Earnings before interest and taxes	$ 0	NZ$700
Interest expense	100	0
Earnings before taxes	−$100	NZ$700

23. **Changes in Economic Exposure.** Walt Disney World built an amusement park in France that opened in 1992. How do you think this project has affected

Disney's economic exposure to exchange rate movements? Think carefully before you give your final answer. There is more than one way in which Disney's cash flows may be affected. Explain.

24. **Lagged Effects of Exchange Rate Movements.** Cornhusker Co. is an exporter of products to Singapore. It wants to know how its stock price is affected by changes in the Singapore dollar's exchange rate. It believes that the impact may occur with a lag of one to three quarters. How could regression analysis be used to assess the impact?

25. **Potential Effects if the United Kingdom Adopted the Euro.** The United Kingdom still has its own currency, the pound. The pound's interest rate has historically been higher than the euro's interest rate. The United Kingdom has considered adopting the euro as its currency. There have been many arguments about whether it should do so.

    Use your knowledge and intuition to discuss the likely effects if the United Kingdom adopts the euro. For each of the 10 statements below, insert either *increase* or *decrease* in the first blank and complete the statement by adding a clear, short explanation (perhaps one to three sentences) of why the United Kingdom's adoption of the euro would have that effect.

    To help you narrow your focus, follow these guidelines. Do not base your answer on whether the pound would have been stronger than the euro in the future. Also, do not base your answer on an unusual change in economic growth in the United Kingdom or in the euro zone if the euro is adopted.

    a. The economic exposure of British firms that are heavy exporters to the euro zone would ________ because ________ .

    b. The translation exposure of firms based in the euro zone that have British subsidiaries would ________ because ________ .

    c. The economic exposure of U.S. firms that conduct substantial business in the United Kingdom and have no other international business would ________ because ________ .

    d. The translation exposure of U.S. firms with British subsidiaries would ________ because ________ .

    e. The economic exposure of U.S. firms that export to the United Kingdom and whose only other international business is importing from firms based in the euro zone would ________ because ________ .

    f. The discount on the forward rate paid by U.S. firms that periodically use the forward market to hedge payables of British imports would ________ because ________ .

    g. The earnings of a foreign exchange department of a British bank that executes foreign exchange transactions desired by its European clients would ________ because ________ .

    h. Assume that the Swiss franc is more highly correlated with the British pound than with the euro. A U.S. firm has substantial monthly exports to the United Kingdom denominated in the British currency and also has substantial monthly imports of Swiss supplies (denominated in Swiss francs). The economic exposure of this firm would ________ because ________ .

    i. Assume that the Swiss franc is more highly correlated with the British pound than with the euro. A U.S. firm has substantial monthly exports to the United Kingdom denominated in the British currency and also has substantial monthly exports to Switzerland (denominated in Swiss francs). The economic exposure of this firm would ________ because ________ .

    j. The British government's reliance on monetary policy (as opposed to fiscal policy) as a means of fine-tuning the economy would ________ because ________ .

26. **Invoicing Policy to Reduce Exposure.** Celtic Co. is a U.S. firm that exports its products to England. It faces competition from many firms in England. Its price to customers in England has generally been lower than those of the competitors, primarily because the British pound has been strong. It has priced its exports in pounds, and then converts the pound receivables into dollars. All of its expenses are in the United States and are paid with dollars. It is concerned about its economic exposure. It considers a change in its pricing policy, in which it will price its products in dollars instead of pounds. Offer your opinion on why this will or will not significantly reduce its economic exposure.

27. **Exposure of an MNC's Subsidiary.** Decko Co. is a U.S. firm with a Chinese subsidiary that produces cell phones in China and sells them in Japan. This

subsidiary pays its wages and its rent in Chinese yuan, which is presently tied to the dollar. The cell phones sold to Japan are denominated in Japanese yen. Assume that Decko Co. expects that the Chinese yuan will continue to stay fixed against the dollar. The subsidiary's main goal is to generate profits for itself and it reinvests the profits. It does not plan to remit any funds to the U.S. parent.

a. Assume that the Japanese yen strengthens against the U.S. dollar over time. How would this be expected to affect the profits earned by the Chinese subsidiary?

b. If Decko Co. had established its subsidiary in Tokyo, Japan instead of China, would its subsidiary's profits be more exposed or less exposed to exchange rate risk?

c. Why do you think that Decko Co. established the subsidiary in China instead of Japan? Assume no major country risk barriers.

d. If the Chinese subsidiary needs to borrow money to finance its expansion and wants to reduce its exchange rate risk, should it borrow U.S. dollars, Chinese yuan, or Japanese yen?

INTERNET APPLICATION

28. **Daily Exchange Rates and Annual Reports** The following website provides daily exchange rate data for several currencies over the last few months: **http://www.federalreserve.gov/releases/**.

a. Use this website to assess the volatility of recent daily exchange rates of the Canadian dollar and Australian dollar over the last two months. Which currency appears to be more volatile? What are the implications for U.S. firms that recently had cash flows denominated in Australian dollars versus Canadian dollars?

b. The following website contains annual reports of many MNCs: **http://www.reportgallery.com**. Review the annual report of your choice. Look for any comments in the report that describe the MNC's transaction exposure, economic exposure, or translation exposure. Summarize the MNC's exposure based on the comments in the annual report.

DISCUSSION IN THE BOARDROOM

This exercise can be found in Appendix E at the back of this textbook.

RUNNING YOUR OWN MNC

This exercise can be found on the Xtra! website at **http://maduraxtra.swlearning.com**.

BLADES, INC. CASE

Assessment of Exchange Rate Exposure

Blades, Inc., is currently exporting roller blades to Thailand and importing certain components needed to manufacture roller blades from that country. Under a fixed contractual agreement, Blades' primary customer in Thailand has committed itself to purchase 180,000 pairs of roller blades annually at a fixed price of 4,594 Thai baht (THB) per pair. Blades is importing rubber and plastic components from various suppliers in Thailand at a cost of approximately THB2,871 per pair, although the exact price (in baht) depends on current market prices. Blades imports materials sufficient to manufacture 72,000 pairs of roller blades from Thailand each year. The decision to import materials from Thailand was reached because rubber and plastic components needed to manufacture Blades' products are inexpensive, yet high quality, in Thailand.

Blades has also conducted business with a Japanese supplier in the past. Although Blades' analysis indicates that the Japanese components are of a lower quality than the Thai components, Blades has occasionally imported components from Japan when the prices were low enough. Currently, Ben Holt, Blades' chief financial officer (CFO), is considering importing components from Japan more frequently. Specifically, he would like to reduce Blades' baht exposure by taking advantage of the recently high correlation between the baht and the yen. Since Blades has net inflows denominated in baht and would have outflows denominated in yen, its net transaction exposure would be reduced if these two currencies were highly correlated. If Blades decides to import components from Japan, it would probably import materials sufficient to manufacture

1,700 pairs of roller blades annually at a price of ¥7,440 per pair.

Holt is also contemplating further expansion into foreign countries. Although he would eventually like to establish a subsidiary or acquire an existing business overseas, his immediate focus is on increasing Blades' foreign sales. Holt's primary reason for this plan is that the profit margin from Blades' imports and exports exceeds 25 percent, while the profit margin from Blades' domestic production is below 15 percent. Consequently, he believes that further foreign expansion will be beneficial to the company's future.

Though Blades' current exporting and importing practices have been profitable, Ben Holt is contemplating extending Blades' trade relationships to countries in different regions of the world. One reason for this decision is that various Thai roller blade manufacturers have recently established subsidiaries in the United States. Furthermore, various Thai roller blade manufacturers have recently targeted the U.S. market by advertising their products over the Internet. As a result of this increased competition from Thailand, Blades is uncertain whether its primary customer in Thailand will renew the current commitment to purchase a fixed number of roller blades annually. The current agreement will terminate in two years. Another reason for engaging in transactions with other, non-Asian, countries is that the Thai baht has depreciated substantially recently, which has somewhat reduced Blades' profit margins. The sale of roller blades to other countries with more stable currencies may increase Blades' profit margins.

While Blades will continue exporting to Thailand under the current agreement for the next two years, it may also export roller blades to Jogs, Ltd., a British retailer. Preliminary negotiations indicate that Jogs would be willing to commit itself to purchase 200,000 pairs of "Speedos," Blades' primary product, for a fixed price of £80 per pair.

Holt is aware that further expansion would increase Blades' exposure to exchange rate fluctuations, but he believes that Blades can supplement its profit margins by expanding. He is vaguely familiar with the different types of exchange rate exposure but has asked you, a financial analyst at Blades, Inc., to help him assess how the contemplated changes would affect Blades' financial position. Among other concerns, Holt is aware that recent economic problems in Thailand have had an effect on Thailand and other Asian countries. Whereas the correlation between Asian currencies such as the Japanese yen and the Thai baht is generally not very high and very unstable, these recent problems have increased the correlation among most Asian currencies. Conversely, the correlation between the British pound and the Asian currencies is quite low.

To aid you in your analysis, Holt has provided you with the following data:

Currency	Expected Exchange Rate	Range of Possible Exchange Rates
British pound	**$1.50**	**$1.47 to $1.53**
Japanese yen	**$0.0083**	**$0.0079 to $0.0087**
Thai baht	**$0.024**	**$0.020 to $0.028**

Holt has asked you to answer the following questions:

1. What type(s) of exposure (i.e., transaction, economic, or translation exposure) is Blades subject to? Why?
2. Using a spreadsheet, conduct a consolidated net cash flow assessment of Blades, Inc., and estimate the range of net inflows and outflows for Blades for the coming year. Assume that Blades enters into the agreement with Jogs, Ltd.
3. If Blades does not enter into the agreement with the British firm and continues to export to Thailand and import from Thailand and Japan, do you think the increased correlations between the Japanese yen and the Thai baht will increase or reduce Blades' transaction exposure?
4. Do you think Blades should import components from Japan to reduce its net transaction exposure in the long run? Why or why not?
5. Assuming Blades enters into the agreement with Jogs, Ltd., how will its overall transaction exposure be affected?
6. Given that Thai roller blade manufacturers located in Thailand have begun targeting the U.S. roller blade market, how do you think Blades' U.S. sales were affected by the depreciation of the Thai baht? How do you think its exports to Thailand and its imports from Thailand and Japan were affected by the depreciation?

SMALL BUSINESS DILEMMA

Assessment of Exchange Rate Exposure by the Sports Exports Company

At the current time, the Sports Exports Company is willing to receive payments in British pounds for the monthly exports it sends to the United Kingdom. While all of its receivables are denominated in pounds, it has no payables in pounds or in any other foreign currency. Jim Logan, owner of the Sports Exports Company, wants to assess his firm's exposure to exchange rate risk.

1. Would you describe the exposure of the Sports Exports Company to exchange rate risk as transaction exposure? Economic exposure? Translation exposure?

2. Jim Logan is considering a change in the pricing policy in which the importer must pay in dollars, so that Jim will not have to worry about converting pounds to dollars every month. If implemented, would this policy eliminate the transaction exposure of the Sports Exports Company? Would it eliminate Sports Exports' economic exposure? Explain.

3. If Jim decides to implement the policy described in the previous question, how would the Sports Exports Company be affected (if at all) by appreciation of the pound? By depreciation of the pound? Would these effects on Sports Exports differ if Jim retained his original policy of pricing the exports in British pounds?

CHAPTER 11

Managing Transaction Exposure

Recall from the previous chapter that a multinational corporation (MNC) is exposed to exchange rate fluctuations in three ways: (1) transaction exposure, (2) economic exposure, and (3) translation exposure. This chapter focuses on the management of transaction exposure, while the following chapter focuses on the management of economic and translation exposure. By managing transaction exposure, financial managers may be able to increase cash flows and enhance the value of their MNCs.

The specific objectives of this chapter are to:

- identify the commonly used techniques for hedging transaction exposure,
- explain how each technique can be used to hedge future payables and receivables,
- compare the advantages and disadvantages of the different hedging techniques, and
- suggest other methods of reducing exchange rate risk when hedging techniques are not available.

Transaction Exposure

Transaction exposure exists when the anticipated future cash transactions of a firm are affected by exchange rate fluctuations. A U.S. firm that purchases Mexican goods may need pesos to buy the goods. Though it may know exactly how many pesos it will need, it doesn't know how many dollars will be needed to be exchanged for those pesos. This uncertainty occurs because the exchange rate between pesos and dollars fluctuates over time. A U.S.-based MNC that will be receiving a foreign currency is exposed because it does not know how many dollars it will obtain when it exchanges the foreign currency for dollars.

If transaction exposure exists, the firm faces three major tasks. First, it must identify its degree of transaction exposure. Second, it must decide whether to hedge this exposure. Finally, if it decides to hedge part or all of the exposure, it must choose among the various hedging techniques available. Each of these tasks is discussed in turn.

Identifying Net Transaction Exposure

Before an MNC makes any decisions related to hedging, it should identify the individual **net transaction exposure** on a currency-by-currency basis. The term *net* here refers to the consolidation of all expected inflows and outflows for a particular time and currency. The management at each subsidiary plays a vital role in reporting its expected inflows and outflows. Then a centralized group consolidates the subsidiary reports to identify, for the MNC as a whole, the expected net positions in each foreign currency during several upcoming periods.

The MNC can identify its exposure by reviewing this consolidation of subsidiary positions. For example, one subsidiary may have net receivables in Mexican pesos three months from now, while a different subsidiary has net payables in pesos. If the peso appreciates, this will be favorable to the first subsidiary and unfavorable to the second subsidiary. For the MNC as a whole, however, the impact is at least partially offset. Each subsidiary may desire to hedge its net currency position in order to avoid the possible adverse impacts on its performance due to fluctuation in the currency's value. The overall performance of the MNC, however, may already be insulated by the offsetting positions between subsidiaries. Therefore, hedging the position of each individual subsidiary may not be necessary.

Adjusting the Invoice Policy to Manage Exposure

In some circumstances, the U.S. firm may be able to modify its pricing policy to hedge against transaction exposure. That is, the firm may be able to invoice (price) its exports in the same currency that will be needed to pay for imports.

MANAGING FOR VALUE

Centralized Management of Exposure

Eastman Kodak Co. uses a centralized currency management approach to manage its transaction exposure. Kodak bills its subsidiaries in their local currencies. The rationale behind this strategy is to shift the foreign exchange exposure from the subsidiaries to the parent company. When the parent was reorganized to concentrate its resources and expert personnel, it centralized its currency exposure management. The parent receives foreign currencies from its subsidiaries overseas and converts them to U.S. dollars. It can maintain the currencies as foreign deposits if it believes the currencies will strengthen against the U.S. dollar in the near future.

Borg-Warner Corp. has set up a central clearinghouse system that also reflects a centralized management approach. Thus, the company assesses and manages its currency exposure on the entire portfolio of all subsidiaries, rather than on each subsidiary individually.

Fiat, the Italian auto manufacturer, implemented a centralized system to monitor 421 subsidiaries dispersed among 55 countries. It uses a comprehensive reporting system that keeps track of its aggregate cash flows in each currency. The net inflow or outflow position for each currency can then be assessed to determine whether and how the position should be balanced out.

DuPont Co. uses a centralized approach to determine its net inflow or outflow in each currecny. Using this approach, it recently anticipated a net inflow position of more than 1 billion British pounds. It used hedging techniques to hedge almost all of its net exposure in pounds. The hedge generated substantial savings for DuPont because the pound's value had declined by the time the pounds were received.

The important point here is that a hedging decision cannot be made until the firm has determined its exposure to a particular currency. The centralized approach enables the MNC to determine its net transaction exposure in each currency so that it can decide whether to hedge these positions.

EXAMPLE

Clarkson, Inc., has continual payables in Mexican pesos because a Mexican exporter sends goods to Clarkson under the condition that the goods be invoiced in Mexican pesos. Clarkson also exports products (invoiced in U.S. dollars) to other corporations in Mexico. If Clarkson changes its invoicing policy from U.S. dollars to pesos, it can use the peso receivables from its exports to pay off its future payables in pesos. It is unlikely, however, that Clarkson would be able to (1) invoice the precise amount of peso receivables to match the peso payables and (2) perfectly time the inflows and outflows to match each other.

Because the matching of inflows and outflows in foreign currencies does have its limitations, an MNC will normally be exposed to some degree of exchange rate risk and, therefore, should consider the various hedging techniques identified next.

Techniques to Eliminate Transaction Exposure

If an MNC decides to hedge part or all of its transaction exposure, it may select from the following hedging techniques:

- Futures hedge
- Forward hedge
- Money market hedge
- Currency option hedge

Before selecting a hedging technique, MNCs normally compare the cash flows that would be expected from each technique. The proper hedging technique can vary over time, as the relative advantages of the various techniques may change over time. Each technique is discussed in turn, with examples provided. After all techniques have been discussed, a comprehensive example illustrates how all the techniques can be compared to determine the appropriate technique to hedge a particular position.

Futures Hedge

Currency futures can be used by firms that desire to hedge transaction exposure.

Purchasing Currency Futures. A firm that buys a currency futures contract is entitled to receive a specified amount in a specified currency for a stated price on a specified date. To hedge a payment on future payables in a foreign currency, the firm may purchase a currency futures contract for the currency it will need in the near future. By holding this contract, it locks in the amount of its home currency needed to make the payment.

http://

http://www.cme.com provides information on the various currency futures contracts that can be used to hedge positions.

Selling Currency Futures. A firm that sells a currency futures contract is entitled to sell a specified amount in a specified currency for a stated price on a specified date. To hedge the home currency value of future receivables in a foreign currency, the firm may sell a currency futures contract for the currency it will be receiving. Therefore, the firm knows how much of its home currency it will receive after converting the foreign currency receivables into its home currency. By locking in the exchange rate at which it will be able to exchange the foreign currency for its home currency, the firm insulates the value of its future receivables from the fluctuations in the foreign currency's spot rate over time.

Forward Hedge

Like futures contracts, forward contracts can be used to lock in the future exchange rate at which a MNC can buy or sell a currency. A forward contract hedge is very similar to a futures contract hedge, except that forward contracts are commonly used for large transactions, whereas futures contracts tend to be used for smaller amounts. Also, MNCs can request forward contracts that specify the exact number of units that they desire, whereas futures contracts represent a standardized number of units for each currency.

Forward contracts are commonly used by large corporations that desire to hedge. For example, DuPont Co. often has the equivalent of $300 million to $500 million in forward contracts at any one time to cover open currency positions. To recognize the uses of forward contracts, consider the following quotations from the annual reports of U.S.-based MNCs:

Outstanding foreign currency forward contracts used as a means of offsetting earnings fluctuations from anticipated foreign currency cash flows totaled $182 million.

Union Carbide

The Company enters into forward currency exchange contracts to hedge its equity investments in certain foreign subsidiaries and to manage its exposure against fluctuations in foreign currency rates. . . . The Company has entered into forward currency exchange contracts to reduce its exposure to currency fluctuations on the proceeds of its sale of its investment in Asahi Fiber Glass Company, Ltd. . . . The Company entered into forward currency exchange contracts to reduce its exposure to currency fluctuations on earnings of certain European subsidiaries.

Owens Corning Co.

USX uses forward currency contracts to reduce exposure to currency price fluctuations when transactions require settlement in a foreign currency.

USX Corp.

Forward Contracts. Recall that forward contracts are negotiated between the firm and a commercial bank and specify the currency, the exchange rate, and the date of the forward transaction. MNCs that need a foreign currency in the future can negotiate a forward contract to purchase the currency forward, thereby locking in the exchange rate at which they will obtain the currency on a future date. MNCs that wish to sell a foreign currency in the future can negotiate a forward contract to sell the currency forward, thereby locking in the exchange rate at which they sell the currency on a future date.

Forward Hedge versus No Hedge on Payables. Although forward contracts are easy to use for hedging, that does not mean that every exposure to exchange rate movements should be hedged. In some cases, an MNC may prefer not to hedge its exposure to exchange rate movements.

USING THE WEB

Forward Rates for Hedging Forward rates are available for the euro, British pound, Canadian dollar, and Japanese yen for 1-month, 3-month, 6-month, and 12-month maturities at http://www.bmo.com/economic/regular/fxrates.html. These forward rates indicate the exchange rates at which positions in these currencies can be hedged for specific time periods.

The decision as to whether to hedge a position with a forward contract or to keep it unhedged can be made by comparing the known result of hedging to the possible results of remaining unhedged.

EXAMPLE

Durham Co. will need £100,000 in 90 days to pay for British imports. Today's 90-day forward rate of the British pound is $1.40. To assess the future value of the British pound, Durham Co. may develop a probability distribution, as shown in Exhibit 11.1. This is graphically illustrated in Exhibit 11.2, which breaks down the probability distribution. Both exhibits can be used to determine the probability that a forward hedge will be more costly than no hedge. This is achieved by estimating the **real cost of hedging** payables (RCH_p). The real cost of hedging measures the additional expenses beyond those incurred without hedging. The real cost of hedging payables is measured as

$$RCH_p = NCH_p - NC_p$$

where

$$NCH_p = \text{nominal cost of hedging payables}$$
$$NC_p = \text{nominal cost of payables without hedging}$$

When the real cost of hedging is negative, this implies that hedging is more favorable than not hedging. The RCH_p is estimated for each scenario in Column 5 of Exhibit 11.1. While NCH_p is certain, NC_p is uncertain, causing RCH_p to be uncertain.

Though Durham Co. doesn't know RCH_p in advance, it can at least use the information in Exhibits 11.1 and 11.2 to decide whether a hedge is feasible. First, it can estimate the expected value of the RCH_p. This expected value is determined by

$$\text{Expected value of } RCH_p = \Sigma P_i RCH_i$$

Exhibit 11.1 Feasibility Analysis for Hedging

Possible Spot Rate of £ in 90 Days	Probability	Nominal Cost of Hedging £100,000	Amount in $ Needed to Buy £100,000 if Firm Remains Unhedged	Real Cost of Hedging £100,000
$1.30	5%	$140,000	$1.30 × 100,000 = $130,000	$10,000
1.32	10	140,000	1.32 × 100,000 = 132,000	8,000
1.34	15	140,000	1.34 × 100,000 = 134,000	6,000
1.36	20	140,000	1.36 × 100,000 = 136,000	4,000
1.38	20	140,000	1.38 × 100,000 = 138,000	2,000
1.40	15	140,000	1.40 × 100,000 = 140,000	0
1.42	10	140,000	1.42 × 100,000 = 142,000	−2,000
1.45	5	140,000	1.45 × 100,000 = 145,000	−5,000

Exhibit 11.2
Comparison of Costs of Hedging versus No Hedge

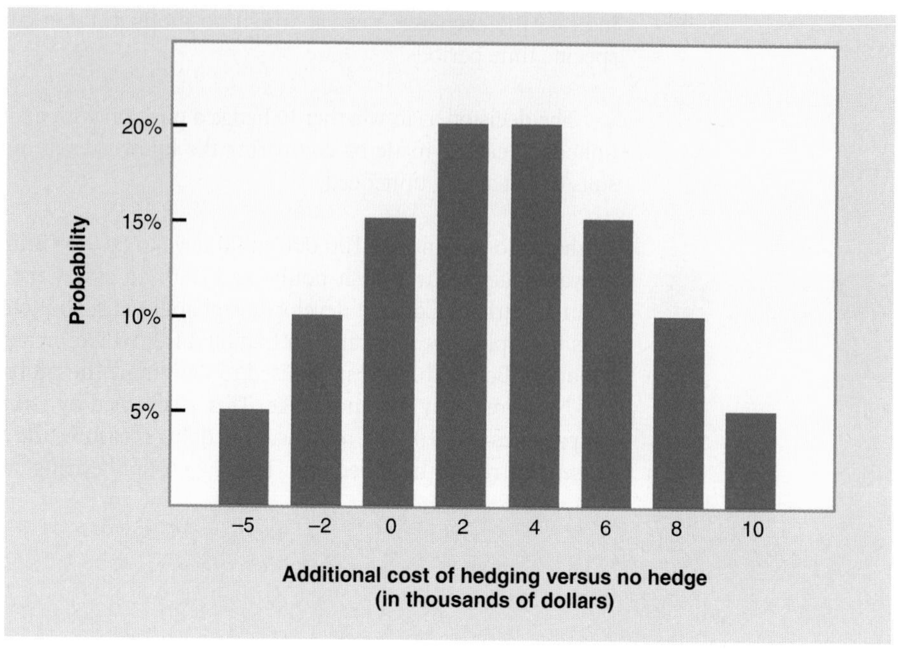

where P_i represents the probability that the ith outcome will occur. In our example, the expected value of the RCH_p can be computed as

$$
\begin{aligned}
E(RCH_p) &= \Sigma P_i RCH_i \\
&= 5\%(\$10{,}000) + 10\%(\$8{,}000) + 15\%(\$6{,}000) \\
&\quad + 20\%(\$4{,}000) + 20\%(\$2{,}000) + 15\%(0) \\
&\quad + 10\%(-\$2{,}000) + 5\%(-\$5{,}000) \\
&= \$500 + \$800 + \$900 \\
&\quad + \$800 + \$400 + 0 \\
&\quad - \$200 - \$250 \\
&= \$2{,}950
\end{aligned}
$$

Although this expected value is useful in assessing RCH_p, it does not clearly indicate the overall probability that hedging will be more costly. A review of Exhibit 11.1 or 11.2. reveals that probability. The data indicate there is a 15 percent chance that the RCH_p will be negative (that the nominal cost of hedging will be lower than remaining unhedged). The probability of incurring a lower cost when remaining unhedged is 85 percent, so Durham decides not to hedge.

The hedge-versus-no-hedge decision is based on the firm's degree of risk aversion. Firms with a greater desire to avoid risk will hedge their open positions in foreign currencies more often than firms that are less concerned about risk.

If the forward rate is an accurate predictor of the future spot rate, the RCH_p will be zero. Because the forward rate often underestimates or overestimates the future spot rate, RCH_p differs from zero. If, however, the forward rate is an unbiased predictor of the future spot rate, RCH_p will be zero on average, as the differences between the forward rate and future spot rate will offset each other over time. If a firm believes that the forward rate is an unbiased predictor of the future spot rate, it will consider hedging its payables, since the forecasted RCH_p is zero, and the transaction exposure can be eliminated.

Forward Hedge versus No Hedge on Receivables. For firms with exposure in receivables, the real cost of hedging receivables (RCH_r) can be estimated as

$$RCH_r = NR_r - NRH_r$$

where

$$NR_r = \text{nominal home currency revenues received without hedging}$$
$$NRH_r = \text{nominal home currency revenues received from hedging}$$

This equation is structured so that the real cost of hedging receivables is positive when hedging results in lower revenue than not hedging. This allows for consistency between RCH_p and RCH_r, in that a negative (positive) value of either indicates that hedging results in a more (less) favorable outcome than not hedging.

As with payable positions, firms can determine whether to hedge receivable positions by first developing a probability distribution for the future spot rate and then using it to develop a probability distribution of RCH_r. If the RCH_r is likely to be negative, hedging is preferred. If the RCH_r is likely to be positive, the firm needs to evaluate whether the potential benefits from remaining unhedged are worth the risk. If the forward rate is believed to be an unbiased predictor of the future spot rate, firms will consider hedging their receivables positions at an expected real cost of zero (ignoring transaction costs).

Measuring the Real Cost of Hedging with Forward Contracts. The *RCH* has been defined here in terms of the MNC's home currency (U.S. dollars, in our example). It can also be expressed as a percentage of the nominal hedged amount. This may be a useful measurement when comparing the *RCH*s for various currencies.

If a U.S. firm is hedging various currencies in different amounts, a comparison of the dollar amount of *RCH* among currencies would be distorted by the dollar amount of payables or receivables hedged. For this reason, the *RCH* for each currency should be measured as a percentage of its respective hedged amount if the *RCH*s are to be compared.

The *RCH* cannot be determined until the payables or receivables period is over. When firms hedge, they should be pleased if the *RCH* turns out to be very low, and especially pleased if it is negative. Conservative firms, however, may feel hedging is worthwhile even if the *RCH* turns out to be high.

The *RCH* for any currency has been positive in some periods and negative in others. In the 2000–2001 period, many currencies such as the euro and the pound weakened against the dollar. Thus, the real cost to a U.S. firm of hedging payables in these currencies was positive in this period, while the real cost of hedging receivables was negative. In the 2002–2003 period, however, these currencies strengthened against the dollar. The real cost of hedging payables in these currencies was negative in this period, while the real cost of hedging receivables was positive.

Money Market Hedge

A **money market hedge** involves taking a money market position to cover a future payables or receivables position. Money market hedges on payables and receivables will be discussed separately.

Money Market Hedge on Payables. If a firm has excess cash, it can create a short-term deposit in the foreign currency that it will need in the future. The first example illustrates a simplified money market hedge, in which the firm has excess cash. Even if a firm does not have excess cash, it can use a money market hedge to hedge payables, as the second example shows.

EXAMPLE

Ashland, Inc., needs $1,000,000 in New Zealand dollars (NZ$) in 30 days, and it can earn 6 percent annualized (.5 percent for 30 days) on a New Zealand security over this period. In this case, the amount needed to purchase a New Zealand one-month security is

$$\text{Deposit amount to hedge NZ\$ payables} = \frac{\text{NZ\$1,000,000}}{1 + .005}$$
$$= \text{NZ\$995,025}$$

Assuming that the New Zealand dollar's spot rate is $.65, then $646,766 is needed to purchase the New Zealand security (computed as NZ$995,025 × $.65). In 30 days, the security will mature and provide NZ$1,000,000 to Ashland, Inc., which can then use this money to cover its payables. Regardless of how the New Zealand dollar exchange rate changes over this period, Ashland's investment in the New Zealand security will be able to cover its payables position.

In many cases, MNCs prefer to hedge payables without using their cash balances. A money market hedge can still be used in this situation, but it requires two money market positions: (1) borrowed funds in the home currency and (2) a short-term investment in the foreign currency.

EXAMPLE

Reconsider the previous example, in which Ashland, Inc., needs NZ$1,000,000 in 30 days. Recall that $646,766 is needed to obtain the investment of NZ$995,025, which in turn will accumulate to the NZ$1,000,000 needed in 30 days. If Ashland has no excess cash, it can borrow $646,766 from a U.S. bank and exchange those dollars for New Zealand dollars in order to purchase the New Zealand security.

Because the New Zealand investment will cover Ashland's future payables position, the firm needs to be concerned only about the dollars owed on the loan in 30 days. The firm's money market hedge used to hedge payables can be summarized as follows:

Step 1. Borrow $646,766 from a U.S. bank; assume a .7 percent interest rate over the 30-day loan period.

Step 2. Convert the $646,766 to NZ$995,025, given the exchange rate of $.65 per New Zealand dollar.

Step 3. Use the New Zealand dollars to purchase a New Zealand security that offers .5 percent over one month.

Step 4. Repay the U.S. loan in 30 days, plus interest; the amount owed is $651,293 (computed as $646,766 × 1.007).

Money Market Hedge on Receivables. If a firm expects receivables in a foreign currency, it can hedge this position by borrowing the currency now and converting it to dollars. The receivables will be used to pay off the loan.

EXAMPLE

Bakersfield Co. is a U.S. firm that transports goods to Singapore and expects to receive 400,000 Singapore dollars (S$) in 90 days. A simplified money market hedge can be implemented if Bakersfield needs to borrow U.S. funds for 90 days anyway. Instead of borrowing U.S. dollars, it can borrow Singapore dollars and convert them into U.S. dollars for use. Assuming an annualized interest rate of 8 percent, or 2 percent over the 90-day period, the amount of Singapore dollars to be borrowed to hedge the future receivables is

$$\text{Borrowed amount to hedge S\$ receivables} = \frac{\text{S\$400,000}}{1 + .02}$$
$$= \text{S\$392,157}$$

If Bakersfield borrows S$392,157 and converts those Singapore dollars to U.S. dollars, then it can use the receivables to pay off the Singapore dollar loan in 90 days. Meanwhile, the proceeds of the loan can be used for whatever purpose Bakersfield Co. desires.

In some cases, MNCs may not need to borrow funds for a 90-day period. In these situations, a money market hedge can still be used to hedge receivables if the firm takes two positions in the money markets: (1) borrow the foreign currency representing future receivables and (2) invest in the home currency.

EXAMPLE

Reconsider the previous example. Even if Bakersfield Co. does not have a use for the S$392,157 borrowed, it can invest the funds in a 90-day U.S. security. Assuming that a Singapore dollar is worth $.55, the Singapore dollars borrowed can be converted to $215,686. Assuming an annualized U.S. interest rate of 7.2 percent (1.8 percent over 90 days) on 90-day securities, the U.S. investment will be worth $219,568 (computed as $215,686 × 1.018) in 90 days. Since the receivables can cover the existing loan, Bakersfield will have $219,568 as a result of enacting the money market hedge.

Hedging with a Money Market Hedge versus a Forward Hedge. Should an MNC implement a forward contract hedge or a money market hedge ? The forward hedge and the money market hedge are directly comparable. Since the results of both hedges are known beforehand, the firm can implement the one that is more feasible. Of course, the firm cannot determine whether either hedge will outperform an unhedged strategy until the period of concern has elapsed.

Implications of IRP for the Money Market Hedge. If interest rate parity (IRP) exists, and transaction costs do not exist, the money market hedge will yield the same results as the forward hedge. This is so because the forward premium on the forward rate reflects the interest rate differential between the two currencies. The hedging of future payables with a forward purchase will be similar to borrowing at the home interest rate and investing at the foreign interest rate.

The hedging of future receivables with a forward sale is similar to borrowing at the foreign interest rate and investing at the home interest rate. Even if the forward premium generally reflects the interest rate differential between countries, the existence of transaction costs may cause the results from a forward hedge to differ from those of the money market hedge.

Currency Option Hedge

Firms recognize that hedging techniques such as the forward hedge and money market hedge can backfire when a payables currency depreciates or a receivables currency appreciates over the hedged period. In these situations, an unhedged strategy would likely outperform the forward hedge or money market hedge. The ideal hedge would insulate the firm from adverse exchange rate movements but allow the firm to benefit from favorable exchange rate movements. Currency options exhibit these attributes. However, a firm must assess whether the advantages of a currency option hedge are worth the price (premium) paid for it. Details on currency options are provided in Chapter 5. The following discussion illustrates how they can be used in hedging.

http://

http://www.phlx.com/products/currency/currency.html provides information on the various currency option contracts that can be used to hedge positions.

Hedging Payables with Currency Call Options. A currency call option provides the right to buy a specified amount of a particular currency at a specified price (the exercise price) within a given period of time. Yet, unlike a futures or forward contract, the currency call option *does not obligate* its owner to buy the currency at that price. If the spot rate of the currency remains lower than the exercise price throughout the life of the option, the firm can let the option expire and simply purchase the currency at the existing spot rate. On the other hand, if the spot rate of the currency appreciates over time, the call option allows the firm to purchase the currency at the exercise price. That is, the firm owning a call option has locked in a maximum price (the exercise price) to pay for the currency. Yet, it also has the flexibility to let the option expire and obtain the currency at the existing spot rate when the currency is to be sent for payment.

EXAMPLE

Clemson Corp. has payables of £100,000, 90 days from now. Assume there is a call option available with an exercise price of $1.60. Assume that the option premium is $.04 per unit. For options that cover the 100,000 units, the total premium is $4,000 (100,000 × $.04). Clemson doesn't have to exercise its call option if it can obtain pounds at a lower spot rate.

Clemson expects the spot rate of the pound to be either $1.58, $1.62, or $1.66 when the payables are due. The effect of each of these scenarios on Clemson's cost of payables is shown in Exhibit 11.3. Columns 1 and 2 simply identify the scenario to be analyzed. Column 3 shows the premium per unit paid on the option, which is the same regardless of the spot rate that occurs when payables are due. Column 4 shows the amount that Clemson would pay per pound for the payables under each scenario, assuming that it owned call options. If Scenario 1 occurs, Clemson will let the options expire and purchase pounds in the spot market for $1.58 each. If Scenario 2 or 3 occurs, Clemson will exercise the options and therefore purchase pounds for $1.60 per unit, and it will use the pounds to make its payment. Column 5, which is the sum of Columns 3 and 4, shows the amount paid per unit when the premium paid on the call option is included. Column 6 converts Column 5 into a total dollar cost, based on the £100,000 hedged.

Exhibit 11.3 Use of Currency Call Options for Hedging British Pound Payables (Exercise Price = $1.60; Premium = $.04)

(1)	(2)	(3)	(4)	(5) = (4) + (3)	(6)
Scenario	Spot Rate When Payables Are Due	Premium per Unit Paid on Call Options	Amount Paid per Unit When Owning Call Options	Total Amount Paid per Unit (Including the Premium) When Owning Call Options	$ Amount Paid for £100,000 When Owning Call Options
1	$1.58	$.04	$1.58	$1.62	$162,000
2	1.62	.04	1.60	1.64	164,000
3	1.66	.04	1.60	1.64	164,000

Hedging Receivables with Currency Put Options. Like currency call options, currency put options can be a valuable hedging device. A currency put option provides the right to sell a specified amount in a particular currency at a specified price (the exercise price) within a given period of time. Firms can use a currency put option to hedge future receivables in foreign currencies, since it guarantees a certain price (the exercise price) at which the future receivables can be sold. The currency put option *does not obligate* its owner to sell the currency at a specified price. If the existing spot rate of the foreign currency is above the exercise price when the firm receives the foreign currency, the firm can sell the currency received at the spot rate and let the put option expire.

EXAMPLE

Knoxville, Inc., transports goods to New Zealand and expects to receive NZ$600,000 in about 90 days. Because it is concerned that the New Zealand dollar may depreciate against the U.S. dollar, Knoxville is considering purchasing put options to cover its receivables. The New Zealand dollar put options considered here have an exercise price of $.50 and a premium of $.03 per unit. Knoxville anticipates that the spot rate in 90 days will be either $.44, $.46, or $.51. The amount to be received as a result of owning currency put options is shown in Exhibit 11.4. Columns 2 through 5 are on a per-unit basis. Column 6 is determined by multiplying the per-unit amount received in Column 5 by 600,000 units.

Exhibit 11.4 Use of Currency Put Options for Hedging New Zealand Dollar Receivables (Exercise Price = $.50; Premium = $.03)

(1)	(2)	(3)	(4)	(5) = (4) − (3)	(6)
Scenario	Spot Rate When Payment on Receivables Is Received	Premium per Unit on Put Options	Amount Received per Unit When Owning Put Options	Net Amount Received per Unit (after Accounting for Premium Paid)	Dollar Amount Received from Hedging NZ$600,000 Receivables with Put Options
1	$.44	$.03	$.50	$.47	$282,000
2	.46	.03	.50	.47	282,000
3	.51	.03	.51	.48	288,000

Hedging Contingent Exposure. Currency call options are also useful for hedging contingent exposure, in which an MNC's exposure is contingent on a specific event happening.

EXAMPLE

Jamie, Inc., of Orlando, Florida, is negotiating to acquire an Australian company in three months, but the deal is contingent on approval by the Australian government. The dollar price that will be paid for the company is dependent on the value of the Australian dollar in three months. Jamie wants to lock in the rate at which it will exchange U.S. dollars for Australian dollars because it is worried that the Australian dollar may appreciate. Yet, it does not want to be obligated to obtain Australian dollars unless the acquisition is approved. It can purchase call options on Australian dollars to hedge its contingent exposure.

Comparison of Hedging Techniques

Each of the hedging techniques is briefly summarized in Exhibit 11.5. When using a futures hedge, forward hedge, or money market hedge, the firm can estimate the funds (denominated in its home currency) that it will need for future payables, or the funds that it will receive after converting foreign currency receivables. Thus, it can compare the costs or revenue and determine which of these hedging techniques is appropriate. In contrast, the cash flow associated with the currency option hedge cannot be determined with certainty because the costs of purchasing payables and the revenue generated from receivables are not known ahead of time. Therefore, firms need to forecast cash flows from the option hedge based on possible exchange rate outcomes.

Comparison of Techniques to Hedge Payables. A comparison of hedging techniques should focus on obtaining a foreign currency at the lowest possible cost. To reinforce an understanding of the hedging techniques, a comprehensive example is provided here.

Exhibit 11.5 Review of Techniques for Hedging Transaction Exposure

Hedging Technique	To Hedge Payables	To Hedge Receivables
1. Futures hedge	Purchase a currency futures contract (or contracts) representing the currency and amount related to the payables.	Sell a currency futures contract (or contracts) representing the currency and amount related to the receivables.
2. Forward hedge	Negotiate a forward contract to purchase the amount of foreign currency needed to cover the payables.	Negotiate a forward contract to sell the amount of foreign currency that will be received as a result of the receivables.
3. Money market hedge	Borrow local currency and convert to currency denominating payables. Invest these funds until they are needed to cover the payables.	Borrow the currency denominating the receivables, convert it to the local currency, and invest it. Then pay off the loan with cash inflows from the receivables.
4. Currency option hedge	Purchase a currency call option (or options) representing the currency and amount related to the payables.	Purchase a currency put option (or options) representing the currency and amount related to the receivables.

EXAMPLE

Assume that Fresno Corp. will need £200,000 in 180 days. It considers using (1) a forward hedge, (2) a money market hedge, (3) an option hedge, or (4) no hedge. Its analysts develop the following information, which can be used to assess the alternative solutions:

- Spot rate of pound as of today = $1.50
- 180-day forward rate of pound as of today = $1.47

Interest rates are as follows:

	U.K.	U.S.
180-day deposit rate	4.5%	4.5%
180-day borrowing rate	5.0%	5.0%

- A call option on pounds that expires in 180 days has an exercise price of $1.48 and a premium of $.03.
- A put option on pounds that expires in 180 days has an exercise price of $1.49 and a premium of $.02.

Fresno Corp. forecasts the future spot rate in 180 days as follows:

Possible Outcome	Probability
$1.43	20%
1.46	70
1.52	10

Fresno Corp. then assesses the alternative solutions, as shown in Exhibit 11.6. Each alternative is analyzed to estimate the nominal dollar cost of paying for the payables denominated in pounds. The cost is known with certainty for the forward rate hedge and money market hedge. When using the call option or remaining unhedged, however, the cost is dependent on the spot rate 180 days from now. The costs of the four alternatives are also compared with the use of probability distributions, as shown in Exhibit 11.7. A review of this exhibit shows that the forward hedge is superior to the money market hedge, since the dollar cost is definitely less. A comparison of the forward hedge with the call option hedge shows that there is an 80 percent chance that the call option hedge will be more expensive. The expected value of the payables when using the currency option hedge is

$$20\%(\$292,000) + 70\%(\$298,000) + 10\%(\$302,000) = \$297,200$$

Since this expected value is higher than the cost of hedging with a forward contract, the forward hedge appears to be the optimal hedge for Fresno Corp.

As for the no-hedge strategy, the expected value of the payables when not hedging is

$$20\%(\$286,000) + 70\%(\$292,000) + 10\%(\$304,000) = \$292,200$$

Exhibit 11.6 Comparison of Hedging Alternatives for Fresno Corp.

Forward Hedge

Purchase pounds 180 days forward.

$$\begin{aligned} \text{Dollars needed in 180 days} &= \text{payables in £} \times \text{forward rate of £} \\ &= £200{,}000 \times \$1.47 \\ &= \$294{,}000 \end{aligned}$$

Money Market Hedge

Borrow \$, convert to £, invest £, repay \$ loan in 180 days.

$$\begin{aligned} \text{Amount in £ to be invested} &= \frac{£200{,}000}{(1 + .045)} \\ &= £191{,}388 \\ \text{Amount in \$ needed to convert into £ for deposit} &= £191{,}388 \times \$1.50 \\ &= \$287{,}082 \\ \text{Interest and principal owed on \$ loan after 180 days} &= \$287{,}082 \times (1 + .05) \\ &= \$301{,}436 \end{aligned}$$

Call Option

Purchase call option (the following computations assume that the option is to be exercised on the day pounds are needed, or not at all. Exercise price = \$1.48, premium = \$.03.)

Possible Spot Rate in 180 days	Premium per Unit Paid for Option	Exercise Option?	Total Price (Including Option Premium) Paid per Unit	Total Price Paid for £200,000	Probability
\$1.43	\$.03	No	\$1.46	\$292,000	20%
1.46	.03	No	1.49	298,000	70
1.52	.03	Yes	1.51	302,000	10

Remain Unhedged

Purchase £200,000 in the spot market 180 days from now.

Future Spot Rate Expected in 180 Days	Dollars Needed to Purchase £200,000	Probability
\$1.43	\$286,000	20%
1.46	292,000	70
1.52	304,000	10

Exhibit 11.7

Nominal Dollar Cost of Pound-Denominated Payables

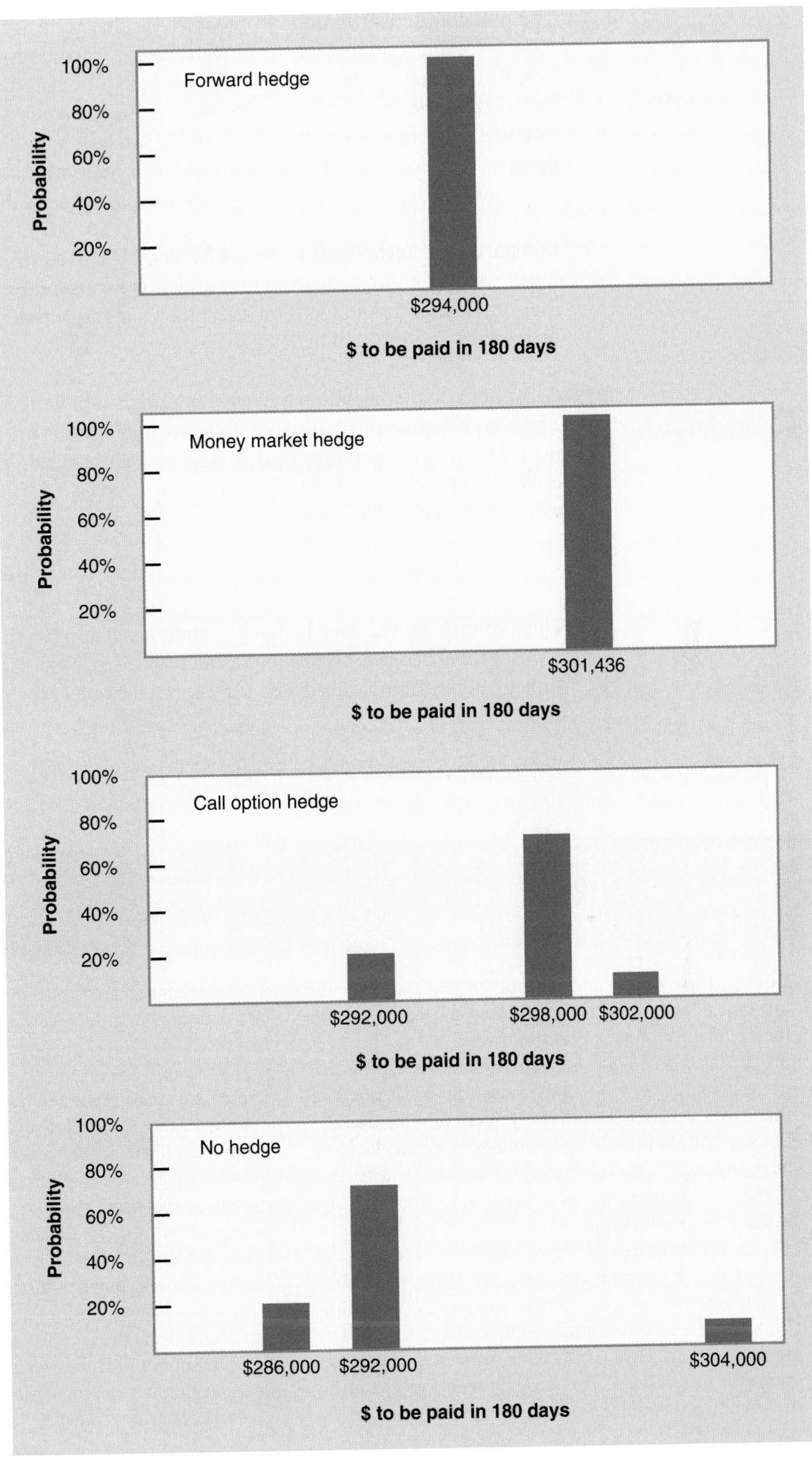

The probability distribution of outcomes for the no-hedge strategy also appears to be more favorable than that for the forward hedge. Thus, Fresno Corp. is likely to perform best if it remains unhedged, but if it prefers to hedge, it should choose the forward hedge. If Fresno does not hedge, it should periodically reassess its hedging decision. For example, after 60 days it should repeat the analysis shown here, based on the applicable spot rate, forward rate, interest rates, call option information, and forecasts of the spot rate 120 days into the future (when the payables are due).

Comparison of Techniques to Hedge Receivables. If a firm desires to hedge receivables, it will conduct a similar analysis of transaction exposure. From a U.S. firm's perspective, the comparison should focus on selecting a technique that will maximize the dollars to be received as a result of hedging.

EXAMPLE

Gator Corp. anticipates no payables in pounds, but it will receive £300,000 in 180 days. The same information on the spot, forward, and options prices is used to compare hedging techniques and an unhedged strategy in Exhibit 11.8. The dollar amounts to be received from each of the four alternatives are compared in Exhibit 11.9. The expected value of the receivables when using the currency option hedge is

$$20\%(\$441{,}000) + 70\%(\$441{,}000) + 10\%(\$450{,}000) = \$441{,}900$$

Thus, comparing the three hedging techniques, it appears that the money market hedge is the optimal hedge for Gator if it decides to hedge. Next, Gator Corp. should assess the strategy of remaining unhedged. The expected value of the receivables when remaining unhedged is

$$20\%(\$429{,}000) + 70\%(\$438{,}000) + 10\%(\$456{,}000) = \$438{,}000$$

MANAGING FOR VALUE

Merck's Hedging Strategy

DuPont, IBM, Merck, and most other MNCs do not use one type of hedging technique exclusively, but determine the optimal technique on a case-by-case basis. The optimal hedging technique is dependent on exchange rate projections. If the projections cause the firm to believe that it will definitely be adversely affected by its transaction exposure, a forward hedge or money market hedge is normally appropriate. Conversely, if the firm believes that it may benefit from its exposure, the currency option hedge is more appropriate (if any hedge is used at all).

Consider the case of Merck, with worldwide sales of over $6 billion per year. Merck has substantial receivables denominated in foreign currencies as a result of exporting. It could use forward or futures contracts to lock in the rate at which those currencies will be converted to dollars. However, it recognizes that hedging with forward or futures contracts could result in an opportunity cost, measured as the amount of funds forgone if the foreign currencies denominating the receivables appreciate by the time the receivables are converted to dollars. Since Merck wants to capitalize on the possible appreciaition of these foreign currencies (weakening of the dollar), it uses put options to hedge its receivables denominated in foreign currencies. If the dollar weakens, Merck lets the put options expire because the receivables are worth more at the prevailing spot rate. Meanwhile, the put options provide insurance in case the dollar strengthens. If Merck feels very confident that the dollar will strengthen, it uses forward or futures contracts instead of put options, because it must pay a premium for the put options. When the future movements in the foreign currencies are uncertain, however, put options are attractive. By making a hedging decision that is consistent with its perceptions of future exchange rate movements, Merck maximizes its value.

Exhibit 11.8 Comparison of Hedging Alternatives for Gator Corp.

Forward Hedge

Sell pounds 180 days forward.

$$\text{Dollars to be received in 180 days} = \text{receivables in £} \times \text{forward rate of £}$$
$$= £300{,}000 \times \$1.47$$
$$= \$441{,}000$$

Money Market Hedge

Borrow £, convert to $, invest $, use receivables to pay off loan in 180 days.

$$\text{Amount in £ borrowed} = \frac{£300{,}000}{(1 + .05)}$$
$$= £285{,}714$$
$$\$ \text{ received from converting £} = £285{,}714 \times \$1.50 \text{ per £}$$
$$= \$428{,}571$$
$$\$ \text{ accumulated after 180 days} = \$482{,}571 \times (1 + .045)$$
$$= \$447{,}857$$

Put Option Hedge

Purchase put option (assume the options are to be exercised on the day pounds are to be received, or not at all. Exercise price = $1.49; premium = $.02.)

Possible Spot Rate in 180 days	Premium per Unit Paid for Option	Exercise Option?	Received per Unit (after Accounting for the Premium)	Total Dollars Received from Converting £300,000	Probability
$1.43	$.02	Yes	$1.47	$441,000	20%
1.46	.02	Yes	1.47	441,000	70
1.52	.02	No	1.50	450,000	10

Remain Unhedged

Possible Spot Rate in 180 Days	Total Dollars Received from Converting £300,000	Probability
$1.43	$429,000	20%
1.46	438,000	70
1.52	456,000	10

Exhibit 11.9
Dollars Received from Pound-Denominated Receivables

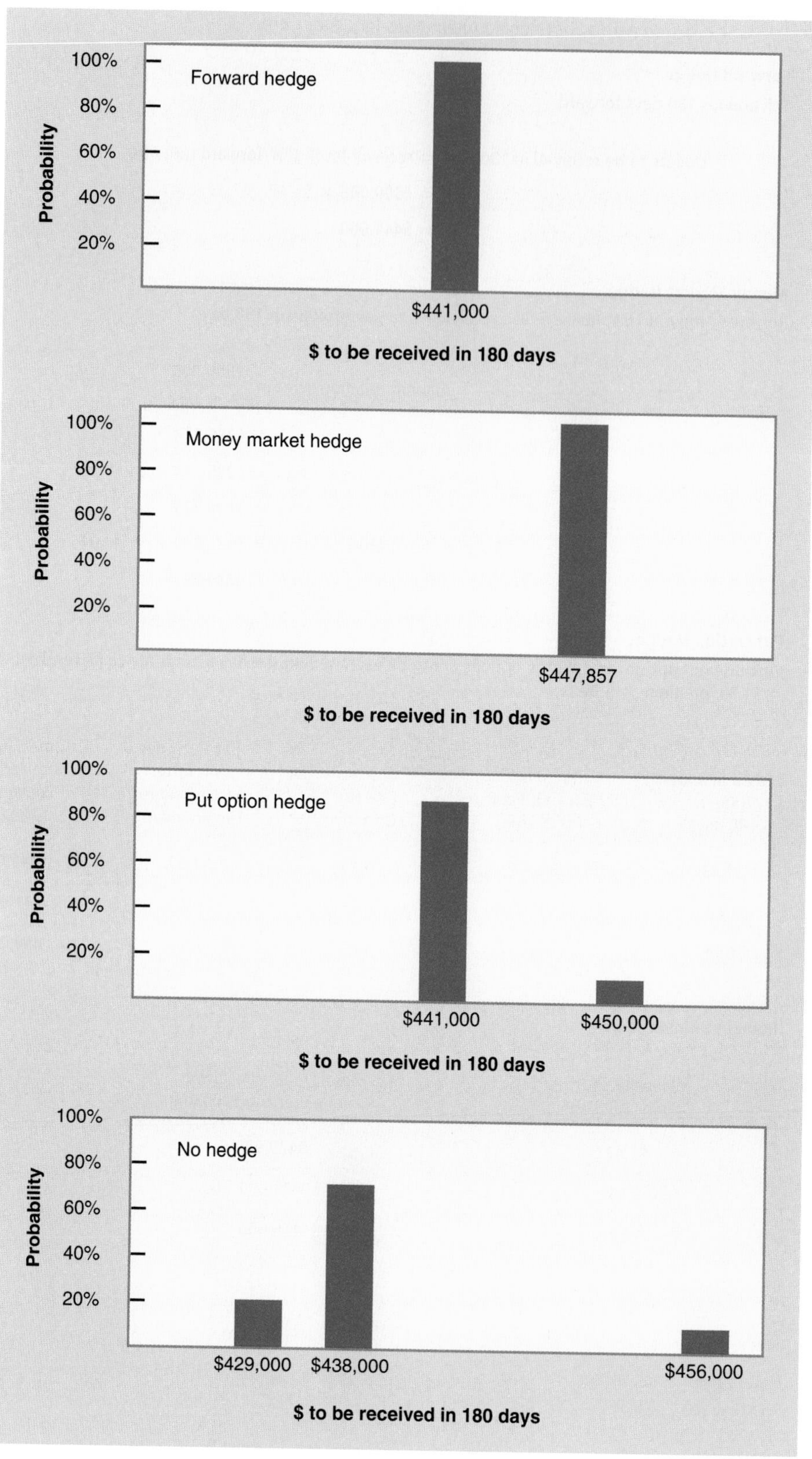

Thus, the expected value if Gator does not hedge is lower than the amount that would be received from using a money market hedge. Although the no-hedge strategy would outperform the money market hedge if the spot rate of the pound in 180 days is $1.52, there is only a 10 percent probability of that outcome. Therefore, Gator Corp. will likely decide to hedge its receivables position.

Comparing Alternative Currency Option Contracts. Although the preceding example assessed only one particular currency option, several alternative currency options are normally available with different exercise prices. When hedging payables, a firm can reduce the premium paid by choosing a call option with a higher exercise price. Of course, the tradeoff is that the maximum amount to be paid for the payables will be higher. Similarly, a firm hedging receivables can reduce the premium paid by choosing a put option with a lower exercise price. In this case, the tradeoff is that the minimum amount to be received for the receivables will be lower. Firms generally compare the available options first to determine which is most appropriate. Then, this particular option is compared to the other hedging techniques to determine which technique (if any) should be used.

When MNCs purchase call options to hedge payables, they can finance their purchase by selling put options.

EXAMPLE

Dido Corp. has payables of 100,000 euros and can purchase call options to cover them. It can finance all or a portion of the premium paid for the call options by selling put options on euros. Assume that call options with an exercise price of $1.14 have a premium of $.03, while put options with an exercise price of $1.10 have a premium of $.03. Dido can sell put options, and use the proceeds to purchase call options. If the spot rate remains between $1.10 and $1.14 until the payables are due, neither option will be exercised. If the spot rate rises above $1.14, Dido can exercise its call options, and the put options will go unexercised. If the spot rate declines below $1.10, the put options will be exercised and Dido will fulfill its obligation by purchasing euros at the exercise price of $1.10. Yet, it needed to purchase euros anyway to pay for its payables. With this strategy, Dido will pay no more than $1.14 for euros and no less than $1.10.

Hedging Policies of MNCs

In general, hedging policies vary with the MNC management's degree of risk aversion. An MNC may choose to hedge most of its exposure, to hedge none of its exposure, or to selectively hedge.

Hedging Most of the Exposure. Some MNCs hedge most of their exposure so that their value is not highly influenced by exchange rates. MNCs that hedge most of their exposure do not necessarily expect that hedging will always be beneficial. In fact, such MNCs may even use some hedges that will likely result in slightly worse outcomes than no hedges at all, just to avoid the possibility of a major adverse movement in exchange rates. They prefer to know what their future cash inflows or outflows in terms of their home currency will be in each period because this improves corporate planning. A hedge allows the firm to know the future cash flows (in terms of the home currency) that will result from any foreign transactions that have already been negotiated.

Hedging None of the Exposure. MNCs that are well diversified across many countries may consider not hedging their exposure. This strategy may be driven by the view that a diversified set of exposures will limit the actual impact that exchange rates will have on the MNC during any period.

http://

See http://www.ibm.com/us/ for an example of an MNC's website. The websites of various MNCs provide financial statements such as annual reports that disclose the use of financial derivatives for the purpose of hedging interest rate risk and foreign exchange rate risk.

Selective Hedging. Many MNCs, such as Black & Decker, Eastman Kodak, and Merck choose to hedge only when they expect the currency to move in a direction that will make hedging feasible. Zenith hedges its imports of Japanese components only when it expects the yen to appreciate. In addition, these MNCs may hedge future receivables if they foresee depreciation in the currency denominating the receivables.

The following quotations from annual reports illustrate the strategy of selective hedging:

The purpose of the Company's foreign currency hedging activities is to reduce the risk that the eventual dollar net cash inflows resulting from sales outside the U.S. will be adversely affected by exchange rates.

The Coca-Cola Co.

Decisions regarding whether or not to hedge a given commitment are made on a case-by-case basis by taking into consideration the amount and duration of the exposure, market volatility, and economic trends.

DuPont Co.

We selectively hedge the potential effect of the foreign currency fluctuations related to operating activities.

General Mills Co.

Selective hedging implies that the MNC prefers to exercise some control over its exposure and makes decisions based on conditions that may affect the currency's future value.

Limitations of Hedging

Although hedging transaction exposure can be effective, there are some limitations that deserve to be mentioned here.

Limitation of Hedging an Uncertain Amount

Some international transactions involve an uncertain amount of goods ordered and therefore involve an uncertain transaction amount in a foreign currency. Consequently, an MNC may create a hedge for a larger number of units than it will acutally need, which causes the opposite form of exposure.

EXAMPLE

Recall the previous example on hedging receivables, which assumed that Gator Corp. will receive £300,000 in 180 days. Now assume that the receivables amount could actually be much lower. If Gator uses the money market hedge on £300,000 and the receivables amount to only £200,000, it will have to make up the difference by purchasing £100,000 in the spot market to achieve the £300,000 needed to pay off the loan. If the pound appreciates over the 180-day period, Gator will need a large amount in dollars to obtain the £100,000.

This example shows how **overhedging** (hedging a larger amount in a currency than the actual transaction amount) can adversely affect a firm. A solution to avoid overhedging is to hedge only the minimum known amount in the future transaction. In our example, if the future receivables could be as low as £200,000, Gator could hedge this amount. Under these conditions, however, the firm may not have completely hedged its position. If the actual transaction amount turns out to be £300,000 as expected, Gator will be only partially hedged and will need to sell the extra £100,000 in the spot market.

Alternatively, Gator may consider hedging the minimum level of receivables with a money market hedge and hedging the additional amount of receivables that may occur with a put option hedge. In this way, it is covered if the receivables exceed the minimum amount. It can let the put option expire if the receivables do not exceed the minimum, or if it is better off exchanging the additional pounds received in the spot market.

Firms commonly face this type of dilemma because the precise amount to be received in a foreign currency at the end of a period can be uncertain, especially for firms heavily involved in exporting. Based on this example, it should be clear that most MNCs cannot completely hedge all of their transactions. Nevertheless, by hedging a portion of those transactions that affect them, they can reduce the sensitivity of their cash flows to exchange rate movements.

Limitation of Repeated Short-Term Hedging

The continual hedging of repeated transactions that are expected to occur in the near future has limited effectiveness over the long run.

EXAMPLE

Winthrop Co. is a U.S. importer that specializes in importing particular CD players in one large shipment per year and then selling them to retail stores throughout the year. Assume that today's exchange rate of the Japanese yen is \$.005 and that the CD players are worth ¥60,000, or \$300. The forward rate of the yen generally exhibits a premium of 2 percent. Exhibit 11.10 shows the dollar/yen exchange rate to be paid by

Exhibit 11.10

Illustration of Repeated Hedging of Foreign Payables When the Foreign Currency Is Appreciating

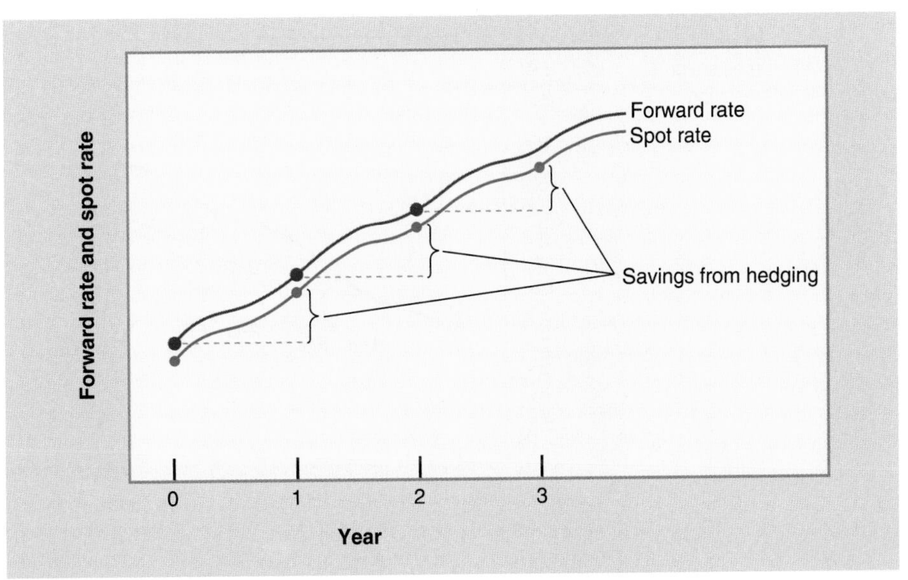

the importer over time. As the spot rate changes, the forward rate will often change by a similar amount. Thus, if the spot rate increases by 10 percent over the year, the forward rate may increase by about the same amount, and the importer will pay 10 percent more for next year's shipment (assuming no change in the yen price quoted by the Japanese exporter). The use of a one-year forward contract during a strong-yen cycle is preferable to no hedge in this case but will still result in subsequent increases in prices paid by the importer each year. This illustrates that the use of short-term hedging techniques does not completely insulate a firm from exchange rate exposure, even if the hedges are used repeatedly over time.

If the hedging techniques can be applied to longer-term periods, they can more effectively insulate the firm from exchange rate risk over the long run. That is, Winthrop Co. could, as of Time 0, create a hedge for shipments to arrive at the end of each of the next several years. The forward rate for each hedge would be based on the spot rate as of today, as shown in Exhibit 11.11. During a strong-yen cycle, such a strategy would save a substantial amount of money.

This strategy faces a limitation, however, in that the amount in yen to be hedged further into the future is more uncertain because the shipment size will be dependent on economic conditions or other factors at that time. If a recession occurs, Winthrop Co. may reduce the number of CD players ordered, but the amount in yen to be received by the importer is dictated by the forward contract that was created. If the CD player manufacturer goes bankrupt, or simply experiences stockouts, Winthrop Co. is still obligated to purchase the yen, even if a shipment is not forthcoming.

Exhibit 11.11
Long-Term Hedging of Payables When the Foreign Currency Is Appreciating

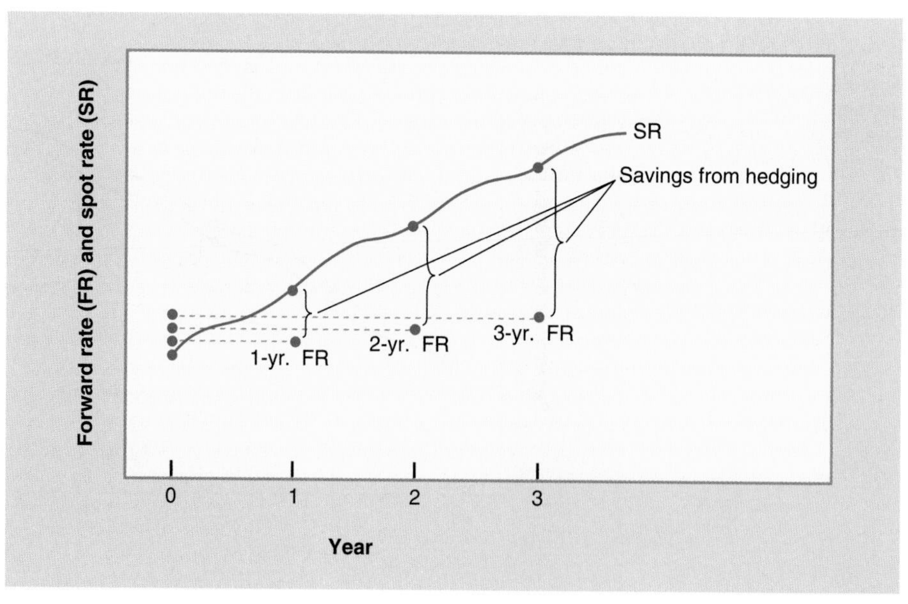

Hedging Long-Term Transaction Exposure

Some MNCs are certain of having cash flows denominated in foreign currencies for several years and attempt to use long-term hedging. For example, Walt Disney Co. hedged its Japanese yen cash flows that will be remitted to the United States (from its Japanese theme park) 20 years ahead. Eastman Kodak Co. and General Electric Co. incorporate foreign exchange management into their long-term corporate planning. Thus, techniques for hedging long-term exchange rate exposure are needed.

Firms that can accurately estimate foreign currency payables or receivables that will occur several years from now commonly use three techniques to hedge such long-term transaction exposure:

- Long-term forward contract
- Currency swap
- Parallel loan

Each technique is discussed in turn.

Long-Term Forward Contract

Until recently, **long-term forward contracts**, or long forwards, were seldom used. Today, the long forward is quite popular. Most large international banks routinely quote forward rates for terms of up to five years for British pounds, Canadian dollars, Japanese yen, and Swiss francs. Long forwards are especially attractive to firms that have set up fixed-price exporting or importing contracts over a long period of time and want to protect their cash flow from exchange rate fluctuations.

Like a short-term forward contract, the long forward can be tailored to accommodate the specific needs of the firm. Maturities of up to 10 years or more can sometimes be set up for the major currencies. Because a bank is trusting that the firm will fulfill its long-term obligation specified in the forward contract, it will consider only very creditworthy customers.

Currency Swap

A **currency swap** is a second technique for hedging long-term transaction exposure to exchange rate fluctuations. It can take many forms. One type of currency swap accommodates two firms that have different long-term needs.

EXAMPLE

Bellevue, Inc., a U.S. firm, is hired to build an oil pipeline in the United Kingdom. It expects to receive payment in British pounds in five years when the job is completed. At the same time, a British firm is hired by a U.S. bank for a long-term consulting project. Assume that this British firm will be paid in U.S. dollars and that much of the payment will occur in five years. Thus, Bellevue, Inc., will be receiving British pounds in five years, and the British firm will be receiving U.S. dollars in five years. These two firms could arrange a currency swap that allows for an exchange of pounds for dollars in five years at some negotiated exchange rate. In this way, Bellevue can lock in the number of U.S. dollars the British pound payment will convert to in five years. Likewise, the British firm can lock in the number of British pounds the U.S. dollar payment will convert to in five years.

To create a currency swap, firms rely on financial intermediaries who can accommodate their needs. Large banks and investment firms employ brokers who act as intermediaries for swaps. Corporations that want to eliminate transaction exposure to specific currencies at certain future dates contact a broker, who then finds one firm that needs the currency another firm wants to dispose of (and vice versa) and matches them up. The broker receives a fee for the service.

Over time, the currency swap obligation may become undesirable to one of the parties involved. Using our example, if the British pound appreciates substantially over time, Bellevue, Inc., will be worse off than if it had been able to obtain its dollars in the spot market. Of course, it did not know this when it engaged in a swap agreement. The swap agreement may require periodic payments from one party to the other to account for exchange rate movements, so as to reduce the possibility that one party will not fulfill its obligation by the time the exchange of currencies is supposed to occur.

Parallel Loan

A **parallel loan** (or "back-to-back loan") involves an exchange of currencies between two parties, with a promise to reexchange currencies at a specified exchange rate and future date. It represents two swaps of currencies, one swap at the inception of the loan contract and another swap at the specified future date. A parallel loan is interpreted by accountants as a loan and is therefore recorded on financial statements.

Alternative Hedging Techniques

When a perfect hedge is not available (or is too expensive) to eliminate transaction exposure, the firm should consider methods to at least reduce exposure. Such methods include the following:

- Leading and lagging
- Cross-hedging
- Currency diversification

Each method is discussed in turn.

Leading and Lagging

Leading and lagging strategies involve adjusting the timing of a payment request or disbursement to reflect expectations about future currency movements.

EXAMPLE

Corvalis Co. is based in the United States and has subsidiaries dispersed around the world. The focus here will be on a subsidiary in the United Kingdom that purchases some of its supplies from a subsidiary in Hungary. These supplies are denominated in Hungary's currency (the forint). If Corvalis Co. expects that the pound will soon depreciate against the forint, it may attempt to expedite the payment to Hungary before the pound depreciates. This strategy is referred to as **leading.**

As a second scenario, assume that the British subsidiary expects the pound to appreciate against the forint soon. In this case, the British subsidiary may attempt to stall its payment until after the pound appreciates. In this way it could use fewer pounds to obtain the forint needed for payment. This strategy is referred to as **lagging**.

General Electric and other well-known MNCs commonly use leading and lagging strategies in countries that allow them. In some countries, the government limits the length of time involved in leading and lagging strategies so that the flow of funds into or out of the country is not disrupted. Consequently, an MNC must be aware of government restrictions in any countries where it conducts business before using these strategies.

Cross-Hedging

Cross-hedging is a common method of reducing transaction exposure when the currency cannot be hedged.

EXAMPLE

Greeley Co., a U.S. firm, has payables in zloty (Poland's currency) 90 days from now. Because it is worried that the zloty may appreciate against the U.S. dollar, it may desire to hedge this position. If forward contracts and other hedging techniques are not possible for the zloty, Greeley may consider cross-hedging. In this case, it needs to first identify a currency that can be hedged and is highly correlated with the zloty. Greeley notices that the euro has recently been moving in tandem with the zloty and decides to set up a 90-day forward contract on the euro. If the movements in the zloty and euro continue to be highly correlated relative to the U.S. dollar (that is, they move in a similar direction and degree against the U.S. dollar), then the exchange rate between these two currencies should be somewhat stable over time. By purchasing euros 90 days forward, Greeley Co. can then exchange euros for the zloty. The effectiveness of this strategy depends on the degree to which these two currencies are positively correlated. The stronger the positive correlation, the more effective will be the cross-hedging strategy.

Currency Diversification

A third method for reducing transaction exposure is **currency diversification**, which can limit the potential effect of any single currency's movements on the value of an MNC. Some MNCs, such as The Coca-Cola Co., PepsiCo, and Altria, claim that their exposure to exchange rate movements is significantly reduced because they diversify their business among numerous countries.

The dollar value of future inflows in foreign currencies will be more stable if the foreign currencies received are *not* highly positively correlated. The reason is that lower positive correlations or negative correlations can reduce the variability of the dollar value of all foreign currency inflows. If the foreign currencies were highly correlated with each other, diversifying among them would not be a very effective way to reduce risk. If one of the currencies substantially depreciated, the others would do so as well, given that all these currencies move in tandem.

SUMMARY

- MNCs use the following techniques to hedge transaction exposure: (1) futures hedge, (2) forward hedge, (3) money market hedge, and (4) currency options hedge.
- To hedge payables, a futures or forward contract on the foreign currency can be purchased. Alternatively, a money market hedge strategy can be used; in this case, the MNC borrows its home currency

and converts the proceeds into the foreign currency that will be needed in the future. Finally, call options on the foreign currency can be purchased.

- To hedge receivables, a futures or forward contract on the foreign currency can be sold. Alternatively, a money market hedge strategy can be used. In this case, the MNC borrows the foreign currency to be received and converts the funds into its home currency; the loan is to be repaid by the receivables. Finally, put options on the foreign currency can be purchased.
- Futures contracts and forward contracts normally yield similar results. Forward contracts are more flexible because they are not standardized. The money market hedge yields results similar to those of the forward hedge if interest rate parity exists. The currency options hedge has an advantage over the other hedging techniques in that the options do not have to be exercised if the MNC would be better off unhedged. A premium must be paid to purchase the currency options, however, so there is a cost for the flexibility they provide.
- When hedging techniques are not available, there are still some methods of reducing transaction exposure, such as leading and lagging, cross-hedging, and currency diversification.

POINT COUNTER-POINT

Should an MNC Risk Overhedging?

Point Yes. MNCs have some "unanticipated" transactions that occur without any advance notice. They should attempt to forecast the net cash flows in each currency due to unanticipated transactions based on the previous net cash flows for that currency in a previous period. Even though it would be impossible to forecast the volume of these unanticipated transactions per day, it may be possible to forecast the volume on a monthly basis. For example, if an MNC has net cash flows between 3,000,000 and 4,000,000 Philippine pesos every month, it may presume that it will receive at least 3,000,000 pesos in each of the next few months unless conditions change. Thus, it can hedge a position of 3,000,0000 in pesos by selling that amount of pesos forward or buying put options on that amount of pesos. Any amount of net cash flows beyond 3,000,000 pesos will not be hedged, but at least the MNC was able to hedge the minimum expected net cash flows.

Counter-Point No. MNCs should not hedge unanticipated transactions. When they overhedge the expected net cash flows in a foreign currency, they are still exposed to exchange rate risk. If they sell more currency short from forward contracts than their net cash flows, they will be adversely affected by an increase in the value of the currency. Their initial reasons for hedging were to protect against the weakness of the currency, but the overhedging described here would cause a shift in their exposure. Overhedging does not insulate an MNC against exchange rate risk. It just changes the means by which the MNC is exposed.

Who Is Correct? Use InfoTrac or some other search engine to learn more about this issue. Offer your own opinion on this issue.

SELF TEST

Answers are provided in Appendix A at the back of the text.

1. Montclair Co., a U.S. firm, plans to use a money market hedge to hedge its payment of 3,000,000 Australian dollars for Australian goods in one year. The U.S. interest rate is 7 percent, while the Australian interest rate is 12 percent. The spot rate of the Australian dollar is $.85, while the one-year forward rate is $.81. Determine the amount of U.S. dollars needed in one year if a money market hedge is used.
2. Using the information in the previous question, would Montclair Co. be better off hedging the payables with a money market hedge or with a forward hedge?
3. Using the information about Montclair from the first question, explain the possible advantage of a currency option hedge over a money market hedge

for Montclair Co. What is a possible disadvantage of the currency option hedge?

4. Sanibel Co. purchases British goods (denominated in pounds) every month. It negotiates a one-month forward contract at the beginning of every month to hedge its payables. Assume the British pound appreciates consistently over the next five years. Will Sanibel be affected? Explain.

5. Using the information from question 4, suggest how Sanibel Co. could more effectively insulate itself from the possible long-term appreciation of the British pound.

6. Hopkins Co. transported goods to Switzerland and will receive 2,000,000 Swiss francs in three months. It believes the three-month forward rate will be an accurate forecast of the future spot rate. The three-month forward rate of the Swiss franc is \$.68. A put option is available with an exercise price of \$.69 and a premium of \$.03. Would Hopkins prefer a put option hedge to no hedge? Explain.

QUESTIONS AND APPLICATIONS

1. **Consolidated Exposure.** Quincy Corp. estimates the following cash flows in 90 days at its subsidiaries as follows:

Net Position in Each Currency Measured in the Parent's Currency (in 1,000s of Units)			
Subsidiary	Currency 1	Currency 2	Currency 3
A	+200	−300	−100
B	+100	−40	−10
C	−180	+200	−40

Determine the consolidated net exposure of the MNC to each currency.

2. **Money Market Hedge on Receivables.** Assume that Stevens Point Co. has net receivables of 100,000 Singapore dollars in 90 days. The spot rate of the S\$ is \$.50, and the Singapore interest rate is 2 percent over 90 days. Suggest how the U.S. firm could implement a money market hedge. Be precise.

3. **Money Market Hedge on Payables.** Assume that Vermont Co. has net payables of 200,000 Mexican pesos in 180 days. The Mexican interest rate is 7 percent over 180 days, and the spot rate of the Mexican peso is \$.10. Suggest how the U.S. firm could implement a money market hedge. Be precise.

4. **Invoicing Strategy.** Assume that Citadel Co. purchases some goods in Chile that are denominated in Chilean pesos. It also sells goods denominated in U.S. dollars to some firms in Chile. At the end of each month, it has a large net payables position in Chilean pesos. How can it use an invoicing strategy to reduce this transaction exposure? List any limitations on the effectiveness of this strategy.

5. **Hedging with Futures.** Explain how a U.S. corporation could hedge net receivables in euros with futures contracts. Explain how a U.S. corporation could hedge net payables in Japanese yen with futures contracts.

6. **Hedging with Forward Contracts.** Explain how a U.S. corporation could hedge net receivables in Malaysian ringgit with a forward contract. Explain how a U.S. corporation could hedge payables in Canadian dollars with a forward contract.

7. **Real Cost of Hedging Payables.** Assume that Loras Corp. imported goods from New Zealand and needs 100,000 New Zealand dollars 180 days from now. It is trying to determine whether to hedge this position. Loras has developed the following probability distribution for the New Zealand dollar:

Possible Value of New Zealand Dollar in 180 Days	Probability
\$.40	5%
.45	10
.48	30
.50	30
.53	20
.55	5

The 180-day forward rate of the New Zealand dollar is $.52. The spot rate of the New Zealand dollar is $.49. Develop a table showing a feasibility analysis for hedging. That is, determine the possible differences between the costs of hedging versus no hedging. What is the probability that hedging will be more costly to the firm than not hedging? Determine the expected value of the additional cost of hedging.

8. **Benefits of Hedging.** If hedging is expected to be more costly than not hedging, why would a firm even consider hedging?

9. **Real Cost of Hedging Payables.** Assume that Suffolk Co. negotiated a forward contract to purchase 200,000 British pounds in 90 days. The 90-day forward rate was $1.40 per British pound. The pounds to be purchased were to be used to purchase British supplies. On the day the pounds were delivered in accordance with the forward contract, the spot rate of the British pound was $1.44. What was the real cost of hedging the payables for this U.S. firm?

10. **Real Cost of Hedging Receivables.** Assume that Bentley Co. negotiated a forward contract to sell 100,000 Canadian dollars in one year. The one-year forward rate on the Canadian dollar was $.80. This strategy was designed to hedge receivables in Canadian dollars. On the day the Canadian dollars were to be sold in accordance with the forward contract, the spot rate of the Canadian dollar was $.83. What was the real cost of hedging receivables for this U.S. firm?

    Repeat the question, except assume that the spot rate of the Canadian dollar was $.75 on the day the Canadian dollars were to be sold in accordance with the forward contract. What was the real cost of hedging receivables in this example?

11. **Forward versus Money Market Hedge on Payables.** Assume the following information:

90-day U.S. interest rate	4%
90-day Malaysian interest rate	3%
90-day forward rate of Malaysian ringgit	$.400
Spot rate of Malaysian ringgit	$.404

    Assume that the Santa Barbara Co. in the United States will need 300,000 ringgit in 90 days. It wishes to hedge this payables position. Would it be better off using a forward hedge or a money market hedge? Substantiate your answer with estimated costs for each type of hedge.

12. **Forward versus Money Market Hedge on Receivables.** Assume the following information:

180-day U.S. interest rate	8%
180-day British interest rate	9%
180-day forward rate of British pound	$1.50
Spot rate of British pound	$1.48

    Assume that Riverside Corp. from the United States will receive 400,000 pounds in 180 days. Would it be better off using a forward hedge or a money market hedge? Substantiate your answer with estimated revenue for each type of hedge.

13. **Currency Options.** Relate the use of currency options to hedging net payables and receivables. That is, when should currency puts be purchased, and when should currency calls be purchased? Why would Cleveland, Inc., consider hedging net payables or net receivables with currency options rather than forward contracts? What are the disadvantages of hedging with currency options as opposed to forward contracts?

14. **Currency Options.** Can Brooklyn Co. determine whether currency options will be more or less expensive than a forward hedge when considering both hedging techniques to cover net payables in euros? Why or why not?

15. **Long-Term Hedging.** How can a firm hedge long-term currency positions? Elaborate on each method.

16. **Leading and Lagging.** Under what conditions would Zona Co.'s subsidiary consider using a "leading" strategy to reduce transaction exposure? Under what conditions would Zona Co.'s subsidiary consider using a "lagging" strategy to reduce transaction exposure?

17. **Cross-Hedging.** Explain how a firm can use cross-hedging to reduce transaction exposure.

18. **Currency Diversification.** Explain how a firm can use currency diversification to reduce transaction exposure.

19. **Hedging with Put Options.** As treasurer of Tucson Corp. (a U.S. exporter to New Zealand), you must decide how to hedge (if at all) future receivables of

250,000 New Zealand dollars 90 days from now. Put options are available for a premium of $.03 per unit and an exercise price of $.49 per New Zealand dollar. The forecasted spot rate of the NZ$ in 90 days follows:

Future Spot Rate	Probability
$.44	30%
.40	50
.38	20

Given that you hedge your position with options, create a probability distribution for U.S. dollars to be received in 90 days.

20. **Forward Hedge.** Would Oregon Co.'s real cost of hedging Australian dollar payables every 90 days have been positive, negative, or about zero on average over a period in which the dollar weakened consistently? What does this imply about the forward rate as an unbiased predictor of the future spot rate? Explain.

21. **Implications of IRP for Hedging.** If interest rate parity exists, would a forward hedge be more favorable, equally favorable, or less favorable than a money market hedge on euro payables? Explain.

22. **Real Cost of Hedging.** Would Montana Co.'s real cost of hedging Japanese yen receivables have been positive, negative, or about zero on average over a period in which the dollar weakened consistently? Explain.

23. **Forward versus Options Hedge on Payables.** If you are a U.S. importer of Mexican goods and you believe that today's forward rate of the peso is a very accurate estimate of the future spot rate, do you think Mexican peso call options would be a more appropriate hedge than the forward hedge? Explain.

24. **Forward versus Options Hedge on Receivables.** You are an exporter of goods to the United Kingdom, and you believe that today's forward rate of the British pound substantially underestimates the future spot rate. Company policy requires you to hedge your British pound receivables in some way. Would a forward hedge or a put option hedge be more appropriate? Explain.

25. **Forward Hedging.** Explain how a Malaysian firm can use the forward market to hedge periodic purchases of U.S. goods denominated in U.S. dollars. Explain how a French firm can use forward contracts to hedge periodic sales of goods sold to the United States that are invoiced in dollars. Explain how a British firm can use the forward market to hedge periodic purchases of Japanese goods denominated in yen.

26. **Continuous Hedging.** Cornell Co. purchases computer chips denominated in euros on a monthly basis from a Dutch supplier. To hedge its exchange rate risk, this U.S. firm negotiates a three-month forward contract three months before the next order will arrive. In other words, Cornell is always covered for the next three monthly shipments. Because Cornell consistently hedges in this manner, it is not concerned with exchange rate movements. Is Cornell insulated from exchange rate movements? Explain.

27. **Hedging Payables with Currency Options.** Malibu, Inc., is a U.S. company that imports British goods. It plans to use call options to hedge payables of 100,000 pounds in 90 days. Three call options are available that have an expiration date 90 days from now. Fill in the number of dollars needed to pay for the payables (including the option premium paid) for each option available under each possible scenario.

Scenario	Spot Rate of Pound 90 Days from Now	Exercise Price = $1.74; Premium = $.06	Exercise Price = $1.76; Premium = $.05	Exercise Price = $1.79; Premium = $.03
1	$1.65			
2	1.70			
3	1.75			
4	1.80			
5	1.85			

If each of the five scenarios had an equal probability of occurrence, which option would you choose? Explain.

28. **Forward Hedging.** Wedco Technology of New Jersey exports plastics products to Europe. Wedco decided to price its exports in dollars. Telematics International, Inc. (of Florida), exports computer network systems to the United Kingdom (denominated in British pounds) and other countries. Telematics decided to use hedging techniques such as forward contracts to hedge its exposure.

    a. Does Wedco's strategy of pricing its materials for European customers in dollars avoid economic exposure? Explain.

    b. Explain why the earnings of Telematics International, Inc., were affected by changes in the value of the pound. Why might Telematics leave its exposure unhedged sometimes?

29. **The Long-Term Hedge Dilemma.** St. Louis, Inc., which relies on exporting, denominates its exports in pesos and receives pesos every month. It expects the peso to weaken over time. St. Louis recognizes the limitation of monthly hedging. It also recognizes that it could remove its transaction exposure by denominating its exports in dollars, but it would still be subject to economic exposure. The long-term hedging techniques are limited, and the firm does not know how many pesos it will receive in the future, so it would have difficulty even if a long-term hedging method was available. How can this business realistically reduce its exposure over the long term?

30. **Long-Term Hedging.** Since Obisbo, Inc., conducts much business in Japan, it is likely to have cash flows in yen that will periodically be remitted by its Japanese subsidiary to the U.S. parent. What are the limitations of hedging these remittances one year in advance over each of the next 20 years? What are the limitations of creating a hedge today that will hedge these remittances over each of the next 20 years?

31. **Hedging during the Asian Crisis.** Describe how the Asian crisis could have reduced the cash flows of a U.S. firm that exported products (denominated in U.S. dollars) to Asian countries. How could a U.S. firm that exported products (denominated in U.S. dollars) to Asia, and anticipated the Asian crisis before it began, have insulated itself from any currency effects while continuing to export to Asia?

ADVANCED QUESTIONS

32. **Comparison of Techniques for Hedging Receivables.**

    a. Assume that Carbondale Co. expects to receive S$500,000 in one year. The existing spot rate of the Singapore dollar is $.60. The one-year forward rate of the Singapore dollar is $.62. Carbondale created a probability distribution for the future spot rate in one year as follows:

Future Spot Rate	Probability
$.61	20%
.63	50
.67	30

Assume that one-year put options on Singapore dollars are available, with an exercise price of $.63 and a premium of $.04 per unit. One-year call options on Singapore dollars are available with an exercise price of $.60 and a premium of $.03 per unit. Assume the following money market rates:

	U.S.	Singapore
Deposit rate	8%	5%
Borrowing rate	9	6

Given this information, determine whether a forward hedge, a money market hedge, or a currency options hedge would be most appropriate. Then compare the most appropriate hedge to an unhedged strategy, and decide whether Carbondale should hedge its receivables position.

    b. Assume that Baton Rouge, Inc., expects to need S$1 million in one year. Using any relevant information in part (a) of this question, determine whether a forward hedge, a money market hedge, or a currency options hedge would be most appropriate. Then, compare the most appropriate hedge to an unhedged strategy, and decide whether Baton Rouge should hedge its payables position.

33. **Comparison of Techniques for Hedging Payables.** SMU Corp. has future receivables of 4,000,000 New Zealand dollars (NZ$) in one year. It must decide whether to use options or a money market hedge to

hedge this position. Use any of the following information to make the decision. Verify your answer by determining the estimate (or probability distribution) of dollar revenue to be received in one year for each type of hedge.

Spot rate of NZ$	**$.54**	
One-year call option	**Exercise price = $.50; premium = $.07**	
One-year put option	**Exercise price = $.52; premium = $.03**	
	U.S.	**New Zealand**
One-year deposit rate	**9%**	**6%**
One-year borrowing rate	**11**	**8**
	Rate	**Probability**
Forecasted spot rate of NZ$	**$.50**	**20%**
	.51	**50**
	.53	**30**

34. **Exposure to September 11.** If you were a U.S. importer of products from Europe, explain whether the September 11, 2001 terrorist attacks on the United States would have caused you to hedge your payables (denominated in euros) due a few months later. Keep in mind that the attack was followed by a reduction in U.S. interest rates.

35. **Hedging with a Bull spread.** (See the chapter appendix.) Evar Imports, Inc., buys chocolate from Switzerland and resells it in the United States. It just purchased chocolate invoiced at SF62,500. Payment for the invoice is due in 30 days. Assume that the current exchange rate of the Swiss franc is $.74. Also assume that three call options for the franc are available. The first option has a strike price of $.74 and a premium of $.03; the second option has a strike price of $.77 and a premium of $.01; the third option has a strike price of $.80 and a premium of $.006. Evar Imports is concerned about a modest appreciation in the Swiss franc.

   a. Describe how Evar Imports could construct a bull spread using the first two options. What is the cost of this hedge? When is this hedge most effective? When is it least effective?

   b. Describe how Evar Imports could construct a bull spread using the first option and the third option. What is the cost of this hedge? When is this hedge most effective? When is it least effective?

   c. Given your answers to parts (a) and (b), what is the tradeoff involved in constructing a bull spread using call options with a higher exercise price?

36. **Hedging with a Bear spread.** (See the chapter appendix.) Marson, Inc., has some customers in Canada and frequently receives payments denominated in Canadian dollars (C$). The current spot rate for the Canadian dollar is $.75. Two call options on Canadian dollars are available. The first option has an exercise price of $.72 and a premium of $.03. The second option has an exercise price of $.74 and a premium of $.01. Marson, Inc., would like to use a bear spread to hedge a receivable position of C$50,000, which is due in one month. Marson is concerned that the Canadian dollar may depreciate to $.73 in one month.

   a. Describe how Marson, Inc., could use a bear spread to hedge its position.

   b. Assume the spot rate of the Canadian dollar in one month is $.73. Was the hedge effective?

37. **Hedging with Forward versus Option Contracts.** As treasurer of Tempe Corp., you are confronted with the following problem. Assume the one-year forward rate of the British pound is $1.59. You plan to receive 1 million pounds in one year. A one-year put option is available. It has an exercise price of $1.61. The spot rate as of today is $1.62, and the option premium is $.04 per unit. Your forecast of the percentage change in the spot rate was determined from the following regression model:

$$e_t = a_0 + a_1 DINF_{t-1} + a_2 DINT_t + \mu$$

where

e_t = percentage change in British pound value over period t

$DINF_{t-1}$ = differential in inflation between the United States and the United Kingdom in period $t - 1$

$DINT_t$ = average differential between U.S. interest rate and British interest rate over period t

a_0, a_1, and a_2 = regression coefficients

μ = error term

The regression model was applied to historical annual data, and the regression coefficients were estimated as follows:

$$a_0 = 0.0$$
$$a_1 = 1.1$$
$$a_2 = 0.6$$

Assume last year's inflation rates were 3 percent for the United States and 8 percent for the United Kingdom. Also assume that the interest rate differential ($DINT_t$) is forecasted as follows for this year:

Forecast of $DINT_t$	Probability
1%	40%
2	50
3	10

Using any of the available information, should the treasurer choose the forward hedge or the put option hedge? Show your work.

38. **Hedging with Straddles.** (See the chapter appendix.) Brooks, Inc., imports wood from Morocco. The Moroccan exporter invoices in Moroccan dirham. The current exchange rate of the dirham is $.10. Brooks just purchased wood for 2 million dirham and should pay for the wood in three months. It is also possible that Brooks will receive 4 million dirham in three months from the sale of refinished wood in Morocco. Brooks is currently in negotiations with a Moroccan importer about the refinished wood. If the negotiations are successful, Brooks will receive the 4 million dirham in three months, for a net cash inflow of 2 million dirham. The following option information is available:

- Call option premium on Moroccan dirham = $.003
- Put option premium on Moroccan dirham = $.002
- Call and put option strike price = $.098
- One option contract represents 500,000 dirham.

a. Describe how Brooks could use a straddle to hedge its possible positions in dirham.

b. Consider three scenarios. In the first scenario, the dirham's spot rate at option expiration is equal to the exercise price of $.098. In the second scenario, the dirham depreciates to $.08. In the third scenario, the dirham appreciates to $.11. For each scenario, consider both the case when the negotiations are successful and the case when the negotiations are not successful. Assess the effectiveness of the long straddle in each of these situations by comparing it to a strategy of using long call options to hedge.

39. **Hedging with Straddles versus Strangles.** (See the chapter appendix.) Refer to the previous problem. Assume that Brooks believes the cost of a long straddle is too high. However, call options with an exercise price of $.105 and a premium of $.002 and put options with an exercise price of $.09 and a premium of $.001 are also available on Moroccan dirham. Describe how Brooks could use a long strangle to hedge its possible dirham positions. What is the tradeoff involved in using a long strangle versus a long straddle to hedge the positions?

40. **Hedging Decision.** You believe that IRP presently exists. The nominal annual interest rate in Mexico is 14 percent. The nominal annual interest rate in the United States is 3 percent. You expect that annual inflation will be about 4 percent in Mexico and 5 percent in the United States The spot rate of the Mexican peso is $0.10. Put options on pesos are available with a one-year expiration date, an exercise price of $0.1008, and a premium of $0.014 per unit.

You will receive 1 million pesos in one year.

a. Determine the expected amount of dollars that you will receive if you use a forward hedge.

b. Determine the expected amount of dollars that you will receive if you do not hedge and believe in purchasing power parity.

c. Determine the amount of dollars that you will expect to receive if you use a currency put option hedge. Account for the premium you would pay on the put option.

INTERNET APPLICATION

41. **Evaluating Exchange Rate Movement** The following website contains annual reports of many MNCs: **http://www.reportgallery.com**.

a. Review the annual report of your choice. Look for any comments in the report that describe the MNC's hedging of transaction exposure. Summarize the MNC's hedging of transaction exposure based on the comments in the annual report.

b. The following website provides exchange rate movements against the dollar over recent months: **http://www.federalreserve.gov/releases/**.

Based on the exposure of the MNC you assessed in part (a), determine whether the exchange rate movements of whatever currency (or currencies) it is exposed to moved in a favorable or unfavorable direction over the last few months.

DISCUSSION IN THE BOARDROOM

This exercise can be found in Appendix E at the back of this textbook.

RUNNING YOUR OWN MNC

This exercise can be found on the Xtra! website at **http://maduraxtra.swlearning.com**.

BLADES, INC. CASE

Management of Transaction Exposure

Blades, Inc., has recently decided to expand its international trade relationship by exporting to the United Kingdom. Jogs, Ltd., a British retailer, has committed itself to the annual purchase of 200,000 pairs of "Speedos," Blades' primary product, for a price of £80 per pair. The agreement is to last for two years, at which time it may be renewed by Blades and Jogs.

In addition to this new international trade relationship, Blades continues to export to Thailand. Its primary customer there, a retailer called Entertainment Products, is committed to the purchase of 180,000 pairs of Speedos annually for another two years at a fixed price of 4,594 Thai baht per pair. When the agreement terminates, it may be renewed by Blades and Entertainment Products.

Blades also incurs costs of goods sold denominated in Thai baht. It imports materials sufficient to manufacture 72,000 pairs of Speedos annually from Thailand. These imports are denominated in baht, and the price depends on current market prices for the rubber and plastic components imported.

Under the two export arrangements, Blades sells quarterly amounts of 50,000 and 45,000 pairs of Speedos to Jogs and Entertainment Products, respectively. Payment for these sales is made on the first of January, April, July, and October. The annual amounts are spread over quarters in order to avoid excessive inventories for the British and Thai retailers. Similarly, in order to avoid excessive inventories, Blades usually imports materials sufficient to manufacture 18,000 pairs of Speedos quarterly from Thailand. Although payment terms call for payment within 60 days of delivery, Blades generally pays for its Thai imports upon delivery on the first day of each quarter in order to maintain its trade relationships with the Thai suppliers. Blades feels that early payment is beneficial, as other customers of the Thai supplier pay for their purchases only when it is required.

Since Blades is relatively new to international trade, Ben Holt, Blades' chief financial officer (CFO), is concerned with the potential impact of exchange rate fluctuations on Blades' financial performance. Holt is vaguely familiar with various techniques available to hedge transaction exposure, but he is not certain whether one technique is superior to the others. Holt would like to know more about the forward, money market, and option hedges and has asked you, a financial analyst at Blades, to help him identify the hedging technique most appropriate for Blades. Unfortunately, no options are available for Thailand, but British call and put options are available for £31,250 per option.

Ben Holt has gathered and provided you with the following information for Thailand and the United Kingdom:

	Thailand	United Kingdom
Current spot rate	$0.0230	$1.50
90-day forward rate	$0.0215	$1.49
Put option premium	Not available	$0.020 per unit
Put option exercise price	Not available	$1.47
Call option premium	Not available	$0.015 per unit
Call option exercise price	Not available	$1.48
90-day borrowing rate (nonannualized)	4%	2%
90-day lending rate (nonannualized)	3.5%	1.8%

In addition to this information, Ben Holt has informed you that the 90-day borrowing and lending rates in the United States are 2.3 percent and 2.1 percent, respectively, on a nonannualized basis. He has also identified the following probability distributions for the exchange rates of the British pound and the Thai baht in 90 days:

Probability	Spot Rate for the British Pound in 90 Days	Spot Rate for the Thai Baht in 90 Days
5%	$1.45	$0.0200
20	1.47	0.0213
30	1.48	0.0217
25	1.49	0.0220
15	1.50	0.0230
5	1.52	0.0235

Blades' next sales to and purchases from Thailand will occur one quarter from now. If Blades decides to hedge, Holt will want to hedge the entire amount subject to exchange rate fluctuations, even if it requires overhedging (i.e., hedging more than the needed amount). Currently, Holt expects the imported components from Thailand to cost approximately 3,000 baht per pair of Speedos. Holt has asked you to answer the following questions for him:

1. Using a spreadsheet, compare the hedging alternatives for the Thai baht with a scenario under which Blades remains unhedged. Do you think Blades should hedge or remain unhedged? If Blades should hedge, which hedge is most appropriate?
2. Using a spreadsheet, compare the hedging alternatives for the British pound receivables with a scenario under which Blades remains unhedged. Do you think Blades should hedge or remain unhedged? Which hedge is the most appropriate for Blades?
3. In general, do you think it is easier for Blades to hedge its inflows or its outflows denominated in foreign currencies? Why?
4. Would any of the hedges you compared in question 2 for the British pounds to be received in 90 days require Blades to overhedge? Given Blades' exporting arrangements, do you think it is subject to overhedging with a money market hedge?
5. Could Blades modify the timing of the Thai imports in order to reduce its transaction exposure? What is the tradeoff of such a modification?
6. Could Blades modify its payment practices for the Thai imports in order to reduce its transaction exposure? What is the tradeoff of such a modification?
7. Given Blades' exporting agreements, are there any long-term hedging techniques Blades could benefit from? For this question only, assume that Blades incurs all of its costs in the United States.

SMALL BUSINESS DILEMMA

Hedging Decisions by the Sports Exports Company

Jim Logan, owner of the Sports Exports Company, will be receiving about 10,000 British pounds about one month from now as payment for exports produced and sent by his firm. Jim is concerned about his exposure because he believes that there are two possible scenarios: (1) the pound will depreciate by 3 percent over the next month or (2) the pound will appreciate by 2 percent over the next month. There is a 70 percent chance that Scenario 1 will occur. There is a 30 percent chance that Scenario 2 will occur.

Jim notices that the prevailing spot rate of the pound is \$1.65, and the one-month forward rate is about \$1.645. Jim can purchase a put option over the counter from a securities firm that has an exercise (strike) price of \$1.645, a premium of \$.025, and an expiration date of one month from now.

1. Determine the amount of dollars received by the Sports Exports Company if the receivables to be received in one month are not hedged under each of the two exchange rate scenarios.
2. Determine the amount of dollars received by the Sports Exports Company if a put option is used to hedge receivables in one month under each of the two exchange rate scenarios.
3. Determine the amount of dollars received by the Sports Exports Company if a forward hedge is used to hedge receivables in one month under each of the two exchange rate scenarios.
4. Summarize the results of dollars received based on an unhedged strategy, a put option strategy, and a forward hedge strategy. Select the strategy that you prefer based on the information provided.

APPENDIX 11

Nontraditional Hedging Techniques

While traditional hedging techniques were covered in the chapter, many other techniques may be appropriate for an MNC's particular situation. Some of these nontraditional techniques are described in this appendix.

Hedging with Currency Straddles

In reality, some MNCs do not know whether they will have net cash inflows or outflows as a result of their transactions in a specific currency over a particular period of time. A long straddle (purchase of a call option and put option with the same exercise price) is an effective tool to hedge under these conditions.

EXAMPLE

Houston Co. conducts business in Mexico and expects to need 4,000,000 Mexican pesos (MXP) to cover specific expenses. If it is unable to renew a business deal with the Mexican government (its biggest customer), it will receive a total of MXP3,000,000 in revenue in one month, which will result in net cash flows of −MXP1,000,000. Conversely, if it is able to renew the business deal with the government, it will receive a total of MXP5,000,000, which will result in net cash flows of +MXP1,000,000. The prevailing spot rate of the Mexican peso is $.09. If Houston has excess pesos in one month, it will convert them to dollars. Conversely, if Houston does not have enough pesos in one month, it will use dollars to obtain the amount that it needs. Houston would like to hedge its exchange rate risk, regardless of which scenario occurs.

Currently, call options for Mexican pesos with expiration dates in one month are available with an exercise price of $.09 and a premium of $.004 per peso. Put options for Mexican pesos with an expiration date of one month are available with an exercise price of $.09 and a premium of $.005 per peso. Options for Mexican pesos are denominated in 250,000 pesos per option contract.

Houston could hedge its possible position of having positive net cash flows of MXP1,000,000 by purchasing put options. It would pay a premium of $5,000 (1,000,000 units × $.005). It could hedge its possible position of needing MXP1,000,000 by purchasing call options. It would pay a premium of $4,000 (1,000,000 units × $.004). Assume that Houston constructs a straddle to hedge both possible outcomes and pays

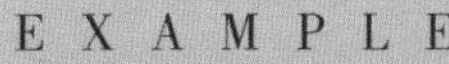

$9,000 for the call options and put options on pesos. Assume that Houston exercises the options in one month, if at all.

Consider the following scenarios that could occur one month from now:

1. If Houston has net cash flows of +MXP1,000,000 and the peso's value is $.10, it would let its put options expire and would convert its pesos to dollars in the spot market, receiving $100,000 (1,000,000 units × $.10) from this transaction. It would also exercise its call option by purchasing 1,000,000 pesos at $.09 and selling them in the spot market for $.10. This transaction would generate a gain of $10,000. Overall, Houston would receive $110,000, minus the $9,000 in premiums paid for the options.
2. If Houston has net cash flows of +MXP1,000,000 and the peso depreciates to $.08, it would exercise its put options and let the call options expire. Overall, Houston would receive $90,000 (1,000,000 units × $.09) from exercising the options, minus the $9,000 in premiums paid for the options.
3. If Houston has net cash flows of +MXP1,000,000 and the peso is $.09, it would let its call and put options expire. It would receive $90,000 (1,000,000 × $.09) from selling pesos in the spot market, minus the $9,000 in premiums paid for the options.
4. If Houston has net cash flows of −MXP1,000,000, and the peso's value is $.10, it would exercise its call options and let its put options expire. Overall, Houston would pay a total of $99,000, which consists of the $90,000 (1,000,000 × $.09) from exercising the call option and the $9,000 in premiums paid for the options.
5. If Houston has net cash flows of −MXP1,000,000 and the peso's value is $.08, it would let its call options expire and buy pesos in the spot market. It would also buy 1,000,000 pesos and then sell them by exercising its put options. This transaction would generate a gain of $10,000. Overall, Houston would pay a total of $79,000, which consists of the $80,000 paid to obtain the pesos it needs, plus the $9,000 in premiums paid for the options, minus the $10,000 gain generated from its put options.
6. If Houston has net cash flows of −MXP1,000,000 and the peso's value is $.09, it would let its call and put options expire. It would pay a total of $99,000, which consists of the $90,000 paid to obtain pesos and the $9,000 in premiums paid for the options.

Many other scenarios could also occur, but a summary of the possible scenarios and the actions taken by Houston appears in Exhibit 11A.1.

Exhibit 11A.1 Possible Scenarios for Houston Co. When Hedging with a Straddle

Panel A: Houston has net cash flows of +MXP1,000,000 in one month.	
MXP value > $.09 in one month	• **Houston converts excess pesos to dollars in the spot market.** • **It lets the put options expire.** • **It exercises its call options and sells the pesos obtained from this transaction in the spot market; the proceeds recapture part of the premiums that were paid for the options.**
MXP value < $.09 in one month	• **Houston converts excess pesos to dollars at $.09, by exercising its put options.** • **It lets the call options expire.**
MXP value = $.09 in one month	• **Houston converts excess pesos to dollars in the spot market.** • **It lets its call options and put options expire.**

Panel B: Houston has net cash flows of −MXP1,000,000 in one month.	
MXP value > $.09 in one month	• Houston converts dollars to pesos by exercising its call options. • It lets the put options expire.
MXP value < $.09 in one month	• It lets the call options expire. • It buys pesos in the spot market and sells pesos obtained by exercising the put options; the proceeds recapture part of the premiums that were paid for the options.
MXP = $.09 in one month	• Houston converts dollars to pesos in the spot market. • It lets its call and put options expire.

Hedging with Currency Strangles

In the hedging example just provided for Houston Co., consider that the expected value of the amount that Houston would pay or receive based on today's spot rate is $90,000 (MXP1,000,000 × $.09). The option premiums paid for the options ($9,000) represent 10 percent of that expected value. Thus, the straddle is an expensive means of hedging. The exercise price at which Houston hedged was equal to the spot rate ("at the money"). If Houston is willing to accept exposure to small exchange rate movements in the peso, it could reduce the premiums paid for the options. Specifically, it would use a *long strangle* by purchasing a call option and a put option that have different exercise prices. By purchasing a call option that has an exercise price higher than $.09, and a put option that has an exercise price lower than $.09, Houston can reduce the premiums it will pay on the options.

EXAMPLE

Reconsider the example in which Houston Co. expects that it will have net cash flows of either +MXP1,000,000 or −MXP1,000,000 in one month. To reduce the premiums it pays for hedging with options, it can purchase options that are out of the money. Assume that it can obtain call options for Mexican pesos with an expiration date of one month, an exercise price of $.095, and a premium of $.002 per peso. It can also obtain put options for Mexican pesos with an expiration date of one month, an exercise price of $.085, and a premium of $.003 per peso.

Houston Co. could hedge its possible position of needing MXP1,000,000 by purchasing call options. It would pay a premium of $2,000 (1,000,000 units × $.002). It could also hedge its possible position of having positive net cash flows of MXP1,000,000 by purchasing put options. It would pay a premium of $3,000 (1,000,000 units × $.003). Overall, Houston would pay $5,000 for the call options and put options on pesos, which is substantially less than the $9,000 it would pay for the straddle in the previous example. However, the options do not offer protection until the spot rate deviates by more than $.005 from its existing level. If the spot rate remains within the range of the two exercise prices (from $.085 to $.095), Houston will not exercise either option.

This example of hedging with a strangle is a compromise between hedging with the straddle in the previous example and no hedge. For the range of possible spot rates between $.085 and $.095, there is no hedge. For scenarios in which the spot rate moves outside the range, Houston is hedged. It will have to pay no more than $.095 if it needs to obtain pesos and will be able to sell pesos for at least $.085 if it has pesos to sell.

Hedging with Currency Bull Spreads

In certain situations, MNCs can use currency bull spreads to hedge their cash outflows denominated in a foreign currency, as the following example illustrates.

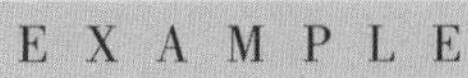

Peak, Inc., needs to order Canadian raw materials to use in its production process. The Canadian exporter typically invoices Peak in Canadian dollars. Assume that the current exchange rate for the Canadian dollar (C$) is $.73 and that Peak needs C$100,000 in three months. Two call options for Canadian dollars with expiration dates in three months and the following additional information are available:

- Call Option 1 premium on Canadian dollars = $.015
- Call Option 2 premium on Canadian dollars = $.008
- Call Option 1 strike price = $.73
- Call Option 2 strike price = $.75
- One option contract represents C$50,000.

To lock into a future price for the C$100,000, Peak could buy two Option 1 contracts, paying 2 × C$50,000 × $.015 = $1,500. This would effectively lock in a maximum price of $.73 that Peak would pay in three months, for a total maximum outflow of $74,500 (C$100,000 × $.73 + $1,500). If the spot price for Canadian dollars at option expiration is below $.73, Peak has the right to let the options expire and buy the C$100,000 in the open market for the lower price. Naturally, Peak would still have paid the $1,500 total premium in this case.

Historically, the Canadian dollar has been relatively stable against the U.S. dollar. If Peak believes that the Canadian dollar will appreciate in the next three months but is very unlikely to appreciate above the higher exercise price of $.75, it should consider constructing a bull spread to hedge its Canadian dollar payables. To do so, Peak would purchase two Option 1 contracts and write two Option 2 contracts. The total cash outflow necessary to construct this bull spread is 2 × C$50,000 × ($.015 − $.008) = $700, since Peak would receive the premiums from writing the two Option 2 contracts. Constructing the bull spread has reduced the cost of hedging by $800 ($1,500 − $700).

If the spot price of the Canadian dollar at option expiration is below the $.75 strike price, the bull spread will have provided an effective hedge. For example, if the spot price at option expiration is $.74, Peak will exercise the two Option 1 contracts it purchased, for a total maximum outflow of $73,700 (C$100,000 × $.73 + $700). The buyer of the two Option 2 contracts Peak wrote would let those options expire. If the Canadian dollar depreciates substantially below the lower strike price of $.73, the hedge will also be effective, as both options will expire worthless. Peak would purchase the Canadian dollars at the prevailing spot rate, having paid the difference in option premiums.

Now consider what will happen if the Canadian dollar appreciates above the higher exercise price of $.75 prior to option expiration. In this case, the bull spread will still reduce the total cash outflow and therefore provide a partial hedge. However, the hedge will be less effective.

To illustrate, assume the Canadian dollar appreciates to a spot price of $.80 in three months. Peak will still exercise the two Option 1 contracts it purchased. However, the two Option 2 contracts it wrote will also be exercised. Recall that this is a situation in which the maximum profit from the bull spread is realized, which is equal to the difference in exercise prices less the difference in the two premiums, or 2 × C$50,000 × ($.75 − $.73 − $.015 + $.008) = $1,300. Importantly, Peak will now have to purchase the C$100,000 it needs in the open market, since it needs to sell the Canadian dollars purchased by exercising the Option 1 contracts to the buyer of the Option 2 contracts it wrote. Therefore, Peak's total cash outflow in three months when it needs the Canadian dollars will be $78,700 (C$100,000 × $.80 − $1,300). While Peak has successfully reduced its cash outflow in three months by $1,300, it would have fared much better by only buying two Option 1 contracts to hedge its payables, which would have resulted in a maximum cash outflow of $74,500. Consequently, MNCs should hedge using bull spreads only for relatively stable currencies that are not expected to appreciate drastically prior to option expiration.

Hedging with Currency Bear Spreads

In certain situations, MNCs can use currency bear spreads to hedge their receivables denominated in a foreign currency.

EXAMPLE

Weber, Inc., has some Canadian customers. Weber typically bills these customers in Canadian dollars. Assume that the current exchange rate for the Canadian dollar (C$) is $.73 and that Weber expects to receive C$50,000 in three months. The following options for Canadian dollars are available.

- Call Option 1 premium on Canadian dollars = $.015
- Call Option 2 premium on Canadian dollars = $.008
- Call Option 1 strike price = $.73
- Call Option 2 strike price = $.75
- One option contract represents C$50,000.

If Weber believes the Canadian dollar will not depreciate much below the lower exercise price of $.75, it can construct a bear spread to hedge the receivable. Weber will buy Call Option 2 and write Call Option 1 to establish this bear spread. The total cash *inflow* resulting from this bear spread is C$50,000 × ($.015 − $.008) = $350. Constructing a bear spread will always result in a net cash inflow, since the spreader writes the call option with the lower exercise price and, therefore, the higher premium.

What will happen if the Canadian dollar appreciates above the higher exercise price of $.75 prior to option expiration? For example, assume that the spot rate for the Canadian dollar is $.80 at option expiration. In this case, the bear spread would result in the maximum loss of $.013 ($.75 − $.73 − $.015 + $.008) per Canadian dollar, for a total maximum loss of $650. However, Weber can now sell the receivables at the prevailing spot rate of $.80, netting $39,350 (C$50,000 × $.80 − $650). Furthermore, while the maximum loss remains at $650 for the bear spread, Weber can benefit if the Canadian dollar appreciates even more.

The bear spread also provides an effective hedge if the spot price of the Canadian dollar at option expiration is above the lower strike price of $.73 but below the higher strike price of $.75. In this case, however, the benefit is reduced. For instance, if the spot price at option expiration is $.74, Weber will let Option 2 expire. The buyer of Option 1 will exercise it, and Weber will sell the receivables at the exercise price of $.73 to fulfill its obligation. This will result in a total cash inflow of $36,850 (C$50,000 × $.73 + $350) after including the net premium received from establishing the spread.

If the Canadian dollar depreciates below the lower strike price of $.73, Weber will realize the maximum gain from the bear spread, but will have to sell the receivables at the low prevailing spot rate. For example, if the spot rate at option expiration is \$.70, both options will expire worthless, but Weber would have received \$350 from establishing the spread. If Weber sells the receivables at the spot rate, the net cash inflow will be \$35,350 (C\$50,000 × \$.70 + \$350).

In summary, MNCs should hedge receivables using bear spreads only for relatively stable currencies that are expected to depreciate modestly, but not drastically, prior to option expiration.

CHAPTER 12

Managing Economic Exposure and Translation Exposure

As the previous chapter described, MNCs can manage the exposure of their international transactions to exchange rate movements (referred to as transaction exposure) in various ways. Nevertheless, cash flows of MNCs may still be sensitive to exchange rate movements (economic exposure) even if anticipated international transactions are hedged. Furthermore, the consolidated financial statements of MNCs may still be exposed to exchange rate movements (translation exposure). By managing economic exposure and translation exposure, financial managers may increase the value of their MNCs.

The specific objectives of this chapter are to:

- explain how an MNC's economic exposure can be hedged, and
- explain how an MNC's translation exposure can be hedged.

In general, it is more difficult to effectively hedge economic or translation exposure than to hedge transaction exposure, for reasons explained in this chapter.

Economic Exposure

From a U.S. firm's perspective, transaction exposure represents only the exchange rate risk when converting net foreign cash inflows to U.S. dollars or when purchasing foreign currencies to send payments. Economic exposure represents any impact of exchange rate fluctuations on a firm's future cash flows. Corporate cash flows can be affected by exchange rate movements in ways not directly associated with foreign transactions. Thus, firms cannot focus just on hedging their foreign currency payables or receivables but must also attempt to determine how all their cash flows will be affected by possible exchange rate movements.

EXAMPLE

Nike's economic exposure comes in various forms. First, it is subject to transaction exposure because of its numerous purchase and sale transactions in foreign currencies, and this transaction exposure is a subset of economic exposure. Second, any remitted earnings from foreign subsidiaries to the U.S. parent also reflect transaction exposure and therefore reflect economic exposure. Third, a change in exchange rates that affects the demand for shoes at other athletic shoe companies (such as Adidas) can indirectly affect the demand for Nike's athletic shoes. Nike attempts to hedge some of its transaction exposure, but it cannot eliminate transaction exposure because it cannot predict all future transactions ahead of time. Moreover, even if it could eliminate its transaction exposure, it cannot perfectly hedge its remaining economic exposure; it is difficult to determine exactly how a specific exchange rate movement will affect the demand for a competitor's athletic shoes and, therefore, how it will indirectly affect the demand for Nike's shoes.

http://

See http://www.ibm.com/us/ as an example of an MNC's website. The websites of various MNCs make available financial statements such as annual reports that describe the use of financial derivatives to hedge interest rate risk and exchange rate risk.

The following comments by PepsiCo summarize the dilemma faced by many MNCs that assess economic exposure.

The economic impact of currency exchange rates on us is complex because such changes are often linked to variability in real growth, inflation, interest rates, governmental actions, and other factors. These changes, if material, can cause us to adjust our financing and operating strategies.

PepsiCo

Use of the Income Statement to Assess Economic Exposure

An MNC must determine its economic exposure before it can manage its exposure. It can determine its exposure to each currency in terms of its cash inflows and cash outflows. The income statements for each subsidiary can be used to derive estimates.

EXAMPLE

Recall from Chapter 10 that Madison, Inc., is subject to economic exposure. Madison can assess its economic exposure to exchange rate movements by determining the sensitivity of its expenses and revenue to various possible exchange rate scenarios. Exhibit 12.1. reproduces Madison's revenue and expense information from Exhibit 10.8 of Chapter 10. The U.S. revenues are assumed to be sensitive to different exchange rate scenarios because of the foreign competition. Regardless of the exchange rate scenario, Canadian sales are expected to be C$4 million, but the dollar amount received from these sales will depend on the scenario. The cost of goods sold attributable to U.S. orders is assumed to be $50 million and insensitive to exchange rate movements. The cost of goods sold attributable to Canadian orders is assumed to be C$200 million. The U.S. dollar amount of this cost varies with the exchange rate scenario. The gross profit shown in Exhibit 12.1 is determined by subtracting the total dollar value of cost of goods sold from the total dollar value of sales.

Operating expenses are separated into fixed and variable categories. The fixed expenses are $30 million per year, while the projected variable expenses are dictated by projected sales. The earnings before interest and taxes are determined by the total U.S. dollar amount of gross profit minus the total U.S. dollar amount of operating expenses. The interest owed to U.S. banks is insensitive to the exchange rate scenario, but the projected amount of dollars needed to pay interest on existing Canadian loans varies with the exchange rate scenario. Earnings before taxes are estimated by subtracting total interest expense from earnings before interest and taxes.

Exhibit 12.1 enables Madison to assess how its income statement items will be affected by different exchange rate movements. A stronger Canadian dollar increases

Exhibit 12.1 Original Impact of Exchange Rate Movements on Earnings: Madison, Inc. (in Millions)

	Exchange Rate Scenario					
	C$ = $.75		C$ = $.80		C$ = $.85	
Sales:						
(1) U.S.		$300.0		$304.00		$307.00
(2) Canadian	C$4 =	3.0	C$4 =	3.20	C$4 =	3.40
(3) Total		$303.0		$307.20		$310.40
Cost of goods sold:						
(4) U.S.		$ 50.0		$ 50.00		$ 50.00
(5) Canadian	C$200 =	150.0	C$200 =	160.00	C$200 =	170.00
(6) Total		$200.0		$210.00		$220.00
(7) Gross profit		$103.0		$ 97.20		$ 90.40
Operating expenses:						
(8) U.S.: Fixed		$ 30.0		$ 30.00		$ 30.00
(9) U.S.: Variable (10% of total sales)		30.3		30.72		31.04
(10) Total		$ 60.3		$ 60.72		$ 61.04
(11) Earnings before interest and taxes		$ 42.7		$ 36.48		$ 29.36
Interest expense:						
(12) U.S.		$ 3.0		$ 3.00		$ 3.00
(13) Canadian	C$10 =	7.5	C$10 =	8.00	C$10 =	8.50
(14) Total		$ 10.5		$ 11.00		$ 11.50
(15) Earnings before taxes		$ 32.2		$ 25.48		$ 17.86

Madison's U.S. sales and the dollar revenue earned from Canadian sales. However, it also increases Madison's cost of materials purchased from Canada and the dollar amount needed to pay interest on loans from Canadian banks. The higher expenses more than offset the higher revenue in this scenario. Thus, the amount of Madison's earnings before taxes is inversely related to the strength of the Canadian dollar.

If the Canadian dollar strengthens consistently over the long run, Madison's cost of goods sold and interest expense likely will rise at a higher rate than its U.S. dollar revenue. Consequently, it may wish to institute some policies to ensure that movements of the Canadian dollar will have a more balanced impact on its revenue and expenses. At the current time, Madison's high exposure to exchange rate movements occurs because its expenses are more susceptible than its revenue to the changing value of the Canadian dollar.

Now that Madison has assessed its exposure, it recognizes that it can reduce this exposure by either increasing Canadian sales or reducing orders of Canadian materials. These actions would allow some offsetting of cash flows and therefore reduce its economic exposure.

How Restructuring Can Reduce Economic Exposure

MNCs may restructure their operations to reduce their economic exposure. The restructuring involves shifting the sources of costs or revenue to other locations in order to match cash inflows and outflows in foreign currencies.

EXAMPLE

Reconsider the previous example of Madison, Inc., which has more cash outflows than cash inflows in Canadian dollars. Madison could create more balance by increasing Canadian sales. It believes that it can achieve Canadian sales of C$20 million if it spends $2 million more on advertising (which is part of its fixed operating expenses). The increased sales will also require an additional expenditure of $10 million on materials from U.S. suppliers. In addition, it plans to reduce its reliance on Canadian suppliers and increase its reliance on U.S. suppliers. Madison anticipates that this strategy will reduce the cost of goods sold attributable to Canadian suppliers by C$100 million and increase the cost of goods sold attributable to U.S. suppliers by $80 million (not including the $10 million increase resulting from increased sales to the Canadian market). Furthermore, it plans to borrow additional funds in the United States and retire some existing loans from Canadian banks. The result will be an additional interest expense of $4 million to U.S. banks and a reduction of C$5 million owed to Canadian banks. Exhibit 12.2 shows the anticipated impact of these strategies on Madison's income statement. For each of the three exchange rate scenarios, the initial projections are in the left column, and the revised projections (as a result of the proposed strategy) are in the right column.

Note first that the projected total sales increase in response to Madison's plan to penetrate the Canadian market. Second, the U.S. cost of goods sold is now $90 million higher as a result of the $10 million increase to accommodate increased Canadian sales and the $80 million increase due to the shift from Canadian suppliers to U.S. suppliers. The Canadian cost of goods sold decreases from C$200 million to C$100 million as a result of this shift. The revised fixed operating expenses of $32 million include the increase in advertising expenses necessary to penetrate the Canadian market. The variable operating expenses are revised because of revised estimates for total sales. The interest expenses are revised because of the increased loans from the U.S. banks and reduced loans from Canadian banks.

If Madison increases its Canadian dollar inflows and reduces its Canadian dollar outflows as proposed, its revenue and expenses will be affected by movements of the Canadian dollar in a somewhat similar manner. Thus, its performance will be less susceptible to movements in the Canadian dollar. Exhibit 12.3 illustrates the sensitivity of Madison's earnings before taxes to the three exchange rate scenarios (derived from Exhibit 12.2). The reduced sensitivity of Madison's proposed restructured operations to exchange rate movements is obvious.

The way a firm restructures its operations to reduce economic exposure to exchange rate risk depends on the form of exposure. For Madison, Inc., future expenses are more sensitive than future revenue to the possible values of a foreign currency. Therefore, it can reduce its economic exposure by increasing the sensitivity of revenue and reducing the sensitivity of expenses to exchange rate movements. Firms that have a greater level of exchange rate-sensitive revenue than expenses, however, would reduce their economic exposure by decreasing the level of exchange rate-sensitive revenue or by increasing the level of exchange rate-sensitive expenses.

Some revenue or expenses may be more sensitive to exchange rates than others. Therefore, simply matching the level of exchange rate-sensitive revenue to the level of exchange rate-sensitive expenses may not completely insulate a firm from exchange rate risk. The firm can best evaluate a proposed restructuring of operations by forecasting various income statement items for various possible exchange rate scenarios (as shown in Exhibit 12.2) and then assessing the sensitivity of earnings to these different scenarios.

Exhibit 12.2 Impact of Possible Exchange Rate Movements on Earnings under Two Alternative Operational Structures (in Millions)

	Exchange Rate Scenario C$ = $.75		Exchange Rate Scenario C$ = $.80		Exchange Rate Scenario C$ = $.85	
	Original Operational Structure	*Proposed Operational Structure*	Original Operational Structure	*Proposed Operational Structure*	Original Operational Structure	*Proposed Operational Structure*
Sales:						
U.S.	$300.0	$300.00	$304.00	$304	$307.00	$307.00
Canadian	C$4 = 3.0	C$20 = 15.00	C$4 = 3.20	C$20 = 16	C$4 = 3.40	C$20 = 17.00
Total	$303.0	$315.00	$307.20	$320	$310.40	$324.00
Cost of goods sold:						
U.S.	$ 50.0	$140.00	$ 50.00	$140	$ 50.00	$140.00
Canadian	C$200 = 150.0	C$100 = 75.00	C$200 = 160.00	C$100 = 80	C$200 = 170.00	C$100 = 85.00
Total	$200.0	$215.00	$210.00	$220	$220.00	$225.00
Gross profit	$103.0	$100.00	$ 97.20	$100	$ 90.40	$ 99.00
Operating expenses:						
U.S.: Fixed	$ 30.0	$ 32.00	$ 30.00	$ 32	$ 30.00	$ 32.00
U.S.: Variable (10% of total sales)	30.3	31.50	30.72	32	31.04	32.40
Total	$ 60.3	$ 63.50	$ 60.72	$ 64	$ 61.04	$ 64.40
Earnings before interest and taxes	$ 42.7	$ 36.50	$ 36.48	$ 36	$ 29.36	$ 34.60
Interest expense:						
U.S.	$ 3.0	$ 7.00	$ 3.00	$ 7	$ 3.00	$ 7.00
Canadian	C$10 = 7.5	C$5 = 3.75	C$10 = 8.00	C$5 = 4	C$10 = 8.50	C$5 = 4.25
Total	$ 10.5	$ 10.75	$ 11.00	$ 11	$ 11.50	$ 11.25
Earnings before taxes	$ 32.2	$ 25.75	$ 25.48	$ 25	$ 17.86	$ 23.35

Exhibit 12.3

Economic Exposure Based on the Original and Proposed Operating Structures

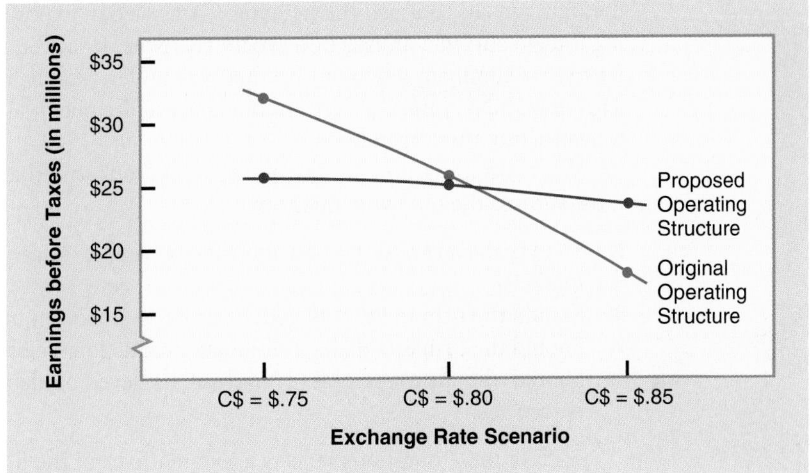

Expediting the Analysis with Computer Spreadsheets. Determining the sensitivity of earnings before taxes to alternative exchange rate scenarios can be expedited by using a computer to create a spreadsheet similar to Exhibit 12.2. The analyst then inputs forecasts for items such as sales, cost of goods sold, and fixed operating expenses. A formula is used to define the remaining items so that the computer can provide estimates after the forecasts are input. For example, the exchange rate forecast influences projections of (1) dollars received from Canadian sales, (2) cost of goods sold attributable to purchases of Canadian materials, and (3) amount in dollars needed to cover the Canadian interest payments. By revising the input to reflect various possible restructurings, the analyst can determine how each operational structure would affect the firm's economic exposure.

EXAMPLE

Recall that Madison, Inc., assessed one alternative operational structure in which it increased Canadian sales by C$16 million, reduced its purchases of Canadian materials by C$100 million, and reduced its interest owed to Canadian banks by C$5 million. By using a computerized spreadsheet, Madison can easily assess the impact of alternative strategies, such as increasing Canadian sales by other amounts and/or reducing the Canadian expenses by other amounts. This provides Madison with more information about its economic exposure under various operational structures and enables it to devise the operational structure that will reduce its economic exposure to the degree desired.

Issues Involved in the Restructuring Decision

Restructuring operations to reduce economic exposure is a more complex task than hedging any single foreign currency transaction, which is why managing economic exposure is normally perceived to be more difficult than managing transaction exposure. By managing economic exposure, however, the firm is developing a long-term solution because once the restructuring is complete, it should reduce economic exposure over the long run. In contrast, the hedging of transaction exposure deals with each upcoming foreign currency transaction separately. Note, however, that it can be very costly to reverse or eliminate restructuring that was undertaken to reduce economic exposure. Therefore, MNCs must be very confident about the potential benefits before they decide to restructure their operations.

When deciding how to restructure operations to reduce economic exposure, one must address the following questions:

- Should the firm attempt to increase or reduce sales in new or existing foreign markets?
- Should the firm increase or reduce its dependency on foreign suppliers?
- Should the firm establish or eliminate production facilities in foreign markets?
- Should the firm increase or reduce its level of debt denominated in foreign currencies?

Each of these questions reflects a different part of the firm's income statement. The first relates to foreign cash inflows and the remaining ones to foreign cash outflows. Some of the more common solutions to balancing a foreign currency's inflows and outflows are summarized in Exhibit 12.4. Any restructuring of operations that can reduce the periodic difference between a foreign currency's inflows and outflows can reduce the firm's economic exposure to that currency's movements.

MNCs that have production and marketing facilities in various countries may be able reduce any adverse impact of economic exposure by shifting the allocation of their operations.

Deland Co. produces products in the United States, Japan, and Mexico and sells these products (denominated in the currency where they are produced) to several countries. If the Japanese yen strengthens against many currencies, Deland may boost production in Mexico, expecting a decline in demand for the Japanese subsidiary's products. Deland may even transfer some machinery from Japan to Mexico and allocate more marketing funds to the Mexican subsidiary at the expense of the Japanese subsidiary. By following this strategy, however, Deland may have to forgo economies of scale that could be achieved if it concentrated production at one subsidiary while other subsidiaries focused on warehousing and distribution.

Exhibit 12.4 How to Restructure Operations to Balance the Impact of Currency Movements on Cash Inflows and Outflows

Type of Operation	Recommended Action When a Foreign Currency Has a Greater Impact on Cash Inflows	Recommended Action When a Foreign Currency Has a Greater Impact on Cash Outflows
Sales in foreign currency units	Reduce foreign sales	Increase foreign sales
Reliance on foreign supplies	Increase foreign supply orders	Reduce foreign supply orders
Proportion of debt structure representing foreign debt	Restructure debt to increase debt payments in foreign currency	Restructure debt to reduce debt payments in foreign currency

MANAGING FOR VALUE

How Auto Manufacturers Restructure to Reduce Exposure

To illustrate how the shifting of production can reduce economic exposure, consider the actual case of Honda, the Japanese automobile producer. By developing plants in the United States to produce automobiles for sale there, Honda not only circumvents possible trade restrictions but also reduces its economic exposure to exchange rate risk. When Honda exported automobiles to the United States, the U.S. demand for Hondas would decline if the yen appreciated because the dollar cost of the autos would increase. Thus, Honda's cash flows were adversely affected when a strong yen reduced demand for its exports. By producing automobiles in the United States and invoicing them in dollars, Honda has reduced the sensitivity of U.S. demand for its automobiles to the value of the Japanese yen. Nevertheless, Honda is not completely insulated from exchange rate risk for two reasons. First, the Honda plants in the United States purchase various components from Japan (invoiced in yen), so the dollar costs of these components rises when the yen appreciates. Second, earnings remitted from Honda's plants in the United States to its parent in Japan convert to a smaller number of yen when the yen appreciates. Nevertheless, by transferring production to the location where the product is sold, Honda has reduced its economic exposure.

Honda's British subsidiary has also restructured to reduce the adverse effects of its economic exposure. When the euro declined against the British pound, consumers throughout Europe reduced their demand for vehicles produced at Honda's subsidiary in the United Kingdom and denominated in pounds. Consequently, Honda shifted some of its supply sources from the United Kingdom to European countries that have adopted the euro. This strategy is intended to reduce the impact of the euro on the performance of Honda's British subsidiary. When the euro declines, the decline in revenue (because of a reduced demand for Hondas produced in the United Kingdom) is partially offset by a decline in the costs of obtaining supplies denominated in euros. When the euro's value increases, Honda's cost of euro-denominated supplies rises, but the demand for its pound-denominated vehicles (and therefore its revenue) also increases (see Exhibit 12.5). By shifting its operations, Honda has reduced its exposure to exchange rate risk, thereby increasing its value.

As a result of Honda's decision to use suppliers in the euro-zone countries to hedge its exposure, it is buying less from suppliers in the United Kingdom. Thus, the U.K. auto suppliers have lost local business because of Honda's desire to offset its exposure. Ironically, these auto suppliers are subject to increased economic exposure as a result of Honda's decision to reduce its exposure.

Exhibit 12.5 Honda's Decision to Obtain Supplies outside the United Kingdom

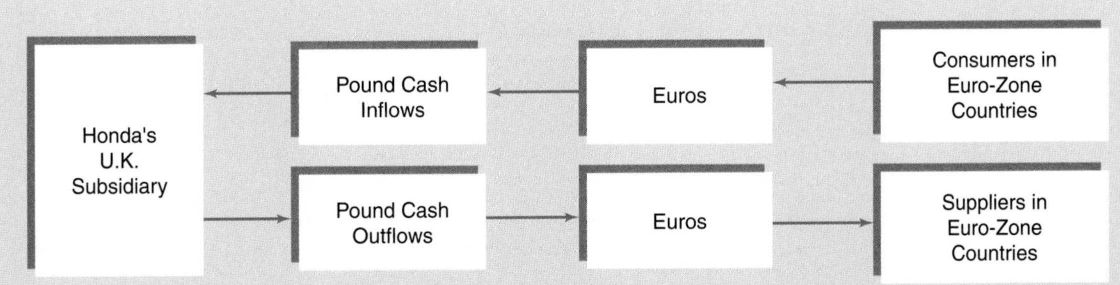

- Weak euro: Weak European demand for Honda's pound-denominated vehicles offset by reduced cost of euro-denominated supplies
- Strong euro: High cost of euro-denominated supplies offset by strong European demand for Honda's pound-denominated vehicles

A Case Study in Hedging Economic Exposure

In reality, most MNCs are not able to reduce their economic exposure as easily as Madison, Inc., in the previous example. First, a MNC's economic exposure may not be so obvious. An analysis of the income statement for an entire MNC may not necessarily detect its economic exposure. The MNC may be composed of various business units, each of which attempts to achieve high performance for its shareholders. Each business unit may have a unique cost and revenue structure. One unit of an MNC may focus on computer consulting services in the United States and have no exposure to exchange rates. Another unit may also focus on sales of personal computers in the United States, but this unit may be adversely affected by weak foreign currencies because its U.S. customers may buy computers from foreign firms.

Although the MNC is mostly concerned with the effect of exchange rates on its performance and value overall, it can more effectively hedge its economic exposure if it can pinpoint the underlying source of the exposure. Yet, even if the MNC can pinpoint the underlying source of the exposure, there may not be a perfect hedge against that exposure. No textbook formula can provide the perfect solution, but a combination of actions may reduce the economic exposure to a tolerable level, as illustrated in the following example. This example is more difficult than the previous example of Madison, Inc., but it may be more realistic for many MNCs.

Savor Co.'s Dilemma

Savor Co., a U.S. firm, is primarily concerned with its exposure to the euro. It wants to pinpoint the source of its exposure so that it can determine how to hedge its exposure. Savor has three units that conduct some business in Europe. Because each unit has established a wide variety of business arrangements, it is not obvious whether all three units have a similar exposure. Each unit tends to be independent of the others, and the managers of each unit are compensated according to that unit's performance. Savor may want to hedge its economic exposure, but it must first determine whether it is exposed and the source of the exposure.

Assessment of Economic Exposure

Because the exact nature of its economic exposure to the euro is not obvious, Savor attempts to assess the relationship between the euro's movements and each unit's cash flows over the last nine quarters. A firm may want to use more data, but nine quarters are sufficient to illustrate the point. The cash flows and movements in the euro are shown in Exhibit 12.6. First, Savor applies regression analysis (as discussed in the previous chapter) to determine whether the percentage change in its total cash flow (*PCF*, shown in Column 5) is related to the percentage change in the euro (%**Δ**euro, shown in Column 6) over time:

$$PCF_t = a_0 + a_1(\%\Delta\text{euro})_t + \mu_t$$

Regression analysis derives the values of the constant, a_0, and the slope coefficient, a_1. The slope coefficient represents the sensitivity of PCF_t to movements in the euro. Based on this analysis, the slope coefficient is positive and statistically significant, which im-

Exhibit 12.6 Assessment of Savor Co.'s Cash Flows and the Euro's Movements

(1) Quarter	(2) % Change in Unit A's Cash Flows	(3) % Change in Unit B's Cash Flows	(4) % Change in Unit C's Cash Flows	(5) % Change in Total Cash Flows	(6) % Change in the Value of the Euro
1	−3	2	1	0	2
2	0	1	3	4	5
3	6	−6	−1	−1	−3
4	−1	1	−1	−1	0
5	−4	0	−1	−5	−2
6	−1	−2	−2	−5	−5
7	1	−3	3	1	4
8	−3	2	1	0	2
9	4	−1	0	3	−4

plies that the cash flows are positively related to the percentage changes in the euro. That is, a negative change in the euro adversely affects Savor's total cash flows. The *R*-squared statistic is .31, which suggests that 31 percent of the variation in Savor's cash flows can be explained by movements in the euro. The evidence presented so far strongly suggests that Savor is exposed to exchange rate movements of the euro, but does not pinpoint the source of the exposure.

Assessment of Each Unit's Exposure

To determine the source of the exposure, Savor applies the regression model separately to each individual unit's cash flows. The results are shown here (apply the regression analysis yourself as an exercise):

Unit	Slope Coefficient
A	Not significant
B	Not significant
C	Coefficient = .45, which is statistically significant (R-squared = .80)

The results suggest that the cash flows of Units A and B are not subject to economic exposure. However, Unit C is subject to economic exposure. Approximately 80 percent of Unit C's cash flows can be explained by movements in the value of the euro over time. The regression coefficient suggests that for a 1 percent decrease in the value of the euro, the unit's cash flows will decline by about .45 percent. Exhibit 12.6, which shows the euro's exchange rate movements and the cash flows for Savor's individual units, confirms the strong relationship between the euro's movements and Unit C's cash flows.

Identifying the Source of the Unit's Exposure

Now that Savor has determined that one unit is the cause of the exposure, it can pinpoint the characteristics of that unit that cause the exposure. Savor believes that the key components that affect Unit C's cash flows are income statement items such as its U.S. revenue, its cost of goods sold, and its operating expenses. This unit conducts all of its production in the United States.

Savor first determines the value of each income statement item that affected the unit's cash flows in each of the last nine quarters. It then applies regression analysis to determine the relationship between the percentage change in the euro and each income statement item over those quarters. Assume that it finds:

- A significant positive relationship between Unit C's revenue and the euro's value.
- No relationship between the unit's cost of goods sold and the euro's value.
- No relationship between the unit's operating expenses and the euro's value.

These results suggest that when the euro weakens, the unit's revenue from U.S. customers declines substantially. Its U.S. customers shift their demand to foreign competitors when the euro weakens and they can obtain imports at a low price. Thus, Savor's economic exposure could be due to foreign competition. A firm's economic exposure is not always obvious, however, and regression analysis may detect exposure that was not suspected by the firm or its individual units. Furthermore, regression analysis can be used to provide a more precise estimate of the degree of economic exposure, which can be useful when deciding how to manage the exposure.

Possible Strategies to Hedge Economic Exposure

Now that Savor has identified the source of its economic exposure, it can develop a strategy to reduce that exposure.

Pricing Policy. Savor recognizes that there will be periods in the future when the euro will depreciate against the dollar. Under these conditions, Unit C may attempt to be more competitive by reducing its prices. If the euro's value declines by 10 percent and this reduces the prices that U.S. customers pay for the foreign products by 10 percent, then Unit C can attempt to remain competitive by discounting its prices by 10 percent. Although this strategy can retain market share, the lower prices will result in less revenue and therefore less cash flows. Therefore, this strategy does not completely eliminate Savor's economic exposure. Nevertheless, this strategy may still be feasible, especially if the unit can charge relatively high prices in periods when the euro is strong and U.S. customers have to pay higher prices for European products. In essence, the strategy might allow the unit to generate abnormally high cash flows in a strong-euro period to offset the abnormally low cash flows in a weak-euro period. The adverse effect during a weak-euro period will still occur, however. Given the limitations of this strategy, other strategies should be considered.

Hedging with Forward Contracts. Savor's Unit C could sell euros forward for the period in which it wants to hedge against the adverse effects of the weak euro. Assume the spot and three-month forward rates on the euro are $1. If the euro weakens, the cash flows from normal operations will still be adversely affected. However, the unit would generate a gain on the forward contract because it will be able to purchase euros at the spot rate at the end of the period at a lower exchange rate than the rate at which it will have to sell those euros to fulfill the forward contract. The weaker the euro, the more pronounced will be the adverse effects on the unit's cash flows from normal operations, but the gains from the forward contract will also be more pronounced.

Using a forward contract has definite limitations, however. Since the economic exposure is likely to continue indefinitely, the use of a forward contract in the manner described here hedges only for the period of the contract. It does not serve as a continuous long-term hedge against economic exposure.

Purchasing Foreign Supplies. Another possibility is for the unit to purchase its materials in Europe, a strategy that would reduce its costs (and enhance its cash flows) during a weak-euro period to offset the adverse effects of the weak euro. However, the cost of buying European materials may be higher than the cost of buying local materials, especially when transportation expenses are considered.

Financing with Foreign Funds. The unit could also reduce its economic exposure by financing a portion of its business with loans in euros. It could convert the loan proceeds to dollars and use the dollars to support its business. It will need to make periodic loan repayments in euros. If the euro weakens, the unit will need fewer dollars to cover the loan repayments. This favorable effect can partially offset the adverse effect of a weak euro on the unit's revenue. If the euro strengthens, the unit will need more dollars to cover the loan repayments, but this adverse effect will be offset by the favorable effect of the strong euro on the unit's revenue. This type of hedge is more effective than the pricing hedge because it can offset the adverse effects of a weak euro in the same period (whereas the pricing policy attempts to make up for lost cash flows once the euro strengthens).

This strategy also has some limitations. First, the strategy only makes sense if Savor needs some debt financing. It should not borrow funds just for the sake of hedging its economic exposure. Second, Savor might not desire this strategy when the euro has a very high interest rate. Though borrowing in euros can reduce its economic exposure, it may not be willing to enact the hedge at a cost of higher interest expenses than it would pay in the United States.

Third, this strategy is unlikely to create a perfect hedge against Savor's economic exposure. Even if the company needs debt financing and the interest rate charged on the foreign loan is low, Savor must attempt to determine the amount of debt financing that will hedge its economic exposure. The amount of foreign debt financing necessary to fully hedge the exposure may exceed the amount of funding that Savor needs.

Revising Operations of Other Units. Given the limitations of hedging Unit C's economic exposure by adjusting the unit's operations, Savor may consider modifying the operations of another unit in a manner that will offset the exposure of Unit C. However, this strategy may require changes in another unit that will not necessarily benefit that unit. For example, assume that Unit C could partially hedge its economic exposure by borrowing euros (as explained above) but that it does not need to borrow as much as would be necessary to fully offset its economic exposure. Savor's top management may suggest that Units A and B also obtain their financing in euros, so that the MNC's overall economic exposure is hedged. Thus, a weak euro would still adversely affect Unit C because the adverse effect on its revenue would not be fully offset by the favorable effect on its financing (debt repayments). Yet, if the other units have borrowed euros as well, the combined favorable effects on financing for Savor overall could offset the adverse effects on Unit C.

However, Units A and B will not necessarily desire to finance their operations in euros. Recall that these units are not subject to economic exposure. Also recall that the managers of each unit are compensated according to the performance of that unit. By agreeing to finance in euros, Units A and B could become exposed to movements in the euro. If the euro strengthens, their cost of financing increases. So, by helping to offset the exposure of Unit C, Units A and B could experience weaker performance, and their managers would receive less compensation.

A solution is still possible if Savor's top managers who are not affiliated with any unit can remove the hedging activity from the compensation formula for the units' managers. That is, top management could instruct Units A and B to borrow funds in euros, but could reward the managers of those units based on an assessment of the units' performance that excludes the effect of the euro on financing costs. In this way, the managers will be more willing to engage in a strategy that increases their economic exposure while reducing Savor's.

Savor's Hedging Solution

In summary, Savor's initial analysis of its units determined that only Unit C was highly subject to economic exposure. Unit C could attempt to use a pricing policy that would maintain market share when the euro weakens, but this strategy would not eliminate the economic exposure because its cash flows would still be adversely affected. Borrowing euros can be an effective strategy to hedge Unit C's exposure, but it does not need to borrow the amount of funds necessary to offset its exposure. The optimal solution for Savor Co. is to instruct its other units to do their financing in euros as well. This strategy effectively increases their exposure, but in the opposite manner of Unit C's exposure, so that the MNC's economic exposure overall is reduced. The units' managers should be willing to cooperate if their compensation is not reduced as a result of increasing the exposure of their individual units.

Limitations of Savor's Optimal Hedging Strategy

Even if Savor Co. is able to achieve the hedge described above, the hedge will still not be perfect. The impact of the euro's movements on Savor's cash outflows needed to repay the loans is known with certainty. But the impact of the euro's movements on Savor's cash inflows (revenue) is uncertain and can change over time. If the amount of foreign competition increases, the sensitivity of Unit C's cash flows to exchange rates would increase. To hedge this increased exposure, it would need to borrow a larger amount of euros. An MNC's economic exposure can change over time in response to shifts in foreign competition or other global conditions, so it must continually assess and manage its economic exposure.

Hedging Exposure to Fixed Assets

Up to this point, the focus has been on how economic exposure can affect periodic cash flows. The effects may extend beyond periodic cash flows, however. When an MNC has fixed assets (such as buildings or machinery) in a foreign country, the dollar cash flows to be received from the ultimate sale of these assets is subject to exchange rate risk.

EXAMPLE

Wagner Co., a U.S. firm, pursued a six-year project in Russia. It purchased a manufacturing plant from the Russian government in April 1998 for 500 million rubles. Since the ruble was worth $.16 at the time of the investment, Wagner needed $80 million to purchase the plant. The Russian government guaranteed that it would repurchase the plant for 500 million rubles in July 2004 when the project was completed. In July 2004, however, the ruble was worth only $.034, so Wagner received only $17 million (computed as 500 million × $.034) from selling the plant. Even though the price of the plant in rubles at the time of the sale was the same as the price at the time of the purchase, the sales price of the plant in dollars at the time of the sale was about 81 percent less than the purchase price.

Some MNCs may not worry about the exchange rate effect on fixed assets because they normally expect to retain the assets for several years. Given the frequent restructuring of global operations, however, MNCs should consider hedging against the possible sale of these assets in the distant future. A sale of fixed assets can be hedged by creating a liability that matches the expected value of the assets at the point in the future when they may be sold. In essence, the sale of the fixed assets generates a foreign currency cash inflow that can be used to pay off the liability that is denominated in the same currency.

EXAMPLE

In the previous example, Wagner could have financed part of its investment in the Russian manufacturing plant by borrowing rubles from a local bank, with the loan structured to have zero interest payments and a lump-sum repayment value equal to the expected sales price set for the date when Wagner expected to sell the plant. Thus, the loan could have been structured to have a lump-sum repayment value of 500 million rubles in July 2004.

The limitations of hedging a sale of fixed assets are that an MNC does not necessarily know the (1) date when it will sell the assets or (2) the price in local currency at which it will sell them. Consequently, it is unable to create a liability that perfectly matches the date and amount of the sale of the fixed assets. Nevertheless, these limitations should not prevent a firm from hedging.

EXAMPLE

Even if the Russian government would not guarantee a purchase price of the plant, Wagner Co. could create a liability that reflects the earliest possible sales date and the lowest expected sales price. If the sales date turns out to be later than the earliest possible sales date, Wagner might be able to extend its loan period to match the sales date. By structuring the lump-sum loan repayment to match the minimum sales price, Wagner will not be perfectly hedged if the fixed assets turn out to be worth more than the minimum expected amount. Nevertheless, Wagner would at least have reduced its exposure by offsetting a portion of the fixed assets with a liability in the same currency.

Long-term forward contracts may also be a possible way to hedge the distant sale of fixed assets in foreign countries, but they may not be available for many emerging market currencies.

Managing Translation Exposure

Translation exposure occurs when an MNC translates each subsidiary's financial data to its home currency for consolidated financial statements. Even if translation exposure does not affect cash flows, it is a concern of many MNCs because it can reduce an MNC's consolidated earnings and thereby cause a decline in its stock price. Thus, some MNCs may consider hedging their translation exposure.

Use of Forward Contracts to Hedge Translation Exposure

MNCs can use forward contracts or futures contracts to hedge translation exposure. Specifically, they can sell the currency forward that their foreign subsidiaries receive as earnings. In this way, they create a cash outflow in the currency to offset the earnings received in that currency.

EXAMPLE

Columbus, Inc., is a U.S.-based MNC with just one subsidiary. As of the beginning of its fiscal year, the subsidiary, which is located in the the United Kingdom, forecasts that its annual earnings will be £20 million. The subsidiary plans to reinvest the entire amount of earnings within the United Kingdom and does not plan to remit any earnings back to the parent in the United States. While there is no foreseeable transaction exposure in the near future from the future earnings (since the pounds will remain in the United Kingdom), Columbus is exposed to translation exposure.

The British earnings will be translated at the weighted average value of the pound over the course of the year. If the British pound is currently worth $1.50 and its value remains constant during the year, the forecasted translation of British earnings into U.S. dollars would be $30 million (computed as £20 million × $1.50 per pound).

The parent of Columbus, Inc., may be concerned that the translated value of the British earnings will be reduced if the pound's exchange rate declines during the year. To hedge this translation exposure, Columbus can implement a forward hedge on the expected earnings by selling £20 million one year forward. Assume the forward rate at that time is $1.50, the same as the spot rate. At the end of the year, Columbus can buy £20 million at the spot rate and fulfill its forward contract obligation to sell £20 million. If the pound depreciates during the fiscal year, then Columbus will be able to purchase pounds at the end of the fiscal year to fulfill the forward contract at a cheaper rate than it can sell them ($1.50 per pound). Thus, it will have generated income that can offset the translation loss.

The precise level of income generated by the forward contract will depend on the spot rate of the pound at the end of the fiscal year. Under conditions in which the pound depreciates, the translation loss will be somewhat offset by the gain generated from the forward contract position.

Limitations of Hedging Translation Exposure

There are four limitations in hedging translation exposure.

Inaccurate Earnings Forecasts. A subsidiary's forecasted earnings for the end of the year are not guaranteed. In the previous example involving Columbus, Inc., British earnings were projected to be £20 million. If the actual earnings turned out to be much higher, and if the pound weakens during the year, the translation loss would likely exceed the gain generated from the forward contract strategy.

Inadequate Forward Contracts for Some Currencies. A second limitation is that forward contracts are not available for all currencies. Thus, an MNC with subsidiaries in some smaller countries may not be able to obtain forward contracts for the currencies of concern.

Accounting Distortions. A third limitation is that the forward rate gain or loss reflects the difference between the forward rate and the future spot rate, whereas the translation gain or loss reflects the difference between the average exchange rate over the period of concern and the future spot rate. In addition, the translation losses are not tax deductible, whereas gains on forward contracts used to hedge translation exposure are taxed.

Increased Transaction Exposure. The fourth and most critical limitation with a hedging strategy (forward or money market hedge) on translation exposure is that the MNC may be increasing its transaction exposure. For example, consider a situation in which the subsidiary's currency appreciates during the fiscal year, resulting in a translation gain. If the MNC enacts a hedge strategy at the start of the fiscal year, this strategy will generate a transaction loss that will somewhat offset the translation gain.

Some MNCs may not be comfortable with this offsetting effect. The translation gain is simply a paper gain; that is, the reported dollar value of earnings is higher due to the subsidiary currency's appreciation. If the subsidiary reinvests the earnings, however, the parent does not receive any more income due to this appreciation. The MNC parent's net cash flow is not affected. Conversely, the loss resulting from a hedge strategy is a *real* loss; that is, the net cash flow to the parent will be reduced due to this loss. Thus, in this situation, the MNC reduces its translation exposure at the expense of increasing its transaction exposure.

SUMMARY

- Economic exposure can be managed by balancing the sensitivity of revenue and expenses to exchange rate fluctuations. To accomplish this, however, the firm must first recognize how its revenue and expenses are affected by exchange rate fluctuations. For some firms, revenue is more susceptible. These firms are most concerned that their home currency will appreciate against foreign currencies, since the unfavorable effects on revenue will more than offset the favorable effects on expenses. Conversely, firms whose expenses are more sensitive to exchange rates than their revenue are most concerned that their home currency will depreciate against foreign currencies. When firms reduce their economic exposure, they reduce not only these unfavorable effects but also the favorable effects if the home currency value moves in the opposite direction.
- Translation exposure can be reduced by selling forward the foreign currency used to measure a subsidiary's income. If the foreign currency depreciates against the home currency, the adverse impact on the consolidated income statement can be offset by the gain on the forward sale in that currency. If the foreign currency appreciates over the time period of concern, there will be a loss on the forward sale that is offset by a favorable effect on the reported consolidated earnings. However, many MNCs would not be satisfied with a "paper gain" that offsets a "cash loss."

POINT COUNTER-POINT

Can an MNC Reduce the Impact of Translation Exposure by Communicating?

Point Yes. Investors commonly use earnings to derive an MNC's expected future cash flows. Investors do not necessarily recognize how an MNC's translation exposure could distort their estimates of the MNC's future cash flows. Therefore, the MNC could clearly communicate in its annual report and elsewhere how the earnings were affected by translation gains and losses in any period. If investors have this information, they will not overreact to earnings changes that are primarily attributed to translation exposure.

Counter-Point No. Investors focus on the bottom line and should ignore any communication regarding the translation exposure. Moreover, they may believe that translation exposure should be accounted for anyway. If foreign earnings are reduced because of a weak currency, the earnings may continue to be weak if the currency remains weak.

Who Is Correct? Use InfoTrac or some other search engine to learn more about this issue. Which argument do you support? Offer your own opinion on this issue.

SELF TEST

Answers are provided in Appendix A at the back of the text.

1. Salem Exporting Co. purchases chemicals from U.S. sources and uses them to make pharmaceutical products that are exported to Canadian hospitals. Salem prices its products in Canadian dollars and is concerned about the possibility of the long-term depreciation of the Canadian dollar against the U.S. dollar. It periodically hedges its exposure with short-term forward contracts, but this does not insulate against the possible trend of continuing Canadian dollar depreciation. How could Salem offset some of its exposure resulting from its export business?
2. Using the information in question 1, give a possible disadvantage of offsetting exchange rate exposure from the export business.
3. Coastal Corp. is a U.S. firm with a subsidiary in the United Kingdom. It expects that the pound will depreciate this year. Explain Coastal's translation exposure. How could Coastal hedge its translation exposure?
4. Arlington Co. has substantial translation exposure in European subsidiaries. The treasurer of Arlington Co. suggests that the translation effects are not relevant because the earnings generated by the European subsidiaries are not being remitted to the U.S. parent, but are simply being reinvested in Europe. Nevertheless, the vice president of finance of Arlington Co. is concerned about translation exposure because the stock price is highly dependent on the consolidated earnings, which are dependent on the exchange rates at which the earnings are translated. Who is correct?
5. Lincolnshire Co. exports 80 percent of its total production of goods in New Mexico to Latin American countries. Kalafa Co. sells all the goods it produces in the United States, but it has a subsidiary in Spain that usually generates about 20 percent of its total earnings. Compare the translation exposure of these two U.S. firms.

QUESTIONS AND APPLICATIONS

1. **Reducing Economic Exposure.** Baltimore, Inc., is a U.S.-based MNC that obtains 10 percent of its supplies from European manufacturers. Sixty percent of its revenues are due to exports to Europe, where its product is invoiced in euros. Explain how Baltimore can attempt to reduce its economic exposure to exchange rate fluctuations in the euro.
2. **Reducing Economic Exposure.** UVA Co. is a U.S.-based MNC that obtains 40 percent of its foreign supplies from Thailand. It also borrows Thailand's currency (the baht) from Thai banks and converts the baht to dollars to support U.S. operations. It currently receives about 10 percent of its revenue from Thai customers. Its sales to Thai customers are denominated in baht. Explain how UVA Co. can reduce its economic exposure to exchange rate fluctuations.
3. **Reducing Economic Exposure.** Albany Corp. is a U.S.-based MNC that has a large government contract with Australia. The contract will continue for several years and generate more than half of Albany's total sales volume. The Australian government pays Albany in Australian dollars. About 10 percent of

Albany's operating expenses are in Australian dollars; all other expenses are in U.S. dollars. Explain how Albany Corp. can reduce its economic exposure to exchange rate fluctuations.

4. **Tradeoffs When Reducing Economic Exposure.** When an MNC restructures its operations to reduce its economic exposure, it may sometimes forgo economies of scale. Explain.

5. **Exchange Rate Effects on Earnings.** Explain how a U.S.-based MNC's consolidated earnings are affected when foreign currencies depreciate.

6. **Hedging Translation Exposure.** Explain how a firm can hedge its translation exposure.

7. **Limitations of Hedging Translation Exposure.** Bartunek Co. is a U.S.-based MNC that has European subsidiaries and wants to hedge its translation exposure to fluctuations in the euro's value. Explain some limitations when it hedges translation exposure.

8. **Effective Hedging of Translation Exposure.** Would a more established MNC or a less established MNC be better able to effectively hedge its given level of translation exposure? Why?

9. **Comparing Degrees of Economic Exposure.** Carlton Co. and Palmer, Inc., are U.S.-based MNCs with subsidiaries in Mexico that distribute medical supplies (produced in the United States) to customers throughout Latin America. Both subsidiaries purchase the products at cost and sell the products at 90 percent markup. The other operating costs of the subsidiaries are very low. Carlton Co. has a research and development center in the United States that focuses on improving its medical technology. Palmer, Inc., has a similar center based in Mexico. The parent of each firm subsidizes its respective research and development center on an annual basis. Which firm is subject to a higher degree of economic exposure? Explain.

10. **Comparing Degrees of Translation Exposure.** Nelson Co. is a U.S. firm with annual export sales to Singapore of about S$800 million. Its main competitor is Mez Co., also based in the United States, with a subsidiary in Singapore that generates about S$800 million in annual sales. Any earnings generated by the subsidiary are reinvested to support its operations. Based on the information provided, which firm is subject to a higher degree of translation exposure? Explain.

ADVANCED QUESTIONS

11. **Managing Economic Exposure.** St. Paul Co. does business in the United States and New Zealand. In attempting to assess its economic exposure, it compiled the following information.

a. St. Paul's U.S. sales are somewhat affected by the value of the New Zealand dollar (NZ$), because it faces competition from New Zealand exporters. It forecasts the U.S. sales based on the following three exchange rate scenarios:

Exchange Rate of NZ$	Revenue from U.S. Business (in millions)
NZ$ = $.48	$100
NZ$ = .50	105
NZ$ = .54	110

b. Its New Zealand dollar revenues on sales to New Zealand invoiced in New Zealand dollars are expected to be NZ$600 million.

c. Its anticipated cost of goods sold is estimated at $200 million from the purchase of U.S. materials and NZ$100 million from the purchase of New Zealand materials.

d. Fixed operating expenses are estimated at $30 million.

e. Variable operating expenses are estimated at 20 percent of total sales (after including New Zealand sales, translated to a dollar amount).

f. Interest expense is estimated at $20 million on existing U.S. loans, and the company has no existing New Zealand loans.

Create a forecasted income statement for St. Paul Co. under each of the three exchange rate scenarios. Explain how St. Paul's projected earnings before taxes are affected by possible exchange rate movements. Explain how it can restructure its operations to reduce the sensitivity of its earnings to exchange rate movements without reducing its volume of business in New Zealand.

12. **Assessing Economic Exposure.** Alaska, Inc., plans to create and finance a subsidiary in Mexico that produces computer components at a low cost and exports them to other countries. It has no other international business. The subsidiary will produce

computers and export them to Caribbean islands and will invoice the products in U.S. dollars. The values of the currencies in the islands are expected to remain very stable against the dollar. The subsidiary will pay wages, rent, and other operating costs in Mexican pesos. The subsidiary will remit earnings monthly to the parent.

a. Would Alaska's cash flows be favorably or unfavorably affected if the Mexican peso depreciates over time?

b. Assume that Alaska considers partial financing of this subsidiary with peso loans from Mexican banks instead of providing all the financing with its own funds. Would this alternative form of financing increase, decrease, or have no effect on the degree to which Alaska is exposed to exchange rate movements of the peso?

13. **Hedging Continual Exposure.** Consider this common real-world dilemma faced by many firms that rely on exporting. Clearlake, Inc., produces its products in its factory in Texas and exports most of the products to Mexico each month. The exports are denominated in pesos. Clearlake recognizes that hedging on a monthly basis does not really protect against long-term movements in exchange rates. It also recognizes that it could eliminate its transaction exposure by denominating the exports in pesos, but that it still would have economic exposure (because Mexican consumers would reduce demand if the peso weakened). Clearlake does not know how many pesos it will receive in the future, so it would have difficulty even if a long-term hedging method was available. How can Clearlake realistically deal with this dilemma and reduce its exposure over the long term? [There is no perfect solution, but in the real world, there rarely are perfect solutions.]

INTERNET APPLICATION

14. **Researching MNCs and Exposure** The following website provides annual reports of numerous MNCs: **http://reportgallery.com**

a. Review an annual report of an MNC of your choice. Look for any comments that relate to the MNC's economic or translation exposure. Does it appear that the MNC hedges its economic exposure or translation exposure? If so, what methods does it uses to hedge its exposure?

b. The following website provides exchange rate movements against the dollar over time: **http://www.oanda.com.**

Based on the translation exposure of the MNC you assessed in exercise (a), determine whether the exchange rate movements of whatever currency (or currencies) it is exposed to moved in a favorable or unfavorable direction over the last few months.

DISCUSSION IN THE BOARDROOM

This exercise can be found in Appendix E at the back of this textbook.

RUNNING YOUR OWN MNC

This exercise can be found on the Xtra! website at **http://maduraxtra.swlearning.com**.

BLADES, INC. CASE

Assessment of Economic Exposure

Blades, Inc., has been exporting to Thailand since its decision to supplement its declining U.S. sales by exporting there. Furthermore, Blades has recently begun exporting to a retailer in the United Kingdom. The suppliers of the components needed by Blades for roller blade production (such as rubber and plastic) are located in the United States and Thailand. Blades decided to use Thai suppliers for rubber and plastic components needed to manufacture roller blades because of cost and quality considerations. All of Blades' exports and imports are denominated in the respective foreign currency; for example, Blades pays for the Thai imports in baht.

The decision to export to Thailand was supported by the fact that Thailand had been one of the world's fastest growing economies in recent years. Furthermore, Blades found an importer in Thailand that was willing to commit itself to the annual purchase of 180,000 pairs of Blades' "Speedos," which are among the highest quality roller blades in the world. The commitment began last year and will last another two years, at which time it may be renewed by the two parties.

Due to this commitment, Blades is selling its roller blades for 4,594 baht per pair (approximately $100 at current exchange rates) instead of the usual $120 per pair. Although this price represents a substantial discount from the regular price for a pair of Speedo blades, it still constitutes a considerable markup above cost. Because importers in other Asian countries were not willing to make this type of commitment, this was a decisive factor in the choice of Thailand for exporting purposes. Although Ben Holt, Blades' chief financial officer (CFO), believes the sports product market in Asia has very high future growth potential, Blades has recently begun exporting to Jogs, Ltd., a British retailer. Jogs has committed itself to purchase 200,000 pair of Speedos annually for a fixed price of £80 per pair.

For the coming year, Blades expects to import rubber and plastic components from Thailand sufficient to manufacture 80,000 pairs of Speedos, at a cost of approximately 3,000 baht per pair of Speedos.

You, as Blades' financial analyst, have pointed out to Ben Holt that recent events in Asia have fundamentally affected the economic condition of Asian countries, including Thailand. For example, you have pointed out that the high level of consumer spending on leisure products such as roller blades has declined considerably. Thus, the Thai retailer may not renew its commitment with Blades in two years. Furthermore, you are worried that the current economic conditions in Thailand may lead to a substantial depreciation of the Thai baht, which would affect Blades negatively.

Despite recent developments, however, Ben Holt remains optimistic; he is convinced that Southeast Asia will exhibit high potential for growth when the impact of recent events in Asia subsides. Consequently, Holt has no doubt that the Thai customer will renew its commitment for another three years when the current agreement terminates. In your opinion, Holt is not considering all of the factors that might directly or indirectly affect Blades. Moreover, you are worried that he is ignoring Blades' future in Thailand even if the Thai importer renews its commitment for another three years. In fact, you believe that a renewal of the existing agreement with the Thai customer may affect Blades negatively due to the high level of inflation in Thailand.

Since Holt is interested in your opinion and wants to assess Blades' economic exposure in Thailand, he has asked you to conduct an analysis of the impact of the value of the baht on next year's earnings to assess Blades' economic exposure. You have gathered the following information:

- Blades has forecasted sales in the United States of 520,000 pairs of Speedos at regular prices; exports to Thailand of 180,000 pairs of Speedos for 4,594 baht a pair; and exports to the United Kingdom of 200,000 pairs of Speedos for £80 per pair.
- Cost of goods sold for 80,000 pairs of Speedos are incurred in Thailand; the remainder is incurred in the United States, where the cost of goods sold per pair of Speedos runs approximately $70.
- Fixed costs are $2 million, and variable operating expenses other than costs of goods sold represent approximately 11 percent of U.S. sales. All fixed and variable operating expenses other than cost of goods sold are incurred in the United States.
- Recent events in Asia have increased the uncertainty regarding certain Asian currencies considerably, making it extremely difficult to forecast the value of the baht at which the Thai revenues will be converted. The current spot rate of the baht is $.022, and the current spot rate of the pound is $1.50. You have created three scenarios and derived an expected value on average for the upcoming year based on each scenario:

Scenario	Effect on the Average Value of Baht	Average Value of Baht	Average Value of Pound
1	No change	$.0220	$1.530
2	Depreciate by 5%	.0209	1.485
3	Depreciate by 10%	.0198	1.500

- Blades currently has no debt in its capital structure. However, it may borrow funds in Thailand if it establishes a subsidiary in the country.

Ben Holt has asked you to answer the following questions:

1. How will Blades be negatively affected by the high level of inflation in Thailand if the Thai customer renews its commitment for another three years?
2. Holt believes that the Thai importer will renew its commitment in two years. Do you think his assessment is correct? Why or why not? Also, assume that the Thai economy returns to the high growth level that existed prior to the recent unfavorable economic events. Under this assumption, how likely is

it that the Thai importer will renew its commitment in two years?

3. For each of the three possible values of the Thai baht and the British pound, use a spreadsheet to construct a pro forma income statement for the next year. Briefly comment on the level of Blades' economic exposure.

4. Now repeat your analysis in question 3 but assume that the British pound and the Thai baht are perfectly correlated. For example, if the baht depreciates by 5 percent, the pound will also depreciate by 5 percent. Under this assumption, is Blades subject to a greater degree of economic exposure? Why or why not?

5. Based on your answers to the previous three questions, what actions could Blades take to reduce its level of economic exposure to Thailand?

SMALL BUSINESS DILEMMA

Hedging the Sports Exports Company's Economic Exposure to Exchange Rate Risk

Jim Logan, owner of the Sports Exports Company, remains concerned about his exposure to exchange rate risk. Even if Jim hedges his transactions from one month to another, he recognizes that a long-term trend of depreciation in the British pound could have a severe impact on his firm. He believes that he must continue to focus on the British market for selling his footballs. However, he plans to consider various ways in which he can reduce his economic exposure. At the current time, he obtains material from a local manufacturer and uses a machine to produce the footballs, which are then exported. He still uses his garage as a place of production and would like to continue using his garage to maintain low operating expenses.

1. How could Jim adjust his operations to reduce his economic exposure? What is a possible disadvantage of such an adjustment?

2. Offer another solution to hedging the economic exposure in the long run as Jim's business grows. What are the disadvantages of this solution?

PART 3

Integrative Problem

Exchange Rate Risk Management

Vogl Co. is a U.S. firm conducting a financial plan for the next year. It has no foreign subsidiaries, but more than half of its sales are from exports. Its foreign cash inflows to be received from exporting and cash outflows to be paid for imported supplies over the next year are shown in the following table:

Currency	Total Inflow	Total Outflow
Canadian dollar (C$)	C$32,000,000	C$2,000,000
New Zealand dollar (NZ$)	NZ$5,000,000	NZ$1,000,000
Mexican peso (MXP)	MXP11,000,000	MXP10,000,000
Singapore dollar (S$)	S$4,000,000	S$8,000,000

The spot rates and one-year forward rates as of today are shown below:

Currency	Spot Rate	One-Year Forward Rate
C$	$.90	$.93
NZ$	.60	.59
MXP	.18	.15
S$	.65	.64

Questions

1. Based on the information provided, determine Vogl's net exposure to each foreign currency in dollars.
2. Assume that today's spot rate is used as a forecast of the future spot rate one year from now. The New Zealand dollar, Mexican peso, and Singapore dollar are expected to move in tandem against the U.S. dollar over the next year. The Canadian dollar's movements are expected to be unrelated to movements of the other currencies. Since exchange rates are difficult to predict, the forecasted net dollar cash flows

per currency may be inaccurate. Do you anticipate any offsetting exchange rate effects from whatever exchange movements do occur? Explain.

3. Given the forecast of the Canadian dollar along with the forward rate of the Canadian dollar, what is the expected increase or decrease in dollar cash flows that would result from hedging the net cash flows in Canadian dollars? Would you hedge the Canadian dollar position?
4. Assume that the Canadian dollar net inflows may range from C$20,000,000 to C$40,000,000 over the next year. Explain the risk of hedging C$30,000,000 in net inflows. How can Vogl Co. avoid such a risk? Is there any tradeoff resulting from your strategy to avoid that risk?
5. Vogl Co. recognizes that its year-to-year hedging strategy hedges the risk only over a given year and does not insulate it from long-term trends in the Canadian dollar's value. It has considered establishing a subsidiary in Canada. The goods would be sent from the United States to the Canadian subsidiary and distributed by the subsidiary. The proceeds received would be reinvested by the Canadian subsidiary in Canada. In this way, Vogl Co. would not have to convert Canadian dollars to U.S. dollars each year. Has Vogl eliminated its exposure to exchange rate risk by using this strategy? Explain.

PART 4

Long-Term Asset and Liability Management

Part 4 (Chapters 13 through 18) focuses on how multinational corporations (MNCs) manage long-term assets and liabilities. Chapter 13 explains how MNCs can benefit from international business. Chapter 14 describes the information MNCs must have when considering multinational projects and demonstrates how the capital budgeting analysis is conducted. Chapter 15 identifies the common forms of multinational restructuring and illustrates how to assess the feasibility of proposed forms of restructuring. Chapter 16 explains how MNCs assess country risk associated with their prevailing projects as well as with their proposed projects. Chapter 17 explains the capital structure decision for MNCs, which affects the cost of financing new projects. Chapter 18 describes the MNC's long-term financing decision.

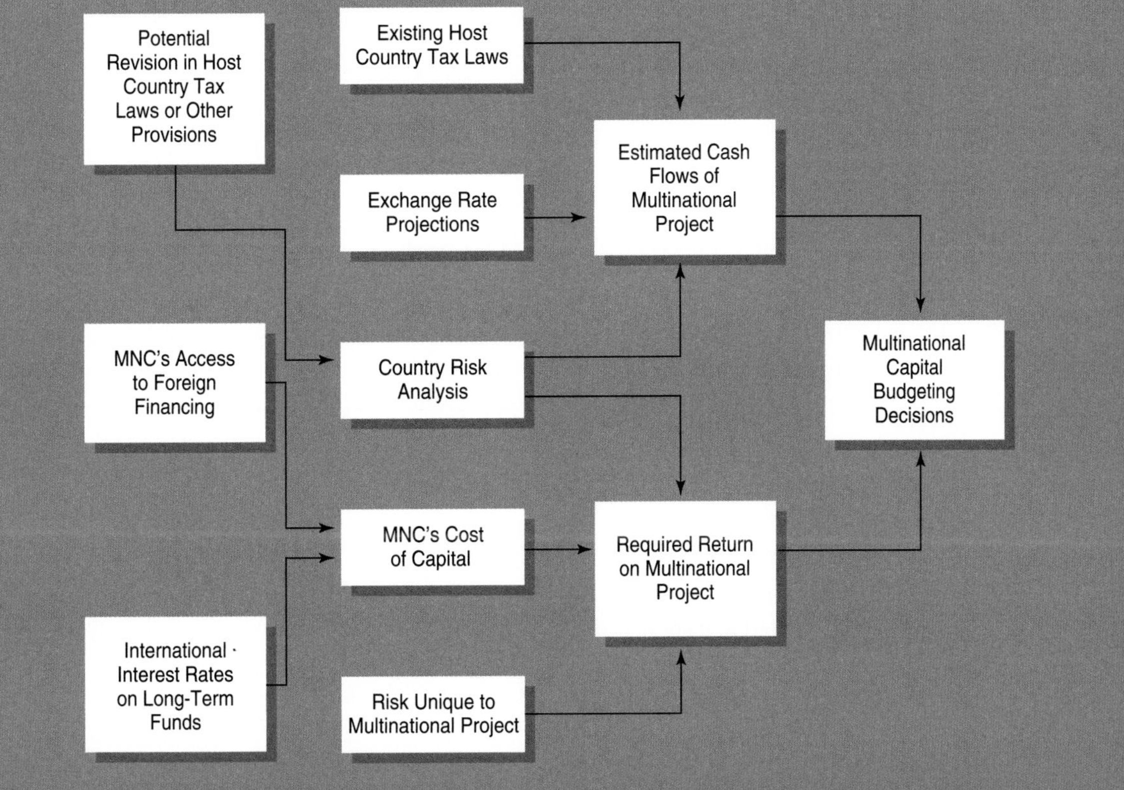

CHAPTER 13

Direct Foreign Investment

MNCs commonly capitalize on foreign business opportunities by engaging in **direct foreign investment (DFI)**, which is investment in real assets (such as land, buildings, or even existing plants) in foreign countries. They engage in joint ventures with foreign firms, acquire foreign firms, and form new foreign subsidiaries. Any of these types of DFI can generate high returns when managed properly. However, DFI requires a substantial investment and can therefore put much capital at risk. Moreover, if the investment does not perform as well as expected, the MNC may have difficulty selling the foreign project it created. Given these return and risk characteristics of DFI, MNCs tend to carefully analyze the potential benefits and costs before implementing any type of DFI. Financial managers must understand the potential return and risk associated with DFI so that they can make investment decisions that maximize the MNC's value.

The specific objectives of this chapter are to:

- describe common motives for initiating direct foreign investment and
- illustrate the benefits of international diversification.

Motives for Direct Foreign Investment

MNCs commonly consider direct foreign investment because it can improve their profitability and enhance shareholder wealth. In most cases, MNCs engage in DFI because they are interested in boosting revenues, reducing costs, or both.

Revenue-Related Motives

The following are typical motives of MNCs that are attempting to boost revenues:

- *Attract new sources of demand.* A corporation often reaches a stage when growth is limited in its home country, possibly because of intense competition. Even if it faces little competition, its market share in its home country may already be near its potential peak. Thus, the firm may consider foreign markets where there is potential demand. Many developing countries, such as Argentina, Chile, Mexico, Hungary, and China, have been perceived as attractive sources of new demand. Many MNCs have penetrated these countries since barriers have been removed. Because the consumers in some countries have historically been restricted from purchasing goods produced by firms outside their countries, the markets for some goods are not well established and offer much potential for penetration by MNCs.

EXAMPLE

Blockbuster Entertainment Corp. has recently established video stores in Australia, Chile, Japan, and several European countries where the video-rental concept is relatively new. With over 2,000 stores in the United States, Blockbuster's growth potential in the United States was limited.

China has also attracted MNCs. Motorola recently invested more than $1 billion in joint ventures in China. The Coca-Cola Co. has invested about $500 million in bottling facilities in China, and PepsiCo has invested about $200 million in bottling facilities. Yum Brands has KFC franchises and Pizza Hut franchises in China. Other MNCs, such as Ford Motor Co., United Technologies, General Electric, Hewlett-Packard, and IBM, have also invested more than $100 million in China to attract demand by consumers there.

- *Enter profitable markets.* If other corporations in the industry have proved that superior earnings can be realized in other markets, an MNC may also decide to sell in those markets. It may plan to undercut the prevailing, excessively high prices. A common problem with this strategy is that previously established sellers in a new market may prevent a new competitor from taking away their business by lowering their prices just when the new competitor attempts to break into this market.
- *Exploit monopolistic advantages.* Firms may become internationalized if they possess resources or skills not available to competing firms. If a firm possesses advanced technology and has exploited this advantage successfully in local markets, the firm may attempt to exploit it internationally as well. In fact, the firm may have a more distinct advantage in markets that have less advanced technology.
- *React to trade restrictions.* In some cases, MNCs use DFI as a defensive rather than an aggressive strategy. Specifically, MNCs may pursue DFI to circumvent trade barriers.

EXAMPLE

Japanese automobile manufacturers established plants in the United States in anticipation that their exports to the United States would be subject to more stringent trade restrictions. Japanese companies recognized that trade barriers could be established that would limit or prohibit their exports. By producing automobiles in the United States, Japanese manufacturers could circumvent trade barriers.

- *Diversify internationally.* Since economies of countries do not move perfectly in tandem over time, net cash flow from sales of products across countries should be more stable than comparable sales of the products in a single country. By diversifying sales (and possibly even production) internationally, a firm can make its net cash flows less volatile. Thus, the possibility of a liquidity deficiency is less likely. In addition, the firm may enjoy a lower cost of capital as shareholders and creditors perceive the MNC's risk to be lower as a result of more stable cash flows. Potential benefits to MNCs that diversify internationally are examined more thoroughly later in the chapter.

EXAMPLE

In 2001, several technology firms experienced weak sales because of reduced U.S. demand for their products. They responded by increasing their expansion in foreign markets. AT&T, Lucent Technologies, and Nortel Networks pursued new business in China. U.S. Technology planned substantial expansion in Europe and Asia. IBM increased its presence in China, India, South Korea, and Taiwan. Cisco Systems expanded substantially in China, Japan, and South Korea. Foreign expansion diversifies an MNC's sources of revenue and thus reduces its reliance on the U.S. economy.

Cost-Related Motives

MNCs also engage in DFI in an effort to reduce costs. The following are typical motives of MNCs that are trying to cut costs:

- *Fully benefit from economies of scale.* A corporation that attempts to sell its primary product in new markets may increase its earnings and shareholder wealth due to **economies of scale** (lower average cost per unit resulting from increased production). Firms that utilize much machinery are most likely to benefit from economies of scale.

EXAMPLE

The removal of trade barriers by the Single European Act allowed MNCs to achieve greater economies of scale. Some U.S.-based MNCs consolidated their European plants because the removal of tariffs between countries in the European Union (EU) enabled firms to achieve economies of scale at a single European plant without incurring excessive exporting costs. The act also enhanced economies of scale by making regulations on television ads, automobile standards, and other products and services uniform across the EU. As a result, Colgate-Palmolive Co. and other MNCs are manufacturing more homogeneous products that can be sold in all EU countries. The adoption of the euro also encouraged consolidation by eliminating exchange rate risk within these countries.

- *Use foreign factors of production.* Labor and land costs can vary dramatically among countries. MNCs often attempt to set up production in locations where land and labor are cheap. Due to market imperfections (as discussed in Chapter 1) such as imperfect information, relocation transaction costs, and barriers to industry entry, specific labor costs do not necessarily become equal among markets. Thus, it is worthwhile for MNCs to survey markets to determine whether they can benefit from cheaper costs by producing in those markets.

EXAMPLE

Many U.S.-based MNCs, including Black & Decker, Eastman Kodak, Ford Motor Co., and General Electric, have established subsidiaries in Mexico to achieve lower labor costs.

Mexico has attracted almost $8 billion in DFI from firms in the automobile industry, primarily because of the low-cost labor. Mexican workers at General Motors' subsidiaries who manufacture sedans and trucks earn daily wages that are less than the average hourly rate for similar workers in the United States. Ford is also producing trucks at subsidiaries based in Mexico.

Non-U.S. automobile manufacturers are also capitalizing on the low-cost labor in Mexico. Volkswagen of Germany produces its Beetle in Mexico. DaimlerChrysler of Germany manufactures its 12-wheeler trucks in Mexico, and Nissan Motor Co. of Japan produces some of its wagons in Mexico.

Other Japanese companies are also increasingly using Mexico and other low-wage countries for production. For example, Sony Corp. recently established a plant in Tijuana. Matsushita Electrical Industrial Co. has a large plant in Tijuana.

Baxter International has established manufacturing plants in Mexico and Malaysia to capitalize on lower costs of production (primarily wage rates). Honeywell has joint ventures in countries such as Korea and India where production costs are low. It has also established subsidiaries in countries where production costs are low, such as Mexico, Malaysia, Hong Kong, and Taiwan.

- *Use foreign raw materials.* Due to transportation costs, a corporation may attempt to avoid importing raw materials from a given country, especially when it plans to sell the finished product back to consumers in that country. Under such circumstances, a more feasible solution may be to develop the product in the country where the raw materials are located.
- *Use foreign technology.* Corporations are increasingly establishing overseas plants or acquiring existing overseas plants to learn the technology of foreign countries. This technology is then used to improve their own production processes and increase production efficiency at all subsidiary plants around the world.
- *React to exchange rate movements.* When a firm perceives that a foreign currency is undervalued, the firm may consider DFI in that country, as the initial outlay should be relatively low.

A related reason for such DFI is to offset the changing demand for a company's exports due to exchange rate fluctuations. For example, when Japanese automobile manufacturers build plants in the United States, they can reduce exposure to exchange rate fluctuations by incurring dollar costs for their production that offset dollar revenues. Although MNCs do not engage in large projects simply as an indirect means of speculating on currencies, the feasibility of proposed projects may be dependent on existing and expected exchange rate movements.

Cost-Related Motives in the Expanded European Union. Several countries that became part of the European Union in 2004 were targeted for new DFI by MNCs that wanted to reduce manufacturing costs.

EXAMPLE

General Motors expanded its production in Poland, Peugot increased its production in the Czech Republic, Toyota expanded its production in Slovakia, Audi expanded in Hungary, and Renault expanded in Romania. Volkswagen recently expanded its capacity in Slovenia, and cut some jobs in Spain. While it originally established operations in Spain because the wages were about half of those in Germany, wages in Slovenia are less than half of those in Spain. The expansion of the EU allows new member countries to transport products throughout Europe at reduced tariffs.

The shifts to low-wage countries will make manufacturers more efficient and competitive, but the tradeoff is thousands of jobs lost in Western Europe. However, it may be argued that the high unionized wages encouraged the firms to seek growth in productivity elsewhere. European labor unions tend to fight layoffs, but recognize that manufacturers might move completely out of the Western European countries where unions have more leverage, and move into the low-wage countries in Eastern Europe.

http://

Visit Morgan Stanley's Global Economic Forum at http://www.morganstanley.com/GEFdata/digests/latest-digest.html for analyses, discussions, statistics, and forecasts related to non-U.S. economies.

Comparing Benefits of DFI among Countries

The optimal way for a firm to penetrate a foreign market is partially dependent on the characteristics of the market. For example, direct foreign investment by U.S. firms is common in Europe but not so common in Asia, where the people are accustomed to purchasing products from Asians. Thus, licensing arrangements or joint ventures may be more appropriate when firms are expanding into Asia.

Exhibit 13.1 summarizes the possible benefits of DFI and explains how MNCs can use DFI to achieve those benefits. Most MNCs pursue DFI based on their expectations of capitalizing on one or more of the potential benefits summarized in Exhibit 13.1. Although most attempts to increase international business are motivated by one or more of the benefits listed here, some disadvantages are also associated with DFI.

USING THE WEB

DFI Indicators Information about economic growth and other macroeconomic indicators used when considering direct foreign investment is provided for each country at http://biz.yahoo.com/ifc/. Click on any country listed, and then click on Country Fact Sheet. Estimates of the country's population, gross domestic product (GDP), GDP growth rate, and GDP per person are shown. In addition, information about the country's political structure and policy issues is provided.

Exhibit 13.1 Summary of Motives for Direct Foreign Investment

	Means of Using DFI to Achieve This Benefit
Revenue-Related Motives	
1. Attract new sources of demand.	Establish a subsidiary or acquire a competitor in a new market.
2. Enter markets where superior profits are possible.	Acquire a competitor that has controlled its local market.
3. Exploit monopolistic advantages.	Establish a subsidiary in a market where competitors are unable to produce the identical product; sell products in that country.
4. React to trade restrictions.	Establish a subsidiary in a market where tougher trade restrictions will adversely affect the firm's export volume.
5. Diversify internationally.	Establish subsidiaries in markets whose business cycles differ from those where existing subsidiaries are based.
Cost-Related Motives	
6. Fully benefit from economies of scale.	Establish a subsidiary in a new market that can sell products produced elsewhere; this allows for increased production and possibly greater production efficiency.
7. Use foreign factors of production.	Establish a subsidiary in a market that has relatively low costs of labor or land; sell the finished product to countries where the cost of production is higher.
8. Use foreign raw materials.	Establish a subsidiary in a market where raw materials are cheap and accessible; sell the finished product to countries where the raw materials are more expensive.
9. Use foreign technology.	Participate in a joint venture in order to learn about a production process or other operations.
10. React to exchange rate movements.	Establish a subsidiary in a new market where the local currency is weak but is expected to strengthen over time.

EXAMPLE

Iowa Co., a large clothing manufacturer, wants to pursue DFI in the Philippines or Mexico because the cost of producing its clothing will be much lower in either country. Iowa Co. determines that the direct costs of production would be lower in the Philippines. However, there are some other indirect costs of DFI that should also be considered. Iowa Co. determines that economic conditions in the Philippines are uncertain, that government restrictions might be imposed on a subsidiary there, and that inflation and exchange rate movements might be unfavorable. Most importantly, the safety of employees who would be sent there to manage the subsidiary might be threatened by terrorist groups. After considering all the costs, Iowa Co. decides not to pursue DFI in Mexico.

USING THE WEB

Direct Foreign Investment Valuable updated country data that can be considered when making DFI decisions is provided at http://www.worldbank.org.

Comparing Benefits of DFI over Time

As conditions change over time, so do possible benefits from pursuing direct foreign investment in various countries. Thus, some countries may become more attractive targets while other countries become less attractive. The choice of target countries for DFI has changed over time. Canada now receives a smaller proportion of total DFI than it received in the past, while Europe, Latin America, and Asia receive a larger proportion than in the past. More than one-half of all DFI by U.S. firms is in European countries. The opening of the Eastern European countries and the expansion of the EU account for some of the increased DFI in Europe, especially Eastern Europe. The increased focus on Latin America is partially attributed to its high economic growth, which has encouraged MNCs to capitalize on new sources of demand for their products. In addition, MNCs have targeted Latin America and Asia to use factors of production that are less expensive in foreign countries than in the United States.

MANAGING FOR VALUE

Yahoo!'s Decision to Expand in Taiwan

Since Yahoo! successfully created a portal in the United States, it has engaged in direct foreign investment so that it can capitalize on its technology in foreign markets. By 2000, it had successfully established portals in Europe and Asia. However, it believed that it could improve its presence in Asia by focusing on the Greater China area. China has much potential because of its population base, but it also imposes restrictions that discourage DFI by firms. Meanwhile, Kimo, a privately held company and the leading portal in Taiwan, was planning to grow throughout Asia. It had 4 million registered users in Taiwan and had considered an initial public offering in the United States to support its growth, but gave up that idea when technology valuations declined substantially, preventing Kimo from offering shares at a high price. In November 2000, Yahoo! agreed to acquire Kimo for about $150 million. Since the acquisition occurred at a time when Internet stock valuations were reduced, Yahoo! was able to purchase Kimo at a relatively low price. With this DFI, Yahoo! not only established a presence in Taiwan, but also established a link to mainland China. By timing its international expansion to a period when the cost (initial outlay) was low, Yahoo! was able to maximize its value.

Last year Georgia Co. contemplated DFI in Thailand, where it would produce and sell cell phones. It decided that costs were too high. Now it is reconsidering because costs in Thailand have declined. Georgia could lease office space at a low cost. It could also purchase a manufacturing plant at a lower cost because factories that recently failed are standing empty. In addition, the Thai baht has depreciated substantially against the dollar recently, so Georgia Co. could invest in Thailand at a time when the dollar can be exchanged at a favorable exchange rate.

Georgia Co. also dicovers, however, that while the cost-related characteristics have improved, the revenue-related characteristics are now less desirable. A new subsidiary in Thailand might not attract new sources of demand due to the country's weak economy. In addition, Georgia might be unable to earn excessive profits there because the weak economy might force existing firms to keep their prices very low in order to survive. Georgia Co. must compare the favorable aspects of DFI in Thailand with the unfavorable aspects by using multinational capital budgeting, which is explained in the following chapter.

Benefits of International Diversification

An international project can reduce a firm's overall risk as a result of international diversification benefits. The key to international diversification is selecting foreign projects whose performance levels are not highly correlated over time. In this way, the various international projects should not experience poor performance simultaneously.

Merrimack Co., a U.S. firm, plans to invest in a new project in either the United States or the United Kingdom. Once the project is completed, it will constitute 30 percent of the firm's total funds invested in itself. The remaining 70 percent of its investment in its business is exclusively in the United States. Characteristics of the proposed project are forecasted for a five-year period for both a U.S. and a British location, as shown in Exhibit 13.2.

Merrimack Co. plans to assess the feasibility of each proposed project based on expected risk and return, using a five-year time horizon. Its expected annual after-tax return on investment on its prevailing business is 20 percent, and its variability of returns (as measured by the standard deviation) is expected to be .10. The firm can assess its expected overall performance based on developing the project in the United States and in

Exhibit 13.2 Evaluation of Proposed Projects in Alternative Locations

	Characteristics of Proposed Project	
	If Located in the United States	If Located in the United Kingdom
Mean expected annual return on investment (after taxes)	25%	25%
Standard deviation of expected annual after-tax returns on investment	.09	.11
Correlation of expected annual after-tax returns on investment with after-tax returns of prevailing U.S. business	.80	.02

the United Kingdom. In doing so, it is essentially comparing two portfolios. In the first portfolio, 70 percent of its total funds are invested in its prevailing U.S. business, with the remaining 30 percent invested in a new project located in the United States. In the second portfolio, again 70 percent of the firm's total funds are invested in its prevailing business, but the remaining 30 percent are invested in a new project located in the United Kingdom. Therefore, 70 percent of the portfolios' investments are identical. The difference is in the remaining 30 percent of funds invested.

If the new project is located in the United States, the firm's overall expected after-tax return (r_p) is

r_p =	[(70%)	×	(20%)]	+	[(30%)	×	(25%)]	=	21.5%
	% of funds invested in prevailing business		**Expected return on prevailing business**		**% of funds invested in new U.S. project**		**Expected return on new U.S. project**		**Firm's overall expected return**

This computation is based on weighting the returns according to the percentage of total funds invested in each investment.

If the firm calculates its overall expected return with the new project located in the United Kingdom instead of the United States, the results are unchanged. This is because the new project's expected return is the same regardless of the country of location. Therefore, in terms of return, neither new project has an advantage.

With regard to risk, the new project is expected to exhibit slightly less variability in returns during the five-year period if it is located in the United States (see Exhibit 13.2). Since firms typically prefer more stable returns on their investments, this is an advantage. However, estimating the risk of the individual project without considering the overall firm would be a mistake. The expected correlation of the new project's returns with those of the prevailing business must also be considered. Recall that portfolio variance is determined by the individual variability of each component as well as their pair-wise correlations. The variance of a portfolio (σ_p^2) composed of only two investments (A and B) is computed as

$$\sigma_p^2 = w_A^2\sigma_A^2 + w_B^2\sigma_B^2 + 2w_A w_B \sigma_A \sigma_B (CORR_{AB})$$

where w_A and w_B represent the percentage of total funds allocated to Investments A and B, respectively; σ_A and σ_B are the standard deviations of returns on Investments A and B, respectively, and $CORR_{AB}$ is the correlation coefficient of returns between Investments A and B. This equation for portfolio variance can be applied to the problem at hand. The portfolio reflects the overall firm. First, compute the overall firm's variance in returns assuming it locates the new project in the United States (based on the information provided in Exhibit 13.2). This variance (σ_p^2) is

$$\begin{aligned}\sigma_p^2 &= (.70)^2(.10)^2 + (.30)^2(.09)^2 + 2(.70)(.30)(.10)(.09)(.80)\\ &= (.49)(.01) + (.09)(.0081) + .003024\\ &= .0049 + .000729 + .003024\\ &= .008653\end{aligned}$$

If Merrimack Co. decides to locate the new project in the United Kingdom instead of the United States, its overall variability in returns will be different, because that project differs from the new U.S. project in terms of individual variability in returns and correlation with the prevailing business. The overall variability of the firm's returns based on locating the new project in the United Kingdom is estimated by variance in the portfolio returns (σ_p^2):

$$\begin{aligned}\sigma_p^2 &= (.70)^2(.10)^2 + (.30)^2(.11)^2 + 2(.70)(.30)(.10)(.11)(.02)\\ &= (.49)(.01) + (.09)(.0121) + .0000924\\ &= .0049 + .001089 + .0000924\\ &= .0060814\end{aligned}$$

Thus, Merrimack will generate more stable returns if the new project is located in the United Kingdom. The firm's overall variability in returns is almost 29.7 percent less if the new project is located in the United Kingdom rather than in the United States.

The variability is reduced when locating in the foreign country because of the correlation of the new project's expected returns with the expected returns of the prevailing business. If the new project is located in Merrimack's home country (the United States), its returns are expected to be more highly correlated with those of the prevailing business than they would be if the project was located in the United Kingdom. When economic conditions of two countries (such as the United States and the United Kingdom) are not highly correlated, then a firm may reduce its risk by diversifying its business in both countries instead of concentrating in just one.

Diversification Analysis of International Projects

Like any investor, an MNC with projects positioned around the world is concerned with the risk and return characteristics of the projects. The portfolio of all projects reflects the MNC in aggregate.

EXAMPLE

Virginia, Inc., considers a global strategy of developing projects as shown in Exhibit 13.3. Each point on the graph reflects a specific project that either has been implemented or is being considered. The return axis may be measured by potential return on assets or return on equity. The risk may be measured by potential fluctuation in the returns generated by each project.

Exhibit 13.3 shows that Project A has the highest expected return of all the projects. While Virginia, Inc., could devote most of its resources toward this project to attempt to achieve such a high return, its risk is possibly too high by itself. In addition, such a project may not be able to absorb all available capital anyway if its potential market for customers is limited. Thus, Virginia, Inc., develops a portfolio of projects. By combining Project A with several other projects, Virginia, Inc., may decrease its expected return. On the other hand, it may also reduce its risk substantially.

If Virginia, Inc., appropriately combines projects, its project portfolio may be able to achieve a risk-return tradeoff exhibited by any of the points on the curve in Exhibit 13.3. This curve represents a frontier of efficient project portfolios that exhibit desirable risk-return characteristics, in that no single project could outperform any of these portfolios. The term *efficient* refers to a minimum risk for a given expected return. Project portfolios outperform the individual projects considered by Virginia, Inc., be-

http://

The CIA's home page at http://www.cia.gov provides a link to the *World Factbook*, which has valuable information about countries that MNCs might be considering for direct foreign investment.

Exhibit 13.3
Risk-Return Analysis of International Projects

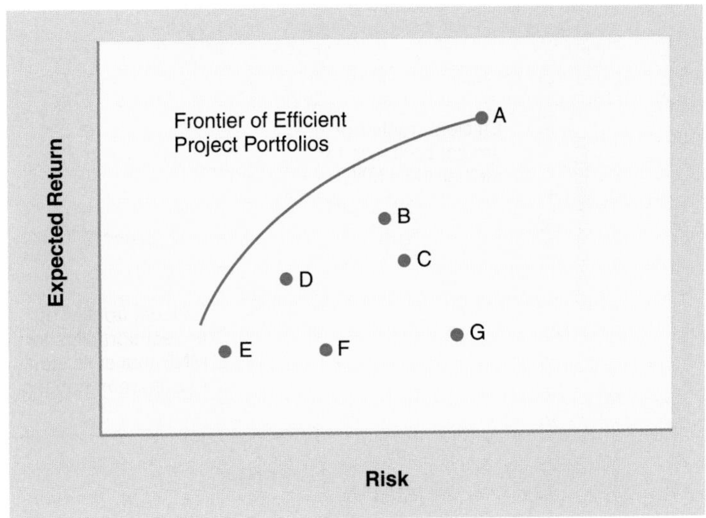

http://

The U.S. Treasury website http://www.treasury.gov has links to international information that should be considered by MNCs that are considering direct foreign investment.

cause of the diversification attributes discussed earlier. The lower, or more negative, the correlation in project returns over time, the lower will be the project portfolio risk. As new projects are proposed, the frontier of efficient project portfolios available to Virginia, Inc., may shift.

Comparing Portfolios along the Frontier. Along the frontier of efficient project portfolios, no portfolio can be singled out as "optimal" for all MNCs. This is because MNCs vary in their willingness to accept risk. If the MNC is very conservative and has the choice of any portfolios represented by the frontier in Exhibit 13.3, it will probably prefer one that exhibits low risk (near the bottom of the frontier). Conversely, a more aggressive strategy would be to implement a portfolio of projects that exhibits risk-return characteristics such as those near the top of the frontier.

Comparing Frontiers among MNCs. The actual location of the frontier of efficient project portfolios depends on the business in which the firm is involved. Some MNCs have frontiers of possible project portfolios that are more desirable than the frontiers of other MNCs.

EXAMPLE

Eurosteel, Inc., sells steel solely to European nations and is considering other related projects. Its frontier of efficient project portfolios exhibits considerable risk (because it sells just one product to countries whose economies move in tandem). In contrast, Global Products, Inc., which sells a wide range of products to countries all over the world, has a lower degree of project portfolio risk. Therefore, its frontier of efficient project portfolios is closer to the vertical axis. This comparison is illustrated in Exhibit 13.4. Of course, this comparison assumes that Global Products, Inc., is knowledgeable about all of its products and the markets where it sells.

Our discussion suggests that MNCs can achieve more desirable risk-return characteristics from their project portfolios if they sufficiently diversify among products and geographic markets. This also relates to the advantage an MNC has over a purely domestic firm with only a local market. The MNC may be able to develop a more efficient portfolio of projects than its domestic counterpart.

Exhibit 13.4
Risk-Return Advantage of a Diversified MNC

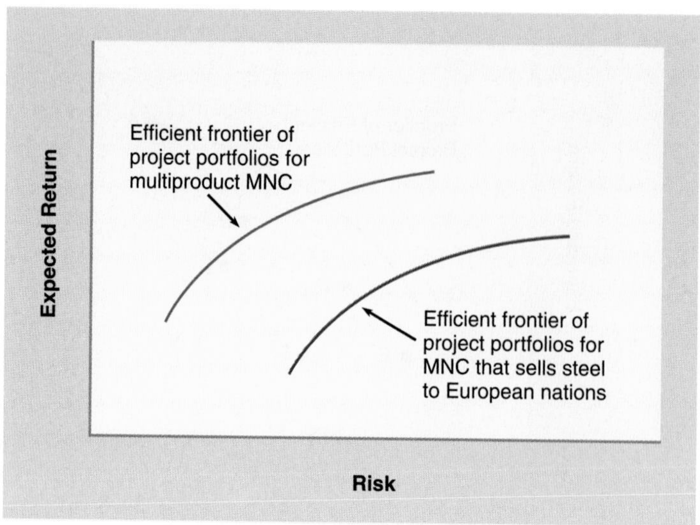

Diversification among Countries

Exhibit 13.5 shows the growth in the inflation-adjusted gross domestic product (GDP) for six major countries. Notice that the growth rates vary among countries, which suggests that MNCs may be able to reduce their exposure to economic conditions by spreading their business among various economies. This strategy reduces the proportion of their business that may be subject to a weak economy at any point in time. In some periods, however, countries may simultaneously experience a recession, so even MNCs that are diversified across countries will be highly exposed to weak economic conditions. Exhibit 13.5 shows that in the 2001–2002 period, most countries experienced relatively weak economic growth.

Decisions Subsequent to DFI

Once direct foreign investment takes place, periodic decisions are necessary to determine whether further expansion should take place in a given location. In addition, as the project generates earnings, the MNC must decide whether to have the funds remitted to the parent or used by the subsidiary. If the subsidiary has a use for the funds that would be of more value than the parent's use, the subsidiary should retain the funds. Of course, a certain percentage of the funds will be needed to maintain operations, but the remaining funds can be sent to the parent, sent to another subsidiary, or reinvested for expansion purposes.

Facts relevant to the decision of whether the subsidiary should reinvest the earnings should be analyzed on a case-by-case basis. The appropriate decision depends on the economic conditions in the subsidiary's country and the parent's country, as well as restrictions imposed by the host country government.

Exhibit 13.5 Comparison of Economic Growth (Annualized) Among Countries

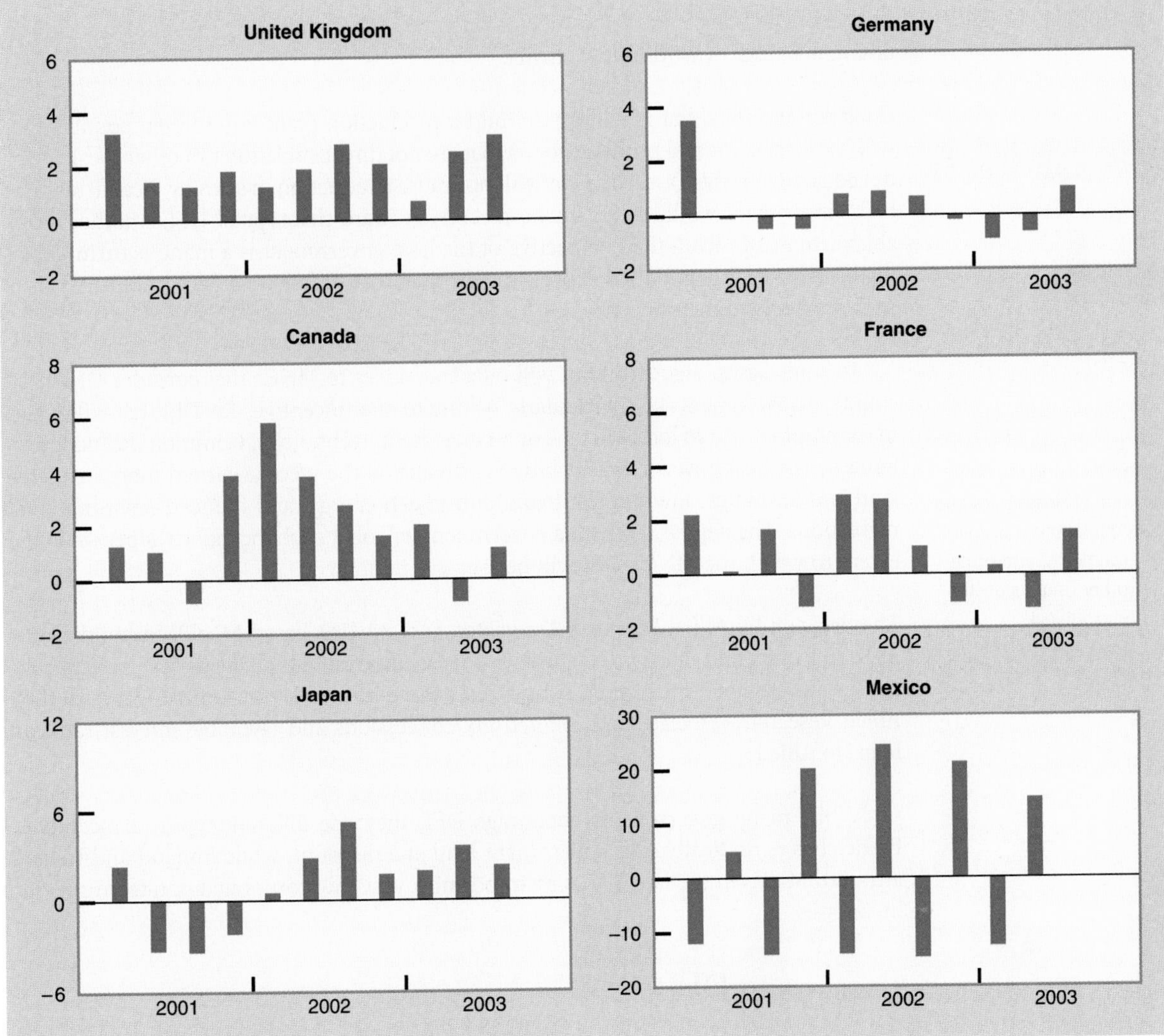

USING THE WEB

DFI Information for a Particular Country Direct foreign investment in specific countries can be assessed by reviewing websites focused on those countries. For example, conditions in China are described at http://www.business-china.com.

Host Government Views of DFI

Each government must weigh the advantages and disadvantages of direct foreign investment in its country. It may provide incentives to encourage some forms of DFI, barriers to prevent other forms of DFI, and impose conditions on some other forms of DFI.

Incentives to Encourage DFI

The ideal DFI solves problems such as unemployment and lack of technology without taking business away from local firms.

EXAMPLE

Consider an MNC that is willing to build a production plant in a foreign country that will use local labor and produce goods that are not direct substitutes of other locally produced goods. In this case, the plant will not cause a reduction in sales by local firms. The host government would normally be receptive toward this type of DFI. Another desirable form of DFI from the perspective of the host government is a manufacturing plant that uses local labor and then exports the products (assuming no other local firm exports such products to the same areas).

http://

The Price Waterhouse Coopers site at http://www.pwcglobal.com provides access to country-specific information such as general business rules and regulations, tax environments, and some other useful statistics and surveys.

In some cases, a government will offer incentives to MNCs that consider DFI in its country. Governments are particularly willing to offer incentives for DFI that will result in the employment of local citizens or an increase in technology. Common incentives offered by the host government include tax breaks on the income earned there, rent-free land and buildings, low-interest loans, subsidized energy, and reduced environmental regulations. The degree to which a government will offer such incentives depends on the extent to which the MNC's DFI will benefit that country.

EXAMPLE

The decision by Allied Research Associates, Inc., (a U.S.-based MNC), to build a production facility and office in Belgium was highly motivated by Belgian government subsidies. The Belgian government subsidized a large portion of the expenses incurred by Allied Research Associates and offered tax concessions and favorable interest rates on loans to Allied.

While many governments encourage DFI, they use different types of incentives. France has periodically sold government land at a discount, while Finland and Ireland attracted MNCs in the late 1990s by imposing a very low corporate tax rate on specific businesses.

Barriers to DFI

Governments are less anxious to encourage DFI that adversely affects locally owned companies, unless they believe that the increased competition is needed to serve consumers. Therefore, they tend to closely regulate any DFI that may affect local firms, consumers, and economic conditions.

Barriers That Protect Local Firms or Consumers. When MNCs consider engaging in DFI by acquiring a foreign company, they may face various barriers imposed by host government agencies. All countries have one or more government agencies that monitor mergers and acquisitions. The acquisition activity in any given country is influenced by the regulations enforced by these agencies.

EXAMPLE

In France, the Treasury can reject any deal if the acquirer is based outside the European Union. The French government may also reject a deal if the target is in some closely monitored industry, such as defense or health care. The Monopolies Commission of France also reviews acquisitions to prevent any combined firms from controlling more than 25 percent of an industry or from severely reducing competition.

The European Union Commission assesses mergers that may affect competition in Europe. The EU Commission rejected the merger between General Electric and Honeywell because it believed that the merger would have resulted in a monopoly.

Acquisitions in Japan are reviewed by the Fair Trade Commission. Japan has historically imposed barriers to discourage international acquisitions. Recently, however, these barriers have been reduced (as long as the Japanese target is agreeable), enabling U.S.-based MNCs such as Corning Glass Works, Data General, Eastman Kodak, and Motorola to acquire Japanese firms.

Acquisitions in the United States are also reviewed by several agencies, including the Securities and Exchange Commission, which regulates the conduct of acquisitions, and the Justice Department and Federal Trade Commission, which analyze the potential impact on competition.

Barriers That Restrict Ownership. Some governments restrict foreign ownership of local firms. Such restrictions may limit or prevent international acquisitions.

EXAMPLE

Many governments in Asia and Latin America have traditionally restricted foreign majority ownership. In recent years, however, these restrictions have been reduced. Governments of Asian countries removed restrictions on international acquisitions during the Asian crisis to encourage MNCs to develop new business there. Mexico also recently announced that it would allow foreign companies to own 100 percent of their subsidiaries established in Mexico.

"Red Tape" Barriers. An implicit barrier to DFI in some countries is the "red tape" involved, such as procedural and documentation requirements. An MNC pursuing DFI is subject to a different set of requirements in each country. Therefore, it is difficult for an MNC to become proficient at the process unless it concentrates on DFI within a single foreign country. The current efforts to make regulations uniform across Europe have simplified the paperwork required to acquire European firms.

Industry Barriers. The local firms of some industries in particular countries have substantial influence on the government and will likely use their influence to prevent competition from MNCs that attempt DFI. MNCs that consider DFI need to recognize the influence that these local firms have on the local government.

Political Instability. The governments of some countries may prevent DFI. If a country is susceptible to abrupt changes in government and political conflicts, the feasibility of DFI may be dependent on the outcome of those conflicts. MNCs want to avoid a situation in which they pursue DFI under a government that is likely to be removed after the DFI occurs.

Government-Imposed Conditions to Engage in DFI

Some governments allow international acquisitions but impose special requirements on MNCs that desire to acquire a local firm. For example, the MNC may be required to ensure pollution control for its manufacturing or to structure the business to export the products it produces so that it does not threaten the market share of other local firms. The MNC may even be required to retain all the employees of the target firm so that unemployment and general economic conditions in the country are not adversely affected.

EXAMPLE

Mexico requires that a specified minimum proportion of parts used to produce automobiles there are made in Mexico. The proportion is lower for automobiles that are to be exported.

Spain's government allowed Ford Motor Co. to set up production facilities in Spain only if it would abide by certain provisions. These included limiting Ford's local sales volume to 10 percent of the previous year's local automobile sales. In addition, two-thirds of the total volume of automobiles produced by Ford in Spain must be exported. The idea behind these provisions was to create jobs for workers in Spain without seriously affecting local competitors. Allowing a subsidiary that primarily exports its product achieved this objective.

Government-imposed conditions do not necessarily prevent an MNC from pursuing DFI in a specific foreign country, but they can be costly. Thus, MNCs should be willing to consider DFI that requires costly conditions only if the potential benefits outweigh the costs.

SUMMARY

- MNCs may be motivated to initiate direct foreign investment in order to attract new sources of demand or to enter markets where superior profits are possible. These two motives are normally based on opportunities to generate more revenue in foreign markets. Other motives for using DFI are typically related to cost efficiency, such as using foreign factors of production, raw materials, or technology. In addition MNCs may engage in DFI to protect their foreign market share, to react to exchange rate movements, or to avoid trade restrictions.
- International diversification is a common motive for direct foreign investment. It allows an MNC to reduce its exposure to domestic economic conditions. In this way, the MNC may be able to stabilize its cash flows and reduce its risk. Such a goal is desirable because it may reduce the firm's cost of financing. International projects may allow MNCs to achieve lower risk than is possible from only domestic projects without reducing their expected returns. International diversification tends to be better able to reduce risk when the DFI is targeted to countries whose economies are somewhat unrelated to an MNC's home country economy.

POINT COUNTER-POINT

Should MNCs Avoid DFI in Countries with Liberal Child Labor Laws?

Point Yes. An MNC should maintain its hiring standards, regardless of what country it is in. Even if a foreign country allows children to work, an MNC should not lower its standards. Although the MNC forgoes the use of low-cost labor, it maintains its global credibility.

Counter-Point No. An MNC will not only benefit its shareholders, but will create employment for some children who need support. The MNC can provide reasonable working conditions and perhaps may even offer educational programs for its employees.

Who Is Correct? Use InfoTrac or some other search engine to learn more about this issue. Which argument do you support? Offer your own opinion on this issue.

SELF TEST

Answers are provided in Appendix A at the back of the text.

1. Offer some reasons why U.S. firms might prefer to direct their direct foreign investment (DFI) to Canada rather than Mexico.
2. Offer some reasons why U.S. firms might prefer to direct their DFI to Mexico rather than Canada.
3. One U.S. executive said that Europe was not considered as a location for DFI because of the euro's value. Interpret this statement.
4. Why do you think U.S. firms commonly use joint ventures as a strategy to enter China?
5. Why would the United States offer a foreign automobile manufacturer large incentives for establishing a production subsidiary in the United States? Isn't this strategy indirectly subsidizing the foreign competitors of U.S. firms?

QUESTIONS AND APPLICATIONS

1. **Motives for DFI.** Describe some potential benefits to an MNC as a result of direct foreign investment (DFI). Elaborate on each type of benefit. Which motives for DFI do you think encouraged Nike to expand its footwear production in Latin America?
2. **Impact of a Weak Currency on Feasibility of DFI.** Packer, Inc., a U.S. producer of computer disks, plans to establish a subsidiary in Mexico in order to penetrate the Mexican market. Packer's executives believe that the Mexican peso's value is relatively strong and will weaken against the dollar over time. If their expectations about the peso value are correct, how will this affect the feasibility of the project? Explain.
3. **DFI to Achieve Economies of Scale.** Bear Co. and Viking, Inc., are automobile manufacturers that desire to benefit from economies of scale. Bear Co. has decided to establish distributorship subsidiaries in various countries, while Viking, Inc., has decided to establish manufacturing subsidiaries in various countries. Which firm is more likely to benefit from economies of scale?
4. **DFI to Reduce Cash Flow Volatility.** Raider Chemical Co. and Ram, Inc., had similar intentions to reduce the volatility of their cash flows. Raider implemented a long-range plan to establish 40 percent of its business in Canada. Ram, Inc., implemented a long-range plan to establish 30 percent of its business in Europe and Asia, scattered among 12 different countries. Which company will more effectively reduce cash flow volatility once the plans are achieved?
5. **Impact of Import Restrictions.** If the United States imposed long-term restrictions on imports, would the amount of DFI by non-U.S. MNCs in the United States increase, decrease, or be unchanged? Explain.
6. **Capitalizing on Low-Cost Labor.** Some MNCs establish a manufacturing facility where there is a relatively low cost of labor. Yet, they sometimes close the facility later because the cost advantage dissipates. Why do you think the relative cost advantage of these countries is reduced over time? (Ignore possible exchange rate effects.)
7. **Opportunities in Less Developed Countries.** Offer your opinion on why economies of some less developed countries with strict restrictions on international trade and DFI are somewhat independent from economies of other countries. Why would MNCs desire to enter such countries? If these countries relaxed their restrictions, would their economies continue to be independent of other economies? Explain.
8. **Effects of September 11.** In August 2001, Ohio, Inc., considered establishing a manufacturing plant in central Asia, which would be used to cover its exports to Japan and Hong Kong. The cost of labor was very low in central Asia. On September 11, 2001, the terrorist attacks on the United States caused Ohio to reassess the potential cost savings.

Why would the estimated expenses of the plant increase after the terrorist attacks?

9. **DFI Strategy.** Bronco Corp. has decided to establish a subsidiary in Taiwan that will produce stereos and sell them there. It expects that its cost of producing these stereos will be one-third the cost of producing them in the United States. Assuming that its production cost estimates are accurate, is Bronco's strategy sensible? Explain.

10. **Risk Resulting from International Business.** This chapter concentrates on possible benefits to a firm that increases its international business.

    a. What are some risks of international business that may not exist for local business?

    b. What does this chapter reveal about the relationship between an MNC's degree of international business and its risk?

11. **Motives for DFI.** Starter Corp. of New Haven, Connecticut, produces sportswear that is licensed by professional sports teams. It recently decided to expand in Europe. What are the potential benefits for this firm from using DFI?

12. **Disney's DFI Motives.** What potential benefits do you think were most important in the decision of the Walt Disney Co. to build a theme park in France?

13. **DFI Strategy.** Once an MNC establishes a subsidiary, DFI remains an ongoing decision. What does this statement mean?

14. **Host Government Incentives for DFI.** Why would foreign governments provide MNCs with incentives to undertake DFI there?

ADVANCED QUESTIONS

15. **DFI Strategy.** J.C. Penney has recognized numerous opportunities to expand in foreign countries and has assessed many foreign markets, including Brazil, Greece, Mexico, Portugal, Singapore, and Thailand. It has opened new stores in Europe, Asia, and Latin America. In each case, the firm was aware that it did not have sufficient understanding of the culture of each country that it had targeted. Consequently, it engaged in joint ventures with local partners who knew the preferences of the local customers.

    a. What comparative advantage does J.C. Penney have when establishing a store in a foreign country, relative to an independent variety store?

    b. Why might the overall risk of J.C. Penney decrease or increase as a result of its recent global expansion?

    c. J.C. Penney has been more cautious about entering China. Explain the potential obstacles associated with entering China.

16. **DFI Location Decision.** Decko Co. is a U.S. firm with a Chinese subsidiary that produces cell phones in China and sells them in Japan. This subsidiary pays its wages and its rent in Chinese yuan, which is presently tied to the dollar. The cell phones sold to Japan are denominated in Japanese yen. Assume that Decko Co. expects that the Chinese yuan will continue to stay fixed against the dollar. The subsidiary's main goal is to generate profits for itself and reinvest the profits. It does not plan to remit any funds to the U.S. parent.

    a. Assume that the Japanese yen strengthens against the U.S. dollar over time. How would this be expected to affect the profits earned by the Chinese subsidiary?

    b. If Decko Co. had established its subsidiary in Tokyo, Japan instead of China, would its subsidiary's profits be more exposed or less exposed to exchange rate risk?

    c. Why do you think that Decko Co. established the subsidiary in China instead of Japan? Assume no major country risk barriers.

    d. If the Chinese subsidiary needs to borrow money to finance its expansion and wants to reduce its exchange rate risk, should it borrow U.S. dollars, Chinese yuan, or Japanese yen?

INTERNET APPLICATION

17. **DFI Online** Information that should be considered when assessing potential DFI is provided at **http://biz.yahoo.com/ifc/**.

    a. Use this site to identify emerging markets that appear to have favorable characteristics.

    b. Review the information for a country of your choice. Explain why you believe this information would or would not attract DFI.

DISCUSSION IN THE BOARDROOM

This exercise can be found in Appendix E at the back of this textbook.

RUNNING YOUR OWN MNC

This exercise can be found on the Xtra! website at **http://maduraxtra.swlearning.com**.

BLADES, INC. CASE

Consideration of Direct Foreign Investment

For the last year, Blades, Inc., has been exporting to Thailand in order to supplement its declining U.S. sales. Under the existing arrangement, Blades sells 180,000 pairs of roller blades annually to Entertainment Products, a Thai retailer, for a fixed price denominated in Thai baht. The agreement will last for another two years. Furthermore, to diversify internationally and to take advantage of an attractive offer by Jogs, Ltd., a British retailer, Blades has recently begun exporting to the United Kingdom. Under the resulting agreement, Jogs will purchase 200,000 pairs of "Speedos," Blades' primary product, annually at a fixed price of £80 per pair.

Blades' suppliers of the needed components for its roller blade production are located primarily in the United States, where Blades incurs the majority of its cost of goods sold. Although prices for inputs needed to manufacture roller blades vary, recent costs have run approximately $70 per pair. Blades also imports components from Thailand because of the relatively low price of rubber and plastic components and because of their high quality. These imports are denominated in Thai baht, and the exact price (in baht) depends on prevailing market prices for these components in Thailand. Currently, inputs sufficient to manufacture a pair of roller blades cost approximately 3,000 Thai baht per pair of roller blades.

Although Thailand had been among the world's fastest growing economies, recent events in Thailand have increased the level of economic uncertainty. Specifically, the Thai baht, which had been pegged to the dollar, is now a freely floating currency and has depreciated substantially in recent months. Furthermore, recent levels of inflation in Thailand have been very high. Hence, future economic conditions in Thailand are highly uncertain.

Ben Holt, Blades' chief financial officer (CFO), is seriously considering DFI in Thailand. He believes that this is a perfect time to either establish a subsidiary or acquire an existing business in Thailand because the uncertain economic conditions and the depreciation of the baht have substantially lowered the initial costs required for DFI. Holt believes the growth potential in Asia will be extremely high once the Thai economy stabilizes.

Although Holt has also considered DFI in the United Kingdom, he would prefer that Blades invest in Thailand as opposed to the United Kingdom. Forecasts indicate that the demand for roller blades in the United Kingdom is similar to that in the United States; since Blades' U.S. sales have recently declined because of the high prices it charges, Holt expects that DFI in the United Kingdom will yield similar results, especially since the components required to manufacture roller blades are more expensive in the United Kingdom than in the United States. Furthermore, both domestic and foreign roller blade manufacturers are relatively well established in the United Kingdom, so the growth potential there is limited. Holt believes the Thai roller blade market offers more growth potential.

Blades can sell its products at a lower price but generate higher profit margins in Thailand than it can in the United States. This is because the Thai customer has committed itself to purchase a fixed number of Blades' products annually only if it can purchase Speedos at a substantial discount from the U.S. price. Nevertheless, since the cost of goods sold incurred in Thailand is substantially below that incurred in the United States, Blades has managed to generate higher profit margins from its Thai exports and imports than in the United States.

As a financial analyst for Blades, Inc., you generally agree with Ben Holt's assessment of the situation. However, you are concerned that Thai consumers have not been affected yet by the unfavorable economic conditions. You believe that they may reduce their spending on leisure products within the next year. Therefore, you think it would be beneficial to wait until next year, when the unfavorable economic conditions in Thailand may subside, to make a decision regarding DFI in Thailand. However, if economic conditions in Thailand improve over the next year, DFI may become more expensive both because target firms will be more expensive and because the baht may appreciate. You are also aware that several of Blades' U.S. competitors are considering expanding into Thailand in the next year.

If Blades acquires an existing business in Thailand or establishes a subsidiary there by the end of next year, it would fulfill its agreement with Entertainment Products for the subsequent year. The Thai retailer has expressed an interest in renewing the contractual agreement with Blades at that time if Blades establishes operations in Thailand. However, Holt believes that Blades could charge a higher price for its products if it establishes its own distribution channels.

Holt has asked you to answer the following questions:

1. Identify and discuss some of the benefits that Blades, Inc., could obtain from DFI.
2. Do you think Blades should wait until next year to undertake DFI in Thailand? What is the tradeoff if Blades undertakes the DFI now?
3. Do you think Blades should renew its agreement with the Thai retailer for another three years? What is the tradeoff if Blades renews the agreement?
4. Assume a high level of unemployment in Thailand and a unique production process employed by Blades, Inc. How do you think the Thai government would view the establishment of a subsidiary in Thailand by firms such as Blades? Do you think the Thai government would be more or less supportive if firms such as Blades acquired existing businesses in Thailand? Why?

SMALL BUSINESS DILEMMA

Direct Foreign Investment Decision by the Sports Exports Company

Jim Logan's business, the Sports Exports Company, continues to grow. His primary product is the footballs he produces and exports to a distributor in the United Kingdom. However, his recent joint venture with a British firm has also been successful. Under this arrangement, a British firm produces other sporting goods for Jim's firm; these goods are then delivered to that distributor. Jim intentionally started his international business by exporting because it was easier and cheaper to export than to establish a place of business in the United Kingdom. However, he is considering establishing a firm in the United Kingdom to produce the footballs there instead of in his garage (in the United States). This firm would also produce the other sporting goods that he now sells, so he would no longer have to rely on another British firm (through the joint venture) to produce those goods.

1. Given the information provided here, what are the advantages to Jim of establishing the firm in the United Kingdom?
2. Given the information provided here, what are the disadvantages to Jim of establishing the firm in the United Kingdom?

CHAPTER 14

Multinational Capital Budgeting

Multinational corporations (MNCs) evaluate international projects by using multinational capital budgeting, which compares the benefits and costs of these projects. Given that many MNCs spend more than $100 million per year on international projects, multinational capital budgeting is a critical function. Many international projects are irreversible and cannot be easily sold to other corporations at a reasonable price. Proper use of multinational capital budgeting can identify the international projects worthy of implementation.

The most popular method of capital budgeting involves determining the project's net present value by estimating the present value of the project's future cash flows and subtracting the initial outlay required for the project. Multinational capital budgeting typically uses a similar process. However, special circumstances of international projects that affect the future cash flows or the discount rate used to discount cash flows make multinational capital budgeting more complex. Financial managers must understand how to apply capital budgeting to international projects, so that they can maximize the value of the MNC.

The specific objectives of this chapter are to:

- compare the capital budgeting analysis of an MNC's subsidiary versus its parent,
- demonstrate how multinational capital budgeting can be applied to determine whether an international project should be implemented, and
- explain how the risk of international projects can be assessed.

Subsidiary versus Parent Perspective

Should capital budgeting for a multinational project be conducted from the viewpoint of the subsidiary that will administer the project or the parent that will most likely finance much of the project? Some would say the subsidiary's perspective should be used because it will be responsible for administering the project. In addition, since the subsidiary is a subset of the MNC, what is good for the subsidiary would appear to be good for the MNC. This reasoning, however, is not necessarily correct. One could argue that if the parent is financing the project, then it should be evaluating the results from its point of view. The feasibility of the capital budgeting analysis can vary with the perspective because the net after-tax cash inflows to the subsidiary can differ substantially from those to the parent. Such differences can be due to several factors, some of which are discussed here.

Tax Differentials

http://

See http://www.kmpg.com for detailed information on the tax regimes, rates, and regulations of over 75 countries.

If the earnings due to the project will someday be remitted to the parent, the MNC needs to consider how the parent's government taxes these earnings. If the parent's government imposes a high tax rate on the remitted funds, the project may be feasible from the subsidiary's point of view, but not from the parent's point of view. Under such a scenario, the parent should not consider implementing the project, even though it appears feasible from the subsidiary's perspective.

Restricted Remittances

Consider a potential project to be implemented in a country where government restrictions require that a percentage of the subsidiary earnings remain in the country. Since the parent may never have access to these funds, the project is not attractive to the parent, although it may be attractive to the subsidiary. One possible solution is to let the subsidiary obtain partial financing for the project within the host country. In this case, the portion of funds not allowed to be sent to the parent can be used to cover the financing costs over time.

USING THE WEB

Foreign Exchange Regulations Information about foreign exchange regulations for each country is provided at http://biz.yahoo.com/ifc/. Click on any country listed, and then click on Forex Regulations. Information is provided about remittances of dividends and earnings, interest and principal, and royalties and fees by subsidiaries based in that country.

Excessive Remittances

Consider a parent that charges its subsidiary very high administrative fees because management is centralized at the headquarters. To the subsidiary, the fees represent an expense. To the parent, the fees represent revenue that may substantially exceed the actual cost of managing the subsidiary. In this case, the project's earnings may appear low from the subsidiary's perspective and high from the parent's perspective. The feasibility of the project again depends on perspective. In most cases, neglecting the parent's perspective will distort the true value of a foreign project.

Exchange Rate Movements

When earnings are remitted to the parent, they are normally converted from the subsidiary's local currency to the parent's currency. The amount received by the parent is therefore influenced by the existing exchange rate. If the subsidiary project is assessed from the subsidiary's perspective, the cash flows forecasted for the subsidiary do not have to be converted to the parent's currency.

Summary of Factors

Exhibit 14.1 illustrates the process from the time earnings are generated by the subsidiary until the parent receives the remitted funds. The exhibit shows that the earnings are reduced initially by corporate taxes paid to the host government. Then, some of the

Exhibit 14.1
Process of Remitting Subsidiary Earnings to the Parent

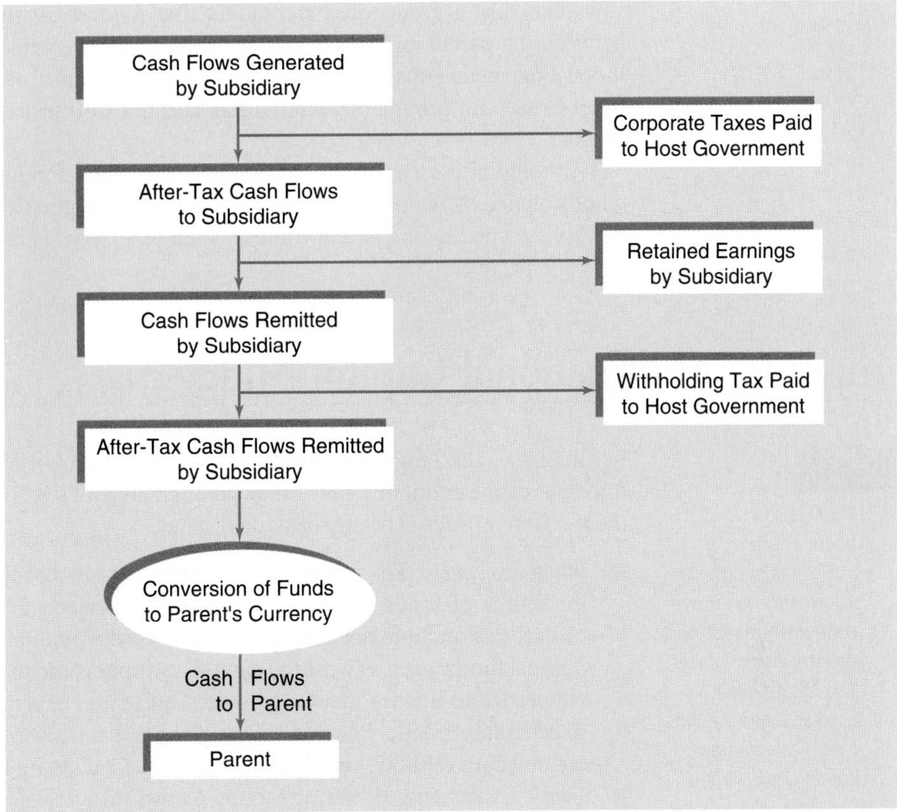

earnings are retained by the subsidiary (either by the subsidiary's choice or according to the host government's rules), with the residual targeted as funds to be remitted. Those funds that are remitted may be subject to a withholding tax by the host government. The remaining funds are converted to the parent's currency (at the prevailing exchange rate) and remitted to the parent.

Given the various factors shown here that can drain subsidiary earnings, the cash flows actually remitted by the subsidiary may represent only a small portion of the earnings it generates. The feasibility of the project from the parent's perspective is dependent not on the subsidiary's cash flows but on the cash flows that the parent ultimately receives.

The parent's perspective is appropriate in attempting to determine whether a project will enhance the firm's value. Given that the parent's shareholders are its owners, it should make decisions that satisfy its shareholders. Each project, whether foreign or domestic, should ultimately generate sufficient cash flows to the parent to enhance shareholder wealth. Any changes in the parent's expenses should also be included in the analysis. The parent may incur additional expenses for monitoring the new foreign subsidiary's management or consolidating the subsidiary's financial statements. Any project that can create a positive net present value for the parent should enhance shareholder wealth.

One exception to the rule of using a parent's perspective occurs when the foreign subsidiary is not wholly owned by the parent and the foreign project is partially financed with retained earnings of the parent and of the subsidiary. In this case, the foreign subsidiary has a group of shareholders that it must satisfy. Any arrangement made between the parent and the subsidiary should be acceptable to the two entities only if the arrangement enhances the values of both. The goal is to make decisions in the interests of both groups of shareholders and not to transfer wealth from one entity to another.

Although this exception occasionally occurs, most foreign subsidiaries of MNCs are wholly owned by the parents. Examples in this text implicitly assume that the subsidiary is wholly owned by the parent (unless noted otherwise) and therefore focus on the parent's perspective.

Input for Multinational Capital Budgeting

http://

The website http://finance.yahoo.com/intlindices?u provides information on the recent performance of country stock indexes. This is sometimes used as a general indication of economic conditions in various countries and may be considered by MNCs that assess the feasibility of foreign projects.

Regardless of the long-term project to be considered, an MNC will normally require forecasts of the economic and financial characteristics related to the project. Each of these characteristics is briefly described here:

- *Initial investment.* The parent's initial investment in a project may constitute the major source of funds to support a particular project. Funds initially invested in a project may include not only whatever is necessary to start the project but also additional funds, such as working capital, to support the project over time. Such funds are needed to finance inventory, wages, and other expenses until the project begins to generate revenue. Because cash inflows will not always be sufficient to cover upcoming cash outflows, working capital is needed throughout a project's lifetime.
- *Consumer demand.* When projecting a cash flow schedule, an accurate forecast of consumer demand for a product is quite valuable, but future demand is often difficult to forecast. For example, if the project is a plant in Germany that produces automobiles, the MNC must forecast what percentage of the auto market in Germany it can pull from prevailing auto producers. Once a market share percentage is forecasted, projected demand can be computed. Demand forecasts can sometimes be aided by historical data on the market share other MNCs in the industry pulled when they entered this market, but historical data are not always an accurate indicator of the future. In addition, many projects reflect a first attempt, so there are no predecessors to review as an indicator of the future.
- *Price.* The price at which the product could be sold can be forecasted using competitive products in the markets as a comparison. A long-term capital budgeting analysis requires projections for not only the upcoming period but the expected lifetime of the project as well. The future prices will most likely be responsive to the future inflation rate in the host country (where the project is to take place), but the future inflation rate is not known. Thus, future inflation rates must be forecasted in order to develop projections of the product price over time.
- *Variable cost.* Like the price estimate, variable-cost forecasts can be developed from assessing prevailing comparative costs of the components (such as hourly labor costs and the cost of materials). Such costs should normally move in tandem with the future inflation rate of the host country. Even if the variable cost per unit can be accurately predicted, the projected total variable cost (variable cost per unit times quantity produced) may be wrong if the demand is inaccurately forecasted.
- *Fixed cost.* On a periodic basis, the fixed cost may be easier to predict than the variable cost since it normally is not sensitive to changes in demand. It is, however, sen-

sitive to any change in the host country's inflation rate from the time the forecast is made until the time the fixed costs are incurred.

- *Project lifetime.* Some projects have indefinite lifetimes that can be difficult to assess, while other projects have designated specific lifetimes, at the end of which they will be liquidated. This makes the capital budgeting analysis easier to apply. It should be recognized that the MNC does not always have complete control over the lifetime decision. In some cases, political events may force the firm to liquidate the project earlier than planned. The probability that such events will occur varies among countries.
- *Salvage (liquidation) value.* The after-tax salvage value of most projects is difficult to forecast. It will depend on several factors, including the success of the project and the attitude of the host government toward the project. As an extreme possibility, the host government could take over the project without adequately compensating the MNC.
- *Restrictions on fund transfers.* In some cases, a host government will prevent a subsidiary from sending its earnings to the parent. This restriction may reflect an attempt to encourage additional local spending or to avoid excessive sales of the local currency in exchange for some other currency. Since the restrictions on fund transfers prevent cash from coming back to the parent, projected net cash flows from the parent's perspective will be affected. If the parent is aware of these restrictions, it can incorporate them when projecting net cash flows. Sometimes, however, the host government adjusts its restrictions over time; in that case, the MNC can only forecast the future restrictions and incorporate these forecasts into the analysis.
- *Tax laws.* The tax laws on earnings generated by a foreign subsidiary or remitted to the MNC's parent vary among countries. Under some circumstances, the MNC receives tax deductions or credits for tax payments by a subsidiary to the host country (see the chapter appendix for more details). Because after-tax cash flows are necessary for an adequate capital budgeting analysis, international tax effects must be determined on any proposed foreign projects.
- *Exchange rates.* Any international project will be affected by exchange rate fluctuations during the life of the project, but these movements are often very difficult to forecast. There are methods of hedging against them, though most hedging techniques are used to cover short-term positions. While it is possible to hedge over longer periods (with long-term forward contracts or currency swap arrangements), the MNC has no way of knowing the amount of funds that it should hedge. This is because it is only guessing at its future costs and revenue due to the project. Thus, the MNC may decide not to hedge the projected foreign currency net cash flows.
- *Required rate of return.* Once the relevant cash flows of a proposed project are estimated, they can be discounted at the project's required rate of return, which may differ from the MNC's cost of capital because of that particular project's risk.

http://

The website http://www.weforum.org provides information on global competitiveness and other details of interest to MNCs that implement projects in foreign countries.

Additional considerations will be discussed after a simplified multinational capital budgeting example is provided. In the real world, magic numbers aren't provided to MNCs for insertion into their computers. The challenge revolves around accurately forecasting the variables relevant to the project evaluation. If garbage (inaccurate forecasts) is input into the computer, the analysis output by the computer will also be garbage. Consequently, an MNC may take on a project by mistake. Since such a mistake may be worth millions of dollars, MNCs need to assess the degree of uncertainty for any input that is used in the project evaluation. This is discussed more thoroughly later in this chapter.

Multinational Capital Budgeting Example

Capital budgeting for the MNC is necessary for all long-term projects that deserve consideration. The projects may range from a small expansion of a subsidiary division to the creation of a new subsidiary. This section presents an example involving the possible development of a new subsidiary. It begins with assumptions that simplify the capital budgeting analysis. Then, additional considerations are introduced to emphasize the potential complexity of such an analysis.

This example illustrates one of many possible methods available that would achieve the same result. Also, keep in mind that a real-world problem may involve more extenuating circumstances than those shown here.

Background

Spartan, Inc., is considering the development of a subsidiary in Singapore that would manufacture and sell tennis rackets locally. Spartan's management has asked various departments to supply relevant information for a capital budgeting analysis. In addition, some Spartan executives have met with government officials in Singapore to discuss the proposed subsidiary. All relevant information follows.

1. *Initial investment.* An estimated 20 million Singapore dollars (S$), which includes funds to support working capital, would be needed for the project. Given the existing spot rate of $.50 per Singapore dollar, the U.S. dollar amount of the parent's initial investment is $10 million.
2. *Project life.* The project is expected to end in four years. The host government of Singapore has promised to purchase the plant from the parent after four years.
3. *Price and demand.* The estimated price and demand schedules during each of the next four years are shown here:

Year	Price per Racket	Demand in Singapore
1	S$350	60,000 units
2	S$350	60,000 units
3	S$360	100,000 units
4	S$380	100,000 units

4. *Costs.* The variable costs (for materials, labor, etc.) per unit have been estimated and consolidated as shown here:

Year	Variable Costs per Racket
1	S$200
2	S$200
3	S$250
4	S$260

The expense of leasing extra office space is S$1 million per year. Other annual overhead expenses are expected to be S$1 million per year.

5. *Exchange rates.* The spot exchange rate of the Singapore dollar is $.50. Spartan uses the spot rate as its best forecast of the exchange rate that will exist in future periods. Thus, the forecasted exchange rate for all future periods is $.50.
6. *Host country taxes on income earned by subsidiary.* The Singapore government will allow Spartan, Inc., to establish the subsidiary and will impose a 20 percent tax rate on income. In addition, it will impose a 10 percent withholding tax on any funds remitted by the subsidiary to the parent.
7. *U.S. government taxes on income earned by Spartan subsidiary.* The U.S. government will allow a tax credit on taxes paid in Singapore; therefore, earnings remitted to the U.S. parent will not be taxed by the U.S. government.
8. *Cash flows from Spartan subsidiary to parent.* The Spartan subsidiary plans to send all net cash flows received back to the parent firm at the end of each year. The Singapore government promises no restrictions on the cash flows to be sent back to the parent firm but does impose a 10 percent withholding tax on any funds sent to the parent, as mentioned earlier.
9. *Depreciation.* The Singapore government will allow Spartan's subsidiary to depreciate the cost of the plant and equipment at a maximum rate of S$2 million per year, which is the rate the subsidiary will use.
10. *Salvage value.* The Singapore government will pay the parent S$12 million to assume ownership of the subsidiary at the end of four years. Assume that there is no capital gains tax on the sale of the subsidiary.
11. *Required rate of return.* Spartan, Inc., requires a 15 percent return on this project.

Analysis

The capital budgeting analysis will be conducted from the parent's perspective, based on the assumption that the subsidiary is intended to generate cash flows that will ultimately be passed on to the parent. Thus, the net present value (*NPV*) from the parent's perspective is based on a comparison of the present value of the cash flows received by the parent to the initial outlay by the parent. As explained earlier in this chapter, an international project's *NPV* is dependent on whether a parent or subsidiary perspective is used. Since the U.S. parent's perspective is used, the cash flows of concern are the dollars ultimately received by the parent as a result of the project.

The initial outlay of concern is the investment by the parent. The required rate of return is based on the cost of capital used by the parent to make its investment, with an adjustment for the risk of the project. For the establishment of the subsidiary to benefit Spartan's parent, the present value of future cash flows (including the salvage value) ultimately received by the parent should exceed the parent's initial outlay.

The capital budgeting analysis to determine whether Spartan, Inc., should establish the subsidiary is provided in Exhibit 14.2 (review this exhibit as you read on). The first step is to incorporate demand and price estimates in order to forecast total revenue (see lines 1 through 3). Then, the expenses are summed up to forecast total expenses (see lines 4 through 9). Next, before-tax earnings are computed (in line 10) by subtracting total expenses from total revenues. Host government taxes (line 11) are then deducted from before-tax earnings to determine after-tax earnings for the subsidiary (line 12).

The depreciation expense is added to the after-tax subsidiary earnings to compute the net cash flow to the subsidiary (line 13). All of these funds are to be remitted by the

Exhibit 14.2 Capital Budgeting Analysis: Spartan, Inc.

	Year 0	Year 1	Year 2	Year 3	Year 4
1. Demand		60,000	60,000	100,000	100,000
2. Price per unit		S$350	S$350	S$360	S$380
3. Total revenue = (1) × (2)		S$21,000,000	S$21,000,000	S$36,000,000	S$38,000,000
4. Variable cost per unit		S$200	S$200	S$250	S$260
5. Total variable cost = (1) × (4)		S$12,000,000	S$12,000,000	S$25,000,000	S$26,000,000
6. Annual lease expense		S$1,000,000	S$1,000,000	S$1,000,000	S$1,000,000
7. Other fixed annual expenses		S$1,000,000	S$1,000,000	S$1,000,000	S$1,000,000
8. Noncash expense (depreciation)		S$2,000,000	S$2,000,000	S$2,000,000	S$2,000,000
9. Total expenses = (5) + (6) + (7) + (8)		S$16,000,000	S$16,000,000	S$29,000,000	S$30,000,000
10. Before-tax earnings of subsidiary = (3) − (9)		S$5,000,000	S$5,000,000	S$7,000,000	S$8,000,000
11. Host government tax (20%)		S$1,000,000	S$1,000,000	S$1,400,000	S$1,600,000
12. After-tax earnings of subsidiary		S$4,000,000	S$4,000,000	S$5,600,000	S$6,400,000
13. Net cash flow to subsidiary = (12) + (8)		S$6,000,000	S$6,000,000	S$7,600,000	S$8,400,000
14. S$ remitted by subsidiary (100% of net cash flow)		S$6,000,000	S$6,000,000	S$7,600,000	S$8,400,000
15. Withholding tax on remitted funds (10%)		S$600,000	S$600,000	S$760,000	S$840,000
16. S$ remitted after withholding taxes		S$5,400,000	S$5,400,000	S$6,840,000	S$7,560,000
17. Salvage value					S$12,000,000
18. Exchange rate of S$		$.50	$.50	$.50	$.50
19. Cash flows to parent		$2,700,000	$2,700,000	$3,420,000	$9,780,000
20. *PV* of parent cash flows (15% discount rate)		$2,347,826	$2,041,588	$2,248,706	$5,591,747
21. Initial investment by parent	$10,000,000				
22. Cumulative *NPV*		−$7,652,174	−$5,610,586	−$3,361,880	$2,229,867

subsidiary, so line 14 is the same as line 13. The subsidiary can afford to send all net cash flow to the parent since the initial investment provided by the parent includes working capital. The funds remitted to the parent are subject to a 10 percent withholding tax (line 15), so the actual amount of funds to be sent after these taxes is shown in line 16. The salvage value of the project is shown in line 17. The funds to be remitted must first be converted into dollars at the exchange rate (line 18) existing at that time.

The parent's cash flow from the subsidiary is shown in line 19. The periodic funds received from the subsidiary are not subject to U.S. corporate taxes since it was assumed that the parent would receive credit for the taxes paid in Singapore that would offset taxes owed to the U.S. government.

Although several capital budgeting techniques are available, a commonly used technique is to estimate the cash flows and salvage value to be received by the parent and compute the *NPV* of the project, as shown here:

$$NPV = -IO + \sum_{t=1}^{n} \frac{CF_t}{(1+k)^t} + \frac{SV_n}{(1+k)^n}$$

where

IO = initial outlay (investment)
CF_t = cash flow in period t
SV_n = salvage value
k = required rate of return on the project
n = lifetime of the project (number of periods)

The *present value (PV)* of each period's net cash flow is computed using a 15 percent discount rate (line 20). The discount rate should reflect the parent's cost of capital with an adjustment for the project's risk. Finally, the cumulative *NPV* (line 22) is determined by consolidating the discounted cash flows for each period and subtracting the initial outlay (in line 21). For example, as of the end of Year 2, the cumulative *NPV* was −\$5,610,586. This was determined by consolidating the \$2,347,826 in Year 1, the \$2,041,588 in Year 2, and subtracting the initial investment of \$10,000,000. The cumulative *NPV* in each period measures how much of the initial outlay has been recovered up to that point by the receipt of discounted cash flows. Thus, it can be used to estimate how many periods it will take to recover the initial outlay. For some projects, the cumulative *NPV* remains negative in all periods, which suggests that the discounted cash flows never exceed the initial outlay. That is, the initial outlay is never fully recovered. The critical value in line 22 is the one for the last period because it reflects the *NPV* of the project.

In our example, the cumulative *NPV* as of the end of the last period is \$2,229,867. Because the *NPV* is positive, Spartan, Inc., may accept this project if the discount rate of 15 percent has fully accounted for the project's risk. If the analysis has not yet accounted for risk, however, Spartan may decide to reject the project. The way an MNC can account for risk in capital budgeting is discussed shortly.

Factors to Consider in Multinational Capital Budgeting

The example of Spartan, Inc., ignored a variety of factors that may affect the capital budgeting analysis, such as:

- Exchange rate fluctuations
- Inflation
- Financing arrangement
- Blocked funds

- Uncertain salvage value
- Impact of project on prevailing cash flows
- Host government incentives
- Real options

Each of these factors is discussed in turn.

Exchange Rate Fluctuations

Recall that Spartan, Inc., uses the Singapore dollar's current spot rate ($.50) as a forecast for all future periods of concern. The company realizes that the exchange rate will typically change over time, but it does not know whether the Singapore dollar will strengthen or weaken in the future. Though the difficulty in accurately forecasting exchange rates is well known, a multinational capital budgeting analysis could at least incorporate other scenarios for exchange rate movements, such as a pessimistic scenario and an optimistic scenario. From the parent's point of view, appreciation of the Singapore dollar would be favorable since the Singapore dollar inflows would someday be converted to more U.S. dollars. Conversely, depreciation would be unfavorable since the weakened Singapore dollars would convert to fewer U.S. dollars over time.

Exhibit 14.3 illustrates both a weak Singapore dollar (weak-S$) scenario and a strong Singapore dollar (strong-S$) scenario. At the top of the table, the anticipated after-tax Singapore dollar cash flows (including salvage value) are shown for the subsidiary from lines 16 and 17 in Exhibit 14.2. The amount in U.S. dollars that these Singapore dollars convert to depends on the exchange rates existing in the various periods when they are converted. The number of Singapore dollars multiplied by the fore-

Exhibit 14.3 Analysis Using Different Exchange Rate Scenarios: Spartan, Inc.

	Year 0	Year 1	Year 2	Year 3	Year 4
S$ remitted after withholding taxes (including salvage value)		**S$5,400,000**	**S$5,400,000**	**S$6,840,000**	**S$19,560,000**
Strong-S$ Scenario					
Exchange rate of S$		**$.54**	**$.57**	**$.61**	**$.65**
Cash flows to parent		**$2,916,000**	**$3,078,000**	**$4,172,400**	**$12,714,000**
***PV* of cash flows (15% discount rate)**		**$2,535,652**	**$2,327,410**	**$2,743,421**	**$7,269,271**
Initial investment by parent	**$10,000,000**				
Cumulative *NPV*		**−$7,464,348**	**−$5,136,938**	**−$2,393,517**	**$4,875,754**
Weak-S$ Scenario					
Exchange rate of S$		**$.47**	**$.45**	**$.40**	**$.37**
Cash flows to parent		**$2,538,000**	**$2,430,000**	**$2,736,000**	**$7,237,200**
***PV* of cash flows (15% discount rate)**		**$2,206,957**	**$1,837,429**	**$1,798,964**	**$4,137,893**
Initial investment by parent	**$10,000,000**				
Cumulative *NPV*		**−$7,793,043**	**−$5,955,614**	**−$4,156,650**	**−$18,757**

casted exchange rate will determine the estimated number of U.S. dollars received by the parent.

Notice from Exhibit 14.3 how the cash flows received by the parent differ depending on the scenario. A strong Singapore dollar is clearly beneficial, as indicated by the increased U.S. dollar value of the cash flows received. The large differences in cash flow received by the parent in the different scenarios illustrate the impact of exchange rate expectations on the feasibility of an international project.

The *NPV* forecasts based on projections for exchange rates are illustrated in Exhibit 14.4. The estimated *NPV* is highest if the Singapore dollar is expected to strengthen and lowest if it is expected to weaken. The estimated *NPV* is negative for the weak-S$ scenario but positive for the stable-S$ and strong-S$ scenarios. This project's true feasibility would depend on the probability distribution of these three scenarios for the

Exhibit 14.4

Sensitivity of the Project's *NPV* to Different Exchange Rate Scenarios: Spartan, Inc.

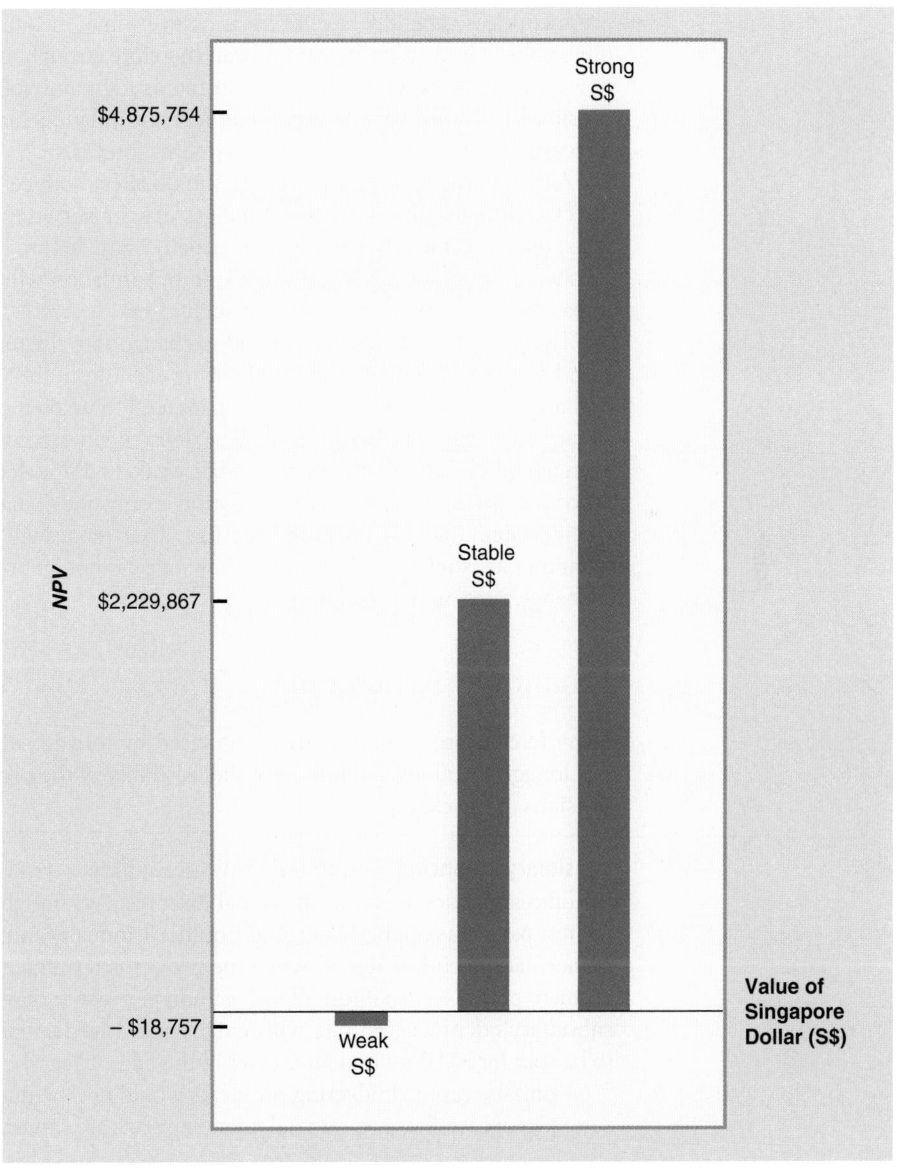

Singapore dollar during the project's lifetime. If there is a high probability that the weak-S$ scenario will occur, this project should not be accepted.

Some U.S.-based MNCs consider projects in countries where the local currency is tied to the dollar. They may conduct a capital budgeting analysis that presumes the exchange rate will remain fixed. It is possible, however, that the local currency will be devalued at some point in the future, which could have a major impact on the cash flows to be received by the parent. Therefore, the MNC may reestimate the project's *NPV* based on a particular devaluation scenario that it believes could possibly occur. If the project is still feasible under this scenario, the MNC may be more comfortable pursuing the project.

Inflation

Capital budgeting analysis implicitly considers inflation, since variable cost per unit and product prices generally have been rising over time. In some countries, inflation can be quite volatile from year to year and can therefore strongly influence a project's net cash flows. In countries where the inflation rate is high and volatile, it will be virtually impossible for a subsidiary to accurately forecast inflation each year. Inaccurate inflation forecasts can lead to inaccurate net cash flow forecasts.

Although fluctuations in inflation should affect both costs and revenues in the same direction, the magnitude of their changes may be very different. This is especially true when the project involves importing partially manufactured components and selling the finished product locally. The local economy's inflation will most likely have a stronger impact on revenues than on costs in such cases.

The joint impact of inflation and exchange rate fluctuations on a subsidiary's net cash flows may produce a partial offsetting effect from the viewpoint of the parent. The exchange rates of highly inflated countries tend to weaken over time. Thus, even if subsidiary earnings are inflated, they will be deflated when converted into the parent's home currency (if the subsidiary's currency has weakened). Such an offsetting effect is not exact or consistent, though. Because inflation is only one of many factors that influence exchange rates, there is no guarantee that a currency will depreciate when the local inflation rate is relatively high. Therefore, one cannot ignore the impact of inflation and exchange rates on net cash flows.

Financing Arrangement

Many foreign projects are partially financed by foreign subsidiaries. To illustrate how this foreign financing can influence the feasibility of the project, consider the following revisions in the example of Spartan, Inc.

Subsidiary Financing. Assume that the subsidiary borrows S$10 million to purchase the offices that are leased in the initial example. Assume that the subsidiary will make interest payments on this loan (of S$1 million) annually and will pay the principal (S$10 million) at the end of Year 4, when the project is terminated. Since the Singapore government permits a maximum of S$2 million per year in depreciation for this project, the subsidiary's depreciation rate will remain unchanged. Assume the offices are expected to be sold for S$10 million after taxes at the end of Year 4.

Domestic capital budgeting problems would not include debt payments in the measurement of cash flows because all financing costs are captured by the discount rate. Foreign projects are more complicated, however, especially when the foreign subsidary partially finances the investment in the foreign project. Although consolidating the initial investments made by the parent and the subsidiary simplifies the capital budgeting process, it can cause significant estimation errors. The estimated foreign cash flows that are ultimately remitted to the parent and are subject to exchange rate risk will be overstated if the foreign interest expenses are not explicitly considered as cash outflows for the foreign subsidiary. Thus, a more accurate approach is to separate the investment made by the subsidiary from the investment made by the parent. The capital budgeting analysis can focus on the parent's perspective by comparing the present value of the cash flows received by the parent to the initial investment by the parent.

Given the revised assumptions, the following revisions must be made to the capital budgeting analysis:

1. Since the subsidiary is borrowing funds to purchase the offices, the lease payments of S$1 million per year will not be necessary. However, the subsidiary will pay interest of S$1 million per year as a result of the loan. Thus, the annual cash outflows for the subsidiary are still the same.
2. The subsidiary must pay the S$10 million in loan principal at the end of four years. However, since the subsidiary expects to receive S$10 million (in 4 years) from the sale of the offices it purchases with the funds provided by the loan, it can use the proceeds of the sale to pay the loan principal.

Since the subsidiary has already taken the maximum depreciation expense allowed by the Singapore government before the offices were considered, it cannot increase its annual depreciation expenses. In this example, the cash flows ultimately received by the parent when the subsidiary obtains financing to purchase offices are similar to the cash flows determined in the original example (when the offices are to be leased). If the numbers were not offsetting, the capital budgeting analysis would be repeated to determine whether the *NPV* from the parent's perspective is higher than in the initial example.

Parent Financing. Consider one more alternative arrangement, in which, instead of the subsidiary leasing the offices or purchasing them with borrowed funds, the parent uses its own funds to purchase the offices. Thus, its initial investment is $15 million, composed of the original $10 million investment as explained earlier, plus an additional $5 million to obtain an extra S$10 million to purchase the offices. This example illustrates how the capital budgeting analysis changes when the parent takes a bigger stake in the investment. If the parent rather than the subsidiary will purchase the offices, the following revisions must be made to the capital budgeting analysis:

1. The subsidiary will not have any loan payments (since it will not need to borrow funds) because the parent will purchase the offices. Since the offices are to be purchased, there will be no lease payments either.
2. The parent's initial investment is $15 million instead of $10 million.
3. The salvage value to be received by the parent is S$22 million instead of S$12 million because the offices are assumed to be sold for S$10 million after taxes at the end of Year 4. The S$10 million to be received from selling the offices can be added to the S$12 million to be received from selling the rest of the subsidiary.

The capital budgeting analysis for Spartan, Inc., under this revised financing strategy in which the parent finances the entire $15 million investment is shown in Exhibit 14.5. This analysis uses our original exchange rate projections of $.50 per Singapore dollar for each period. The numbers that are directly affected by the revised

Exhibit 14.5 Analysis with an Alternative Financing Arrangement: Spartan, Inc.

	Year 0	Year 1	Year 2	Year 3	Year 4
1. Demand		60,000	60,000	100,000	100,000
2. Price per unit		S$350	S$350	S$360	S$380
3. Total revenue = (1) × (2)		S$21,000,000	S$21,000,000	S$36,000,000	S$38,000,000
4. Variable cost per unit		S$200	S$200	S$250	S$260
5. Total variable cost = (1) × (4)		S$12,000,000	S$12,000,000	S$25,000,000	S$26,000,000
6. Annual lease expense		[S$ 0]	[S$ 0]	[S$ 0]	[S$ 0]
7. Other fixed annual expenses		S$1,000,000	S$1,000,000	S$1,000,000	S$1,000,000
8. Noncash expense (depreciation)		S$2,000,000	S$2,000,000	S$2,000,000	S$2,000,000
9. Total expenses = (5) + (6) + (7) + (8)		S$15,000,000	S$15,000,000	S$28,000,000	S$29,000,000
10. Before-tax earnings of subsidiary = (3) − (9)		S$6,000,000	S$6,000,000	S$8,000,000	S$9,000,000
11. Host government tax (20%)		S$1,200,000	S$1,200,000	S$1,600,000	S$1,800,000
12. After-tax earnings of subsidiary		S$4,800,000	S$4,800,000	S$6,400,000	S$7,200,000
13. Net cash flow to subsidiary = (12) + (8)		S$6,800,000	S$6,800,000	S$8,400,000	S$9,200,000
14. S$ remitted by subsidiary (100% of S$)		S$6,800,000	S$6,800,000	S$8,400,000	S$9,200,000
15. Withholding tax on remitted funds (10%)		S$680,000	S$680,000	S$840,000	S$920,000
16. S$ remitted after withholding taxes		S$6,120,000	S$6,120,000	S$7,560,000	S$8,280,000
17. Salvage value					[S$22,000,000]
18. Exchange rate of S$		$.50	$.50	$.50	$.50
19. Cash flows to parent		$3,060,000	$3,060,000	$3,780,000	$15,140,000
20. PV of parent cash flows (15% discount rate)		$2,660,870	$2,313,800	$2,485,411	$8,656,344
21. Initial investment by parent	[$15,000,000]				
22. Cumulative *NPV*		−$12,339,130	−$10,025,330	−$7,539,919	$1,116,425

financing arrangement are bracketed. Other numbers are also affected indirectly as a result. For example, the subsidiary's after-tax earnings increase as a result of avoiding interest or lease payments on its offices. The *NPV* of the project under this alternative financing arrangement is positive but less than in the original arrangement. Given the higher initial outlay of the parent and the lower *NPV*, this arrangement is not as feasible as the arrangement in which the subsidiary either leases the offices or purchases them with borrowed funds.

Comparison of Parent versus Subsidiary Financing. One reason that the subsidiary financing is more feasible than complete parent financing is that the financing rate on the loan is lower than the parent's required rate of return on funds provided to the subsidiary. If local loans had a relatively high interest rate, however, the use of local financing would likely not be as attractive.

In general, this revised example shows that the increased investment by the parent increases the parent's exchange rate exposure for the following reasons. First, since the parent provides the entire investment, no foreign financing is required. Consequently, the subsidiary makes no interest payments and therefore remits larger cash flows to the parent. Second, the salvage value to be remitted to the parent is larger. Given the larger payments to the parent, the cash flows ultimately received by the parent are more susceptible to exchange rate movements.

The parent's exposure is not as large when the subsidiary purchases the offices because the subsidiary incurs some of the financing expenses. The subsidiary financing essentially shifts some of the expenses to the same currency that the subsidiary will receive and therefore reduces the amount that will ultimately be converted into dollars for remittance to the parent.

Financing with Other Subsidiaries' Retained Earnings. Some foreign projects are completely financed with retained earnings of existing foreign subsidiaries. These projects are difficult to assess from the parent's perspective because their direct effects are normally felt by the subsidiaries. One approach is to view a subsidiary's investment in a project as an opportunity cost, since the funds could be remitted to the parent rather than invested in the foreign project. Thus, the initial outlay from the parent's perspective is the amount of funds it would have received from the subsidiary if the funds had been remitted rather than invested in this project. The cash flows from the parent's perspective reflect those cash flows ultimately received by the parent as a result of the foreign project.

Even if the project generates earnings for the subsidiary that are reinvested by the subsidiary, the key cash flows from the parent's perspective are those that it ultimately receives from the project. In this way, any international factors that will affect the cash flows (such as withholding taxes and exchange rate movements) are incorporated into the capital budgeting process.

Blocked Funds

In some cases, the host country may block funds that the subsidiary attempts to send to the parent. Some countries require that earnings generated by the subsidiary be reinvested locally for at least three years before they can be remitted. Such restrictions can affect the accept/reject decision on a project.

Exhibit 14.6 Capital Budgeting with Blocked Funds: Spartan, Inc.

	Year 0	Year 1	Year 2	Year 3	Year 4
S$ to be remitted by subsidiary		S$6,000,000	S$6,000,000	S$7,600,000	S$8,400,000
					S$7,980,000
S$ accumulated by reinvesting funds to be remitted					S$6,615,000 S$6,945,750 S$29,940,750
Withholding tax (10%)					S$2,994,075
S$ remitted after withholding tax					S$26,946,675
Salvage value					S$12,000,000
Exchange rate					$.50
Cash flows to parent					$19,473,338
PV of parent cash flows (15% discount rate)					$11,133,944
Initial investment by parent	$10,000,000				
Cumulative *NPV*		−$10,000,000	−$10,000,000	−$10,000,000	$1,133,944

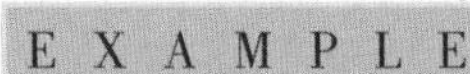

Reconsider the example of Spartan, Inc., assuming that all funds are blocked until the subsidiary is sold. Thus, the subsidiary must reinvest those funds until that time. Blocked funds penalize a project if the return on the reinvested funds is less than the required rate of return on the project.

Assume that the subsidiary uses the funds to purchase marketable securities that are expected to yield 5 percent annually after taxes. A reevaluation of Spartan's cash flows (from Exhibit 14.2) to incorporate the blocked-funds restriction is shown in Exhibit 14.6. The withholding tax is not applied until the funds are remitted to the parent, which is in Year 4. The original exchange rate projections are used here. All parent cash flows depend on the exchange rate four years from now. The *NPV* of the project with blocked funds is still positive, but it is substantially less than the *NPV* in the original example.

If the foreign subsidiary has a loan outstanding, it may be able to better utilize the blocked funds by repaying the local loan. For example, the S$6 million at the end of Year 1 could be used to reduce the outstanding loan balance instead of being invested in marketable securities, assuming that the lending bank allows early repayment.

Uncertain Salvage Value

The salvage value of an MNC's project typically has a significant impact on the project's *NPV*. When the salvage value is uncertain, the MNC may incorporate various possible outcomes for the salvage value and reestimate the *NPV* based on each possible outcome. It may even estimate the break-even salvage value (also called break-even terminal value), which is the salvage value necessary to achieve a zero *NPV* for the project. If the actual salvage value is expected to equal or exceed the break-even salvage value, the project is feasible. The break-even salvage value (called SV_n) can be determined by setting NPV equal to zero and rearranging the capital budgeting equation, as follows:

$$NPV = -IO + \sum_{t=1}^{n} \frac{CF_t}{(1+k)^t} + \frac{SV_n}{(1+k)^n}$$

$$0 = -IO + \sum_{t=1}^{n} \frac{CF_t}{(1+k)^t} + \frac{SV_n}{(1+k)^n}$$

$$\left[IO - \sum_{t=1}^{n} \frac{CF_t}{(1+k)^t}\right] = \frac{SV_n}{(1+k)^n}$$

$$\left[IO - \sum_{t=1}^{n} \frac{CF_t}{(1+k)^t}\right](1+k)^n = SV_n$$

EXAMPLE

Reconsider the Spartan, Inc., example and assume that Spartan is not guaranteed a price for the project. The break-even salvage value for the project can be determined by (1) estimating the present value of future cash flows (excluding the salvage value), (2) subtracting the discounted cash flows from the initial outlay, and (3) multiplying the difference times $(1 + k)^n$. Using the original cash flow information from Exhibit 14.2, the present value of cash flows can be determined:

$$\begin{aligned} PV \text{ of parent cash flows} &= \frac{\$2{,}700{,}000}{(1.15)^1} + \frac{\$2{,}700{,}000}{(1.15)^2} + \frac{\$3{,}420{,}000}{(1.15)^3} + \frac{\$3{,}780{,}000}{(1.15)^4} \\ &= \$2{,}347{,}826 + \$2{,}041{,}588 + \$2{,}248{,}706 + \$2{,}161{,}227 \\ &= \$8{,}799{,}347 \end{aligned}$$

Given the present value of cash flows and the estimated initial outlay, the break-even salvage value is determined this way:

$$\begin{aligned} SV_n &= \left[IO - \sum \frac{CF_t}{(1+k)^t}\right](1+k)^n \\ &= (\$10{,}000{,}000 - \$8{,}799{,}347)(1.15)^4 \\ &= \$2{,}099{,}950 \end{aligned}$$

Given the original information in Exhibit 14.2, Spartan, Inc., will accept the project only if the salvage value is estimated to be at least \$2,099,950 (assuming that the project's required rate of return is 15 percent).

Assuming the forecasted exchange rate of \$.50 per Singapore dollar (2 Singapore dollars per U.S. dollar), the project must sell for more than S\$4,199,900 (computed as \$2,099,950 divided by \$.50) to exhibit a positive *NPV* (assuming no taxes are paid on this amount). If Spartan did not have a guarantee from the Singapore government, it could assess the probability that the subsidiary would sell for more than the break-even salvage value and then incorporate this assessment into its decision to accept or reject the project.

Impact of Project on Prevailing Cash Flows

Thus far, in our example, we have assumed that the new project has no impact on prevailing cash flows. In reality, however, there may often be an impact.

Reconsider the Spartan, Inc., example, assuming this time that (1) Spartan currently exports tennis rackets from its U.S. plant to Singapore; (2) Spartan, Inc., still considers establishing a subsidiary in Singapore because it expects production costs to be lower in Singapore than in the United States; and (3) without a subsidiary, Spartan's export business to Singapore is expected to generate net cash flows of $1 million over the next four years. With a subsidiary, these cash flows would be forgone. The effects of these assumptions are shown in Exhibit 14.7. The previously estimated cash flows to the parent from the subsidiary (drawn from Exhibit 14.2) are restated in Exhibit 14.7. These estimates do not account for forgone cash flows since the possible export business was not considered. If the export business is established, however, the forgone cash flows attributable to this business must be considered, as shown in Exhibit 14.7. The adjusted cash flows to the parent account for the project's impact on prevailing cash flows.

The present value of adjusted cash flows and cumulative *NPV* are also shown in Exhibit 14.7. The project's *NPV* is now negative as a result of the adverse effect on prevailing cash flows. Thus, the project will not be feasible if the exporting business to Singapore is eliminated.

Some foreign projects may have a favorable impact on prevailing cash flows. For example, if a manufacturer of computer components establishes a foreign subsidiary to manufacture computers, the subsidiary might order the components from the parent. In this case, the sales volume of the parent would increase.

Host Government Incentives

Foreign projects proposed by MNCs may have a favorable impact on economic conditions in the host country and are therefore encouraged by the host government. Any incentives offered by the host government must be incorporated into the capital budgeting analysis. For example, a low-rate host government loan or a reduced tax rate offered to the subsidiary will enhance periodic cash flows. If the government subsidizes the initial establishment of the subsidiary, the MNC's initial investment will be reduced.

Exhibit 14.7 Capital Budgeting When Prevailing Cash Flows Are Affected: Spartan, Inc.

	Year 0	Year 1	Year 2	Year 3	Year 4
Cash flows to parent, ignoring impact on prevailing cash flows		$2,700,000	$2,700,000	$3,420,000	$9,780,000
Impact of project on prevailing cash flows		−$1,000,000	−$1,000,000	−$1,000,000	−$1,000,000
Cash flows to parent, incorporating impact on prevailing cash flows		$1,700,000	$1,700,000	$2,420,000	$8,780,000
PV of cash flows to parent (15% discount rate)		$1,478,261	$1,285,444	$1,591,189	$5,019,994
Initial investment	$10,000,000				
Cumulative *NPV*		−$8,521,739	−$7,236,295	−$5,645,106	−$625,112

Real Options

Some capital budgeting projects contain real options, in that they may allow for additional business opportunities. Since these opportunities can generate cash flows, they can enhance the value of a project.

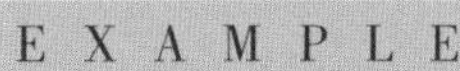

Topeka, Inc., considers undertaking a project requested by the government of Ukraine. This specific project would require a significant outlay for materials. Topeka determines that this project has a slight negative *NPV*. However, the project would allow Topeka to establish a relationship with the Ukrainian government, so that it would be well positioned to expand its business in Ukraine if the country's economy becomes more market oriented over time. Without a business relationship with the government, Topeka will not be positioned to expand in Ukraine. Thus, the government contract contains an implicit call option (to expand its business in Ukraine) that Topeka could exercise someday if Ukraine's economy becomes more market oriented. When the value of this real option is considered, the *NPV* of the government project becomes positive. Therefore, Topeka decides to undertake the project.

The value of a real option within a project is primarily influenced by two factors: (1) the probability that the real option will be exercised and (2) the *NPV* that will result from exercising the real option. In the previous example, Topeka's real option is influenced by (1) the probability that Ukraine's economy will become market oriented and (2) the *NPV* of opportunities that would be pursued under this condition.

Adjusting Project Assessment for Risk

If an MNC is unsure of the estimated cash flows of a proposed project, it needs to incorporate an adjustment for this risk. Three methods are commonly used to adjust the evaluation for risk:

- Risk-adjusted discount rate
- Sensitivity analysis
- Simulation

Each method is described in turn.

Risk-Adjusted Discount Rate

The greater the uncertainty about a project's forecasted cash flows, the larger should be the discount rate applied to cash flows, other things being equal. This risk-adjusted discount rate tends to reduce the worth of a project by a degree that reflects the risk the project exhibits. This approach is easy to use, but it is criticized for being somewhat arbitrary. In addition, an equal adjustment to the discount rate over all periods does not reflect differences in the degree of uncertainty from one period to another. If the projected cash flows among periods have different degrees of uncertainty, the risk adjustment of the cash flows should vary also.

Consider a country where the political situation is slowly destabilizing. The probability of blocked funds, expropriation, and other adverse events is increasing over time. Thus, cash flows sent to the parent are less certain in the distant future than they are in the near future. A different discount rate should therefore be applied to each period in accordance with its corresponding risk. Even so, the adjustment will be subjective and may not accurately reflect the risk.

Despite its subjectivity, the risk-adjusted discount rate is a commonly used technique, perhaps because of the ease with which it can be arbitrarily adjusted. In addition, there is no alternative technique that will perfectly adjust for risk, although in certain cases some others (discussed next) may better reflect a project's risk.

Sensitivity Analysis

Once the MNC has estimated the *NPV* of a proposed project, it may want to consider alternative estimates for its input variables.

EXAMPLE

Recall that the demand for the Spartan subsidiary's tennis rackets (in our earlier example) was estimated to be 60,000 in the first two years and 100,000 in the next two years. If demand turns out to be 60,000 in all four years, how will the *NPV* results change? Alternatively, what if demand is 100,000 in all four years? Use of such *what-if* scenarios is referred to as **sensitivity analysis.** The objective is to determine how sensitive the *NPV* is to alternative values of the input variables. The estimates of any input variables can be revised to create new estimates for *NPV*. If the *NPV* is consistently positive during these revisions, then the MNC should feel more comfortable about the project. If it is negative in many cases, the accept/reject decision for the project becomes more difficult.

The two exchange rate scenarios developed earlier represent a form of sensitivity analysis. Sensitivity analysis can be more useful than simple point estimates because it reassesses the project based on various circumstances that may occur. Many computer software packages are available to perform sensitivity analysis.

Simulation

Simulation can be used for a variety of tasks, including the generation of a probability distribution for *NPV* based on a range of possible values for one or more input variables. Simulation is typically performed with the aid of a computer package.

EXAMPLE

Reconsider Spartan, Inc., and assume that it expects the exchange rate to depreciate by 3 to 7 percent per year (with an equal probability of all values in this range occurring). Unlike a single point estimate, simulation can consider the range of possibilities for the Singapore dollar's exchange rate at the end of each year. It considers all point estimates for the other variables and randomly picks one of the possible values of the Singapore dollar's depreciation level for each of the four years. Based on this random selection process, the *NPV* is determined.

The procedure just described represents one iteration. Then the process is repeated: the Singapore dollar's depreciation for each year is again randomly selected (within the range of possibilities assumed earlier), and the *NPV* of the project is computed. The simulation program may be run for, say, 100 iterations. This means that 100 different possible scenarios are created for the possible exchange rates of the Singapore dollar during the four-year project period. Each iteration reflects a different scenario. The *NPV* of the project based on each scenario is then computed. Thus, simulation generates a distribution of *NPVs* for the project. The major advantage of simulation is that the MNC can examine the range of possible *NPVs* that may occur. From the information, it can determine the probability that the *NPV* will be positive or greater than a particular level. The greater the uncertainty of the exchange rate, the greater will be the uncertainty of the *NPV*. The risk of a project will be greater if it involves transactions in more volatile currencies, other things being equal.

In reality, many or all of the input variables necessary for multinational capital budgeting may be uncertain in the future. Probability distributions can be developed for all variables with uncertain future values. The final result is a distribution of possible *NPVs* that might occur for the project. The simulation technique does not put all of its emphasis on any one particular *NPV* forecast but instead provides a distribution of the possible outcomes that may occur.

The project's cost of capital can be used as a discount rate when simulation is performed. The probability that the project will be successful can be estimated by measuring the area within the probability distribution in which the $NPV > 0$. This area represents the probability that the present value of future cash flows will exceed the initial outlay. An MNC can also use the probability distribution to estimate the probability that the project will backfire by measuring the area in which $NPV < 0$.

Simulation is difficult to do manually because of the iterations necessary to develop a distribution of *NPVs*. Computer programs can run 100 iterations and generate results within a matter of seconds. The user of a simulation program must provide the probability distributions for the input variables that will affect the project's *NPV*. As with any model, the accuracy of results generated by simulation will be determined by the accuracy of the input.

MANAGING FOR VALUE

Wal-Mart's Decision to Expand in Germany

In recent years, Wal-Mart has grown substantially by penetrating foreign markets. It now has about 170 stores in Canada, 500 stores in South America (mostly in Mexico), 240 stores in the United Kingdom, 50 stores in Germany, and 13 stores in Asia. From a capital budgeting perspective, Wal-Mart pursues direct foreign investment because it expects to generate sufficient cash flows from applying its business model to foreign countries. In the United States, it has been very successful at using its size to buy products from wholesalers in bulk at low prices, employing its employees efficiently, using its brand name to attract demand for its products, and satisfying customers to gain repeat business.

Recently, Wal-Mart engaged in direct foreign investment in Germany by making two large acquisitions to expand its stores there. These acquisitions illustrate the difficulty of estimating the cash flows to be generated from a foreign target. First, the retail industry is subject to more regulation in Germany than in the United States. The German government frowned on Wal-Mart's aggressive strategy of gaining market share by offering lower prices than local competitors. Second, Wal-Mart's brand name is not as well known in Germany as in the United States. Third, economic conditions in Germany have been weaker than expected. Fourth, Wal-Mart's ability to use its employees efficiently is limited by the strong unions in Germany. Such country-specific characteristics have caused Wal-Mart's net cash flows to be less than expected.

In summary, Wal-Mart's performance in Germany has been limited due to economic conditions, political conditions, and industry conditions. When it assessed the feasibility of penetrating the European market, however, Wal-Mart used a long-term perspective and recognized that the full benefits of its expansion in Germany might not be realized for many years. The use of this long-term perspective to make international expansion decisions allowed Wal-Mart to maximize its value.

SUMMARY

- Capital budgeting may generate different results and a different conclusion depending on whether it is conducted from the perspective of an MNC's subsidiary or from the perspective of the MNC's parent. The subsidiary's perspective does not consider possible exchange rate and tax effects on cash flows transferred by the subsidiary to the parent. When a parent is deciding whether to implement an international project, it should determine whether the project is feasible from its own perspective.
- Multinational capital budgeting requires any input that will help estimate the initial outlay, periodic cash flows, salvage value, and required rate of return on the project. Once these factors are estimated, the international project's net present value can be estimated, just as if it were a domestic project. However, it is normally more difficult to estimate these factors for an international project. Exchange rates create an additional source of uncertainty because they affect the cash flows ultimately received by the parent as a result of the project. Other international conditions that can influence the cash flows ultimately received by the parent include the financing arrangement (parent versus subsidiary financing of the project), blocked funds by the host government, and host government incentives.
- The risk of international projects can be accounted for by adjusting the discount rate used to estimate the project's net present value. However, the adjustment to the discount rate is subjective. An alternative method is to estimate the net present value based on various possible scenarios for exchange rates or any other uncertain factors. This method is facilitated by the use of sensitivity analysis or simulation.

POINT COUNTER-POINT

Should MNCs Use Forward Rates to Estimate Dollar Cash Flows of Foreign Projects?

Point Yes. An MNC's parent should use the forward rate for each year in which it will receive net cash flows in a foreign currency. The forward rate is market-determined and serves as a useful forecast for future years.

Counter-Point No. An MNC should use its own forecasts for each year in which it will receive net cash flows in a foreign currency. If the forward rates for future time periods are higher than the MNC's expected spot rates, the MNC may accept a project that it should not accept.

Who Is Correct? Use InfoTrac or some other search engine to learn more about this issue. Which argument do you support? Offer your own opinion on this issue.

SELF TEST

Answers are provided in Appendix A at the back of the text.

1. Two managers of Marshall, Inc., assessed a proposed project in Jamaica. Each manager used exactly the same estimates of the earnings to be generated by the project, as these estimates were provided by other employees. The managers agree on the proportion of funds to be remitted each year, the life of the project, and the discount rate to be applied. Both managers also assessed the project from the U.S. parent's perspective. Nevertheless, one manager determined that this project had a large net present value, while the other manager determined that the project had a negative net present value. Explain the possible reasons for such a difference.
2. Pinpoint the parts of a multinational capital budgeting analysis for a proposed sales distribution center in Ireland that are sensitive when the forecast of a stable economy in Ireland is revised to predict a recession.
3. New Orleans Exporting Co. produces small computer components, which are then sold to Mexico. It plans to expand by establishing a plant in Mexico that will produce the components and sell them lo-

cally. This plant will reduce the amount of goods that are transported from New Orleans. The firm has determined that the cash flows to be earned in Mexico would yield a positive net present value after accounting for tax and exchange rate effects, converting cash flows to dollars, and discounting them at the proper discount rate. What other major factor must be considered to estimate the project's *NPV*?

4. Explain how the present value of the salvage value of an Indonesian subsidiary will be affected (from the U.S. parent's perspective) by (a) an increase in the risk of the foreign subsidiary and (b) an expectation that Indonesia's currency (rupiah) will depreciate against the dollar over time.

5. Wilmette Co. and Niles Co. (both from the United States) are assessing the acquisition of the same firm in Thailand and have obtained the future cash flow estimates (in Thailand's currency, baht) from the firm. Wilmette would use its retained earnings from U.S. operations to acquire the subsidiary. Niles Co. would finance the acquisition mostly with a term loan (in baht) from Thai banks. Neither firm has any other business in Thailand. Which firm's dollar cash flows would be affected more by future changes in the value of the baht (assuming that the Thai firm is acquired)?

6. Review the capital budgeting example of Spartan, Inc., discussed in this chapter. Identify the specific variables assessed in the process of estimating a foreign project's net present value (from a U.S. perspective) that would cause the most uncertainty about the *NPV*.

QUESTIONS AND APPLICATIONS

1. **MNC Parent's Perspective.** Why should capital budgeting for subsidiary projects be assessed from the parent's perspective? What additional factors that normally are not relevant for a purely domestic project deserve consideration in multinational capital budgeting?

2. **Accounting for Risk.** What is the limitation of using point estimates of exchange rates in the capital budgeting analysis?

   List the various techniques for adjusting risk in multinational capital budgeting. Describe any advantages or disadvantages of each technique.

   Explain how simulation can be used in multinational capital budgeting. What can it do that other risk adjustment techniques cannot?

3. **Uncertainty of Cash Flows.** Using the capital budgeting framework discussed in this chapter, explain the sources of uncertainty surrounding a proposed project in Hungary by a U.S. firm. In what ways is the estimated net present value of this project more uncertain than that of a similar project in a more developed European country?

4. **Accounting for Risk.** Your employees have estimated the net present value of project X to be $1.2 million. Their report says that they have not accounted for risk, but that with such a large *NPV*, the project should be accepted since even a risk-adjusted *NPV* would likely be positive. You have the final decision as to whether to accept or reject the project. What is your decision?

5. **Impact of Exchange Rates on *NPV*.**

   a. Describe in general terms how future appreciation of the euro will likely affect the value (from the parent's perspective) of a project established in Germany today by a U.S.-based MNC. Will the sensitivity of the project value be affected by the percentage of earnings remitted to the parent each year?

   b. Repeat this question, but assume the future depreciation of the euro.

6. **Impact of Financing on *NPV*.** Explain how the financing decision can influence the sensitivity of the net present value to exchange rate forecasts.

7. **September 11 Effects on *NPV*.** In August 2001, Woodsen, Inc., of Pittsburgh, Pennsylvania, considered the development of a large subsidiary in Greece. In response to the September 11, 2001 terrorist attack on the United States, its expected cash flows and earnings from this acquisition were reduced only slightly. Yet, the firm decided to retract its offer because of an increase in its required rate of return on the project, which caused the *NPV* to be negative. Explain why the required rate of return on its project may have increased after the attack.

8. **Assessing a Foreign Project.** Huskie Industries, a U.S.-based MNC, considers purchasing a small manufacturing company in France that sells products only within France. Huskie has no other existing business in France and no cash flows in euros. Would the proposed acquisition likely be more feasible if the euro is expected to appreciate or depreciate over the long run? Explain.

9. **Relevant Cash Flows in Disney's French Theme Park.** When Walt Disney World considered establishing a theme park in France, were the forecasted revenues and costs associated with the French park sufficient to assess the feasibility of this project? Were there any other "relevant cash flows" that deserved to be considered?

10. **Capital Budgeting Logic.** Athens, Inc., established a subsidiary in the United Kingdom that was independent of its operations in the United States. The subsidiary's performance was well above what was expected. Consequently, when a British firm approached Athens about the possibility of acquiring the subsidiary, Athens' chief financial officer implied that the subsidiary was performing so well that it was not for sale. Comment on this strategy.

11. **Capital Budgeting Logic.** Lehigh Co. established a subsidiary in Switzerland that was performing below the cash flow projections developed before the subsidiary was established. Lehigh anticipated that future cash flows would also be lower than the original cash flow projections. Consequently, Lehigh decided to inform several potential acquiring firms of its plan to sell the subsidiary. Lehigh then received a few bids. Even the highest bid was very low, but Lehigh accepted the offer. It justified its decision by stating that any existing project whose cash flows are not sufficient to recover the initial investment should be divested. Comment on this statement.

12. **Impact of Reinvested Foreign Earnings on *NPV*.** Flagstaff Corp. is a U.S.-based firm with a subsidiary in Mexico. It plans to reinvest its earnings in Mexican government securities for the next 10 years since the interest rate earned on these securities is so high. Then, after 10 years, it will remit all accumulated earnings to the United States. What is a drawback of using this approach? (Assume the securities have no default or interest rate risk.)

13. **Capital Budgeting Example.** Brower, Inc., just constructed a manufacturing plant in Ghana. The construction cost 9 billion Ghanian cedi. Brower intends to leave the plant open for three years. During the three years of operation, cedi cash flows are expected to be 3 billion cedi, 3 billion cedi, and 2 billion cedi, respectively. Operating cash flows will begin one year from today and are remitted back to the parent at the end of each year. At the end of the third year, Brower expects to sell the plant for 5 billion cedi. Brower has a required rate of return of 17 percent. It currently takes 8,700 cedi to buy one U.S. dollar, and the cedi is expected to depreciate by 5 percent per year.

    a. Determine the *NPV* for this project. Should Brower build the plant?

    b. How would your answer change if the value of the cedi was expected to remain unchanged from its current value of 8,700 cedi per U.S. dollar over the course of the three years? Should Brower construct the plant then?

14. **Impact of Financing on *NPV*.** Ventura Corp., a U.S.-based MNC, plans to establish a subsidiary in Japan. It is very confident that the Japanese yen will appreciate against the dollar over time. The subsidiary will retain only enough revenue to cover expenses and will remit the rest to the parent each year. Will Ventura benefit more from exchange rate effects if its parent provides equity financing for the subsidiary or if the subsidiary is financed by local banks in Japan? Explain.

15. **Accounting for Changes in Risk.** Santa Monica Co., a U.S.-based MNC, was considering establishing a consumer products division in Germany, which would be financed by German banks. Santa Monica completed its capital budgeting analysis in August. Then, in November, the government leadership stabilized and political conditions improved in Germany. In response, Santa Monica increased its expected cash flows by 20 percent but did not adjust the discount rate applied to the project. Should the discount rate be affected by the change in political conditions?

16. **Estimating the *NPV*.** Assume that a less developed country called LDC encourages direct foreign investment (DFI) in order to reduce its unemployment rate, currently at 15 percent. Also assume that

several MNCs are likely to consider DFI in this country. The inflation rate in recent years has averaged 4 percent. The hourly wage in LDC for manufacturing work is the equivalent of about $5 per hour. When Piedmont Co. developes cash flow forecasts to perform a capital budgeting analysis for a project in LDC, it assumes a wage rate of $5 in Year 1 and applies a 4 percent increase for each of the next 10 years. The components produced are to be exported to Piedmont's headquarters in the United States, where they will be used in the production of computers. Do you think Piedmont will overestimate or underestimate the net present value of this project? Why? (Assume that LDC's currency is tied to the dollar and will remain that way.)

17. **PepsiCo's Project in Brazil.** PepsiCo recently decided to invest more than $300 million for expansion in Brazil. Brazil offers considerable potential because it has 150 million people and their demand for soft drinks is increasing. However, the soft drink consumption is still only about one-fifth of the soft drink consumption in the United States. PepsiCo's initial outlay was used to purchase three production plants and a distribution network of almost 1,000 trucks to distribute its products to retail stores in Brazil. The expansion in Brazil was expected to make PepsiCo's products more accessible to Brazilian consumers.

    a. Given that PepsiCo's investment in Brazil was entirely in dollars, describe its exposure to exchange rate risk resulting from the project. Explain how the size of the parent's initial investment and the exchange rate risk would have been affected if PepsiCo had financed much of the investment with loans from banks in Brazil.

    b. Describe the factors that PepsiCo likely considered when estimating the future cash flows of the project in Brazil.

    c. What factors did PepsiCo likely consider in deriving its required rate of return on the project in Brazil?

    d. Describe the uncertainty that surrounds the estimate of future cash flows from the perspective of the U.S. parent.

    e. PepsiCo's parent was responsible for assessing the expansion in Brazil. Yet, PepsiCo already had some existing operations in Brazil. When capital budgeting analysis was used to determine the feasibility of this project, should the project have been assessed from a Brazilian perspective or a U.S. perspective? Explain.

18. **Impact of Asian Crisis.** Assume that Fordham Co. was evaluating a project in Thailand (to be financed with U.S. dollars). All cash flows generated from the project were to be reinvested in Thailand for several years. Explain how the Asian crisis would have affected the expected cash flows of this project and the required rate of return on this project. If the cash flows were to be remitted to the U.S. parent, explain how the Asian crisis would have affected the expected cash flows of this project.

19. **Tax Effects on *NPV*.** When considering the implementation of a project in one of various possible countries, what types of tax characteristics should be assessed among the countries? (See the chapter appendix.)

20. **Capital Budgeting Analysis.** A project in South Korea requires an initial investment of 2 billion South Korean won. The project is expected to generate net cash flows to the subsidiary of 3 billion and 4 billion won in the two years of operation, respectively. The project has no salvage value. The current value of the won is 1,100 won per U.S. dollar, and the value of the won is expected to remain constant over the next two years.

    a. What is the *NPV* of this project if the required rate of return is 13 percent?

    b. Repeat the question, except assume that the value of the won is expected to be 1,200 won per U.S. dollar after two years. Further assume that the funds are blocked and that the parent company will only be able to remit them back to the United States in two years. How does this affect the *NPV* of the project?

21. **Accounting for Exchange Rate Risk.** Carson Co. is considering a 10-year project in Hong Kong, where the Hong Kong dollar is tied to the U.S. dollar. Carson Co. uses sensitivity analysis that allows for alternative exchange rate scenarios. Why would Carson use this approach rather than using the pegged exchange rate as its exchange rate forecast in every year?

22. **Decisions Based on Capital Budgeting.** Marathon, Inc., considers a one-year project with the Belgian government. Its euro revenue would be guaranteed. Its consultant states that the percentage change in the euro is represented by a normal distribution and that based on a 95 percent confidence interval, the percentage change in the euro is expected to be between 0 percent and 6 percent. Marathon uses this information to create five scenarios: 0 percent, 3 percent, and 6 percent for the euro. It derives an estimated *NPV* based on each scenario and then determines the mean *NPV*. The *NPV* was positive for the 3 percent and 6 percent scenarios, but was slightly negative for the 0 percent scenario. This led Marathon to reject the project. Its manager stated that it did not want to pursue a project that had a one-in-three chance of having a negative *NPV*. Do you agree with the manager's interpretation of the analysis? Explain.

23. **Estimating Cash Flows of a Foreign Project.** Assume that Nike decides to build a shoe factory in Brazil; half the initial outlay will be funded by the parent's equity and half by borrowing funds in Brazil. Assume that Nike wants to assess the project from its own perspective to determine whether the project's future cash flows will provide a sufficient return to the parent to warrant the initial investment. Why will the estimated cash flows be different from the estimated cash flows of Nike's shoe factory in New Hampshire? Why will the initial outlay be different? Explain how Nike can conduct multinational capital budgeting in a manner that will achieve its objective.

ADVANCED QUESTIONS

24. **Break-even Salvage Value.** A project in Malaysia costs $4,000,000. Over the next three years, the project will generate total operating cash flows of $3,500,000, measured in today's dollars using a required rate of return of 14 percent. What is the break-even salvage value of this project?

25. **Capital Budgeting Analysis.** Zistine Co. considers a one-year project in New Zealand so that it can capitalize on its technology. It is risk-averse, but is attracted to the project because of a government guarantee. The project will generate a guaranteed NZ$8 million in revenue, paid by the New Zealand government at the end of the year. The payment by the New Zealand government is also guaranteed by a credible U.S. bank. The cash flows earned on the project will be converted to U.S. dollars and remitted to the parent in one year. The prevailing nominal one-year interest rate in New Zealand is 8 percent while the nominal one-year interest rate in the United States is 2 percent. Zistine's chief executive officer believes that the movement in the New Zealand dollar is highly uncertain over the next year, but his best guess is that the change in its value will be in accordance with the international Fisher effect (IFE). He also believes that interest rate parity holds. He provides this information to three recent finance graduates that he just hired as managers and asks them for their input.

a. The first manager states that due to the parity conditions, the feasibility of the project will be the same whether the cash flows are hedged with a forward contract or are not hedged. Is this manager correct? Explain.

b. The second manager states that the project should not be hedged. Based on the interest rates, the IFE suggests that Zistine Co. will benefit from the future exchange rate movements, so the project will generate a higher *NPV* if Zistine does not hedge. Is this manager correct? Explain.

c. The third manager states that the project should be hedged because the forward rate contains a premium and, therefore, the forward rate will generate more U.S. dollar cash flows than the expected amount of dollar cash flows if the firm remains unhedged. Is this manager correct? Explain.

26. **Accounting for Uncertain Cash Flows.** Blustream, Inc., considers a project in which it will sell the use of its technology to firms in Mexico. It already has received orders from Mexican firms that will generate MXP3,000,000 in revenue at the end of the next year. However, it might also receive a contract to provide this technology to the Mexican government. In this case, it will generate a total of MXP5,000,000 at the end of the next year. It will not know whether it will receive the government order until the end of the year.

Today's spot rate of the peso is $.14. The one-year forward rate is $.12. Blustream expects that the spot rate of the peso will be $.13 one year from now. The only initial outlay will be $300,000 to cover development expenses (regardless of whether the Mexican government purchases the technology). Blustream will pursue the project only if it can satisfy its required rate of return of 18 percent. Ignore possible tax effects. It decides to hedge the maximum amount of revenue that it will receive from the project.

a. Determine the *NPV* if Blustream receives the government contract.

b. If Blustream does not receive the contract, it will have hedged more than it needed to and will offset the excess forward sales by purchasing pesos in the spot market at the time the forward sale is executed. Determine the *NPV* of the project assuming that Blustream does not receive the government contract.

c. Now consider an alternative strategy in which Blustream only hedges the minimum peso revenue that it will receive. In this case, any revenue due to the government contract would not be hedged. Determine the *NPV* based on this alternative strategy and assume that Blustream receives the government contract.

d. If Blustream uses the alternative strategy of only hedging the minimum peso revenue that it will receive, determine the *NPV* assuming that it does not receive the government contract.

e. If there is a 50 percent chance that Blustream will receive the government contract, would you advise Blustream to hedge the maximum amount or the minimum amount of revenue that it may receive? Explain.

f. Blustream recognizes that it is exposed to exchange rate risk whether it hedges the minimum amount or the maximum amount of revenue it will receive. It considers a new strategy of hedging the minimum amount it will receive with a forward contract and hedging the additional revenue it might receive with a put option on Mexican pesos. The one-year put option has an exercise price of $.125 and a premium of $.01. Determine the *NPV* if Blustream uses this strategy and receives the government contract. Also, determine the *NPV* if Blustream uses this strategy and does not receive the government contract. Given that there is a 50 percent probability that Blustream will receive the government contract, would you use this new strategy or the strategy that you selected in question (e)?

27. **Capital Budgeting Analysis.** Wolverine Corp. currently has no existing business in New Zealand but is considering establishing a subsidiary there. The following information has been gathered to assess this project:

- The initial investment required is $50 million in New Zealand dollars (NZ$). Given the existing spot rate of $.50 per New Zealand dollar, the initial investment in U.S. dollars is $25 million. In addition to the NZ$50 million initial investment for plant and equipment, NZ$20 million is needed for working capital and will be borrowed by the subsidiary from a New Zealand bank. The New Zealand subsidiary will pay interest only on the loan each year, at an interest rate of 14 percent. The loan principal is to be paid in 10 years.
- The project will be terminated at the end of Year 3, when the subsidiary will be sold.
- The price, demand, and variable cost of the product in New Zealand are as follows:

Year	Price	Demand	Variable Cost
1	NZ$500	40,000 units	NZ$30
2	NZ$511	50,000 units	NZ$35
3	NZ$530	60,000 units	NZ$40

- The fixed costs, such as overhead expenses, are estimated to be NZ$6 million per year.
- The exchange rate of the New Zealand dollar is expected to be $.52 at the end of Year 1, $.54 at the end of Year 2, and $.56 at the end of Year 3.
- The New Zealand government will impose an income tax of 30 percent on income. In addition, it will impose a withholding tax of 10 percent on earnings remitted by the subsidiary. The U.S. government will allow a tax credit on the remitted earnings and will not impose any additional taxes.
- All cash flows received by the subsidiary are to be sent to the parent at the end of each year. The subsidiary will use its working capital to support ongoing operations.
- The plant and equipment are depreciated over 10 years using the straight-line depreciation method. Since the plant and equipment are initially valued at

NZ$50 million, the annual depreciation expense is NZ$5 million.

- In three years, the subsidiary is to be sold. Wolverine plans to let the acquiring firm assume the existing New Zealand loan. The working capital will not be liquidated but will be used by the acquiring firm that buys the subsidiary. Wolverine expects to receive NZ$52 million after subtracting capital gains taxes. Assume that this amount is not subject to a withholding tax.
- Wolverine requires a 20 percent rate of return on this project.

a. Determine the net present value of this project. Should Wolverine accept this project?

b. Assume that Wolverine is also considering an alternative financing arrangement, in which the parent would invest an additional $10 million to cover the working capital requirements so that the subsidiary would avoid the New Zealand loan. If this arrangement is used, the selling price of the subsidiary (after subtracting any capital gains taxes) is expected to be NZ$18 million higher. Is this alternative financing arrangement more feasible for the parent than the original proposal? Explain.

c. From the parent's perspective, would the *NPV* of this project be more sensitive to exchange rate movements if the subsidiary uses New Zealand financing to cover the working capital or if the parent invests more of its own funds to cover the working capital? Explain.

d. Assume Wolverine used the original financing proposal and that funds are blocked until the subsidiary is sold. The funds to be remitted are reinvested at a rate of 6 percent (after taxes) until the end of Year 3. How is the project's *NPV* affected?

e. What is the break-even salvage value of this project if Wolverine uses the original financing proposal and funds are not blocked?

f. Assume that Wolverine decides to implement the project, using the original financing proposal. Also assume that after one year, a New Zealand firm offers Wolverine a price of $27 million after taxes for the subsidiary and that Wolverine's original forecasts for Years 2 and 3 have not changed. Compare the present value of the expected cash flows if Wolverine keeps the subsidiary to the selling price. Should Wolverine divest the subsidiary? Explain.

28. **Capital Budgeting With Hedging.** Baxter Co. considers a project with Thailand's government. If it accepts the project, it will definitely receive one lump sum cash flow of 10 million Thai baht in five years. The spot rate of the Thai baht is presently $0.03. The annualized interest rate for a 5-year period is 4 percent in the United States and 17 percent in Thailand. Interest rate parity exists. Baxter plans to hedge its cash flows with a forward contract. What is the dollar amount of cash flows that Baxter will receive in five years if it accepts this project?

29. **Capital Budgeting and Financing.** Cantoon Co. is considering the acquisition of a unit from the French government. Its initial outlay would be $4 million. It will reinvest all the earnings in the unit. It expects that at the end of 8 years, it will sell the unit for 12 million euros after capital gains taxes are paid. The spot rate of the euro is $1.20 and is used as the forecast of the euro in the future years. Cantoon has no plans to hedge its exposure to exchange rate risk. The annualized U.S. risk-free interest rate is 5 percent regardless of the maturity of the debt, and the annualized risk-free interest rate on euros is 7 percent, regardless of the maturity of debt. Assume that interest rate parity exists. Cantoon's cost of capital is 20 percent. It plans to use cash to make the acquisition.

a. Determine the NPV under these conditions.

b. Rather than use all cash, Cantoon could partially finance the acquisition. It could obtain a loan of 3 million euros today that would be used to cover a portion of the acquisition. In this case, it would have to pay a lump sum total of 7 million euros at the end of 8 years to repay the loan. There are no interest payments on this debt. The way in which this financing deal is structured, none of the payment is tax-deductible. Determine the NPV if Cantoon uses the forward rate instead of the spot rate to forecast the future spot rate of the euro, and elects to partially finance the acquisition. You need to derive the 8-year forward rate for this specific question.

INTERNET APPLICATION

30. **MNC Cashflows in Portugal** The following website offers regional and country-specific information: **http://biz.yahoo.com/ifc/**. Go to the section on country-specific information on Europe, and then link to Portugal. Explain how the most recent conditions described for Portugal would possibly cause

an MNC to revise its expected cash flows from a project it considered six months ago. That is, identify any factors in the environment that would affect estimates of an MNC's future cash flows on proposed projects in Portugal. State whether the recent environmental changes would cause expected cash flows estimated as of today to be lower or higher than estimates made six months ago.

DISCUSSION IN THE BOARDROOM

This exercise can be found in Appendix E at the back of this textbook.

RUNNING YOUR OWN MNC

This exercise can be found on the Xtra! website at **http://maduraxtra.swlearning.com**.

BLADES, INC. CASE

Decision by Blades, Inc., to Invest in Thailand

Since Ben Holt, Blades' chief financial officer (CFO), believes the growth potential for the roller blade market in Thailand is very high, he, together with Blades' board of directors, has decided to invest in Thailand. The investment would involve establishing a subsidiary in Bangkok consisting of a manufacturing plant to produce "Speedos," Blades' high-quality roller blades. Holt believes that economic conditions in Thailand will be relatively strong in 10 years, when he expects to sell the subsidiary.

Blades will continue exporting to the United Kingdom under an existing agreement with Jogs, Ltd., a British retailer. Furthermore, it will continue its sales in the United States. Under an existing agreement with Entertainment Products, Inc., a Thai retailer, Blades is committed to selling 180,000 pairs of Speedos to the retailer at a fixed price of 4,594 Thai baht per pair. Once operations in Thailand commence, the agreement will last another year, at which time it may be renewed. Thus, during its first year of operations in Thailand, Blades will sell 180,000 pairs of roller blades to Entertainment Products under the existing agreement whether it has operations in the country or not. If it establishes the plant in Thailand, Blades will produce 108,000 of the 180,000 Entertainment Products Speedos at the plant during the last year of the agreement. Therefore, the new subsidiary would need to import 72,000 pairs of speedos from the United States so that it can accommodate its agreement with Entertainment Products. It will save the equivalent of 300 baht per pair in varible costs on the 108,000 pairs not previously manufactured in Thailand.

Entertainment Products has already declared its willingness to renew the agreement for another three years under identical terms. Because of recent delivery delays, however, it is willing to renew the agreement only if Blades has operations in Thailand. Moreover, if Blades has a subsidiary in Thailand, Entertainment Products will keep renewing the existing agreement as long as Blades operates in Thailand. If the agreement is renewed, Blades expects to sell a total of 300,000 pairs of Speedos annually during its first two years of operation in Thailand to various retailers, including 180,000 pairs to Entertainment Products. After this time, it expects to sell 400,000 pairs annually (including 180,000 to Entertainment Products). If the agreement is not renewed, Blades will be able to sell only 5,000 pairs to Entertainment Products annually, but not at a fixed price. Thus, if the agreement is not renewed, Blades expects to sell a total of 125,000 pairs of Speedos annually during its first two years of operation in Thailand and 225,000 pairs annually thereafter. Pairs not sold under the contractual agreement with Entertainment Products will be sold for 5,000 Thai baht per pair, since Entertainment Products had required a lower price to compensate it for the risk of being unable to sell the pairs it purchased from Blades.

Ben Holt wishes to analyze the financial feasibility of establishing a subsidiary in Thailand. As a Blades' financial analyst, you have been given the task of analyzing the proposed project. Since future economic conditions in Thailand are highly uncertain, Holt has also asked you to conduct some sensitivity analyses. Fortunately, he has provided most of the information you need to conduct a capital budgeting analysis. This information is detailed here:

- The building and equipment needed will cost 550 million Thai baht. This amount includes additional funds to support working capital.
- The plant and equipment, valued at 300 million baht, will be depreciated using straight-line depreciation. Thus, 30 million baht will be depreciated annually for 10 years.

- The variable costs needed to manufacture Speedos are estimated to be 3,500 baht per pair next year.
- Blades' fixed operating expenses, such as administrative salaries, will be 25 million baht next year.
- The current spot exchange rate of the Thai baht is $0.023. Blades expects the baht to depreciate by an average of 2 percent per year for the next 10 years.
- The Thai government will impose a 25 percent tax rate on income and a 10 percent withholding tax on any funds remitted by the subsidiary to Blades. Any earnings remitted to the United States will not be taxed again.
- After 10 years, Blades expects to sell its Thai subsidiary. It expects to sell the subsidiary for about 650 million baht, after considering any capital gains taxes.
- The average annual inflation in Thailand is expected to be 12 percent. Unless prices are contractually fixed, revenue, variable costs, and fixed costs are subject to inflation and are expected to change by the same annual rate as the inflation rate.

Blades could continue its current operations of exporting to and importing from Thailand, which have generated a return of about 20 percent. Blades requires a return of 25 percent on this project in order to justify its investment in Thailand. All excess funds generated by the Thai subsidiary will be remitted to Blades and will be used to support U.S. operations.

Ben Holt has asked you to answer the following questions:

1. Should the sales and the associated costs of 180,000 pairs of roller blades to be sold in Thailand under the existing agreement be included in the capital budgeting analysis to decide whether Blades should establish a subsidiary in Thailand? Should the sales resulting from a renewed agreement be included? Why or why not?
2. Using a spreadsheet, conduct a capital budgeting analysis for the proposed project, assuming that Blades renews the agreement with Entertainment Products. Should Blades establish a subsidiary in Thailand under these conditions?
3. Using a spreadsheet, conduct a capital budgeting analysis for the proposed project assuming that Blades does not renew the agreement with Entertainment Products. Should Blades establish a subsidiary in Thailand under these conditions? Should Blades renew the agreement with Entertainment Products?
4. Since future economic conditions in Thailand are uncertain, Ben Holt would like to know how critical the salvage value is in the alternative you think is most feasible.
5. The future value of the baht is highly uncertain. Under a worst case scenario, the baht may depreciate by as much as 5 percent annually. Revise your spreadsheet to illustrate how this would affect Blades' decision to establish a subsidiary in Thailand. (Use the capital budgeting analysis you have identified as the most favorable from questions 2 and 3 to answer this question.)

SMALL BUSINESS DILEMMA

Multinational Capital Budgeting by the Sports Exports Company

Jim Logan, owner of the Sports Exports Company, has been pleased with his success in the United Kingdom. He began his business by producing footballs and exporting them to the United Kingdom. While American-style football is still not nearly as popular in the United Kingdom as it is in the United States, his firm controls the market in the United Kingdom. Jim is considering an application of the same business in Mexico. He would produce the footballs in the United States and export them to a distributor of sporting goods in Mexico, who would sell the footballs to retail stores. The distributor likely would want to pay for the product each month in Mexican pesos. Jim would need to hire one full-time employee in the United States to produce the footballs. He would also need to lease one more warehouse.

1. Describe the capital budgeting steps that would be necessary to determine whether this proposed project is feasible, as related to this specific situation.
2. Explain why there is uncertainty surrounding the cash flows of this project.

APPENDIX 14

Incorporating International Tax Laws in Multinational Capital Budgeting

Tax laws can vary among countries in many ways, but any type of tax causes an MNC's after-tax cash flows to differ from its before-tax cash flows. To estimate the future cash flows that are to be generated by a proposed foreign project (such as the establishment of a new subsidiary or the acquisition of a foreign firm), MNCs must first estimate the taxes that they will incur due to the foreign project. This appendix provides a general background on some of the more important international tax characteristics that an MNC must consider when assessing foreign projects. Financial managers do not necessarily have to be international tax experts because they may be able to rely on the MNC's international tax department or on independent tax consultants for guidance. Nevertheless, they should at least be aware of international tax characteristics that can affect the cash flows of a foreign project and recognize how those characteristics can vary among the countries where foreign projects are considered.

Variation in Tax Laws among Countries

Each country generates tax revenue in different ways. The United States relies on corporate and individual income taxes for federal revenue. Other countries may depend more on a *value-added tax (VAT)* or excise taxes. Since each country has its own philosophy on whom to tax and how much, it is not surprising that the tax treatment of corporations differs among countries. Because each country has a unique tax system and tax rates, MNCs need to recognize the various tax provisions of each country where they consider investing in a foreign project. The more important tax characteristics of a country to be considered in an MNC's international tax assessment are (1) corporate income taxes, (2) withholding taxes, (3) personal and excise tax rates, (4) provision for carrybacks and carryforwards, (5) tax treaties, (6) tax credits, and (7) taxes on income from intercompany transactions. A discussion of each characteristic follows.

Corporate Income Taxes

In general, countries impose taxes on corporate income generated within their borders, even if the parents of those corporations are based in other countries. Each country has its unique corporate income tax laws. The United States, for example, taxes the worldwide income of U.S. *persons*, a term that includes corporations. As a general rule, however, foreign income of a foreign subsidiary of a U.S. company is not taxed until it is transferred to the U.S. parent by payment of dividends or a liquidation distribution. This is the concept of deferral.

http://

The Price Waterhouse Coopers site at http://www.pwcglobal.com provides access to country-specific information such as general business rules and regulations and tax environments.

An MNC planning direct foreign investment in foreign countries must determine how the anticipated earnings from a foreign project will be affected. Tax rates imposed on income earned by businesses (including foreign subsidiaries of MNCs) or income remitted to a parent are shown in Exhibit 14A.1 for several countries. The tax rates may be lower than what is shown for corporations that have relatively low levels of earnings. This exhibit shows the extent to which corporate income tax rates can vary among host countries and illustrates why MNCs closely assess the tax guidelines in any foreign country where they consider conducting direct foreign investment. Given differences in tax deductions, depreciation, business subsidies, and other factors, corporate tax differentials cannot be measured simply by comparing quoted tax rates across countries.

Corporate tax rates can also differ within a country, depending on whether the entity is a domestic corporation. Also, if an unregistered foreign corporation is considered to have a permanent establishment in a country, it may be subject to that country's tax laws on income earned within its borders. Generally, a permanent establishment includes an office or fixed place of business or a specified kind of agency (*independent* agents are normally excluded) through which active and continuous business is conducted. In some cases, the tax depends on the industry or on the form of business used (e.g., corporation, branch, partnership).

Exhibit 14A.1

Comparison of Tax Characteristics among Countries

Country	Corporate Income Tax	Country	Corporate Income Tax
Argentina	35%	Israel	36
Australia	30	Italy	37
Austria	34	Japan	42
Belgium	34	Korea	30
Brazil	34	Malaysia	28
Canada	36	Mexico	33
Chile	17	Netherlands	35
China	33	New Zealand	33
Czech Republic	28	Singapore	22
France	34	Spain	35
Germany	38	Switzerland	24
Hong Kong	17	Taiwan	25
Hungary	16	United Kingdom	30
India	36	United States	35
Indonesia	30	Venezuela	34
Ireland	13		

Source: Worldwide Corporate Tax Guide, Ernst & Young. The numbers provided are for illustrative purposes only, as the actual tax rate may depend on specific characteristics of the MNC.

Withholding Taxes

The following types of payments by an MNC's subsidiary are commonly subject to a withholding tax by the host government: (1) A subsidiary may remit a portion of its earnings, referred to as *dividends*, to its parent since the parent is the shareholder of the subsidiary. (2) The subsidiary may pay interest to the parent or to other nonresident debtholders from which it received loans. (3) The subsidiary may make payments to the parent or to other nonresident firms in return for the use of patents (such as technology) or other rights. The payment of dividends reduces the amount of reinvestment by the subsidiary in the host country. The payments by the subsidiary to nonresident firms to cover interest or patents reflect expenses by the subsidiary, which will normally reduce its taxable income and therefore will reduce the corporate income taxes paid to the host government. Thus, withholding taxes may be a way for host governments to tax MNCs that make interest or patent payments to nonresident firms.

Since withholding taxes imposed on the subsidiary can reduce the funds remitted by the subsidiary to the parent, the withholding taxes must be accounted for in a capital budgeting analysis conducted by the parent. As with corporate tax rates, the withholding tax rate can vary substantially among countries.

Reducing Exposure to Withholding Taxes. Withholding taxes can be reduced by income tax treaties (discussed shortly). Because of tax treaties between some countries, the withholding taxes may be lower when the MNC's parent is based in a county participating in the treaties.

If the host country government of a particular subsidiary imposes a high withholding tax on subsidiary earnings remitted to the parent, the parent of the MNC may instruct the subsidiary to temporarily refrain from remitting earnings and to reinvest them in the host country instead. As an alternative approach, the MNC may instruct the subsidiary to set up a research and development division that will enhance subsidiaries elsewhere. The main purpose behind this strategy is to efficiently use the funds abroad when the funds cannot be sent to the parent without excessive taxation. Since international tax laws can influence the timing of the transfer of funds to the parent, they affect the timing of cash flows on proposed foreign projects. Therefore, the international tax implications must be understood before the cash flows of a foreign project can be estimated.

Personal and Excise Tax Rates

An MNC is more likely to be concerned with corporate tax rates and withholding tax rates than individual tax rates because its cash flows are directly affected by the taxes incurred. However, a country's individual tax rates can indirectly affect an MNC's cash flows because the MNC may have to pay higher wages to employees in countries (such as in Europe) where personal income is taxed at a relatively high rate. In addition, a country's value-added tax or excise tax may affect cash flows to be generated from a foreign project because it may make the products less competitive on a global basis (reducing the expected quantity of products to be sold).

Provision for Carrybacks and Carryforwards

Negative earnings from operations can often be carried back or forward to offset earnings in other years. The laws pertaining to these so-called **net operating loss carrybacks** and **carryforwards** can vary among countries. An MNC generally does not plan to generate negative earnings in foreign countries. If negative earnings do occur, however, it is desirable to be able to use them to offset other years of positive earnings. Most foreign countries do not allow negative earnings to be carried back but allow some flexibility in carrying losses forward. Since many foreign projects are expected to result in negative earnings in the early years, the tax laws for the country of concern will affect the future tax deductions resulting from these losses and will therefore affect the future cash flows of the foreign project.

Tax Treaties

Countries often establish income tax treaties, whereby one partner will reduce its taxes by granting a credit for taxes imposed on corporations operating within the other treaty partner's tax jurisdiction. Income tax treaties help corporations avoid exposure to double taxation. Some treaties apply to taxes paid on income earned by MNCs in foreign countries. Other treaties apply to withholding taxes imposed by the host country on foreign earnings that are remitted to the parent.

Without such treaties, subsidiary earnings could be taxed by the host country and then again by the parent's country when received by the parent. To the extent that the parent uses some of these earnings to provide cash dividends for shareholders, triple taxation could result (since the dividend income is also taxed at the shareholder level). Because income tax treaties reduce taxes on earnings generated by MNCs, they help stimulate direct foreign investment. Many foreign projects that are perceived as feasible would not be feasible without income tax treaties because the expected cash flows would be reduced by excessive taxation.

Tax Credits

Even without income tax treaties, an MNC may be allowed a credit for income and withholding taxes paid in one country against taxes owed by the parent if it meets certain requirements. Like income tax treaties, tax credits help to avoid double taxation and stimulate direct foreign investment.

Tax credit policies vary somewhat among countries, but they generally work like this. Consider a U.S.-based MNC subject to a U.S. tax rate of 35 percent. Assume that a foreign subsidiary of this corporation has generated earnings taxed at less than 35 percent by the host country's government. The earnings remitted to the parent from the subsidiary will be subject to an additional amount of U.S. tax to bring the total tax up to 35 percent. From the parent's point of view, the tax on its subsidiary's remitted earnings are 35 percent overall, so it does not matter whether the host country of the subsidiary or the United States receives most of the taxes. From the perspective of the governments of these two countries, however, the allocation of taxes is very important. If subsidiaries of U.S. corporations are established in foreign countries, and if these countries tax income at a rate close to 35 percent, they can generate large tax revenues from income earned by the subsidiaries. The host countries receive the tax revenues at the expense of the parent's country (the United States, in this case).

If the corporate income tax rate in a foreign country is greater than 35 percent, the United States generally does not impose any additional taxes on earnings remitted to a U.S. parent by foreign subsidiaries in that country. In fact, under current law, the United States allows the excess foreign tax to be credited against other taxes owed by the parent, due on the same type of income generated by subsidiaries in other lower-tax countries. In a sense, this suggests that some host countries could charge abnormally high corporate income tax rates to foreign subsidiaries and still attract direct foreign investment. If the MNC in our example has subsidiaries located in some countries with low corporate income taxes, the U.S. tax on earnings remitted to the U.S. parent will normally bring the total tax up to 35 percent. Yet, credits against excessive income taxes by high-tax countries on foreign subsidiaries could offset these taxes that would otherwise be paid to the U.S. government. Due to tax credits, therefore, an MNC might be more willing to invest in a project in a country with excessive tax rates.

Basic information on a country's current taxes may not be sufficient for determining the tax effects of a particular foreign project because tax incentives may be offered in particular circumstances, and tax rates can change over time. Consider an MNC that plans to establish a manufacturing plant in Country Y rather than Country X. Assume that while many economic characteristics favor Country X, the current tax rates in Country Y are lower. However, whereas tax rates in Country X have been historically stable and are expected to continue that way, they have been changing every few years in Country Y. In this case, the MNC must assess the future uncertainty of the tax rates. It cannot treat the current tax rate of Country Y as a constant when conducting a capital budgeting analysis. Instead, it must consider possible changes in the tax rates over time and, based on these possibilities, determine whether Country Y's projected tax advantages *over time* sufficiently outweigh the advantages of Country X. One approach to account for possible changes in the tax rates is to use sensitivity analysis, which measures the sensitivity of the net present value (*NPV*) of after-tax cash flows to various possible tax changes over time. For each tax scenario, a different *NPV* is projected. By accounting for each possible tax scenario, the MNC can develop a distribution of possible *NPV*s that may occur and can then compare these for each country.

Two critical, broadly defined functions are necessary to determine how international tax laws affect the cash flows of a foreign project. The first is to be aware of all the current (and possible future) tax laws that exist for each country where the MNC does (or plans to do) business. The second is to take the information generated from the first function and apply it to forecasted earnings and remittances to determine the taxes, so that the proposed project's cash flows can be estimated.

Taxes on Income from Intercompany Transactions

Many of an MNC's proposed foreign projects will involve intercompany transactions. For example, a U.S-based MNC may consider acquiring a foreign firm that will produce and deliver supplies to its U.S. subsidiaries. Under these conditions, the MNC must use transfer pricing, which involves pricing the transactions between two entities (such as subsidiaries) of the same corporation. When MNCs consider new foreign projects, they must incorporate their transfer pricing to properly estimate cash flows that will be generated from these projects. Therefore, before the feasibility of a foreign project can be determined, transfer pricing decisions must be made on any anticipated intercompany transactions that would result from the new project. MNCs are subject to some guidelines on transfer pricing, but they usually have some flexibility and tend to use a transfer pricing policy that will minimize taxes while satisfying the guidelines.

EXAMPLE

Oakland Corp. has established two subsidiaries to capitalize on low production costs. One of these subsidiaries (called Hitax Sub) is located in a country whose government imposes a 50 percent tax rate on before-tax earnings. Hitax Sub produces partially finished products and sends them to the other subsidiary (called Lotax Sub) where the final assembly takes place. The host government of Lotax Sub imposes a 20 percent tax on before-tax earnings. To simplify the example, assume that no dividends are to be remitted to the parent in the near future. Given this information, pro forma income statements would be as shown in the top part of Exhibit 14A.2 for Hitax Sub (second column), Lotax Sub (third column), and the combined subsidiaries (last column). The income statement items are reported in U.S. dollars to more easily illustrate how a revised transfer pricing policy can affect earnings and cash flows.

The sales level shown for Hitax Sub matches the cost of goods sold for Lotax Sub, indicating that all Hitax Sub sales are to Lotax Sub. The additional expenses incurred by Lotax Sub to complete the product are classified as operating expenses.

Exhibit 14A.2 Impact of Transfer Pricing Adjustment on Pro Forma Earnings and Taxes: Oakland Corp. (in Thousands)

	Original Estimates		
	Hitax Sub	Lotax Sub	Combined[1]
Sales	$100,000	$150,000	$250,000
Less: Cost of goods sold	50,000	100,000	150,000
Gross profit	50,000	50,000	100,000
Less: Operating expenses	20,000	20,000	40,000
Earnings before interest and taxes	30,000	30,000	60,000
Interest expense	5,000	5,000	10,000
Earnings before taxes	25,000	25,000	50,000
Taxes (50% for Hitax and 20% for Lotax)	12,500	5,000	17,500
Earnings after taxes	$ 12,500	$ 20,000	$ 32,500
	Revised Estimates Based on Adjusting Transfer Pricing Policy		
	Hitax Sub	Lotax Sub	Combined[1]
Sales	$80,000	$150,000	$230,000
Less: Cost of goods sold	50,000	80,000	130,000
Gross profit	30,000	70,000	100,000
Less: Operating expenses	20,000	20,000	40,000
Earnings before interest and taxes	10,000	50,000	60,000
Interest expense	5,000	5,000	10,000
Earnings before taxes	5,000	45,000	50,000
Taxes (50% for Hitax and 20% for Lotax)	2,500	9,000	11,500
Earnings after taxes	$ 2,500	$ 36,000	$ 38,500

[1]The combined numbers are shown here for illustrative purposes only and do not reflect the firm's official consolidated financial statements. When consolidating sales for financial statements, intercompany transactions (between subsidiaries) would be eliminated. This example is intended simply to illustrate how total taxes paid by subsidiaries are lower when transfer pricing is structured to shift some gross profit from a high-tax subsidiary to a low-tax subsidiary.

Notice from Exhibit 14A.2 that both subsidiaries have the same earnings before taxes. Yet, because of the different tax rates, Hitax Sub's after-tax income is $7.5 million less than Lotax Sub's. If Oakland Corp. can revise its transfer pricing, its combined earnings after taxes will be increased. To illustrate, suppose that the price of products sent from Hitax Sub to Lotax Sub is reduced, causing Hitax Sub's sales to decline from $100 million to $80 million. This also reduces Lotax Sub's cost of goods sold by $20 million. The revised pro forma income statement resulting from the change in the transfer pricing policy is shown in the bottom part of Exhibit 14A.2. The two subsidiaries' forecasted earnings before taxes now differ by $40 million, although the combined amount has not changed. Because earnings have been shifted from Hitax Sub to Lotax Sub, the total tax payments are reduced to $11.5 million from the original estimate of $17.5 million. Thus, the corporate taxes imposed on earnings are now forecasted to be $6 million lower than originally expected.

It should be mentioned that possible adjustments in the transfer pricing policies may be limited because host governments may restrict such practices when the intent is to avoid taxes. Transactions between subsidiaries of a firm are supposed to be priced using the principle of "arm's-length" transactions. That is, the price should be set as if the buyer is unrelated to the seller and should not be adjusted simply to shift tax burdens. Nevertheless, there is some flexibility on transfer pricing policies, enabling MNCs from all countries to attempt to establish policies that are within legal limits, but also reduce tax burdens. Even if the transfer price reflects the "fair" price that would normally be charged in the market, one subsidiary can still charge another for technology transfers, research and development expenses, or other forms of overhead expenses incurred.

The actual mechanics of international transfer pricing go far beyond the example provided here. The U.S. laws in this area are particularly strict. Nevertheless, there are various ways that MNCs can justify increasing prices at one subsidiary and reducing them at another.

There is substantial evidence that MNCs based in numerous countries use transfer pricing strategies to reduce their taxes. Moreover, transfer pricing restrictions can be circumvented in several ways. Various fees can be implemented for services, research and development, royalties, and administrative duties. Although the fees may be imposed to shift earnings and minimize taxes, they have the effect of distorting the actual performance of each subsidiary. To correct for any distortion, the MNC can use a centralized approach to account for the transfer pricing strategy when assessing the performance of each subsidiary.

USING THE WEB

Country Corporate Tax Rates An MNC must determine a country's corporate tax rates before it can properly estimate its cash flows from establishing direct foreign investment there. Information about taxes imposed by each country is provided at http://biz.yahoo.com/ifc/. Click on any country listed, then click on Tax Regulations. Detailed information about how an MNC would be taxed on various forms of income is available through various links, including Corporate Income Taxes, Dividend Withholding Tax, Interest Withholding Tax, and Royalties and Fees Withholding Tax.

CHAPTER 15

Multinational Restructuring

Multinational corporations (MNCs) commonly engage in **multinational restructuring**, which involves restructuring the composition of their multinational assets or liabilities. Thus, multinational restructuring decisions not only determine the types of assets, but also the countries where those assets are located. Financial managers must understand how to assess restructuring alternatives so that they can make restructuring decisions that maximize the value of the MNC.

The specific objectives of this chapter are to:

- provide a background on how MNCs use international acquisitions as a form of multinational restructuring,
- explain how MNCs conduct valuations of foreign target firms,
- explain why valuations of a target firm vary among MNCs that plan to restructure by acquiring a target, and
- identify other types of multinational restructuring besides international acquisitions.

Background on Multinational Restructuring

Decisions by an MNC to build a new subsidiary in the Netherlands, to acquire a company in Italy, to sell its Singapore subsidiary, to downsize its operations in New Zealand, or to shift some production from its British subsidiary to its Mexican subsidiary all represent forms of multinational restructuring. Even the most successful MNCs continuously assess possible forms of multinational restructuring so that they can capitalize on changing economic, political, or industry conditions across countries.

MNCs reevaluate their existing businesses and other proposed projects when determining the ideal composition of assets to employ and the locations where the assets are employed. Even if an existing business adds value to the MNC, it may be worthwhile to assess whether the business would generate more value to the MNC if it was restructured.

Trends in International Acquisitions

The volume of foreign acquisitions of U.S. firms has increased consistently since 1993. In particular, European firms have been attractive targets for U.S. firms attempting to establish a presence in Europe due to the more uniform regulations across countries in the European Union, the momentum for free enterprise in Eastern Europe, and the inception of the euro. U.S. firms acquire more targets in the United Kingdom than in any other country. British and Canadian firms are the most common non-U.S. acquirers of U.S. targets.

Model for Valuing a Foreign Target

http://

http://www.cia.gov provides a link to the *World Factbook,* which has valuable information about countries that would be considered by MNCs that may attempt to acquire foreign targets.

An MNC's decision to invest in a foreign company is similar to the decision to invest in other projects, in that it is based on a comparison of benefits and costs as measured by net present value. From an MNC's parent's perspective, the foreign target's value can be estimated as the present value of cash flows that it would receive from the target, as the target would become a foreign subsidiary owned by the parent.

The MNC's parent would consider investing in the target only if the estimated present value of the cash flows it would ultimately receive from the target over time exceeds the initial outlay necessary to purchase the target. Thus, capital budgeting analysis can be used to determine whether a firm should be acquired. The net present value of a company from the acquiring firm's perspective (NPV_a) is

$$NPV_a = -IO_a + \sum_{t=1}^{n} \frac{CF_{a,t}}{(1+k)^t} + \frac{SV_a}{(1+k)^n}$$

MANAGING FOR VALUE

International Acquisitions

An international acquisition of a firm is similar to other international projects in that it requires an initial outlay and is expected to generate cash flows whose present value will exceed the initial outlay. Many international acquisitions are motivated by the desire to increase global market share or to capitalize on economies of scale through global consolidation. Many U.S.-based MNCs including Rockwell International, Ford Motor Co., Scott Paper Co., Borden, Inc., and Dow Chemical Co. have recently engaged in international acquisitions.

MNCs may view international acquisitions as a better form of direct foreign investment (DFI) than establishing a new subsidiary. However, there are distinct differences between these two forms of DFI. Through an international acquisition, the firm can immediately expand its international business since the target is already in place. Establishing a new subsidiary requires time. Second, an international acquisition can benefit from the customer relationships that have already been established. These advantages of an international acquisition over the establishment of a foreign subsidiary must be weighed against the higher costs of the acquisition. When viewed as a project, the international acquisition usually generates quicker and larger cash flows than the establishment of a new subsidiary, but it also requires a larger initial outlay. International acquisitions also necessitate the integration of the parent's management style with that of the foreign target.

where

IO_a = initial outlay needed by the acquiring firm to acquire the target
$CF_{a,t}$ = cash flow to be generated by the target for the acquiring firm
k = required rate of return on the acquisition of the target
SV_a = salvage value of the target (expected selling price of the target at a point in the future)
n = time when the target will be sold by the acquiring firm

The capital budgeting analysis of a foreign target must account for the exchange rate of concern. For example, consider a U.S.-based MNC that assesses the acquisition of a foreign company. The dollar initial outlay ($IO_{U.S.}$) needed by the U.S. firm is determined by the acquisition price in foreign currency units (IO_f) and the spot rate of the foreign currency (S):

$$IO_{U.S.} = IO_f(S)$$

The dollar amount of cash flows to the U.S. firm is determined by the foreign currency cash flows ($CF_{f,t}$) per period remitted to the United States and the spot rate at that time (S_t):

$$CF_{a,t} = (CF_{f,t})S_t$$

This ignores any withholding taxes or blocked-funds restrictions imposed by the host government and any income taxes imposed by the U.S. government. The dollar amount of salvage value to the U.S. firm is determined by the salvage value in foreign currency units (SV_f) and the spot rate at the time (period n) when it is converted to dollars (S_n):

$$SV_a = (SV_f)S_n$$

The net present value of a foreign target can be derived by substituting the equalities just described in the capital budgeting equation:

$$\begin{aligned} NPV_a &= -IO_a + \sum_{t=1}^{n} \frac{CF_{a,t}}{(1+k)^t} + \frac{SV_a}{(1+k)^n} \\ &= -(IO_f)S + \sum_{t=1}^{n} \frac{(CF_{f,t})S_t}{(1+k)^t} + \frac{(SV_f)S_n}{(1+k)^n} \end{aligned}$$

http://

Visit the World Bank's website at http://www.worldbank.org for data on socioeconomic development and performance indicators as well as links to statistical and project-oriented publications and analyses.

Assessing Potential Acquisitions after the Asian Crisis

Although the Asian crisis had devastating effects, it created an opportunity for some MNCs to pursue new business in Asia. The initial outlay for acquiring a firm in Asia was lower as a result of the crisis. First, property values in Asia had declined. Second, the parent's currency (for parents in the United States or Europe) had more purchasing power due to the weakening of the Asian currencies. Third, many firms in Asia were near bankruptcy and were unable to obtain necessary funding. Fourth, the governments in these countries were more willing to allow foreign acquisitions of local firms (especially those that were failing) as a means of resolving the crisis. Consequently, some U.S. and European firms pursued direct foreign investment in Asia during the Asian crisis.

In the first six months of 1998, U.S. firms invested more than $8 billion in Asia—more than double the amount they had invested there in all of 1997. Procter & Gamble agreed to acquire Sanyong Paper (a large conglomerate in South Korea) during the crisis. Citicorp obtained a large stake of First City Bank in Thailand.

Firms that made aquistions had to consider the obvious adverse effects of the crisis in their capital budgeting analysis. The lower economic growth meant that most Asian projects would generate lower cash flows, and the weak currencies reduced the amount of cash flows (in the parent's currency) that would ultimately be received as a return on the parent's investment.

To the extent that the firms believed that the Asian currency values had hit bottom and would rebound, they could assume that any new acquisitions of Asian firms would benefit from future exchange rate movements. Firms could initiate their investment in Asia by investing their home currency in exchange for the weak Asian currency. Then, if the Asian currency appreciated over time, the earnings generated there would be worth more (in terms of the parent's currency) when remitted to the parent.

Assessing Potential Acquisitions in Europe

Before the adoption of the euro, a U.S.-based MNC had to separately consider the exchange rate effects from acquiring firms in different European countries. For example, Italy's currency (the lira) was considered more likely to weaken against the dollar than some of the other European currencies, and this could affect the decision of whether to acquire an Italian firm versus a firm in Germany or France. The adoption of the euro as the local currency by several European countries has simplified the analysis for an MNC that is comparing possible target firms in those countries. The U.S.-based MNC can still be affected by future movements in the euro's value against the dollar, but those effects will occur regardless of whether the MNC purchases a firm in Italy or in any other eurozone country. Thus, the MNC can make its decision on which firm to acquire within these countries without being concerned about differential exchange rate effects. If the MNC is also considering firms in European countries that have not adopted the euro as their currency, however, it will still have to compare the potential exchange rate effects that could result from the acquisition.

Factors That Affect the Expected Cash Flows of the Foreign Target

When an MNC estimates the future cash flows that it will ultimately receive after acquiring a foreign target, it considers several factors that reflect either conditions in the country of concern or conditions of the target itself.

Target-Specific Factors

The following characteristics of the foreign target are typically considered when estimating the cash flows that the target will provide to the parent.

Target's Previous Cash Flows. Since the foreign target has been conducting business, it has a history of cash flows that it has generated. The recent cash flows per period may serve as an initial base from which future cash flows per period can be estimated after accounting for other factors. Since the target firm has already been conducting business, it may be easier to estimate the cash flows it will generate than to estimate the cash flows to be generated from a new foreign subsidiary.

A company's previous cash flows are not necessarily an accurate indicator of future cash flows, however, especially when the target's future cash flows would have to be converted into the acquirer's home currency as they are remitted to the parent. Therefore, the MNC needs to carefully consider all the factors that could influence the cash flows that will be generated from a foreign target.

Managerial Talent of the Target. An acquiring firm must assess the target's existing management so that it can determine how the target firm will be managed after the acquisition. The way the acquirer plans to deal with the managerial talent will affect the estimated cash flows to be generated by the target.

If the MNC acquires the target, it may allow the target firm to be managed as it was before the acquisition. Under these conditions, however, the acquiring firm may have less potential for enhancing the target's cash flows.

A second alternative for the MNC is to downsize the target firm after acquiring it. For example, if the acquiring firm introduces new technology that reduces the need for some of the target's employees, it can attempt to downsize the target. Downsizing reduces expenses but may also reduce productivity and revenue, so the effect on cash flows can vary with the situation. In addition, an MNC may encounter significant barriers to increasing efficiency by downsizing in several countries. Governments of some countries are likely to intervene and prevent the acquisition if downsizing is anticipated.

A third alternative for the MNC is to maintain the existing employees of the target but restructure the operations so that labor is used more efficiently. For example, the MNC may infuse its own technology into the target firm and then restructure operations so that many of the employees receive new job assignments. This strategy may cause the acquirer to incur some additional expenses, but there is potential for improved cash flows over time.

Country-Specific Factors

An MNC typically considers the following country-specific factors when estimating the cash flows that will be provided by the foreign target to the parent.

Target's Local Economic Conditions. Potential targets in countries where economic conditions are strong are more likely to experience strong demand for their products in the future and may generate higher cash flows. However, some firms are more sensitive to economic conditions than others. Also, some acquisitions of firms are intended to focus on exporting from the target's home country, so the economic conditions in the target's country may not be as important. Economic conditions are difficult to predict over a long-term period, especially for emerging countries.

Target's Local Political Conditions. Potential targets in countries where political conditions are favorable are less likely to experience adverse shocks to their cash flows. The sensitivity of cash flows to political conditions is dependent on the firm's type of business. Political conditions are also difficult to predict over a long-term period, especially for emerging countries.

Target's Industry Conditions. Industry conditions within a country can cause some targets to be more desirable than others. Some industries in a particular country may be extremely competitive while others are not. In addition, some industries exhibit strong potential for growth in a particular country, while others exhibit very little potential. When an MNC assesses targets among countries, it would prefer a country where the growth potential for its industry is high and the competition within the industry is not excessive.

http://

Visit Fred, the Federal Reserve's data bank, at http://research.stlouisfed.org/fred2 for numerous economic and financial time series, e.g., on balance-of-payments statistics, interest rates, and foreign exchange rates.

Target's Currency Conditions. If a U.S.-based MNC plans to acquire a foreign target, it must consider how future exchange rate movements may affect the target's local currency cash flows. It must also consider how exchange rates will affect the conversion of the target's remitted earnings to the U.S. parent. In the typical case, ideally the foreign currency would be weak at the time of the acquisition (so that the MNC's initial outlay is low) but strengthen over time as funds are periodically remitted to the U.S. parent. There can be exceptions to this general statement, but the point is that the MNC forecasts future exchange rates and then applies those forecasts to determine the impact on cash flows.

Target's Local Stock Market Conditions. Potential target firms that are publicly held are continuously valued in the market, so their stock prices can change rapidly. As the target firm's stock price changes, the acceptable bid price necessary to buy that firm will likely change as well. Thus, there can be substantial swings in the purchase price that would be acceptable to a target. This is especially true for publicly traded firms in emerging markets in Asia, Eastern Europe, and Latin America where stock prices commonly change by 5 percent or more in a week. Therefore, an MNC that plans to acquire a target would prefer to make its bid at a time when the local stock market prices are generally low.

Taxes Applicable to the Target. When an MNC assesses a foreign target, it must estimate the expected after-tax cash flows that it will ultimately receive in the form of funds remitted to the parent. Thus, the tax laws applicable to the foreign target are used to derive the after-tax cash flows. First, the applicable corporate tax rates are applied to the estimated future earnings of the target to determine the after-tax earnings. Second, the after-tax proceeds are determined by applying any withholding tax rates to the funds that are expected to be remitted to the parent in each period. Third, if the acquiring firm's government imposes an additional tax on remitted earnings or allows a tax credit, that tax or credit must be applied.

Example of the Valuation Process

Lincoln Co. desires to expand in Latin America or Canada. The methods Lincoln uses to initially screen targets in various countries and then to estimate a target's value are discussed next.

International Screening Process

Lincoln Co. considers the factors just described when it conducts an initial screening of prospective targets. It has identified prospective targets in Mexico, Brazil, Colombia, and Canada, as shown in Exhibit 15.1. The target in Mexico has no plans to sell its business

Exhibit 15.1 Example of Process Used to Screen Foreign Targets

Target Based in:	Is the Target Receptive to an Acquisition?	Local Economic and Industry Conditions	Local Political Conditions	Local Currency Conditions	Prevailing Stock Market Prices	Tax Laws
Mexico	No	Favorable	OK	OK	OK	May change
Brazil	Maybe	OK	OK	OK	Too high	May change
Colombia	Yes	Favorable	Volatile	Favorable	OK	Reasonable
Canada	Yes	OK	Favorable	Slightly unfavorable	OK	Reasonable

and is unwilling to even consider an offer from Lincoln Co. Therefore, this firm is no longer considered. Lincoln anticipates potential political problems that could create barriers to an acquisition in Colombia, even though the Colombian target is willing to be acquired. Stock market conditions are not favorable in Brazil, as the stock prices of most Brazilian companies have recently risen substantially. Lincoln does not want to pay as much as the Brazilian target is now worth based on its prevailing market value.

Based on this screening process, the only foreign target that deserves a closer assessment is the target in Canada. According to Lincoln's assessment, Canadian currency conditions are slightly unfavorable, but this is not a reason to eliminate the target from further consideration. Thus, the next step would be for Lincoln to obtain as much information as possible about the target and conditions in Canada. Then Lincoln can use this information to derive the target's expected cash flows and to determine whether the target's value exceeds the initial outlay that would be required to purchase it, as explained next.

Estimating the Target's Value

Once Lincoln Co. has completed its initial screening of targets, it conducts a valuation of all targets that passed the screening process. Lincoln can estimate the present value of future cash flows that would result from acquiring the target. This estimation is then used to determine whether the target should be acquired.

Continuing with our simplified example, Lincoln's screening process resulted in only one eligible target, a Canadian firm. Assume the Canadian firm has conducted all of its business locally. Assume also that Lincoln expects that it can obtain materials at a lower cost than the target can because of its relationships with some Canadian suppliers and that it also expects to implement a more efficient production process. Lincoln also plans to use its existing managerial talent to manage the target and thereby reduce the administrative and marketing expenses incurred by the target. It also expects that the target's revenue will increase when its products are sold under Lincoln's name. Lincoln expects to maintain prices of the products as they are.

The target's expected cash flows can be measured by first determining the revenue and expense levels in recent years and then adjusting those levels to reflect the changes that would occur after the acquisition.

Revenue. The target's annual revenue has ranged between C$80 million and C$90 million in Canadian dollars (C$) over the last four years. Lincoln Co. expects that it can im-

Exhibit 15.2
Valuation of Canadian Target Based on the Assumptions Provided (in Millions of Dollars)

	Last Year	Year 1	Year 2	Year 3
Revenue	C$90	C$100	C$93.3	C$121
Cost of goods sold	C$45	C$40	C$37.3	C$ 48.4
Gross profit	C$45	C$60	C$56	C$ 72.6
Selling & administrative expenses	C$20	C$15	C$15	C$15
Depreciation	C$10	C$10	C$10	C$10
Earnings before taxes	C$15	C$35	C$31	C$47.6
Tax (30%)	C$ 4.5	C$10.5	C$ 9.3	C$14.28
Earnings after taxes	C$10.5	C$24.5	C$21.7	C$33.32
+Depreciation		C$10	C$10	C$10
−Funds to reinvest		C$5	C$5	C$5
Sale of firm		—	—	C$230
Cash flows in C$		C$29.5	C$26.7	C$268.32
Exchange rate of C$		$ .80	$ .80	$ .80
Cash flows in $		$23.6	$21.36	$214.66
PV (20% discount rate)		$19.67	$14.83	$124.22
Cumulative *PV*		$19.67	$34.50	$158.72

prove sales, and forecasts revenue to be C$ 100 million next year, C$93.3 million in the following year, and $121 million in the year after. The cost of goods sold has been about 50 percent of the revenue in the past, but Lincoln expects it will fall to 40 percent of revenue because of improvements in efficiency. The estimates are shown in Exhibit 15.2.

Expenses. Selling and administrative expenses have been about C$20 million annually, but Lincoln believes that through restructuring it can reduce these expenses to C$15 million in each of the next three years. Depreciation expenses have been about C$10 million in the past and are expected to remain at that level for the next three years. The Canadian tax rate on the target's earnings is expected to be 30 percent.

Earnings and Cash Flows. Given the information assumed here, the after-tax earnings that the target would generate under Lincoln's ownership are estimated in Exhibit 15.2. The cash flows generated by the target are determined by adding the depreciation expenses back to the after-tax earnings. Assume that the target will need C$5 million in cash each year to support existing operations (including the repair of existing machinery) and that the remaining cash flow can be remitted to the U.S. parent. Assume that the target firm is financially supported only by its equity. It currently has 10 million shares of stock outstanding that are priced at C$17 per share.

Cash Flows to Parent. Since Lincoln's parent wishes to assess the target from its own perspective, it focuses on the dollar cash flows that it expects to receive. Assuming no additional taxes, the expected cash flows generated in Canada that are to be remitted to Lincoln's parent are converted into U.S. dollars at the expected exchange rate at the end of each year. Lincoln uses the prevailing exchange rate of the Canadian dollar (which is $.80) as the expected exchange rate for the Canadian dollar in future years.

Estimating the Target's Future Sales Price. If Lincoln purchases the target, it will sell the target in three years, after improving the target's performance. Lincoln expects to receive C$230 million (after capital gains taxes) from the sale. The price at which the target can actually be sold will depend on its expected future cash flows from that point forward, but those expected cash flows are partially dependent on its performance prior to that time. Thus, Lincoln can enhance the sales price by improving the target's performance over the three years it plans to own the target.

Valuing the Target Based on Estimated Cash Flows. The expected U.S. dollar cash flows to Lincoln's parent over the next three years are shown in Exhibit 15.2. The high cash flow in Year 3 is due to Lincoln's plans to sell the target at that time. Assuming that Lincoln has a required rate of return of 20 percent on this project, the cash flows are discounted at that rate to derive the present value of target cash flows. From Lincoln's perspective, the present value of the target is about $158.72 million.

Given that the target's shares are currently valued at C$17 per share, the 10 million shares are worth C$170 million. At the prevailing exchange rate of $.80 per dollar, the target is currently valued at $136 million by the market (computed as C$170 million × $.80). Lincoln's valuation of the target of about $159 million is about 17 percent above the market valuation. However, Lincoln will have to pay a premium on the shares to persuade the target's board of directors to approve the acquisition. Premiums commonly range from 10 percent to 40 percent of the market price. If Lincoln allows for a premium of 10 percent above the prevailing stock price of C$17 per share, it would pay C$18.7 per share for the target. At this price per share, the price paid for the Canadian firm would be C$187 million, or $149.6 million at the existing exchange rate. This price is less than the perceived net present value of the target, so Lincoln may be willing to pay this amount.

Lincoln recognizes that the target may reject its offer of a 10 percent premium and ask for a higher premium, but it will not pay more than its estimate of the target's net present value. Since Lincoln values the target at about $159 million, it will not pay more than about C$199 million at the prevailing exchange rate (computed as $159 million divided by $.80 per Canadian dollar), or a share price of C$19.90 (computed as C$199 million divided by 10 million shares).

Sources of Uncertainty. This example shows how the acquisition of a publicly traded foreign firm differs from the creation of a new foreign subsidiary. Although the valuation of a publicly traded foreign firm can utilize information about an existing business, the cash flows resulting from the acquisition are still subject to uncertainty for several reasons, which can be identified by reviewing the assumptions made in the valuation process. First, the growth rate of revenue is subject to uncertainty. If this rate is overestimated (perhaps because Canadian economic growth is overestimated), the earnings generated in Canada will be lower, and cash flows remitted to the U.S. parent will be lower as well.

Second, the cost of goods sold could exceed the assumed level of 40 percent of revenue, which would reduce cash flows remitted to the parent. Third, the selling and administrative expenses could exceed the assumed amount of C$15 million, especially when considering that the annual expenses were C$20 million prior to the acquisition. Fourth, Canada's corporate tax rate could increase, which would reduce the cash flows remitted to the parent. Fifth, the exchange rate of the Canadian dollar may be weaker than assumed, which would reduce the cash flows received by the parent. Sixth, the estimated selling price of the target three years from now could be incorrect for any of these five reasons, and this estimate is very influential on the valuation of the target today.

Since one or more of these conditions could occur, the estimated net present value of the target could be overestimated. Consequently, it is possible for Lincoln to acquire the target at a purchase price exceeding its actual value. In particular, the future cash flows are very sensitive to exchange rate movements. This can be illustrated by using sensitivity analysis and reestimating the value of the target based on different scenarios for the exchange rate over time.

Changes in Valuation over Time

If Lincoln Co. decides not to bid for the target at this time, it will need to redo its analysis if it later reconsiders acquiring the target. As the factors that affect the expected cash flows or the required rate of return from investing in the target change, so will the value of the target.

Impact of Stock Market Conditions. A change in stock market conditions affects the price per share of each stock in that market. Thus, the value of publicly traded firms in that market will change. Remember that an acquirer needs to pay a premium above the market valuation to acquire a foreign firm.

Continuing with our example involving Lincoln Co.'s pursuit of a Canadian target, assume that the target firm has a market price of C$17 per share, representing a valuation of C$170 million, but that before Lincoln makes its decision to acquire the target, the Canadian stock market level rises by 20 percent. If the target's stock price rises by this same percentage, the firm is now valued at

$$\begin{aligned}\text{New stock price} &= \text{C\$170 million} \times 1.2\\ &= \text{C\$204 million}\end{aligned}$$

Using the 10 percent premium assumed in the earlier example, Lincoln must now pay C$224.4 million (computed as C$204 million × 1.1) if it wants to acquire the target. This example illustrates how the price paid for the target can change abruptly simply because of a change in the general level of the stock market.

Impact of Stock Market Conditions on the Value of Private Firms. Even if a target is privately held, general stock market conditions will affect the amount that an acquirer has to pay for the target because a privately held company's value is influenced by the market price multiples of related firms in the same country. A simple method of valuing a private company is to apply the price-earnings (P/E) ratios of publicly traded firms in the same industry to the private company's annual earnings.

For example, if the annual earnings of a private Canadian company are C$8 million and the average P/E ratio of publicly traded Canadian firms in the same industry is 15, the company's market valuation can be estimated as

$$\begin{aligned}\text{Market valuation} &= \text{earnings} \times \text{average P/E ratio}\\ &= \text{C\$8 million} \times 15\\ &= \text{C\$120 million}\end{aligned}$$

Exhibit 15.3

Influence of Czech Stock Market and Currency Conditions on the Cost of Acquiring a Czech Target

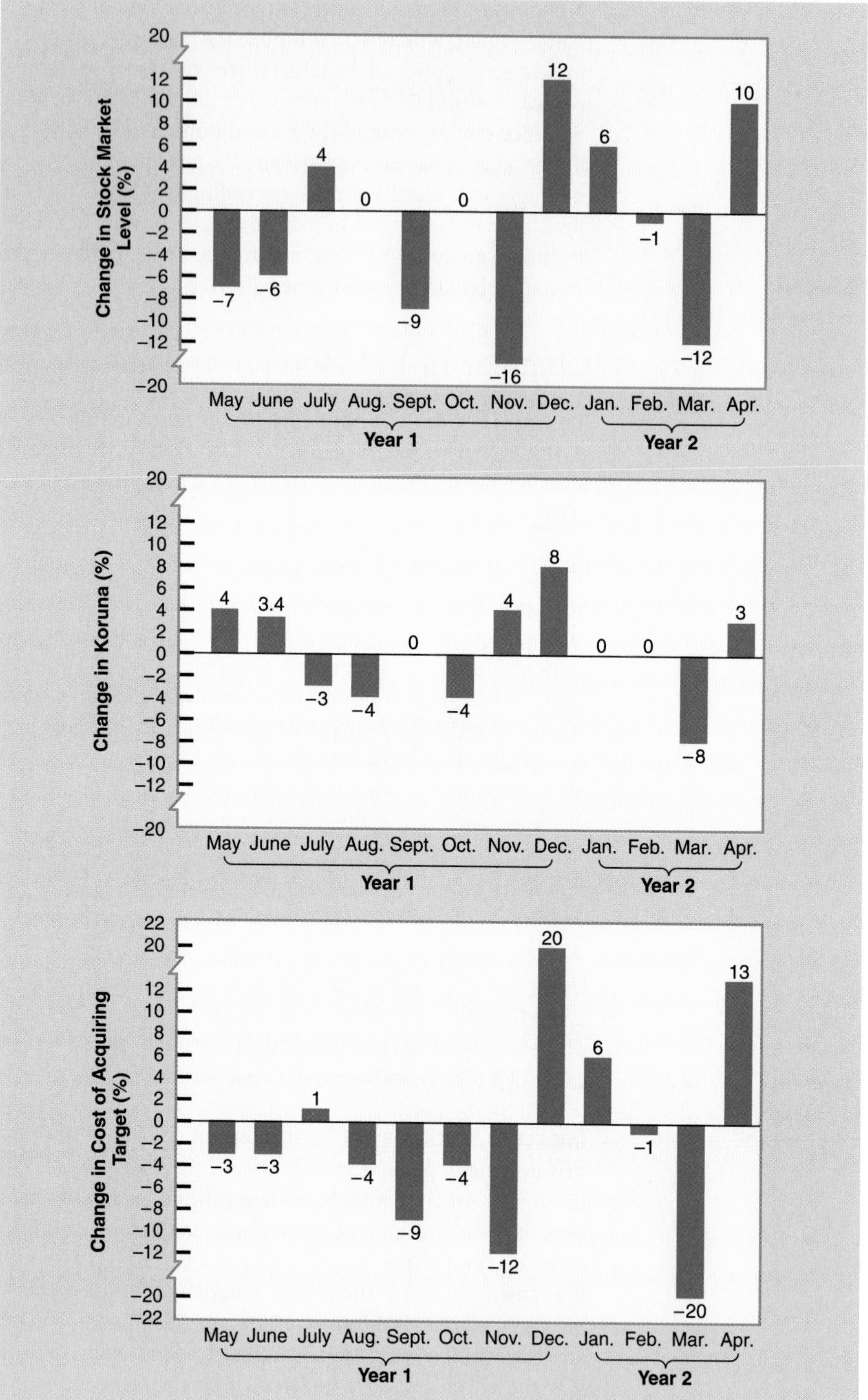

If the stock market level rises by 20 percent, the average P/E ratio of the firms in the same industry will likely rise by about 20 percent, which represents an increase in the P/E ratio from 15 to 18. The new market valuation of the Canadian firm will be

$$\begin{aligned}\text{New market valuation} &= \text{C\$8 million} \times 18 \\ &= \text{C\$144 million}\end{aligned}$$

As this example illustrates, private companies also become more expensive targets when local stock market conditions improve.

Impact of Exchange Rates. Whether a foreign target is publicly traded or private, a U.S. acquirer must convert dollars to the local currency to purchase the target. If the foreign currency appreciates by the time the acquirer makes payment, the acquisition will be more costly. The cost of the acquisition changes in the same proportion as the change in the exchange rate.

Combined Stock Market and Exchange Rate Effects. In reality, stock market levels and exchange rates change simultaneously. The effects on the cost of acquiring a foreign target are especially pronounced in emerging markets where stock and currency values are volatile.

For example, assume that Mizner, Inc., a U.S. firm, wants to acquire a firm in the Czech Republic so that it can expand its business in Eastern Europe. Also assume that the Czech target's valuation moves in tandem with general Czech stock market conditions. Exhibit 15.3, which is based on actual data from a recent period, shows how the cost to Mizner of acquiring the Czech target could change over time, even though the performance of the firm itself does not change. During the period shown, the cost of acquisition could have increased by 20 percent in a single month (December of Year 1) as a result of a very strong stock market in that month and also appreciation of the Czech currency (koruna). At the other extreme, the cost of the acquisition declined by 20 percent in a single month (March of Year 2) as a result of a weakening stock market and koruna over that month. This exhibit illustrates how sensitive the cost of an acquisition of a foreign target is to foreign market conditions.

Impact of Market Anticipation regarding the Target. The stock price of the target may increase if investors anticipate that the target will be acquired, since they are aware that stock prices of targets rise abruptly after a bid by the acquiring firm. Thus, it is important that Lincoln keep its intentions about acquiring the target confidential.

Why Valuations of a Target May Vary among MNCs

Most MNCs that consider acquiring a specific target will use a somewhat similar process for valuing the target. Nevertheless, their valuations will differ because of differences in the way the MNC's estimate the key determinants of a given target's valuation: (1) cash flows to be generated by the target, (2) exchange rate effects on funds remitted to the MNC's parent, and (3) the required rate of return when investing in the target.

Estimated Cash Flows of the Foreign Target

The target's expected future cash flows will vary among MNCs because the cash flows will be dependent on the MNC's management or oversight of the target's operations. If an MNC can improve the production efficiency of the target without reducing the target's production volume, it can improve the target's cash flows.

Each MNC may have a different plan as to how the target will fit within its structure and how the target will conduct future operations. The target's expected cash flows will be influenced by the way it is utilized. An MNC with production plants in Asia that purchases another Asian production plant may simply be attempting to increase its market share and production capacity. This MNC's cash flows change because of a higher production and sales level. Conversely, an MNC with all of its production plants in the United States may purchase an Asian production plant to shift its production where costs are lower. This MNC's cash flows change because of lower expenses.

Tax laws can create competitive advantages for acquirers based in some countries. Acquirers based in low-tax countries may be able to generate higher cash flows from acquiring a foreign target than acquirers in high-tax countries simply because they are subject to lower taxes on the future earnings remitted by the target (after it is acquired).

Exchange Rate Effects on the Funds Remitted

The valuation of a target can vary among MNCs simply because of differences in the exchange rate effects on funds remitted by the foreign target to the MNC's parent. If the target remits funds frequently in the near future, its value will be partially dependent on the expected exchange rate of the target's local currency in the near future. If the target does not remit funds in the near future, its value is more dependent on its local growth strategy and on exchange rates in the distant future.

Required Return of Acquirer

The valuation of the target could also vary among MNCs because of differences in their required rate of return from investing funds to acquire the target. If an MNC targets a successful foreign company with plans to continue the target's local business in a more efficient manner, the risk of the business will be relatively low, and therefore the MNC's required return from acquiring the target will be relatively low. Conversely, if an MNC targets the company because it plans to turn the company into a major exporter, the risk is much higher. The target has not established itself in foreign markets, so the cash flows that would result from the exporting business are very uncertain. Thus, the required return to acquire the target company will be relatively high as well.

If potential acquirers are based in different countries, their required rates of return from a specific target will vary even if they plan to use the target in similar ways. Recall that an MNC's required rate of return on any project is dependent on the local risk-free interest rate (since that influences the cost of funds for that MNC). Therefore, the required rate of return for MNCs based in countries with relatively high interest rates such as Brazil and Venezuela may differ from MNCs based in low-interest-rate countries such as the United States or Japan. The higher required rate of return for MNCs based in Latin American countries will not necessarily lead to a lower valuation. The target's currency might be expected to appreciate substantially against Latin American currencies (since some Latin American currencies have consistently weakened over time), which would enhance the amount of cash flows received as a result of remitted funds and could possibly offset the effects of the higher required rate of return.

Other Types of Multinational Restructuring

Besides acquiring foreign firms, MNCs can engage in multinational restructuring through international partial acquisitions, acquisitions of privatized businesses, international alliances, and international divestitures. Each type is described in turn.

International Partial Acquisitions

In many cases, an MNC may consider a partial international acquisition of a firm, in which it purchases part of the existing stock of a foreign firm. A partial international acquisition requires less funds because only a portion of the foreign target's shares are purchased. With this type of investment, the foreign target normally continues operating and may not experience the employee turnover that commonly occurs after a target's ownership changes. Nevertheless, by acquiring a substantial fraction of the shares, the MNC may have some influence on the target's management and be in a position to complete the acquisition in the future. Some MNCs buy substantial stakes in foreign companies to have some control over their operations. For example, Coca-Cola has purchased stakes in many foreign bottling companies that bottle its syrup. In this way, it can ensure that the bottling operations meet its standards.

Valuation of a Foreign Firm That May Be Partially Acquired. When an MNC considers a partial acquisition in which it will purchase sufficient shares so that it can control the firm, the MNC can conduct its valuation of the target in much the same way as when it purchases the entire firm. If the MNC buys only a small proportion of the firm's shares, however, the MNC cannot restructure the firm's operations to make it more efficient. Therefore, its estimates of the firm's cash flows must be made from the perspective of a passive investor rather than as a decision maker for the firm.

International Acquisitions of Privatized Businesses

In recent years, government-owned businesses of many developing countries in Eastern Europe and South America have been sold to individuals or corporations. Many MNCs have capitalized on this wave of so-called privatization by acquiring businesses being sold by governments. These businesses may be attractive because of the potential for MNCs to increase their efficiency.

Valuation of a Privatized Business. An MNC can conduct a valuation of a foreign business that was owned by the government in a developing country by using capital budgeting analysis, as illustrated earlier. However, the valuation of such businesses is difficult for the following reasons:

- The future cash flows are very uncertain because the businesses were previously operating in environments of little or no competition. Thus, previous sales volume figures may not be useful indicators of future sales.

- Data concerning what businesses are worth are very limited in some countries because there are not many publicly traded firms in their markets, and there is limited disclosure of prices paid for targets in other acquisitions. Consequently, there may not be any benchmarks to use when valuing a business.
- Economic conditions in these countries are very uncertain during the transition to a market-oriented economy.
- Political conditions tend to be volatile during the transition, as government policies for businesses are sometimes unclear or subject to abrupt changes.
- If the government retains a portion of the firm's equity, it may attempt to exert some control over the firm. Its objectives may be very different from those of the acquirer, a situation that could lead to conflict.

Despite these difficulties, MNCs such as Gerber Products and PepsiCo have acquired privatized businesses as a means of entering new markets. Hungary serves as a model country for privatizations. More than 25,000 MNCs have a foreign stake in Hungary's businesses. Hungary's government has been quick and efficient at selling off its assets to MNCs.

International Alliances

MNCs commonly engage in international alliances such as joint ventures and licensing agreements with foreign firms. International alliances are quite different from international acquisitions. The initial outlay is typically smaller because the MNC is not acquiring a foreign firm, and the cash flows to be received are typically smaller as well.

EXAMPLE

Laredo, Inc., plans to provide a Mexican firm with technology. In return, the Mexican firm will pay royalties amounting to 10 percent of its future sales of products resulting from use of this technology over the next five years. Laredo's initial outlay for this international alliance is the initial expense incurred as a result of providing the technology. Laredo can estimate the cash flows to be received from the Mexican firm by first forecasting the Mexican firm's annual sales (in pesos) of products based on the technology. Laredo will receive 10 percent of this amount. Then, it must forecast the value of the peso over each of the next five years so that it can determine the dollar cash flows resulting from these royalties. It must also consider any tax effects.

International Divestitures

An MNC should periodically reassess its direct foreign investments to determine whether they should be retained or sold (divested). Some foreign projects may no longer be feasible as a result of the MNC's increased cost of capital, increased host government taxes, increased political risk in the host country, or revised projections of exchange rates. Many divestitures occur as a result of a revised assessment of industry or economic conditions. For example, Warner-Lambert Co., Johnson & Johnson, and several other U.S.-based MNCs recently divested some of their Latin American subsidiaries when economic conditions deteriorated there.

Assessing Whether to Divest Existing Operations in Asia. During the Asian crisis in the 1997–1998 period, some MNCs with direct foreign investment in Asia reassessed the feasibility of their existing operations. The expected cash flows that these operations would generate for the parent had declined in many cases for two obvious reasons. First, the rate of economic growth in Asia declined, which led to a decline in expected local sales by the foreign subsidiaries and therefore a decline in the expected level of foreign currency cash flow. Second, the weak currencies of Asian countries led to a decline in the expected amount of the parent's currency to be received when foreign subsidiaries in Asian countries remitted funds. At the same time, however, market valuations had declined so much that any operations could be divested only if the parent was willing to sell them at a low price. The low prices deterred some divestitures.

Valuation of an International Project That May Be Divested. The valuation of a proposed international divestiture can be determined by comparing the present value of the cash flows if the project is continued to the proceeds that would be received (after taxes) if the project is divested.

EXAMPLE

Reconsider the example from the previous chapter in which Spartan, Inc., considered establishing a Singapore subsidiary. Assume that the Singapore subsidiary was created and, after two years, the spot rate of the Singapore dollar (S$) is $.46. In addition, forecasts have been revised for the remaining two years of the project, indicating that the Singapore dollar should be worth $.44 in Year 3 and $.40 in the project's final year. Because these forecasted exchange rates have an adverse effect on the project, Spartan, Inc., considers divesting the subsidiary. For simplicity, assume that the original forecasts of the other variables remain unchanged and that a potential acquirer has offered S$13 million (after adjusting for any capital gains taxes) for the subsidiary if the acquirer can retain the existing working capital.

Spartan can conduct a divestiture analysis by comparing the after-tax proceeds from the possible sale of the project (in U.S. dollars) to the present value of the expected U.S. dollar inflows that the project will generate if it is not sold. This comparison will determine the net present value of the divestiture (NPV_d), as illustrated in Exhibit 15.4. Since the present value of the subsidiary's cash flows from Spartan's perspective exceeds the price at which it can sell the subsidiary, the divestiture is not feasible. Thus, Spartan should not divest the subsidiary at the price offered. Spartan may still search for another firm that is willing to acquire the subsidiary for a price that exceeds its present value.

Exhibit 15.4 Divestiture Analysis: Spartan, Inc.

	End of Year 2 (Today)	End of Year 3 (One Year from Today)	End of Year 4 (Two Years from Today)
S$ remitted after withholding taxes		S$6,840,000	S$19,560,000
Selling price	S$13,000,000		
Exchange rate	$.46	$.44	$.40
Cash flow received from divestiture	$5,980,000		
Cash flows forgone due to divestiture		$3,009,600	$7,824,000
PV of forgone cash flows (15% discount rate)		$2,617,044	$5,916,068
NPV_d = \$5,980,000 − (\$2,617,044 + \$5,916,068) = \$5,980,000 − \$8,533,112 = −\$2,553,112			

Restructuring Decisions as Real Options

Some restructuring issues faced by MNCs involve **real options**, or implicit options on real assets (such as buildings, machinery, and other assets used by MNCs to facilitate their production). A real option can be classified as a call option on real assets or a put option on real assets, as explained next.

Call Option on Real Assets

A **call option on real assets** represents a proposed project that contains an option of pursuing an additional venture. Some possible forms of restructuring by MNCs contain a call option on real assets. Multinational capital budgeting can be conducted in a manner to account for the option.

EXAMPLE

Coral, Inc., an Internet firm in the United States, is considering the acquisition of an Internet business in Mexico. Coral estimates and discounts the expected dollar cash flows that would result from acquiring this business and compares them to the initial outlay. At this time, the present value of the future cash flows that are directly attributable to the Mexican business is slightly lower than the initial outlay that would be required to purchase that business, so the business appears to be an infeasible investment.

A Brazilian Internet firm is also for sale, but its owners will only sell the business to a firm that they know and trust, and Coral, Inc., has no relationship with this business. A possible advantage of the Mexican firm that is not measured by the traditional multinational capital budgeting analysis is that it frequently does business with the Brazilian Internet firm and could use its relationship to help Coral acquire the Brazilian firm. Thus, if Coral purchases the Mexican business, it will have an option to also acquire the Internet firm in Brazil. In essence, Coral will have a call option on real assets (of the Brazilian firm), because it will have the option (not the obligation) to purchase the Brazilian firm. The expected purchase price of the Brazilian firm over the next few months serves as the exercise price in the call option on real assets. If Coral acquires the Brazilian firm, it now has a second initial outlay and will generate a second stream of cash flows.

When the call option on real assets is considered, the acquisition of the Mexican Internet firm may now be feasible, even though it was not feasible when considering only the cash flows directly attributable to that firm. The project can be analyzed by segmenting it into two scenarios. In the first scenario, Coral, Inc., acquires the Mexican firm but, after taking a closer look at the Brazilian firm, decides not to exercise its call option (decides not to purchase the Brazilian firm). The net present value in this scenario is simply a measure of the present value of expected dollar cash flows directly attributable to the Mexican firm minus the initial outlay necessary to purchase the Mexican firm. In the second scenario, Coral, Inc., acquires the Mexican firm and then exercises its option by also purchasing the Brazilian firm. In this case, the present value of combined (Mexican firm plus Brazilian firm) cash flow streams (in dollars) would be compared to the combined initial outlays.

If the outlay necessary to acquire the Brazilian firm was made after the initial outlay of the Mexican firm, the outlay for the Brazilian firm should be discounted. If Coral, Inc., knows the probability of these two scenarios, it can determine the probability of each scenario and then determine the expected value of the net present value of the proposed project by summing the products of the probability of each scenario times the respective net present value for that scenario.

MANAGING FOR VALUE

Mazda's Decision to Restructure

Mazda's main production facilities are based in Japan, but it relies heavily on exports to the United States and Europe. In 1996, Ford Motor Co. purchased about one-third of Mazda's shares. In the late 1990s, Mazda's performance was weak despite Ford's efforts to improve its operations. It had an excessive amount of debt. It was also highly susceptible to the weakness of the euro in the 1999–2000 period. When the euro weakened against the yen, the European demand for exports made in Japan (and priced in Japanese yen) was reduced. Mazda's costs of producing its vehicles in Japan were not reduced, however, because those costs were denominated in yen. In the first six months of 2000, Mazda experienced losses of more than $9 billion yen (about $90 million), and much of the loss was attributed to the euro's weakness.

In November 2000, Mazda decided to engage in major multinational restructuring to resolve its financial problems. It shifted some of its production from Japan to Europe so that its expenses and revenue from its sales in Europe would be denominated in the same currency. This strategy reduced Mazda's exposure to exchange rate risk because it could sell the cars in Europe at a markup above the cost (in euros) necessary to produce them. The euro's movements against other currencies would not have a direct effect on the European demand for Mazdas. This multinational restructuring was politically tense because it required the closing of some facilities in Japan, which resulted in layoffs. Since the restructuring, however, the value of the firm has increased; thus, the shareholders have benefited from Mazda's decision.

Put Option on Real Assets

A **put option on real assets** represents a proposed project that contains an option of divesting part or all of the project. As with a call option on real assets, a put option on real assets can be accounted for by multinational capital budgeting.

EXAMPLE

Jade, Inc., an office supply firm in the United States, is considering the acquisition of a similar business in Italy. Jade, Inc., believes that if future economic conditions in Italy are favorable, the net present value of this project is positive. However, given that weak economic conditions in Italy are more likely, the proposed project appears to be infeasible.

Assume now that Jade, Inc., knows that it can sell the Italian firm at a specified price to another firm over the next four years. In this case, Jade has an implied put option attached to the project.

The feasibility of this project can be assessed by determining the net present value under both the scenario of strong economic conditions and the scenario of weak economic conditions. The expected value of the net present value of this project can be estimated as the sum of the products of the probability of each scenario times its respective net present value. If economic conditions are favorable, the net present value is positive. If economic conditions are weak, Jade, Inc., may sell the Italian firm at the locked-in sales price (which resembles the exercise price of a put option) and therefore may still achieve a positive net present value over the short time that it owned the Italian firm. Thus, the put option on real assets may turn an infeasible project into a feasible project.

SUMMARY

- International acquisitions are one of the most common types of multinational restructuring. MNCs can use capital budgeting to determine whether a foreign target is worth acquiring. The expected cash flows of a foreign target are affected by target-specific factors (such as the target's previous cash flows and its managerial talent) and country-specific factors (such as economic conditions, political conditions, currency conditions, and stock market conditions).
- In the typical valuation process, an MNC initially screens prospective targets based on willingness to be acquired and country barriers. Then, each prospective target is valued by estimating its cash flows, based on target-specific characteristics and the target's country characteristics, and by discounting the expected cash flows. Then the perceived value is compared to the target's market value to determine whether the target can be purchased at a price that is below the perceived value from the MNC's perspective.
- Valuations of a foreign target may vary among potential acquirers because of differences in estimates of the target's cash flows or exchange rate movements or differences in the required rate of return among acquirers. These differences may be especially pronounced when the acquirers are from different countries.
- Besides international acquisitions of firms, the more common types of multinational restructuring include international partial acquisitions, international acquisitions of privatized businesses, international alliances (such as international licensing or joint ventures), and international divestitures. Each of these types of multinational restructuring can be assessed by applying multinational capital budgeting.

POINT COUNTER-POINT

Can a Foreign Target Be Assessed Like Any Other Asset?

Point Yes. The value of a foreign target to an MNC is the present value of the future cash flows to the MNC. The process of estimating a foreign target's value is the same as the process of estimating a machine's value. A target has expected cash flows, which can be derived from information about previous cash flows.

Counter-Point No. A target's behavior will change after it is acquired by an MNC. Its efficiency may improve depending on the ability of the MNC to integrate the target with its own operations. The morale of the target employees could either improve or worsen after the acquisition, depending on the treatment by the acquirer. Thus, a proper estimate of cash flows generated by the target must consider the changes in the target due to the acquisition.

Who Is Correct? Use InfoTrac or some other search engine to learn more about this issue. Which argument do you support? Offer your own opinion on this issue.

SELF TEST

Answers are provided in Appendix A at the back of the text.

1. Explain why more acquisitions have taken place in Europe in recent years.
2. What are some of the barriers to international acquisitions?
3. Why might a U.S.-based MNC prefer to establish a foreign subsidiary rather than acquire an existing firm in a foreign country?
4. Provo, Inc. (based in Utah), has been considering the divestiture of a Swedish subsidiary that produces ski equipment and sells it locally. A Swedish firm has already offered to acquire this Swedish subsidiary. Assume that the U.S. parent has just revised its projections of the Swedish krona's value downward. Will the proposed divestiture now seem more or less feasible than it did before? Explain.

QUESTIONS AND APPLICATIONS

1. **Motives for Restructuring.** Why do you think MNCs continuously assess possible forms of multinational restructuring, such as foreign acquisitions or downsizing of a foreign subsidiary?

2. **Exposure to Country Regulations.** Maude, Inc., a U.S.-based MNC, has recently acquired a firm in Singapore. To eliminate inefficiencies, Maude downsized the target substantially, eliminating two-thirds of the workforce. Why might this action affect the regulations imposed on the subsidiary's business by the Singapore government?

3. **Global Expansion Strategy.** Poki, Inc., a U.S.-based MNC, is considering expanding into Thailand because of decreasing profit margins in the United States. The demand for Poki's product in Thailand is very strong. However, forecasts indicate that the baht is expected to depreciate substantially over the next three years. Should Poki expand into Thailand? What factors may affect its decision?

4. **Alternatives to International Acquisitions.** Rastell, Inc., a U.S.-based MNC, is considering the acquisition of a Russian target to produce personal computers (PCs) and market them throughout Russia, where demand for PCs has increased substantially in recent years. Assume that the stock market conditions are not favorable in Russia, as the stock prices of most Russian companies rose substantially just prior to Rastell's assessment of the target. What are some alternatives available to Rastell?

5. **Comparing International Projects.** Savannah, Inc., a manufacturer of clothing, wants to increase its market share by acquiring a target producing a popular clothing line in Europe. This clothing line is well established. Forecasts indicate a relatively stable euro over the life of the project. Marquette, Inc., wants to increase its market share in the personal computer market by acquiring a target in Thailand that currently produces radios and converting the operations to produce PCs. Forecasts indicate a depreciation of the baht over the life of the project. Funds resulting from both projects will be remitted to the respective U.S. parent on a regular basis. Which target do you think will result in a higher net present value? Why?

6. **Privatized Business Valuations.** Why are valuations of privatized businesses previously owned by the governments of developing countries more difficult than valuations of existing firms in developed countries?

7. **Valuing a Foreign Target.** Blore, Inc., a U.S.-based MNC, has screened several targets. Based on economic and political considerations, only one eligible target remains in Malaysia. Blore would like you to value this target and has provided you with the following information:

- Blore expects to keep the target for three years, at which time it expects to sell the firm for 300 million Malaysian ringgit (MYR) after any taxes.
- Blore expects a strong Malaysian economy. The estimates for revenue for the next year are MYR200 million. Revenues are expected to increase by 8 percent in each of the following two years.
- Cost of goods sold are expected to be 50 percent of revenue.
- Selling and administrative expenses are expected to be MYR30 million in each of the next three years.
- The Malaysian tax rate on the target's earnings is expected to be 35 percent.
- Depreciation expenses are expected to be MYR20 million per year for each of the next three years.
- The target will need MYR7 million in cash each year to support existing operations.
- The target's stock price is currently MYR30 per share. The target has 9 million shares outstanding.
- Any remaining cash flows will be remitted by the target to Blore, Inc. Blore uses the prevailing exchange rate of the Malaysian ringgit as the expected exchange rate for the next three years. This exchange rate is currently $.25.
- Blore's required rate of return on similar projects is 20%.

   a. Prepare a worksheet to estimate the value of the Malaysian target based on the information provided.

   b. Will Blore, Inc., be able to acquire the Malaysian target for a price lower than its valuation of the target?

8. **Uncertainty Surrounding a Foreign Target.** Refer to question 7. What are some of the key sources of

uncertainty in Blore's valuation of the target? Identify two reasons why the expected cash flows from an Asian subsidiary of a U.S.-based MNC would have been lower as a result of the Asian crisis.

9. **Divestiture Strategy.** The reduction in expected cash flows of Asian subsidiaries as a result of the Asian crisis likely resulted in a reduced valuation of these subsidiaries from the parent's perspective. Explain why a U.S.-based MNC might not have sold its Asian subsidiaries.

10. **Why a Foreign Acquisition May Backfire.** Provide two reasons why an MNC's strategy of acquiring a foreign target will backfire. That is, explain why the acquisition might result in a negative NPV.

ADVANCED QUESTIONS

11. **Pricing a Foreign Target.** Alaska, Inc., would like to acquire Estoya Corp., which is located in Peru. In initial negotiations, Estoya has asked for a purchase price of 1 billion Peruvian new sol. If Alaska completes the purchase, it would keep Estoya's operations for two years and then sell the company. In the recent past, Estoya has generated annual cash flows of 500 million new sol per year, but Alaska believes that it can increase these cash flows by 5 percent each year by improving the operations of the plant. Given these improvements, Alaska believes it will be able to resell Estoya in two years for 1.2 billion new sol. The current exchange rate of the new sol is $.29, and exchange rate forecasts for the next two years indicate values of $.29 and $.27, respectively. Given these facts, should Alaska, Inc., pay 1 billion new sol for Estoya Corp. if the required rate of return is 18 percent? What is the maximum price Alaska should be willing to pay?

12. **Global Strategy.** Senser Co. established a subsidiary in Russia two years ago. Under its original plans, Senser intended to operate the subsidiary for a total of four years. However, it would like to reassess the situation, since exchange rate forecasts for the Russian ruble indicate that it may depreciate from its current level of $.033 to $.028 next year and to $.025 in the following year. Senser could sell the subsidiary today for 5 million rubles to a potential acquirer. If Senser continues to operate the subsidiary, it will generate cash flows of 3 million rubles next year and 4 million rubles in the following year. These cash flows would be remitted back to the parent in the United States. The required rate of return of the project is 16 percent. Should Senser continue operating the Russian subsidiary?

13. **Divestiture Decision.** Colorado Springs Co. plans to divest either its Singapore or its Canadian subsidiary. Assume that if exchange rates remain constant, the dollar cash flows each of these subsidiaries would provide to the parent over time would be somewhat similar. However, the firm expects the Singapore dollar to depreciate against the U.S. dollar, and the Canadian dollar to appreciate against the U.S. dollar. The firm can sell either subsidiary for about the same price today. Which one should it sell?

14. **Divestiture Decision.** San Gabriel Corp. recently considered divesting its Italian subsidiary and determined that the divestiture was not feasible. The required rate of return on this subsidiary was 17 percent. In the last week, San Gabriel's required return on that subsidiary increased to 21 percent. If the sales price of the subsidiary has not changed, explain why the divestiture may now be feasible.

15. **Divestiture Decision.** Ethridge Co. of Atlanta, Georgia, has a subsidiary in India that produces products and sells them throughout Asia. In response to the September 11, 2001 terrorist attack on the United States, Ethridge Co. decided to conduct a capital budgeting analysis to determine whether it should divest the subsidiary. Why might this decision be different after the attack as opposed to before the attack? Describe the general method for determining whether the divestiture is financially feasible.

16. **Feasibility of a Divestiture.** Florida, Inc., has a subsidiary in Bulgaria that it fully finances with its own equity. Last week, a firm offered to buy the subsidiary from Florida for $60 million in cash, and the offer is still available this week as well. The annualized long-term risk-free rate in the United States increased from 7 percent to 8 percent this week. The expected monthly cash flows to be generated by the subsidiary have not changed since last week. The risk premium that Florida applies to its projects in Bulgaria was reduced from 11.3 percent to 10.9 percent this week. The annualized long-term risk-free rate in Bulgaria declined from 23 percent to 21 percent this week. Would the *NPV* to Florida, Inc., from divesting this unit be more or less than

the *NPV* determined last week? Why? [No analysis is necessary, but make sure that your explanation is very clear.]

17. **Accounting for Government Restrictions.** Sunbelt, Inc., plans to purchase a firm in Indonesia. It believes that it can install its operating procedure in this firm, which would significantly reduce the firm's operating expenses. However, the Indonesian government may approve the acquisition only if Sunbelt does not lay off any workers. How can Sunbelt possibly increase efficiency without laying off workers? How can Sunbelt account for the Indonesian government's position as it assesses the *NPV* of this possible acquisition?

INTERNET APPLICATION

18. **Current Events Affecting MNCs** Use an online news source to review international events in the last week. Select three economic events that could affect economic or political conditions in foreign countries and explain how an MNC might restructure its business in response to these events. Would the MNC increase or reduce its business in that country due to that event?

DISCUSSION IN THE BOARDROOM

This exercise can be found in Appendix E at the back of this textbook.

RUNNING YOUR OWN MNC

This exercise can be found on the Xtra! website at **http://maduraxtra.swlearning.com**.

BLADES, INC. CASE

Assessment of an Acquisition in Thailand

Recall that Ben Holt, Blades' chief financial officer (CFO), has suggested to the board of directors that Blades proceed with the establishment of a subsidiary in Thailand. Due to the high growth potential of the roller blade market in Thailand, his analysis suggests that the venture will be profitable. Specifically, his view is that Blades should establish a subsidiary in Thailand to manufacture roller blades, whether an existing agreement with Entertainment Products (a Thai retailer) is renewed or not. Under this agreement, Entertainment Products is committed to the purchase of 180,000 pairs of "Speedos," Blades' primary product, annually. The agreement was initially for three years and will expire two years from now. At this time, the agreement may be renewed. Due to delivery delays, Entertainment Products has indicated that it will renew the agreement only if Blades establishes a subsidiary in Thailand. In this case, the price per pair of roller blades would be fixed at 4,594 Thai baht per pair. If Blades decides not to renew the agreement, Entertainment Products has indicated that it would purchase only 5,000 pairs of Speedos annually at prevailing market prices.

According to Ben Holt's analysis, renewing the agreement with Entertainment Products and establishing a subsidiary in Thailand will result in a net present value (*NPV*) of $2,638,735. Conversely, if the agreement is not renewed and a subsidiary is established, the resulting *NPV* is $8,746,688. Consequently, Holt has suggested to the board of directors that Blades establish a subsidiary without renewing the existing agreement with Entertainment Products.

Recently, a Thai roller blade manufacturer called Skates'n'Stuff contacted Holt regarding the potential sale of the company to Blades. Skates'n'Stuff entered the Thai roller blade market a decade ago and has generated a profit in every year of operation. Furthermore, Skates'n'Stuff has established distribution channels in Thailand. Consequently, if Blades acquires the company, it could begin sales immediately and would not require an additional year to build the plant in Thailand. Initial forecasts indicate that Blades would be able to sell 280,000 pairs of roller blades annually. These sales are incremental to the acquisition of Skates'n'Stuff. Furthermore, all sales resulting from the acquisition would be made to retailers in Thailand. Blades' fixed expenses would be 20 million baht annually. Although Holt has not previously considered the acquisition of an existing business, he is now wondering whether aquiring Skates'n'Stuff may be a better course of action than building a subsidiary in Thailand.

Holt is also aware of some disadvantages associated with such an acquisition. Skates'n'Stuff's CFO has indicated that he would be willing to accept a price of 1 billion baht in payment for the company, which is clearly more expensive than the 550 million baht outlay that would be required to establish a subsidiary in Thailand. However, Skates'n'Stuff's CFO has indicated that it is willing to negotiate. Furthermore, Blades' employs a high-quality production process, which enables it to charge relatively high prices for roller blades produced in its plants. If Blades acquires Skates'n'Stuff, which uses an inferior production process (resulting in lower quality roller blades), it would have to charge a lower price for the roller blades it produces there. Initial forecasts indicate that Blades will be able to charge a price of 4,500 Thai baht per pair of roller blades without affecting demand. However, because Skates'n'Stuff uses a production process that results in lower quality roller blades than Blades' Speedos, operating costs incurred would be similar to the amount incurred if Blades establishes a subsidiary in Thailand. Thus, Blades estimates that it would incur operating costs of about 3,500 baht per pair of roller blades.

Ben Holt has asked you, a financial analyst for Blades, Inc., to determine whether the acquisition of Skates'n'Stuff is a better course of action for Blades than the establishment of a subsidiary in Thailand. Acquiring Skates'n'Stuff will be more favorable than establishing a subsidiary if the present value of the cash flows generated by the company exceeds the purchase price by more than $8,746,688, the *NPV* of establishing a new subsidiary. Thus, Holt has asked you to construct a spreadsheet that determines the *NPV* of the acquisition.

To aid you in your analysis, Holt has provided the following additional information, which he gathered from various sources, including unaudited financial statements of Skates'n'Stuff for the last three years:

- Blades, Inc., requires a return on the Thai acquisition of 25 percent, the same rate of return it would require if it established a subsidiary in Thailand.
- If Skates'n'Stuff is acquired, Blades, Inc., will operate the company for 10 years, at which time Skates'n'Stuff will be sold for an estimated 1.1 million baht.
- Of the 1 billion baht purchase price, 600 million baht constitutes the cost of the plant and equipment. These items are depreciated using straight-line depreciation. Thus, 60 million baht will be depreciated annually for 10 years.
- Sales of 280,000 pairs of roller blades annually will begin immediately at a price of 4,500 baht per pair.
- Variable costs per pair of roller blades will be 3,500 per pair.
- Fixed operating costs, including salaries and administrative expenses, will be 20 million baht annually.
- The current spot rate of the Thai baht is $0.023. Blades expects the baht to depreciate by an average of 2 percent per year for the next 10 years.
- The Thai government will impose a 25 percent tax on income and a 10 percent withholding tax on any funds remitted by Skates'n'Stuff to Blades, Inc. Any earnings remitted to the United States will not be taxed again in the United States All earnings generated by Skates'n'Stuff will be remitted to Blades, Inc.
- The average inflation rate in Thailand is expected to be 12 percent annually. Revenues, variable costs, and fixed costs are subject to inflation and are expected to change by the same annual rate as the inflation rate.

In addition to the information outlined above, Ben Holt has informed you that Blades, Inc., will need to manufacture all of the 180,000 pairs to be delivered to Entertainment Products this year and next year in Thailand. Since Blades previously only used components from Thailand (which are of a lower quality but cheaper than U.S. components) sufficient to manufacture 72,000 pairs annually, it will incur cost savings of 32.4 million baht this year and next year. However, since Blades will sell 180,000 pairs of Speedos annually to Entertainment Products this year and next year whether it acquires Skates'n'Stuff or not, Holt has urged you not to include these sales in your analysis. The agreement with Entertainment Product will not be renewed at the end of next year.

Ben Holt would like you to answer the following questions:

1. Using a spreadsheet, determine the *NPV* of the acquisition of Skates'n'Stuff. Based on your numerical analysis, should Blades establish a subsidiary in Thailand or acquire Skates'n'Stuff?
2. If Blades negotiates with Skates'n'Stuff, what is the

maximum amount (in Thai baht) Blades should be willing to pay?

3. Are there any other factors Blades should consider in making its decision? In your answer, you should consider the price Skates'n'Stuff is asking relative to your analysis in question 1, other potential businesses for sale in Thailand, the source of the information your analysis is based on, the production process that will be employed by the target in the future, and the future management of Skates'n'Stuff.

SMALL BUSINESS DILEMMA

Multinational Restructuring by the Sports Exports Company

The Sports Exports Company has been successful in producing footballs in the United States and exporting them to the United Kingdom. Recently, Jim Logan (owner of the Sports Exports Company) has considered restructuring his company by expanding throughout Europe. He plans to export footballs and other sporting goods that were not already popular in Europe to one large sporting goods distributor in Germany; the goods will then be distributed to any retail sporting goods stores throughout Europe that are willing to purchase these goods. This distributor will make payments in euros to the Sports Exports Company.

1. Are there any reasons why the business that has been so successful in the United Kingdom will not necessarily be successful in other European countries?
2. If the business is diversified throughout Europe, will this substantially reduce the exposure of the Sports Exports Company to exchange rate risk?
3. Now that several countries in Europe participate a single currency system, will this affect the performance of new expansion throughout Europe?

CHAPTER 16

Country Risk Analysis

An MNC conducts country risk analysis when assessing whether to continue conducting business in a particular country. The analysis can also be used when determining whether to implement new projects in foreign countries. Country risk can be partitioned into the country's political risk and its financial risk. Financial managers must understand how to measure country risk so that they can make investment decisions that maximize their MNC's value.

The specific objectives of this chapter are to:

- identify the common factors used by MNCs to measure a country's political risk,
- identify the common factors used by MNCs to measure a country's financial risk,
- explain the techniques used to measure country risk, and
- explain how MNCs use the assessment of country risk when making financial decisions.

Why Country Risk Analysis Is Important

Country risk is the potentially adverse impact of a country's environment on an MNC's cash flows. Country risk analysis can be used to monitor countries where the MNC is currently doing business. If the country risk level of a particular country begins to increase, the MNC may consider divesting its subsidiaries located there. MNCs can also use country risk analysis as a screening device to avoid conducting business in countries with excessive risk. Events that heighten country risk tend to discourage U.S. direct foreign investment in that particular country.

Country risk analysis is not restricted to predicting major crises. An MNC may also use this analysis to revise its investment or financing decisions in light of recent events. In any given week, the following unrelated international events might occur around the world:

- A terrorist attack
- A major labor strike in an industry
- A political crisis due to a scandal within a country
- Concern about a country's banking system that may cause a major outflow of funds
- The imposition of trade restrictions on imports

Any of these events could affect the potential cash flows to be generated by an MNC or the cost of financing projects and therefore affect the value of the MNC.

Even if an MNC reduces its exposure to all such events in a given week, a new set of events will occur in the following week. For each of these events, an MNC must consider whether its cash flows will be affected and whether there has been a change in policy to which it should respond. Country risk analysis is an ongoing process. Most MNCs will not be affected by every event, but they will pay close attention to any events that may have an impact on the industries or countries in which they do business. They also recognize that they cannot eliminate their exposure to all events but may at least attempt to limit their exposure to any single country-specific event.

Political Risk Factors

An MNC must assess country risk not only in countries where it currently does business but also in those where it expects to export or establish subsidiaries. Several risk characteristics of a country may significantly affect performance, and the MNC should be concerned about the likely degree of impact for each. The September 11, 2001 terrorist attack on the United States heightened the awareness of political risk.

As one might expect, many country characteristics related to the political environment can influence an MNC. An extreme form of political risk is the possibility that the host country will take over a subsidiary. In some cases of expropriation, some compensation (the amount decided by the host country government) is awarded. In other cases, the assets are confiscated and no compensation is provided. Expropriation can take place peacefully or by force. The folllowing are some of the more common forms of political risk:

- Attitude of consumers in the host country
- Actions of host government
- Blockage of fund transfers
- Currency inconvertibility
- War
- Bureaucracy
- Corruption

Each of these characteristics will be examined.

Attitude of Consumers in the Host Country

A mild form of political risk (to an exporter) is a tendency of residents to purchase only locally produced goods. Even if the exporter decides to set up a subsidiary in the foreign country, this philosophy could prevent its success. All countries tend to exert some pressure on consumers to purchase from locally owned manufacturers. (In the United States, consumers are encouraged to look for the "Made in the U.S.A." label.) MNCs that consider entering a foreign market (or have already entered that market) must monitor the general loyalty of consumers toward locally produced products. If consumers are very loyal to local products, a joint venture with a local company may be more feasible than an exporting strategy. The September 11, 2001 terrorist attack caused some consumers to pay more attention to the country where products are produced.

http://

The website http://www.cia.gov provides valuable information about political risk that should be considered by MNCs that engage in direct foreign investment.

Actions of Host Government

Various actions of a host government can affect the cash flow of an MNC. For example, a host government might impose pollution control standards (which affect costs) and additional corporate taxes (which affect after-tax earnings) as well as withholding taxes and fund transfer restrictions (which affect after-tax cash flows sent to the parent).

EXAMPLE

In 2004, the Chinese government enacted a law requiring computer chips to include security technology that is licensed by Chinese firms. In addition, China imposes a 17 percent tax on computer chips sold there, but provides a rebate of up to 14 percent for chips produced locally. This may discourage chip manufacturers such as Intel and Broadcom from selling chips in China.

Some MNCs use turnover in government members or philosophy as a proxy for a country's political risk. While this can significantly influence the MNC's future cash flows, it alone does not serve as a suitable representation of political risk. A subsidiary will not necessarily be affected by changing governments. Furthermore, a subsidiary can be affected by new policies of the host government or by a changed attitude toward the subsidiary's home country (and therefore the subsidiary), even when the host government has no risk of being overthrown.

A host government can use various means to make an MNC's operations coincide with its own goals. It may, for example, require the use of local employees for managerial positions at a subsidiary. In addition, it may require social facilities (such as an exercise room or nonsmoking areas) or special environmental controls (such as air pollution controls). Furthermore, it is not uncommon for a host government to require special permits, impose extra taxes, or subsidize competitors. All of these actions represent political risk, in that they reflect a country's political characteristics and could influence an MNC's cash flows.

EXAMPLE

In March 2004, antitrust regulators representing the European Union countries decided to fine Microsoft about 500 million euros (equivalent to about $610 million at the time) for abusing its monopolistic position in computer software. They also imposed restrictions on how Microsoft can bundle its Windows MediaPlayer (needed to access music or videos) in its portable computer sold in Europe. Microsoft argued that the fine is unfair because it is not subject to such restrictions in its home country, the United States. Some critics argue, however, that the European regulators are not being too strict, but rather that the U.S. regulators are being too lenient.

Lack of Restrictions. In some cases, MNCs are adversely affected by a lack of restrictions in a host country, which allows illegitimate business behavior to take market share. One of the most troubling issues for MNCs is the failure by host governments to enforce copyright laws against local firms that illegally copy the MNC's product. For example, local firms in Asia commonly copy software produced by MNCs and sell it to customers at lower prices. Software producers lose an estimated $3 billion in sales annually in Asia for this reason. Furthermore, the legal systems in some countries do not adequately protect a firm against copyright violations or other illegal means of obtaining market share.

Blockage of Fund Transfers

Subsidiaries of MNCs often send funds back to the headquarters for loan repayments, purchases of supplies, administrative fees, remitted earnings, or other purposes. In some cases, a host government may block fund transfers, which could force subsidiaries to undertake projects that are not optimal (just to make use of the funds). Alternatively, the MNC may invest the funds in local securities that provide some return while the funds are blocked. But this return may be inferior to what could have been earned on funds remitted to the parent.

Currency Inconvertibility

Some governments do not allow the home currency to be exchanged into other currencies. Thus, the earnings generated by a subsidiary in these countries cannot be remitted to the parent through currency conversion. When the currency is inconvertible, an MNC's parent may need to exchange it for goods to extract benefits from projects in that country.

War

Some countries tend to engage in constant conflicts with neighboring countries or experience internal turmoil. This can affect the safety of employees hired by an MNC's subsidiary or by salespeople who attempt to establish export markets for the MNC. In addition, countries plagued by the threat of war typically have volatile business cycles, which make the MNC's cash flows generated from such countries more uncertain. The terrorist attack on the United States on September 11, 2001, aroused the expectation that the United States would be involved in a war. MNCs were adversely affected by their potential exposure to terrorist attacks, especially if their subsidiaries were located in countries where there might be anti-U.S. sentiment. Even if an MNC is not directly damaged due to a war, it may incur costs from ensuring the safety of its employees.

The 2003 War in Iraq. As a result of the 2003 war in Iraq, MNCs' cash flows were affected in various ways. The war caused friction between the United States and some countries in the Middle East. Consequently, MNCs faced the possibility that their buildings or offices overseas might be destroyed and that their employees might be attacked. Furthermore, demand for U.S. products and services by consumers in the Middle East declined. In addition, because of friction between the United States and France over how the situation in Iraq should be handled, French demand for some products produced by U.S.-based MNCs also declined. To a lesser extent, there were protests by citizens in other countries, which could have reduced the demand for products produced by U.S. firms. This form of country risk is not limited to U.S.-based MNCs. Friction periodically arises between many countries. Just as French consumers reduced their demand for U.S. products during the war, U.S. consumers reduced their demand for French wine and reduced their travel to France. The French Government Tourist Office estimated that revenue received in France due to U.S. tourism in 2003 was about $500 million less than in the previous year.

Even if MNCs were not directly affected by the various protests, there was substantial uncertainty about how the war might adversely affect MNCs by weakening economic conditions. There was concern that oil prices would rise because of the possible destruction of oil wells, and higher oil prices have a direct impact on transportation and energy costs. Higher interest rates were feared because of the substantial funding needed to finance the military spending. Some of the more pessimistic predictions suggested there would be a major world recession combined with high inflation. Thus, MNCs were concerned about the potential higher costs of supplies and the potential impact of high U.S. inflation or interest rates on exchange rates. Given all this uncertainty, MNCs restricted their expansion until the impact of the war on oil prices, the U.S. budget deficit, and the political relationships between the United States and other countries was clear.

Bureaucracy

Another country risk factor is government bureaucracy, which can complicate an MNC's business. Although this factor may seem irrelevant, it was a major deterrent for MNCs that considered projects in Eastern Europe in the early 1990s. Many of the Eastern European governments were not experienced at facilitating the entrance of MNCs into their markets.

USING THE WEB

Political Risk Ratings If an MNC wants to review an assessment of various political risk characteristics by outside evaluators, it can obtain this information at http://biz.yahoo.com/ifc/.

Corruption

Corruption can adversely affect an MNC's international business because it can increase the cost of conducting business or it can reduce revenue. Various forms of corruption can occur between firms or between a firm and the government. For example, an MNC may lose revenue because a government contract is awarded to a local firm that paid off a government official. Laws and their enforcement vary among countries, however. For example, in the United States, it is illegal to make a payment to a high-ranking government official in return for political favors, but it is legal for U.S. firms to contribute to a politician's election campaign.

A corruption index is derived for most countries by Transparency International (see **http://www.transparency.org**). The index for selected countries is shown in Exhibit 16.1.

Financial Risk Factors

Along with political factors, financial factors should be considered when assessing country risk. One of the most obvious financial factors is the current and potential state of the country's economy. An MNC that exports to a country or develops a subsidiary in a country is highly concerned about that country's demand for its products. This demand is, of course, strongly influenced by the country's economy. A recession in the country could severely reduce demand for the MNC's exports or products sold by the MNC's local subsidiary. In the early 1990s and again in the 2000–2002 period, the European business performance of Ford Motor Co., Nike, Walt Disney Co., and many other U.S.-based MNCs was adversely affected by a weak European economy.

Exhibit 16.1
Corruption Index Ratings for Selected Countries (Maximum rating = 10. High ratings indicate low corruption.)

Country	Index Rating	Country	Index Rating
Finland	9.7	Chile	7.4
Denmark	9.6	France	6.9
New Zealand	9.5	Spain	6.9
Singapore	9.4	Taiwan	5.7
Sweden	9.3	Uruguay	5.5
Netherlands	8.9	Italy	5.3
Switzerland	8.8	Malaysia	5.2
Canada	8.7	Hungary	4.8
United Kingdom	8.7	Greece	4.3
Austria	8.0	Brazil	3.9
Hong Kong	8.0	Czech Republic	3.9
Germany	7.7	Mexico	3.6
Belgium	7.6	China	3.4
Ireland	7.6	India	2.8
United States	7.5	Russia	2.7

Source: Transparency International, 2003.

Indicators of Economic Growth

http://

The website http://www.heritage.org offers interesting insight into international political risk issues that should be considered by MNCs conducting international business.

A country's economic growth is dependent on several financial factors:

- *Interest rates.* Higher interest rates tend to slow the growth of an economy and reduce demand for the MNC's products. Lower interest rates often stimulate the economy and increase demand for the MNC's products.
- *Exchange rates.* Exchange rates can influence the demand for the country's exports, which in turn affects the country's production and income level. A strong currency may reduce demand for the country's exports, increase the volume of products imported by the country, and therefore reduce the country's production and national income. A very weak currency can cause speculative outflows and reduce the amount of funds available to finance growth by businesses.
- *Inflation.* Inflation can affect consumers' purchasing power and therefore their demand for an MNC's goods. It also indirectly affects a country's financial condition by influencing the country's interest rates and currency value. A high level of inflation may also lead to a decline in economic growth.

Most financial factors that affect a country's economic conditions are difficult to forecast. Thus, even if an MNC considers them in its country risk assessment, it may still make poor decisions because of an improper forecast of the country's financial factors.

Some financial conditions may be caused by political risk. For example, the September 11, 2001 terrorist attack on the United States affected U.S.-based MNCs because of political risk and financial risk. Political uncertainty caused uncertainty about economic conditions, which resulted in a reduction in spending by consumers and, therefore, a reduction in cash flows of MNCs.

Types of Country Risk Assessment

Although there is no consensus as to how country risk can best be assessed, some guidelines have been developed. The first step is to recognize the difference between (1) an overall risk assessment of a country without consideration of the MNC's business and (2) the risk assessment of a country as it relates to the MNC's type of business. The first type can be referred to as **macroassessment** of country risk and the latter type as a **microassessment**. Each type is discussed in turn.

Macroassessment of Country Risk

http://

Visit http://lcweb2.loc.gov/frd/cs/cshome.html for detailed studies of 85 countries provided by the Library of Congress.

A macroassessment involves consideration of all variables that affect country risk except those unique to a particular firm or industry. This type of risk is convenient in that it remains the same for a given country, regardless of the firm or industry of concern; however, it excludes relevant information that could improve the accuracy of the assessment. Although a macroassessment of country risk is not ideal for any individual MNC, it serves as a foundation that can then be modified to reflect the particular business of the MNC.

Any macroassessment model should consider both political and financial characteristics of the country being assessed:

- *Political factors.* Political factors include the relationship of the host government with the MNC's home country government, the attitude of people in the host country toward the MNC's government, the historical stability of the host government, the vulnerability of the host government to political takeovers, and the probability of war between the host country and neighboring countries. Consideration of such political factors will indicate the probability of political events that may affect an MNC and the magnitude of the impact. The September 11, 2001 terrorist attack on the United States caused more concern about political risk for U.S.-based MNCs because of all the factors cited here.
- *Financial factors.* The financial factors of a macroassessment model should include GDP growth, inflation trends, government budget levels (and the government deficit), interest rates, unemployment, the country's reliance on export income, the balance of trade, and foreign exchange controls. The list of financial factors could easily be extended several pages. The factors listed here represent just a subset of the financial factors considered when evaluating the financial strength of a country.

http://

The U.S. Department of Commerce Web page at http://www.stat-usa.gov provides access to a variety of microeconomic and macroeconomic data on emerging markets.

Uncertainty Surrounding a Macroassessment. There is clearly a degree of subjectivity in identifying the relevant political and financial factors for a macroassessment of country risk. There is also some subjectivity in determining the importance of each factor for the overall macroassessment for a particular country. For instance, one assessor may assign a much higher weight (degree of importance) to real GDP growth than another assessor. Finally, there is some subjectivity in predicting these financial factors. Because of these various types of subjectivity, it is not surprising that risk assessors often arrive at different opinions after completing a macroassessment of country risk.

Microassessment of Country Risk

While a macroassessment of country risk provides an indication of the country's overall status, it does not assess country risk from the perspective of the particular business of concern. A microassessment of country risk is needed to determine how the country risk relates to the specific MNC.

EXAMPLE

Since Nike conducts a large amount of international business, it must monitor country risk in many countries. Nike could be affected by country risk in several ways. First, a conflict between the United States and a specific foreign country could cause either the foreign country's government or its people to vent their anger against a Nike subsidiary in that country. Thus, Nike could be a target simply because it is viewed as a U.S. company, even if all the employees at that subsidiary are locals. Second, a change in a foreign government could result in new tax laws and other restrictions imposed on subsidiaries of U.S. firms or firms from any other country that are based there. Third, other local shoe manufacturers could possibly use government ties to impose more restrictions against Nike so that they could have a competitive advantage in the country of concern. Fourth, Nike's subsidiary could be adversely affected by other political problems that cause a deterioration in economic conditions in that country. Any of these events could cause an increase in the subsidiary's expenses or a decline in its revenue.

The specific impact of a particular form of country risk can affect MNCs in different ways.

EXAMPLE

Country Z has been assigned a relatively low macroassessment by most experts due to its poor financial condition. Two MNCs are deciding whether to set up subsidiaries in Country Z. Carco, Inc., is considering developing a subsidiary that would produce automobiles and sell them locally, while Milco, Inc., plans to build a subsidiary that would produce military supplies. Carco's plan to build an automobile subsidiary does not appear to be feasible, unless Country Z does not have a sufficient number of automobile producers already.

Country Z's government may be committed to purchasing a given amount of military supplies, regardless of how weak the economy is. Thus, Milco's plan to build a military supply subsidiary may still be feasible, even though Country Z's financial condition is poor.

It is possible, however, that Country Z's government will order its military supplies from a locally owned firm because it wants its supply needs to remain confidential. This possibility is an element of country risk because it is a country characteristic (or attitude) that can affect the feasibility of a project. Yet, this specific characteristic is relevant only to Milco, Inc., and not to Carco, Inc.

This example illustrates how an appropriate country risk assessment varies with the firm, industry, and project of concern and therefore why a macroassessment of country risk has its limitations. A microassessment is also necessary when evaluating the country risk related to a particular project proposed by a particular firm.

In addition to political variables, financial variables must also be included in a microassessment of country risk. Microfactors include the sensitivity of the firm's business to real GDP growth, inflation trends, interest rates, and other factors. Due to differences in business characteristics, some firms are more susceptible to the host country's economy than others.

In summary, the overall assessment of country risk consists of four parts:

1. Macropolitical risk
2. Macrofinancial risk
3. Micropolitical risk
4. Microfinancial risk

Although these parts can be consolidated to generate a single country risk rating, it may be useful to keep them separate so that an MNC can identify the various ways its direct foreign investment or exporting operations are exposed to country risk.

Techniques to Assess Country Risk

Once a firm identifies all the macro- and microfactors that deserve consideration in the country risk assessment, it may wish to implement a system for evaluating these factors and determining a country risk rating. Various techniques are available to achieve this objective. The following are some of the more popular techniques:

- Checklist approach
- Delphi technique
- Quantitative analysis
- Inspection visits
- Combination of techniques

Each technique is briefly discussed in turn.

Checklist Approach

A checklist approach involves making a judgment on all the political and financial factors (both macro and micro) that contribute to a firm's assessment of country risk. Ratings are assigned to a list of various financial and political factors, and these ratings are then consolidated to derive an overall assessment of country risk. Some factors (such as real GDP growth) can be measured from available data, while others (such as probability of entering a war) must be subjectively measured.

A substantial amount of information about countries is available on the Internet. This information can be used to develop ratings of various factors used to assess country risk. The factors are then converted to some numerical rating in order to assess a particular country. Those factors thought to have a greater influence on country risk should be assigned greater weights. Both the measurement of some factors and the weighting scheme implemented are subjective.

Delphi Technique

The **Delphi technique** involves the collection of independent opinions on country risk without group discussion by the assessors (such as employees or outside consultants) who provide these opinions. Though the Delphi technique can be useful, it is based on subjective opinions, which may vary among assessors. The MNC can average these opinions in some manner and even assess the degree of disagreement by measuring the dispersion of opinions.

Quantitative Analysis

Once the financial and political variables have been measured for a period of time, models for quantitative analysis can attempt to identify the characteristics that influence the level of country risk. For example, regression analysis may be used to assess risk, since it can measure the sensitivity of one variable to other variables. A firm could regress a measure of its business activity (such as its percentage increase in sales) against country characteristics (such as real growth in GDP) over a series of previous months or quarters. Results from such an analysis will indicate the susceptibility of a particular business to a country's economy. This is valuable information to incorporate into the overall evaluation of country risk.

Although quantitative models can quantify the impact of variables on each other, they do not necessarily indicate a country's problems before they actually occur (preferably before the firm's decision to pursue a project in that country). Nor can they evaluate subjective data that cannot be quantified. In addition, historical trends of various country characteristics are not always useful for anticipating an upcoming crisis.

Inspection Visits

Inspection visits involve traveling to a country and meeting with government officials, business executives, and/or consumers. Such meetings can help clarify any uncertain opinions the firm has about a country. Indeed, some variables, such as intercountry relationships, may be difficult to assess without a trip to the host country.

Combination of Techniques

A survey of 193 corporations heavily involved in foreign business found that about half of them have no formal method of assessing country risk. This does not mean that they neglect to assess country risk, but rather that there is no proven method to use. Consequently, many MNCs use a variety of techniques, possibly using a checklist approach to develop an overall country risk rating and then using the Delphi technique, quantitative analysis, and inspection visits to assign ratings to the various factors.

Missouri, Inc., recognizes that it must consider several financial and political factors in its country risk analysis of Mexico, where it plans to establish a subsidiary. Missouri creates a checklist of several factors and assigns a rating to each factor. It uses the Delphi technique to rate various political factors. It uses quantitative analysis to predict future economic conditions in Mexico so that it can rate various financial factors. It conducts an inspection visit to complement its assessment of the financial and political factors.

Measuring Country Risk

Deriving an overall country risk rating using a checklist approach requires separate ratings for political and financial risk. First, the political factors are assigned values within some arbitrarily chosen range (such as values from 1 to 5, where 5 is the best value/lowest risk). Next, these political factors are assigned weights (representing degree of importance), which should add up to 100 percent. The assigned values of the factors times their respective weights can then be summed to derive a political risk rating.

The process is then repeated to derive the financial risk rating. All financial factors are assigned values (from 1 to 5, where 5 is the best value/lowest risk). Then the assigned values of the factors times their respective weights can be summed to derive a financial risk rating.

Once the political and financial ratings have been derived, a country's overall country risk rating as it relates to a specific project can be determined by assigning weights to the political and financial ratings according to their perceived importance. The importance of political risk versus financial risk varies with the intent of the MNC. An MNC considering direct foreign investment to attract demand in that country must be highly concerned about financial risk. An MNC establishing a foreign manufacturing plant and planning to export the goods from there should be more concerned with political risk.

If the political risk is thought to be much more influential on a particular project than the financial risk, it will receive a higher weight than the financial risk rating (together both weights must total 100 percent). The political and financial ratings multiplied by their respective weights will determine the overall country risk rating for a country as it relates to a particular project.

EXAMPLE

Assume that Cougar Co. plans to build a steel plant in the Mexico. It has used the Delphi technique and quantitative analysis to derive ratings for various political and financial factors. The discussion here focuses on how to consolidate the ratings to derive an overall country risk rating.

Exhibit 16.2 illustrates Cougar's country risk assessment of Mexico. Notice in Exhibit 16.2 that two political factors and five financial factors contribute to the overall country risk rating in this example. Cougar Co. will consider projects only in countries that have a country risk rating of 3.5 or higher, based on its country risk rating.

Cougar Co. has assigned the values and weights to the factors as shown in Exhibit 16.3. In this example, the company generally assigns the financial factors higher

Exhibit 16.2

Determining the Overall Country Risk Rating

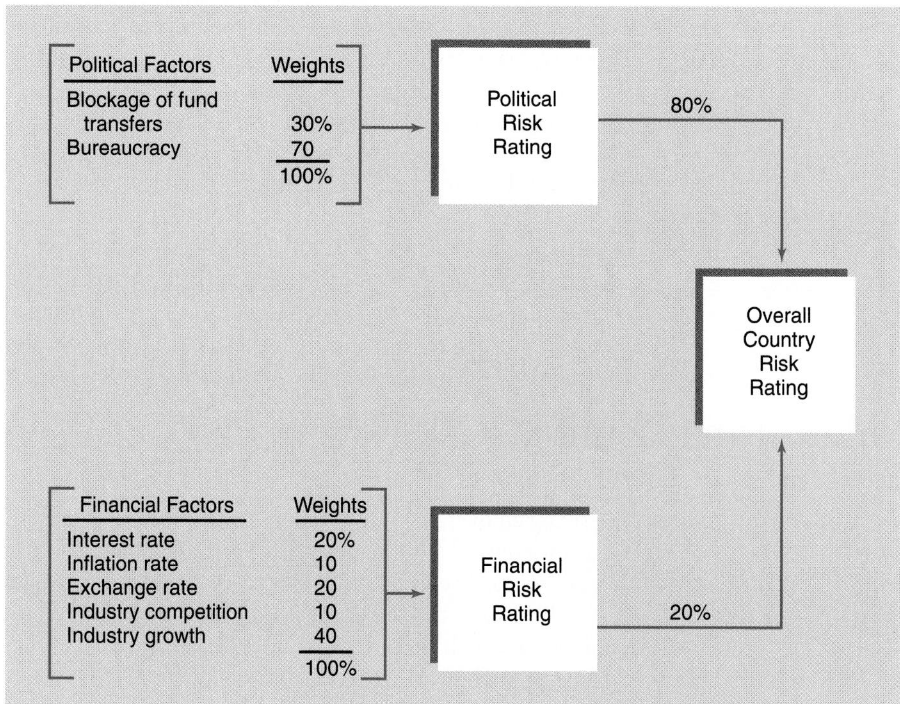

Exhibit 16.3 Derivation of the Overall Country Risk Rating Based on Assumed Information

(1)	(2)	(3)	(4) = (2) × (3)
Political Risk Factors	Rating Assigned by Company to Factor (within a Range of 1–5)	Weight Assigned by Company to Factor According to Importance	Weighted Value of Factor
Blockage of fund transfers	4	30%	1.2
Bureaucracy	3	70	2.1
		100%	3.3 = Political risk rating
Financial Risk Factors			
Interest rate	5	20%	1.0
Inflation rate	4	10	.4
Exchange rate	4	20	.8
Industry competition	5	10	.5
Industry growth	3	40	1.2
		100%	3.9 = Financial risk rating
(1)	(2)	(3)	(4) = (2) × (3)
Category	Rating as Determined Above	Weight Assigned by Company to Each Risk Category	Weighted Rating
Political risk	3.3	80%	2.64
Financial risk	3.9	20	.78
		100%	3.42 = Overall country risk rating

ratings than the political factors. The financial condition of Mexico has therefore been assessed more favorably than the political condition. Industry growth is the most important financial factor in Mexico, based on its 40 percent weighting. The bureaucracy is thought to be the most important political factor, based on a weighting of 70 percent; regulation of international fund transfers receives the remaining 30 percent weighting. The political risk rating is estimated at 3.3 by adding the products of the assigned ratings (Column 2) and weights (Column 3) of the political risk factors.

The financial risk is computed to be 3.9, based on adding the products of the assigned ratings and the weights of the financial risk factors. Once the political and financial ratings are determined, the overall country risk rating can be derived (as shown at the bottom of Exhibit 16.3), given the weights assigned to political and financial risk. Column 3 at the bottom of Exhibit 16.3 indicates that Cougar perceives political risk (receiving an 80 percent weight) to be much more important than financial risk (receiving a 20 percent weight) in Mexico for the proposed project. The overall country risk rating of 3.42 may appear low given the individual category ratings. This is due to the heavy weighting given to political risk, which in this example is critical from the firm's perspective. In particular, Cougar views Mexico's bureaucracy as a critical factor and assigns it a low rating. Given that Cougar considers projects only in countries that have a rating of at least 3.5, it decides not to pursue the project in Mexico.

Variation in Methods of Measuring Country Risk

Country risk assessors have their own individual procedures for quantifying country risk. The procedure described here is just one of many. Most procedures are similar, though, in that they somehow assign ratings and weights to all individual characteristics relevant to country risk assessment.

The number of relevant factors comprising both the political risk and the financial risk categories will vary with the country being assessed and the type of corporate operations planned for that country. The assignment of values to the factors, along with the degree of importance (weights) assigned to the factors, will also vary with the country being assessed and the type of corporate operations planned for that country.

Using the Country Risk Rating for Decision Making

If the country risk is too high, then the firm does not need to analyze the feasibility of the proposed project any further. Some firms may contend that no risk is too high when considering a project. Their reasoning is that if the potential return is high enough, the project is worth undertaking. When employee safety is a concern, however, the project may be rejected regardless of its potential return.

Even after a project is accepted and implemented, the MNC must continue to monitor country risk. With a labor-intensive MNC, the host country may feel it is benefiting from a subsidiary's existence (due to the subsidiary's employment of local people), and the chance of expropriation may be low. Nevertheless, several other forms of country risk could suddenly make the MNC consider divesting the project. Furthermore, decisions regarding subsidiary expansion, fund transfers to the parent, and sources of financing can all be affected by any changes in country risk. Since country risk can change dramatically over time, periodic reassessment is required, especially for less stable countries.

Regardless of how country risk analysis is conducted, MNCs are often unable to predict crises in various countries. MNCs should recognize their limitations when assessing country risk and consider ways they might limit their exposure to a possible increase in that risk.

Comparing Risk Ratings among Countries

An MNC may evaluate country risk for several countries, perhaps to determine where to establish a subsidiary. One approach to comparing political and financial ratings among countries, advocated by some foreign risk managers, is a **foreign investment risk matrix (FIRM),** which displays the financial (or economic) and political risk by intervals ranging across the matrix from "poor" to "good." Each country can be positioned in its appropriate location on the matrix based on its political rating and financial rating.

USING THE WEB

Country Risk Ratings If an MNC wants to consider a country risk assessment by outside evaluators, it can obtain a country risk rating for any country at http://biz.yahoo.com/ifc/. For each country, various components used to derive the overall country risk rating are rated, including the country's political risk and economic risk.

Actual Country Risk Ratings across Countries

http://

Visit http://www.duke.edu/~charvey for the results of Campbell R. Harvey's political, economic, and financial country risk analysis.

Country risk ratings are shown in Exhibit 16.4. This exhibit is not necessarily applicable to a particular MNC that wants to pursue international business because the risk assessment here may not focus on the factors that are relevant to that MNC. Nevertheless, the exhibit illustrates how the risk rating can vary substantially among countries. Many industrialized countries have high ratings, indicating low risk. Emerging countries tend to have lower ratings. Country risk ratings change over time in response to the factors that influence a country's rating.

Incorporating Country Risk in Capital Budgeting

If the risk rating of a country is in the tolerable range, any project related to that country deserves further consideration. Country risk can be incorporated in the capital budgeting analysis of a proposed project by adjusting the discount rate or by adjusting the estimated cash flows. Each method is discussed here.

Adjustment of the Discount Rate

The discount rate of a proposed project is supposed to reflect the required rate of return on that project. Thus, the discount rate can be adjusted to account for the country risk. The lower the country risk rating, the higher the perceived risk and the higher the discount rate applied to the project's cash flows. This approach is convenient in that one adjustment to the capital budgeting analysis can capture country risk. However, there is no precise formula for adjusting the discount rate to incorporate country risk. The adjustment is somewhat arbitrary and may therefore cause feasible projects to be rejected or infeasible projects to be accepted.

MANAGING FOR VALUE

TheStreet.com's Decision to Close Its British Subsidiary

TheStreet.com is a U.S.-based Internet firm that provides financial information on its website. In February 2000, it decided to expand its operations into the United Kingdom where it created a website specific to British investors. One country characteristic in its favor was that many individual investors in Europe are based in the United Kingdom. A key characteristic of any country, however, is the preferences of its consumers, which affect the demand for a firm's products.

It appears that TheStreet.com's assessment of the United Kingdom's environment was overly optimistic. The Internet and online brokerage accounts are not used as much in the United Kingdom as in some other European countries. Therefore, TheStreet.com attracted fewer customers than it had expected. In November 2000, TheStreet.com decided to close its operations in the United Kingdom because the website was costly to maintain and was not generating sufficient advertising revenue.

This example illustrates the danger of generalizing about Europe rather than recognizing the specific characteristics of each European country. Although there are more individual investors in the United Kingdom, individuals in Germany and the Scandinavian countries use the Internet more. TheStreet.com's decision to close its operations in the United Kingdom enhanced its value because it discontinued a value-decreasing project.

Exhibit 16.4 Country Risk Ratings among Countries

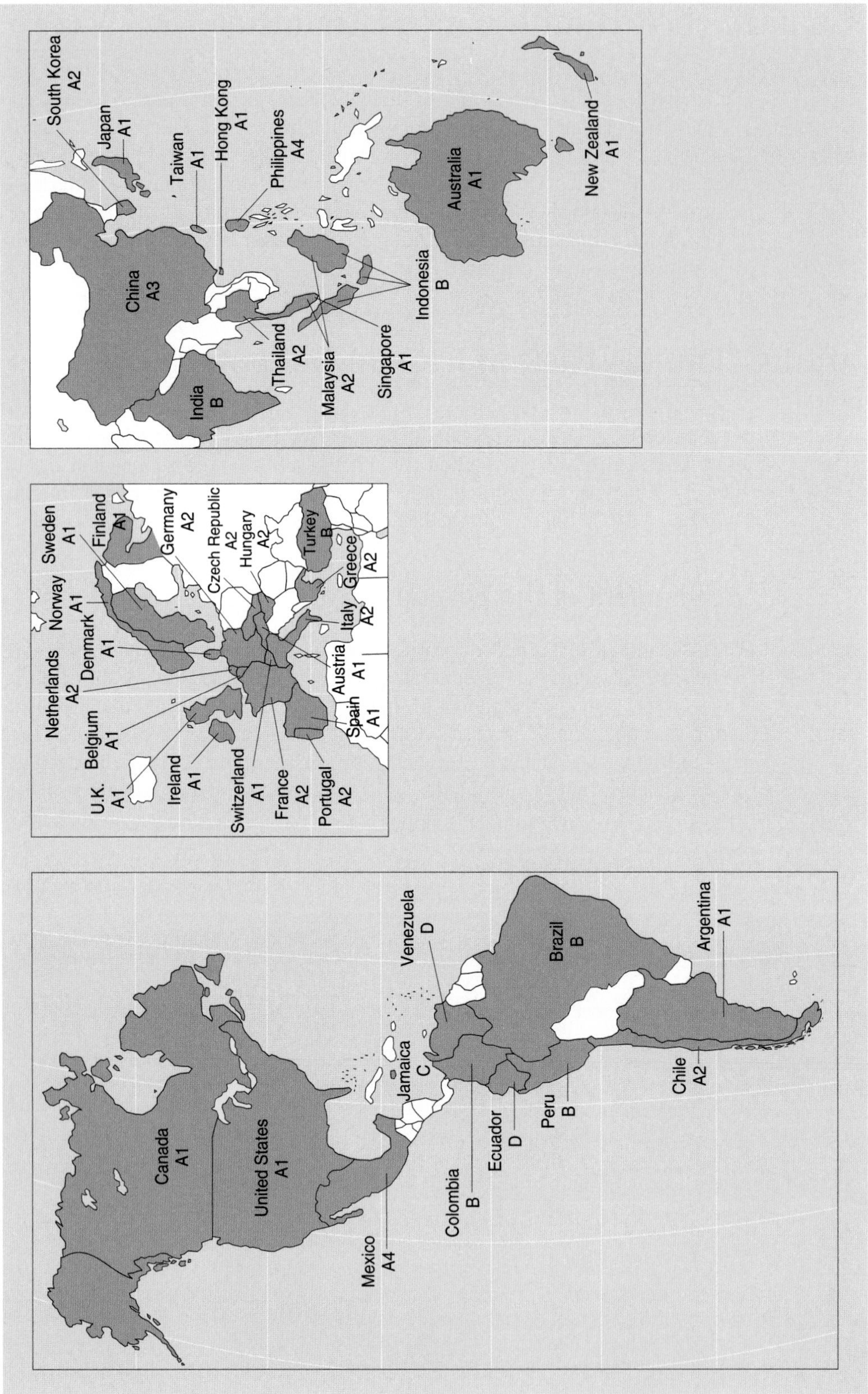

Source: Coface, 2004. Ratings range from a high of A1 to a low of D.

Adjustment of the Estimated Cash Flows

Perhaps the most appropriate method for incorporating forms of country risk in a capital budgeting analysis is to estimate how the cash flows would be affected by each form of risk. For example, if there is a 20 percent probability that the host government will temporarily block funds from the subsidiary to the parent, the MNC should estimate the project's net present value (*NPV*) under these circumstances, realizing that there is a 20 percent chance that this *NPV* will occur.

If there is a chance that a host government takeover will occur, the foreign project's *NPV* under these conditions should be estimated. Each possible form of risk has an estimated impact on the foreign project's cash flows and therefore on the project's *NPV*. By analyzing each possible impact, the MNC can determine the probability distribution of *NPV*s for the project. Its accept/reject decision on the project will be based on its assessment of the probability that the project will generate a positive *NPV*, as well as the size of possible *NPV* outcomes. Though this procedure may seem somewhat tedious, it directly incorporates forms of country risk into the cash flow estimates and explicitly illustrates the possible results from implementing the project. The more convenient method of adjusting the discount rate in accordance with the country risk rating does not indicate the probability distribution of possible outcomes.

EXAMPLE

Reconsider the example of Spartan, Inc., that was discussed in Chapter 14. Assume for the moment that all the initial assumptions regarding Spartan's initial investment, project life, pricing policy, exchange rate projections, and so on still apply. Now, however, we will incorporate two country risk characteristics that were not included in the initial analysis. First, assume that there is a 30 percent chance that the withholding tax imposed by the Singapore government will be at a 20 percent rate rather than a 10 percent rate. Second, assume that there is a 40 percent chance that the Singapore government will provide Spartan a payment (salvage value) of S$7 million rather than S$12 million. These two possibilities represent a form of country risk.

Assume that these two possible situations are unrelated. To determine how the *NPV* is affected by each of these scenarios, a capital budgeting analysis similar to that shown in Exhibit 14.2 in Chapter 14 can be used. If this analysis is already on a spreadsheet, the *NPV* can easily be estimated by adjusting line items no. 15 (withholding tax on remitted funds) and no. 17 (salvage value). The capital budgeting analysis measures the effect of a 20 percent withholding tax rate in Exhibit 16.5. Since items before line no. 14 are not affected, these items are not shown here. If the 20 percent withholding tax rate is imposed, the *NPV* of the four-year project is $1,252,160.

Now consider the possibility of the lower salvage value, while using the initial assumption of a 10 percent withholding tax rate. The capital budgeting analysis accounts for the lower salvage value in Exhibit 16.6. The estimated *NPV* is $800,484, based on this scenario.

Finally, consider the possibility that both the higher withholding tax and the lower salvage value occur. The capital budgeting analysis in Exhibit 16.7 accounts for both of these situations. The *NPV* is estimated to be −$177,223.

Once estimates for the *NVP* are derived for each scenario, Spartan, Inc., can attempt to determine whether the project is feasible. There are two country risk variables that are uncertain, and there are four possible *NVP* outcomes, as illustrated in Exhibit 16.8. Given the probability of each possible situation and the assumption that the withholding tax outcome is independent from the salvage value outcome, joint probabilities can be determined for each pair of outcomes by multiplying the probabilities of the two

Exhibit 16.5 Analysis of Project Based on a 20 Percent Withholding Tax: Spartan, Inc.

	Year 0	Year 1	Year 2	Year 3	Year 4
14. S$ remitted by subsidiary		S$6,000,000	S$6,000,000	S$7,600,000	S$8,400,000
15. Withholding tax imposed on remitted funds (20%)		S$1,200,000	S$1,200,000	S$1,520,000	S$1,680,000
16. S$ remitted after withholding taxes		S$4,800,000	S$4,800,000	S$6,080,000	S$6,720,000
17. Salvage value					S$12,000,000
18. Exchange rate of S$		$.50	$.50	$.50	$.50
19. Cash flows to parent		$2,400,000	$2,400,000	$3,040,000	$9,360,000
20. *PV* of parent cash flows (15% discount rate)		$2,086,956	$1,814,745	$1,998,849	$5,351,610
21. Initial investment by parent	$10,000,000				
22. Cumulative *NPV*		−$7,913,044	−$6,098,299	−$4,099,450	$1,252,160

Exhibit 16.6 Analysis of Project Based on a Reduced Salvage Value: Spartan, Inc.

	Year 0	Year 1	Year 2	Year 3	Year 4
14. S$ remitted by subsidiary		S$6,000,000	S$6,000,000	S$7,600,000	S$8,400,000
15. Withholding tax imposed on remitted funds (10%)		S$600,000	S$600,000	S$760,000	S$840,000
16. S$ remitted after withholding taxes		S$5,400,000	S$5,400,000	S$6,840,000	S$7,560,000
17. Salvage value					S$7,000,000
18. Exchange rate of S$		$.50	$.50	$.50	$.50
19. Cash flows to parent		$2,700,000	$2,700,000	$3,420,000	$7,280,000
20. PV of parent cash flows (15% discount rate)		$2,347,826	$2,041,588	$2,248,706	$4,162,364
21. Initial investment by parent	$10,000,000				
22. Cumulative *NPV*		−$7,652,174	−$5,610,586	−$3,361,880	$800,484

outcomes of concern. Since the probability of a 20 percent withholding tax is 30 percent, the probability of a 10 percent withholding tax is 70 percent. Given that the probability of a lower salvage value is 40 percent, the probability of the initial estimate for the salvage value is 60 percent. Thus, scenario no. 1 (10 percent withholding tax and S$12 million salvage value) created in Chapter 14 has a joint probability (probability that both outcomes will occur) of 70% × 60% = 42%.

In Exhibit 16.8, scenario no. 4 is the only scenario in which there is a negative *NVP*. Since this scenario has a 12 percent chance of occurring, there is a 12 percent chance that the project will adversely affect the value of the firm. Put another way, there is an

Exhibit 16.7 Analysis of Project Based on a 20 Percent Withholding Tax and a Reduced Salvage Value: Spartan, Inc.

	Year 0	Year 1	Year 2	Year 3	Year 4
14. S$ remitted by subsidiary		S$6,000,000	S$6,000,000	S$7,600,000	S$8,400,000
15. Withholding tax imposed on remitted funds (20%)		S$1,200,000	S$1,200,000	S$1,520,000	S$1,680,000
16. S$ remitted after withholding taxes		S$4,800,000	S$4,800,000	S$6,080,000	S$6,720,000
17. Salvage value					S$7,000,000
18. Exchange rate of S$		$.50	$.50	$.50	$.50
19. Cash flows to parent		$2,400,000	$2,400,000	$3,040,000	$6,860,000
20. *PV* of parent cash flows (15% discount rate)		$2,086,956	$1,814,745	$1,998,849	$3,922,227
21. Initial investment by parent	$10,000,000				
22. Cumulative *NPV*		−$7,913,044	−$6,098,299	−$4,099,450	−$177,223

Exhibit 16.8 Summary of Estimated *NPV*s across the Possible Scenarios: Spartan, Inc.

Scenario	Withholding Tax Imposed by Singapore Government	Salvage Value of Project	*NPV*	Probability
1	10%	S$12,000,000	$2,229,867	(70%)(60%) = 42%
2	20%	S$12,000,000	$1,252,160	(30%)(60%) = 18%
3	10%	S$7,000,000	$800,484	(70%)(40%) = 28%
4	20%	S$7,000,000	−$177,223	(30%)(40%) = 12%

E(*NPV*) = $2,229,867(42%)
+ $1,252,160(18%)
+ $800,484(28%)
− $177,223(12%)
= $1,364,801

88 percent chance that the project will enhance the firm's value. The expected value of the project's *NVP* can be measured as the sum of each scenario's estimated *NVP* multiplied by its respective probability across all four scenarios, as shown at the bottom of Exhibit 16.8. Most MNCs would accept the proposed project, given the likelihood that the project will have a positive *NVP* and the limited loss that would occur under even the worst case scenario.

Using an Electronic Spreadsheet to Account for Uncertainty. In the previous example, the initial assumptions for most input variables were used as if they were known with certainty. However, Spartan, Inc., could account for the uncertainty of country risk characteristics (as in our current example) while also allowing for uncertainty in the other variables as well. This process can be facilitated if the analysis is on a computer spreadsheet.

EXAMPLE

If Spartan, Inc., wishes to allow for three possible exchange rate trends, it can adjust the exchange rate projections for each of the four scenarios assessed in the current example. Each scenario will reflect a specific withholding tax outcome, a specific salvage value outcome, and a specific exchange rate trend. There will be a total of 12 scenarios, with each scenario having an estimated *NPV* and a probability of occurrence. Based on the estimated *NPV* and the probability of each scenario, Spartan, Inc., can then measure the expected value of the *NPV* and the probability that the *NPV* will be positive, which leads to a decision regarding whether the project is feasible.

How Country Risk Affects Financial Decisions

When incorporating country risk into the capital budgeting analysis, some projects are no longer feasible, and MNCs reduced their involvement in politically tense countries.

Gulf War. As a result of the crisis that culminated in the Gulf War in 1991, many MNCs attempted to reassess country risk. Terrorism became a major concern. MNCs used various methods to protect against terrorism. Cross-country travel by executives was reduced, as MNCs used teleconference calls instead. Some MNCs with subsidiaries in Saudi Arabia temporarily closed some of their operations, allowing employees from other countries to return home. Some projects that were being considered for countries that could be subject to terrorist attacks were postponed. Even projects that appeared to be feasible from a financial perspective were postponed because of the potential danger to employees.

In addition to the threat of terrorism, the crisis influenced cash flows of MNCs in many other ways. The effects varied with the characteristics of each MNC. The more obvious effects of the crisis were reduced travel and higher oil prices. The reduction in travel adversely affected airlines, hotels, restaurants, luggage manufacturers, tourist attractions, rental car agencies, and cruise lines.

Asian Crisis. As a result of the 1997–1998 Asian crisis, MNCs realized that they had underestimated the potential financial problems that could occur in the high-growth Asian countries. Country risk analysts had concentrated on the high degree of economic growth, even though the Asian countries had high debt levels and their commercial banks had massive loan problems. The loan problems were not obvious because commercial banks were typically not required to disclose much information about their loans. Some MNCs recognized the potential problems in Asia, though, and discontinued their exports to those Asian businesses that were not willing to pay in advance.

Terrorist Attack on United States. Following the September 11, 2001 attack on the United States, some MNCs reduced their exposure to various forms of country risk by discontinuing business in countries where U.S. firms might be subject to more terrorist attacks. Some MNCs also reduced employee travel to protect employees from attacks. MNCs recognize that some unpredictable events will unfold that will affect their exposure to country risk. Yet, they can at least be prepared to revise their operations in order to reduce their exposure.

Reducing Exposure to Host Government Takeovers

Although direct foreign investment offers several possible benefits, country risk can offset such benefits. The most severe country risk is a host government takeover. This type of takeover may result in major losses, especially when the MNC does not have any power to negotiate with the host government.

The following are the most common strategies used to reduce exposure to a host government takeover:

- Use a short-term horizon.
- Rely on unique supplies or technology.
- Hire local labor.
- Borrow local funds.
- Purchase insurance.
- Use project finance.

Use a Short-Term Horizon

An MNC may concentrate on recovering cash flow quickly so that in the event of expropriation, losses are minimized. An MNC would also exert only a minimum effort to replace worn-out equipment and machinery at the subsidiary. It may even phase out its overseas investment by selling off its assets to local investors or the government in stages over time.

Rely on Unique Supplies or Technology

If the subsidiary can bring in supplies from its headquarters (or a sister subsidiary) that cannot be duplicated locally, the host government will not be able to take over and operate the subsidiary without those supplies. Also the MNC can cut off the supplies if the subsidiary is treated unfairly.

If the subsidiary can hide the technology in its production process, a government takeover will be less likely. A takeover would be successful in this case only if the MNC would provide the necessary technology, and the MNC would do so only under conditions of a friendly takeover that would ensure that it received adequate compensation.

Hire Local Labor

If local employees of the subsidiary would be affected by the host government's takeover, they can pressure their government to avoid such action. However, the government could still keep those employees after taking over the subsidiary. Thus, this strategy has only limited effectiveness in avoiding or limiting a government takeover.

Borrow Local Funds

If the subsidiary borrows funds locally, local banks will be concerned about its future performance. If for any reason a government takeover would reduce the probability that the banks would receive their loan repayments promptly, they might attempt to prevent a takeover by the host government. However, the host government may guarantee repayment to the banks, so this strategy has only limited effectiveness. Nevertheless, it could still be preferable to a situation in which the MNC not only loses the subsidiary but also still owes home country creditors.

Purchase Insurance

Insurance can be purchased to cover the risk of expropriation. For example, the U.S. government provides insurance through the Overseas Private Investment Corporation (OPIC). The insurance premiums paid by a firm depend on the degree of insurance coverage and the risk associated with the firm. Typically, however, any insurance policy will cover only a portion of the company's total exposure to country risk.

Many home countries of MNCs have investment guarantee programs that insure to some extent the risks of expropriation, wars, or currency blockage. Some guarantee programs have a one-year waiting period or longer before compensation is paid on losses due to expropriation. Also, some insurance policies do not cover all forms of expropriation. Furthermore, to be eligible for such insurance, the subsidiary might be required by the country to concentrate on exporting rather than on local sales. Even if a subsidiary qualifies for insurance, there is a cost. Any insurance will typically cover only a portion of the assets and may specify a maximum duration of coverage, such as 15 or 20 years. A subsidiary must weigh the benefits of this insurance against the cost of the policy's premiums and potential losses in excess of coverage. The insurance can be helpful, but it does not by itself prevent losses due to expropriation.

In 1993, Russia established an insurance fund to protect MNCs against various forms of country risk. The Russian government took this action to encourage more direct foreign investment in Russia.

The World Bank has established an affiliate called the Multilateral Investment Guarantee Agency (MIGA) to provide political insurance for MNCs with direct foreign investment in less developed countries. MIGA offers insurance against expropriation, breach of contract, currency inconvertibility, war, and civil disturbances.

Use Project Finance

Many of the world's largest infrastructure projects are structured as "project finance" deals, which limit the exposure of the MNCs. First, project finance deals are heavily financed with credit. Thus, the MNC's exposure is limited because it invests only a limited amount of equity in the project. Second, a bank may guarantee the payments to the MNC. Third, project finance deals are unique in that they are secured by the project's future revenues from production. That is, the project is separate from the MNC that manages the project. The loans are "nonrecourse" in that the creditor cannot pursue the MNC for payment but only the assets and cash flows of the project itself. Thus, the cash flows of the project are relevant, and not the credit risk of the borrower. Because of the transparency of the process arising from the single purpose and finite plan for termination, project finance allows projects to be financed that otherwise would likely not obtain financing under conventional terms. A host government is unlikely to take over this type of project because it would have to assume the existing liabilities due to the credit arrangement.

The largest project financed by the International Financial Corp. (IFC) is the $1.34 billion Mozal aluminum smelter in Mozambique. The IFC's investment in the smelter involves the extension of $133 million of credit, which is more than Mozambique's annual

GDP. The credit risk of the government of Mozambique is very high, as is the political risk inherent in the project, especially since the country has experienced 20 years of civil war. The project is managed by Mitsubishi, BHB Billiton, and the Industrial Development Corp. of South Africa. The plant and the aluminum output serve as collateral for the loan. The project has had a major impact on the economy of Mozambique.

SUMMARY

- The factors used by MNCs to measure a country's political risk include the attitude of consumers toward purchasing locally produced goods, the host government's actions toward the MNC, the blockage of fund transfers, currency inconvertibility, war, bureaucracy, and corruption. These factors can increase the costs of international business.
- The factors used by MNCs to measure a country's financial risk are the country's interest rates, exchange rates, and inflation rates.
- The techniques typically used by MNCs to measure the country risk are the checklist approach, the Delphi technique, quantitative analysis, and inspection visits. Since no one technique covers all aspects of country risk, a combination of these techniques is commonly used. The measurement of country risk is essentially a weighted average of the political or financial factors that are perceived to comprise country risk. Each MNC has its own view as to the weights that should be assigned to each factor. Thus, the overall rating for a country may vary among MNCs.
- Once country risk is measured, it can be incorporated into a capital budgeting analysis by adjustment of the discount rate. The adjustment is somewhat arbitrary, however, and may lead to improper decision making. An alternative method of incorporating country risk analysis into capital budgeting is to explicitly account for each factor that affects country risk. For each possible form of risk, the MNC can recalculate the foreign project's net present value under the condition that the event (such as blocked funds, increased taxes, etc.) occurs.

POINT COUNTER-POINT

Does Country Risk Matter for U.S. Projects?

Point No. U.S.-based MNCs should consider country risk for foreign projects only. A U.S.-based MNC can account for U.S. economic conditions when estimating cash flows of a U.S. project or deriving the required rate of return on a project, but it does not need to consider country risk.

Counter-Point Yes. Country risk should be considered for U.S. projects. Country risk can indirectly affect the cash flows of a U.S. project. Consider a U.S. project in which supplies are produced and sent to a U.S. exporter. The demand for the supplies will be dependent on the demand for the exports over time, and the demand for exports over time may be dependent on country risk.

Who Is Correct? Use InfoTrac or some other search engine to learn more about this issue. Which argument do you support? Offer your own opinion on this issue.

SELF TEST

Answers are provided in Appendix A at the back of the text.

1. Key West Co. exports highly advanced phone system components to its subsidiary shops on islands in the Caribbean. The components are purchased by consumers to improve their phone systems. These components are not produced in other countries. Explain how political risk factors could adversely affect the profitability of Key West Co.

2. Using the information in question 1, explain how financial risk factors could adversely affect the profitability of Key West Co.

3. Given the information in question 1, do you expect that Key West Co. is more concerned about the adverse effects of political risk or of financial risk?

4. Explain what types of firms would be most concerned about an increase in country risk as a result of the terrorist attack on the United States on September 11, 2001.

5. Rockford Co. plans to expand its successful business by establishing a subsidiary in Canada. However, it is concerned that after two years the Canadian government will either impose a special tax on any income sent back to the U.S. parent or order the subsidiary to be sold at that time. The executives have estimated that either of these scenarios has a 15 percent chance of occurring. They have decided to add four percentage points to the project's required rate of return to incorporate the country risk that they are concerned about in the capital budgeting analysis. Is there a better way to more precisely incorporate the country risk of concern here?

QUESTIONS AND APPLICATIONS

1. **Forms of Country Risk.** List some forms of country risk other than a takeover of a subsidiary by the host government, and briefly elaborate on how each factor can affect the risk to the MNC. Identify common financial factors for an MNC to consider when assessing country risk. Briefly elaborate on how each factor can affect the risk to the MNC.

2. **Country Risk Assessment.** Describe the steps involved in assessing country risk once all relevant information has been gathered.

3. **Uncertainty Surrounding the Country Risk Assessment.** Describe the possible errors involved in assessing country risk. In other words, explain why country risk analysis is not always accurate.

4. **Diversifying Away Country Risk.** Why do you think that an MNC's strategy of diversifying projects internationally could achieve low exposure to country risk?

5. **Monitoring Country Risk.** Once a project is accepted, country risk analysis for the foreign country involved is no longer necessary, assuming that no other proposed projects are being evaluated for that country. Do you agree with this statement? Why or why not?

6. **Country Risk Analysis.** If the potential return is high enough, any degree of country risk can be tolerated. Do you agree with this statement? Why or why not? Do you think that a proper country risk analysis can replace a capital budgeting analysis of a project considered for a foreign country? Explain.

7. **Country Risk Analysis.** Niagra, Inc., has decided to call a well-known country risk consultant to conduct a country risk analysis in a small country where it plans to develop a large subsidiary. Niagra prefers to hire the consultant since it plans to use its employees for other important corporate functions. The consultant uses a computer program that has assigned weights of importance linked to the various factors. The consultant will evaluate the factors for this small country and insert a rating for each factor into the computer. The weights assigned to the factors are not adjusted by the computer, but the factor ratings are adjusted for each country that the consultant assesses. Do you think Niagra, Inc., should use this consultant? Why or why not?

8. **Microassessment.** Explain the microassessment of country risk.

9. **Incorporating Country Risk in Capital Budgeting.** How could a country risk assessment be used to adjust a project's required rate of return? How could such an assessment be used instead to adjust a project's estimated cash flows?

10. **Reducing Country Risk.** Explain some methods of reducing exposure to existing country risk, while maintaining the same amount of business within a particular country.

11. **Managing Country Risk.** Why do some subsidiaries maintain a low profile as to where their parents are located?

12. **Country Risk Analysis.** When NYU Corp. considered establishing a subsidiary in Zenland, it performed a country risk analysis to help make the decision. It first retrieved a country risk analysis performed about one year earlier, when it had planned to begin a major exporting business to Zenland firms. Then it updated the analysis by incorporating all current information on the key variables that were used in that analysis, such as Zenland's willingness to accept exports, its existing quotas, and existing tariff laws. Is this country risk analysis adequate? Explain.

13. **Reducing Country Risk.** MNCs such as Alcoa, DuPont, Heinz, and IBM donated products and technology to foreign countries where they had subsidiaries. How could these actions have reduced some forms of country risk?

14. **Country Risk Ratings.** Assauer, Inc., would like to assess the country risk of Glovanskia. Assauer has identified various political and financial risk factors, as shown below.

Political Risk Factor	Assigned Rating	Assigned Weight
Blockage of fund transfers	5	40%
Bureaucracy	3	60%

Financial Risk Factor	Assigned Rating	Assigned Weight
Interest rate	1	10%
Inflation	4	20%
Exchange rate	5	30%
Competition	4	20%
Growth	5	20%

Assauer has assigned an overall rating of 80 percent to political risk factors and of 20 percent to financial risk factors. Assauer is not willing to consider Glovanskia for investment if the country risk rating is below 4.0. Should Assauer consider Glovanskia for investment?

15. **Effects of September 11.** Arkansas, Inc., exports to various less developed countries, and its receivables are denominated in the foreign currencies of the importers. It considers reducing its exchange rate risk by establishing small subsidiaries to produce products. By incurring some expenses in the countries where it generates revenue, it reduces its exposure to exchange rate risk. Since September 11, 2001, when terrorists attacked the United States, it has questioned whether it should restructure its operations. Its CEO believes that its cash flows may be less exposed to exchange rate risk but more exposed to other types of risk as a result of restructuring. What is your opinion?

ADVANCED QUESTIONS

16. **How Country Risk Affects *NVP*.** Hoosier, Inc., is planning a project in the United Kingdom. It would lease space for one year in a shopping mall to sell expensive clothes manufactured in the United States. The project would end in one year, when all earnings would be remitted to Hoosier, Inc. Assume that no additional corporate taxes are incurred beyond those imposed by the British government. Since Hoosier, Inc., would rent space, it would not have any long-term assets in the United Kingdom and expects the salvage (terminal) value of the project to be about zero.

    Assume that the project's required rate of return is 18 percent. Also assume that the initial outlay required by the parent to fill the store with clothes is $200,000. The pretax earnings are expected to the £300,000 at the end of one year. The British pound is expected to be worth $1.60 at the end of one year, when the after-tax earnings are converted to dollars and remitted to the United States. The following forms of country risk must be considered:

    - The British economy may weaken (probability = 30 percent), which would cause the expected pretax earnings to be £200,000.
    - The British corporate tax rate on income earned by U.S. firms may increase from 40 percent to 50 percent (probability = 20 percent).

    These two forms of country risk are independent. Calculate the expected value of the project's net present value (*NPV*) and determine the probability that the project will have a negative *NPV*.

17. **How Country Risk Affects *NVP*.** Explain how the capital budgeting analysis in the previous question would need to be adjusted if there were three possible outcomes for the British pound along with the possible outcomes for the British economy and corporate tax rate.

18. **J.C. Penney's Country Risk Analysis.** Recently, J.C. Penney decided to consider expanding into various foreign countries; it applied a comprehensive country risk analysis before making its expansion decisions. Initial screenings of 30 foreign countries were based on political and economic factors that contribute to country risk. For the remaining 20 countries where country risk was considered to be tolerable, specific country risk characteristics of each country were considered. One of J.C. Penney's biggest targets is Mexico, where it planned to build and operate seven large stores.

    a. Identify the political factors that you think may possibly affect the performance of the J.C. Penney stores in Mexico.

    b. Explain why the J.C. Penney stores in Mexico and in other foreign markets are subject to financial risk (a subset of country risk).

    c. Assume that J.C. Penney anticipated that there was a 10 percent chance that the Mexican government would temporarily prevent conversion of peso profits into dollars because of political conditions. This event would prevent J.C. Penney from remitting earnings generated in Mexico and could adversely affect the performance of these stores (from the U.S. perspective). Offer a way in which this type of political risk could be explicitly incorporated into a capital budgeting analysis when assessing the feasibility of these projects.

    d. Assume that J.C. Penney decides to use dollars to finance the expansion of stores in Mexico. Second, assume that J.C. Penney decides to use one set of dollar cash flow estimates for any project that it assesses. Third, assume that the stores in Mexico are not subject to political risk. Do you think that the required rate of return on these projects would differ from the required rate of return on stores built in the United States at that same time? Explain.

    e. Based on your answer to the previous question, does this mean that proposals for any new stores in the United States have a higher probability of being accepted than proposals for any new stores in Mexico?

19. **How Country Risk Affects *NVP*.** Monk, Inc., is considering a capital budgeting project in Tunisia. The project requires an initial outlay of 1 million Tunisian dinar; the dinar is currently valued at $.70. In the first and second years of operation, the project will generate 700,000 dinar in each year. After two years, Monk will terminate the project, and the expected salvage value is 300,000 dinar. Monk has assigned a discount rate of 12 percent to this project. The following additional information is available:

    - There is currently no withholding tax on remittances to the United States, but there is a 20 percent chance that the Tunisian government will impose a withholding tax of 10 percent beginning next year.
    - There is a 50 percent chance that the Tunisian government will pay Monk 100,000 dinar after two years instead of the 300,000 dinar it expects.
    - The value of the dinar is expected to remain unchanged over the next two years.

    a. Determine the net present value (*NPV*) of the project in each of the four possible scenarios.

    b. Determine the joint probability of each scenario.

    c. Compute the expected *NPV* of the project and make a recommendation to Monk regarding its feasibility.

20. **How Country Risk Affects *NVP*.** In the previous question, assume that instead of adjusting the estimated cash flows of the project, Monk had decided to adjust the discount rate from 12 percent to 17 percent. Reevaluate the *NPV* of the project's expected scenario using this adjusted discount rate.

21. **The Risk and Cost of Potential Kidnapping.** In 2004 following the war in Iraq, some MNCs capitalized on opportunities to rebuild Iraq. However, in April 2004, some employees were kidnapped by local militant groups. How should an MNC account for this potential risk when it considers direct foreign investment (DFI) in any particular country? Should it avoid DFI in any country in which such an event could occur? If so, how would it screen the countries to determine which are acceptable? For whatever countries that it is willing to consider, should it adjust its feasibility analysis to account for the possibility of kidnapping? Should it attach a cost to reflect this possibility or increase the discount rate when estimating the net present value? Explain.

22. **Integrating Country Risk and Capital Budgeting.** Tovar Co. is a U.S. firm that has been asked to provide consulting services to help Grecia Company (in Greece) improve its performance. Tovar would need to spend $300,000 today on expenses related

to this project. In one year, Tovar will receive payment from Grecia, which will be tied to Grecia's performance during the year. There is uncertainty about Grecia's performance and about Grecia's tendency for corruption.

Tovar expects that it will receive 400,000 euros if Grecia achieves strong performance following the consulting job. However, there are two forms of country risk that are a concern to Tovar Co. There is an 80 percent chance that Grecia will achieve strong performance. There is a 20 percent chance that Grecia will perform poorly, and in this case, Tovar will receive a payment of only 200,000 euros.

While there is a 90 percent chance that Grecia will make its payment to Tovar, there is a 10 percent chance that Grecia will become corrupt, and in this case, Grecia will not submit any payment to Tovar.

Assume that the outcome of Grecia's performance is independent of whether Grecia becomes corrupt. The prevailing spot rate of the euro is $1.30, but Tovar expects that the euro will depreciate by 10 percent in one year, regardless of Grecia's performance or whether it is corrupt.

Tovar's cost of capital is 26 percent. Determine the expected value of the project's net present value. Determine the probability that the project's *NVP* will be negative.

INTERNET APPLICATION

23. **Political Considerations** Go to the website of the CIA *World Factbook* at **http://www.cia.gov/cia/publications/factbook/**. Select a country and review the information about the country's political conditions. Explain whether these conditions would likely discourage an MNC from engaging in direct foreign investment. Explain how the political conditions could adversely affect the cash flows of the MNC.

DISCUSSION IN THE BOARDROOM

This exercise can be found in Appendix E at the back of this textbook.

RUNNING YOUR OWN MNC

This exercise can be found on the Xtra! website at **http://maduraxtra.swlearning.com**.

BLADES, INC. CASE

Country Risk Assessment

Recently, Ben Holt, Blades' chief financial officer (CFO), has assessed whether it would be more beneficial for Blades to establish a subsidiary in Thailand to manufacture roller blades or to acquire an existing manufacturer, Skates'n'Stuff, which has offered to sell the business to Blades for 1 billion Thai baht. In Holt's view, establishing a subsidiary in Thailand yields a higher net present value (*NPV*) than acquiring the existing business. Furthermore, the Thai manufacturer has rejected an offer by Blades, Inc., for 900 million baht. A purchase price of 900 million baht for Skates'n'Stuff would make the acquisition as attractive as the establishment of a subsidiary in Thailand in terms of *NPV*. Skates'n'Stuff has indicated that it is not willing to accept less than 950 million baht.

Although Holt is confident that the *NPV* analysis was conducted correctly, he is troubled by the fact that the same discount rate, 25 percent, was used in each analysis. In his view, establishing a subsidiary in Thailand may be associated with a higher level of country risk than acquiring Skates'n'Stuff. Although either approach would result in approximately the same level of financial risk, the political risk associated with establishing a subsidiary in Thailand may be higher then the political risk of operating Skates'n'Stuff. If the establishment of a subsidiary in Thailand is associated with a higher level of country risk overall, then a higher discount rate should have been used in the analysis. Based on these considerations, Holt wants to measure the country risk associated with Thailand on both a macro and a micro level and then to reexamine the feasibility of both approaches.

First, Holt has gathered some more detailed political information for Thailand. For example, he believes that consumers in Asian countries prefer to purchase goods produced by Asians, which might prevent a subsidiary in Thailand from being successful. This cultural characteristic might not prevent an acquisition of Skates'n'Stuff from succeeding, however, especially if Blades retains the company's management and employees. Furthermore, the subsidiary would have to apply for various licenses and permits to be allowed to operate in Thailand, while Skates'n'Stuff obtained these licenses and permits long ago. However, the number of licenses required for Blades' industry is relatively low compared to other industries. Moreover, there is a high possibility that the Thai government will implement capital controls in the near future, which would prevent funds from leaving Thailand. Since Blades, Inc., has planned to remit all earnings generated by its subsidiary or by Skates'n'Stuff back to the United States, regardless of which approach to direct foreign investment it takes, capital controls may force Blades to reinvest funds in Thailand.

Ben Holt has also gathered some information regarding the financial risk of operating in Thailand. Thailand's economy has been weak lately, and recent forecasts indicate that a recovery may be slow. A weak economy may affect the demand for Blades' products, roller blades. The state of the economy is of particular concern to Blades since it produces a leisure product. In the case of an economic turndown, consumers will first eliminate these types of purchases. Holt is also worried about the high interest rates in Thailand, which may further slow economic growth if Thai citizens begin saving more. Furthermore, Holt is also aware that inflation levels in Thailand are expected to remain high. These high inflation levels can affect the purchasing power of Thai consumers, who may adjust their spending habits to purchase more essential products than roller blades. However, high levels of inflation also indicate that consumers in Thailand are still spending a relatively high proportion of their earnings.

Another financial factor that may affect Blades' operations in Thailand is the baht-dollar exchange rate. Current forecasts indicate that the Thai baht may depreciate in the future. However, recall that Blades will sell all roller blades produced in Thailand to Thai consumers. Therefore, Blades is not subject to a lower level of U.S. demand resulting from a weak baht. Blades will remit the earnings generated in Thailand back to the United States, however, and a weak baht would reduce the dollar amount of these translated earnings.

Based on these initial considerations, Holt feels that the level of political risk of operating may be higher if Blades decides to establish a subsidiary to manufacture roller blades (as opposed to acquiring Skates'n'Stuff). Conversely, the financial risk of operating in Thailand will be roughly the same whether Blades establishes a subsidiary or acquires Skates'n'Stuff. Holt is not satisfied with this initial assessment, however, and would like to have numbers at hand when he meets with the board of directors next week. Thus, he would like to conduct a quantitative analysis of the country risk associated with operating in Thailand. He has asked you, a financial analyst at Blades, to develop a country risk analysis for Thailand and to adjust the discount rate for the riskier venture (i.e., establishing a subsidiary or acquiring Skates'n'Stuff). Holt has provided the following information for your analysis:

- Since Blades produces leisure products, it is more susceptible to financial risk factors than political risk factors. You should use weights of 60 percent for financial risk factors and 40 percent for political risk factors in your analysis.
- You should use the attitude of Thai consumers, capital controls, and bureaucracy as political risk factors in your analysis. Holt perceives capital controls as the most important political risk factor. In his view, the consumer attitude and bureaucracy factors are of equal importance.
- You should use interest rates, inflation levels, and exchange rates as the financial risk factors in your analysis. In Holt's view, exchange rates and interest rates in Thailand are of equal importance, while inflation levels are slightly less important.
- Each factor used in your analysis should be assigned a rating in a range of 1 to 5, where 5 indicates the most unfavorable rating.

Ben Holt has asked you to provide answers to the following questions for him, which he will use in his meeting with the board of directors:

1. Based on the information provided in the case, do you think the political risk associated with Thailand is higher or lower for a manufacturer of leisure products such as Blades as opposed to, say, a food producer? That is, conduct a microassessment of political risk for Blades, Inc.
2. Do you think the financial risk associated with Thailand is higher or lower for a manufacturer of leisure products such as Blades as opposed to, say, a food producer? That is, conduct a microassessment of financial risk for Blades, Inc. Do you think a leisure product manufacturer such as Blades will be more affected by political or financial risk factors?
3. Without using a numerical analysis, do you think establishing a subsidiary in Thailand or acquiring Skates'n'Stuff will result in a higher assessment of political risk? Of financial risk? Substantiate your answer.

4. Using a spreadsheet, conduct a quantitative country risk analysis for Blades, Inc., using the information Ben Holt has provided for you. Use your judgment to assign weights and ratings to each political and financial risk factor and determine an overall country risk rating for Thailand. Conduct two separate analyses for (a) the establishment of a subsidiary in Thailand and (b) the acquisition of Skates'n'Stuff.

5. Which method of direct foreign investment should utilize a higher discount rate in the capital budgeting analysis? Would this strengthen or weaken the tentative decision of establishing a subsidiary in Thailand?

SMALL BUSINESS DILEMMA

Country Risk Analysis at the Sports Exports Company

The Sports Exports Company produces footballs in the United States and exports them to the United Kingdom. It also has an ongoing joint venture with a British firm that produces some sporting goods for a fee. The Sports Exports Company is considering the establishment of a small subsidiary in the United Kingdom.

1. Under the current conditions, is the Sports Exports Company subject to country risk?

2. If the firm does decide to develop a small subsidiary in the United Kingdom, will its exposure to country risk change? If so, how?

CHAPTER 17

Multinational Cost of Capital and Capital Structure

An MNC finances its operations by using a capital structure (proportion of debt versus equity financing) that can minimize its cost of capital. By minimizing the cost of capital used to finance a given level of operations, financial managers minimize the required rate of return necessary to make the foreign operations feasible and therefore maximize the value of those operations.

The specific objectives of this chapter are to:

- explain how corporate and country characteristics influence an MNC's cost of capital,
- explain why there are differences in the costs of capital among countries, and
- explain how corporate and country characteristics are considered by an MNC when it establishes its capital structure.

Background on Cost of Capital

A firm's capital consists of equity (retained earnings and funds obtained by issuing stock) and debt (borrowed funds). The firm's cost of retained earnings reflects an opportunity cost: what the existing shareholders could have earned if they had received the earnings as dividends and invested the funds themselves. The firm's cost of new common equity (issuing new stock) also reflects an opportunity cost: what the new shareholders could have earned if they had invested their funds elsewhere instead of in the stock. This cost exceeds that of retained earnings because it also includes the expenses associated with selling the new stock (flotation costs).

The firm's cost of debt is easier to measure because the firm incurs interest expenses as a result of borrowing funds. Firms attempt to use a specific capital structure, or mix of capital components, that will minimize their cost of capital. The lower a firm's cost of capital, the lower is its required rate of return on a given proposed project. Firms estimate their cost of capital before they conduct capital budgeting, because the net present value of any project is partially dependent on the cost of capital.

Comparing the Costs of Equity and Debt

A firm's weighted average cost of capital (referred to as k_c) can be measured as

$$k_c = \left(\frac{D}{D + E}\right)k_d(1 - t) + \left(\frac{E}{D + E}\right)k_e$$

where D is the amount of the firm's debt, k_d is the before-tax cost of its debt, t is the corporate tax rate, E is the firm's equity, and k_e is the cost of financing with equity. These ratios reflect the percentage of capital represented by debt and equity, respectively.

There is an advantage to using debt rather than equity as capital because the interest payments on debt are tax deductible. The greater the use of debt, however, the greater the interest expense and the higher the probability that the firm will be unable to meet its expenses. Consequently, the rate of return required by potential new shareholders or creditors will increase to reflect the higher probability of bankruptcy.

The tradeoff between debt's advantage (tax deductibility of interest payments) and its disadvantage (increased probability of bankruptcy) is illustrated in Exhibit 17.1. As the exhibit shows, the firm's cost of capital initially decreases as the ratio of debt to total capital increases. However, after some point (labeled X in Exhibit 17.1), the cost of capital rises as the ratio of debt to total capital increases. This suggests that the firm should increase its use of debt financing until the point at which the bankruptcy probability becomes large enough to offset the tax advantage of using debt. To go beyond that point would increase the firm's overall cost of capital.

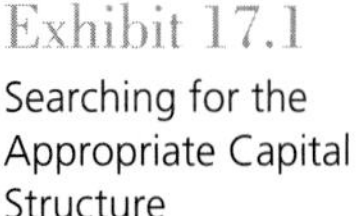

Exhibit 17.1
Searching for the Appropriate Capital Structure

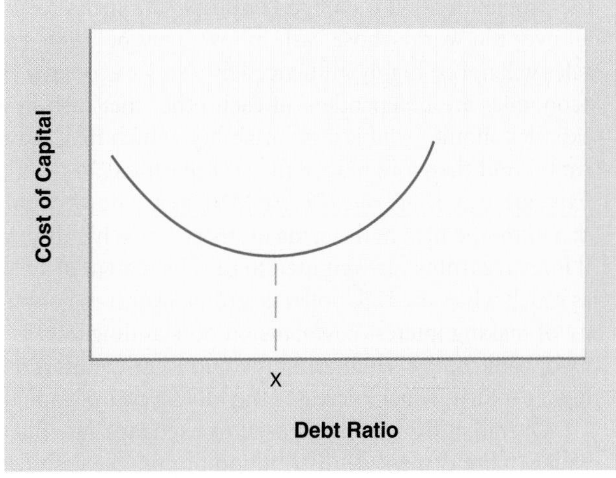

Cost of Capital for MNCs

The cost of capital for MNCs may differ from that for domestic firms because of the following characteristics that differentiate MNCs from domestic firms:

- *Size of firm*. An MNC that often borrows substantial amounts may receive preferential treatment from creditors, thereby reducing its cost of capital. Furthermore, its relatively large issues of stocks or bonds allow for reduced flotation costs (as a percentage of the amount of financing). Note, however, that these advantages are due to the MNC's size and not to its internationalized business. A domestic corporation may receive the same treatment if it is large enough. Nevertheless, a firm's growth is more restricted if it is not willing to operate internationally. Because MNCs may more easily achieve growth, they may be more able than purely domestic firms to reach the necessary size to receive preferential treatment from creditors.
- *Access to international capital markets*. MNCs are normally able to obtain funds through the international capital markets. Since the cost of funds can vary among markets, the MNC's access to the international capital markets may allow it to obtain funds at a lower cost than that paid by domestic firms. In addition, subsidiaries may be able to obtain funds locally at a lower cost than that available to the parent if the prevailing interest rates in the host country are relatively low.

The Coca-Cola Co.'s recent annual report stated: "Our global presence and strong capital position afford us easy access to key financial markets around the world, enabling us to raise funds with a low effective cost. This posture, coupled with the aggressive management of our mix of short-term and long-term debt, results in a lower overall cost of borrowing."

The use of foreign funds will not necessarily increase the MNC's exposure to exchange rate risk since the revenues generated by the subsidiary will most likely be denominated in the same currency. In this case, the subsidiary is not relying on the parent for financing, although some centralized managerial support from the parent will most likely still exist.

- *International diversification*. As explained earlier, a firm's cost of capital is affected by the probability that it will go bankrupt. If a firm's cash inflows come from sources all over the world, those cash inflows may be more stable because the firm's total sales will not be highly influenced by a single economy. To the extent that individual economies are independent of each other, net cash flows from a portfolio of subsidiaries should exhibit less variability, which may reduce the probability of bankruptcy and therefore reduce the cost of capital.
- *Exposure to exchange rate risk*. An MNC's cash flows could be more volatile than those of a domestic firm in the same industry if it is highly exposed to exchange rate risk. If foreign earnings are remitted to the U.S. parent of an MNC, they will not be worth as much when the U.S. dollar is strong against major currencies. Thus, the capability of making interest payments on outstanding debt is reduced, and the probability of bankruptcy is higher. This could force creditors and shareholders to require a higher return, which increases the MNC's cost of capital.

  Overall, a firm more exposed to exchange rate fluctuations will usually have a wider (more dispersed) distribution of possible cash flows in future periods. Since the cost of capital should reflect that possibility, and since the possibility of bankruptcy will be higher if the cash flow expectations are more uncertain, exposure to exchange rate fluctuations could lead to a higher cost of capital.

- *Exposure to country risk.* An MNC that establishes foreign subsidiaries is subject to the possibility that a host country government may seize a subsidiary's assets. The probability of such an occurrence is influenced by many factors, including the attitude of the host country government and the industry of concern. If assets are seized and fair compensation is not provided, the probability of the MNC's going bankrupt increases. The higher the percentage of an MNC's assets invested in foreign countries and the higher the overall country risk of operating in these countries, the higher will be the MNC's probability of bankruptcy (and therefore its cost of capital), other things being equal.

  Other forms of country risk, such as changes in a host government's tax laws, could also affect an MNC's subsidiary's cash flows. These risks are not necessarily incorporated into the cash flow projections because there is no reason to believe that they will arise. Nevertheless, there is a possibility that these events will occur, so the capital budgeting process should incorporate such risk.

ExxonMobil has much experience in assessing the feasibility of potential projects in foreign countries. If it detects a radical change in government or tax policy, it adds a premium to the required return of related projects. The adjustment also reflects a possible increase in its cost of capital.

The five factors that distinguish the cost of capital for an MNC and the cost for a domestic firm in a particular industry are summarized in Exhibit 17.2. In general, the first

Exhibit 17.2

Summary of Factors That Cause the Cost of Capital of MNCs to Differ from That of Domestic Firms

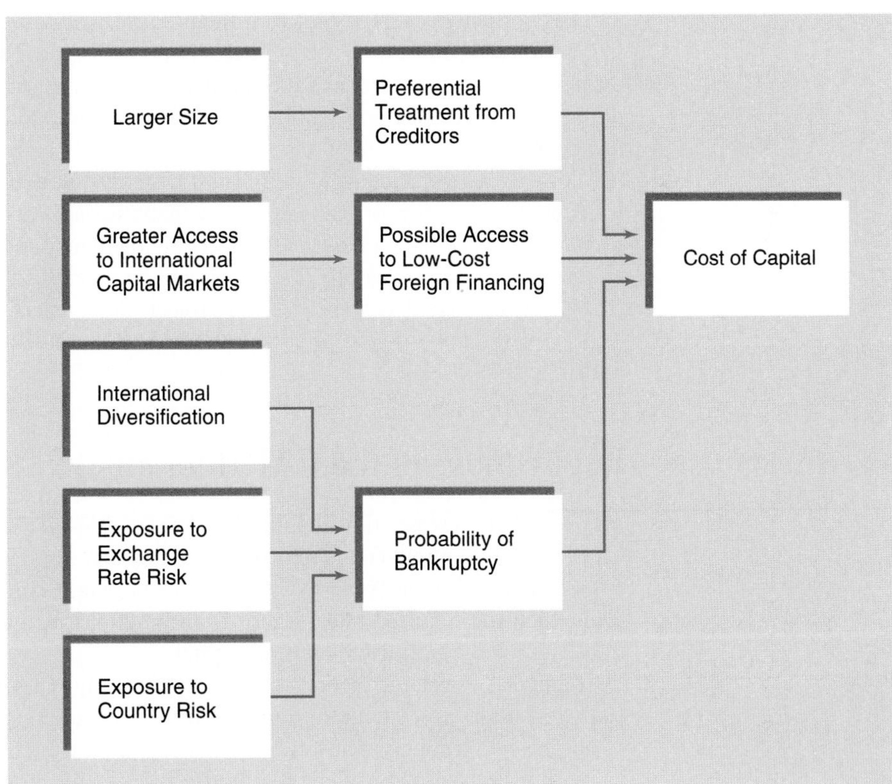

http://

The Price Waterhouse Coopers website at http://www.pwcglobal.com provides access to country-specific information such as general business rules and regulations, tax environments, and other useful statistics and surveys.

three factors listed (size, access to international capital markets, and international diversification) have a favorable effect on an MNC's cost of capital, while exchange rate risk and country risk have an unfavorable effect. It is impossible to generalize as to whether MNCs have an overall cost-of-capital advantage over domestic firms. Each MNC should be assessed separately to determine whether the net effects of its international operations on the cost of capital are favorable.

Cost-of-Equity Comparison Using the CAPM

To assess how required rates of return of MNCs differ from those of purely domestic firms, the capital asset pricing model (CAPM) can be applied. It defines the required return (k_e) on a stock as

$$k_e = R_f + B(R_m - R_f)$$

where

$$R_f = \text{risk-free rate of return}$$
$$R_m = \text{market return}$$
$$B = \text{beta of stock}$$

The CAPM suggests that the required return on a firm's stock is a positive function of (1) the risk-free rate of interest, (2) the market rate of return, and (3) the stock's beta. The beta represents the sensitivity of the stock's returns to market returns (a stock index is normally used as a proxy for the market). Advocates of the CAPM may suggest that a project's beta can be used to determine the required rate of return for that project. A project's beta represents the sensitivity of the project's cash flow to market conditions. A project whose cash flow is insulated from market conditions will exhibit a low beta.

For a well-diversified firm with cash flows generated by several projects, each project contains two types of risk: (1) unsystematic variability in cash flows unique to the firm and (2) systematic risk. Capital asset pricing theory suggests that the unsystematic risk of projects can be ignored because it will be diversified away. However, systematic risk is not diversified away because all projects are similarly affected. The lower a project's beta, the lower is the project's systematic risk and the lower its required rate of return.

Implications of the CAPM for an MNC's Risk

An MNC that increases the amount of its foreign sales may be able to reduce its stock's beta and therefore reduce the return required by investors. In this way, it will reduce its cost of capital. If projects of MNCs exhibit lower betas than projects of purely domestic firms, then the required rates of return on the MNCs' projects should be lower. This translates into a lower overall cost of capital.

Capital asset pricing theory would most likely suggest that the cost of capital is generally lower for MNCs than for domestic firms for the reasons just presented. It should be emphasized, though, that some MNCs consider unsystematic project risk to be relevant. And if it is also considered within the assessment of a project's risk, the required rate of return will not necessarily be lower for MNCs' projects than for projects of domestic firms. In fact, many MNCs would perceive a large project in a less developed country with very volatile economic conditions and a high degree of country risk as being very risky, even if the project's expected cash flows are uncorrelated with the U.S. market. This indicates that MNCs may consider unsystematic risk to be an important factor when determining a foreign project's required rate of return.

When assuming that financial markets are segmented, it is acceptable to use the U.S. market when measuring a U.S.-based MNC's project beta. If U.S. investors invest mostly in the United States, their investments are systematically affected by the U.S. market. MNCs that adopt projects with low betas may be able to reduce their own betas (the sensitivity of their stock returns to market returns). U.S. investors consider such firms desirable because they offer more diversification benefits due to their low betas.

Since markets are becoming more integrated over time, one could argue that a world market is more appropriate than a U.S. market for determining the betas of U.S.-based MNCs. That is, if investors purchase stocks across many countries, their stocks will be substantially affected by world market conditions, not just U.S. market conditions. Consequently, to achieve more diversification benefits, they will prefer to invest in firms that have low sensitivity to world market conditions. MNCs that adopt projects that are somewhat isolated from world market conditions may be able to reduce their overall sensitivity to these conditions and therefore could be viewed as desirable investments by investors.

Though markets are becoming more integrated, U.S. investors still tend to focus on U.S. stocks and to capitalize on lower transaction and information costs. Thus, their investments are systematically affected by U.S. market conditions; this causes them to be most concerned about the sensitivity of investments to the U.S. market.

In summary, we cannot say with certainty whether an MNC will have a lower cost of capital than a purely domestic firm in the same industry. However, we can use this discussion to understand how an MNC may attempt to take full advantage of the favorable aspects that reduce its cost of capital, while minimizing exposure to the unfavorable aspects that increase its cost of capital.

Costs of Capital across Countries

An understanding of why the cost of capital can vary among countries is relevant for three reasons. First, it can explain why MNCs based in some countries may have a competitive advantage over others. Just as technology and resources differ across countries, so does the cost of capital. MNCs based in some countries will have a larger set of feasible (positive net present value) projects because their cost of capital is lower; thus, these MNCs can more easily increase their world market share. MNCs operating in countries with a high cost of capital will be forced to decline projects that might be feasible for MNCs operating in countries with a low cost of capital.

Second, MNCs may be able to adjust their international operations and sources of funds to capitalize on differences in the cost of capital among countries. Third, differences in the costs of each capital component (debt and equity) can help explain why MNCs based in some countries tend to use a more debt-intensive capital structure than MNCs based elsewhere. Country differences in the cost of debt are discussed next, followed by country differences in the cost of equity.

Country Differences in the Cost of Debt

The cost of debt to a firm is primarily determined by the prevailing risk-free interest rate in the currency borrowed and the risk premium required by creditors. The cost of debt for firms is higher in some countries than in others because the corresponding risk-free rate is higher at a specific point in time or because the risk premium is higher. Explanations for country differences in the risk-free rate and in the risk premium follow.

Differences in the Risk-Free Rate. The risk-free rate is determined by the interaction of the supply of and demand for funds. Any factors that influence the supply and/or demand will affect the risk-free rate. These factors include tax laws, demographics, monetary policies, and economic conditions, all of which differ among countries.

http://

Visit http://www.bloomberg.com for the latest information from financial markets around the world.

Tax laws in some countries offer more incentives to save than those in others, which can influence the supply of savings and, therefore, interest rates. A country's corporate tax laws related to depreciation and investment tax credits can also affect interest rates through their influence on the corporate demand for funds.

A country's demographics influence the supply of savings available and the amount of loanable funds demanded. Since demographics differ among countries, so will supply and demand conditions and, therefore, nominal interest rates. Countries with younger populations are likely to experience higher interest rates because younger households tend to save less and borrow more.

The monetary policy implemented by a country's central bank influences the supply of loanable funds and therefore influences interest rates. Each central bank implements its own monetary policy, and this can cause interest rates to differ among countries. One exception is the set of European countries that rely on the European Central Bank to control the supply of euros. All of these countries now have the same risk-free rate because they use the same currrency.

Since economic conditions influence interest rates, they can cause interest rates to vary across countries. The cost of debt is much higher in many less developed countries than in industrialized countries, primarily because of economic conditions. Countries such as Brazil and Russia commonly have a high risk-free interest rate, which is partially attributed to high inflation. Investors in these countries will invest in a firm's debt securities only if they are compensated beyond the degree to which prices of products are expected to increase.

Differences in the Risk Premium. The risk premium on debt must be large enough to compensate creditors for the risk that the borrower may be unable to meet its payment obligations. This risk can vary among countries because of differences in economic conditions, relationships between corporations and creditors, government intervention, and degree of financial leverage.

http://

Morgan Stanley's Global Economic Forum at http://www.morganstanley.com/GEFdata/digests/latest-digest.html provides analysis, discussions, statistics, and forecasts related to non-U.S. economies.

When a country's economic conditions tend to be stable, the risk of a recession in that country is relatively low. Thus, the probability that a firm might not meet its obligations is lower, allowing for a lower risk premium.

Corporations and creditors have closer relationships in some countries than in others. In Japan, creditors stand ready to extend credit in the event of a corporation's financial distress, which reduces the risk of illiquidity. The cost of a Japanese firm's financial problems may be shared in various ways by the firm's management, business customers, and consumers. Since the financial problems are not borne entirely by creditors, all parties involved have more incentive to see that the problems are resolved. Thus, there is less likelihood (for a given level of debt) that Japanese firms will go bankrupt, allowing for a lower risk premium on the debt of Japanese firms.

Governments in some countries are more willing to intervene and rescue failing firms. For example, in the United Kingdom many firms are partially owned by the government. It may be in the government's best interest to rescue firms that it partially owns. Even if the government is not a partial owner, it may provide direct subsidies or extend loans to failing firms. In the United States, government rescues are less likely because taxpayers prefer not to bear the cost of corporate mismanagement. Although the government has intervened occasionally in the United States to protect particular industries, the probability that a failing firm will be rescued by the government is lower there than in other countries. Therefore, the risk premium on a given level of debt may be higher for U.S. firms than for firms of other countries.

Firms in some countries have greater borrowing capacity because their creditors are willing to tolerate a higher degree of financial leverage. For example, firms in Japan and Germany have a higher degree of financial leverage than firms in the United States. If all other factors were equal, these high-leverage firms would have to pay a higher risk premium. However, all other factors are not equal. In fact, these firms are allowed to use a higher degree of financial leverage because of their unique relationships with the creditors and governments.

Comparative Costs of Debt across Countries. The before-tax cost of debt (as measured by high-rated corporate bond yields) for various countries is displayed in Exhibit 17.3.

Exhibit 17.3 Costs of Debt across Countries

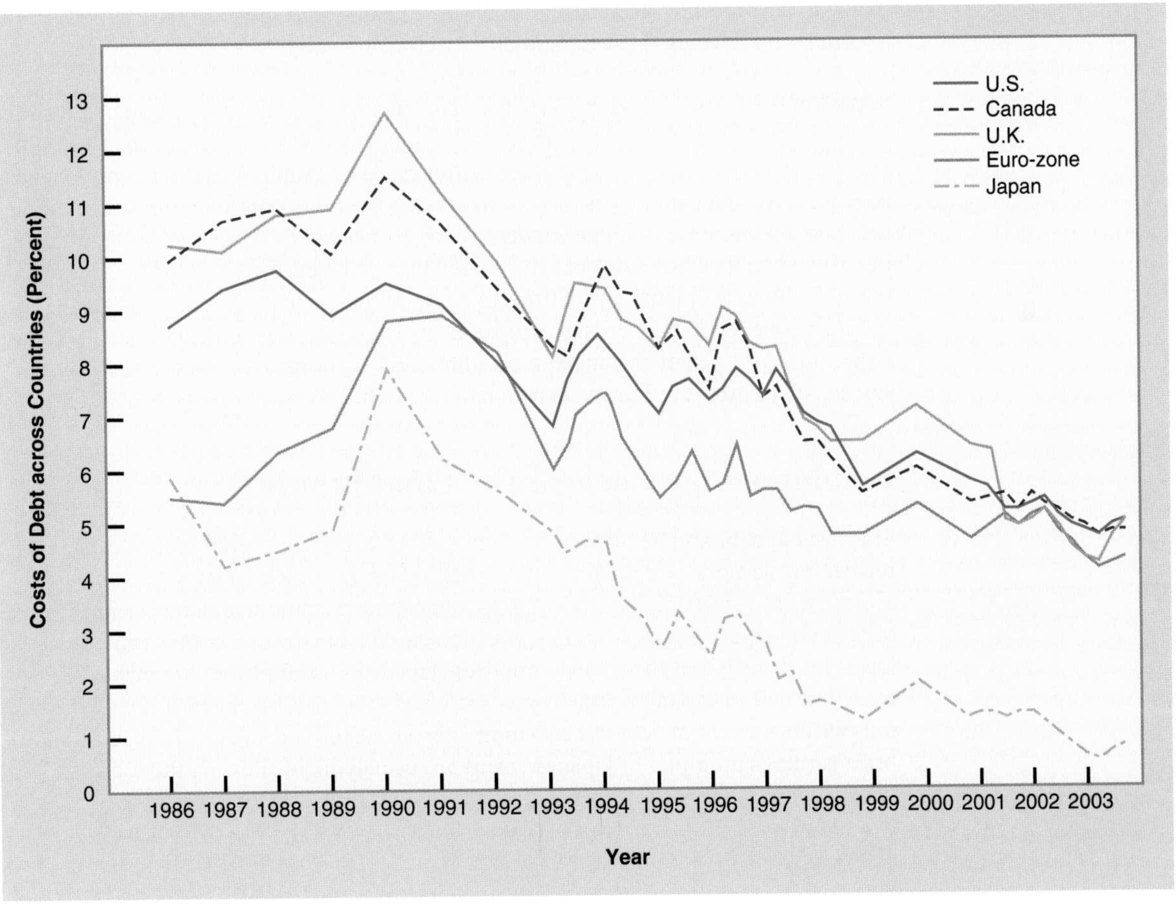

There is some positive correlation between country cost-of-debt levels over time. The nominal cost of debt for firms in many countries declined in 2001–2002 due to a global recession. However, some rates declined more than others. The disparity in the cost of debt among the countries is due primarily to the disparity in their risk-free interest rates.

Country Differences in the Cost of Equity

A firm's cost of equity represents an opportunity cost: what shareholders could earn on investments with similar risk if the equity funds were distributed to them. This return on equity can be measured as a risk-free interest rate that could have been earned by shareholders, plus a premium to reflect the risk of the firm. As risk-free interest rates vary among countries, so does the cost of equity.

The cost of equity is also based on investment opportunities in the country of concern. In a country with many investment opportunities, potential returns may be relatively high, resulting in a high opportunity cost of funds and, therefore, a high cost of equity. According to McCauley and Zimmer, a firm's cost of equity in a particular country can be estimated by first applying the price-earnings multiple to a given stream of earnings.[1]

The price-earnings multiple is related to the cost of capital because it reflects the share price of the firm in proportion to the firm's performance (as measured by earnings). A high price-earnings multiple implies that the firm receives a high price when selling new stock for a given level of earnings, which means that the cost of equity financing is low. The price-earnings multiple must be adjusted for the effects of a country's inflation, earnings growth, and other factors, however.

Impact of the Euro. The adoption of the euro has facilitated the integration of European stock markets because investors from each country are more willing to invest in other countries where the euro is used as the currency. As demand for shares by investors has increased, trading volume has increased, making the European stock markets more liquid. Investors in one euro-zone country no longer need to be concerned about exchange rate risk when they buy stock of a firm based in another euro-zone country. In addition, the euro allows the valuations of firms to be more transparent because firms throughout the euro-zone can be more easily compared since their values are all denominated in the same currency. Given the increased willingness of European investors to invest in stocks, MNCs based in Europe may obtain equity financing at a lower cost.

Combining the Costs of Debt and Equity

The costs of debt and equity can be combined to derive an overall cost of capital. The relative proportions of debt and equity used by firms in each country must be applied as weights to reasonably estimate this cost of capital. Given the differences in the costs of debt and equity across countries, it is understandable that the cost of capital may be lower for firms based in specific countries. Japan, for example, commonly has a relatively low cost of capital. It usually has a relatively low risk-free interest rate, which not only affects the cost of debt but also indirectly affects the cost of equity. In addition, the price-earnings multiples of Japanese firms are usually high, allowing these firms to ob-

[1] Robert N. McCauley and Steven A. Zimmer, "Explaining International Differences in the Cost of Capital," *FRBNY Quarterly Review* (Summer 1989): 7–28.

tain equity funding at a relatively low cost. MNCs can attempt to access capital from countries where capital costs are low, but when the capital is used to support operations in other countries, the cost of using that capital is exposed to exchange rate risk. Thus, the cost of capital may ultimately turn out to be higher than expected.

Estimating the Cost of Debt and Equity

When financing new projects, MNCs estimate their cost of debt and equity from various sources. They consider these estimates when they decide on the capital structure to use for financing the projects.

The after-tax cost of debt can be estimated with reasonable accuracy using public information on the present costs of debt (bond yields) incurred by other firms whose risk level is similar to that of the project. The cost of equity is an opportunity cost: what investors could earn on alternative equity investments with similar risk. The MNC can attempt to measure the expected return on a set of stocks that exhibit the same risk as its project. This expected return can serve as the cost of equity. The required rate of return on the project will be the project's weighted cost of capital, based on the estimates as explained here.

EXAMPLE

Lexon Co., a successful U.S.-based MNC, is considering how to obtain funding for a project in Argentina during the next year. It considers the following information:

- U.S. risk-free rate = 6%.
- Argentine risk-free rate = 10%.
- Risk premium on dollar-denominated debt provided by U.S. creditors = 3%.
- Risk premium on Argentine peso-denominated debt provided by Argentine creditors = 5%.
- Beta of project (expected sensitivity of project returns to U.S. investors in response to the U.S. market) = 1.5.
- Expected U.S. market return = 14%.
- U.S. corporate tax rate = 30%.
- Argentine corporate tax rate = 30%.
- Creditors will likely allow no more than 50 percent of the financing to be in the form of debt, which implies that equity must provide at least half of the financing.

Lexon's Cost of Each Component of Capital
Cost of dollar-denominated debt = (6% + 3%) × (1 − .3) = 6.3%
Cost of Argentine peso-denominated debt = (10% + 5%) × (1 − .3) = 10.5%
Cost of dollar-denominated equity = 6% + 1.5(14% − 6%) = 18%

Notice that Lexon's cheapest source of funds is dollar-denominated debt. However, creditors have imposed restrictions on the total amount of debt funding that Lexon can obtain.

Lexon considers four different capital structures for this new project, as shown in Exhibit 17.4. Its weighted average cost of capital (WACC) for this project can be derived by summing the products of the weight times the cost for each component of capital. The weight assigned to each component is the proportion of total funds obtained from that component.

Exhibit 17.4 Lexon's Estimated Weighted Average Cost of Capital (WACC) for Financing a Project

Possible Capital Structure	U.S. Debt (Cost = 6.3%)	Argentine Debt (Cost = 10.5%)	Equity (Cost = 18%)	Estimated WACC
30% U.S. debt, 70% equity	30% × 6.3% = 1.89%		70% × 18% = 12.6%	14.49%
50% U.S. debt, 50% U.S. equity	50% × 6.3% = 3.15%		50% × 18% = 9%	12.15%
20% U.S. debt, 30% Argentine debt, 50% U.S. equity	20% × 6.3% = 1.26%	30% × 10.5% = 3.15%	50% × 18% = 9%	13.41%
50% Argentine debt, 50% U.S. equity		50% × 10.5% = 5.25%	50% × 18% = 9%	14.25%

The exhibit shows that lowest estimate of the WACC results from a capital structure of 50 percent U.S. debt and 50 percent equity. Although it is useful to estimate the costs of possible capital structures as shown here, the estimated WACC does not account for the exposure to exchange rate risk. Thus, Lexon will not necessarily choose the capital structure with the lowest estimated WACC. Lexon can attempt to incorporate the exchange rate effects in various ways, as explained in the following section.

Using the Cost of Capital for Assessing Foreign Projects

When an MNC's parent proposes an investment in a foreign project that has the same risk as the MNC itself, it can use its weighted average cost of capital as the required rate of return for the project. However, many foreign projects exhibit different risk levels than the risk of the MNC. There are various ways for an MNC to account for the risk differential in its capital budgeting process.

Derive Net Present Values Based on the Weighted Average Cost of Capital

EXAMPLE

Recall that Lexon estimated that its WACC will be 12.15 percent if it uses 50 percent dollar-denominated debt and 50 percent equity. It considers assessing the project in Argentina based on a required rate of return of 12.15 percent. Yet, by financing the Argentine project completely with dollars, Lexon will likely be highly exposed to exchange rate movements. It can attempt to account for how expected exchange rate movements will affect its cash flows when it conducts its capital budgeting analysis.

Furthermore, Lexon could account for the risk within its cash flow estimates. Many possible values for each input variable (such as demand, price, labor cost, etc.) can be incorporated to estimate net present values (*NPVs*) under alternative scenarios and then derive a probability distribution of the *NPVs*. When the WACC is used as the required rate of return, the probability distribution of *NPVs* can be assessed to determine the probability that the foreign project will generate a return that is at least equal to the firm's WACC. If the probability distribution contains some possible negative *NPV*s, this suggests that the project could backfire.

This method is useful in accounting for risk because it explicitly incorporates the various possible scenarios in the *NPV* estimation and therefore can measure the probability that a project may backfire. Computer software programs that perform sensitivity analysis and simulation can be used to facilitate the process.

Adjust the Weighted Average Cost of Capital for the Risk Differential

An alternative method of accounting for a foreign project's risk is to adjust the firm's weighted average cost of capital for the risk differential. For example, if the foreign project is thought to exhibit more risk than the MNC exhibits, a premium can be added to the WACC to derive the required rate of return on the project. Then, the capital budgeting process will incorporate this required rate of return as the discount rate. If the foreign project exhibits lower risk, the MNC will use a required rate of return on the project that is less than its WACC.

Lexon estimated that its WACC will be 12.15 percent if it uses the capital structure of 50 percent dollar-denominated debt and 50 percent equity. But it recognizes that its Argentine project will be exposed to exchange rate risk and that this project is exposed to more risk than its normal operations. Lexon considers adding a risk premium of 6 percentage points to the estimated WACC to derive the required rate of return. In this case, the required rate of return would be 12.15% + 6% = 18.15%.

The usefulness of this method is limited because the risk premium is arbitrarily determined and is subject to error. The risk premium is dependent on the manager who conducts the analysis. Thus, the decision to accept or reject the foreign project, which is based on the estimated *NPV* of the project, could be dependent on the manager's arbitrary decision about the risk premium to use within the required rate of return.

Derive the Net Present Value of the Equity Investment

The two methods described up to this point discount cash flows based on the total cost of the project's capital. That is, they compare the *NPV* of the project's cash flows to the initial capital outlay. They ignore debt payments because the cost of debt is captured within the required rate of return on the capital to be invested in the project. When an MNC is considering financing a portion of the foreign project within that country, these methods are less effective because they do not measure how the debt payments could affect dollar cash flows. Some of the MNC's debt payments in the foreign country may reduce its exposure to exchange rate risk, which affects the cash flows that will ultimately be received by the parent.

To explicitly account for the exchange rate effects, an MNC can assess the project by measuring the *NPV* of the equity investment in the project. All debt payments are explicitly accounted for when using this method, so the analysis fully accounts for the effects of expected exchange rate movements. Then, the present value of all cash flows received by the parent can be compared to the parent's initial equity investment in the project. The MNC can conduct this same analysis for various financing alternatives to determine the one that yields the most favorable *NPV* for the project.

To illustrate, reconsider Lexon Co., which might finance the Argentine project with partial financing from Argentina. More details are needed to illustrate this point. Assume that Lexon would need to invest 80 million Argentine pesos (AP) in the project. Since the peso is currently worth $.50, Lexon needs the equivalent of $40 million. It will use equity for 50 percent of the funds needed, or $20 million. It will use debt to obtain the remaining capital. For its debt financing, Lexon decides that it will either borrow dollars and convert the funds into pesos or borrow pesos. The project will be terminated in one year; at that time, the debt will be repaid, and any earnings generated by the project will be remitted to Lexon's parent in the United States. The project is expected to result in revenue of AP200 million, and operating expenses in Argentina will be AP10 million. Lexon expects that the Argentine peso will be valued at $.40 in one year.

This project will not generate any revenue in the United States, but Lexon does expect to incur operating expenses of $10 million in the United States. It will also incur dollar-denominated interest expenses if it finances the project with dollar-denominated debt. Any dollar-denominated expenses provide tax benefits, as the expenses will reduce U.S. taxable income from other operations. The amount of debt used in each country affects the interest payments incurred and the taxes paid in that country.

The previous two methods are not effective for analyzing this type of financing decision. To compare the two financing alternatives, the analysis needs to incorporate the debt payments directly into the cash flow estimates. Consequently, the focus is on comparing the present value of dollar cash flows earned on the equity investment to the initial equity outlay. If neither alternative has a positive *NPV*, the proposed project will not be undertaken. If both alternatives have positive *NPVs*, the project will be financed with the capital structure that is expected to generate a higher *NPV*.

As with the capital budgeting analysis in Chapter 14, it is necessary to assess the project from the perspective of the parent's local equity holders. A project should be considered only if it is beneficial to the parent's shareholders. The payments from Lexon to any creditors in the United States or in a foreign country should be explicitly accounted for in order to measure the cash flows that flow back to the parent's shareholders after payments have been made to creditors. This allows for a more accurate measure of the remitted cash flows that are exposed to exchange rate movements. Cash flows to the parent are discounted at the parent's cost of equity, which represents the required rate of return on the project by the parent's shareholders. Since the debt payments are explicitly accounted for, the analysis compares the present value of the project's cash flows to the initial equity investment that would be invested in the project.

The analysis of the two financing alternatives is provided in Exhibit 17.5. If Lexon uses dollar-denominated debt, a larger amount of funds will be remitted and thus will be subject to the exchange rate effect. Conversely, if Lexon uses peso-denominated debt, the amount of remitted funds is smaller. The analysis shows that the project generates an *NPV* of $1.135 million if the project is partially financed with dollar-denominated debt versus an *NPV* of $4.17 million if it is partially financed with peso-denominated debt. Since the peso is expected to depreciate significantly over the year, Lexon will be better off using the more expensive peso-denominated debt than the dollar-denominated debt. That is, the higher cost of the debt is more than offset by the reduced exposure to adverse exchange rate effects. Consequently, Lexon should finance this project with a capital structure that includes the peso-denominated debt, even though the interest rate on this debt is high.

Relationship between Project's Net Present Value and Capital Structure. The *NPV* of the foreign project is dependent on the project's capital structure for two reasons. First, the capital structure can affect the cost of capital. Second, the capital structure influences

Exhibit 17.5 Analysis of Lexon's Project Based on Two Financing Alternatives (Numbers are in millions.)

	Rely on U.S. Debt ($20 Million Borrowed) and Equity of $20 Million	Rely on Argentine Debt (40 Million Pesos Borrowed) and Equity of $20 Million
Argentine revenue	AP200	AP200
− Argentine operating expenses	−AP10	−AP10
− Argentine interest expenses (15% rate)	−AP0	−AP6
= Argentine earnings before taxes	= AP190	= AP184
− Taxes (30% tax rate)	−AP57	−AP55.2
= Argentine earnings after taxes	= AP133	= AP128.8
− Principal payments on Argentine debt	−AP0	−AP40
= Amount of pesos to be remitted	= AP133	= AP88.8
× Expected exchange rate of AP	×$.40	×$.40
= Amount of dollars received from converting pesos	= $53.2	= $35.52
− U.S. operating expenses	−$10	−$10
− U.S. interest expenses (9% rate)	−$1.8	−$0
+ U.S. tax benefits on U.S. expenses (based on 30% tax rate)	+$3.54	+$3
− Principal payments on U.S. debt	−$20	−$0
= Dollar cash flows	= $24.94	= $28.52
Present value of dollar cash flows, discounted at the cost of equity (assumed to be 18%)	$21.135	$24.17
− Initial equity outlay	$20	$20
= *NPV*	= $1.135	= $4.17

the amount of cash flows that are distributed to creditors in the local country before taxes are imposed and funds are remitted to the parent. Since the capital structure influences the tax and exchange rate effects, it affects the cash flows that are ultimately received by the parent.

Tradeoff When Financing in Developing Countries. The results here do not imply that foreign debt should always be used to finance a foreign project. The advantage of using foreign debt to offset foreign revenue (reduce exchange rate risk) must be weighed against the cost of that debt. Many developing countries commonly have high interest rates on debt, but their local currencies tend to weaken against the dollar. Thus, U.S.-based MNCs must either tolerate a high cost of local debt financing or borrow in dollars but be exposed to significant exchange rate risk. The tradeoff can best be assessed by estimating the *NPV* of the MNC's equity investment under each financing alternative, as illustrated in the previous example.

Accounting for Multiple Periods. The preceding example focused on just one period to illustrate how the analysis is conducted. The analysis can easily be adapted to assess multiple periods, however. The same analysis shown for a single year in Exhibit 17.5 could be applied to multiple years. For each year, the revenue and expenses would be recorded, with the debt payments explicitly accounted for. The tax and exchange rate effects would be measured to derive the amount of cash flows received in each year. A discount rate that reflects the required rate of return on equity would be applied to measure the present value of the cash flows to be received by the parent.

Comparing Alternative Debt Compositions. In this example, the focus was on whether the debt should be in pesos or in dollars. Other debt compositions could also have been considered, such as the following:

- 75 percent of the debt denominated in Argentine pesos, and the remaining debt denominated in dollars.
- 50 percent of the debt denominated in Argentine pesos, and the remaining debt denominated in dollars.
- 25 percent of the debt denominated in Argentine pesos, and the remaining debt denominated in dollars.

The analysis can also account for different debt maturity structures. For example, if an MNC is considering a short-term Argentine loan that would be paid off in one year, it can estimate the cash outflow payments associated with the debt repayment. If it is considering a medium-term or long-term loan denominated in pesos, the payments will be spread out more and incorporated within the cash outflows over time. The analysis can easily account for a combination of short-term loans in Argentina and long-term loans in the United States or vice versa. It can account for floating-rate loans that adjust to market interest rates by developing one or more scenarios for how market interest rates will change in the future. The key is that all interest and principal payments on the debt are accounted for, along with any other cash flows. Then the present value of the cash flows can be compared to the initial outlay to determine whether the equity investment is feasible.

Comparing Alternative Capital Structures. In the example of Lexon Co., the proportion of debt versus equity was held constant for both alternatives that were analyzed. In reality, the capital structure decision will consider not only the composition of the debt, but also the proportion of equity versus debt that should be obtained. The same type of analysis could have been used to compare different capital structures, such as the following:

- 50 percent equity and 50 percent debt.
- 60 percent equity and 40 percent debt.
- 70 percent equity and 30 percent debt.

If Lexon in the previous example used more U.S. equity, there would be two obvious effects:

1. A higher initial equity investment would be needed.
2. With the lower debt level, the cash outflows needed to make debt payments would be reduced, so the present value of cash flows would increase.

The first effect would reduce the *NPV* of the equity investment in the project, whereas the second effect would increase it. As in the previous example, an analysis would have to be conducted to determine whether using more equity would result in a higher *NPV* generated by the equity investment.

Assessing Alternative Exchange Rate Scenarios. The example used only one exchange rate scenario, which may not be realistic. A spreadsheet can easily compare the *NPV*s of the two alternatives based on other exchange rate projections. This type of analysis would show that because of the greater exposure, the *NPV* of the project will be more sensitive to exchange rate scenarios if the project is financed with dollar-denominated debt than if it is financed with peso-denominated debt. The values of other variables such as the assumed level of revenue or operating expenses could also be changed to allow for alternative scenarios.

Considering Foreign Stock Ownership. Some capital structure decisions also include foreign shareholders, but the analysis can still be conducted in the same manner. The analysis becomes complicated only if the foreign ownership changes the corporate governance in some way that affects the firm's cash flows. Many U.S-based MNCs have issued stock in foreign countries where they do business. They will consider issuing stock only in countries where there is a sufficient demand for it. When there is not sufficient foreign demand, an MNC can more easily place its stock in the U.S. market. Research has found that U.S.-based MNCs that issue stock on a global basis (in more than one country) are more capable of issuing new stock at the stock's prevailing market price than MNCs that issue stock only in their home country. However, the results can vary for a particular MNC. Those MNCs that have established global name recognition may be better able to place shares in foreign countries.

Normally, an MNC will focus its stock offerings in a few countries where it does most of its business. The stock will be listed on the local stock exchange in the countries where the shares are issued and will be denominated in the local currency. The listing is necessary to create a secondary market for the stock in the foreign country. Many investors will consider purchasing a stock only if there is a local secondary market where they can easily sell their shares.

The MNC's Capital Structure Decision

An MNC's capital structure decision involves the choice of debt versus equity financing within all of its subsidiaries. Thus, its overall capital structure is essentially a combination of all of its subsidiaries' capital structures. MNCs recognize the tradeoff between using debt and using equity for financing their operations. The advantages of using debt as opposed to equity vary with corporate characteristics specific to each MNC and specific to the countries where the MNC has established subsidiaries. Some of the more relevant corporate characteristics specific to an MNC that can affect its capital structure are identified first, followed by country characteristics.

http://

Visit http://www.worldbank.org for country profiles, analyses, and sectoral surveys.

Influence of Corporate Characteristics

Characteristics unique to each MNC can influence its capital structure. Some of the more common firm-specific characteristics that affect the MNC's capital structure are identified here.

Stability of MNC's Cash Flows. MNCs with more stable cash flows can handle more debt because there is a constant stream of cash inflows to cover periodic interest payments. Conversely, MNCs with erratic cash flows may prefer less debt because they are not assured of generating enough cash in each period to make larger interest payments on debt. MNCs that are diversified across several countries may have more stable cash flows since the conditions in any single country should not have a major impact on their cash flows. Consequently, these MNCs may be able to handle a more debt-intensive capital structure.

MNC's Credit Risk. MNCs that have lower credit risk (risk of default on loans provided by creditors) have more access to credit. Any factors that influence credit risk can affect an MNC's choice of using debt versus equity. For example, if an MNC's management is thought to be strong and competent, the MNC's credit risk may be low, allowing for easier access to debt. MNCs with assets that serve as acceptable collateral (such as buildings, trucks, and adaptable machinery) are more able to obtain loans and may prefer to emphasize debt financing. Conversely, MNCs with assets that are not marketable have less acceptable collateral and may need to use a higher proportion of equity financing.

MNC's Access to Retained Earnings. Highly profitable MNCs may be able to finance most of their investment with retained earnings and therefore use an equity-intensive capital structure. Conversely, MNCs that have small levels of retained earnings may rely on debt financing. Growth-oriented MNCs are less able to finance their expansion with retained earnings and tend to rely on debt financing. MNCs with less growth need less new financing and may rely on retained earnings (equity) rather than debt.

MNC's Guarantees on Debt. If the parent backs the debt of its subsidiary, the subsidiary's borrowing capacity might be increased. Therefore, the subsidiary might need less equity financing. At the same time, however, the parent's borrowing capacity might be reduced, as creditors will be less willing to provide funds to the parent if those funds might be needed to rescue the subsidiary.

MNC's Agency Problems. If a subsidiary in a foreign country cannot easily be monitored by investors from the parent's country, agency costs are higher. To maximize the firm's stock price, the parent may induce the subsidiary to issue stock rather than debt in the local market so that its managers there will be monitored. In this case, the foreign subsidiary is referred to as "partially owned" rather than "wholly owned" by the MNC's parent. This strategy can affect the MNC's capital structure. It may be feasible when the MNC's parent can enhance the subsidiary's image and presence in the host country or can motivate the subsidiary's managers by allowing them partial ownership.

One concern about a partially owned foreign subsidiary is a potential conflict of interest, especially when its managers are minority shareholders. These managers may make decisions that can benefit the subsidiary at the expense of the MNC overall. For example, they may use funds for projects that are feasible from their perspective but not from the parent's perspective.

Influence of Country Characteristics

In addition to characteristics unique to each MNC, the characteristics unique to each host country can influence the MNC's choice of debt versus equity financing and therefore influence the MNC's capital structure. Specific country characteristics that can influence an MNC's choice of equity versus debt financing are described here.

Stock Restrictions in Host Countries. In some countries, governments allow investors to invest only in local stocks. Even when investors are allowed to invest in other countries, they may not have complete information about stocks of companies outside their home countries. This represents an implicit barrier to cross-border investing. Furthermore, potential adverse exchange rate effects and tax effects can discourage investors from investing outside their home countries. Such impediments to worldwide investing can cause some investors to have fewer stock investment opportunities than others. Consequently, an MNC operating in countries where investors have fewer investment opportunities may be able to raise equity in those countries at a relatively low cost. This could entice the MNC to use more equity by issuing stock in these countries to finance its operations.

USING THE WEB

Stock Market Conditions If an MNC's subsidiary is considering issuing its own stock to local investors as a means of obtaining equity, it should assess the general stock market conditions of the country. Information about stock market conditions for each country is provided at http://biz.yahoo.com/ifc/. Click on any country listed. Then click on Equity Consensus.

Interest Rates in Host Countries. Because of government-imposed barriers on capital flows along with potential adverse exchange rate, tax, and country risk effects, loanable funds do not always flow to where they are needed most. Thus, the price of loanable funds (the interest rate) can vary across countries. MNCs may be able to obtain loanable funds (debt) at a relatively low cost in specific countries, while the cost of debt in other countries may be very high. Consequently, an MNC's preference for debt may depend on the costs of debt in the countries where it operates. If markets are somewhat segmented and the cost of funds in the subsidiary's country appears excessive, the parent may use its own equity to support projects implemented by the subsidiary.

Strength of Host Country Currencies. If an MNC is concerned about the potential weakness of the currencies in its subsidiaries' host countries, it may attempt to finance a large proportion of its foreign operations by borrowing those currencies instead of relying on parent funds. In this way, the subsidiaries will remit a smaller amount in earnings because they will be making interest payments on local debt. This strategy reduces the MNC's exposure to exchange rate risk.

If the parent believes that a subsidiary's local currency will appreciate against the parent's currency, it may have the subsidiary retain and reinvest more of its earnings. The parent may also provide an immediate cash infusion to finance growth in the subsidiary. As a result, there will be a transfer of internal funds from the parent to the subsidiary, possibly resulting in more external financing by the parent and less debt financing by the subsidiary.

Country Risk in Host Countries. A relatively mild form of country risk is the possibility that the host government will temporarily block funds to be remitted by the subsidiary to the parent. Subsidiaries that are prevented from remitting earnings over a period may prefer to use local debt financing. This strategy reduces the amount of funds that are blocked because the subsidiary can use some of the funds to pay interest on local debt.

If an MNC's subsidiary is exposed to risk that a host government might confiscate its assets, the subsidiary may use much debt financing in that host country. Then local creditors that have lent funds will have a genuine interest in ensuring that the subsidiary is treated fairly by the host government. In addition, if the MNC's operations in a foreign country are terminated by the host government, it will not lose as much if its operations are financed by local creditors. Under these circumstances, the local creditors will have to negotiate with the host government to obtain all or part of the funds they have lent after the host government liquidates the assets it confiscates from the MNC.

A less likely way to reduce exposure to a high degree of country risk is for the subsidiary to issue stock in the host country. Minority shareholders benefit directly from a profitable subsidiary. Therefore, they could pressure their government to refrain from imposing excessive taxes, environmental constraints, or any other provisions that would reduce the profits of the subsidiary. Having local investors own a minority interest in a subsidiary may also offer some protection against threats of adverse actions by the host government. Another advantage of a partially owned subsidiary is that it may open up additional opportunities in the host country. The subsidiary's name will become better known when its shares are acquired by minority shareholders in that country.

Tax Laws in Host Countries. Foreign subsidiaries of an MNC may be subject to a withholding tax when they remit earnings. By using local debt financing instead of relying on parent financing, they will have to make interest payments on the local debt and thus may be able to reduce the amount to be remitted periodically. Thus, they may reduce the withholding taxes by using more local debt financing. Foreign subsidiaries may also consider using local debt if the host governments impose high corporate tax rates on foreign earnings; in this way, the subsidiaries can benefit from the tax advantage of using debt where taxes are high (unless the higher taxes paid would be fully offset by tax credits received by the parent).

Revising the Capital Structure in Response to Changing Conditions

As economic and political conditions in a country change or an MNC's business changes, the costs or benefits of each component cost of capital can change as well. An MNC may revise its capital structure in response to the changing conditions.

EXAMPLE

1. A firm discontinues its business in Argentina and decides to reduce its Argentine debt. It no longer has Argentine peso revenue that it used to offset to reduce exchange rate risk.
2. The U.S. government reduces taxes on dividends, which makes stocks more attractive to investors than investing in debt securities. Thus, the cost of equity has decreased, causing some MNCs to shift their capital structure.
3. Interest rates in Europe increase, causing some U.S.-based MNCs to support their European operations with dollar-denominated debt.
4. Interest rates in Singapore decrease, causing some U.S.-based MNCs with operations in Singapore to increase their use of debt denominated in Singapore dollars.
5. Political risk in Peru increases, causing some U.S.-based MNCs to finance more of their business there with local debt so that they have some support from local institutions with political connections.

In recent years, MNCs have revised their capital structures to reduce their withholding taxes on remitted earnings by subsidiaries.

EXAMPLE

Clayton, Inc., is a U.S.-based MNC whose parent plans to raise $50 million of capital in the United States by issuing stock in the United States. The parent plans to convert the $50 million into 70 million Australian dollars (A$) and use the funds to build a subsidiary in Australia. Since the parent may need some return on this capital to pay its shareholders' dividends, it will require that its Australian subsidiary remit A$2 million per year. Assume that the Australian government will impose a withholding tax of 10 percent on the remitted earnings, which will amount to A$200,000 per year. Clayton, Inc., can revise its capital structure in several different ways to reduce or avoid this tax. Most solutions involve reducing the reliance of the subsidiary on the parent's capital.

First, Clayton's Australian subsidiary could borrow funds in Australia as its main source of capital instead of relying on the U.S. parent. Thus, it would use some of its earnings to pay its local creditors interest instead of remitting a large amount of earnings to the U.S. parent. This financing strategy minimizes the amount of funds that would be remitted and can therefore minimize the withholding taxes that would be paid to the Australian government. In addition, the subsidiary would not need as much equity investment from the parent. One limitation of this strategy is that the subsidiary may increase its debt to an excessive level.

If Clayton prefers not to increase the subsidiary's debt, the subsidiary could raise funds by issuing stock in the host country. In this case, the subsidiary would use a portion of its funds to pay dividends to local shareholders rather than remit those funds to the parent. Once again, withholding taxes are minimized because the subsidiary would not remit much money to the parent. The issuance of stock would create a minority ownership in Australia, which reduces the parent's control over the subsidiary. The parent could retain control, however, by instructing the subsidiary to issue nonvoting stock.

Both strategies minimize Clayton's withholding tax, but the first strategy reflects a more debt-intensive capital structure while the second strategy reflects a more equity-intensive capital structure. The two strategies are illustrated in Exhibit 17.6. These strategies could also have been used to reduce Clayton's exposure to exchange rate risk because they minimize the amount of Australian dollars that will be converted into U.S. dollars.

Interaction between Subsidiary and Parent Financing Decisions

The decision by a subsidiary to use internal equity financing (retaining and reinvesting its earnings) or obtain debt financing can affect its degree of reliance on parent financing and the amount of funds that it can remit to the parent. Thus, its financing decisions should be made in consultation with the parent. The potential impact of two common subsidiary financing situations on the parent's capital structure are explained next.

USING THE WEB

Capital Structure Regulations When an MNC revises its capital structure by ordering a subsidiary to remit some of the capital back to the parent, it needs to review the country's regulations. The capital repatriation regulations imposed by each country are provided at http://biz.yahoo.com/ifc/.

Exhibit 17.6
Adjusting the Multinational Capital Structure to Reduce Withholding Taxes

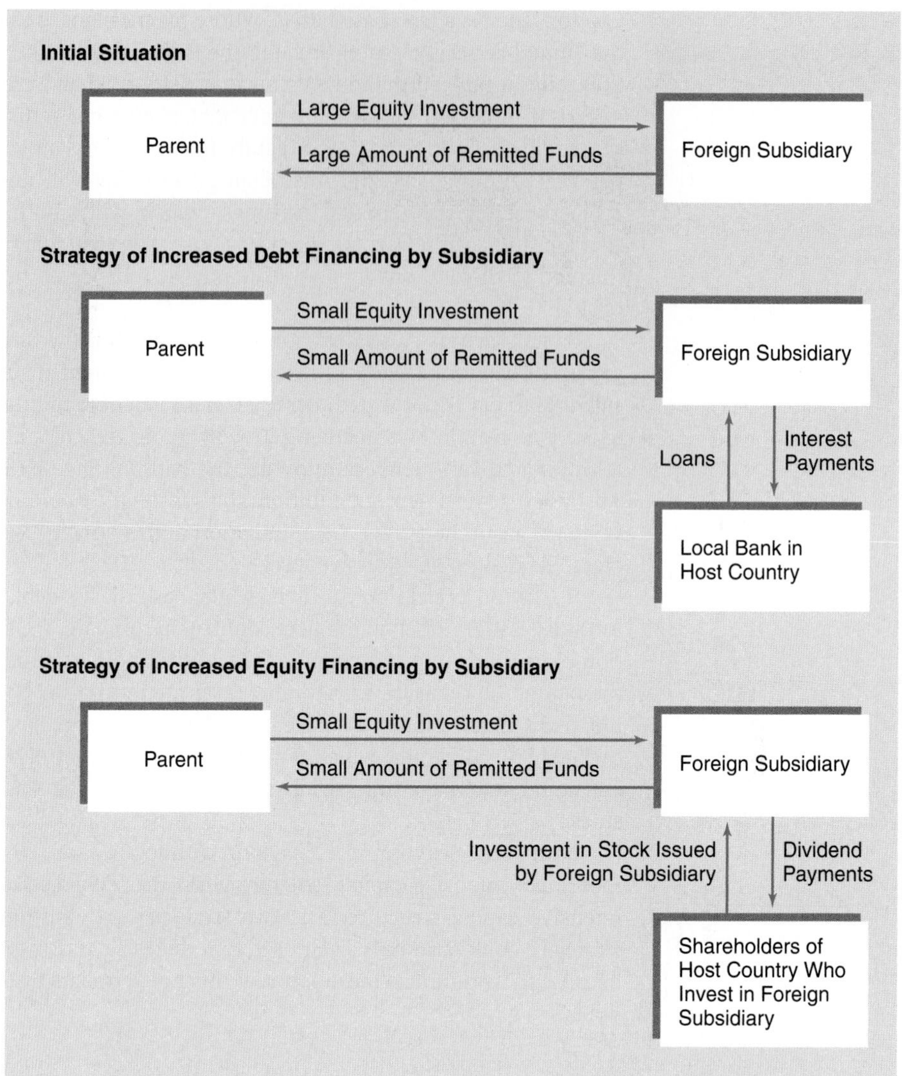

Impact of Increased Debt Financing by the Subsidiary

When global conditions increase a subsidiary's debt financing, the amount of internal equity financing needed by the subsidiary is reduced. As these extra internal funds are remitted to the parent, the parent will have a larger amount of internal funds to use for financing before resorting to external financing. Assuming that the parent's operations absorb all internal funds and require some debt financing, there are offsetting effects on the capital structures of the subsidiary and the parent. The increased use of debt financing by the subsidiary is offset by the reduced debt financing of the parent. Nevertheless, the cost of capital for the MNC overall could have changed for two reasons. First, the revised composition of debt financing (more by the subsidiary, less by the parent) could affect the interest charged on the debt. Second, it could affect the MNC's overall exposure to exchange rate risk and therefore influence the risk premium on capital.

In some situations, the subsidiary's increased use of debt financing will not be offset by the parent's reduced debt financing. For example, if there are any restrictions or excessive taxes on remitted funds, the parent may not be able to rely on the subsidiary and may need some debt financing as well. In this case, international conditions that encourage increased use of debt financing by the subsidiary will result in a more debt-intensive capital structure for the MNC. Again, for reasons already mentioned, the cost of capital to the MNC could be affected by the subsidiary's increased debt financing. In addition, the use of a higher proportion of debt financing for the MNC overall would also affect the cost of capital.

Impact of Reduced Debt Financing by the Subsidiary

When global conditions encourage the subsidiary to use less debt financing, the subsidiary will need to use more internal financing. Consequently, it will remit fewer funds to the parent, reducing the amount of internal funds available to the parent. If the parent's operations absorb all internal funds and require some debt financing, there are offsetting effects on the capital structures of the subsidiary and parent. The subsidiary's reduced use of debt financing is offset by the parent's increased use. For reasons expressed earlier, the cost of capital may change even if the MNC's overall capital structure does not.

If the parent's operations can be fully financed with internal funds, the parent will not use debt financing. Thus, the subsidiary's reduced debt financing is not offset by the parent's increased debt financing, and the MNC's overall capital structure becomes more equity-intensive.

Summary of Interaction between Subsidiary and Parent Financing Decisions

Exhibit 17.7 provides a summary of some of the more relevant characteristics of the host country that can affect a subsidiary's preference for debt or equity financing. The decision by a subsidiary to finance with local debt affects the amount of funds remitted to the parent and therefore affects the amount of internal financing available to the parent.

Exhibit 17.7 Effect of Global Conditions on Financing

Host Country Conditions	Amount of Local Debt Financing by Subsidiary	Amount of Internal Funds Available to Parent	Amount of Debt Financing Provided by Parent
Higher country risk	Higher	Higher	Lower
Higher interest rates	Lower	Lower	Higher
Lower interest rates	Higher	Higher	Lower
Expected weakness of local currency	Higher	Higher	Lower
Expected strength of local currency	Lower	Lower	Higher
Blocked funds	Higher	Higher	Lower
High withholding taxes	Higher	Higher	Lower
Higher corporate taxes	Higher	Higher	Lower

Since the subsidiary's local debt financing decisions are influenced by country-specific characteristics like those shown in Exhibit 17.7, the MNC's overall capital structure is partially influenced by the locations of the foreign subsidiaries.

Local versus Global Target Capital Structure

An MNC may deviate from its "local" target capital structure in each country where financing is obtained, yet still achieve its "global" target capital structure (based on consolidating the capital structures of all its subsidiaries). The following examples of particular foreign country conditions illustrate the motive behind deviating from a local target capital structure while still satisfying a global target capital structure.

Offsetting a Subsidiary's High Degree of Financial Leverage

First, consider that Country A does not allow MNCs with headquarters elsewhere to list their stocks on its local stock exchange. Under these conditions, an MNC's subsidiary that desires to expand its operations will likely decide to borrow funds by issuing bonds or obtaining bank loans rather than by issuing stock in this country. By being forced to use debt financing here, the MNC may deviate from its target capital structure, which could raise its overall cost of capital. The parent might offset this concentration in debt by using more equity financing for its own operations.

Alternatively, consider an MNC that desires financing in Country B, which is experiencing political turmoil. The use of local bank loans would be most appropriate since local banks may be able to prevent the subsidiary's operations from being affected by political conditions in that country. If the local banks serve as creditors to the MNC's subsidiary, it is in their interest to ensure that the subsidiary's operations are sufficiently profitable to repay its loans. Since the subsidiary may have more financial leverage than is desired for the MNC overall, the parent may use less financial leverage to finance its own operations in order to achieve its overall ("global") target capital structure.

Offsetting a Subsidiary's Low Degree of Financial Leverage

Suppose that Country C allows the MNC's subsidiary to issue stock there and list its stock on its local exchange. Also assume that the project to be implemented in that country will not generate net cash flows for five years, thereby limiting the subsidiary's ability to generate internal financing. In this case, equity financing by the subsidiary may be more appropriate. The subsidiary could issue stock, and, by paying low or zero dividends, it could avoid any major cash outflows for the next five years. The parent might offset the subsidiary's concentration in equity by instructing one of its other foreign subsidiaries in some other host country to use mostly debt financing. Alternatively, the parent could use more debt financing to support its own operations.

Limitations in Offsetting a Subsidiary's Abnormal Degree of Financial Leverage

The examples provided up to this point suggest that the parent can offset the imbalance created by a foreign subsidiary by adjusting the way it finances its own operations. However, the revision of the parent's capital structure may result in a higher cost of capital for the parent. Given that the subsidiary's financing decision could affect the parent's capital structure and therefore affect the parent's cost of capital, the subsidiary must consider the impact of its decision on the parent. The subsidiary's decision to use an unusually high or low degree of financial leverage should be made only if the benefits outweigh any costs for the MNC overall.

The strategy of ignoring a "local" target capital structure in favor of a "global" target capital structure is rational as long as it is acceptable to foreign creditors and investors. However, if foreign creditors and investors monitor each subsidiary's local capital structure, they may require a higher rate of return on funds provided to the MNC. For example, the "local" target capital structures for the subsidiaries based in Country A (from the earlier example) and in Country B are debt-intensive. Creditors in these two countries may penalize the subsidiary for its highly leveraged local capital structure, even though the MNC's global capital structure is more balanced, because they believe that the subsidiary may be unable to meet its high debt repayments. If the parent plans to back the subsidiaries, however, it could guarantee debt repayment to the creditors in the foreign countries, which might reduce their risk perception and lower the cost of the debt. Many MNC parents stand ready to financially back their subsidiaries because, if they did not, their subsidiaries would be unable to obtain adequate financing.

SUMMARY

- The cost of capital may be lower for an MNC than for a domestic firm because of characteristics peculiar to the MNC, including its size, its access to international capital markets, and its degree of international diversification. Yet, some characteristics peculiar to an MNC can increase the MNC's cost of capital, such as exposure to exchange rate risk and to country risk.
- Costs of capital vary across countries because of country differences in the components that comprise the cost of capital. Specifically, there are differences in the risk-free rate, the risk premium on debt, and the cost of equity among countries. Countries with a higher risk-free rate tend to exhibit a higher cost of capital.
- An MNC's capital structure decision is influenced by corporate characteristics such as the stability of the MNC's cash flows, its credit risk, and its access to earnings. The capital structure is also influenced by characteristics of the countries where the MNC conducts business, such as stock restrictions, interest rates, strength of local currencies, country risk, and tax laws. Some characteristics favor an equity-intensive capital structure because they discourage the use of debt. Other characteristics favor a debt-intensive structure because of the desire to protect against risks by creating foreign debt. Given that the relative costs of capital components vary among countries, the MNC's capital structure may be dependent on the specific mix of countries in which it conducts operations.

POINT COUNTER-POINT

Should the Reduced Tax Rate on Dividends Affect an MNC's Capital Structure?

Point No. The change in the tax law reduces the taxes that investors pay on dividends. It does not change the taxes paid by the MNC. Thus, it should not affect the capital structure of the MNC.

Counter-Point A dividend income tax reduction may encourage a U.S.-based MNC to offer dividends to its shareholders or to increase the dividend payment. This strategy reflects an increase in the cash outflows of the MNC. To offset these outflows, the MNC may have to adjust its capital structure. For example, the next time that it raises funds, it may prefer to use equity rather than debt so that it could free up some cash outflows (the outflows to cover dividends would be less than outflows associated with debt).

Who Is Correct? Use InfoTrac or some other search engine to learn more about this issue. Which argument do you support? Offer your own opinion on this issue.

SELF TEST

Answers are provided in Appendix A at the back of the text.

1. When Goshen, Inc., focused only on domestic business in the United States, it had a low debt level. As it expanded into other countries, it increased its degree of financial leverage (on a consolidated basis). What factors would have caused Goshen to increase its financial leverage (assuming that country risk was not a concern)?
2. Lynde Co. is a U.S.-based MNC with a large subsidiary in the Philippines financed with equity from the parent. In response to news about a possible change in the Philippine government, the subsidiary revised its capital structure by borrowing from local banks and transferring the equity investment back to the U.S. parent. Explain the likely motive behind these actions.
3. Duever Co. (a U.S. firm) noticed that its financial leverage was substantially lower than that of most successful firms in Germany and Japan in the same industry. Is Duever's capital structure less than optimal?
4. Atlanta, Inc., has a large subsidiary in Venezuela, where interest rates are very high and the currency is expected to weaken. Assume that Atlanta perceives the country risk to be high. Explain the tradeoff involved in financing the subsidiary with local debt versus an equity investment from the parent.
5. Reno, Inc., is considering a project to establish a plant for producing and selling consumer goods in an undeveloped country. Assume that the host country's economy is very dependent on oil prices, the local currency of the country is very volatile, and the country risk is very high. Also assume that the country's economic conditions are unrelated to U.S. conditions. Should the required rate of return (and therefore the risk premium) on the project be higher or lower than that of other alternative projects in the United States?

QUESTIONS AND APPLICATIONS

1. **Capital Structure of MNCs.** Present an argument in support of an MNC's favoring a debt-intensive capital structure. Present an argument in support of an MNC's favoring an equity-intensive capital structure.
2. **Optimal Financing.** Wizard, Inc., has a subsidiary in a country where the government allows only a small amount of earnings to be remitted to the United States each year. Should Wizard finance the subsidiary with debt financing by the parent, equity

financing by the parent, or financing by local banks in the foreign country?

3. **Country Differences.** Describe general differences between the capital structures of firms based in the United States and those of firms based in Japan. Offer an explanation for these differences.

4. **Local versus Global Capital Structure.** Why might a firm use a "local" capital structure at a particular subsidiary that differs substantially from its "global" capital structure?

5. **Cost of Capital.** Explain how characteristics of MNCs can affect the cost of capital.

6. **Capital Structure and Agency Issues.** Explain why managers of a wholly owned subsidiary may be more likely to satisfy the shareholders of the MNC.

7. **Target Capital Structure.** LaSalle Corp. is a U.S.-based MNC with subsidiaries in various less developed countries where stock markets are not well established. How can LaSalle still achieve its "global" target capital structure of 50 percent debt and 50 percent equity, if it plans to use only debt financing for the subsidiaries in these countries?

8. **Financing Decision.** Drexel Co. is a U.S.-based company that is establishing a project in a politically unstable country. It is considering two possible sources of financing. Either the parent could provide most of the financing, or the subsidiary could be supported by local loans from banks in that country. Which financing alternative is more appropriate to protect the subsidiary?

9. **Financing Decision.** Veer Co. is a U.S.-based MNC that has most of its operations in Japan. Since the Japanese companies with which it competes use more financial leverage, it has decided to adjust its financial leverage to be in line with theirs. With this heavy emphasis on debt, Veer should reap more tax advantages. It believes that the market's perception of its risk will remain unchanged, since its financial leverage will still be no higher than that of its Japanese competitors. Comment on this strategy.

10. **Financing Tradeoffs.** Pullman, Inc., a U.S. firm, has been highly profitable, but prefers not to pay out higher dividends because its shareholders want the funds to be reinvested. It plans for large growth in several less developed countries. Pullman would like to finance the growth with local debt in the host countries of concern to reduce its exposure to country risk. Explain the dilemma faced by Pullman, and offer possible solutions.

11. **Costs of Capital across Countries.** Explain why the cost of capital for a U.S.-based MNC with a large subsidiary in Brazil is higher than for a U.S.-based MNC in the same industry with a large subsidiary in Japan. Assume that the subsidiary operations for each MNC are financed with local debt in the host country.

12. **WACC.** An MNC has total assets of $100 million and debt of $20 million. The firm's before-tax cost of debt is 12 percent, and its cost of financing with equity is 15 percent. The MNC has a corporate tax rate of 40 percent. What is this firm's weighted average cost of capital?

13. **Cost of Equity.** Wiley, Inc., an MNC, has a beta of 1.3. The U.S. stock market is expected to generate an annual return of 11 percent. Currently, Treasury bonds yield 2 percent. Based on this information, what is Wiley's estimated cost of equity?

14. **WACC.** Blues, Inc., is an MNC located in the United States. Blues would like to estimate its weighted average cost of capital. On average, bonds issued by Blues yield 9 percent. Currently, T-bill rates are 3 percent. Furthermore, Blues' stock has a beta of 1.5, and the return on the Wilshire 5000 stock index is expected to be 10 percent. Blues' target capital structure is 30 percent debt and 70 percent equity. If Blues is in the 35 percent tax bracket, what is its weighted average cost of capital?

15. **Effects of September 11.** Rose, Inc., of Dallas, Texas, needed to infuse capital into its foreign subsidiaries to support their expansion. As of August 2001, it planned to issue stock in the United States. However, after the September 11, 2001 terrorist attack, it decided that long-term debt was a cheaper source of capital. Explain how the terrorist attack could have altered the two forms of capital.

16. **Nike's Cost of Capital.** If Nike decides to expand further in South America, why might its capital structure be affected? Why will its overall cost of capital be affected?

ADVANCED QUESTIONS

17. **Interaction between Financing and Investment.** Charleston Corp. is considering establishing a subsidiary in either Germany or the United Kingdom. The subsidiary will be mostly financed with loans from the local banks in the host country chosen. Charleston has determined that the revenue generated from the British subsidiary will be slightly more favorable than the revenue generated by the German subsidiary, even after considering tax and exchange rate effects. The initial outlay will be the same, and both countries appear to be politically stable. Charleston decides to establish the subsidiary in the United Kingdom because of the revenue advantage. Do you agree with its decision? Explain.

18. **Financing Decision.** In recent years, several U.S. firms have penetrated Mexico's market. One of the biggest challenges is the cost of capital to finance businesses in Mexico. Mexican interest rates tend to be much higher than U.S. interest rates. In some periods, the Mexican government does not attempt to lower the interest rates because higher rates may attract foreign investment in Mexican securities.

    a. How might U.S.-based MNCs expand in Mexico without incurring the high Mexican interest expenses when financing the expansion? Are any disadvantages associated with this strategy?

    b. Are there any additional alternatives for the Mexican subsidiary to finance its business itself after it has been well established? How might this strategy affect the subsidiary's capital structure?

19. **Financing Decision.** Forest Co. produces goods in the United States, Germany, and Australia and sells the goods in the areas where they are produced. Foreign earnings are periodically remitted to the U.S. parent. As the euro's interest rates have declined to a very low level, Forest has decided to finance its German operations with borrowed funds in place of the parent's equity investment. Forest will transfer the U.S. parent's equity investment in the German subsidiary over to its Australian subsidiary. These funds will be used to pay off a floating-rate loan, as Australian interest rates have been high and are rising. Explain the expected effects of these actions on the consolidated capital structure and cost of capital of Forest Co.

    Given the strategy to be used by Forest, explain how its exposure to exchange rate risk may have changed.

20. **Financing in a High-Interest-Rate Country.** Fairfield Corp., a U.S. firm, recently established a subsidiary in a less developed country that consistently experiences an annual inflation rate of 80 percent or more. The country does not have an established stock market, but loans by local banks are available with a 90 percent interest rate. Fairfield has decided to use a strategy in which the subsidiary is financed entirely with funds from the parent. It believes that in this way it can avoid the excessive interest rate in the host country. What is a key disadvantage of using this strategy that may cause Fairfield to be no better off than if it paid the 90 percent interest rate?

21. **Cost of Foreign Debt versus Equity.** Carazona, Inc., is a U.S. firm that has a large subsidiary in Indonesia. It wants to finance the subsidiary's operations in Indonesia. However, the cost of debt is currently about 30 percent there for firms like Carazona or government agencies that have a very strong credit rating. A consultant suggests to Carazona that it should use equity financing there to avoid the high interest expense. He suggests that since Carazona's cost of equity in the United States is about 14 percent, the Indonesian investors should be satisfied with a return of about 14 percent as well. Clearly explain why the consultant's advice is not logical. That is, explain why Carazona's cost of equity in Indonesia would not be less than Carazona's cost of debt in Indonesia.

22. **Integrating Cost of Capital and Capitial Budgeting.** Zylon Co. is a U.S. firm that provides technology software for the government of Singapore. It will be paid S$7,000,000 at the end of each of the next five years. The entire amount of the payment represents earnings since Zylon created the technology software years ago. Zylon is subject to a 30 percent corporate income tax rate in the United States. Its other cash inflows (such as revenue) are expected to be offset by its other cash outflows (due to operating expenses) each year, so its profits on the Singapore contract represent its expected annual net cash flows. Its financing costs are not considered within its estimate of cash flows. The Singapore dollar (S$) is presently worth $.60, and Zylon uses that spot exchange rate as a forecast of future exchange rates.

The risk-free interest rate in the United States is 6 percent while the risk-free interest rate in Singapore is 14 percent. Zylon's capital structure is 60 percent debt and 40 percent equity. Zylon is charged an interest rate of 12 percent on its debt. Zylon's cost of equity is based on the CAPM. It expects that the U.S. annual market return will be 12 percent per year. Its beta is 1.5.

Quiso Co., a U.S. firm, wants to acquire Zylon and offers Zylon a price of $10,000,000.

Zylon's owner must decide whether to sell the business at this price and hires you to make a recommendation. Estimate the NPV to Zylon as a result of selling the business, and make a recommendation about whether Zylon's owner should sell the business at the price offered.

INTERNET APPLICATION

23. **The Cost of Debt.** The Bloomberg website provides interest rate data for many countries and various maturities. Its address is **http://www.bloomberg.com**.

Go to the "Markets" section and then to "International Yield Curves." Assume that an MNC would pay 1 percent more on borrowed funds than the risk-free (government) rates shown at the Bloomberg website. Determine the cost of debt (use a 10-year maturity) for the U.S. parent that borrows dollars. Then determine the cost of funds for a foreign subsidiary in Japan that borrows funds locally. Then determine the cost of debt for a subsidiary in Germany that borrows funds locally. Offer some explanations as to why the cost of debt may vary among the three countries.

DISCUSSION IN THE BOARDROOM

This exercise can be found in Appendix E at the back of this textbook.

RUNNING YOUR OWN MNC

This exercise can be found on the Xtra! website at **http://maduraxtra.swlearning.com**.

BLADES, INC. CASE

Assessment of Cost of Capital

Recall that Blades has tentatively decided to establish a subsidiary in Thailand to manufacture roller blades. The new plant will be utilized to produce "Speedos," Blades' primary product. Once the subsidiary has been established in Thailand, it will be operated for 10 years, at which time it is expected to be sold. Ben Holt, Blades' chief financial officer (CFO), believes the growth potential in Thailand will be extremely high over the next few years. However, his optimism is not shared by most economic forecasters, who predict a slow recovery of the Thai economy, which has been very negatively affected by recent events in that country. Furthermore, forecasts for the future value of the baht indicate that the currency may continue to depreciate over the next few years.

Despite the pessimistic forecasts, Ben Holt believes Thailand is a good international target for Blades' products because of the high growth potential and lack of competitors in Thailand. At a recent meeting of the board of directors, Holt presented his capital budgeting analysis and pointed out that the establishment of a subsidiary in Thailand had a net present value (*NPV*) of over $8 million even when a 25 percent required rate of return is used to discount the cash flows resulting from the project. Blades' board of directors, while favorable to the idea of international expansion, remained skeptical. Specifically, the directors wondered where Holt obtained the 25 percent discount rate to conduct his capital budgeting analysis and whether this discount rate was high enough. Consequently, the decision to establish a subsidiary in Thailand has been delayed until the directors' meeting next month.

The directors also asked Holt to determine how operating a subsidiary in Thailand would affect Blades' required rate of return and its cost of capital. The directors would like to know how Blades' characteristics would affect its cost of capital relative to roller blade manufacturers operating solely in the United States. Furthermore, the capital asset pricing model (CAPM) was mentioned by two directors, who would like to know how Blades' systematic risk would be affected by expanding into Thailand. Another issue that was raised is how the cost of debt and equity in Thailand differ from the corresponding costs in the United States, and whether these differences would affect Blades' cost of capital. The last issue that was raised during the meeting was whether Blades' capital structure would be affected by expanding into Thailand. The directors have asked Holt to conduct a thorough analysis of these issues and report back to them at their next meeting.

Ben Holt's knowledge of cost of capital and capital structure decisions is somewhat limited, and he requires your help. You are a financial analyst for Blades, Inc. Holt has gathered some information regarding Blades' characteristics that distinguish it from roller blade manufacturers operating solely in the United States, its systematic risk, and the costs of debt and equity in Thailand, and he wants to know whether and how this information will affect Blades' cost of capital and its capital structure decision.

Regarding Blades' characteristics, Holt has gathered information regarding Blades' size, its access to the Thai capital markets, its diversification benefits from a Thai expansion, its exposure to exchange rate risk, and its exposure to country risk. Although Blades' expansion into Thailand classifies the company as an MNC, Blades is still relatively small compared to U.S. roller blade manufacturers. Also, Blades' expansion into Thailand will give it access to the capital and money markets there. However, negotiations with various commercial banks in Thailand indicate that Blades will be able to borrow at interest rates of approximately 15 percent, versus 8 percent in the United States.

Expanding into Thailand will diversify Blades' operations. As a result of this expansion, Blades would be subject to economic conditions in Thailand as well as the United States. Ben Holt sees this as a major advantage since Blades' cash flows would no longer be solely dependent on the U.S. economy. Consequently, he believes that Blades' probability of bankruptcy would be reduced. Nevertheless, if Blades establishes a subsidiary in Thailand, all of the subsidiary's earnings will be remitted back to the U.S. parent, which would create a high level of exchange rate risk. This is of particular concern because current economic forecasts for Thailand indicate that the baht will depreciate further over the next few years. Furthermore, Holt has already conducted a country risk analysis for Thailand, which resulted in an unfavorable country risk rating.

Regarding Blades' level of systematic risk, Holt has determined how Blades' beta, which measures systematic risk, would be affected by the establishment of a subsidiary in Thailand. Holt believes that Blades' beta would drop from its current level of 2.0 to 1.8 because the firm's exposure to U.S. market conditions would be reduced by the expansion into Thailand. Moreover, Holt estimates that the risk-free interest rate is 5 percent and the required return on the market is 12 percent.

Holt has also determined that the costs of both debt and equity are higher in Thailand than in the United States. Lenders such as commercial banks in Thailand require interest rates higher than U.S. rates. This is partially attributed to a higher risk premium, which reflects the larger degree of economic uncertainty in Thailand. The cost of equity is also higher in Thailand than in the United States. Thailand is not as developed as the United States in many ways, and various investment opportunities are available to Thai investors, which increases the opportunity cost. However, Holt is not sure that this higher cost of equity in Thailand would affect Blades, as all of Blades' shareholders are located in the United States.

Ben Holt has asked you to analyze this information and to determine how it may affect Blades' cost of capital and its capital structure. To help you in your analysis, Holt would like you to provide answers to the following questions:

1. If Blades expands into Thailand, do you think its cost of capital will be higher or lower than the cost of capital of roller blade manufacturers operating solely in the United States? Substantiate your answer by outlining how Blades' characteristics distinguish it from domestic roller blade manufacturers.
2. According to the CAPM, how would Blades' required rate of return be affected by an expansion into Thailand? How do you reconcile this result with your answer to question 1? Do you think Blades should use the required rate of return resulting from the CAPM to discount the cash flows of the Thai subsidiary to determine its *NPV*?
3. If Blades borrows funds in Thailand to support its Thai subsidiary, how would this affect its cost of capital? Why?
4. Given the high level of interest rates in Thailand, the high level of exchange rate risk, and the high (perceived) level of country risk, do you think Blades will be more or less likely to use debt in its capital structure as a result of its expansion into Thailand? Why?

SMALL BUSINESS DILEMMA

Multinational Capital Structure Decision at the Sports Exports Company

The Sports Exports Company has considered a variety of projects, but all of its business is still in the United Kingdom. Since most of its business comes from exporting footballs (denominated in pounds), it remains exposed to exchange rate risk. On the favorable side, the British demand for its footballs has risen consistently every month. Jim Logan, the owner of the Sports Exports Company, has retained more than \$100,000 (after the pounds were converted into dollars) in earnings since he began his business. At this point in time, his capital structure is mostly his own equity, with very little debt. Jim has periodically considered establishing a very small subsidiary in the United Kingdom to produce the footballs there (so that he would not have to export them from the United States). If he does establish this subsidiary, he has several options for the capital structure that would be used to support it: (1) use all of his equity to invest in the firm, (2) use pound-denominated long-term debt, or (3) use dollar-denominated long-term debt. The interest rate on British long-term debt is slightly higher than the interest rate on U.S. long-term debt.

1. What is an advantage of using equity to support the subsidiary? What is a disadvantage?
2. If Jim decides to use long-term debt as the primary form of capital to support this subsidiary, should he use dollar-denominated debt or pound-denominated debt?
3. How can the equity proportion of this firm's capital structure increase over time after it is established?

CHAPTER 18

Long-Term Financing

Multinational corporations (MNCs) typically use long-term sources of funds to finance long-term projects. They have access to both domestic and foreign sources of funds. It is worthwhile for MNCs to consider all possible forms of financing before making their final decisions. Financial managers must be aware of their sources of long-term funds so that they can finance international projects in a manner that maximizes the wealth of the MNC.

The specific objectives of this chapter are to:

- explain why MNCs consider long-term financing in foreign currencies,
- explain how to assess the feasibility of long-term financing in foreign currencies, and
- explain how the assessment of long-term financing in foreign currencies is adjusted for bonds with floating interest rates.

Long-Term Financing Decision

Since MNCs commonly invest in long-term projects, they rely heavily on long-term financing. The decision to use equity versus debt was covered in the previous chapter. Once that decision is made, the MNC must consider the possible sources of equity or debt and the cost and risk associated with each source.

Sources of Equity

MNCs may consider a domestic equity offering in their home country, in which the funds are denominated in their local currency. Second, they may consider a global equity offering, in which they issue stock in their home country and in one or more foreign countries. They may consider this approach to obtain partial funding in a currency that they need to finance a foreign subsidiary's operations. In addition, the global offering may provide them with some name recognition. Investors in a foreign country will be more interested in a global offering if the MNC places a sufficient number of shares in that country to provide liquidity. The stock will be listed on an exchange in the foreign country so that investors there can sell their holdings of the stock.

Third, MNCs may offer a private placement of equity to financial institutions in their home country. Fourth, they may offer a private placement of equity to financial institutions in the foreign country where they are expanding. Private placements are beneficial because they may reduce transaction costs. However, MNCs may not be able to obtain all the funds that they need with a private placement. The funding must come from a limited number of large investors who are willing to maintain the investment for a long period of time, because the equity has very limited liquidity.

Sources of Debt

When MNCs consider debt financing, they have a similar set of options. They can engage in a public placement of debt in their own country or a global debt offering. In addition, they can engage in a private placement of debt in their own country or in the foreign country where they are expanding.

Most MNCs obtain equity funding in their home country. In contrast, debt financing is frequently done in foreign countries. Thus, the focus of this chapter is on how debt financing decisions can affect the MNC's cost of capital and risk.

Cost of Debt Financing

An MNC's long-term financing decision is commonly influenced by the different interest rates that exist among currencies. The actual cost of long-term financing is based on both the quoted interest rate and the percentage change in the exchange rate of the currency borrowed over the loan life. Just as interest rates on short-term bank loans vary among currencies, so do bond yields. Exhibit 18.1 illustrates the long-term bond yields for several different countries. The wide differentials in bond yields among countries reflect a different cost of debt financing for firms in different countries.

Because bonds denominated in foreign currencies sometimes have lower yields, U.S. corporations often consider issuing bonds denominated in those currencies. For example, Hewlett-Packard, IBM, PepsiCo, and Walt Disney recently issued bonds denominated in Japanese yen to capitalize on low Japanese interest rates. Since the actual financing cost to a U.S. corporation issuing a foreign currency-denominated bond is affected by that currency's value relative to the U.S. dollar during the financing period, there is no guarantee that the bond will be less costly than a U.S. dollar-denominated bond. The borrowing firm must make coupon payments in the currency denominating the bond. If this currency appreciates against the firm's home currency, more funds will be needed to make the coupon payments. For this reason, a firm will not always denominate debt in a currency that exhibits a low interest rate.

To make the long-term financing decision, the MNC must (1) determine the amount of funds needed, (2) forecast the price at which it can issue the bond, and (3) forecast periodic exchange rate values for the currency denominating the bond. This information can be used to determine the bond's financing costs, which can be compared with

Exhibit 18.1
Annualized Bond Yields among Countries

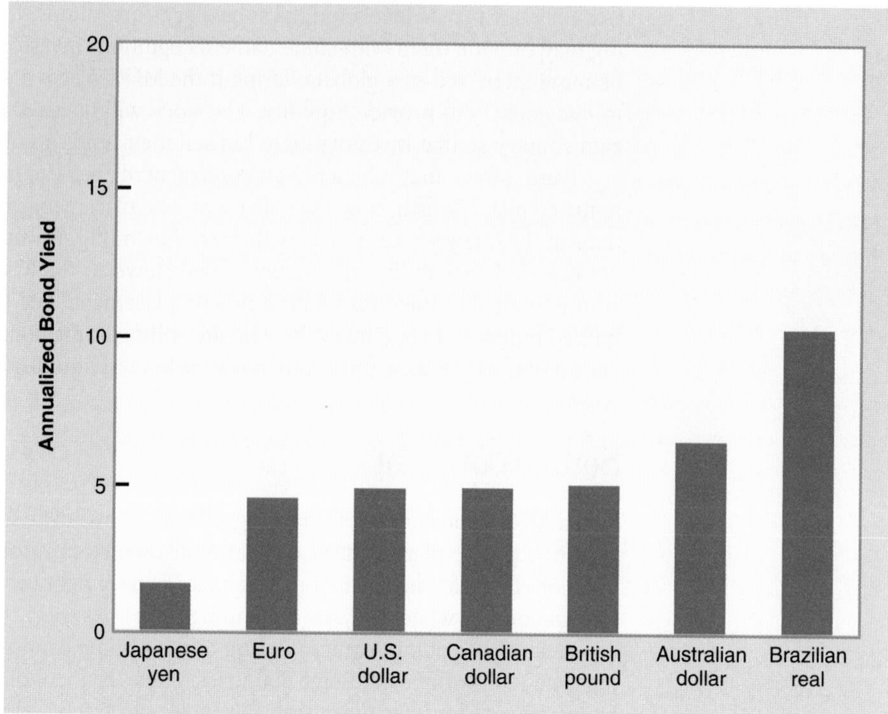

the financing costs the firm would incur using its home currency. The uncertainty of the actual financing costs to be incurred from foreign financing must be accounted for as well.

Measuring the Cost of Financing

From a U.S.-based MNC's perspective, the cost of financing in a foreign currency is influenced by the value of that currency when the MNC makes coupon payments to its bondholders and when it pays off the principal at the time the bond reaches maturity.

EXAMPLE

Piedmont Co. needs to borrow $1 million over a three-year period. This reflects a relatively small amount of funds and a short time period for bond financing but will allow for a more simplified example. Piedmont believes it can sell dollar-denominated bonds at par value if it provides a coupon rate of 14 percent. It also has the alternative of denominating the bonds in Singapore dollars (S$), in which case it would convert its borrowed Singapore dollars to U.S. dollars to use as needed. Then, it would need to obtain Singapore dollars annually to make the coupon payments. Assume that the current exchange rate of the Singapore dollar is $.50.

Piedmont needs S$2 million (computed as $1million/$.50 per Singapore dollar) to obtain the $1 million it initially needs. It believes it can sell the Sinapore dollar-denominated bonds at par value if it provides a coupon rate of 10 percent.

The costs of both financing alternatives are illustrated in Exhibit 18.2, which provides the outflow payment schedule of each financing method. The outflow payments if Piedmont finances with U.S. dollar-denominated bonds are known. In addition, if Piedmont finances with Singapore dollar-denominated bonds, the number of Singapore dollars needed at the end of each period is known. Yet, because the future exchange rate of

Exhibit 18.2
Financing with Bonds Denominated in U.S.Dollars versus Singapore Dollars

Financing Alternative	End of Year: 1	2	3	Annual Cost of Financing
(1) U.S. dollar–denominated bonds (coupon rate = 14%)	$140,000	$140,000	$1,140,000	14%
(2) Singapore dollar–denominated bonds (coupon rate = 10%)	S$200,000	S$200,000	S$2,200,000	—
Forecasted exchange rate of S$	$.50	$.50	$.50	—
Payments in dollars	$100,000	$100,000	$1,100,000	10%

the Singapore dollar is uncertain, the number of dollars needed to obtain the Singapore dollars each year is uncertain. If exchange rates do not change, the annual cost of financing with Singapore dollars is 10 percent, which is less than the 14 percent annual cost of financing with U.S. dollars.

A comparison between the costs of financing with the two different currencies can be conducted by determining the annual cost of financing with each bond, from Piedmont's perspective. The comparison is shown in the last column of Exhibit 18.2. The annual cost of financing represents the discount rate at which the future outflow payments must be discounted so that their present value equals the amount borrowed. This is similar to the so-called yield to maturity but is assessed here from the borrower's perspective rather than from the investor's perspective. When the price at which the bonds are initially issued equals the par value and there is no exchange rate adjustment, the annual cost of financing is simply equal to the coupon rate. Thus, the annual cost of financing for the U.S. dollar-denominated bonds would be 14 percent.

For Piedmont, the Singapore dollar-denominated debt appears to be less costly. However, it is unrealistic to assume that the Singapore dollar will remain stable over time. Consequently, some MNCs may choose to issue U.S. dollar-denominated debt, even though it appears more costly. The potential savings from issuing bonds denominated in a foreign currency must be weighed against the potential risk of such a method. In this example, risk reflects the possibility that the Singapore dollar will appreciate to a degree that causes Singapore dollar-denominated bonds to be more costly than U.S. dollar-denominated bonds.

Normally, exchange rates are more difficult to predict over longer time horizons. Thus, the time when the principal is to be repaid may be so far away that it is virtually impossible to have a reliable estimate of the exchange rate at that time. For this reason, some firms may be uncomfortable issuing bonds denominated in foreign currencies.

Impact of a Strong Currency on Financing Costs. If the currency that was borrowed appreciates over time, an MNC will need more funds to cover the coupon or principal payments. This type of exchange rate movement increases the MNC's financing costs.

EXAMPLE

After Piedmont decides to issue Singapore dollar-denominated bonds, assume that the Singapore dollar appreciates from $.50 to $.55 at the end of Year 1, to $.60 at the end of Year 2, and to $.65 by the end of Year 3. In this case, the payments made by Piedmont are displayed in Exhibit 18.3. By comparing the dollar outflows in this scenario with the outflows that would have occurred from a U.S. dollar-denominated bond, the risk to a

Exhibit 18.3
Financing with Singapore Dollars during a Strong-S$ Period

	End of Year:			Annual Cost of Financing
	1	2	3	
Payments in Singapore dollars	S$200,000	S$200,000	S$2,200,000	—
Forecasted exchange rate of Singapore dollar	$.55	$.60	$.65	—
Payments in dollars	$110,000	$120,000	$1,430,000	20.11%

firm from denominating a bond in a foreign currency is evident. The period of the last payment is particularly crucial for bond financing in foreign currencies because it includes not only the final coupon payment but the principal as well. Based on the exchange rate movements assumed here, financing with Singapore dollars was more expensive than financing with U.S. dollars would have been.

Impact of a Weak Currency on Financing Costs. Whereas an appreciating currency increases the periodic outflow payments of the bond issuer, a depreciating currency will reduce the issuer's outflow payments and therefore reduce its financing costs.

EXAMPLE

Reconsider the case of Piedmont Co., except assume that the Singapore dollar depreciates from $.50 to $.48 at the end of Year 1, to $.46 at the end of Year 2, and to $.40 by the end of Year 3. In this case, the payments made by Piedmont are shown in Exhibit 18.4. When one compares the dollar outflows in this scenario with the outflows that would have occurred from a U.S. dollar-denominated bond, the potential savings from foreign financing are evident.

Exhibit 18.5 compares the effects of a weak currency on financing costs to the effects of a stable or a strong currency. An MNC that denominates bonds in a foreign cur-

Exhibit 18.4
Financing with Singapore Dollars during a Weak-S$ Period

	End of Year:			Annual Cost of Financing
	1	2	3	
Payments in Singapore dollars	S$200,000	S$200,000	S$2,200,000	—
Forecasted exchange rate of Singapore dollar	$.48	$.46	$.40	—
Payments in dollars	$96,000	$92,000	$880,000	2.44%

Exhibit 18.5
Exchange Rate Effects on Outflow Payments for Singapore Dollar-Denominated Bonds

	Payment in U.S. Dollars at End of Year:			Annual Cost of Financing
Exchange Rate Scenario	1	2	3	
Scenario 1: No change in S$ value	$100,000	$100,000	$1,100,000	10.00%
Scenario 2: Strong S$	$110,000	$120,000	$1,430,000	20.11%
Scenario 3: Weak S$	$96,000	$92,000	$880,000	2.44%

rency may achieve a major reduction in costs, but could incur high costs if the currency denominating the bonds appreciates over time.

USING THE WEB

Country Debt Situation When an MNC subsidiary borrows funds locally, its financing rate will be affected by the risk-free rate at the time it borrows funds. The future risk-free rate is partially influenced by the country's debt situation. Information on the debt situation for each country is provided at http://biz.yahoo.com/ifc/.

Click on any country listed. Then click on Country Risk, and then click on Debt Outlook. An increase in the budget deficit affects the demand for loanable funds by the government and can place upward pressure on interest rates.

Actual Effects of Exchange Rate Movements on Financing Costs

To recognize how exchange rate movements have affected the cost of bonds denominated in a foreign currency, consider the following example, which uses actual exchange rate data for the British pound from 1980 to 2004.

EXAMPLE

In January 1980, Parkside, Inc., sold bonds denominated in British pounds with a par value of £10 million and a 10 percent coupon rate, thereby requiring coupon payments of £1 million at the end of each year. Assume that this U.S. firm had no existing business in the United Kingdom and therefore needed to exchange dollars for pounds to make the coupon payments each year. Exhibit 18.6 shows how the dollar payments would fluctuate each year according to the actual exchange rate at that time.

In 1980, when the pound was worth $2.3950, the coupon payment was $2,395,000. Just four years later, the pound was worth $1.1592, causing the coupon payment to be $1,159,200. Thus, the firm's dollar coupon payment in 1984 was less than half of that paid in 1980, even though the same number of pounds was needed (£1 million) each year.

In general, the dollar coupon payments increased during the late 1980s (as the pound appreciated) and then declined during the early 1990s (as the pound depreciated). The pound was less volatile in the middle and late 1990s, so its effect on the coupon payment was not so pronounced. As the pound appreciated in 2002 and 2003, the dollar coupon payments increased again. The influence of exchange rate movements on the cost of financing with bonds denominated in a foreign currency is very obvious in this exhibit. The actual effects would vary with the currency of denomination, since exchange rates do not move in perfect tandem against the dollar.

Assessing the Exchange Rate Risk of Debt Financing

Given the importance of the exchange rate when issuing bonds in a foreign currency, an MNC needs a reliable method to account for the potential impact of exchange rate fluctuations. It can use a point estimate exchange rate forecast of the currency used to denominate its bonds for each period in which an outflow payment will be provided to bondholders. However, a point estimate forecast does not account for uncertainty surrounding the forecast, which varies depending on the volatility of the currency. From a U.S. borrower's perspective, for example, a bond denominated in Canadian dollars is subject to less exchange rate risk than a bond denominated in most other foreign

Exhibit 18.6

Actual Costs of Annual Financing with Pound-Denominated Bonds from a U.S. Perspective

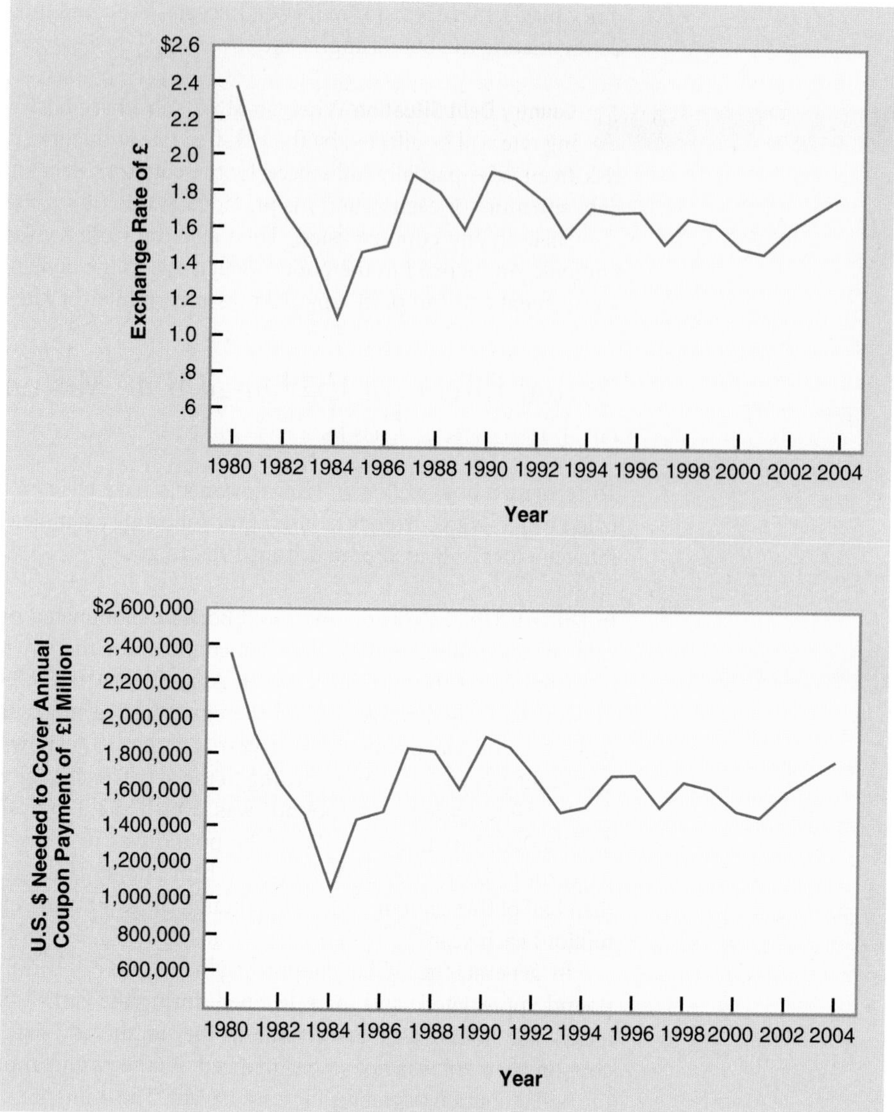

currencies (assuming the borrower has no offsetting position in these currencies). The Canadian dollar exhibits less variability against the U.S. dollar over time and therefore is less likely to deviate far from its projected future exchange rate. The uncertainty surrounding a point estimate forecast can be accounted for by using probabilities or simulation, as described next.

Use of Exchange Rate Probabilities

One approach to using point estimates of future exchange rates is to develop a probability distribution for an exchange rate for each period in which payments will be made to bondholders. The *expected value* of the exchange rate can be computed for each period by multiplying each possible exchange rate by its associated probability and totaling the products. Then, the exchange rate's expected value can be used to forecast the cash outflows necessary to pay bondholders over each period. The exchange rate's expected value may vary from one period to another. After developing probability distributions and computing the expected values, the MNC can estimate the expected cost of financing and compare that with the cost of financing with a bond denominated in the home currency.

Using this approach, a single outflow estimate is derived for each payment period, and a single estimate is derived for the annual cost of financing over the life of the bond. This approach does not indicate the range of possible results that may occur, however, so it does not measure the probability that a bond denominated in a foreign currency will be more costly than a bond denominated in the home currency.

Use of Simulation

After an MNC has developed its probability distributions of the foreign currency's exchange rate at the end of each period, as just described, it can feed those probability distributions into a computer simulation program. The program will randomly draw one possible value from the exchange rate distribution for the end of each year and determine the outflow payments based on those exchange rates. Consequently, the cost of financing is determined. The procedure described up to this point represents one iteration.

Next, the program will repeat the procedure by again randomly drawing one possible value from the exchange rate distribution at the end of each year. This will provide a new schedule of outflow payments reflecting those randomly selected exchange rates. The cost of financing for this second iteration is also determined. The simulation program continually repeats this procedure, perhaps 100 times or so (as many times as desired).

Every iteration provides a possible scenario of future exchange rates, which is then used to determine the annual cost of financing if that scenario occurs. Thus, the simulation generates a probability distribution of annual financing costs that can then be compared with the known cost of financing if the bond is denominated in U.S. dollars (the home currency). Through this comparison, the MNC can determine the probability that issuing bonds denominated in a foreign currency will be cheaper than dollar-denominated bonds.

Reducing Exchange Rate Risk

The exchange rate risk from financing with bonds in foreign currencies can be reduced by using one of the alternative strategies described next.

Offsetting Cash Inflows

Some firms may have inflow payments in particular currencies, which could offset their outflow payments related to bond financing. Thus, a firm may be able to finance with bonds denominated in a foreign currency that exhibits a lower coupon rate without becoming exposed to exchange rate risk. Nevertheless, it is unlikely that the firm would be able to perfectly match the timing and amount of the outflows in the foreign currency denominating the bond to the inflows in that currency. Therefore, some exposure to exchange rate fluctuations will exist. The exposure can be substantially reduced, though,

MANAGING FOR VALUE

General Electric's Decision to Rely on Global Financial Markets

General Electric is a well-diversified MNC that produces lighting products, automation devices, electrical equipment, and many other products. It has subsidiaries scattered throughout the world, which produce products that are sold locally. General Electric obtains funds from many different markets to finance a portion of its investment in foreign countries. It has issued bonds denominated in Australian dollars, British pounds, Japanese yen, New Zealand dollars, and Polish zloty to finance its foreign operations. Its subsidiaries in Australia use Australian dollar inflows to pay off their Australian debt. Its subsidiaries in Japan use Japanese yen inflows to pay off their yen-denominated debt. By using various debt markets, General Electric can match its cash inflows and outflows in a particular currency. The decision to obtain debt in currencies where it receives cash inflows reduces the company's exposure to exchange rate risk. If it used dollars to finance all of its foreign investment, the subsidiaries would have to convert much of the local currency they receive to dollars to repay their debt. During periods when the foreign currencies depreciate against the dollar, General Electric would need more foreign currency to pay off the dollar-denominated debt. Thus, by considering its source of cash inflows, General Electric is able to make financing decisions that reduce its exposure to exchange rate risk and maximize its value.

if the firm receives inflows in the particular currency denominating the bond. This can help to stabilize the firm's cash flow.

EXAMPLE

Many MNCs, including Honeywell and The Coca-Cola Co., issue bonds in some of the foreign currencies that they receive from operations. PepsiCo issues bonds in several foreign currencies and uses proceeds in those same currencies resulting from foreign operations to make interest and principal payments. Nike issued bonds denominated in yen at low interest rates and uses yen-denominated revenue to make the interest payments.

Offsetting Cash Flows with High-Yield Debt. U.S.-based MNCs that generate earnings in countries where yields on debt are typically high may be able to offset their exposure to exchange rate risk by issuing bonds denominated in the local currency. Issuing debt denominated in the currencies of some developing countries such as Brazil, Indonesia, Malaysia, and Thailand is an example. If a U.S.-based MNC issues bonds denominated in the local currency in one of those countries, there may be a natural offsetting effect that will reduce the MNC's exposure to exchange rate risk because it can use its cash inflows in that currency to repay the debt.

Alternatively, the MNC might obtain debt financing in dollars at a lower interest rate, but it will not be able to offset its earnings in the foreign currency. Recall that countries where bond yields are high tend to have a high risk-free interest rate and that a high risk-free interest rate usually occurs where inflation is high (the Fisher effect). Also consider that the currencies of countries with relatively high inflation tend to weaken over time (as suggested by purchasing power parity). Thus, the U.S.-based MNC could be highly exposed to exchange rate risk when using dollar-denominated debt to finance business in a country with high costs of local debt because it would have to convert cash inflows generated in a potentially depreciated currency to cover the debt repayments. Thus, U.S.-based MNCs face a dilemma when they consider obtaining long-term financing: issue debt in the local currency and reduce exposure to exchange rate risk, or issue dollar-denominated debt at a lower interest rate but with considerable exposure to exchange rate risk. Neither solution is especially desirable.

Implications of the Euro for Financing to Offset Cash Inflows. The decision of several European countries to adopt the euro as their currency has important implications for MNCs that require long-term financing and wish to offset some of their cash inflows with debt payments. MNCs that have cash inflows in many of the participating European countries can now issue bonds denominated in euros and then use their cash inflows from operations in these countries to make the debt payments.

Prior to the adoption of the euro, an MNC might have preferred to finance in the currency of each European country where it was conducting business so that it could cover its financing payments with cash inflows in the same currency. This strategy would have reduced the MNC's ability to use bonds because it might not have needed enough financing in every country to justify bond offerings in each of several currencies. Thus, the MNC might have had to use local bank financing in each country instead of bond financing, even when local bank financing was more expensive. Now, however, the MNC can issue bonds denominated in euros to cover its financing needs in all eurozone countries where it has operations, distribute the proceeds for use among these countries, and then aggregate cash inflows from these countries to cover the financing payments. In this way, the adoption of the euro has increased the use of bond financing and reduce the cost of financing for MNCs conducting business in Europe.

In addition, since countries such as Italy and Spain have adopted the euro, their interest rates are similar to those of the other participating countries. Thus, MNCs are able to finance projects in these countries and use cash inflows to cover their debt payments while achieving lower financing costs than when those countries had their own currencies.

The Eurobond market has historically been dominated by government bond offerings. Recently, however, corporations have increased their use of the Eurobond market by issuing bonds denominated in euros to offset their euro cash inflows. The difference in yields paid (and therefore cost of financing) on these bonds by the issuing firms is primarily determined by the credit risk of the issuer.

Forward Contracts

When a bond denominated in a foreign currency has a lower coupon rate than the firm's home currency, the firm may consider issuing bonds denominated in that currency and simultaneously hedging its exchange rate risk through the forward market. Because the forward market can sometimes accommodate requests of five years or longer, such an approach may be possible. The firm could arrange to purchase the foreign currency forward for each time at which payments are required. However, the forward rate for each horizon will most likely be above the spot rate. Consequently, hedging these future outflow payments may not be less costly than the outflow payments needed if a dollar-denominated bond were issued. The relationship implied here reflects the concept of interest rate parity, which was discussed in earlier chapters, except that the point of view in this chapter is long term rather than short term.

Currency Swaps

A currency swap enables firms to exchange currencies at periodic intervals. Ford Motor Co., Johnson & Johnson, General Motors, and many other MNCs use currency swaps.

EXAMPLE

Miller Co., a U.S. firm, desires to issue a bond denominated in euros because it could make payments with euro inflows to be generated from existing operations. However, Miller Co. is not well known to investors who would consider purchasing euro-denominated bonds. Meanwhile Beck Co. of Germany desires to issue dollar-denominated bonds because its inflow payments are mostly in dollars. However, it is not well known to the investors who would purchase these bonds.

If Miller is known in the dollar-denominated market while Beck is known in the euro-denominated market, the following transactions are appropriate. Miller issues dollar-denominated bonds, while Beck issues euro-denominated bonds. Miller will provide euro payments to Beck in exchange for dollar payments. This swap of currencies allows the companies to make payments to their respective bondholders without concern about exchange rate risk. This type of currency swap is illustrated in Exhibit 18.7.

The swap just described was successful in eliminating exchange rate risk for both Miller Co. and Beck Co. Miller essentially passes the euros it receives from ongoing operations through to Beck and passes the dollars it receives from Beck through to the investors in the dollar-denominated bonds. Thus, even though Miller receives euros from its ongoing operations, it is able to make dollar payments to the investors without having to be concerned about exchange rate risk. The same logic applies to Beck Co. on the other side of the transaction.

Many MNCs simultaneously swap interest payments and currencies. The Gillette Co. engaged in swap agreements that converted $500 million in fixed rate dollar-

Exhibit 18.7
Illustration of a Currency Swap

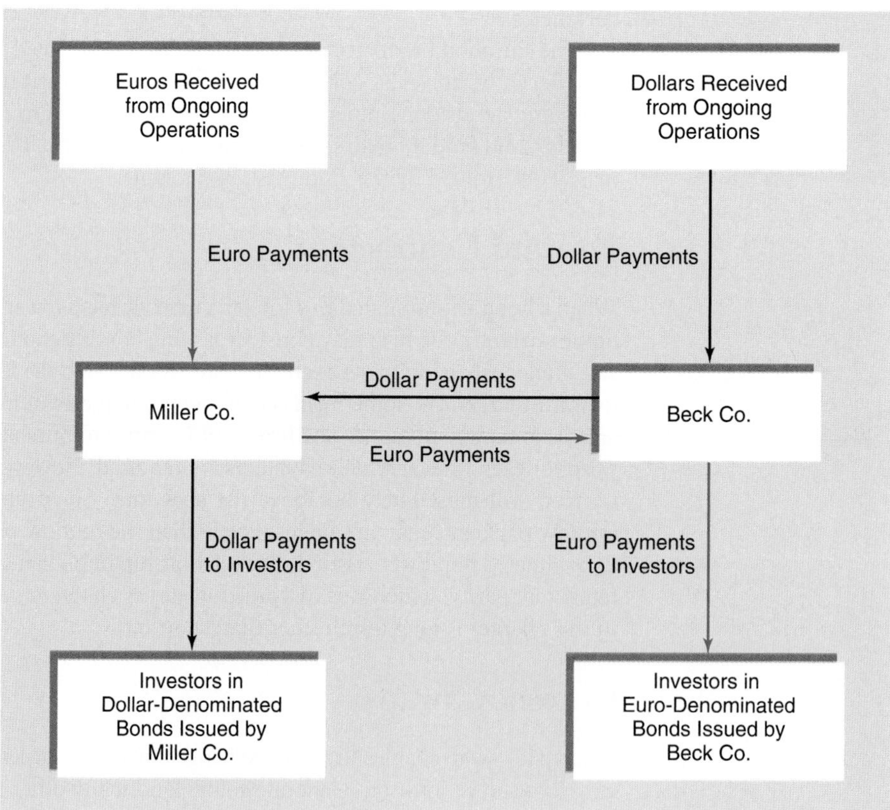

denominated debt into multiple currency variable rate debt. PepsiCo enters into interest rate swaps and currency swaps to reduce borrowing costs.

The large commercial banks that serve as financial intermediaries for currency swaps sometimes take positions. That is, they may agree to swap currencies with firms, rather than simply search for suitable swap candidates.

Parallel Loans

Firms can also obtain financing in a foreign currency through a parallel (or back-to-back) loan, which occurs when two parties provide simultaneous loans with an agreement to repay at a specified point in the future.

EXAMPLE

The parent of Ann Arbor Co. desires to expand its British subsidiary, while the parent of a British-based MNC desires to expand its American subsidiary. The British parent provides pounds to the British subsidiary of Ann Arbor Co., while the parent of Ann Arbor Co. provides dollars to the American subsidiary of the British-based MNC (as shown in Exhibit 18.8). At the time specified by the loan contract, the loans are repaid. The British subsidiary of Ann Arbor Co. uses pound-denominated revenues to repay the British company that provided the loan. At the same time, the American subsidiary of the British-based MNC uses dollar-denominated revenues to repay the U.S. company that provided the loan.

Using Parallel Loans to Hedge Exchange Rate Risk for Foreign Projects. The ability to reduce or eliminate exchange rate risk can also affect the attractiveness of projects in foreign countries. Sometimes, parallel loans can function as a useful alternative to forward or futures contracts as a way to finance foreign projects. The use of parallel loans is particularly attractive if the MNC is conducting a project in a foreign country, will receive the cash flows in the foreign currency, and is worried that the foreign currency will depreciate substantially. If the foreign currency is not heavily traded, other hedging alternatives, such as forward or futures contracts, may not be available, and the project may have a negative net present value (*NPV*) if the cash flows remain unhedged.

Exhibit 18.8
Illustration of a Parallel Loan

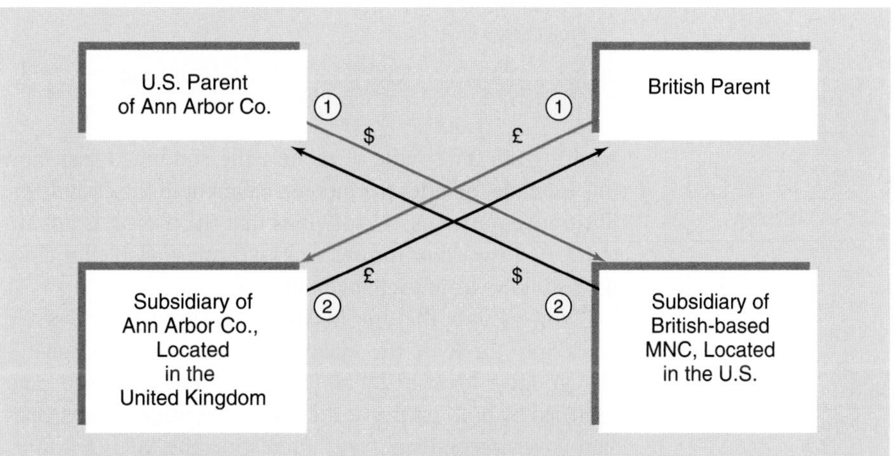

EXAMPLE

Schnell, Inc., has been approached by the government of Malaysia to engage in a project there over the next year. The investment in the project totals 1 million Malaysian ringgit (MR), and the project is expected to generate cash flows of MR1.4 million next year. The project will terminate at that time.

The current value of the ringgit is $.25, but Schnell believes that the ringgit will depreciate substantially over the next year. Specifically, it believes the ringgit will have a value of either $.20 or $.15 next year. Furthermore, Schnell will have to borrow the funds necessary to undertake the project and will incur financing costs of 13 percent.

If Schnell undertakes the project, it will incur a net outflow now of MR1,000,000 × $.25 = $250,000. Next year, it will also have to pay the financing costs of $250,000 × 13% = $32,500. If the ringgit depreciates to $.20, then Schnell will receive MR1,400,000 × $.20 = $280,000 next year. If the ringgit depreciates to $.15, it will receive MR1,400,000 × $.15 = $210,000 next year. For each year, the cash flows are summarized below.

Scenario 1: Ringgit Depreciates to $.20

	Year 0	Year 1
Investment	−$250,000	
Interest payment		−$32,500
Project cash flow	0	$280,000
Net	−$250,000	$247,500

Ignoring the time value of money, the combined cash flows are −$2,500.

Scenario 2: Ringgit Depreciates to $.15

	Year 0	Year 1
Investment	−$250,000	
Interest payment		−$32,500
Project cash flow	0	$210,000
Net	−$250,000	$177,500

Ignoring the time value of money, the combined cash flows are −$72,500. Although this example includes the interest payment in the cash flows and ignores discounting for illustrative purposes, it is obvious that the project is not attractive for Schnell. Furthermore, no forward or futures contracts are available for ringgit, so Schnell cannot hedge its cash flows from exchange rate risk.

Now assume that the Malaysian government offers a parallel loan to Schnell. According to the loan, the Malaysian government will give Schnell MR1,000,000 in exchange for a loan in dollars at the current exchange rate. The same amount will be returned by both parties at the end of the project. Next year, Schnell will pay the Malaysian government 15 percent interest on the MR1,000,000, and the Malaysian government will pay Schnell 7 percent interest on the dollar loan. Graphically, the parallel loan would be as follows:

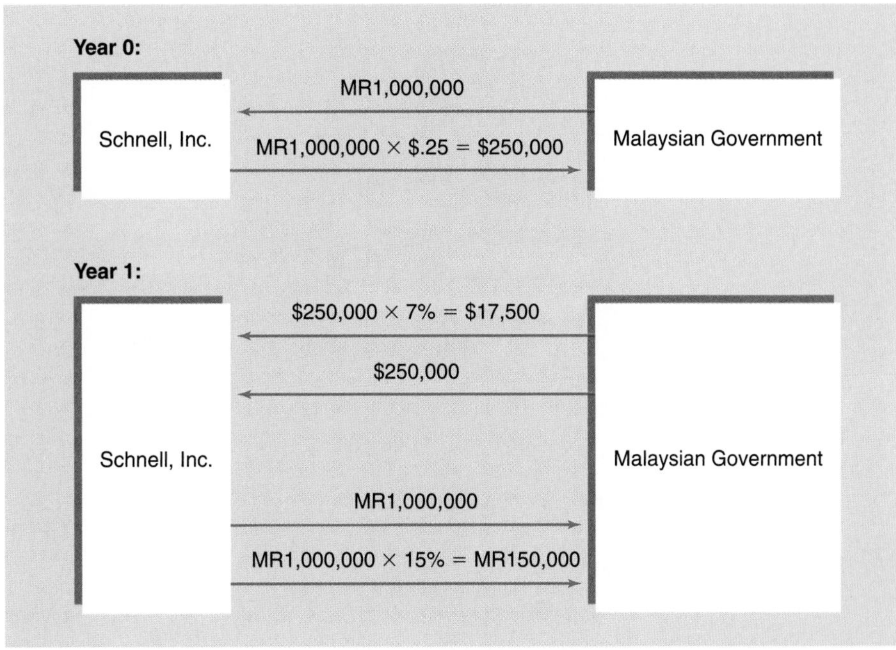

By using the parallel loan, Schnell is able to reduce the net cash flows denominated in Malaysian ringgit it will receive in one year. Consider both the dollar and ringgit cash flows:

Schnell's Cash Flows

	Dollar Cash Flows	
	Year 0	**Year 1**
Loan to Malaysia	**−$250,000**	
Interest payment		**−$32,500**
Interest received on swap ($250,000 × 7%)		**$17,500**
Return of loan	______	**$250,000**
Net cash flow	**−$250,000**	**$235,000**

	Ringgit Cash Flows	
	Year 0	**Year 1**
Loan from Malaysia	**MR1,000,000**	
Investment in project	**−MR1,000,000**	
Interest paid on swap (MR1,000,000 × 15%)		**−MR150,000**
Return of loan		**−MR1,000,000**
Project cash flow	______	**MR1,400,000**
Net cash flow	**0**	**MR250,000**

Scenario 1: Ringgit Depreciates to $.20

The net cash flow in Year 1 of MR250,000 is converted to dollars at the $.20 spot rate to generate MR250,000 × $.20 = $50,000. Thus, the total dollar cash flows using the parallel loan are as follows:

	Year 0	Year 1
Dollar cash flows	−$250,000	$235,000
Converted ringgit cash flows	______	$50,000
Net cash flow	−$250,000	$285,000

Again ignoring time value, the combined cash flows over both years are now $35,000.

Scenario 2: Ringgit Depreciates to $.15

The net cash flow in Year 1 of MR 250,000 is converted to dollars at the $.15 spot rate to generate MR250,000 × $.15 = $37,500. Thus, the total dollar cash flows using the parallel loan are as follows:

	Year 0	Year 1
Dollar cash flows	−$250,000	$235,000
Converted ringgit cash flows	______	$37,500
Net cash flow	−$250,000	$272,500

The combined cash flows over both years are $22,500 in this scenario.

Notice that the cash flows have improved dramatically by using the parallel loan, as the following table illustrates:

	Scenario 1	Scenario 2
Total cash flow without swap	−$2,500	−$72,500
Total cash flow with swap	$35,000	$22,500

Not only was Schnell able to reduce its exchange rate risk by financing the project through the loan, but it was also able to generate positive total cash flows. The reason for this is that the very large expected percentage depreciation in the ringgit (20 percent or 40 percent) exceeds the incremental cost of financing (15 percent − 7 percent = 8 percent). By using the parallel loan, Schnell has reduced the ringgit amount it must convert to dollars at project termination from MR1.4 million to MR250,000. It was therefore able to reduce the amount of its cash flows that would be subject to the expected depreciation of the ringgit.

The Malaysian government also benefits from the loan because it receives incremental interest payments of 8 percent from the arrangements. Of course, the Malaysian government also incurs the implicit cost of the depreciating ringgit since it must reexchange ringgit for dollars after one year. Nevertheless, it may offer such a loan if its expectations for the ringgit's value differ from those of Schnell. That is, the government may expect the ringgit to appreciate or to depreciate by less than Schnell expects. In addition, the government may not have many other options for completing the project if local companies do not have the expertise to perform the work.

Diversifying among Currencies

A U.S. firm may denominate bonds in several foreign currencies, rather than a single foreign currency, so that substantial appreciation of any one currency will not drastically increase the number of dollars needed to cover the financing payments.

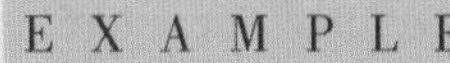

Nevada, Inc., a U.S.-based MNC, is considering four alternatives for issuing bonds to support its U.S. operations:

1. Issue bonds denominated in U.S. dollars.
2. Issue bonds denominated in Japanese yen.
3. Issue bonds denominated in Canadian dollars.
4. Issue some bonds denominated in Japanese yen and some bonds denominated in Canadian dollars.

Nevada, Inc., has no net exposure in either Japanese yen or Canadian dollars. The coupon rate for a U.S. dollar-denominated bond is 14 percent, while the coupon rate is 8 percent for a yen- or Canadian dollar-denominated bond. It is expected that any of these bonds could be sold at par value.

If the Canadian dollar appreciates against the U.S. dollar, Nevada's actual financing cost from issuing Canadian dollar-denominated bonds may be higher than that of the U.S. dollar-denominated bonds. If the Japanese yen appreciates substantially against the U.S. dollar, Nevada's actual financing cost from issuing yen-denominated bonds may be higher than that of the U.S. dollar-denominated bonds. If the exchange rates of the Canadian dollar and Japanese yen move in opposite directions against the U.S. dollar, then both types of bonds could not simultaneously be more costly than U.S. dollar-denominated bonds, so financing with both types of bonds would almost ensure that the Nevada's overall financing cost would be less than the cost from issuing U.S. dollar-denominated bonds.

There is no guarantee that the exchange rates of the Canadian dollar and Japanese yen will move in opposite directions. The movements of these two currencies are not highly correlated, however, so it is unlikely that both currencies will simultaneously appreciate to an extent that will offset their lower coupon rate advantages. Therefore, financing in bonds denominated in more than one foreign currency can increase the probability that the overall cost of foreign financing will be less than that of financing with the dollars. Nevada decides to issue bonds denominated in Canadian dollars and in yen.

The preceding example involved only two foreign currencies. In reality, a firm may consider several currencies that exhibit lower interest rates and issue a portion of its bonds in each of these currencies. Such a strategy can increase the other costs (advertising, printing, etc.) of issuing bonds, but those costs may be offset by a reduction in cash outflows to bondholders.

Currency Cocktail Bonds. A firm can finance in several currencies without issuing various types of bonds (thus avoiding higher transaction costs) by developing a **currency cocktail bond,** denominated in not one, but a mixture (or "cocktail") of currencies. A currency cocktail simply reflects a multicurrency unit of account. Several currency cocktails have been developed to denominate international bonds, and some have already been used in this manner. One of the more popular currency cocktails is the **Special Drawing Right (SDR)**, which was originally devised as an alternative foreign reserve asset but is now used to denominate bonds and bank deposits and to price various services.

With the creation of the euro, the use of currency cocktail bonds in Europe is limited because numerous European countries now use a single currency.

Interest Rate Risk from Debt Financing

Regardless of the currency that an MNC uses to finance its international operations, it must also decide on the maturity that it should use for its debt. Its goal is to use a maturity that will minimize the total payments on the debt needed for each business unit. Normally, an MNC will not use a maturity that exceeds the expected life of the business in that country.

When it uses a relatively short maturity, the MNC is exposed to interest rate risk, or the risk that interest rates will rise, forcing it to refinance at a higher interest rate. It can avoid this exposure by issuing a long-term bond (with a fixed interest rate) that matches the expected life of the operations in the foreign country. The disadvantage of this strategy is that long-term interest rates may decline in the near future, but the MNC will be obligated to continue making its debt payments at the higher rate. There is no perfect solution, but the MNC should consider the expected life of the business and the yield curve of the country in question when weighing the tradeoff. The yield curve is shaped by the demand for and supply of funds at various maturity levels in a country's debt market.

The Debt Maturity Decision

Before making the debt maturity decision, MNCs assess the yield curves of the countries in which they need funds. Examples of yield curves as of February 2004 for six different countries are shown in Exhibit 18.9. First, notice that at any given debt maturity, the interest rate varies among countries. Second, notice that the shape of the yield curve can vary among countries. For example, the United States typically has an upward-sloping yield curve, which means that the annualized yields are lower for short-term debt than for long-term debt. One argument for the upward slope is that investors may require a higher rate of return on long-term debt as compensation for lower liquidity. The market value of long-term debt is more sensitive to market interest rate movements, so investors face a greater risk of a loss if they need to sell the debt before its maturity. Even in the United States, the yield curve is not always upward sloping because other forces such as interest rate expectations may affect the demand and supply conditions for debt at various maturity levels. In some countries, the yield curve is commonly flat or downward sloping for longer maturities.

Some MNCs may use a country's yield curve to compare annualized rates among debt maturities, so that they can choose a maturity that has a relatively low rate. Other MNCs use a yield curve to assess the prevailing market demand for and supply of funds for particular debt maturities, which may indicate the future movement in interest rates. This type of information may help an MNC decide whether to lock in a long-term rate or borrow for a short-term period and refinance in the near future.

Washington Co. expects to generate earnings in Indonesia, Malaysia, and Thailand for the next 10 years. It expects that the Indonesian rupiah and Malaysian ringgit will weaken substantially against the dollar over that period, and therefore plans to finance

Exhibit 18.9 Yield Curves among Foreign Countries (as of February 8, 2004)

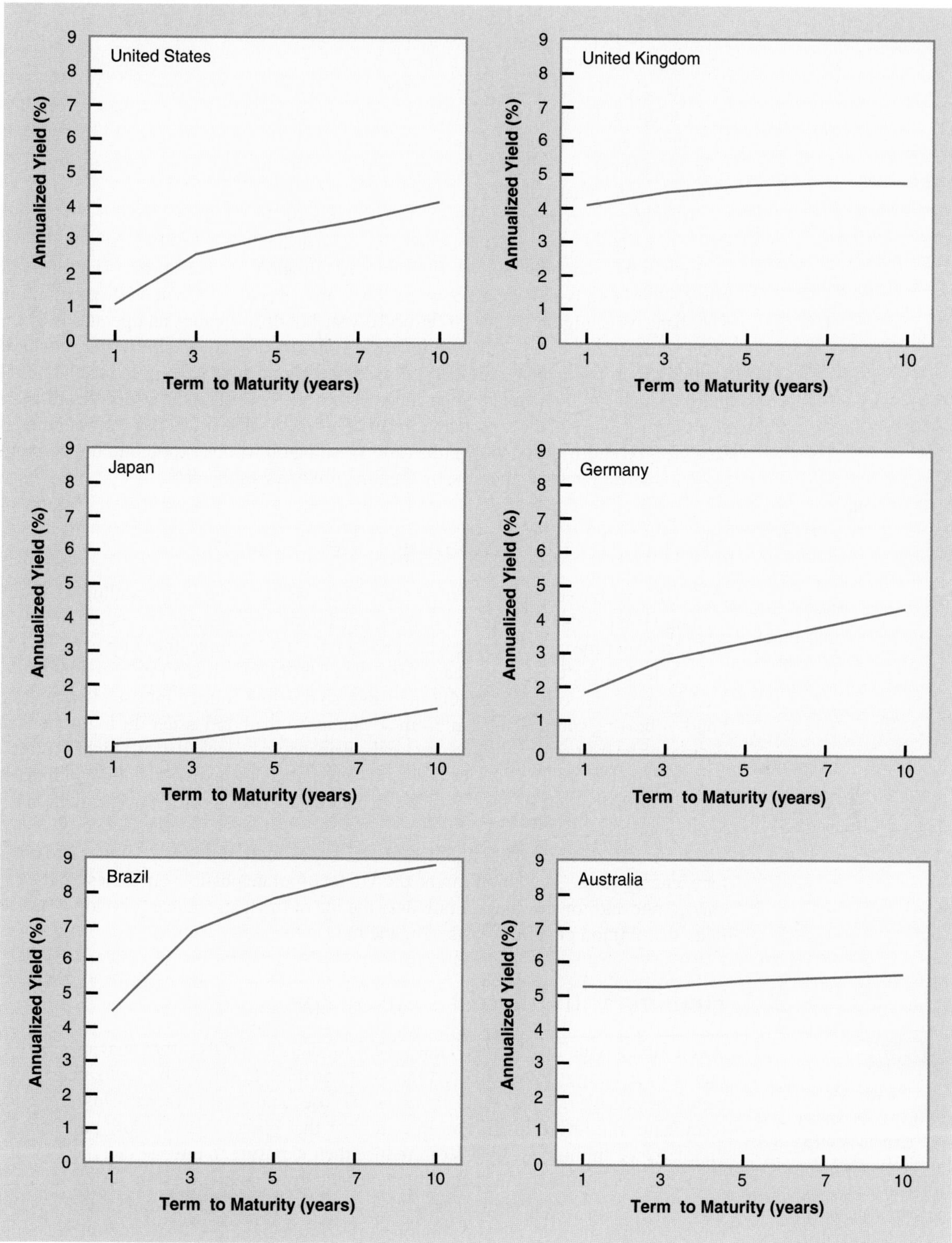

the respective operations with local debt from those countries. Its earnings from Thailand may be discontinued in five years when a contract with the Thai government expires. Washington's best guess is that the Thai baht's future value will be similar to today's spot rate, but it is concerned about the exchange rate risk of its baht-denominated revenue. The 10-year bond yield is about 12 percent for each country, but the yield curve is upward sloping (implying lower annualized yields for shorter debt maturities) in Malaysia and Thailand and downward sloping (higher annualized yields for shorter debt maturities) in Indonesia. It expects that future interest rates in these countries should be somewhat stable over time.

Washington Co. decides to issue Thai notes with a maturity of five years to finance the Thai operations because it does not want to have debt in the business beyond the period when its operations may be discontinued. In addition, the upward-sloping yield curve allows it to issue 5-year notes at a lower annualized yield than a 10-year bond in Thai baht. Washington decides to issue 10-year bonds to finance its operations in Indonesia; because the yield curve is downward sloping, if it issued shorter-term debt, it would have to pay a higher annualized yield and would then be exposed to the possibility of higher interest rates when it refinances the debt. Finally, it decides to issue short-term debt to finance its operations in Malaysia because it will pay a lower annualized yield on short-term debt. In this case, Washington will be exposed to the possibility that interest rates will increase by the time it refinances the debt.

The Fixed versus Floating Rate Decision

MNCs that wish to use a long-term maturity but wish to avoid the prevailing fixed rate on long-term bonds may consider floating rate bonds. In this case, the coupon rate will fluctuate over time in accordance with interest rates. For example, the coupon rate is frequently tied to the **London Interbank Offer Rate (LIBOR)**, which is a rate at which banks lend funds to each other. As LIBOR increases, so does the coupon rate of a floating rate bond. A floating coupon rate can be an advantage to the bond issuer during periods of decreasing interest rates, when otherwise the firm would be locked in at a higher coupon rate over the life of the bond. It can be a disadvantage during periods of rising interest rates. In some countries, such as those in South America, most long-term debt has a floating interest rate.

If the coupon rate is floating, then forecasts are required for interest rates as well as for exchange rates. Simulation can be used to incorporate possible outcomes for the exchange rate and for the coupon rate over the life of the loan and can develop a probability distribution of annual costs of financing.

Hedging with Interest Rate Swaps

http://

The web site http://www.bloomberg.com commonly offers information about international financing, including the issuance of debt in international markets.

When MNCs issue bonds that expose them to interest rate risk, they may use interest rate *swaps* to hedge the risk. Interest rate swaps enable a firm to exchange fixed rate payments for variable rate payments. Bonds issuers use interest rate swaps because they may reconfigure the future cash flows in a manner that offsets their outflow payments to bondholders. In this way, MNCs can reduce their exposure to interest rate movements.

Financial institutions such as commercial and investment banks and insurance companies often act as dealers in interest rate swaps. Financial institutions can also act as brokers in the interest rate swap market. As a broker, the financial institution simply arranges an interest rate swap between two parties, charging a fee for the service, but does not actually take a position in the swap. MNCs frequently engage in interest rate swaps to hedge or to reduce financing costs.

Plain Vanilla Swap

A plain vanilla swap is a standard contract without any unusual contract additions. In a plain vanilla swap, the floating rate payer is typically highly sensitive to interest rate changes and seeks to reduce interest rate risk. A firm with a large amount of highly interest rate–sensitive assets may seek to exchange floating rate payments for fixed rate payments. In general, the floating rate payer believes interest rates are going to decline. The fixed rate payer in a plain vanilla interest rate swap, on the other hand, expects interest rates to rise and would prefer to make fixed rate payments. Fixed rate payers may include firms with a large amount of highly interest rate–sensitive liabilities or a relatively large proportion of fixed rate assets.

EXAMPLE

Two firms plan to issue bonds:

- Quality Co. is a highly rated firm that prefers to borrow at a variable interest rate.
- Risky Co. is a low-rated firm that prefers to borrow at a fixed interest rate.

Assume that the rates these companies would pay for issuing either floating (variable) rate or fixed rate bonds are as follows:

	Fixed Rate Bond	Floating Rate Bond
Quality Co.	9%	LIBOR + 1/2%
Risky Co.	10 1/2%	LIBOR + 1%

LIBOR changes over time. Based on the information given, Quality Co. has an advantage when issuing either fixed rate or variable rate bonds, but more of an advantage with fixed rate bonds. Quality Co. could issue fixed rate bonds while Risky Co. issues variable rate bonds; then, Quality could provide variable rate payments to Risky in exchange for fixed rate payments.

Assume that Quality Co. negotiates with Risky Co. to provide variable rate payments at LIBOR + 1/2 percent in exchange for fixed rate payments of 9 1/2 percent. The interest rate swap arrangement is shown in Exhibit 18.10. Quality Co. benefits because the fixed rate payments it receives on the swap exceed the payments it owes to bondholders by 1/2 percent. Its variable rate payments to Risky Co. are the same as what it would have paid if it had issued variable rate bonds. Risky Co. is receiving LIBOR + 1/2 percent on the swap, which is 1/2 percent less than what it must pay on its variable rate bonds. Yet, it is making fixed rate payments of 9 1/2 percent, which is 1 percent less than what it would have paid if it had issued fixed rate bonds. Overall, Risky Co. saves 1/2 percent per year of financing costs.

Determining Swap Payments. The payments in an interest rate swap are typically determined using some **notional value** agreed upon by the parties to the swap and established contractually. Importantly, the notional amount itself is never exchanged between the parties, but is used only to determine the swap payments. Once the swap payments have been determined using the notional amount, the parties periodically exchange only

Exhibit 18.10
Illustration of an Interest Rate Swap

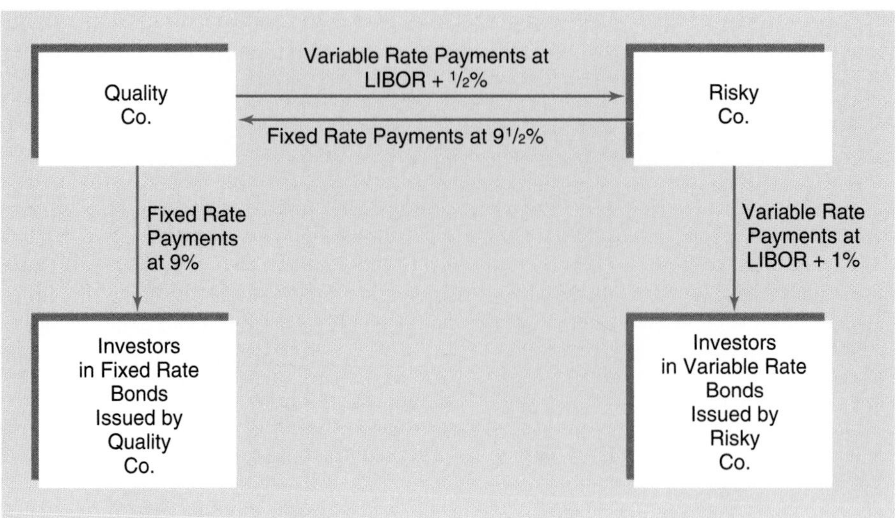

the net amount owed instead of all payments. Payments are typically exchanged either annually or semiannually.

EXAMPLE

Continuing with the previous example involving Quality Co. and Risky Co., assume that the notional value agreed upon by the parties is $50 million and that the two firms exchange net payments annually.

From Quality Co.'s viewpoint, the complete swap arrangement now involves payment of LIBOR + ½ percent annually, based on a notional value of $50 million. From Risky Co.'s viewpoint, the swap arrangement involves a fixed payment of 9½ percent annually based on a notional value of $50 million. The following table below illustrates the payments based on LIBOR over time.

Year	LIBOR	Quality Co.'s Payment	Risky Co.'s Payment	Net Payment
1	8.0%	8.5% × $50 million = $4.25 million	9.5% × $50 million = $4.75 million	Risky pays Quality $.5 million.
2	7.0%	7.5% × $50 million = $3.75 million	9.5% × $50 million = $4.75 million	Risky pays Quality $1 million.
3	5.5%	6.0% × $50 million = $3 million	9.5% × $50 million = $4.75 million	Risky pays Quality $1.75 million.
4	9.0%	9.5% × $50 million = $4.75 million	9.5% × $50 million = $4.75 million	No payment is made.
5	10.0%	10.5% × $50 million = $5.25 million	9.5% × $50 million = $4.75 million	Quality pays Risky $.5 million.

Two limitations of the swap just described are worth mentioning. First, there is a cost of time and resources associated with searching for a suitable swap candidate and negotiating the swap terms. Second, each swap participant faces the risk that the counterparticipant could default on payments. For this reason, financial intermediaries are usually involved in swap agreements. They match up participants and also assume the default risk involved. For their role, they charge a fee, which would reduce the estimated benefits in the preceding example, but their involvement is critical to effectively match up swap participants and reduce concern about default risk.

Ashland, Inc., Campbell Soup Co., Intel Corp., Johnson Controls, Union Carbide, and many other MNCs commonly use interest rate swaps. Ashland, Inc., commonly issues fixed rate debt and uses interest rate swaps to achieve lower borrowing costs on variable rate debt. Campbell Soup Co. uses interest rate swaps to minimize its worldwide financing costs and to achieve a targeted proportion of fixed rate versus variable rate debt. GTE (now part of Verizon) used interest rate swaps to convert more than $500 million of variable rate debt into fixed rate debt.

Other Types of Interest Rate Swaps. Continuing financial innovation has resulted in various additional types of interest rate swaps in recent years. Listed below are some examples:

- *Accretion swap.* An accretion swap is a swap in which the notional value is increased over time.
- *Amortizing swap.* An amortizing swap is essentially the opposite of an accretion swap. In an amortizing swap, the notional value is reduced over time.
- *Basis (floating-for-floating) swap.* A basis swap involves the exchange of two floating rate payments. For example, a swap between one-year LIBOR and six-month LIBOR is a basis swap.
- *Callable swap.* As the name suggests, a callable swap gives the fixed rate payer the right to terminate the swap. The fixed rate payer would exercise this right if interest rates fall substantially.
- *Forward swap.* A forward swap is an interest rate swap that is entered into today. However, the swap payments start at a specific future point in time.
- *Putable swap.* A putable swap gives the floating rate payer the right to terminate the swap. The floating rate payer would exercise this right if interest rates rise substantially.
- *Zero-coupon swap.* In a zero-coupon swap, all fixed interest payments are postponed until maturity and are paid in one lump sum when the swap matures. However, the floating rate payments are due periodically.
- *Swaption.* A swaption gives its owner the right to enter into a swap. The exercise price of a swaption is a specified fixed interest rate at which the swaption owner can enter the swap at a specified future date. A payer swaption gives its owner the right to switch from paying floating to paying fixed interest rates at the exercise price. A receiver swaption gives its owner the right to switch from receiving floating rate to receiving fixed rate payments at the exercise price.

Standardization of the Swap Market. As the swap market has grown in recent years, one association in particular is frequently credited with its standardization. The **International Swaps and Derivatives Association (ISDA)** is a global trade association representing leading participants in the privately negotiated derivatives industry. This encompasses interest rate, currency, commodity, credit, and equity swaps, as well as related products such as caps, collars, floors, and swaptions. The ISDA was chartered in 1985, after a group of 18 swap dealers began work in 1984 to develop standard terms for interest rate swaps. Today, the ISDA has over 600 member institutions from 46 countries. These members include most of the world's major institutions that deal in derivative instruments, as well as leading end-users of privately negotiated derivatives and associated service providers and consultants.

Since its inception, the ISDA has pioneered efforts to identify and reduce the sources of risk in the derivatives and risk management business. The ISDA's two primary objectives are (1) the development and maintenance of derivatives documentation to promote efficient business conduct practices and (2) the promotion of the development of sound risk management practices.

One of the ISDA's most notable accomplishments is the development of the ISDA **Master Agreement**. This agreement provides participants in the private derivatives markets with the opportunity to establish the legal and credit terms between them for an ongoing business relationship. The key advantage of such an agreement is that the general legal and credit terms do not have to be renegotiated each time the parties enter into a transaction. Consequently, the ISDA Master Agreement has contributed greatly to the standardization of the derivatives market.[1]

USING THE WEB

Long-Term Foreign Interest Rates Long-term interest rates for major currencies such as the Canadian dollar, Japanese yen, and British pound for various maturities are provided at http://www.bloomberg.com. You can develop a yield curve from this information.

SUMMARY

- Some MNCs may consider long-term financing in foreign currencies to offset future cash inflows in those currencies and therefore reduce exposure to exchange rate risk. Other MNCs may consider long-term financing in foreign currencies to reduce financing costs. If a foreign interest rate is relatively low or the foreign currency borrowed depreciates over the financing period, long-term financing in that currency can result in low financing costs.
- An MNC can assess the feasibility of financing in foreign currencies by applying exchange rate forecasts to the periodic coupon payments and the principal payment. In this way, it determines the amount of its home currency that is necessary per period to cover the payments. The annual cost of financing can be estimated by determining of the discount rate that equates the periodic payments on the foreign financing to the initial amount borrowed (as measured in the domestic currency). The discount rate derived from this exercise represents the annual cost of financing in the foreign currency, which can be compared to the cost of domestic financing. The cost of long-term financing in a foreign currency is dependent on the currency's exchange rate over the financing period and therefore is uncertain. Thus, the MNC will not automatically finance with a foreign currency that has a lower interest rate, since its exchange rate forecasts are subject to error. For this reason, the MNC may estimate the costs of foreign financing under various exchange rate scenarios over time.
- For bonds that have floating interest rates, the coupon payment to be paid to investors is uncertain. This creates another uncertain variable (along with exchange rates) in estimating the amount in the firm's domestic currency that is required per period to make the payments. This uncertainty can be accounted for by estimating the coupon payment amount necessary under various interest rate scenarios over time. Then, with the use of these estimates, the amount of the firm's domestic currency required to make the payments can be estimated, based on various exchange rate scenarios over time.

[1]For more information about interest rate swaps, see the following: Robert A. Strong, *Derivatives: An Introduction,* 2e (Mason, Ohio: South-Western, 2005); Student Accountant, at **http://www.accademy.com/publications/studentaccountant/36955**; BACA-Group, at **http://www.treasury.at/zinsprodukte/english/content/interestrateswapbeschr4.htm**; and the ISDA, at **http://www.isda.org**.

POINT COUNTER-POINT

Will Currency Swaps Result in Low Financing Costs?

Point Yes. Currency swaps have created greater participation by firms that need to exchange their currencies in the future. Thus, firms that finance in a low-interest-rate currency can more easily establish an agreement to obtain the currency that has the low interest rate.

Counter-Point No. Currency swaps will establish an exchange rate that is based on market forces. If a forward rate exists for a future period, the swap rate should be somewhat similar to the forward rate. If it was not as attractive as the forward rate, the participants would use the forward market instead. If a forward market does not exist for the currency, the swap rate should still reflect market forces. The exchange rate at which a low-interest currency could be purchased will be higher than the prevailing spot rate, since otherwise MNCs would borrow the low-interest currency and simultaneously purchase the currency forward so that they could hedge their future interest payments.

Who Is Correct? Use InfoTrac or some other search engine to learn more about this issue. Which argument do you support? Offer your own opinion on this issue.

SELF TEST

Answers are provided in Appendix A at the back of the text.

1. Explain why a firm may issue a bond denominated in a currency different from its home currency to finance local operations. Explain the risk involved.
2. Tulane, Inc. (based in Louisiana), is considering issuing a 20-year Swiss franc-denominated bond. The proceeds are to be converted to British pounds to support the firm's British operations. Tulane, Inc., has no Swiss operations but prefers to issue the bond in francs rather than pounds because the coupon rate is 2 percentage points lower. Explain the risk involved in this strategy. Do you think the risk here is greater or less than it would be if the bond proceeds were used to finance U.S. operations? Why?
3. Some large companies based in Latin American countries could borrow funds (through issuing bonds or borrowing from U.S. banks) at an interest rate that would be substantially less than the interest rates in their own countries. Assuming that they are perceived to be creditworthy in the United States, why might they still prefer to borrow in their local countries when financing local projects (even if they incur interest rates of 80 percent or more)?
4. A respected economist recently predicted that even though Japanese inflation would not rise, Japanese interest rates would rise consistently over the next five years. Paxson Co., a U.S. firm with no foreign operations, has recently issued a Japanese yen-denominated bond to finance U.S. operations. It chose the yen denomination because the coupon rate was low. Its vice president stated, "I'm not concerned about the prediction because we issued fixed rate bonds and are therefore insulated from risk." Do you agree? Explain.
5. Long-term interest rates in some Latin American countries commonly exceed 100 percent annually. Offer your opinion as to why these interest rates are so much higher than those of industrialized countries and why some projects in these countries are feasible for local firms, even though the cost of funding the projects is so high.

QUESTIONS AND APPLICATIONS

1. **Floating Rate Bonds.**

   a. What factors should be considered by a U.S. firm that plans to issue a floating rate bond denominated in a foreign currency?

   b. Is the risk of issuing a floating rate bond higher or lower than the risk of issuing a fixed rate bond? Explain.

   c. How would an investing firm differ from a borrowing firm in the features (i.e., interest rate and currency's future exchange rates) it would prefer a floating rate foreign currency-denominated bond to exhibit?

2. **Risk from Issuing Foreign Currency-Denominated Bonds.** What is the advantage of using simulation to assess the bond financing position?

3. **Exchange Rate Effects.**

   a. Explain the difference in the cost of financing with foreign currencies during a strong-dollar period versus a weak-dollar period for a U.S. firm.

   b. Explain how a U.S.-based MNC issuing bonds denominated in euros may be able to offset a portion of its exchange rate risk.

4. **Bond Offering Decision.** Columbia Corp. is a U.S. company with no foreign currency cash flows. It plans to issue either a bond denominated in euros with a fixed interest rate or a bond denominated in U.S. dollars with a floating interest rate. It estimates its periodic dollar cash flows for each bond. Which bond do you think would have greater uncertainty surrounding these future dollar cash flows? Explain.

5. **Currency Diversification.** Why would a U.S. firm consider issuing bonds denominated in multiple currencies?

6. **Financing That Reduces Exchange Rate Risk.** Kerr, Inc., a major U.S. exporter of products to Japan, denominates its exports in dollars and has no other international business. It can borrow dollars at 9 percent to finance its operations or borrow yen at 3 percent. If it borrows yen, it will be exposed to exchange rate risk. How can Kerr borrow yen and possibly reduce its economic exposure to exchange rate risk?

7. **Exchange Rate Effects.** Katina, Inc., is a U.S. firm that plans to finance with bonds denominated in euros to obtain a lower interest rate than is available on dollar-denominated bonds. What is the most critical point in time when the exchange rate will have the greatest impact?

8. **Financing Decision.** Ivax Corp. (based in Miami) is a U.S. drug company that has attempted to capitalize on new opportunities to expand in Eastern Europe. The production costs in most Eastern European countries are very low, often less than one-fourth of the cost in Germany or Switzerland. Furthermore, there is a strong demand for drugs in Eastern Europe. Ivax penetrated Eastern Europe by purchasing a 60 percent stake in Galena AS, a Czech firm that produces drugs.

   a. Should Ivax finance its investment in the Czech firm by borrowing dollars from a U.S. bank that would then be converted into koruna (the Czech currency) or by borrowing koruna from a local Czech bank? What information do you need to know to answer this question?

   b. How can borrowing koruna locally from a Czech bank reduce the exposure of Ivax to exchange rate risk?

   c. How can borrowing koruna locally from a Czech bank reduce the exposure of Ivax to political risk caused by government regulations?

ADVANCED QUESTIONS

9. **Bond Financing Analysis.** Sambuka, Inc., can issue bonds in either U.S. dollars or in Swiss francs. Dollar-denominated bonds would have a coupon rate of 15 percent; Swiss franc-denominated bonds would have a coupon rate of 12 percent. Assuming that Sambuka can issue bonds worth $10,000,000 in either currency, that the current exchange rate of the Swiss franc is $.70, and that the forecasted exchange rate of the franc in each of the next three years is $.75, what is the annual cost of financing for the franc-denominated bonds? Which type of bond should Sambuka issue?

10. **Bond Financing Analysis.** Hawaii Co. just agreed to a long-term deal in which it will export products to

Japan. It needs funds to finance the production of the products that it will export. The products will be denominated in dollars. The prevailing U.S. long-term interest rate is 9 percent versus 3 percent in Japan. Assume that interest rate parity exists, and that Hawaii Co. believes that the international Fisher effect holds.

a. Should Hawaii Co. finance its production with yen and leave itself open to exchange rate risk? Explain.

b. Should Hawaii Co. finance its production with yen and simultaneously engage in forward contracts to hedge its exposure to exchange rate risk?

c. How could Hawaii Co. achieve low-cost financing while eliminating its exposure to exchange rate risk?

11. **Cost of Financing.** Assume that Seminole, Inc., considers issuing a Singapore dollar-denominated bond at its present coupon rate of 7 percent, even though it has no incoming cash flows to cover the bond payments. It is attracted to the low financing rate, since U.S. dollar-denominated bonds issued in the United States would have a coupon rate of 12 percent. Assume that either type of bond would have a four-year maturity and could be issued at par value. Seminole needs to borrow $10 million. Therefore, it will issue either U.S. dollar-denominated bonds with a par value of $10 million or bonds denominated in Singapore dollars with a par value of S$20 million. The spot rate of the Singapore dollar is $.50. Seminole has forecasted the Singapore dollar's value at the end of each of the next four years, when coupon payments are to be paid:

End of Year	Exchange Rate of Singapore Dollar
1	$.52
2	.56
3	.58
4	.53

Determine the expected annual cost of financing with Singapore dollars. Should Seminole, Inc., issue bonds denominated in U.S. dollars or Singapore dollars? Explain.

12. **Interaction between Financing and Invoicing Policies.** Assume that Hurricane, Inc., is a U.S. company that exports products to the United Kingdom, invoiced in dollars. It also exports products to Denmark, invoiced in dollars. It currently has no cash outflows in foreign currencies, and it plans to issue bonds in the near future. Hurricane could likely issue bonds at par value in (1) dollars with a coupon rate of 12 percent, (2) Danish kroner with a coupon rate of 9 percent, or (3) pounds with a coupon rate of 15 percent. It expects the kroner and pound to strengthen over time. How could Hurricane revise its invoicing policy and make its bond denomination decision to achieve low financing costs without excessive exposure to exchange rate fluctuations?

13. **Swap Agreement.** Grant, Inc., is a well-known U.S. firm that needs to borrow 10 million British pounds to support a new business in the United Kingdom. However, it cannot obtain financing from British banks because it is not yet established within the United Kingdom. It decides to issue dollar-denominated debt (at par value) in the United States, for which it will pay an annual coupon rate of 10 percent. It then will convert the dollar proceeds from the debt issue into British pounds at the prevailing spot rate (the prevailing spot rate is one pound = $1.70). Over each of the next three years, it plans to use the revenue in pounds from the new business in the United Kingdom to make its annual debt payment. Grant, Inc., engages in a currency swap in which it will convert pounds to dollars at an exchange rate of $1.70 per pound at the end of each of the next three years. How many dollars must be borrowed initially to support the new business in the United Kingdom? How many pounds should Grant, Inc., specify in the swap agreement that it will swap over each of the next three years in exchange for dollars so that it can make its annual coupon payments to the U.S. creditors?

14. **Interest Rate Swap.** Janutis Co. has just issued fixed rate debt at 10 percent. Yet, it prefers to convert its financing to incur a floating rate on its debt. It engages in an interest rate swap in which it swaps variable rate payments of LIBOR plus 1 percent in exchange for payments of 10 percent. The interest rates are applied to an amount that represents the principal from its recent debt issue in order to determine the interest payments due at the end of each year for the next three years. Janutis Co. expects that the LIBOR will be 9 percent at the end of the first year, 8.5 percent at the end of the second

year, and 7 percent at the end of the third year. Determine the financing rate that Janutis Co. expects to pay on its debt after considering the effect of the interest rate swap.

INTERNET APPLICATION

15. **Long-term Cost of Debt.** The Bloomberg website provides interest rate data for many countries and various maturities. Its address is **http://www.bloomberg.com**.

    Go to the "Markets" section of the website and then to "International Yield Curves." Consider a subsidiary of a U.S.-based MNC that is located in Australia. Assume that when it borrows in Australian dollars, it would pay 1 percent more than the risk-free (government) rates shown on the website. What rate would the subsidiary pay for 1-year debt? For 5-year debt? For 10-year debt? Assuming that it needs funds for 10 years, do you think it should use 1-year debt, 5-year debt, or 10-year debt? Explain your answer.

DISCUSSION IN THE BOARDROOM

This exercise can be found in Appendix E at the back of this textbook.

RUNNING YOUR OWN MNC

This exercise can be found on the Xtra! website at **http://maduraxtra.swlearning.com**.

BLADES, INC. CASE

Use of Long-Term Foreign Financing

Recall that Blades, Inc., is considering the establishment of a subsidiary in Thailand to manufacture "Speedos," Blades' primary roller blade product. Alternatively, Blades could acquire an existing manufacturer of roller blades in Thailand, Skates'n'Stuff. At the most recent meeting of the board of directors of Blades, Inc., the directors voted to establish a subsidiary in Thailand because of the relatively high level of control it would afford Blades.

The Thai subsidiary is expected to begin production by early next year, and the construction of the plant in Thailand and the purchase of necessary equipment to manufacture Speedos are to commence immediately. Initial estimates of the plant and equipment required to establish the subsidiary in Bangkok indicate costs of approximately 550 million Thai baht. Since the current exchange rate of the baht is $0.023, this translates to a dollar cost of $12.65 million. Blades currently has $2.65 million available in cash to cover a portion of the costs. The remaining $10 million (434,782,609 baht), however, will have to be obtained from other sources.

The board of directors has asked Ben Holt, Blades' chief financial officer (CFO), to line up the necessary financing to cover the remaining construction costs and purchase of equipment. Holt realizes that Blades is a relatively small company whose stock is not widely held. Furthermore, he believes that Blades' stock is currently undervalued because the company's expansion into Thailand has not been widely publicized at this point. Because of these considerations, Holt would prefer debt to equity financing to raise the funds necessary to complete construction of the Thai plant.

Ben Holt has identified two alternatives for debt financing: issue the equivalent of $10 million yen-denominated notes or issue the equivalent of approximately $10 million baht-denominated notes. Both types of notes would have a maturity of five years. In the fifth year, the face value of the notes will be repaid together with the last annual interest payment. Notes denominated in yen (¥) are available in increments of ¥125,000, while baht-denominated notes are issued in increments of 50,000 baht. Since the baht-denominated notes are issued in increments of 50,000 baht (THB), Blades needs to issue THB434,782,609/50,000 = 8,696 baht-denominated notes. Furthermore, since the current exchange rate of the yen in baht is THB0.347826/¥, Blades needs to obtain THB434,782,609/THB0.347826 = ¥1,250,000,313. Since yen-denominated notes would be issued in increments of 125,000 yen, Blades would have to issue ¥1,250,000,313/¥125,000 = 10,000 yen-denominated notes.

Due to recent unfavorable economic events in Thailand, expansion into Thailand is viewed as relatively risky; Holt's research indicates that Blades would have to offer a coupon rate of approximately 10 percent on the yen-denominated notes to induce investors to purchase these notes. Conversely, Blades could issue baht-denominated notes at a coupon rate of 15 percent. Whether Blades decides to issue baht- or yen-denominated notes, it would use the cash flows generated by the Thai subsidiary to pay the interest on the notes and to repay the principal in five years. For example, if Blades decides to issue yen-denominated notes, it would convert baht into yen to pay the interest on these notes and to repay the principal in five years.

Although Blades can finance with a lower coupon rate by issuing yen-denominated notes, Ben Holt suspects that the effective financing rate for the yen-denominated notes may actually be higher than for the baht-denominated notes. This is because forecasts for the future value of the yen indicate an appreciation of the yen (versus the baht) in the future. Although the precise future value of the yen is uncertain, Holt has compiled the following probability distribution for the annual percentage change of the yen versus the baht:

Annual % Change in Yen (versus the baht)	Probability
0%	20%
2	50
3	30

Holt suspects that the effective financing cost of the yen-denominated notes may actually be higher than for the baht-denominated notes once the expected appreciation of the yen (versus the baht) is taken into consideration.

Holt has asked you, a financial analyst at Blades, Inc., to answer the following questions for him:

1. Given that Blades expects to use the cash flows generated by the Thai subsidiary to pay the interest and principal of the notes, would the effective financing cost of the baht-denominated notes be affected by exchange rate movements? Would the effective financing cost of the yen-denominated notes be affected by exchange rate movements? How?
2. Construct a spreadsheet to determine the annual effective financing percentage cost of the yen-denominated notes issued in each of the three scenarios for the future value of the yen. What is the probability that the financing cost of issuing yen-denominated notes is higher than the cost of issuing baht-denominated notes?
3. Using a spreadsheet, determine the expected annual effective financing percentage cost of issuing yen-denominated notes. How does this expected financing cost compare with the expected financing cost of the baht-denominated notes?
4. Based on your answers to the previous questions, do you think Blades should issue yen- or baht-denominated notes?
5. What is the tradeoff involved?

SMALL BUSINESS DILEMMA

Long-Term Financing Decision by the Sports Exports Company

The Sports Exports Company continues to focus on producing footballs in the United States and exporting them to the United Kingdom. The exports are denominated in pounds, which has continually exposed the firm to exchange rate risk. It is now considering a new form of expansion where it would sell specialty sporting goods in the United States. If it pursues this U.S. project, it will need to borrow long-term funds. The dollar-denominated debt has an interest rate that is slightly lower than the pound-denominated debt.

1. Jim Logan, owner of the Sports Exports Company, needs to determine whether dollar-denominated debt or pound-denominated debt would be most appropriate for financing this expansion, if he does expand. He is leaning toward financing the U.S.

project with dollar-denominated debt, since his goal is to avoid exchange rate risk. Is there any reason why he should consider using pound-denominated debt to reduce exchange rate risk?

2. Assume that Jim decides to finance his proposed U.S. business with dollar-denominated debt, if he does implement the U.S. business idea. How could he use a currency swap along with the debt to reduce the firm's exposure to exchange rate risk?

PART 4

Integrative Problem

Long-Term Asset and Liability Management

Gandor Co. is a U.S. firm that is considering a joint venture with a Chinese firm to produce and sell videocassettes. Gandor will invest $12 million in this project, which will help to finance the Chinese firm's production. For each of the first three years, 50 percent of the total profits will be distributed to the Chinese firm, while the remaining 50 percent will be converted to dollars to be sent to the United States. The Chinese government intends to impose a 20 percent income tax on the profits distributed to Gandor. The Chinese government has guaranteed that the after-tax profits (denominated in yuan, the Chinese currency) can be converted to U.S. dollars at an exchange rate of $.20 per yuan and sent to Gandor Co. each year. At the current time, no withholding tax is imposed on profits sent to the United States as a result of joint ventures in China. Assume that after considering the taxes paid in China, an additional 10 percent tax is imposed by the U.S. government on profits received by Gandor Co. After the first three years, all profits earned are allocated to the Chinese firm.

The expected total profits resulting from the joint venture per year are as follows:

Year	Total Profits From Joint Venture (in yuan)
1	60 million
2	80 million
3	100 million

Gandor's average cost of debt is 13.8 percent before taxes. Its average cost of equity is 18 percent. Assume that the corporate income tax rate imposed on Gandor is normally 30 percent. Gandor uses a capital structure composed of 60 percent debt and 40 percent equity. Gandor automatically adds 4 percentage points to its cost of capital when deriving its required rate of return on international joint ventures. Though this project has particular forms of country risk that are unique, Gandor plans to account for these forms of risk within its estimation of cash flows.

Gandor is concerned about two forms of country risk. First, there is the risk that the Chinese government will increase the corporate income tax rate from 20 percent to 40 percent (20 percent probability). If this occurs, additional tax credits will be allowed, resulting in no U.S. taxes on the profits from this joint venture. Second, there is the risk that the Chinese government will impose a withholding tax of 10 percent on the profits that are sent to the United States (20 percent probability). In this case, additional tax credits will not be allowed, and Gandor will still be subject to a 10 percent U.S. tax on profits received from China. Assume that the two types of country risk are mutually exclusive. That is, the Chinese government will adjust only one of its taxes (the income tax or the withholding tax), if any.

Questions

1. Determine Gandor's cost of capital. Also, determine Gandor's required rate of return for the joint venture in China.
2. Determine the probability distribution of Gandor's net present values for the joint venture. Capital budgeting analyses should be conducted for these three scenarios:
   - *Scenario 1.* Based on original assumptions.
   - *Scenario 2.* Based on an increase in the corporate income tax by the Chinese government.
   - *Scenario 3.* Based on the imposition of a withholding tax by the Chinese government.
3. Would you recommend that Gandor participate in the joint venture? Explain.
4. What do you think would be the key underlying factor that would have the most influence on the profits earned in China as a result of the joint venture?
5. Is there any reason for Gandor to revise the composition of its capital (debt and equity) obtained from the United States when financing joint ventures like this?
6. When Gandor was assessing this proposed joint venture, some of its managers recommended that Gandor borrow the Chinese currency rather than dollars to obtain some of the necessary capital for its initial investment. They suggested that such a strategy could reduce Gandor's exchange rate risk. Do you agree? Explain.

PART 5

Short-Term Asset and Liability Management

Part 5 (Chapters 19 through 21) focuses on the MNC's management of short-term assets and liabilities. Chapter 19 describes methods by which MNCs can finance their international trade. Chapter 20 identifies sources of short-term funds and explains the criteria used by MNCs to make their short-term financing decisions. Chapter 21 describes how MNCs optimize their cash flows and explains the criteria used to make their short-term investment decisions.

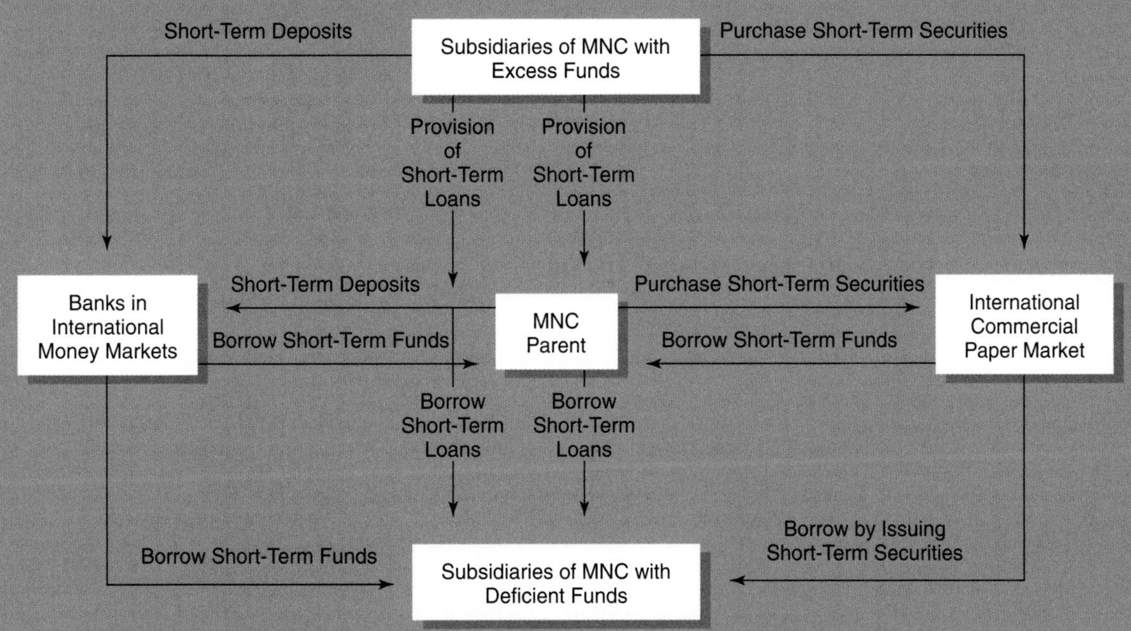

CHAPTER 19

Financing International Trade

The international trade activities of MNCs have grown in importance over time. This trend is attributable to the increased globalization of the world economies and the availability of trade finance from the international banking community. Although banks also finance domestic trade, their role in financing international trade is more critical due to the additional complications involved. First, the exporter might question the importer's ability to make payment. Second, even if the importer is creditworthy, the government might impose exchange controls that prevent payment to the exporter. Third, the importer might not trust the exporter to ship the goods ordered. Fourth, even if the exporter does ship the goods, trade barriers or time lags in international transportation might delay arrival time. Financial managers must recognize methods that they can use to finance international trade so that they can conduct exporting or importing in a manner that maximizes the value of an MNC.

The specific objectives of this chapter are to:

- describe methods of payment for international trade,
- explain common trade finance methods, and
- describe the major agencies that facilitate international trade with export insurance and/or loan programs.

Payment Methods for International Trade

In any international trade transaction, credit is provided by either the supplier (exporter), the buyer (importer), one or more financial institutions, or any combination of these. The supplier may have sufficient cash flow to finance the entire trade cycle, beginning with the production of the product until payment is eventually made by the buyer. This form of credit is known as **supplier credit**. In some cases, the exporter may require bank financing to augment its cash flow. On the other hand, the supplier may not desire to provide financing, in which case the buyer will have to finance the transaction itself, either internally or externally, through its bank. Banks on both sides of the transaction can thus play an integral role in trade financing.

Exhibit 19.1 Comparison of Payment Methods

Method	Usual Time of Payment	Goods Available to Buyers	Risk to Exporter	Risk to Importer
Prepayment	Before shipment	After payment	None	Relies completely on exporter to ship goods as ordered
Letter of credit	When shipment is made	After payment	Very little or none, depending on credit terms	Assured shipment made, but relies on exporter to ship goods described in documents
Sight draft; documents against payment	On presentation of draft to buyer	After payment	If draft unpaid, must dispose of goods	Same as above unless importer can inspect goods before payment
Time draft; documents against acceptance	On maturity of drafts	Before payment	Relies on buyer to pay drafts	Same as above
Consignment	At time of sale by buyer	Before payment	Allows importer to sell inventory before paying exporter	None; improves cash flow of buyer
Open account	As agreed	Before payment	Relies completely on buyer to pay account as agreed	None

In general, five basic methods of payment are used to settle international transactions, each with a different degree of risk to the exporter and importer (Exhibit 19.1):

- Prepayment
- Letters of credit
- Drafts (sight/time)
- Consignment
- Open account

Prepayment

Under the **prepayment** method, the exporter will not ship the goods until the buyer has remitted payment to the exporter. Payment is usually made in the form of an international wire transfer to the exporter's bank account or foreign bank draft. As technology progresses, electronic commerce will allow firms engaged in international trade to make electronic credits and debits through an intermediary bank. This method affords the supplier the greatest degree of protection, and it is normally requested of first-time buyers whose creditworthiness is unknown or whose countries are in financial difficulty. Most buyers, however, are not willing to bear all the risk by prepaying an order.

Letters of Credit (L/C)

A **letter of credit (L/C)** is an instrument issued by a bank on behalf of the importer (buyer) promising to pay the exporter (beneficiary) upon presentation of shipping documents in compliance with the terms stipulated therein. In effect, the bank is substituting its

http://

Many banks have a website that explains the variety of trade financing that they can provide for firms. See, for example, http://www.huntington.com/bas/HNB2740.htm.

credit for that of the buyer. This method is a compromise between seller and buyer because it affords certain advantages to both parties. The exporter is assured of receiving payment from the issuing bank as long as it presents documents in accordance with the L/C. An important feature of an L/C is that the issuing bank is obligated to honor drawings under the L/C regardless of the buyer's ability or willingness to pay. On the other hand, the importer does not have to pay for the goods until shipment has been made and the documents are presented in good order. However, the importer must still rely upon the exporter to ship the goods as described in the documents, since the L/C does not guarantee that the goods purchased will be those invoiced and shipped. Letters of credit will be described in greater detail later in this chapter.

Drafts

A **draft** (or **bill of exchange**) is an unconditional promise drawn by one party, usually the exporter, instructing the buyer to pay the face amount of the draft upon presentation. The draft represents the exporter's formal demand for payment from the buyer. A draft affords the exporter less protection than an L/C, because the banks are not obligated to honor payments on the buyer's behalf.

Most trade transactions handled on a draft basis are processed through banking channels. In banking terminology, these transactions are known as **documentary collections**. In a documentary collection transaction, banks on both ends act as intermediaries in the processing of shipping documents and the collection of payment. If shipment is made under a sight draft, the exporter is paid once shipment has been made and the draft is presented to the buyer for payment. The buyer's bank will not release the shipping documents to the buyer until the buyer has paid the draft. This is known as **documents against payment**. It provides the exporter with some protection, since the banks will release the shipping documents only according to the exporter's instructions. The buyer needs the shipping documents to pick up the merchandise. The buyer does not have to pay for the merchandise until the draft has been presented.

If a shipment is made under a time draft, the exporter instructs the buyer's bank to release the shipping documents against acceptance (signing) of the draft. This method of payment is sometimes referred to as **documents against acceptance**. By accepting the draft, the buyer is promising to pay the exporter at the specified future date. This accepted draft is also known as a **trade acceptance**, which is different from a banker's acceptance (disussed later in the chapter). In this type of transaction, the buyer is able to obtain the merchandise prior to paying for it.

The exporter is providing the financing and is dependent upon the buyer's financial integrity to pay the draft at maturity. Shipping on a time draft basis provides some added comfort in that banks at both ends are used as collection agents. In addition, a draft serves as a binding financial obligation in case the exporter wishes to pursue litigation on uncollected receivables. The added risk is that if the buyer fails to pay the draft at maturity, the bank is not obligated to honor payment. The exporter is assuming all the risk and must analyze the buyer accordingly.

Consignment

Under a **consignment** arrangement, the exporter ships the goods to the importer while still retaining actual title to the merchandise. The importer has access to the inventory but does not have to pay for the goods until they have been sold to a third party. The exporter is trusting the importer to remit payment for the goods sold at that time. If the importer fails to pay, the exporter has limited recourse because no draft is involved and the goods have already been sold. As a result of the high risk, consignments are seldom used except by affiliated and subsidiary companies trading with the parent company. Some equipment suppliers allow importers to hold some equipment on the sales floor as demonstrator models. Once the models are sold or after a specified period, payment is sent to the supplier.

Open Account

The opposite of prepayment is the **open account transaction** in which the exporter ships the merchandise and expects the buyer to remit payment according to the agreed-upon terms. The exporter is relying fully upon the financial creditworthiness, integrity, and reputation of the buyer. As might be expected, this method is used when the seller and buyer have mutual trust and a great deal of experience with each other. Despite the risks, open account transactions are widely utilized, particularly among the industrialized countries in North America and Europe.

Trade Finance Methods

As mentioned in the previous section, banks on both sides of the transaction play a critical role in financing international trade. The following are some of the more popular methods of financing international trade:

- Accounts receivable financing
- Factoring
- Letters of credit (L/Cs)
- Banker's acceptances
- Working capital financing
- Medium-term capital goods financing (forfaiting)
- Countertrade

Each of these methods is described in turn.

Accounts Receivable Financing

http://

The Bankers' Association for Finance and Trade has a website http://www.baft.org/jsps/ that provides useful information about bankers' acceptances and the financing of foreign trade.

In some cases, the exporter of goods may be willing to ship goods to the importer without an assurance of payment from a bank. This could take the form of an open account shipment or a time draft. Prior to shipment, the exporter should have conducted its own credit check on the importer to determine creditworthiness. If the exporter is willing to wait for payment, it will extend credit to the buyer.

If the exporter needs funds immediately, it may require financing from a bank. In what is referred to as **accounts receivable financing**, the bank will provide a loan to the exporter secured by an assignment of the account receivable. The bank's loan is made to the exporter based on its creditworthiness. In the event the buyer fails to pay the exporter for whatever reason, the exporter is still responsible for repaying the bank.

Accounts receivable financing involves additional risks, such as government restrictions and exchange controls, that may prevent the buyer from paying the exporter. As a result, the loan rate is often higher than domestic accounts receivable financing. The length of a financing term is usually one to six months. To mitigate the additional risk of a foreign receivable, exporters and banks often require export credit insurance before financing foreign receivables.

Factoring

When an exporter ships goods before receiving payment, the accounts receivable balance increases. Unless the exporter has received a loan from a bank, it is initially financing the transaction and must monitor the collections of receivables. Since there is a danger that the buyer will never pay at all, the exporting firm may consider selling the accounts receivable to a third party, known as a **factor**. In this type of financing, the exporter sells the accounts receivable without recourse. The factor then assumes all administrative responsibilities involved in collecting from the buyer and the associated credit exposure. The factor performs its own credit approval process on the foreign buyer before purchasing the receivable. For providing this service, the factor usually purchases the receivable at a discount and also receives a flat processing fee.

Factoring provides several benefits to the exporter. First, by selling the accounts receivable, the exporter does not have to worry about the administrative duties involved in maintaining and monitoring an accounts receivable accounting ledger. Second, the factor assumes the credit exposure to the buyer, so the exporter does not have to maintain personnel to assess the creditworthiness of foreign buyers. Finally, by selling the receivable to the factor, the exporter receives immediate payment and improves its cash flow.

Since it is the importer who must be creditworthy from a factor's point of view, **cross-border factoring** is often used. This involves a network of factors in various countries who assess credit risk. The exporter's factor contacts a correspondent factor in the buyer's country to assess the importer's creditworthiness and handle the collection of the receivable. Factoring services are usually provided by the factoring subsidiaries of commercial banks, commercial finance companies, and other specialized finance houses. Factors often utilize export credit insurance to mitigate the additional risk of a foreign receivable.

Letters of Credit (L/C)

Introduced earlier, the letter of credit (L/C) is one of the oldest forms of trade finance still in existence. Because of the protection and benefits it accords to both exporter and importer, it is a critical component of many international trade transactions. The L/C is an undertaking by a bank to make payments on behalf of a specified party to a beneficiary under specified conditions. The beneficiary (exporter) is paid upon presentation of the required documents in compliance with the terms of the L/C. The L/C process normally involves two banks, the exporter's bank and the importer's bank. The issuing bank is substituting its credit for that of the importer. It has essentially guaranteed payment to the exporter, provided the exporter complies with the terms and conditions of the L/C.

Sometimes the exporter is uncomfortable with the issuing bank's promise to pay because the bank is located in a foreign country. Even if the issuing bank is well known worldwide, the exporter may be concerned that the foreign government will impose exchange controls or other restrictions that would prevent payment by the issuing bank.

For this reason, the exporter may request that a local bank confirm the L/C and thus assure that all the responsibilities of the issuing bank will be met. The confirming bank is obligated to honor drawings made by the beneficiary in compliance with the L/C regardless of the issuing bank's ability to make that payment. Consequently, the confirming bank is trusting that the foreign bank issuing the L/C is sound. The exporter, however, need worry only about the credibility of the confirming bank.

EXAMPLE

Nike can attribute part of its international business growth in the 1970s to the use of L/Cs. In 1971, Nike (which was then called BSR) was not well known to businesses in Japan or anywhere else. Nevertheless, by using L/Cs, it was still able to subcontract the production of athletic shoes in Japan. The L/Cs assured the Japanese shoe producer that it would receive payment for the shoes it would send to the United States and thus facilitated the flow of trade without concern about credit risk. Banks served as the guarantors in the event that the Japanese shoe company was not paid in full after transporting shoes to the United States. Thus, because of the backing of the banks, the L/Cs allowed the Japanese shoe company to do international business without having to worry that the counterparty in its agreement would not fulfill its obligation. Without such agreements, Nike (and many other firms) would not be able to order shipments of goods.

Types of Letters of Credit. Trade-related letters of credit are known as **commercial letters of credit** or **import/export letters of credit**. There are basically two types: revocable and irrevocable. A **revocable letter of credit** can be canceled or revoked at any time without prior notification to the beneficiary, and it is seldom used. An **irrevocable letter of credit** (see Exhibit 19.2) cannot be canceled or amended without the beneficiary's consent. The bank issuing the L/C is known as the **"issuing" bank**. The correspondent bank in the beneficiary's country to which the issuing bank sends the L/C is commonly referred to as the **"advising" bank**. An irrevocable L/C obligates the issuing bank to honor all drawings presented in conformity with the terms of the L/C. Letters of credit are normally issued in accordance with the provisions contained in "Uniform Customs

Exhibit 19.2

Example of an Irrevocable Letter of Credit

Name of issuing bank

Address of issuing bank

Name of exporter

Address of exporter

We establish our irrevocable letter of credit:
for the account of (*importer name*),
in the amount of (*value of exports*),
expiring (*date*),
available by your draft at (*time period*) days sight and accompanied by: (any invoices, packing lists, bills of lading, etc., that need to be presented with the letter of credit)
Insurance provided by (*exporter or importer*)
covering shipment of (*merchandise description*)
From: (*port of shipment*)
To: (*port of arrival*)

(Authorized Signature)

____

and Practice for Documentary Credits," published by the International Chamber of Commerce.

The bank issuing the L/C makes payment once the required documentation has been presented in accordance with the payment terms. The importer must pay the issuing bank the amount of the L/C plus accrued fees associated with obtaining the L/C. The importer usually has established an account at the issuing bank to be drawn upon for payment, so that the issuing bank does not tie up its own funds. However, if the importer does not have sufficient funds in its account, the issuing bank is still obligated to honor all valid drawings against the L/C. This is why the bank's decision to issue an L/C on behalf of an importer involves an analysis of the importer's creditworthiness and is analogous to the decision to make a loan. The documentary credit procedure is depicted in the flowchart in Exhibit 19.3. In what is commonly referred to as a *refinancing of a sight L/C,* the bank arranges to fund a loan to pay out the L/C instead of charging the importer's account immediately. The importer is responsible for repaying the bank both the principal and interest at maturity. This is just another method of providing extended payment terms to a buyer when the exporter insists upon payment at sight.

The bank issuing the L/C makes payment to the beneficiary (exporter) upon presentation of documents that meet the conditions stipulated in the L/C. Letters of credit are payable either at sight (upon presentation of documents) or at a specified future date. The typical documentation required under an L/C includes a draft (sight or time), a commercial invoice, and a bill of lading. Depending upon the agreement, product, or country, other documents (such as a certificate of origin, inspection certificate, packing list, or insurance certificate) might be required. The three most common L/C documents are as follows.

Draft. Also known as a **bill of exchange**, a draft (introduced earlier) is an unconditional promise drawn by one party, usually the exporter, requesting the importer to pay the face amount of the draft at sight or at a specified future date. If the draft is drawn at sight,

Exhibit 19.3 Documentary Credit Procedure

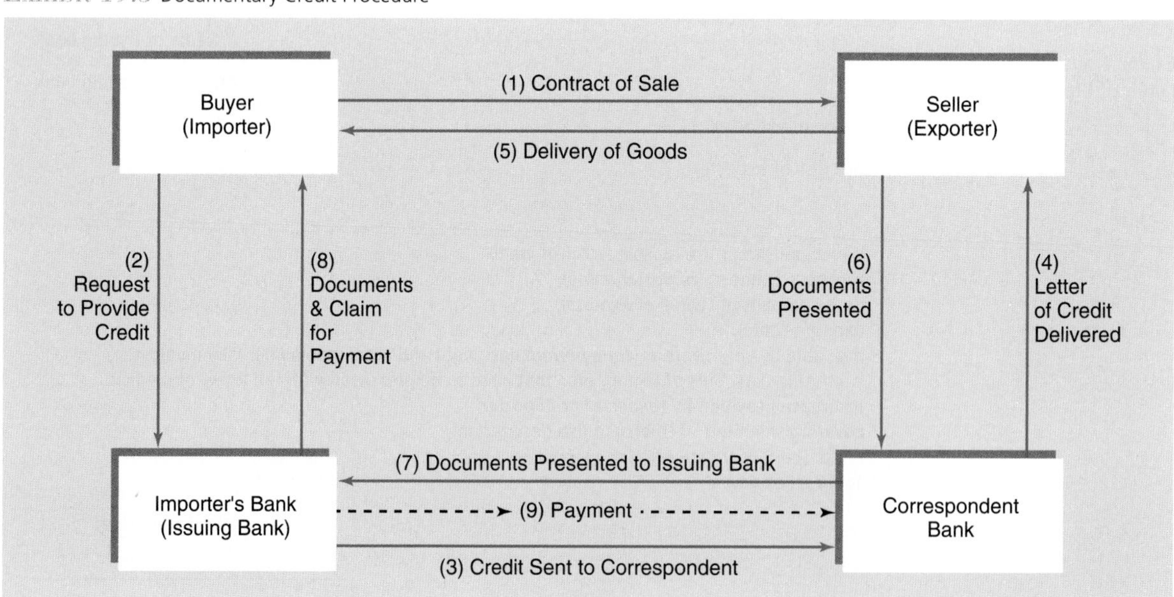

it is payable upon presentation of documents. If it is payable at a specified future date (a time draft) and is accepted by the importer, it is known as a trade acceptance. A **banker's acceptance** is a time draft drawn on and accepted by a bank. When presented under an L/C, the draft represents the exporter's formal demand for payment. The time period, or **tenor**, of most time drafts is usually anywhere from 30 to 180 days.

Bill of Lading. The key document in an international shipment under an L/C is the **bill of lading (B/L)**. It serves as a receipt for shipment and a summary of freight charges; most importantly, it conveys title to the merchandise. If the merchandise is to be shipped by boat, the carrier will issue what is known as an **ocean bill of lading.** When the merchandise is shipped by air, the carrier will issue an **airway bill**. The carrier presents the bill to the exporter (shipper), who in turn presents it to the bank along with the other required documents.

A significant feature of a B/L is its negotiability. A straight B/L is consigned directly to the importer. Since it does not represent title to the merchandise, the importer does not need it to pick up the merchandise. When a B/L is made out to order, however, it is said to be in negotiable form. The exporter normally endorses the B/L to the bank once payment is received from the bank.

The bank will not endorse the B/L over to the importer until payment has been made. The importer needs the original B/L to pick up the merchandise. With a **negotiable B/L**, title passes to the holder of the endorsed B/L. Because a negotiable B/L grants title to the holder, banks can take the merchandise as collateral. A B/L usually includes the following provisions:

- A description of the merchandise
- Identification marks on the merchandise
- Evidence of loading (receiving) ports
- Name of the exporter (shipper)
- Name of the importer
- Status of freight charges (prepaid or collect)
- Date of shipment

Commercial Invoice. The exporter's (seller's) description of the merchandise being sold to the buyer is the **commercial invoice**, which normally contains the following information:

- Name and address of seller
- Name and address of buyer
- Date
- Terms of payment
- Price, including freight, handling, and insurance if applicable
- Quantity, weight, packaging, etc.
- Shipping information

Under an L/C shipment, the description of the merchandise outlined in the invoice must correspond exactly to that contained in the L/C.

Variations of the L/C. There are several variations of the L/C that are useful in financing trade. A **standby letter of credit** can be used to guarantee invoice payments to a supplier. It promises to pay the beneficiary if the buyer fails to pay as agreed. Internationally, standby L/Cs often are used with government-related contracts and serve as bid bonds, performance bonds, or advance payment guarantees. In an international or domestic trade transaction, the seller will agree to ship to the buyer on standard open account terms as long as the buyer provides a standby L/C for a specified amount and term. As long as the buyer pays the seller as agreed, the standby L/C is never funded. However, if the buyer fails to pay, the exporter may present documents under the L/C and request payment from the bank. The buyer's bank is essentially guaranteeing that the buyer will make payment to the seller.

A **transferable letter of credit** is a variation of the standard commercial L/C that allows the first beneficiary to transfer all or a part of the original L/C to a third party. The new beneficiary has the same rights and protection as the original beneficiary. This type of L/C is used extensively by brokers, who are not the actual suppliers.

EXAMPLE

The broker asks the foreign buyer to issue an L/C for $100,000 in his favor. The L/C must contain a clause stating that the L/C is transferable. The broker has located an end supplier who will provide the product for $80,000, but requests payment in advance from the broker. With a transferable L/C, the broker can transfer $80,000 of the original L/C to the end supplier under the same terms and conditions, except for the amount, the latest shipment date, the invoice, and the period of validity. When the end supplier ships the product, it presents its documents to the bank. When the bank pays the L/C, $80,000 is paid to the end supplier and $20,000 goes to the broker. In effect, the broker has utilized the credit of the buyer to finance the entire transaction.

Another type of L/C is the **assignment of proceeds**. In this case, the original beneficiary of the L/C pledges (or assigns) the proceeds under an L/C to the end supplier. The end supplier has assurance from the bank that if and when documents are presented in compliance with the terms of the L/C, the bank will pay the end supplier according to the assignment instructions. This assignment is valid only if the beneficiary presents documents that comply with the L/C. The end supplier must recognize that the issuing bank is under no obligation to pay the end supplier if the original beneficiary never ships the goods or fails to comply with the terms of the L/C.

Banker's Acceptance

Introduced earlier, a banker's acceptance (shown in Exhibit 19.4) is a bill of exchange, or time draft, drawn on and accepted by a bank. It is the accepting bank's obligation to pay the holder of the draft at maturity.

In the first step in creating a banker's acceptance, the importer orders goods from the exporter. The importer then requests its local bank to issue an L/C on its behalf. The L/C will allow the exporter to draw a time draft on the bank in payment for the exported goods. The exporter presents the time draft along with shipping documents to its local bank, and the exporter's bank sends the time draft along with shipping documents to the importer's bank. The importer's bank accepts the draft, thereby creating the banker's acceptance. If the exporter does not want to wait until the specified date to receive payment, it can request that the banker's acceptance be sold in the money market. By doing so, the exporter will receive less funds from the sale of the banker's acceptance than if it had waited to receive payment. This discount reflects the time value of money.

A money market investor may be willing to buy the banker's acceptance at a discount and hold it until payment is due. This investor will then receive full payment be-

Exhibit 19.4
Banker's Acceptance

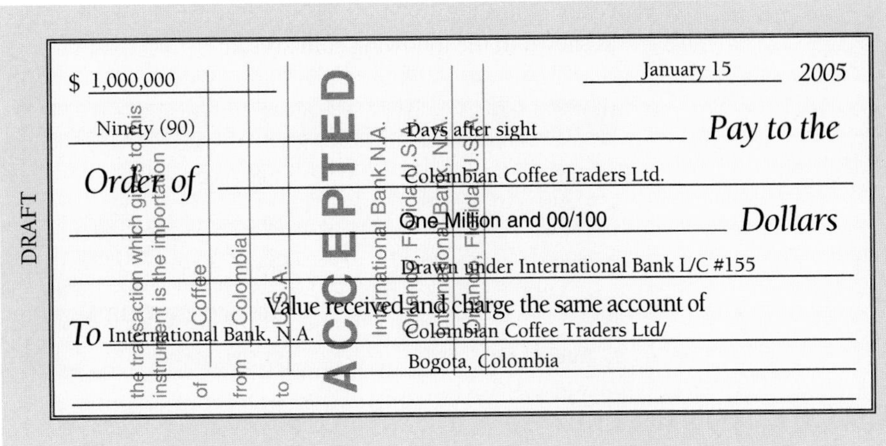

DRAFT

$ 1,000,000 January 15 2005

Ninety (90) Days after sight Pay to the

Order of Colombian Coffee Traders Ltd.

One Million and 00/100 Dollars

Drawn under International Bank L/C #155

Value received and charge the same account of

To International Bank, N.A. Colombian Coffee Traders Ltd/

Bogota, Colombia

the transaction which gives rise to this instrument is the importation of Coffee from Colombia to U.S.A.

ACCEPTED

International Bank N.A. Orlando, Florida U.S.A.

International Bank, N.A. Orlando, Florida U.S.A.

cause the banker's acceptance represents a future claim on funds of the bank represented by the acceptance. The bank will make full payment at the date specified because it expects to receive this amount plus an additional fee from the importer.

If the exporter holds the acceptance until maturity, it provides the financing for the importer as it does with accounts receivable financing. In this case, the key difference between a banker's acceptance and accounts receivable financing is that a banker's acceptance guarantees payment to the exporter by a bank. If the exporter sells the banker's acceptance in the secondary market, however, it is no longer providing the financing for the importer. The holder of the banker's acceptance is financing instead.

A banker's acceptance can be beneficial to the exporter, importer, and issuing bank. The exporter does not need to worry about the credit risk of the importer and can therefore penetrate new foreign markets without concern about the credit risk of potential customers. In addition, the exporter faces little exposure to political risk or to exchange controls imposed by a government because banks normally are allowed to meet their payment commitments even if controls are imposed. In contrast, controls could prevent an importer from paying, so without a banker's acceptance, an exporter might not receive payment even though the importer is willing to pay. Finally, the exporter can sell the banker's acceptance at a discount before payment is due and thus obtain funds up front from the issuing bank.

The importer benefits from a banker's acceptance by obtaining greater access to foreign markets when purchasing supplies and other products. Without banker's acceptances, exporters may be unwilling to accept the credit risk of importers. In addition, due to the documents presented along with the acceptance, the importer is assured that goods have been shipped. Even though the importer has not paid in advance, this assurance is valuable because it lets the importer know if and when supplies and other products will arrive. Finally, because the banker's acceptance allows the importer to pay at a later date, the importer's payment is financed until the maturity date of the banker's acceptance. Without an acceptance, the importer would likely be forced to pay in advance, thereby tying up funds.

The bank accepting the drafts benefits in that it earns a commission for creating an acceptance. The commission that the bank charges the customer reflects the customer's perceived creditworthiness. The interest rate charged the customer, commonly referred to as the **all-in-rate,** consists of the discount rate plus the acceptance commission. In general, the all-in-rate for acceptance financing is lower than prime-based borrowings, as shown in the following comparison:

	Loan	Acceptance
Amount:	$1,000,000	$1,000,000
Term:	180 days	180 days
Rate:	Prime + 1.5%	BA rate + 1.5%
	10.0% + 1.5% = 11.5%	7.60% + 1.5% = 9.10%
Interest cost:	$57,500	$45,500

In this case, the interest savings for a six-month period is $12,000. Since the banker's acceptance is a marketable instrument with an active secondary market, the rates on acceptances usually fall between the rates on short-term Treasury bills and the rates on commercial paper. Investors are usually willing to purchase acceptances as an investment because of their yield, safety, and liquidity. When a bank creates, accepts, and sells the acceptance, it is actually using the investor's money to finance the bank's customer. As a result, the bank has created an asset at one price, sold it at another, and retained a commission (spread) as its fee.

Banker's acceptance financing can also be arranged through the refinancing of a sight letter of credit. In this case, the beneficiary of the L/C (the exporter) may insist on payment at sight. The bank arranges to finance the payment of the sight L/C under a separate acceptance-financing agreement. The importer (borrower) simply draws drafts upon the bank, which in turn accepts and discounts the drafts. The proceeds are used to pay the exporter. At maturity, the importer is responsible for repayment to the bank.

Acceptance financing can also be arranged without the use of an L/C under a separate acceptance agreement. Similar to a regular loan agreement, it stipulates the terms and conditions under which the bank is prepared to finance the borrower using acceptances instead of promissory notes. As long as the acceptances meet one of the underlying transaction requirements, the bank and borrower can utilize banker's acceptances as an alternative financing mechanism. The life cycle of a banker's acceptance is illustrated in Exhibit 19.5.

Working Capital Financing

As just explained, a banker's acceptance can allow an exporter to receive funds immediately, yet allow an importer to delay its payment until a future date. The bank may even provide short-term loans beyond the banker's acceptance period. In the case of an importer, the purchase from overseas usually represents the acquisition of inventory. The loan finances the working capital cycle that begins with the purchase of inventory and continues with the sale of the goods, creation of an account receivable, and conversion to cash. With an exporter, the short-term loan might finance the manufacture of the merchandise destined for export (pre-export financing) or the time period from when the sale is made until payment is received from the buyer. For example, the firm may have imported foreign beer, which it plans to distribute to grocery and liquor stores. The bank can not only provide a letter of credit for trade finance, but it can also finance the importer's cost from the time of distribution and collection of payment.

Exhibit 19.5 Life Cycle of a Typical Banker's Acceptance (B/A)

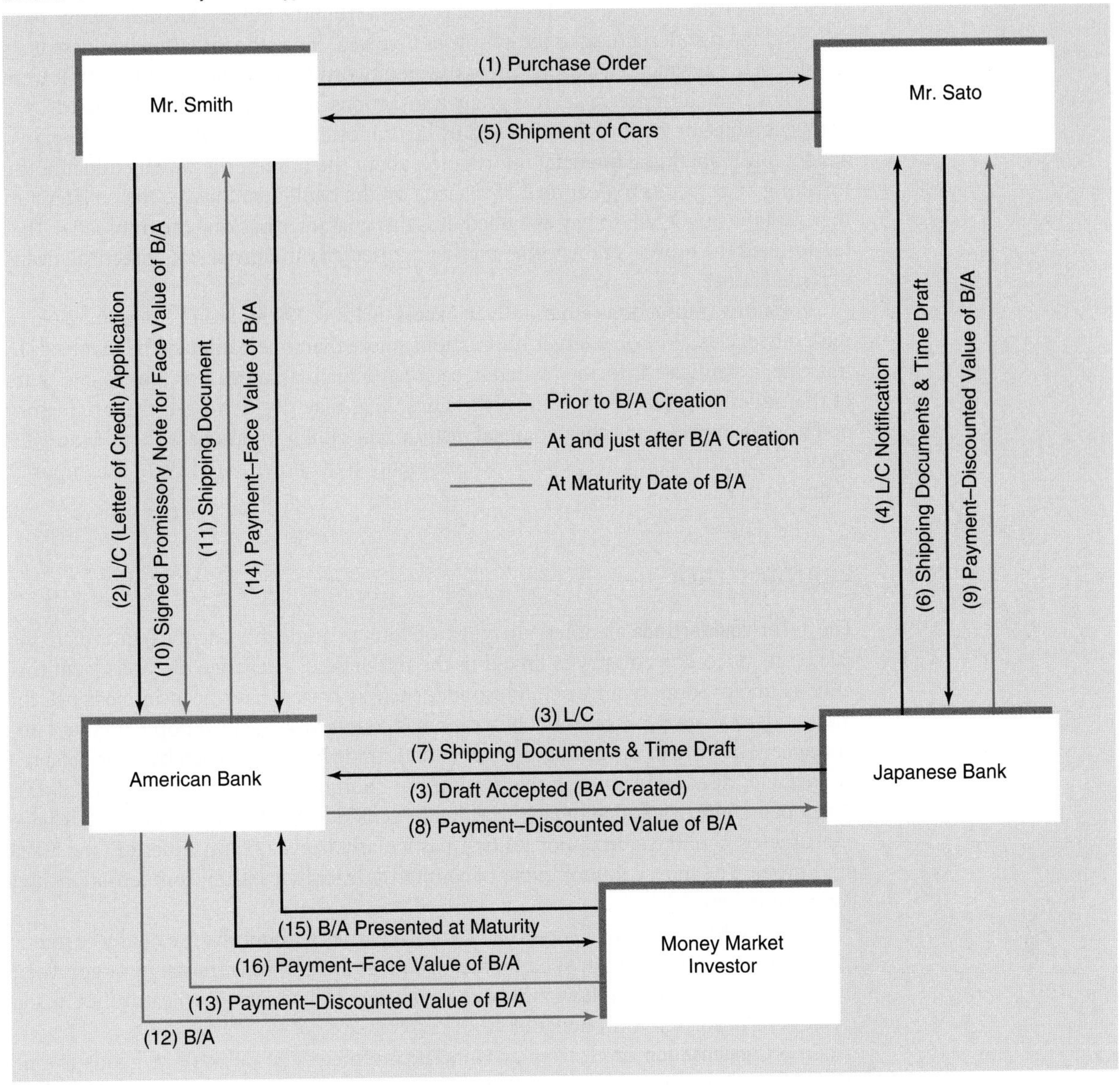

Mr. Smith
(1) Purchase Order
Mr. Sato
(5) Shipment of Cars
(2) L/C (Letter of Credit) Application
(10) Signed Promissory Note for Face Value of B/A
(11) Shipping Document
(14) Payment–Face Value of B/A
Prior to B/A Creation
At and just after B/A Creation
At Maturity Date of B/A
(4) L/C Notification
(6) Shipping Documents & Time Draft
(9) Payment–Discounted Value of B/A
(3) L/C
American Bank
(7) Shipping Documents & Time Draft
Japanese Bank
(3) Draft Accepted (BA Created)
(8) Payment–Discounted Value of B/A
(15) B/A Presented at Maturity
Money Market Investor
(16) Payment–Face Value of B/A
(13) Payment–Discounted Value of B/A
(12) B/A

Medium-Term Capital Goods Financing (Forfaiting)

Because capital goods are often quite expensive, an importer may not be able to make payment on the goods within a short time period. Thus, longer-term financing may be required here. The exporter might be able to provide financing for the importer but may not desire to do so, since the financing may extend over several years. In this case, a type of trade finance known as **forfaiting** could be used. Forfaiting refers to the purchase of financial obligations, such as bills of exchange or promissory notes, without recourse to the original holder, usually the exporter. In a forfait transaction, the importer issues a promissory note to pay the exporter for the imported goods over a period that generally ranges from three to seven years. The exporter then sells the notes, without recourse, to the forfaiting bank.

In some respects, forfaiting is similar to factoring, in that the forfaiter (or factor) assumes responsibility for the collection of payment from the buyer, the underlying credit risk, and the risk pertaining to the countries involved. Since the forfaiting bank assumes the risk of nonpayment, it should assess the creditworthiness of the importer as if it were extending a medium-term loan. Forfait transactions normally are collateralized by a bank guarantee or letter of credit issued by the importer's bank for the term of the transaction. Since obtaining financial information about the importer is usually difficult, the forfaiting bank places a great deal of reliance on the bank guarantee as the collateral in the event the buyer fails to pay as agreed. It is this guarantee backing the transaction that has fostered the growth of the forfait market, particularly in Europe, as a practical means of trade finance.

Forfaiting transactions are usually in excess of $500,000 and can be denominated in most currencies. For some larger transactions, more than one bank may be involved. In this case, a syndicate is formed wherein each participant assumes a proportionate share of the underlying risk and profit. A forfaiting firm may decide to sell the promissory notes of the importer to other financial institutions willing to purchase them. However, the forfaiting firm is still responsible for payment on the notes in the event the importer is unable to pay.

Countertrade

The term **countertrade** denotes all types of foreign trade transactions in which the sale of goods to one country is linked to the purchase or exchange of goods from that same country. Some types of countertrade, such as barter, have been in existence for thousands of years. Only recently, however, has countertrade gained popularity and importance. The growth in various types of countertrade has been fueled by large balance-of-payment disequilibriums, foreign currency shortages, the debt problems of less developed countries and stagnant worldwide demand. As a result, many MNCs have encountered countertrade opportunities, particularly in Asia, Latin America, and Eastern Europe. The most common types of countertrade include barter, compensation, and counterpurchase.

Barter is the exchange of goods between two parties without the use of any currency as a medium of exchange. Most barter arrangements are one-time transactions governed by one contract. An example would be the exchange of 100 tons of wheat from Canada for 20 tons of shrimp from Ecuador.

In a **compensation** or clearing-account arrangement, the delivery of goods to one party is compensated for by the seller's buying back a certain amount of the product from that same party. The transaction is governed by one contract, and the value of the goods is expressed in monetary terms. The buy-back arrangement could be for a fraction of the original sale (**partial compensation**) or more than 100 percent of the original sale (**full compensation**). An example of compensation would be the sale of phosphate from Morocco to France in exchange for purchasing a certain percentage of fertilizer. In some countries, this is also referred to as an industrial cooperation arrangement. Such arrangements often involve the construction of large projects, such as power plants, in exchange for the purchase of the project's output over an extended period of time. For example, Brazil sold a hydroelectric plant to Argentina and in exchange purchased a percentage of the plant's output under a long-term contract.

The term **counterpurchase** denotes the exchange of goods between two parties under two distinct contracts expressed in monetary terms. Delivery and payment of both goods are technically separate transactions.

Despite the economic inefficiencies of countertrade, it has become much more important in recent years. The primary participants are governments and MNCs, with assistance provided by specialists in the field, such as attorneys, financial institutions, and trading companies. The transactions are usually large and very complex. Many variations of countertrade exist, and the terminology used by the various market participants is still forming as the countertrade market continues to develop.

Agencies That Motivate International Trade

Due to the inherent risks of international trade, government institutions and the private sector offer various forms of export credit, export finance, and guarantee programs to reduce risk and stimulate foreign trade.

Three prominent agencies provide these services in the United States:

- Export-Import Bank of the United States (Ex-Imbank)
- Private Export Funding Corporation (PEFCO)
- Overseas Private Investment Corporation (OPIC)

Each of these agencies is described in turn.

http://

Visit http://www.exim.gov, the site of the Export-Import Bank of the United States, for interest rates charged by an export credit agency.

Export-Import Bank of the United States

The Export-Import Bank was established in 1934 with the original goal of facilitating Soviet-American trade. Its mission today is to finance and facilitate the export of American goods and services and maintain the competitiveness of American companies in overseas markets. It operates as an independent agency of the U.S. government and, as such, carries the full faith and credit of the United States.

MANAGING FOR VALUE

Engelhard's Selection of a Bank to Service Export Collections

Engelhard Corp. is a large chemical manufacturer in New Jersey. It is one of the largest exporters in the United States and frequently uses banks to facilitate its trade. On a typical day, it may have 15 to 20 letters of credit (L/Cs). As it searched for a bank to facilitate its international trade financing, Engelhard established a set of requirements that the bank must meet:

- The bank must provide a workstation where L/Cs are stored as separate records.
- The bank must be capable of electronically transferring L/C information to various sites and to the workstation.
- The workstation must be accessible so that the firm can check payment information on a timely basis.
- The workstation must be able to retrieve L/C information pertaining to Engelhard's business with any firm over any particular period.

Several banks bid for Engelhard's business and assured the company that they could provide the services needed. As a result of Engelhard's efforts to communicate its needs, it now has electronic access to much more information and can easily monitor its trade financing positions with each of its importers. This allows it to make more informed decisions about the terms of trade that it negotiates with each customer and thus enables it to maximize its value.

The Ex-Imbank's programs are typically designed to encourage the private sector to finance export trade by assuming some of the underlying credit risk and providing direct financing to foreign importers when private lenders are unwilling to do so. To satisfy these objectives, the Ex-Imbank offers programs that are classified as (1) guarantees, (2) loans, (3) bank insurance, and (4) export credit insurance.

Guarantee Programs. The two most widely used guarantee programs are the **Working Capital Guarantee Program** and the **Medium-Term Guarantee Program**. The Working Capital Guarantee Program encourages commercial banks to extend short-term export financing to eligible exporters by providing a comprehensive guarantee that covers 90 to 100 percent of the loan's principal and interest. This guarantee protects the lender against the risk of default by the exporter. It does not protect the exporter against the risk of nonpayment by the foreign buyer. The loans are fully collateralized by export receivables and export inventory and require the payment of guarantee fees to the Ex-Imbank. The export receivables are usually supported with export credit insurance or a letter of credit.

The Guarantee Program encourages commercial lenders to finance the sale of U.S. capital equipment and services to approved foreign buyers. The Ex-Imbank guarantees 100 perent of the loan's principal and interest. The financed amount cannot exceed 85 percent of the contract price. This program is designed to finance products sold on a medium-term basis, with repayment terms of generally between one and five years. The guarantee fees paid to the Ex-Imbank are determined by the repayment terms and the buyer's risk. The Ex-Imbank now offers a leasing program to finance capital equipment and related services.

http://

The website http://www.bloomberg.com has a section on international markets that offers quotations of short-term foreign interest rates. This information is useful to an MNC that needs to finance its short-term liquidity needs.

Loan Programs. Two of the most popular loan programs are the **Direct Loan Program** and the **Project Finance Loan Program**. Under the Direct Loan Program, Ex-Imbank offers fixed rate loans directly to the foreign buyer to purchase U.S. capital equipment and services on a medium-term or long-term basis. The total financed amount cannot exceed 85 percent of the contract price. Repayment terms depend upon the amount but are typically one to five years for medium-term transactions and seven to ten years for long-term transactions. The Ex-Imbank's lending rates are generally below market rates.

The Project Finance Loan Program allows banks, the Ex-Imbank, or a combination of both to extend long-term financing for capital equipment and related services for major projects. These are typically large infrastructure projects, such as power generation projects, whose repayment depends on project cash flow. Major U.S. corporations are often involved in these types of projects. The program typically requires a 15 percent cash payment by the foreign buyer and allows for guarantees of up to 85 percent of the contract amount. The fees and interest rates vary depending on the project risk.

Bank Insurance Programs. The Ex-Imbank offers several insurance policies to banks. The most widely used is the **Bank Letter of Credit Policy**. This policy enables banks to confirm letters of credit issued by foreign banks supporting a purchase of U.S. exports. Without this insurance, some banks would not be willing to assume the underlying commercial and political risk associated with confirming an L/C. The banks are insured up to 100 percent for sovereign (government) banks and 95 percent for all other banks. The insurance premium is based on the type of buyer, repayment term, and country.

The **Financial Institution Buyer Credit Policy** is issued in the name of the bank. This policy provides insurance coverage for loans by banks to foreign buyers on a short-term basis. A variety of short-term and medium-term insurance policies are available to exporters, banks, and other eligible applicants. Basically, all the policies provide insurance protection against the risk of nonpayment by foreign buyers. If the foreign buyer fails to pay the exporter because of commercial reasons such as cash flow problems or insolvency, the Ex-Imbank will reimburse the exporter between 90 and 100 percent of the insured amount, depending on the type of policy and buyer.

If the loss is due to political factors, such as foreign exchange controls or war, the Ex-Imbank will reimburse the exporter for 100 percent of the insured amount. Exporters can use the insurance policies as a marketing tool because the insurance enables them to offer more competitive terms while protecting them against the risk of nonpayment. An exporter can also use the insurance policy as a financing tool by assigning the proceeds of the policy to a bank as collateral. Certain restrictions may apply to particular countries, depending on the Ex-Imbank's experience, as well as existing economic and political conditions.

Export Credit Insurance. The **Small Business Policy** provides enhanced coverage to new exporters and small businesses. The policy insures short-term credit sales (under 180 days) to approved foreign buyers. In addition to providing 95 percent coverage against commercial risk defaults and 100 percent against political risk, the policy offers lower premiums and no annual commercial risk loss deductible. The exporter can assign the policy to a bank as collateral.

The **Umbrella Policy** operates in a slightly different manner. The policy itself is issued to an "administrator," such as a bank, trading company, insurance broker, or government agency. The policyholder administers the policy for multiple exporters and relieves the exporters of the administrative responsibilities associated with the policy. The short-term insurance protection is similar to that provided by the Small Business Policy and does not have a commercial risk deductible. The proceeds of the policy may be assigned to a bank for financing purposes.

The **Multi-Buyer Policy** is used primarily by experienced exporters. It provides insurance coverage on short-term export sales to many different buyers. Premiums are based on an exporter's sales profile, credit history, terms of repayment, country, and other factors. Based on the exporter's experience and the buyer's creditworthiness, the Ex-Imbank may grant the exporter authority to preapprove specific buyers up to a certain limit.

The **Single-Buyer Policy** allows an exporter to selectively insure certain short-term transactions to preapproved buyers. Premiums are based on repayment terms and transaction risk. There is also a Medium-Term Policy to cover sales to a single buyer for terms of between one and five years.

The Ex-Imbank has also entered into partnership arrangements with more than 30 states to disseminate government trade promotion services to a broader audience. For example, in Florida, the Florida Export Finance Corp. provides export credit insurance consulting, trade finance, and guarantees to exporters based in Florida.

Several private insurance carriers, such as AIG, also provide various types of insurance policies that may be used to mitigate risk. They are frequently employed when Ex-Imbank insurance is not available or desirable.

Private Export Funding Corporation (PEFCO)

PEFCO, a private corporation, is owned by a consortium of commercial banks and industrial companies. In cooperation with the Ex-Imbank, PEFCO provides medium- and long-term fixed rate financing to foreign buyers. The Ex-Imbank guarantees all export loans made by PEFCO. Most PEFCO loans are to finance large projects, such as aircraft and power generation equipment, and as a result have very long terms (5 to 25 years). Since commercial banks usually do not extend such long terms, PEFCO fills a void in the market. PEFCO also serves as a secondary market buyer of export loans originated by U.S. banks. PEFCO raises its funds in the capital markets through the issuance of long-term bonds. These bonds are readily marketable since they are in effect secured by Ex-Imbank-guaranteed loans.

Overseas Private Investment Corporation (OPIC)

OPIC, formed in 1971, is a self-sustaining federal agency responsible for insuring direct U.S. investments in foreign countries against the risks of currency inconvertibility, expropriation, and other political risks. Through the direct loan or guaranty program, OPIC will provide medium- to long-term financing to U.S. investors undertaking an overseas venture. In addition to the general insurance and finance programs, OPIC offers specific types of coverage for exporters bidding on or performing foreign contracts. American contractors can insure themselves against contractual disputes and even the wrongful calling of standby letters of credit.

SUMMARY

- The common methods of payment for international trade are (1) prepayment (before goods are sent), (2) letters of credit, (3) drafts, (4) consignment, and (5) open account.
- The most popular methods of financing international trade are (1) accounts receivable financing, (2) factoring, (3) letters of credit, (4) banker's acceptances, (5) working capital financing, (6) medium-term capital goods financing (forfaiting), and (7) countertrade.
- The major agencies that facilitate international trade with export insurance and/or loan programs are (1) Export-Import Bank, (2) Private Export Funding Corporation, and (3) Overseas Private Investment Corporation.

POINT COUNTER-POINT

Do Agencies That Facilitate International Trade Prevent Free Trade?

Point Yes. The Export-Import Bank of the United States provides many programs to help U.S. exporters conduct international trade. The government is essentially subsidizing the exports. Governments in other countries have various programs as well. Thus, some countries may have a trade advantage because their exporters are subsidized in various ways. These subsidies distort the notion of free trade.

Counter-Point No. It is natural for any government to facilitate exporting for relatively inexperienced exporting firms. All governments provide a variety of services for their firms, including public services, and tax breaks for producing products that are ultimately exported. There is a difference between facilitating the exporting process and protecting an industry from foreign competition. The protection of an industry violates the notion of free trade, but facilitating the exporting process does not.

Who Is Correct? Use InfoTrac or some other search engine to learn more about this issue. Which argument do you support? Offer your own opinion on this issue.

SELF TEST

Answers are provided in Appendix A at the back of the text.

1. Explain why so many international transactions require international trade credit facilitated by commercial banks.
2. Explain the difference in the risk to the exporter between accounts receivable financing and factoring.
3. Explain how the Export-Import Bank can encourage U.S. firms to export to less developed countries where there is political risk.

QUESTIONS AND APPLICATIONS

1. **Banker's Acceptances.**

   a. Describe how foreign trade would be affected if banks did not provide trade-related services.

   b. How can a banker's acceptance be beneficial to an exporter, an importer, and a bank?

2. **Export Financing.**

   a. Why would an exporter provide financing for an importer?

   b. Is there much risk in this activity? Explain.

3. **Role of Factors.**

   a. What is the role of a factor in international trade transactions?

4. **Export-Import Bank.**

   a. What is the role today of the Export-Import Bank of the United States?

   b. Describe the Direct Loan Program administered by the Export-Import Bank.

5. **Bills of Lading.** What are bills of lading, and how do they facilitate international trade transactions?
6. **Forfaiting.** What is forfaiting? Specify the type of traded goods for which forfaiting is applied.
7. **PEFCO.** Briefly describe the role of the Private Export Funding Corporation (PEFCO).
8. **Government Programs.** This chapter described many forms of government insurance and guarantee programs. What motivates a government to establish so many programs?
9. **Countertrade.** What is countertrade?
10. **Impact of September 11.** Every quarter, Bronx Co. ships computer chips to a firm in central Asia. It has not used any trade financing because the importing firm always pays its bill in a timely manner upon receipt of the computer chips. After the September 11, 2001 terrorist attack on the United States, Bronx reconsidered whether it should use some form of trade financing that would ensure that it would be paid for its exports upon delivery. Offer a suggestion to Bronx Co. on how it could achieve its goal.
11. **Working Capital Guarantee Program.** Briefly describe the Working Capital Guarantee Program administered by the Export-Import Bank.
12. **Small Business Policy.** Describe the Small Business Policy.
13. **OPIC.** Describe the role of the Overseas Private Investment Corporation (OPIC).

ADVANCED QUESTIONS

14. **Letters of Credit.** Ocean Traders of North America is a firm based in Mobile, Alabama, that specializes in seafood exports and commonly uses letters of credit (L/Cs) to ensure payment. It recently experienced a problem, however. Ocean Traders had an irrevocable L/C issued by a Russian bank to ensure that it would receive payment upon shipment of 16,000 tons of fish to a Russian firm. This bank backed out of its obligation, however, stating that it was not authorized to guarantee commercial transactions.

    a. Explain how an irrevocable L/C would normally facilitate the business transaction between the Russian importer and Ocean Traders of North America (the U.S. exporter).

    b. Explain how the cancellation of the L/C could create a trade crisis between the U.S. and Russian firms.

c. Why do you think situations like this (the cancellation of the L/C) are rare in industrialized countries?

d. Can you think of any alternative strategy that the U.S. exporter could have used to protect itself better when dealing with a Russian importer?

INTERNET APPLICATION

15. **Trade and the Import-Export Bank.** The website of the Export-Import Bank of the United States offers information about trade financing. Its address is **http://www.exim.gov**. Summarize what the Ex-Imbank does to facilitate trade by businesses.

DISCUSSION IN THE BOARDROOM

This exercise can be found in Appendix E at the back of this textbook.

RUNNING YOUR OWN MNC

This exercise can be found on the Xtra! website at **http://maduraxtra.swlearning.com**.

BLADES, INC. CASE

Assessment of International Trade Financing in Thailand

Blades, Inc., has recently decided to establish a subsidiary in Thailand to produce "Speedos," Blades' primary roller blade product. In establishing the subsidiary in Thailand, Blades was motivated by the high growth potential of the Thai roller blade market. Furthermore, Blades has decided to establish a subsidiary, as opposed to acquiring an existing Thai roller blade manufacturer for sale, in order to maintain its flexibility and control over the operations in Thailand. Moreover, Blades has decided to issue yen-denominated notes to partially finance the cost of establishing the subsidiary. Blades has decided to issue notes denominated in yen instead of baht to avoid the high effective interest rates associated with the baht-denominated notes.

Currently, Blades plans to sell all roller blades manufactured in Thailand to retailers in Thailand. Furthermore, Blades plans to purchase all components for roller blades manufactured in Thailand from Thai suppliers. Similarly, all of Blades' roller blades manufactured in the United States will be sold to retailers in the United States and all components needed for Blades' U.S. production will be purchased from suppliers in the United States. Consequently, Blades will have no exports and imports once the plant in Thailand is operational, which is expected to occur early next year.

Construction of the plant in Thailand has already begun, and Blades is currently in the process of purchasing the machinery necessary to produce Speedos. Besides these activities, Ben Holt, Blades' chief financial officer (CFO), has been actively lining up suppliers of the needed rubber and plastic components in Thailand and identifying Thai customers, which will consist of various sports product retailers in Thailand.

Although Holt has been successful in locating both interested suppliers and interested customers, he is discovering that he has neglected certain precautions for operating a subsidiary in Thailand. First, although Blades is relatively well known in the United States, it is not recognized internationally. Consequently, the suppliers Blades would like to use in Thailand are not familiar with the firm and have no information about its reputation. Moreover, Blades' previous activities in Thailand were restricted to the export of a fixed number of Speedos annually to one customer, a Thai retailer called Entertainment Products. Holt has little information about the potential Thai customers that would buy the roller blades produced by the new plant. He is aware, however, that although letters of credit (L/Cs) and drafts are usually employed for exporting purposes, these instruments are also used for trade within a country between relatively unknown parties.

Of the various potential customers Blades has identified in Thailand, four retailers of sports products appear particularly interested. Because Blades is not familiar with these firms and their reputations, it would like to receive payment from them as soon as possible. Ideally, Blades would like its customers to prepay for their purchases, as this would involve the least risk for Blades. Unfortunately, none of the four potential customers have agreed to a prepayment arrangement. In fact, one potential customer, Cool Runnings, Inc., insists on an open account transaction. Payment terms in Thailand for purchases of this type are typically "net 60," indicating that payment for the roller blades would be due approximately two months after a purchase was made. Two of the remaining three retailers, Sports Equipment, Inc., and Major Leagues, Inc., have indicated that they would also prefer an open account transaction; however, both of these retailers have indicated that their banks would act as intermediaries for a time draft. The fourth retailer, Sports Gear, Inc., is indifferent as to the specific payment method but has indicated to Blades that it finds a prepayment arrangement unacceptable.

Blades also needs a suitable arrangement with its various potential suppliers of rubber and plastic components in Thailand. Because Blades' financing of the Thai subsidiary involved a U.S. bank, it has virtually no contacts in the Thai banking system. Because Blades is relatively unknown in Thailand, Thai suppliers have indicated that they would prefer prepayment or at least a guarantee from a Thai bank that Blades will be able to make payment within 30 days of purchase. Blades does not currently have accounts receivable in Thailand. It does, however, have accounts receivable in the United States resulting from its U.S. sales.

Ben Holt would like to please Blades' Thai customers and suppliers in order to establish strong business relationships in Thailand. However, he is worried that Blades may be at a disadvantage if it accepts all of the Thai firms' demands. Consequently, he has asked you, a financial analyst for Blades, Inc., to provide him with some guidance regarding international trade financing. Specifically, Holt has asked you to answer the following questions for him:

1. Assuming that banks in Thailand issue a time draft on behalf of Sports Equipment, Inc., and Major Leagues, Inc., would Blades receive payment for its roller blades before it delivers them? Do the banks issuing the time drafts guarantee payment on behalf of the Thai retailers if they default on the payment?
2. What payment method should Blades suggest to Sports Gear, Inc.? Substantiate your answer.
3. What organization could Blades contact in order to insure its sales to the Thai retailers? What type of insurance does this organization provide?
4. How could Blades use accounts receivable financing or factoring, considering that it does not currently have accounts receivable in Thailand? If Blades uses a Thai bank to obtain this financing, how do you think the fact that Blades does not have receivables in Thailand would affect the terms of the financing?
5. Assuming that Blades is unable to locate a Thai bank that is willing to issue an L/C on Blades' behalf, can you think of a way Blades could utilize its bank in the United States to effectively obtain an L/C from a Thai bank?
6. What organizations could Blades contact to obtain working capital financing? If Blades is unable to obtain working capital financing from these organizations, what are its other options to finance its working capital needs in Thailand?

SMALL BUSINESS DILEMMA

Ensuring Payment for Products Exported by the Sports Exports Company

The Sports Exports Company produces footballs and exports them to a distributor in the United Kingdom. It typically sends footballs in bulk and then receives payment after the distributor receives the shipment. The business relationship with the distributor is based on trust. Although the relationship has worked thus far, Jim Logan (owner of the Sports Exports Company) is concerned about the possibility that the distributor will not make its payment.

1. How could Jim use a letter of credit to ensure that he will be paid for the products he exports?
2. Jim has discussed the possibility of expanding his export business through a second sporting goods distributor in the United Kingdom; this second distributor would cover a different territory than the first distributor. The second distributor is only willing to engage in a consignment arrangement when selling footballs to retail stores. Explain the risk to Jim beyond the typical types of risk he incurs when dealing with the first distributor. Should Jim pursue this type of business?

CHAPTER 20

Short-Term Financing

All firms make short-term financing decisions periodically. Beyond the trade financing discussed in the previous chapter, MNCs obtain short-term financing to support other operations as well. Because MNCs have access to additional sources of funds, their short-term financing decisions are more complex than those of other companies. Financial managers must understand the possible advantages and disadvantages of short-term financing with foreign currencies so that they can make short-term financing decisions that maximize the value of the MNC.

The specific objectives of this chapter are to:

- explain why MNCs consider foreign financing,
- explain how MNCs determine whether to use foreign financing, and
- illustrate the possible benefits of financing with a portfolio of currencies.

Sources of Short-Term Financing

MNC parents and their subsidiaries typically use various methods of obtaining short-term funds to satisfy their liquidity needs.

Euronotes

One method increasingly used in recent years is the issuing of **Euronotes**, or unsecured debt securities. The interest rates on these notes are based on LIBOR (the interest rate Eurobanks charge on interbank loans). Euronotes typically have maturities of one, three, or six months. Some MNCs continually roll them over as a form of intermediate-term financing. Commercial banks underwrite the notes for MNCs, and some commercial banks purchase them for their own investment portfolios.

Euro-Commercial Paper

In addition to Euronotes, MNCs also issue **Euro-commercial paper** to obtain short-term financing. Dealers issue this paper for MNCs without the backing of an underwriting syndicate, so a selling price is not guaranteed to the issuers. Maturities can be tailored to the issuer's preferences. Dealers make a secondary market by offering to repurchase Euro-commercial paper before maturity.

Eurobank Loans

Direct loans from Eurobanks, which are typically utilized to maintain a relationship with Eurobanks, are another popular source of short-term funds for MNCs. If other sources of short-term funds become unavailable, MNCs rely more heavily on direct loans from Eurobanks. Most MNCs maintain credit arrangements with various banks around the world. Some MNCs have credit arrangements with more than 100 foreign and domestic banks.

Internal Financing by MNCs

Before an MNC's parent or subsidiary in need of funds searches for outside funding, it should check other subsidiaries' cash flow positions to determine whether any internal funds are available.

The Canadian subsidiary of Shreveport, Inc., has experienced strong earnings and invested a portion of the earnings locally in money market securities. Meanwhile, Shreveport's Mexican subsidiary has generated lower earnings recently but needs funding to support expansion. The U.S. parent of Shreveport can instruct the Canadian subsidiary to loan some of its excess funds to the Mexican subsidiary.

This process is especially feasible during periods when the cost of obtaining funds in the parent's home country is relatively high.

Parents of MNCs can also attempt to obtain financing from their subsidiaries by increasing the markups on supplies they send to the subsidiaries. In this case, the funds the subsidiary gives to the parent will never be returned. This method of supporting the parent can sometimes be more feasible than obtaining loans from the subsidiary because it may circumvent restrictions or taxes imposed by national governments. In some cases, though, this method itself may be restricted or limited by host governments where subsidiaries are located.

Why MNCs Consider Foreign Financing

Regardless of whether an MNC parent or subsidiary decides to obtain financing from subsidiaries or from some other source, it must also decide which currency to borrow. Even if it needs its home currency, it may prefer to borrow a foreign currency. Reasons for this preference follow.

Foreign Financing to Offset Foreign Currency Inflows

A large firm may finance in a foreign currency to offset a net receivables position in that foreign currency.

EXAMPLE

Penn, Inc., has net receivables denominated in euros and needs dollars now for liquidity purposes. It can borrow euros and convert them to U.S. dollars to obtain the needed funds. Then, the net receivables in euros will be used to pay off the loan. In this example, financing in a foreign currency reduces the firm's exposure to fluctuating exchange rates. This strategy is especially appealing if the interest rate of the foreign currency is low.

How Avon Used Foreign Financing during the Asian Crisis. During the Asian crisis in 1997 and 1998, many MNCs with Asian subsidiaries were adversely affected by the weakening of Asian currencies against the dollar. Avon Products, Inc., used various methods to reduce its economic exposure to the weak Asian currencies. Given that Avon had more cash inflows than cash outflows in Asian currencies, it used strategies that reduced the excess of cash inflows denominated in those currencies. First, it purchased more materials locally. Second, it borrowed funds locally to finance its operations so that it could use some of its cash inflows in Asian currencies to repay the debt. Third, it hired more local salespeople (rather than relying on marketing from the United States) to help sell its products locally. Fourth, it began to remit its earnings more frequently so that excess cash flows denominated in Asian currencies would not accumulate.

Foreign Financing to Reduce Costs

http://

Morgan Stanley's Economic Forum at http://www.morganstanley.com/GEFdata/digests/latest-digest.html provides analysis discussions, statistics, and forecasts related to non-U.S. economies.

Even when an MNC parent or subsidiary is not attempting to cover foreign net receivables, it may still consider borrowing foreign currencies if the interest rates on those currencies are relatively low. Since interest rates vary among currencies, the cost of borrowing can vary substantially among countries. MNCs that conduct business in countries with high interest rates incur a high cost of short-term financing if they finance in the local currency. Thus, they may consider financing with another currency that has a lower interest rate. By shaving 1 percentage point off its financing rate, an MNC can save $1 million annually on debt of $100 million. Thus, MNCs are motivated to consider various currencies when financing their operations.

Exhibit 20.1 compares short-term interest rates among countries for a given point in time. In most periods, the interest rate in Japan is relatively low, while the interest rates in many developing countries are relatively high. Countries with a high rate of inflation tend to have high interest rates.

EXAMPLE

Salem, Inc., is a U.S. firm that needs dollars to expand its U.S. operations. Assume the dollar financing rate is 9 percent, while the Japanese yen financing rate is 4 percent. Salem can borrow Japanese yen and immediately convert those yen to dollars for use. When the loan repayment is due, Salem will need to obtain Japanese yen to pay off the loan. If the value of the Japanese yen in terms of U.S. dollars has not changed since the time Salem obtained the loan, it will pay 4 percent on that loan.

Exhibit 20.1
Comparison of Interest Rates among Countries (as of February 2004)

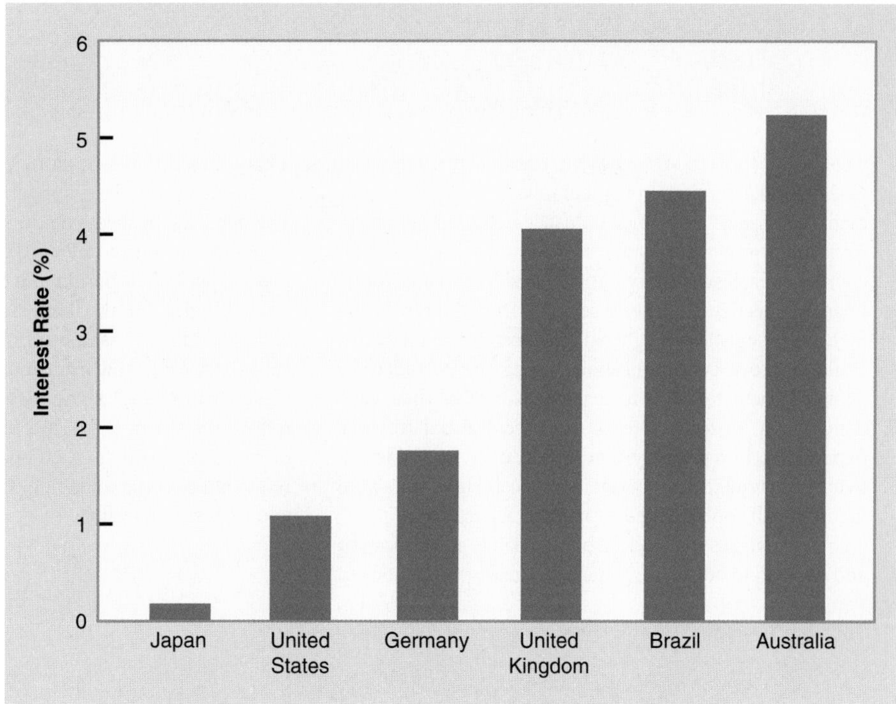

USING THE WEB

Forecasts of Interest Rates When an MNC borrows funds in a specific currency, its choice of a maturity is partially based on expectations of future interest rates in that country. Forecasts of interest rates in the near future for each country are provided at http://biz.yahoo.com/ifc/. Click on any country listed, and then click on Interest Rate Consensus. Also, click on Analysis to review the factors that could affect that country's interest rates in the near future.

Determining the Effective Financing Rate

http://

Visit http://www.bloomberg.com for the latest information from financial markets around the world.

In reality, the value of the currency borrowed will most likely change with respect to the borrower's local currency over time. The actual cost of financing by the debtor firm will depend on (1) the interest rate charged by the bank that provided the loan and (2) the movement in the borrowed currency's value over the life of the loan. Thus, the actual or "effective" financing rate may differ from the quoted interest rate. This point is illustrated in the following example.

EXAMPLE

Dearborn, Inc. (based in Michigan), obtains a one-year loan of $1,000,000 in New Zealand dollars (NZ$) at the quoted interest rate of 8 percent. When Dearborn receives the loan, it converts the New Zealand dollars to U.S. dollars to pay a supplier for materials. The exchange rate at that time is $.50 per New Zealand dollars, so the NZ$1,000,000 is converted to $500,000 (computed as NZ$1,000,000 × $.50 per NZ$ = $500,000). One year later, Dearborn pays back the loan of NZ$1,000,000 plus interest of NZ$80,000 (interest computed as 8% × NZ$1,000,000). Thus, the total

MANAGING FOR VALUE

Financing and Treasury Decisions by GeoLogistics

GeoLogistics, a U.S.-based MNC created in 1996, provides logistics services in the technology, business equipment, aerospace, and other industries. As it experienced substantial growth, it established subsidiaries in several countries. Each subsidiary initially used local banks for its financing needs, as if it were separate from the rest of the MNC. GeoLogistics recognized that a centralized network could improve communication among the subsidiaries, allowing them to work as a team to resolve their cash deficiencies. It decided to set up a centralized treasury department in a country that would offer favorable tax treatment, limited regulations, and local banks that were familiar with sophisticated treasury practices.

GeoLogistics selected Dublin, Ireland, as its location and decided to outsource some of its treasury functions to a bank based there. In particular, the bank is responsible for the firm's lending, foreign exchange, and reporting. The bank established a netting system so that only the net payments owed by one subsidiary to another are made over a particular period. This has reduced transaction costs. In addition, the bank established a network so that each subsidiary's cash position is known; this enables one subsidiary to borrow from another that has cash available. GeoLogistics adopted a policy of having the subsidiaries reduce their debt levels and use either other subsidiaries or the Dublin bank for their financing. These changes have reduced the firm's financing costs, improved its liquidity, and increased its value.

amount in New Zealand dollars needed by Dearborn is NZ$1,000,000 + NZ$80,000 = NZ$1,080,000. Assume the New Zealand dollar appreciates from $.50 to $.60 by the time the loan is to be repaid. Dearborn will need to convert $648,000 (computed as NZ$1,080,000 × $.60 per NZ$) to have the necessary number of New Zealand dollars for loan repayment.

To compute the effective financing rate, first determine the amount in U.S. dollars beyond the amount borrowed that was paid back. Then divide by the number of U.S. dollars borrowed (after converting the New Zealand dollars to U.S. dollars). Given that Dearborn borrowed the equivalent of $500,000 and paid back $648,000 for the loan, the effective financing rate in this case is $148,000/$500,000 = 29.6%. If the exchange rate had remained constant throughout the life of the loan, the total loan repayment would have been $540,000, representing an effective rate of $40,000/$500,000 = 8%. Since the New Zealand dollar appreciated substantially in this example, the effective financing rate was very high. If Dearborn, Inc., had anticipated the New Zealand dollar's substantial appreciation, it would not have borrowed the New Zealand dollars.

The effective financing rate (called r_f) is derived as follows:

$$r_f = (1 + i_f)\left[1 + \left(\frac{S_{t+1} - S}{S}\right)\right] - 1$$

where i_f represents the interest rate of the foreign currency and S and S_{t+1} represent the spot rate of the foreign currency at the beginning and end of the financing period, respectively. Since the terms in parentheses reflect the percentage change in the foreign currency's spot rate (denoted as e_f), the preceding equation can be rewritten as

$$r_f = (1 + i_f)(1 + e_f) - 1$$

In this example, e_f reflects the percentage change in the New Zealand dollar (against the U.S. dollar) from the day the New Zealand dollars were borrowed until the day they were paid back by Dearborn. The New Zealand dollar appreciated from $.50 to $.60, or by 20 percent, over the life of the loan. With this information and the quoted interest rate of 8 percent, Dearborn's effective financing rate on the New Zealand dollars can be computed as

$$\begin{aligned} r_f &= (1 + i_f)(1 + e_f) - 1 \\ &= (1 + .08)(1 + .20) - 1 \\ &= .296, \text{ or } 29.6\% \end{aligned}$$

which is the same rate determined from the alternative computational approach.

To test your understanding of financing in a foreign currency, consider a second example involving Dearborn.

EXAMPLE

Assuming that the quoted interest rate for the New Zealand dollar is 8 percent and that the New Zealand dollar depreciates from $.50 (on the day the funds were borrowed) to $.45 (on the day of loan repayment), what is the effective financing rate of a one-year loan from Dearborn's viewpoint? The answer can be determined by first computing the percentage change in the New Zealand dollar's value: ($.45 − $.50)/$.50 = −10%. Next, the quoted interest rate (i_f) of 8 percent and the percentage change in the New Zealand dollar (e_f) of −10 percent can be inserted into the formula for the effective financing rate (r_f):

$$\begin{aligned} r_f &= (1 + .08)[1 + (-.10)] - 1 \\ &= [(1.08)(.9)] - 1 \\ &= -.028, \text{ or } -2.8\% \end{aligned}$$

A *negative* effective financing rate indicates that Dearborn actually paid fewer dollars to repay the loan than it borrowed. Such a result can occur if the New Zealand dollar depreciates substantially over the life of the loan. This does not mean that a loan will basically be "free" whenever the currency borrowed depreciates over the life of the loan. Nevertheless, depreciation of any amount will cause the effective financing rate to be lower than the quoted interest rate, as can be substantiated by reviewing the formula for the effective financing rate.

The examples provided so far suggest that when choosing which currency to borrow, a firm should consider the expected rate of appreciation or depreciation as well as the quoted interest rates of foreign currencies.

USING THE WEB

Short-Term Foreign Interest Rates Short-term interest rates for major currencies such as the Canadian dollar, Japanese yen, and British pound for various maturities are provided at http://www.bloomberg.com. The short-term interest rates provided at this site reflect the government cost of borrowing; an MNC would have to pay a slightly higher interest rate than the rate shown. A review of the data illustrates how short-term interest rates can vary among currencies at a given point in time.

Criteria Considered for Foreign Financing

An MNC must consider various criteria in its international financing decision, including the following:

- Interest rate parity
- The forward rate as a forecast
- Exchange rate forecasts

These criteria can influence the MNC's decision regarding which currency or currencies to borrow. Each is discussed in turn.

Interest Rate Parity

Recall that covered interest arbitrage was described as a short-term foreign investment with a simultaneous forward sale of the foreign currency denominating the foreign investment. From a financing perspective, covered interest arbitrage can be conducted as follows. First, borrow a foreign currency and convert that currency to the home currency for use. Also, simultaneously purchase the foreign currency forward to lock in the exchange rate of the currency needed to pay off the loan. If the foreign currency's interest rate is low, this may appear to be a feasible strategy. However, such a currency normally will exhibit a forward premium that offsets the differential between its interest rate and the home interest rate.

This can be shown by recognizing that the financing firm will no longer be affected by the percentage change in exchange rates but instead by the percentage difference between the spot rate at which the foreign currency was converted to the local currency and the forward rate at which the foreign currency was repurchased. The difference reflects the forward premium (unannualized). The unannualized forward premium (p) can substitute for e_f in the equation introduced earlier to determine the effective financing rate when covering in the forward market under conditions of interest rate parity:

$$r_f = (1 + i_f)(1 + p) - 1$$

If interest rate parity exists, the forward premium is

$$p = \frac{(1 + i_h)}{(1 + i_f)} - 1$$

where i_h represents the home currency's interest rate. When this equation is used to reflect financing rates, we can substitute the formula for p to determine the effective financing rate of a foreign currency under conditions of interest rate parity:

$$\begin{aligned} r_f &= (1 + i_f)(1 + p) - 1 \\ &= (1 + i_f)\left[1 + \frac{(1 + i_h)}{(1 + i_f)} - 1\right] - 1 \\ &= i_h \end{aligned}$$

Exhibit 20.2
Implications of Interest Rate Parity for Financing

Scenario	Implications
1. Interest rate parity holds.	Foreign financing and a simultaneous hedge of that position in the forward market will result in financing costs similar to those incurred in domestic financing.
2. Interest rate parity holds, and the forward rate is an accurate forecast of the future spot rate.	Uncovered foreign financing will result in financing costs similar to those incurred in domestic financing.
3. Interest rate parity holds, and the forward rate is expected to overestimate the future spot rate.	Uncovered foreign financing is expected to result in lower financing costs than those incurred in domestic financing.
4. Interest rate parity holds, and the forward rate is expected to underestimate the future spot rate.	Uncovered foreign financing is expected to result in higher financing costs than those incurred in domestic financing.
5. Interest rate parity does not hold; the forward premium (discount) exceeds (is less than) the interest rate differential.	Foreign financing with a simultaneous hedge of that position in the forward market results in higher financing costs than those incurred in domestic financing.
6. Interest rate parity does not hold; the forward premium (discount) is less than (exceeds) the interest rate differential.	Foreign financing with a simultaneous hedge of that position in the forward market results in lower financing costs than those incurred in domestic financing.

Thus, if interest rate parity exists, the attempt of covered interest arbitrage to finance with a low-interest-rate currency will result in an effective financing rate similar to the domestic interest rate.

Exhibit 20.2 summarizes the implications of a variety of scenarios relating to interest rate parity. Even if interest rate parity exists, financing with a foreign currency may still be feasible, but it would have to be conducted on an uncovered basis (without use of a forward hedge). In other words, foreign financing may result in a lower financing cost than domestic financing, but it cannot be guaranteed (unless the firm has receivables in that same currency).

The Forward Rate as a Forecast

Assume the forward rate (F) of the foreign currency borrowed is used by firms as a predictor of the spot rate that will exist at the end of the financing period. The expected effective financing rate from borrowing a foreign currency can be forecasted by substituting F for S_{t+1} in the following equation:

$$r_f = (1 + i_f)\left[1 + \frac{S_{t+1} - S}{S}\right] - 1$$

$$r_f = (1 + i_f)\left[1 + \frac{F - S}{S}\right] - 1$$

As already shown, the right side of this equation is equal to the home currency financing rate if interest rate parity exists. If the forward rate is an accurate estimator of the future spot rate S_{t+1}, the foreign financing rate will be similar to the home financing rate.

When interest rate parity exists here, the forward rate can be used as a break-even point to assess the financing decision. When a firm is financing with the foreign currency (and not covering the foreign currency position), the effective financing rate will be less than the domestic rate if the future spot rate of the foreign currency (spot rate at the time of loan repayment) is less than the forward rate (at the time the loan is granted). Conversely, the effective financing rate in a foreign loan will be greater than the domestic rate if the future spot rate of the foreign currency turns out to be greater than the forward rate.

If the forward rate is an unbiased predictor of the future spot rate, then the effective financing rate of a foreign currency will on average be equal to the domestic financing rate. In this case, firms that consistently borrow foreign currencies will not achieve lower financing costs. Although the effective financing rate may turn out to be lower than the domestic rate in some periods, it will be higher in other periods, causing an offsetting effect. Firms that believe the forward rate is an unbiased predictor of the future spot rate will prefer borrowing their home currency, where the financing rate is known with certainty and is not expected to be any higher on average than foreign financing.

Exchange Rate Forecasts

While the forecasting capabilities of firms are somewhat limited, some firms may make decisions based on cycles in currency movements. Firms may use the recent movements as a forecast of future movements to determine whether they should borrow a foreign currency. This strategy would have been successful on average if utilized in the past. It will be successful in the future if currency movements continue to move in one direction for long periods of time.

Once the firm develops a forecast for the exchange rate's percentage change over the financing period (e_f), it can use this forecast along with the foreign interest rate to forecast the effective financing rate of a foreign currency. The forecasted rate can then be compared to the domestic financing rate.

EXAMPLE

Sarasota, Inc., needs funds for one year and is aware that the one-year interest rate in U.S. dollars is 12 percent while the interest rate from borrowing Swiss francs is 8 percent. Sarasota forecasts that the Swiss franc will appreciate from its current rate of \$.45 to \$.459, or by 2 percent over the next year. The expected value for e_f [written as $E(e_f)$] will therefore be 2 percent. Thus, the expected effective financing rate [$E(r_f)$] will be

$$\begin{aligned} E(r_f) &= (1 + i_f)[1 + E(e_f)] - 1 \\ &= (1 + .08)(1 + .02) - 1 \\ &= .1016, \text{ or } 10.16\% \end{aligned}$$

In this example, financing in Swiss francs is expected to be less expensive than financing in U.S. dollars. However, the value for e_f is forecasted and therefore is not known with certainty. Thus, there is no guarantee that foreign financing will truly be less costly.

Deriving a Value for e_f That Equates Domestic and Foreign Rates. Continuing from the previous example, Sarasota, Inc., may attempt at least to determine what value of e_f would make the effective rate from foreign financing the same as domestic financing. To determine this value, begin with the effective financing rate formula and solve for e_f as shown:

$$r_f = (1 + i_f)(1 + e_f) - 1$$
$$(1 + r_f) = (1 + i_f)(1 + e_f)$$
$$\frac{(1 + r_f)}{(1 + i_f)} = (1 + e_f)$$
$$\frac{(1 + r_f)}{(1 + i_f)} - 1 = e_f$$

Since the U.S. financing rate is 12 percent in our previous example, that rate is plugged in for r_f. We can also plug in 8 percent for i_f, so the break-even value of e_f is

$$\begin{aligned} e_f &= \frac{(1 + r_f)}{(1 + i_f)} - 1 \\ &= \frac{(1 + .12)}{(1 + .08)} - 1 \\ &= .037037, \text{ or } 3.703\% \end{aligned}$$

This suggests that the Swiss franc would have to appreciate by about 3.7 percent over the loan period to make the Swiss franc loan as costly as a loan in U.S. dollars. Any smaller degree of appreciation would make the Swiss franc loan less costly. Sarasota, Inc., can use this information when determining whether to borrow U.S. dollars or Swiss francs. If it expects the Swiss franc to appreciate by more than 3.7 percent over the loan life, it should prefer borrowing in U.S. dollars. If it expects the Swiss franc to appreciate by less than 3.7 percent or to depreciate, its decision is more complex. If the potential savings from financing with the foreign currency outweigh the risk involved, then the firm should choose that route. The final decision here will be influenced by Sarasota's degree of risk aversion.

Use of Probability Distributions. To gain more insight about the financing decision, a firm may wish to develop a probability distribution for the percentage change in value for a particular foreign currency over the financing horizon. Since forecasts are not always accurate, it is sometimes useful to develop a probability distribution instead of relying on a single point estimate. Using the probability distribution of possible percentage changes in the currency's value, along with the currency's interest rate, the firm can determine the probability distribution of the possible effective financing rates for the currency. Then, it can compare this distribution to the known financing rate of the home currency in order to make its financing decision.

Carolina Co. is deciding whether to borrow Swiss francs for one year. It finds that the quoted interest rate for the Swiss franc is 8 percent and the quoted rate for the U.S. dollar is 15 percent. It then develops a probability distribution for the Swiss franc's possible percentage change in value over the life of the loan.

Exhibit 20.3

Analysis of Financing with a Foreign Currency

Possible Rate of Change in the Swiss Franc over the Life of the Loan (e_f)	Probability of Occurrence	Effective Financing Rate If This Rate of Change in the Swiss Franc Does Occur (r_f)
−6%	5%	(1.08)[1 + (−6%)] − 1 = 1.52%
−4	10	(1.08)[1 + (−4%)] − 1 = 3.68
−1	15	(1.08)[1 + (−1%)] − 1 = 6.92
+1	20	(1.08)[1 + (1%)] − 1 = 9.08
+4	20	(1.08)[1 + (4%)] − 1 = 12.32
+6	15	(1.08)[1 + (6%)] − 1 = 14.48
+8	10	(1.08)[1 + (8%)] − 1 = 16.64
+10	5	(1.08)[1 + (10%)] − 1 = 18.80
	100%	

The probability distribution is displayed in Exhibit 20.3. The first row in Exhibit 20.3 shows that there is a 5 percent probability of a 6 percent depreciation in the Swiss franc over the loan life. If the Swiss franc does depreciate by 6 percent, the effective financing rate would be 1.52 percent. Thus, there is a 5 percent probability that Carolina will incur a 1.52 percent effective financing rate on its loan. The second row shows that there is a 10 percent probability of a 4 percent depreciation in the Swiss franc over the loan life. If the Swiss franc does depreciate by 4 percent, the effective financing rate would be 3.68 percent. Thus, there is a 10 percent probability that Carolina will incur a 3.68 percent effective financing rate on its loan.

For each possible percentage change in the Swiss franc's value, there is a corresponding effective financing rate. We can associate each possible effective financing rate (third column) with its probability of occurring (second column). By multiplying each possible effective financing rate by its associated probability, we can compute an expected value for the effective financing rate of the Swiss franc. Based on the information in Exhibit 20.3, the expected value of the effective financing rate, referred to as $E(r_f)$, is computed as

$$\begin{aligned} E(r_f) &= 5\%(1.52\%) + 10\%(3.68\%) + 15\%(6.92\%) + 20\%(9.08\%) \\ &\quad + 20\%(12.32\%) + 15\%(14.48\%) \\ &\quad + 10\%(16.64\%) + 5\%(18.80\%) \\ &= .076\% + .368\% + 1.038\% + 1.816\% \\ &\quad + 2.464\% + 2.172\% + 1.664\% + .94\% \\ &= 10.538\% \end{aligned}$$

Thus, the decision for Carolina is whether to borrow U.S. dollars (at 15 percent interest) or Swiss francs (with an expected value of 10.538 percent for the effective financing rate). Using Exhibit 20.3, the risk reflects the 5 percent chance (probability) that the effective financing rate on Swiss francs will be 18.8 percent and the 10 percent chance

Exhibit 20.4
Probability Distribution of Effective Financing Rates

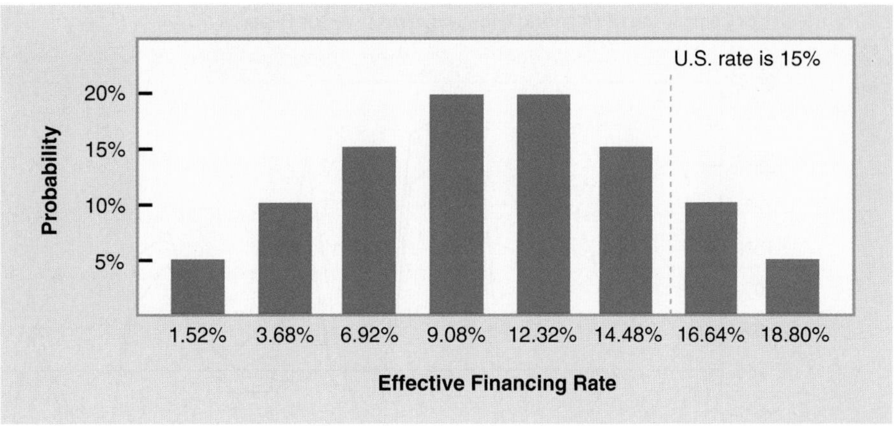

that the effective financing rate on Swiss francs will be 16.64 percent. Either of these possibilities represents a greater expense to Carolina than it would incur if it borrowed U.S. dollars.

To further assess the decision regarding which currency to borrow, the information in the second and third columns of Exhibit 20.3 is used to develop the probability distribution in Exhibit 20.4. This exhibit illustrates the probability of each possible effective financing rate that may occur if Carolina borrows Swiss francs. Notice that the U.S. interest rate (15 percent) is included in Exhibit 20.4 for comparison purposes. There is no distribution of possible outcomes for the U.S. rate since the rate of 15 percent is known with certainty (no exchange rate risk exists). There is a 15 percent probability that the U.S. rate will be lower than the effective rate on Swiss francs and an 85 percent chance that the U.S. rate will be higher than the effective rate on Swiss francs. This information can assist the firm in its financing decision. Given the potential savings relative to the small degree of risk, Carolina decides to borrow Swiss francs.

Actual Results from Foreign Financing

The fact that some firms utilize foreign financing suggests that they believe reduced financing costs can be achieved. To assess this issue, the effective financing rates of the Swiss franc and the U.S. dollar are compared in Exhibit 20.5 from the perspective of a U.S. firm. The data are segmented into annual periods.

http://

http://Commerzbank.com offers much information about how it provides financing services to firms, and also provides its prevailing view about conditions in the foreign exchange market.

In the 1999–2000 period, the Swiss franc weakened against the dollar, and a U.S. firm that borrowed Swiss francs would have incurred a negative effective financing rate. In the 2002–2003 period, however, the Swiss franc appreciated against the dollar. The effective financing rate of Swiss francs from a U.S. perspective was 22 percent in 2002 and 11 percent in 2003. These rates were much higher than the U.S. interest rate and illustrate the risk to an MNC that finances operations with a foreign currency.

Exhibit 20.5 demonstrates the potential savings in financing costs that can be achieved if the foreign currency depreciates against the firm's home currency. It also demonstrates how the foreign financing can backfire if the firm's expectations are incorrect and the foreign currency appreciates over the financing period.

Exhibit 20.5 Comparison of Financing with Swiss Francs versus Dollars

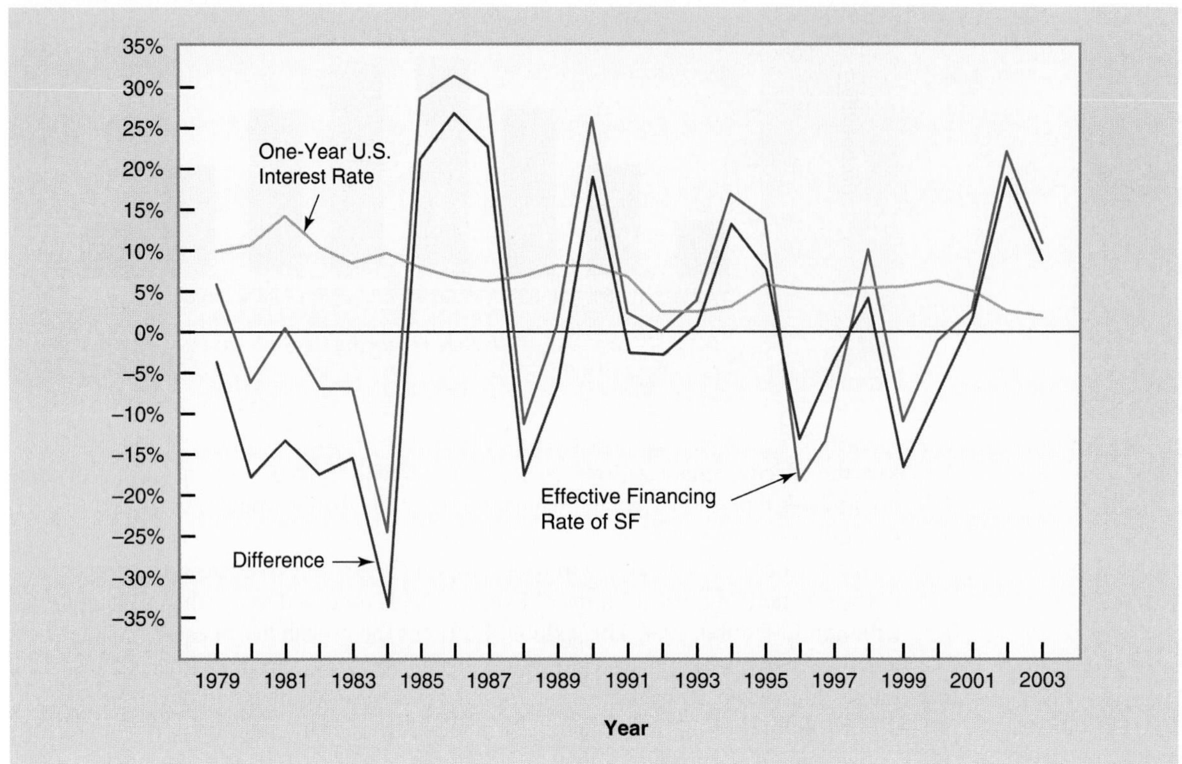

Financing with a Portfolio of Currencies

Although foreign financing can result in significantly lower financing costs, the variance in foreign financing costs over time is higher. MNCs may be able to achieve lower financing costs without excessive risk by financing with a portfolio of foreign currencies, as demonstrated here.

EXAMPLE

Nevada, Inc., needs to borrow $100,000 for one year and obtains the following interest rate quotes:

- Interest rate for a one-year loan in U.S. dollars = 15%
- Interest rate for a one-year loan in Swiss francs = 8%
- Interest rate for a one-year loan in Japanese yen = 9%

Since the quotes for a loan in Swiss francs or Japanese yen are relatively low, Nevada may desire to borrow in a foreign currency. If Nevada decides to use foreign financing, it has three choices based on the information given: (1) borrow only Swiss francs, (2) borrow only Japanese yen, or (3) borrow a portfolio of Swiss francs and Japanese yen. Assume that Nevada, Inc., has established possible percentage changes in the spot rate for both the Swiss franc and the Japanese yen from the time the loan would begin until loan repayment, as shown in the second column of Exhibit 20.6. The third column shows the probability that each possible percentage change might occur.

Exhibit 20.6 Derivation of Possible Effective Financing Rates

Currency	Possible Percentage Change in the Spot Rate over the Loan Life	Probability of That Percentage Change in the Spot Rate Occurring	Computation of Effective Financing Rate Based on That Percentage Change in the Spot Rate
Swiss franc	1%	30%	(1.08)[1 + (.01)] − 1 = .0908, or 9.08%
Swiss franc	3	50	(1.08)[1 + (.03)] − 1 = .1124, or 11.24%
Swiss franc	9	20	(1.08)[1 + (.09)] − 1 = .1772, or 17.72%
		100%	
Japanese yen	−1%	35%	(1.09)[1 + (−.01)] − 1 = .0791, or 7.91%
Japanese yen	3	40	(1.09)[1 + (.03)] − 1 = .1227, or 12.27%
Japanese yen	7	25	(1.09)[1 + (.07)] − 1 = .1663, or 16.63%
		100%	

Based on the assumed interest rate of 8 percent for the Swiss franc, the effective financing rate is computed for each possible percentage change in the Swiss franc's spot rate over the loan life. There is a 30 percent chance that the Swiss franc will appreciate by 1 percent over the loan life. In that case, the effective financing rate will be 9.08 percent. Thus, there is a 30 percent chance that the effective financing rate will be 9.08 percent. Furthermore, there is a 50 percent chance that the effective financing rate will be 11.24 percent and a 20 percent chance that it will be 17.72 percent. Given that the U.S. loan rate is 15 percent, there is only a 20 percent chance that financing in Swiss francs will be more expensive than domestic financing.

The lower section of Exhibit 20.6 provides information on the Japanese yen. For example, the yen has a 35 percent chance of depreciating by 1 percent over the loan life, and so on. Based on the assumed 9 percent interest rate and the exchange rate fluctuation forecasts, there is a 35 percent chance that the effective financing rate will be 7.91 percent, a 40 percent chance that it will be 12.27 percent, and a 25 percent chance that it will be 16.63 percent. Given the 15 percent rate on U.S. dollar financing, there is a 25 percent chance that financing in Japanese yen will be more costly than domestic financing. Before examining the third possible foreign financing strategy (the portfolio approach), determine the expected value of the effective financing rate for each foreign currency by itself. This is accomplished by totaling the products of each possible effective financing rate and its associated probability as follows:

Currency	Computation of Expected Value of Effective Financing Rate
Swiss francs	30%(9.08%) + 50%(11.24%) + 20%(17.72%) = 11.888%
Japanese yen	35%(7.91%) + 40%(12.27%) + 25%(16.63%) = 11.834%

The expected financing costs of the two currencies are almost the same. The individual degree of risk (that the costs of financing will turn out to be higher than domestic financing) is about the same for each currency. If Nevada, Inc., chooses to finance with only one of these foreign currencies, it is difficult to pinpoint (based on our analysis) which currency is more appropriate. Now, consider the third and final foreign financing strategy: the portfolio approach.

Based on the information in Exhibit 20.6, there are three possibilities for the Swiss franc's effective financing rate. The same holds true for the Japanese yen. If Nevada, Inc., borrows half of its needed funds in each of the foreign currencies, then there will be nine possibilities for this portfolio's effective financing rate, as shown in Exhibit 20.7. Columns 1 and 2 list all possible joint effective financing rates. Column 3 computes the joint probability of that occurrence assuming that exchange rate movements of the Swiss franc and Japanese yen are independent. Column 4 shows the computation of the portfolio's effective financing rate based on the possible rates shown for the individual currencies.

An examination of the top row will help to clarify the table. This row indicates that one possible outcome of borrowing both Swiss francs and Japanese yen is that they will exhibit effective financing rates of 9.08 percent and 7.91 percent, respectively. The probability of the Swiss franc's effective financing rate occurring is 30 percent, while the probability of the Japanese yen rate occurring is 35 percent. Recall that these percentages were given in Exhibit 20.6. The joint probability that both of these rates will occur simultaneously is (30%)(35%) = 10.5%. Assuming that half (50%) of the funds needed are to be borrowed from each currency, the portfolio's effective financing rate will be .5(9.08%) + .5(7.91%) = 8.495% (if those individual effective financing rates occur for each currency).

A similar procedure was used to develop the remaining eight rows in Exhibit 20.7. From this table, there is a 10.5 percent chance that the portfolio's effective financing rate will be 8.495 percent, a 12 percent chance that it will be 10.675 percent, and so on.

Exhibit 20.7 Analysis of Financing with Two Foreign Currencies

(1)	(2)	(3)	(4)
Possible Joint Effective Financing Rates		Computation of Joint Probability	Computation of Effective Financing Rate of Portfolio (50% of Total Funds Borrowed in Each Currency)
Swiss Franc	Japanese Yen		
9.08%	7.91%	(30%)(35%) = 10.5%	.5(9.08%) + .5(7.91%) = 8.495%
9.08	12.27	(30%)(40%) = 12.0	.5(9.08%) + .5(12.27%) = 10.675
9.08	16.63	(30%)(25%) = 7.5	.5(9.08%) + .5(16.63%) = 12.855
11.24	7.91	(50%)(35%) = 17.5	.5(11.24%) + .5(7.91%) = 9.575
11.24	12.27	(50%)(40%) = 20.0	.5(11.24%) + .5(12.27%) = 11.755
11.24	16.63	(50%)(25%) = 12.5	.5(11.24%) + .5(16.63%) = 13.935
17.72	7.91	(20%)(35%) = 7.0	.5(17.72%) + .5(7.91%) = 12.815
17.72	12.27	(20%)(40%) = 8.0	.5(17.72%) + .5(12.27%) = 14.995
17.72	16.63	(20%)(25%) = 5.0	.5(17.72%) + .5(16.63%) = 17.175
		100.0%	

Exhibit 20.8 Probability Distribution of the Portfolio's Effective Financing Rate

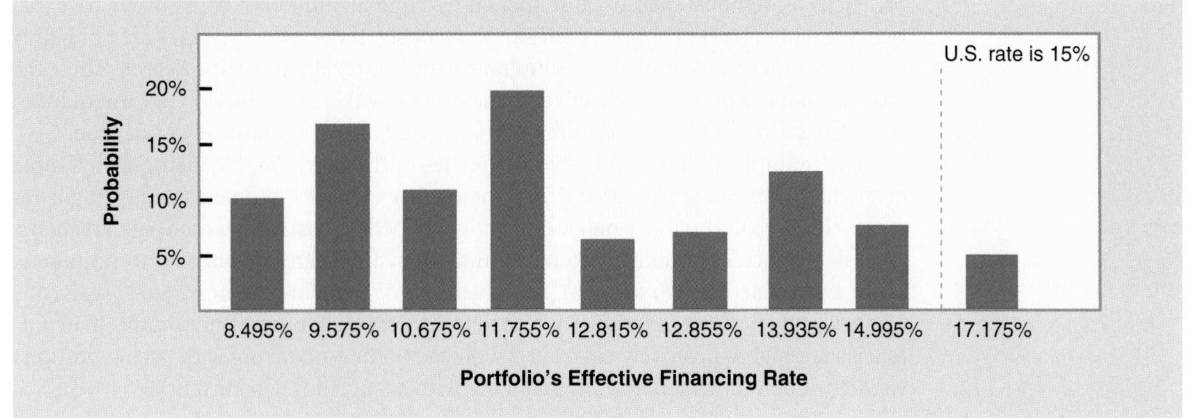

Exhibit 20.8 displays the probability distribution for the portfolio's effective financing rate that was derived in Exhibit 20.7. This exhibit shows that financing with a portfolio (50 percent financed in Swiss francs with the remaining 50 percent financed in Japanese yen) has only a 5 percent chance of being more costly than domestic financing. These results are more favorable than those of either individual foreign currency Therefore, Nevada, Inc., decides to borrow the portfolio of currencies.

Portfolio Diversification Effects

When both foreign currencies are borrowed, the only way the portfolio will exhibit a higher effective financing rate than the domestic rate is if *both* currencies experience their maximum possible level of appreciation (which is 9 percent for the Swiss franc and 7 percent for the Japanese yen). If only one does, the severity of its appreciation will be somewhat offset by the other currency's not appreciating to such a large extent. The probability of maximum appreciation is 20 percent for the Swiss franc and 25 percent for the Japanese yen. The joint probability of both of these events occurring simultaneously is (20%)(25%) = 5%. This is an advantage of financing in a portfolio of foreign currencies. Nevada, Inc., has a 95 percent chance of attaining lower costs with the foreign portfolio than with domestic financing.

The expected value of the effective financing rate for the portfolio can be determined by multiplying the percentage financed in each currency by the expected value of that currency's individual effective financing rate. Recall that the expected value was 11.888 percent for the Swiss franc and 11.834 percent for the Japanese yen. Thus, for a portfolio representing 50 percent of funds borrowed in each currency, the expected value of the effective financing rate is .5(11.888%) + .5(11.834%) = 11.861%. Based on an overall comparison, the expected value of the portfolio's effective financing rate is very similar to that from financing solely in either foreign currency. However, the risk (of incurring a higher effective financing rate than the domestic rate) is substantially less when financing with the portfolio.

In the example, the computation of joint probabilities requires the assumption that the two currencies move independently. If movements of the two currencies are actually highly positively correlated, then financing with a portfolio of currencies will not be as beneficial as demonstrated because there is a strong likelihood of both currencies experiencing a high level of appreciation simultaneously. If the two currencies are not highly correlated, they are less likely to simultaneously appreciate to such a degree. Thus, the chances that the portfolio's effective financing rate will exceed the U.S. rate are reduced when the currencies included in the portfolio are not highly positively correlated.

The example included only two currencies in the portfolio. Financing with a more diversified portfolio of additional currencies that exhibit low interest rates might increase the probability that foreign financing will be less costly than domestic financing; several currencies are unlikely to move in tandem and therefore unlikely to simultaneously appreciate enough to offset the advantage of their low interest rates. Again, the degree to which these currencies are correlated with each other is important. If all currencies are highly positively correlated with each other, financing with such a portfolio would not be very different from financing with a single foreign currency.

Repeated Financing with a Currency Portfolio

A firm that repeatedly finances with a currency portfolio would normally prefer to compose a financing package that exhibits a somewhat predictable effective financing rate on a periodic basis. The more volatile a portfolio's effective financing rate over time, the more uncertainty (risk) there is about the effective financing rate that will exist in any period. The degree of volatility depends on the standard deviations and paired correlations of effective financing rates of the individual currencies within the portfolio.

We can use the portfolio variance as a measure of the degree of volatility. The variance of a two-currency portfolio's effective financing rate [$VAR(r_p)$] over time is computed as

$$VAR(r_p) = w_A^2\sigma_A^2 + w_B^2\sigma_B^2 + 2w_Aw_B\sigma_A\sigma_B CORR_{AB}$$

where w_A^2 and w_B^2 represent the percentage of total funds financed from Currencies A and B, respectively; σ_A^2 and σ_B^2 represent the individual variances of each currency's effective financing rate over time, and $CORR_{AB}$ reflects the correlation coefficient of the two currencies' effective financing rates. Since the percentage change in the exchange rate plays an important role in influencing the effective financing rate, it should not be surprising that $CORR_{AB}$ is strongly affected by the correlation between the exchange rate fluctuations of the two currencies. A low correlation between movements of the two currencies may force $CORR_{AB}$ to be low.

EXAMPLE

Valparaiso, Inc., considers borrowing a portfolio of Japanese yen and Swiss francs to finance its U.S. operations. Half of the needed funding would come from each currency. To determine how the variance in this portfolio's effective financing rate is related to characteristics of the component currencies, assume the following information based on historical information for several three-month periods:

- Mean effective financing rate of Swiss franc for three months = 3%
- Mean effective financing rate of Japanese yen for three months = 2%
- Standard deviation of Swiss franc's effective financing rate = .04
- Standard deviation of Japanese yen's effective financing rate = .09
- Correlation coefficient of effective financing rates of these two currencies = .10

Given this information, the mean effective rate on a portfolio (r_p) of funds financed 50 percent by Swiss francs and 50 percent by Japanese yen is determined by totaling the weighted individual effective financing rates:

$$\begin{aligned} r_p &= w_A r_A + w_B r_B \\ &= .5(.03) + .5(.02) \\ &= .015 + .01 \\ &= .025, \text{ or } 2.5\% \end{aligned}$$

The variance of this portfolio's effective financing rate over time is

$$\begin{aligned} VAR(r_p) &= .5^2(.04)^2 + .5^2(.09)^2 + 2(.5)(.5)(.04)(.09)(.10) \\ &= .25(.0016) + .25(.0081) + .00018 \\ &= .0004 + .002025 + .00018 \\ &= .002605 \end{aligned}$$

Valparaiso can use this same process to compare various financing packages to see which package would be most appropriate. It may be more interested in estimating the mean return and variability for repeated financing in a particular portfolio in the future. There is no guarantee that past data will be indicative of the future. Yet, if the individual variability and paired correlations are somewhat stable over time, the historical variability of the portfolio's effective financing rate should provide a reasonable forecast.

To recognize the benefits from financing with two currencies that are not highly correlated, reconsider how the variance of the portfolio's effective financing rate would have been affected if the correlation between the two currencies was .90 (very high correlation) instead of .10. The variance would be .004045, which is more than 50 percent higher than the variance when the correlation was assumed to be .10.

The assessment of a currency portfolio's effective financing rate and variance is not restricted to just two currencies. The mean effective financing rate for a currency portfolio of any size will be determined by totaling the respective individual effective financing rates weighted by the percentage of funds financed with each currency. Solving the variance of a portfolio's effective financing rate becomes more complex as more currencies are added to the portfolio, but computer software packages are commonly applied to more easily determine the solution.

SUMMARY

- MNCs may use foreign financing to offset anticipated cash inflows in foreign currencies so that exposure to exchange rate risk will be minimized. Alternatively, some MNCs may use foreign financing in an attempt to reduce their financing costs. Foreign financing costs may be lower if the foreign interest rate is relatively low or if the foreign currency borrowed depreciates over the financing period.
- MNCs can determine whether to use foreign financing by estimating the effective financing rate for any foreign currency over the period in which financing will be needed. The expected effective financing rate is dependent on the quoted interest rate of the foreign currency and the forecasted percentage change in the currency's value over the financing period.
- When MNCs borrow a portfolio of currencies that have low interest rates, they can increase the probability of achieving relatively low financing costs if the currencies' values are not highly correlated.

POINT COUNTER-POINT

Do MNCs Increase Their Risk When Borrowing Foreign Currencies?

Point Yes. MNCs should borrow the currency that matches their cash inflows. If they borrow a foreign currency to finance business in a different currency, they are essentially speculating on the future exchange rate movements. The results of the strategy are uncertain, which represents risk to the MNC and its shareholders.

Counter-Point No. If MNCs expect that they can reduce the effective financing rate by borrowing a foreign currency, they should consider borrowing that currency. This enables them to achieve lower costs and improves their ability to compete. If they take the most conservative approach by borrowing whatever currency matches their inflows, they may incur higher costs and have a greater chance of failure.

Who Is Correct? Use InfoTrac or some other search engine to learn more about this issue. Which argument do you support? Offer your own opinion on this issue.

SELF TEST

Answers are provided in Appendix A at the back of the text.

1. Assume that the interest rate in New Zealand is 9 percent. A U.S. firm plans to borrow New Zealand dollars, convert them to U.S. dollars, and repay the loan in one year. What will be the effective financing rate if the New Zealand dollar depreciates by 6 percent? If the New Zealand dollar appreciates by 3 percent?
2. Using the information in question 1 and assuming a 50 percent chance of either scenario occurring, determine the expected value of the effective financing rate.
3. Assume that the Japanese one-year interest rate is 5 percent, while the U.S. one-year interest rate is 8 percent. What percentage change in the Japanese yen would cause a U.S. firm borrowing yen to incur the same effective financing rate as it would if it borrowed dollars?
4. The spot rate of the Australian dollar is \$.62. The one-year forward rate of the Australian dollar is \$.60. The Australian one-year interest rate is 9 percent. Assume that the forward rate is used to forecast the future spot rate. Determine the expected effective financing rate for a U.S. firm that borrows Australian dollars to finance its U.S. business.
5. Omaha, Inc., plans to finance its U.S. operations by repeatedly borrowing two currencies with low interest rates whose exchange rate movements are highly correlated. Will the variance of the two-currency portfolio's effective financing rate be much lower than the variance of either individual currency's effective financing rate? Explain.

QUESTIONS AND APPLICATIONS

1. **Financing from Subsidiaries.** Explain why an MNC parent would consider financing from its subsidiaries.
2. **Foreign Financing.**

   a. Explain how a firm's degree of risk aversion enters into its decision of whether to finance in a foreign currency or a local currency.

   b. Discuss the use of specifying a break-even point when financing in a foreign currency.
3. **Probability Distribution.**

   a. Discuss the development of a probability distribution of effective financing rates when financing in a foreign currency. How is this distribution developed?

   b. Once the probability distribution of effective financing rates from financing in a foreign currency is developed, how can this distribution be used in deciding whether to finance in the foreign currency or the home currency?

4. **Financing and Exchange Rate Risk.** How can a U.S. firm finance in euros and not necessarily be exposed to exchange rate risk?

5. **Short-Term Financing Analysis.** Assume that Tulsa, Inc., needs $3 million for a one-year period. Within one year, it will generate enough U.S. dollars to pay off the loan. It is considering three options: (1) borrowing U.S. dollars at an interest rate of 6 percent, (2) borrowing Japanese yen at an interest rate of 3 percent, or (3) borrowing Canadian dollars at an interest rate of 4 percent. Tulsa expects that the Japanese yen will appreciate by 1 percent over the next year and that the Canadian dollar will appreciate by 3 percent. What is the expected "effective" financing rate for each of the three options? Which option appears to be most feasible? Why might Tulsa, Inc., not necessarily choose the option reflecting the lowest effective financing rate?

6. **Effective Financing Rate.** How is it possible for a firm to incur a negative effective financing rate?

7. **IRP Application to Short-term Financing.**

   a. If interest rate parity does not hold, what strategy should Connecticut Co. consider when it needs short-term financing?

   b. Assume that Connecticut Co. needs dollars. It borrows euros at a lower interest rate than that for dollars. If interest rate parity exists and if the forward rate of the euro is a reliable predictor of the future spot rate, what does this suggest about the feasibility of such a strategy?

   c. If Connecticut Co. expects the current spot rate to be a more reliable predictor of the future spot rate, what does this suggest about the feasibility of such a strategy?

8. **Break-Even Financing.** Akron Co. needs dollars. Assume that the local one-year loan rate is 15 percent, while a one-year loan rate on euros is 7 percent. By how much must the euro appreciate to cause the loan in euros to be more costly than a U.S. dollar loan?

9. **IRP Application to Short-Term Financing.** Assume that interest rate parity exists. If a firm believes that the forward rate is an unbiased predictor of the future spot rate, will it expect to achieve lower financing costs by consistently borrowing a foreign currency with a low interest rate?

10. **Effective Financing Rate.** Boca, Inc., needs $4 million for one year. It currently has no business in Japan but plans to borrow Japanese yen from a Japanese bank because the Japanese interest rate is three percentage points lower than the U.S. rate. Assume that interest rate parity exists; also assume that Boca believes that the one-year forward rate of the Japanese yen will exceed the future spot rate one year from now. Will the expected effective financing rate be higher, lower, or the same as financing with dollars? Explain.

11. **IRP Application to Short-Term Financing.** Assume that the U.S. interest rate is 7 percent and the euro's interest rate is 4 percent. Assume that the euro's forward rate has a premium of 4 percent. Determine whether the following statement is true: "Interest rate parity does not hold; therefore, U.S. firms could lock in a lower financing cost by borrowing euros and purchasing euros forward for one year." Explain your answer.

12. **Break-Even Financing.** Orlando, Inc., is a U.S.-based MNC with a subsidiary in Mexico. Its Mexican subsidiary needs a one-year loan of 10 million pesos for operating expenses. Since the Mexican interest rate is 70 percent, Orlando is considering borrowing dollars, which it would convert to pesos to cover the operating expenses. By how much would the dollar have to appreciate against the peso to cause such a strategy to backfire? (The one-year U.S. interest rate is 9 percent.)

13. **Financing since the Asian Crisis.** Bradenton, Inc., has a foreign subsidiary in Asia that commonly obtained short-term financing from local banks prior to the Asian crisis. Explain why the firm may not be able to easily obtain funds from the local banks since the crisis.

14. **Effects of September 11.** Homewood Co. commonly finances some of its U.S. expansion by borrowing foreign currencies (such as Japanese yen) that have low interest rates. Describe how the potential return and risk of this strategy may have changed after the September 11, 2001 terrorist attack on the United States.

ADVANCED QUESTIONS

15. **Probability Distribution of Financing Costs.** Missoula, Inc., decides to borrow Japanese yen for one year.

The interest rate on the borrowed yen is 8 percent. Missoula has developed the following probability distribution for the yen's degree of fluctuation against the dollar:

Possible Degree of Fluctuation of Yen against the Dollar	Percentage Probability
−4%	20%
−1	30
0	10
3	40

Given this information, what is the expected value of the effective financing rate of the Japanese yen from Missoula's perspective?

16. **Analysis of Short-Term Financing.** Jacksonville Corp. is a U.S.-based firm that needs $600,000. It has no business in Japan but is considering one-year financing with Japanese yen because the annual interest rate would be 5 percent versus 9 percent in the United States. Assume that interest rate parity exists.

a. Can Jacksonville benefit from borrowing Japanese yen and simultaneously purchasing yen one year forward to avoid exchange rate risk? Explain.

b. Assume that Jacksonville does not cover its exposure and uses the forward rate to forecast the future spot rate. Determine the expected effective financing rate. Should Jacksonville finance with Japanese yen? Explain.

c. Assume that Jacksonville does not cover its exposure and expects that the Japanese yen will appreciate by either 5 percent, 3 percent, or 2 percent, and with equal probability of each occurrence. Use this information to determine the probability distribution of the effective financing rate. Should Jacksonville finance with Japanese yen? Explain.

17. **Financing with a Portfolio.** Pepperdine, Inc., considers obtaining 40 percent of its one-year financing in Canadian dollars and 60 percent in Japanese yen. The forecasts of appreciation in the Canadian dollar and Japanese yen for the next year are as follows:

Currency	Possible Percentage Change in the Spot Rate over the Loan Life	Probability of That Percentage Change in the Spot Rate Occurring
Canadian dollar	4%	70%
Canadian dollar	7	30
Japanese yen	6	50
Japanese yen	9	50

The interest rate on the Canadian dollar is 9 percent, and the interest rate on the Japanese yen is 7 percent. Develop the possible effective financing rates of the overall portfolio and the probability of each possibility based on the use of joint probabilities.

18. **Financing with a Portfolio.**

a. Does borrowing a portfolio of currencies offer any possible advantages over the borrowing of a single foreign currency?

b. If a firm borrows a portfolio of currencies, what characteristics of the currencies will affect the potential variability of the portfolio's effective financing rate? What characteristics would be desirable from a borrowing firm's perspective?

19. **Financing with a Portfolio.** Raleigh Corp. needs to borrow funds for one year to finance an expenditure in the United States. The following interest rates are available:

	Borrowing Rate
U.S.	10%
Canada	6
Japan	5

The percentage changes in the spot rates of the Canadian dollar and Japanese yen over the next year are as follows:

Canadian Dollar		Japanese Yen	
Probability	Percentage Change in Spot Rate	Probability	Percentage Change in Spot Rate
10%	5%	20%	6%
90	2	80	1

If Raleigh Corp. borrows a portfolio, 50 percent of funds from Canadian dollars and 50 percent of funds from yen, determine the probability distribution of the effective financing rate of the portfolio. What is the probability that Raleigh will incur a higher effective financing rate from borrowing this portfolio than from borrowing U.S. dollars?

INTERNET APPLICATION

20. **Yields for Foreign Currencies.** The Bloomberg website provides interest rate data for many different foreign currencies over various maturities. Its address is: **http://www.bloomberg.com**.

a. Go to the section that shows yields for different foreign currencies. Review the three-month yields of currencies. Assume that you could borrow at a rate 1 percentage point above the quoted yield for each currency. Which currency would offer you the lowest quoted yield?

b. As a cash manager of a U.S.-based MNC that needs dollars to support U.S. operations, where would you borrow funds for the next three months? Explain.

DISCUSSION IN THE BOARDROOM

This exercise can be found in Appendix E at the back of this textbook.

RUNNING YOUR OWN MNC

This exercise can be found on the Xtra! website at **http://maduraxtra.swlearning.com**.

BLADES, INC. CASE

Use of Foreign Short-Term Financing

Blades, Inc., just received a special order for 120,000 pairs of "Speedos," its primary roller blade product. Ben Holt, Blades' chief financial officer (CFO), needs short-term financing to finance this large order from the time Blades orders its supplies until the time it will receive payment. Blades will charge a price of 5,000 baht per pair of Speedos. The materials needed to manufacture these 120,000 pairs will be purchased from Thai suppliers. Blades expects the cost of the components for one pair of Speedos to be approximately 3,500 baht in its first year of operating the Thai subsidiary.

Because Blades is relatively unknown in Thailand, its suppliers have indicated that they would like to receive payment as early as possible. The customer that placed this order insists on open account transactions, which means that Blades will receive payment for the roller blades approximately three months subsequent to the sale. Furthermore, the production cycle necessary to produce Speedos, from purchase of the materials to the eventual sale of the product, is approximately three months. Because of these considerations, Blades expects to collect its revenues approximately six months after it has paid for the materials, such as rubber and plastic components, needed to manufacture Speedos.

Ben Holt has identified at least two alternatives for satisfying Blades' financing needs. First, Blades could borrow Japanese yen for six months, convert the yen to Thai baht, and use the baht to pay the Thai suppliers. When the accounts receivable in Thailand are collected, Blades would convert the baht received to yen and repay the Japanese yen loan. Second, Blades could borrow Thai baht for six months in order to pay its Thai suppliers. When Blades collects its accounts receivable, it would use these receipts to repay the baht loan. Thus, Blades will use revenue generated in Thailand to repay the loan, whether it borrows the money in yen or in baht.

Holt's initial research indicates that the 180-day interest rates available to Blades in Japan and in Thailand are 4 percent and 6 percent, respectively. Consequently, Holt favors borrowing the Japanese yen, as he believes this loan will be cheaper than the baht-denominated loan. He is aware that he should somehow incorporate the future movements of the yen-baht exchange rate in his analysis, but he is unsure how to accomplish this. However, he has identified the following probability distribution of the change in the value of the Japanese yen with respect to the Thai baht and of the change in the value of the Thai baht with respect to the dollar over the six-month period of the loan:

Possible Rate of Change in the Japanese Yen Relative to the Thai Baht over the Life of the Loan	Possible Rate of Change in the Thai Baht Relative to the Dollar over the Life of the Loan	Probability of Occurrence
2%	−3%	30%
1	−2	30
0	−1	20
1	0	15
2	1	5

Holt has also informed you that the current spot rate of the yen (in baht) is THB.347826, while the current spot rate of the baht (in dollars) is $.0023.

As a financial analyst for Blades, you have been asked to answer the following questions for Ben Holt:

1. What is the amount, in baht, that Blades needs to borrow to cover the payments due to the Thai suppliers? What is the amount, in yen, that Blades needs to borrow to cover the payments due to the Thai suppliers?
2. Given that Blades will use the receipts from the receivables in Thailand to repay the loan and that Blades plans to remit all baht-denominated cash flows to the U.S. parent whether it borrows in baht or yen, does the future value of the yen with respect to the baht affect the cost of the loan if Blades borrows in yen?
3. Using a spreadsheet, compute the expected amount (in U.S. dollars) that will be remitted to the United States in six months if Blades finances its working capital requirements by borrowing baht versus borrowing yen. Based on your analysis, should Blades obtain a yen- or baht-denominated loan?

SMALL BUSINESS DILEMMA

Short-Term Financing by the Sports Exports Company

At the current time, the Sports Exports Company focuses on producing footballs and exporting them to a distributor in the United Kingdom. The exports are denominated in British pounds. Jim Logan, the owner, plans to develop other sporting goods products besides the footballs that he produces. His entire expansion will be focused on the United Kingdom, where he is trying to make a name for his firm. He remains concerned about his firm's exposure to exchange rate risk but does not plan to let that get in the way of his expansion plans because he believes that his firm can continue to penetrate the British sporting goods market. He has just negotiated a joint venture with a British firm that will produce other sporting goods products that are more popular in the United States (such as basketballs) but will be sold in the United Kingdom. Jim will pay the British manufacturer in British pounds. These products will be delivered directly to the British distributor rather than to Jim, and the distributor will pay Jim with British pounds.

Jim's expansion plans will result in the need for additional funding. Jim would prefer to borrow on a short-term basis now. Jim has an excellent credit rating and collateral and therefore should be able to obtain short-term financing. The British interest rate is one-fourth of a percentage point above the U.S. interest rate.

1. Should Jim borrow dollars or pounds to finance his joint venture business? Why?
2. Jim could also borrow euros at an interest rate that is lower than the U.S. or British rate. The values of the euro and pound tend to move in the same direction against the dollar but not always by the same degree. Would borrowing euros to support the British joint venture result in more exposure to exchange rate risk than borrowing pounds? Would it result in more exposure to exchange rate risk than borrowing dollars?

CHAPTER 21

International Cash Management

The term **cash management** can be broadly defined to mean optimization of cash flows and investment of excess cash. From an international perspective, cash management is very complex because laws pertaining to cross-border cash transfers differ among countries. In addition, exchange rate fluctuations can affect the value of cross-border cash transfers. Financial managers need to understand the advantages and disadvantages of investing cash in foreign markets so that they can make international cash management decisions that maximize the value of the MNC.

The specific objectives of this chapter are to:

- explain the difference in analyzing cash flows from a subsidiary perspective and from a parent perspective,
- explain the various techniques used to optimize cash flows,
- explain common complications in optimizing cash flows, and
- explain the potential benefits and risks from foreign investing.

Cash Flow Analysis: Subsidiary Perspective

The management of working capital (such as inventory, accounts receivable, and cash) has a direct influence on the amount and timing of cash flow. Working capital management and the management of cash flow are integrated. We discuss them here first before focusing on cash management.

Subsidiary Expenses

Begin with outflow payments by the subsidiary to purchase raw materials or supplies. The subsidiary will normally have a more difficult time forecasting future outflow payments if its purchases are international rather than domestic because of exchange rate fluctuations. In addition, there is a possibility that payments will be substantially higher due to appreciation of the invoice currency. Consequently, the firm may wish to maintain a large inventory of supplies and raw materials so that it can draw from its inventory and cut down on purchases if the invoice currency appreciates. Still another possibility is that imported goods from another country could be restricted by the host government (through quotas, etc.). In this event, a larger inventory would give a firm more time to search for alternative sources of supplies or raw materials. A subsidiary with domestic supply sources would not experience such a problem and therefore would not need such a large inventory.

Outflow payments for supplies will be influenced by future sales. If the sales volume is substantially influenced by exchange rate fluctuations, its future level becomes more uncertain, which makes its need for supplies more uncertain. Such uncertainty may force the subsidiary to maintain larger cash balances to cover any unexpected increase in supply requirements.

Subsidiary Revenue

If subsidiaries export their products, their sales volume may be more volatile than if the goods were only sold domestically. This volatility could be due to the fluctuating exchange rate of the invoice currency. Importers' demand for these finished goods will most likely decrease if the invoice currency appreciates. The sales volume of exports is also susceptible to business cycles of the importing countries. If the goods were sold domestically, the exchange rate fluctuations would not have a direct impact on sales, although they would still have an indirect impact since the fluctuations would influence prices paid by local customers for imports from foreign competitors.

Sales can often be increased when credit standards are relaxed. However, it is important to focus on cash inflows due to sales rather than on sales themselves. Looser credit standards may cause a slowdown in cash inflows from sales, which could offset the benefits of increased sales. Accounts receivable management is an important part of the subsidiary's working capital management because of its potential impact on cash inflows.

Subsidiary Dividend Payments

The subsidiary may be expected to periodically send dividend payments and other fees to the parent. These fees could represent royalties or charges for overhead costs incurred by the parent that benefit the subsidiary. An example is research and development costs incurred by the parent, which improve the quality of goods produced by the subsidiary. Whatever the reason, payments by the subsidiary to the parent are often necessary. When dividend payments and fees are known in advance and denominated in the subsidiary's currency, forecasting cash flows is easier for the subsidiary. The level of dividends paid by subsidiaries to the parent is dependent on the liquidity needs of each subsidiary, potential uses of funds at various subsidiary locations, expected movements in the currencies of the subsidiaries, and regulations of the host country government.

Subsidiary Liquidity Management

After accounting for all outflow and inflow payments, the subsidiary will find itself with either excess or deficient cash. It uses liquidity management to either invest its excess cash or borrow to cover its cash deficiencies. If it anticipates a cash deficiency, short-term financing is necessary, as described in the previous chapter. If it anticipates excess cash, it must determine how the excess cash should be used. Investing in foreign currencies can sometimes be attractive, but exchange rate risk makes the effective yield uncertain. This issue is discussed later in this chapter.

Liquidity management is a crucial component of a subsidiary's working capital management. Subsidiaries commonly have access to numerous lines of credit and overdraft facilities in various currencies. Therefore, they may maintain adequate liquidity without substantial cash balances. While liquidity is important for the overall MNC, it cannot be properly measured by liquidity ratios. Potential access to funds is more relevant than cash on hand.

Centralized Cash Management

Each subsidiary should manage its working capital by simultaneously considering all of the points discussed thus far. Often, though, each subsidiary is more concerned with its own operations than with the overall operations of the MNC. Thus, a **centralized cash management** group may need to monitor, and possibly manage, the parent-subsidiary and intersubsidiary cash flows. This role is critical since it can often benefit individual subsidiaries in need of funds or overly exposed to exchange rate risk.

EXAMPLE

The treasury department of Kraft Foods is centralized to manage liquidity, funding, and foreign exchange requirements of its global operations. And Monsanto has a centralized system for pooling different currency balances from various subsidiaries in Asia that saves hundreds of thousands of dollars per year.

Exhibit 21.1 is a complement to the following discussion of cash flow management. It is a simplified cash flow diagram for an MNC with two subsidiaries in different countries. Although each MNC may handle its payments in a different manner, Exhibit 21.1 is based on simplified assumptions that will help illustrate some key concepts of international cash management. The exhibit reflects the assumption that the two subsidiaries periodically send loan repayments and dividends to the parent or send excess cash to the parent (where the centralized cash management process is assumed to take place). These cash flows represent the incoming cash to the parent from the subsidiaries. The parent's cash outflows to the subsidiaries can include loans and the return of cash previously invested by the subsidiaries. The subsidiaries also have cash flows between themselves because they purchase supplies from each other.

While each subsidiary is managing its working capital, there is a need to monitor and manage the cash flows between the parent and the subsidiaries, as well as between the individual subsidiaries. This task of international cash management should be delegated to a centralized cash management group. International cash management can be segmented into two functions: (1) optimizing cash flow movements and (2) investing excess cash. These two functions are discussed in turn.

The centralized cash management division of an MNC cannot always accurately forecast events that affect parent-subsidiary or intersubsidiary cash flows. It should, however, be ready to react to any event by considering (1) any potential adverse impact on cash flows and (2) how to avoid such an adverse impact. If the cash flow situation between the parent and subsidiaries results in a cash squeeze on the parent, it should have sources of funds (credit lines) available. On the other hand, if it has excess cash after considering all outflow payments, it must consider where to invest funds. This decision is thoroughly examined shortly.

Exhibit 21.1 Cash Flow of the Overall MNC

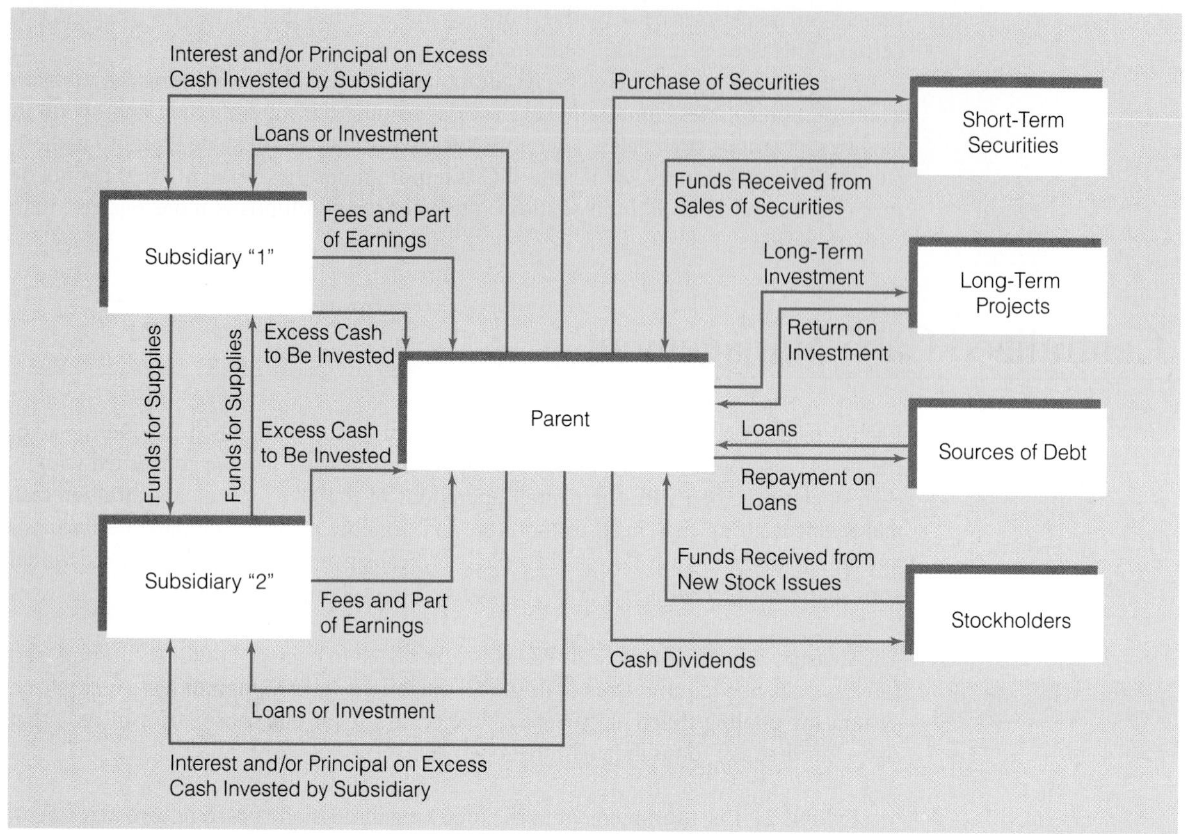

MANAGING FOR VALUE

Flexsys's Decision to Use a Multibank Payments System

Flexsys is a large chemical company with more than 20 subsidiaries in Europe, the United States, and Asia. To improve its liquidity, it wanted to create a system that would enable its treasury department to continuously monitor all payments at each subsidiary. Since the inception of the euro, Flexsys has had euro balances at several subsidiaries and consolidates these balances so that it can maximize the interest earned on the balances. It uses technology that allows all payments due to be recorded and transmitted to the treasury department. The treasury nets all payments due between subsidiaries so that only net payments need to be made to cover the payments due between subsidiaries. Flexsys's system is especially effective because it is "transparent," meaning that the payments due at each subsidiary can be easily monitored by the subsidiaries.

Flexsys uses multiple banks rather than branches of a single bank so that each subsidiary can use the bank it prefers. Having a multibank system complicates the reporting of payments, but allows each subsidiary to choose the bank that provides it with the best service. Thus, Flexsys's decision to use a multibank system can ensure optimal service at its subsidiaries. At the same time, however, its centralized payments network ensures that cash is utilized properly so that it can maximize its value.

Techniques to Optimize Cash Flows

Cash inflows can be optimized by the following techniques:

- Accelerating cash inflows
- Minimizing currency conversion costs
- Managing blocked funds
- Managing intersubsidiary cash transfers

Each of these techniques is discussed in turn.

Accelerating Cash Inflows

The first goal in international cash management is to accelerate cash inflows, since the more quickly the inflows are received, the more quickly they can be invested or used for other purposes. Several managerial practices are advocated for this endeavor, some of which may be implemented by the individual subsidiaries. First, a corporation may establish **lockboxes** around the world, which are post office boxes to which customers are instructed to send payment. When set up in appropriate locations, lockboxes can help reduce mailing time (**mail float**). A bank usually processes incoming checks at a lockbox on a daily basis. Second, cash inflows can be accelerated by using **preauthorized payments**, which allow a corporation to charge a customer's bank account up to some limit. Both preauthorized payments and lockboxes are also used in a domestic setting. Because international transactions may have a relatively long mailing time, these methods of accelerating cash inflows can be quite valuable for an MNC.

Minimizing Currency Conversion Costs

Another technique for optimizing cash flow movements, **netting**, can be implemented with the joint effort of subsidiaries or by the centralized cash management group. This technique optimizes cash flows by reducing the administrative and transaction costs that result from currency conversion.

EXAMPLE

Montana, Inc., has subsidiaries located in France and in Hungary. Whenever the French subsidiary needs to purchase supplies from the Hungarian subsidiary, it needs to convert euros into Hungary's currency (the forint) to make payment. Hungary's subsidiary must convert its forint into euros when purchasing supplies from the French subsidiary. Montana, Inc., has instructed both subsidiaries to net their transactions on a monthly basis so that only one net payment is made at the end of each month. By using this approach, both subsidiaries avoid (or at least reduce) the transaction costs of currency conversion.

Over time, netting has become increasingly popular because it offers several key benefits. First, it reduces the number of cross-border transactions between subsidiaries, thereby reducing the overall administrative cost of such cash transfers. Second, it reduces the need for foreign exchange conversion since transactions occur less frequently, thereby reducing the transaction costs associated with foreign exchange conversion. Third, the netting process imposes tight control over information on transactions between subsidiaries. Thus, all subsidiaries engage in a more coordinated effort to accurately report and settle their various accounts. Finally, cash flow forecasting is easier since only net cash transfers are made at the end of each period, rather than individual cash transfers throughout the period. Improved cash flow forecasting can enhance financing and investment decisions.

A **bilateral netting system** involves transactions between two units: between the parent and a subsidiary, or between two subsidiaries. A **multilateral netting system** usually involves a more complex interchange among the parent and several subsidiaries. For most large MNCs, a multilateral netting system would be necessary to effectively reduce administrative and currency conversion costs. Such a system is normally centralized so that all necessary information is consolidated. From the consolidated cash flow information, net cash flow positions for each pair of units (subsidiaries, or whatever) are determined, and the actual reconciliation at the end of each period can be dictated. The centralized group may even maintain inventories of various currencies so that currency conversions for the end-of-period net payments can be completed without significant transaction costs.

MNCs commonly monitor the cash flows between their subsidiaries with the use of an intersubsidiary payments matrix.

EXAMPLE

Exhibit 21.2 is an example of an intersubsidiary payments matrix that totals each subsidiary's individual payments to each of the other subsidiaries. The first row indicates that the Canadian subsidiary owes the equivalent of $40,000 to the French subsidiary, the equivalent of $90,000 to the Japanese subsidiary, and so on. During this same period, these subsidiaries have also received goods from the Canadian subsidiary, for which payment is due. The second column (under Canada) shows that the Canadian

Exhibit 21.2
Intersubsidiary Payments Matrix

Payments Owed by Subsidiary Located in:	U.S. Dollar Value (in Thousands) Owed to Subsidiary Located in:				
	Canada	*France*	*Japan*	*Switzerland*	*U.S.*
Canada	—	40	90	20	40
France	60	—	30	60	50
Japan	100	30	—	20	30
Switzerland	10	50	10	—	50
U.S.	10	60	20	20	—

Exhibit 21.3
Netting Schedule

Net Payments to Be Made by Subsidiary Located in:	Net U.S. Dollar Value (in Thousands) Owed to Subsidiary Located in:				
	Canada	*France*	*Japan*	*Switzerland*	*U.S.*
Canada	—	0	0	10	30
France	20	—	0	10	0
Japan	10	0	—	10	10
Switzerland	0	0	0	—	30
U.S.	0	10	0	0	—

subsidiary is owed the equivalent of $60,000 by the French subsidiary, the equivalent of $100,000 by the Japanese subsidiary, and so on.

Since subsidiaries owe each other, currency conversion costs can be reduced by requiring that only the net payment be extended. Using the intersubsidiary table, the schedule of net payments is determined as shown in Exhibit 21.3. Since the Canadian subsidiary owes the French subsidiary the equivalent of $40,000 but is owed the equivalent of $60,000 by the French subsidiary, the net payment required is the equivalent of $20,000 from the French subsidiary to the Canadian subsidiary. Exhibits 21.2 and 21.3 convert all figures to U.S. dollar equivalents to allow for consolidating payments in both directions so the net payment can be determined.

There can be some limitations to multilateral netting due to foreign exchange controls. Although the major industrialized countries typically do not impose such controls, some other countries do, and some countries prohibit netting altogether. Thus, an MNC with subsidiaries around the world may not be able to include all of its subsidiaries in its multilateral netting system. Obviously, this will limit the degree to which the netting system can reduce administration and transaction costs.

Managing Blocked Funds

Cash flows can also be affected by a host government's blockage of funds, which might occur if the government requires all funds to remain within the country in order to create jobs and reduce unemployment. To deal with funds blockage, the MNC may implement the same strategies used when a host country government imposes high taxes. To make efficient use of these funds, the MNC may instruct the subsidiary to set up a research and development division, which incurs costs and possibly generates revenues for other subsidiaries.

Another strategy is to use transfer pricing in a manner that will increase the expenses incurred by the subsidiary. A host country government is likely to be more lenient on funds sent to cover expenses than on earnings remitted to the parent.

When subsidiaries are restricted from transferring funds to the parent, the parent may instruct the subsidiary to obtain financing from a local bank rather than from the parent. By borrowing through a local intermediary, the subsidiary is assured that its earnings can be distributed to pay off previous financing. Overall, most methods of managing blocked funds are intended to make efficient use of the funds by using them to cover expenses that are transferred to that country.

EXAMPLE

Wittenberg, Inc., a U.S.-based MNC, has a subsidiary in the Philippines. During a turbulent period, the subsidiary was prevented from exchanging its Philippine pesos into U.S. dollars to be sent home. Wittenberg held its corporate meeting in Manila so that it could use the pesos to pay the expenses of the meeting (hotel, food, etc.) in pesos. In this way, it was able to use local funds to cover an expense that it would have incurred anyway. Ordinarily, the corporate meeting would have been held in the parent's country, and the parent would have paid the expenses.

Managing Intersubsidiary Cash Transfers

Proper management of cash flows can also be beneficial to a subsidiary in need of funds.

Texas, Inc., has two foreign subsidiaries called Short Sub and Long Sub. Short Sub needs funds, while Long Sub has excess funds. If Long Sub purchases supplies from Short Sub, it can provide financing by paying for its supplies earlier than necessary. This technique is often called **leading**. Alternatively, if Long Sub sells supplies to Short Sub, it can provide financing by allowing Short Sub to lag its payments. This technique is called **lagging**.

The leading or lagging strategy can make efficient use of cash and thereby reduce debt. Some host governments prohibit the practice by requiring that a payment between subsidiaries occur at the time the goods are transferred. Thus, an MNC needs to be aware of any laws that restrict the use of this strategy.

Complications in Optimizing Cash Flow

Most complications encountered in optimizing cash flow can be classified into three categories:

- Company-related characteristics
- Government restrictions
- Characteristics of banking systems

Each complication is discussed in turn.

Company-Related Characteristics

In some cases, optimizing cash flow can become complicated due to characteristics of the MNC. If one of the subsidiaries delays payments to other subsidiaries for supplies received, the other subsidiaries may be forced to borrow until the payments arrive. A centralized approach that monitors all intersubsidiary payments should be able to minimize such problems.

Government Restrictions

The existence of government restrictions can disrupt a cash flow optimization policy. Some governments prohibit the use of a netting system, as noted earlier. In addition, some countries periodically prevent cash from leaving the country, thereby preventing net payments from being made. These problems can arise even for MNCs that do not experience any company-related problems. Countries in Latin America commonly impose restrictions that affect an MNC's cash flows.

Characteristics of Banking Systems

The abilities of banks to facilitate cash transfers for MNCs vary among countries. Banks in the United States are advanced in this field, but banks in some other countries do not offer services. MNCs prefer some form of zero-balance account, where excess funds can be used to make payments but earn interest until they are used. In addition, some MNCs benefit from the use of lockboxes. Such services are not available in some countries.

In addition, a bank may not update the MNC's bank account information sufficiently or provide a detailed breakdown of fees for banking services. Without full use of banking resources and information, the effectiveness of international cash management is limited. In addition, an MNC with subsidiaries in, say, eight different countries will typically be dealing with eight different banking systems. Much progress has been made in foreign banking systems in recent years. As time passes and a more uniform global banking system emerges, such problems may be alleviated.

Investing Excess Cash

Many MNCs have at least $100 million in cash balances across banks in various countries. If they can find a way to earn an extra 1 percent on those funds, they will generate an extra $1 million each year on cash balances of $100 million. Thus, their short-term investment decision affects the amount of their cash inflows. Their excess funds can be invested in domestic or foreign short-term securities. In some periods, foreign short-term securities will have higher interest rates than domestic interest rates. The differential can be substantial, as illustrated in Exhibit 21.4. However, firms must account for the possible exchange rate movements when assessing the potential yield on foreign investments.

How to Invest Excess Cash

International money markets have grown to accommodate corporate investments of excess cash. MNCs may use international money markets in an attempt to earn higher returns than they can achieve domestically.

Exhibit 21.4

Short-Term Annualized Interest Rates among Countries (as of February 2004)

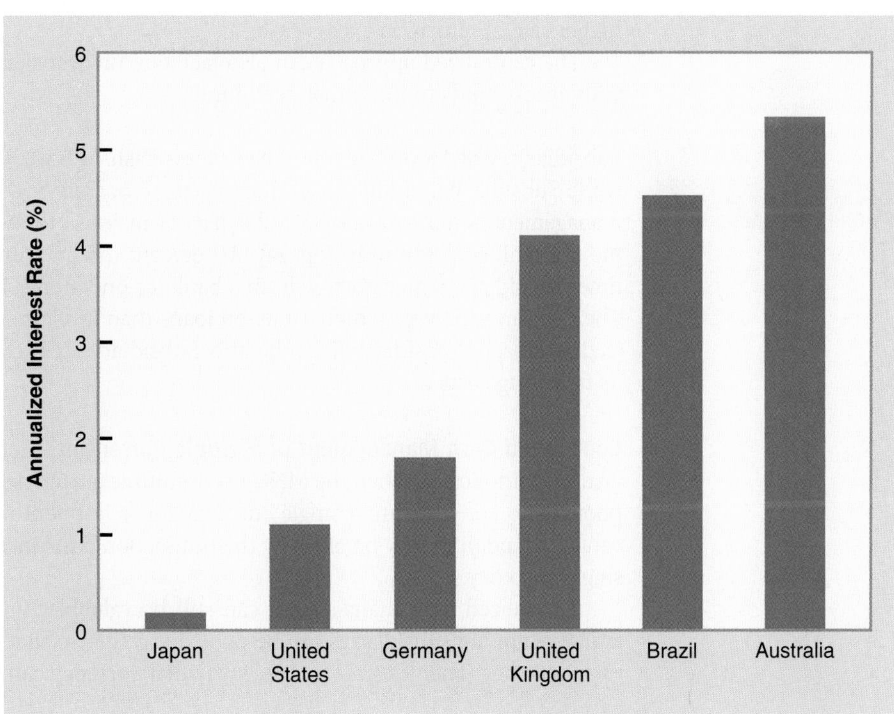

Eurocurrency deposits are one of the most commonly used international money market instruments. Many MNCs establish large deposits in various currencies in the Eurocurrency market, with Eurodollar deposits being the most popular. The dollar volume of Eurodollar deposits has more than doubled since 1980. Eurodollar deposits commonly offer MNCs a slightly higher yield than bank deposits in the United States. Though Eurodollar deposits still dominate the market, the relative importance of non-dollar currencies has increased over time.

In addition to using the Eurocurrency market, MNCs can also purchase foreign Treasury bills and commercial paper. Improved telecommunications systems have increased access to these securities in foreign markets and allow for a greater degree of integration among money markets in various countries.

Centralized Cash Management

An MNC's short-term investing policy can either maintain separate investments for all subsidiaries or employ a centralized approach. Recall that the function of optimizing cash flows can be improved by a centralized approach, since all subsidiary cash positions can be monitored simultaneously. With regard to the investing function, centralization allows for more efficient usage of funds and possibly higher returns. Here the term *centralized* means that excess cash from each subsidiary is pooled until it is needed by a particular subsidiary.

Centralization When Subsidiaries Use the Same Currency. To understand the advantages of a centralized system, consider that the rates paid on short-term investments such as bank deposits are often higher for larger amounts. Thus, if two subsidiaries have excess cash of $50,000 each for one month, the rates on their individual bank deposits may be lower than the rate they could obtain if they pooled their funds into a single $100,000 bank deposit. In this manner, the centralized (pooling) approach generates a higher rate of return on excess cash.

The centralized approach can also facilitate the transfer of funds from subsidiaries with excess funds to those that need funds.

EXAMPLE

Subsidiary A of Moorhead, Inc., has excess cash of $50,000 during the next month, while Subsidiary B of Moorhead, Inc., needs to borrow $50,000 for one month. If cash management is not centralized, Subsidiary A may use the $50,000 to purchase a one-month bank certificate earning, say, 10 percent (on an annualized basis). At the same time, Subsidiary B may borrow from a bank for one month at a rate of, say, 12 percent. The bank must charge a higher rate on loans than it offers on deposits. With a centralized approach, Subsidiary B can borrow Subsidiary A's excess funds, thereby reducing its financing costs.

Centralized Cash Management of Multiple Currencies. Centralized cash management is more complicated when the MNC uses multiple currencies. All excess funds could be pooled and converted to a single currency for investment purposes. However, the advantage of pooling may be offset by the transaction costs incurred when converting to a single currency.

Centralized cash management can still be valuable, though. The short-term cash available among subsidiaries can be pooled together so that there is a separate pool for each currency. Then excess cash in a particular currency can still be used to satisfy other subsidiary deficiencies in that currency. In this way, funds can be transferred from one subsidiary to another without incurring transaction costs that banks charge for exchanging currencies. This strategy is especially feasible when all subsidiary funds are deposited in branches of a single bank so that the funds can easily be transferred among subsidiaries.

Another possible function of centralized cash management is to invest funds in securities denominated in the foreign currencies that will be needed by the subsidiaries in the future. MNCs can use excess cash to invest cash in international money market instruments so that they can cover any payables positions in specific foreign currencies. If they have payables in foreign currencies that are expected to appreciate, they can cover such positions by creating short-term deposits in those currencies. The maturity of a deposit would ideally coincide with the date at which the funds are needed.

Impact of Technology on Centralized Cash Management. International cash management requires timely information across subsidiaries regarding each subsidiary's cash positions in each currency, along with interest rate information about each currency. A centralized cash management system needs a continual flow of information about currency positions so that it can determine whether one subsidiary's shortage of cash can be covered by another subsidiary's excess cash in that currency. Given the major improvements in online technology in recent years, all MNCs can easily and efficiently create a multinational communications network among their subsidiaries to ensure that information about cash positions is continually updated.

EXAMPLE

To understand how such a communications network works, consider Jax Co., which creates a cash balances website that specifies the cash balance of every currency for each subsidiary. Near the end of each day, each subsidiary revises the website to provide the latest update of its cash balance for each currency. Each subsidiary also specifies the period of time in which the excess or deficiency will persist. The parent's treasury department monitors the updated data and determines whether any cash needs identified by a subsidiary in a particular currency can be accommodated by another subsidiary that has excess cash in that same currency. The treasury department then e-mails instructions to the subsidiaries about fund transfers. If it notices that the Canadian subsidiary has an excess of Canadian dollars for the next 26 days, and the Belgian subsidiary needs Canadian dollars tomorrow (but will have inflows of Canadian dollars in 17 days), it provides the following instructions: "The Canadian subsidiary should transfer C$60,000 to the Belgian subsidiary and will be repaid by the Belgian subsidiary in 17 days." The fund transfers are essentially short-term loans, so a subsidiary that borrows funds will repay them with interest. The interest charged on a loan creates an incentive for subsidiaries to make their excess cash available and an incentive for subsidiaries with cash deficiencies to return the funds as soon as possible.

The electronic communications network may be more sophisticated than the one described here, but this description illustrates how easy it is for an MNC's parent to continuously monitor the cash balances of each subsidiary and communicate instructions among subsidiaries. The process of transferring funds among subsidiaries may be especially easy when all the MNC's subsidiaries use branches of the same bank. A communications network allows the MNC to make the best use of each subsidiary's cash, which can reduce the amount of external financing needed and reduce the MNC's exchange rate risk.

Determining the Effective Yield

Firms commonly consider investing in a deposit denominated in a currency with a high interest rate and then converting the funds back to dollars when the deposit matures. This strategy will not necessarily be feasible, since the currency denominating the deposit may depreciate over the life of the deposit. If it does, the advantage of a higher interest rate may be more than offset by the depreciation in the currency representing the deposit.

Consequently, it is the deposit's **effective yield**, not its interest rate, that is most important to the cash manager. The effective yield of a bank deposit considers both the interest rate and the rate of appreciation (or depreciation) of the currency denominating the deposit and can therefore be very different from the quoted interest rate on a deposit denominated in a foreign currency. An example follows to illustrate this point.

EXAMPLE

Quant Co., a large U.S. corporation with $1,000,000 in excess cash, could invest in a one-year deposit at 6 percent but is attracted to higher interest rates in Australia. It creates a one-year deposit denominated in Australian dollars (A$) at 9 percent. The exchange rate of the Australian dollar at the time of the deposit is $.68. The U.S. dollars are first converted to A$1,470,588 (since $1,000,000/$.68 = $1,470,588) and then deposited in a bank.

One year later, Quant Co. receives A$1,602,941, which is equal to the initial deposit plus 9 percent interest on the deposit. At this time, Quant Co. has no use for Australian dollars and converts them into U.S. dollars. Assume that the exchange rate at this time is $.72. The funds will convert to $1,154,118 (computed as A$1,602,941 × $.72 per A$). Thus, the yield on this investment to the U.S. corporation is

$$\frac{\$1{,}154{,}118 - \$1{,}000{,}000}{\$1{,}000{,}000} = .1541, \text{ or } 15.41\%$$

The high yield is attributed to the relatively high interest rate earned on the deposit, plus the appreciation in the currency denominating the deposit over the investment period.

If the currency had depreciated over the investment period, however, the effective yield to Quant Co. would have been less than the interest rate on the deposit and could even have been lower than the interest rate available on U.S. investments. For example, if the Australian dollar had depreciated from $.68 at the beginning of the investment period to $.65 by the end of the investment period, Quant Co. would have received $1,041,912 (computed as A$1,602,941 × $.65 per A$). In this case, the yield on the investment to the U.S. corporation would have been

$$\frac{\$1{,}041{,}912 - \$1{,}000{,}000}{\$1{,}000{,}000} = .0419, \text{ or } 4.19\%$$

The preceeding example illustrates how appreciation of the currency denominating a foreign deposit over the deposit period will force the effective yield to be above the quoted interest rate. Conversely, depreciation will create the opposite effect.

The previous computation of the effective yield on foreign deposits was conducted in a logical manner. A quicker method is shown here:

$$r = (1 + i_f)(1 + e_f) - 1$$

http://

Visit http://www.bloomberg.com for the latest information from financial markets around the world.

The effective yield on the foreign deposit is represented by r, i_f is the quoted interest rate, and e_f is the percentage change (from the day of deposit to the day of withdrawal) in the value of the currency representing the foreign deposit. The term i_f was used in Chapter 20 to represent the interest rate when borrowing a foreign currency. In this chapter, the interest rate of concern is the deposit rate on the foreign currency.

EXAMPLE

Given the information for Quant Co., the effective yield on the Australian deposit can be estimated. The term e_f represents the percentage change in the Australian dollar (against the U.S. dollar) from the date Australian dollars are purchased (and deposited) until the day they are withdrawn (and converted back to U.S. dollars). The Australian dollar appreciated from \$.68 to \$.72, or by 5.88 percent over the life of the deposit. Using this information as well as the quoted deposit rate of 9 percent, the effective yield to the U.S. firm on this deposit denominated in Australian dollars is

$$\begin{aligned} r &= (1 + i_f)(1 + e_f) - 1 \\ &= (1 + .09)[1 + (.0588)] - 1 \\ &= .1541, \text{ or } 15.41\% \end{aligned}$$

This estimate of the effective yield corresponds with the return on investment determined earlier for Quant Co.

If the currency had depreciated, Quant Co. would have earned an effective yield that was less than the interest rate.

In the revised example for Quant Co., the Australian dollar depreciated from \$.68 to \$.65, or by 4.41 percent. Based on the quoted interest rate of 9 percent and the depreciation of 4.41 percent, the effective yield is

$$\begin{aligned} r &= (1 + i_f)(1 + e_f) - 1 \\ &= (1 + .09)[1 + (.0441)] - 1 \\ &= .0419, \text{ or } 4.19\% \end{aligned}$$

which is the same rate computed earlier for this revised example.

The effective yield can be negative if the currency denominating the deposit depreciates to an extent that more than offsets the interest accrued from the deposit.

EXAMPLE

Nebraska, Inc., invests in a bank deposit denominated in euros that provides a yield of 9 percent. The euro depreciates against the dollar by 12 percent over the one-year period. The effective yield is

$$\begin{aligned} r &= (1 + .09)[1 + (-.12)] - 1 \\ &= -.0408, \text{ or } -4.08\% \end{aligned}$$

This result indicates that Nebraska, Inc., will end up with 4.08 percent less in funds than it initially deposited.

As with bank deposits, the effective yield on all other securities denominated in a foreign currency is influenced by the fluctuation of that currency's exchange rate. Our discussion will continue to focus on bank deposits for short-term foreign investment, but the implications of the discussion can be applied to other short-term securities as well.

Implications of Interest Rate Parity

Recall that covered interest arbitrage is described as a short-term foreign investment with a simultaneous forward sale of the foreign currency denominating the foreign investment. One might think that a foreign currency with a high interest rate would be an ideal candidate for covered interest arbitrage. However, such a currency will normally exhibit a forward discount that reflects the differential between its interest rate and the investor's home interest rate. This relationship is based on the theory of interest rate parity. Investors cannot lock in a higher return when attempting covered interest arbitrage if interest rate parity exists.

Even if interest rate parity does exist, short-term foreign investing may still be feasible but would have to be conducted on an uncovered basis (without use of the forward market). That is, short-term foreign investing may result in a higher effective yield than domestic investing, but it cannot be guaranteed.

Use of the Forward Rate as a Forecast

If interest rate parity exists, the forward rate serves as a break-even point to assess the short-term investment decision. When investing in the foreign currency (and not covering the foreign currency position), the effective yield will be more than the domestic yield if the spot rate of the foreign currency after one year is more than the forward rate at the time the investment is undertaken. Conversely, the yield of a foreign investment will be lower than the domestic yield if the spot rate of the foreign currency after one year turns out to be less than the forward rate at the time the investment is undertaken.

http://

Visit http://ciber.msu.edu for links to numerous sites related to international business.

Relationship with the International Fisher Effect. When interest rate parity exists, MNCs that use the forward rate as a predictor of the future spot rate expect the yield on foreign deposits to equal that on U.S. deposits. Though the forward rate is not necessarily an accurate predictor, it may provide unbiased forecasts of the future spot rate. If the forward rate is unbiased, it does not consistently underestimate or overestimate the future spot rate with equal frequency. Thus, the effective yield on foreign deposits is equal to the domestic yield, on average. MNCs that consistently invest in foreign short-term securities would earn a yield similar on average to what they could earn on domestic securities.

Our discussion here is closely related to the international Fisher effect (IFE). Recall that the IFE suggests that the exchange rate of a foreign currency is expected to change by an amount reflecting the differential between its interest rate and the U.S. interest rate. The rationale behind this theory is that a high nominal interest rate reflects an expectation of high inflation, which could weaken the currency (according to purchasing power parity).

If interest rate parity exists, the forward premium or discount reflects that interest rate differential and represents the expected percentage change in the currency's value when the forward rate is used as a predictor of the future spot rate. The IFE suggests that firms cannot consistently earn short-term yields on foreign securities that are higher than those on domestic securities because the exchange rate is expected to adjust to the interest rate differential on average. If interest rate parity holds and the forward rate is an unbiased predictor of the future spot rate, we can expect the IFE to hold.

A look back in time reveals that the IFE is supported for some currencies in some periods. Moreover, it may be difficult for an MNC to anticipate when the IFE will hold and when it will not. For virtually any currency, it is possible to identify previous periods when the forward rate substantially underestimated the future spot rate, and an MNC would have earned very high returns from investing short-term funds in a foreign money market security. However, it is also possible to identify other periods when the forward rate substantially overestimated the future spot rate, and the MNC would have earned low or even negative returns from investing in that same foreign money market security.

Conclusions about the Forward Rate. The key implications of interest rate parity and the forward rate as a predictor of future spot rates for foreign investing are summarized in Exhibit 21.5. This exhibit explains the conditions in which investment in foreign short-term securities is feasible.

Use of Exchange Rate Forecasts

Although MNCs do not know how a currency's value will change over the investment horizon, they can use the formula for the effective yield provided earlier in this chapter and plug in their forecast for the percentage change in the foreign currency's exchange rate (e_f). Since the interest rate of the foreign currency deposit (i_f) is known, the

Exhibit 21.5
Considerations When Investing Excess Cash

Scenario	Implications for Investing in Foreign Money Markets
1. Interest rate parity exists.	Covered interest arbitrage is not worthwhile.
2. Interest rate parity exists, and the forward rate is an accurate forecast of the future spot rate.	An uncovered investment in a foreign security is not worthwhile.
3. Interest rate parity exists, and the forward rate is an unbiased forecast of the future spot rate.	An uncovered investment in a foreign security will on average earn an effective yield similar to an investment in a domestic security.
4. Interest rate parity exists, and the forward rate is expected to overestimate the future spot rate.	An uncovered investment in a foreign security is expected to earn a lower effective yield than an investment in a domestic security.
5. Interest rate parity exists, and the forward rate is expected to underestimate the future spot rate.	An uncovered investment in a foreign security is expected to earn a higher effective yield than an investment in a domestic security.
6. Interest rate parity does not exist; the forward premium (discount) exceeds (is less than) the interest rate differential.	Covered interest arbitrage is feasible for investors residing in the home country.
7. Interest rate parity does not exist; the forward premium (discount) is less than (exceeds) the interest rate differential.	Covered interest arbitrage is feasible for foreign investors but not for investors residing in the home country.

effective yield can be forecasted given a forecast of e_f. This projected effective yield on a foreign deposit can then be compared with the yield when investing in the firm's local currency.

EXAMPLE

Latrobe, Inc., is a U.S. firm with funds available to invest for one year. It is aware that the one-year interest rate on a U.S. dollar deposit is 11 percent and the interest rate on an Australian deposit is 14 percent. Assume that the U.S. firm forecasts that the Australian deposit will depreciate from its current rate of \$.1600 to \$.1584, or a 1 percent decrease. The expected value for e_f $[E(e_f)]$ will therefore be -1 percent. Thus, the expected effective yield $[E(r)]$ on an Australian dollar-denominated deposit is

$$\begin{aligned} E(r) &= (1 + i_f)[1 + E(e_f)] - 1 \\ &= (1 + 14\%)[1 + (-1\%)] - 1 \\ &= 12.86\% \end{aligned}$$

Thus, this example, investing in an Australian dollar deposit is expected to be more rewarding than investing in a U.S. dollar deposit.

Keep in mind that the value for e_f is forecasted and therefore is not known with certainty. Thus, there is no guarantee that foreign investing will truly be more lucrative.

Deriving the Value of e_f That Equates Foreign and Domestic Yields. From the preceding example, Latrobe may attempt to at least determine what value of e_f would make the effective yield from foreign investing the same as that from investing in a U.S. dollar deposit. To determine this value, begin with the effective yield formula and solve for e_f as follows:

$$\begin{aligned} r &= (1 + i_f)(1 + e_f) - 1 \\ (1 + r) &= (1 + i_f)(1 + e_f) \\ \frac{(1 + r)}{(1 + i_f)} &= (1 + e_f) \\ \frac{(1 + r)}{(1 + i_f)} - 1 &= e_f \end{aligned}$$

Since the U.S. deposit rate was 11 percent in our previous example, that is the rate to be plugged in for r. We can also plug in 14 percent for i_f, so the break-even value of e_f would be

$$\begin{aligned} e_f &= \frac{(1 + r)}{(1 + i_f)} - 1 \\ &= \frac{(1 + 11\%)}{(1 + 14\%)} - 1 \\ &= -2.63\% \end{aligned}$$

This suggests that the Australian dollar must depreciate by about 2.63 percent to make the Australian dollar deposit generate the same effective yield as a deposit in U.S. dollars. With any smaller degree of depreciation, the Australian dollar deposit would be more rewarding. Latrobe, Inc., can use this information when determining whether to invest in a U.S. dollar or Australian dollar deposit. If it expects the Australian dollar to depreciate by more than 2.63 percent over the deposit period, it will prefer investing in U.S. dollars. If it expects the Australian dollar to depreciate by less than 2.63 percent, or to appreciate, its decision is more complex. If the potential reward from investing in the foreign currency outweighs the risk involved, then the firm should choose that route. The final decision here will be influenced by the firm's degree of risk aversion.

Use of Probability Distributions. Since even expert forecasts are not always accurate, it is sometimes useful to develop a probability distribution instead of relying on a single prediction. An example of how a probability distribution is applied follows.

EXAMPLE

Ohio, Inc., is deciding whether to invest in Australian dollars for one year. It finds that the quoted interest rate for the Australian dollar is 14 percent, and the quoted interest rate for a U.S. dollar deposit is 11 percent. It then develops a probability distribution for the Australian dollar's possible percentage change in value over the life of the deposit.

The probability distribution is displayed in Exhibit 21.6. From the first row in the exhibit, we see that there is a 5 percent probability of a 10 percent depreciation in the Australian dollar over the deposit's life. If the Australian dollar does depreciate by 10 percent, the effective yield will be 2.60 percent. This indicates that there is a 5 percent probability that Ohio, Inc., will earn a 2.60 percent effective yield on its funds. From the second row in the exhibit, there is a 10 percent probability of an 8 percent depreciation in the Australian dollar over the deposit period. If the Australian dollar does depreciate by 8 percent, the effective yield will be 4.88 percent, which means there is a 10 percent probability that Ohio will generate a 4.88 percent effective yield on this deposit.

For each possible percentage change in the Australian dollar's value, there is a corresponding effective yield. Each possible effective yield (third column) is associated with a probability of that yield occurring (second column). An *expected value* of the effective

Exhibit 21.6

Analysis of Investing in a Foreign Currency

Possible Rate of Change in the Australian Dollar over the Life of the Investment (e_f)	Probability of Occurrence	Effective Yield If This Rate of Change in the Australian Dollar Does Occur
−10%	5%	(1.14) [1 + (−.10)] − 1 = .0260, or 2.60%
−8	10	(1.14) [1 + (−.08)] − 1 = .0488, or 4.88%
−4	15	(1.14) [1 + (−.04)] − 1 = .0944, or 9.44%
−2	20	(1.14) [1 + (−.02)] − 1 = .1172, or 11.72%
+1	20	(1.14) [1 + (.01)] − 1 = .1514, or 15.14%
+2	15	(1.14) [1 + (.02)] − 1 = .1628, or 16.28%
+3	10	(1.14) [1 + (.03)] − 1 = .1742, or 17.42%
+4	5	(1.14) [1 + (.04)] − 1 = .1856, or 18.56%
	100%	

yield of the Australian dollar is derived by multiplying each possible effective yield by its corresponding probability. Based on the information in Exhibit 21.6, the expected value of the effective yield, referred to as $E(r)$, is computed this way:

$$\begin{aligned} E(r_f) &= 5\%(2.60\%) + 10\%(4.88\%) + 15\%(9.44\%) + 20\%(11.72\%) \\ &\quad + 20\%(15.14\%) + 15\%(16.28\%) + 10\%(17.42\%) \\ &\quad + 5\%(18.56\%) \\ &= .13\% + .488\% + 1.416\% + 2.344\% + 3.028\% + 2.442\% \\ &\quad + 1.742\% + .928\% \\ &= 12.518\% \end{aligned}$$

Thus, the expected value of the effective yield when investing in Australian dollars is approximately 12.5 percent.

To further assess the question of which currency to invest in, the information in the second and third columns from Exhibit 21.6 is used to develop a probability distribution in Exhibit 21.7, which illustrates the probability of each possible effective yield that may occur if Ohio, Inc., invests in Australian dollars. Notice that the U.S. interest rate (11 percent) is known with certainty and is included in Exhibit 21.7 for comparison purposes. A comparison of the Australian dollar's probability distribution against the U.S. interest rate suggests that there is a 30 percent probability that the U.S. rate will be

Exhibit 21.7 Probability Distribution of Effective Yields

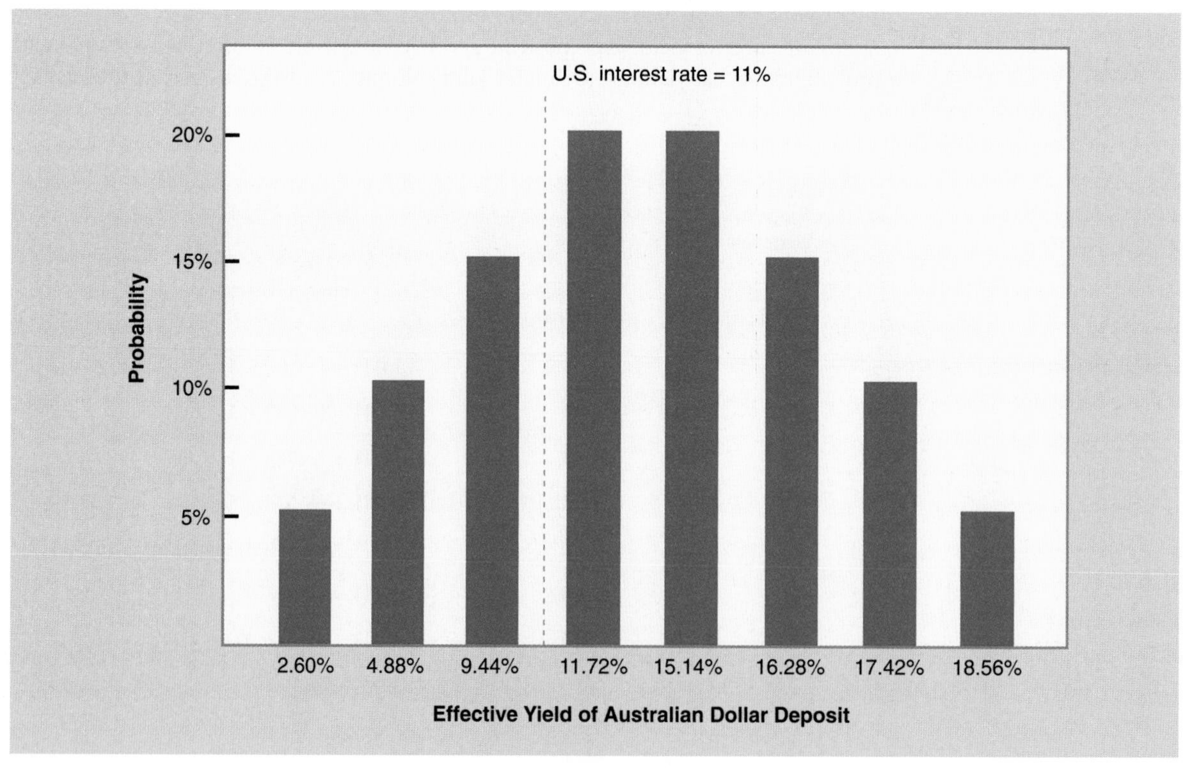

more than the effective yield from investing in Australian dollars and a 70 percent chance that it will be less.

If Ohio, Inc., invests in a U.S. dollar deposit, it knows with certainty the yield it will earn from its investment. If it invests in Australian dollars, its risk is the 5 percent chance (probability) that the effective yield on the Australian dollar deposit will be 2.60 percent, or the 10 percent chance that the effective yield on the Australian dollar deposit will be 4.88 percent, or the 15 percent chance that the effective yield on Australian dollars will be 9.44 percent. Each of these possibilities represents a lower return to Ohio, Inc., than what it would have earned had it invested in a U.S. dollar deposit. Ohio, Inc., concludes that the potential return on the Australian deposit is not high enough to compensate for the risk and decides to invest in the U.S. deposit.

Diversifying Cash across Currencies

Because an MNC is not sure how exchange rates will change over time, it may prefer to diversify cash among securities denominated in different currencies. Limiting the percentage of excess cash invested in each currency will reduce the MNC's exposure to exchange rate risk.

The degree to which a portfolio of investments denominated in various currencies will reduce risk depends on the currency correlations. Ideally, the currencies represented within the portfolio will exhibit low or negative correlations with each other. When currencies are likely to be affected by the same underlying event, their movements tend to be more highly correlated, and diversification among these types of currencies does not substantially reduce exposure to exchange rate risk.

EXAMPLE

In 1997, the interest rates in most Asian countries were higher than the interest rate in the United States. However, Asian currencies, such as the Indonesian rupiah, the Malaysian ringgit, the South Korean won, and the Thailand baht, depreciated by more than 50 percent against the U.S. dollar in less than one year. Consequently, subsidiaries based outside Asia that attempted to benefit from the high Asian interest rates earned negative effective yields on their investments, so they received less than what they initially invested. Diversification of cash among these currencies was not beneficial in this case because all of the currencies weakened in response to the Asian crisis. The potential benefits from investing in a portfolio of currencies are more thoroughly discussed in Appendix 21.

Dynamic Hedging

Some MNCs continually adjust their short-term positions in currencies in response to revised expectations of each currency's future movement. They may engage in **dynamic hedging**, which is a strategy of applying a hedge when the currencies held are expected to depreciate and removing the hedge when the currencies held are expected to appreciate. In essence, the objective is to protect against downside risk while benefiting from the favorable movement of exchange rates.

For example, consider a treasurer of a U.S. firm who plans to invest in British money market securities. If the British pound begins to decline and is expected to depreciate further, the treasurer may sell pounds forward in the foreign exchange market for a future date at which the pound's value is expected to turn upward. If the treasurer is very confident that the pound will depreciate in the short run, most or all of the position will be hedged.

Now assume that the pound begins to appreciate before the forward contract date. Since the contract will preclude the potential benefits from the pound's appreciation, the treasurer may buy pounds forward to offset the existing forward sale contracts. In this way, the treasurer has removed the existing hedge. Of course, if the forward rate at the time of the forward purchase exceeds the forward rate that existed at the time of the forward sale, a cost is incurred to offset the hedge.

The treasurer may decide to remove only part of the hedge, offsetting only some of the existing forward sales with forward purchases. With this approach, the position is still partially protected if the pound depreciates further. Overall, the performance from using dynamic hedging is dependent on the treasurer's ability to forecast the direction of exchange rate movements.

SUMMARY

- Each subsidiary of an MNC can assess its cash flows by estimating expected cash inflows and outflows to forecast its balance in each currency. This will indicate whether it will have excess cash to invest or a cash deficiency. The MNC's parent may prefer to use a centralized perspective, which consolidates the cash flow positions of all subsidiaries. In this way, funds can be transferred among subsidiaries to accommodate cash deficiencies at particular subsidiaries.
- The common techniques to optimize cash flows are (1) accelerating cash inflows, (2) minimizing currency conversion costs, (3) managing blocked funds, and (4) implementing intersubsidiary cash transfers.
- The efforts by MNCs to optimize cash flows are complicated by (1) company-related characteristics, (2) government restrictions, and (3) characteristics of banking systems.
- MNCs can possibly achieve higher returns when investing excess cash in foreign currencies that either have relatively high interest rates or may appreciate over the investment period. If the foreign currency depreciates over the investment period, however, this may offset any interest rate advantage of that currency.

POINT COUNTER-POINT

Should Interest Rate Parity Prevent MNCs from Investing in Foreign Currencies?

Point Yes. Currencies with high interest rates have large forward discounts according to interest rate parity. To the extent that the forward rate is a reasonable forecast of the future spot rate, investing in a foreign country is not feasible.

Counter-Point No. Even if interest rate parity holds, MNCs should still consider investing in a foreign currency. The key is their expectations of the future spot rate. If their expectations of the future spot rate are higher than the forward rate, the MNCs would benefit from investing in a foreign currency.

Who Is Correct? Use InfoTrac or some other search engine to learn more about this issue. Which argument do you support? Offer your own opinion on this issue.

SELF TEST

Answers are provided in Appendix A at the back of the text.

1. Country X typically has a high interest rate, and its currency is expected to strengthen against the dollar over time. Country Y typically has a low interest rate, and its currency is expected to weaken against the dollar over time. Both countries have imposed a "blocked funds" restriction over the next four years on the two subsidiaries owned by a U.S. firm. Which subsidiary will be more adversely affected by the blocked funds, assuming that there are limited opportunities for corporate expansion in both countries?

2. Assume that the Australian one-year interest rate is 14 percent. Also assume that the Australian dollar is expected to appreciate by 8 percent over the next year against the U.S. dollar. What is the expected effective yield on a one-year deposit in Australia by a U.S. firm?

3. Assume that the one-year forward rate is used as the forecast of the future spot rate. The Malaysian ringgit's spot rate is $.20, while its one-year forward rate is $.19. The Malaysian one-year interest rate is 11 percent. What is the expected effective yield on a one-year deposit in Malaysia by a U.S. firm?

4. Assume that the Venezuelan one-year interest rate is 90 percent, while the U.S. one-year interest rate is 6 percent. Determine the break-even value for the percentage change in Venezuela's currency (the bolivar) that would cause the effective yield to be the same for a one-year deposit in Venezuela as for a one-year deposit in the United States.

5. Assume interest rate parity exists. Would U.S. firms possibly consider placing deposits in countries with high interest rates? Explain.

QUESTIONS AND APPLICATIONS

1. **International Cash Management.** Discuss the general functions involved in international cash management. Explain how the MNC's optimization of cash flow can distort the profits of each subsidiary.

2. **Netting.** Explain the benefits of netting. How can a centralized cash management system be beneficial to the MNC?

3. **Leading and Lagging.** How can an MNC implement leading and lagging techniques to help subsidiaries in need of funds?

4. **International Fisher Effect.** If a U.S. firm believes that the international Fisher effect holds, what are the implications regarding a strategy of continually attempting to generate high returns from investing in currencies with high interest rates?

5. **Investing Strategy.** Tallahassee Co. has $2 million in excess cash that it has invested in Mexico at an annual interest rate of 60 percent. The U.S. interest rate is 9 percent. By how much would the Mexican peso have to depreciate to cause such a strategy to backfire?

6. **Investing Strategy.** Why would a U.S. firm consider investing short-term funds in euros even when it does not have any future cash outflows in euros?

7. **Covered Interest Arbitrage.** Evansville, Inc., has $2 million in cash available for 90 days. It is considering the use of covered interest arbitrage, since the euro's 90-day interest rate is higher than the U.S. interest rate. What will determine whether this strategy is feasible?

8. **Effective Yield.** Fort Collins, Inc., has $1 million in cash available for 30 days. It can earn 1 percent on a 30-day investment in the United States. Alternatively, if it converts the dollars to Mexican pesos, it can earn 1½ percent on a Mexican deposit. The spot rate of the Mexican peso is $.12. The spot rate 30 days from now is expected to be $.10. Should Fort Collins invest its cash in the United States or in Mexico? Substantiate your answer.

9. **Effective Yield.** Rollins, Inc., has $3 million in cash available for 180 days. It can earn 7 percent on a U.S. Treasury bill or 9 percent on a British Treasury

bill. The British investment does require conversion of dollars to British pounds. Assume that interest rate parity holds and that Rollins believes the 180-day forward rate is a reliable predictor of the spot rate to be realized 180 days from now. Would the British investment provide an effective yield that is below, above, or equal to the yield on the U.S. investment? Explain your answer.

10. **Effective Yield.** Repeat question 9, but this time assume that Rollins, Inc., expects the 180-day forward rate of the pound to substantially overestimate the spot rate to be realized in 180 days.

11. **Effective Yield.** Repeat question 9, but this time assume that the Rollins, Inc., expects the 180-day forward rate of the pound to substantially underestimate the spot rate to be realized in 180 days.

12. **Effective Yield.** Assume that the one-year U.S. interest rate is 10 percent and the one-year Canadian interest rate is 13 percent. If a U.S. firm invests its funds in Canada, by what percentage will the Canadian dollar have to depreciate to make its effective yield the same as the U.S. interest rate from the U.S. firm's perspective?

13. **Investing in a Currency Portfolio.** Why would a firm consider investing in a portfolio of foreign currencies instead of just a single foreign currency?

14. **Interest Rate Parity.** Dallas Co. has determined that the interest rate on euros is 16 percent while the U.S. interest rate is 11 percent for one-year Treasury bills. The one-year forward rate of the euro has a discount of 7 percent. Does interest rate parity exist? Can Dallas achieve a higher effective yield by using covered interest arbitrage than by investing in U.S. Treasury bills? Explain.

15. **Diversified Investments.** Hofstra, Inc., has no European business and has cash invested in six European countries, each of which uses the euro as its local currency. Are Hofstra's short-term investments well diversified and subject to a low degree of exchange rate risk? Explain.

16. **Investing Strategy.** Should McNeese Co. consider investing funds in Latin American countries where it may expand facilities? The interest rates are high, and the proceeds from the investments could be used to help support the expansion. When would this strategy backfire?

17. **Impact of September 11.** Palos Co. commonly invests some of its excess dollars in foreign government short-term securities in order to earn a higher short-term interest rate on its cash. Describe how the potential return and risk of this strategy may have changed after the September 11, 2001 terrorist attack on the United States.

ADVANCED QUESTIONS

18. **Investing in a Portfolio.** Pittsburgh Co. plans to invest its excess cash in Mexican pesos for one year. The one-year Mexican interest rate is 19 percent. The probability of the peso's percentage change in value during the next year is shown below:

Possible Rate of Change in the Mexican Peso over the Life of the Investment	Probability of Occurrence
−15%	20%
−4	50
0	30

What is the expected value of the effective yield based on this information? Given that the U.S. interest rate for one year is 7 percent, what is the probability that a one-year investment in pesos will generate a lower effective yield than could be generated if Pittsburgh Co. simply invested domestically?

19. **Effective Yield of Portfolio.** Ithaca Co. considers placing 30 percent of its excess funds in a one-year Singapore dollar deposit and the remaining 70 percent of its funds in a one-year Canadian dollar deposit. The Singapore one-year interest rate is 15 percent, while the Canadian one-year interest rate is 13 percent. The possible percentage changes in the two currencies for the next year are forecasted as follows:

Currency	Possible Percentage Change in the Spot Rate over the Investment Horizon	Probability of That Change in the Spot Rate Occurring
Singapore dollar	−2%	20%
Singapore dollar	1	60
Singapore dollar	3	20
Canadian dollar	1	50
Canadian dollar	4	40
Canadian dollar	6	10

Given this information, determine the possible effective yields of the portfolio and the probability associated with each possible portfolio yield. Given a one-year U.S. interest rate of 8 percent, what is the probability that the portfolio's effective yield will be lower than the yield achieved from investing in the United States? (See Appendix 21.)

INTERNET APPLICATION

20. **Foreign Currency Yields.** The Bloomberg website provides interest rate data for many different foreign currencies over various maturities. Its address is **http://www.bloomberg.com**.

a. Go to the section that shows yields for different foreign currencies. Review the one-year yields of currencies. Assume that you could borrow at a rate 1 percentage point above the quoted yield for each currency. Which currency would offer you the highest quoted yield?

b. As a cash manager of an MNC based in the United States that has extra dollars that can be invested for one year, where would you invest funds for the next year? Explain.

c. If you were working for a foreign subsidiary based in Japan and could invest Japanese yen for one year until the yen are needed to support local operations, where would you invest the yen? Explain.

DISCUSSION IN THE BOARDROOM

This exercise can be found in Appendix E at the back of this textbook.

RUNNING YOUR OWN MNC

This exercise can be found on the Xtra! website at **http://maduraxtra.swlearning.com**.

BLADES, INC. CASE

International Cash Management

Recall from Chapter 20 that the new Thailand subsidiary of Blades, Inc., received a one-time order from a customer for 120,000 pairs of "Speedos," Blades' primary product. There is a six-month lag between the time when Blades needs funds to purchase material for the production of the Speedos and the time when it will be paid by the customer. Ben Holt, Blades' chief financial officer (CFO), has decided to finance the cost by borrowing Thai baht at an interest rate of 6 percent over a six-month period. Since the average cost per pair of Speedos is approximately 3,500 baht, Blades will borrow 420 million baht. The payment for the order will be used to repay the loan's principal and interest.

Ben Holt is currently planning to instruct the Thai subsidiary to remit any remaining baht-denominated cash flows back to the United States. Just before Blades receives payment for the large order, however, Holt notices that interest rates in Thailand have increased substantially. Blades would be able to invest funds in Thailand at a relatively high interest rate compared to the U.S. rate. Specifically, Blades could invest the remaining baht-denominated funds for one year in Thailand at an interest rate of 15 percent.

If the funds are remitted back to the U.S. parent, the excess dollar volume resulting from the conversion of baht will either be used to support the U.S. production of Speedos, if needed, or be invested in the United States. Specifically, the funds will be used to cover cost of goods sold in the U.S. manufacturing plant, located in Omaha, Nebraska. Since Blades used a significant amount of cash to finance the initial investment to build the plant in Thailand and purchase the necessary equipment, its U.S. operations are strapped for cash. Consequently, if the subsidiary's earnings are not remitted back to the United States, Blades will have to borrow funds at an interest rate of 10 percent to support its U.S. operations. Any funds remitted by the subsidiary that are not used to support U.S. operations will be invested in the United States at an interest rate of 8 percent. Holt estimates that approximately 60 percent of the remitted funds will be needed to support U.S. operations and that the remaining 40 percent will be invested in the United States.

Consequently, Holt must choose between two alternative plans. First, he could instruct the Thai subsidiary to repay the baht loan (with interest) and invest any remaining funds in Thailand at an interest rate of 15 percent. Second, he could instruct the Thai subsidiary to repay the baht loan and remit any remaining funds back to the United States, where 60 percent of the funds would be used to support U.S. operations and 40 percent would be invested at an interest rate of

8 percent. Assume no income or withholding taxes on the earnings generated in Thailand.

Ben Holt has contacted you, a financial analyst at Blades, Inc., to help him analyze these two options. Holt has informed you that the current spot rate of the Thai baht is .0225 and that the baht is expected to depreciate by 5 percent over the coming year. He has provided you with the following list of questions he would like you to answer.

1. There is a tradeoff between the higher interest rates in Thailand and the delayed conversion of baht into dollars. Explain what this means.
2. If the net baht received from the Thailand subsidiary are invested in Thailand, how will U.S. operations be affected?
3. Construct a spreadsheet that compares the cash flows resulting from the two plans. Under the first plan, net baht-denominated cash flows (received today) will be invested in Thailand at 15 percent for a one-year period, after which the baht will be converted to dollars. Under the second plan, net baht-denominated cash flows are converted to dollars immediately and 60 percent of the funds will be used to support U.S. operations, while 40 percent are invested in the United States for one year at 8 percent. Which plan is superior given the expectation of the baht's value in one year?

SMALL BUSINESS DILEMMA

Cash Management at the Sports Exports Company

Ever since Jim Logan began his Sports Exports Company, he has been concerned about his exposure to exchange rate risk. The firm produces footballs and exports them to a distributor in the United Kingdom, with the exports being denominated in British pounds. Jim has just entered into a joint venture in the United Kingdom in which a British firm produces sporting goods for Jim's firm and sells the goods to the British distributor. The distributor pays pounds to Jim's firm for these products. Jim recently borrowed pounds to finance this venture, which created some cash outflows (interest payments) that partially offset his cash inflows in pounds. The interest paid on this loan is equal to the British Treasury bill rate plus 3 percentage points. His original business of exporting has been very successful recently, which has caused him to have revenue (in pounds) that will be retained as excess cash. Jim must decide whether to pay off part of the existing British loan, invest the cash in the U.S. Treasury bills, or invest the cash in British Treasury bills.

1. If Jim invests the excess cash in U.S. Treasury bills, would this reduce the firm's exposure to exchange rate risk?
2. Jim decided to use the excess cash to pay off the British loan. However, a friend advised him to invest the cash in British Treasury bills, stating that "the loan provides an offset to the pound receivables, so you would be better off investing in British Treasury bills than paying off the loan." Is Jim's friend correct? What should Jim do?

APPENDIX 21

Investing in a Portfolio of Currencies

Large financial corporations may consider investing in a portfolio of currencies, as illustrated in the following example.

Assume that MacFarland Co., a U.S. firm, needs to invest $100,000 for one year and obtains these interest rate quotes:

- Interest rate for a one-year deposit in U.S. dollars = 11%
- Interest rate for a one-year deposit in Singapore dollars = 14%
- Interest rate for a one-year deposit in British pounds = 13%

Due to the relatively high quotes for a deposit in Singapore dollars or British pounds, it is understandable that MacFarland Co. may desire to invest in a foreign currency. If the firm decides to use foreign investing, it has three choices based on the information given here:

- Invest in only Singapore dollars
- Invest in only British pounds
- Invest in a mixture (or portfolio) of Singapore dollars and pounds

Assume that MacFarland Co. has established possible percentage changes in the spot rate from the time the deposit would begin until maturity for both the Singapore dollar and the British pound, as shown in the second column of Exhibit 21A.1. We shall first discuss the Singapore dollar. For each possible percentage change that might occur, a probability of that occurrence is shown in the third column. Based on the assumed interest rate of 14 percent for the Singapore dollar, the effective yield is computed for each possible percentage change in the Singapore dollar's spot rate over the loan life. In Exhibit 21A.1, there is a 20 percent chance the Singapore dollar will depreciate by 4 percent during the deposit period. If it does, the effective yield will be 9.44 percent. Furthermore, there is a 50 percent chance the effective yield will be 12.86 percent and a 30 percent chance it will be 16.28 percent. Given that the U.S. deposit rate is 11 percent, there is a 20 percent chance that investing in Singapore dollars will result in a lower effective yield than investing in a U.S. dollar deposit.

The lower section of Exhibit 21A.1 provides information on the British pound. The pound has a 30 percent chance of depreciating by 3 percent during the deposit period, and so on. Based on the 13 percent interest rate for a British pound deposit, there is a

Exhibit 21A.1 Development of Possible Effective Yields

Currency	Possible Percentage Change in the Spot Rate over the Deposit Life	Probability of That Percentage Change in the Spot Rate Occurring	Computation of Effective Yield Based on That Percentage Change in the Spot Rate
Singapore dollar	−4%	20%	(1.14) [1 + (−4%)] − 1 = 9.44%
Singapore dollar	−1	50	(1.14) [1 + (−1%)] − 1 = 12.86%
Singapore dollar	+2	30	(1.14) [1 + (2%)] − 1 = 16.28%
		100%	
British pound	−3	30	(1.13) [1 + (−3%)] − 1 = 9.61%
British pound	0	30	(1.13) [1 + (0%)] − 1 = 13.00%
British pound	2	40	(1.13) [1 + (2%)] − 1 = 15.26%
		100%	

30 percent chance the effective yield will be 9.61 percent, a 30 percent chance it will be 13 percent, and a 40 percent chance it will be 15.26 percent. Keeping in mind the 11 percent rate on a U.S. dollar deposit, there is a 30 percent chance that investing in British pounds will be less rewarding than investing in a U.S. dollar deposit.

Before examining the third possible foreign investing strategy (the portfolio approach) available here, determine the expected value of the effective yield for each foreign currency, summing up the products of each possible effective yield and its associated probability as follows:

Currency	Computation of Expected Value of Effective Yield
Singapore dollar	(20%)(9.44%) + 50%(12.86%) + 30%(16.28%) = 13.202%
British pound	(30%)(9.61%) + 30%(13.00%) + 40%(15.26%) = 12.887%

The expected value of the Singapore dollar's yield is slightly higher. In addition, the individual degree of risk (the chance the return on investment will be lower than the return on a U.S. deposit) is higher for the pound. If MacFarland Co. does choose to invest in only one of these foreign currencies, it may choose the Singapore dollar since its risk and return characteristics are more favorable. Before making its decision, however, the firm should consider the possibility of investing in a currency portfolio.

The information in Exhibit 21A.1 shows three possibilities for the Singapore dollar's effective yield. The same holds true for the British pound. If MacFarland Co. invests half of its available funds in each of the foreign currencies, then there will be nine possibilities for this portfolio's effective yield. These possibilities are shown in Exhibit 21A.2. The first two columns list all possible joint effective yields. The third column computes the joint probability of each possible occurrence. The fourth column shows the computation of the portfolio's effective yield based on the possible rates for the individual currencies shown in the first two columns. The top row of the table indicates that one possible outcome of investing in both Singapore dollars and British pounds is an effective yield of 9.44 percent and 9.61 percent, respectively. The probability that the

Exhibit 21A.2 Analysis of Investing in Two Foreign Currencies

Possible Joint Effective Yield			
Singapore Dollar	British Pound	Computation of Joint Probability	Computation of Effective Yield of Portfolio (50% of Total Funds Invested in Each Currency)
9.44%	9.61%	(20%)(30%) = 6%	.5(9.44%) + .5(9.61%) = 9.525%
9.44	13.00	(20%)(30%) = 6	.5(9.44%) + .5(13.00%) = 11.22%
9.44	15.26	(20%)(40%) = 8	.5(9.44%) + .5(15.26%) = 12.35%
12.86	9.61	(50%)(30%) = 15	.5(12.86%) + .5(9.61%) = 11.235%
12.86	13.00	(50%)(30%) = 15	.5(12.86%) + .5(13.00%) = 12.93%
12.86	15.26	(50%)(40%) = 20	.5 (12.86%) + .5(15.26%) =14.06%
16.28	9.61	(30%)(30%) = 9	.5(16.28%) + .5(9.61%) = 12.945%
16.28	13.00	(30%)(30%) = 9	.5(16.28%) + .5(13.00%) = 14.64%
16.28	15.26	(30%)(40%) = 12	.5(16.28%) + .5(15.26%) = 15.77%
		100%	

Singapore dollar's effective yield will occur is 20 percent, while the probability that the British pound's effective yield will occur is 30 percent. The joint probability that both of these effective yields will occur simultaneously is (20%)(30%) = 6%. Assuming that half (50%) of the funds available are invested in each currency, the portfolio's effective yields will be .5(9.44%) + .5(9.61%) = 9.525% (if those individual effective yields do occur).

A similar procedure was used to develop the remaining eight rows in Exhibit 21A.2. There is a 6 percent chance the portfolio's effective yield will be 11.22 percent, an 8 percent chance that it will be 12.35 percent, and so on.

Exhibit 21A.2 shows that investing in the portfolio will likely be more rewarding than investing in a U.S. dollar deposit. While there is a 6 percent chance the portfolio's effective yield will be 9.525 percent, all other possible portfolio yields (see the fourth column) are more than the U.S. deposit rate of 11 percent.

Recall that investing solely in Singapore dollars has a 20 percent chance of being less rewarding than investing in the U.S. deposit, while investing solely in British pounds has a 30 percent chance of being less rewarding. The analysis in Exhibit 21A.2 suggests that investing in a portfolio (50 percent invested in Singapore dollars, with the remaining 50 percent invested in British pounds) has only a 6 percent chance of being less rewarding than domestic investing. These results will be explained.

When an investment is made in both currencies, the only time the portfolio will exhibit a lower yield than the U.S. deposit is when *both* currencies experience their maximum possible levels of depreciation (which is 4 percent depreciation for the Singapore dollar and 3 percent depreciation for the British pound). If only one of these events occurs, its severity will be somewhat offset by the other currency's not depreciating to such a large extent.

In our example, the computation of joint probabilities requires the assumption that the movements in the two currencies are independent. If movements of the two currencies were actually highly correlated, then investing in a portfolio of currencies would not be as beneficial as demonstrated here because there would be a strong likelihood that both currencies would experience a high level of depreciation simultaneously. If the two currencies are not highly correlated, they will not be expected to simultaneously depreciate to such a degree.

The current example includes two currencies in the portfolio. Investing in a more diversified portfolio of additional currencies that exhibit high interest rates can increase the probability that foreign investing will be more rewarding than the U.S. deposit. This is due to the low probability that all currencies will move in tandem and therefore simultaneously depreciate to offset their high interest rate advantages. Again, the degree to which these currencies are correlated with each other is important. If all currencies are highly positively correlated with each other, investing in such a portfolio will not be very different from investing in a single foreign currency.

Repeated Investing in a Currency Portfolio

A firm that repeatedly invests in foreign currencies usually prefers to compose a portfolio package that will exhibit a somewhat predictable effective yield on a periodic basis. The more volatile a portfolio's effective yield over time, the more uncertainty (risk) there is about the yield that portfolio will exhibit in any period. The portfolio's variability depends on the standard deviations and paired correlations of effective yields of the individual currencies within the portfolio.

We can use the portfolio variance as a measurement for degree of volatility. The variance of a two-currency portfolio's effective yield σ_p^2 over time is computed as

$$\sigma_p^2 = w_A^2\sigma_A^2 + w_B^2\sigma_B^2 + 2w_Aw_B\sigma_A\sigma_B CORR_{AB}$$

where w_A and w_B represent the percentage of total funds invested in Currencies A and B, respectively, σ_A^2 and σ_B^2 represent the individual variances of each currency's effective yield over time, and $CORR_{AB}$ reflects the correlation coefficient of the two currencies' effective yields. Since the percentage change in the exchange rate plays an important role in influencing the effective yield, it should not be surprising that $CORR_{AB}$ is strongly affected by the correlation between the exchange rate fluctuations of the two currencies. A low correlation between currency fluctuations can force $CORR_{AB}$ to be low.

To illustrate how the variance in a portfolio's effective yield is related to characteristics of the component currencies, consider the following example. The following information is based on several three-month periods:

- Mean effective yield of British pound over three months = 4%
- Mean effective yield of Singapore dollar over three months = 5%
- Standard deviation of British pound's effective yield = .06
- Standard deviation of Singapore dollar's effective yield = .10
- Correlation coefficient of effective yields of these two currencies = .20

Given the previous information, the mean effective yield on a portfolio (r_p) of funds invested 50 percent into British pounds and 50 percent into Singapore dollars is determined by summing up the weighted individual effective yields:

$$\begin{aligned} r_p &= .5(.04) + .5(.05) \\ &= .02 + .025 \\ &= .045, \text{ or } 4.5\% \end{aligned}$$

The variance of this portfolio's effective financing rate over time is

$$\begin{aligned}\sigma_p^2 &= .5^2(.06)^2 + .5^2(.10)^2 + 2(.5)(.5)(.06)(.10)(.20)\\ &= .25(.0036) + .25(.01) + .5(.0012)\\ &= .0009 + .0025 + .0006\\ &= .004\end{aligned}$$

There is no guarantee that past data will be indicative of the future. Yet, if the individual variability and paired correlations are somewhat stable over time, the historical variability of the portfolio's effective yield should be a reasonable forecast of the future portfolio variability.

PART 5

Integrative Problem

Short-Term Asset and Liability Management

Kent Co. is a large U.S. firm with no international business. It has two branches within the United States, an eastern branch and a western branch. Each branch currently makes investing or financing decisions independently, as if it were a separate entity. The eastern branch has excess cash of $15 million to invest for the next year. It can invest its funds in Treasury bills denominated in dollars or in any of four foreign currencies. The only restriction enforced by the parent is that a maximum of $5 million can be invested or financed in any foreign currency.

The western branch needs to borrow $15 million over one year to support its U.S. operations. It can borrow funds in any of these same currencies (although any foreign funds borrowed would need to be converted to dollars to finance the U.S. operations). The only restriction enforced by the parent is that a maximum equivalent of $5 million can be borrowed in any single currency. A large bank serving the international money market has offered Kent Co. the following terms:

Currency	Annual Interest Rate on Deposits	Annual Interest Rate Charged on Loans
U.S. dollar	6%	9%
Australian dollar	11	14
Canadian dollar	7	10
New Zealand dollar	9	12
Japanese yen	8	11

The parent of Kent Co. has created one-year forecasts of each currency for the branches to use in making their investing or financing decisions:

Currency	Today's Spot Exchange Rate	Forecasted Annual Percentage Change in Exchange Rate
Australian dollar	$.70	−4%
Canadian dollar	.80	−2
New Zealand dollar	.60	+3
Japanese yen	.008	0

Questions

1. Determine the investment portfolio composition for Kent's eastern branch that would maximize the expected effective yield while satisfying the restriction imposed by the parent.
2. What is the expected effective yield of the investment portfolio?
3. Based on the expected effective yield for the portfolio and the initial investment amount of $15 million, determine the annual interest to be earned on the portfolio.
4. Determine the financing portfolio composition for Kent's western branch that would minimize the expected effective financing rate while satisfying the restriction imposed by the parent.
5. What is the expected effective financing rate of the total amount borrowed?
6. Based on the expected effective financing rate for the portfolio and the total amount of $15 million borrowed, determine the expected loan repayment amount beyond the principal borrowed.
7. When the expected interest received by the eastern branch and paid by the western branch of Kent Co. are consolidated, what is the net amount of interest received?
8. If the eastern branch and the western branch worked together, the eastern branch could loan its $15 million to the western branch. Nevertheless, one could argue that the branches could not take advantage of interest rate differentials or expected exchange rate effects among currencies. Given the data provided in this example, would you recommend that the two branches make their short-term investment or financing decisions independently, or should the eastern branch lend its excess cash to the western branch? Explain.

APPENDIX A
Answers to Self Test Questions

Answers to Self Test Questions for Chapter 1

1. MNCs can capitalize on comparative advantages (such as a technology or cost of labor) that they have relative to firms in other countries, which allows them to penetrate those other countries' markets. Given a world of imperfect markets, comparative advantages across countries are not freely transferable. Therefore, MNCs may be able to capitalize on comparative advantages. Many MNCs initially penetrate markets by exporting but ultimately establish a subsidiary in foreign markets and attempt to differentiate their products as other firms enter those markets (product cycle theory).
2. In the late 1980s and 1990s, Western European countries removed many barriers, which allowed more potential for efficient expansion throughout Europe. Consequently, U.S. firms may be able to expand across European countries at a lower cost than before.

   During the same period, Eastern European countries opened their markets to foreign firms and privatized many of the state-owned firms. This allowed U.S. firms to penetrate these countries to offer products that previously had been unavailable.
3. First, there is the risk of poor economic conditions in the foreign country. Second, there is country risk, which reflects the risk of changing government or public attitudes toward the MNC. Third, there is exchange rate risk, which can affect the performance of the MNC in the foreign country.

Answers to Self Test Questions for Chapter 2

1. Each of the economic factors is described, holding other factors constant.

   a. *Inflation*. A relatively high U.S. inflation rate relative to other countries can make U.S. goods less attractive to U.S. and non-U.S. consumers, which results in fewer U.S. exports, more U.S. imports, and a lower (or more negative) current account balance. A relatively low U.S. inflation rate would have the opposite effect.
   b. *National income*. A relatively high increase in the U.S. national income (compared to other countries) tends to cause a large increase in demand for imports and can cause a lower (or more negative) current account balance. A relatively low increase in the U.S. national income would have the opposite effect.

c. *Exchange rates.* A weaker dollar tends to make U.S. products cheaper to non-U.S. firms and makes non-U.S. products expensive to U.S. firms. Thus, U.S. exports are expected to increase, while U.S. imports are expected to decrease. However, some conditions can prevent these effects from occurring, as explained in the chapter. Normally, a stronger dollar causes U.S. exports to decrease and U.S. imports to increase because it makes U.S. goods more expensive to non-U.S. firms and makes non-U.S. goods less expensive to U.S. firms.
d. *Government restrictions.* When the U.S. government imposes new barriers on imports, U.S. imports decline, causing the U.S. balance of trade to increase (or be less negative). When non-U.S. governments impose new barriers on imports from the United States, the U.S. balance of trade may decrease (or be more negative). When governments remove trade barriers, the opposite effects are expected.

2. When the United States imposes tariffs on imported goods, foreign countries may retaliate by imposing tariffs on goods exported by the United States. Thus, there is a decline in U.S. exports that may offset any decline in U.S. imports.
3. The Asian crisis caused a decline in Asian income levels and therefore resulted in a reduced demand for U.S. exports. In addition, Asian exporters experienced problems, and some U.S. importers discontinued their relationships with the Asian exporters.

Answers to Self Test Questions for Chapter 3

1. (\$.80 − 784)/\$.80 = .02 or 2%
2. (\$.19 − \$.188)/\$.19 = .0105 or 1.05%
3. MNCs use the spot foreign exchange market to exchange currencies for immediate delivery. They use the forward foreign exchange market and the currency futures market to lock in the exchange rate at which currencies will be exchanged at a future point in time. They use the currency options market when they wish to lock in the maximum (minimum) amount to be paid (received) in a future currency transaction but maintain flexibility in the event of favorable exchange rate movements.

   MNCs use the Eurocurrency market to engage in short-term investing or financing or the Eurocredit market to engage in medium-term financing. They can obtain long-term financing by issuing bonds in the Eurobond market or by issuing stock in the international markets.

Answers to Self Test Questions for Chapter 4

1. Economic factors affect the yen's value as follows:

   a. If U.S. inflation is higher than Japanese inflation, the U.S. demand for Japanese goods may increase (to avoid the higher U.S. prices), and the Japanese demand for U.S. goods may decrease (to avoid the higher U.S. prices). Consequently, there is upward pressure on the value of the yen.
   b. If U.S. interest rates increase and exceed Japanese interest rates, the U.S. demand for Japanese interest-bearing securities may decline (since U.S. interest-bearing

securities are more attractive), while the Japanese demand for U.S. interest-bearing securities may rise. Both forces place downward pressure on the yen's value.

c. If U.S. national income increases more than Japanese national income, the U.S. demand for Japanese goods may increase more than the Japanese demand for U.S. goods. Assuming that the change in national income levels does not affect exchange rates indirectly through effects on relative interest rates, the forces should place upward pressure on the yen's value.

d. If government controls reduce the U.S. demand for Japanese goods, they place downward pressure on the yen's value. If the controls reduce the Japanese demand for U.S. goods, they place upward pressure on the yen's value.

The opposite scenarios of those described here would cause the expected pressure to be in the opposite direction.

2. U.S. capital flows with Country A may be larger than U.S. capital flows with Country B. Therefore, the change in the interest rate differential has a larger effect on the capital flows with Country A, causing the exchange rate to change. If the capital flows with Country B are nonexistent, interest rate changes do not change the capital flows and therefore do not change the demand and supply conditions in the foreign exchange market.
3. Smart Banking Corp. should not pursue the strategy because a loss would result, as shown here.

a. Borrow $5 million.

b. Convert $5 million to C$5,263,158 (based on the spot exchange rate of $.95 per C$).

c. Invest the C$ at 9 percent annualized, which represents a return of .15 percent over six days, so the C$ received after six days = C$5,271,053 (computed as C$5,263,158 × [1 + .0015]).

d. Convert the C$ received back to U.S. dollars after six days: C$5,271,053 = $4,954,789 (based on anticipated exchange rate of $.94 per C$ after six days).

e. The interest rate owed on the U.S. dollar loan is .10 percent over the six-day period. Thus, the amount owed as a result of the loan is $5,005,000 (computed as $5,000,000 × [1 + .001]).

f. The strategy is expected to cause a gain of ($4,954,789 − $5,005,000) = −$50,211.

Answers to Self Test Questions for Chapter 5

1. The net profit to the speculator is −$.01 per unit.

   The net profit to the speculator for one contract is −$500 (computed as −$.01 × 50,000 units).

   The spot rate would need to be $.66 for the speculator to break even.

   The net profit to the seller of the call option is $.01 per unit.
2. The speculator should exercise the option.

   The net profit to the speculator is $.04 per unit.

   The net profit to the seller of the put option is −$.04 per unit.

3. The premium paid is higher for options with longer expiration dates (other things being equal). Firms may prefer not to pay such high premiums.

Answers to Self Test Questions for Chapter 6

1. Market forces cause the demand and supply of yen in the foreign exchange market to change, which causes a change in the equilibrium exchange rate. The central banks could intervene to affect the demand or supply conditions in the foreign exchange market, but they would not always be able to offset the changing market forces. For example, if there were a large increase in the U.S. demand for yen and no increase in the supply of yen for sale, the central banks would have to increase the supply of yen in the foreign exchange market to offset the increased demand.
2. The Fed could use direct intervention by selling some of its dollar reserves in exchange for pesos in the foreign exchange market. It could also use indirect intervention by attempting to reduce U.S. interest rates through monetary policy. Specifically, it could increase the U.S. money supply, which places downward pressure on U.S. interest rates (assuming that inflationary expectations do not change). The lower U.S. interest rates should discourage foreign investment in the United States and encourage increased investment by U.S. investors in foreign securities. Both forces tend to weaken the dollar's value.
3. A weaker dollar tends to increase the demand for U.S. goods because the price paid for a specified amount in dollars by non-U.S. firms is reduced. In addition, the U.S. demand for foreign goods is reduced because it takes more dollars to obtain a specified amount in foreign currency once the dollar weakens. Both forces tend to stimulate the U.S. economy and therefore improve productivity and reduce unemployment in the United States.

Answers to Self Test Questions for Chapter 7

1. No. The cross exchange rate between the pound and the C$ is appropriate, based on the other exchange rates. There is no discrepancy to capitalize on.
2. No. Covered interest arbitrage involves the exchange of dollars for pounds. Assuming that the investors begin with $1 million (the starting amount will not affect the final conclusion), the dollars would be converted to pounds as shown here:

   $$\$1\text{ million}/\$1.60\text{ per }£ = £625{,}000$$

   The British investment would accumulate interest over the 180-day period, resulting in

   $$£625{,}000 \times 1.04 = £650{,}000$$

   After 180 days, the pounds would be converted to dollars:

   $$£650{,}000 \times \$1.56\text{ per pound} = \$1{,}014{,}000$$

This amount reflects a return of 1.4 percent above the amount U.S. investors initially started with. The investors could simply invest the funds in the United States at 3 percent. Thus, U.S. investors would earn less using the covered interest arbitrage strategy than investing in the United States.

3. No. The forward rate discount on the pound does not perfectly offset the interest rate differential. In fact, the discount is 2.5 percent, which is larger than the interest rate differential. U.S. investors do worse when attempting covered interest arbitrage than when investing their funds in the United States because the interest rate advantage on the British investment is more than offset by the forward discount.

   Further clarification may be helpful here. While the U.S. investors could not benefit from covered interest arbitrage, British investors could capitalize on covered interest arbitrage. While British investors would earn 1 percent interest less on the U.S. investment, they would be purchasing pounds forward at a discount of 2.5 percent at the end of the investment period. When interest rate parity does not exist, investors from only one of the two countries of concern could benefit from using covered interest arbitrage.
4. If there is a discrepancy in the pricing of a currency, one may capitalize on it by using the various forms of arbitrage described in the chapter. As arbitrage occurs, the exchange rates will be pushed toward their appropriate levels because arbitrageurs will buy an underpriced currency in the foreign exchange market (increase in demand for currency places upward pressure on its value) and will sell an overpriced currency in the foreign exchange market (increase in the supply of currency for sale places downward pressure on its value).
5. The one-year forward discount on pounds would become more pronounced (by about one percentage point more than before) because the spread between the British interest rates and U.S. interest rates would increase.

Answers to Self Test Questions for Chapter 8

1. If the Japanese prices rise because of Japanese inflation, the value of the yen should decline. Thus, even though the importer might need to pay more yen, it would benefit from a weaker yen value (it would pay fewer dollars for a given amount in yen). Thus, there could be an offsetting effect if PPP holds.
2. Purchasing power parity does not necessarily hold. In our example, Japanese inflation could rise (causing the importer to pay more yen), and yet the Japanese yen would not necessarily depreciate by an offsetting amount, or at all. Therefore, the dollar amount to be paid for Japanese supplies could increase over time.
3. High inflation will cause a balance of trade adjustment, whereby the United States will reduce its purchases of goods in these countries, while the demand for U.S. goods by these countries should increase (according to PPP). Consequently, there will be downward pressure on the values of these currencies.
4.
$$\begin{aligned} e_f &= I_h - I_f \\ &= 3\% - 4\% \\ &= -.01 \text{ or } -1\% \\ S_{t+1} &= S(1 + e_f) \\ &= \$.85[1 + (-.01)] \\ &= \$.8415 \end{aligned}$$

5. $$e_f = \frac{(1 + i_h)}{(1 + i_f)} - 1$$
$$= \frac{(1 + .06)}{(1 + .11)} - 1$$
$$\cong -.045, \text{ or } -4.5\%$$
$$S_{t+1} = S(1 + e_f)$$
$$= \$.90[1 + (-.045)]$$
$$= \$.8595$$

6. According to the IFE, the increase in interest rates by 5 percentage points reflects an increase in expected inflation by 5 percentage points.

   If the inflation adjustment occurs, the balance of trade should be affected, as Australian demand for U.S. goods rises while the U.S. demand for Australian goods declines. Thus, the Australian dollar should weaken.

   If U.S. investors believed in the IFE, they would not attempt to capitalize on higher Australian interest rates because they would expect the Australian dollar to depreciate over time.

Answers to Self Test Questions for Chapter 9

1. U.S. four-year interest rate = $(1 + .07)^4$ = 131.08% or 1.3108. Mexican four-year interest rate = $(1 + .20)^4$ = 207.36% or 2.0736.
$$p = \frac{(1 + i_h)}{(1 + i_f)} - 1 = \frac{1.3108}{2.0736} - 1$$
$$= -.3679 \text{ or } -36.79\%.$$

2. Canadian dollar $\frac{|\$.80 - \$.82|}{\$.82} = 2.44\%$

   Japanese yen $\frac{|\$.012 - \$.011|}{\$.011} = 9.09\%$

   The forecast error was larger for the Japanese yen.

3. The forward rate of the peso would have overestimated the future spot rate because the spot rate would have declined by the end of each month.
4. Semistrong-form efficiency would be refuted since the currency values do not adjust immediately to useful public information.
5. The peso would be expected to depreciate because the forward rate of the peso would exhibit a discount (be less than the spot rate). Thus, the forecast derived from the forward rate is less than the spot rate, which implies anticipated depreciation of the peso.
6. As the chapter suggests, forecasts of currencies are subject to a high degree of error. Thus, if a project's success is very sensitive to the future value of the bolivar, there is much uncertainty. This project could easily backfire because the future value of the bolivar is very uncertain.

Answers to Self Test Questions for Chapter 10

1. Managers have more information about the firm's exposure to exchange rate risk than do shareholders and may be able to hedge it more easily than shareholders could. Shareholders may prefer that the managers hedge for them. Also, cash flows may be stabilized as a result of hedging, which can reduce the firm's cost of financing.
2. The Canadian supplies would have less exposure to exchange rate risk because the Canadian dollar is less volatile than the Mexican peso.
3. The Mexican source would be preferable because the firm could use peso inflows to make payments for material that is imported.
4. No. If exports are priced in dollars, the dollar cash flows received from exporting will depend on Mexico's demand, which will be influenced by the peso's value. If the peso depreciates, Mexican demand for the exports would likely decrease.
5. The earnings generated by the European subsidiaries will be translated to a smaller amount in dollar earnings if the dollar strengthens. Thus, the consolidated earnings of the U.S.-based MNCs will be reduced.

Answers to Self Test Questions for Chapter 11

1. Amount of A$ to be invested today = A$3,000,000/(1 + .12)
   = A$2,678,571

   Amount of U.S. $ to be borrowed to convert to A$ = A$2,678,571 × $.85
   = $2,276,785

   Amount of U.S. $ needed in one year to pay off loan = $2,276,785 × (1 + .07)
   = $2,436,160
2. The forward hedge would be more appropriate. Given a forward rate of $.81, Montclair would need $2,430,000 in one year (computed as A$3,000,000 × $.81) when using a forward hedge.
3. Montclair could purchase currency call options in Australian dollars. The option could hedge against the possible appreciation of the Australian dollar. Yet, if the Australian dollar depreciates, Montclair could let the option expire and purchase the Australian dollars at the spot rate at the time it needs to send payment. A disadvantage of the currency call option is that a premium must be paid for it. Thus, if Montclair expects the Australian dollar to appreciate over the year, the money market hedge would probably be a better choice, since the flexibility provided by the option would not be useful in this case.
4. Even though Sanibel Co. is insulated from the beginning of a month to the end of the month, the forward rate will become higher each month because the forward rate moves with the spot rate. Thus, the firm will pay more dollars each month, even though it is hedged during the month. Sanibel will be adversely affected by the consistent appreciation of the pound.
5. Sanibel Co. could engage in a series of forward contracts today to cover the payments in each successive month. In this way, it locks in the future payments today and does not have to agree to the higher forward rates that may exist in future months.

6. A put option on SF2,000,000 would cost $60,000. If the spot rate of the SF reached $.68 as expected, the put option would be exercised, which would yield $1,380,000 (computed as SF2,000,000 × $.69). Accounting for the premium costs of $60,000, the receivables amount would convert to $1,320,000. If Hopkins remains unhedged, it expects to receive $1,360,000 (computed as SF2,000,000 × $.68). Thus, the unhedged strategy is preferable.

Answers to Self Test Questions for Chapter 12

1. Salem could attempt to purchase its chemicals from Canadian sources. Then, if the C$ depreciates, the reduction in dollar inflows resulting from its exports to Canada will be partially offset by a reduction in dollar outflows needed to pay for the Canadian imports.

   An alternative possibility for Salem is to finance its business with Canadian dollars, but this would probably be a less efficient solution.
2. A possible disadvantage is that Salem would forgo some of the benefits if the C$ appreciated over time.
3. The consolidated earnings of Coastal Corp. will be adversely affected if the pound depreciates because the British earnings will be translated into dollar earnings for the consolidated income statement at a lower exchange rate. Coastal could attempt to hedge its translation exposure by selling pounds forward. If the pound depreciates, it will benefit from its forward position, which could help offset the translation effect.
4. This argument has no perfect solution. It appears that shareholders penalize the firm for poor earnings even when the reason for poor earnings is a weak euro that has adverse translation effects. It is possible that translation effects could be hedged to stabilize earnings, but Arlington may consider informing the shareholders that the major earnings changes have been due to translation effects and not to changes in consumer demand or other factors. Perhaps shareholders would not respond so strongly to earnings changes if they were well aware that the changes were primarily caused by translation effects.
5. Lincolnshire has no translation exposure since it has no foreign subsidiaries. Kalafa has translation exposure resulting from its subsidiary in Spain.

Answers to Self Test Questions for Chapter 13

1. Possible reasons may include
   - More demand for the product (depending on the product)
   - Better technology in Canada
   - Fewer restrictions (less political interference)
2. Possible reasons may include
   - More demand for the product (depending on the product)
   - Greater probability of earning superior profits (since many goods have not been marketed in Mexico in the past)
   - Cheaper factors of production (such as land and labor)
   - Possible exploitation of monopolistic advantages

3. U.S. firms prefer to enter a country when the foreign country's currency is weak. U.S. firms normally would prefer that the foreign currency appreciate after they invest their dollars to develop the subsidiary. The executive's comment suggests that the euro is too strong, so any U.S. investment of dollars into Europe will not convert into enough euros to make the investment worthwhile.
4. It may be easier to engage in a joint venture with a Chinese firm, which is already well established in China, to circumvent barriers.
5. The government may attempt to stimulate the economy in this way.

Answers to Self Test Questions for Chapter 14

1. In addition to earnings generated in Jamaica, the *NPV* is based on some factors not controlled by the firm, such as the expected host government tax on profits, the withholding tax imposed by the host government, and the salvage value to be received when the project is terminated. Furthermore, the exchange rate projections will affect the estimates of dollar cash flows received by the parent as earnings are remitted.
2. The most obvious effect is on the cash flows that will be generated by the sales distribution center in Ireland. These cash flow estimates will likely be revised downward (due to lower sales estimates). It is also possible that the estimated salvage value could be reduced. Exchange rate estimates could be revised as a result of revised economic conditions. Estimated tax rates imposed on the center by the Irish government could also be affected by the revised economic conditions.
3. New Orleans Exporting Co. must account for the cash flows that will be forgone as a result of the plant, because some of the cash flows that used to be received by the parent through its exporting operation will be eliminated. The *NPV* estimate will be reduced after this factor is accounted for.
4. a. An increase in the risk will cause an increase in the required rate of return on the subsidiary, which results in a lower discounted value of the subsidiary's salvage value.
   b. If the rupiah depreciates over time, the subsidiary's salvage value will be reduced because the proceeds will convert to fewer dollars.
5. The dollar cash flows of Wilmette Co. would be affected more because the periodic remitted earnings from Thailand to be converted to dollars would be larger. The dollar cash flows of Niles would not be affected so much because interest payments would be made on the Thai loans before earnings could be remitted to the United States. Thus, a smaller amount in earnings would be remitted.
6. The demand for the product in the foreign country may be very uncertain, causing the total revenue to be uncertain. The exchange rates can be very uncertain, creating uncertainty about the dollar cash flows received by the U.S. parent. The salvage value may be very uncertain; this will have a larger effect if the lifetime of the project is short (for projects with a very long life, the discounted value of the salvage value is small anyway).

Answers to Self Test Questions for Chapter 15

1. Acquisitions have increased in Europe to capitalize on the inception of the euro, which created a single European currency for many European countries. This has not only eliminated the exchange rate risk on transactions between the participating European countries, but it has also made it easier to compare valuations among European countries to determine where targets are undervalued.
2. Common restrictions include government regulations, such as antitrust restrictions, environmental restrictions, and red tape.
3. The establishment of a new subsidiary allows an MNC to create the subsidiary it desires without assuming existing facilities or employees. However, the process of building a new subsidiary and hiring employees will normally take longer than the process of acquiring an existing foreign firm.
4. The divestiture is now more feasible because the dollar cash flows to be received by the U.S. parent are reduced as a result of the revised projections of the krona's value.

Answers to Self Test Questions for Chapter 16

1. First, consumers on the islands could develop a philosophy of purchasing homemade goods. Second, they could discontinue their purchases of exports by Key West Co. as a form of protest against specific U.S. government actions. Third, the host governments could impose severe restrictions on the subsidiary shops owned by Key West Co. (including the blockage of funds to be remitted to the U.S. parent).
2. First, the islands could experience poor economic conditions, which would cause lower income for some residents. Second, residents could be subject to higher inflation or higher interest rates, which would reduce the income that they could allocate toward exports. Depreciation of the local currencies could also raise the local prices to be paid for goods exported from the United States. All factors described here could reduce the demand for goods exported by Key West Co.
3. Financial risk is probably a bigger concern. The political risk factors are unlikely, based on the product produced by Key West Co. and the absence of substitute products available in other countries. The financial risk factors deserve serious consideration.
4. This event has heightened the perceived country risk for any firms that have offices in populated areas (especially next to government or military offices). It has also heightened the risk for firms whose employees commonly travel to other countries and for firms that provide office services or travel services.
5. Rockford Co. could estimate the net present value (*NPV*) of the project under three scenarios: (1) include a special tax when estimating cash flows back to the parent (probability of scenario = 15%), (2) assume the project ends in two years and include a salvage value when estimating the *NPV* (probability of scenario = 15%), and (3) assume no Canadian government intervention (probability = 70%). This results in three estimates of *NPV*, one for each scenario. This method is less arbitrary than the one considered by Rockford's executives.

Answers to Self Test Questions for Chapter 17

1. Growth may have caused Goshen to require a large amount for financing that could not be completely provided by retained earnings. In addition, the interest rates may have been low in these foreign countries to make debt financing an attractive alternative. Finally, the use of foreign debt can reduce the exchange rate risk since the amount in periodic remitted earnings is reduced when interest payments are required on foreign debt.
2. If country risk has increased, Lynde can attempt to reduce its exposure to that risk by removing its equity investment from the subsidiary. When the subsidiary is financed with local funds, the local creditors have more to lose than the parent if the host government imposes any severe restrictions on the subsidiary.
3. Not necessarily. German and Japanese firms tend to have more support from other firms or from the government if they experience cash flow problems and can therefore afford to use a higher degree of financial leverage than firms from the same industry in the United States.
4. Local debt financing is favorable because it can reduce the MNC's exposure to country risk and exchange rate risk. However, the high interest rates will make the local debt very expensive. If the parent makes an equity investment in the subsidiary to avoid the high cost of local debt, it will be more exposed to country risk and exchange rate risk.
5. The answer to this question is dependent on whether you believe unsystematic risk is relevant. If the CAPM is used as a framework for measuring the risk of a project, the risk of the foreign project is determined to be low, because the systematic risk is low. That is, the risk is specific to the host country and is not related to U.S. market conditions. However, if the project's unsystematic risk is relevant, the project is considered to have a high degree of risk. The project's cash flows are very uncertain, even though the systematic risk is low.

Answers to Self Test Questions for Chapter 18

1. A firm may be able to obtain a lower coupon rate by issuing bonds denominated in a different currency. The firm converts the proceeds from issuing the bond to its local currency to finance local operations. Yet, there is exchange rate risk because the firm will need to make coupon payments and the principal payment in the currency denominating the bond. If that currency appreciates against the firm's local currency, the financing costs could become larger than expected.
2. The risk is that the Swiss franc would appreciate against the pound over time since the British subsidiary will periodically convert some of its pound cash flows to francs to make the coupon payments.

   The risk here is less than it would be if the proceeds were used to finance U.S. operations. The Swiss franc's movement against the dollar is much more volatile than the Swiss franc's movement against the pound. The Swiss franc and the pound have historically moved in tandem to some degree against the dollar, which means that there is a somewhat stable exchange rate between the two currencies.

3. If these firms borrow U.S. dollars and convert them to finance local projects, they will need to use their own currencies to obtain dollars and make coupon payments. These firms would be highly exposed to exchange rate risk.
4. Paxson Co. is exposed to exchange rate risk. If the yen appreciates, the number of dollars needed for conversion into yen will increase. To the extent that the yen strengthens, Paxson's cost of financing when financing with yen could be higher than when financing with dollars.
5. The nominal interest rate incorporates expected inflation (according to the so-called Fisher effect). Therefore, the high interest rates reflect high expected inflation. Cash flows can be enhanced by inflation because a given profit margin converts into larger profits as a result of inflation, even if costs increase at the same rate as revenues.

Answers to Self Test Questions for Chapter 19

1. The exporter may not trust the importer or may be concerned that the government will impose exchange controls that prevent payment to the exporter. Meanwhile, the importer may not trust that the exporter will ship the goods ordered and therefore may not pay until the goods are received. Commercial banks can help by providing guarantees to the exporter in case the importer does not pay.
2. In accounts receivable financing, the bank provides a loan to the exporter secured by the accounts receivable. If the importer fails to pay the exporter, the exporter is still responsible to repay the bank. Factoring involves the sales of accounts receivable by the exporter to a so-called factor, so that the exporter is no longer responsible for the importer's payment.
3. The guarantee programs of the Export-Import Bank provide medium-term protection against the risk of nonpayment by the foreign buyer due to political risk.

Answers to Self Test Questions for Chapter 20

1. $r_f = (1 + i_f)(1 + e_f) - 1$

   If $e_f = -6\%$, $r_f = (1 + .09)[1 + (-.06)] - 1$
   $= .0246$, or 2.46%

   If $e_f = 3\%$, $r_f = (1 + .09)(1 + .03) - 1$
   $= .1227$, or 12.27%

2. $E(r_f) = 50\%(2.46\%) + 50\%(12.27\%)$
   $= 1.23\% + 6.135\%$
   $= 7.365\%$

3. $$e_f = \frac{(1 + r_f)}{(1 + i)} - 1$$
   $$= \frac{(1 + .08)}{(1 + .05)} - 1$$
   $= .0286$, or 2.86%

4. $E(e_f)$ = (Forward rate–Spot rate)/Spot rate
 = (\$.60 − \$.62)/\$.62
 = −.0322, or 3.22%
 $E(r_f) = (1 + i_f)[1 + E(e_f)] - 1$
 $= (1 + .09)[1 + (-.0322)] - 1$
 = .0548, or 5.48%
5. The two-currency portfolio will not exhibit much lower variance than either individual currency because the currencies tend to move together. Thus, the diversification effect is limited.

Answers to Self Test Questions for Chapter 21

1. The subsidiary in Country Y should be more adversely affected because the blocked funds will not earn as much interest over time. In addition, the funds will likely be converted to dollars at an unfavorable exchange rate because the currency is expected to weaken over time.
2. $E(r) = (1 + i_f)[1 + E(e_f)] - 1$
 $= (1 + .14)(1 + .08) - 1$
 = .2312, or 23.12%
3. $E(e_f)$ = (Forward rate – Spot rate)/Spot rate
 = (\$.19 − \$.20)/\$.20
 = −.05, or −5%
 $E(r) = (1 + i_f)[1 + E(e_f)] - 1$
 $= (1 + .11)[1 + (-.05)] - 1$
 = .0545, or 5.45%
4. $$e_f = \frac{(1 + r)}{(1 + i_f)} - 1$$
 $$= \frac{(1 + .06)}{(1 + .90)} - 1$$
 = −.4421, or −44.21%

 If the bolivar depreciates by less than 44.21 percent against the dollar over the one-year period, a one-year deposit in Venezuela will generate a higher effective yield than a one-year U.S. deposit.
5. Yes. Interest rate parity would discourage U.S. firms only from covering their investments in foreign deposits by using forward contracts. As long as the firms believe that the currency will not depreciate to offset the interest rate advantage, they may consider investing in countries with high interest rates.

APPENDIX B
Supplemental Cases

Chapter 1 Ranger Supply Company

Motivation for International Business

Ranger Supply Company is a large manufacturer and distributor of office supplies. It is based in New York but sends supplies to firms throughout the United States. It markets its supplies through periodic mass mailings of catalogues to those firms. Its clients can make orders over the phone, and Ranger ships the supplies upon demand. Ranger has had very high production efficiency in the past. This is attributed partly to low employee turnover and high morale, as employees are guaranteed job security until retirement.

Ranger already holds a large proportion of the market share in distributing office supplies in the United States. Its main competition in the United States comes from one U.S. firm and one Canadian firm. A British firm has a small share of the U.S. market but is at a disadvantage because of its distance. The British firm's marketing and transportation costs in the U.S. market are relatively high.

Although Ranger's office supplies are somewhat similar to those of its competitors, it has been able to capture most of the U.S. market because its high efficiency enables it to charge low prices to retail stores. It expects a decline in the aggregate demand for office supplies in the United States in future years. However, it anticipates strong demand for office supplies in Canada and in Eastern Europe over the next several years. Ranger's executives have begun to consider exporting as a method of offsetting the possible decline in domestic demand for its products.

a. Ranger Supply Company plans to attempt penetrating either the Canadian market or the Eastern European market through exporting. What factors deserve to be considered in deciding which market is more feasible?
b. One financial manager has been responsible for developing a contingency plan in case whichever market is chosen imposes export barriers over time. This manager proposed that Ranger should establish a subsidiary in the country of concern under such conditions. Is this a reasonable strategy? Are there any obvious reasons why this strategy could fail?

Chapter 2 MapleLeaf Paper Company

Assessing the Effects of Changing Trade Barriers

MapleLeaf Paper Company is a Canadian firm that produces a particular type of paper not produced in the United States. It focuses most of its sales in the United States. In the past year, for example, 180,000 of its 200,000 rolls of paper were sold to the United States, and the remaining 20,000 rolls were sold in Canada. It has a niche in the United States, but because there are some substitutes, the U.S. demand for the product is sensitive to any changes in price. In fact, MapleLeaf has estimated that the U.S. demand rises (declines) 3 percent for every 1 percent decrease (increase) in the price paid by U.S. consumers, other things held constant.

A 12 percent tariff had historically been imposed on exports to the United States. Then on January 2, a free trade agreement between the United States and Canada was implemented, eliminating the tariff. MapleLeaf was ecstatic about the news, as it had been lobbying for the free trade agreement for several years.

At that time, the Canadian dollar was worth $.76. MapleLeaf hired a consulting firm to forecast the value of the Canadian dollar in the future. The firm expects the Canadian dollar to be worth about $.86 by the end of the year and then stabilize after that. The expectations of a stronger Canadian dollar are driven by an anticipation that Canadian firms will capitalize on the free trade agreement more than U.S. firms, which will cause the increase in the U.S. demand for Canadian goods to be much higher than the increase in the Canadian demand for U.S. goods. (However, no other Canadian firms are expected to penetrate the U.S. paper market.) MapleLeaf expects no major changes in the aggregate demand for paper in the U.S. paper industry. It is also confident that its only competition will continue to be two U.S. manufacturers that produce imperfect substitutes for its paper. Its sales in Canada are expected to grow by about 20 percent by the end of the year because of an increase in the overall Canadian demand for paper and then remain level after that. MapleLeaf invoices its exports in Canadian dollars and plans to maintain its present pricing schedule, since its costs of production are relatively stable. Its U.S. competitors will also continue their pricing schedule. MapleLeaf is confident that the free trade agreement will be permanent. It immediately begins to assess its long-run prospects in the United States.

a. Based on the information provided, develop a forecast of MapleLeaf's annual production (in rolls) needed to accommodate demand in the future. Since orders for this year have already occurred, focus on the years following this year.
b. Explain the underlying reasons for the change in the demand and the implications.
c. Will the general effects on MapleLeaf be similar to the effects on a U.S. paper producer that exports paper to Canada? Explain.

Chapter 3 Gretz Tool Company

Using International Financial Markets

Gretz Tool Company is a large U.S.-based multinational corporation with subsidiaries in eight different countries. The parent of Gretz provided an initial cash infusion to establish each subsidiary. However, each subsidiary has had to finance its own growth since then. The parent and subsidiaries of Gretz typically use Citicorp (the largest bank in the United States, with branches in numerous countries) when possible to facilitate any flow of funds necessary.

a. Explain the various ways in which Citicorp could facilitate Gretz's flow of funds, and identify the type of financial market where that flow of funds occurs. For each type of financing transaction, specify whether Citicorp would serve as the creditor or would simply be facilitating the flow of funds to Gretz.
b. Recently, the British subsidiary called on Citicorp for a medium-term loan and was offered the following alternatives:

Loan Denominated In	Annualized Rate
British pounds	13%
U.S. dollars	11%
Canadian dollars	10%
Japanese yen	8%

What characteristics do you think would help the British subsidiary determine which currency to borrow?

Chapter 4 Bruin Aircraft, Inc.

Factors Affecting Exchange Rates

Bruin Aircraft, Inc., is a designer and manufacturer of airplane parts. Its production plant is based in California. About one-third of its sales are exports to the United Kingdom. Though Bruin invoices its exports in dollars, the demand for its exports is highly sensitive to the value of the British pound. In order to maintain its parts inventory at a proper level, it must forecast the total demand for its parts, which is somewhat dependent on the forecasted value of the pound. The treasurer of Bruin was assigned the task of forecasting the value of the pound (against the dollar) for each of the next five years. He was planning to request from the firm's chief economist forecasts on all the relevant factors that could affect the pound's future exchange rate. He decided to organize his worksheet by separating demand-related factors from supply-related factors, as illustrated by the headings below:

Factors that can affect the value of the pound	Check (✓) here if the factor influences the U.S. demand for pounds	Check (✓) here if the factor influences the supply of pounds for sale

Help the treasurer by identifying the factors in the first column and then checking the second or third (or both) columns. Include any possible government-related factors and be specific (tie your description to the specific case background provided here).

Chapter 5 Capital Crystal, Inc.

Using Currency Futures and Options

Capital Crystal, Inc., is a major importer of crystal from the United Kingdom. The crystal is sold to prestigious retail stores throughout the United States. The imports are denominated in British pounds (£). Every quarter, Capital needs £500 million. It is currently attempting to determine whether it should use currency futures or currency options to hedge imports three months from now, if it will hedge at all. The spot rate of the pound is $1.60. A three-month futures contract on the pound is available for $1.59 per unit. A call option on the pound is available with a three-month expiration date and an exercise price of $1.60. The premium to be paid on the call option is $.01 per unit.

Capital is very confident that the value of the pound will rise to at least $1.62 in three months. Its previous forecasts of the pound's value have been very accurate. The management style of Capital is very risk-averse. Managers receive a bonus at the end of the year if they satisfy minimal performance standards. The bonus is fixed, regardless of how high above the minimum level one's performance is. If performance is below the minimum, there is no bonus, and future advancement within the company is unlikely.

a. As a financial manager of Capital, you have been assigned the task of choosing among three possible strategies: (1) hedge the £ position by purchasing futures, (2) hedge the £ position by purchasing call options, or (3) do not hedge. Offer your recommendation and justify it.
b. Assume the previous information that was provided, except for this difference: Capital has revised its forecast of the pound to be worth $1.57 three months from now. Given this revision, recommend whether Capital should (1) hedge the £ position by purchasing futures, (2) hedge the £ position by purchasing call options, or (3) not hedge. Justify your recommendation. Is your recommendation consistent with maximizing shareholder wealth?

Chapter 6 Hull Importing Company

Effects of Intervention on Import Expenses

Hull Importing Company is a U.S.-based firm that imports small gift items and sells them to retail gift shops across the United States. About half of the value of Hull's purchases comes from the United Kingdom, while the remaining purchases are from Mexico. The imported goods are denominated in the currency of the country where they are produced. Hull normally does not hedge its purchases.

In previous years, the Mexican peso and pound fluctuated substantially against the dollar (although not by the same degree). Hull's expenses are directly tied to these currency values because all of its products are imported. It has been successful because the imported gift items are somewhat unique and are attractive to U.S. consumers. However, Hull has been unable to pass on higher costs (due to a weaker dollar) to its consumers, because consumers would then switch to different gift items sold at other stores.

a. Hull expects that Mexico's central bank will increase interest rates, and that Mexico's inflation will not be affected. Offer any insight on how the peso's value may change and how Hull's profits would be affected as a result.

b. Hull used to closely monitor government intervention by the Bank of England (the British central bank) on the value of the pound. Assume that the Bank of England intervenes to strengthen the pound's value with respect to the dollar by 5 percent. Would this have a favorable or unfavorable effect on Hull's business?

Chapter 7 Zuber, Inc.

Using Covered Interest Arbitrage

Zuber, Inc., is a U.S.-based MNC that has been aggressively pursuing business in Eastern Europe since the Iron Curtain was lifted in 1989. Poland has allowed its currency's value to be market determined. The spot rate of the Polish zloty is $.40. Poland also has begun to allow investments by foreign investors, as a method of attracting funds to help build its economy. Its interest rate on one-year securities issued by the federal government is 14 percent, which is substantially higher than the 9 percent rate currently offered on one-year U.S. Treasury securities.

A local bank has begun to create a forward market for the zloty. This bank was recently privatized and has been trying to make a name for itself in international business. The bank has quoted a one-year forward rate of $.39 for the zloty. As an employee in Zuber's international money market division, you have been asked to assess the possibility of investing short-term funds in Poland. You are in charge of investing $10 million over the next year. Your objective is to earn the highest return possible while maintaining safety (since the firm will need the funds next year).

Since the exchange rate has just become market determined, there is a high probability that the zloty's value will be very volatile for several years as it seeks its true equilibrium value. The expected value of the zloty in one year is $.40, but there is a high degree of uncertainty about this. The actual value in one year may be as much as 40 percent above or below this expected value.

a. Would you be willing to invest the funds in Poland without covering your position? Explain.
b. Suggest how you could attempt covered interest arbitrage. What is the expected return from using covered interest arbitrage?
c. What risks are involved in using covered interest arbitrage here?
d. If you had to choose between investing your funds in U.S. Treasury bills at 9 percent or using covered interest arbitrage, what would be your choice? Defend your answer.

Chapter 8 Flame Fixtures, Inc.

Business Application of Purchasing Power Parity

Flame Fixtures, Inc., is a small U.S. business in Arizona that produces and sells lamp fixtures. Its costs and revenues have been very stable over time. Its profits have been adequate, but Flame has been searching for means of increasing profits in the future. It has recently been negotiating with a Mexican firm called Corón Company, from which it will purchase some of the necessary parts. Every three months, Corón Company will send a specified number of parts with the bill invoiced in Mexican pesos. By having the parts produced by Corón, Flame expects to save about 20 percent on production costs. Corón is only willing to work out a deal if it is assured that it will receive a minimum specified amount of orders every three months over the next ten years, for a minimum specified amount. Flame will be required to use its assets to serve as collateral in case it does not fulfill its obligation.

The price of the parts will change over time in response to the costs of production. Flame recognizes that the cost to Corón will increase substantially over time as a result of the very high inflation rate in Mexico. Therefore, the price charged in pesos likely will rise substantially every three months. However, Flame feels that, because of the concept of purchasing power parity (PPP), its dollar payments to Corón will be very stable. According to PPP, if Mexican inflation is much higher than U.S. inflation, the peso will weaken against the dollar by that difference. Since Flame does not have much liquidity, it could experience a severe cash shortage if its expenses are much higher than anticipated.

The demand for Flame's product has been very stable and is expected to continue that way. Since the U.S. inflation rate is expected to be very low, Flame likely will continue pricing its lamps at today's prices (in dollars). It believes that by saving 20 percent on production costs it will substantially increase its profits. It is about ready to sign a contract with Corón Company.

a. Describe a scenario that could cause Flame to save even more than 20 percent on production costs.
b. Describe a scenario that could cause Flame to actually incur higher production costs than if it simply had the parts produced in the United States.
c. Do you think that Flame will experience stable dollar outflow payments to Corón over time? Explain. (Assume that the number of parts ordered is constant over time.)
d. Do you think that Flame's risk changes at all as a result of its new relationship with Corón Company? Explain.

Chapter 9 Whaler Publishing Co.

Forecasting Exchange Rates

Whaler Publishing Co. specializes in producing textbooks in the United States and marketing these books in foreign universities where the English language is used. Its sales are invoiced in the currency of the country where the textbooks are sold. The expected revenues from textbooks sold to university bookstores are shown in Exhibit B.1.

Whaler is comfortable with the estimated foreign currency revenues in each country. However, it is very uncertain about the U.S. dollar revenues to be received from each country. At this time (which is the beginning of Year 16), Whaler is using today's spot rate as its best guess of the exchange rate at which the revenues from each country will be converted into U.S. dollars at the end of this year (which implies a zero percentage change in the value of each currency). Yet, it recognizes the potential error associated with this type of forecast. Therefore, it desires to incorporate the risk surrounding each currency forecast by creating confidence intervals for each currency. First, it must derive the annual percentage change in the exchange rate over each of the last 15 years for

Exhibit B.1

Expected Revenues from Textbooks Sold to University Bookstores

University Bookstores in	Local Currency	Today's Spot Exchange Rate	Expected Revenues from Bookstores This Year
Australia	Australian dollars (A$)	$ .7671	A$38,000,000
Canada	Canadian dollars (C$)	.8625	C$35,000,000
New Zealand	New Zealand dollars (N$)	.5985	N$33,000,000
United Kingdom	Pounds (£)	1.9382	£34,000,000

each currency to derive a standard deviation in the percentage change of each foreign currency. By assuming that the percentage changes in exchange rates are normally distributed, it plans to develop two ranges of forecasts for the annual percentage change in each currency: (1) one standard deviation in each direction from its best guess to develop a 68 percent confidence interval, and (2) two standard deviations in each direction from its best guess to develop a 95 percent confidence interval. These confidence intervals can then be applied to today's spot rates to develop confidence intervals for the future spot rate one year from today.

The exchange rates at the beginning of each of the last 16 years for each currency (with respect to the U.S. dollar) are shown here:

Beginning of Year	Australian $	Canadian $	New Zealand $	British Pound
1	$1.2571	$.9839	$1.0437	£2.0235
2	1.0864	.9908	.9500	1.7024
3	1.1414	.9137	1.0197	1.9060
4	1.1505	.8432	1.0666	2.0345
5	1.1055	.8561	.9862	2.2240
6	1.1807	.8370	.9623	2.3850
7	1.1279	.8432	.8244	1.9080
8	.9806	.8137	.7325	1.6145
9	.9020	.8038	.6546	1.4506
10	.8278	.7570	.4776	1.1565
11	.6809	.7153	.4985	1.4445
12	.6648	.7241	.5235	1.4745
13	.7225	.8130	.6575	1.8715
14	.8555	.8382	.6283	1.8095
15	.7831	.8518	.5876	1.5772
16	.7671	.8625	.5985	1.9382

The confidence intervals for each currency can be applied to the expected book revenues to derive confidence intervals in U.S. dollars to be received from each country. Complete this assignment for Whaler Publishing Co., and also rank the currencies in terms of uncertainty (degree of volatility). Since the exchange rate data provided are real, the analysis will indicate (1) how volatile currencies can be, (2) how much more volatile some currencies are than others, and (3) how estimated revenues can be subject to a high degree of uncertainty as a result of uncertain exchange rates. [If you use a spreadsheet to do this case, you may want to retain it, since the case in the following chapter is an extension of this case.]

Chapter 10 Whaler Publishing Co.

Measuring Exposure to Exchange Rate Risk

Recall the situation of Whaler Publishing Co. from the previous chapter. Whaler needed to develop confidence intervals of four exchange rates in order to derive confidence intervals for U.S. dollar cash flows to be received from four different countries. Each confidence interval was isolated on a particular country.

Assume that Whaler would like to estimate the range of its aggregate dollar cash flows to be generated from other countries. A computer spreadsheet should be developed to facilitate this exercise. Whaler plans to simulate the conversion of the expected currency cash flows to dollars, using each of the previous years as a possible scenario (recall that exchange rate data are provided in the original case in Chapter 9). Specifically, Whaler will determine the annual percentage change in the spot rate of each currency for a given year. Then, it will apply that percentage to the respective existing spot rates to determine a possible spot rate in one year for each currency. Recall that today's spot rates are assumed to be as follows:

- Australian dollar = $.7671
- Canadian dollar = $.8625
- New Zealand dollar = $.5985
- British pound = £1.9382

Once the spot rate is forecasted for one year ahead for each currency, the U.S. dollar revenues received from each country can be forecasted. For example, from Year 1 to Year 2, the Australian dollar declined by about 13.6 percent. If this percentage change occurs this year, the spot rate of the Australian dollar will decline from today's rate of $.7671 to about $.6629. In this case, the A$38,000,000 to be received would convert to $25,190,200. The same tasks must be done for the other three currencies as well in order to estimate the aggregate dollar cash flows under this scenario.

This process can be repeated, using each of the previous years as a possible future scenario. There will be 15 possible scenarios, or 15 forecasts of the aggregate U.S. dollar cash flows. Each of these scenarios is expected to have an equal probability of occurring. By assuming that these cash flows are normally distributed, Whaler uses the standard deviation of the possible aggregate cash flows for all 15 scenarios to develop 68 percent and 95 percent confidence intervals surrounding the "expected value" of the aggregate level of U.S. dollar cash flows to be received in one year.

a. Perform these tasks for Whaler in order to determine these confidence intervals on the aggregate level of U.S. dollar cash flows to be received. Whaler uses the methodology described here, rather than simply combining the results for individual countries (from the previous chapter), because exchange rate movements may be correlated.

b. Review the annual percentage changes in the four exchange rates. Do they appear to be positively correlated? Estimate the correlation coefficient between exchange rate movements with either a calculator or a spreadsheet package. Based on this analysis, you can fill out the following correlation coefficient matrix:

	A$	C$	NZ$	£
A$	1.00			
C$		1.00		
NZ$			1.00	
£				1.00

Would aggregate dollar cash flows to be received by Whaler be more risky than they would if the exchange rate movements were completely independent? Explain.

c. One Whaler executive has suggested that a more efficient way of deriving the confidence intervals would be to use the exchange rates instead of the percentage changes as the scenarios and derive U.S. dollar cash flow estimates directly from them. Do you think this method would be as accurate as the method now used by Whaler? Explain.

Chapter 11 Blackhawk Company

Forecasting Exchange Rates and the Hedging Decision

This case is intended to illustrate how forecasting exchange rates and hedging decisions are related. Blackhawk Company imports goods from New Zealand and plans to purchase NZ$800,000 one quarter from now to pay for imports. As the treasurer of Blackhawk, you are responsible for determining whether and how to hedge this payables position. Several tasks will need to be completed before you can make these decisions. The entire analysis can be performed using LOTUS or Excel spreadsheets.

- Your first goal is to assess three different models for forecasting the value of NZ$ at the end of the quarter (also called the future spot rate, or FSR):
- Using the forward rate (FR) at the beginning of the quarter. Using the spot rate (SR) at the beginning of the quarter.
- Estimating the historical influence of the inflation differential during each quarter on the percentage change in the NZ$ (which leads to a forecast of the FSR of the NZ$).

The historical data to be used for this analysis are provided in Exhibit B.2.

a. Use regression analysis to determine whether the forward rate is an unbiased estimator of the spot rate at the end of the quarter.

b. Use the simplified approach of assessing the signs of forecast errors over time. Do you detect any bias when using the FR to forecast? Explain.

c. Determine the average absolute forecast error when using the forward rate to forecast.

Exhibit B.2 Historical Data for Analysis

Quarter	Spot Rate of NZ$ at Beginning of Quarter	90-Day Forward Rate of NZ$ at Beginning of Quarter	Spot Rate of NZ$ at End of Quarter	Last Quarter's Inflation Differential	Percentage Change in NZ$ over Quarter
1	$.3177	$.3250	$.3233	−.05%	1.76%
2	.3233	.3272	.3267	−.46	1.05
3	.3267	.3285	.3746	.66	14.66
4	.3746	.3778	.4063	.94	8.46
5	.4063	.4093	.4315	.58	6.20
6	.4315	.4344	.4548	.23	5.40
7	.4548	.4572	.4949	.02	8.82
8	.4949	.4966	.5153	1.26	4.12
9	.5153	.5169	.5540	.86	7.51
10	.5540	.5574	.5465	.54	−1.35
11	.5465	.5510	.5440	1.00	−.46
12	.5440	.5488	.6309	1.09	15.97
13	.6309	.6365	.6027	.78	−4.47
14	.6027	.6081	.5409	.23	−10.25
15	.5491	.5538	.5320	.71	−3.11
16	.5320	.5365	.5617	1.18	5.58
17	.5617	.5667	.5283	.70	−5.95
18	.5283	.5334	.5122	−.31	−3.05
19	.5122	.5149	.5352	.62	4.49
20	.5352	.5372	.5890	.87	10.05
21 (Now)	.5890	.5878	(to be forecasted)	.28	(to be forecasted)

d. Determine whether the spot rate of the NZ$ at the beginning of the quarter is an unbiased estimator of the spot rate at the end of the quarter using regression analysis.

e. Use the simplified approach of assessing the signs of forecast errors over time. Do you detect any bias when using the SR to forecast? Explain.

f. Determine the average absolute forecast error when using the spot rate to forecast. Is the spot rate or the forward rate a more accurate forecast of the future spot rate (FSR)? Explain.

g. Use the following regression model to determine the relationship between the inflation differential (called *DIFF* and defined as the U.S. inflation minus New Zealand inflation) and the percentage change in the NZ$ (called PNZ$):

$$\text{PNZ\$} = b_0 + b_1 DIFF$$

Once you have determined the coefficients b_0 and b_1, use them to forecast PNZ$ based on a forecast of 2 percent for *DIFF* in the upcoming quarter. Then, apply your forecast for PNZ$ to the prevailing spot rate (which is $.589) to derive the expected FSR of the NZ$.

h. Blackhawk plans to develop a probability distribution for the FSR. First, it will assign a 40 percent probability to the forecast of FSR derived from the regression analysis in the previous question. Second, it will assign a 40 percent probability to the forecast of FSR based on either the forward rate or the spot rate (whichever was more accurate according to your earlier analysis). Third, it will assign a 20 percent probability to the forecast of FSR based on either the forward rate or the spot rate (whichever was less accurate according to your earlier analysis).

Fill in the table that follows:

Probability	FSR
40%	
40	
20	

i. Assuming that Blackhawk does not hedge, fill in the following table.

Probability	Forecasted Dollar Amount Needed to Pay for Imports in 90 Days
40%	
40	
20	

j. Based on the probability distribution for the FSR, use the table that follows to determine the probability distribution for the real cost of hedging if a forward contract is used for hedging (recall that the prevailing 90-day forward rate is $.5878).

Probability	Forecasted Dollar Amount Needed If Hedged with a Forward Contract	Forecasted Amount Needed If Unhedged	Forecasted Real Cost of Hedging Payables
40%			
40			
20			

k. If Blackhawk hedges its position, it will use either a 90-day forward rate, a money market hedge, or a call option. The following data are available at the time of its decision.

- Spot rate = $.589
- 90-day forward rate = $.5878
- 90-day U.S. borrowing rate = 2.5%
- 90-day U.S. investing rate = 2.3%
- 90-day New Zealand borrowing rate = 2.4%
- 90-day New Zealand investing rate = 2.1%
- Call option on NZ$ has a premium of $.01 per unit.
- Call option on NZ$ has an exercise price of $.60.

Determine the probability distribution of dollars needed for a call option if used (include the premium paid) by filling out the following table:

Probability	FSR	Dollars Needed to Pay for Payables
40%		
40		
20		

l. Compare the forward hedge to the money market hedge. Which is superior? Why?

m. Compare either the forward hedge or the money market hedge (whichever is better) to the call option hedge. If you hedge, which technique should you use? Why?

n. Compare the hedge you believe is the best to an unhedged strategy. Should you hedge or remain unhedged? Explain.

Chapter 12 Madison, Inc.

Assessing Economic Exposure

The situation for Madison, Inc., was described in this chapter to illustrate how alternative operational structures could affect economic exposure to exchange rate movements. Ken Moore, the vice president of finance at Madison, Inc., was seriously considering a shift to the proposed operational structure described in the text. He was determined to stabilize the earnings before taxes and believed that the proposed approach would achieve this objective. The firm expected that the Canadian dollar would consistently depreciate over the next several years. Over time, its forecasts have been very accurate. Moore paid little attention to the forecasts, stating that regardless of how the Canadian dollar changed, future earnings would be more stable under the proposed operational structure. He also was constantly reminded of how the strengthened Canadian dollar in some years had adversely affected the firm's earnings. In fact, he was somewhat concerned that he might even lose his job if the adverse effects from economic exposure continued.

a. Would a revised operational structure at this time be in the best interests of the shareholders? Would it be in the best interests of the vice president?
b. How could a revised operational structure possibly be feasible from the vice president's perspective but not from the shareholders' perspective? Explain how the firm might be able to ensure that the vice president will make decisions related to economic exposure that are in the best interests of the shareholders.

Chapter 13 Blues Corporation

Capitalizing on the Opening of Eastern European Borders

Having done business in the United States for over 50 years, Blues Corporation has an established reputation. Most of Blues' business is in the United States. It has a subsidiary in the western section of Germany, which produces goods and exports them to other European countries. Blues Corporation produces many consumer goods that could possibly be produced or marketed in Eastern European countries. The following issues were raised at a recent executive meeting. Offer your comments about each issue.

a. Blues Corporation is considering shifting its European production facility from western Germany to eastern Germany. There are two key factors motivating this shift. First, the labor cost is lower in eastern Germany. Second, there is an existing facility (currently government owned) in the former East Germany that is for sale. Blues would like to transform the facility and use its technology to increase production efficiency. It estimates that it would need only one-fourth of the workers in that facility. What other factors deserve to be considered before the decision is made?
b. Blues Corporation believes that it could penetrate the Eastern European markets. It would need to invest considerable funds in promoting its consumer goods in Eastern Europe, since its goods are not well known in that area. Yet, it believes that this strategy could pay off in the long run because Blues could underprice the competition. At the current time, the main competition consists of businesses that are perceived to be inefficiently run. The lack of competitive pricing in this market is the primary reason for Blues Corporation to consider marketing its product in Eastern Europe. What other factors deserve to be considered before a decision is made?
c. Blues Corporation is currently experiencing a cash squeeze because of a reduced demand for its goods in the United States (although management expects the demand in the United States to increase soon). It is currently near its debt capacity and prefers not to issue stock at this time. Blues Corporation will purchase a facility in Eastern Europe or implement a heavy promotion program in Eastern Europe only if it can raise funds by divesting a significant amount of its U.S. assets. The market values of its assets are temporarily depressed, but some of the executives think an immediate move is necessary to fully capitalize on the Eastern European market. Would you recommend that Blues Corporation divest some of its U.S. assets? Explain.

Chapter 14 North Star Company

Capital Budgeting

This case is intended to illustrate that the value of an international project is sensitive to various types of input. It also is intended to show how a computer spreadsheet format can facilitate capital budgeting decisions that involve uncertainty.

This case can be performed using an electronic spreadsheet such as Excel. The following present value factors may be helpful input for discounting cash flows:

Years from Now	Present Value Interest Factor at 18%
1	.8475
2	.7182
3	.6086
4	.5158
5	.4371
6	.3704

For consistency in discussion of this case, you should develop your computer spreadsheet in a format somewhat similar to that in the Capital Budgeting chapter, with each year representing a column across the top. The use of a computer spreadsheet will significantly reduce the time needed to complete this case.

North Star Company is considering establishing a subsidiary to manufacture clothing in Singapore. Its sales would be invoiced in Singapore dollars (S$). It has forecasted net cash flows to the subsidiary as follows:

Year	Net Cash Flows to Subsidiary
1	S$ 8,000,000
2	10,000,000
3	14,000,000
4	16,000,000
5	16,000,000
6	16,000,000

These cash flows do not include financing costs (interest expenses) on any funds borrowed in Singapore. North Star Company also expects to receive S$30 million after taxes as a result of selling the subsidiary at the end of Year 6. Assume that there will not be any withholding taxes imposed on this amount.

The exchange rate of the Singapore dollar is forecasted in Exhibit B.3 based on three possible scenarios of economic conditions.

Exhibit B.3
Three Scenarios of Economic Conditions

End of Year	Scenario I: Somewhat Stable S$	Scenario II: Weak S$	Scenario III: Strong S$
1	.50	.49	.52
2	.51	.46	.55
3	.48	.45	.59
4	.50	.43	.64
5	.52	.43	.67
6	.48	.41	.71

The probability of each scenario is shown below:

	Somewhat Stable S$	Weak S$	Strong S$
Probability	60%	30%	10%

Fifty percent of the net cash flows to the subsidiary would be remitted to the parent, while the remaining 50 percent would be reinvested to support ongoing operations at the subsidiary. North Star Company anticipates a 10 percent withholding tax on funds remitted to the United States.

The initial investment (including investment in working capital) by North Star in the subsidiary would be S$40 million. Any investment in working capital (such as accounts receivable, inventory, etc.) is to be assumed by the buyer in Year 6. The expected salvage value has already accounted for this transfer of working capital to the buyer in Year 6. The initial investment could be financed completely by the parent ($20 million, converted at the present exchange rate of $.50 per Singapore dollar to achieve S$40 million). North Star Company will go forward with its intentions to build the subsidiary only if it expects to achieve a return on its capital of 18 percent or more.

The parent is considering an alternative financing arrangement. With this arrangement, the parent would provide $10 million (S$20 million), which means that the subsidiary would need to borrow S$20 million. Under this scenario, the subsidiary would obtain a 20-year loan and pay interest on the loan each year. The interest payments are S$1.6 million per year. In addition, the forecasted proceeds to be received from selling the subsidiary (after taxes) at the end of six years would be S$20 million (the forecast of proceeds is revised downward here because the equity investment of the subsidiary is less; the buyer would be assuming more debt if part of the initial investment in the subsidiary were supported by local bank loans). Assume the parent's required rate of return would still be 18 percent.

a. Which of the two financing arrangements would you recommend for the parent? Assess the forecasted *NPV* for each exchange rate scenario to compare the two financing arrangements and substantiate your recommendation.
b. In the first question, an alternative financing arrangement of partial financing by the subsidiary was considered, with an assumption that the required rate of return by the parent would not be affected. Is there any reason why the parent's required rate of return might increase when using this financing arrangement?

Explain. How would you revise the analysis in the previous question under this situation? (This question requires discussion, not analysis.)

c. Would you recommend that North Star Company establish the subsidiary even if the withholding tax is 20 percent?

d. Assume that there is some concern about the economic conditions in Singapore, which could cause a reduction in the net cash flows to the subsidiary. Explain how Excel could be used to reevaluate the project based on alternative cash flow scenarios. That is, how can this form of country risk be incorporated into the capital budgeting decision? (This question requires discussion, not analysis.)

e. Assume that North Star Company does implement the project, investing $10 million of its own funds with the remainder borrowed by the subsidiary. Two years later, a U.S.-based corporation notifies North Star that it would like to purchase the subsidiary. Assume that the exchange rate forecasts for the somewhat stable scenario are appropriate for Years 3 through 6. Also assume that the other information already provided on net cash flows, financing costs, the 10 percent withholding tax, the salvage value, and the parent's required rate of return is still appropriate. What would be the minimum dollar price (after taxes) that North Star should receive to divest the subsidiary? Substantiate your opinion.

Chapter 15 Redwing Technology Company

Assessing Subsidiary Performance

Redwing Technology Company is a U.S.-based firm that makes a variety of high-tech components. Five years ago, it established subsidiaries in Canada, South Africa, and Japan. The earnings generated by each subsidiary as translated (at the average annual exchange rate) into U.S. dollars per year are shown in Exhibit B.4.

Each subsidiary had an equivalent amount in resources with which to conduct operations. The wage rates for the labor needed were similar across countries. The inflation rates, economic growth, and degree of competition were somewhat similar across countries. The average exchange rates of the respective currencies over the last five years are disclosed below:

Years Ago	Canadian Dollar	South African Rand	Japanese Yen
5	$.84	$.10	$.0040
4	.83	.12	.0043
3	.81	.16	.0046
2	.81	.20	.0055
1	.79	.24	.0064

The earnings generated by each country were reinvested rather than remitted. There were no plans to remit any future earnings either.

A committee of vice presidents met to determine the performance of each subsidiary in the last five years. The assessment was to be used to determine whether Redwing

Exhibit B.4
Translated Dollar Value of Annual Earnings in Each Subsidiary (in millions of $)

Years Ago	Canada	South Africa	Japan
5	$20	$21	$30
4	24	24	32
3	28	24	35
2	32	36	41
1	36	42	46

should be restructured to focus future growth on any particular subsidiary or to divest any subsidiaries that might experience poor performance. Since exchange rates of the related currencies were affected by so many different factors, the treasurer acknowledged that there was much uncertainty about their future direction. The treasurer did suggest, however, that last year's average exchange rate would probably serve as at least a reasonable guess of exchange rates in future years. He did not anticipate that any of the currencies would experience consistent appreciation or depreciation.

a. Use whatever means you think are appropriate to rank the performance of each subsidiary. That is, which subsidiary did the best job over the five-year period, in your opinion? Justify your opinion.
b. Use whatever means you think are appropriate to determine which subsidiary deserves additional funds from the parent to push for additional growth. (Assume no constraint on potential growth in any country.) Where would you recommend the parent's excess funds be invested, based on the information available? Justify your opinion.
c. Repeat question (b), but assume that all earnings generated from the parent's investment will be remitted to the parent every year. Would your recommendation change? Explain.
d. A final task of the committee was to recommend whether any of the subsidiaries should be divested. One vice president suggested that a review of the earnings translated into dollars shows that the performances of the Canadian and South African subsidiaries are very highly correlated. She concluded that having both of these subsidiaries did not achieve much in diversification benefits and suggested that either the Canadian or the South African subsidiary could be sold without forgoing any diversification benefits. Do you agree? Explain.

Chapter 16 King, Inc.

Country Risk Analysis

King, Inc., a U.S. firm, is considering the establishment of a small subsidiary in Bulgaria that would produce food products. All ingredients can be obtained or produced in Bulgaria. The final products to be produced by the subsidiary would be sold in Bulgaria and other Eastern European countries. King, Inc., is very interested in this project, as there is little competition in that area. Three high-level managers of King, Inc., have been assigned the task of assessing the country risk of Bulgaria. Specifically, the managers were asked to list all characteristics of Bulgaria that could adversely affect the performance of this project. The decision as to whether to undertake this project will be made only after this country risk analysis is completed and accounted for in the capital budgeting analysis. Since King, Inc., has focused exclusively on domestic business in the past, it is not accustomed to country risk analysis.

a. What factors related to Bulgaria's government deserve to be considered?
b. What country-related factors can affect the demand for the food products to be produced by King, Inc.?
c. What country-related factors can affect the cost of production?

Chapter 17 Sabre Computer Corporation

Cost of Capital

Sabre Computer Corporation is a U.S.-based company that plans to participate in joint ventures in Mexico and in Hungary. Each joint venture involves the development of a small subsidiary that helps produce computers. Sabre's main contributions are the technology and a few key computer components used in the production process. The joint venture in Mexico specifies joint production of computers with a Mexican company owned by the government. The computers have already been ordered by educational institutions and government agencies throughout Mexico. Sabre has a contract to sell all the computers it produces in Mexico to these institutions and agencies at a price that is tied to inflation. Given the very high and volatile inflation levels in Mexico, Sabre wanted to assure that the contracted price would adjust to cover rising costs over time.

The venture will require a temporary transfer of several managers to Mexico plus the manufacturing of key computer components in a leased Mexican plant. Most of these costs will be incurred in Mexico and will therefore require payment in pesos. Sabre will receive 30 percent of the revenue generated (in pesos) from computer sales. The Mexican partner will receive the remainder.

The joint venture in Hungary specifies joint production of personal computers with a Hungarian computer manufacturer. The computers will then be marketed to consumers throughout Eastern Europe. Similar computers are produced by some competitors, but Sabre believes it can penetrate these markets because its products will be competitively priced. Although the economies of the Eastern European countries are expected to be somewhat stagnant, demand for personal computers is reasonably strong. The computers will be priced in Hungary's currency, the forint, and Sabre will receive 30 percent of the revenue generated from sales.

a. Assume that Sabre plans to finance most of its investment in the Mexican subsidiary by borrowing Mexican pesos and to finance most of its investment in the Hungarian subsidiary by borrowing forint. The cost of financing is influenced by the risk-free rates in the respective countries and the risk premiums on funds borrowed. Explain how these factors will affect the relative costs of financing both ventures. Address this question from the perspective of the subsidiary, not from the perspective of Sabre's parent.
b. Will the joint venture experiencing the higher cost of financing (as determined in the previous question) necessarily experience lower returns to the subsidiary? Explain.

c. The Hungarian subsidiary has a high degree of financial leverage. Yet, the parent's capital structure is mostly equity. What will determine whether the creditors of the Hungarian subsidiary charge a high-risk premium on borrowed funds because of the high degree of financial leverage?
d. One Sabre executive has suggested that since the cost of debt financing by highly leveraged Hungarian-owned companies is about 14 percent, its Hungarian subsidiary should be able to borrow at about the same interest rate. Do you agree? Explain. (Assume that the chances of the subsidiary's experiencing financial problems are the same as those for these other Hungarian-owned firms.)
e. There is some concern that the economy in Hungary could become inflated. Assess the relative magnitude of an increase in inflation on (1) the cost of funds, (2) the cost of production, and (3) revenue from selling the computers.

Chapter 18 Devil VCR Corporation

Long-Term Financing

Devil VCR Corporation is a U.S.-based company that produces videocassette recorders. Three years ago, Devil established a production facility in the United Kingdom, since it sells VCRs there. Devil has excess capacity there and will use that facility to produce the VCRs that are to be marketed in Singapore. The VCRs will be sold to distributors in Singapore and invoiced in Singapore dollars (S$). If the exporting program is very successful, Devil Corporation will probably build a facility in Singapore, but it plans to wait at least 10 years.

Prior to this exporting program, Devil Corporation decided to develop a hedging strategy to hedge any cash flows to the U.S. parent. Its plan is to issue bonds to finance the entire investment in the exporting program. Virtually all expenses associated with this program are denominated in pounds. Yet, the revenue generated by the program is denominated in Singapore dollars. Any revenue above and beyond expenses is to be remitted to the United States on an annual basis. Aside from the exporting program, the British subsidiary will generate just enough in cash flows to cover expenses and therefore will not be remitting any earnings to the parent. Devil Corporation is considering three different ways to finance the program for 10 years:

- Issue 10-year, Singapore dollar–denominated bonds at par value; coupon rate = 11%.
- Issue 10-year, pound-denominated bonds at par value; coupon rate = 14%.
- Issue 10-year, U.S. dollar–denominated bonds at par value; coupon rate = 11%.

a. Describe the exchange rate risk if Devil finances with Singapore dollars.
b. Describe the exchange rate risk if Devil finances with British pounds.
c. Describe the exchange rate risk if Devil finances with U.S. dollars.

Chapter 19 Ryco Chemical Company

Using Countertrade

Ryco Chemical Company produces a wide variety of chemical products that are sold to manufacturing firms. Some of the chemicals used in its production process are imported from Concellos Chemical Company in Brazil. Concellos uses some chemicals in its production process that are produced by Ryco (although Concellos has historically purchased these chemicals from another U.S. chemical company rather than from Ryco). The Brazilian real has been depreciating continuously against the dollar, so Concellos' cost of obtaining chemicals is always rising. Concellos will probably pay twice as much for these chemicals this year because of the weak real. It probably will attempt to pass on most of its higher costs to its customers in the form of higher prices. However, it may not always be able to pass on higher costs from a weak real: Its competitors make all their chemicals locally, and their costs are directly tied to Brazil's inflation. Its competitors sell all their goods locally. This year, Concellos planned to charge Ryco a price in real that was substantially above last year's price.

Representatives from Ryco are flying to Brazil to discuss its trade problems with Concellos. Specifically, Ryco wants to avoid its exposure to the high inflation rate in Brazil. This adverse effect is somewhat offset by the consistent decline in the value of the real, which allows Ryco to obtain more real with a given amount of dollars every year. However, the offset is not perfect, and Ryco wants to create a better hedge against Brazilian inflation.

a. Describe a countertrade strategy that could reduce Ryco's exposure to Brazilian inflation.
b. Would Concellos be willing to consider this strategy? Is there any favorable effect on Concellos that may motivate it to accept the strategy?
c. Assume that both parties agree on countertrade. Why would the cost of obtaining imports still rise over time for Concellos? Would Concellos earn lower profits as a result?

Chapter 20 Flyer Company

Composing the Optimal Currency Portfolio for Financing

As treasurer for Flyer Company, you must develop a strategy for short-term financing. The firm, based in the United States, currently has no transaction exposure to currency movements. Assume the following data as of today:

Currency	Spot Exchange Rate	Annualized Interest Rate
Australian dollar	$.75	13.0%
British pound	1.70	12.5
Canadian dollar	.86	11.0
Japanese yen	.006	8.0
Mexican peso	.17	11.5
New Zealand dollar	.60	7.0
Singapore dollar	.50	6.0
South African rand	.16	9.0
U.S. dollar	1.00	9.0
Venezuelan bolivar	.0008	12.0

Your forecasting department has provided you with the following forecasts of the spot rates one year from now:

	Strong $ Scenario	Stable $ Scenario	Weak $ Scenario
Australian dollar	$ .66	$ .76	$ .85
British pound	1.58	1.73	1.83
Canadian dollar	.85	.85	.91
Japanese yen	.0055	.0062	.0072
Mexican peso	.14	.173	.18
New Zealand dollar	.53	.59	.63
Singapore dollar	.45	.48	.52
South African rand	.15	.155	.17
U.S. dollar	1.00	1.00	1.00
Venezuelan bolivar	.00073	.00079	.00086

The probability of the strong dollar scenario is 30 percent, the probability of the stable dollar scenario is 40 percent, and the probability of the weak dollar scenario is 30 percent. Based on the information provided, prescribe the composition of the portfolio that would achieve the minimum expected effective financing rate based on each of the following risk preferences:

1. *Risk-neutral* — Focus on minimizing the expected value of your effective financing rate, without any constraints.
2. *Balanced* — Borrow no more than 25 percent in any foreign currency.
3. *Conservative* — Borrow at least 60 percent U.S. dollars and no more than 10 percent of the funds from any individual foreign currency.
4. *Ultraconservative* — Do not create any exposure to exchange rate risk.

Fill out the following table:

Risk Preference	Portfolio's Effective Financing Rate Based on: Strong $ Scenario	Stable $ Scenario	Weak $ Scenario	Expected Value of Effective Financing Rate
Risk-neutral portfolio				
Balanced portfolio				
Conservative portfolio				
Ultraconservative portfolio				

Which portfolio would you prescribe for your firm? Why?

Chapter 21 Islander Corporation

Composing the Optimal Currency Portfolio for Investing

As treasurer for the Islander Corporation, you must develop a strategy for investing the excess cash that will be available for the next year. The firm, based in the United States, currently has no transaction exposure to foreign currency movements. Assume the following data as of today:

Currency	Spot Exchange Rate	Annualized Interest Rate
Australian dollar	.75	13.00
British pound	1.70	12.5
Canadian dollar	.86	11.0
Japanese yen	.006	8.0
U.S. dollar	1.00	9.0

Your forecasting department has provided you with the following forecasts of the spot rates one year from now:

	Strong $ Scenario	Somewhat Stable $ Scenario	Weak $ Scenario
Australian dollar	$ .66	$ .76	$ .85
British pound	1.58	1.73	1.83
Canadian dollar	.85	.85	.91
Japanese yen	.0055	.0062	.0072
U.S. dollar	1.00	1.00	1.00

The probability of the strong dollar scenario is 30 percent, the probability of the somewhat stable dollar scenario is 40 percent, and the probability of the weak dollar scenario is 30 percent. Based on the information provided, prescribe the composition of the investment portfolio that would maximize the expected value of the effective yield for each of four possible risk preferences:

1. *Risk-neutral* — Focus on maximizing the expected value of your effective yield, without any constraints.
2. *Balanced* — Invest no more than 25 percent in any foreign currency.
3. *Conservative* — Invest at least 50 percent of the funds in the U.S. dollar and no more than 10 percent of the funds in any individual foreign currency.
4. *Ultraconservative* — Do not create any exposure to exchange rate risk.

Fill out the following table:

Risk Preference	Forecasted Effective Yield for:			
	Strong $ Scenario	Somewhat Stable $ Scenario	Weak $ Scenario	Expected Value of Effective Yield
Risk-neutral portfolio				
Balanced portfolio				
Conservative portfolio				
Ultraconservative portfolio				

Which portfolio would you prescribe for your firm? Why? (You may find it helpful to draw bar charts that show the probability distribution of effective yields for each of the portfolios, placing one bar chart above another.)

APPENDIX C

Fundamentals of Regression Analysis

Businesses often use **regression analysis** to measure relationships between variables when establishing policies. For example, a firm may measure the historical relationship between its sales and its accounts receivable. Using the relationship detected, it can then forecast the future level of accounts receivable based on a forecast of sales. Alternatively, it may measure the sensitivity of its sales to economic growth and interest rates so that it can assess how susceptible its sales are to future changes in these economic variables. In international financial management, regression analysis can be used to measure the sensitivity of a firm's performance (using sales or earnings or stock price as a proxy) to currency movements or economic growth of various countries.

Regression analysis can be applied to measure the sensitivity of exports to various economic variables. This example will be used to explain the fundamentals of regression analysis. The main steps involved in regression analysis are

1. Specifying the regression model
2. Compiling the data
3. Estimating the regression coefficients
4. Interpreting the regression results

Specifying the Regression Model

Assume that your main goal is to determine the relationship between percentage changes in U.S. exports to Australia (called *CEXP*) and percentage changes in the value of the Australian dollar (called *CAUS*). The percentage change in the exports to Australia is the **dependent variable** since it is hypothesized to be influenced by another variable. Although you are most concerned with how *CAUS* affects *CEXP*, the regression model should include any other factors (or so-called **independent variables**) that could also affect *CEXP*. Assume that the percentage change in the Australian GDP (called *CGDP*) is also hypothesized to influence *CEXP*. This factor should also be included in the regression model. To simplify the example, assume that *CAUS* and *CGDP* are the only factors expected to influence *CEXP*. Also assume that there is a lagged impact of one quarter. In this case, the regression model can be specified as

$$CEXP_t = b_0 + b_1(CAUS_{t-1}) + b_2(CGDP_{t-1}) + \mu_t$$

where

b_0 = a constant

b_1 = regression coefficient that measures the sensitivity of $CEXP_t$ to $CAUS_{t-1}$

b_2 = regression coefficient that measures the sensitivity of $CEXP_t$ to $CGDP_{t-1}$

μ_t = an error term

The t subscript represents the time period. Some models, such as this one, specify a lagged impact of an independent variable on the dependent variable and therefore use a $t-1$ subscript.

Compiling the Data

Now that the model has been specified, data on the variables must be compiled. The data are normally input onto a spreadsheet as follows:

Period (*t*)	*CEXP*	*CAUS*	*CGDP*
1	.03	−.01	.04
2	−.01	.02	−.01
3	−.04	.03	−.02
4	.00	.02	−.01
5	.01	−.02	.02
.	...	...	...
.	...	...	...
.	...	...	...

The column specifying the period is not necessary to run the regression model but is normally included in the data set for convenience.

The difference between the number of observations (periods) and the regression coefficients (including the constant) represents the degrees of freedom. For our example, assume that the data covered 40 quarterly periods. The degrees of freedom for this example are $40 - 3 = 37$. As a general rule, analysts usually try to have at least 30 degrees of freedom when using regression analysis.

Some regression models involve only a single period. For example, if you desired to determine whether there was a relationship between a firm's degree of international sales (as a percentage of total sales) and earnings per share of MNCs, last year's data on these two variables could be gathered for many MNCs, and regression analysis could be applied. This example is referred to as **cross-sectional analysis**, whereas our original example is referred to as a **time-series analysis**.

Estimating the Regression Coefficients

Once the data have been input into a data file, a regression program can be applied to the data to estimate the **regression coefficients**. There are various packages such as Excel and Lotus that contain a regression analysis application.

The actual steps conducted to estimate regression coefficients are somewhat complex. For more details on how regression coefficients are estimated, see any econometrics textbook.

Interpreting the Regression Results

Most regression programs provide estimates of the regression coefficients along with additional statistics. For our example, assume that the following information was provided by the regression program:

	Estimated Regression Coefficient	Standard Error of Regression Coefficient	*t*-statistic
Constant	.002		
$CAUS_{t-1}$	.80	.32	2.50
$CGDP_{t-1}$	.36	.50	.72
Coefficient of determination (R^2) = .33			

The independent variable $CAUS_{t-1}$ has an estimated regression coefficient of .80, which suggests that a 1 percent increase in *CAUS* is associated with an .8 percent increase in the dependent variable *CEXP* in the following period. This implies a positive relationship between $CAUS_{t-1}$ and $CEXP_t$. The independent variable $CGDP_{t-1}$ has an estimated coefficient of .36, which suggests that a 1 percent increase in the Australian GDP is associated with a .36 percent increase in *CEXP* one period later.

Many analysts attempt to determine whether a coefficient is statistically different from zero. Regression coefficients may be different from zero simply because of a coincidental relationship between the independent variable of concern and the dependent variable. One can have more confidence that a negative or positive relationship exists by testing the coefficient for significance. A *t*-test is commonly used for this purpose, as follows:

Test to determine whether $CAUS_{t-1}$ affects $CEXP_t$

$$\begin{array}{c}\text{Calculated}\\ t\text{-statistic}\end{array} = \frac{\begin{array}{c}\text{Estimated}\\ \text{regression coefficient}\\ \text{for } CAUS_{t-1}\end{array}}{\begin{array}{c}\text{Standard error of}\\ \text{the regression coefficient}\end{array}} = \frac{.80}{.32} = 2.50$$

Test to determine whether $CGDP_{t-1}$ affects $CEXP_t$

$$\text{Calculated } t\text{-statistic} = \frac{\text{Estimated regression coefficient for } CGDP_{t-1}}{\text{Standard error of the regression coefficient}} = \frac{.36}{.50} = .72$$

The calculated t-statistic is sometimes provided within the regression results. It can be compared to the critical t-statistic to determine whether the coefficient is significant. The critical t-statistic is dependent on the degrees of freedom and confidence level chosen. For our example, assume that there are 37 degrees of freedom and that a 95 confidence level is desired. The critical t-statistic would be 2.02, which can be verified by using a t-table from any statistics book. Based on the regression results, the coefficient of $CAUS_{t-1}$ is significantly different from zero, while $CGDP_{t-1}$ is not. This implies that one can be confident of a positive relationship between $CAUS_{t-1}$ and $CEXP_t$, but the positive relationship between $CGDP_{t-1}$ and $CEXP_t$ may have occurred simply by chance.

In some particular cases, one may be interested in determining whether the regression coefficient differs significantly from some value other than zero. In these cases, the t-statistic reported in the regression results would not be appropriate. See an econometrics text for more information on this subject.

The regression results indicate the **coefficient of determination** (called R^2) of a regression model, which measures the percentage of variation in the dependent variable that can be explained by the regression model. R^2 can range from 0 to 100 percent. It is unusual for regression models to generate an R^2 of close to 100 percent, since the movement in a given dependent variable is partially random and not associated with movements in independent variables. In our example, R^2 is 33 percent, suggesting that one-third of the variation in *CEXP* can be explained by movements in $CAUS_{t-1}$ and $CGDP_{t-1}$.

Some analysts use regression analysis to forecast. For our example, the regression results could be used along with data for *CAUS* and *CGDP* to forecast *CEXP*. Assume that *CAUS* was 5 percent in the most recent period, while *CGDP* was −1 percent in the most recent period. The forecast of *CEXP* in the following period is derived from inserting this information into the regression model as follows:

$$\begin{aligned} CEXP_t &= b_0 + b_1(CAUS_{t-1}) + b_2(CGDP_{t-1}) \\ &= .002 + (.80)(.05) + (.36)(-.01) \\ &= .002 + .0400 - .0036 \\ &= .0420 - .0036 \\ &= .0384 \end{aligned}$$

Thus, the *CEXP* is forecasted to be 3.84 percent in the following period. Some analysts might eliminate $CGDP_{t-1}$ from the model because its regression coefficient was not significantly different from zero. This would alter the forecasted value of *CEXP*.

When there is not a lagged relationship between independent variables and the dependent variable, the independent variables must be forecasted in order to derive a forecast of the dependent variable. In this case, an analyst might derive a poor forecast of the dependent variable even when the regression model is properly specified, if the forecasts of the independent variables are inaccurate.

As with most statistical techniques, there are some limitations that should be recognized when using regression analysis. These limitations are described in most statistics and econometrics textbooks.

Using Excel to Conduct Regression Analysis

Various software packages are available to run regression analysis. The following example is run on Excel to illustrate the ease with which regression analysis can be run. Assume that a firm wants to assess the influence of changes in the value of the Australian dollar on changes in its exports to Australia based on the following data:

Period	Value (in Thousands of Dollars) of Exports to Australia	Average Exchange Rate of Australian Dollar over That Period
1	110	$.50
2	125	.54
3	130	.57
4	142	.60
5	129	.55
6	113	.49
7	108	.46
8	103	.42
9	109	.43
10	118	.48
11	125	.49
12	130	.50
13	134	.52
14	138	.50
15	144	.53
16	149	.55
17	156	.58
18	160	.62
19	165	.66
20	170	.67
21	160	.62
22	158	.62
23	155	.61
24	167	.66

Assume that the firm applies the following regression model to the data:

$$CEXP = b_0 + b_1 CAUS + \mu$$

where

$CEXP$ = percentage change in the firm's export value from one period to the next

$CAUS$ = percentage change in the average exchange rate from one period to the next

μ = error term

The first step is to input the data for the two variables in two columns on a file using Excel. Then, the data can be converted into percentage changes. This can be easily performed with a COMPUTE statement in the third column (Column C) to derive *CEXP* and another COMPUTE statement in the fourth column (Column D) to derive *CAUS*. These two columns will have a blank first row, since the percentage change cannot be computed without the previous period's data. Many students already know how to use Excel to create a COMPUTE statement and to apply the COMPUTE statement to all of the data within a column. If you do not, ask a friend for a few minutes of help.

Once you have derived *CEXP* and *CAUS* from the raw data, you can perform regression analysis as follows. On the main menu, select "Tools." This leads to a new menu, in which you should click on "Data Analysis." Next to the "Input Y Range," identify the range C2 to C24 for the dependent variable as C2:C24. Next to the "Input X Range," identify the range D2 to D24 for the independent variable as D2:D24. The "Output Range" specifies the location on the screen where the output of the regression analysis should be displayed. In our example, F1 would be an appropriate location, representing the upper-left section of the output. Then, click on OK, and within a few seconds, the regression analysis will be complete. For our example, the output is listed below:

SUMMARY OUTPUT

Regression Statistics	
Multiple R	0.8852
R Square	0.7836
Adjusted R Square	0.7733
Standard Error	2.9115
Observations	23.0000

ANOVA

	df	*SS*	*MS*	*F*	*Significance F*
Regression	1.0000	644.6262	644.6262	76.0461	0.0000
Residual	21.0000	178.0125	8.4768		
Total	22.0000	822.6387			

	Coefficients	*Standard Error*	*t Stat*	*P-value*
Intercept	**0.7951**	**0.6229**	**1.2763**	**0.2158**
***X* Variable 1**	**0.8678**	**0.0995**	**8.7204**	**0.0000**

	Lower 95%	*Upper 95%*	*Lower 95.0%*	*Upper 95.0%*
Intercept	**−0.5004**	**2.0905**	**−0.5004**	**2.0905**
***X* Variable 1**	**0.6608**	**1.0747**	**0.6608**	**1.0747**

The estimate of the so-called slope coefficient is about .8678, which suggests that every 1 percent change in the Australian dollar's exchange rate is associated with a .8678 percent change (in the same direction) in the firm's exports to Australia. The *t*-statistic is also estimated to determine whether the slope coefficient is significantly different than zero. Since the standard error of the slope coefficient is about .0995, the *t*-statistic is (.8678/.0995) = 8.72. This would imply that there is a significant relationship between *CAUS* and *CEXP*. The R-Square statistic suggests that about 78 percent of the variation in *CEXP* is explained by *CAUS*. The correlation between *CEXP* and *CAUS* can also be measured by the correlation coefficient, which is the square root of the R-Square statistic.

If you have more than one independent variable (multiple regression), you should place the independent variables next to each other in the file. Then, for the X-RANGE, identify this block of data. The output for the regression model will display the coefficient, standard error, and *t*-statistic for each of the independent variables. For multiple regression, the R-Square statistic is interpreted as the percentage of variation in the dependent variable explained by the model as a whole.

Using the "COPY" Command

If you need to repeat a particular type of computation for several different cells, you can use the COPY command. You must highlight the particular cells in which the computation is performed and instruct Excel (by clicking on "Edit") to copy that computation to whatever range of cells you desire.

APPENDIX D

International Investing Project

Note to the Professor: *You may want to assign this as a project to be completed by the end of the semester. This project helps students to understand the factors that influence the performance of MNCs and foreign stocks. This project can also be done with teams of students and may be used for class presentations near the end of the semester. If you allow students to share their results in class, the students will learn that relationships cannot necessarily be generalized, as some MNCs are more exposed than others to economic conditions and exchange rate movements. The focus in grading this project will be on the explanations provided by the students, not on the movements in the stock prices or exchange rates.*

This project allows you to learn more about international investing and about firms that compete in the global arena. You will be asked to create a stock portfolio of at least two U.S.-based multinational corporations (MNCs) and two foreign stocks. You will monitor the performance of your portfolio over the school term and ultimately will attempt to explain why your portfolio performed well or poorly relative to the portfolios created by other students in your class. The explanations will offer insight on what is driving the valuations of the U.S.-based MNCs and the foreign stocks over time.

Select two stocks of U.S.-based MNCs that you want to include in your portfolio. If you want to review a list of possible stocks or do not know the ticker symbol of the stocks you want to invest in, go to the website **http://biz.yahoo.com/i/**, which lists stocks alphabetically, or to **http://biz.yahoo.com/p/**, which lists stocks by sectors or industries. Make sure that your firms conduct a substantial amount of international business.

Next, select two foreign stocks that are traded on U.S. stock exchanges and are not from the same foreign country. Many foreign stocks are traded on U.S. stock exchanges as American depository receipts (ADRs), which are certificates that represent ownership of foreign stock. ADRs are denominated in dollars, but reflect the value of a foreign stock, so an increase in the value of the foreign currency can have a favorable effect on the ADR's value. To review a list of ADRs in which you may invest, go to **http://www.adr.com/entry_disclaimer.html**. Go to the site map, and click on "ADR Universe." Click on any industry listed to see a list of foreign companies within that industry that offer ADRs and the country where each foreign company is based. You should select ADRs of firms that are based in any of the countries shown on the website **http://finance.yahoo.com/intlindices**. Click on any company listed to review background information, including a description of its business and its stock price trend over the last year. It is assumed that you will invest $10,000 in each stock that you purchase.

List your portfolio in the following format:

U.S.-Based MNCs			
Name of Firm	Ticker Symbol	Amount of Your Investment	Price per Share at Which You Purchased the Stock
		$10,000	
		$10,000	

Foreign Stocks (ADRs)				
Name of Firm	Ticker Symbol	Country Where Firm Is Based	Amount of Your Investment	Price per Share of ADR at Which You Purchased the Stock
			$10,000	
			$10,000	

You can easily monitor your portfolio using various Internet tools. If you do not already use a specific website for this purpose, go to **http://finance.yahoo.com/?u** and register for free. Follow the instructions, and in a few minutes you can create your own portfolio tracking system. This system not only updates the values of your stocks, but also provides charts and recent news and other information on the stocks in your portfolio.

Evaluation

At the end of each month during the school term (or a date specified by your professor), you should evaluate the performance and behavior of your stocks.

1. a. Determine the percentage increase or decrease in each of your stocks over the period of your investment and provide that percentage in a table like the one below. In addition, offer the primary reason for this change in the stock price based on news about that stock or your own intuition. To review the recent news about each of your stocks, click on **http://finance.yahoo.com/?u** and insert the ticker symbol for each firm. Recent news is provided at the bottom of the screen.

Name of Firm	Percentage Change in Stock Price	Primary Reason
1.		
2.		
3.		
4.		
Portfolio (average)		

b. How does your portfolio's performance compare to the portfolios of some other students? (Your professor may survey the class on their performances so that you can see how your performance differs from those of other students.) Why do you think your performance was relatively high or low compared to other students' performances? Was it because of the markets where your firms do their business or because of firm-specific conditions?

2. Determine whether the performance of each of your U.S.-based MNCs is driven by the U.S. market. Go to the site **http://finance.yahoo.com/?u** and insert the symbol for your stock. Once the quote is provided, click on "Chart." Click on the box marked S&P (which represents the S&P 500 Index). Then, click on "Compare" and assess the relationship between the U.S. market index movements and the stock's price movements. Explain whether the stock's price movements appear to be driven by U.S. market conditions. Repeat this task for each U.S.-based MNC in which you invested.
3. a. Determine whether the performance of each of your foreign stocks is driven by the corresponding market where the firm is based. First, go to the site **http://finance.yahoo.com/intlindices?u** and look up the symbol for the country index of concern. For example, Brazil's index is ^BVSP. Next, go to the site **http://finance.yahoo.com/?u** and insert the symbol for your stock. Click on "Chart"; at the bottom of the chart, insert the corresponding market index symbol (make sure you include the ^ if it is part of the index symbol) in the box. Then, click on "Compare" and assess the relationship between the market index movements and the stock's price movements. Explain whether the stock's price movements appear to be driven by the local market conditions. Repeat this exercise for each foreign stock in which you invested.
   b. Determine whether your foreign stock prices are highly correlated. Repeat the process described above, except insert the symbol representing one of the foreign stocks you own in the box below the chart.
   c. Determine whether your foreign stock's performance is driven by the U.S. market (using the S&P 500 as a market proxy). Erase the symbol you typed into the box below the chart, and click on "S&P" just to the right.
4. a. Review annual reports and news about each of your U.S.-based MNCs to determine where it does most of its business and the foreign currency to which it is most exposed. Determine whether your U.S.-based MNC's stock performance is influenced by the exchange rate movements of the foreign currency (against the U.S. dollar) to which it is most exposed. Go to **http://www.oanda.com** and click on "FXHistory." You can convert the foreign currency to which the MNC is highly exposed to U.S. dollars and determine the exchange rate movements over the period in which you invested in the stock. Provide your assessment of the relationship between the currency's exchange rate movements and the performance of the stock over the investment period. Attempt to explain the relationship that you just found.
   b. Repeat the steps in 4a for each U.S.-based MNC in which you invested.
5. a. Determine whether the stock performance of each of your foreign firms is influenced by the exchange rate movements of the firm's local currency against the U.S. dollar. You can obtain this information from **http://www.oanda.com**. You can convert the foreign currency of concern to U.S. dollars and determine the exchange rate movements over the period in which you invested in the stock. Provide your assessment of the relationship between the currency's exchange rate movements and the performance of the stock over the investment period. Attempt to explain the relationship that you just found.
   b. Repeat the steps in 5a for each of the foreign stocks in which you invested.

APPENDIX E

Discussion in the Boardroom

This exercise is intended to apply many of the key concepts presented in the text to broad issues that are discussed by managers who make financial decisions. It does not replace the more detailed questions and problems at the end of the chapters. Instead, it focuses on broad financial issues to facilitate class discussion and simulate a boardroom discussion. It serves as a running case in which concepts from every chapter are applied to the same business throughout the school term. The exercise not only enables students to apply concepts to the real world, but also develops their intuitive and communication skills.

This exercise can be used in a course in several ways:

1. Apply it on a chapter-by-chapter basis to ensure that the broad chapter concepts are understood before moving to the next chapter.
2. Use it to encourage online discussion for courses taught online.
3. Use it as a review before each exam, covering all chapters assigned for that exam.
4. Use it as a comprehensive case discussion near the end of the semester, as a means of reviewing the key concepts that were described throughout the course.
5. Use it for presentations, in which individuals or teams present their views on the questions that were assigned to them.

This exercise has been placed on the course website so that students can download it and insert their answers after the questions. By the end of the course, students will have applied all the major concepts of the text to a single firm. The focus on a single firm will allow students to recognize how some of their decisions in the earlier chapters interact with decisions to be made in later chapters.

Background

One of the best ways to learn the broad concepts presented in this text is to put yourself in the position of an MNC manager or board member and apply the concepts to financial decisions. Although board members normally do not make the decisions discussed here, they must have the conceptual skills to monitor the policies that are implemented by the MNC's managers. Thus, they must frequently consider what they would do if they were making the managerial decisions or setting corporate policies.

This exercise is based on a business that you could easily create: a business that teaches individuals in a non-U.S. country to speak English. Although this business is very basic, it still requires the same types of decisions faced by large MNCs.

Assume that you live in the United States and invest $60,000 to establish a language school called Escuela de Inglés in Mexico City, Mexico. You set up a small subsidiary in Mexico, with an office and an attached classroom that you lease. You hire local individuals in Mexico who can speak English and teach it to others. Your school offers two types of courses: a one-month structured course in English and a one-week intensive course for individuals who already know English but want to improve their skills before visiting the United States. You advertise both types of teaching services in the local newspapers.

All revenue and expenses associated with your business are denominated in Mexican pesos. Your subsidiary sends most of the profits from the business in Mexico to you at the end of each month. Although your expenses are somewhat stable, your revenue varies with the number of clients who sign up for the courses in Mexico.

This background is sufficient to enable you to answer the questions that are asked about your business throughout the term. Answer each question as if you were serving on the board or as a manager of the business. The questions in the early chapters force you to assess the firm's opportunities and exposure, while the later chapters force you to consider potential strategies that your business might pursue.

Chapter 1

a. Discuss the corporate control of your business. Explain why your business in Mexico is exposed to agency problems.
b. How would you attempt to monitor the ongoing operations of the business?
c. Explain how you might be able to use a compensation plan to limit the potential agency problems.
d. Assume that you have been approached by a competitor in Mexico to engage in a joint venture. The competitor would provide the classroom facilities (so you would not need to rent classroom space), while your employees would teach the classes. You and the competitor would split the profits. Discuss how your potential return and your risk would change if you pursue the joint venture.
e. Explain the conditions that would cause your business to be adversely affected by exchange rate movements.
f. Explain how your business could be adversely affected by political risk.

Chapter 2

Your business provides cassettes for free to customers who pay for the English courses that you offer in Mexico. You are considering mass-producing the cassettes in the United States so that you can sell (export) them to distributors or to retail stores throughout Mexico. You would price the cassettes in dollars when exporting them. The cassettes are less effective without the teaching, but still can be useful to individuals who want to learn the basics of the English language.

a. If you pursue this idea, explain how the factors that affect international trade flows (identified in Chapter 2) could affect the Mexican demand for your cassettes. Which of these factors would likely have the largest impact on the Mexican demand for your cassettes? What other factors would affect the Mexican demand for the cassettes?

b. Suppose that you believe the Mexican government will impose a tariff on the cassettes exported to Mexico. How could you still execute this business idea at a relatively low cost while avoiding the tariff? Describe any disadvantages of this idea to avoid the tariff.

Chapter 3

Assume that the business in Mexico grows. Explain how financial markets could help to finance the growth of the business.

Chapter 4

Given the factors that affect the value of a foreign currency, describe the type of economic or other conditions in Mexico that could cause the Mexican peso to weaken and thereby to adversely affect your business.

Chapter 5

Explain how currency futures could be used to hedge your business in Mexico. Explain how currency options could be used to hedge your business in Mexico.

Chapter 6

a. Explain how your business will likely be affected (at least in the short run) if the central bank of Mexico intervenes in the foreign exchange market by exchanging Mexican pesos for dollars.
b. Explain how your business will likely be affected if the central bank of Mexico uses indirect intervention by lowering Mexican interest rates (assume inflationary expectations have not changed).

Chapter 7

Mexican interest rates are normally substantially higher than U.S. interest rates.

a. What does this imply about the forward premium or discount of the Mexican peso?
b. What does this imply about your business using forward or futures contracts to hedge your periodic profits in pesos that must be converted into dollars?
c. Do you think you would frequently hedge your exposure to Mexican pesos? Explain your answer.

Chapter 8

Mexican interest rates are normally substantially higher than U.S. interest rates.

a. What does this imply about the inflation differential (Mexico inflation minus U.S. inflation), assuming that the real interest rate is the same in both countries? Does this imply that the Mexican peso will appreciate or depreciate? Explain.
b. It might be argued that the high Mexican interest rates should entice U.S. investors to invest in Mexican money market securities, which could cause the peso to appreciate. Reconcile this theory with your answer in part (a). If you believe that the high Mexican interest rates will not entice U.S. investors, explain your reasoning.
c. Assume that the difference between Mexican and U.S. interest rates is typically attributed to a difference in expected inflation in the two countries. Also assume that purchasing power parity holds. Do you think that your business cash flows will be adversely affected? In reality, purchasing power parity does not hold consistently. Assume that the inflation differential (Mexico inflation minus U.S. inflation) is not fully offset by the exchange rate movement of the peso. Will this benefit or hurt your business? Now assume that the inflation differential is more than offset by the exchange rate movement of the peso. Will this benefit or hurt your business?
d. Assume that the nominal interest rate in Mexico is currently much higher than the U.S. interest rate and that this difference is due to a high rate of expected inflation in Mexico. You are considering hiring a local firm to promote your business, but you would have to borrow funds to finance this marketing campaign. A consultant advises you to delay the marketing campaign for a year so that you can capitalize on the high nominal interest rate in Mexico. He suggests that you retain the profits that you would normally have remitted to the United States and deposit them in a Mexican bank. The Mexican peso cash flows that your business deposits will grow at a high rate of interest over the year. Should you follow the advice of the consultant?

Chapter 9

a. Mexican interest rates are normally substantially higher than U.S. interest rates. What does this imply about the forward rate as a forecast of the future spot rate?
b. Does the forward rate reflect a forecast of appreciation or depreciation of the Mexican peso? Explain how the degree of the expected change implied by the forward rate forecast is tied to the interest rate differential.
c. Do you think that today's forward rate or today's spot rate of the peso provides a better forecast of the future spot rate of the peso?

Chapter 10

Recall that your Mexican business invoices in Mexican pesos.

a. You are already aware that a decline in the value of the peso could reduce your dollar cash flows. Yet, according to purchasing power parity, a weak peso should occur only in response to a high level of Mexican inflation, and such high inflation should increase your profits. If this theory holds precisely, your cash flows would not really be exposed. Should you be concerned about your exposure, or not? Explain.

b. If you change your policy and invoice only in dollars, how will your transaction exposure be affected?
c. Why might the demand for your business change if you change your invoice policy? What are the implications for your economic exposure?

Chapter 11

Mexican interest rates are normally substantially higher than U.S. interest rates.

a. Assuming that interest rate parity exists, do you think hedging with a forward rate will be beneficial if the spot rate of the Mexican peso is expected to decline slightly over time?
b. Will hedging with a money market hedge be beneficial if the spot rate of the Mexican peso is expected to decline slightly over time (assume zero transaction costs)? Explain.
c. What are some limitations on using currency futures or options that may make it difficult for you to perfectly hedge against exchange rate risk over the next year or so?
d. In general, not many long-term currency futures and options on the Mexican peso are available. A consultant suggests that this is not a problem because you can hedge your position a quarter at a time. In other words, the profits that you remit at any point in the future can be hedged by taking a currency futures or options position three months or so before that time. Thus, although the consultant recognizes that the peso could weaken substantially in the long term, she sees no reason why you should worry about its decline as long as you continually create a short-term hedge. Do you agree?

Chapter 12

a. Explain how your business is subject to translation exposure.
b. How could you hedge against this translation exposure?
c. Is it worthwhile for your business to hedge the translation exposure?

Chapter 13

Assume that you want to expand your English teaching business to other non-U.S. countries where some individuals may want to learn to speak English.

a. Explain why you might be able to stabilize the profits of your total business in this manner. Review the motives for direct foreign investment that are identified in this chapter. Which of these motives are most important?
b. Why would a city such as Montreal be a less desirable site for your business than a city such as Mexico City?

c. Describe the conditions in which your total business would experience weak effects even if the business was spread across three or four countries.
d. What factors affect the probability that the conditions you identified in part (c) might occur? (In other words, explain why the conditions could occur in one set of countries, but not another set of countries.)
e. What data would you review to assess the probability that these conditions will occur?
f. Assume that your business has already created some pamphlets and cassettes that translate common Spanish terms into English to supplement your primary service of teaching individuals in Mexico to speak English. How could you expand your business in a manner that might allow you to benefit from economies of scale (and perhaps even benefit from your existing business reputation)? When you attempt to benefit from economies of scale, do you forgo diversification benefits? Explain.
g. How would you come to a decision on whether to pursue business expansion that capitalizes on economies of scale even though it would mean forgoing diversification benefits? Do you think economies of scale would be more or less important than diversification for your business?
h. Is there any way to achieve both economies of scale and diversification benefits?

Chapter 14

a. Review the different items that are used in the multinational capital budgeting example (Spartan, Inc.). Describe the items that you would include on a spreadsheet if you conducted a multinational capital budgeting analysis of investing dollars to expand your existing language business in a different location.
b. Assume that you recognize your limitations in predicting the future exchange rate of the invoice currency for your expanded business. You think that there are several possible exchange rate scenarios, each with equal probability of occurrence. Explain how you could use this information to estimate the future net present value (*NPV*) and make a decision about whether to accept or reject the project.
c. Now assume that there is also much uncertainty about individuals' demand for your service in the new location. Explain how you can incorporate this uncertainty along with the uncertainty of exchange rate movements so that you can make a decision about whether to accept or reject the project.
d. Explain how you would derive a required rate of return for your capital budgeting analysis. What type of information would you use to derive the required rate of return?

Chapter 15

You have an opportunity to purchase a private competitor called Fernand in Mexico. If you decide to purchase the company, you will use only your own funds.

a. When you attempt to determine the value of this company, how will you derive your required rate of return? Specifically, should you use the U.S. or the Mexican risk-free rate as a base when deriving your required rate of return? Why?

b. Another Mexican firm called Vascon is also considering acquiring this firm. Explain why Vascon's required rate of return may be higher than your required rate of return. Is there any reason why Vascon's required rate of return may be lower than your required rate of return?
c. Assume that you and Vascon have the same expectations regarding the Mexican cash flows that will be generated by Fernand. Fernand's owner is willing to sell the company for 2 million Mexican pesos. You and Vascon use a similar process to determine the feasibility of acquiring the target. You both compare the present value of the target's cash flows to the purchase price. Based on your analysis, Fernand would generate a positive net present value (*NPV*) for your firm. Based on Vascon's analysis, Fernand would generate a negative *NPV* for Vascon. How could you determine that the acquisition of Fernand is feasible, while Vascon determines that the acquisition is not feasible?
d. Repeat part (c), but reverse the assumptions. That is, you determine that Fernand would generate a negative *NPV* for your firm, whereas Vascon determines that Fernand would generate a positive *NPV*. How could you determine that the acquisition of Fernand is not feasible, while Vascon determines that the acquisition of Fernand is feasible?

Chapter 16

a. Review the political risk factors, and identify those that could possibly affect your business. Explain how your cash flows could be affected.
b. Explain why threats of terrorism due to friction between two countries could possibly affect your business, even though the terrorism has no effect on the relations between the United States and Mexico.
c. Assume that an upcoming election in Mexico may result in a complete change in government. Explain why the election could have significant effects on your cash flows.

Chapter 17

a. Assume that your business is considering expanding in Mexico. You plan to invest a small amount of U.S. dollar equity into this project and finance the remainder with debt. You can obtain debt financing for the expansion in Mexico, but Mexican interest rates are higher than U.S. rates. Yet, if you use mostly U.S. debt financing, you will be more exposed to exchange rate risk. Explain why.
b. You want to assess the feasibility of the new project in Mexico if you use mostly U.S. debt financing versus mostly Mexican debt financing. You also want to capture possible exchange rate effects on your cash flows over time. How can you use capital budgeting to conduct your comparison?
c. You prefer to avoid using Mexican debt to finance your expansion in Mexico because the interest rates are high. A consultant suggests that you seek one or more investors in Mexico who would be willing to take an equity position in your business. You would provide them with periodic dividends, and they would be partial owners of your company. The consultant suggests that this strategy would circumvent the high

cost of capital in Mexico because it uses equity financing instead of debt financing. Is the consultant correct?

Chapter 18

Recall from the previous chapter that your business is considering expansion within Mexico. Recall that you plan to invest a small amount of U.S. dollar equity into this project and finance the remainder with debt. You can obtain debt financing for the expansion in Mexico, but Mexican interest rates are higher than U.S. rates. Today, you receive credit offers from different banks. You can obtain a fixed rate loan in the United States at 8 percent for the life of this project or a floating rate loan (rate changes each year in response to market interest rates) in Mexico at 10 percent. Explain how you could estimate the net present value (*NPV*) of the project for each alternative financing method. Include an explanation of how you would account for the uncertainty of future movements of Mexican interest rates.

Chapter 19

Recall that your business provides cassettes that complement the teaching provided by your employees in Mexico. Assume that you decide to capitalize on these cassettes by selling them to a large retail store based in Mexico. The cassettes are less effective without the teaching, but still can be useful to individuals who want to learn the basics of the English language. You do not want to take the risk of sending a case of cassettes to the retail store unless you can be sure of receiving payment. Explain how you can ensure payment for the cassettes.

Chapter 20

You are considering a major marketing campaign in Mexico. If you implement it, you will incur high expenses in Mexican pesos and will need to finance the cost. To cover the cost, you can either borrow dollars at a low interest rate and convert them to Mexican pesos or borrow Mexican pesos. You expect to pay off the loan on a monthly basis over the next year by using a portion of the revenue you generate from your business in Mexico.

a. Will your business be more exposed to exchange rate risk if you borrow dollars or Mexican pesos?
b. Explain how you would make the decision to borrow dollars versus Mexican pesos. What is the key factor (other than the interest rate of each currency) that will determine whether you borrow dollars or Mexican pesos?

Chapter 21

Assume that this year you decide not to implement the marketing campaign that you considered in the previous chapter. Instead, you will invest some of this year's profits in money market investments and then use this money to cover the campaign next year. You can retain the profits earned this year by investing them in a Mexican bank where interest rates are high. Alternatively, you could invest the profits in a dollar-denominated bank account. That is, you could convert your Mexican peso profits to dollars periodically and accumulate the dollars over the year. At the end of the year, you could convert the dollars back to Mexican pesos to pay for the marketing campaign. Explain how you would decide between these two alternatives.

Glossary

A

absolute form of purchasing power parity This theory explains how inflation differentials affect exchange rates. It suggests that prices of two products of different countries should be equal when measured by a common currency.

accounts receivable financing indirect financing provided by an exporter for an importer by exporting goods and allowing for payment to be made at a later date.

advising bank corresponding bank in the beneficiary's country to which the issuing bank sends the letter of credit.

agency problem conflict of goals between a firm's shareholders and its managers.

airway bill receipt for a shipment by air, which includes freight charges and title to the merchandise.

all-in-rate rate used in charging customers for accepting banker's acceptances, consisting of the discount interest rate plus the commission.

American depository receipts (ADRs) certificates representing ownership of foreign stocks, which are traded on stock exchanges in the United States.

appreciation increase in the value of a currency.

arbitrage action to capitalize on a discrepancy in quoted prices; in many cases, there is no investment of funds tied up for any length of time.

Asian dollar market market in Asia in which banks collect deposits and make loans denominated in U.S. dollars.

ask price price at which a trader of foreign exchange (typically a bank) is willing to sell a particular currency.

assignment of proceeds arrangement that allows the original beneficiary of a letter of credit to pledge or assign proceeds to an end supplier.

B

balance of payments statement of inflow and outflow payments for a particular country.

balance of trade difference between the value of merchandise exports and merchandise imports.

balance on goods and services balance of trade, plus the net amount of payments of interest and dividends to foreign investors and from investment, as well as receipts and payments resulting from international tourism and other transactions.

Bank for International Settlements (BIS) institution that facilitates cooperation among countries involved in international transactions and provides assistance to countries experiencing international payment problems.

Bank Letter of Credit Policy policy that enables banks to confirm letters of credit by foreign banks supporting the purchase of U.S. exports.

banker's acceptance bill of exchange drawn on and accepted by a banking institution; it is commonly used to guarantee exporters that they will receive payment on goods delivered to importers.

barter exchange of goods between two parties without the use of any currency as a medium of exchange.

Basel Accord agreement among country representatives in 1988 to establish standardized risk-based capital requirements for banks across countries.

bid price price that a trader of foreign exchange (typically a bank) is willing to pay for a particular currency.

bid/ask spread difference between the price at which a bank is willing to buy a currency and the price at which it will sell that currency.

bilateral netting system netting method used for transactions between two units.

bill of exchange (draft) promise drawn by one party (usually an exporter) to pay a specified amount to another party at a specified future date, or upon presentation of the draft.

bill of lading document serving as a receipt for shipment and a summary of freight charges and conveying title to the merchandise.

Bretton Woods Agreement conference held in Bretton Woods, New Hampshire, in 1944, resulting in an agreement to maintain exchange rates of currencies within very narrow boundaries; this agreement lasted until 1971.

C

call see *currency call option*.

call option on real assets project that contains an option of pursuing an additional venture.

capital account account reflecting changes in country ownership of long-term and short-term financial assets.

carryforwards tax losses that are applied in a future year to offset income in the future year.

cash management optimization of cash flows and investment of excess cash.

central exchange rate exchange rate established between two European currencies through the European Monetary System arrangement; the exchange rate between the two currencies is allowed to move within bands around that central exchange rate.

centralized cash flow management policy that consolidates cash management decisions for all MNC units, usually at the parent's location.

coefficient of determination measure of the percentage variation in the dependent variable that can be explained by the independent variables when using regression analysis.

cofinancing agreements arrangement in which the World Bank participates along with other agencies or lenders in providing funds to developing countries.

commercial invoice exporter's description of merchandise being sold to the buyer.

commercial letters of credit trade-related letters of credit.

comparative advantage theory suggesting that specialization by countries can increase worldwide production.

compensation arrangement in which the delivery of goods to a party is compensated for by buying back a certain amount of the product from that same party.

Compensatory Financing Facility (CFF) facility that attempts to reduce the impact of export instability on country economies.

consignment arrangement in which the exporter ships goods to the importer while still retaining title to the merchandise.

contingency graph graph showing the net profit to a speculator in currency options under various exchange rate scenarios.

counterpurchase exchange of goods between two parties under two distinct contracts expressed in monetary terms.

countertrade sale of goods to one country that is linked to the purchase or exchange of goods from that same country.

country risk characteristics of the host country, including political and financial conditions, that can affect an MNC's cash flows.

covered interest arbitrage investment in a foreign money market security with a simultaneous forward sale of the currency denominating that security.

cross exchange rate exchange rate between currency A and currency B, given the values of currencies A and B with respect to a third currency.

cross-border factoring factoring by a network of factors across borders. The exporter's factor can contact correspondent factors in other countries to handle the collections of accounts receivable.

cross-hedging hedging an open position in one currency with a hedge on another currency that is highly correlated with the first currency. This occurs when for some reason the common hedging techniques cannot be applied to the first currency. A cross-hedge is not a perfect hedge, but can substantially reduce the exposure.

cross-sectional analysis analysis of relationships among a cross section of firms, countries, or some other variable at a given point in time.

currency board system for maintaining the value of the local currency with respect to some other specified currency.

currency call option contract that grants the right to purchase a specific currency at a specific price (exchange rate) within a specific period of time.

currency cocktail bond bond denominated in a mixture (or cocktail) of currencies.

currency diversification process of using more than one currency as an investing or financing strategy. Exposure to a diversified currency portfolio typically results in less exchange rate risk than if all of the exposure was in a single foreign currency.

currency futures contract contract specifying a standard volume of a particular currency to be exchanged on a specific settlement date.

currency put option contract granting the right to sell a particular currency at a specified price (exchange rate) within a specified period of time.

currency swap agreement to exchange one currency for another at a specified exchange rate and date. Banks commonly serve as intermediaries between two parties who wish to engage in a currency swap.

current account broad measure of a country's international trade in goods and services.

D

Delphi technique collection of independent opinions without group discussion by the assessors who provide the opinions; used for various types of assessments (such as country risk assessment).

dependent variable term used in regression analysis to represent the variable that is dependent on one or more other variables.

depreciation decrease in the value of a currency.

direct foreign investment (DFI) investment in real assets (such as land, buildings, or even existing plants) in foreign countries.

Direct Loan Program program in which the Ex-Im Bank offers fixed-rate loans directly to the foreign buyer to purchase U.S. capital equipment and services.

direct quotations exchange rate quotations representing the value measured by number of dollars per unit.

discount as related to forward rates, represents the percentage amount by which the forward rate is less than the spot rate.

documentary collections trade transactions handled on a draft basis.

documents against acceptance situation in which the buyer's bank does not release shipping documents to the buyer until the buyer has accepted (signed) the draft.

documents against payment shipping documents that are released to the buyer once the buyer has paid for the draft.

double-entry bookkeeping accounting method in which each transaction is recorded as both a credit and a debit.

draft (bill of exchange) unconditional promise drawn by one party (usually the exporter) instructing the buyer to pay the face amount of the draft upon presentation.

dumping selling products overseas at unfairly low prices (a practice perceived to result from subsidies provided to the firm by its government).

dynamic hedging strategy of hedging in those periods when existing currency positions are expected to be adversely affected, and remaining unhedged in other periods when currency positions are expected to be favorably affected.

E

economic exposure degree to which a firm's present value of future cash flows can be influenced by exchange rate fluctuations.

economies of scale achievement of lower average cost per unit by means of increased production.

effective yield yield or return to an MNC on a short-term investment after adjustment for the change in exchange rates over the period of concern.

efficient frontier set of points reflecting risk-return combinations achieved by particular portfolios (so-called efficient portfolios) of assets.

equilibrium exchange rate exchange rate at which demand for a currency is equal to the supply of the currency for sale.

Eurobanks commercial banks that participate as financial intermediaries in the Eurocurrency market.

Eurobonds bonds sold in countries other than the country represented by the currency denominating them.

Euro-clear telecommunications network that informs all traders about outstanding issues of Eurobonds for sale.

Euro-commercial paper debt securities issued by MNCs for short-term financing.

Eurocredit loans loans of one year or longer extended by Eurobanks.

Eurocredit market collection of banks that accept deposits and provide loans in large denominations and in a variety of currencies. The banks that comprise this market are the same banks that comprise the Eurocurrency market; the difference is that the Eurocredit loans are longer term than so-called Eurocurrency loans.

Eurocurrency market collection of banks that accept deposits and provide loans in large denominations and in a variety of currencies.

Eurodollar term used to describe U.S. dollar deposits placed in banks located in Europe.

Euronotes unsecured debt securities issued by MNCs for short-term financing.

European Central Bank (ECB) central bank created to conduct the monetary policy for the countries participating in the single European currency, the euro.

European Currency Unit (ECU) unit of account representing a weighted average of exchange rates of member countries within the European Monetary System.

exchange rate mechanism method of linking European currency values with the European Currency Unit (ECU).

exercise price (strike price) price (exchange rate) at which the owner of a currency call option is allowed to buy a specified currency; or the price (exchange rate) at which the owner of a currency put option is allowed to sell a specified currency.

Export-Import Bank (Ex-Im Bank) bank that attempts to strengthen the competitiveness of U.S. industries involved in foreign trade.

F

factor firm specializing in collection on accounts receivable; exporters sometimes sell their accounts receivable to a factor at a discount.

factoring purchase of receivables of an exporter by a factor without recourse to the exporter.

Financial Institution Buyer Credit Policy policy that provides insurance coverage for loans by banks to foreign buyers of exports.

Fisher effect theory that nominal interest rates are composed of a real interest rate and anticipated inflation.

fixed exchange rate system monetary system in which exchange rates are either held constant or allowed to fluctuate only within very narrow boundaries.

floating rate notes (FRNs) provision of some Eurobonds, in which the coupon rate is adjusted over time according to prevailing market rates.

foreign bond bond issued by a borrower foreign to the country where the bond is placed.

foreign exchange market market composed primarily of banks, serving firms and consumers who wish to buy or sell various currencies.

foreign investment risk matrix (FIRM) graph that displays financial and political risk by intervals, so that each country can be positioned according to its risk ratings.

forfaiting method of financing international trade of capital goods.

forward contract agreement between a commercial bank and a client about an exchange of two currencies to be made at a future point in time at a specified exchange rate.

forward discount percentage by which the forward rate is less than the spot rate; typically quoted on an annualized basis.

forward premium percentage by which the forward rate exceeds the spot rate; typically quoted on an annualized basis.

forward rate rate at which a bank is willing to exchange one currency for another at some specified date in the future.

franchising agreement by which a firm provides a specialized sales or service strategy, support assistance, and possibly an initial investment in the franchise in exchange for periodic fees.

freely floating exchange rate system monetary system in which exchange rates are allowed to move due to market forces without intervention by country governments.

full compensation an arrangement in which the delivery of goods to one party is fully compensated for by buying back more than 100 percent of the value that was originally sold.

fundamental forecasting forecasting based on fundamental relationships between economic variables and exchange rates.

G

General Agreement on Tariffs and Trade (GATT) agreement allowing for trade restrictions only in retaliation against illegal trade actions of other countries.

gold standard era in which each currency was convertible into gold at a specified rate, allowing the exchange rate between two currencies to be determined by their relative convertibility rates per ounce of gold.

H

hedge to insulate a firm from exposure to exchange rate fluctuations.

hostile takeovers acquisitions not desired by the target firms.

I

imperfect market the condition where, due to the costs to transfer labor and other resources used for production, firms may attempt to use foreign factors of production when they are less costly than local factors.

import/export letters of credit trade-related letters of credit.

independent variable term used in regression analysis to represent the variable that is expected to influence another (the "dependent") variable.

indirect quotations exchange rate quotations representing the value measured by number of units per dollar.

interbank market market that facilitates the exchange of currencies between banks.

Interest Equalization Tax (IET) tax imposed by the U.S. government in 1963 to discourage U.S. investors from investing in foreign securities.

interest rate parity theory specifying that the forward premium (or discount) is equal to the interest rate differential between the two currencies of concern.

interest rate parity (IRP) line diagonal line depicting all points on a four-quadrant graph that represent a state of interest rate parity.

interest rate parity theory theory suggesting that the forward rate differs from the spot rate by an amount that reflects the interest differential between two currencies.

interest rate swap agreement to swap interest payments, whereby interest payments based on a fixed interest rate are exchanged for interest payments based on a floating interest rate.

International Bank for Reconstruction and Development (IBRD) bank established in 1944 to enhance economic development by providing loans to countries. Also referred to as the World Bank.

International Development Association (IDA) association established to stimulate country development; it was especially suited for less prosperous nations, since it provided loans at low interest rates.

International Financial Corporation (IFC) firm established to promote private enterprise within countries; it can provide loans to and purchase stock of corporations.

international Fisher effect theory specifying that a currency's exchange rate will depreciate against another currency when its interest rate (and therefore expected inflation rate) is higher than that of the other currency.

international Fisher effect (IFE) line diagonal line on a graph that reflects points at which the interest rate differential between two countries is equal to the percentage change in the exchange rate between their two respective currencies.

International Monetary Fund (IMF) agency established in 1944 to promote and facilitate international trade and financing.

international mutual funds (IMFs) mutual funds containing securities of foreign firms.

intracompany trade international trade between subsidiaries that are under the same ownership.

irrevocable letter of credit letter of credit issued by a bank that cannot be canceled or amended without the beneficiary's approval.

issuing bank bank that issues a letter of credit.

J

J-curve effect effect of a weaker dollar on the U.S. trade balance, in which the trade balance initially deteriorates; it only improves once U.S. and non-U.S. importers respond to the change in purchasing power that is caused by the weaker dollar.

joint venture venture between two or more firms in which responsibilities and earnings are shared.

L

lagging strategy used by a firm to stall payments, normally in response to exchange rate projections.

leading strategy used by a firm to accelerate payments, normally in response to exchange rate expectations.

letter of credit (L/C) agreement by a bank to make payments on behalf of a specified party under specified conditions.

licensing arrangement in which a local firm in the host country produces goods in accordance with another firm's (the licensing firm's) specifications; as the goods are sold, the local firm can retain part of the earnings.

locational arbitrage action to capitalize on a discrepancy in quoted exchange rates between banks.

lockbox post office box number to which customers are instructed to send payment.

London Interbank Offer Rate (LIBOR) interest rate commonly charged for loans between Eurobanks.

long-term forward contracts contracts that state any exchange rate at which a specified amount of a specified currency can be exchanged at a future date (more than one year from today). Also called long forwards.

Louvre Accord 1987 agreement between countries to attempt to stabilize the value of the U.S. dollar.

M

macroassessment overall risk assessment of a country without considering the MNC's business.

mail float mailing time involved in sending payments by mail.

managed float exchange rate system in which currencies have no explicit boundaries, but central banks may intervene to influence exchange rate movements.

margin requirement deposit placed on a contract (such as a currency futures contract) to cover the fluctuations in the value of that contract; this minimizes the risk of the contract to the counterparty.

market-based forecasting use of a market-determined exchange rate (such as the spot rate or forward rate) to forecast the spot rate in the future.

Medium-Term Guarantee Program program conducted by the Ex-Im Bank in which commercial lenders are encouraged to finance the sale of U.S. capital equipment and services to approved foreign buyers; the Ex-Im Bank guarantees the loan's principal and interest on these loans.

microassessment the risk assessment of a country as related to the MNC's type of business.

mixed forecasting development of forecasts based on a mixture of forecasting techniques.

money market hedge use of international money markets to match future cash inflows and outflows in a given currency.

multibuyer policy policy administered by the Ex-Im Bank that provides credit risk insurance on export sales to many different buyers.

Multilateral Investment Guarantee Agency (MIGA) agency established by the World Bank that offers various forms of political risk insurance to corporations.

multilateral netting system complex interchange for netting between a parent and several subsidiaries.

multinational restructuring restructuring of the composition of an MNC's assets or liabilities.

N

negotiable bill of lading contract that grants title of merchandise to the holder, which allows banks to use the merchandise as collateral.

net operating loss carrybacks practice of applying losses to offset earnings in previous years.

net operating loss carryforwards practice of applying losses to offset earnings in future years.

netting combining of future cash receipts and payments to determine the net amount to be owed by one subsidiary to another.

net transaction exposure consideration of inflows and outflows in a given currency to determine the exposure after offsetting inflows against outflows.

non-deliverable forward contracts (NDFs) like a forward contract, represents an agreement regarding a position in a specified currency, a specified exchange rate, and a specified future settlement date, but does not result in delivery of currencies. Instead, a payment is made by one party in the agreement to the other party based on the exchange rate at the future date.

nonsterilized intervention intervention in the foreign exchange market without adjusting for the change in money supply.

O

ocean bill of lading receipt for a shipment by boat, which includes freight charges and title to the merchandise.

open account transaction sale in which the exporter ships the merchandise and expects the buyer to remit payment according to agreed-upon terms.

overhedging hedging an amount in a currency larger than the actual transaction amount.

P

parallel bonds bonds placed in different countries and denominated in the respective currencies of the countries where they are placed.

parallel loan loan involving an exchange of currencies between two parties, with a promise to reexchange the currencies at a specified exchange rate and future date.

partial compensation an arrangement in which the delivery of goods to one party is partially compensated for by buying back a certain amount of product from the same party.

pegged exchange rate exchange rate whose value is pegged to another currency's value or to a unit of account.

perfect forecast line a 45-degree line on a graph that matches the forecast of an exchange rate with the actual exchange rate.

petrodollars deposits of dollars by countries that receive dollar revenues due to the sale of petroleum to other countries; the term commonly refers to OPEC deposits of dollars in the Eurocurrency market.

Plaza Accord agreement among country representatives in 1985 to implement a coordinated program to weaken the dollar.

political risk political actions taken by the host government or the public that affect the MNC's cash flows.

preauthorized payment method of accelerating cash inflows by receiving authorization to charge a customer's bank account.

premium as related to forward rates, represents the percentage amount by which the forward rate exceeds the spot rate. As related to currency options, represents the price of a currency option.

prepayment method that exporter uses to receive payment before shipping goods.

price-elastic sensitive to price changes.

privatization conversion of government-owned businesses to ownership by shareholders or individuals.

product cycle theory theory suggesting that a firm initially establish itself locally and expand into foreign markets in response to foreign demand for its product; over time, the MNC will grow in foreign markets; after some point, its foreign business may decline unless it can differentiate its product from competitors.

Project Finance Loan Program program that allows banks, the Ex-Im Bank, or a combination of both to extend long-term financing for capital equipment and related services for major projects.

purchasing power parity (PPP) line diagonal line on a graph that reflects points at which the inflation differential between two countries is equal to the percentage change in the exchange rate between the two respective currencies.

purchasing power parity (PPP) theory theory suggesting that exchange rates will adjust over time to reflect the differential in inflation rates in the two countries; in this way, the purchasing power of consumers when purchasing domestic goods will be the same as that when they purchase foreign goods.

put see *currency put option*.

put option on real assets project that contains an option of divesting part or all of the project.

Q

quota maximum limit imposed by the government on goods allowed to be imported into a country.

R

real cost of hedging the additional cost of hedging when compared to not hedging (a negative real cost would imply that hedging was more favorable than not hedging).

real interest rate nominal (or quoted) interest rate minus the inflation rate.

real options implicit options on real assets.

regression analysis statistical technique used to measure the relationship between variables and the sensitivity of a variable to one or more other variables.

regression coefficient term measured by regression analysis to estimate the sensitivity of the dependent variable to a particular independent variable.

reinvoicing center facility that centralizes payments and charges subsidiaries fees for its function; this can effectively shift profits to subsidiaries where tax rates are low.

relative form of purchasing power parity theory stating that the rate of change in the prices of products should be somewhat similar when measured in a common currency, as long as transportation costs and trade barriers are unchanged.

revocable letter of credit letter of credit issued by a bank that can be canceled at any time without prior notification to the beneficiary.

S

semistrong-form efficient description of foreign exchange markets, implying that all relevant public information is already reflected in prevailing spot exchange rates.

sensitivity analysis technique for assessing uncertainty whereby various possibilities are input to determine possible outcomes.

simulation technique for assessing the degree of uncertainty. Probability distributions are developed for the input variables; simulation uses this information to generate possible outcomes.

Single-Buyer Policy policy administered by the Ex-Im Bank that allows the exporter to selectively insure certain transactions.

Single European Act act intended to remove numerous barriers imposed on trade and capital flows between European countries.

Small Business Policy policy providing enhanced coverage to new exporters and small businesses.

Smithsonian Agreement conference between nations in 1971 that resulted in a devaluation of the dollar against major currencies and a widening of boundaries (2 percent in either direction) around the newly established exchange rates.

snake arrangement established in 1972, whereby European currencies were tied to each other within specified limits.

special drawing rights (SDRs) reserves established by the International Monetary Fund; they are used only for intergovernment transactions; the SDR also serves as a unit of account (determined by the values of five major currencies) that is used to denominate some internationally traded goods and services, as well as some foreign bank deposits and loans.

spot market market in which exchange transactions occur for immediate exchange.

spot rate current exchange rate of currency.

standby letter of credit document used to guarantee invoice payments to a supplier; it promises to pay the beneficiary if the buyer fails to pay.

sterilized intervention intervention by the Federal Reserve in the foreign exchange market, with simultaneous intervention in the Treasury securities markets to offset any effects on the dollar money supply; thus, the intervention in the foreign exchange market is achieved without affecting the existing dollar money supply.

straddle combination of a put option and a call option.

strike price See *exercise price*.

strong-form efficient description of foreign exchange markets, implying that all relevant public information and private information is already reflected in prevailing spot exchange rates.

Structural Adjustment Loan Facility (SAL) facility established in 1980 by the World Bank to enhance a country's long-term economic growth through financing projects.

supplier credit credit provided by the supplier to itself to fund its operations.

syndicate group of banks that participate in loans.

syndicated Eurocredit loans loans provided by a group (or syndicate) of banks in the Eurocredit market.

T

target zones implicit boundaries established by central banks on exchange rates.

tariff tax imposed by a government on imported goods.

technical forecasting development of forecasts using historical prices or trends.

tenor time period of drafts.

time-series analysis analysis of relationships between two or more variables over periods of time.

time-series models models that examine series of historical data; sometimes used as a means of technical forecasting by examining moving averages.

trade acceptance draft that allows the buyer to obtain merchandise prior to paying for it.

transaction exposure degree to which the value of future cash transactions can be affected by exchange rate fluctuations.

transfer pricing policy for pricing goods sent by either the parent or a subsidiary to a subsidiary of an MNC.

transferable letter of credit document that allows the first beneficiary on a standby letter of credit to transfer all or part of the original letter of credit to a third party.

translation exposure degree to which a firm's consolidated financial statements are exposed to fluctuations in exchange rates.

triangular arbitrage action to capitalize on a discrepancy where the quoted cross exchange rate is not equal to the rate that should exist at equilibrium.

U

umbrella policy policy issued to a bank or trading company to insure exports of an exporter and handle all administrative requirements.

unilateral transfers accounting for government and private gifts and grants.

W

weak-form efficient description of foreign exchange markets, implying that all historical and current exchange rate information is already reflected in prevailing spot exchange rates.

Working Capital Guarantee Program program conducted by the Ex-Im Bank that encourages commercial banks to extend short-term export financing to eligible exporters; the Ex-Im Bank provides a guarantee of the loan's principal and interest.

World Bank bank established in 1944 to enhance economic development by providing loans to countries.

World Trade Organization (WTO) organization established to provide a forum for multilateral trade negotiations and to settle trade disputes related to the GATT accord.

writer seller of an option.

Y

Yankee stock offerings offerings of stock by non-U.S. firms in the U.S. markets.

Index

A

B

C

D

E

F

Q

R

S

T